P9-CFO-706

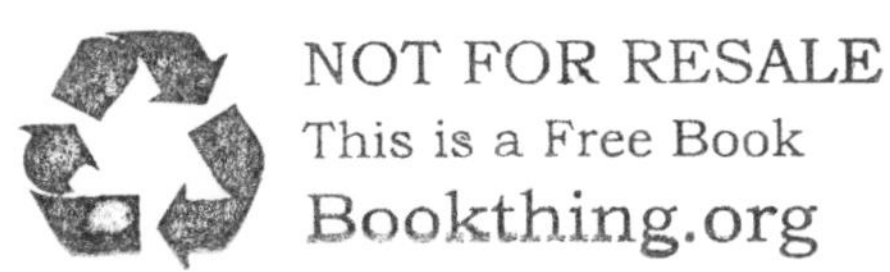
NOT FOR RESALE
This is a Free Book
Bookthing.org

Praise for *Core Security Patterns*

"Java provides the application developer with essential security mechanisms and support in avoiding critical security bugs common in other languages. A language, however, can only go so far. The developer must understand the security requirements of the application and how to use the features Java provides in order to meet those requirements. *Core Security Patterns* addresses both aspects of security and will be a guide to developers everywhere in creating more secure applications."

—Whitfield Diffie, inventor of Public-Key Cryptography

"A comprehensive book on Security Patterns, which are critical for secure programming."

—Li Gong, former Chief Java Security Architect, Sun Microsystems, and coauthor of *Inside Java 2 Platform Security*

"As developers of existing applications, or future innovators that will drive the next generation of highly distributed applications, the patterns and best practices outlined in this book will be an important asset to your development efforts."

—Joe Uniejewski, Chief Technology Officer and Senior Vice President, RSA Security, Inc.

"This book makes an important case for taking a proactive approach to security rather than relying on the reactive security approach common in the software industry."

—Judy Lin, Executive Vice President, VeriSign, Inc.

"*Core Security Patterns* provides a comprehensive patterns-driven approach and methodology for effectively incorporating security into your applications. I recommend that every application developer keep a copy of this indispensable security reference by their side."

—Bill Hamilton, author of *ADO.NET Cookbook*, *ADO.NET in a Nutshell*, and *NUnit Pocket Reference*

"As a trusted advisor, this book will serve as a Java developer's security handbook, providing applied patterns and design strategies for securing Java applications."

—Shaheen Nasirudheen, CISSP, Senior Technology Officer, JPMorgan Chase

Core Security Patterns

PRENTICE HALL CORE SERIES

Core J2EE Patterns, Second Edition, Alur/Malks/Crupi

Core PHP Programming, Third Edition, Atkinson/Suraski

Core Lego Mindstorms, Bagnall

Core Python Programming, Second Edition, Chun

Core Internet Application Development with ASP.NET 2.0, Connolly

Core JSTL, Geary

Core JavaServer Faces, Second Edition, Geary/Horstmann

Core Web Programming, Second Edition, Hall/Brown

Core Servlets and JavaServer Pages, Volume 1: Core Technologies, Second Edition, Hall/Brown

Core Servlets and JavaServer Pages, Volume 2: Advanced Technologies, Second Edition, Hall/Brown

Core Java™ 2, Volume I—Fundamentals, Eighth Edition, Horstmann/Cornell

Core Java™ 2, Volume II—Advanced Features, Eighth Edition, Horstmann/Cornell

Core C# and .NET, Perry

Core CSS, Second Edition, Schengili-Roberts

Core Security Patterns, Steel/Nagappan/Lai

Core Java Data Objects, Tyagi/Vorburger/McCammon/Bobzin

Core Web Application Development with PHP and MySQL, Wandschneider

Core Security Patterns

Best Practices and Strategies for J2EE,™ Web Services, and Identity Management

Christopher Steel
Ramesh Nagappan
Ray Lai

Upper Saddle River, NJ • Boston• Indianapolis • San Francisco
New York • Toronto • Montreal • London • Munich • Paris • Madrid
Capetown • Sydney • Tokyo • Singapore • Mexico City

The publisher offers excellent discounts on this book when ordered in quantity for bulk purchases or special sales, which may include electronic versions and/or custom covers and content particular to your business, training goals, marketing focus, and branding interests. For more information, please contact: U. S. Corporate and Government Sales, (800) 382-3419, corpsales@pearsontechgroup.com.

For sales outside the U. S., please contact: International Sales, international@pearsoned.com

Visit us on the Web: www.phptr.com

Library of Congress Cataloging-in-Publication Data

Steel, Christopher, 1968-

Core security patterns : best practices and strategies for J2EE, Web services and identity management / Christopher Steel, Ramesh Nagappan, Ray Lai.

p. cm.

Includes bibliographical references and index.

ISBN 0-13-146307-1 (pbk. : alk. paper)

1. Java (Computer program language) 2. Computer security. I. Nagappan, Ramesh. II. Lai, Ray. III. Title.

QA76.73.J3S834 2005

005.8-dc22

2005020502

ISBN 0131463071

Text printed in the United States on recycled paper at Courier Westford in Westford, Massachusetts.

4th Printing January 2009

To Kristin, Brandon, Ian, and Alec—
For your love and support in making this possible
C. S.

To Joyce, Roger, and Kaitlyn—
For all your love, inspiration, and sacrifice
R. N

To Johanan and Angela—
Love never fails (1 Corinthians 13:8)
R. L.

Contents

Foreword

On May 10, 1869 the tracks of the Union Pacific and Central Pacific Railroads were joined to create the Transcontinental Railroad. The first public railway, the Liverpool and Manchester railway, had opened less than forty years earlier on a track only thirty-five miles long. A journey from New York to San Francisco could now be completed in days rather than months.

The railroad was the Internet of its day. The benefits of fast, cheap, and reliable transport were obvious to all, but so was the challenge of building an iron road thousands of miles long through mountains and over rivers. Even though few people doubted that a railroad spanning the North American continent would eventually be completed, it took real vision and courage to make the attempt.

The railway age is often compared to the Internet since both technologies played a key role in transforming the economy and society of their day. Perhaps for this reason both began with public skepticism that rapidly changed into enthusiasm, a speculative mania, and despair. If the railway mania of 1845 had been the end of railway building, the transcontinental would never have been built.

The building of an Internet infrastructure for business applications represents the transcontinental railroad of the Internet age. Every day millions of workers sit at computers generating orders, invoices, and the like that are then sent on to yet more millions of workers who spend most of their time entering the information into yet more computers.

Ten years ago practically all businesses worked that way. Today a significant proportion of business takes place through the Web. Consumers are used to ordering books, clothes, and travel online and expect the improvements in customer service that this makes possible.

During the dotcom era it was fashionable to speak of "e-commerce" as if the Internet would create a completely new and separate form of commerce that would quickly replace traditional businesses. Despite the failure of many companies founded on this faulty premise, Internet commerce has never been stronger. In the peak year of the dotcom boom, 2000, VeriSign issued 275,000 SSL certificates and processed 35 million payments in transactions totaling $1.3 billion. In 2003 VeriSign issued 390,000 certificates and processed 345 million payments in transactions totaling $25 billion.

It is now understood that defining a class of "e-commerce" businesses is as meaningless as trying to distinguish "telephone commerce" or "fax commerce" businesses. Businesses of every size and in every sector of the economy are now using the Internet and the Web. It is no longer unusual to find a plumber or carpenter advertising their services through a Web site.

It is clear that the emerging Internet business infrastructures will eventually connect, and electronic processes that are largely automated will replace the current fax gap. It is also apparent that when this connection is finally achieved it will enable a transformation of commerce as fundamental as the railroads. Before this can happen, however, two key problems must be solved.

The first problem is complexity. Despite the many practical difficulties that had to be overcome to make online retail successful, a standard business process for mail order sales had been established for over a century. Allowing orders to be placed through a Web site rather than by mail or telephone required a modification of an established process that was already well understood. Coding systems to support business-to-business transactions is considerably more challenging than producing a system to support online retail. Business-to-business transactions vary greatly as do the internal processes that enterprises have established to support them.

The railroad engineers addressed a similar problem through standardization. An engine built to a bespoke design had to be maintained by a specialist. If a part broke it might be necessary for a replacement to be made using the original jigs in a factory a thousand miles away. The theory of interchangeable parts meant that an engine that broke down could be repaired using a part from standard stock.

Software reuse strategies that are desirable in building any application become essential when coding business-to-business applications. In addition to taking longer and costing more to build, a system that is built using bespoke techniques will be harder to administer, maintain, and extend.

Software patterns provide a ready-made template for building systems. Industry standards ensure that software will interoperate across implementation platforms.

Interoperability becomes essential when the business systems of one enterprise must talk to those of a partner.

The second challenge that must be addressed is security. A business will not risk either its reputation or its assets to an online transaction system unless it is convinced that it fully understands the risks.

It is rarely sufficient for an electronic system to provide security that is merely as good as existing systems deliver. Whether fairly or unfairly, electronic systems are invariably held to a higher standard of security than the paper processes they replace.

Today, rail is one of the safest ways to travel. This has not always been the case. Railway safety was at one time considered as intractable a problem as some consider Internet safety today. Victorian trains came off their rails with alarming frequency, bridges collapsed, cargoes caught fire, almost anything that might go wrong did. Eventually engineers began to see these accidents as failures of design rather than merely the result of unlucky chance. Safety became a central consideration in railway engineering rather than an afterthought.

The use of standardized, interchangeable parts played a significant role in the transformation of railway safety. Whether an engineer was designing a trestle for a bridge or a brake for a carriage, the use of a book of standard engineering design patterns was faster and less error prone.

The security field has long accepted the argument that a published specification that has been widely reviewed is less likely to fail than one that has had little external review. The use of standard security protocols such as SSL or SAML represents the modern day software engineering equivalent of the books of standard engineering parts of the past.

This book is timely because it addresses the major challenges facing deployment of Internet business infrastructure. Security patterns describe a means of delivering security in an application that is both repeatable and reliable. It is by adopting the principle of standardized software patterns that the engines to drive Internet business will be built.

In particular this book makes an important case for taking a proactive approach to security rather than relying on the reactive security approach common in the software industry. Most security problems are subject to a 'last mover advantage'—that is, whichever side made the last response is likely to win. Relying on the reactive approach to security cedes the initiative and thus the advantage to the attacker. A proactive approach to security is necessary to ensure that problems are solved before they become serious.

The recent upsurge in spam and spam-related frauds (so called spam-scams) show the result of relying on a reactive approach to security. By the time the system has grown large enough to be profitably attacked, any measures intended to react to the challenge must work within the constraints set by the deployed base.

Despite the numerous applications of email and the Web, email remains at base a messaging protocol, the Web a publishing protocol. The security requirements are well understood and common to all users. The challenges faced in creating an Internet business infrastructure are considerably more complex and difficult. It is clear that every software developer must have access to the best security expertise, but how can that be possible when the best expertise is by definition a scarce resource?

Reuse of well-understood security components in an application design allows every application designer to apply the experience and knowledge of the foremost experts in the industry to control risk. In addition it allows a systematic framework to be applied, providing better predictability and reducing development cost.

Computer network architectures are moving beyond the perimeter security model. This does not mean that firewalls will disappear or that perimeter security will cease to have relevance. But at the same time what happens across the firewall between enterprises will become as important from a security perspective as what takes place within the security perimeter. It is important then that the end-to-end security model and its appropriate application are understood.

In the railway age businesses discovered that certain important security tasks such as moving money from place to place were better left to specialists. The same applies in the computer security world—it is neither necessary nor desirable for every company to connect to payments infrastructures, operate a PKI or other identity infrastructure, manage its own security infrastructure, or perform one of hundreds of other security-related tasks itself. The use of standard Web Services infrastructure makes it possible to delegate these security sensitive tasks to specialists.

The benefits of an infrastructure for business applications are now widely understood. I believe that this book will provide readers with the tools they need to build that infrastructure with security built into its fabric.

—Judy Lin
Executive Vice President, VeriSign

Foreword

The last twenty years have brought dramatic changes to computing architectures and technologies, at both the network level and the application level. Much has been done at the network infrastructure layer, with intrusion detection, anti-virus, firewalls, VPNs, Quality of Service, policy management and enforcement, Denial of Service detection and prevention, and end point security. This is necessary, but not sufficient—more emphasis must now be placed on designing security into applications and in deploying application security infrastructure. While network security focuses on detecting, defending, and protecting, application security is more concerned with enablement and potentially with regulatory compliance (Sarbanes-Oxley, HIPPA, GLB, and so on).

Application security is an imperative not only for technology, but also for business. Companies with better security will gain competitive advantage, reduce costs, reach new markets, and improve end-user experience. This is true for both B2B (e.g., supply chain) and B2C (e.g., financial services, e-tail) applications. With global network connectivity and ever-increasing bandwidth, we have seen business transformation and unprecedented access to information and resources. Security is now at the forefront of the challenges facing users, enterprises, governments, and application providers and developers.

Loosely coupled distributed applications based on J2EE and Web Services have become the preferred model for multivendor, standards-based application development, and the leading application development and deployment platforms have evolved to provide increasing levels of security. Security can no longer be viewed as a layer (or multiple layers) that is added as problems or vulnerabilities arise; it must be an initial design consideration and an essential application development priority. Security should be a first thought, not an afterthought.

This book provides a comprehensive description of the various elements and considerations that must be accounted for in developing an overall application security strategy and implementation. Sun Microsystems—as a pioneer and leader in network computing, distributed applications, and the Java system—is uniquely positioned to cover this important area. As developers of existing applications, or future innovators that will drive the next generation of highly distributed applications, the information and best practices outlined in this book will be an important asset to your development efforts. We are counting on you to ensure that businesses and end users can confidently, and securely, experience the promise and power of the Internet.

—Joseph Uniejewski
CTO and Senior Vice President of Corporate Development, RSA Security

Preface

"The problems that exist in the world today cannot be solved by the level of thinking that created them."
—Albert Einstein

Security now has unprecedented importance in the information industry. It compels every business and organization to adopt proactive or reactive measures that protect data, processes, communication, and resources throughout the information lifecycle. In a continuous evolution, every day a new breed of business systems is finding its place and changes to existing systems are becoming common in the industry. These changes are designed to improve organizational efficiency and cost effectiveness and to increase consumer satisfaction. These improvements are often accompanied by newer security risks, to which businesses must respond with appropriate security strategies and processes. At the outset, securing an organization's information requires a thorough understanding of its security-related business challenges, potential threats, and best practices for mitigation of risks by means of appropriate safeguards and countermeasures. More importantly, it becomes essential that organizations adopt trusted proactive security approaches and enforce them at all levels—information processing, information transmittal, and information storage.

What This Book Is About

This book is meant to be a hands-on practitioner's guide to security. It captures a wealth of experience about using patterns-driven and best practices-based approaches to building trustworthy IT applications and services. The primary focus of the book is on the introduction of a security design methodology using a proven set of reusable patterns, best practices, reality checks, defensive strategies, and assessment checklists that can be applied to securing J2EE applications, Web Services, Identity Management, Service Provisioning, and Personal Identification. The book presents a catalog of 23 new security patterns and 101 best practices, identifying use case scenarios, architectural models, design strategies, applied technologies, and validation processes. The best practices and reality checks provide hints on real-world deployment and end-user experience of what works and what does not. The book also describes the architecture, mechanisms, standards, technologies, and implementation principles of applying security in J2EE applications, Web Services, Identity Management, Service Provisioning, and Personal Identification and explains the required fundamentals from the ground up.

Starting with an overview of today's business challenges, including the identification of security threats and exploits and an analysis of the importance of information security, security compliance, basic security concepts, and technologies, the book focuses in depth on the following topics:

- Security mechanisms in J2SE, J2EE, J2ME, and Java Card platforms
- Web Services security standards and technologies
- Identity Management standards and technologies
- Security design methodology, patterns, best practices, and reality checks
- Security patterns and design strategies for J2EE applications
- Security patterns and design strategies for Web Services
- Security patterns and design strategies for Identity Management
- Security patterns and design strategies for Service Provisioning
- Building an end-to-end security architecture—case study
- Secure Personal Identification strategies for using Smart Cards and Biometrics

The book emphasizes the use of the Java platform and stresses its importance in developing and deploying secure applications and services.

What This Book Is Not

While this book is heavily based on Java technologies, we do not describe the specific Java APIs intended for basic J2EE application development (e.g., JSPs, Servlets, and EJB). If you wish to learn the individual API technologies, we highly recommend the J2EE blueprints, tutorials, and recommended books on the official Java home page at http://java.sun.com.

We use UML diagrams to document the patterns and implementation strategies. If you wish to learn the UML basics, please refer to *The Unified Modeling Language User Guide* by Grady Booch, James Rumbaugh, and Ivar Jacobson (Addison-Wesley, 1999).

Who Should Read This Book?

This book is meant for all security enthusiasts, architects, Java developers, and technical project managers who are involved with securing information systems and business applications. The book is also valuable for those who wish to learn basic security concepts and technologies related to Java applications, Web Services, Identity Management, Service Provisioning, and Personal Identification using Smart Cards and Biometrics.

The book presumes that the reader has a basic conceptual knowledge of development and deployment of business applications using Java. We have attempted to write this book as an introduction to all security mechanisms used in the design, architecture, and development of applications using the Java platform. We intended our use of the methodology, patterns, best practices, and pitfalls to be an invaluable resource for answering the real-world IT security problems that software architects and developers face every day.

Most of us no longer have time to read a software development book from cover to cover. Therefore, we have broken this book into different technology parts; the book may thus be read in almost in any sequence according to the reader's specific interests.

How This Book Is Organized

The content of this book is organized into seven parts:

Part I: Introduction

Part I introduces the current state of the industry, business challenges, and various application security issues and strategies. It then presents the basics of security.

Chapter 1: Security by Default

This first chapter describes current business challenges, the weakest links of security, and critical application flaws and exploits. It introduces the security design strategies, concepts of patterns-driven security development, best practices, and reality checks. It also highlights the importance of security compliance, Identity Management, the Java platform, and Personal Identification technologies such as

Smart Cards and Biometrics. In addition, this chapter presents security from a business perspective and offers recommendations for making a case for security as a business enabler that delivers specific benefits.

Chapter 2: Basics of Security

This chapter introduces the fundamentals of security, including the background and guiding principles of various security technologies. It also provides a high-level introduction to securing applications by using popular cryptographic techniques. In addition, it discusses basic concepts about the role of directory services and identity management in security.

Part II: Java Security Architecture and Technologies

Part II provides in-depth coverage and demonstration of security practices using J2SE, J2EE, J2ME, and Java Card technologies. It delves into the intricate details of Java platform security architecture and its contribution to the end-to-end security of Java-based application solutions.

Chapter 3: The Java 2 Platform Security

This chapter explores the inherent security features of the various Java platforms and the enabling of Java security in stand-alone Java applications, applets, Java Web start (JNLP) applications, J2ME MIDlets, and Java Card applets. It also explores how to use Java security management tools to manage keys and certificates. This chapter also discusses the importance of applying Java code obfuscation techniques.

Chapter 4: Java Extensible Security Architecture and APIs

This chapter provides an in-depth discussion of the Java extensible security architecture and its API framework as well as how to utilize those API implementations for building end-to-end security in Java-based application solutions. In particular, the chapter illustrates how to use Java security APIs for applying cryptographic mechanisms and public-key infrastructure, how to secure application communication, and how to plug in third-party security providers in Java-based applications.

Chapter 5: J2EE Security Architecture

This chapter explains the J2EE security architecture and mechanisms and then illustrates how to apply them in the different application tiers and components. It features in-depth coverage of the J2EE security mechanisms applied to Web components (JSPs, Servlets, and JSFs), business components (EJBs), and integration components (JMS, JDBC, and J2EE connectors). This chapter also highlights

J2EE-based Web services security and relevant technologies. In addition, it illustrates the different architectural options for designing a DMZ network topology that delivers security to J2EE applications in production.

Part III: Web Services Security and Identity Management

Part III concentrates on the industry-standard initiatives and technologies used to enable Web services security and identity management.

Chapter 6: Web Services Security–Standards and Technologies

This chapter explains the Web services architecture, its core building blocks, common Web services security threats and vulnerabilities, Web services security requirements and Web services security standards and technologies. It provides in-depth details about how to represent XML-based security using industry-standard initiatives such as XML Signature, XML Encryption, XKMS, WS-Security, SAML Profile, REL Profile and WS-I Basic Security Profile. In addition, this chapter also introduces the Java-based Web services infrastructure providers and XML-aware security appliances that facilitate support for enabling security in Web services.

Chapter 7: Identity Management–Standards and Technologies

This chapter provides an in-depth look at the standards and technologies essential for managing identity information. It highlights the identity management challenges and then introduces the architectural models for implementing standards-based identity management. It illustrates how to represent XML standards such as SAML, XACML and Liberty Alliance (ID-*) specifications for enabling federated identity management and identity-enabled services.

Part IV: Security Design Methodology, Patterns, and Reality Checks

Part IV describes a security design methodology and introduces a patterns-driven security design approach that can be adopted as part of a software design and development process.

Chapter 8: The Alchemy of Security Design–Security Methodology, Patterns, and Reality Checks

This chapter begins with a high-level discussion about the importance of using a security design methodology and then details a security design process for identifying and applying security practices throughout the software life cycle including architecture, design, development, deployment, production, and retirement. The chapter describes various roles and responsibilities and explains core security analysis processes required for the analysis of risks, trade-offs, effects, factors, tier options, threat profiling, and trust modeling. This chapter also introduces the security design patterns catalog and security assessment checklists that can be applied during application development to address security requirements or provide solutions.

Part V: Design Strategies and Best Practices

Part V presents the security patterns, strategies, and best practices categorized specific to J2EE application tiers, Web services, Identity Management, and Service Provisioning.

Chapter 9: Securing the Web Tier–Design Strategies and Best Practices

This chapter presents seven security patterns that pertain to designing and deploying J2EE Web-tier and presentation components such as JSPs, servlets, and other related components. Each pattern addresses a common problem associated with the Web-tier or presentation logic and describes a design solution illustrating numerous implementation strategies. It describes the results of using the pattern, highlights security factors and their associated risks when using the pattern, and demonstrates verification of pattern applicability through the use of reality checks. The chapter also provides a comprehensive list of best practices for securing J2EE Web components and Web-based applications.

Chapter 10: Securing the Business Tier–Design Strategies and Best Practices

This chapter presents seven security patterns that pertain to designing and deploying J2EE Business-tier components such as EJBs, JMS, and other related components. Each pattern addresses a set of security problems associated with the Business tier and describes a design solution illustrating numerous implementation strategies along with the results of using the pattern. It highlights security factors and associated risks of using the Business-tier security pattern and finally verifies pattern applicability through the use of reality checks. The chapter also provides a comprehensive list of best practices and pitfalls in securing J2EE business components.

Chapter 11: Securing Web Services–Design Strategies and Best Practices

This chapter presents three security patterns that pertain to designing and deploying Web services. The chapter begins with a discussion of the Web services security infrastructure and key components that contribute to security. Then it describes each pattern, addresses the security problems associated with Web services, and describes a design solution illustrating numerous implementation strategies and consequences of using the Web services pattern. It also highlights security factors and associated risks using the pattern and verifies pattern applicability using reality checks. Finally, the chapter provides a comprehensive list of best practices and pitfalls in securing Web services.

Chapter 12: Securing the Identity–Design Strategies and Best Practices

This chapter presents three security patterns that pertain to Identity Management. Each pattern addresses an Identity Management-specific issue, describes a design solution illustrating implementation strategies, presents the results of using the pattern, and then highlights security factors and associated risks using the pattern. Finally, the chapter verifies pattern applicability using reality checks. It also provides a comprehensive list of best practices in Identity Management.

Chapter 13: Secure Service Provisioning–Design Strategies and Best Practices

This chapter begins with a high-level discussion of business challenges, the scope of Service Provisioning, and the relationship of Service Provisioning to Identity Management. Then it details the process for user account provisioning and discusses various architecture and application scenarios. It presents a security pattern that applies to user account provisioning and illustrates implementation strategies and the results of using the pattern. Then it highlights security factors and associated risks involved with using the pattern and verify pattern applicability using reality checks. This chapter also introduces SPML and its relevance in Service Provisioning. Finally, the chapter provides a comprehensive list of best practices for Service Provisioning.

Part VI: Putting It All Together

Part VI presents a case study that illustrates a real-world security implementation scenario and describes how to put the security design process to work using the patterns and best practices.

Chapter 14: Building an End-to-End Security Architecture–Case Study

This chapter uses a real-world example of a Web portal that shows how to define and implement an end-to-end security solution using the security design methodology, design patterns, and best practices introduced in this book. The chapter walks through the security design process, illustrating how to analyze and identify risks, how to balance trade-offs, how to identify and apply security patterns, and how to perform factor analysis, tier analysis, threat profiling, and reality checks.

The chapter also provides details about how to adopt a patterns-driven security design process, the pertinent do's and don'ts, and describes how to align security in different logical tiers together to deliver end-to-end security.

Part VII: Personal Identification Using Smart Cards and Biometrics

Part VII provides in-depth coverage on Personal Identification using Smart Cards and Biometrics. It delves into the enabling technologies, architecture, implementation strategies of using Smart Cards, Biometrics and combination of both.

Chapter 15: Secure Personal Identification Using Smart Cards and Biometrics

This chapter explores the concepts, technologies, architectural strategies, and best practices for implementing secure Personal Identification and authentication using Smart Cards and Biometrics. The chapter begins with a discussion of the importance of converging physical and logical access control and the role of using Smart Cards and Biometrics in Personal Identification. This chapter illustrates the architecture and implementation strategies for enabling Smart Cards and Biometrics-based authentication in J2EE–based enterprise applications, UNIX, and Windows environments as well as how to combine these in multifactor authentication. Finally, the chapter provides a comprehensive list of best practices for using Smart Cards and Biometrics in secure Personal Identification.

Companion Web Site

The official companion Web site for this book is www.coresecuritypatterns.com. All example illustrations found within this book can be downloaded from that site. The site will also include errata, changes, updates, and additional reading recommendations and references.

The Prentice Hall Web site for this book is http://www.phptr.com/title/ 0131463071.

Feedback

The authors would like to receive reader feedback, so we encourage you to post questions using the discussion forum linked to the Web site. You can also contact the authors at their prospective email addresses. Contact information can be found at www.coresecuritypatterns.com. The Web site also includes a reader's forum for public subscription and participation. Readers may also post their questions, share their views, and discuss related topics.

Welcome to ***Core Security Patterns***. We hope you enjoy reading this book as much as we enjoyed writing it. We trust that you will be able to adopt the theory, concepts, techniques, and approaches that we have discussed as you design, deploy, and upgrade the security of your IT systems—and keep those systems immune from all security risks and vulnerabilities in the future.

Chris, Ramesh, and Ray
www.coresecuritypatterns.com

Acknowledgments

"The learning and knowledge that we have,
is, at the most, but little compared with
that of which we are ignorant."
—Plato (427–347 B.C.)

The authors would like to extend their thanks to the Prentice Hall publishing team, including Greg Doench, Ralph Moore, Bonnie Granat, and Lara Wysong for their constant help and support in the process of creating this work.

We also thank Judy Lin, Joe Uniejewski, Whitfield Diffie, Li Gong, John Crupi, Danny Malks, Deepak Alur, Radia Perlman, Glenn Brunette, Bill Hamilton, and Shaheen Nasirudheen for their initial feedback and for sharing their best thoughts and advice.

Numerous others furnished us with in-depth reviews of the book and supported us with their invaluable expertise. Without their assistance, this book would not have become a reality. Our gratitude extends to Seth Proctor, Anne Anderson, Tommy Szeto, Dwight Hare, Eve Maler, Sang Shin, Sameer Tyagi, Rafat Alvi, Tejash Shah, Robert Skoczylas, Matthew MacLeod, Bruce Chapman, Tom Duell, Annie Kuo, Reid Williams, Frank Hurley, Jason Miller, Aprameya Puduthonse, Michael Howard, Tao Huang, and Sen Zhang.

We are indebted to our friends at Sun Microsystems, RSA Security, VeriSign, Microsoft, Oracle, Agilent Technologies, JPMorganChase, FortMoon Consulting, AC Technology, Advanced Biometric Controls, and the U. S. Treasury's Pay.Gov project for all their direct and indirect support and encouragement.

Chris Steel

I wish to thank all of the many people who contributed to my effort. First, I would like to thank the individuals that directly contributed content to my work.

- Frank Hurley, who single-handedly wrote Chapter 2 and who contributed a lot of material and references to the discussion of security fundamentals. Without Frank, I would have missed a lot of the security basics.
- Aprameya Paduthonse, who contributed several patterns across the Web and Business tiers. He also reviewed several chapters and was able to add content and fill in a lot of gaps quickly. Without Aprameya, I would have been even further behind schedule.
- Jason Miller, who contributed vast amounts of knowledge about the Web tier and who was responsible for the technical details about how the Web-tier patterns fit together. His understanding of Struts and Web tier frameworks is unsurpassed.

I also wish to express my deepest gratitude to our many reviewers. Their time and dedication to reviewing the book is what has kept this book on track.

In particular, my thanks go to Robert Skoczylas, whose thorough reviews and many suggestions to the chapters about Web tier and Business tier patterns have made my work much more cohesive and understandable. I have not had a better reviewer than Robert.

Ramesh Nagappan

Security has been one of my favorite subjects ever since I started working at Sun Microsystems. Although I worked mostly on Java distributed computing, I had plenty of opportunities to experiment with security technologies. With my passion for writing, a book on security has always been one of my goals, and now it has become a reality with the completion of this mammoth project.

It is always fun to have a look back and recall the genesis of this book: It was Sun's JavaSmart Day—Developer's conference in Boston (September 16, 2002), and after presenting to a huge audience on Web services security, Chris and I came out, tired and hungry. We sat down at The Cheesecake Factory, and while we refreshed ourselves, we came up with the idea of writing an applied security book for Java developers that would allow us to share our best kept secrets, tips, and techniques we'd been hiding up our sleeves. Over the course of the next few days, we created the proposal for this book. Greg Doench at Prentice Hall readily accepted our proposal, but Chris and I had a tough time keeping pace with the schedule. At one point, Greg asked me "Will the manuscript be ready before the Red Sox win the World Series—again?" Because Chris and I wanted to cover additional relevant topics in the book, it soon became an effort of much greater scope than initially planned. After a few months of increasing the scope of the book, Chris and I decided to invite Ray Lai to contribute to this book. That's how our writing journey began. During the course of writing, it's been great fun having a midnight conference call to discuss and share our thoughts and resolve issues. After more than two years of work on this book, I'm actually a bit surprised that it's done. It's a great feeling to see it turn out much beyond our thoughts as we envisioned back at The Cheesecake Factory.

First, I would like to thank and recognize the people who have directly or indirectly influenced me by providing me with opportunities to learn and to gain experience in working with security technologies. I would not have been able to gain the expertise necessary for the writing of this book without those opportunities. Thus, my thanks are extended to:

- Gary Lippert, Dave DiMillo, Li Gong, and Chris Steel, for giving me the opportunity to work with Java security technologies and J2EE application security projects.
- Sunil Mathew and William Olsen, for introducing me to real-world Web services projects and providing me with opportunities to test-drive my Web services security prototypes.
- Doug Bunting, for having introduced me to participation in Web services standards initiatives, particularly the OASIS WS-CAF and WS-Security working groups.
- Wayne Ashworth and Dan Fisher for giving me access to the world of Smart Cards and opportunities to work on Smart Card application prototypes.
- Art Sands, Chris Sands, Tuomo Lampinen, Jeff Groves, and Travis Hatmaker for allowing me to play with Biometric technologies and for providing opportunities to work on biometrics integration with Sun Identity Management products.
- Luc Wijns, Charles Andres, Sujeet Vasudevan for all the trust and confidence on my expertise and giving me a opportunity to prototype the Java Card-based Identity Management solution for a prestigious national ID project.

Second, I was fortunate enough to have an excellent team of reviewers whose insightful comments and suggestions considerably increased the quality of my work.

My sincere thanks go to Glenn Brunette, Shaheen Nasirudeen, Tommy Szeto, Sang Shin, Robert Skoczylas, Tejash Shah, Eve Maler, Rafat Alvi, Sameer Tyagi, Bruce Chapman, Tom Duell, Annie Kuo, and Reid Williams for all the excellent review comments that I incorporated into the chapters.

My special thanks go to Patric Chang and Matthew MacLeod for all their encouragement and recognition during my work on this book.

Finally, the largest share of credit goes to my loving wife Joyce, my son Roger, my little girl Kaitlyn 'Minmini,' and my parents for all their love, inspiration, and endless support. Only through their love and support was I able to accomplish this goal.

Ray Lai

I want to give thanks to God, who answered my prayer to complete this book, and to my family, who waited for me every night and weekend while I was writing.

I would like to also express thanks to the following individuals for their support:

- Dr. Glen Reece, Kumar Swaminathan, and Samir Patel for their management and moral support.
- Rafat Alvi, Glenn Brunette, Dwight Hare, Eve Maler, and Seth Procter, for their critical and honest review to ensure technical accuracy of the manuscript.
- Anne Anderson, for her critical review and suggestions for Chapter 7.

About the Authors

Christopher Steel, CISSP, ISSAP, is the President and CEO of FortMoon Consulting and was recently the chief architect on the U.S. Treasury's Pay.gov project. He has more than fifteen years experience in distributed enterprise computing with a strong focus on application security, patterns, and methodologies. Some of his clients include the U.S. Navy, Raytheon, Fleet, CVS Pharmacy, Nextel, Verizon, AOL, KPMG, MCI, and GTE. He presents regularly at local and industry conferences on topics of security.

Ramesh Nagappan is a Java Technology Architect at Sun Microsystems. With extensive industry experience, he specializes in Java distributed computing and Security architectures for mission-critical applications. Prior to this work, he has co-authored three best selling books on J2EE, EAI, and Web Services. He is an active contributor to open-source applications and industry standard initiatives. He frequently speaks at industry conferences related to Java, XML and Security. His current technology focus is on Web Services Security, Identity Management, and Secure Personal Identification technologies using Smart Cards and Biometrics.

Ray Lai is a Principal Engineer with Sun Microsystems, and is currently working in Sun's Chief Technology Office. He has developed and architected enterprise applications for leading multinational companies including HSBC, Visa, American

Express, UBS, Daiwa Securities, DHL, and Cathay Pacific Airway around the globe. He is also the author of *J2EE Platform Web Services* (Prentice Hall, 2004) and a frequent international conference speaker. His current technology focus includes application security, policy and service provisioning.

Part I

Introduction

Security by Default

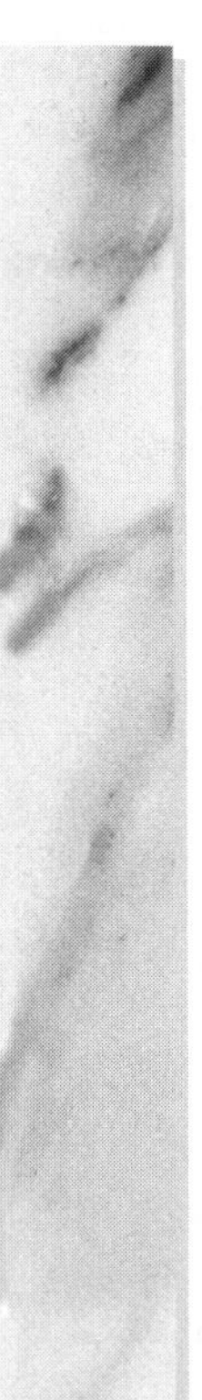

Topics in This Chapter

- Business Challenges Around Security
- What Are the Weakest Links?
- The Impact of Application Security
- The Four W's
- Strategies for Building Robust Security
- Proactive and Reactive Security
- The Importance of Security Compliance
- The Importance of Identity Management
- Secure Personal Identification
- The Importance of Java Technology
- Making Security a "Business Enabler"

Chapter 1

Security by Default

In today's world, everyone relies on information from a variety of sources and tends to depend on its accuracy and reliability in making their own business decisions. The rapid adoption of computing systems and network technologies in critical businesses and industry sectors has brought newer threats and risks such as service interruptions, unauthorized access, stealing and altering of information, impersonation, the spreading of viruses, and so on. This heightens the importance of security and presents every business and organization with the ethical and legal responsibility to properly secure its information by using appropriate measures and processes. Enforcing security at all levels ensures that information is processed, stored, or transmitted with reliability and that it is available to all authorized entities.

The unfortunate reality, however, is that security today is often considered as a post-deployment event at the end of the development phase or as an after-the-fact reactive action when something goes wrong. While most businesses and organizations recognize the importance of information security, it is alarming to note that very few have implemented strategies and processes to proactively identify and counter the myriad risks they face. Adopting security in a reactive and risk-averse way often results in businesses and organizations suffering huge financial losses and losing customer confidence. For instance, according to a recent FBI/Computer Security Institute survey (refer to [CSI2003] and [CSI2004] for details), the financial loss worldwide as a result of malicious code attacks was about $455.8 million in 2002, $201 million in 2003, and $141 million in 2004. In

2003, denial-of-service attacks were the source of a $65 million loss, and the theft of proprietary information averaged $2.7 million per incident. With the number of cyber crimes constantly increasing, the cost of security attacks can be highly damaging to both businesses and their customers. The most troubling problem is that most business applications and services are not designed for security and are deployed without eliminating their inherent risks. Architects and developers have chosen to adopt a physical security solution during deployment and have then used a reactive approach for handling post-deployment security issues. In some organizations, there is a huge cognitive disconnect between the importance of information security and its alignment with their key business objectives. This cognitive disconnect seriously affects actual business security, because security is not seen as a business enabler until the potential losses due to threats and vulnerabilities are understood—usually by an actual financial loss.

Every business and organization must understand the critical importance of information security. Then it must adopt a proactive and holistic approach that can help it reduce and manage the risks associated with network applications and services throughout the business cycle. In simpler terms, it is critically important to understand what security represents to us and to know the challenges that are involved in building robust security into a business service. Those common challenges include answering the following questions:

- How do we identify risks?
- How do we protect resources?
- How do we build application or service level defense mechanisms?
- How do we enforce authentication and authorization?
- How do we prevent identity theft?
- How do we establish access control policies?
- How do we resist internal and external attacks?
- How do we detect malicious code?
- How do we overcome service interruptions?
- How do we assess and test countermeasures?
- How do we monitor and audit for threats and vulnerabilities?

This book introduces a radical approach called *Security by Default* that delivers robust security architecture from the ground up and proactively assists in implementing appropriate countermeasures and safeguards. This approach adopts security as a key component of the software development life cycle—from design and development through post-production operations. It is based on a structured security design methodology, is pattern-driven, and adopts industry best practices that help security architects and developers identify situations of *what, why, when, where* and *how* to evolve and apply end-to-end security measures during the application design process as well as in the production or operations environment.

This chapter discusses current business challenges, the weakest links in security, and critical application flaws and exploits. Then it introduces the basic concepts behind *Security by Default* and addresses the importance of a security design process methodology, pattern-driven security development, best practices, and reality checks. Because this book focuses on Java platform-based applications and services, this chapter introduces an overview of the Java platform security. It also highlights the importance of identity management and other emerging security technologies. Finally, it discusses how to make a case for security as a business enabler and reviews the potential benefits brought by approaching security in this way.

Business Challenges Around Security

The overwhelming adoption of Internet- and network-centric applications and services offered unlimited opportunities for businesses and organizations to offer customers, partners, and employees convenient access to the information they need. The result has been increased efficiency, mobility, and collaboration—all at a reduced cost. However, this innovative action has opened the door to malicious activities, exploits, and attacks by hackers, disgruntled employees, and cyber criminals. Businesses and organizations are now facing a growing number of security threats and vulnerabilities—both internally and externally—and there are, unfortunately, no easy answers or solutions. The causes of today's increasing vulnerability of businesses are primarily related to the current methods of meeting business challenges and their ineffectiveness in implementing security.

The key factors that contribute to the ineffectiveness of current methods of meeting business challenges are as follows:

- *Security as an add-on*: Applying security features is often considered as the last effort of the deployment phase in a typical software development cycle. This is the result of a failure to adopt proactive approaches in the design phase. When security is an afterthought, the system remains unprotected from many threats and associated risks.
- *Architectural inefficiencies*: The failure to analyze security risks and tradeoffs during the architectural design process results in an inefficient system

architecture that is vulnerable to more exploits and attacks than would be the case had security been considered during the design process.

- *Security patches and upgrades*: The failure to install and configure security-related patches and upgrades leaves all of the existing security loopholes in place in the deployment infrastructure.
- *Proprietary solutions and compatibility*: Adopting proprietary security solutions often results in compatibility issues that affect interoperability with other standards-based systems environments. This problem also affects further scalability and extensibility of the overall security infrastructure.
- *Poor infrastructure choices*: Choosing a platform infrastructure that has known security bugs and flaws increases platform-specific threats and vulnerabilities.
- *Poor operational practices*: Lack of audit and control over production operations leads to failures in detecting malicious activities and vulnerabilities.
- *Poor identification and verification processes*: Lack of identification and verification processes in business applications leads to identity theft, impersonation, and identity fraud.
- *Poor configuration management*: Improper security configuration and the failure to verify configuration parameters and settings affects operational efficiency and increases the likelihood of an attack.
- *Poor security policies and controls*: Lack of security policies related to business applications and failure to exercise tighter access control impairs data confidentiality and can adversely affect the target data and its associated owners.
- *Lack of expertise*: Most security administrators focus on network and infrastructure security and tend to ignore application-specific and content-level vulnerabilities. This leads to application and content-level attacks such as malicious code injection, cross-site scripting, XML attacks, and so on.
- *Awareness and training issues*: Lack of security awareness among personnel leads to unintended disclosure of confidential data and processes. The failure to train business staff leads to accidental security issues and potential abuses of the infrastructure.
- *Lack of management priorities:* Poor management focus on security matters and improper handling of security-related incidents adversely affects the business, causing it to incur losses because of its inappropriate choices and wrong directives.

In addition to the above challenges, there are still many technical and management issues that remain unaddressed. These issues will be the roadblocks in identifying the nature and degree of potential threats and implementing efficient safeguards against those threats and vulnerabilities.

What Are the Weakest Links?

Security is like a chain—it is only as strong as its weakest link. The concept of building and achieving end-to-end security encompasses all IT systems' infrastructure components such as hosts, applications, users, network devices, client applications, communications, and so on. From a security standpoint, every resource in an IT system's infrastructure is vulnerable to security breaches and malicious activities. The overall security architecture of an IT system's infrastructure relies on three fundamental IT infrastructure components: the network services, the host operating system, and the target application. Any security loophole or flaw in any one of these three components can be exploited. In the worst case, a hacker can compromise the entire IT infrastructure. These three components could be the weakest links in the chain that secures an IT system's infrastructure end-to-end.

The Network Services

A network is a group of computers or information devices and associated peripherals connected by a communications channel capable of sharing information and resources between computers, applications, users, and other networks. A typical network uses routers, switches, and firewalls. Contributors to the security of a network include network firewalls, Intrusion Detection Systems (IDS), Router Access Control Lists (ACL), Virtual Private Networks (VPN), and SSL/Cryptographic accelerator appliances. These devices enforce access control by examining and filtering the inbound and outbound traffic routed between the networks. The network-level security is limited to protecting the network resources from IP connection attacks and to packet filtering for unauthorized ports, protocols, and services. Because of this limitation, resources are still publicly accessible and vulnerable to attacks via the network communication channels that are open for inbound and outbound traffic to support, for example, Web servers that use the HTTP protocol and mail servers that use the SMTP protocol. For example, in Web services communications, the XML traffic tunnels through using the HTTP and HTTP/SSL ports of a firewall. Such access allows hackers and criminals to abuse the network by attacking content-level vulnerabilities with malicious code injection, virus attachments, buffer overflow, content-based denial-of-service, and so on.

The Host Operating System (OS)

The OS plays a vital role in running, managing, and controlling hardware and software applications and in interacting with other hosts and with network-enabled applications. An OS consists of surplus functionalities and services such as tools and utilities that support administration, application deployment, and end users. The typical out-of-the-box OS provides for an insecure configuration that uses a default security policy. Such a configuration leaves the OS open to exploitation and attack by hackers. Information theft, spreading viruses, trojan horses, software buffer overflows, password cracking, and so on are all invited by the default configuration. Applying OS Hardening and minimization techniques reduces the risks by establishing an OS-level security policy, eliminating non-essential utilities and tools, disabling unused services and ports, updating the environment with security-specific patches and upgrades, and so on. The end result of OS hardening and minimization is a bastion host—a host with improved resistance that provides safeguards against all known threats. Without implementing an OS hardening and minimization process or adopting a trusted OS environment, a network-connected host will always be vulnerable to security threats.

The Application or Service

An application or service is a software program composed of one or more components that act as executable business functions, processes, or user presentation interfaces running within one or more hosts in a network. An application is vulnerable to security breaches if it is not protected against all known threats to functions, deployments, and operations. A risk or a flaw can be exploited by a hacker if it exists in any low-level area: code, data, input/output validation, exception handling, sign-on, access control, library linking, configuration management, session handling, connection, communication, or program execution.

The Impact of Application Security

A Gartner Group report [CSO online] estimates that employees of companies are responsible for more than 70% of the unauthorized access to information systems in those companies. It is also employees of companies who perpetrate more than 95% of the information systems intrusions that cause significant financial losses. The survey also highlights that a majority of organizations tend to see the importance of security only after actually suffering damage from security breaches. Real-life experience must generally occur before these organizations will allow architects and application developers to get involved with instituting security measures. Businesses are becoming more aware that computer security incidents can originate inside the organization as well as outside. Insider attacks are worse than outside attacks and are usually more malicious. The attacker abuses user privileges or steals application-specific administrator rights and then gains access to resources such as financial applications and other confidential information repositories. With the wide adoption of Internet-enabled applications, businesses and organizations are experiencing a growing rate of security-related damage, such as denial-of-access, exposure of confidential data, unauthorized transactions, identity theft, and data corruption. Most of these issues are more associated with application-specific security flaws and the failure of applications to defend against known threats.

According to an FBI survey [eWeek] of 500 companies, 90 percent said they'd had a computer security breach, and 80 percent of those said they'd suffered financial loss as a result. A 2003 Federal Trade Commission survey [FTC findings] found that 27.3 million Americans have been victims of identity theft in the last five years, including 9.9 million people in 2002 alone. According to the survey, businesses and financial institutions in 2002 lost nearly $48 billion due to identity theft; consumer victims reported losses of $5 billion. After some prodding, the University of Washington Medical Center [AMNews] acknowledged that a hacker had infiltrated its computer system and stolen the confidential records of thousands of patients. Another interesting story [online-kasino] comes from an online gambling casino, where a hacker gained access to the gaming application and corrupted the game so that gamblers could not lose. In just a few hours, gamblers racked up winnings of $1.9 million dollars.

In most organizations, the importance of application-level security is often underestimated until an application faces a major security breach that causes a serious loss or downtime. Most of the time it is clear that the probable cause of the failure is related to deficiencies in the application architecture and design, the programming, the coding security, the runtime platform, and the tools and utilities used. The primary responsibility, of course, belongs to the application architects and developers who contributed to the application design and program code. As a result, today it is mandatory to adopt a proactive security approach during the application development life cycle that identifies critical security aspects. Architects and developers today must design security into their applications proactively.

Let's now take a look at how the most common application-specific security flaws and exploits compromise the security of an application or service.

Critical Application Security Flaws and Exploits

In this section, we will see the most common application flaws that are critical to security and how they can be exploited by hackers.

Input Validation Failures

Validating the input parameters before accepting the request and resuming the process is critical to application security. It is also a good practice to validate all inputs—from both trusted and untrusted resources. This practice will help in avoiding application-level failures and attacks from both intentional hackers and unintentional abusers. Input validation is a mechanism for validating data such as data type (string, integer), format, length, range, null-value handling, verifying for character-set, locale, patterns, context, legal values and validity, and so on. For example, if a form-based Web application fails to encode square brackets ("[" and "]"), a remote user can create a specially crafted URL that will cause the target user's browser to execute some arbitrary scripting code when the URL is loaded. This can cause a malicious code injection attack, depending on the impact of the scripting code executed. If an application relies on client-side data validation, any flaw may be exploited by a hacker. It is always a good practice to re-verify and validate input, even after client-side validation. From a security perspective, it is very important that all input data are validated prior to application processing. Refer to [InputValidation] for details.

Output Sanitation

Re-displaying or echoing the data values entered by users is a potential security threat because it provides a hacker with a means to match the given input and its output. This provides a way to insert malicious data inputs. With Web pages, if the page generated by a user's request is not properly sanitized before it is displayed, a hacker may be able to identify a weakness in the generated output. Then the hacker can design malicious HTML tags to create pop-up banners; at the worst, hackers may be able to change the content originally displayed by the site. To prevent these issues from arising, the generated output must be verified for all known values. Any unknown values not intended for display must be eliminated. All comments and identifiers in the output response must also be removed.

Buffer Overflow

When an application or process tries to store more data in a data storage or memory buffer than its fixed length or its capacity can handle, the extra information is likely to go somewhere in adjacent buffers. This event causes corruption or overwrite in the buffer that holds the valid data and can abruptly end the process, causing the application to crash. To design this kind of attack, a hacker passes malicious input by tampering or manipulating the input parameters to force an application buffer overflow. Such an act usually leads to denial-of-service attacks. Buffer overflow attacks are typically carried out using application weaknesses related to input validation, output sanitization, and data injection flaws.

Data Injection Flaw

Security intruders can piggyback user data or inject malicious code together with user data while exploiting a weakness in the user data input environment. Data injection flaws are often found in browsers with pop-up windows (window injection vulnerability) or in SQL statements when external input is transmitted directly into SQL (SQL injection vulnerability). In a window injection flaw scenario, security intruders can "hijack" a named Web browser window after a user opens both a malicious Web site and a trusted Web site in separate browser windows. This assumes that the trusted Web site opens up a pop-up window and that the malicious Web site is aware of the name of the pop-up window. To avoid data injection flaws, it is important to enforce thorough input validation; that is, all input values, query strings, form fields, cookies, client-side scripts must be validated for known and valid values only. The rest of them must be rejected. Refer to [SQLInjection] and [InjectionFlaw] for details.

Cross-Site Scripting (XSS)

With XSS, a Web application can gather information by using a hyperlink or script that contains malicious content. An attacker typically uses this mechanism to inject malicious code into a target Web server or to deliver to users a malicious link that redirects them to another Web server. The attackers frequently use JavaScript, VBScript, ActiveX, HTML, or Flash in a vulnerable Web application to gather data from the current user. Based on the user interaction with the target Web server, the script may hijack the user's account information, change user privileges, steal cookie or session information, poison the user-specific content, and so on. Thus, it is important to diagnose and test the application for XSS risks and vulnerabilities.

Improper Error Handling

Most applications are susceptible to security issues related to error handling when they display detailed internal error messages about application conditions such as out of memory, null pointer exceptions, system call failure, database access failure, network timeout, and so on. This information usually reveals internal details of implementation, failure conditions, and the runtime environment. Hackers can make use of this information to locate a weak point in the application and design an attack. This information helps hackers crash applications or cause them to throw error messages by sending invalid data that forces the applications to access non-existent databases or resources. Adopting proper error handling mechanisms will display error messages as user-specific messages based on user input; no internal details related to the application environment or its components will be revealed. All user-specific error messages are mapped to underlying application-specific error conditions and stored as log files for auditing. In the event of an attack, the log files provide diagnostic information for verifying the errors and for further auditing.

Insecure Data Transit or Storage

Confidentiality of data in transit or storage is very important, because most security is compromised when data is represented in plain text. Adopting cryptographic mechanisms and data encryption techniques helps ensure the integrity and confidentiality of data in transit or storage.

Weak Session Identifiers

Issuing or using session identifiers before authentication or over unencrypted communication channels allows hackers to steal session information and then hijack the associated user sessions for unauthorized business transactions. Representing the session identifiers as cleartext helps the hacker to spoof the user identity information using the session attributes. This weakness intensifies if the service provider or Web applications do not validate the identity information obtained from the session identifier of the service requester or if they do not set an expiry time for the session. To prevent these issues, the application should issue encrypted session identifiers after initiating a secure communication channel using SSL that ensures confidentiality and integrity of the session information.

Weak Security Tokens

Weak security tokens refer to the use of password security tokens that allow hackers to guess passwords by using a dictionary or token decrypting tools and to impersonate the user. Some Web applications may also echo back their passwords as Base64 values that are susceptible to an attack and are easily reproducible. If the HTML scripts or Web applications echo the password or security token, hackers may intercept them and then impersonate the user for unauthorized access. A weak security token is a common security problem in authentication and application session management. To address the vulnerabilities they cause, adopting strong authentication or multifactor authentication mechanisms using digital certificates, biometrics, or smart cards are usually considered. Thus, it is important to protect the password files and also ensure that the passwords being used on accounts cannot easily be guessed or cracked by hackers.

Weak Password Exploits

Passwords are the weakest mechanisms for user authentication because they can be easily guessed or compromised by a hacker who is watching the keystrokes or using password-cracking tools to obtain data from password files. When a password is stolen, it is very difficult to identify the culprit while an application is being abused or attacked. Thus, it is important to protect password files by using encrypted files and to ensure that the stored passwords cannot be retrieved, easily guessed, or cracked by hackers. Adoption of strong authentication or multifactor authentication mechanisms using digital certificates, biometrics, or smart cards is strongly recommended. Weak password exploits are one of the most common security issues in network-enabled applications. Refer to [PasswordExploit] for an example.

Weak Encryption

Encryption allows the scrambling of data from plaintext to ciphertext by means of cryptographic algorithms. Using computers with lots of processing power can compromise weaker algorithms. Algorithm key-lengths exceeding 56 bits are considered strong encryption, but in most cases, using 128-bits and above is usually recommended.

Session Theft

Also referred to as session hijacking, session theft occurs when attackers create a new session or reuse an existing session. Session theft hijacks a client-to-server or server-to-server session and bypasses the authentication. Hackers do not need to intercept or inject data into the communication between hosts. Web applications that use a single SessionID for multiple client-server sessions are also susceptible to session theft, where session theft can be at the Web application session level, the host session level, or the TCP protocol. In a TCP communication, session hijacking is done via IP spoofing techniques, where an attacker uses source-routed IP packets to insert commands into an active TCP communication between the two communicating systems and disguises himself as one of the authenticated users. In Web-based applications, session hijacking is done via forging or guessing SessionIDs and stealing SessionID cookies. Preventing session hijacking is one of the first steps in hardening Web application security, because session information usually carries sensitive data such as credit card numbers, PINs, passwords, and so on. To prevent session theft, always invalidating a session after a logout, adopting PKI solutions for encrypting session information, and adopting a secure communication channel (such as SSL/TLS) are often considered best practices. Refer to [SessionHijack] for details.

Insecure Configuration Data

A variety of configuration-related issues in the application or its server infrastructure impact the security of business applications, particularly in the Web Tier and the Business Tier. The most common examples are misconfigured SSL certificates and encryption settings, use of default certificates, default accounts with default passwords, and misconfigured Web server plug-ins. To prevent issues, it is important to test and verify the environment for configuration-related weaknesses. Refer to [InsecureConfig] for details.

Broken Authentication

Broken authentication is caused by improper configuration of authentication mechanisms and flawed credential management that compromise application authentication through password change, forgotten password, account digital update, certificate issues, and so on. Attackers compromise vulnerable applications by manipulating credentials such as user passwords, keys, session cookies, or security tokens and then impersonating a user. To prevent broken authentication, the application must verify its authentication mechanisms and enforce reauthentication by verifying the requesting user's credentials prior to granting access to the application. Refer to [BrokenAuth] for details.

Broken Access Control

Access control determines an authenticated user's rights and privileges for access to an application or data. Any access control failure leads to loss of confidential information and unauthorized disclosure of protected resources such as application data, functions, files, folders, databases, and so on. Access control problems are directly related to the failure to enforce application-specific security policies and the lack of policy enforcement in application design. To prevent access control failures, it is important to verify the application-specific access control lists for all known risks and to run a penetration test to identify potential failures. Refer to [ACLFailure] for details.

Policy Failures

Security policy provides rules and conditions that are used to determine what actions should be taken in response to defined events. In general, business and organizations adopt security policies to enforce access control in IT applications, firewalls, anti-spam processing, message routing, service provisioning, and so on. If there are insufficient or missing rules, invalid conditions or prerequisites, or conflicting rules, the security policy processing will not be able to enforce the defined security rules. Applications can thus be vulnerable due to policy failures. With such failures, hackers can discover and exploit any resource loophole. Policy failure is a security issue for application design and policy management.

Audit and Logging Failures

Auditing and logging mechanisms facilitate non-repudiation services that provide irrefutable evidence about all application events. They help to record all key application events. Any audit or logging failure can cripple the ability of an application to diagnose suspicious activity and foil malicious attacks. Applications also cannot trace exceptions and specific bugs if audit and logging failure is present. Monitoring of auditing and logging processes of applications with high-availability is vital. Log files must be secured by restricted access.

Denial of Service (DOS) and Distributed DOS (DDOS)

DOS and DDOS are the worst form of network-level attacks. They can affect applications in many ways, including excessive consumption of nonrenewable resources such as network bandwidth, memory, CPU utilization, storage, and so on. They can also cause destruction of host configuration information, resulting in application failures and OS crashes. Traditional DOS is an attack by a single machine on another machine; DDOS initiates an attack by distributing and coordinating it from several machines. Hackers initiate DOS or DDOS attacks by exploiting application weaknesses and flaws related to resource management, authentication, error handling and application configuration. Web-based applications are highly susceptible to DOS and DDOS attacks, and in some cases it is impossible to identify whether the incoming service request is an attack or ordinary traffic. It is extremely difficult to adopt preventive measures for DOS and DDOS, although possible approaches include hostname verification and implementation of router filtering to drop connections from attacks initiated from untrusted hosts and networks. Refer to [DOS] for details.

Man-in-the-Middle (MITM)

A MITM attack is a security attack in which the hacker is able to read or modify business transactions or messages between two parties without either party knowing about it. Attackers may execute man-in-the-middle attacks by spoofing the business transactions, stealing user credentials, or exploiting a flaw in the underlying public key infrastructure or Web browser. For example, Krawczyk illustrates a man-in-the-middle attack on a user using Microsoft Internet Explorer while connecting to an SSL server. Man-in-the-middle is a security issue in application design and application infrastructure. Refer to [Krawczyk] for details.

Multiple Sign-On Issues

Multiple sign-on is a common issue in an enterprise application integration environment. It requires a user to log on multiple times because the integrated application does not share a common sign-on mechanism within the environment. This makes an application vulnerable due to the required multiple sign-on actions. When a user switches applications within a server, hackers can compromise security by using credentials from previous sign-on sessions. In addition, users are required to explicitly sign off from every application session within the server. This can result in an increase in human error, loss of productivity, and frequent failure to access all the applications in which they have access rights.

Adopting Single Sign-On (SSO) mechanisms solves these problems by eliminating the need for users to remember usernames and passwords other than their initial application login. SSO also increases productivity, because users no longer need to physically enter repetitive usernames and passwords or other forms of authentication credentials.

Deployment Problems

Many security exposure issues and vulnerabilities occur by chance because of application deployment problems. These include inconsistencies within and conflicts between application configuration data and the deployment infrastructure (hosts, network environment, and so on). Human error in policy implementation also contributes to these problems. In some cases, deployment problems are due to application design flaws and related issues. To prevent these problems, it is important to review and test all infrastructure security policies and to make sure application-level security policies reflect the infrastructure security policies, and vice versa. Where there are conflicts, the two policies will need to be reconciled.

Some trade-offs in constraints and restrictions related to OS administration, services, protocols, and so on may need to be made.

Coding Problems

Coding practices greatly influence application security. Coding issues also cause flaws and erroneous conditions in programming and application program flow. Other issues related to input validation, race conditions, exceptions, runtime failures, and so on may also be present. To ensure better coding practices are followed, it is always recommended to adopt a coding review methodology followed by source code scanning so that all potential risks and vulnerabilities can be identified and corrected.

The Four W's

Critical security flaws and exploits can exist across multiple server or application components. This fact reinforces the critical importance of end-to-end security—not just security for a server or a specific application component. However, how should security architects and developers begin establishing end-to-end security? We can get started from the perspective of the four W's:

- Which applications are we protecting?
- Who are we protecting the applications from?
- Where should we protect them?
- Why are we protecting them?

End-to-end security requires a particular scope and has implications based on deployment environment constraints such as network services, operating systems, and the application and identity infrastructure. The four W's can help us to identify and define those boundary constraints that are relevant to a particular deployment environment.

Which Applications Are We Protecting?

Business applications and mission-critical business services require protection from unauthorized access, and they use different levels of security access control. It is important to identify and determine which application resources need security and access control. To do so, security and access control may need to be designed based on:

- Network applications
- Network boundaries
- Business data or messages
- Required user-specific operations and transactions
- Required administrative tasks

Who Are We Protecting the Applications From?

Applications and resources that contain personal data or sensitive business transactions require protection from users other than the owner. In other words, the system needs to protect these applications and resources from the public Internet and unauthorized users. It is important for security architects and developers to consider the possibility of protecting these applications and resources by categorizing users in their organization by rights and privileges granted. Users can then be grouped based on their access rights. Security architects and developers should also consider giving access to highly confidential data or strategic resources to only a few trusted administrators. It may be prudent not to allow administrators to access data or resources unless they have an active user account specifically defined to carry out only selected operations. Throughout the application life-cycle, logging, monitoring, and auditing user access and application events is necessary.

Where Should We Protect Them?

Understanding which applications need protection and from whom is not sufficient for end-to-end security. The next important consideration is where we should protect them. The protection should address all the aspects of an application and its associated resources, including its different tiers, components, users, hosts, and network infrastructure. The enforced protection can be based on architecturally significant security criteria such as the specific location (e.g., single or multiple server machine, intranet, or Internet), type of connection (e.g., TCP/IP or SOAP), nature of the objects or resource (e.g., database objects), communication (e.g., SSL/TLS, IPSec), client infrastructure, and so on.

Why Are We Protecting Them?

A fault in the system security of business applications may cause great damage to an organization or to individual clients. Understanding the potential for damage from security breaches will help security architects and developers protect business applications and resources properly. Thus, it is important to understand the threat levels and vulnerabilities and then plan and establish a service recovery and continuity program for all potential failures.

Strategies for Building Robust Security

The four W's of security help us define the outline of what end-to-end security may entail. End-to-end security requires a proactive approach—the essential security strategies and decisions for the application must be made and adopted during the design and architecture phases, not at the time of deployment. Security by default mechanisms must be implemented by using a structured methodology, patterns-driven design, adoption of best practices, risk verification through reality checks, and proactive assessment of deployment architecture. The robustness of security also needs to be enhanced by using defensive strategies, security profiling, and security recovery and continuity strategies.

Let's take a look at some of the concepts and strategies that contribute to building robust security architecture and design.

Unified Process for Security Design

Unified Process (UP) is the de facto standard for the software application development process. It addresses all disciplines of the application development life cycle—from requirements gathering to deployment. In addition, it provides a set of supporting disciplines such as configuration management, project management, environment, operations, and support. However, it does not have specific guidelines for security. It would be extremely useful if security design principles were incorporated as a discipline in the UP-based application development life cycle. Chapter 8, "The Alchemy of Security Design–Methodology, Patterns, and Reality Checks," introduces such a UP-based security design methodology.

Design Patterns

A design pattern is a reusable solution to a recurring design problem. Design patterns are usually considered successful solution strategies and best practices for resolving common software design problems. In a typical security solution, they allow application-level security design with reusable security components and frameworks. In a typical security design scenario, patterns help architects and developers to communicate security knowledge, to define a new design paradigm or architectural style, and to identify risks that have traditionally been identified only by prototyping or experience.

Best Practices

Best practices are selected principles and guidelines derived from real-world experience that have been identified by industry experts as applicable practices. They are considered exceptionally well-suited to contributing to the improvement of design and implementation techniques. They are also promoted for adoption in the performance of a process or an activity within a process. They are usually represented as do's and don'ts.

Reality Checks

Reality checks are a collection of review items used to identify specific application behavior. They assist in the analysis of whether the applied design principles are practicable, feasible, and effective under all required circumstances. There are many grand design principles and theories in the application security area, but some of them may not be practical. Reality checks can help identify alternatives that have fewer penalties but achieve the same goals.

Proactive Assessment

Proactive assessment is a process of using existing security knowledge and experience and then applying it in order to prevent the same problems from recurring. It also predicts what is likely to occur if preventive measures are not implemented.

Profiling

A complementary strategy to proactive assessment is security profiling and optimization. Using featured tools, it helps in identifying risks and vulnerabilities and in verifying mandated regulatory or compliance requirements on an ongoing basis. These tools execute a set of scripts that detect existing vulnerabilities and mitigate risks by means of required changes or patches.

Defensive Strategies

Defensive strategies are a set of proactive and reactive actions that thwart security breaches. They are usually represented by a plan of action that helps to identify and restrict a security violation early—while it is still at a low level. These strategies should present explicit instructions for their use and should also present instructions for use when a low-level breach is missed and the attack has progressed to a higher level.

Recovery and Continuity Strategies

Despite the presence of proactive assessment and defensive strategies, there are still unknown security issues that one may encounter. These can cause serious application failures and service shutdown. It is therefore important to have a recovery and continuity plan for those services that support recovery and business continuity. A comprehensive recovery and continuity plan can reduce operational risks by reducing downtime.

Proactive and Reactive Security

Adopting proactive security measures means actively improving application design and implementation as well as using preventive measures to avoid security breaches. For example, using firewall appliances in the DMZ environment, implementing security design using design patterns, and using best practices are proactive strategies. Security architects and developers often need to defend such a strategy by presenting a business case that clearly explains its benefits. Doing so is not always easy.

Adopting reactive security measures means performing a series of post-incident remedial or corrective actions that address security threats and their resulting damage. Reactive security measures are a response to an actual security breach after it has occurred: identifying the problem, determining the possible cause, and restricting further damage. Examples of reactive security measures include using service continuity and recovery strategies, antivirus tools, patch management, and so on.

In practice, it is important to strike a balance between proactive and reactive security options by studying the trade-offs and effects based on business requirements such as regulatory mandates, technological dependencies and potential operating costs.

The Importance of Security Compliance

An emerging business driver for proactive security comes from federal and state government regulatory compliance requirements. These laws and regulations define high-level requirements for the protection of information. All organizations must comply with them. As a result, awareness about security compliance is increasing in every industry worldwide. Businesses face mandatory compliance with those legislative and regulatory requirements, and therefore they must protect their critical business and identity information, operations, systems, and applications. Some laws and regulations suggest guidelines and best practices by referring to industry standards and frameworks from NIST, COBIT, ISO 17779, and FFIEC.

Let's take a look at some of the core objectives of the major laws and regulations.

Sarbanes-Oxley Act

The Sarbanes-Oxley Act of 2002 (SOX) is a United States federal law designed to rebuild public trust in corporate business and reporting practices and to prevent the recent corporate ethics scandals and governance problems from recurring. SOX requires all public U.S. companies to comply with a set of mandatory regulations dealing with financial reporting and corporate accountability. Any failure to comply with this law can result in federal penalties.

While SOX does not prescribe a solution to the compliance issue, it does make clear what obligations a company is under in order to be compliant. Section 404(a) of the Act requires establishing "adequate internal controls" around financial reporting and its governance. The term "internal controls" refers to a series of processes that companies must adhere to in the preparation of financial reports as well as in the protection of the financial information that goes into making the reports. This financial information must also be protected as stored in various locations throughout the enterprise (including enterprise applications, database tools, and even accounting spreadsheets). The information technology and its related processes generate the majority of data that makes up financial reports, and as such, it is critical that the effectiveness of these processes can be verified. The security and identity management aspects of IT play a critical part in ensuring that a company is in compliance with the law. If they do not properly work, the risk to the corporation and the potential personal liability of its executives can be significant.

From an IT security perspective, as mentioned in the previous paragraph, the SOX Act does not explicitly contain any prescriptive processes and definitions. It also does not articulate what "adequate internal controls" means or what solutions must be implemented in order to create them. However, by drawing from industry best practices for security and control of other types of information, several inferences can be made.

According to industry experts, a quick review of the legislation reveals the following common requirements for internal control:

- A readily available, verifiable audit trail and auditable evidence of all events, privileges, and so on should be established.

- Immediate notification of audit policy violations, exceptions, and anomalies must be made.
- Real-time and accurate disclosure must be made for all material events within 48 hours.
- Access rights in distributed and networked environments should be effectively controlled and managed.
- Companies should be able to remove terminated employees' or contractors' access to applications and systems immediately.
- Companies should be able to confirm that only authorized users have access to sensitive information and systems.
- Control over access to multiuser information systems should be put in place—including the elimination of multiple user IDs and accounts for individual persons.
- The allocation of passwords should be managed, and password security policies must be enforced.
- Appropriate measures must be taken to prevent unauthorized access to computer system resources and the information held in application systems.

The SOX Act has certainly raised the bar and the level of interest in the role of information security in improving application and system capabilities. Refer to [SOX1] and [SOX2] for details.

Gramm-Leach-Bliley Act

The Gramm-Leach-Bliley Act (GLB), which was previously known as the Financial Services Modernization Act, is a United States federal law that was passed in 1999. The GLB Act was established primarily to repeal restrictions on banks affiliated with securities firms, but it also requires financial institutions to adopt strict privacy measures relating to customer data. The law applies to any organization that works with people who prepare income tax returns, consumer credit reporting agencies, real estate transaction settlement services, debt collection agencies, and people who receive protected information from financial institutions.

From an IT security perspective, there are three provisions of the GLB Act that restrict the collection and use of consumer data. The first two, the Financial Privacy Rule and the Pretexting Provisions, detail responsible business practices and are mainly outside the scope of information security duties. The third provision, the Safeguards Rule, went into effect during 2003 and requires subject institutions to take proactive steps to ensure the security of customer information.

While financial institutions have traditionally been more security-conscious than institutions in other industries, the GLB Act requires financial institutions to reevaluate their security policies and take action if deficiencies are discovered.

The following are key information security actions that financial institutions must perform under the GLB Act:

- Evaluate IT environments and understand their security risks; define internal and external risks to the organization.
- Establish information security policies to assess and control risks; these include authentication, access control, and encryption systems.
- Conduct independent assessments—third-party testing of the institution's information security infrastructure.
- Provide training and security awareness programs for employees.
- Scrutinize business relationships to ensure they have adequate security.
- Establish procedures to upgrade security programs that are in place.

From a technical perspective, the security requirements set forth in the GLB Act seem to be enormous, but these requirements can be met by a robust security policy that is enforced across the enterprise. Refer to [GrammLeach1] and [GrammLeach2] for details.

HIPPA

HIPPA refers to the Health Insurance Privacy and Portability Act of 1996. HIPPA requires that institutions take steps to protect the confidentiality of patient information. Achieving HIPPA compliance means implementing security standards that govern how healthcare plans, providers, and clearinghouses transmit, access, and store protected health information in electronic form. HIPPA privacy regulations require that the use of personal health information (PHI) be limited to that which is minimally necessary to administer treatment. Such limitations must be based on the requirements of various HIPPA provisions regarding parents and minors; information used in marketing, research, and payment processes; and government access to authorization decisions. HIPPA security regulations further impose requirements to develop and enforce "formal security policies and procedures for granting different levels of access to PHI." This includes authorization to access PHI, the establishment of account access privileges, and modifications to account privileges. Furthermore, the HIPPA security regulations require the deployment of mechanisms for obtaining consent to use and disclose PHI. With regard to security, HIPPA defines technical security services in terms of the following:

- Entity authentication—Proving your identity to gain access.
- Access control—What you can access.
- Audit control—What you have accessed.
- Authorization control—What you can do once you have access.
- Message authentication—Ensuring the data integrity and confidentiality of data.
- Alarms/Notifications—Notifies out-of-compliance security policy enforcement.
- Availability of PHI—Ensures high availability of PHI within a secure infrastructure.

These mandatory security requirements are intended to prevent deliberate or accidental access to PHI and to address concerns over the privacy of patient data. While most organizations that deal with patient records have implemented HIPPA in one form or another, the recent acceleration of e-mail viruses, spyware introduction, and personal data theft should prompt security architects and developers to reexamine their applications and systems. Refer to [HIPPA] for details.

The Children's Online Privacy Protection Act

The Children's Online Privacy Protection Act (COPPA) establishes privacy protection requirements for any organization holding information about children. If an organization releases personal data about a child (such as name, age, sex, or home address) and that information is used to support a crime involving that child, the organization can be prosecuted. Refer to [COPPA] for more information.

EU Directive on Data Protection

The European Union (EU) passed a data protection law called Data Protection Directive 95/46/EC in October 1995. Under the Directive (refer to [EU95] for details), a set of rules addresses the handling of all types of personal data. In essence, the EU countries that have enacted national legislation enabling the EU Directive on Data Protection generally impose the following obligations on enterprises that conduct business within their jurisdictions:

- Personal data must be kept confidential.
- Individuals need to know in advance, and in detail, what information will be collected about them, who will use it, how it will be used, where it will

be stored, what procedure to follow to verify and update it, and how to effectively remove it.

The Directive also states that the baseline controls appropriate to achieve the required level of confidentiality and privacy of the identity should be drawn from the industry in which the subject organization operates. Thus, if an industry is generally pursuing ISO 17799 as a security baseline, then ISO 17799 will be the standard against which compliance will be measured.

California's Notice of Security Breach (1798.29)

California Civil Code Section 1798.29 requires organizations to disclose security breaches that result in compromise of personal information, identity theft, or loss of customer data in a timely fashion. The law defines a breach of the security of a system as a system breach that results in the disclosure of any personal information, particularly Social Security numbers, California driver's license or ID card numbers, financial account numbers, and credit or debit card numbers. Upon a security breach, the organization must notify the government in the most expedient time possible and without unreasonable delay when any California residents' personal information has been acquired, or believed to have been acquired, without authorization. Refer to [1798] for details.

Security Compliance in Other Countries

Canada has regulations similar to those of the Sarbanes-Oxley Act. The Canadian Public Accountability Board issued similar standards and guidelines for audit and control. In late 2002, the Ontario government introduced Bill 198, which allowed the Ontario Securities Commission to introduce new corporate governance requirements. Refer to [KMPG] for a comparison between the Sarbanes-Oxley Act and the local Canadian regulations. Canada also has a Privacy Act, which is similar to the Gramm-Leach-Bliley Act. Refer to [CanadaPrivacy] for details.

There are similar data privacy laws in many Asia-Pacific countries. The data privacy security requirements and risk implications are quite similar. Caslon Analytics Privacy Guide [Caslon] depicts a summary of these data privacy laws in Asian countries. For example, China (Hong Kong) has passed a Personal Data (Privacy) Ordinance based on the EU Directive. This ordinance sets forth specific guidelines about how positive and negative personal credit data can be shared electronically among financial services institutions.

The Importance of Identity Management

In this age of the network economy, businesses and organizations are in pursuit of new opportunities and are finding new ways of conducting business using the Internet. They must, at the same time, ensure that their exposed information assets remain secure. The increasing numbers of customers, employees, partners, and suppliers have forced businesses and organizations to provide virtually global-level access to their critical informational resources while they protect sensitive information from competitors and hackers. With the potential for business that these new opportunities present, organizations and users are more involved in accessing more and more disparate resources. With that access comes a greater risk of compromising the security of business information. To overcome these challenges, an effective identity management infrastructure solution becomes essential. Identity management is the only method by which organizations can achieve the levels of integration, security, service, streamlined operations—all at reduced costs—that the virtual enterprise demands.

A typical identity management infrastructure solution would provide the following capabilities as services.

Identity Provisioning Services

Automated identity provisioning (also referred to as User Account Provisioning) and management greatly reduces the time it takes to get users up and running productively, to change their access privileges as their roles change, and to instantly and securely revoke their accounts when their relationships with the company end. Solutions that use role- and rule-based provisioning provide a degree of flexibility in the setting of provisioning rules for users, organizations, resources, roles, or groups. Such solutions ensure that policies are enforced. Finally, a dynamic workflow component supports multistep, complex provisioning and automates the process of making changes in identity data.

Identity Data Synchronization Services

Automatically synchronizing identity data (also referred to as User Account Synchronization) across a wide range of heterogeneous applications, directories, databases, and other data stores will improve operational efficiencies. Automatic synchronization eliminates the need for data to be synchronized manually and ensures data accuracy and consistency across systems.

Access Management Services

To efficiently achieve the levels of security and user service that are necessary, it is critical that an identity management solution secure the delivery of essential identity and application information, enabling single sign-on (SSO). The SSO access to applications and services must provide support for heterogeneous applications, Web services, and resources running on diverse platforms residing locally or across networks.

Federation Services

Identity management federation services incorporate the industry standards (i.e., Liberty) for providing a federated framework and authentication-sharing mechanism that is interoperable with existing enterprise systems. This allows an authenticated identity to be recognized and enables the user associated with that identity to participate in personalized services across multiple domains. Employees, customers, and partners can seamlessly and securely access multiple applications and outsourced services without interruption, which enhances the user experience.

Directory Services

In the quest for secure consolidation of processes and resources, companies are increasingly adopting centralized or decentralized directories to enhance security, improve performance, and enable enterprise-wide integration. The right directory-based solution should deliver benefits above and beyond a basic LDAP directory—externalizing identity information, making "globally centric" information from key sources of authority, and making relevant information centrally available to both off-the-shelf applications and custom-written corporate applications. An effective directory solution must provide, at a minimum, high performance, security, and availability; full interoperability across other vendor directories; and ease of management and administration.

Auditing and Reporting Services

Comprehensive audit and reporting of user profile data, change history, and user permissions ensure that security risks are detected so that administrators can respond proactively. The ability to review the status of access privileges at any time improves audit performance and helps achieve compliance with governmental mandates. Finally, reporting on items such as usage of self-service password resets and time to provision or de-provision users provides visibility into key operational metrics and possible operational improvements.

Secure Personal Identification

With the growth of network-centric businesses and services, everyone connects with a great deal of trust to a faceless application channel to access information and do transactions. Everyone is required to confirm his or her identity by verification and validation using a set of credentials. However, identity theft, identity fraud, and impersonation crimes are increasing because someone has wrongfully obtained and abused another person's identity information for economic or personal gain. It is surprising to note that most identities are stolen from trusted insiders such as employees, colleagues, friends, and even family members who have easy access to private information. These fraudulent acts include unauthorized access to confidential information, bank accounts, transactions, and so on.

According to The 9/11 Commission Report (page 401) ". . . terrorists use evasive methods, such as altered and counterfeit passports and visas, specific travel methods and routes, liaisons with corrupt government officials, human smuggling networks, supportive travel agencies, and immigration and identity fraud." The stealing and forging of magnetic-strip credit cards are also on the rise and have caused many people losses that have led to bankruptcy. *The Christian Science Monitor*, October 7, 2004, reported that Phishing has victimized some 1.8 million consumers and cost banks and credit-card issuers nearly $1.2 billion in the past year. The most common reasons for the success of identity-theft related crimes are poor personal identification and verification processes, stolen passwords, inaccurate authentication mechanisms, counterfeiting, and impersonation. Some of those issues are due to processes that are more susceptible to error, particularly when they rely on manual verification. Traditional identification technologies and authentication mechanisms are not adequate to counter and prevent identity-theft related crimes. For example, traditional identification mechanisms such as passwords, PINs (magnetic-stripe cards), and driver's licenses can be lost or stolen, and these credentials can be hacked, manipulated, or forged.

Personal Identification and Authentication

From a technical perspective, most of us get confused when we try to distinguish between identification and authentication processes. Identification is a process of assigning an identity to a specific entity (i.e., a person) and authentication is a process of verifying an identity. The requesting identity can be identified and authenticated by using his or her information credentials and/or his or her possessions and physical characteristics, particularly what he or she knows (e.g., PIN, passwords), what he or she owns (e.g., smart card), or what his or her human characteristics are (e.g., biometrics). Adoption of identification and authentication technologies using smart cards, biometrics, RFID tags, digital certificates, or a combination of any of them has proven to be a viable method of thwarting mostly identity-theft related crimes.

Let's take a high-level look at using smart cards and biometrics for personal identification and verification.

Smart Card Identity

Smart cards are credit-card sized computing devices that can act as tokens to enable services that require security. A smart card is a plastic card with an integrated circuit (IC) chip embedded within the plastic substrate of its body. The smart card IC chip is meant for processing, data transmission, and storage. Smart cards do not contain power supply, display, or keyboard. For communication, it makes use of a card acceptance device (CAD), also referred to as a smart card reader, that is connected to a computer via USB or serial port. A smart card may also have a magnetic strip on the other face of the card. Smart cards can be divided into groups as microprocessor and memory cards. They can be further categorized as contact cards and contactless cards based on the difference in the card access mechanism. The physical appearance of a smart card is defined in ISO 7816, which set the standards for the smart card industry. With industry support, Sun Microsystems introduced Java Card specifications that define a Java runtime environment for smart cards as a Java technology platform for developing smart card applications. The platform also supports smart card manufacturers, card issuers, and related communities. We will discuss the Java Card platform and its security features in Chapter 3, "The Java 2 Platform Security." Figure 1–1 illustrates the physical appearance of a smart card (from Sun Microsystems).

Microprocessor cards, as the name implies, contain a processor. The microprocessor performs data handling, processing, and memory access according to a given set of conditions (PINs, encryptions, and so on). Microprocessor-based cards are widely used for access control, banking, wireless telecommunication, and so on. Memory cards contain memory chips with non-programmable logic and do not contain a processor. Memory cards are typically used for prepaid phone cards, for gift cards, and for buying goods sold based on prepayment. Since memory cards do not contain a processor, they cannot be reprogrammed or reused. Contact cards must be inserted in a CAD reader to communicate with a

Figure 1–1 The Java Card (Source: Sun Microsystems)

user or an application. Contactless cards makes use of an antenna, and the power can be provided by the internal or collected by the antenna. Typically, contactless cards transmit data to the CAD reader through electromagnetic fields. One limitation of contactless cards is the requirement that they be used within a certain distance of the CAD reader.

The Role of Smart Cards in Personal Identification

With the built-in power of a processor and storage, smart cards offer security and portability in support of personal identification. Smart cards are resistant to cyber-attacks and hackers, because they do not connect with vulnerable external resources. Any attack on a smart card requires physical possession of the card and specialized expertise to verify it. In addition, accessing a smart card usually requires the card holder's PIN (personal identification number), which prevents the card from being used by an unauthorized person. Using cryptographic algorithms can further strengthen the security features of smart cards, allowing storing the data as encrypted in memory. The data exchanged between the card and CAD readers can be encrypted as well using mutual authentication.

Today, smart cards are commonly adopted by various industries, particularly for personal identification and authentication. Smart cards are considered as secure alternatives to traditional identification documents such as driver's licenses, national IDs, and visas. Unlike traditional identification cards, smart cards are often impossible to forge or copy. Personal confidential information and images can be securely stored into the card and protected by using cryptographic algorithms. By setting up the access conditions, such as PIN and passwords, only authorized persons or authorities can access the secured information. Smart cards also allow storage of digital certificates representing a person that can be used to digitally sign documents and request logical access to applications. The smart card store certificates can be verified for validity using CRLs (Certificate Revocation Lists) and OCSP (Online Certificate Status Protocol) services facilitated by a Certificate Authority (CA).

Combined with biometric technologies, smart cards also offer a highly assured and trusted personal identification solution to counter identity theft and related crimes. Biometric information about the cardholder can also be stored on the card. With biometrics information on the card, in addition to providing password/PIN, the cardholder must use a biometrics scanner device to identify or verify the biometric sample, whether the cardholder owns the card or not.

Biometric Identity

Biometric identity refers to the use of physiological or behavioral characteristics of a human being to identify a person. It verifies a person's identity based on his or her unique physical attributes, referred to as biometric samples, such as fingerprints, face geometry, hand geometry, retinal information, iris information, and so on. The biometric identification system stores the biometric samples of the identity during registration and then matches it every time the identity is claimed. Biometric identification systems typically work using pattern-recognition algorithms that determine the authenticity of the provided physiological or behavioral characteristic sample. Popular biometric identification systems based on physical and behavioral characteristics are as follows:

- **Fingerprint Verification**: Based on the uniqueness of a series of ridges and furrows found on the surface of a human finger as well as its minutiae points. A minutiae point is a point that occurs at either a ridge bifurcation or a ridge ending.
- **Retinal Analysis**: Based on the blood vessel patterns in the back of the eye, the vessels' thickness, and the number of branching points, and so on.
- **Facial Recognition**: Based on the spatial geometry of the key features of the face measured as distance between eyes, nose, jaw edges, etc.
- **Iris Verification**: Based on the iris pattern, which is the colored part of the eye.
- **Hand Geometry**: Based on the measurement of the dimensions of a hand, including the fingers, and examining the spatial geometry of the distinctive features.
- **Voice Verification**: Based on the vocal characteristics to identify individuals using a pass-phrase.

- **Signature Verification**: The verification done based on the shape, stroke, pen pressure, speed, and time taken during the signature.

Figure 1–2 shows a biometric facial recognition solution (BiObex).

Industry standards and specifications are available for developing and representing biometric information. The key standards are as follows:

- **BioAPI**: The BioAPI is an industry consortium effort for a standardized application programming interface for developing compatible biometric solutions. It provides BioAPI specifications and a reference implementation to support a wide range of biometric technology solutions. For more information, refer to the BioAPI web site at http://www.bioapi.org/.
- **OASIS XCBF**: The OASIS XML Common Biometric Format (XCBF) is an industry effort for XML representation of descriptive biometric infor-

Figure 1–2 BiObex—Biometric identification using facial recognition (Courtesy: AC Technology, Inc.)

mation for verifying an identity based on human characteristics such as DNA, fingerprints, iris scans, and hand geometry. For more information, refer to [XCBF].

- **CBEFF (Common Biometric Exchange File Format)**: CBEFF is a standard defined by NIST (National Institute of Standards and Technology) for handling different biometric techniques, versions, and data structures in a common way to facilitate ease of data exchange and interoperability. For more information, refer to [CBEFF].

Security by Default

The Role of Biometric Identity in Secure Identification

Biometric identification is not a new mechanism or even considered as an emerging technology solution. In 1870, French criminologist Alphonse Bertillon invented a method for identifying criminals. The method used measurements and characteristics based on morphological representation of bony parts of the human body, descriptions of peculiar marks, and mental or moral qualities [Forensic-evidence]. Although many experts feel that biometric techniques are still in their infancy, it has already been shown that adoption of biometric technologies leads to more accurate and reliable identification and authentication than any other mechanisms.

Biometric identification provides a strong alternative to manual verification, where passwords and PINs may be forgotten, lost, or stolen and smart cards can be shared, stolen, or lost. A biometric sample cannot be stolen or lost. Adopting biometrics in multifactor authentication is becoming the de facto standard for securing security-sensitive applications and resources. Today, biometric identification solutions are widely deployed in forensic investigation, intelligence, government, military, homeland security, financial institutions, and casinos. These solutions play a vital role in criminal identification, terrorist identification, access control, and security-sensitive information systems. With the increasing adoption, acceptance, and availability of biometric identification solutions and tools, biometrics is expected to become a standard identification and authentication solution for the prevention of identity-theft related crimes and for all security-sensitive applications and services.

In a *Security by Default* strategy, secure personal identification using smart cards and biometrics plays a vital role in providing highly secure logical access control to security-sensitive applications. For more information about the architecture and implementation of secure personal identification solutions using smart card and biometric technologies, refer to Chapter 15, "Secure Personal Identification Using Smart Cards and Biometrics."

RFID-Based Identity

Radio Frequency Identification (RFID) provides a mechanism for identification services using radio frequencies. It makes use of an RFID tag, comprised of an integrated circuit chip and an antenna. The RFID tag stores a unique Electronic Product Code (EPC) and uses an antenna to receive the radio frequency for emitting and transmitting the EPC data as signals to the RFID readers. When an RFID passes through an electromagnetic zone, the RFID tag is activated and sends signals to the RFID reader. The RFID reader receives and decodes the signals and then communicates the EPC to the RFID server that provides the Object Name Service (ONS). The ONS identifies the object by interpreting the EPC and sends it for further processing. The EPC data may provide information related to the identification, location, and other specifics related to the identified object. The standards and specifications related to RFID systems are defined by EPCglobal (www.epcglobalinc.org) an industry standard initiative with participation by leading firms and industries promoting RFID technologies. Figure 1–3 illustrates the transmission of EPC data from the RFID tag to the RFID reader.

RFID tags are available in a wide variety of shapes and sizes. RFID tags can be categorized as active or passive. Active RFID tags have a power source that supports read/write, longer read range frequencies, and larger storage (operating up to 1 Mb). Passive RFID tags do not contain any power source; they generate power by using the incoming radio frequency energy induced in the antenna to transfer the EPC from the RFID tag to the RFID reader. Passive RFID tags are usually less expensive than active tags and are commonly adopted to support shorter read ranges.

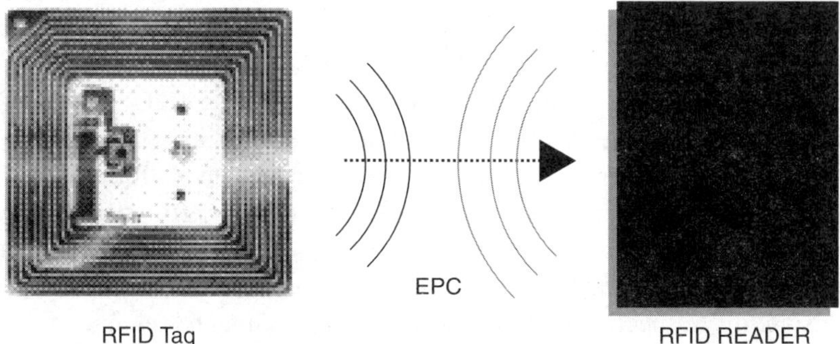

Figure 1–3 RFID Tag and Reader

The Role of RFID in Secure Identification

RFID was originally intended to replace product bar codes such as UPC and EAN due to their limitations. The uniqueness of RFID tags and their flexibility in identifying any object presented a promising solution to the industry, particularly for supporting identification and tracking of objects, combat thefts, and so on. Today, RFID-based systems are best suited to detect unauthorized access and theft in organizations, to manage the supply chain in retail stores by speeding up restocking and reducing shrinkage, to manage book inventories in libraries that use self check-out procedures, to identify expired products in food industries, to track patients and matching prescriptions in hospitals and pharmacies, to track passenger baggage in commercial airlines, and to identify livestock and track animals.

While RFID technologies are gaining momentum in a lot of industries, they are also becoming controversial because of security concerns related to information privacy. The EPCglobal standards define privacy-related guidelines for the use of RFID in consumer industries. These guidelines require notifying consumers about the presence of EPC and advising them to discard, deactivate, or remove EPC tags. At the time of writing this book, the EPCglobal standards committee is working on network and information-level security specifications to support all of the security aspects related to RFID tags, tag discovery, and network security.

The Importance of Java Technology

Java is one of the most popular software technologies in the industry today. With the power of platform-independence, portability, and vendor-independence, Java has become a vital component of most IT infrastructures in businesses, organizations, and communities worldwide. Sun Microsystems has achieved Java support on every possible computing device by defining different platform editions, such Java 2 Standard Edition (J2SE), Java 2 Enterprise Edition (J2EE), Java 2 Micro Edition (J2ME), and the Java Card Platform Edition. With overwhelming successes, the Java 2 Enterprise Edition (J2EE) platform is the platform of choice for developing and deploying large-scale Web-centric enterprise-class application solutions. The Java 2 Micro Edition and Java Card Platform have become the de facto platforms for enabling and delivering application solutions on microdevices and smart cards, respectively. Widely adopted as a secure and reliable middleware platform in the software industry, Java runs on a variety of platforms and devices—from wallet-sized smart cards to huge mainframe computers to power-up mission-critical applications that deliver secure network communications. Java technology has also been well-accepted in industries involved with gaming, automobiles, space-based telemetry, embedded devices, and real-time processing.

Today, Java provides the software industry with a standardized platform that is continuously evolving through an open community-based process (Java Community Process). This process engages a variety of enterprise computing vendors to ensure that the platform meets the widest possible range of industry and business requirements. As a result, Java addresses the core issues that impede organizations' efforts to maintain a competitive pace in the exploding information economy.

Security in the Java Platform

Java was originally designed for network-based computing, and so security measures were an integral part of Java's design from the beginning. Java's security model differs greatly from traditional approaches and competing platforms. First, most operating systems permit applications to access system resources, and it is the administrator's or the users' responsibility to set permissions and protect the exposed resources from unauthorized access. More importantly, users must verify the application's authenticity before executing it and must assume it does not contain any viruses or malicious programs. These are the common drawbacks in popular operating systems; they rely on the end user to perform the application verification and trust before executing it. In comparison, Java takes a proactive approach by addressing security as an integral part of its core platform. It allows users to download and execute untrusted applications without any undue risk by restricting such code to their own sandbox. This sandbox mechanism protects the resources from potential vulnerabilities so that the downloaded program cannot access or alter the user's resources beyond the sandbox. Java also provides end-to-end security of an application beyond its underlying platform, ensuring security at all levels, including its users, components, services, and communications.

Because a key focus of this book is the security of Java-based applications and services, we will study and explore the details of Java security architecture in the next few chapters.

Making Security a "Business Enabler"

Economic pressures compel businesses and organizations to look for technology solutions that reduce costs and improve efficiency. They seek to do this, of course, without sacrificing the quality and productivity of the existing system. The heightened risk of security not only relates to the security of the assets involving buildings and people, but also relates to the security of the organizational technology and its managed business processes. Ironically, investing in security is often considered as a capital investment and is not considered as a contributor to business productivity. More interestingly, IT architects and developers focus on the technical elegance of new security technologies as a defensive mechanism to protect the applications and infrastructure without realizing the potential cost benefits from them. From an IT management and business investor's perspective, security infrastructure and solutions for a business case is not justifiable without reference to how security contributes to overcoming technological and economical obstacles and risks faced by an organization.

With security gaining significant importance in every business and organizational process, it is often challenging to explain how security addresses an organizational goal such as improving operational efficiency or reducing costs. Equally difficult to explain is how security contributes to Return On Investment (ROI). Let's take a look at some examples of security measures and how they function as "business enablers" in an organization.

Case 1–Justifying Identity and Access Management

Identity and access management provides compelling business benefits by reducing costs, risks, and complexity in the enforcement of organizational security policies and practices. In a nutshell, an identity management solution facilitates an organization by the following:

- Centralized management of identity and policy information.
- Centralized or decentralized authentication and authorization services.
- Delegated identity administration and control.
- Ability to securely exchange data across trusted networks of partners, suppliers, and customers.
- Enforcement of single sign-on capabilities over heterogeneous applications and services.
- Federated sign-on and sign-out capabilities over trusted networks of partners, suppliers, and customers.
- Automated processes and instant change in identity privileges and relationships.
- Elimination of duplicate user accounts.
- Visualization of who has access to what resources at any given time.

- From an organization cost benefits and ROI perspective, a typical identity and access management solution would offer the following:
  - The time required for registering a user to access his or her privileged application is significantly reduced.
  - Enforcement of single sign-on capabilities offers dramatic reduction of help desk calls for resetting passwords and time savings for help desk administrators.

Case 2–Justifying Proactive Security Approaches

McLean and Brown in their ROI study for security (refer to [McLeanBrown] for details) discuss an ROI estimation model for security architecture investment. Table 1–1 shows a slightly modified version to illustrate potential ROI with implementation of end-to-end security for J2EE and Web services applications. In this example, a medium-sized firm intends to estimate the cost of implementing J2EE and Web services security architecture using single sign-on architecture. The firm has some existing security infrastructure in place. To simplify the sample scenario, we present a list of assumptions following the table. We have used a three-year cost estimate to compute the ROI per year. Note that the financial exposure is likely to be greater than the security investment, and we estimate an ROI of $683,333 per year. Thus, it is justifiable to implement a proactive security architecture design using J2EE and Web services technologies.

Table 1–1 Sample ROI Estimate for Justifying Proactive Security

Potential threat	*Description*	*Estimated Loss US$*
A. Financial Exposure (Qualitative)		
Denial-of-service attacks, or single point of failure	Access to network, system resources, and application resources is denied due to hacker attacks, or system unavailability due to system failure.	$1.4 million
Man-in-the-middle attacks or replay attacks	Security attacks by spoofing the business transactions in the network, or replaying the business transactions with tampered transaction information.	N/A

(continues)

Table 1–1 Sample ROI Estimate for Justifying Proactive Security (*continued*)

Potential threat	*Description*	*Estimated Loss US$*
B. Inefficient Processes (Quantitative)		
Password resets (that is, no single sign-on capability)	The cost of resetting user passwords or user administration as a result of not having single sign-on capability.	$25,000
C. Intangible Cost (Qualitative)		
Loss to public image, loss of reputation, denial to network resources	Loss of confidence of reputation due to publicized security breach.	$25,000
D. Total Security Exposure Cost (yearly)	A + B + C	$1,450,000
E. Investment in Security (One-time)		
Infrastructural platform security	Investment in firewall, proxies, and directory server.	N/A
Intrusion detection	Cost of implementing and executing intrusion detection system to monitor any suspicious network activities.	N/A
Antivirus protection	Cost of antivirus software to protect network and system resources against viruses.	N/A
Implementing J2EE and Web services security	Internal cost for implementing J2EE and Web services security.	$1,500,000
Implementing single sign-on architecture	Additional hardware and software cost of implementing single sign-on architecture.	$1,000,000

(*continues*)

Table 1–1 Sample ROI Estimate for Justifying Proactive Security (*continued*)

Potential threat	*Description*	*Estimated Loss US$*
Reengineering inefficient security administration processes	Internal cost of addressing the inefficient security administration processes.	N/A
	Total one-time investment	$2.5 million
F. Annual Maintenance Cost – Hardware and software	This includes the single sign-on architecture only.	$100,000
G. Total Security Cost for 3 years	E (one-time) + F (annual) * 3 years	$2,300,000
H. Estimated Return	ROI = D – (E /3) – F	
First year cost	$766,666	
Second year cost	$766,666	
Third year cost	$766,666	
	ROI per year	$683,333

Assumptions

- Only denial-of-service attack is included in this ROI estimate. The cost estimate of the denial-of-service attack assumes the average cost per incident (refer to the CSI report in [CSI2003] p. 20 for details).
- Most of the investment in security is already in place. This includes infrastructure platform, intrusion detection, and virus protection.
- Ten percent of the workforce require password reset (1,000 cases per year), assuming $25 per password reset incident will be incurred by the outsourcing data center.
- Intangible security cost for loss to public image, loss of reputation, and denial to network resources assumes five days of lost sales, amounting to $25,000.
- Maintenance cost assumes 10 percent of the hardware and software cost.
- As a simple illustration of the ROI concept, this example does not calculate and display the present value of the security investment and returns. In a real-life scenario, the present value would be used.

Case 3–Justifying Security Compliance

Security compliance is a strong business enabler in terms of enhancing consumer confidence and improving the operational efficiency of an organization's information systems and processes. It also ensures an organization will follow an auditable process and use reporting mechanisms that help protect them from errors and fraudulent practices. For example, in January 2004 the Bank of Scotland was fined about $2.5 million for failing to keep proper records of customer identification as stipulated by the UK Financial Services Authority's money laundering regulations [ExpressComputer].

By achieving compliance, the organization can meet its responsibilities as specified by the government regulations and avoid issues related to negligence and compliance failures—fines, sanctions, and jail terms for corporate executives and board members. Achieving security compliance also helps organizations to do the following:

- Evaluate and test their organizational security practices and controls.
- Mitigate the risks.
- Implement safeguards and countermeasures.
- Increase operational efficiency and cost-effectiveness.

Compliance with regulatory requirements often drives the need for implementing effective security procedures and identity management solutions that provide proof of compliance. It also improves organizational productivity and customer trust.

Summary

Security has taken unprecedented importance in many industries today, and every organization must adopt proactive security measures for data, processes, and resources throughout the information life cycle. Thus, an organization must have a thorough understanding of the business challenges related to security, critical security threats, exploits, and how to mitigate risk and implement safeguards and countermeasures. Adopting security by using proactive approaches becomes essential to organizational health and well-being. Such approaches may well also increase operational efficiency and cost effectiveness.

In this chapter, we have had an overview of security strategies and key technologies as well as the importance of delivering end-to-end security to an IT system. In particular, we discussed the key constituents that contributes to achieving "Security-by-Default," such as:

- Understanding the weakest links in an IT ecosystem
- Understanding the boundaries of end-to-end security
- Understanding the impact of application security
- Strategies for building robust security architecture
- Understanding the importance of security compliance
- Understanding the importance of identity management
- Understanding the importance of secure personal identification
- Understanding the importance of Java technology
- How to justify security as a business enabler

We've just looked at the importance of proactive security approaches and strategies. Now we'll start our detailed journey with a closer look at key security technologies. Then we'll look at how to achieve *Security by Default* by adopting radical approaches based on well-defined security design methodology, pattern catalogs, best practices, and reality checks.

References

[1798] California Office of Privacy Protection. "Notice of Security Breach—Civil Code Sections 1798-29, 1798-82 and 1798-84."

http://www.privacy.ca.gov/code/cc1798.291798.82.htm

[ACLFailure] Open Web Application Security Project. "A2. Broken Access Control."

http://www.owasp.org/documentation/topten/a2.html

[AMNews] Security Breach: Hacker Gets Medical Records

http://www.ama-assn.org/amednews/2001/01/29/tesa0129.htm

[BrokenAuth] The Open Web Application Security Project. "A3. Broken Authentication and Session Management."

http://www.owasp.org/documentation/topten/a3.html

[CanadaPrivacy] Department of Justice, Canada. "Privacy Act—Chapter P-21."

http://laws.justice.gc.ca/en/P-21/94799.html

[Caslon] Caslon Analytics. Caslon Analytics Privacy Guide.
http://www.caslon.com.au/privacyguide6.htm

[CBEFF] Common Biometric Exchange File Format.
http://www.itl.nist.gov/div895/isis/bc/cbeff/.

[CNET] Matt Hines. "Gartner: Phishing on the Rise."
http://news.com.com/2100-7349_3-5234155.html

[ComputerWeek134554] "IBM Offers Companies Monthly Security Report."
http://www.computerweekly.com/Article134554.htm

[COPPA] Children Online Privacy Protection Act.
http://www.ftc.gov/os/1999/10/64fr59888.htm

[CSI2003] Robert Richardson. 2003 CSI / FBI Computer Crime and Security Survey. Computer Security Institute, 2003.
http://www.gocsi.cpactourom/forms/fbi/pdf.jhtml

[CSI2004] Lawrence A. Gordon, Martin P. Loeb, William Lucyshyn, and Robert Richardson. "2004 CSI / FBI Computer Crime and Security Survey." Computer Security Institute, 2004.
http://www.gocsi.com

[CSO Online] Richard Mogul. "Danger Within—Protecting Your Company from Internal Security Attacks (Gartner Report)."
http://www.csoonline.com/analyst/report400.html

[DataMon2003] Datamonitor. "Financial Sector Opts for J2EE." The Register, June 4, 2003.
http://theregister.com/content/53/31021.html

[DOS] The Open Web Application Security Project. "A9. Denial of Service."
http://www.owasp.org/documentation/topten/a9.html

[EU95] European Parliament. Data Protection Directive 95/46/EC. October 24, 1995.
http://europa.eu.int/comm/internal_market/privacy/index_en.htm

[ExpressComputer] Identity Management Market at Crossroads. April 19, 2004.
http://www.expresscomputeronline.com/20040419/securespace01.shtml

[FTC] Gramm-Leach-Bliley Act. Federal Trade Commission.

http://www.ftc.gov/privacy/glbact/glbsub1.htm

[FTC findings] FTC Releases Survey of Identity Theft.

http://www.ftc.gov/opa/2003/09/idtheft.htm

[Gartner Reports] Security reports from Gartner at:

http://www.gartner.com/security

[GrammLeach1] Federal Trade Commission. "Gramm-Leach-Bliley Act." 1999.

http://www.ftc.gov/privacy/glbact/glbsub1.htm

[GrammLeach2] US Senate Committee on Banking, Housing, and Urban Affairs. "Information Regarding the Gramm-Leach-Bliley Act of 1999."

http://banking.senate.gov/conf/

[Hewitt] Tim Hilgenberg and John A. Hansen. "Building a Highly Robust, Secure Web Services Conference Architecture to Process 4 Million Transactions per Day." IBM developerWorks Live! 2002.

[HIPPA] Achieving HIPPA Compliance with Identity Management from Sun.

http://www.sun.com/software/products/identity/wp_HIPPA_identity_mgmt.pdf

[ImproperDataHandling] The Open Web Application Security Project. "A7. Improper Data Handling."

http://www.owasp.org/documentation/topten/a7.html

[InputValidation] Security Tracker. "Lotus Notes/Domino Square Bracket Encoding failure Lets Remote Users Conduct Cross-site Scripting Attacks."

http://securitytracker.com/alerts/2004/Oct/1011779.html

[InjectionFlaw] Secunia. "Multiple Browsers Window Injection Vulnerability Test."

http://secunia.com/multiple_browsers_window_injection_vulnerability_test/

[InsecureConfig] The Open Web Application Security Project. "A10. Insecure Configuration Management."

http://www.owasp.org/documentation/topten/a10.html

[KMPG] KMPG. "Comparison of U.S. and Canadian Regulatory Changes."

http://www.kpmg.ca/en/services/audit/documents/USCDNRegulatory.pdf

[Krawczyk] Pawel Krawczyk. "Practical Demonstration of the MSIE6 Certificate Path Vulnerability." IPSec.pl

http://www.ipsec.pl/msiemitm/msiemitm.en.php

[Lai] Ray Lai. *J2EE™ Platform Web Services*. Prentice Hall, 2003.

[LiGong] Li Gong. "Java Security Architecture." in "Java™ 2 SDK, Standard Edition Documentation Version 1.4.2." Sun Microsystems, 2003.

http://java.sun.com/j2se/1.4.2/docs/guide/security/spec/security-spec.doc1.html

and

http://java.sun.com/j2se/1.4.2/docs/guide/security/spec/security-spec.doc2.html.

[McLeanBrown] Greg McLean and Jason Brown. "Determining the ROI in IT Security." April 2003.

http://www.cica.ca/index.cfm/ci_id/14138/la_id/1.htm

[Online-Kasino] Online Kasinos Info.

http://www.onlinekasinos.info/

[PasswordExploit] Esther Shein, editor. "Worm Targets Network Shares with Weak Passwords." eSecurityPlanet.com.

http://www.esecurityplanet.com/alerts/article.php/3298791

[PHP3_errorLog] Security Advisory. "FreeBSD: 'PHP' Ports Vulnerability." LinuxSecurity.com. November 20, 2000.

http://www.linuxsecurity.com/content/view/102698/103/

[PICC] IDC. "People's Insurance Company of China: eBusiness Portal Attracts New Customers and Reduces Costs." IDC eBusiness Case Study.

http://www.sun.com/service/about/success/recent/PICC_English_IDC.pdf

[SDTimes057] Alan Zeichick. ".NET Advancing Quickly on J2EE, but Research Shows Java Maintains Strong Position." SD Times. July 1, 2002.

http://www.sdtimes.com/news/057/story7.htm

[SessionHijack] Kevin Lam, David LeBlanc, and Ben Smith. "Theft on the Web: Prevent Session Hijacking." Microsoft TechNet Magazine. Winter 2005.

http://www.microsoft.com/technet/technetmag/issues/2005/01/sessionhijacking/default.aspx

[SOX1] U.S. Congress. Sarbanes-Oxley Act. H.R. 3763. July 30, 2002.

http://www.law.uc.edu/CCL/SOact/soact.pdf

[SOX2] "The Role of Identity Management in Sarbanes-Oxley Compliance."

http://www.sun.com/software/products/identity/wp_identity_mgmt_sarbanes_oxley.pdf

[SQLInjection] Shawna McAlearney. "Automated SQL Injection: What Your Enterprise Needs to Know." SearchSecurity.com. July 26, 2004.

http://searchsecurity.techtarget.com/originalContent/0,289142,sid14_gci995325,00.html

[XCBF] OASIS XCBF Technical Committee Web Site.

http://www.oasis-open.org/committees/tc_home.php?wg_abbrev=xcbf

[XSiteScript] The Open Web Application Security Project. "A4. Cross-Site (XSS) Flaws."

http://www.owasp.org/documentation/topten/a4.html

Basics of Security

Topics in This Chapter

- Security Requirements and Goals
- The Role of Cryptography in Security
- The Role of Secure Socket Layer (SSL)
- The Importance and Role of LDAP in Security
- Common Challenges in Cryptography
- Threat Modeling
- Identity Management

Chapter 2

The quickest and most reliable way to secure your computer is to not turn it on. Because that's not a viable option, you are left with a variety of complex possibilities. As a software developer, you must completely understand the basics of security before beginning the software design. Security is a broad term that includes all physical and logical access to business locations, resources, and data. As a software developer, you must have an equally broad knowledge of the environment that you need to secure. For example, securing an application doesn't require implementation of authentication and access control functionalities alone. It also requires a range of other things—from securing the host on which that application resides to securing the client that accesses the application over a network. In simpler terms, the five major goals of information security are as follows:

- Confidentiality
- Integrity
- Authentication
- Authorization
- Non-repudiation

These five goals serve as the basis for incorporating security in software applications and for delivering trustworthy business applications and services. This chapter provides a tutorial on basic security concepts. It introduces the fundamentals of security requirements, the role of cryptography and identity management technologies, and the common challenges posed by using these technologies.

Security Requirements and Goals

Security is a key issue with many implications, and it is critical throughout software systems. Thus, when we speak of security in software, it can refer to many areas of the system—applications, data, networks, communications, users, host systems, and so forth. Within each of these areas are common security requirements and goals that involve the protection of data. Data that is passed over communication paths that may be open to unauthorized viewers needs to be protected; this is the concept of **confidentiality**. This same data must be protected from unauthorized changes during transit; this is the concept of **data integrity**. Users, whether human or programmatic, must be able to prove their identities before being allowed access to the data; this is the concept of **authentication**. Once authenticated, the system needs to ascertain what type of access the user has to the data; this is the concept of **authorization**. When a user does perform an action on data, such as approving a document, that action must be bound with the user in such a way that the user cannot deny performing the action; this is the concept of **non-repudiation**. Each of these concepts is explained further in the sections that follow.

Confidentiality

Confidentiality is the concept of protecting sensitive data from being viewable by an unauthorized entity. A wide variety of information falls under the category of sensitive data. Some sensitive data may be illegal to compromise, such as a patient's medical history or a customer's credit card number. Other sensitive data may divulge too much information about the application. For example, a Web application that keeps a user's state via a cookie value may be more susceptible to compromise if a malicious adversary can derive certain information from the cookie value. With the increased use of legacy systems exposed via Web services over the Internet, ensuring the confidentiality of sensitive data becomes an especially high priority.

However, communication links are not the only area that needs solutions to ensure confidentiality. An internal database holding thousands of medical histories and credit card numbers is an enticing target to a malicious adversary. Securing the confidentiality of this data reduces the probability of exposure in the event the application itself is compromised.

To protect the confidentiality of sensitive data during its transit or in storage, one needs to render the data unreadable except by authorized users. This is accomplished by using encryption algorithms, or **ciphers**. Ciphers are secret ways of representing messages. There are a wide variety of ciphers at the software developer's disposal; these are discussed later in this chapter.

Integrity

Integrity is the concept of ensuring that data has not been altered by an unknown entity during it transit or storage. For example, it is possible for an e-mail containing sensitive data such as a contractual agreement to be modified before it reaches the recipient. Similarly, a purchase request sent to a Web service could be altered en route to the server, or a software package available for downloading could be altered to introduce code with malicious intent (a "trojan horse"). Checking data integrity ensures that data has not been compromised.

Many communications protocols, including TCP/IP, employ checksum or CRC (cyclic-redundancy check) algorithms to verify data integrity, but an intelligent adversary easily overcomes these. For example, suppose a downloadable software package has a published CRC associated with it, and this package is available at many mirror sites. An adversary with control over one of the mirrors installs a Trojan horse in the program; now the CRC has changed. The attacker can alter other insignificant parts of the code so that the CRC calculates to what it was before the alteration.

To counter this threat, cryptographically strong one-way hash functions have been developed that make it computationally infeasible to create the same hash value from two different inputs. There are quite a few such hash functions available in the public domain; details are discussed later in this chapter.

Authentication

Authentication is the concept of ensuring that a user's identity is truly what the user claims it to be. This is generally accomplished by having the user first state his identity and then present a piece of information that could only be produced from that user.

The oldest and most common form of user authentication is password authentication. However, passwords may be intercepted if sent on an unsecured line, where their confidentiality is not ensured. Passwords can be exposed by a variety of other means as well. Passwords are often written down and left in places too easily discovered by others. Also, people often use the same password for different services, so exposure of one password opens up multiple targets for potential abuse. Passwords are an example of authentication based on "what you know."

In response to the issues with password-type authentication, alternatives have been developed that are based on other factors. One approach requires the user to enter a different password for each login. This can be accomplished by giving the user a device that is used during the authentication process. When the user logs in, the server sends a "challenge" string that the user keys into her security device. The device displays a response to the challenge string, which the user sends back to the server. If the response is correct, the user has been successfully authenticated. Unlike passwords, this authentication is based on "what you have," rather than "what you know." Alternatively, instead of sending a challenge string, the server and the security device may be time-synchronized so that the user only needs to type in the display on the security device. Generally, such security devices use cryptographic techniques; for example, the device will have a unique internal key value that is known by the server, and the user's response will be derived from an encrypt function of the challenge string or current time. One of the more popular security device-based authentication solutions is SecureID, which uses a time-synchronized device to display a one-time password. Additionally, SecureID requires the user to prepend the one-time password with a regular password of the user's choosing, combining "what you have" with "what you know" to create a strong authentication solution.

Along with "what you know" and "what you have," there are authentication methods based on "what you are"—biometrics. Biometric authentication products check fingerprints, retina patterns, voice patterns, and facial infrared patterns, among others, to verify the identity of the user. However, even these methods can be fooled [Schneier02], so a best practice is to combine biometrics with additional authentication (such as a password). The role of biometrics in personal identification and authentication is discussed in Chapter 15, "Secure Personal Identification Strategies Using Smart Cards and Biometrics."

Authorization

Authorization is the concept of determining what actions a user is allowed to perform after being allowed access to the system.

Authorization methods and techniques vary greatly from system to system. One common method employs access control lists (ACLs), which list all users and their access privileges, such as read-only, read and modify, and so forth. Another technique is to assign each user a role or group identification, and the rest of the application checks this to determine what actions the user may perform. On UNIX operating systems, the owner of each file determines access to that file by others. Each system presents unique requirements that affect the design of authorization methods for that system.

Non-Repudiation

Non-repudiation is the concept that when a user performs an action on data, such as approving a document, that action must be bound with the user in such a way that the user cannot deny performing the action. Non-repudiation is generally associated with digital signatures; more details are presented later in this chapter.

The Role of Cryptography in Security

The past few years have seen major advances in security technologies, especially in the area of cryptography. The advent of the one-way digitally signed hash algorithm opened up opportunities for both verifying data integrity (with algorithms such as MD5 and SHA-1) and, to a lesser extent, protecting data through obfuscation (as with UNIX passwords using "crypt"). Encryption algorithms such as symmetric ciphers have evolved from the government-endorsed DES (Data Encryption Standard), a mainstay from the seventies through today in many government and commercial systems, to the latest algorithms such as RC4, IDEA, Blowfish, and the newly government-endorsed AES (Advanced Encryption standard), a.k.a. Rijndael.

But perhaps the most compelling recent achievement in cryptography has been the advent of asymmetric ciphers (also known as "public key cryptography"). Before asymmetric ciphers, the sender of a message that is secured with a symmetric cipher would need to communicate the key value used to encrypt the message to the receiver via a separate secure communications channel. In 1976, Whitfield Diffie and Martin Hellman developed a method that would allow two parties to communicate over an unsecured communications channel (for example, e-mail) and derive a secret key value that would be known only to them, even if others were eavesdropping on the communication [DiffieHellman]. In 1977, Ron Rivest, Adi Shamir, and Leonard Adleman developed the RSA asymmetric cipher, where one key value is used to encrypt a message but another key value is used to decrypt the message. The technology is based on the inability to quickly factor large prime numbers. The exact details are beyond the scope of this book. Suffice it to say that with asymmetric ciphers, the headache of key management is greatly reduced. Let's take a closer look at the popular cryptographic algorithms and how their use contributes to achieving security goals.

Cryptographic Algorithms

Although cryptography has been studied for years, its value has only recently—with the tremendous increase in the use of networking—been recognized. One normally associates cryptography with confidentiality via data encryption, but some cryptographic algorithms, such as the one-way hash function and digital signatures, are more concerned with data integrity than confidentiality.

This chapter will introduce you to the following cryptographic algorithms: one-way hash functions, symmetric ciphers, asymmetric ciphers, digital signatures, and digital certificates. For more information about understanding and implementing cryptographic algorithms in Java, refer to Chapter 4.

One-Way Hash Function Algorithms

One-way hash functions are algorithms that take as input a message (any string of bytes, such as a text string, a Word document, a JPG file) and generate as output a fixed-size number referred to as the "hash value" or "message digest." The size of the hash value depends on the algorithm used, but it is usually between 128 and 256 bits.

The purpose of a one-way hash function is to create a short digest that can be used to verify the integrity of a message. In communication protocols such as TCP/IP, message integrity is often verified using a checksum or CRC (cyclic-redundancy check). The sender of the message calculates the checksum of the message and sends it along with the message, and the receiver recalculates the checksum and compares it to the checksum that was sent. If they do not match, the receiver assumes the message was corrupted during transit and requests that the sender resend the message. These methods are fine when the expected cause of the corruption is due to electronic glitches or some other natural phenomena, but if the expected cause is an intelligent adversary with malicious intent, something stronger is needed. That is where cryptographically strong one-way hash functions come in.

A cryptographically strong one-way hash function is designed in such a way that it is computationally infeasible to find two messages that compute to the same hash value. With a checksum, a modestly intelligent adversary can fairly easily alter the message so that the checksum calculates to the same value as the original message's checksum. Doing the same with a CRC is not much more difficult. But a cryptographically strong one-way hash function makes this task all but impossible.

Two examples of cryptographically strong one-way hash algorithms are MD5 and SHA-1. MD5 was created by Ron Rivest (of RSA fame) in 1992 [RFC1321] and produces a 128-bit hash value. SHA-1 was created by the National Institute of Standards and Technology (NIST) in 1995 [FIPS1801] and produces a 160-bit hash value. SHA-1 is slower to compute than MD5 but is considered stronger because it creates a larger hash value. For references to other hash algorithms with various hash value sizes, see [Hashfunc01].

The Breaking of the SHA-1 One-Way Hash Algorithm

In February 2005, researchers at China's Shandong University released a preliminary paper demonstrating the ability to find two messages that, when run through the SHA-1 algorithm, produce the same hash value; this is known as a "collision." The purpose and benefit of one-way hash algorithms are that they produce unique hash values for different messages, and finding collisions should be impossible without trying all possibilities, which is known as a "brute force" attack. A brute force attack against SHA-1 would involve trying 2**80 (about 10**24, or 1 million billion billion) hash operations. The new research shows that it is possible to find a collision with SHA-1 in 2**69 (about 5 x 10**20, or 500 billion billion) hash operations.

For practical purposes, this is no big deal. For example, no one is going to be able to change your Web address on your X.509 certificate and have it still look like you signed it. But it is a kink in the armor, and more kinks will appear as better attacks against all cryptographic algorithms are researched. The general advice is that one should start thinking about avoiding using SHA-1 and opt for newer one-way hash algorithms, such as SHA-256 or SHA-512.

As an example of using a hash function, suppose an open-source development project posts its product, which is available for download, on the Web at several mirror sites. On their main site, they also have available the result of an MD5 hash performed on the whole download file. If an attacker breaks into one of the mirror sites, and inserts some malicious code into the product, he would need to be able to adjust other parts of the code so that the output of the MD5 would be the same as it was before. With a checksum or CRC, the attacker could do it, but MD5 is specifically designed to prevent this. Anyone who downloads the altered file and checks the MD5 hash will be able to detect that the file is not the original.

Another example: Suppose two parties are communicating over a TCP/IP connection. TCP uses a CRC check on its messages, but as discussed earlier, a CRC can be defeated. So, for additional security, suppose that the two parties are using an application protocol on top of TCP that attaches an MD5 hash value at the end of each message. Suppose an attacker lies at a point in between the two communicating parties in such a way that he can change the contents of the TCP stream. Would he be able to defeat the MD5 check?

It turns out he can. The attacker simply alters the data stream, and then recalculates the MD5 hash on the new data and attaches that. The two communicating parties have no other resource against which to check the MD5 value, because the communicating data could be anything, such as an on-the-fly conversation over an instant message channel. To prevent this, one combines a hash function with a secret key value. A standard way to do this is defined as the HMAC [RFC2104].

With hash functions, as with any cryptographic algorithm, the wise developer uses a tried-and-true published algorithm instead of developing one from scratch. The tried-and-true algorithms have undergone much scrutiny, and for every MD5 and SHA-1 there are many others that have fallen because of vulnerabilities and weaknesses.

We will discuss ciphers next. There are two types of ciphers, symmetric and asymmetric. We will start with symmetric ciphers, which have been around for centuries and are the cornerstone of data privacy.

Symmetric Ciphers

Symmetric ciphers are mechanisms that transform text in order to conceal its meaning. Symmetric ciphers provide two functions: message encryption and message decryption. They are referred to as **symmetric** because both the sender and the receiver must share the same key to encrypt and then decrypt the data. The encryption function takes as input a message and a key value. It then generates as output a seemingly random sequence of bytes roughly the same length as the input message. The decryption function is just as important as the encryption function. The decryption function takes as input the same seemingly random sequence of bytes output by the first function and the same key value, and generates as output the original message. The term "symmetric" refers to the fact that the same key value used to encrypt the message must be used to successfully decrypt it.

The purpose of a symmetric cipher is to provide message confidentiality. For example, if Alice needs to send Bob a confidential document, she could use e-mail; however, e-mail messages have about the same privacy as a postcard. To prevent the message from being disclosed to parties unknown, Alice can encrypt the message using a symmetric cipher and an appropriate key value and e-mail that. Anyone looking at the message en route to Bob will see the aforementioned seemingly random sequence of bytes instead of the confidential document. When Bob receives the encrypted message, he feeds it and the same key value used by Alice into the decrypt function of the same symmetric cipher used by Alice, which will produce the original message—the confidential document (see Figure 2–1).

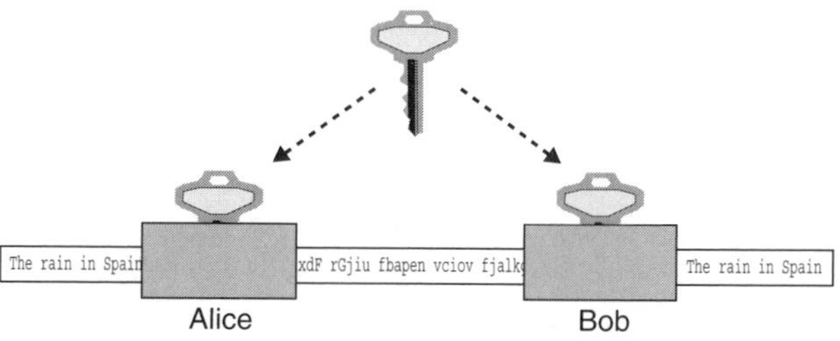

Figure 2–1 Encryption using a symmetric cipher

An example of a simple symmetric key cipher is the rotate, or Caesar, cipher. With the rotate cipher, a message is encrypted by substituting one letter at a time with a letter *n* positions ahead in the alphabet. If, for example, the value of *n* (the "key value" in a loose sense) is 3, then the letter A would be substituted with the letter D, B with E, C with F, and so on. Letters at the end would "wrap around" to the beginning; W would be substituted with Z, X would be substituted with A, Y with B, Z with C, and so on. So, a plaintext message of "WINNERS USE JAVA" encrypted with the rotate cipher with a key value of 7 would result in the ciphertext "DPUULYZ BZL QHCH." Even without the aid of a computer, the rotate cipher is quite easily broken; one need only try all possible key values, of which there are 26, to crack the code.

However, there are plenty of published symmetric ciphers from which to choose that have held up to a great deal of scrutiny. Some examples include DES, IDEA, AES (Rijndael), Twofish, and RC2. For references to these and other symmetric ciphers, see [WeiDai01], which is also a great starting point for other cryptographic references.

With symmetric ciphers, as with any cryptographic algorithm, the wise developer uses a tried-and-true published algorithm instead of developing one from scratch. The tried-and-true algorithms have undergone much scrutiny, and for every Rijndael and Twofish, there are many others that have fallen because of vulnerabilities and weaknesses [RSA02].

Symmetric ciphers are available in two types: block ciphers and stream ciphers. Block ciphers encrypt blocks of data (blocks are typically 8 bytes or 16 bytes) at a time. Stream ciphers are relatively new and are generally faster than block ciphers. However, it seems that block ciphers are more popular, probably because they have been around longer, and there are many free choices available [RSA02]. Examples of block ciphers include DES, IDEA, AES (Rijndael), and Blowfish. Examples of stream ciphers are RC4 and WAKE. Ron Rivest's RC4 leads the stream cipher popularity contest, because it is used with SSL in all Web browsers, but it can only be used via a license with RSA. Also, block ciphers can be used in modes where they can emulate stream cipher behavior [FIPS81]. An excellent free reference on the use of the modes, as well as cryptography in general, is available at [RSA01].

Advanced Encryption Standard (AES)

Among the symmetric ciphers, the AES deserves extra attention because it replaced DES as the symmetric cipher standard endorsed by the United States government. The AES algorithm, known as "Rijndael," was developed by Belgian cryptographers Joan Daemen and Vincent Rijmen and was selected from 21 entries in a contest held by NIST (National Institute of Standards and Technology).

Since 1977, DES has been the U.S. federal government's standard method for encrypting sensitive information [AES01]. But as computing power increased, DES was in danger of being too easily compromised. In 1987, the U.S. government started Capstone, a project to standardize encryption that included an algorithm called Skipjack. However, the algorithm was kept secret, so cryptographers could not openly analyze it for weaknesses. Due to these and other circumstances [RSA03], Skipjack's popularity never got off the ground, although the algorithm was finally published in 1998 [Schneier04].

In 1997, NIST announced that the replacement for DES, called AES, would be an algorithm selected from an open number of entries. Anyone could submit an algorithm, all algorithms would be made public, and the winner would be selected on a number of factors, including speed and ease of implementation. On October 2, 2000, the Rijndael algorithm was selected over finalists such as Bruce Schneier's Twofish and Ron Rivest's RC6. Rijndael is a block cipher with a key length of 128, 192, or 256 bits and a block length of 128, 192, or 256 bits.

The AES contest was a landmark activity in computer security, because it demonstrated the acceptance of the concept that open scrutiny of an encryption algorithm offered better security in the long run than a secretly developed algorithm. To understand how to use AES in Java applications, refer to Chapter 4.

Asymmetric Ciphers

Asymmetric ciphers provide the same two functions as symmetric ciphers: message encryption and message decryption. There are two major differences, however. First, the key value used in message decryption is different than the key value used for message encryption. Second, asymmetric ciphers are thousands of times slower than symmetric key ciphers. But asymmetric ciphers offer a phenomenal advantage in secure communications over symmetric ciphers.

To explain this advantage, let's review the earlier example of using a symmetric cipher. Alice encrypts a message using key K and sends it to Bob. When Bob receives the encrypted message, he uses key K to decrypt the encrypted message and recover the original message. This scenario introduces the question of how Alice sends the key value used to encrypt the message to Bob. The answer is that Alice must use a separate communication channel, one that is known to be secure (that is, no one can listen in on the communication), when she sends the key value to Bob.

The requirement for a separate, secure channel for key exchanges using symmetric ciphers invites even more questions. First, if a separate, secure channel exists, why not send the original message over that? The usual answer is that the secure channel has limited bandwidth, such as a secure phone line or a trusted courier. Second, how long can Alice and Bob assume that their key value has not been compromised (that is, become known to someone other than themselves) and when should they exchange a fresh key value? Dealing with these questions and issues falls within the realm of key management.

Key management is the single most vexing problem in using cryptography. Key management involves not only the secure distribution of key values to all communication parties, but also management of the lifetime of the keys, determination of what actions to take if a key is compromised, and so on. Alice and Bob's key management needs may not be too complicated; they could exchange a password over the phone (if they were certain that no one was listening in) or via registered mail. But suppose Alice needed to securely communicate not just with Bob but with hundreds of other people. She would need to exchange (via trusted phone or registered mail) a key value with each of these people and manage this list of keys, including keeping track of when to exchange a fresh key, handling key compromises, handling key mismatches (when the receiver cannot decrypt the message because he has the wrong key), and so on. Of course, these issues would apply not just to Alice but to Bob and everyone else; they all would need to exchange keys and endure these key management headaches (there actually exists an ANSI standard (X9.17) [ANSIX9.17] on key management for DES.)

To make matters worse, if Alice needs to send a message to hundreds of people, she will have to encrypt each message with its own key value. For example, to send an announcement to 200 people, Alice would need to encrypt the message 200 times, one encryption for each recipient. Obviously, symmetric ciphers for secure communications require quite a bit of overhead.

The major advantage of the asymmetric cipher is that it uses *two* key values instead of one: one for message encryption and one for message decryption. The two keys are created during the same process and are known as a key pair. The one for message encryption is known as the public key; the one for message decryption is known as the private key. Messages encrypted with the public key can only be decrypted with its associated private key. The private key is kept secret by the owner and shared with no one. The public key, on the other hand, may be given out over an unsecured communication channel or published in a directory.

Using the earlier example of Alice needing to send Bob a confidential document via e-mail, we can show how the exchange works with an asymmetric cipher. First, Bob e-mails Alice his public key. Alice then encrypts the document with Bob's public key, and sends the encrypted message via e-mail to Bob. Because any message encrypted with Bob's public key can only be decrypted with Bob's private key, the message is secure from prying eyes, even if those prying eyes know Bob's public key. When Bob receives the encrypted message, he decrypts it using his private key and recovers the original document.

Figure 2–2 illustrates the process of encrypting and decrypting with the public and private keys.

If Bob needs to send some edits on the document back to Alice, he can do so by having Alice send him her public key; he then encrypts the edited document using Alice's public key and e-mails the secured document back to Alice. Again, the message is secure from eavesdroppers, because only Alice's private key can decrypt the message, and only Alice has her private key.

Note the very important difference between using an asymmetric cipher and a symmetric cipher: No separate, secure channel is needed for Alice and Bob to exchange a key value to be used to secure the message. This solves the major problem of key management with symmetric ciphers: getting the key value communicated to the other party. With asymmetric ciphers, the key value used to send

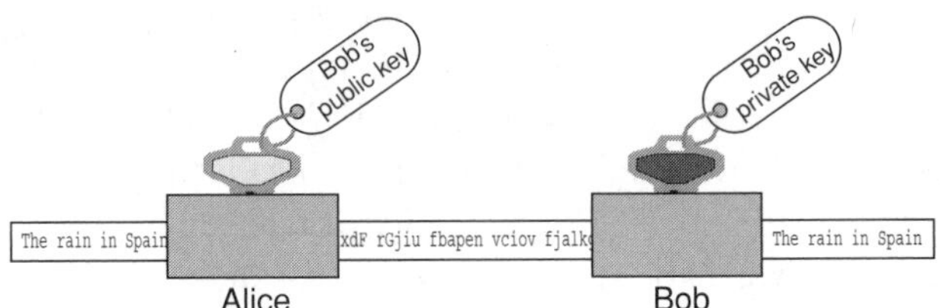

Figure 2–2 Encryption using an asymmetric cipher

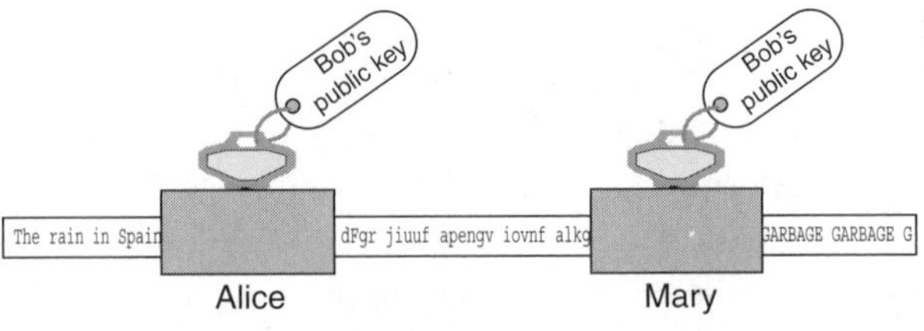

Figure 2–3 Bob's public key cannot decrypt what it encrypted

someone a message is published for all to see. This also solves another symmetric key management headache: having to exchange a key value with each party with whom one wishes to communicate. Anyone who wants to send a secure message to Alice uses Alice's public key.

Recall that one of the differences between asymmetric and symmetric ciphers is that asymmetric ciphers are much slower, up to thousands of times slower [WeiDai02]. This issue is resolved in practice by using the asymmetric cipher to communicate an ephemeral symmetric key value and then using a symmetric cipher and the ephemeral key to encrypt the actual message. The symmetric key is referred to as ephemeral (meaning to last for a brief time) because it is only used once, for that exchange. It is not persisted or reused, the way traditional symmetric key mechanisms require. Going back to the earlier example of Alice e-mailing a confidential document to Bob, Alice would first create an ephemeral key value to encrypt the document with a symmetric cipher. Then she would create another message, encrypting the ephemeral key value with Bob's public key, and then send both messages to Bob. Upon receipt, Bob would first decrypt the ephemeral key value with his private key and then decrypt the secured document with the ephemeral key value (using the symmetric cipher) to recover the original document.

Figure 2–4 depicts using a combination of asymmetric and symmetric ciphers.

Some examples of asymmetric ciphers are RSA, Elgamal, and ECC (elliptic-curve cryptography). RSA is by far the most popular in use today. Elgamal is another popular asymmetric cipher. It was developed in 1985 by Taher Elgamal and is based on the Diffie-Hellman key exchange, which allows two parties to communicate publicly yet derive a secret key value known only to them [Diffie-Hellman].

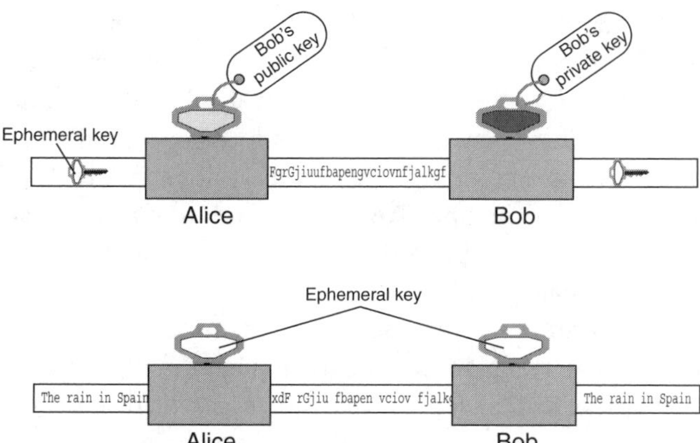

Figure 2–4 Using a combination of asymmetric and symmetric ciphers

Diffie-Hellman, developed by Whitfield Diffie and Martin Hellman in 1976, is considered the first asymmetric cipher, though the concept of an asymmetric cipher may have been invented in the U. K. six years earlier. Diffie-Hellman is different from RSA in that it is not an encryption method; it creates a secure numeric value that can be used as a symmetric key. In a Diffie-Hellman exchange, the sender and receiver each generate a random number (kept private) and value derived from the random number (made public). The two parties then exchange the public values. The power behind the Diffie-Hellman algorithm is its ability to generate a shared secret. Once the public values have been exchanged, each party can then use its private number and the other's public value to generate a symmetric key, known as the shared secret, which is identical to the other's. This key can then be used to encrypt data using a symmetric cipher. One advantage Diffie-Hellman has over RSA is that every time keys are exchanged, a new set of values is used. With RSA, if an attacker managed to capture your private key, they could decrypt all your future messages as well as any message exchange captured in the past. However, RSA keys can be authenticated (as with X.509 certificates), preventing man-in-the-middle attacks, to which a Diffie-Hellman exchange is susceptible.

Digital Signature

Digital signatures are used to guarantee the integrity of the message sent to a recipient by representing the identity of the message sender. This is done by signing the message using a digital signature, which is the unique by-product of asymmetric ciphers. Although the public key of an asymmetric cipher generally performs message encryption and the private key generally performs message decryption, the reverse is also possible. The private key can be used to encrypt a message, which would require the public key to decrypt it. So, Alice could encrypt a message using her private key, and that message could be decrypted by anyone with access to Alice's public key. Obviously, this behavior does not secure the message; by definition, anyone has access to Alice's public key (it could be posted in a directory) so anyone can decrypt it. However, Alice's private key, by definition, is known to no one but Alice; therefore, a message that is decrypted with Alice's public key could not have come from anyone but Alice. This is the idea behind digital signatures.

Digital signatures are the only mechanisms that make it possible to ascertain the source of a message using an asymmetric cipher. Encrypting a message with a private key is a form of digital signature. However, as we discussed before, asymmetric ciphers are quite slow. Alice could use the technique presented in the previous section of creating an ephemeral key to encrypt the message, and then encrypt the ephemeral key with her private key. But encrypting the message is a wasted effort, because anyone can decrypt it. Besides, the point of the exercise is not to secure the message but to prove it came from Alice.

The solution is to perform a one-way hash function on the message, and encrypt the hash value with the private key. For example, Alice wants to confirm a contract with Bob. Alice can edit the contract's dotted line with "I agree," then perform an MD5 hash on the documents, encrypt the MD5 hash value with her private key, and send the document with the encrypted hash value (the digital signature) to Bob. Bob can verify that Alice has agreed to the documents by checking the digital signature; he also performs an MD5 hash on the document, and then he decrypts the digital signature with Alice's public key. If the MD5 hash value computed from the document contents equals the decrypted digital signature, then Bob has verified that it was Alice who digitally signed the document.

Figure 2–5 shows how a digital signature is created.

Figure 2–6 shows the process of verifying a digital signature.

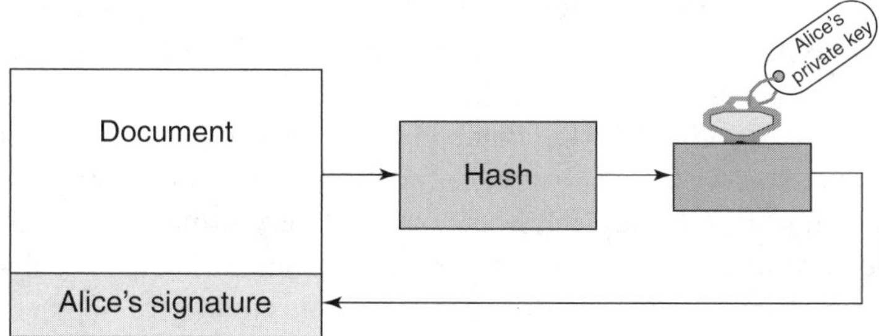

Figure 2–5 Digital signature

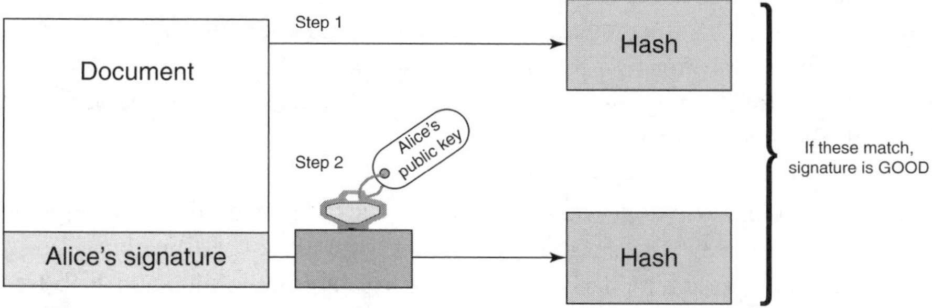

Figure 2–6 Verifying a digital signature

Moreover, Alice cannot say that she never signed the document; she cannot refute the signature, because only she holds the private key that could have produced the digital signature. This ensures non-repudiation.

Digital Certificates

A digital certificate is a document that uniquely identifies information about a party. It contains a party's public key plus other identification information that is digitally signed and issued by a trusted third party, also referred to as a **Certificate Authority (CA)**. A digital certificate is also known as an **X.509 certificate** and is commonly used to solve problems associated with key management.

As explained earlier in this chapter, the advent of asymmetric ciphers has greatly reduced the problem of key management. Instead of requiring that each party exchange a different key value with every other party with whom they wish to communicate over separate, secure communication channels, one simply exchanges public keys with the other parties or posts public keys in a directory.

However, another problem arises: How is one sure that the public key really belongs to Alice? In other words, how is the identity of the public key's owner *verified*? Within a controlled environment, such as within a company, a central directory may have security controls that ensure that the identities of public keys' owners have been verified by the company. But what if Alice runs a commerce Web site, and Bob wishes to securely send Alice his credit card number. Alice may send Bob her public key, but Mary (an adversary sitting on the communication between Alice and Bob) may intercept the communication and substitute her public key in place of Alice's. When Bob sends his credit card number using the received public key, he is unwittingly handing it to Mary, not Alice.

One method to verify Alice's public key is to call Alice and ask her directly to verify her public key, but because public keys are large (typically 1024 bits, or 128 bytes), for Alice to recite her public key value would prove too cumbersome and is prone to error. Alice could also verify her public key *fingerprint*, which is the output of a hash function performed on her public key. If one uses the MD5 hash function for this purpose, the hash value is 128 bits or 16 bytes, which would be a little more manageable.

But suppose Bob does not know Alice personally and therefore could not ascertain her identity with a phone call? Bob needs a trusted third party to vouch for Alice's public key. This need is met, in part, by a digital certificate.

For example, assume Charlie is a third party that both Alice and Bob trust. Alice sends Charlie her public key, plus other identifying information such as her name, address, and Web site URL. Charlie verifies Alice's public key, perhaps by calling her on the phone and having her recite her public key fingerprint. Then

Charlie creates a document that includes Alice's public key and identification, and digitally signs it using his private key, and sends it back to Alice. This signed document is the digital certificate of Alice's public key and identification, vouched for by Charlie.

Now, when Bob goes to Alice's Web site and wants to securely send his credit card number, Alice sends Bob her digital certificate. Bob verifies Charlie's signature on the certificate using Charlie's public key (assume Bob has already verified Charlie's public key), and if the signature is good, Bob can be assured that, according to Charlie, the public key within the certificate is associated with the identification within the certificate—namely, Alice's name, address, and Web site URL. Bob can encrypt his credit card number using the public key with confidence that only Alice can decrypt it.

Figure 2–7 illustrates how a digital certificate is used to verify Alice's identity.

Suppose Mary (an adversary) decides to intercept the communication between Alice and Bob, and replaces Alice's public key with her own within the digital certificate. When Bob verifies Charlie's signature, the verification will fail because the contents of the certificate has changed. Recall that to check a digital signature, one decrypts the signature with the signer's public key, and the result should equal the output of the hash function performed on the document. Because the document has changed, the hash value will not be the same as the one Charlie encrypted with his private key.

Figure 2–8 shows what happens if an adversary (Mary) tries to alter Alice's certificate.

Verification of a digital certificate can also be a multilevel process; this is known as **verifying a certificate chain**. In the previous example, it was assumed that Bob had already verified Charlie's public key. Let's now assume that Bob does not know Charlie or Alice but does have in his possession the pre-verified public key of Victor, and that Charlie has obtained a digital certificate from Victor.

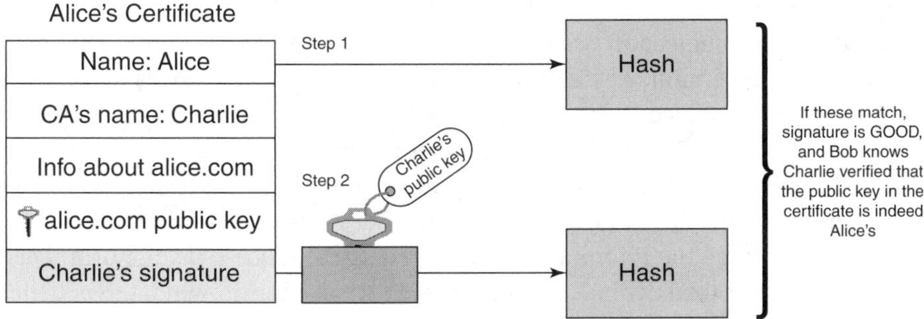

Figure 2–7 Verifying an identity using a digital certificate

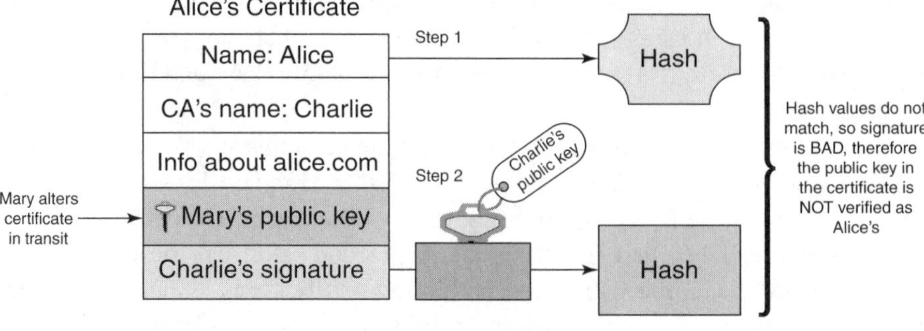

Figure 2–8 Adversary (Mary) alters certificate

When Bob needs to secure information being sent to Alice, Alice sends Bob not only her digital certificate signed by Charlie, but Charlie's certificate signed by Victor. Bob verifies Charlie's signature on Alice's certificate using Charlie's public key, and then verifies Victor's signature on Charlie's public key using Victor's public key. If all signatures are good, Bob can be assured that Victor vouches for Charlie and that Charlie vouches for Alice.

In practice, Victor's public key will be distributed as a certificate that was self-signed. A self-signed certificate is known as a *root certificate.* So in the example, there are really three certificates involved: Alice's certificate signed by Charlie, Charlie's certificate signed by Victor, and Victor's certificate, also signed by Victor. These three certificates make up the certificate chain.

Figure 2–9 shows how certificates can be chained together to verify identity.

In this example, Victor acts as a CA. He is in the business of being a trusted authority who verifies an individual's identification, verifies that individual's public key, and binds them together in a document that he digitally signs. CAs play an important part in the issuance and revocation of digital certificates.

The Role of CA in Issuing Certificates

In a trusted communication using digital certificates, a CA plays the role of the entity that issues a public key certificate. The certificate is the CA's assertion that the public key contained in the certificate belongs to a specific person, associated organization, or server host. Other information related to the person noted in the certificate is also provided. The CA is obligated to verify the information when a user requests a certificate and sends a Certificate Signing Request (CSR) to the CA. After verifying the information, the CA signs the requests and returns a certificate to the user (usually in X.509 certificate format). It is important to note that the relying parties also trust the certificate information issued by the CA. The

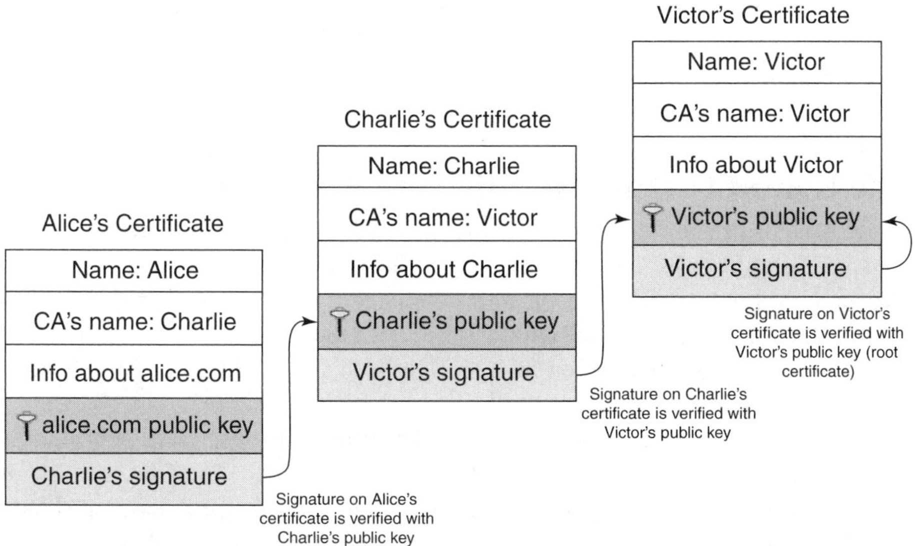

Figure 2–9 A certificate chain

relying party can decrypt the CA's signature using the CA's public key, which assures the relying party that the certificate was issued by the CA mentioned in the certificate.

In order to trust a certificate, the relying party has to trust the root certificate in its hierarchical chain. The CA, therefore, provides the trusted root certificate, and the CA is responsible for verifying the identities (out-of-band) of the certificates it signs. The reason digital certificates are so pervasive on the Web today is because many CA root certificates come bundled in the Web browsers. This eliminates the need for Web users to import and verify root certificates, though often this must be done with employees in organizations that have their own root certificates that are not bundled by default in the browsers. One of the most popular certificate authorities is VeriSign. Most of the secure Web sites on the Internet have their certificates verified (and signed) by VeriSign.

All Web browsers that support HTTPS employ the SSL (Secure Socket Layer) protocol, which in turn uses X.509 certificates. S/MIME (Secure MIME) and PEM (Privacy Enhanced Mail), both used to secure e-mail, also use X.509 certificates. Along with the public key and identification information, X.509 certificates include validity dates that indicate from what point in time the certificate is valid and when it expires. Other information is included as well; see [RFC2459]. The examples in this chapter have described the X.509 certificate structure, which is a hierarchical trust model; a signing authority signs each digital certificate once, and the top authority self-signs his certificate. Other certificate structures use different trust models; PGP (Pretty Good Privacy), which is another program used to secure e-mail, uses its own type of digital certificate that can be signed more than once. Trust models are discussed later in this chapter.

The Role of CA in Revocation of Certificates

The CA is also responsible for revoking the certificates if the CA discovers that the issued certificate is falsely verified or the identified user does not adhere to the CA-mandated policy requirements or has violated its policies. In addition, revoking certificates is also necessary for a variety of other reasons. A user may leave an organization, an organization with an SSL Web site might go out of business, or a private key may be compromised.

As part of the revocation process, the CA maintains the user certificate and its serial number as part of a certificate revocation list (CRL). The CRL is a list of certificates that are considered revoked, that are no longer valid, and that should not be trusted by any system or users. It is important to note that when a revoked certificate's expiration date occurs, the certificate will be automatically removed from the CRL.

Using Certificate Revocation Lists (CRL)

To verify a certificate, it is quite important to use the appropriate CRL to make sure the signer's certificate has not been revoked. CRLs are usually maintained as repositories identified with a URL for sites containing the latest CRLs. It is also possible to download CA-listed CRLs by subscribing to the repositories and creating an in-house CRL repository to make CRL searches for verifying the signer's information. Most Web servers and Web browsers provide a facility for verifying the certificates using CRLs.

Using the Online Certificate Status Protocol (OCSP)

Another alternative for verifying certificates using CA-maintained CRLs is the Online Certificate Status Protocol (OCSP) defined in RFC 2560 [RFC2560]. In this method, the CA publishes the revoked certificate lists to an OSCP-enabled directory. This could be done using a CRL or an LDAP update. The CA then maintains an OCSP responder application that will use the data in the OCSP directory to respond to a query for a particular certificate with a "good," "revoked," or "unknown" response. This allows CAs to create plug-ins for Web browsers that can automatically check for certificate revocations. Application developers can also write code to query the OSCP responder, because it is a standard protocol. The drawbacks to OSCP are that it does not allow for out-of-band verification and that it may be slow, because each response must be signed by the CA and the CA may get overwhelmed with requests as the number of users hitting it and the number of revoked certificates grows.

The Role of Secure Sockets Layer (SSL)

SSL was developed by Netscape in 1996 [Netscape01] for the purpose of securing HTTP data between the Web user and Web server. However, the design of SSL allows it to secure not just HTTP, but any data communicated over any connection-oriented, end-to-end reliable protocol (such as TCP/IP). The protocol uses a combination of public-key algorithms and symmetric-key algorithms to authenticate the server side, optionally authenticate the client side, and secure all communications using encryption between the two sides.

During an SSL connection, the communicating parties exchange all messages using the SSL Record protocol. There are four types of messages:

- Handshake
- Alert
- Change cipher spec
- Application data

Handshake messages negotiate the SSL session parameters, which include authentication information, data encryption algorithm, and so forth. Alert messages indicate an error condition and are either warnings or fatal errors. The ChangeCipherSpec message tells the receiving party that all subsequent messages will be secured using the previously negotiated parameters. Application data represents the data that is being secured by the SSL protocol.

An SSL connection maintains two types of state: session state and connection state. The session state contains the security parameters negotiated by the communicating parties, including authentication information such as certificates, encryption algorithms, and a master "secret" value. A connection state is created for each separate connection (for example, each HTTP GET) and maintains security parameters for that connection, such as encryption key values and sequence numbers.

The idea behind the two states is to avoid the overhead of authentication every time a new connection is set up between the communicating parties. One of the parameters of the session state is a master secret value that is agreed upon after authentication and negotiation of security parameters have occurred. Using this shared secret, the communicating parties can derive new key values for securing new connections, thereby implicitly reauthenticating each other.

When an SSL connection is started, the first order of business is for the communicating parties to negotiate security parameters such as authentication and encryption algorithms. These parameters are referred to in SSL as the CipherSuite, which is represented as an integer. For example, the integer *4* refers to CipherSuite SSL_RSA_WITH_RC4_128_MD5 (authentication using RSA public-key certificate, data encryption using 128-bit RC4, and data integrity using an MD5 hash). A full list of CipherSuite assignments is available in the spec [Netscape01].

The first message sent in this negotiation comes from the client (the initiator of the secure connection) and is known as the ClientHello. The ClientHello contains a list of CipherSuite options that are acceptable to the client for securing the connection. The server responds with either a ServerHello message indicating the CipherSuite to be used or with a fatal alert indicating that none of the client's options were acceptable. The ServerHello also contains a session identifier that can be used by the client for creating future SSL connections. The next messages depend on the selected CipherSuite, but most require server authentication, so the server sends its digital certificate.

The public-key value in the certificate will be used to authenticate the server. The client then generates a random value, encrypts it with the server's public key, and sends it back to the server in the form of the ClientKeyExchange message. The random value is then known by both parties and is used to calculate the session's master secret, from which key values are derived for securing communication data, both for the current connection and future ones. This is also the major step in authenticating the server. Unless the server is the true owner of the public key, it will be unable to create the key values necessary to communicate later in the process.

Lastly, both client and server send a ChangeCipherSpec message, indicating that from this point onward, all messages will be secured using the negotiated security parameters. Both sides then send a "Finished" message, the first message secured with the negotiated security parameters. The Finished message contains a value that is the result of the negotiated hash function value computed on all handshake messages. Both communicating parties ensure that the hash value is correct, and then they continue sending application data secured with the negotiated security.

Figure 2–10 illustrates an SSL handshake.

When the client wants to create a new network connection with the same server, the overhead of exchanging certificates and key values can be skipped. When sending the ClientHello message, the client can specify the session identifier returned by the ServerHello during the initial connection setup. If the server

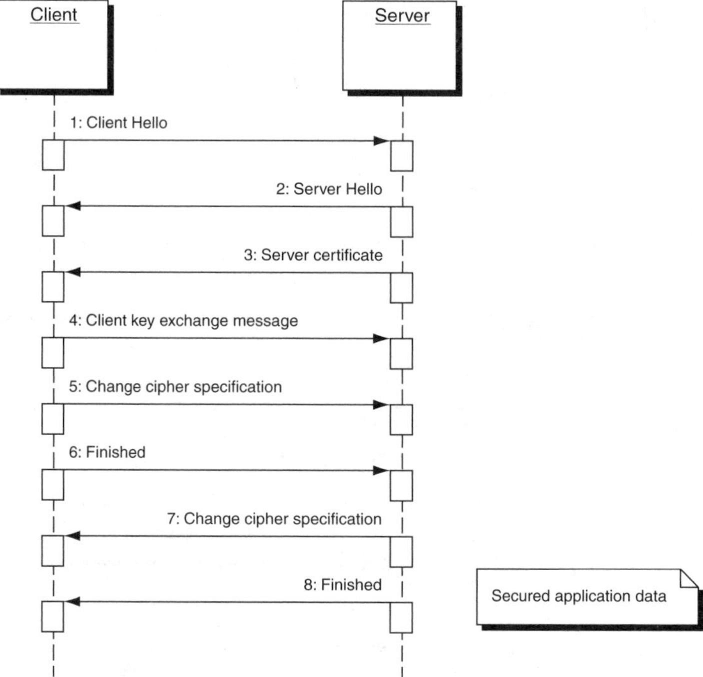

Figure 2–10 An SSL handshake

still has the session information associated with that session identifier, it will send a ChangeCipherSpec to the client, indicating that it still has the session info and has created the pertinent key values to secure this new connection. The client will then send a ChangeCipherSpec message. The two parties can then continue sending secured application data. (See Figure 2–11.)

Transport Layer Security (TLS)

The TLS specification was authored in 1999 by Certicom, mostly as an attempt to create an official IETF standard protocol out of SSL 3.0. However, TLS and SSL are not exactly the same. The TLS specification [RFC2246] describes TLS as being based on the SSL 3.0 Protocol Specification as published by Netscape. The differences between this protocol and SSL 3.0 are not dramatic, but they are significant enough that TLS 1.0 and SSL 3.0 do not interoperate (although TLS 1.0 does incorporate a mechanism by which a TLS implementation can back down to SSL 3.0). As the saying goes, the great thing about standards is that there are so many to choose from.

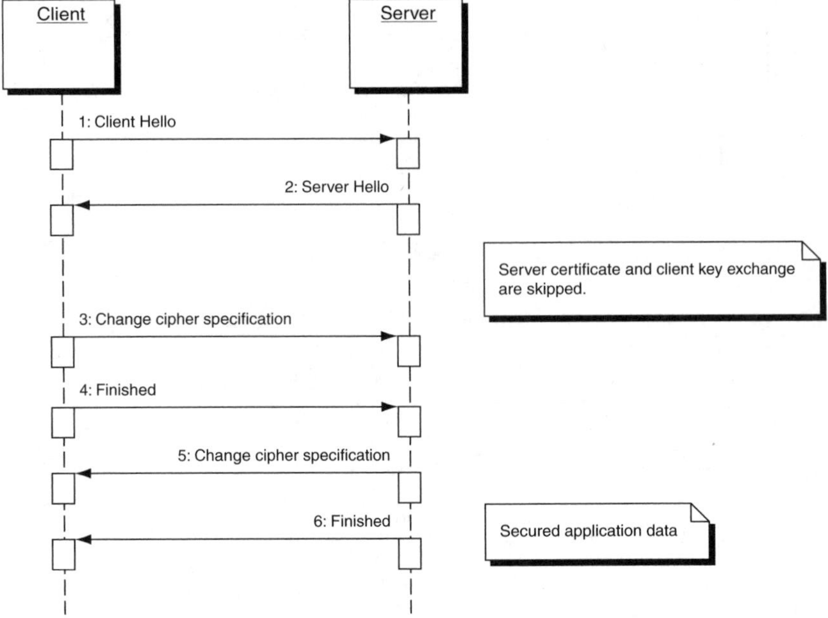

Figure 2–11 SSL connection reuse of session information

Fortunately, the two protocols are so alike that, despite the fact that they do not interoperate, the mechanism by which a TLS implementation can back down to SSL 3.0 is pretty simple. In fact, TLS identifies itself as version 3.1 to differentiate itself from SSL 3.0 and the older, broken SSL 2.0. The differences between the two protocols include: TLS and SSL 3.0 use a slightly different keyed MAC algorithm (TLS uses the new HMAC [RFC2104], which is very similar to the keyed MAC used in SSL 3.0), TLS chooses more data to include in the MAC (it includes the protocol version along with the data and data type), and TLS does not support FORTEZZA, a hardware-based security token based on the ill-received and mostly unused Skipjack security infrastructure. All of the basic principles of the SSL protocol described in the previous section, such as ClientHello messages and ChangeCipherSpec messages, are the same in both protocols.

Security Issues with SSL/TLS

SSL is a fully disclosed, open protocol that has been reviewed by some of the best in the business [Schneier01]. Despite that, SSL has been reported as "broken" (a session could be hijacked) or similar more than once since its inception. As discussed later in this chapter, Ian Goldberg and David Wagner ten years ago described how they could eavesdrop on a secured SSL session with Netscape version 1.2 and recover the communication being secured in a matter of minutes [Goldberg01]. This demonstrated how an error in the implementation of SSL could undermine its security.

More recently, it was discovered in 2003 that certain browsers allowed SSL communications using the CipherSuite SSL_NULL_WITH_NULL_NULL. This is the initial CipherSuite in SSL communications, the expectation being that the only communication using this CipherSuite are the exchanges described earlier to negotiate one of the secure CipherSuites. However, a malicious Web site, for example, could negotiate use of this CipherSuite, and the client would assume that normal SSL security was in place (the browser would show the lock icon, indicating an SSL session, which would be accurate) even though all communications were actually "in the clear" (unencrypted). Moreover, the malicious Web site could impersonate another, legitimate, Web site, and there would be no name mismatch warning because the CipherSuite SSL_NULL_WITH_NULL_NULL does not require a certificate. (Most browsers raise a warning if the server presents a valid certificate but the name on the certificate does not match the Web site name.)

The Importance and Role of LDAP in Security

Every organization requires a mechanism that keeps track of entities within the organization, such as individual employees, departments of employees, and assets such as buildings, meeting rooms, equipment, and so on. This structure often exists in the form of a directory, which provides contact information for all members of the organization. Before computers were ubiquitous in the business world, these directories often were just private telephone books that presented one view of the organizational structure, usually an alphabetical list of employees and associated contact information. If the organization was large enough, a section might have been included listing departments, sections of a building, phone numbers for conference rooms, and so forth. Publishing such a directory was frequently the responsibility of a single person or team; the larger the organization, the more daunting the task.

With the increased use of electronic business tools such as pagers, cell phones, and e-mail, maintaining such a directory became even more daunting. Employees today do not have just a phone number—they have several pieces of contact information. The need arose for an electronic directory that could hold various types of contact information and be structurally flexible so that maintenance could easily be performed.

LDAP (Lightweight Directory Access Protocol), based on the X.500 directory standard, is a standard directory structure and protocol. LDAP provides a standard electronic directory service that is implemented by many vendors and used by many companies. The X.500 directory standard came about in 1988 through the work of the International Organization for Standards (ISO) and the International Telecommunication Union (ITU). One of the main concepts in X.500 is that a directory is a hierarchical structure of objects, where an object represents an employee, an asset such as a piece of equipment, or any other entity. Another concept is that the directory is structured in such a way that each section of an organization is responsible for maintaining only its piece of the directory structure. Related to this decentralization is the hierarchical structure, which guarantees that each object has a "parent" responsible for creating and maintaining the object. This is an important point, because one of the pieces of information associated with an employee may be a public key (discussed earlier in this chapter).

The communication between users and the directory structure employs the Directory Access Protocol (DAP). However, the X.500 standard and associated DAP protocol was deemed by many to be far too complicated to implement. LDAP was developed at the University of Michigan in 1995 to offer a lightweight version of the DAP for accessing X.500 directories over TCP/IP. LDAP has quickly become the de facto electronic directory standard.

Earlier in this chapter, the discussion of asymmetric ciphers included the use of public keys and the difficulties in verifying the owner of a public key. One method for assuring the authenticity of the public key and verifying its owner's identity is to present the public key in the form of a digital certificate, where a trusted third party vouches for the owner's identity and binds a digital certificate to the owner's public key. This is done by digitally signing a document that contains the owner's identity and public key. The challenge, then, is to publish or make available the certificate to the public.

LDAP's flexibility makes it possible to store digital certificates along with the rest of an employee's information. It can also be used to publish a digital certificate chain structure for all members of an organization. The LDAP protocol's roots stem from the X.500 directory standard. That is the same standard from which the X.509 digital certificate (widely used by SSL and S/MIME protocols) comes. The two technologies thus work together smoothly.

Figure 2–12 presents a simple example of an organizational hierarchy with digital certificates for each member. Each member's public key (contained within the digital certificate) is signed (and is assumed to be verified) by the "parent" member in the hierarchy. The certificate authority of the organization verifies the

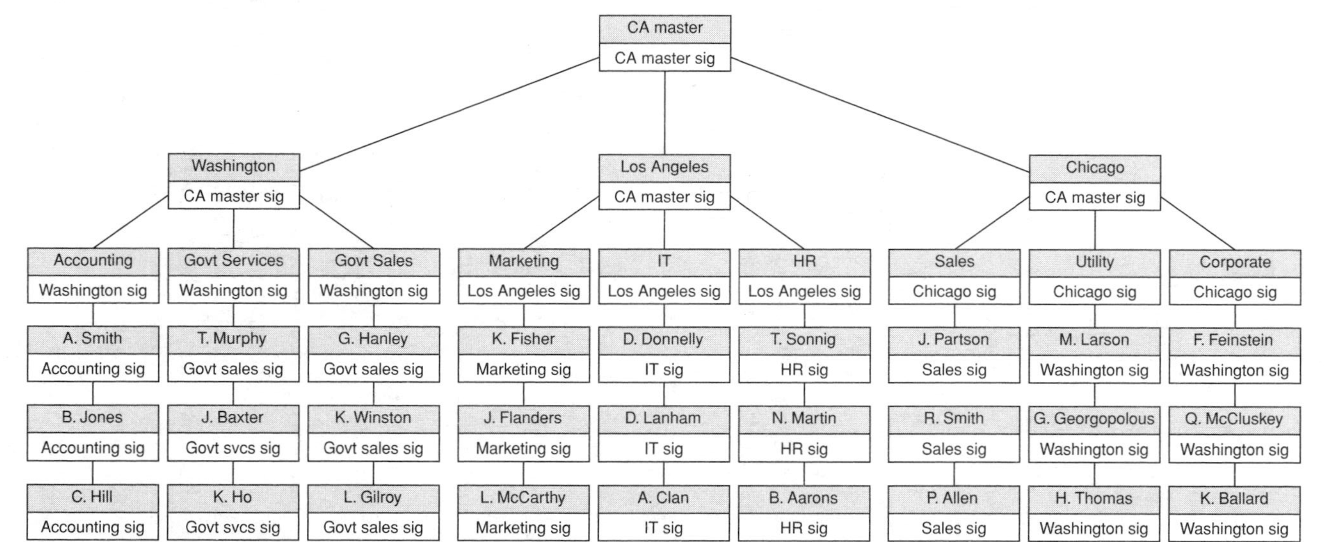

Figure 2–12 Example LDAP Hierarchy

public key for the different offices in the organization, such as Washington, Los Angeles, and Chicago. Each office, in turn, is responsible for its portion of the directory structure, including digital certificates. For example, the Los Angeles office maintains departments within its area—Marketing, IT, and Human Resources. Each of these departments' digital certificates are signed by an authority for the entire office. Marketing, in turn, maintains the employee directory structure within its area, and therefore the head of Marketing signs each of that department's employees' certificates.

Note that at the top of the hierarchy is the certificate authority, which has no parent node. Its digital certificate is signed by itself and therefore is the root certificate. The root certificate is widely distributed, and its public key value is well-known; from it, all other certificates can be verified.

As an example, suppose Q. McCluskey in Corporate needs to send a secure e-mail to L. Gilroy in Government Services. Q. McCluskey verifies L. Gilroy's certificate by obtaining a certificate chain that includes L. Gilroy's certificate, Government Services' certificate, Washington's certificate, and the CA master certificate. If each certificate signature checks out, L. Gilroy's certificate is validated.

The Role of LDAP in J2EE

LDAP also plays an important role in Java 2 Enterprise Edition (J2EE) applications. LDAP is the preferred directory service provider for J2EE's Java Naming and Directory Interface (JNDI) requirements. JNDI is an enterprise Java API that provides naming and directory functionality using a common set of classes and interfaces that are independent of a specific naming and directory service implementation [Moraes]. The J2EE specification requires that JNDI be used for the application component's naming environment. For instance, remote interfaces to Enterprise Java Beans (EJBs) can be obtained across a J2EE cluster by retrieving them using a JNDI API call to a common LDAP store. This allows Java objects in one instance of an application server to locate and invoke operations on Enterprise Java Beans (EJBs) in another instance. Other service providers, such as Databases, can be used as well, but LDAP is best suited for the task based on its market share and the fact that it is generally the best performing service provider.

LDAP is also commonly used to store policies, access control lists, and user information in J2EE applications. Many application servers ship with built-in LDAP directories, and all support external LDAP directories. Access control information is often stored in LDAP alongside the user information. Because of LDAP's universality, LDAP-enabled directories have become the de facto standard for managing user information across the enterprise.

Common Challenges in Cryptography

In applying security to a computing system such as a Web application server, the security designer must overcome challenges involved with using the security tools discussed earlier in this chapter. When implementing cryptographic algorithms such as symmetric ciphers, the designer must study the tool and avoid its weaknesses. For example, some ciphers have a set of "weak" keys, which are key values that lend themselves to easier compromise by an intelligent adversary. Challenges the security designer faces when using security solutions include proper random number generation for key values, key management, certificate revocation issues, trust models, and threat modeling.

Random Number Generation

In 1995, Ian Goldberg and David Wagner published a paper [Goldberg01] describing how they could eavesdrop on a secured SSL session with Netscape version 1.2 and recover the communication being secured in a matter of minutes. Netscape had implemented SSL and the associated cryptographic tools correctly, except for one thing: the key values they were creating were easily determined because the random number generation technique they were using was predictable.

Bad random numbers can kill security. When one creates a key value for use with a cipher that is meant only for one session, the key value must be as random as possible. In Netscape's case, they were deriving the random number from the current daytime clock value, process id, and parent process id. An intelligent adversary needed only to go through all the possible combinations before hitting on the right millisecond that created the key value; even if the clock's resolution was down to the millisecond, the key could be recovered within minutes. Netscape finally fixed the problem by looking at more sources of entropy, or true randomness, to create their key values. Ideas for creating random numbers are offered by Eastlake [RFC1750].

Many modern operating systems support cryptographically strong pseudo-random number generators. Bruce Schneier's Yarrow [Schneier03] offers a platform-independent method of producing strong pseudo-random numbers; many UNIX-style systems use Yarrow to support the device /dev/random, from which an indefinite string of random bytes can be read.

Key Management

As mentioned earlier in this chapter, key management is the single most vexing problem in cryptography use. To secure data via encryption, one must exchange a key value to be used with the encryption process. If the communicating parties only have a publicly accessible communications link, exchanging this key value securely is impossible.

Fortunately, asymmetric ciphers, also known as public key encryption, resolve this issue by providing a mechanism for exchanging key values for use with a symmetric cipher. However, with asymmetric ciphers, a new problem arises: how to verify the identities of the communicating parties. This is resolved through trust models, most notably digital certificates. X.509 digital certificates offer a hierarchical trust model, and X.509 is the most popular protocol due to its use in SSL for securing Web transactions. But other types of trust models exist, each with their own advantages and disadvantages.

Certificate Revocation Issues

A major stumbling block in the area of key management within a public key infrastructure (PKI) is that a digital certificate can be valid one day and then become invalid the next day. For example, say a certificate authority such as VeriSign signs a digital certificate for a company that plans to use SSL to secure transactions over the Web. Suppose the next day, VeriSign discovers that although due diligence was performed in verifying the company's information, somehow the information turned out to be falsified. The certificate in and of itself indicates that it is valid; it has a valid signature from a trusted certificate authority, and it has not expired—yet it is an invalid certificate. This is a *revoked* certificate.

To revoke a certificate, a certificate authority must add the certificate to a published certificate revocation list (CRL). The CRL is a digitally signed list that contains an identifier for the revoked certificate and the date and time at which it was revoked. This list is analogous to a list that a store owner may have of bad customers from whom no checks should be accepted and to whom no credit should be extended. So when verifying a certificate, after the signatures of the certificate chain (for X.509 certificates) have all checked out, the CRL should be consulted to check if the certificate has been revoked.

Unfortunately, checking certificate revocation has not been built into many of the security protocols that use digital certificates, including SSL [SSL01], which is widely used to secure Web pages. Browsers such as Mozilla, Firefox, and Microsoft's Internet Explorer have implemented solutions to check CRLs for server certificates, but often this check is optional and turned off by default. Another problem is that CRLs are updated periodically, so that one may check a certificate that has in fact been revoked but just has not yet been put on the list. However, Cisco and VeriSign have developed a certificate protocol that includes checking certificate revocations; it is currently a proposed IETF standard [SCEP01].

Trust Models

A trust model is the mechanism used by a security architecture to verify the identity of an entity and its associated data, such as name, public key, and so on. An example of a trust model is the X.509 certificate structure discussed earlier in this chapter. Identities are vouched for through a hierarchical structure that culminates at the root certificate, which is self-signed by a well-known certificate authority (see Figure 2–13). Other trust models exist, including the PGP trust model.

PGP (Pretty Good Privacy) uses a "web of trust" model instead of a hierarchical trust model. Developed by Phil Zimmerman in 1991, PGP is a program that uses a combination of the RSA asymmetric cipher and the IDEA symmetric cipher to secure e-mail, specifically. PGP supports the concept of a digital certificate, but a PGP certificate may contain many signatures, unlike the X.509 certificate that contains exactly one signature. As with X.509 certificates, a signature represents an entity that vouches for the identity and the associated public key within the certificate. With X.509 certificates, this entity is a single authority; with PGP, this entity can be any person or organization. The information in the PGP certificate can be verified using any one of the many signatures, and the verifier can choose which signature is trusted the most.

For example, suppose Alice creates a PGP key pair. She then creates a digital certificate containing her public key and identification information, typically her name and e-mail address. Alice then immediately signs the certificate herself; this is to protect the information within the certificate from being altered before being signed by anyone else. Alice then calls her good friends Andy, Aaron, and Albert, tells them her public key fingerprint, and asks them to sign her public key certificate, which she mails to each of them. All three verify Alice's public key by checking the fingerprint, and then each signs her public key certificate. Figure 2–14 illustrates a PGP certificate with multiple signatures.

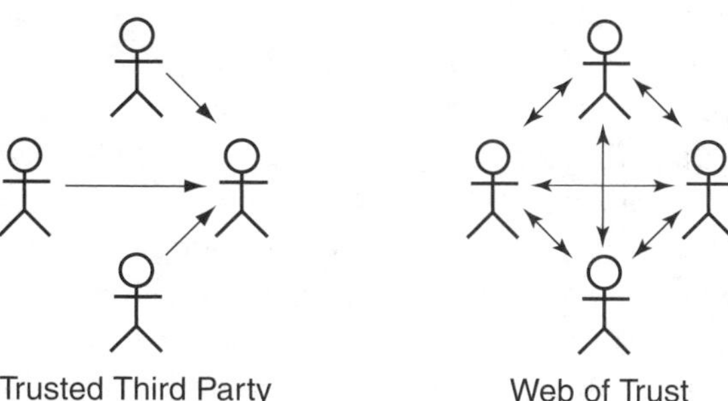

Figure 2–13 Different trust models

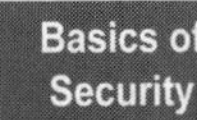

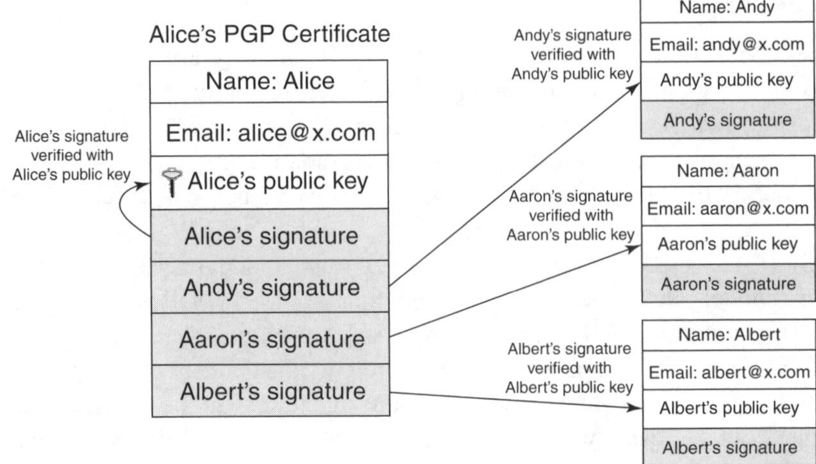

Figure 2–14 PGP certificate with multiple signatures

If Bob wants to send a secure e-mail to Alice, he looks up Alice's public key certificate. Bob then checks the signatures to see if any of them are from entities that he trusts. If Bob knows Andy and has verified Andy's public key, and if he trusts Andy to correctly verify someone else's public key certificate, then if Andy's signature checks out on Alice's public key certificate, Bob can be assured that he indeed has Alice's public key, and can use it to send Alice secure e-mail.

Furthermore, even if Bob does not trust any of the signatures on Alice's public key certificate, he may still be able to verify Alice's information. Bob can look up the certificates of Alice's signatories and check if any of their certificates are signed by someone he trusts. So, if Bob looks up Aaron's certificate, which is signed by Bart, whom Bob knows and trusts, then Bob can verify Aaron's certificate with Bart's signature, and then in turn verify Alice's certificate with Aaron's signature. This can be seen in Figure 2–15.

As with the X.509 certificate structure, the PGP web of trust assumes that the signer of a certificate performs due diligence in verifying the information contained in the certificate. However, X.509 offers a controlled hierarchy of signatories; in the case where the information in an X.509 certificate is incorrect or falsified, the signatory of the certificate can be pinpointed and held responsible for repercussions (for example, VeriSign could have legal action taken against it if it signed a certificate for a bogus company's secure Web site). The PGP web of trust model is more "loose" in that no organizational or legal relationship between signatories and certificate holders is required. There is no concept of a certificate authority in the PGP web of trust. Because of this, PGP allows the user to label the "trust

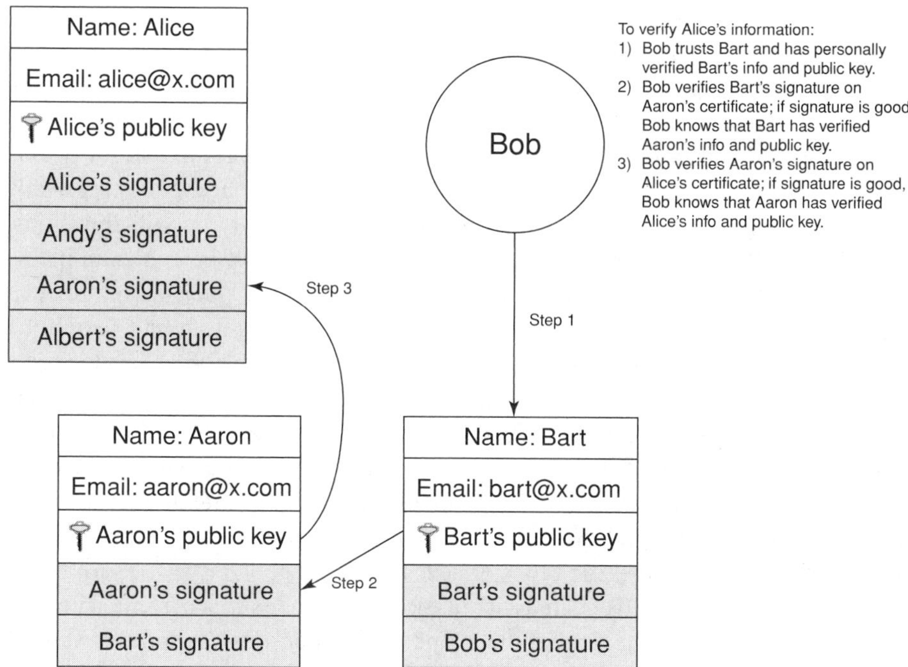

Figure 2–15 Indirect verification of a PGP certificate

level" of a public key certificate. Thus, referring to the earlier scenario, if Bob really doesn't know Andy all that well, he may label Alice's public key as "marginal." Obviously, for business purposes, a key must be trusted or not trusted, which explains the widespread use of X.509 certificates for situations like e-commerce. Newer versions of PGP now support use of X.509 certificates. This allows better interoperability for security providers.

Threat Modeling

Threat modeling involves determining who would be most likely to attack a system and what possible ways an attacker could compromise the system. The results of a threat modeling exercise help determine what risks the threats are to a system and what security precautions should be taken to protect the system. In Chapter 8 we will look at how threat profiling plays an integral part in the security development methodology.

Web applications and all computing systems use security procedures and tools to provide access to the system for legitimate users and to prevent unauthorized users from accessing the system. Different users are often allowed different types of access to a system. For example, a Web application may allow read-only access to the public and allow only authorized users to perform updates to data. A potential attacker wanting to compromise a system must look at what avenues are available in accessing the system, and then he must try to exploit any vulnerabilities. For example, if an attacker has only public read-only access, he can examine as much of the Web site as possible and try various attacks, such as malformed URLs, various FORM attacks, and so forth. Perhaps, after a thorough search, he may find the only attack he can perform is to fill up some customer service rep's mailbox. But if the attacker discovers a legitimate logon account, further possibilities for attack open up to him. Once logged in as an authorized user, he is allowed access to more of the Web site, which allows him to try attacks at more points in the application. Perhaps he can now deface the Web site or alter data in a database. A threat model allows an assessment of what damage can be inflicted by an attacker who has specific types of access.

Attack trees [Schneier01] can assist in modeling threats to a system. The root node of an attack tree is the goal of the attack; child nodes represent direct actions that can attain the attack's goal. These actions may or may not be directly achievable. If they are achievable, they are leaf nodes in the tree. If they are not achievable, the necessary preliminary actions are listed as child nodes under them. Figure 2–16 shows a simple example of an attack tree for reading someone's e-mail.

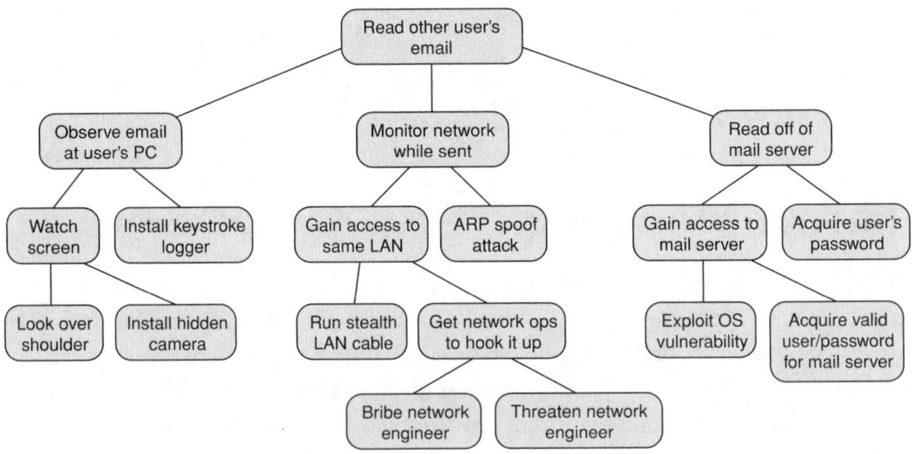

Figure 2–16 Example of an attack tree

Note that the root node represents the goal of the attack, to read some other user's e-mail. The nodes directly under the root node describe direct actions that can accomplish the goal. For example, the middle node under the root indicates that one can monitor the network on which the user is sending and receiving the e-mail. The nodes directly under that node describe possible methods of monitoring the target user's network traffic. The process continues until a leaf node is reached, which is an action that requires no prerequisite action. Ideally, the attack tree illustrates the possible avenues an attacker can follow, starting from any one of the leaf nodes and moving on up until the goal of the attack at the root node is accomplished.

Once an attack tree's nodes have been identified, each node can be assigned a cost. Looking over the shoulder of the target, for example, is less expensive than installing a hidden camera. However, the cost does not need to be monetary; perhaps looking over the target's shoulder carries too much risk of being caught for the attacker, and thus that risk is worth the price of installing a hidden camera. Various costs, or weightings, can be applied to each node. These include ease of execution, legality, intrusiveness, probability of success, and so forth [Schneier01].

As one applies costs to each of the nodes in the attack tree, one can start to see the path that has the least cost and is therefore more likely to be used by an attacker. The probability of likely paths and the risk value associated with the goal of the attack determine how much effort needs to be directed at securing those paths.

Identity Management

An increasingly important issue in today's online world is identity management. How do we protect and manage our credentials across a plethora of network applications that have different authentication methods and requirements? If you have ever been locked out of one application because you continuously tried a password that you later realized was your password for a different application, you understand why there is a need for identity management.

Identity management is a problem that confronts security professionals because users tend to circumvent security measures when they become annoyed with the necessity of managing an increasing number of identities across applications. Ease of use has always been a corollary to a good security architecture. The fewer identities the user has to manage, or the easier it is for the user to manage those identities, the more the user will voluntarily adhere to specified security requirements of the applications owning those identities.

Several approaches to identity management exist. Modern Web browsers have rudimentary identity management built in or available as add-ons, with Identity Management as a value-add. Features such as Google's AutoFill on a user's toolbar allows that user to store profile information and manage passwords across multiple applications. By allowing the user to remember and manage one centralized password, this approach reduces the tendency for users to reuse passwords across applications and thereby reduces the risk of one compromised password being used to impersonate the user across many applications.

A common buzz term in the media today is "identity theft." It refers to the theft of a user's credentials in order to impersonate the user, or steal the identity of that user. Popular sites such as eBay, Amazon, and PayPal are common targets for identity thieves. An attacker will send out an e-mail supposedly from a PayPal administrator requesting that the user follow an embedded URL to log in to PayPal and perform some sort of account maintenance. The URL in reality, however, directs the unknowing user to the attacker's PayPal look-alike site where the attacker is then able to capture the user's id and password. The attacker can then use that id and password to log in to PayPal and transfer money from the user to his own account through some laundering scheme. A variant of that attack is one that uses a Web site that sells items, to redirect users to a phony payment site in order to gain the user's id and password to the legitimate payment site.

Single Sign-on (SSO)

The proliferation of Web applications and Web services has created the need for single sign-on (SSO). SSO refers to the ability of a user to log in once to multiple applications that would ordinarily require their own separate logins. Many Web-based applications are constructed as aggregations of finer-grained services. These services can be accessed individually or in a larger context.

Consider a portal, for instance. It allows users to define a set of disparate services that can be accessed via a centralized interface, or portal. Each of these services may require users to authenticate. The portal adds value by enabling SSO across all of its aggregated services, thus eliminating the need for the user to constantly log in.

SSO is considered a requirement in most Web applications today. Whether the application is a traditional browser-based Web application or a true Web service, SSO is absolutely necessary for user-friendliness. One thing is certain: Users hate to log in any more than they have to. And the more frequently they have to log in, the easier to guess they will make their passwords, thus reducing overall security.

SSO through a Portal

SSO dictates that when the user is authenticated for a particular resource, any subsequent access to that resource must be granted without requiring the user to log in again. The most common approach to enabling SSO in a portal is to implement a security token that is presented upon each request throughout the portal. The portal can then use the security token to verify the user's identity across the applications contained in it.

This approach can be used by employing an intercepting agent such as the one defined in the Intercepting Web Agent pattern in Chapter 8 (see Table 8–5). The agent intercepts requests and checks for the token's presence. If the token exists, it is validated, and then the request is allowed through. If the token is invalid or expired, the interceptor will forward the request to the authentication service, which will prompt the user to log in.

Additional information, such as session data, can be stored in the token as well. The portal can use this session information instead of persisting it itself. Implementation of such a token will most often be provided in the form of a secure cookie. If the user disables cookies, the token can be provided as an encrypted value in a hidden field.

The industry has yet to standardize one mechanism for authenticating and authorizing Web service requests. To date, a lot of work has been done by OASIS; the result is the Security Assertion Markup Language (SAML). SAML enables SSO across multiple application servers and allows unrelated applications to make assertions based on trusted third parties. Future development will center on SAML as an alternative to the SSO mechanisms currently used by portals today. For now, third-party products are using a mixture of standard and proprietary approaches to providing SSO.

Cross-Domain SSO

As discussed earlier, traditional Web application SSO is accomplished using cookies. One drawback to this approach is that applications can only set and read cookies from their own domains. Obviously, this prevents straightforward SSO between services in a.com and services in b.com.

Cross-domain SSO (CDSSO) enables SSO across domains and allows users to authenticate in one domain and then use applications in other domains without having to reauthenticate. This is a critical issue today for Web applications that require SSO for their browser-based clients. When Web services become dominant, and SAML is king, this will no longer be an issue. Until then, it is important to understand the problem and the technology that's available to solve it.

CDSSO provides both cost and management savings across the enterprise. These savings are realized when the enterprise uses cross-domain access SSO that doesn't require implementation of homogenous platforms or authentication products. Existing systems can be aggregated without reengineering them to use proprietary mechanisms or even, in the radical case, to share a domain.

How It Works

The various implementations of CDSSO use one basic high-level approach that contains the following major components:

- Cross-Domain Controller
- Cross-Domain Single Sign-On Component

The controller is responsible for redirecting a request to the authentication service or the CDSSO component. The CDSSO component is responsible for setting the cookie information for its particular domain. A CDSSO component must be present in every domain that participates in the SSO federation.

Federated SSO

The goal of the enterprise today is to provide seamless employee access to the multitude of internal and externally hosted Web applications that exist in the corporate world. But not all of these applications are managed or maintained by a central authority. That fact, though, should not require employees to know whether an application is internal or external. They should be able to access a service without being required to log in again or having to maintain an additional account. Without a way to federate SSO across services and domains, users will be forced to manage an increasing number of identities and perform more and more logins as they jump from service to service.

The solution to this problem is federation. An SSO Federation provides a means for unifying SSO across a number of services without requiring each service provider to participate directly in the authentication process. Previously, we discussed SSO and CDSSO. We assumed the participating parties were each responsible for authenticating users for each other. The burden upon each service provider increases at a nonlinear rate as the number of services grows and the number of users increases. To alleviate the burden on each service provider to authenticate and authorize participating users, a centralized Identity Provider is used to off-load the work.

The Identity Provider acts as a central authority for authentication and authorization. It authenticates users and then provides users with tokens that can be verified by participating service providers. This method frees service providers from performing authentication and authorization of users. Some users are known by service providers, and others are known only to partner service providers. These users are those who have access to a particular service provider through some temporary partnering agreement. In Figure 2–17, we see how service providers can share identity information through a common identity provider and thus form a federation.

Organizations have struggled with the need to aggregate their users into a single repository in order to reduce costs related to the management and complexity of multiple user stores. Applications have also moved to a centralized user repository in order to implement centralized authentication and authorization. Organizations that are consolidating services via a portal have done the same.

Identity Provider federations provide a centralized aggregation of users and the capability of acting as a centralized authentication service. Service providers

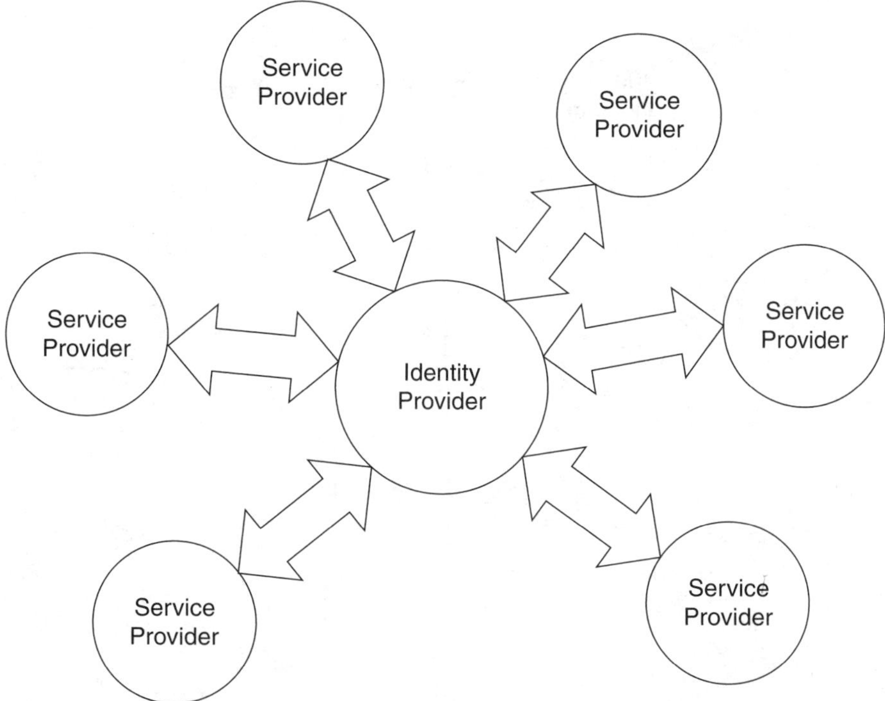

Figure 2–17 Federation of Service Providers with one Identity Provider

can delegate authentication and authorization to the Identity Provider. Doing this reduces the burden on a service to provide user management and reduces system complexity.

Cross-Domain Federations

Cross-domain federations are the most complex and most powerful architectures. They allow each Identity Provider to act both as a producer and consumer of identity assertions. Cross-domain federations allow a virtually unlimited topological range of identity propagation—not just across the enterprise, but globally. Someday you may see one central digital warehouse that propagates and verifies your identity information to any service—anywhere—that you want to access. That is the goal of Identity Management.

Figure 2–18 shows how Identity Providers can communicate with each other to create cross-domain federations.

For more information about understanding and implementing identity management, refer to Chapter 7, "Identity Architecture and Its Technologies," and

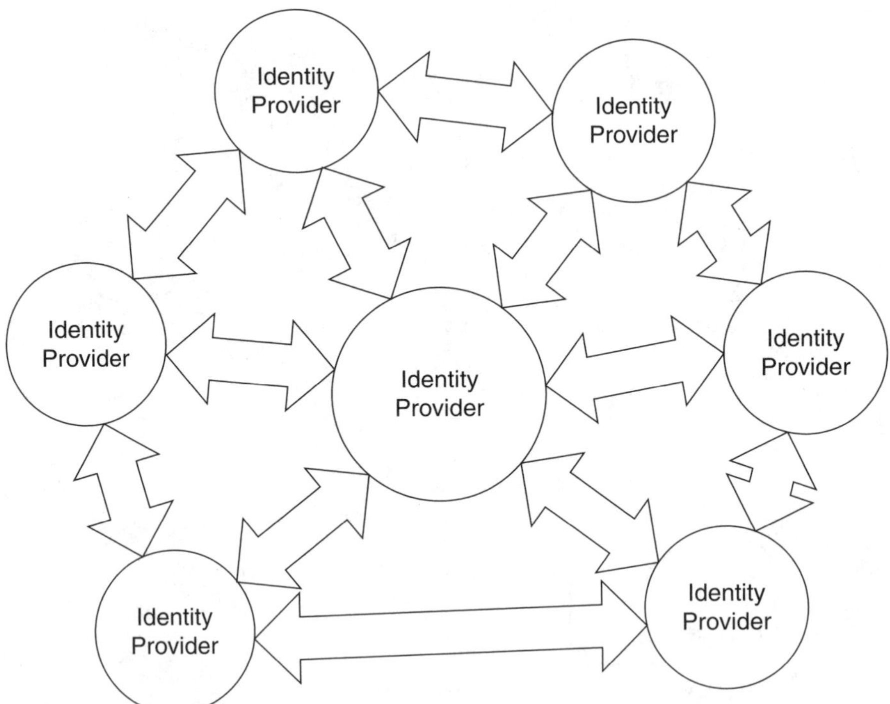

Figure 2–18 Federation of cross-domain Identity Providers

Chapter 12, "Securing the Identity: Design Strategies and Best Practices." We will discuss in those chapters the technologies, patterns, and best practices for enabling Identity Management in enterprise applications.

Summary

This chapter has provided some of the basics of security—from the fundamentals of cryptography to the challenges in identity management. We have explored the security goals and challenges of securing applications and the different cryptographic mechanisms that are used. We have also discussed other problems that arise from these approaches, such as identity management, single sign-ons, and federated sign-ons.

In the following chapters, we will illustrate how these fundamental requirements are met using Java technologies that provide an end-to-end security architectural foundation. We will also discuss security methodology, patterns, and best practices that contribute to providing secure enterprise computing. We will wrap up by putting all of it together into a set of case studies that demonstrate an end-to-end security architecture using patterns and best practices.

References

[DiffieHellman] W. Diffie and M.E. Hellman. "New Directions in Cryptography," IEEE Transactions on Information Theory 22, 1976.

[FIPS81] NIST. "DES Modes of Operation." Federal Information Processing Standards Publication 81.

http://www.itl.nist.gov/fipspubs/fip81.htm

[Schneier01] B. Schneier. "Attack Trees: Modeling Security Threats." *Dr. Dobb's Journal* 306, December 1999.

http://www.schneier.com/paper-attacktrees-ddj-ft.html

[Schneier02] B. Schneier. *Cryptogram*, May 2002.

http://www.schneier.com/crypto-gram-0205.html#5

[Schneier03] B. Schneier. "Yarrow: A Secure Pseudorandom Number Generator."

http://www.schneier.com/yarrow.html

[Schneier04] B. Schneier. "Declassifying Skipjack." *Cryptogram*, July 1998.

http://www.schneier.com/crypto-gram-9807.html#skip

[Hashfunc01] H. Lipma. "Hash Functions."
http://www.cs.ut.ee/~helger/crypto/link/hash/

[RSA01] RSA Security. "Frequently Asked Questions About Today's Cryptography."
http://www.rsasecurity.com/rsalabs/faq/sections.html

[RSA02] RSA Security. "What Are Some other Blocks Ciphers."
http://www.rsasecurity.com/rsalabs/faq/3-6-7.html

[RSA03] RSA Security. "What Is Capstone."
http://www.rsasecurity.com/rsalabs/faq/6-2-3.html

[AES01] E. Roback and M. Dworkin. "First AES Candidate Conference Report," August 1998.
http://csrc.nist.gov/CryptoToolkit/aes/round1/conf1/j41ce-rob.pdf

[WeiDai01] Wei Dai. Crypto++ TM Library 5.0 Reference Manual.
http://cryptopp.sourceforge.net/docs/ref5/

[WeiDai02] Wei Dai. Crypto++ 5.1 Benchmarks, July 2003.
http://www.eskimo.com/~weidai/benchmarks.html

[Kaufman] Charlie Kaufman, Radia Perman, and Mike Speciner. *Network Security: Private Communication in a Public World*. Prentice Hall, 2002.

[Goldberg01] Ian Goldberg and David Wagner. "Randomness and the Netscape Browser," *Dr. Dobbs' Journal*, January 1996.
http://www.cs.berkeley.edu/~daw/papers/ddj-netscape.html

[RFC1750] D. Eastlake, et al. "Randomness Recommendations for Security," December 1994.
http://www.ietf.org/rfc/rfc1750.txt

[SCEP01] Cisco. Simple Certificate Enrollment Protocol.
http://www.cisco.com/warp/public/cc/pd/sqsw/tech/scep_wp.html

[RFC2459] R. Housley, W. Ford, W. Polk, and D. Solo. "Internet X.509 Public Key Infrastructure Certificate and CRL Profile." The Internet Society, January 1999.
http://www.ietf.org/rfc/rfc2459.txt.

[Moraes] Ian Moraes, Ph.D. "The Use of JNDI in Enterprise Java APIs." JDJ SYS-CON Media, August 1, 2000.
http://jdj.sys-con.com/read/36454.htm

[Netscape01] A. Frier, P. Karlton, and P. Kocher. The SSL Protocol, Version 3.0, 1996.

http://wp.netscape.com/eng/ssl3/ssl-toc.html

[RFC2246] T. Dierks and C. Allen. "The TLS Protocol Version 1.0," January 1999.

http://www.ietf.org/rfc/rfc2246.txt

[RFC2104] H. Krawczyk, et al. "HMAC: Keyed-Hashing for Message Authentication," February 1997.

http://www.ietf.org/rfc/rfc2104.txt

[ANSIX9.17] American National Standards Institute. American National Standard X9.17: Financial Institution Key Management (Wholesale), 1985.

[SSL01] Alan O. Freier, et al. "The SSL Protocol Version 3.0," November 18, 1996.

http://wp.netscape.com/eng/ssl3/draft302.txt

[RFC2560] M. Meyers et al. "X509 Internet Public Key Infrastructure Online Certificate Status Protocol–OCSP," June 1999.

http://www.ietf.org/rfc/rfc2560.txt

Part II

Java Security Architecture and Technologies

The Java 2 Platform Security

Topics in This Chapter

- Java Security Architecture
- Java Applet Security
- Java Web Start Security
- Java Security Management Tools
- J2ME Security Architecture
- Java Card Security Architecture
- Securing the Java Code

Chapter 3

The Java 2 Platform Security

Sun's Java philosophy of "Write Once, Run Anywhere" has been an evolving success story since its inception, and it has revolutionized the computing industry by delivering to us the most capable platform for building and running a wide range of applications and services. In general, the Java platform provides a general-purpose object-oriented programming language and a standard runtime environment for developing and delivering secure, cross-platform application solutions that can be accessed and dynamically loaded over the network or run locally.

With the release of the Java 2 Platform, Sun categorized the Java technologies under three key major editions in order to simplify software development and deployment. The Java 2 Standard Edition (J2SE) provides the runtime environment and API technologies for developing and executing basic Java applications, and it also serves as the secure foundation for running Java enterprise applications. The Java 2 Enterprise Edition (J2EE), or the J2EE Platform, is a set of standards and API technologies for developing and deploying multi-tier business applications. To support Java on microdevices and embedded systems, Java 2 Micro Edition (J2ME) provides the runtime environment and API technologies for addressing the needs of consumer electronics and devices. With its widespread adoption, today Java technology is enabled and executed from smart cards to microdevices, handhelds to desktops, workstations to enterprise servers, mainframes to supercomputers, and so on.

To facilitate end-to-end security of the Java platform-based application solutions, the Java runtime environment (JRE) and the Java language provide a solid security foundation from the ground up by imposing strong format and structural constraints on the code and its execution environment. This distinguishes the Java platform from other application programming languages—it has a well-defined security architectural model for programming Java-based solutions and their secure execution.

In this chapter, we will explore the various Java platforms and the intricate details of their security architecture that contribute to the end-to-end security of Java-based application solutions. In particular, we will study Java security and the inherent features of the following technologies:

- J2SE security
- Java applet security
- Java Web start security
- Java security management tools
- J2ME security
- Java Card security
- Java Code obfuscation

Java Security Architecture

Security has been an integral part of Java technology from day one. Security is also an evolving design goal of the Java community—building and running secure and robust Java-based network applications. The primary reason for Java's success today as a secure execution environment is the intrinsic security of its architectural foundation—the Java Virtual Machine (JVM) and the Java language. This foundation achieves the basic Java security goal and its definitive ways for extending security capabilities to ensure features such as confidentiality, integrity, trust, and so forth. A second reason for its success is its ability to deliver an interoperable and platform-neutral security infrastructure that can be integrated with the security of the underlying operating system and services.

The Java Virtual Machine (JVM)

The JVM is an abstract computing engine that resides on a host computer. It is the execution environment for the Java programming language and has the primary responsibility for executing the compiled code by interpreting it in a machine-independent and cross-platform fashion. The JVM is often referred to as the Java runtime environment. While executing a Java program running on top of the JVM, the JVM insulates the application from the underlying differences of the operating systems, networks, and system hardware, thus ensuring cross-platform compatibility among all of the implementations of the Java platform.

The Java language allows creation of general-purpose programs called Java classes that represent a Java program or an application. The Java classes compile into a format called Java's executable bytecodes, which are quite similar to the machine language that can run on top of a JVM. The JVM also allows users to download and execute untrusted programs and applications from remote resources or over a network. To support delivery of Java components over the network, the JVM controls the primary security layer by protecting users and the environment from malicious programs. To enable security, the JVM enforces stringent measures ensuring systems security on the host client machine and its target server environments.

Distributing the executable Java bytecode over a network or running automatically inside a Web browser or a client's machine leads to different security risks and attacks, such as disclosure of the target environment to the untrusted applications and damage or modification of the client's private information and data. For example, Java applets downloaded from a network are not allowed to have access to, read from, or write to a local file system. They are also not allowed to create network connections to any host system except the one where they are deployed. On the other hand, stand-alone Java applications that reside and run locally as trusted applications are not subjected to these security features. The key issue is that allowing untrusted applications such as Java applets to be downloaded from a network via a Web browser and letting them access certain resources on the host computer paves the way for security breaches and becomes a potential avenue for the spread of viruses. To prevent known security breaches and threats, the JVM provides a built-in Java security architecture model, configurable security policies, access control mechanisms, and security extensions. Because of the built-in JVM safety features, Java programs can run safely and are more securely protected from known vulnerabilities.

The Java Language

Java is a general-purpose object-oriented programming language similar to C++. It delivers platform-neutral compiled code that can be executed using a JVM and is intended for use in distributed application environments, heterogeneous systems, and diverse network environments. The Java language is also designed to provide for the security and integrity of the application and its underlying systems at all levels—from the Java language constructs to the JVM runtime and from the class library to the complete application.

The several inherent features of the Java language that provide for the secure Java platform are as follows:

- The language defines all primitives with a specific size and all operations are defined to be in a specific order of execution. Thus, the code executed in different JVMs will not differ from the specified order of execution.
- The language provides access-control functionality on variables and methods in the object by defining name space management for type and procedure names. This secures the program by restricting access to its critical objects from untrusted code. For example, access is restricted by qualifying the type members as public, protected, private, package, etc.
- The Java language does not allow defining or dereferencing pointers, which means that programmers cannot forge a pointer to the memory or create code defining offset points to memory. All references to methods and instance variables in the class file are done via symbolic names. The elimination of pointers helps to prevent malicious programs like computer viruses and misuse of pointers such as accessing private methods directly by using a pointer starting from the object's pointer, or running off the end of an array.
- The Java object encapsulation supports "programming by contract," which allows the reuse of code that has already been tested.
- The Java language is a strongly typed language. During compile time, the Java compiler does extensive type checking for type mismatches. This mechanism guarantees that the runtime data type variables are compatible and consistent with the compile time information.
- The language allows declaring classes or methods as final. Any classes or methods that are declared as final cannot be overridden. This helps to protect the code from malicious attacks such as creating a subclass and substituting it for the original class and override methods.
- The Java Garbage Collection mechanism contributes to secure Java programs by providing a transparent storage allocation and recovering unused memory instead of deallocating the memory using manual intervention. This ensures program integrity during execution and prevents programmatic access to accidental and incorrect freeing of memory resulting in a JVM crash.

With these features, Java fulfills the promise of providing a secure programming language that gives the programmer the freedom to write and execute code locally or distribute it over a network.

Java Built-in Security Model

In the previous two sections, we briefly looked at the basic security features provided by the JVM and the Java language. As part of its security architecture, Java has a built-in policy-driven, domain-based security model. This allows implementing security policies, protecting/controlling access to resources, rule-based class loading, signing code and assigning levels of capability, and maintaining content privacy.

In the first release of the Sun Java Platform, the Java Development Kit 1.0.x (JDK) introduced the notion of a sandbox-based security model. This primarily supports downloading and running Java applets securely and avoids any potential risks to the user's resources. With the JDK 1.0 sandbox security model, all Java applications (excluding Java applets) executed locally can have full access to the resources available to the JVM. Application code downloaded from remote resources, such as Java applets, will have access only to the restricted resources provided within its sandbox. This sandbox security protects the Java applet user from potential risks because the downloaded applet cannot access or alter the user's resources beyond the sandbox.

The release of JDK 1.1.x introduced the notion of signed applets, which allowed downloading and executing applets as trusted code after verifying the applet signer's information. To facilitate signed applets, JDK 1.1.x added support for cryptographic algorithms that provide digital signature capabilities. With this support, a Java applet class could be signed with digital signatures in the Java archive format (JAR file). The JDK runtime will use the trusted public keys to verify the signers of the downloaded applet and then treat it as a trusted local application, granting access to its resources. Figure 3–1 shows the representation of a sandbox in the JDK 1.1 security model.

Java 2 Security Model

The release of J2SE [J2SE] introduced a number of significant enhancements to JDK 1.1 and added such features as security extensions providing cryptographic services, digital certificate management, PKI management, and related tools. Some of the major changes in the Java 2 security architecture are as follows:

- Policy-driven restricted access control to JVM resources.
- Rules-based class loading and verification of byte code.

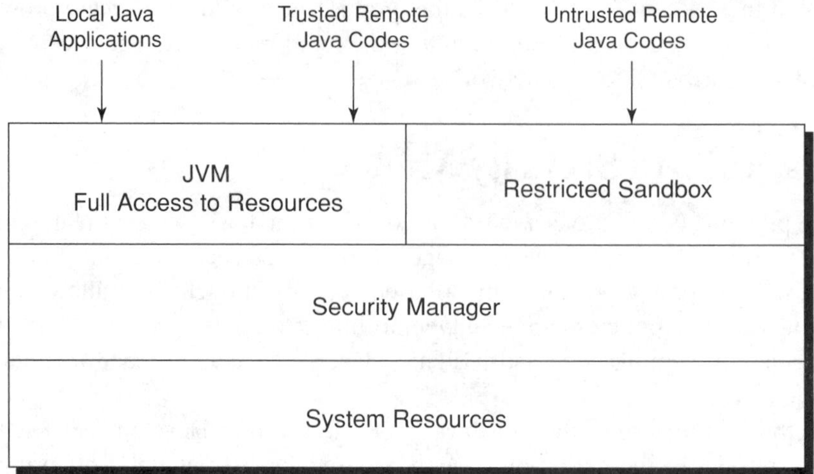

Figure 3–1 JDK 1.1 security model

- System for signing code and assigning levels of capability.
- Policy-driven access to Java applets downloaded by a Web browser.

In the Java 2 security architecture, all code—regardless of whether it is run locally or downloaded remotely—can be subjected to a security policy configured by a JVM user or administrator. All code is configured to use a particular domain (equivalent to a sandbox) and a security policy that dictates whether the code can be run on a particular domain or not. Figure 3–2 illustrates the J2SE security architecture and its basic elements.

Let's take a more detailed look at those core elements of the Java 2 security architecture.

Protection Domains (java.security.ProtectionDomain): In J2SE, all local Java applications run unrestricted as trusted applications by default, but they can also be configured with access-control policies similar to what is defined in applets and remote applications. This is done by configuring a ProtectionDomain, which allows grouping of classes and instances and then associating them with a set of permissions between the resources. Protection domains are generally categorized as two domains: "system domain" and "application domain." All protected external resources, such as the file systems, networks, and so forth, are accessible only via system domains. The resources that are part of the single execution thread are considered an application domain. So in reality, an application that requires access to an external resource may have an application domain as well as a sys-

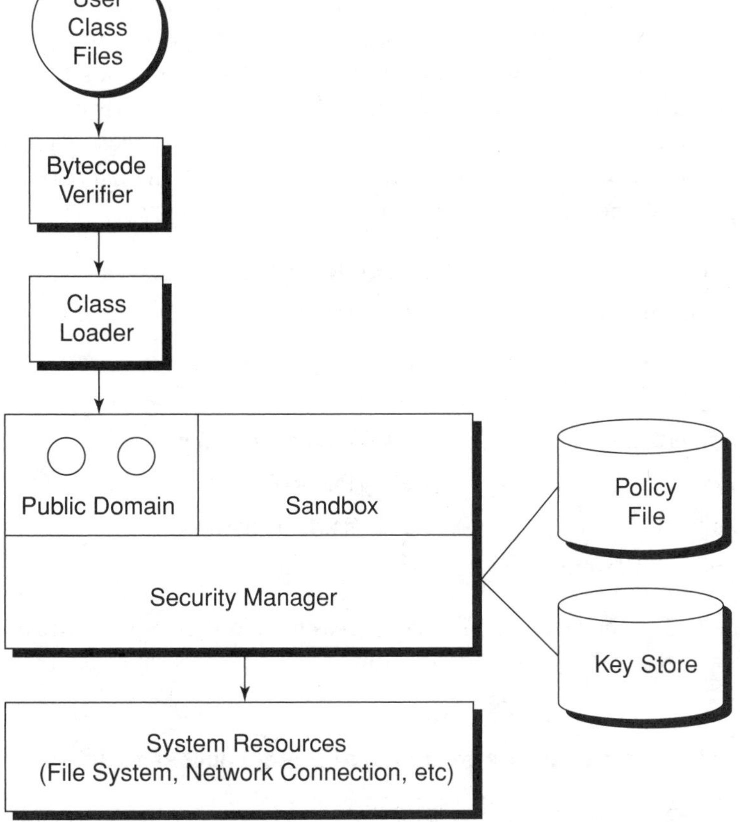

Figure 3–2 Java 2 Security architecture and basic elements

tem domain. While executing code, the Java runtime maintains a mapping from code to protection domain and then to its permissions.

Protection domains are determined by the current security policy defined for a Java runtime environment. The domains are characterized using a set of permissions associated with a code source and location. The java.security.ProtectionDomain class encapsulates the characteristics of a protected domain, which encloses a set of classes and its granted set of permissions when being executed on behalf of a user.

Permissions (java.security.Permission): In essence, permissions determine whether access to a resource of the JVM is granted or denied. To be more precise, they give specified resources or classes running in that instance of the JVM the ability to permit or deny certain runtime operations. An applet or an application using a security manager can obtain access to a system resource only if it has permission. The Java Security API defines a hierarchy for Permission classes that can be used to configure a security policy. At the root, java.security.Permission is the abstract class, which represents access to a target resource; it can also include a set of operations to construct access on a particular resource. The Permission class contains several subclasses that represent access to different types of resources. The subclasses belong to their own packages that represent the APIs for the particular resource. Some of the commonly used Permission classes are as follows:

For wildcard permissions	-java.security.AllPermission
For named permissions	-java.security.BasicPermission
For file system	-java.io.FilePermission
For network	-java.net.SocketPermission
For properties	-java.lang.PropertyPermission
For runtime resources	-java.lang.RuntimePermission
For authentication	-java.security.NetPermission
For graphical resources	-java.awt.AWTPermission

Example 3–1 shows how to protect access to an object using permissions. The code shows the caller application with the required permission to access an object.

Example 3–1 Using Java permissions to protect access to an object

```
// Create the object that requires protection
String protectedObj = "For trusted eyes only";

// create the required permission that will
// protect the object.
// Guard, represents an object that is used to protect
// access to another object.

 Guard myGuard = new PropertyPermission
                              ("java.home", "read");

// Create the guard
GuardedObject gobj =
                new GuardedObject(protectedObj, myGuard);

// Get the guarded object
try {
```

```
    Object o = gobj.getObject();
} catch (AccessControlException e) {
    // Cannot access the object
}
```

Permissions can also be defined using security policy configuration files (java.policy). For example, to grant access to read a file in "c:\temp\" (on Windows), the FilePermission can be defined in a security policy file (see Example 3–2).

Example 3–2 Setting Java permissions in policy configuration file

```
grant{
   permission java.io.FilePermission
                        "c:\\temp\\testFile", "read";
};
```


Policy: The Java 2 security policy defines the protection domains for all running Java code with access privileges and a set of permissions such as read and write access or making a connection to a host. The policy for a Java application is represented by a Policy object, which provides a way to declare permissions for granting access to its required resources. In general, all JVMs have security mechanisms built in that allow you to define permissions through a Java security policy file. A JVM makes use of a policy-driven access-control mechanism by dynamically mapping a static set of permissions defined in one or more policy configuration files. These entries are often referred to as grant entries. A user or an administrator externally configures the policy file for a J2SE runtime environment using an ASCII text file or a serialized binary file representing a Policy class. In a J2SE environment, the default system-wide security policy file java.policy is located at <JRE_HOME>/lib/security/ directory. The policy file location is defined in the security properties file with a java.security setting, which is located at <JRE_HOME>/lib/security/java.security.

Example 3–3 is a policy configuration file that specifies the permission for a signed JAR file loaded from "http://coresecuritypatterns.com/*" and signed by "javaguy," and then grants read/write access to all files in /export/home/test.

Example 3–3 Setting codebase and permissions in policy configuration file

```
grant signedBy "javaguy",
  codebase "http://coresecuritypatterns.com/*"   {
 permission java.io.FilePermission
"/export/home/test/*", "read,write";
};
```

The J2SE environment also provides a GUI-based tool called "policytool" for editing a security policy file, which is located at "<JAVA_HOME>/bin/policytool."

By default, the Java runtime uses the policy files located in:

```
${java.home}/jre/lib/security/java.policy
${user.home}/.java.policy
```

These policy files are specified in the default security file:

```
${java.home}/jre/lib/security/java.security
```


The effective policy of the JVM runtime environment will be the union of all permissions in all policy files. To specify an additional policy file, you can set the java.security.policy system property at the command line:

```
java -Djava.security.manager
                    -Djava.security.policy=myURL MyClass
```

To ignore the policies in the java.security file and only use the custom policy, use `==' instead of `=':

```
java -Djava.security.manager
          -Djava.security.policy==Mylocation/My.policy
                                                 MyClass
```

SecurityManager (java.lang.SecurityManager): Each Java application can have its own security manager that acts as its primary security guard against malicious attacks. The security manager enforces the required security policy of an application by performing runtime checks and authorizing access, thereby protecting resources from malicious operations. Under the hood, it uses the Java security policy file to decide which set of permissions are granted to the classes. However, when untrusted classes and third-party applications use the JVM, the Java security manager applies the security policy associated with the JVM to identify malicious operations. In many cases, where the threat model does not include malicious code being run in the JVM, the Java security manager is unnecessary. In cases where the SecurityManager detects a security policy violation, the JVM will throw an AccessControlException or a SecurityException.

In a Java application, the security manager is set by the setSecurityManager method in class System. And the current security manager is obtained via the getSecurityManager method (see Example 3–4).

Example 3–4 Using SecurityManager

```
 SecurityManager mySecurityMgr =
                       System.getSecurityManager();
if (mySecurityMgr != null) {
     mySecurityMgr.checkWrite(name);
   }
```

The class java.lang.SecurityManager consists of a number of checkXXXX methods like checkRead (String file) to determine access privileges to a file. The check methods call the SecurityManager.checkPermission method to find whether the calling application has permissions to perform the requested operation, based on the security policy file. If not, it throws a SecurityException.

If you wish to have your applications use a SecurityManager and security policy, start up the JVM with the -Djava.security.manager option and you can also specify a security policy file using the policies in the -Djava.security.policy option as JVM arguments. If you enable the Java Security Manager in your application but do not specify a security policy file, then the Java Security Manager uses the default security policies defined in the java.policy file in the $JAVA_HOME/jre/lib/security directory. Example 3–5 programmatically enables the security manager.

Example 3–5 Using SecurityManager for restricting access control

```
// Before the security manager is enabled,
// this call is possible
System.setProperty("java.version","Malicious: Delete");

try {
    // Enable the security manager
    SecurityManager sm = new SecurityManager();
    System.setSecurityManager(sm);
} catch (SecurityException se) {
    // SecurityManager already set
}

// After the security manager is enabled:
// This call is no longer possible;
// an AccessControlException is thrown

System.setProperty ("java.version", "Malicious: Delete");
```

The security manager can also be installed from the command-line interface:

```
java -Djava.security.manager <ClassName>
```

AccessController (java.security.AccessController): The access controller mechanism performs a dynamic inspection and decides whether the access to a particular resource can be allowed or denied. From a programmer's standpoint, the Java access controller encapsulates the location, code source, and permissions to perform the particular operation. In a typical process, when a program executes an operation, it calls through the security manager, which delegates the request to the access controller, and then finally it gets access or denial to the resources. In the java.security.AccessController class, the checkPermission method is used to determine whether the access to the required resource is granted or denied. If a requested access is granted, the checkPermission method returns true; otherwise, the method throws an AccessControlException.

For example, to check read and write permission for a directory in the file system, you would use the code shown in Example 3–6.

Example 3–6 Using AccessController

```
 try {
AccessController.checkPermission
         (new FilePermission("/var/temp/*", "read,write"));

   } catch (SecurityException e) {
      // Does not have permission to access the directory
   }
```

Codebase: A URL location of class or JAR files are specified using codebase. The URL may refer to a location of a directory in the local file system or on the Internet. Example 3–7 retrieves all the permissions granted to a particular class that's been loaded from a code base. The permissions are effective only if the security manager is installed. The loaded class uses those permissions by executing Class.getProtectionDomain() and Policy.getPermissions().

Example 3–7 Using codebase class

```
URL codebase = null;
try {
  // Get permissions for a URL
  codebase = new URL("http://coresecuritypatterns.com/");

} catch (MalformedURLException e) {
} catch (IOException e) {
}

// Construct a code source with the code base
CodeSource cs = new CodeSource(codebase, null);
```

```
// Get all granted permissions
PermissionCollection pcoll =
            Policy.getPolicy().getPermissions(cs);

// View each permission in the permission collection
Enumeration enum = pcoll.elements();
for (; enum.hasMoreElements(); ) {
    Permission p = (Permission)enum.nextElement();
        System.out.println("Permission " + p);

}
```


To test Example 3–7, Example 3–8 is the policy file (test.policy), which provides permission to read all system properties.

Example 3–8 Policy file for testing permissions to a codebase

```
grant codebase "http://coresecuritypatterns.com/-" {
    // Give permission to read all system properties
    permission java.util.PropertyPermission "*", "read";
};
```

To ignore the default policies in the java.security file, and only use the specified policy, use `==' instead of `='. With the policy just presented, you may run the following:

```
java -Djava.security.policy==test.policy TestClass
```

CodeSource: The CodeSource allows representation of a URL from which a class was loaded and the certificate keys that were used to sign that class. It provides the same notion as codebase, but it encapsulates the codebase (URL) of the code where it is loaded and also the certificate keys that were used to verify the signed code. The CodeSource class and its two arguments to specify the code location and its associated certificate keys are as follows:

```
CodeSource(URL url, java.security.cert.Certificate certs[]);
```

To construct a code source with the code base and without using certificates, you would use the following:

```
CodeSource cs = new CodeSource(codebase, null);
```

Bytecode verifier: The Java bytecode verifier is an integral part of the JVM that plays the important role of verifying the code prior to execution. It ensures that the code was produced consistent with specifications by a trustworthy compiler, confirms the format of the class file, and proves that the series of Java byte codes are legal. With bytecode verification, the code is proved to be internally consistent following many of the rules and constraints defined by the Java language compiler. The bytecode verifier may also detect inconsistencies related to certain cases of array bound-checking and object-casting through runtime enforcement.

To manually control the level of bytecode verification, the options to the Java command with the V1.2 JRE are as follows:

- -Xverify:remote runs verification process on classes loaded over network (default)
- -Xverify:all verifies all classes loaded
- -Xverify:none does no verification

ClassLoader: The ClassLoader plays a distinct role in Java security, because it is primarily responsible for loading the Java classes into the JVM and then converting the raw data of a class into an internal data structure representing the class. From a security standpoint, class loaders can be used to establish security policies before executing untrusted code, to verify digital signatures, and so on. To enforce security, the class loader coordinates with the security manager and access controller of the JVM to determine the security policies of a Java application. The class loader further enforces security by defining the namespace separation between classes that are loaded from different locations, including networks. This ensures that classes loaded from multiple hosts will not communicate within the same JVM space, thus making it impossible for untrusted code to get information from trusted code. The class loader finds out the Java application's access privileges using the security manager, which applies the required security policy based on the requesting context of the caller application.

With the Java 2 platform, all Java applications have the capability of loading bootstrap classes, system classes, and application classes initially using an internal class loader (also referred to as primordial class loader). The primordial class loader uses a special class loader SecureClassLoader to protect the JVM from loading malicious classes. This java.security.SecureClassLoader class has a protected constructor that associates a loaded class to a protection domain. The SecureClassLoader also makes use of permissions set for the codebase. For instance, URLClassLoader is a subclass of the SecureClassLoader. URLClassLoader allows loading a class or location specified with a URL.

Refer to Example 3–9, which shows how a URLClassLoader can be used to load classes from a directory.

Example 3–9 Using URLClassLoader

```
// Create a File object on the root of the
// directory containing the class file

File file = new File("c:\\myclasses\\");

try {
    // Convert File to a URL
    URL url = file.toURL();
    URL[] urls = new URL[]{url};

    // Create a new class loader with the directory
    ClassLoader myclassloader = new URLClassLoader(urls);

    // Load in the class;
    // MyClass.class should be located in
    // the directory file:/c:/myclasses/com/security

Class myclass
 = myclassloader.loadClass("com.security.MySecureClass");
} catch (MalformedURLException e) {
 } catch (ClassNotFoundException e) {
}
```

Keystore and Keytool: The Java 2 platform provides a password-protected database facility for storing trusted certificate entries and key entries. The keytool allows the users to create, manage, and administer their own public/private key pairs and associated certificates that are intended for use in authentication services and in representing digital signatures.

We will take a look in greater detail at the usage of the Java keystore and keytool and how these tools help Java security in the section entitled "Java Security Management Tools," later in this chapter.

Java Applet Security

A Java applet downloaded from the Web runs in either a Java-enabled Web browser or a Java appletviewer, which is provided in the J2SE bundle. From a security standpoint, Java applets downloaded from the Internet or from any remote sources are restricted from reading and writing files and making network connections on client host systems. They are also restricted from starting other programs, loading libraries, or making native calls on the client host system. In general, applets downloaded from a network or remote sources are considered untrusted. An applet can be considered trusted, based on the following factors:

- Applets installed on a local filesystem or executed on a localhost.
- Signed applets provide a way to verify that the applet is downloaded from a reliable source and can be trusted to run with the permissions granted in the policy file.

In a Web browser, a Java plug-in provides a common framework and enables secure deployment of applets in the browser using the JRE. While downloading an applet, the Java plug-in enables the browser to install all the class files and then render the applet. A security manager (SecurityManager implementation) will be automatically installed during startup whenever an applet starts running in a Java-enabled Web browser. No downloaded applets are allowed to access resources in the client host unless they are explicitly granted permission using an entry in a Java security policy file.

Example 3–10 is source code for an applet named WriteFileApplet that attempts to create and to write to a file named AppletGenrtdFile in the local directory.

Example 3–10 WriteFileApplet.java

```
import java.awt.*;
import java.io.*;
import java.lang.*;
import java.applet.*;

public class WriteFileApplet extends Applet {

    String myFile = "/tmp/AppletGenrtdFile";
    File f = new File(myFile);
    DataOutputStream dos;

  public void init() {

    String osname = System.getProperty("os.name");
    if (osname.indexof("Windows") != -1) {
      myFile="C:" + file.separator + "AppletGenrtdFile";
    }
  }
```

```
  public void paint(Graphics g) {

    try {
        dos = new DataOutputStream(new BufferedOutputStream
                     (new FileOutputStream(myFile),128));
         dos.writeChars("This is an Applet generated file\n");
         dos.flush();
         g.drawString("Success: Writing file"
                                   + myFile, 10, 10);
       }
       catch (SecurityException se) {
         g.drawString("Write Failed: Security exception:
                                         " + se, 10, 10);
         }
       catch (IOException ioe) {
     g.drawString("Write Failed:I/O exception" + ioe, 10, 10);
         }
   }
}
```

To run the applet, you need to compile the source code using javac and then you may choose to deploy this applet class along with an HTML page in a Web server. To do so, create an HTML file (see Example 3–11) called WriteFileApplet.html.

Example 3–11 WriteFileApplet.html

```
<html><head>
<title> Core Security Patterns Example: Applet Security</title></head><body>
<h1> WriteFileApplet: Writing Files in the Client host </h1>
<hr>
<APPLET CODE = WriteFileApplet.class WIDTH=400 HEIGHT=40>
</APPLET>
<hr></body>
</html>
```

To execute this applet using an appletviewer, run the following :

```
appletviewer
   http://coresecuritypatterns.com/WriteFileApplet.html
```

When executing this applet, you should receive the SecurityException in the applet window. This applet shouldn't be able to write the file, because it does not have a security policy with a file permission to write in the user's home directory.

Now, let's use the following policy file WriteAppletPolicy, which grants a write permission. To do so, create a policy file (see Example 3–12) called WriteAppletPolicy.policy in the working directory:

Example 3–12 WriteAppletPolicy.policy

```
grant {
  permission java.io.FilePermission "<<ALL FILES>>","write";
};
```


To test the applet using an appletviewer, you may choose to use the -J-Djava.security.policy=WriteAppletPolicy.policy option on the JVM command line, or you can explicitly specify your policy file in the JVM security properties file in the <JAVA_HOME>/jre/lib/security directory:

```
policy.url.3=file:/export/xyz/WriteAppletpolicy.policy
```

Example 3–13 shows running the WriteFileApplet applet with the WriteAppletPolicy policy file from the command-line interface.

Example 3–13 Running appletviewer using a Java security policy

```
appletviewer
 -J-Djava.security.policy=WriteAppletPolicy.policy
      http://coresecuritypatterns.com/WriteFileApplet.html
```

You should be able to run the WriteFileApplet applet successfully without a SecurityException, and it should also be able to create and write the file AppletGenrtdFile in the client's local directory.

Now let's explore the concept of signed applets.

Signed Applets

The Java 2 platform introduced the notion of signed applets. Signing an applet ensures that an applet's origin and its integrity are guaranteed by a certificate authority (CA) and that it can be trusted to run with the permissions granted in the policy file. The J2SE bundle provides a set of security tools that allows the end users and administrators to sign applets and applications, and also to define local security policy. This is done by attaching a digital signature to the applet that indicates who developed the applet and by specifying a local security policy in a policy file mentioning the required access to local system resources.

The Java 2 platform requires an executable applet class to be packaged into a JAR file before it is signed. The JAR file is signed using the private key of the applet creator. The signature is verified using its public key by the client user of the JAR file. The public key certificate is sent along with the JAR file to any client recipients who will use the applet. The client who receives the certificate uses it to authenticate the signature on the JAR file. To sign the applet, we need to obtain a certificate that is capable of code signing. For all production purposes, you must always obtain a certificate from a CA such as VeriSign, Thawte, or some other CA.

The Java 2 platform introduced new key management tools to facilitate support for creating signed applets:

- The keytool is used to create pairs of public and private keys, to import and display certificate chains, to export certificates, and to generate X.509 v1 self-signed certificates.
- The jarsigner tool is used to sign JAR files and also to verify the authenticity of the signature(s) of signed JAR files.
- The policytool is used to create and modify the security policy configuration files.

Let's take a look at the procedure involved in creating a signed applet using our previous WriteFileApplet applet example. The following steps are involved on the originating host environment responsible for developing and deploying the signed applet:

1. **Compile the Applet source code to an executable class**. Use the javac command to compile the WritefileApplet.java class. The output from the javac command is the WriteFileApplet.class.

   ```
   javac WriteFileApplet.java
   ```

2. **Package the compiled class into a JAR file**. Use the jar utility with the cvf option to create a new JAR file with verbose mode (v), and specify the archive file name (f).

   ```
   jar cvf WriteFileApplet.jar WriteFileApplet.class
   ```

3. **Generate key pairs**. Using the keytool utility, create the key pair and self-signed certificate (for testing purposes only). The JAR file is signed with the creator's private key and the signature is verified by the communicating peer of the JAR file with the public key in the pair.

   ```
   keytool -genkey -alias signapplet -keystore mykeystore
   -keypass mykeypass
   -storepass mystorepass
   ```

This keytool -genkey command generates a key pair that is identified by the alias signapplet. Subsequent keytool commands are required to use this alias and the key password (-keypass mykeypass) to access the private key in the generated pair.

The generated key pair is stored in a keystore database called mykeystore (-keystore mykeystore) in the current directory and is accessed with the mystorepass password (-storepass mystorepass). The command also prompts the signer to input information about the certificate, such as name, organization, location, and so forth.

4. **Sign the JAR file**. Using the jarsigner utility (see Example 3–14), sign the JAR file and verify the signature on the JAR files.

   Example 3–14 Signing an applet using jarsigner tool

   ```
   jarsigner -keystore mykeystore -storepass mystorepass
   -keypass mykeypass -signedjar  SignedWriteFileApplet.jar
   WriteFileApplet.jar signapplet
   ```

   The -storepass mystorepass and -keystore mykeystore options specify the keystore database and password where the private key for signing the JAR file is stored. The -keypass mykeypass option is the password to the private key, SignedWriteFileApplet.jar is the name of the signed JAR file, and signapplet is the alias to the private key. jarsigner extracts the certificate from the keystore and attaches it to the generated signature of the signed JAR file.

5. **Export the public key certificate**. The public key certificate will be sent with the JAR file to the end user who will use it to authenticate the signed applet. To have trusted interactions, the end user must have a copy of those public keys in its keystore. This is accomplished by exporting the public key certificate from the originating JAR signer keystore as a binary certificate file and then importing it into the client's keystore as a trusted certificate.

   Using the keytool, export the certificate from mykeystore to a file named mycertificate.cer as follows:

   ```
   keytool -export -keystore mykeystore
   -storepass mystorepass
           -alias signapplet -file mycertificate.cer
   ```

6. **Deploy the JAR and certificate files**. They should be deployed to a distribution directory on a Web server. Additionally, create a Web page embedding the applet and the JAR. As shown in Example 3–15, the applet tag must use the following syntax.

Example 3–15 Deploying a signedapplet Jar

```
<applet code=WriteFileApplet.class
archive="SignedWriteFileApplet.jar" codebase="/export/home/ws/"
                          width=400 height=40>
</applet>
```

In addition to the previous steps, the following steps are involved in the client's environment:

7. **Import certificate as a trusted certificate.** To download and execute the signed applet, you must import the trusted public key certificate (provided by the issuer) into a keystore database. The Java runtime will use this client-side keystore to store its trusted certificates and to authenticate the signed applet. Using the Keytool utility, import the trusted certificate provided by the issuer (see Example 3–16).

Example 3–16 Importing a certificate

```
keytool -import -alias clientcer -file mycertificate.cer
            -keystore clientstore -storepass clientpass
```

8. **Create the policy file.** Create a policy file client.policy, which grants the applet to have permission for creating and writing to the file "AppletGenrtdFile" in the client's local directory (see Example 3–17).

Example 3–17 Sample policy file (Client.policy)

```
keystore "/export/home/clientstore";
grant SignedBy "clientcer" {
  permission java.io.FilePermission "<<ALL FILES>>",   "write";
};
```

9. **Run and test the applet using appletviewer.** The appletviewer tool runs the HTML document specified in the URL, which displays the applet in its own window. To run the applet using the client policy file, enter the following at the command line (see Example 3–18).

Example 3–18 Testing the applet using the client policy

```
appletviewer -J-Djava.security.policy=client.policy
       http://coresecuritypatterns.com/SignedWriteFileApplet.html
```

Java Web Start Security

Java Web Start (JWS) is a full-fledged Java application that allows Java client applications to be deployed, launched, and updated from a Web server. It provides a mechanism for application distribution through a Web server and facilitates Java rich-client access to applications over a network. The underlying technology of JWS is the Java Network Launch protocol (JNLP), which provides a standard way for packaging and provisioning the Java programs (as JAR files) and then launching Java programs over a network. The JNLP-packaged applications are typically started from a Web browser that launches the client-side JWS software, which downloads, caches, and then executes the application locally. Once the application is downloaded, it does not need to be downloaded again unless newer updates are made available in the server. These updates are done automatically in an incremental fashion during the client application startup. Applications launched using JWS are typically cached on the user's machine and can also be run offline. Since the release of J2SE 1.4, JWS has been an integral part of the J2SE bundle, and it does not require a separate download [JWS].

JWS Security Model

Typical to a stand-alone Java application, JWS applications run outside a Web browser using the sandbox features of the underlying Java platform. JWS also allows defining security attributes for client-side Java applications and their access to local resources, such as file system access, making network connections, and so on. These security attributes are specified using XML tags in the JNLP descriptor file. The JNLP descriptor defines the application access privileges to the local and network resources. In addition, JWS allows the use of digital signatures for signing JAR files in order to verify the application origin and its integrity so that it can be trusted before it is downloaded to a client machine. The certificate used to sign the JAR files is verified using the trusted certificates in the client keystore. This helps users avoid starting malicious applications and inadvertent downloads without knowing the originating source of the application.

When downloading signed JARs, JWS displays a dialog box that mentions the source of the application and the signer's information before the application is executed. This allows users to make decisions regarding whether to grant additional privileges to the application or not. When downloading unsigned applications (unsigned JARs) that require access to local resources, JWS throws a "Security Advisory" dialog box notifying the user that an application requires access to the local resources and prompts the user with a question "Do you want to allow this action?" JWS will allow the user to grant the client application access to the local resources by clicking the "Yes" button in the Security Advisory dialog box.

Signing a JWS application is quite similar to the steps involved in signing an applet, as we saw in the previous section. To sign a JWS application for production, you must obtain a certificate from a certificate authority such as VeriSign and Thawte. For testing purposes, you may choose to use the key management tools provided with the J2SE bundle.

JNLP Settings for Security

To deploy a JWS application, in addition to JAR files, adding a .jnlp file is required. The JNLP file is an XML-based document that describes the application classes (JAR files), their location in a Web server, JRE version, and how to launch in the client environment. The client user downloads the JNLP file from the server, which automatically launches the JWS application on the client side. The JNLP file uses XML elements to describe a JWS application. The root element is tagged as <jnlp>, which contains the four core sub-elements: information, security, resources, and application-desc.

To enforce security, the <security> element is used to specify the required permissions. The security element provides two permission options: <all-permissions/> to provide an application with full access to the client's local computing resources, and <j2ee-application-client-permissions/> to provide a selected set of permissions that includes socket permissions, clipboard access permission, printing permission, and so forth. Example 3–19 is a JNLP file that shows putting all the elements including a <security> element setting with all permissions.

Example 3–19 JNLP file showing <security> elements

```
<?xml version="1.0" encoding="UTF-8"?>
<jnlp spec="1.0+" codebase="file:///c:/testarea/jnlp/">
  <information>
<title>My Signed Jar</title>
<vendor>Core Security Patterns</vendor>
  <homepage href="http://www.sec-patterns.com/signed" />
<description>Java Web start example</description>
</information>
<offline-allowed/>
<security>
  <all-permission/>
</security>
<resources>
  <j2se version="1.2+" />
```

```
  <jar href="SignedClientApp.jar"/>
</resources>
<application-desc main-class="SignedClientApp" />
</jnlp>
```

Java Security Management Tools

As part of the J2SE bundle, the Java 2 platform provides a set of tools that helps Java developers and security administrators to administer security policies, create keys (for testing purposes only), manage keys and certificates, sign JAR files, verify signatures, and support other functions related to key management.

The following tools and utilities are provided as part of the J2SE bundle.

Java Keystore

The keystore is a protected database that stores keys and trusted certificate entries for those keys. A keystore stores all the certificate information related to verifying and proving an identity of a person or an application. It contains a private key and a chain of certificates that allows establishing authentication with corresponding public keys. Each entry in the keystore is identified by a unique alias. All stored key entries can also be protected using a password. The Java keystore follows the RSA cryptographic standard known as PKCS#12, which provides a way to securely store multiple keys and certificates in a password-protected file. Unless specified by default, the key entries are stored in a .keystore file and the trusted CA certificate entries are stored in a cacerts file, which resides in the JRE security directory.

Keytool

Keytool is a key and certificate management tool that allows users and administrators to administer their own private/public key pairs and associated certificates. This tool is intended for use with authentication services and verifying data integrity using digital signatures. The keytool is provided with the J2SE bundle as a command-line utility, which can be used to create JKS (Java keystore) and JCEKS (Java Cryptographic Extensions Keystore) keystores, generate and store keys and their associated X.509v1 certificates, generate Certificate Signing Requests (CSR), import and store trusted certificates, and perform maintenance on keystore entries.

The keytool utility uses the X.509 certificate standard, which is encoded using the Abstract Syntax Notation 1 (ASN.1) standard to describe data and the Definite Encoding Rules (DER) standard to identify how the information is to be stored and transmitted. The X.509 certificate takes the values of subject and issuer fields from the X.500 Distinguished Name (DN) standard.

Let's take a look at the most common operations performed using the keytool utility:

Creating a keystore database. A keystore is created whenever you use keytool with options to add entries to a non-existent keystore. The following options automatically create a keystore when the specified keystore does not exist in the user's directory:

- -genkey option is used to generate private/public key pairs.
- -import option is used to import a trusted certificate.
- -identitydb is used to import data from a legacy JDK 1.1.

By default, the keytool creates a keystore as a file named .keystore in the user's home directory, but a name can be specified using the –keystore option.

Generating private/public key pairs. When a keytool is used to generate a private/public key pair, each entry contains a private key and an associated certificate "chain." The first certificate in the chain contains the public key corresponding to the private key.

A pair of public and private keys can be generated and added to the keystore using the keytool -genkey command. The -genkey option creates a public/private key pair and then wraps the public key in a self-signed certificate. The following example will generate a key pair wrapped in a X.509 self-signed certificate and stored in a single-element certificate chain. In this command, we also need to specify passwords for the keys and the keystore, the algorithm to use (RSA), and the alias (see Example 3–20).

Example 3–20 Generating key pairs using keytool

```
keytool -genkey -alias myalias -keyalg RSA
      -keypass mykeypass -keystore mykeystore
                          -storepass mystorepass
```

In the command shown in Example 3–20, the -genkey option is used to generate the key pair, and all other options are used in support of this command. The key pair is identified with an alias myalias with a password of mykeypass. Both the alias and the keypass are required for all the subsequent commands and operations when we access the particular key pair in the keystore. The other options that can be used are as follows:

- -keyalg -- specifies the encryption algorithm used for the key (example: RSA). An additional "–keysize" option would allow us to specify the bit size for the key; if not specified, the keytool uses the default value of 1024 bits.
- -keypass -- specifies the password for the key generated.
- -keystore -- specifies the name of the keystore to store the keys, which is a binary file. If it is not specified, a new file will be created and saved as a .keystore file.
- -storepass -- specifies the password used to control access to the keystore. After keystore creation, all modifications to the keystore will require you to use the password whenever accessing the keystore.

When you execute these command and options, you will also be prompted with questions to supply the following names for creating subcomponents of the X.500 Distinguished Name standard:

```
CN - First and Last name
OU - Organizational unit
O - Organization
L - City or Locality
ST - State or Province
C - Country code
```

Example 3–21 is a sample output generated using these command and options.

Example 3–21 Generating keypairs using Keytool

```
$ keytool -genkey -alias myalias -keyalg RSA
        -keystore mykeystore  -keypass mykeypass
                     -storepass mystorepass
What is your first and last name?
  [Unknown]:  Roger R
What is the name of your organizational unit?
  [Unknown]:  Java developer
What is the name of your organization?
  [Unknown]:  Java Day care
What is the name of your City or Locality?
```

```
  [Unknown]:  Boston
What is the name of your State or Province?
  [Unknown]:  Massachusetts
What is the two-letter country code for this unit?
  [Unknown]:  US
Is CN=Roger R, OU=Java developer,
O=Java Day care, L=Boston, ST=Massachusetts, C=US correct?
  [no]:  yes
```

With all the questions answered, the keytool generates the keys and the certificate and stores them in the specified keystore file.

Listing the entries of a keystore. The keytool with the -list option is used to list all the entries of a keystore, and also to look at the contents of an entry associated with an alias. Example 3–22 is a command that lists all the entries of a keystore named mykeystore. This command also requires us to enter the keystore password.

Example 3–22 Using keytool to list entries of a Java keystore

```
$ keytool -list -keystore mykeystore
Enter keystore password:  mystorepass

Keystore type: jks
Keystore provider: SUN

Your keystore contains 1 entry
myalias, Sep 5, 2003, keyEntry,
Certificate fingerprint (MD5):
68:A2:CA:0C:D5:C6:D2:96:D5:DC:EA:8D:E3:A1:AB:9B
```

To display the contents of a keystore entry when identified with an alias, the list command prints the MD5 fingerprint of a certificate. If the -v option is specified, the certificate is printed in a human-readable format. If the -rfc option is specified, the certificate is output in the Base 64 encoding format. The following command (see Example 3–23) lists the contents of a keystore entry in a human-readable format for alias "myalias."

Example 3–23 Using keytool to list contents of a Java keystore

```
$ keytool -list -alias myalias -keystore mykeystore -v
Enter keystore password:  mystorepass
Alias name: myalias
Creation date: Sep 5, 2003
Entry type: keyEntry
```

```
Certificate chain length: 1
Certificate[1]:
Owner: CN=Roger R, OU=Java developer,
O=Java Day care, L=Boston, ST=MA, C=US
Issuer: CN=Roger R, OU=Java developer,
O=Java Day care, L=Boston, ST=MA, C=US
Serial number: 3f58edda
Valid from: Fri Sep 05 16:11:06 EDT 2003
until: Thu Dec 04 15:11:06 EST 2003
Certificate fingerprints:
MD5:  68:A2:CA:0C:D5:C6:D2:96:D5:DC:EA:8D:E3:A1:AB:9B
SHA1: 2E:E1:36:ED:D0:E8:EF:85:E5:6B:92:AD:9D:AE:28:82:25:8C:CC:9F
```


Exporting a certificate entry from a keystore. To have trusted interactions, the communicating client peer needs to have a copy of the public keys from the original signer in the keystore. This is done by exporting the certificate (containing the public key and signer information) to a binary certificate file and then importing them as a trusted certificate into the client peer's keystore.

To export the certificate to a binary certificate file (see Example 3–24), the keytool -export and -file options are used. The following command exports a certificate entry identified with alias myalias in keystore mykeystore to a file mycertificate.cer. This command requires entering the keystore password.

Example 3–24 Exporting a certificate from a Java keystore

```
$ keytool -export -alias myalias -file mycertificate.cer -keystore
mykeystore
Enter keystore password:  mystorepass
Certificate stored in file <mycertificate.cer>
```

Importing a trusted certificate. The keytool -import option is used to import a trusted certificate into a keystore database and to associate it with a unique alias. This is executed in the environment of a client who wishes to trust this certificate and to have trusted client interactions with that communicating peer.

When a new certificate is imported into the keystore, the keytool utility verifies that the certificate has integrity and authenticity. The keytool utility attempts this verification by building a chain of trust from that certificate to the self-signed certificate that belongs to the issuer. The lists of trusted certificates are stored in the cacerts file.

To execute the import in a keystore (see Example 3–25), you need to provide the certificate entry with a unique alias and key password. For example, the following command imports a certificate entry from a file mycertificate.cer and identifies the entry with myclientalias and key password clientkeypass in keystore clientkeystore with keystore password clientpass. As a last step, the command displays the owner and issuer information of the certificate and prompts the user to trust the certificate:

Example 3–25 Importing a trusted certificate to a Java keystore

```
$ keytool -import -alias myclientalias -file
            mycertificate.cer -keypass clientkeypass
           -keystore clientstore -storepass clientpass
Owner: CN=Roger R, OU=Java developer,
O=Java Day care, L=Boston, ST=MA, C=US
Issuer: CN=Roger R, OU=Java developer,
O=Java Day care, L=Boston, ST=MA, C=US
Serial number: 3f58edda
Valid from: Fri Sep 05 16:11:06 EDT 2003
until: Thu Dec 04 15:11:06 EST 2003
Certificate fingerprints:
MD5:  68:A2:CA:0C:D5:C6:D2:96:D5:DC:EA:8D:E3:A1:AB:9B
SHA1: 2E:E1:36:ED:D0:E8:EF:85:E5:6B:92:AD:9D:AE:28:82:25:8C:CC:9F
Trust this certificate? [no]:  yes
Certificate was added to keystore
```

The Java 2 Platform Security

Printing certificate information. The keytool –printcert option is used to display the contents of a certificate that has been exported from a keystore and made available as a file. To execute this command, no associated keystore database or password is required, because the certificate contains the information as a certificate file (.cer), which is not imported into the keystore.

You would use Example 3–26 to display the contents of a binary certificate file.

Example 3–26 Displaying contents of a certificate

```
$ keytool -printcert -file mycertificate.cer
Owner: CN=Roger R, OU=Java developer,
O=Java Day care, L=Boston, ST=MA, C=US
Issuer: CN=Roger R, OU=Java developer,
O=Java Day care, L=Boston, ST=MA, C=US
Serial number: 3f58edda
Valid from: Fri Sep 05 16:11:06 EDT 2003 until: Thu Dec
 04 15:11:06 EST 2003
Certificate fingerprints:
MD5:  68:A2:CA:0C:D5:C6:D2:96:D5:DC:EA:8D:E3:A1:AB:9B
SHA1: 2E:E1:36:ED:D0:E8:EF:85:E5:6B:92:AD:9D:AE:28:82:25:8C:CC:9F
```

Creating a Certificate Signing Request (CSR). The Keytool -certreq option allows you to generate a certificate authentication request for a certificate from a Certificate Authority (CA). The -certreq option (see Example 3–27) creates a CSR for the certificate and places the CSR in a file named certreq_file.csr, where certreq_file.csr is the name of the file that is to be sent to the CA for authentication. If a CA considers the certificate to be valid, it issues a certificate reply and places the reply in a file named cert_reply.cer, where cert_reply.cer is the file returned by the CA that holds the results of the CSR authorizations that were submitted in the certreq_file.csr file.

Example 3–27 Creating a CSR

```
keytool -certReq -keystore mykeystore
            -file myCSR.csr -alias mycsralias
```

Deleting a keystore. To delete a keystore, use an operating system delete command to delete the keystore files.

Changing password in the keystore. To change the keystore password, use keytool -storepassword -new options to set a new password (see Example 3–28).

Example 3–28 Changing keystore password

```
keytool -storepasswd -new newstorepass
     -keystore mykeystore -storepass mystorepass
```

Example 3–28 shows how the password for the keystore mykeystore is changed from mystorepass to newstorepass.

Smart Cards and Cryptographic Devices Based Keystores

With the release of J2SE 5.0 [J2SE5], Java provides support for using smart cards and cryptographic devices as keystores. J2SE 5.0 introduced the support for RSA Cryptographic Token Interface Standard (referred to as PKCS#11) which defines native programming interfaces to cryptographic tokens, such as hardware cryptographic accelerators and smart cards. Integrating smart card based keystores is accomplished by configuring the smart card PKCS#11 module as a security provider. To facilitate the integration using PKCS#11 interfaces, J2SE 5.0 provides a new cryptographic provider (SunPKCS11). The SunPKCS11 provider enables existing applications written to the JCA and JCE APIs to access native PKCS#11-based smart cards and cryptographic devices. To enable this, the JRE must be configured with the PKCS#11 provider in the java.security file located at $JAVA_HOME/jre/lib/security/java.security.

For a detailed example about how to configure the smart card as Java keystore, refer to the section "Using Smart Cards as Keystores" in Chapter 4, "Java Extensible Security Architecture and APIs."

Policytool

The policytool is a utility that provides a menu-driven user-friendly interface for creating and viewing Java security policy configuration files. The policytool menu options enable you to read and edit policy files by adding policy and permission entries, assigning a keystore, and creating a new policy configuration file.

To start the Policy Tool utility, simply type the following at the command line:

```
policytool
```

For more information about using policytool menu options, refer to the policytool documentation provided with the J2SE bundle.

Jarsigner

The jarsigner tool is used to digitally sign the Java archives (JAR files) and to verify the signature and its integrity. The jarsigner can sign and verify only the JAR file created by the JAR utility provided with the J2SE bundle.

Signing a JAR file

The jarsigner uses the private key information from the signer's keystore to generate digital signatures for signing the JAR files. After signing, the signed JAR file includes a copy of the public key from the keystore that corresponds to the private key used to sign the file. The jarsigner can also verify the signer's information in the signed JAR file.

Example 3–29 shows what you would use to sign a JAR file named myJar.jar and then name the signed JAR file as mySignedJar.jar.

Example 3–29 Using jarsigner to sign a jar file

```
jarsigner
     -keystore /home/nr/mykeystore
     -storepass mykeystorepass
      -keypass mykeypass
     -signedjar mySignedJar.jar
        myJar.jar myPrivateKeyalias
```

Verifying a Signed JAR

To verify a signed JAR file, and to verify that the signature is valid and the JAR file has not been tampered with, you would use the command shown in Example 3–30.

Example 3–30 Using jarsigner to verify signature a signed jar

```
jarsigner -keystore /home/nr/mykeystore
          -verify -certs mySignedJar.jar
```


The J2SE environment also provides support for cryptographic services, secure communication services using SSL and TLS protocols, and certificate management services. The J2SE 5.0 is the newest release of the Java platform. It includes numerous feature and security updates to the Java language and the JVM. J2SE 5.0 also offers significant security enhancements compared to the previous release of J2SE 1.4.x. These will be discussed in Chapter 4, "Java Extensible Security Architecture and APIs."

J2ME Security Architecture

The Java 2 Micro Edition (J2ME) is designed to deliver the benefits of Java technology on microdevices and embedded systems with limited constraints on their resources, such as memory size, display size, processing power, network bandwidth, and battery life. The J2ME platform provides the runtime environment and API technologies to support a broad range of consumer electronics, embedded devices, and personal mobile devices such as cellular phones, personal digital assistants (PDAs), TV set-top boxes, telematic systems, electronic appliances, and so forth. J2ME offers a rich graphical user interface, storage, networking, security, and other capabilities that include browsing Web applications and running mobile gaming applications. J2ME is also designed to produce portable code and to establish portability of applications across device groups such as PDAs and smartphones. With its security and portability benefits, today J2ME is widely adopted as a core platform for building customized services on a variety of devices and for running mobile applications.

In general, J2ME is a slimmed-down version of J2SE. To enable J2ME applications to meet the device resource constraints and to run efficiently, many API components have been removed from the core Java platform. Figure 3–3 illustrates the J2ME platform architecture and its elements.

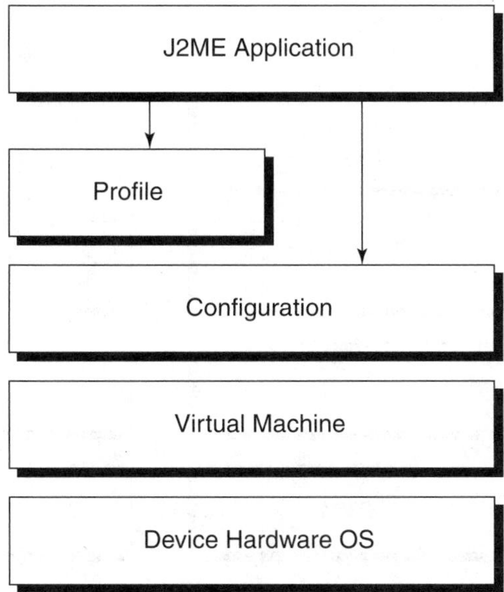

Figure 3–3 J2ME platform architecture and core elements

J2ME defines the notion of configurations and profiles to represent the characteristics of supported devices. These configurations and profiles are developed by the industry groups participating in the Java community process.

J2ME Configurations

A J2ME configuration defines Java runtime and API technologies that satisfy the needs of a broad range of devices. Configurations are defined based on the device limitations and the characteristics of memory, display, processing power, network connectivity, and so forth.

The current J2ME specification defines two types of configurations: Connected Device Configuration (CDC) and Connected Limited Device Configuration (CLDC).

CDC

CDC targets high-end consumer devices with TCP/IP network connectivity and higher bandwidth. It requires at least 2Mb memory available for the Java platform. It defines a full-featured JVM that includes all the functionality of a Java runtime environment residing on a standard desktop system. The low-level interfaces for

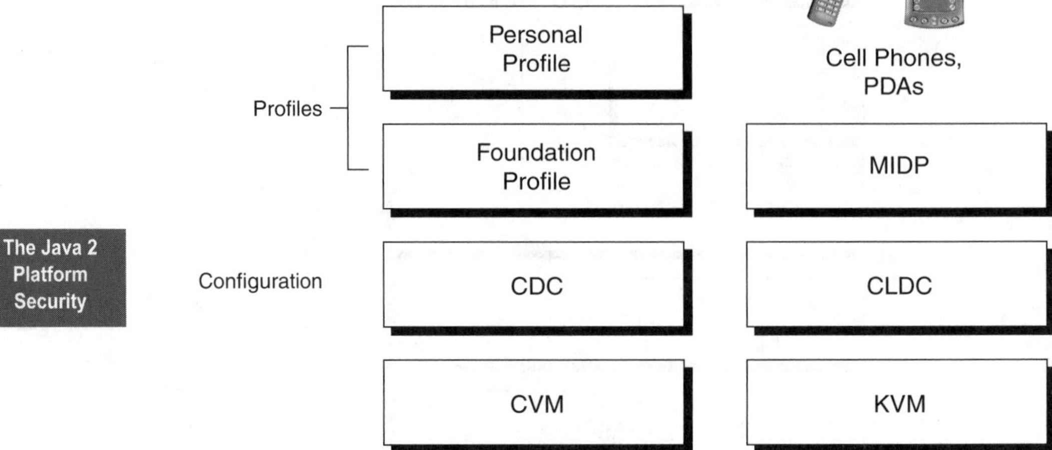

Figure 3–4 J2ME platform configuration and profiles

calling native code (JNI), connecting to debuggers (JVMDI), and profiling code (JVMPI) are optional. Vendors may adopt them based on device requirements.

CDC provides a full-featured Java security model and associated mechanisms of a J2SE environment:

- All code runs in a sandbox without exposing the user's system to risk. All classes are loaded with full byte-code verification and Java language features.
- Signed classes verify the integrity and originating source of the Java classes when the JVM attempts to load it.
- Security policy provides fine-grained access control over the resources using a user-defined set of permissions and policies.
- Support for Java cryptography to secure programs, data, communication, and retrieval is provided.

In short, CDC offers all the security benefits leveraging a standard J2SE environment and gives architects and developers the flexibility to use different Java security API capabilities for building secure applications. J2ME runtime implementations built on the CDC may utilize the standard JVM bundled with the J2SE or the Compact Virtual Machine (CVM) depending on the size of the device for which the implementation is being developed.

CLDC

CLDC targets low-end consumer devices, with only 128–512 kilobytes of memory required for the Java platform and running applications. It features a subset of a standard JVM with limited API and supporting libraries.

When compared to the J2SE implementation, J2ME differs as follows:

- Limited security model
- New class verification mechanism
- No user-defined class loaders
- No support for thread groups or daemon threads
- No support for weak references
- Limited error handling
- No finalization
- No reflection support
- New connection framework for networking

CLDC runs on top of Sun's K Virtual Machine (KVM), which is a JVM designed specifically for supporting resource-limited devices. KVM is the core component of the J2ME platform for CLDC devices. CLDC defines two levels of security: Low-level KVM security and application-level security.

Low-level KVM security: An application running in the KVM must not be able to harm the device in any way. Such security is guaranteed by a pre-verification process that rejects invalid class files and ensures that a class does not contain any references to invalid memory locations. The preverify tool is responsible for the verification process, and it inserts some special attributes into the Java class file. After pre-verification, the KVM does an in-device verification process, which ensures that the class is pre-verified. Figure 3–5 illustrates a CLDC verification process.

Application-level security: The KVM defines a sandbox model that is quite different from the J2SE sandbox model. The sandbox requires that all Java classes are verified and guaranteed to be valid Java applications. It limits all but a predefined set of APIs from becoming available to the application as required by the CLDC specifications and supporting profiles. The downloading and management of applications take place at the native code level, and application programmers cannot define their own classloader or override the classloader or system classes and associated packages of the KVM. Application programmers also cannot

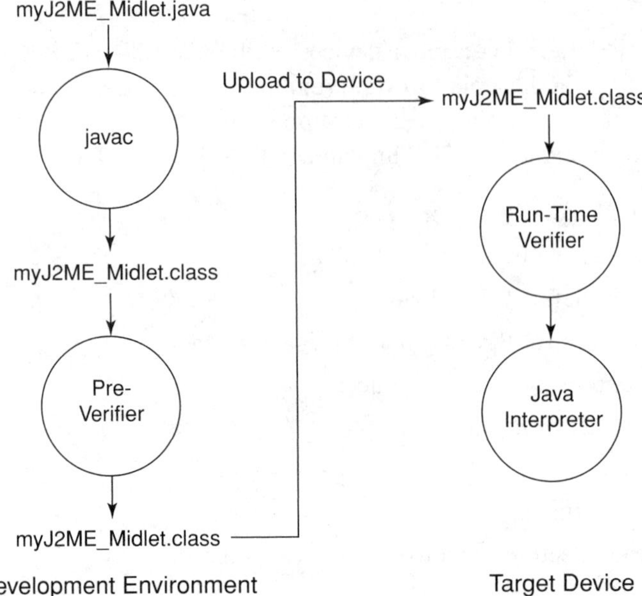

Figure 3–5 Pre-verification process–KVM low-level security

download or add any native libraries that contain code and functionality that are not part of the CLDC supported libraries.

J2ME Profiles

J2ME profiles define a broader set of Java API technologies that are suited to a specific device class or a targeted class of devices. Profiles are built on top of J2ME configurations and define API libraries that enable specific types of applications that are suitable for the target devices. Each J2ME configuration supports one or more J2ME profiles. For the smallest of devices, the Mobile Information Device Profile (MIDP) is one such profile that is built on top of the CLDC configuration. The other class of devices based on CDC configuration use the Foundation Profile. The Foundation profile and its API libraries are based on J2SE 1.3.

Understanding MIDP and MIDlets

MIDP is designed for the family of limited computing devices that have wireless network connectivity and mechanisms for user input and display. The MIDP combined with the CLDC provides the execution environment and application functionality, which includes the user interface, application management, network connectivity, local data storage, and application life-cycle management. The CLDC and MIDP are packaged as a standardized J2ME runtime environment along with the API libraries and are deployed on the native operating system of the device. The OEM-specific classes are provided by the device manufacturer.

A MIDlet is a J2ME application designed to run on a mobile device. In simple terms, a MIDlet is a Java applet, except that it runs on a mobile device rather than in a Web browser. The mobile device provides an Application Management utility that is responsible for installing, executing, and removing MIDlet suites. The Java 2 Micro Edition Wireless Toolkit (J2ME WTK) provides a MIDlet development environment for creating and testing MIDP applications. Aside from the basics of building and packaging MIDlet suites, it includes tools for setting MIDlet security permission attributes, cryptographically signing MIDlet suites, and working with MIDP protection domains. The J2ME toolkit download is available for free from http://java.sun.com/j2me.

A MIDlet suite consists of one or more MIDlets packaged together as a JAR file. A packaged MIDlet will generally consist of compiled and pre-verified Java classes and other files, including images and application-related data. In addition to those files, a manifest file (manifest.mf) is also stored as part of the JAR file. The manifest file stores the MIDlet name, version, and MIDlet vendor-specific attributes. When running the JAR utility, it is important to use the -m option along with the manifest file in the arguments. Example 3–31 shows a manifest file.

Example 3–31 MIDlet JAR–manifest file

```
MIDlet-1: SecMidlet, /icons/csp.png, com.csp.SecMidlet
MMIDlet-Description: Example Manifest file illustration
MIDlet-Name: Example Secure Midlet
MIDlet-Permissions:
MIDlet-Vendor: Coresecuritypatterns.com
MIDlet-Version: 2.0
MicroEdition-Configuration: CLDC-1.0
MicroEdition-Profile: MIDP-2.0
```

In addition to a JAR file, a Java Application Descriptor (JAD) file is also required to be available as part of the MIDlet suite to provide information about the MIDlet(s) bundled in the JAR file. The JAD file provides information to the mobile device's application manager about the contents of the JAR file and also provides a way to pass parameters required by the MIDlet(s). The application manager requires that the JAD file have an extension of .jad. Example 3–32 shows an example of a JAD file.

Example 3–32 JAD file

```
MIDlet-1: SecMidlet,/icons/csp.png, com.csp.SecureMidlet
MMIDlet-Description: Example Manifest file illustration
MIDlet-Jar-URL: SecureMidlet.jar
MIDlet-Name: Example Secure Midlet
MIDlet-Permissions:
MIDlet-Vendor: Coresecuritypatterns.com
MIDlet-Version: 2.0
MicroEdition-Configuration: CLDC-1.0
MicroEdition-Profile: MIDP-2.0
MIDlet-Jar-Size: 19250
```


Use the ktoolbar GUI tool provided with the J2ME WTK to load the JAD file and the JAR file containing the MIDlet suite from a local filesystem.

MIDlet Security

The MIDP 1.0 specification introduced the basic security feature that restricts all MIDlet suites to operate within a sandbox-based security model. This was primarily done to ensure that MIDlets prevent access to sensitive APIs and functions of devices, and to avoid any risks to the device resources.

The MIDP 2.0 introduced the notion of trusted MIDlets to provide a flexible and consistent security model with access-control mechanisms defined by a domain policy. The device enforces access control on a MIDlet suite as trusted MIDlets in accordance with the defined domain policy. A MIDlet suite is identified as untrusted when the origin and integrity of the MIDlet suite's JAR file cannot be verified and trusted by the device. The MIDP 2.0 also specifies how MIDlet suites can be cryptographically signed so that their authenticity and originating source can be validated.

Trusted MIDlets

The MIDP defines a security model for trusted MIDlets based on a notion referred to as Protection Domains. Each protection domain associates a MIDlet with a set of permissions and related interaction modes, which allows a MIDlet to access the domain based on the permissions granted. A protection domain contains allowed and user permissions.

- The allowed permissions define a set of actions that should be allowed without any user interaction.

- The user permissions define a set of permissions that require explicit user approval. The MIDlet is bound by the protection domain and will allow or deny access to functions after prompting the user and obtaining their permissions.

In the case of user permissions, a MIDlet needs permission at the first time of access and asks the user whether the permission should be granted or denied. The user permission is defined to grant allow or deny permissions to specific API functions with the following three interaction modes.

- **Blanket**: The MIDlet is valid for every invocation until its permission is revoked by the user or the MIDlet is deleted from the device.
- **Session**: The MIDlet is valid for every invocation of the MIDlet suite until it terminates. It prompts the user for every initiated session on or before its first invocation.
- **Oneshot**: The MIDlet is valid for a single invocation of a restricted method and prompts the user on each such invocation.

All user permission has a default interaction mode with an optional set of available interaction modes. These interaction modes are determined by the security policy. A policy consists of the definitions of domains and aliases. Each domain consists of the definition of granted permissions and user permissions. Aliases permit groups of named permissions to be reused in more than one domain and help keep the policy compact. Aliases may only be defined and used within a single policy file.

A domain is defined with a domain identifier and a sequence of permissions. The domain identifier is implementation-specific. Each permission line begins with allowing or denying user permissions and indicates the interaction modes, such as blanket, session, and oneshot for the specified list of permissions that follow. Example 3–33 shows a policy file.

Example 3–33 MIDlet policy file

```
domain: O="MIDlet Underwriters, Inc.", C=US
allow: javax.microedition.io.HttpConnection
oneshot(oneshot): javax.microedition.io.CommConnection

alias: client_connections
 javax.microedition.io.SocketConnection,
      javax.microedition.io.SecureConnection,
      javax.microedition.io.HttpConnection,
      javax.microedition.io.HttpsConnection
```

```
 domain: O=Acme Wireless, OU=Software Assurance
 allow: client_connections
 allow: javax.microedition.io.ServerSocketConnection,

               javax.microedition.io.UDPDatagramConnection
oneshot(oneshot): javax.microedition.io.CommConnection

domain: allnet
blanket(session): client_connections
oneshot: javax.microedition.io.CommConnection
```


To request permissions for executing a MIDlet suite, we will make use of attributes such as MIDlet-Permissions and MIDlet-Permissions-opt in a JAD descriptor file that signals a MIDlet suite's dependence on requiring certain permissions. These special JAD attributes represent the MIDlet suite and provide a device at installation time with access control information about which particular operations the MIDlet suite will be attempting. For example, suppose the MIDlet suite will attempt to make an HTTP connection and optionally make socket connections. The attributes in the JAD descriptor file would look like this:

```
MIDlet-Permissions: javax.microedition.io.Connector.http
MIDlet-Permissions-opt:
                     javax.microedition.io.Connector.socket
```

If a device attempts to install a MIDlet suite into a protection domain that doesn't allow the required permissions specified in the MIDlet suite's JAD file, the installation fails automatically. Thus, the trusted MIDlet provides the mechanisms that protect the device from poorly or maliciously written Java code that can render a device inoperable.

Signed MIDlet Suite

Since MIDP 2.0, a MIDlet suite can be cryptographically signed and its authenticity and originating source can be validated as trusted. This is an enhanced security model for MIDP applications, which is handled via digital signatures and PKI support. As with any PKI authentication, it requires zero or more root CA certificates that are used to verify other certificates. Signing a MIDlet suite is quite similar to signing applets that involve a signer and public key certificates. The signer of the MIDlet is responsible for distributing and supporting the MIDlets. The signer needs to have a public key certificate that can be validated by one of the protection domain root certificates on the device. A signed MIDlet suite usually includes a certificate issued by a well-known certificate authority. It is important to note that signing a MIDlet suite isn't useful unless client devices can verify the signature.

From a developer standpoint, signing a MIDlet suite is the process of adding the signer certificates and the digital signature of the JAR file to a JAD file. Signing a MIDlet suite adds new attributes to the JAD file, represented using Base 64 encoded values.

```
MIDlet-Certificate: <Base64 encoded value of certificate>
MIDlet-Jar-RSA-SHA1: <Base64 encoded value of signatures>
```


The J2ME Wireless Toolkit enables a signer to either sign a MIDlet suite with an existing public and private key pair obtained from a certificate authority or with a new key pair that can be generated as a self-signed certificate for testing purposes only. Each key pair is associated with a certificate. Assigning a security domain to the certificate designates the level of trust that the certificate holder has to access protected APIs and the level of access to those APIs.

The JADTool is a command-line interface provided with the J2ME toolkit for signing MIDlet suites. The JADTool only uses certificates and keys from J2SE keystores, discussed earlier in this chapter. As we discussed previously, the J2SE bundle provides key management tools for managing keystores.

The JADTool utility is packaged in a JAR file. To run it from the command line interface, change your current directory to {j2metoolkit-dir}\bin, and execute the following command:

```
java -jar JADTool.jar <command-options> <JAD file>
```

Example 3–34 would add the certificate of the key pair from the given J2SE keystore to the specified JAD file.

Example 3–34 Adding a certificate to a JAD file

```
java -jar JADTool.jar -addcert -keystore <mykeystore>
    -storepass <storepassword> -alias <alias>
    -inputjad <input_jadfile>
    -outputjad <output_jadfile>
```

Example 3–35 adds the digital signature of the given JAR file to the specified JAD file.

Example 3–35 Adding a digital signature to a JAD file

```
java -jar JADTool.jar -addjarsig -jarfile <jarfile>
  -keystore <mykeystore>  -storepass <storepassword>
```

```
-alias <alias>
-inputjad <input_jadfile>
-outputjad <output_jadfile>
```

Example 3–36 displays a list of certificates in a given JAD file.

Example 3–36 Displaying list of certificates for a given JAD file

```
java -jar JADTool.jar -showcert
                  -inputJAD <input_jadfile>
```


If you don't wish to use the JADTool command-line utility, the J2ME toolkit also provides a GUI-based utility (Ktoolbar) that enables you to complete the entire signing process without having to use the command-line options. Finally, you may also choose to use the Ktoolbar tool to publish and then directly install the MIDlet suite in the device using Over-The-Air (OTA) provisioning techniques commonly adopted in wireless service deployment. The OTA provisioning mechanisms allow deploying applications wirelessly, the same way they send and receive messages or browse the Internet.

The J2ME platform [J2ME] also provides mechanisms for using cryptographic algorithms and securing network communication using SSL/TLS protocols as well as ensuring source authentication, integrity, and confidentiality. This will be discussed in Chapter 4. "Java Extensible Security Architecture and APIs."

Java Card Security Architecture

The Java Card technology enables smart cards and other devices with limited memory to run Java-based applications. Java Card technology brings a whole set of advantages to smart cards by offering a secure execution environment, platform-independence, the ability to store and update multiple applications, and compatibility with existing smart-card standards. It is also important to note that the Java Card technology [JavaCard] was developed specifically to enhance the security of smart cards.

Understanding Smart Cards

A smart card looks like a typical credit card but is much more powerful than the traditional magnetic stripe card. Smart cards make use of an embedded microprocessor chip. One of the primary advantages of smart cards over magnetic stripe cards is their ability to run small applications that perform computations. They

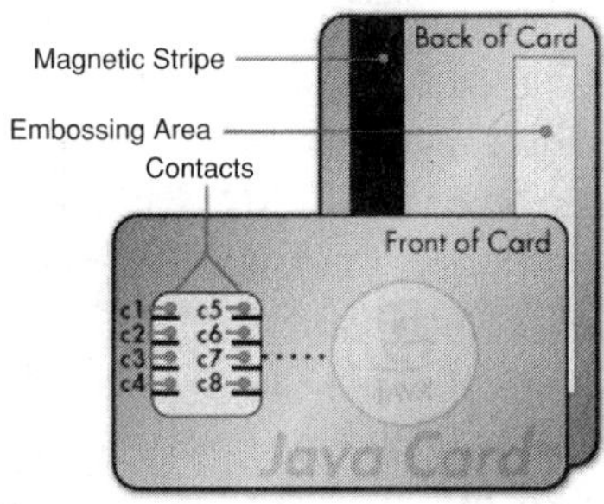

Figure 3–6 The Java Card (Source: Sun Microsystems)

are, in a sense, small computers. Smart cards are also compatible with a variety of portable electronic devices, such as cellular phones, personal digital assistants (PDAs), and other consumer devices.

Smart card technology is quickly becoming a replacement for several current technologies—from ID badges to credit cards. Financial companies are considering smart cards as a mechanism for delivering services at a lower cost to businesses and consumers. A common service would be an electronic purse service that allows bank customers to transfer money from their bank accounts to their smart cards in the form of secure electronic cash. The electronic cash can then be used to purchase products, pay bills, or pay bridge tolls. Smart cards can be used as a form of ID in a variety of industries. Smart cards can hold information commonly found on an ID card, driver's license, or in a patient's medical records. For example, a doctor can create a record of a patient's treatment history by writing information to his or her smart card. This allows the patient, or another doctor, to have medical information available at any time. A smart card can also act as an employee access badge (by containing encrypted security information such as user names and passwords) that allows an employee access into a company's building or computer network.

Smart Card Components

Each smart card solution requires a number of hardware and software components (operating systems, APIs, and applications) and protocols (for communication between tiers and between components on a tier). There can be four or more hardware components in an enterprise smart card solution. The hardware components are the smart card, the card reader or card acceptance device (CAD), the terminal, and the back-end business applications. All smart cards contain some amount of memory—ROM, RAM, and EEPROM (that is, electrically erasable programmable read-only memory). Both memory cards and processor cards can store much more information than traditional magnetic stripe cards. ROM is used to hold the operating system and other software that you cannot modify. RAM is a volatile memory and any information in RAM is lost when the card is disconnected from the reader. Like ROM, EEPROM is used to store information that persists after power is disconnected. The CAD is a card reader that enables access to and communication with a smart card. It can also enable developers to build applications that are smart card capable. The card reader provides a "path" for your application to send and receive commands from the card. The card reader is connected to a terminal that is usually an electronic device—from common computer workstations and desktop computers (PCs) to small embedded devices, such as screen phones, set-top boxes, and cellular phones. The back-end technologies provide the information, database, or processing system to facilitate any number of smart-card enterprise solutions. Smart cards solve many of the security problems that occur in a network environment. At the center of the solution is the promising fact that a smart card requires a user PIN (Personal Identification Number) to get access to a system.

Java Card Technology in Smart Cards

Java Card technology makes it possible to create and download new applications and services to smart-card consumers. In general, a Java Card is a smart card that is capable of running Java applets. From a security standpoint, the Java Card technology maintains the built-in security of the Java platform and makes the smart card a safe way to conduct consumer transactions over such insecure networks as the Internet and public telephone systems. Thus, Java Card technology preserves many of the existing benefits of the Java programming language, such as security, robustness, and portability.

Java Card technology was designed based on the smart-card specification standard, ISO7816. This standard specifies that communication between a host application and a smart card occur through Application Protocol Data Units (APDUs). An APDU is a packet of data that conforms to a specific format. There are two types of APDUs: command APDUs and response APDUs. In Java Card technology, the host application sends a command APDU, and a Java Card applet responds with a response APDU. The Java Card technology defines a Java Card runtime environment (JCRE) on top of the hardware and the smart-card native system.

The JCRE acts as an intermediary between the native smart card system and the Java Card applet. The command APDU is transmitted to the JCRE, which sends it to the appropriate Java Card applet for processing. After processing the

Java Card Runtime Environment and APIs

The JCRE provides a high-level standard interface to smart-card applications. It provides a secure execution environment with a virtual firewall between different applications in the same card. This allows different applications on the same card to function separately and independently from each other, as if they were on separate cards.

The Java Card API is a subset of the Java platform that allows development using object-oriented programming to create secure smart applications. By contrast, traditional smart-card application programming uses assembly language or the C programming language, which forces security evaluation of the application and also requires looking at the entire application as a unit to verify the behavior.

The Java Card API is a standard set of APIs and software classes that will run on any existing smart card. It is ISO7816-4 compliant, and compatible with formal international standards such as ISO7816 and industry-specific standards such as Europay/MasterCard/Visa (EMV). It also provides Java Card issuers with interoperable services through logical channel support defined by standards organizations, such as the European Telecommunications Standards Institute (ETSI), Third Generation Partner Project (3GPP), and Wireless Access Protocol (WAP).

Let's look at the Java Card platform security features in greater detail.

New in Java SE 6: The Java SE 6 (SDK) includes a smart card I/O API (as defined by JSR 268) and also a provider implementation that supports PC/SC integration with a host. This allows Java applications to communicate with a smart card using ISO 7816 APDUs.

Java Card Platform Security Model

The Java Card platform provides a number of security features that can be enforced at every level at the inception of application development. They are characterized as follows:

- The Java Card technology supports a subset of the Java programming language and JVM specifications, inheriting the security features built into the supported subset.
- The Java Card platform stores the objects and data in memory. During a power loss or unexpected failure, the platform makes sure that the objects and data are stored to its previous state before such failures.

- The Java Card applets are verified to ensure their integrity, because they can be downloaded over an unsecured network. A trusted third party can also cryptographically sign Java Card applets. The digital signature of an applet can be verified during on-card installation to further ensure the safety of the code.
- In the Java Card runtime, the notion of a sandbox is implemented via the applet firewall mechanism. The firewall essentially assigns an object space, called a context, to each applet on the card. Data access within a context is allowed, but the access to an applet in a different context is prohibited by the firewall. Applets residing in different contexts can share objects using secure object-sharing mechanisms by implementing a shareable interface.
- The Java Card applets are not allowed to execute native methods except for the card's vendor-issued applets. This means that applets installed after issuance of the card are restricted from running native methods.
- The Java Card technology embraces techniques using compressed archive files with cryptographic signatures to provide tamperproof distribution and installation procedures for Java class files and Java Card applets.

Java Card Applets

A Java Card applet is a smart card application written using the Java Card APIs and is able to run within a JCRE. It is important to note that Java Card applets are not intended to run in a Web browser environment. Multiple applets can be loaded and coexist on a Java Card and can have multiple instances. Each applet instance is uniquely identified by an application identifier (AID). Similar to any persistent objects, applets installed on a Java Card live throughout the entire lifetime of the Java Card as long as the card is usable. The applets will terminate only if they are uninstalled. The process of applet installation to a card (also referred to as masking) is done through the proprietary tools provided by the Java Card manufacturer.

Java Card Applet Development and Installation

To study Java Card security, it is very important to understand the process of developing and installing Java Card applets. Figure 3–7 illustrates the steps involved in developing and installing a Java Card applet.

The development of a Java Card applet typically starts like developing any other Java program and compiling the source file to produce Java class files. The resulting class files are tested and debugged using a Java Card simulator environment that simulates the applet using the Java Card runtime environment running

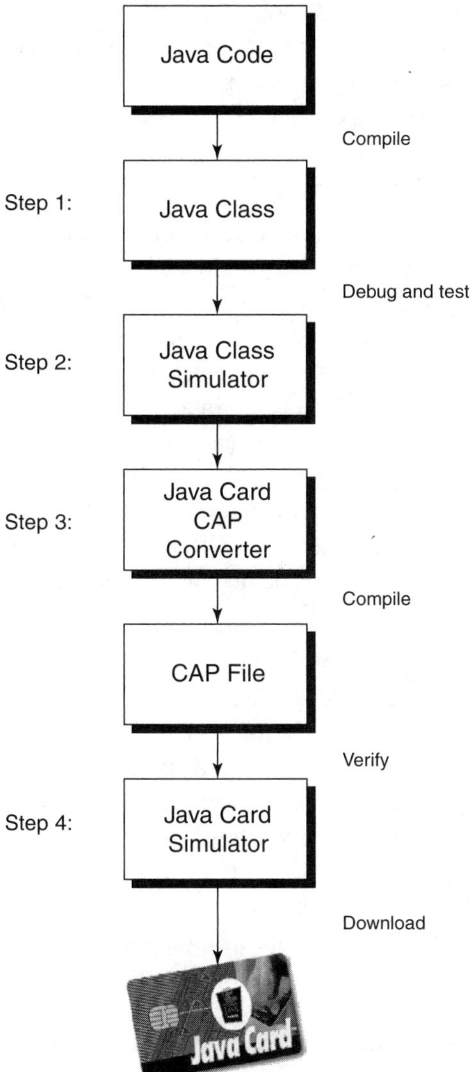

Figure 3–7 Java Card applet development and installation

on a development workstation. The simulator helps the developer to study the behavior and results prior to deploying on a Java Card. Then the class files that make up the applet are converted to a Converted Applet (CAP) file using a Java Card CAP converter tool. As a package, the resulting CAP files represent a Java Card applet. These CAP files are further tested using a Java Card emulator tool in the development environment to identify the expected behavior of the applet in a real Java Card. Finally, the tested applet comprised of all the CAP files is downloaded into the Java Card using a proprietary tool provided by the Java Card vendor. To secure the applets (using vendor-provided tools), it is possible to sign the applet code and allow the Java Card to verify the signatures.

Java Card Applet Security

The Java Card provides a multi-application smart card environment that allows multiple applets to coexist on a Java Card and also provides the flexibility to download applets after manufacture or issuance. The Java Card provides a virtual applet firewall protection mechanism that isolates an applet package to its designated firewall partition (referred to as context). The context mechanism disallows object access from another applet located in a different context. To support cooperative applications running on a single card, it provides a secure object sharing mechanism. The sharing mechanism under specific conditions enables one context to access objects belonging to another context by performing a context switch. When an object is accessed, the JCRE enforces access control, and if the contexts do not match, the access is denied and results in a SecurityException.

Java Card Development Kit

Sun Microsystems provides a Java Card development kit that contains components and tools that you need to develop Java Card applets. The development kit provides a set of tools that support Java Card applet development and deployment onto a smart card. It provides a Java Card Workstation Development Environment (JCWDE) that simulates a Java Card runtime environment using a JVM. It provides a Converter utility, which does off-card verification processes, including class loading, linking, name resolution, bytecode verification, optimization, and conversion of an applet to a smart-card installation format. For more information about the Java Card Development Kit, refer to the Web site at http://java.sun.com/products/javacard.

In summary, a Java Card is a portable computing device about the size of a credit card that is often used as a secure storage device; beyond that, it can be used for a variety of security and identity-management solutions. Some common examples are as follows:

- Secure storage for personal and confidential information
- Prepaid GSM phone SIM cards offering a cash-free and anti-fraud mechanism
- Secure identity cards for personal identification, physical access, user authentication, and access control

- Bank credit cards that cannot be copied and misused like magnetic stripe cards

We will take a look at Java Card strategies for secure personal identification in Chapter 15, "Secure Personal Identification Using Smart Cards and Biometrics."

Securing the Java Code

The threat of reverse engineering is a well-known security problem for Java applications. By default, the byte code generated by the Java compiler contains much symbolic information, including the actual Java source of the executable and debugging information. Using reverse engineering mechanisms, it is possible to disassemble and decompile the executable Java bytecode into actual Java source code. This fact highlights the vulnerabilities of Java applications and makes clear the risks of someone having the ability to do the following:

- Modify code and data
- Determine the flow of program execution
- Determine algorithms
- Construct a fraudulent application
- Steal intellectual property
- Apply code-level security breaches

Reverse Engineering: Disassembling and Decompiling

The process of reverse engineering the Java program is done by disassembling the executable classes to an intermediate assembly code and then decompiling the assembly code to obtain the higher-level abstractions of the byte code. This higher-level abstraction contains significant source code, including variables, methods, and so forth. When compared with the actual source code, the noticeable difference is the absence of comments. It is also noted that the reverse engineering process does not provide source code with accuracy. There are many commercial and freeware tools available that provide disassembling and decompiling capabilities.

From a security standpoint, it is very important to realize the threats posed by the use of disassembling and decompiling techniques to reverse engineer the Java executable. With these techniques, a hacker can reconstruct an application with modified code and disrupt the original application by attacking its underlying resources. To counter these issues, there are several tools and techniques that allow protecting the source code from prying eyes by making it difficult to apply any reverse engineering mechanisms.

The possible ways to prevent reverse engineering of Java executables and to protect the source code are as follows:

- **Code authentication**: This approach adopts evaluation and verification of executable code for trusted sources, runtime checks, predictable behavior, and output. This ensures that code is not executed from an unauthorized host, not modified to produce any unpredicted output, and not duplicated to act as an original application.
- **Encryption and decryption**: Using encryption and decryption of executable code in transmission ensures that the code is not accessible or tampered with during its transit. This approach limits portability of the application but works well in scenarios where applications are made available via server-side invocations.
- **Code obfuscation**: This approach uses a transformation mechanism that changes the program and generates Java code with obscure references. The obfuscated code is understood by compilers but difficult to read by humans. This is the most popular way to prevent the success of reverse engineering capabilities on executable code.

Code Obfuscation

Code obfuscation is the process of transforming the executable in a manner that affects reverse engineering mechanisms by making the generated code more complex and harder to understand. It decouples the relationship between the executable code and its original source, which ultimately makes the decompiled code ineffective. With all those changes, the obfuscated program still works in a functionally identical way compared to the original executable. There are several transformation mechanisms that allow obfuscation of Java code, and the most common techniques [Obfuscation] are as follows:

- **Structural or layout transformation**: This transforms the lexical structure of the code by scrambling and renaming the identifiers of methods and variables.
- **Data transformation**: This transformation affects the data structures represented in the program. For example, it changes the data represented in the

memory from a local to a global variable, converting a two-dimensional array into a one-dimensional array and vice-versa, changing the order of data in a list, and so forth.

- **Control transformation**: This transformation affects the flow control represented in the program. For example, it changes the grouping of statements as inline procedures, order of execution, and so forth.
- **Tamper-proofing and preventive transformation**: This transformation makes the decompiler fail to extract the actual program, and the generated code is unusable. Refer to [PrevTransform] for more detailed information.
- **String encryption**: This mechanism encrypts all string literals within the executable code, and during runtime invocation it decrypts them for use.
- **Watermarking**: This mechanism embeds a secret message in the executable that identifies the copy of the executable and allows you to trace the hacker who exploited the generated code.

With little performance overhead, the code obfuscation process restricts the abuse of decompilation mechanisms and offers portability without affecting the deployment platforms. Adopting code obfuscators is a good choice to make in the attempt to reduce the risks of reverse engineering. They prevent loss of intellectual property and offer protection of Java code from malicious attacks. The Java code obfuscators are publicly available in the form of freeware, shareware, and commercial applications.

Summary

This chapter explained the Java 2 platform architecture and its security features as they apply to building Java applications. In particular, it described the various Java platforms and the core security features that contribute to the end-to-end security of Java-based applications running on various systems—from servers to stand-alone computers, computers to devices, and devices to smart cards. It discussed securing Java applets, JNLP-based Java Web start applications and code obfuscation strategies.

The chapter also described how to use the different security mechanisms, tools, and strategies for implementing the following:

Java application security

Java applet security

Java Web start security

J2ME Platform security

Java Card Platform security

Java code obfuscation

In the next chapter, we will explore the Java extensible security architecture and API mechanisms that allow preserving confidentiality, integrity, authentication, and nonrepudiation in Java-based applications.

References

[J2SE] Li Gong. "Java Security Architecture." Java™ 2 SDK, Standard Edition Documentation Version 1.4.2. Sun Microsystems, 2003.

http://java.sun.com/j2se/1.4.2/docs/guide/security/spec/security-spec.doc1.html

and

http://java.sun.com/j2se/1.4.2/docs/guide/security/spec/security-spec.doc2.html.

[J2SE5] "J2SE 5.0 Platform Specifications," Sun Microsystems, 2004.

http://java.sun.com/j2se/1.5.0/docs/api/

[J2ME] "J2ME Platform Specifications," Sun Microsystems, 2003.

http://java.sun.com/j2me/

[JavaCard] "Java Card Platform Specifications," Sun Microsystems, 2003.

http://java.sun.com/products/javacard/

[JWS] "Java Web Start Technology Specifications," Sun Microsystems, 2003.

http://java.sun.com/products/javawebstart/.

[Obfuscation] Christian Collberg and Clark Thomborson. "Watermarking, Tamper-proofing, and Obfuscation—Tools for Software Protection." IEEE Transactions on Software Engineering 28:8, 735-746, August 2002

[PrevTransform] Christian Collberg, Clark Thomborson, and Douglas Low. "A Taxonomy of Obfuscating Transformations." Technical Report 148, Department of Computer Science, University of Auckland, New Zealand, July 1997.

http://www.cs.auckland.ac.nz/~collberg/Research/Publications/CollbergThomborsonLow97a/index.html

Java Extensible Security Architecture and APIs

Java Extensible Security

Topics in This Chapter

- Java Extensible Security Architecture
- Java Cryptography Architecture (JCA)
- Java Cryptographic Extensions (JCE)
- Java Certification Path API (CertPath)
- Java Secure Socket Extension (JSSE)
- Java Authentication and Authorization Service (JAAS)
- Java Generic Secure Services API (JGSS)
- Simple Authentication and Security Layer (SASL)

Chapter 4

Java Extensible Security

Building end-to-end security of an application mandates a security architecture beyond the application's underlying runtime platform. Security must be extended at all levels, including users, components, services, and communications. Without any compromise, the application security infrastructure must address the core security requirements of maintaining integrity, confidentiality, and privacy of data during communication and storage as well as preventing unauthorized access or damage caused by any unprivileged user(s) and their associated risks. Accordingly, when an organization plans to build Internet-based business applications or enable their applications over a network, it becomes very important to ensure that such applications are built to meet all security requirements beyond their runtime execution environment.

In the previous chapter, we looked at the core Java platform security architecture, which provides a secure and restricted runtime environment for applications to execute safely and reliably. In addition to runtime security, the Java platform provides an extensible security architecture to support a variety of security infrastructure services, including cryptographic services; certificate interfaces and classes for managing digital certificates; Public Key Infrastructure (PKI) interfaces and classes to access, modify, and manage the key repository; certificates and secure socket communication to protect the privacy and integrity of data transited over the network; services for authentication and access control; and mechanisms for single sign-on access to underlying applications.

This chapter expands on the Java extensible security architecture and its API framework and discusses how to utilize those provider implementations and APIs for building security infrastructure in Java-based solutions. In particular, we will be taking an in-depth look at the core Java security API solutions and implementation strategies that contribute to building end-to-end security of Java-based application solutions. In addition, this chapter will also discuss the new Java security enhancements made in the release of J2SE 5.0.

Java Extensible Security Architecture

The Java platform facilitates an extensible security architectural model via standards-based security API technologies that provide platform independence and allow interoperability among vendor implementations. These API technologies add a variety of security features to the core Java platform by integrating technologies to support cryptography, certificate management, authentication and authorization, secure communication, and other custom security mechanisms.

Figure 4–1 illustrates the Java extensible security architecture and its core API mechanisms.

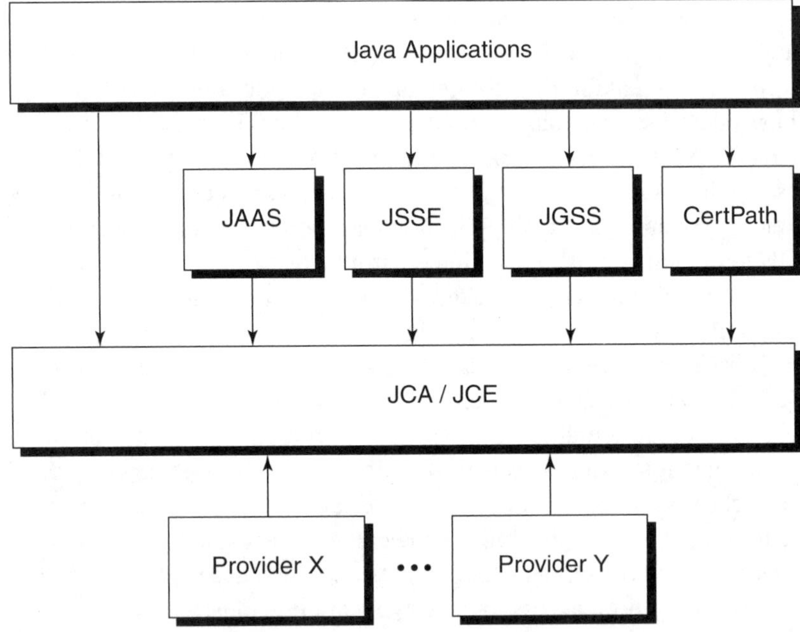

Figure 4–1 Java extensible security architecture and its core APIs

As part of the J2SE bundle, the Java extensible security architecture provides the following set of API frameworks and their implementations, which contributes to the end-to-end security of Java-based applications.

- **Java Cryptography Architecture (JCA)**: Provides basic cryptographic services and algorithms, which include support for digital signatures and message digests.
- **Java Cryptographic Extension (JCE)**: Augments JCA functionalities with added cryptographic services that are subjected to U.S. export control regulations and includes support for encryption and decryption operations, secret key generation and agreement, and message authentication code (MAC) algorithms.
- **Java Certification Path API (CertPath)**: Provides the functionality of checking, verifying, and validating the authenticity of certificate chains.
- **Java Secure Socket Extension (JSSE)**: Facilitates secure communication by protecting the integrity and confidentiality of data exchanged using SSL/TLS protocols.
- **Java Authentication and Authorization Service (JAAS)**: Provides the mechanisms to verify the identity of a user or a device to determine its accuracy and trustworthiness and then provide access rights and privileges depending on the requesting identity. It facilitates the adoption of pluggable authentication mechanisms and user-based authorization.
- **Java Generic Secure Services (JGSS)**: Provides functionalities to develop applications using a unified API to support a variety of authentication mechanisms such as Kerberos based authentication and also facilitates single sign-on.

These Java security APIs are made available as part of J2SE 1.4 and later. They were also made available as optional security API packages for use with earlier versions of J2SE. We will take a closer look at each of these API mechanisms in the next sections.

Java Cryptography Architecture (JCA)

In J2SE, the JCA provides the Java platform with cryptographic services and algorithms to secure messages. JCA defines a notion of provider implementation and a generic API framework for accessing cryptographic services and implementing related functionalities. JCA is also designed to provide algorithm and

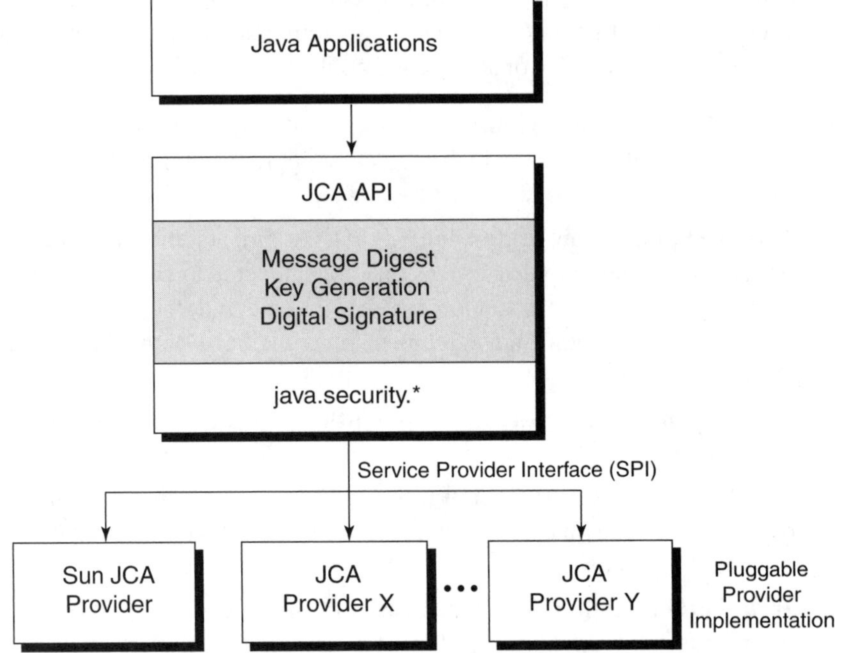

Figure 4–2 JCA architectural model and its cryptographic services

implementation independence via a standardized API framework and provider implementation.

Figure 4–2 illustrates the JCA and its cryptographic services.

JCA Cryptographic Services

JCA provides support for various cryptographic algorithms by defining the types and functionalities of cryptographic services. The cryptographic services include support for message digests and digital signatures. JCA also ensures interoperability among the provider implementations using a standardized set of APIs, which implements those required cryptographic algorithms and services. For example, using the same algorithms, a key generated by one provider can be usable by another provider; likewise, a digital signature generated by one provider can be verified using another provider.

Let's take a closer look at the JCA provider architecture, its core API classes, and its programming model.

JCA Cryptographic Service Provider

JCA introduces the notion of a *Cryptographic Service Provider*, which is an API package containing a set of packages that implements cryptographic services. A JCA provider package can contain one or more digital signature algorithms, message digest algorithms, and key generation algorithms, as well as services related to keys and keystore creation and management, certificate management, and algorithm parameter generation and management.

As part of the J2SE bundle, the JCA framework includes a default provider implementation named *SUN*, which provides the following features:

- Implementation of Digital Signature Algorithm (DSA) and Message Digest Algorithms (MD5 and SHA1)
- DSA key pair generator for generating public and private keys based on DSA
- DSA algorithm parameter generator and manager
- DSA key factory to provide conversations between public and private keys
- Certificate path builder and validator for X.509 certificates
- Certificate factory for X.509 certificates and revocation lists
- Keystore implementation named JKS, which allows managing a repository of keys and certificates

JCA Classes and Interfaces

In J2SE, the JCA framework provides the core classes and interfaces of the Java platform security package related to cryptography. It exists as part of java.security package.

JCA Provider Classes

The JCA API provides a specific set of Java security APIs that allow interacting with the cryptographic services of the provider.

- **Provider (java.security.Provider)**: This class represents a cryptographic service provider that implements some or all parts of Java cryptographic functions such as Algorithms (such as DSA, RSA, MD5, or SHA-1), key generation, conversion, and management. It also contains methods for registering other security services and accessing the provider name, version, and other provider-specific information. The types of services implemented by the provider are represented using an Engine class.

- **Security** (java.security.Security): This class manages all installed providers and security properties. It provides static methods for adding providers, removing providers, and setting and maintaining security properties. These methods can only be executed by a trusted application. The J2SE security policy configuration file (i.e., security.policy) specifies the security properties of the trusted application.

Example 4–1 shows a JCA code fragment for retrieving the list of available cryptographic service providers.

Example 4–1 Listing available cryptographic service providers

```
Provider[] csps = Security.getProviders();
for (int i=0; i < csps.length, i++) {
   System.out.println (csps[i].getName());
}
```

JCA Engine Classes

The JCA also defines a set of engine classes. An engine class represents a cryptographic service associated with a particular algorithm and provides interfaces to the functionality of the service. The application interfaces provided by an engine class are implemented as Service Provider Interfaces (SPIs). For each engine API class, JCA has a corresponding SPI class for which the cryptographic service provider must provide an implementation. Let's take a look at some of the most important engine classes.

- **MessageDigest** (java.security.MessageDigest): Defines the functionality of using a message digest algorithm such as MD5 or SHA. Message digests are secure one-way hash functions that take arbitrary-sized data and output a fixed-length hash value.
- **Signature** (java.security.Signature): Defines the functionality of using a digital signature algorithm. Digital signatures are mainly used for authentication validation and integrity assurance of digital data.
- **KeyPairGenerator** (java.security.KeyPairGenerator): Defines the functionality for generating pairs of public and private keys for a chosen algorithm.
- **KeyFactory** (java.security.KeyFactory): Defines the functionality for converting opaque cryptographic keys into key specifications, and vice-versa.
- **CertificateFactory** (java.security.cert.CertificateFactory): Defines the functionality for generating certificates along with certification path (CertPath) and certificate revocation list (CRL) objects.

- **KeyStore** (java.security.KeyStore): Defines the functionality for creating and managing a keystore. A keystore represents an in-memory collection of keys and certificates. It stores them as key and certificate entries.
- **AlgorithmParameters** (java.security.AlgorithmParameters): Used to manage the parameters of a particular algorithm, which includes its encoding and decoding.
- **AlgorithmParameterGenerator** (java.security.AlgorithmParameterGenerator): Defines the functionality for generating a set of parameters suitable for a specified algorithm.
- **SecureRandom** (java.security.SecureRandom): Defines the functionality for generating cryptographically strong random or pseudo-random numbers.

Now, let's take a look at the programming model for some of these classes.

Understanding JCA API Programming Model

JCA provides flexible API mechanisms to install one or more JCA provider implementations. This allows for the use of a variety of cryptographic services and algorithms provided by different vendor implementations. For example, to get the cryptographic service provider that implements a specified algorithm, the getInstance() method is used. The service providers can be used independently or in combination with one another to achieve the required level of cryptographic security. JCA also provides API mechanisms to support the JCA provider—cryptographic operations such as computing message digests, generating key pairs, and generating and verifying digital signatures. Let's take a closer look at the supported cryptographic operations and how to use those APIs.

Message Digests

Message digest is a one-way secure hash function. Its computed values are referred to as message digests or hash values and act as fingerprints of messages. The message digest values are computationally impossible to reverse and thus protect the original message from being derived.

As a cryptographic technique, message digests are applied for preserving the secrecy of messages, files, and objects. In conjunction with digital signature, message digests are used to support integrity, authentication, and non-repudiation of messages during transmission or storage. Message digest functions are publicly available and use no keys. In J2SE, the JCA provider supports two message digest algorithms: Message Digest 5 (MD5) and secure hash algorithm (SHA-1). MD5 produces a 128-bit (16-byte) hash and SHA-1 produces a 160-bit message digest value.

Computing a Message Digest Object

Message digests are represented using the Engine class java.security.MessageDigest as byte arrays. The MessageDigest.getInstance(algorithm) creates an instance of a message digest object implementing the given algorithm, if this algorithm is available with the provider. The MessageDigest.update method updates the digest using the data specified as byte array and the MessageDigest.digest method computes the hash value and returns a byte array.

Example 4–2 would compute a message digest with MD5.

Example 4–2 Computing a message digest using MD5

```
try {
     MessageDigest md5 = MessageDigest.getInstance("MD5");
     byte[] testdata = { 1,2,3,4,5 };
     md5.update(testdata);
     byte []  myhash =  md5.digest();
     } catch (NoSuchAlgorithmException e) {
   }
```

Example 4–3 computes a message digest with SHA-1.

Example 4–3 Computing a message digest using SHA-1

```
try {
     MessageDigest sha = MessageDigest.getInstance("SHA-1");
     byte[] testdata = { 1,2,3,4,5 };
     sha.update(testdata);
     byte []  myhash =  sha.digest();
     } catch (NoSuchAlgorithmException e) {
   }
```

Key Pair Generation

Generating key pairs and securely distributing them is one of the major challenges in implementing cryptographic security. JCA provides the ability to generate key pairs using digital signature algorithms such as DSA, RSA, and Diffie-Hellman. JCA also supports using random number algorithms to add a high degree of randomness, which makes it computationally difficult to predict and determine the generated values.

The key is represented using the java.security.Key interface, which provides three methods: getAlgorithm() for obtaining the associated key algorithm, getEncoded() for returning the key as a byte array in its primary encoded format, and getFormat() for returning the format in which the key is encoded. The key interface is extended by

PrivateKey and PublicKey interfaces that are used to identify the private and public keys as key pairs representing asymmetric algorithms.

The java.security.KeyPairGenerator is an abstract class that provides the functionality for creating both public and private key pairs using public key algorithms.

- To generate a public/private key pair, use the KeyPairGenerator.getInstance (algorithm) to create an instance of the KeyPairGenerator object implementing the given algorithm:

```
KeyPairGenerator kpg
          = KeyPairGenerator.getInstance("DSA");
```

- Use the KeyPairGenerator.initialize(bitSize) method to initialize the key generator specifying the size of the key in bits (for DSA, the size should be between 512 and 1024 with a multiple of 64) and to securely randomize the key generation in an unpredictable fashion:

```
kpg.initialize(1024);
```

- To generate the key pair, use KeyPairGenerator.genKeyPair() to create the KeyPair object. To obtain the private and public keys, use the KeyPair.getPrivate() and KeyPair.getPublic() methods, respectively.

Example 4–4 is a code fragment showing generation of a key pair for public/private key algorithms such as "DSA" and "DH".

Example 4–4 Key pair generation using DSA and DH algorithms

```
try {
    //1024-bit Digital Signature Algorithm(DSA) key pairs
    KeyPairGenerator keyGen
            = KeyPairGenerator.getInstance("DSA");
    keyGen.initialize(1024);
    KeyPair keypair = keyGen.genKeyPair();
    PrivateKey privateKey = keypair.getPrivate();
    PublicKey publicKey = keypair.getPublic();

    //576-bit DiffieHellman key pair
    keyGen = KeyPairGenerator.getInstance("DH");
    keyGen.initialize(576);
    keypair = keyGen.genKeyPair();
    privateKey = keypair.getPrivate();
    publicKey = keypair.getPublic();
    } catch (java.security.NoSuchAlgorithmException e) {
   }
```

Digital Signature Generation

A digital signature is computed using public-key cryptographic techniques. The sender signs a message using a private key and the receiver decodes the message using the public key. This allows the receiver to verify the source or signer of the message and guarantee its integrity and authenticity.

The java.security.Signature class provides the functionalities for digitally signing and verifying a message during its transmission or its storage.

To generate a signature object, Signature.getInstance(algorithm) creates an instance of the Signature object implementing the given algorithm. To sign the message, the Signature.initSign(key) method is used with a private key as an input, Signature.update (message) updates the message to be signed using the specified byte array, and finally, Signature.sign() finishes the operation resulting in the signature bytes.

Example 4–5 shows how to apply a signature to a message using a private key.

Example 4–5 Applying digital signature using a private key

```
try {
       byte[] testdata = { 1,2,3,4,5 };
       Signature dsig
            = Signature.getInstance(privateKey.getAlgorithm());
       dsig.initSign(privateKey);
       dsig.update(testdata);
       byte[] signedData = dsig.sign();
        } catch (SignatureException e) {
          } catch (InvalidKeyException e) {
           } catch (NoSuchAlgorithmException e) {
    }
```

To verify a digital signature object using a public key, use the Signature.getInstance(algorithm), which creates an instance of Signature implementing the algorithm, if such an algorithm is available with the provider. To verify the message, the Signature.initVerify(key) method is used with a public key as an input, Signature.update(message) takes the signed message to be verified using the specified byte array, and finally, Signature.verify(signature) takes the signature as a byte array for verification and results in a boolean value indicating success or failure. The signature verification will be successful only if the signature corresponds to the message and its public key.

Example 4–6 shows how to verify a digital signature on a message using a public key.

Example 4–6 Verifying digital signature using a public key

```
try {
  Signature dsig
    = Signature.getInstance(myPublicKey.getAlgorithm());
  dsig.initVerify(publicKey);
  dsig.update(signedData);
  boolean result = dsig.verify(signatureToVerify);
} catch (SignatureException e) {
} catch (InvalidKeyException e) {
} catch (NoSuchAlgorithmException e) {
}
```


So far we have looked at JCA and the use of standard-based cryptographic services. Now, let's explore Java Cryptographic Extensions (JCE), an enhancement to JCA that has additional features and capabilities.

Java Cryptographic Extensions (JCE)

JCE was originally developed as an extension package to include APIs and implementations for cryptographic services that were subject to U.S. export control regulations. JCE provides a provider implementation and related set of API packages to provide support for encryption and decryption, secret key generation, and agreement and message authentication code (MAC) algorithms. The encryption and decryption support includes symmetric, asymmetric, block, and stream ciphers. JCE also provides support for secure streams and sealed objects.

Initially, JCE was made available as an optional package to the JSDK versions 1.2.x and 1.3.x in accordance with U.S. regulations specific to the export of cryptography. Due to changes in the U.S. regulations related to the export of cryptography, JCE has now been integrated into J2SE 1.4.

JCE facilitates the Java platform with cryptographic services and algorithms by providing implementations and interfaces for the following:

- Cryptographic ciphers used for encryption and decryption
- Password-based encryption
- Secret key generation used for symmetric algorithms
- Creation of sealed objects that are serialized and encrypted
- Key agreement for encrypted communication among multiple parties
- MAC algorithms to validate information transmitted between parties

- Support for PKCS#11 (RSA Cryptographic Token Interface Standard), which allows devices to store cryptographic information and perform cryptographic services. This feature is available in J2SE 5.0 and later versions.

Like JCA, JCE also has the notion of provider implementations and a generic API framework for accessing JCE-supported cryptographic services and implementing related functionalities. It is also designed to provide algorithm- and implementation-independence via a standardized API framework.

Figure 4–3 illustrates the architectural representation of JCE and its cryptographic services.

Let's take a closer look at the JCE provider architecture, core API classes, and its programming model.

JCE Cryptographic Service Provider

Because JCE's design is based on the architectural principles of JCA, like JCA it allows for integration of *Cryptographic Service Providers*, which implements the JCE-defined cryptographic services from a vendor. JCE also facilitates a pluggable framework architecture that allows qualified JCE providers to be plugged in. As part of the J2SE bundle, the JCE framework provides a default provider imple-

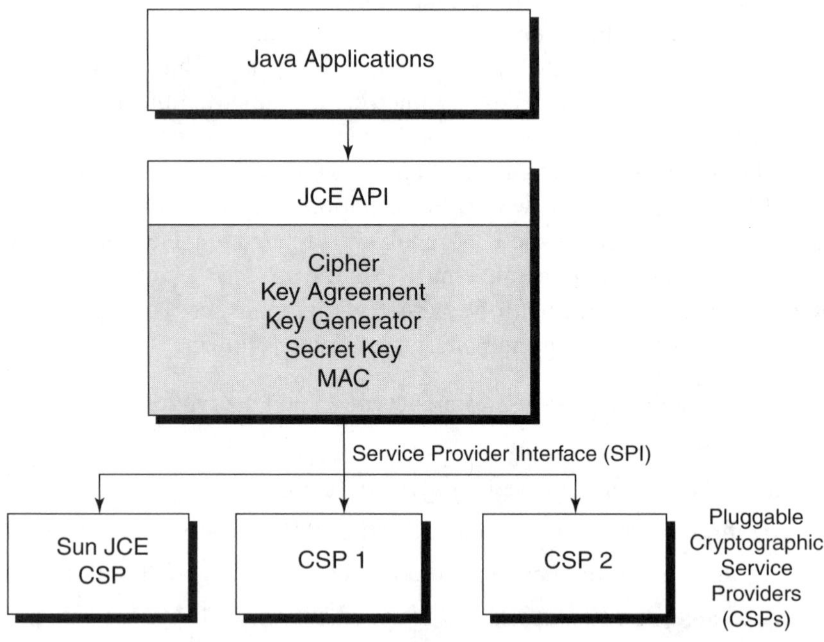

Figure 4–3 JCE architectural model and its cryptographic services

mentation named *SunJCE*, which provides the following cryptographic services and algorithms.

- Implementation of Ciphers and Encryption algorithms such as DES (FIPS PUB 46-1), Triple DES, and Blowfish
- Modes include Electronic Code Book (ECB), Cipher Block Chaining (CBC), Cipher Feedback (CFB), Output Feedback (OFB), and Propagating Cipher Block Chaining (PCBC)
- Implementation of MAC algorithms such as HMAC-MD5 and HMAC-SHA1 algorithms
- Key generators for DES, Triple DES, Blowfish, HMAC-MD5, and HMAC-SHA1 algorithms
- Implementation of the MD5 with DES-CBC password-based encryption (PBE) algorithm
- Implementation of key agreement protocols based on Diffie-Hellman
- Implementation of Padding scheme as per PKCS#5
- Algorithm parameter managers for Diffie-Hellman, DES, Triple DES, Blowfish, and PBE
- Support for Advanced Encryption Standard (AES)
- A keystore implementation named JCEKS

The following services and algorithms are introduced as J2SE 5.0 security enhancements:

- Support for PKCS#11 standard
- Support for ECC algorithm
- Support for XML Encryption RSA-OAEP algorithm
- Integration with Solaris Cryptographic Framework
- Support for "PBEWithSHA1AndDESede" and "PBEWithSHA1AndRC2_40" Ciphers
- Support for RC2ParameterSpec
- Support for RSA encryption to SunJCE provider
- Support for RC2 and ARCFOUR Ciphers to SunJCE provider
- Support for HmacSHA256, HmacSHA384 and HmacSHA512

New in Java SE 6: The Java SE 6 (SDK) includes a SunMSCAPI JCE provider that allows Java applications to interact with Microsoft Crypto API (CAPI) and perform RSA cryptographic functions.

JCE Classes and Interfaces

In J2SE, the JCE API framework exists as part of the javax.crypto package.

JCE Provider classes

JCE employs JCA provider classes, particularly the java.security.Provider and java.security.Security classes that allow querying the cryptographic services offered by the provider. The type of services implemented by the provider are represented using an *Engine* class available as part of the javax.crypto package.

JCE Engine classes

Like JCA, JCE defines a set of engine classes that provide interfaces to the functionality of cryptographic services. The application interfaces of the engine class implements the SPI. Each engine API class has a corresponding SPI class for which the cryptographic service provider provides an implementation.

The following JCE engine classes are available within J2SE:

- **Cipher (javax.crypto.Cipher)**: The core of the JCE API, which provides the functionality of a cryptographic cipher for doing encryption and decryption.
- **Cipher Stream classes (javax.crypto.CipherInputStream and javax.crypto.CipherOutputStream)**: JCE introduced the notion of secure streams, which combine the inputstream and outputstream of a Cipher object.
- **Mac (javax.crypto.Mac)**: Provides the functionality of a MAC algorithm, which is used to check the integrity of a message based on a secret key transmitted over a network or stored in an unreliable medium
- **KeyGenerator (javax.crypto.KeyGenerator)**: Provides the functionality of a symmetric key (secret key) generator.
- **SecretKeyFactory (javax.crypto.SecretKeyFactory)**: Acts as a factory class for SecretKey; operates only on symmetric keys.
- **SealedObject (javax.crypto.SealedObject)**: Allows creating a serialized object and protects its confidentiality using a cryptographic algorithm.
- **KeyAgreement (javax.crypto.KeyAgreement)**: Provides the functionality of using KeyAgreement protocols; allows the creation of a KeyAgreement object for each party involved in the key agreement.

Additionally, the javax.crypto.interfaces package provides interfaces for Diffie-Hellman keys, and the javax.crypto.spec provides the key and parameter specifications for the different algorithms such as DES, BlowFish, and Diffie-Hellman.

Understanding the JCE API Programming Model

Let's explore the JCE API programming model and the steps involved in using important JCE API classes and mechanisms. Although the details of using specific algorithms and operations vary, the common steps are as follows:

1. Get the cryptographic provider.
2. Obtain the specified Cipher using the getInstance() method.
3. Get the key generator; use SecretKeyFactory and KeyGenerator to generate the Key object. Random classes and Key specification classes can be used as additional input to the algorithm.
4. Initialize the Cipher with the init() method.
5. Encrypt or decrypt the message using update() methods.
6. Depending about how it was initialized, the process will be finished using the doFinal() method.

In the next section, we will take a look at some commonly applied JCE cryptographic operations such as encryption and decryption with symmetric keys, using block and stream ciphers, password-based encryption, AES, and computing MAC digests.

Encryption and Decryption

Encryption is a cryptographic technique for scrambling a message or files or programs by changing each character string, byte, or bit to another using a mathematical algorithm. A message that is not encrypted is referred to as plaintext or cleartext, and an encrypted message is called ciphertext. Decryption is the reverse process of encryption, which converts the ciphertext back into plaintext. This process generally requires a cryptographic key or code.

Let's walk through the steps involved in using JCE to perform basic encryption and decryption operations. First, we will take a look at the process of generating a Data Encryption Standard (DES) key, creating and initializing a cipher object, encrypting a file, and then decrypting it.

- **Generate a DES Key**: To create a DES key, instantiate a KeyGenerator using the getInstance("DES"), and then, to generate the key, use the generateKey() method:

```
KeyGenerator kg = KeyGenerator.getInstance("DES");
SecretKey sKey = kg.generateKey();
```

- **Create the Cipher**: Use the getInstance() factory method of the Cipher class and specify the name of the requested transformation (algorithm/mode/padding) as input. In the example shown here, we use the *DES* algorithm, ECB (Electronic code book mode), "PKCS5Padding" PKCS#5 padding:

```
Cipher myCipher =
  Cipher.getInstance("DES/ECB/PKCS5Padding");
```

- **Initialize the Cipher for encryption**: Use the init() method of the Cipher class and initialize the cipher object encryption with ENCRYPT_MODE and secret key. For this example, we use a String object as test data. Use the dofinal() to finish the encrypt operation:


```
   myCipher.init(Cipher.ENCRYPT_MODE, sKey);
  // Test data
 String testdata
          = "Understanding Encryption & Decryption";
   byte[] testBytes = testdata.getBytes();
  // Encrypt the testBytes
   byte[] myCipherText = myCipher.doFinal(testBytes);
```

- **Initialize the Cipher for decryption**: Use the init() method of the Cipher class and initialize the cipher object decryption with DECRYPT_MODE and secret key. For this example, use the dofinal() to finish the decrypt operation.

```
myCipher.init(Cipher.DECRYPT_MODE, sKey);

// Decrypt the byte array
  byte[] myCipherText
     = myCipher.doFinal(encryptedText);
```

Example 4–7 is a full code example (EncryptDecryptWithBlowFish.java) showing encryption and decryption using the Blowfish algorithm.

Example 4–7 EncryptDecryptWithBlowFish.java

```
package com.csp.ch4;
import java.security.*;
import javax.crypto.*;

public class EncryptDecryptWithBlowFish {

 public static void main (String[] args)
                             throws Exception {
```

```
 if (args.length != 1) {
    System.err.println ("Usage: java
          EncryptDecryptWithBlowFish <Enter text> ");
    System.exit(1);
  }
 String testData = args[0];
 System.out.println("Generating a Blowfish key...");

 // Create a key using "Blowfish"
   KeyGenerator myKeyGenerator
              = KeyGenerator.getInstance("Blowfish");
   keyGenerator.init(128);   // specifying keysize as 128
   Key myKey = myKeyGenerator.generateKey();
   System.out.println("Key generation Done.");

 // Create a cipher using the key
   Cipher myCipher
      = Cipher.getInstance("Blowfish/ECB/PKCS5Padding");
   myCipher.init(Cipher.ENCRYPT_MODE, myKey);
   byte[] testBytes = testData.getBytes();

 // Perform  encryption
   byte[] encryptedText = cipher.doFinal(testBytes);

 // Printing out the encrypted data
     System.out.println
        ("Encryption Done:" + new String(encryptedText));

 // Initialize the cipher for DECRYPTION mode
     cipher.init(Cipher.DECRYPT_MODE, myKey);

// Performing decryption
   byte[] decryptedText = cipher.doFinal(encryptedText);
   // Printing out the decrypted data
   System.out.println("Decryption Done:"
                        + new String(decryptedText));
   }
}
```

Using Block Ciphers

A block cipher is a symmetric-key encryption algorithm that encrypts and decrypts a fixed-length block of data (usually 64 bits long) into a block of ciphertext of the same length. To implement block ciphers it becomes important that the data required to be encrypted must be in the multiple of the block size. To fill in the reminder block and to derive the required block size, block ciphers makes use of padding.

Padding defines how to fill out the reminder of a block with random data. During decryption, the encrypted data will be retrieved to the original data and removing the padding. PKCS#5 specifies one of the popular padding schemes and it is defined as a standard by RSA. In the SunJCEProvider the PKCS#5 padding scheme is represented using PKCS5Padding.

In block ciphers to encrypt bigger blocks of data, it makes use of operation "Modes." The modes define how the blocks of plaintext are encrypted to ciphertext and decrypted from ciphertext to plaintext. The SunJCEprovider provides support for commonly used modes such as ECB (Electronic Code Book), OFB (Output feedback), CFB (Cipher Feedback), CBC (Cipher-block chaining), PCBC (Propagating Cipher Block Chaining). For more information about these modes and their characteristics, refer to RSA Security Web site on Cryptography standards [RSASecurity].

Example 4–8 is a Java code fragment showing how to represent an encryption and decryption using a block cipher.

Example 4–8 Encryption and Decryption using a Block cipher

```
//  Encryption using DES, ECB Mode and PKCS5Padding Scheme

try {

// 1. Create the cipher using DES algorithm
//    ECB Mode and PKCS5Padding scheme
      Cipher myCipher =
           Cipher.getInstance("DES/ECB/PKCS5Padding");

  // 2. Initialize the Cipher
      myCipher.init(Cipher.ENCRYPT_MODE, key);

 //  3.  Represent the Plaintext
  byte[] plaintext =
  "Eye for an Eye makes the Whole world blind".getBytes();

 // 4. Encrypt the Plaintext
      byte[] myciphertext = myCipher.doFinal(plaintext);

 // 5. Return the cipher text as String
      return getString( myciphertext );
}
```

```
catch( Exception e ) {
      e.printStackTrace();
    }

. . .
//  Decryption using DES, ECB Mode and PKCS5Padding Scheme

try {

. . .

  // 1. Create the cipher using DES algorithm
  //    ECB Mode and PKCS5Padding scheme
      Cipher myCipher =
         Cipher.getInstance("DES/ECB/PKCS5Padding");

  // 2. Get the ciphertext
      byte[] ciphertext = getBytes( myciphertext );

  // 3. Initialize the cipher for decryption
      myCipher.init(Cipher.DECRYPT_MODE, key);

  // 4. Decrypt the ciphertext
      byte[] plaintext = myCipher.doFinal(ciphertext);

  // 5. Return the plaintext as string
      return new String( plaintext );
    }
    catch( Exception ex ) {
      ex.printStackTrace();
    }
```


Using Stream Ciphers

Stream ciphers are composed of I/O streams and ciphers. They provide the convenience of reading and writing from underlying InputStream and OutputStream additionally processed by the ciphers. For example, if the cipher is initialized for encryption, the CipherOutputStream will attempt to encrypt data before writing out the encrypted data, and if the cipher is initialized for decryption, the CipherInputStream will attempt to read in data and decrypt them, before returning the decrypted data.

Example 4–9 is a code fragment showing reading a text file *myTextFile*, encrypting. the text using a stream cipher, and then writing it using CipherOutputStream to the file *CipherTextFile*.

Example 4–9 Using stream ciphers to encrypt a file

```
FileInputStream inputFile
                = new FileInputStream(myTextFile);
FileOutputStream outputFile
             = new FileOutputStream(cipherTextFile);
CipherOutputStream cipherOutputStream
    = new CipherOutputStream(outputFile, myCipher);

int i = 0;
    while (i=inputFile.read() != -1) {
            cipherOutputStream.write(i);
    }
 cipherOutputStream.close();
 outputFile.close();
 inputFile.close();
```


Sealed Object

JCE introduced the notion of creating sealed objects. A Sealed object is all about encrypting a serializable object using a cipher. Sealed objects provide confidentiality and helps preventing unauthorized viewing of contents of the object by restricting de-serialization.

From a programming standpoint, the sealed object creates a copy of given object by serializing the object to an embedded byte array, and then encrypt them using a cipher. To retrieve the original object, the object can be unsealed using the cipher that had been used for sealing the object. Example 4–10 shows how to create a sealed object.

Example 4–10 Creating a sealed object

```
//  Creating a Sealed Object
ObjectOutputStream oos
        = new ObjectOutputStream(mySocket.getOutputStream());
Cipher myCipher
         = Cipher.getInstance("DES/ECB/PKCS5Padding");
myCipher.init(Cipher.ENCRYPT_MODE, mykey);

SealedObject mySealedObject
         = new SealedObject(myObject, myCipher);

oos.writeObject(mySealedObject);

. . .
```

```
// To deserialize a Sealed object and retrieve its contents

ObjectInputStream ois
        = new ObjectInputStream(mySocket.getInputStream());
SealedObject mso = (SealedObject)ois.readObject();
Cipher mc
         = Cipher.getInstance("DES/ECB/PKCS5Padding");
mc.init(Cipher.DECRYPT_MODE, mykey);

Object myObject = mso.getObject(mc);
```


Password-Based Encryption (PBE)

Password-Based Encryption (PBE) is a technique that derives an encryption key from a password, which helps in combating dictionary attacks by hackers and other related vulnerabilities. To use PBE, we have to use a salt (a very large random number also referred to as seed) and an iteration count, which will be specified as parameters with PBEParameterSpec. The salt and iteration count used for encryption must be the same as the ones used for decryption.

Example 4–11 is a code fragment that reads a user password from a prompt, stores it in a char array, and then converts it into a SecretKey object using PBEKeySpec and SecretKeyFactory. The PBEKeySpec parameters are specified with the salt and iteration count using PBEParameterSpec. To create the PBE cipher for encryption, we use the *PBEWithMD5AndDES* algorithm and initialize it with the PBEKey and PBEParameterSpec.

Example 4–11 Password-based encryption using PBEWithMD5AndDES algorithm

```
    PBEKeySpec pbeKeySpec;
    PBEParameterSpec pbeParamSpec;
    SecretKeyFactory keyFac;

   //Encryption password is obtained
   //via prompt ex: args[0]
    char[] password = args[0].toCharArray();

    // Salt
    byte[] salt = {
        (byte)0xc7, (byte)0x73, (byte)0x21, (byte)0x8c,
        (byte)0x7e, (byte)0xc8, (byte)0xee, (byte)0x99
    };

    // Iteration count
```

```
int count = 20;

// Create PBE parameter set
pbeParamSpec = new PBEParameterSpec(salt, count);


// Collect user password as char array, and convert
// it into a SecretKey object, using a PBE key
// factory.

pbeKeySpec = new PBEKeySpec(password);
keyFac
  = SecretKeyFactory.getInstance("PBEWithMD5AndDES");
SecretKey pbeKey
  = keyFac.generateSecret(pbeKeySpec);

// Create PBE Cipher
Cipher pbeCipher
        = Cipher.getInstance("PBEWithMD5AndDES");

// Initialize PBE Cipher with key and parameters
pbeCipher.init(Cipher.ENCRYPT_MODE,
                         pbeKey, pbeParamSpec);

// Text to encrypt
String textForEncryption
                    = "This is a test message";

byte[] myText = textForEncryption.getBytes();

// Encrypt the text using PBE Cipher
byte[] ciphertext = pbeCipher.doFinal(myText);
```

Advanced Encryption Standard (AES)

AES is a new cryptographic algorithm that can be used to protect electronic data. More specifically, AES is a symmetric-key block cipher that can use keys of 128, 192, and 256 bits, and encrypts and decrypts data in blocks of 128 bits (16 bytes).

AES has been approved by NIST as a standard to replace the DES algorithms. The AES algorithm is based on the Rijndael algorithm (Developed by Vincent Rijmen and Joan Daemen). AES can also encrypt data much faster than Triple-DES, and it is getting wider acceptance for encrypting data used in business applications, telecommunications, and private and federal government information. As part of the Java platform (J2SE 1.4.2 and later), the JCE provider (SunJCE) implementation provides support for the AES algorithm. The AES algorithm can be used like any other cipher such as DES or Blowfish. The programming model and steps involved are also same as those for other ciphers.

Example 4–12 is a full code example showing encryption and decryption using the AES algorithm.

Example 4–12 Encryption and decryption using AES algorithm

```
package com.csp.ch4;
import java.security.*;
import javax.crypto.*;
public class EncryptDecryptWithAES {

 public static void main (String[] args)
                            throws Exception   {
 if (args.length != 1) {

 System.err.println("Usage: java
                EncryptDecryptWithAES <Enter text> ");
 System.exit(1);

 }
   String testData = args[0];
   System.out.println("Generating a AES based key...");

   // Create a key using "AES"
   KeyGenerator myKeyGenerator
              = KeyGenerator.getInstance("AES");
   keyGenerator.init(128);   // specifying keysize as 128
   SecretKey myKey = myKeyGenerator.generateKey();
   byte[] encodeKey = myKey.getEncoded();

   SecretKeySpec myKeySpec
                 = new SecretKeySpec(encodeKey, "AES");
   System.out.println("Key generation Done.");

  // Create a cipher using the key
   Cipher myCipher = Cipher.getInstance("AES");
   myCipher.init(Cipher.ENCRYPT_MODE, myKeySpec);
   byte[] testBytes = testData.getBytes();

  // Perform  encryption
     byte[] encryptedText = cipher.doFinal(testBytes);
```

```
  // Printing out the encrypted data
     System.out.println("Encryption Done:"
                          + new String(encryptedText));

 // Initialize the cipher for DECRYPTION mode
     cipher.init(Cipher.DECRYPT_MODE, myKeySpec);

 // Performing decryption
   byte[] decryptedText = cipher.doFinal(encryptedText);

   // Printing out the decrypted data
   System.out.println("Decryption Done:"
                         + new String(decryptedText));
   }
}
```


Computing Message Authentication Code (MAC) objects

Message Authentication Code (MAC) is generally used for checking the integrity and validity of the information based on a secret key. MAC uses a secret key to generate the hash code for a sequence of specific bytes arrays.

Example 4–13 is a code fragment that shows computing a MAC object using the HMAC-MD5 algorithm.

Example 4–13 Computing a MAC object using HMAC-MD5 algorithm

```
import java.security.*;
import javax.crypto.*;
import javax.crypto.spec.*;
import java.util.*;

// This is for BASE64 encoding and decoding
import sun.misc.*;
   //...

    try {
        // Generate a key using HMAC-MD5
        KeyGenerator keyGen
                   = KeyGenerator.getInstance("HmacMD5");
        SecretKey mySecretkey = keyGen.generateKey();

        // Create a MAC object and initialize
```

```
        Mac mac = Mac.getInstance(key.getAlgorithm());
        mac.init(mySecretkey);

        String testString
             = "This is a test message for MAC digest";

      // Encode the string into bytes and digest it
        byte[] testBytes = testString.getBytes();
        byte[] macDigest = mac.doFinal(testBytes);

     // convert the digest into a string
        String digestB64
         = new       sun.misc.BASE64Encoder().encode(macDigest);

      System.out.println("Printing MAC Digest as String:"
                  + digestB64);
    } catch (InvalidKeyException e) {
    } catch (NoSuchAlgorithmException e) {
    }
```


Using Key Agreement Protocols

A key agreement protocol is a process that allows carrying out an encrypted communication between two or more parties by securely exchanging a secret key over a network. The Diffie-Hellman (DH) key agreement protocol allows two users to exchange a secret key over an insecure medium without any prior secrets. JCE provides support for the Diffie-Hellman key agreement protocol.

To create a Diffie-Hellman KeyAgreement object, instantiate a KeyAgreement object using the getInstance("DH") and then initialize it using the init() method.

```
KeyAgreement keyAgreement
                  = KeyAgreement.getInstance("DH");
```

If two or more parties are involved in a key agreement, all corresponding parties must create and initialize a KeyAgreement object. After creating and initializing the KeyAgreement object, the corresponding parties execute the different phases specific to the KeyAgreement protocol. The DHParameterSpec constructs a parameter set for Diffie-Hellman, using a prime modulus p, a base generator g, and the size in bits l, of the random exponent (private value).

Example 4–14 is a code fragment showing the steps involved in using the Diffie-Hellman KeyAgreement protocol.

Example 4–14 Using Diffie-Hellman Keyagreement protocol

```
try {
       //1. Use the values to generate a key pair
       KeyPairGenerator keyGen
                = KeyPairGenerator.getInstance("DH");
       DHParameterSpec dhSpec
                = new DHParameterSpec(p, g, l);
       keyGen.initialize(dhSpec);
       KeyPair keypair = keyGen.generateKeyPair();

       //2. Get the generated public and private keys
       PrivateKey privateKey = keypair.getPrivate();
       PublicKey publicKey = keypair.getPublic();

       //3. Send the public key bytes to the
       // other party...
       byte[] publicKeyBytes = publicKey.getEncoded();

       //4. Retrieve the public key bytes
       // of the other party
       publicKeyBytes = ...;

       //5. Convert the public key bytes
       // into a X.509 PublicKey object
       X509EncodedKeySpec x509KeySpec
          = new X509EncodedKeySpec(publicKeyBytes);
       KeyFactory keyFact
          = KeyFactory.getInstance("DH");
       publicKey = keyFact.generatePublic(x509KeySpec);

       //6. Prepare to generate the secret key
        // with the private key and
        // public key of the other party
       KeyAgreement ka = KeyAgreement.getInstance("DH");
       ka.init(privateKey);

       ka.doPhase(publicKey, true);

       //7. Specify the type of key to generate;
       String algorithm = "DES";

       //8. Generate the secret key
       SecretKey secretKey
                  =  ka.generateSecret(algorithm);
```

```
        //9. Use the secret key to encrypt/decrypt data;
        /...
    } catch (java.security.InvalidKeyException e) {
} catch(java.security.spec.InvalidKeySpecException e) {
    } catch (java.security.InvalidAlgorithmParameterException e) {
    } catch (java.security.NoSuchAlgorithmException e) {
    }
```

JCE Hardware Acceleration and Smart Card Support

With the release of J2SE 5.0, JCE provides support for the PKCS#11 standard that allows the following:

- Using hardware cryptographic accelerators for enhancing performance of cryptographic operations.
- Using smart cards as key stores for key and trust management.

To use these services, it is necessary to install a PKCS#11 implementation provided by the hardware accelerator and smart card vendors. As part of the J2SE 5.0 bundle, Sun facilitates a SunPKCS#11 provider.

Installing PKCS#11

To install the PKCS#11 provider statically, edit the Java security properties file located at <JAVA_HOME>/jre/lib/security/java.security. For example, to install the Sun PKCS#11 provider with the configuration file /opt/hwcryptocfg/pkcs11.cfg, add the following in the Java security properties file:

```
security.provider.7=sun.security.pkcs11.SunPKCS11 \
                          /opt/hwcryptocfg/pkcs11.cfg
```

To install the provider dynamically (see Example 4–15), create an instance of the provider with the appropriate configuration filename and then install it.

Example 4–15 Programmatically installing a PKCS#11 provider

```
String configName ="/opt/hwcryptocfg/pkcs11.cfg";
Provider provider = new
         sun.security.pkcs11.SunPKCS11(configName);
Security.addProvider(provider);
```

Using Smart Cards as Java Key Stores

To use a smart card as a keystore or trust store, set the javax.net.ssl.keyStoreType and javax.net.ssl.trustStoreType system properties to "pkcs11", and set the javax.net.ssl.keyStore and javax.net.ssl.trustStore system properties to NONE. To specify the use of a vendor smart-card provider, use the javax.net.ssl.keyStoreProvider and javax.net.ssl.trustStoreProvider system properties to identify them. (For example: "SunPKCS11-smart card"). By setting these properties, you can configure an application to use a smart-card keystore with no changes to the application that previously accessed a file-based keystore.

Configuring a Smart card as a Java Keystore

The following example shows how to configure OpenSC supported smart card as a Java keystore and list the certificates using the keytool utility. The OpenSC framework can be downloaded from http://www.opensc.org.

1. Add the OpenSC PKCS#11 module as the keystore provider in java.security file located at $JAVA_HOME/jre/lib/security/java.security.

```
security.provider.8=sun.security.pkcs11.SunPKCS11 \
                    /opt/openSC/openscpkcs11-solaris.cfg
```

2. Create the OpenSC PKCS#11 configuration file. For example, the openscpkcs11-solaris.cfg looks like as follows:

```
name = OpenSC-PKCS11
description = SunPKCS11 w/ OpenSC Smart card Framework
library = /usr/lib/pkcs11/opensc-pkcs11.so
```

With the above settings, it is possible to use the smart card as a keystore and retrieve information about the certificates. For example (see Example 4–16). Using keytool to list the certificate will look like as follows.

Example 4–16 Using keytool to list certificate entries from a smart card

```
$ keytool -keystore NONE -storetype PKCS11 \
        -providerName SunPKCS11-OpenSC -list -v
Enter keystore password: <PIN>

Keystore type: PKCS11
Keystore provider: SunPKCS11-OpenSC

Your keystore contains 4 entries
```

```
Alias name: Signature
Entry type: keyEntry
Certificate chain length: 1
Certificate[1]:
Owner: SERIALNUMBER=79797900036, GIVENNAME=Nagappan Expir?e1779,
SURNAME=R, CN=Nagappan (Signature), C=US
Issuer: CN=Nagappan OpenSSL CA, C=BE
Serial number: 1000000000102fdf39941
Valid from: Fri Apr 01 15:29:22 EST 2005 until: Wed Jun 01 15:29:22 EST 2005
Certificate fingerprints:
         MD5:  12:20:AC:2F:F2:F5:5E:91:0A:53:7A:4B:8A:F7:39:4F
         SHA1:
77:76:48:DA:EC:5E:9C:26:A2:63:A9:EC:A0:14:42:BF:90:53:0F:BC


Alias name: Root
Entry type: trustedCertEntry

Owner: CN=Nagappan OpenSSL Root CA, C=US
Issuer: CN=Nagappan OpenSSL Root CA, C=US
Serial number: 111111111111111111111111111112
Valid from: Wed Aug 13 11:00:00 EST 2003 until: Mon Jan 27 00:00:00 EST 2014
Certificate fingerprints:
         MD5:  5A:0F:FD:DB:4F:FC:37:D4:CD:95:17:D5:04:01:6E:73
         SHA1:
6A:5F:FD:25:7E:85:DC:60:81:82:8D:D1:69:AA:30:4E:7E:37:DD:3B

Alias name: Authentication
Entry type: keyEntry
Certificate chain length: 1
Certificate[1]:
Owner: SERIALNUMBER=79797900036, GIVENNAME=Nagappan Expir?e1779,
SURNAME=R, CN=NAGAPPAN, C=US
Issuer: CN=Nagappan OpenSSL CA, C=US
Serial number: 1000000000102fd10d2d9
Valid from: Fri Apr 01 11:21:40 EST 2005 until: Wed Jun 01 11:21:40 EST 2005
Certificate fingerprints:
         MD5:  29:7E:8A:5C:91:34:9B:05:52:21:4E:49:5B:45:F8:C4
         SHA1:
15:B7:EA:27:E1:0E:9D:94:4E:7B:3B:79:00:48:A2:31:7E:9D:72:1A
```

Using Keytool and Jarsigner with Smart Card Tokens

If the Sun PKCS#11 provider (for using a smart card) has been configured in the java.security security properties file, then keytool and jarsigner can be used to operate on the PKCS#11 token by specifying the following options.

- -keystore NONE
- -storetype PKCS11

Here is an example of a command to list the contents of the configured PKCS#11 on a smart-card token.


```
keytool -keystore NONE -storetype PKCS11 -list
```

The smart-card token PIN can be specified using the -storepass option. If it is not specified, then the keytool and jarsigner tool will prompt the user for the PIN. If the token has a protected authentication path (such as a dedicated PIN-pad or a biometric reader), then the -protected option must be specified, and no password options can be specified. For more information about installing PKCS#11 providers, refer to the JCE PKCS#11 documentation available at http://java.sun.com/j2se/1.5.0/docs/guide/security/p11guide.html.

Strong versus Unlimited Strength Cryptography

By default, JCA allows the use of strong cryptography (128-bit key size). To use 192- and 256-bit key sizes, you are required to use unlimited strength cryptography policy files, which are available as part of a separate download of JCE. U.S. export laws restrict the export and use of JCE with unlimited strength cryptography. Those living in eligible countries may download the unlimited strength version and replace the strong cryptography jar files with the unlimited strength files. Using JCE with unlimited strength cryptography is also subject to the import control restrictions of certain countries. For more information on U.S. export laws related to cryptography, refer to The Bureau of Industry and Security's Web site (U.S. Department of Commerce) at http://www.bxa.doc.gov and the Java Cryptography Extension (JCE) Web site at http://java.sun.com/products/jce/.

To summarize, the JCE implementation and API framework feature an enhancement to JCA that provides a full range of cryptographic services, including support for encryption and decryption and key agreement protocols. It also maintains interoperability with other cryptographic provider implementations. In the next section, we will explore the Java CertPath API, which defines an API framework for creating, building, and validating digital certification paths.

Java Certification Path API (CertPath)

CertPath provides a full-fledged API framework for application developers who wish to integrate the functionality of checking, verifying, and validating digital certificates into their applications.

Digital certificates play the role of establishing trust and credentials when conducting business or other transactions. Issued by a Certification Authority (CA), a digital certificate defines a binding data structure containing the holder name, a serial number, expiration dates, a public key, and the digital signature of the CA so that a recipient can verify the authenticity of the certificate. CAs usually obtain their certificates from their own higher-level authority. Typically in a certificate binding, a chain of certificates (referred to as a certification chain) starts from the certificate holder, is followed by zero or more certificates of intermediate CAs, and ends with a root-certificate of some top-level CA. So the process of reading, verifying, and validating certificate chains becomes important in PKI certificate-enabled applications and systems. In J2SE, Java CertPath APIs provides API-based mechanisms for parsing and managing certificates, certificate revocation lists (CRLs), and certification paths (also referred to as certificate chains). The API implementations can be plugged into any J2SE environment, because the same JCA provider interfaces are used. The API includes algorithm-specific classes for building and validating X.509 certification paths according to IETF-defined PKIX standards.

With the release of J2SE 5.0, CertPath provides client-side support for the Online Certificate Status Protocol (OCSP) as per RFC2560 that allows determining the current status of a certificate without requiring CRLs. The J2SE 5.0 CertPath implementation has also passed the compliance tests of the Public Key Interoperability Test Suite (PKITS) defined by NIST in conjunction with DigitalNet and NSA.

Let's take a closer look at the Java CertPath API and its core classes, interfaces, and programming model.

Java CertPath–Classes and Interfaces

In J2SE, the Java CertPath API is an extension of the JCA, and it exists as part of the java.security.cert.* package. The core classes fit into four basic categories: Basic Certification path classes, Certification path Validation classes, Certification path Building classes, and Certificate/CRL Storage classes.

Let's take a look at some of the most important classes from the Java CertPath API.

- **CertPath** (java.security.cert.CertPath): Defines an abstract class for certification paths that represents a certificate chain and defines all related functionality of certification path objects.
- **CertificateFactory** (java.security.cert.CertificateFactory): Defines an engine class that defines the functionality to generate certificate and CRL objects from their encodings.
- **CertPathBuilder** (java.security.cert.CertPathBuilder): Defines an engine class that enables building certificate chains (CertPath objects) using a provider implementation.
- **CertPathValidator** (java.security.cert.CertPathValidator): Defines an engine class that enables validation of certificate chains.
- **CertStore** (java.security.cert.CertStore): Defines an object used to retrieve Certificates and CRLs from a repository.
- **TrustAnchor** (java.security.cert.TrustAnchor): Represents the end point of most-trusted CA (root certificates of the CA), which is used as a trust anchor for validating X.509 certification paths during verification.
- **PKIXParameters** (java.security.cert.PKIXParameters): Describes the set of input parameters defined by the PKIX certification path validation algorithm.

Java CertPath API Programming Model

Let's explore the CertPath API programming model and the steps involved in using those important classes and mechanisms. Although the details of using specific algorithms and operations vary, the common steps are discussed in the code fragments shown in the following sections.

Create a Certificate Chain Using CertPath

The following is an example code fragment (see Example 4–17) that demonstrates the steps involved in creating a CertPath object for a specified list of certificates:

Example 4–17 Creating a certificate chain for a list of certificates

```
CertPath
   createCertPath(java.security.cert.Certificate[] certs) {

  try {
```

```
    //1. Instantiate CertificateFactory for X.509
     CertificateFactory certFact
               = CertificateFactory.getInstance("X.509");

    // 2. Generate a Certificate chain
    // for the specified list of certificates
     CertPath path
       = certFact.generateCertPath(Arrays.asList(certs));

    return path;

  } catch(java.security.cert.CertificateEncodingException e)
      {
      } catch (CertificateException e) {
      }
      return null;
  }
```


Validate a Certificate Chain Using CertPath

Example 4–18 is an example code fragment that demonstrates the steps involved in validating a CertPath object using a trusted CA in the trusted certificate keystore (cacerts). Before using this code snippet, make sure a CertPath object is created and available for validation.

Example 4–18 Validating a certificate chain

```
try {

    // 1. Load the J2SE cacerts truststore file
  String filename
   = System.getProperty("java.home") +
     "/lib/security/cacerts".replace('/',
                              File.separatorChar);
    FileInputStream is = new FileInputStream(filename);

    // 2. Load the default keystore
    KeyStore keystore
       = KeyStore.getInstance(KeyStore.getDefaultType());
    String password = "changeit";
    keystore.load(is, password.toCharArray());

    // 3. Create the parameters for the validator
    PKIXParameters params = new PKIXParameters(keystore);
```

```
        // 4. Disable CRL checking
        // as we are not supplying any CRLs
        params.setRevocationEnabled(false);

        // 5. Create the validator and validate
        // the specified certpath
        CertPathValidator certPathValidator
          = CertPathValidator.getInstance
                    (CertPathValidator.getDefaultType());
        CertPathValidatorResult result
              = certPathValidator.validate(certPath, params);

        // 6. Get the CA used to validate this path
        PKIXCertPathValidatorResult pkixResult
                    = (PKIXCertPathValidatorResult)result;
        TrustAnchor ta = pkixResult.getTrustAnchor();
        X509Certificate cert = ta.getTrustedCert();

    } catch (CertificateException ce) {
    } catch (KeyStoreException ke) {
    } catch (NoSuchAlgorithmException ne) {
    } catch (InvalidAlgorithmParameterException ie) {
    } catch (CertPathValidatorException cpe) {
        // Validation failed
    }
```


In the next section, we will explore Java Secure Socket Extensions (JSSE), which defines an API framework to secure communications over the network using standardized protocols.

Java Secure Socket Extension (JSSE)

Protecting the integrity and confidentiality of data exchanged in network communications is one of the key security challenges of network security. During communication, the potential vulnerability is that the data exchanged can be accessed or modified by someone with a malicious intent or who is not an intended client recipient. Secure Socket Layer (SSL) and Transport Layer Security (TLS) are application-independent protocols developed by IETF that provide critical security features for end-to-end application communication by protecting the privacy and integrity of exchanged data. They establish authenticity, trust, and reliability between the communicating partners. SSL/TLS operates on top of the TCP/IP stack, which secures communication through features like data encryption, server authentication, message integrity, and optional client authentication. For data encryption, SSL uses both public-key and secret-key cryptography. It uses secret-key cryptography to bulk-encrypt the data exchanged between two applications.

JSSE enables end-to-end communication security for client/server-based network communications by providing a standardized API framework and mechanisms for client-server communications. JSSE provides support for SSL and TLS protocols and includes functionalities related to data encryption, message integrity, and peer authentication.

Figure 4–4 illustrates JSSE-based secure communication using the SSL/TLS protocols.

With JSSE, it is possible to develop client and server applications that use secure transport protocols, which include:

- Secure HTTP (HTTP over SSL)
- Secure Shell (Telnet over SSL)
- Secure SMTP (SMTP over SSL)
- IPSEC (Secure IP)
- Secure RMI or RMI/IIOP (RMI over SSL)

Like other security packages, JSSE also features a provider architecture and service-provider interface that enables different JSSE-compliant providers to be plugged into the J2SE environment.

JSSE Provider (*SunJSSE*)

The J2SE (from J2SE 1.4 and later versions) includes a full-featured JSSE provider named *SunJSSE* which is pre-installed and pre-configured with JCA. Starting with the release of J2SE 5.0 and later, the *SunJSSE* provider uses the *SunJCE* implementation for all its cryptographic needs. You can use other vendor JCA/JCE providers by statically registering them before the *SunJCE* provider using the java.security properties file located at <java-home>/jre/lib/security/java.security. JSSE providers

Figure 4–4 Secure communication using SSL/TLS protocols

can also be registered programmatically using the addProvider or insertProviderAt method in the java.security.Security class. With the release of Java SE 6, JSSE allows to plug-in third-party JSSE providers that implements proprietary Cipher suites.

The SunJSSE provider facilitates the Java platform with the following services:

- Implementation of SSL 3.0 and TLS 1.0 protocols.
- Implementation of SSL/TLS state machine (SSLEngine), which allows processing of data in the buffer to produce SSL/TLS encoded data (J2SE 5.0 and later).
- Implementation of key factory and key generators to support RSA algorithms.
- Implementation of the most common SSL and TLS Cipher suites to support authentication, key agreement, encryption, and integrity protection.
- X.509-based key manager for managing keys of supporting JCA KeyStore.
- X.509-based trust manager, implementing support for verifying and validating certificate chains.
- Support for Kerberos Cipher suites if the underlying OS provides it (J2SE 5.0 and later).
- Support for hardware acceleration and smart-card tokens using JCE PKCS#11 provider (J2SE 5.0 and later).
- With the release of Java SE 6, the SunJSSE provider supports FIPS-140 compliant mode and appropriate FIPS-140 certified PKCS#11 tokens.

Let's take a closer look at the JSSE API mechanisms, core classes, interfaces, and the programming model.

JSSE Classes and Interfaces

The JSSE API framework exists as part of the following packages:

- **javax.net.***: This package contains the set of core classes and interfaces for creating basic client and server sockets.
- **javax.net.ssl.***: This package contains the set of core classes and interfaces for creating secure client and server SSL sockets, and for creating secure HTTP URL connections.
- **javax.security.cert.***: This package is the same as the Java certification path API, which supports JSSE with basic certificate management functions.

Let's take a look at some of the most important classes from the JSSE API framework:

- **SocketFactory (javax.net.SocketFactory)**: A factory class for creating Socket objects. The ServerSocketFactory is analogous to the SocketFactory class, but it is specific to creating server sockets.
- **SSLSocket (javax.net.ssl.SSLSocket)**: Represents a Socket that supports SSL and TLS protocols.
- **SSLServerSocket**: Extends the ServerSocket and provides secure server sockets using protocols such as the Secure Sockets Layer (SSL) or Transport Layer Security (TLS) protocols.
- **SSLEngine**: An abstract class that allows implementing transport-independent secure communications using SSL/TLS protocols. This class is available from J2SE 5.0 and later.
- **SSLSocketFactory (javax.net.ssl.SSLSocketFactory)**: A factory class for creating SSLSocket objects. To create an SSLSocket, the JSSE provider must be configured by setting appropriate values to the ssl.SocketFactory.provider property in java.security properties. The SSLServerSocketFactory is analogous to the SSLSocketFactory class, but it is specific to creating SSL-based server sockets.
- **SSLSession (javax.net.ssl.SSLSession)**: Represents the session attributes that describe the session negotiated between two communicating peers. The session context contains attributes such as the shared master secret key, network address of the remote peer, time, usage, and so forth.
- **SSLSessionContext (javax.net.ssl.SSLSessionContext)**: Represents a set of SSLSession objects associated with a communicating peer, which can be a server or a client.
- **SSLSessionBindingEvent (javax.net.ssl.SSLSessionBindingEvent)**: Represents an event object that encapsulates SSL session binding and unbinding objects.
- **SSLSessionBindingListener (javax.net.ssl.SSLSessionBindingListener)**: Represents a listener interface, implemented by objects, which listens to SSLSession binding or unbinding events.
- **TrustManager (javax.net.ssl.TrustManager)**: Represents an interface to determine whether the presented authentication credentials from the remote identity should be trusted or not trusted.
- **TrustManagerFactory (javax.net.ssl.TrustManagerFactory)**: An engine class for a JSSE provider that acts as a factory for one or more TrustManager objects. For SunJSSE provider, it returns a basic X.509 trust manager.
- **HttpsURLConnection (javax.net.ssl.HttpsURLConnection)**: Represents an HttpURLConnection that supports the SSL and TLS protocols.

- **HostnameVerifier** (javax.net.ssl.HostnameVerifier): Represents an interface class for hostname verification used for verifying the authenticity of the requests from the originating host. In an SSL handshake, if the URL's hostname and the server's identification hostname mismatch, the verification mechanism uses this interface to verify the authenticity of the connection and its originating host.

Understanding the JSSE API Programming Model

For more information about the JSSE API programming model and the steps involved, we will take a look at some common JSSE usage scenarios, such as secure socket connection using SSL, client and server mutual authentication, proxy tunneling, HTTP over SSL communication, and peer host name verification.

Secure Socket Connection Using SSL

Let's take a look at a client and server communication scenario using the SSL and J2SE default keystore and truststore for storing certificates. The SSL server uses the keystore that contains its private key and corresponding public key. The SSL client uses the server's certificate stored in the truststore to verify the authenticity of a communicating peer. For more information about setting up KeyStore and TrustStore and generating public and private keys using the KeyTool utility, refer to the section entitled "KeyTool" in Chapter 3.

JSSE Client-side Communication

The programming steps involved in creating an SSL socket for a client-side application to communicate with a server using SSL is as follows:

1. Register the JSSE provider.
2. Create an instance of the SSLSocketFactory.
3. Create an SSLSocket specifying the hostname and port.
4. Create streams to securely send and receive data to and from the server.
5. Close the streams.
6. Close the socket.

When an SSL client socket connects to an SSL server, it receives a certificate of authentication from the server. The client socket then validates the certificate against a set of certificates in its truststore. The default truststore is <java-home>/jre/

lib/security/cacerts, and a user-specific truststore can also be specified using the javax.net.ssl.trustStore system property. To validate the server's certificate on the client side, the server's certificate must be imported to the truststore before trying out the connection.

The following example MySSLClient.java (see Example 4–19) shows a client establishing an SSL connection with a server to send and receive messages.

Example 4–19 MySSLClient.java

```
import java.io.*;
import javax.net.ssl.*;
import com.sun.net.ssl.*;

public class MySSLClient
{
  public static void main(String [] args)
                              throws Exception {

   String servername = "localhost";
   int sslport = "443";

   // Register to use Sun JSSE as SSL provider
   // Specify the Client truststore and its password
   static {
    Security.addProvider(new
         com.sun.net.ssl.internal.ssl.Provider());
   System.setProperty ("javax.net.ssl.trustStore",
                                       "cacerts");
  System.setProperty ("javax.net.ssl.trustStorePassword",
                              "changeit");
 }

try {
     // Create an instance of a SocketFactory
    SSLSocketFactory sslsocketfactory =
      (SSLSocketFactory) SSLSocketFactory.getDefault();

  // Create a Socket
  SSLSocket sslsocket
   = (SSLSocket)sslsocketfactory.createSocket(servername,
                                           sslport);
  System.out.println("SSL Connection Established
                                    with server");
```

```
  // Create the streams to send and receive data
  // using Socket
     OutputStream out = sslSocket.getOutputStream();
     InputStream in = sslSocket.getInputStream();

// Send messages to the server using the OutputStream
// Receive messages from the server using the InputStream

       //...

    }
     catch (Exception e) {
      e.printStackTrace();
     }
  }
}
```


JSSE Server-side Communication

The programming steps involved in creating an application that acts as a server and communicates with a client using secure sockets are as follows:

1. Register the JSSE provider.
2. Create an instance of the SSLServerSocket Factory.
3. Create an SSL Server Socket specifying the port.
4. Listen for client SSL connections.
5. Create streams to securely send and receive data to and from the client.
6. Close the streams.
7. Close the socket.

Creating an SSL server socket requires that the server has certificates that it will send to clients for authentication. The certificates must be contained in a keystore explicitly specified using the javax.net.ssl.keyStore system property.

The following code fragment example (see Example 4–20) describes how to create an SSL server socket and listen to client connections.

Example 4–20 MySSLServer.java

```
import java.io.*;
import javax.net.ssl.*;
import com.sun.net.ssl.*;
```

```
public class MySSLServer {

public static void main(String [] args)
                                  throws Exception {

 int sslport = "443";

   // Register to use Sun JSSE as SSL provider
   // Specify the server's keystore and its password
   static {
     Security.addProvider(new
           com.sun.net.ssl.internal.ssl.Provider());
     System.setProperty("javax.net.ssl.keyStore",
                                        "keystore");
     System.setProperty("javax.net.ssl.keyStorePassword",
                                           "changeit");
   }

 try {

  // Create an instance of an SSL Server SocketFactory
   SSLServerSocketFactory sslServerSocketfactory
         = (SSLServerSocketFactory)
                SSLServerSocketFactory.getDefault();

  // Create an SSL Server Socket
   SSLServerSocket sslServerSocket
    = (SSLServerSocket)
      sslServerSocketfactory.createServerSocket(sslport);

  while (true) {
     // Accept client connection
       SSLSocket sslsocket =
            (SSLSocket)sslServerSocket.accept();

      InputStream inputstream
                        =  sslsocket.getInputStream();
      InputStreamReader inputstreamreader
                   = new InputStreamReader(inputstream);
      BufferedReader bufferedreader
               = new BufferedReader(inputstreamreader);

      String test;
```

```
    while((test = bufferedreader.readLine()) != null){
       System.out.println(test);
      }
    }
    }
    catch (Exception e) {
         e.printStackTrace();
    }
   }
}
```


Mutual Authentication

The mutual authentication in a secure communication adds the value of a client being able to authenticate a server. This provides a means whereby a client can verify a server's authenticity and trust the data exchanged from the server.

In a mutual authentication process, both client and server exchange their certificates and thereby create a trusted communication channel between them. When an SSL client socket connects to an SSL server, it receives a certificate of authentication from the server. The client socket validates the certificate against a set of certificates in its truststore. Then the client sends its certificate of authentication to the server, which the server validates against a set of certificates in its truststore. Upon successful validation, a secure communication is established. To validate the server's certificate on the client side and the client's certificate on the server side, the server's certificate must be imported beforehand to the client's truststore and the client's certificate must be imported to the server's truststore.

In JSSE, enabling client-based mutual authentication to authenticate the server can be done by setting SSLServerSocket.setNeedClientAuth(true). To enforce client authentication, requesting the client to furnish the peer client certificate is done by setting SSLServerSocket.setWantClientAuth(true).

The following code fragment (see Example 4–21) shows how to force SSL server socket connections that request client certificate authentication (mutual authentication).

Example 4–21 Establishing mutual authentication using client certificates

```
// 1. Create an SSL Server Socket
 SSLServerSocket sslServerSocket = (SSLServerSocket)
     sslServerSocketfactory.createServerSocket(sslport);

// 2. To force requesting client's certificate from server
     sslServerSocket.setWantClientAuth(true);
```

Additionally, we need to specify KeyStore and TrustStore properties as command-line options or system properties (see Example 4–22) in both client and server environments. For example (in the client environment):

Example 4–22 Setting up the Keystore and Truststore properties

```
java -Djavax.net.ssl.trustStore=client-cacerts \
-Djavax.net.ssl.trustStorePassword=changeit \
-Djavax.net.ssl.trustStoreType=JCEKS \
-Djavax.net.ssl.keyStore=client-keys \
-Djavax.net.ssl.keyStorePassword=changeit \
-Djavax.net.ssl.keyStoreType=JCEKS MySSLClient
```


HTTP Over SSL (HTTPS) Using JSSE

HTTP over SSL allows establishing secure HTTP communications using SSL/TLS sockets. With JSSE, the procedure for creating HTTPS connections is similar to that for HTTP connections, except that you must register the JSSE provider and its associated HTTPS protocol handler and configure SSL parameters before trying out the connection.

The following code fragment (see Example 4–23) walks through the steps involved in creating a client that's required to open an HTTPS connection with an SSL-enabled HTTP server capable of handling https:// URLs.

Example 4–23 Creating an HTTP/SSL connection from a client

```
    HttpsURLConnection urlConnection = null;

  // 1.Dynamically register the JSSE provider.
    java.security.Security.addProvider(new
             com.sun.net.ssl.internal.ssl.Provider());

  // 2.Use Sun's JSSE implementation of the HTTPS handler
     System.setProperty("java.protocol.handler.pkgs",
              "com.sun.net.ssl.internal.www.protocol");

 // 3.Get the handle to HTTPS URL and its connection
  url = new URL("https://www.coresecuritypatterns.com");
  urlConnection
         = (HttpsURLConnection)url.openConnection();
```

Setting Timeouts in a URLConnection

With the release of J2SE 5.0, the JSSE API now provides a way of setting timeouts on connect and read operations for protocol handlers. This will benefit any

HTTP client application that must behave robustly in the event of server failure. The new methods for setting and getting timeouts are included with URLConnection as setConnectTimeout(int timeout), int getConnectTimeout(), setReadTimeout(int timeout), and int getReadTimeout().

Proxy Tunneling

Proxy tunneling provides a new level of communication security when two parties decide on communicating across the Internet. When the communication layer and data exchanged is not encrypted, it becomes easy to attack and identify the communication endpoints, sender/receiver information, and the conversation from the packets. Proxy tunneling provides a mechanism that allows access to a resource behind a firewall via a proxy server. The proxy server hides the addresses of the communicating hosts on its subnet from the outside attackers and protects the communication from those attacks.

JSSE provides proxy tunneling support for accessing applications behind a firewall. This allows access using HTTP only via a proxy server. To enable proxy tunneling, the JSSE requires the application to specify the https.ProxyHost and https.ProxyPort as system properties. To exclude selected hosts to connect without using a proxy, add http.nonProxyHosts as a system property.

Let's take a look at the following code example (HTTPSClientUsingProxyTunnel.java) that walks through the steps involved in tunneling through a proxy server using HttpsURLConnection (HTTP over SSL connection) with an SSL-enabled HTTP server:

Example 4–24 HTTPSClientUsingProxyTunnel.java

```
public class HTTPSClientUsingProxyTunnel {

     String proxyHost = "myproxy.com";
     String proxyPort = "8080";

  public static void main(String[] args)
                              throws Exception {

   // Register the JSSE provider and HTTPS handlers
   // Specify client truststore properties
   static {
     Security.addProvider(new
          com.sun.net.ssl.internal.ssl.Provider());

     System.setProperty("javax.net.ssl.trustStore",
                                          "cacerts");
```

```
    System.setProperty
        ("javax.net.ssl.trustStorePassword",
                                "changeit");
    System.setProperty("java.protocol.handler.pkgs",
            "com.sun.net.ssl.internal.www.protocol");
   }

  URL httpsURL = new URL("https://www.verisign.com");

  // Open a HTTPS Connection

  URLConnection urlConnection
                        = httpsURL.openConnection();
  if(urlConnection instanceof
     com.sun.net.ssl.HttpsURLConnection) {
((com.sun.net.ssl.HttpsURLConnection)urlConnection).
      SetSSLSocketFactory(new
         SSLTunnelSocketFactory(proxyHost,proxyPort));
     }

  BufferedReader in = new BufferedReader(new
     InputStreamReader(urlConnection.getInputStream()));

  String input;
     while ((input = in.readLine()) != null)
     System.out.println(input);
     in.close();
    }
 }
```


Host Name Verification Using JSSE

Host name verification is a mechanism that helps prevent man-in-the-middle attacks by validating that the host to which an SSL connection is made is the intended or authorized party or a trusted host. Host name verifier is quite useful when a client or a server instance is acting as an SSL client for another server. During an SSL handshake, if the URL's host name and the identified host name mismatch, the verification mechanism can call back to determine if this connection should be allowed.

In a JSSE-based SSL communication, host name verification can be enabled by setting HttpsURLConnection.setHostnameVerifier(HostnameVerifier hnv). The following code snippet (see Example 4–25) shows how to set a HostnameVerifier in a JSSE-based SSL connection to verify a peer host.

Example 4–25 Enabling Host name verification in SSL communication

```
URL url = new URL("https://myserver.sunnyday.com");
HttpsURLConnection mycon
         = (HttpsURLConnection) url.openConnection();

// Set the host name verifier
  mycon.setHostnameVerifier(new HostnameVerifier() {

// Verify the SSL Peer
 public boolean verify( String urlHost,
                                SSLSession ssls ){
 if( !urlHost.equals( ssls.getPeerHost() ) ){
    System.out.println( "Alert: SSL host "
       + ssls.getPeerHost() + "does not match URL host"
                                          + urlHost);
   }
  return true;
 } } );

mycon.setDoInput(true);
mycon.setDoOutput(true);
mycon.setUseCaches(false);
mycon.setDefaultUseCaches(false);
return mycon;
```


SSLEngine and Non-Blocking I/O

In the release of J2SE 5.0, JSSE introduced a new abstraction class that allows applications to use the SSL/TLS protocols in a transport-independent way, thus freeing applications to choose transport, I/O, and threading models that best meet their needs. This allows applications to use a wide variety of I/O types, such as non-blocking I/O (polling), selectable non-blocking I/O, Socket and the traditional Input/OutputStreams, local ByteBuffers or byte arrays, and so forth.

Using the SSLEngine

An SSLEngine is created by calling SSLContext.createSSLEngine() from an initialized SSLContext. All configuration parameters should be set before initiating the call to wrap(), unwrap(), or beginHandshake(). These methods all trigger the initial handshake. Data moves through the engine by calling wrap() or unwrap() on outbound or inbound data, respectively. Depending on the state of the SSLEngine, a wrap() call may consume application data from the source buffer and may produce network data in the destination buffer. The outbound data may contain application and/or handshake data. A call to unwrap() will examine the source buffer and may advance the handshake if the data is handshaking information, or may place application data in the destination buffer if the data is application information. The state of the underlying SSL/TLS algorithm will determine when data is consumed and produced.

Example 4–26 shows the steps in typical usage.

Example 4–26 Using SSLEngine

```
// 1. Use KeyManager to identify the key to use.
KeyManagerFactory kmf =
    KeyManagerFactory.getInstance("SunX509");
kmf.init(ksKeys, passphrase);

// 2. Use TrustManager's to allow connections.
TrustManagerFactory tmf =
    TrustManagerFactory.getInstance("SunX509");
tmf.init(ksTrust);

// 3. Initialize the SSLContext with key material

sslContext = SSLContext.getInstance("TLS");
sslContext.init(
    kmf.getKeyManagers(), tmf.getTrustManagers(), null);

// 4. Create the SSLEngine.
SSLEngine engine = sslContext.createSSLengine(hostname, port);

// 5. Use as client
engine.setUseClientMode(true);


// 6. Create a non-blocking socket channel
SocketChannel socketChannel = SocketChannel.open();
socketChannel.configureBlocking(false);
socketChannel.connect(new InetSocketAddress(hostname, port));

// 7. Complete connection
while (!socketChannel.finishedConnect()) {
    // do something until connect completed
}

// 8. Use byte buffers to hold application/encoded data
SSLSession session = engine.getSession();
```

```
ByteBuffer myAppData =
 ByteBuffer.allocate(session.getApplicationBufferSize());
ByteBuffer myNetData =
   ByteBuffer.allocate(session.getPacketBufferSize());
ByteBuffer peerAppData =
 ByteBuffer.allocate(session.getApplicationBufferSize());
ByteBuffer peerNetData =
  ByteBuffer.allocate(session.getPacketBufferSize());

// 9. Do initial handshake
doHandshake(socketChannel, engine, myNetData, peerNetData);

myAppData.put("hello world".getBytes());
myAppData.flip();

while (myAppData.hasRemaining()) {

// 10. Generate SSL/TLS encoded data
//     (handshake or application data)
    SSLEngineResult res = engine.wrap(myAppData, myNetData);

    // Process status of call
}
```


The SSLEngine produces or consumes complete SSL/TLS packets only and it does not store application data internally between calls to wrap() or unwrap(). Thus, input and output ByteBuffers must be sized appropriately to hold the maximum record that can be produced. Calls to SSLSession.getPacketBufferSize() and SSLSession.getApplicationBufferSize() should be used to determine the appropriate buffer sizes. The size of the outbound application data buffer generally does not matter. If buffer conditions do not allow for the proper consumption/production of data, the application must determine the problem using SSLEngineResult, correct the problem, and then retry the call again. Unlike SSLSocket, all methods of SSLEngine are non-blocking. SSLEngine implementations may cause the results of tasks that may take an extended period of time to complete, or may be seemingly blocking or slow. For any operation which may potentially block, the SSLEngine will create a runnable delegated task using a thread depending on the design strategy.

To shut down an SSL/TLS connection, the SSL/TLS protocols require the transmission of close messages. Therefore, when an application is done with the SSL/TLS connection, it should first obtain the close messages from the SSLEngine, transmit them to the communicating peer using its transport mechanism, and then finally shut down the transport mechanism.

So far we have looked at JSSE and how to use its secure communication services. Now, let's explore the Java Authentication and Authorization Service (JAAS), which provides API mechanisms for authentication and authorization services.

Java Authentication and Authorization Service (JAAS)

Authentication is the process of verifying the identity of a user or a device to determine its accuracy and trustworthiness. Authorization provides access rights and privileges depending on the requesting identity's granted permissions to access a resource or execute a required functionality.

JAAS provides API mechanisms and services for enabling authentication and authorization in Java-based application solutions. JAAS is the Java implementation of the Pluggable Authentication Module (PAM) framework originally developed for Sun's Solaris operating system. PAM enables the plugging in of authentication mechanisms, which allows applications to remain independent from the underlying authentication technologies. Using PAM, JAAS Authentication modules allow integrating authentication technologies such as Kerberos, RSA, smart cards, and biometric authentication systems. Figure 4–5 illustrates JAAS-based authentication and authorization using pluggable authentication modules.

In an end-to-end application security model, JAAS provides authentication and authorization mechanisms to the Java applications and also enables them to remain independent from JAAS provider implementations. The JAAS API framework features can be categorized into two concepts:

- ***Authentication***: JAAS provides reliable and secure API mechanisms to verify and determine the identity of who is executing the code.
- ***Authorization***: Based on an authenticated identity, JAAS applies access control rights and privileges to execute the required functions. JAAS extends the Java platform access control based on code signers and codebases with fine-grained access control mechanisms based on identities.

Like other security packages, JAAS also features a provider architecture and service-provider interface that allows different JAAS-based authentication and authorization provider modules to be plugged into a J2SE environment. With the release of Java SE 6, JAAS includes a login module that allows Java applications to perform LDAP authentication.

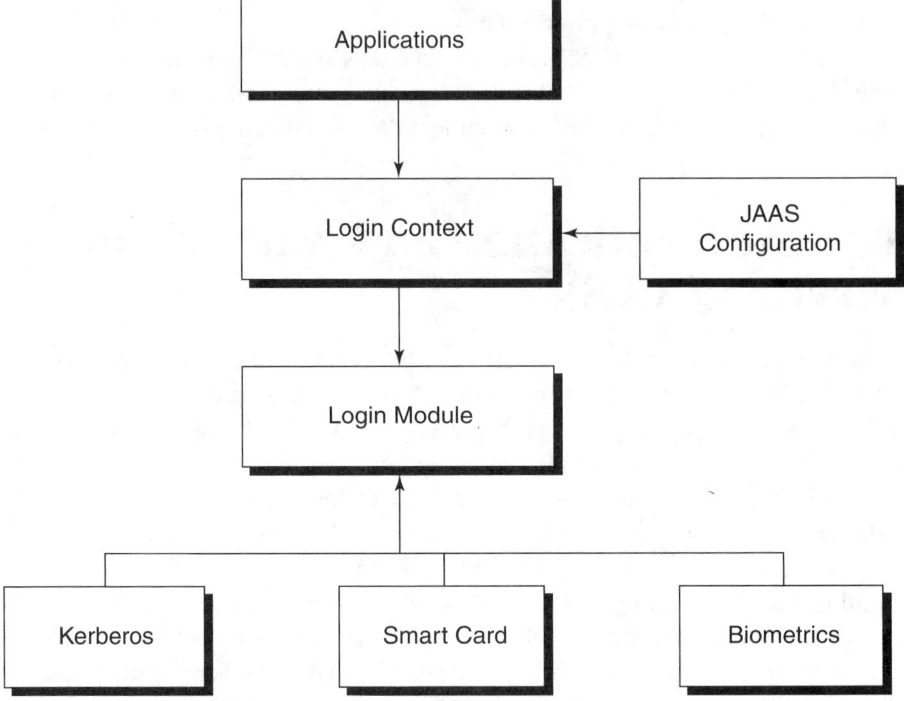

Figure 4–5 JAAS architectural model and pluggable authentication

JAAS Classes and Interfaces

In J2SE, the core classes and interfaces of the JAAS framework are available in the following packages:

- **javax.security.auth.***: Contains the base classes and interfaces for authentication and authorization mechanisms.
- **javax.security.auth.callback.***: Contains the classes and interfaces for defining authentication credentials of the application.
- **javax.security.auth.login.***: Contains the classes for logging in and out of an application domain.
- **javax.security.auth.spi.***: Contains interfaces for a JAAS provider for implementing JAAS modules.

The classes and interfaces are further classified into three categories: Common, Authentication, and Authorization. Let's take a look at some of the important classes and interfaces from these categories.

Common Classes

- **Subject** (**javax.security.auth.Subject**): Represents a group of related entities, such as people, organizations, or services with a set of security credentials. Once authenticated, a Subject is populated with associated identities, or Principals. The authorization actions will be made based on the Subject.
- **Principal** (**java.security.Principal**): An interface that represents an authenticated entity, such as an individual, organization, service, and so forth.

Authentication Classes

- **LoginContext** (**javax.security.auth.login.LoginContext**): Provides the basic methods to authenticate Subjects. Once the caller has instantiated a LoginContext, the LoginContext invokes the login method to authenticate a Subject. It is also responsible for loading the Configuration and instantiating the appropriate LoginModules.
- **LoginModule** (**javax.security.auth.spi.LoginModule**): This interface is primarily meant for JAAS providers. It allows JAAS providers to implement and plug in authentication mechanisms as login modules. LoginModules are plugged into an application environment to provide a particular type of authentication. In an authentication process, each LoginModule is initialized with a Subject, a CallbackHandler, shared LoginModule state, and LoginModule-specific options. The LoginModule uses the CallbackHandler to communicate with the user. J2SE 1.4 provides a number of LoginModules bundled under the com.sun.security.auth.module package.
- **Configuration** (**javax.security.auth.login.Configuration**): Represents the configuration of LoginModule(s) for use with a particular login application.
- **CallbackHandler** (**javax.security.auth.callback.CallbackHandler**): Defines an interface that allows interaction with a user identity to retrieve authentication-related data such as username/password, biometric samples, smart card-based credentials, and so forth. Applications implement the CallbackHandler and pass it to the LoginContext, which forwards it directly to the underlying LoginModule.

Authorization Classes

- **Policy** (**java.security.Policy**): Represents the system-wide access control policy for authorization based on an authenticated subject.

- **AuthPermission** (javax.security.auth.AuthPermission): Encapsulates the basic permissions required for a JAAS authorization and guards the access to the Policy, Subject, LoginContext, and Configuration objects.
- **PrivateCredentialsPermission** (javax.security.auth.PrivateCredentialsPermission): Encapsulates the permissions for accessing the private credentials of a Subject.

Understanding the JAAS API Programming Model

To understand the JAAS API programming model and the steps involved, let's take a look at some common JAAS authentication and authorization usage scenarios.

JAAS Authentication

In a JAAS authentication process, the client applications initiate authentication by instantiating a LoginContext object. The LoginContext then communicates with the LoginModule, which performs the actual authentication process. As the LoginContext uses the generic interface provided by a LoginModule, changing authentication providers during runtime becomes simpler without any changes in the LoginContext. A typical LoginModule will prompt for and verify a username and password or interface with authentication providers such as RSA SecureID, smart cards, and biometrics. LoginModules use a CallbackHandler to communicate with the clients to perform user interaction to obtain authentication information and to notify login process and authentication events.

Implementing a JAAS LoginModule

The following programming steps are required for implementing a JAAS LoginModule:

1. Define a class that represents your LoginModule (for example, *MyTestLoginModule*). The LoginModule class implements the LoginModule interface (see Example 4–27).

Example 4–27 Implementing a JAAS LoginModule

```
import javax.security.auth.*;
   import javax.security.auth.login.*;
      import javax.security.auth.callback.*;
      import javax.security.auth.spi.*;
   import java.security.*;
      import java.io.*;
      import java.util.*;
```

```
public class MyTestLoginModule implements
                              LoginModule {

Boolean loginVerification = false;
Subject  subject;
      CallbackHandler CallbackHandler;
      Map sharedState;
      Map options;
      String myName;
      String myPassword;
      DemoPrincipal myNamePrincipal;

....
// LoginModule methods

}
```


2. Implement the LoginModule interface methods:
   - **initialize()**: The initialize() method initializes the authentication scheme and its state information (see Example 4–28).

Example 4–28 Implementing a JAAS LoginModule–initialize() method

```
/** Implement the LoginModule initialize() method */
    public void
        initialize(Subject subject,
                    CallbackHandler callbackHandler,
                     Map sharedState,
                     Map options) {
        this.subject = subject;
        this.callbackHandler = callbackHandler;
        this.sharedState = sharedState;
        this.options = options;
    }
```

   - **login()**: The login() method performs the actual authentication process. For example, the login() method is responsible for prompting the client for a username and password, and then attempting to verify the password against a password repository. It makes use of callbacks to prompt the client user to provide the username and password information. The login() method (see Example 4–29) returns a Boolean value of true if the requested authentication is successful; if authentication is not successful, it returns false with a LoginExeption such as FailedLoginException.

Example 4–29 Implementing a JAAS LoginModule–login() method

```
/** Implement LoginModule login() method */
 public boolean login() throws LoginException {

    boolean loginVerification = false;

    try {

  // Setup the callbacks to obtain
  // user authentication information

   Callback myCallback[] = new Callback[2];
   myCallback[0] =
         new NameCallback(" Enter Username:" );
   myCallback[1] =
   new PasswordCallback("Enter Password:", false);

  // Invoke the handle() method
  // in the Callbackhandler

   CallbackHandler.handle(myCallback);

   // Get the username and password from the callback
   // populate them

   myName = ((NameCallback) myCallback[0]).getName();
   myPassword
     = new String ((PasswordCallback)
                 myCallback[1]).getPassword());

// Perform a simple verification

     If (( myName.equals("ramesh"))
           && (myPassword.equals("javaguy"))) {
           loginVerification = true;
       }
      else {
           loginVerification = false;
       }
```

```
        } catch (Exception e) {
            throw new LoginException("Login failed")
        }
    }
```

- **commit()**: If the user is successfully authenticated (see Example 4–30), the commit() method adds the Principal from the corresponding authentication state information and populates the Subject with the Principal. If the authentication fails, the commit() method returns false and destroys the authentication state information.

Example 4–30 Implementing a JAAS LoginModule–commit() method

```
/** Implement LoginModule commit() method */
  public boolean commit() throws LoginException {

 if (loginVerification) {

     // Add Principal to the Subject
      myNamePrincipal = new DemoPrincipal();
      myNamePrincipal = setName(myName);
      subject.getPrincipals().add(myNamePrincipal);
    }
      myName = null;
      myPassword = null;
     return loginVerification;
 }
```

- **abort()**: If the authentication fails, the abort() method exits the LoginModule and cleans up all the corresponding user state information (see Example 4–31).

Example 4–31 Implementing a JAAS LoginModule–abort() method

```
/** Implement LoginModule abort() method */
  public boolean abort() throws LoginException {

  boolean myReturnValue = false;

 if (!(loginVerification)) {

     // Clear out all state information
      myName = null;
      myPassword = null;
      loginVerification = false;
```

```
    }
     else {
subject.getPrincipals().remove(myNamePrincipal);
myName = null;
myPassword = null;
myReturnValue = true;
}
return myReturnValue;
       }
```

- **logout()**: The logout() clears the subject and cleans up all Principal settings of the subject in the LoginModule. It returns true if the logout() process succeeds (see Example 4–32).

Example 4–32 Implementing a JAAS LoginModule–logout() method

```
/** Implement LoginModule logout() method */
    public boolean logout() throws LoginException {

    boolean myReturnValue = false;

   // Clear all
   if (loginVerification) {
subject.getPrincipals().remove(myNamePrincipal);
myName = null;
myPassword = null;
myReturnValue = false;
}
return true;
       }
} // End of LoginModule
```

Configuring JAAS LoginModule Providers

JAAS LoginModules are configured in the java.security properties file, which is located in the <java.home>/jre/lib/security directory. To configure JAAS LoginModules in a J2SE environment, the following security properties are required:

- Authentication configuration Properties

  ```
  login.configuration.provider
  login.config.url.n
  ```

  The login.configuration.provider identifies the JAAS LoginModule provider, and the login.config.url.n identifies the JAAS LoginModule configuration file.

For example (see Example 4–33), the JAAS provider can be represented in the java.security properties.

Example 4–33 Configuring a JAAS Provider in java.security properties

```
login.configuration.provider=com.csp.JAASprovider
login.config.url.1=/export/home/my-jaas.conf
```

To enable the JAAS LoginModule at runtime, the JAAS configuration file can also be specified as Java command-line options (see Example 4–34).

Example 4–34 Enabling a JAAS Provider as Java runtime options

```
java
 -Djava.security.auth.login.config==/export/home/my-jaas.conf
Myapplication
```


Configuring JAAS LoginModule for an application

The JAAS LoginModules are configured with an application using a JAAS configuration file (e.g., my-jaas.conf), which identifies one or more JAAS LoginModules intended for authentication. Each entry in the configuration file is identified by an application name, and contains a list of LoginModules configured for that application. Each LoginModule is specified via its fully qualified class name and an authentication *Flag* value that controls the overall authentication behavior. The authentication process proceeds down the specified list of entries in the configuration file. The following is the list of authentication flag values:

- **Required**: Defines that the associated login module must succeed with authentication. Even if it succeeds or fails, the authentication still continues to proceed down the LoginModule list.
- **Requisite**: Defines that the associated login module must succeed for the overall authentication to be considered as successful. If it succeeds, the authentication still continues to proceed down the LoginModule list; otherwise, it terminates authentication and returns to the application.
- **Sufficient**: Defines the associated login module's successful authentication sufficient for the overall authentication. If the authentication is successful, the control is returned back to the application and it is not required to proceed down the LoginModule list. If the authentication fails, then the authentication still continues down the list of other login modules.
- **Optional**: Defines that the associated login module authentication is not required to succeed. Even if the authentication succeeds or fails, the authentication still continues down the list of other login modules.

If the Sufficient flag value is not specified, the overall authentication succeeds only if all Required and Requisite LoginModules are successful. If no Required or Requisite LoginModules are specified, then at least one Sufficient or Optional LoginModule must succeed. In addition to flags, you can also specify module-specific options as name-value pairs that can be passed directly to the underlying LoginModules.

Example 4–35 shows an example configuration file based on the preceding syntax.

Example 4–35 JAAS Authentication configuration file

```
BiometricLogin {
   com.csp.jaasmodule.BioLoginModule sufficient;
   com.csp.jaasmodule.JavaCardLoginModule
                              required matchOnCard="true";
};
```

The preceding example specifies that an application named BiometricLogin requires users to first authenticate using the com.csp.jaasmodule.BioLoginModule, which is required to succeed. Even if the BioLoginModule authentication fails, the com.csp.jaasmodule.JavaCardLoginModule still gets invoked. This helps hide the source of failure during authentication. Also note that the LoginModule-specific option, matchOnCache="true" is passed to the JavaCardLoginModule as a custom attribute required for processing.

Implementing JAAS Authentication in a Client

To implement JAAS-based authentication in a client application, the following steps are required:

1. The client application instantiates a LoginContext.
2. The LoginContext loads the LoginModule(s) specified in the JAAS Configuration file.
3. The client application invokes the LoginContext's login() method. The login() method calls the loaded LoginModule and then attempts to authenticate the Subject. Upon success, the LoginModule associates the initiating client credentials (such as username/password or tokens) with the Subject.
4. Finally, the LoginContext returns the authentication status to the application. If the authentication succeeds, the application retrieves the authenticated Subject from the LoginContext.

Let's walk through the steps for building a client using JAAS authentication when a username and password are required to grant access to an application.

- **Create a LoginContext**: To instantiate a new LoginContext, a JAAS configuration file is required. The JAAS configuration file specifies the class that implements the authentication mechanisms and has a reference to its CallbackHandler. The LoginContext instantiates the configured LoginModule (see Example 4–36, MyTestLoginModule) and initializes it with this new Subject and a CallbackHandler (in our example, MyTestCallbackHandler).

Example 4–36 Creating the JAAS LoginContext

```
LoginContext loginContext = null;
      try {

        loginContext
           = new LoginContext("MyTestLoginModule",
                         new MyTestCallbackHandler());

     } catch (LoginException le) {
          System.err.println("Cannot create
                       LoginContext. " + le.getMessage());
          System.exit(-1);
      } catch (SecurityException se) {
          System.err.println("Cannot create LoginContext. "
              + se.getMessage());
          System.exit(-1);
      }
```

The following JAAS configuration file MyTestLoginModule.conf specifies the authentication module MyTestLoginModule from the com.csp.jaasmodule package that implements the authentication mechanisms.

```
MyTestLoginApp {
    com.csp.jaasmodule.MyTestLoginModule required;
};
```

- **Logging In**: After instantiating the LoginContext, the login process is performed by invoking the login() method (see Example 4–37).

Example 4–37 Invoking the login() method

```
try {
      loginContext.login();
    } catch (LoginException le) {
```

```
        System.err.println("Authentication failed:");
        System.err.println("  " + le.getMessage());
    }
```

The LoginContext's login method calls methods in the MyTestLoginModule to perform the login and authentication.

- **Implement the** CallbackHandler: The LoginModule invokes a CallbackHandler to perform the user interaction and to obtain the authentication credentials (such as username/password, smart-card tokens). In the following example (see Example 4–38), the MyTestLoginModule utilizes the handle() method of TextCallbackHandler to obtain the username and password. The MyTestLoginModule passes the CallbackHandler handle() method with an array of appropriate Callbacks such as NameCallback for the username and a PasswordCallback for the password, which allows the CallbackHandler to perform the client interaction for authentication data and then set appropriate values in the Callbacks.

Example 4–38 Implementing the Callbackhandler handle() method

```
public void handle(Callback[] callbacks)
    throws IOException, UnsupportedCallbackException {

   for (int i = 0; i < callbacks.length; i++) {

     if (callbacks[i] instanceof TextOutputCallback) {

    // Display the message according
    // to the specified type
         //..

    }
  } else if (callbacks[i] instanceof NameCallback) {

    // prompt the user for a User Name
    NameCallback nc = (NameCallback)callbacks[i];

    System.err.print(nc.getPrompt());
    System.err.flush();
    nc.setName((new BufferedReader
       (new InputStreamReader(System.in))).readLine());

     } else if (callbacks[i] instanceof
                                  PasswordCallback) {
```

```
        // prompt the user for Password information
        PasswordCallback pc
                  = (PasswordCallback)callbacks[i];
        System.err.print(pc.getPrompt());
        System.err.flush();

        // Uses readPassword method
        pc.setPassword(readPassword(System.in));

      } else {
        throw new UnsupportedCallbackException
           (callbacks[i], " Callback Unrecognized ");
          }
      }
}
```

The MyTestLoginModule then authenticates the user by verifying the user inputs. If authentication is successful, MyTestLoginModule populates the Subject with a Principal representing the user. The calling application can retrieve the authenticated Subject by calling the LoginContext's getSubject method.

- **Logging Out**: It is always good practice to log out the user as soon as the user-specific actions have been performed, or at least before exiting the application. To perform logout, invoke the logout() method in the LoginContext. The logout() method of the LoginContext calls the logout() method of the login module being used. (see Example 4–39).

Example 4–39 Invoking the logout() method

```
try {
   loginContext.logout();
}
catch (LoginException e) {
    System.out.println(e.getMessage());
}
```

To run the client application, it is necessary to specify the login module configuration with the following:

```
-Djava.security.auth.login.config==MyTestLoginModule.conf
```

This option can be set as a command-line option or a system property. For authorization policies, it is necessary to specify a policy file that defines a security policy. For example:

```
java
-Djava.security.auth.login.config==MyTestLoginModule.conf
    -Djava.security.policy==security.policy
                           MyTestAuthenticationClient
```

JAAS Authorization

JAAS authorization enhances the Java security model by adding user, group, and role-based access control mechanisms. It allows setting user and operational level privileges for enforcing access control on who is executing the code.

When a Subject is created as a result of an authentication process, the Subject represents an authenticated entity. A Subject usually contains a set of Principals, where each Principal represents a caller of an application. Permissions are granted using the policy for selective Principals. Once the user logged in is authenticated, the application associates the Subject with the Principal based on the user's access control context.

Implementing JAAS Authorization

To implement JAAS-based client authorization, the following is required:

- The caller must be successfully authenticated with a Subject.
- A policy file has to be configured with Principal-based entries and allowed permissions.
- The caller's Subject must be associated with the current access control object.

Now, let's walk through the steps involved in implementing authorization.

- **Configuring a Principal-based policy file**: The JAAS Principal-based policy file provides grant statements to include one or more Principal fields. Adding Principal fields in the policy file defines the user or entities with designated permissions to execute the specific application code or other privileges associated with the application or resources. The basic format of a grant statement (see Example 4–40) is as follows.

Example 4–40 JAAS authorization policy file–grant statement

```
grant <signer(s) field>, <codeBase URL>
  <Principal field(s)> {
    permission class_name "target_name", "action1";
     ....
    permission class_name "target_name", "action2";
  };
```

The signer field usually defines the application codebase and is followed by a codebase location. The Principal field defines the Principal_class defined by the authentication module and the associated user name. If multiple Principal fields are provided, then the Permissions in that grant statement are granted only if the Subject associated with the current access control context contains all of those as authenticated Principals. To grant the same set of Permissions to multiple Principals, create multiple grant statements listing all the permissions and containing a single Principal field designating one of the Principals. Example 4–41 is a sample JAAS Principal-based policy file defining the access control policies.

Example 4–41 Sample JAAS authorization policy file

```
grant codebase "file:/export/rn/MyTestLoginModule.jar" {
    permission javax.security.auth.AuthPermission
                                "modifyPrincipals";
};
grant codebase "file:/export/rn/MyTestAction.jar" {
   permission javax.security.auth.AuthPermission
                               "MyTestAction.class";
   permission javax.security.auth.AuthPermission
                               "doAsPrivileged";
};

/** User-Based Access Control Policy

grant   codebase "file:/export/rn/MyTestAction.jar",
      Principal sample.principal.SamplePrincipal
                                    "testUser" {

  permission java.util.PropertyPermission "java.home",
                                          "read";
  permission java.util.PropertyPermission "user.home",
                                          "read";
  permission java.io.FilePermission "cspaction.txt",
                                          "read";
};
```

- **Associating the Subject with access control**: To associate a Subject with the access control context (see Example 4–42), we need to authenticate the user with JAAS authentication.

```
Subject mySubject = loginContext.getSubject();
```

Example 4–42 will find out the Principals part of the authenticated Subject.

Example 4–42 Obtaining the user principal information from the subject

```
Iterator principalIterator
        = mySubject.getPrincipals().iterator();
System.out.println("Authenticated user
                        has Principals:");
while (principalIterator.hasNext()) {
    Principal p = (Principal)principalIterator.next();
    System.out.println("\t" + p.toString());
}
```


Then we can call the doAs() method available in the Subject class, passing the authenticated subject and either a java.security.PrivilegedAction or java.security.PrivilegedExceptionAction object. The doAs() method associates the Subject with the current access control context and invokes the run() method from the action, which contains all the necessary code to be executed. The doAsPrivileged() method from the Subject class can be called instead of the doAs() method, with the AccessControlContext as an additional parameter. This enables the Subject to associate with only the AccessControlContext provided.

Example 4–43 Using doAs() and doAsPrivileged()

```
// Authorize the execution of TestAction
//as the authenticated Subject

  PrivilegedAction action = new MyTestAction();
  Subject.doAs(mySubject, action);

  // To associate with an AccessControlContext
  //   Subject.doAsPrivileged(mySubject, action,
                         accessControlContext);
```

Example 4–44 is sample code for the PrivilegedAction to be executed after associating the Subject with the current access control context. Upon successful authentication, the action defined in the MyTestAction class will be executed based on the user access privileges defined in the policy file providing grant permissions.

Example 4–44 MyTestAction.java

```
import java.security.PrivilegedAction;

    public class MyTestAction implements
                             PrivilegedAction {

    public Object run() {
    try {
      FileOutputStream fos
             = new FileOutputStream("cspaction.txt");
      fos.write("Java Rules");
      fos.close();
      } catch (IOException ioe) {
      }
      }
  }
```

To run the client application using JAAS-based authentication and authorization, it is necessary to include the CLASSPATH containing the LoginModule and to specify the login module configuration file and JAAS principal-based policy file as command-line options or as system properties (see Example 4–45).

Example 4–45 Representing JAAS authentication and authorization policies

```
java
  -Djava.security.auth.login.config
                             ==MyTestLoginModule.conf
  -Djava.security.policy==MyJaasAction.policy
                                         MyTestClient
```

Single Sign-On (SSO) Using the JAAS Shared State

The JAAS shared state provides sharing of security credentials (such as username/password, shared secrets, and so forth) across multiple authentication modules. This enables SSO access to multiple applications by sharing of security credentials between the LoginModules used for multiple applications. JAAS provides a shared state mechanism that allows a login module to put the authentication credentials into a shared map and then pass it to other login modules defined in the configuration file. In a typical SSO scenario, multiple applications are required to have a unified authentication solution that enables a user to log in once to access multiple applications. In JAAS, to achieve SSO, all corresponding login modules of the applications participating in an SSO must be defined in the JAAS configuration file. The LoginModules can make use of a sharedState parameter specified in the configuration file, which ensures the authentication result of a LoginModule will be shared with other configured login modules. For example, when LoginModules are configured with sharedState, it allows username and password to be shared with multiple LoginModules, thus ensuring the user only enters the password once though authenticating to multiple LoginModules.

In a JAAS client authentication process, the login() method in the LoginContext iterates through the configured list of LoginModules by calling the login() method implemented in each LoginModule. Example 4–46 shows instantiating a LoginModule.

Example 4–46 Initializing the LoginModule with shared state

```
// Instantiate  the module
 LoginModule loginmodule =
(LoginModule)(Class.forName(moduleName).newInstance());
 loginmodule.initialize(subject_,
         callbackHandler_, sharedStateMap, options);
```

The Subject is populated with principal and credential information by the login module, CallBackHandler is used by the login module for capturing user credential information (such as username/password), sharedStateMap will be used for passing user security information between login modules, and options are additional name/value pairs defined in the configuration file and are meaningful only for that particular login module. The LoginContext determines the authentication result by consulting the configuration file and also combining the returned results of each LoginModule. For example (see Example 4–47), the JAAS configuration file that lists multiple LoginModules will look like the following.

Example 4–47 Setting SharedState attribute in the JAAS configuration file

```
MyTestLoginModule {
      com.csp.jaasmodule.MyPortalLoginModule required;
      com.csp.jaasmodule.MyApplicationLoginModule
                           required useSharedState=true;

  };
```

If the useSharedState attribute is specified, the LoginModule stores and retrieves the username and password from the shared state, using javax.security.auth.login.name and javax.security.auth.login.password as the respective keys. The retrieved values, such as username and password, can be used again by other listed LoginModules.

So far we have looked at JAAS and how to use its authentication and authorization services. Now, let's explore Java Generic Secure Services (JGSS), which enables uniform access to security services over a variety of underlying authentication mechanisms.

Java Generic Secure Services API (JGSS)

The Generic Security Services API (GSS-API) is a standardized API developed by the Internet Engineering Task Force (IETF) to provide a generic authentication and secure messaging interface that supports a variety of pluggable security mechanisms. The GSS-API is also designed to insulate its users from the underlying security mechanisms by allowing the development of application authentication using a generic interface. GSS-API Version 2 is also defined in a language-independent format.

Sun introduced the Java GSS-API (JGSS) as an optional security package for J2SE 1.4 that provides the Java bindings for the GSS-API. This allows development of applications that enable uniform access to security services over a variety of underlying authentication mechanisms, including Kerberos.

Comparing JGSS with JSSE and JAAS

JGSS-API shares many features with JAAS and JSSE, particularly with regard to client-server authentication, data encryption, and integrity. However, there are some distinguishable differences you should be aware of before choosing JGSS as an appropriate mechanism to use:

- **Single Sign-On Support**: JGSS contains support for Kerberos as the key authentication mechanism, which allows building single sign-on, thus avoiding multiple user login requirements using Kerberos. With the release of Java SE 6, JGSS provides support for SPENEGO (Simple and Protected GSSAPI Negotiation Mechanism) protocol for enabling Microsoft NTLM v2 and Active Directory authentication.
- **Communication**: JGSS is a token-based API that relies on the application to handle the communication. This allows an application to use the transport protocols of its choice, such as TCP sockets, UDP datagrams, or any other transport for communicating JGSS-generated tokens. JSSE provides a socket-based API and allows applications to communicate using TCP sockets only.
- **Credential Delegation**: Using Kerberos mechanisms, JGSS allows the client to delegate its credentials to the server applications deployed in a multi-tier environment. JAAS also supports similar delegation support using Kerberos mechanisms.

- **Encryption**: JGSS is token-based and also allows a choice of encryption types depending upon the application needs to intersperse plaintext and ciphertext messages. This feature is not supported by other Java security APIs.
  - Support for Kerberos AES and RC4-HMAC encryption.

The Java GSS-API classes and interfaces are available in the org.ietf.jgss.* package, available as part of J2SE 1.4. Kerberos V5 GSS-API is available as the default instance of org.ietf.jgss.GSSManager. To use JGSS, it is necessary to have an installation of Kerberos realm and also a Kerberos Key Distribution Center (KDC). The KDC is part of a Kerberos installation and is not provided with J2SE bundle.

For more information about using JGSS with Kerberos, refer to http://java.sun.com/j2se/1.4.2/docs/guide/security/jgss/single-signon.html.

Simple Authentication and Security Layer (SASL)

SASL defines a protocol for authentication and optional establishment of a security layer between client and server applications. SASL defines how authentication data is to be exchanged but does not itself specify the contents of that data. It is a framework into which specific authentication mechanisms that specify the contents and semantics of the authentication data can fit. SASL is a standard defined by RFC 2222. SASL is used by protocols such as the Lightweight Directory Access Protocol, version 3 (LDAP v3) and the Internet Message Access Protocol, version 4 (IMAP v4) to enable pluggable authentication. Instead of hardwiring an authentication method into the protocol, LDAP v3 and IMAP v4 use SASL to perform authentication via various SASL mechanisms.

Java SASL

Java SASL was introduced in the release of J2SE 5.0. It defines Java API mechanisms with an authentication mechanism-neutral solution so the application that uses the API need not be hard-wired to use any particular SASL mechanism. The API facilitates both client and server applications. It allows applications to select the mechanism to use based on desired security features, such as whether they are susceptible to passive dictionary attacks or whether they accept anonymous authentication. The Java SASL API supports developers creating their own custom SASL mechanisms. SASL mechanisms are installed by using the JCA.

SASL provides a pluggable authentication solution and security layer for network applications. It works together with other API solutions such as JSSE and Java GSS. For example, an application can use JSSE for establishing a secure channel and then use SASL for client, username/password-based authentication. Similarly, SASL mechanisms can be layered on top of GSS-API mechanisms to support the SASL GSS-API/Kerberos v5 mechanism that is used with LDAP.

Java SASL–API Overview

The Java SASL API has two interfaces, SaslClient and SaslServer, that represent client-side and server-side mechanisms, respectively. The application interacts with the SASL mechanisms using a challenge-response protocol with byte arrays that represent the challenges and responses. The server-side mechanism iterates, issuing challenges and processing responses, until it is satisfied, while the client-side mechanism iterates, evaluating challenges and issuing responses, until the server is satisfied. The application that is using the mechanism drives each iteration. That is, it extracts the challenge or response from a protocol packet and supplies it to the mechanism. Then it puts the response or challenge returned by the mechanism into a protocol packet and sends it to the peer. In many protocols that use SASL, the server advertises (either statically or dynamically) a list of SASL mechanisms that it supports. The client then selects one of these based on its security requirements.

The Sasl class is used for creating instances of SaslClient and SaslServer. Here is an example of how an application creates an SASL client mechanism using a list of possible SASL mechanisms. Let's take a look at some code fragments that show how to use Java SASL API mechanisms.

An application or library can locate and instantiate an SASL server or client using the Sasl class. For example (see Example 4–48), to locate and instantiate an SASL client, you would proceed as follows.

Java Extensible Security

Example 4–48 Creating a SASL client

```
SaslClient sc =
  Sasl.createSaslClient(mechanisms,authorizationId,
      protocol, serverName, props,callbackHandler);
```

Then the SASL Client can proceed for LDAP authentication (see Example 4–49).

Example 4–49 Using the SASL client for LDAP authentication

```
// Get initial response and send to server
 byte[] response =
    (sc.hasInitialResponse() ?
```

```
          sc.evaluateChallenge(new byte[0]) :
                                              null);
LdapResult res
    = ldap.sendBindRequest(dn, sc.getName(), response);

 while (!sc.isComplete() &&
  (res.status == SASL_BIND_IN_PROGRESS
               || res.status == SUCCESS)) {
     response = sc.evaluateChallenge(res.getBytes());

    if (res.status == SUCCESS) {
         // we're done here;
        // Don't expect to send another BIND

    if (response != null) {
       throw new SaslException("Protocol error");
      }
         break;
     }
     res = ldap.sendBindRequest(dn, sc.getName(),
                                            response);
   }
   if (sc.isComplete() && res.status == SUCCESS) {
    String qop = (String)
        sc.getNegotiatedProperty(Sasl.QOP);
    if (qop != null
        && (qop.equalsIgnoreCase("auth-int")
            || qop.equalsIgnoreCase("auth-conf"))) {

      // Use SaslClient.wrap() and SaslClient.unwrap()
      // for future
      // communication with server
        ldap.in = new SecureInputStream(sc, ldap.in);
        ldap.out = new SecureOutputStream(sc, ldap.out);
    }
 }
```

Similarly, a server creates an SASL server as shown in Example 4–50.

Example 4–50 Creating a SASL server

```
SaslServer ss = Sasl.createSaslServer(mechanism,
          protocol, serverName, props, callbackHandler);
```

The SASL server can proceed for authentication (i.e., assuming the LDAP server received an LDAP BIND request containing the name of the SASL mechanism and an (optional) initial response). The server will initiate authentication as follows (see Example 4–51).

Example 4–51 SASL server for authentication after LDAP BIND request

```
while (!ss.isComplete()) {
  try {
   byte[] challenge = ss.evaluateResponse(response);
   if (ss.isComplete()) {
     status = ldap.sendBindResponse(mechanism,
                          challenge, SUCCESS);
        } else {
     status = ldap.sendBindResponse(mechanism,
              challenge, SASL_BIND_IN_PROGRESS);

              response = ldap.readBindRequest();
        }
     } catch (SaslException e) {
            status = ldap.sendErrorResponse(e);
            break;
     }
 }
 if (ss.isComplete() && status == SUCCESS) {
    String qop = (String)
         sc.getNegotiatedProperty(Sasl.QOP);
    if (qop != null
        && (qop.equalsIgnoreCase("auth-int")
            || qop.equalsIgnoreCase("auth-conf"))) {

      // Use SaslServer.wrap()
      // and SaslServer.unwrap() for future
      // communication with client

ldap.in = new SecureInputStream(ss, ldap.in);
ldap.out = new SecureOutputStream(ss, ldap.out);
    }
 }
```

Installing Java SASL

The SASL security providers provide SASL mechanism implementations. Each provider implementation may support one or more SASL mechanisms that can be registered with JCA. By default in J2SE 5.0, the SunSASL provider is automatically registered as a JCA provider in the Java Security Properties file at ($JAVA_HOME/jre/lib/security/java.security).

```
security.provider.7=com.sun.security.sasl.Provider
```

The Sun Java SASL provider (SunSASL) provides support for several SASL mechanisms used in popular protocols such as LDAP, IMAP, and SMTP. This includes support for the following client and server authentication mechanisms as well:

Client Mechanisms

- PLAIN (RFC 2595): Supports cleartext username/password authentication.
- CRAM-MD5 (RFC 2195). Supports a hashed username/password authentication scheme.
- DIGEST-MD5 (RFC 2831). Defines how HTTP Digest Authentication can be used as an SASL mechanism.
- GSSAPI (RFC 2222). Uses the GSSAPI for obtaining authentication information. It supports Kerberos v5 authentication.
- EXTERNAL (RFC 2222). To obtain authentication information from an external channel (such as TLS or IPsec).

Server Mechanisms

- CRAM-MD5
- DIGEST-MD5
- GSSAPI (Kerberos v5)

For more information about using Java SASL, refer to http://java.sun.com/j2se/1.5.0/docs/guide/security/sasl/sasl-refguide.html.

Summary

This chapter offered a tour of the Java extensible security architecture and its core API technologies that contribute to building an end-to-end security infrastructure for Java-based application solutions. We studied the various Java security API technologies that provide support for the following:

- Using cryptographic services in Java
- Using certificate interfaces and classes for managing digital certificates

- Using Public Key Infrastructure (PKI) interfaces and classes to manage the key repository and certificates
- Using secure socket communication to protect the privacy and integrity of data transmitted over the network
- Using hardware accelerators and smart card based keystores
- Using authentication and authorization mechanisms for enabling single sign-on access to underlying applications

We also looked at the security enhancements available from J2SE 5.0. In particular, we looked at the API mechanisms and programming techniques of the following Java extensible security technologies:

- The Java Extensible Security Architecture
- Java Cryptographic Architecture (JCA)
- Java Cryptographic Extensions (JCE)
- Java Certification API (Java CertPath)
- Java Secure Socket Communication (JSSE)
- Java Authentication and Authorization Services (JAAS)
- Java Generic Secure Services (JGSS)
- Java Simple Authentication and Security Layer (Java SASL)

It is important to know these technologies, because they serve as the foundation for delivering end-to-end security to Java-based applications and Web services.

In the next chapter, we will explore the security techniques and mechanisms available for securing J2EE-based applications and Web services.

References

"Java Security Architecture," in "Java™ 2 SDK, Standard Edition Documentation Version 1.4.2." Sun Microsystems, 2003.

http://java.sun.com/j2se/1.4.2/docs/guide/security/spec/security-spec.doc1.html and http://java.sun.com/j2se/1.4.2/docs/guide/security/spec/security-spec.doc2.html.

Java Security Guide for "Java™ 2 SDK, Standard Edition Documentation Version 1.4.2." Sun Microsystems, 2003.

http://java.sun.com/j2se/1.4.2/docs/guide/security/

"Security Enhancements in the Java 2 Platform Standard Edition 5.0," Sun Microsystems, 2004.

http://java.sun.com/j2se/1.5.0/docs/guide/security/enhancements15.html

[RSASecurity] CryptoFAQ.

http://www.rsasecurity.com/rsalabs/node.asp?id=2168

J2EE Security Architecture

Topics in This Chapter

- J2EE Architecture and Its Logical Tiers
- J2EE Security Definitions
- J2EE Security Infrastructure
- J2EE Container-Based Security
- J2EE Component/Tier-Level Security
- J2EE Client Security
- EJB Tier or Business Component Security
- EIS Integration Tier–Overview
- J2EE Architecture–Network Topology
- J2EE Web Services Security–Overview

Chapter 5

The J2EE platform provides a multi-tier application infrastructure solution for developing and deploying portable and scalable distributed computing applications. It is essentially a set of Java technologies that can span from the client tier to the presentation tier to the business logic and finally to back-end resources. The J2EE platform is also designed to provide a full-fledged security architectural model that addresses the core security requirements of a multi-tier application infrastructure.

The key challenges of implementing end-to-end security across multiple tiers of J2EE application architecture involve ensuring security of every component that contributes to the infrastructure—from its network services to the ultimate client of the target resource. Accordingly, the security of the infrastructure must meet the critical security requirements of maintaining the integrity and the confidentiality of data and transport; preventing unauthorized use or damage caused by any unprivileged user(s); and avoiding the associated potential risks.

To achieve end-to-end security of the J2EE infrastructure, security is addressed in all deployed components and associated container services, allowing propagation of security in all logical tiers of the application and its exposed Web services. J2EE leverages on the underlying Java platform security and its extensible security architecture APIs with additional features provided by the J2EE container services and components.

Over the course of this chapter, we will study J2EE security architecture and mechanisms provided by the J2EE server container and components. In particular, we will take a closer look at the J2EE security mechanisms available to the logical tiers and components that contribute to building end-to-end security for J2EE-based applications and Web services. At the time of writing this book, the J2EE 1.4 specification has been released as a public specification, and this chapter addresses that version of J2EE.

This chapter assumes that you have worked with J2EE components such as JSPs, Servlets, and EJBs for J2EE application servers.

J2EE Architecture and Its Logical Tiers

The J2EE platform is essentially a Java-based distributed computing environment that defines the multi-tier application architecture best suited for building enterprise applications. The multi-tiered architecture is based on the notion of logical partitioning of self-contained components. The logical partitioning encapsulates related functional components of unique responsibility and delivers their functionalities through well-defined interfaces (see Figure 5–1 J2EE Platform and its logical tiers).

The J2EE platform is generally represented with the following logical tiers shown in Figure 5–1:

- **Client Tier**: The client tier represents the J2EE platform's user interface or its application clients that interact with the J2EE platform-based application or system. A typical client can be a Java application (J2SE/J2ME),

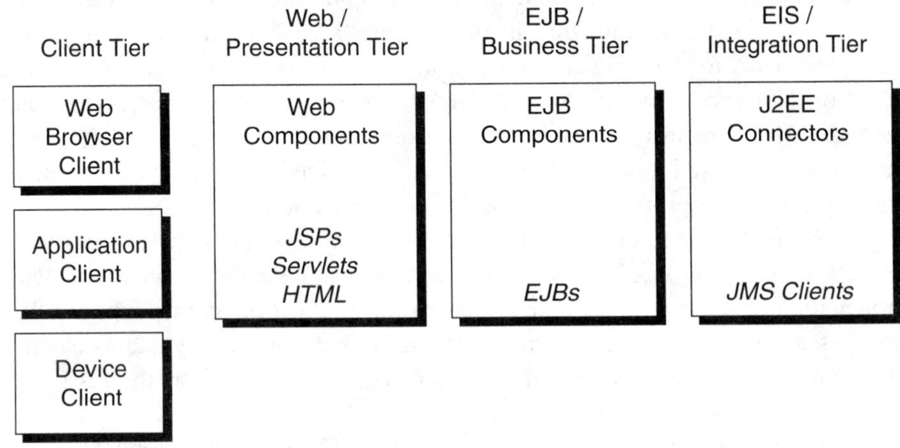

Figure 5–1 J2EE Platform and its logical tiers

Java applet, Web browser, Web service, Java enabled device, or Java-based network application.

- **Web or Presentation Tier**: The presentation tier represents the presentation logic components required to access the J2EE application and its business services. It handles the requests and responses, session management, device-independent content delivery, and invocation of business components. From a security standpoint, it delivers client login sessions and establishes single sign-on access control to underlying application components. J2EE components such as JSPs, Servlets, and Java Server Faces (JSF) reside in the Web container, which delivers user interfaces to clients. In J2EE 1.4, Web services-based communication can also be delivered using Web components such as Servlets.
- **Business or Application Tier**: The Business Tier represents the core business logic processing required. It typically deals with business functions, and transactions with back-end resources, or workflow automation. In some cases, it acts as a business wrapper when the underlying resources handle the actual business logic. EJB components such as Session Beans, Entity Beans, and Message-driven Beans reside in this tier. In J2EE 1.4, Stateless EJB components can be exposed as Web services and can be invoked using SOAP-based Web services communication.
- **Integration or EIS Tier**: The Integration Tier represents the connection and communication with back-end resources such as Enterprise-information systems (EISs), database applications, and legacy or mainframe applications. The business-tier components are tightly coupled with the Integration Tier in order to facilitate data query and retrieval from back-end resources. J2EE components such as JMS, J2EE connectors, and JDBC components reside in this tier.
- **Resources Tier**: The resources tier represents the back-end application resources that contain data and services. These resources can be database applications, EIS systems, mainframe applications, and other network-based services.

The components in these tiers are executed inside of component-specific containers such as a Web container or an EJB container. Containers provide the environment in which the components can be executed in a controlled and managed way. They also provide an abstraction layer through which the components see the underlying services and the architecture.

The J2EE platform provides a full-fledged security infrastructure and container-based security services that address the end-to-end security requirements of the different application tiers and their resources. To define security at all levels, the J2EE platform defines contracts that establish the security roles and responsibilities involved in the development, deployment, and management of a J2EE application. In accordance with J2EE specifications, the security roles and responsibilities involve the following:

- **J2EE Platform Provider**: The J2EE server vendor who is responsible for implementing the J2EE security infrastructure and mechanisms.
- **J2EE Application Developer**: The application developer who is responsible for specifying the application roles and role-based access restrictions to the components.
- **J2EE Application Assembler**: The component builder who is responsible for assembling the components and defining the security view identifying the security dependencies in the component.
- **J2EE Application Deployer**: The component deployer who is responsible for assigning the users and groups to the roles and who establishes the security deployment scenarios.

The above roles and responsibilities ensure security at every stage of development and deployment of all components and their residing application tiers.

Before we delve into the J2EE security mechanisms, let's take a look at the J2EE security definitions, which are used to describe the security of a J2EE environment.

J2EE Security Definitions

The J2EE platform uses a set of standard terms and definitions that describe the J2EE environment's specific security requirements such as roles, users, policies and related technologies. The definitions are as follows:

- **Principal**: A principal is an entity (a person or an application client) that can be authenticated by an authentication service or a security realm. As a result of authentication, the principal is identified with a unique name and its associated data.
- **Security Realm or Policy Domain**: A security realm provides common security policies and mechanisms that can be enforced by a security service for protecting J2EE platform-managed resources.
- **Security Provider**: A security provider provides security technologies and associated services to enforce a security policy that protects applica-

tions and resources. Usually, J2EE vendors provide support for third-party or standards-based security providers that can be plugged into a J2EE server security realm.

- **Security Attributes**: The security attributes are data-specific to a principal that allows or denies access to resources and to auditing of the principal.
- **Security Credential**: The security credential contains information related to authentication of a principal. The contents and format of a security credential vary depending on the authentication mechanisms in use.

Now let's take a closer look at the J2EE platform security infrastructure and mechanisms.

J2EE Security Infrastructure

All J2EE components, regardless of whether they are Web (presentation components) or EJB (business components), must be assembled and deployed in the appropriate container of the J2EE server infrastructure. The J2EE platform vendors implement the J2EE component container and services that act as the server infrastructure for executing these components. In addition to providing an execution environment, the J2EE server also provides managed services such as security, transactions, persistence, connection, resource pooling, and so forth.

In a J2EE server infrastructure, the J2EE security services ensure that the security of the application data accessed is protected over the different logical tiers, between the requests and responses, and across the components and resources. The J2EE server-facilitated security infrastructure takes much of the burden of securing the application from the application developers, allowing them to concentrate on implementing the business logic of the application.

In general, most J2EE application servers provide the following security services:

- Security realms to protect server resources representing a logical group of users, groups, and access control lists (ACLs).
- Authentication mechanisms to identify the user requesting access to J2EE server-managed resources. Authentication can be accomplished using a username/password combination or digital certificates, with which a client is authenticated using the identity of the X.509 certificate provided to the server as part of an SSL authentication.
- Authorization of users and groups through ACLs, which allows policy enforcement and access restriction to specific users and resources.

- Data integrity and confidentiality by securing communication using SSL/TLS protocols. Clients can establish secure communication with the server via SSL sessions using HTTP or RMI/IIOP over SSL.
- Auditing and logging of events for identification of failed login attempts, authentication requests, rejected digital certificates, and invalid ACLs.
- Client connection filtering for the purpose of accepting or rejecting client requests based on the origin (Host name or network address verification) or protocol of the client.
- Support for pluggable JAAS-based authentication and authorization services.
- Support for pluggable authorization using Java Authorization Contract for Containers (JACC).
- Support for third-party security services via pluggable security provider agents to provide support for Web servers, portals, and other business applications.
- Implementation of Java-extensible security architecture and APIs such as JSSE, JCE, and so forth.
- Realm and User Directory Support using File, LDAP, and Relational databases.
- Support for single sign-on across all J2EE applications within a single security domain.

Some of these security infrastructure services are mandated by the J2EE specification, and it is the application server vendor's responsibility to ensure that these technologies are integrated into the J2EE server environment.

In addition to the J2EE security infrastructure provided by the server vendors, the J2EE specification dictates that a standardized security model be applied to the J2EE components within the logical tiers using the J2EE container-based security mechanisms.

J2EE Container-Based Security

The J2EE container-based security services primarily address the security requirements of the application tiers and components. They provide authentication and authorization mechanisms by which callers and service providers prove each other's identities, and then they provide access control over the resources to which an identified user or system has access.

A J2EE container supports two kinds of security mechanisms. Declarative security allows enforcement of security using a declarative syntax applied during the application's deployment. Programmatic security allows expressing and enforcing security decisions at the application's invoked methods and its associated parameters.

Declaring Security Using Annotations in Java EE 5

The new release of Java EE 5 provides a means of specifying security configuration parameters and values directly in the application code using "Annotations" (as per JSR-175). This option replaces the use of a deployment descriptor for declaring security and its dependencies.

Declarative Security

In a declarative security model, the application security is expressed using rules and permissions in a declarative syntax specific to the J2EE application environment. The security rules and permissions will be defined in a deployment descriptor document packaged along with the application component. The application deployer is responsible for assigning the required rules and permissions granted to the application in the deployment descriptor. Figure 5–2 shows the deployment descriptors meant for different J2EE components.

Example 5–1 is an XML snippet from a Web application deployment descriptor (web.xml) that represents a security constraint defining an access control policy for a Web application resource (/products/apply-discount) and specifies the access privileges for a role (employee).

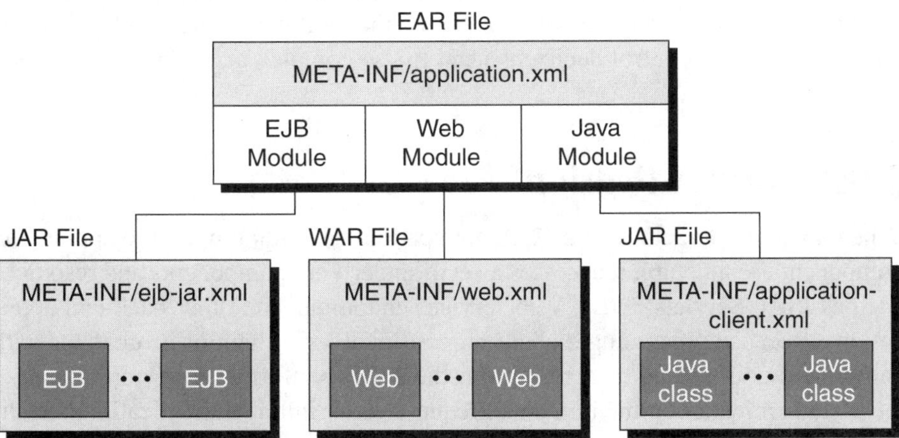

Figure 5–2 J2EE deployment descriptors

Example 5–1 Security constraints in Web application deployment descriptor

```
<security-constraint>
   <web-resource-collection>
<web-resource-name>apply-discount</web-resource-name>
 <url-pattern>/products/apply-discount</url-pattern>
        <http-method>POST</http-method>
        <http-method>GET</http-method>
    </web-resource-collection>
    <auth-constraint>
        <role-name>employee</role-name>
    </auth-constraint>
</security-constraint>
```


Programmatic Security

In a programmatic security model, the J2EE container makes security decisions based on the invoked business methods to determine whether the caller has been granted a privilege to access or deny a resource. This determination is based on the parameters of the call, its internal state, or other factors based on the time of the call or its processed data.

For example, an application component can perform fine-grained access control with the identity of its caller by using EJBContext.getCallerPrincipal (EJB component) or HttpServletRequest.getUserPrincipal (Web component) and by using EJBContext.isCallerInRole (EJB component) and HttpServletRequest.isUserInRole (Web component). This allows determining whether the identity of the caller has the privileged role to execute a method for accessing a protected resource.

Using programmatic security helps when declarative security is not sufficient to build the security requirements of the application component and where the component access control decisions need to use complex and dynamic rules and policies.

J2EE Authentication

When a client interacts with a J2EE application, depending upon the application component architecture, it accesses a set of underlying components and resources such as JSPs, Servlets, EJBs, Web services endpoints, and other back-end applications. Because processing a client request involves a chain of invocations with subsequent components and resources, the J2EE platform allows introducing a client authentication at the initial call request. After initial authentication, the client identity and its credentials can be propagated to the subsequent chain of calls.

The J2EE platform allows establishing user authentication in all application tiers and components. The J2EE environment provides support for the following three types of authentication services:

- Container-based authentication
- Application-based authentication
- Agent-based authentication

Container-Based Authentication

This is the standard authentication service provided by the J2EE server infrastructure. This allows the J2EE environment to authenticate users for access to its deployed applications. The J2EE specification mandates Web container support for four authentication types, which include the following:

HTTP Basic Authentication

The Web container component authenticates a principal using a username and password dialog from the Web client.

Form-Based Authentication

Similar to Basic Authentication, but the login dialog is customized as a form to pass the username and password to the Web container.

Client/Server Mutual Authentication

Both the client and server use X.509 certificates to establish their identities, and this authentication usually occurs over a secure communication channel using SSL/TLS protocols.

HTTP Digest Authentication

With HTTP digest authentication, the client authenticates to the server using a message digest containing the client password and sends it with the HTTP request message.

These authentication types can also be performed in the EJB Business Tier, which involves a Web component that receives a user request and then invokes an EJB component on the EJB Tier. In a Web component-to-EJB interaction scenario, the application uses a Web component in front of the EJB component to provide authentication. While integrating with back-end enterprise applications such as EIS and databases, the J2EE environment provides a container-managed resource manager sign-on authentication. This allows engaging authentication with the client caller, including Web and Business Tier components.

Application-Based Authentication

In application-based authentication, the application relies on a programmatic security approach to collect the user credentials and verifies the identity against the security realm. In a Web-component–based application, the servlet adopts the authentication mechanisms from the J2EE container services and then uses declarative security mechanisms to map the user principal to a security role defined in the deployment descriptor.

Agent-Based Authentication

This allows J2EE applications to use third-party security providers for authentication. The security providers provide pluggable agents typically to provide a single sign-on solution to portals, J2EE-managed business applications, and so forth. The agent usually resides as a proxy that intercepts the user requests to the J2EE server.

Typically, to support agent-based authentication, the J2EE server infrastructure uses JAAS-based authentication modules to integrate custom authentication technologies.

Protection Domains

In the J2EE platform, the container provides an authentication boundary between the external callers and the deployed components. It is the container's responsibility to enforce the security within its boundary and ensure that calls entering are authenticated and identified within the boundary for all interactions. Interactions within the container-managed boundary are managed as protection domains, which maintain the identity proof for the interacting components to trust each other. Figure 5–3 illustrates the notion of protection domains.

When a user makes an inbound request to the container to invoke a J2EE component, it is the container's responsibility to ensure that the authentication information is available to the component as a credential. Similarly, in the case of outbound calls, it is the container's responsibility to maintain the caller's identity to enforce the protection domain to the called components.

In a J2EE component deployment, this is done by declaring the resource references (e.g., `resource-ref` element) in the deployment descriptor of the J2EE component that interacts with other components and external resources managed by the container.

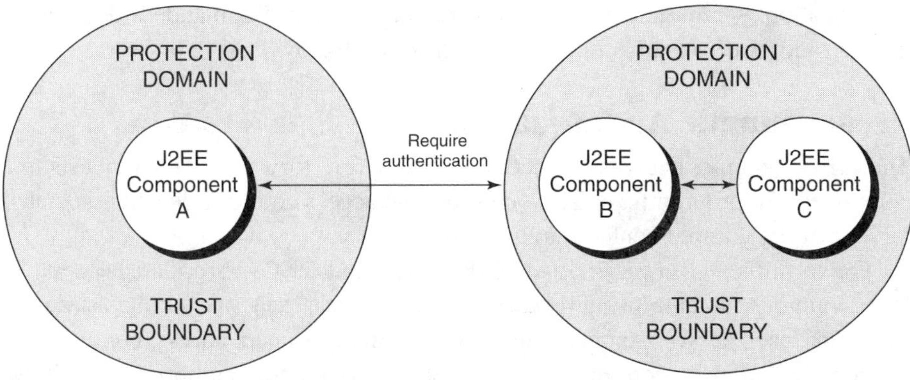

Figure 5–3 Protection domains

J2EE Authorization

J2EE uses a role-based authorization model to restrict access control with components and resources. The role is a logical grouping of users defined by the application assembler. The application deployer maps the users to roles in the target environment. In a J2EE environment, the container serves as the authentication boundary between the components and its caller clients. When a client initiates a request with a successful authentication, the container verifies the security attributes from the client's credentials and identifies the access control rules for the target resource. If the rules are satisfied, the container allows the caller to access the resource; otherwise, it denies the request.

The J2EE platform provides the following two types of authorization mechanisms:

- Declarative authorization
- Programmatic authorization

Declarative Authorization

In a J2EE environment, the application deployer specifies the enforced rules and permissions associated with an application. The rules and resources are listed in the application deployment descriptor along with a list of roles that are able to access the resource. These roles are mapped to specific users by the application deployer.

In Web components such as JSPs and Servlets, access can be protected at the URL level, and it can be further protected down to GET or POST methods. In EJB components, permissions can be specified down to specific class methods. Because declarative authorization is based on a static policy, it has limitations when the enforcing of dynamic access rules, multi-role access, and content-level authorization is required. Unless these requirements are demanded, declarative authorizations are usually preferred and easier to deploy.

Programmatic Authorization

The J2EE container decides on access control before forwarding the requests to a component. In programmatic authorization, the access control rule and associated logic is directly implemented into the application.

For example: Using EJBContext.isCallerInRole() and EJBContext.getCallerPrincipal() in EJB components and using HttpServletRequest.isUserInRole() and HttpServletRequest.getUserPrincipal() in Web components provide finer-grained access control than declarative authorization provides. Using programmatic authorization allows implementing security-aware J2EE applications that can enforce access control mechanisms such as dynamic access rules, multi-role access, and content-level authorization.

Java Authorization Contract for Client Containers (JACC)

Java Authorization Contract for Containers (JACC) defines a set of security contracts between the J2EE application containers and authorization policy modules. These contracts specify how the pluggable authorization policy providers are installed, configured, and used in access decisions.

JACC was introduced as a mandatory part of the J2EE 1.4 platform, which defines a new set of java.security.Permission classes that support role-based authorization. The JACC provider is set as a <security-service> element in the J2EE environment config file. For example, in Sun J2EE 1.4 reference implementation (Sun Java System Application Server 8–Platform Edition), using a simple file-based JACC authorization engine is shown in the domain.xml as shown in Example 5–2.

Example 5–2 File-based JACC authorization engine configuration

```
<security-service jacc="default">
   <jacc-provider name="default
   policy-provider= "com.sun.enterprise.security.provider.PolicyWrapper"
policy-configuration-factory-provider=
"com.sun.enterprise.security.provider.PolicyConfigurationFactoryImpl">
    <property name="repository"
          value="jesdomain/mypolicy"/>
  </jacc-provider>
</security-service>
```

Transport Layer Security

The J2EE platform facilitates secure communication by adopting transport layer integrity and confidentiality mechanisms based on SSL/TLS protocols. This ensures a tamperproof encrypted message between the communicating entities. The SSL/TLS transport security properties are configured at the container level and will be applied to communication during the creation of the connection. In addition, J2EE provides configuration features that enforce protected communication and reject unprotected requests and responses.

SSL/TLS-based communication security can be specified for Web components and EJB components, including their Web services endpoints. It is the responsibility of the J2EE application assembler to identify the components with method calls whose parameters or return values should be protected for integrity or confidentiality. The component's deployment descriptor is used to represent this information.

To secure communication with Web components such as Servlets and JSP pages, the transport-guarantee sub-element of the user-data-constraint sub-element of a security-constraint is used. In cases where a component's interactions with an external resource are known to carry sensitive information, these sensitivities should be described in the description sub-element of the corresponding resource-ref. In EJB components, this is done in a description sub-element of the target EJB component. Example 5–3 illustrates a Web deployment descriptor snippet (web.xml) showing the <transport-guarantee> sub-element.

Example 5–3 Web deployment descriptor showing the <transport-guarantee> sub-element

```
<security-constraint>
    . . .
    <user-data-constraint>
       <transport-guarantee>
          CONFIDENTIAL
       </transport-guarantee>
    </user-data-constraint>
    . . .
</security-constraint>
```

In the previous sections, we briefly looked at the different security mechanisms and services made available by the J2EE environment. Now, we will look over the different component-level security mechanisms that encompass all the logical tiers and components.

J2EE Component/Tier-Level Security

J2EE-based applications and Web services applications are made up of discrete components that build a multi-tier enterprise application. Although these components run in different component containers, the J2EE specification mandates that J2EE server vendors deliver mechanisms for securing each tier and its associated components, clients, and users.

In an end-to-end J2EE application practice, JSPs and Servlets form the presentation-tier components, EJBs will form the business logic behind presentation components, and connectors and other drivers will form the integration-tier components. When a Web component interacts with a client user, it collects the security credentials about the user for authentication against the J2EE server's security infrastructure. After identifying the user, it forwards the authenticated identity to determine the access to the required components. When the authenticated identity attempts to carry out that particular operation, the container first determines whether the identity has the privileges to access or deny the operation based on the assigned role and its access rights. So in J2EE security practice, before implementing the component-level security, it is crucial to understand the mechanisms that contribute to the access control and how to represent users, groups, roles, and realms. This helps to achieve the applied J2EE security in the operational environment with an adequate degree of authentication and authorization that addresses the security requirements of the different component tiers and their users.

Users, Groups, Roles, and Realms

In a J2EE environment, security privileges and access control rights are defined by linking users, groups, roles, and realms to JSP/Servlet/EJB methods, URLs, or Web-service endpoints. This allows applying security privileges either at the application level, by mapping privileges to deployed components and their implemented methods, or at the system environment level, by mapping privileges to the operational environment and services.

User: Represents the end user of the application or a software client or service that interacts with a J2EE-based application environment. As a result of authentication, a user is assigned with a Principal. Users may represent a group associated with security roles, or they can be directly associated with roles.

Group: Represents a set of authenticated users, categorized based on logical characteristics. Groups allow addressing a number of users who assume a role or typically functions as one entity.

Roles: Represents security permissions or privileges granted to users or groups to access or restrict a particular set of resources or operations. Roles are represented dynamically to users and groups based on conditions, and roles can be scoped to represent a single application or multiple applications and their underlying resources.

Realms: Represents a collection of users, groups, and roles used for protecting a single application or multiple applications and their underlying resources. Realms also provide mechanisms for implementing security constraints to protect applications and resources by integrating users, groups, and roles. In a J2EE environment, realms allow security management for applications and resources by mapping security mechanisms to applications and users, mapping one or more users to groups, and mapping one or more groups or users to roles. J2EE server vendors provide support for configuring realms using user information directories such as LDAP, RDBMS, and custom file formats. Using realms also allows implementing authentication and authorization based on user-specific information and the user's mapping role. Configuring a realm is vendor-specific; refer to the J2EE vendor administration guide for configuration procedures.

Web- or Presentation-Tier Security

In a J2EE environment, the Web tier represents the presentation components, which interact between the end user Web clients and the underlying application's business logic. The Web-tier components generally consist of JSPs, Servlets, Java Applets, Static HTML files, and associated helper classes that are packaged and deployed as a single Web application or as multiple application components running in a J2EE application server or a Servlet engine. A Web application file is packaged as a (`.war`) file containing all of the class files and resources for the Web application, along with an XML-based deployment descriptor file that contains the configuration information for the application.

The Web tier typically produces content to its end users, which can be of any content type, including HTML, XML, Image, or Sound, and more importantly, the Web tier delivers the content to a Web browser or a device that has the ability to access the application. While business logic is often implemented as Enterprise Java Beans (EJB), it can also be implemented entirely within the Web tier using Web components such as JSPs, Servlets, and JSF, along with helper classes.

The Web container provides multilayer security mechanisms for the Web-tier components to enforce security and controlled access to operations and their underlying resources. The security features include authentication, authorization, user login mechanisms, secure session handling, securing the client interactions, transport-layer security, single sign-on access for integrating multiple applications, and so forth. Let's take a closer look at these features in order to understand how they contribute to the end-to-end security of a J2EE-based application.

Web-Tier Authentication Mechanisms

To protect and control access to Web applications, the Web container facilitates authentication mechanisms that can be configured for a Web application prior to its deployment. When an unauthenticated user attempts to access a protected Web application, the Web container will prompt the user to authenticate with the Web container using the configured authentication mechanisms. The user's request will not be accepted by the Web container until the user has been authenticated to the Web container with its required credentials and identified to be one of the users with granted permission to access the application and its resources. Most J2EE platform vendors provide the Web container with the following authentication mechanisms:

HTTP Basic Authentication

The Web container authenticates the requesting identity using username and password information. When a Web application is configured with Basic Authentication, the Web container requests the interacting user's browser to capture the username and password using a dialog and then send those values to the server as part of the request. To secure a Web application using HTTP Basic Authentication login, the login-config element in the Web component deployment descriptor is configured. The login-config element includes auth-method and realm-name sub-elements, which contain the element values BASIC and the realm name to be used for login. Example 5–4 is a code snippet of the deployment descriptor illustrating the declaration of HTTP Basic Authentication.

Example 5–4 Deployment descriptor for setting HTTP basic authentication

```
<web-app>
. . .
   security-constraint>. . .</security-constraint>
 <login-config>
        <auth-method>BASIC</auth-method>
        <realm-name>myrealm</realm-name>
   </login-config>
. . .
</web-app>
```

Realm name applies only when the authentication method is BASIC. It provides the name of the security realm in which the user is required to log in and authenticate.

Form-Based Authentication

This allows specifying a custom login interface using a JSP/Servlet/HTML page to authenticate a user who is trying to access a protected Web application. It also allows configuring a custom login error page to display an invalid authentication request. To set up Form-based Authentication, it is necessary to configure login-config and form-login-config elements in the Web component deployment descriptor. The form-login-config element includes form-login-page and form-error-page sub-elements, which contain the element values referring to the URL pages to be displayed for login and error. Example 5–5 is a code snippet of the deployment descriptor illustrating the declaration of Form-based Authentication.

Example 5–5 Deployment descriptor for setting form-based authentication

```
<web-app>
 . . .
    <security-constraint>. . .</security-constraint>
 <login-config>
    <auth-method>FORM</auth-method>
   <form-login-config>
    <form-login-page>myLogin.jsp</form-login-page>
    <form-error-page>myError.jsp</form-error-page>
  </form-login-config>
    </login-config>
. . .
</web-app>
```

In addition to configuring the Web deployment descriptor, the JSP and Servlet specifications mandate that the custom login interface (using JSP, Servlet, or HTML) be implemented with the special action attribute j_security_check as well as the name attributes j_username (username field) and j_password (password field) when obtaining the username and password inputs. Example 5–6 is a JSP example of myLogin.jsp, illustrating a Form-based Authentication login page.

Example 5–6 Form-based authentication–sample login page

```
<%@ page contentType="test/html" %>
<html><body>
<head>
  <title>Form based login page</title>
</head>
  <h2>Enter your user name and password:</h2>
<p>
<form method="POST" action="j_security_check">
```

```
<table border=1>
  <tr>
    <td>Username:</td>
    <td><input type="text" name="j_username"></td>
  </tr>
  <tr>
   <td>Password:</td>
   <td><input type="password" name="j_password"></td>
  </tr>
  <tr>
   <td colspan=2 align=right>
    <input type=submit   value="Submit"></td>
  </tr>
</table>
</form>
</body></html>
```


To display login failures and error conditions, it is also necessary to define an error page. Example 5–7 is a JSP example of myError.jsp that illustrates an error page that will display after an authentication request is made by a user who is not authorized to access the protected Web application.

Example 5–7 Error page to display after an authentication failure

```
<%@ page contentType="test/html" %>
<html>
<body>
<h1> Error - Invalid username or password</h1>
<p>To retry, Try
     <a href="/myLogin.jsp">Login</a> or
     <a href="/logout.jsp">Logout</a>
</p>
</body>
</html>
```

Form-based Authentication mechanisms can also be used for GUI clients, including Swing- and AWT-based applet clients. The implementation steps are the same, except the Swing- or AWT-based applets are required to use a Client application component that provides Form-based Authentication. In the case of rich clients using RMI/IIOP communication, the client may choose to use JNDI lookup for creating an InitialContext and then do authentication by passing the username and password information. Alternatively, use JAAS authentication and custom

CallbackHandler for login, and then use the Security.runAs() method inside the Swing event thread and its children.

HTTP Basic or Form-Based Authentication over SSL (HTTPS)

Both HTTP Basic and Form-based authentication use Base64 encoding, which is generally considered insecure because it exposes username and password information if someone intercepts the communication and decodes them. HTTP Basic and Form-based Authentication over SSL (HTTPS) is considered the best approach, because they ensure secure communication using digital certificates (encrypting the data sent and then decrypting the data upon receipt). HTTPS ensures a secure communication channel using the SSL/TLS protocol before initiating the HTTP authentication request. This allows establishing confidentiality and data integrity during communication using public-key certificates and SSL/TLS configuration done at the J2EE server or Web container provider. To configure HTTP Basic or Form-based Authentication over SSL, it is necessary to use the transport-guarantee element in the Web deployment descriptor. To configure HTTP Basic or Form-based Authentication over SSL in the transport-guarantee element, specify the value as CONFIDENTIAL when the Web application requires that the data to be transmitted is secured from viewing during transmission, or specify INTEGRAL as the value when the Web application requires that the data be sent between client and server in such a way that it cannot be tampered with during transit. Example 5–8 is an example Web deployment descriptor configuring HTTPS for Form-based Authentication.

Example 5–8 Deployment descriptor for HTTPS in form-based authentication

```
<web-app>
    . . .
    <security-constraint>
      . . .
      <user-data-constraint>
            <description>
               Secure transmission using HTTP/SSL.
            </description>
      <transport-guarantee>
            CONFIDENTIAL
       </transport-guarantee>
     </user-data-constraint>
      . . .
    </security-constraint>
```

```
    <login-config>
        <auth-method>FORM</auth-method>
        <form-login-config>
        <form-login-page>/myLogin.jsp</form-login-page>
        <form-error-page>/myError.jsp</form-error-page>
        </form-login-config>
    </login-config>
  . . .
</web-app>
```


Client-Certificate or Mutual Authentication

This allows configuring the Web container or Servlet engine to accept HTTP requests using bidirectional SSL and authenticate client users' public-key certificates issued by a trusted certificate authority (CA). This facilitates a strong-authentication mechanism whereby both the client and server use their digital certificates to prove their identities over a bidirectional SSL connection. To secure a Web application using Client-Certificate or Mutual Authentication-based login access, configure the login-config element in the Web component deployment descriptor. The login-config element includes auth-method, which contains the element value CLIENT-CERT (see Example 5–9).

Example 5–9 Deployment descriptor for client-certificate authentication

```
<web-app>
. . .
    security-constraint>. . .</security-constraint>
 <login-config>
        <auth-method>CLIENT-CERT</auth-method>
    </login-config>
. . .
</web-app>
```

Digest Authentication

This allows a Web client to authenticate a Web container by sending a message digest along with its HTTP request message. Digest-based authentication is also deemed to be insecure because an attacker can intercept and capture the hashed password and resend it as a replay attack. Using digests over SSL should be considered so that the communication remains secure and tamperproof.

Digest authentication is quite similar to HTTP Basic Authentication, except that requesting the user's password is represented as a scrambled text using a one-way hash algorithm (message digest). To secure a Web application using Digest

Authentication-based login access, configure the login-config element in the Web component deployment descriptor. The login-config element includes auth-method, which contains the element value DIGEST, which tells the client to transmit the username and password encrypted using a message digest (see Example 5–10).

Example 5–10 Deployment descriptor for digest authentication

```
<web-app>
. . .
    security-constraint>. . .</security-constraint>
 <login-config>
        <auth-method>DIGEST</auth-method>
    </login-config>

. . .
</web-app>
```

It is very important to note that very few Web browsers support Digest Authentication and that the JSP and Servlet specifications do not mandate this method either.

Using JAAS for Web-Tier Authentication

The introduction of JAAS to the J2EE platform allows enforcing authentication and access controls based on user identity in a Web container and its components. Using JAAS facilitates using a pluggable login module and ensures that applications remain independent of their authentication mechanisms. This allows the creation of custom login modules for Web applications that support multiple client types and devices and the use of authentication interfaces using smart card or biometric sensors. It also permits use of custom user repositories based on Flat-file, LDAP, NT Realm, RDBMS, and so forth. JAAS also provides a single sign-on security architecture solution for handling multiple Web applications with a unified login access to authenticate the identity and to determine its user access privileges.

Most J2EE vendors and Servlet container providers implement support for JAAS-based authentication and authorization mechanisms. To implement JAAS-based authentication and authorization for Web applications, it is necessary to use JAAS LoginModules built using JAAS APIs. In a J2EE environment, JAAS LoginModules are usually configured as a Realm. Using the JAAS LoginModule, the Realm governs the authentication process of the application by mapping the user, group, security role, security policy, and other credential information. To learn more about JAAS APIs and the programming model, refer to "Java Authentication and Authorization Service" in Chapter 4, "Java Extensible Security Architecture and APIs." For more information about how to plug in JAAS providers in a J2EE environment, follow your J2EE vendor-provided administration guide procedure for installing a JAAS provider.

Single Sign-On Authentication for Web Applications

Single sign-on authentication in the Web Tier allows multiple applications that require the same user sign-on information to share this information among themselves rather than requiring the user to sign on separately for each application. When a user first accesses an application, the person is required to log in once. When needed, the authentication information is propagated to all other involved applications. Once authenticated, the roles associated with this user are used for access-control decisions across all associated Web applications; the user is not asked to authenticate to each application individually. When the user logs out of one Web application (for example, by invalidating or timing out the corresponding session if Form-based login is used), the user's sessions in all Web applications are invalidated. Any subsequent attempt to access a protected resource in any application requires the user to reauthenticate. Traditionally, the single sign-on feature for Web applications utilizes HTTP cookies (discussed later in this chapter) to transmit a token that associates each request with the saved user identity, so single sign-on can only be used in client environments that support cookies.

Using JAAS also allows enabling single sign-on authentication for Web applications. When multiple Web applications are deployed on a J2EE application server, usually each application authenticates its client user by using a user repository such as LDAP or RDBMS. To establish single sign-on, each application will define its own JAAS LoginModule for its authentication provider. All login modules are stacked together and configured using a JAAS configuration file. From a programming standpoint, JAAS LoginContext executes all configured authentication provider LoginModule instances and is responsible for managing those configured authentication providers. Once the caller has instantiated a LoginContext, it invokes the login method to authenticate a Subject. This login method iterates through all the configured LoginModules and invokes the login method for each LoginModule assigned to the application. This allows determination of the overall authentication result by combining the successful login results returned from each login module. Each LoginModule maintains the state of remembering whether or not its login or commit method previously succeeded or failed. To establish single sign-on, JAAS uses the shared-state mechanism, which allows passing the authentication information between login modules and results in a unified sign-on for the user, who now has access to all configured applications. To log out, the caller client invokes the logout method, which in turn invokes the logout method of the LoginModules configured for the applications.

Refer to the section "Java Authentication and Authorization Service" in Chapter 4, "Java Extensible Security Architecture and APIs," for information about the JAAS programming and login module configuration.

Agent-based Authentication for Web-Tier Applications

Most J2EE application server vendors and Web containers provide authentication support via agents from third-party security or identity infrastructure providers. The use of these security or identity provider infrastructures allows enforcement of authentication and access control policies regardless of whether the caller client is a browser, device, or Java/Non-Java application. In addition, the application no longer needs to use its own container-based mechanisms to perform authentication. This also adds value to the application by making it independent of the type of authentication mechanism used. This means that the authentication mechanism can be changed without affecting the Web application. Figure 5–4 represents an agent-based authentication model for securing Web-tier applications.

In a typical usage scenario, the Web agent installed in the Web server intercepts the caller's request before forwarding it to a J2EE server or its Web container. After interception, it verifies the caller's request for authentication credentials. If there are no authentication credentials present or the existing

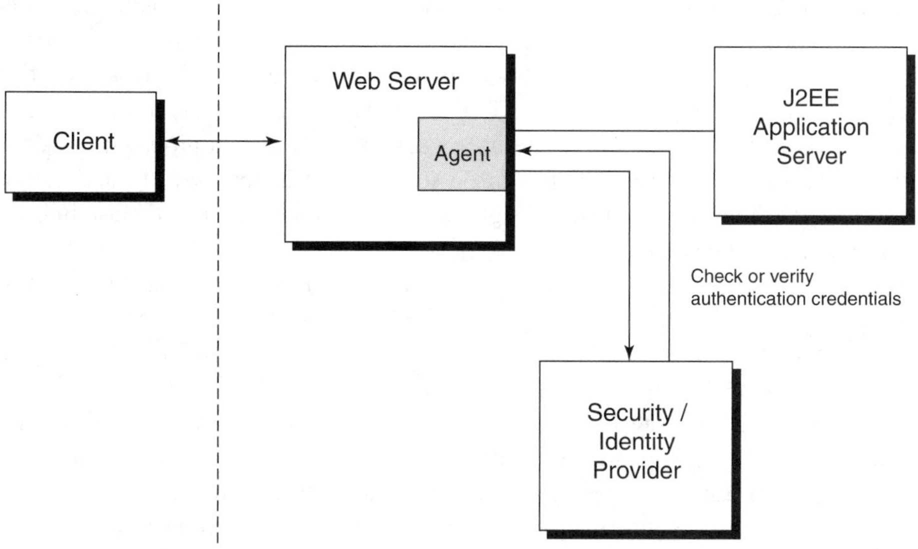

Figure 5–4 Agent-based authentication

authentication credentials are found to be insufficient, then the security provider's authentication service will present a login page or a login challenge window. The login page prompts the user for credentials such as username and password. After proper authentication, the agent examines all the roles assigned to the user. Based on the policies assigned to the user, the client will be either allowed or denied access to the Web application or its protected URL.

HTTP Session Tracking Using Cookies and URL Rewriting

An HTTP session (Session) is a series of user requests from a Web browser client during a definite period of time. An HTTP session usually corresponds to one user who accesses a Web application through a Web browser. Using an HTTP session allows you to identify and track users and maintain their Web application requests as a conversational state. The Web container uses Session objects to maintain the user-specific information from user requests over JSPs, Servlets, and even from HTML pages. An example would be a Shopping Cart application saving the state of a user's shopping cart transactions across requests. To handle HTTP sessions, the Web browser-based clients are usually required to support cookies or URL rewriting mechanisms for maintaining the client session state. With traditional Java clients, managing session state is a responsibility of the client applications because they can cache and manipulate substantial amounts of session state in memory.

Session state maintenance has an enormous impact on application security, performance, availability, and scalability. When designing a Web application, it is quite important to identify the risks and associated mitigation options in order to manage the state and effectively track the current saved state. From a Web-tier security infrastructure standpoint, HTTP sessions play a vital role in maintaining security-specific information in the user's session state and in propagating security context in Web-based single sign-on scenarios. It is necessary to maintain a relatively high level of control and tight security over session information in both server and client environments.

In J2EE application servers, the Web-tier HTTP sessions can be tracked, maintained, and managed via cookies, URL rewriting, and hidden fields in HTML forms or with a combination of cookies and/or URL rewriting. In the case of cookie-disabled Web browsers, it is the responsibility of the Web application or the server infrastructure to enable session tracking via URL rewriting. With URL rewriting, the client appends the additional data to the end of each URL to identify the session, and the server associates the data to the stored session.

To ensure session information security, make sure the cookies are encrypted and URLs are encoded in case of URL rewriting. Refer to the J2EE vendor security administration guide for configuration procedures.

Using HTTP sessions in Web applications is relatively simple. It involves looking up attributes associated with an HTTP request, creating a session object, looking up and storing user-specific information with a session, and terminating completed or abandoned sessions.

Creating and Assessing an HTTP Session

In a J2EE environment, Sessions are represented using javax.servlet.http.HttpSession objects that usually reside in the Web container. HTTPSession objects are associated with a user through cookies or URL rewriting or a combination of both. The Web container uses the HTTPSession interface to create an HTTP session between a Web browser client and a Web server. The created session usually persists in the Web container for the specific period of time defined in the Web application configuration. It also allows viewing and manipulating information about a user request, such as user's session identifier, session state, session created time, and last accessed time. It also allows binding user-specific objects to sessions and persisting them across multiple connections.

To create a new HTTP session or to obtain access to an existing session, use the HttpServletRequest method's getSession()method, as shown in Example 5–11.

Example 5–11 Creating an HTTP session

```
HttpSession mySession = request.getSession();
```

The getSession() method returns the valid session object associated with the user's HTTP request, which is identified in the session cookie that is encapsulated in the request object. Calling the method with no arguments creates a new HTTP session if one does not already exist. Calling the method with a Boolean argument creates a session only if the argument is true. Example 5–12 is a snippet showing a doPost() method from a servlet that performs the servlet's functions if the HTTP session is present. This means that the false parameter to getSession() prevents the servlet from creating a new session if one does not already exist, as shown in Example 5–12 Servlet showing how to prevent creating new session if one exists.

Example 5–12 Servlet showing how to prevent creating new session if one exists

```
public void doPost (HttpServletRequest req,
                              HttpServletResponse res)
          throws ServletException, IOException  {
  if ( HttpSession session = req.getSession(false) )
  {
```

```
    // HTTP session present, continuing
    // servlet operations
    }
    else
       // HTTP session not available,
        // return an error page

    }
}
```


Examining HTTP Session Properties

Once an HTTP session is created, we can set session attributes by name. The session attributes are stored as state information in the request related to the session. This can be examined by using the public methods in the HTTPSession interface. Example 5–13 would obtain the session attributes stored by a Web application.

Example 5–13 Obtaining session attributes from HTTP session

```
HttpSession mySession = request.getSession();
// To obtain the Session ID
String myName = mySession.getAttribute("name");
```

Invalidating an HTTP Session

Once the client interaction is completed, it is the responsibility of the Web application to clean up the existing HTTP session state and to remove any client-specific session information. Leaving stale sessions on the server often leads to security breaches involving session hijacking, client-side trojans, and eavesdropping on subsequent sessions. To invalidate an HTTP session on the server side, use the invalidate() method. Example 5–14 would invalidate a session stored by a Web application.

Example 5–14 Invalidating an HTTP session

```
HttpSession mySession = request.getSession();
// . . .
// Use HTTP Session attributes
// Finally invalidate the session
   mySession.invalidate();
```

HTTP Session Timeout

In the case of Web applications with a very large number of users, the server would be overburdened with the task of keeping a huge number of session objects alive. This would usually tax system resources in terms of memory, storage, and CPU capacity, thus reducing their efficiency. It is important to track user sessions after a period of inactivity, because there is no option for an HTTP client to signal a server that it no longer needs a session. So session timeout becomes a mandatory event, and each session has an associated timeout so that its resources can be reclaimed. From a security standpoint, if the user is missing after a period of user inactivity, the session timeout must automatically occur and the missing user needs to be logged out. The user can access the requested resource only after providing new credentials.

To enable the HTTP session timeout, the Web application is required to set a default session timeout period in the Web application deployment descriptor (web.xml), as shown in Example 5–15.

Example 5–15 Deployment descriptor setting for default session timeout

```
<session-config>
   <session-timeout>30</session-timeout>
<session-config>
```

With this setting, the user's session will automatically be deactivated after 30 minutes of inactivity.

The timeout period can also be controlled by using HTTPSession getMaxInactiveInterval and setMaxInactiveInterval methods, which allows to programmatically specify timeout in seconds. The snippet in Example 5–16 will invalidate a user's session after a period of inactivity in timeoutInSeconds seconds.

Example 5–16 Session invalidation after inactivity

```
session.setmaxinactiveinternal(int timeOutInSeconds);
```

Web-Tier Authorization Mechanisms

The J2EE Web container adopts role-based authorization mechanisms to restrict access control for Web components and their associated resources. When a Web-tier client initiates a request with a successful authentication, the Web container verifies the security attributes from the client's credentials and identifies the access control rules for the target resource. If the rules are satisfied, the container allows the caller to access the resource; otherwise, it denies the request. If the protected Web resource is accessed by an unauthenticated user, the Web container will direct the application to prompt the user to request the authentication credentials. The Web container will only allow the request after the user has been authenticated with appropriate credentials that grant permission to access the requested resources.

Security Context and Access Control

Once the Web container performs the authentication and obtains the security credentials of an authenticated principal, it maintains them as part of the user session. This information is usually referred to as a security context. The security context will be used and enforced whenever the user attempts to access a protected Web resource. The container uses the roles known to be associated with the authenticated user in conjunction with the roles authorized to access the component, as defined in the Web deployment descriptor, to either permit access or deny it. For example, the container will allow an authenticated user "securityguy," who belongs to the "admin" role, to access a Web application component with a deployment descriptor setting that specifies "admin," which defines the role to authorize access to the particular resource.

With annotations (in Java EE 5), the security roles and the mapping security role permissions can be declared within the Web application code using @DeclareRoles and @RolesAllowed annotations, respectively.

The Web-tier authorization follows the general J2EE security mechanisms using both declarative and programmatic security models.

Declaring Security and Authorization Constraints

In Web application components, using a <security-constraint> in the Web application deployment descriptor performs authorization and enforces role-based access control. The <security-constraint> and its <auth-constraint> sub-element determines who is authorized to access protected Web resources that include Web components such as JSPs, Servlets, URL patterns, and HTTP methods.

The security constraints work only on the original Web application request URI initiated by the caller and not on calls made from the service methods via a RequestDispatcher (which include <jsp:include> and <jsp:forward>). This means that inside the application, the application has access control over all required resources, and it would not forward a user's request to access a resource unless the requesting user had privileges to access them.

In addition, after authentication, the container retrieves the specified security roles for the authenticated user and checks to see if the user belongs to one of the roles defined in the <auth-constraint> tag of the Web deployment descriptor. If the user does not belong to the specified roles for the Web resource, the request is terminated with an error message.

The Web deployment descriptor code snippet in Example 5–17 shows the representation of security and authorization constraints (web.xml).

Example 5–17 Representation of security and authorization constraints

```
<web-app>
 . . .
  <security-constraint>
    <web-resource-collection>
     <web-resource-name>
          My Secure Resource
     </web-resource-name>

<!—Define context-relative URL(s) to be secured -->
    <url-pattern>
           /export/home/jsp/security/mysecure-resource/*
  </url-pattern>

<!—Define the HTTP methods, to be protected -->
          <http-method>DELETE</http-method>
          <http-method>GET</http-method>
          <http-method>POST</http-method>
          <http-method>PUT</http-method>
      </web-resource-collection>

 <!—Define the roles that may access this resource -->

      <auth-constraint>
          <role-name>authors</role-name>
          <role-name>readers</role-name>
          <role-name>publishers</role-name>
      </auth-constraint>
   </security-constraint>
   . . .
</web-app>
```


Web-Tier Programmatic Authorization

Programmatic authorization is used to enforce access control mechanisms such as dynamic access rules within an application, multi-role access, and content-level authorization. It is also used when the access-control policies using declarative options are not sufficient to express the Web application security requirements.

In the Web Tier, the programmatic authorization can be done using the following methods of the HttpServletRequest interface.

- getRemoteUser(): This method returns the name of the authenticated user who is making the request to the application (see Example 5–18).

Example 5–18 Obtaining the user name from the request

```
String userName = request.getRemoteUser();
```

- isUserInRole(): This method determines whether an authenticated user belongs to the specified role. It returns true or false indicating whether the user is included in the role (see Example 5–19).

Example 5–19 Determining the user role from the request

```
if (httpRequest.isUserInRole("SecurityRole")) {
      // Do some functions
   } else if
      // Unauthorized, display error
          }
```


When using the isUserInRole(role) method, the string role is mapped to the role name defined in the <role-name> element nested within the <security-role-ref> element of a Web deployment descriptor. It is also important to note that the <role-link> element must match a <role-name> defined in the <security-role> element of the Web deployment descriptor. The web.xml will be as shown in Example 5–20.

Example 5–20 Deployment descriptor showing the security role mapping

```
<web-app>
. . .
<servlet>
   ...
  <security-role-ref>
    <role-name>author</role-name>
    <role-link>cspAuthor</role-link>
  </security-role-ref>
   ...
</servlet>

<security-role>
   <role-name>cspAuthor</role-name>
</security-role>
. . .
<web-app>
```

- **getUserPrincipal()**: This method returns a java.security.Principal object for the current authenticated user. This method is used to check whether the user has logged in to the Web application and launched a specific action (see Example 5–21).

Example 5–21 Obtaining the principal of the authenticated user

```
if ((request.getUserPrincipal() != null) &&
        (request.getUserPrincipal().getName()
                        .equals("ramesh")) {
    // Do something
}
```

J2EE Client Security

Stand-alone clients, rich clients, or Java applets are commonly used as alternatives to Web-based clients. These clients are adopted particularly to support dynamic content and client-side business scenarios as well as to overcome limitations of Web pages. Clients are usually not considered J2EE components, because they don't make use of the J2EE container services provided by the J2EE server environment. In most scenarios, clients connect with the J2EE server-deployed applications via HTTP connections, remote-method invocation, or asynchronous messaging. Typically rich clients use HTTP as a transport to interact with JSP or Servlet components, RMI-IIOP for interacting with EJB components, and JAX-RPC (SOAP-RPC) for interacting with J2EE Web services components.

In a J2EE environment, a Java client depends on an application client container (ACC) to provide the client-specific artifacts and services for looking up and then communicating with server-deployed components, particularly EJBs, JMS Queues, data sources, and so forth. An application client container is usually packaged as a JAR file that includes a deployment descriptor (application-client.xml) specifying the J2EE deployed components and their associated resources. If the J2EE components are secured, the client can make use of the deployment descriptor to specify security-specific information.

In general, to enforce J2EE security mechanisms from a Java client, the following options are considered.

HTTPS Connection

Using JSSE mechanisms, clients can create HTTP/SSL-based URL connections with J2EE-deployed components such as JSPs and Servlets. Using two-way SSL allows the client to confirm the user identity with the J2EE component by verifying client's certificates issued by a CA listed in the server's list of trusted CAs. Using JSSE for HTTPS connection, it is necessary to import the trusted certificates into the respective client and server keystores.

The code snippet in Example 5–22 shows how to use HTTP/SSL in a Java client code.

Example 5–22 Using HTTPS connection from a Java client code

```
// Dynamically add Sun's SSL provider
Security.addProvider(new
         com.sun.net.ssl.internal.ssl.Provider());

// Set the system property for Sun's implementation of
// HTTPS URL handler
System.setProperty("java.protocol.handler.pkgs",
           "com.sun.net.ssl.internal.www.protocol");
URL securesite = new URL("https://www.verisign.com/");
      BufferedReader in = new BufferedReader(
                  new InputStreamReader(
                     securesite.openStream()));

      String inputLine;

      while ((inputLine = in.readLine()) != null)
         System.out.println(inputLine);

      in.close();
```

If the client uses a proxy server, the proxy-specific properties can be set as shown in Example 5–23.

Example 5–23 Setting proxy-specific properties in client code

```
// set name of proxy server
      System.setProperty("https.proxyHost", "proxy");

// set port number for proxy server
      System.setProperty("https.proxyPort", "8080");
```

For more information about JSSE API mechanisms, refer to Chapter 4, "Java Extensible Security Architecture and APIs."

JAAS Client-Side Callbacks

A client can make use of the JAAS callback handlers to interact with a JAAS LoginModule plugged in a J2EE application environment. A typical JAAS LoginModule implements the javax.security.auth.callback.CallbackHandler interface for obtaining client input such as username and password to perform authentication. For example, the implementation of a callback handler using a Java GUI application might prompt the user with a GUI window to provide user credentials, or the implementation of a callback handler for a command-line tool might simply prompt the user for input directly from the OS prompt. In a typical scenario, the JAAS LoginModule initiates an array of callbacks to the callback handler's handle method (e.g., a NameCallback for the username and a PasswordCallback for the password), and the callback handler performs the requested user interaction and sets appropriate values in the callbacks. To support this, the client-side callback initiates the client login prompt to obtain the username and password. The snippet in Example 5–24 shows a JAAS client that uses a callback handler to perform authentication before invoking a J2EE component.

Example 5–24 J2EE client using a JAAS Client callback handler

```
LoginContext lc = null;
// Create a LoginContext
try {
lc = new  LoginContext("MyJAASClient",
      new MyCallbackHandler(username, password, url));
} catch  (LoginException le) {
System.err.println("Failed:
         Creating LoginContext. "+ le.getMessage());
System.exit(-1);
} catch  (SecurityException se) {
System.err.println("Failed:
         Creating LoginContext. " + se.getMessage());
System.exit(-1);
  }
 // Call the login method of the LoginModule

    try {
         loginContext.login( );
      } catch (Exception e) {

      }
  //  Now create the initial context
  //  for Looking up the J2EE component
Initial  Context ic = new InitialContext();

    // Invoke the J2EE component
```

For more information about implementing JAAS LoginModules and JAAS Clients, refer to Chapter 4, "Java Extensible Security Architecture and APIs."

Secure J2ME Clients

J2ME clients may interact remotely with a J2EE application server and access its deployed components. However, since J2ME clients have limited GUI capabilities compared to traditional Java clients, J2ME clients should only be considered when mobility and remote access are key deployment requirements.

With MIDP 2.0 implementation, J2ME devices support using HTTP/SSL communication, specifically the TLS 1.0, SSLv3, WTLS (Wireless Transport Layer Security), and WAP TLS Profile and Tunneling Specifications. This allows establishing HTTPS connections with J2EE Web-tier components and ensures authentication, integrity, and confidentiality of all data exchanged between the J2ME device and the J2EE server. MIDP 2.0 provides a javax.microedition.io.HttpsConnection interface, an extension of the HttpConnection. This interface includes a getSecurityInfo() method that returns an instance of another interface, SecurityInfo. The SecurityInfo interface provides methods that return information about a secure connection—details such as protocol name, protocol version, cipher suite, server certificate, and so forth. When using client-side artifacts such as an application client container, it is important to note that the provisioned component must comply with the appropriate J2ME profile.

The snippet in Example 5–25 illustrates how a J2EE client establishes an SSL connection and obtain the server certificate information.

Example 5–25 J2ME client using an SSL connection

```
String url = "https://www.cspsecurity.org/";

// Create an HTTPS connection
  HttpsConnection hc = null;

// Use the Connector.open method
      hc = (HttpsConnection)Connector.open(url);

// Obtain the security information
       SecurityInfo info = hc.getSecurityInfo();
        Certificate c = info.getServerCertificate();
   String name = c.getIssuer();
```

MIDP 2.0 also introduced the concept of trusted MIDlets that can be digitally signed and verified. With signed MIDlets, it is possible to authenticate and verify the integrity of the MIDlet suite. For more information about MIDlet security features, refer to Chapter 3, "The Java 2 Platform Security."

EJB Tier or Business Component Security

In a J2EE environment, the EJB tier represents the business components. It generally resides between the Web-tier or application-client components and the underlying database or EIS-tier components. The EJB tier typically consists of Session Beans, Entity Beans, and Message-driven Beans, along with associated helper classes. Each bean is typically packaged and deployed as a single component (.jar) file. A J2EE application can also be packaged to include multiple EJB components, Web components, and other resources as a J2EE application (.ear) file, along with an XML-based deployment descriptor file that contains the configuration information of the EJB component or J2EE application.

The EJB security model is a subset of J2EE security and follows security strategies that are similar to those applied to other J2EE components. While similar to Web components in terms of authentication and authorization models, the EJB specifications do not specify any supported authentication schemes and leave the responsibility of providing them to the J2EE vendor. EJB security options are more focused on authorization and access control. In a J2EE server, the EJB container implements the security services for the deployed EJB components. The security policies specified for the EJB components are enforced by the EJB container. Like Web components, the security policies of EJB components are expressed in terms of roles and permissions for accessible EJB methods. During runtime, when a client session makes an EJB invocation, the EJB container verifies the caller and determines its required method invocations. This is done by verification of whether the caller principal is mapped to a security role that is granted to execute specific methods.

The J2EE server allows us to protect the EJB-tier components and associated resources, adopting declarative or programmatic security.

EJB Declarative Authorization

With EJB declarative security, also referred to as declarative authorization, the EJB deployer defines the access control rules and policies externally, using a deployment descriptor, and then associates them with an EJB component. In practice, declarative authorization allows declaring security roles and then associating them with EJB method permissions. The EJB container takes responsibility for granting permissions to access bean methods for callers representing the defined security role and at least possessing one of the privileges associated with the bean method. The EJB deployer is responsible for mapping a list of roles to caller identities (principals) via J2EE vendor-specific descriptor mechanisms. Thus, defining a security policy declaratively for an EJB refers to defining which methods can be executed by which roles.

In an EJB deployment, the EJB deployment descriptor represents security roles and associated method permissions. The deployment descriptor can contain zero or more <method-permission> elements defined within an <assembly-descriptor> element to provide role-to-method access control mappings. A <method-permission> element can contain one or more <role-name> elements, and one or more <method> elements. The <role-name> elements contain the role name values that have been defined in a <role-name> element contained within the <security-role> elements. The <method> element identifies the EJB method(s) for which it is necessary to define access control permissions. Example 5–26 shows two method permissions: the first <method-permission> represents all the methods of the bean interfaces (including remote, home, local, and local home). The second <method-permission> applies to the specified <security-role>.

Using annotations (in Jave EE 5), the security roles and the mapping security role permissions can be declared in the EJB application code using @DeclareRoles and @RolesAllowed annotations, respectively.

Example 5–26 Declaring role and associated method permissions

```
<ejb-jar>
. . .
 <assembly-descriptor>
.. .
<security-role>admin</security-role>
    <method-permission>
        <role-name>*</role-name>
        <method>
          <ejb-name>CSPSecureService</ejb-name>
          <method-name>create</method-name>
        </method>
  </method-permission>
  <method-permission>
        <role-name>admin</role-name>
        <method>
          <ejb-name>CSPSecureService</ejb-name>
          <method-name>adminService</method-name>
        </method>
  </method-permission>
          ...
</assembly-descriptor>
. . .
</ejb-jar>
```

In addition to the <role-name> element, a <role-link> element can be defined within a <security-role-ref> element. Like Web components, this element value can be defined to establish EJB relationships using role names from one EJB to another.

There may be cases where you need to restrict a client from executing a list of methods of an EJB. In such cases, you can indicate the methods that should not be invoked using the <exclude-list> element. The methods listed under the <exclude-list> element are not callable—regardless of the role, and in cases where a method is specified in both <exclude-list> as well as <method-permission> elements. Example 5–27 shows two methods that cannot be called because they are specified within an <exclude-list>.

Example 5–27 Declaring exclude lists for restricting EJB methods

```
<ejb-jar>
. . .
 <assembly-descriptor>
.. .
    <exclude-list>
        <method>
        <ejb-name>OldPartsCatalog</ejb-name>
        <method-name>checkModelNo</method-name>
        </method>
        <method>
        <ejb-name>OldPriceList</ejb-name>
        <method-name>checkLastPrice</method-name>
        </method>
  </exclude-list>
         ...
</assembly-descriptor>
. . .
</ejb-jar>
```

EJB Programmatic Authorization

The EJB programmatic authorization allows dynamic invocation of business methods based on the remote caller's security role. The programmatic authorization mechanism allows performing fine-grained access control using dynamic access rules when declarative options are not sufficient for expressing the EJB component security requirements. In practice, the EJB component can use programmatic methods to determine whether a caller has been granted a privilege based on the parameters of the call, the internal state of the component, or other factors such as the time of the invocation.

In the EJB tier, the programmatic authorization can be accomplished using the following methods of the EJBContext interface:

- **isCallerInRole()**: This method determines whether the caller of the EJB belongs to the specified role. It returns true or false, indicating whether or not the user is included in the role. The code in Example 5–28 checks whether the bean caller belongs to role "admin."

  Example 5–28 Verifying an EJB caller's associated role

  ```
  Boolean privilegedCaller
              = ejbContext.isCallerInRole("admin");
  ```

- **getCallerPrincipal()**: This method returns a java.security.Principal object that contains the name of the current authenticated user making the call. This method is used to verify the caller's identity; if the identity verified is equivalent to the caller's identity, then the container will allow the caller to proceed with the invocation. If the identity verified is not equivalent to the caller's identity, the container denies further interaction. The code in Example 5–29 shows how to obtain the caller identity in the EJB using the ejbContext.getCallerPrincipal().getName() method.

  Example 5–29 Obtaining the EJB caller identity

  ```
    public String getCallerIdentity() {
          return
        ejbContext.getCallerPrincipal().getName();

  }
  ```

Anonymous or Unprotected EJB Resources

If the EJB caller need not be authenticated and access is allowed to anonymous callers, then it is categorized as an unprotected EJB method. In the EJB tier, unrestricted access can be provided to EJB methods by using an unchecked element in the method permissions. The snippet in Example 5–30 shows how to use the <unchecked> element.

Example 5–30 Unrestricting access to EJB methods

```
<method-permission>
    <unchecked/>
```

```
    <method>
      <ejb-name>ProductCatalogue</ejb-name>
        <method-name>listBeverages</method-name>
    </method>
    <method>
    ...
</method-permission>
```

Principal Delegation in EJBs

In a chain of invocations between one EJB and another, it is very important that the principal identity of the EJB that initiated the call is propagated to the other EJBs in the chain. This means that the principal identity associated with the original EJB must remain constant in all EJB method invocations and across other EJB servers (see Figure 5–5).

In general, the client principal of an EJB method that is invoked is associated with that subsequent invocation across other EJBs. If the EJB component of the other container has to use the caller's identity from the originating EJB container, the <user-caller-identity> option has to be specified to instruct the container. If the EJB method makes a call to another EJB and its defined principal is not the original caller, then to delegate the principal, each EJB has to be assigned with a <run-as> role and principal.

To better understand identity propagation (see Figure 5–5), let's consider a scenario where a client principal identity roleA calls an EJB MyEJB1.methodA() as principal roleA in EJB Server A and then calls EJB MySecureEJB2.methodB() to EJB server B. If both MyEJB1 and MyEJB2 have their security identity set to the <user-caller-identity>, then both MyEJB1.methodA() and MyEJB2.methodB() will execute using caller's principal roleA as its identity. To support this scenario, the EJB deployment descriptor will look like Example 5–31.

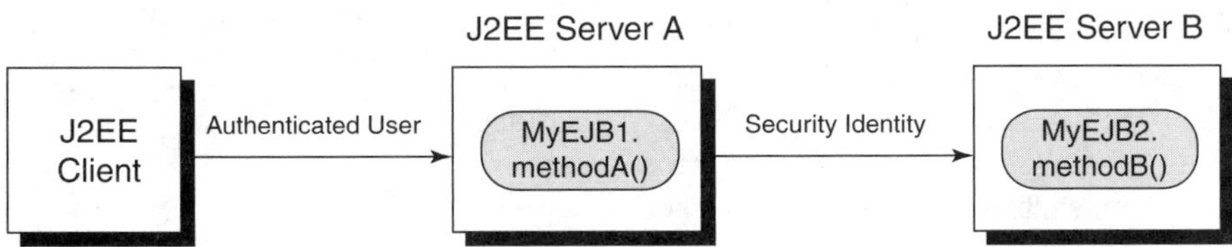

Figure 5–5 Principal delegation in EJBs

Example 5–31 EJB principal delegation using <user-caller-identity>

```
<ejb-jar>
<enterprise-beans>
   <session>
      <ejb-name>MyEJB1</ejb-name>
      <home>com.csp.MyEJB1Home</home>
      <remote> com.csp.MyEJB1</remote>
      <ejb-class> com.csp.MyEJB1Bean</ejb-class>
      <session-type>Stateful</session-type>
     <transaction-type>Bean</transaction-type>
      <security-identity>
         <user-caller-identity></user-caller-identity>
      </security-identity>
   </session>
</enterprise-beans>
</ejb-jar>
```

Run-As

To make the originating EJB call on other EJB components use a different principal identity, it is necessary to use the <run-as> identity option. If the <run-as> identity option is specified, the container establishes the identity of the bean using the specified role name and propagates the <run-as> principal identity when it calls on other EJBs as a whole, including all methods of the home and the remote interfaces. Example 5–32 illustrates <run-as> identity in the EJB deployment descriptor in order to execute MyEJB2 using "roleB."

Example 5–32 EJB deployment descriptor for run-as different principal

```
<ejb-jar>
<enterprise-beans>
   <session>
      <ejb-name>MyEJB2</ejb-name>
      <home>com.csp.MyEJB2Home</home>
      <remote> com.csp.MyEJB2</remote>
      <ejb-class> com.csp.MyEJB2Bean</ejb-class>
      <session-type>Stateful</session-type>
     <transaction-type>Bean</transaction-type>
      <security-identity>
         <run-as>roleB</run-as>
      </security-identity>
   </session>
</enterprise-beans>
</ejb-jar>
```

Using <run-as> identity is very useful when the business functionality requires delegation of certain operations without transferring complete access privileges to the caller principal. An example for its use is when an EJB is required to run privileged administrative tasks that make use of methods from another administrative EJB. Assigning the EJB with <run-as> identity will enable use of the administrative EJB without compromising the security and access privileges.

Security Context Propagation from Web Tier to EJB Tier

In a J2EE environment, it is quite common for EJB components to rely on the authentication mechanisms provided by the Web container. The Web container provides the user interface for obtaining the caller security credentials and vouches for the identity of users and their access privileges. It is the container's responsibility to set and maintain the authentication boundary between callers and the components deployed in the container. The container also maintains the security context that encapsulates all the authentication information. J2EE uses the notion of protection domains to manage all of the component interactions within the container boundary and to maintain the principal so that the interacting components can trust each other. Figure 5–6 illustrates the security context propagation from the Web tier to the EJB tier.

When a Web client invokes an EJB method, the container propagates the security context via the EJB stubs and skeletons. The security context propagation is initiated from the Web container as part of the inbound call, which interacts with

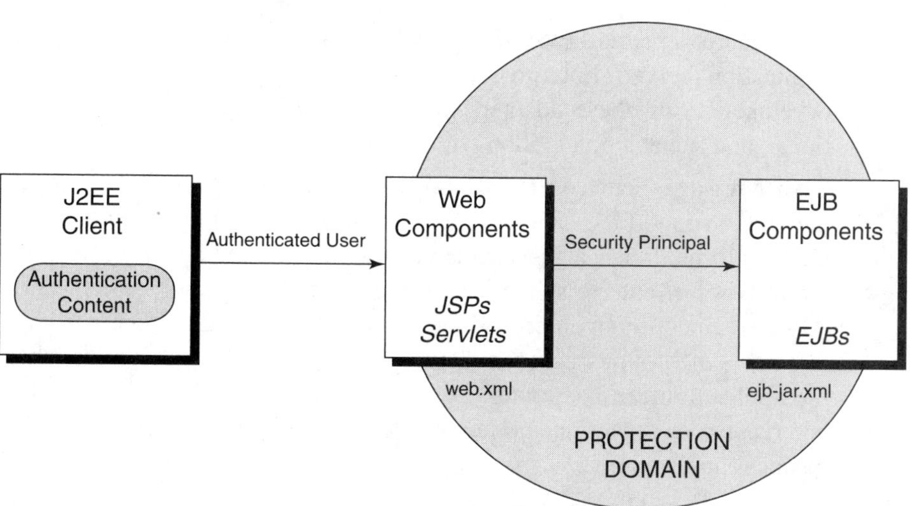

Figure 5–6 Security context propagation from Web tier to EJB tier

the EJBs. It is the EJB container's responsibility to make the representation of the caller's principal identity available to the invoked EJB component. This means that once the user is authenticated in the Web Tier, the authenticated principal identity is applied to the protection domain that manages the container authentication boundary and in turn it makes the principal identity available to the deployed Web and EJB components.

In the case of CORBA- and RMI/IIOP-based clients, the security context propagation among the EJB components and CORBA applications occurs via interoperability, because J2EE-compliant containers support all the requirements of Conformance Level 0 of the Common Security Interoperability version 2 (CSIv2) specifications from Object Management Group (OMG).

EIS Integration Tier–Overview

J2EE offers a standards-based integration infrastructure that facilitates enterprise application integration and provides mechanisms for establishing communication and exchange data with heterogeneous back-end business resources such as relational databases, EIS systems, and JMS messaging providers. The key integration technologies that are part of a J2EE environment are as follows:

- **J2EE Connector Architecture (J2EE CA)**: The J2EE CA provides a standards-based infrastructure for integrating J2EE applications with existing EISs and business applications. J2EE CA provides resource adapters for external EISs that can be plugged into a J2EE-compliant application server. Enterprise-class business applications can then be developed using these adapters to support and manage secure, transactional, and scalable integration with EISs and back-end systems.
- **Java Message Service (JMS)**: JMS is a Java-based API infrastructure defined to support message-oriented middleware and enterprise messaging systems. It facilitates a generic messaging API that can be used across different types of enterprise messaging providers. Applications use the JMS API to connect to an enterprise messaging system using either asynchronous or synchronous communication. Once a connection is established, the application can use a messaging provider (via the JMS API) to send and receive messages and communicate asynchronously with one or more business applications.
- **Java Database Connectivity (JDBC)**: The JDBC API defines a Java API for integration with relational database systems. A Java application uses the JDBC API for obtaining database connections, retrieving database

records, executing database queries and stored procedures, and performing other database functions.

Let's take a closer look at these technologies and the security mechanisms available for securing the Integration Tier of a J2EE environment.

Securing J2EE Connector and EIS

The J2EE Connector Architecture (J2EE CA) provides security management services that define the security mechanisms between the application server and the EIS resource. In general, it offers a variety of security mechanisms used to protect an EIS against unauthorized access and other security threats. These security mechanisms include:

- User identification, authentication, and authorization of principals.
- Secure communication between the application server and the EIS resource, using open network communication security protocols like Kerberos that provide end-to-end security with authentication and confidentiality services.
- Enabling EIS-specific proprietary security mechanisms that exist in EIS systems such as SAP, BAAN, and Oracle.
- Under the hood, the J2EE Connector establishes a security contract between the J2EE server and the EIS resource adapter that extends the connection management mechanisms to support secure communication with protocols that provide authentication, integrity, and confidentiality services. The Connector allows support for different security mechanisms to protect the underlying EIS against security threats such as unauthorized access and loss or corruption of information. Figure 5–7 illustrates the representation of a J2EE Connector security contract with J2EE components.

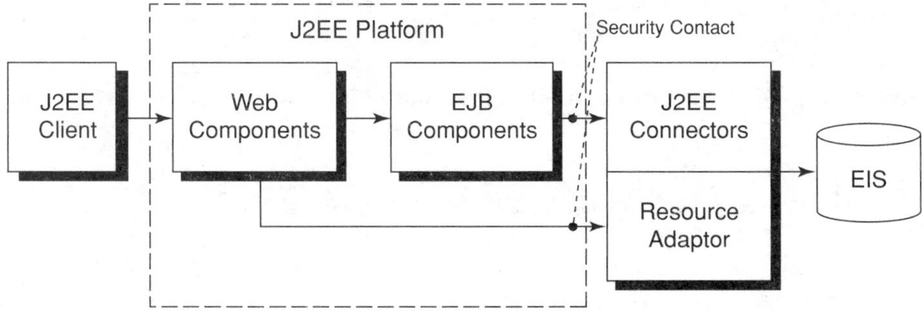

Figure 5–7 J2EE Connector security contract with the J2EE platform

In a typical usage scenario, the application component makes a request to establish a connection with the underlying EIS layer. To serve the request, the resource adapter security services authenticate the caller using the credentials and then establish a connection with the underlying EIS layer. After authentication, the security service determines the access privileges for the authenticated user in order to determine whether the user is permitted to access the EIS resource. All subsequent invocations that the application component makes to the EIS instance occur using the security context of the caller's principal identity.

Establishing a Secure EIS Connection

The J2EE CA provider has two choices for implementing the EIS connections:

- **Container-Managed Sign-On**: The application component lets the container take the responsibility of configuring and managing the EIS sign-on. The container determines the username and password to establish the connection to an EIS instance.
- **Component-Managed Sign-On**: The application component code manages the EIS sign-on by including code that performs the sign-on process to an EIS.

Let's take a closer look at these two approaches.

Container-Managed Sign-On

With container-managed sign-on, the application developer assigns the responsibility of managing the EIS sign-on to the J2EE application server and the application deployer to be responsible for managing the EIS sign-on. To represent this, the application developer sets the res-auth element in the Connector deployment descriptor to Container. The deployer sets up and configures the EIS sign-on configuration with the required username and password for establishing the connection. The snippet in Example 5–33 represents the res-auth element in the connector module deployment descriptor.

Example 5–33 Declaring container managed sign-on

```
. . .
<resource-ref>
   <res-ref-name>eis/PeopleSoft</res-ref-name>
<res-type>javax.resource.cci.ConnectionFactory
</res-type>
        <res-auth>Container</res-auth>
        <res-sharing-scope>Shareable</res-sharing-scope>
```

```
    </resource-ref>
    . . .
```

In the application code, when the component invokes the getConnection method on the ConnectionFactory instance, it does not need to pass any security credentials. The application using the container managed sign-on will look like Example 5–34.

Example 5–34 Establishing EIS connection using container managed sign-on

```
// Perform JNDI lookup and obtain a connection factory
javax.resource.cci.ConnectionFactory cxf =
            (javax.resource.cci.ConnectionFactory)
        ctx.lookup("java:comp/env/eis/PeoplesftCxFactory");

// Invoke factory to obtain a connection
javax.resource.cci.Connection cx= cxf.getConnection();
```


Component-Managed Sign-On

With component-managed sign-on, the application developer includes the code that is responsible for managing the EIS sign-on. To represent this, the application developer sets the res-auth element in the Connector deployment descriptor to Application. This indicates that the component code is designed to perform a programmatic sign-on to the EIS. The application developer must pass the required credentials, such as username and password, to establish the connection. The snippet in Example 5–35 represents the use of the res-auth element in the Connector module deployment descriptor.

Example 5–35 Declaring component managed sign-on

```
. . .
    <resource-ref>
    <res-ref-name>eis/PeopleSoft</res-ref-name>
    <res-type>javax.resource.cci.ConnectionFactory</res-type>
        <res-auth>Application</res-auth>
        <res-sharing-scope>Shareable</res-sharing-scope>
    </resource-ref>
    . . .
```

In the application code, when the component invokes the getConnection method on the ConnectionFactory instance, it is necessary to pass the required security credentials. The application using the component-managed sign-on will look like Example 5–36.

Example 5–36 Establishing EIS connection using component-managed sign-on

```
// Perform JNDI lookup and Obtain a connection factory
javax.resource.cci.ConnectionFactory cxf =
             (javax.resource.cci.ConnectionFactory)
          ctx.lookup("java:comp/env/eis/PeoplesftCxFactory");

//Get a new ConnectionSpec
   com.eis.ConnectionSpecImpl myEIS = //../

// Invoke factory to obtain a connection
myEIS.setUserName("javaman");
myEIS.setPassword("javarules");
javax.resource.cci.Connection cx= cxf.getConnection(myEIS);
```


EIS Sign-On Process

The creation of a new EIS connection usually involves the creation of a sign-on process. Implementing an EIS sign-on requires one or more of the following steps:

- Determine the resource principal (identity of the initiating caller) under whose security context a new connection to an EIS will be established.
- Authenticate the resource principal if the connection is not already authenticated.
- Establish a secure association between the application server and the EIS. Additional mechanisms like SSL or Kerberos can also be deployed.

Once the EIS sign-on is established, the connection is associated with the security context of the initiating user. Subsequently, all application-level invocations of an EIS instance occur under the security context of that principal identity.

When deploying an application that uses a J2EE Connector, the deployer configures the security credentials required to create the connections to the underlying EIS systems. The deployer performs the principal mapping configuration to ensure that all connections are established under the security context of the EIS user who is the resource principal of the underlying EIS. The J2EE application server takes the responsibility of handling the principal mapping for all the authenticated caller principals. Thus, a user accesses the EIS under the security context of the configured resource principal.

Securing JMS

Java Message Service (JMS) is an integral part of the J2EE platform. It provides a standard set of Java APIs that allow J2EE applications to send and receive messages asynchronously. It also allows access to the common features of any JMS-compliant enterprise messaging system (typical to message brokers). JMS defines a loosely coupled, reliable application communication mechanism for enabling J2EE components to send and receive messages with enterprise applications and legacy systems. The JMS specification primarily aims at defining a Java-based messaging API designed to support a wide range of enterprise messaging vendor products. It leaves the responsibility of adding security features to the JMS provider vendors.

From a security viewpoint, a JMS-based application security solution requires support for authentication, authorization, encryption, confidentiality, data integrity, and non-repudiation. Most messaging vendors provide support for some of these features:

- JMS provider authentication and access control
- JMS queues protection so that the destinations are available for access to privileged applications
- JMS message and transport security

It is also important to note that the JMS specification does not address these security requirements but leaves it to the JMS provider vendors to implement its requirements. So the features discussed in the following sections may differ among vendor implementations.

JMS Provider Authentication

Most JMS providers allow JMS clients to authenticate themselves with the JMS provider and target destinations. The authentication occurs either using a username/password combination or using digital certificates. In some vendor implementations, the JMS provider makes use of a repository such as LDAP or a relational database for storing privileged users or digital certificates.

Access Control for JMS Destinations

Establishing access control for JMS destinations allows rules and policies to be set with the JMS clients so that they are secure and accessed by designated systems. This requires that an access control list (ACL) be created to define the security policies for sending and receiving messages from a target destination (Queue or

Topic). Most JMS providers facilitate support for setting access control on JMS destinations by applying ACLs that grant permissions to send and receive messages.

JMS Transport Security

The JMS specification does not address the choice of protocols to transport JMS messages. To secure JMS transport, most providers facilitate secure communication by adopting transport-layer integrity and confidentiality mechanisms based on SSL/TLS protocols. These transport-specific properties are configured at the JMS provider level and are applied to communication during the creation of the JMS connection.

Securing JDBC

JDBC technology is an API (included in both J2SE and J2EE releases) that provides a cross-DBMS connectivity supporting a wide range of data sources, including SQL databases and tabular data sources such as spreadsheets or flat files. With JDBC API mechanisms, Java-based applications are able to send SQL or other statements to data sources running on heterogeneous platforms. To access these data sources, JDBC makes use of appropriate JDBC-enabled drivers provided by the database vendor. The JDBC specification leaves the responsibility of providing security features to the JDBC drivers and the database implementation. With the introduction of JDBC 3.0 specification, JDBC provides compatibility with the J2EE Connector architecture. This means that JDBC drivers can be implemented as J2EE Connectors (Resource Adapters). They are packaged and deployed as a resource adopter that allows a J2EE container to integrate its connection, transaction, and security management services with the underlying data source.

So far there are no standard JDBC security mechanisms, but most of the major database and JDBC driver vendors offer custom security mechanisms to provide the following:

- Secure communication between the application and the underlying database system using HTTP over SSL/TLS protocols
- Data encryption mechanisms
- Support for data integrity checking mechanisms
- Support for secure rich-client communication to databases via Firewall
- Support for security auditing and reporting on data access

These mechanisms are represented in the JDBC driver properties by setting appropriate configuration parameters; there is no need to change code.

J2EE Architecture–Network Topology

J2EE security architects are frequently faced with questions related to network topology design options and strategies for deploying J2EE applications in a production DMZ environment. The network design defines the security of the J2EE application deployment in a DMZ environment by the way it addresses architectural capabilities such as availability, reliability, scalability, manageability, and performance. In particular, these capabilities are greatly influenced by the network environment and characteristics of deployed J2EE components such as JSP/Servlets and EJBs. The key characteristics are as follows:

Stateless/stateful transactions: The availability and scalability characteristics are determined by considering the nature of transactions between the client and server. If the nature of transactions are idempotent (that is, stateless, where the order of transactions is not dependent on any transaction), then the availability strategies are trivial. If the transactions between the client and server mandate a state has to be maintained between the individual client HTTP requests and server HTTP responses, then the production deployment architecture must provide high-availability strategies that include session failover and fault-tolerance. This adds a bit more complexity as it requires a state-aware multilayer switch with load-balancing capabilities and the ability to switch based on session IDs and cookies.

Partitioning: The J2EE application itself might make better use of resources by segregating the Web tier from applications. If an application makes use of heavy static-content Web pages and then JSP/Servlets and EJBs for business logic, it might make sense to use Web servers to render static content and then use application servers for dynamic content that requires business-logic processing.

Security level: Separating the Web tier, Business tier, and Integration tier with a firewall creates a more secure solution. The potential drawbacks include hardware and software costs, increased communication latencies between servlet and EJB communication, and increased manageability costs.

Failover and fault-tolerance: The J2EE application server failover and fault-tolerance capabilities play a vital role in the infrastructure configuration. The failover capabilities forward requests from failed instances to available server instances without interrupting the service to the client. Fault-tolerance insulates applications from failures and without other coexisting application server instances.

Performance: In some cases, architects are willing to forego tight security advantages for increased performance. For example, the firewall between the Web tier, the Business tier, and the Integration tier might be considered as overkill because the incoming traffic is already firewalled in front of the Web tier.

Scalability: J2EE applications can be partitioned and deployed based on two scalability models. In a horizontally scaled environment, many small separate server infrastructures are utilized for multiple instances of Web servers and application servers to cater to the different tiers. In a vertically scaled environment, a few monolithic systems (large-scale servers) are able to support many instances of Web servers and application servers.

Manageability: In general, the fewer the number of servers, the lower the total cost of operation (TCO).

Demilitarized Zone (DMZ) is a logical location between two sets of firewalls. The assumption is that infrastructure residing in the DMZ needs to be accessed directly and therefore will be more likely to be compromised. The second firewall layer is used to protect attackers who have compromised servers in the DMZ from gaining access to back-end servers such as application servers. By necessity, the front layer will allow traffic on port 80, 443, 21, and other commonly attacked ports. But the second layer firewall will only allow traffic on ports needed by the back-end servers.

Designing for Security with Horizontal Scalability

Figure 5–8 represents a logical network architecture (horizontally scaled) showing a horizontally partitioned J2EE application as Web-tier (JSP/Servlets), Application-tier (EJB components), and Back-end resources. The horizontal scalability is achieved by adding servers to run multiple instances of Web servers and application servers. The Web-server tier and the applications tier are separated with a firewall. This enhances the security, because the traffic between the Web server and the application servers is required to pass through the firewall. This may increase the reliability, availability, and performance of the overall infrastructure, because it depends on the load-balancing and nature of transactions. Horizontal scalability decreases the manageability because it increases the cost of operations manageability. A single point of failure will not lead to an overall system failure. This architectural model is usually not suitable for applications that have relatively intensive servlet-to-EJB communications and back-end transactions.

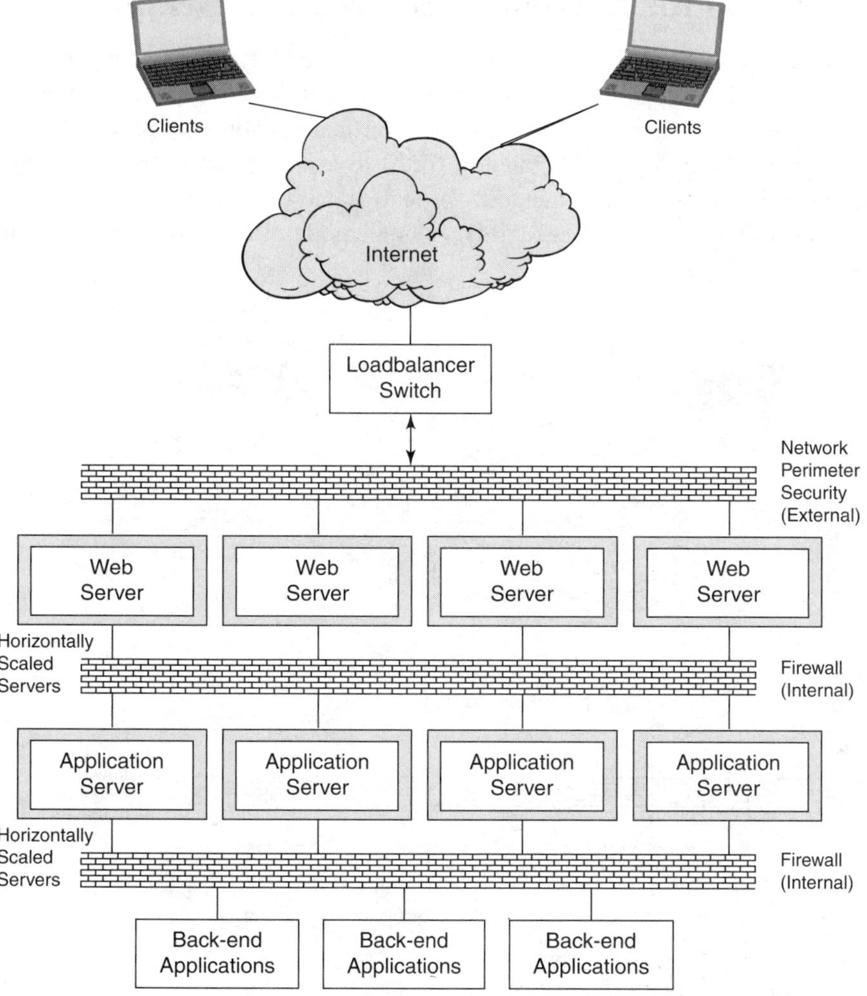

Figure 5–8 Logical network architecture for horizontal scalability

Another potential disadvantage includes increased latency between Web-tier and application-tier communication.

To decouple the Web tier from applications, the Web server is configured with a reverse-proxy, which receives the HTTP requests from a client on the incoming network side and then opens another socket connection on the application server side to perform business application processing. This architectural model is suitable for applications that have relatively intensive servlet-to-EJB communications and less stringent security requirements.

Designing for Security with Vertical Scalability

Figure 5–9 represents a logical network architecture (vertically scaled) showing a partitioned J2EE application as Web-tier (JSP/Servlets), Application-tier (EJB components), and Back-end resources. The vertical scalability is achieved by adding capacity (memory, CPUs, and so forth) to existing servers without making any system infrastructure changes. Vertical scalability increases manageability and reduces the cost of manageability. A single point of failure at the server infra-

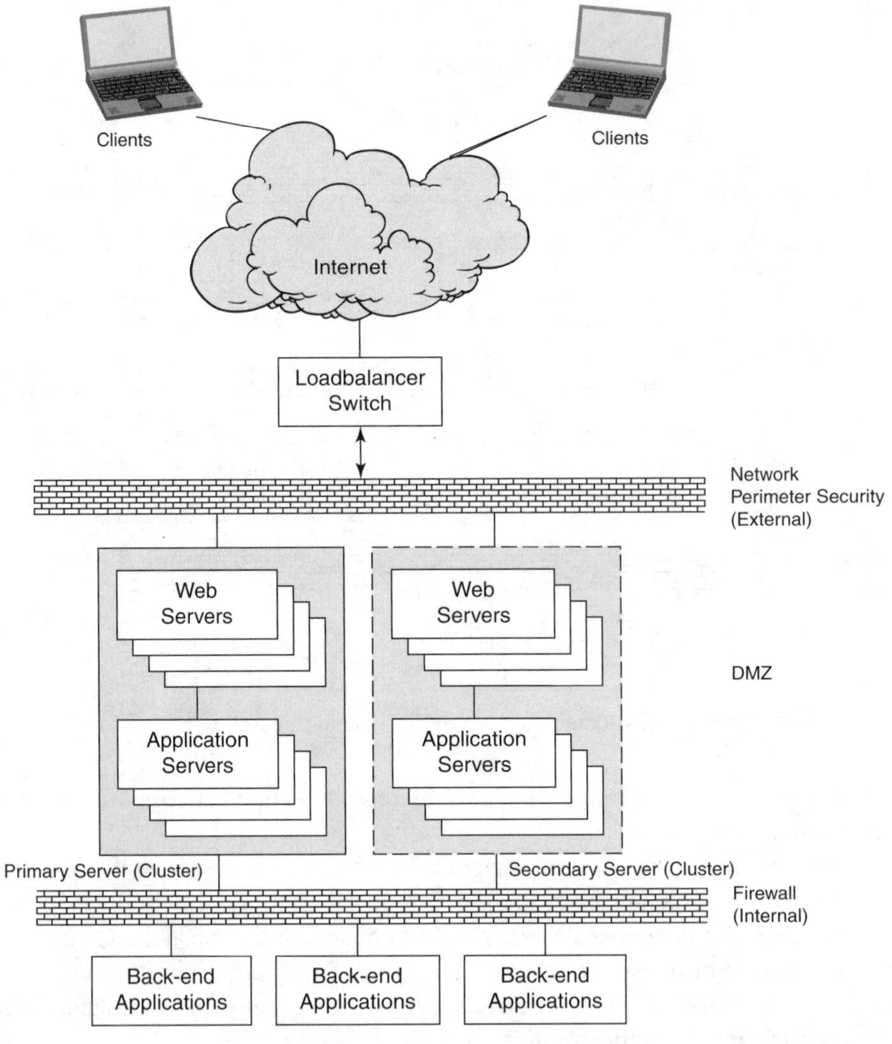

Figure 5–9 Logical network architecture for vertical scalability

structure may likely lead to an overall system failure. To overcome such failures, a high-availability (HA) cluster configuration becomes mandatory. This means that all the processes and the configuration associated with the Web servers and applications must be up and active in both primary and secondary servers of the HA cluster. The HA cluster provides resilience for the Web server and application-server infrastructure in the event of local hardware and software failures.

To decouple Web tier with applications, the Web server is configured with a reverse-proxy, which receives the HTTP requests from a client on the incoming network side and then forwards the request to the application server side to perform business application processing.

J2EE Web Services Security–Overview

Web services are based on the concept of Service-Oriented Architecture (SOA), which enables software components, including application functions, objects, and processes from different systems to be exposed as Web services. Web services represent a composable application solution model based on XML standards such as SOAP, WSDL, UDDI, and standards-based technologies. Web services are self-describing and modular applications that expose their business logic and functionality as services over the Internet. They also provide ways to find, subscribe, and invoke services accessible through the Internet by anyone, anytime, at any location, and using any platform. This ensures that the implementation of Web services applications is compliant with industry standards and enables interoperability and ease of integration with other standards-compliant Web services applications.

With the release of the J2EE 1.4 specification, the J2EE platform introduced newer technologies for enabling J2EE components to participate in Web services and built upon its earlier technologies for its Web services support. J2EE 1.4 is designed to facilitate development and deployment of Web services-based application solutions by supporting Web services providers, requestors, and registries. To develop and deliver Web services, the J2EE platform supports XML-based standards such as SOAP, WSDL, and UDDI using Java technologies such as JAX-RPC (Java API for XML-based RPC), SAAJ (SOAP With Attachment API for Java), and JAXR (Java API for XML Registry). The J2EE platform-based Web services also meet the interoperability and security requirements and standards specified by WS-I Basic profile 1.0.

From a security perspective, ensuring integrity, confidentiality, and trust of a Web service by applying a well-defined security model is very important for implementing Web services—for both providers and consumers. Many efforts are currently under way to develop an industry standard for securing XML-based Web services. The most prominent XML security standards (currently available as final or in progress) and their associated standards bodies are:

- XML Encryption—W3C
- XML Signature (XML DSIG)—W3C
- WS-Security (WSS)—OASIS
- Security Assertions Markup Language (SAML)—OASIS
- XML Access Control Markup Language (XACML)—OASIS
- XML Key Management Services (XKMS)—W3C
- Service Provisioning Markup Language—OASIS
- Extensible Rights Management Language (XrML)
- XML Common Biometric Format (XCBF)—OASIS

In J2EE-based Web services, defining a comprehensive Web services security model involves integration of Java security mechanisms and technologies with the evolving set of Web services security technologies. The J2EE Web service security model builds on the core J2EE security mechanisms and services used for securing Web-tier and EJB-tier components. It leverages the existing J2EE platform's authentication and access control mechanisms for securing Web services applications while maintaining the integrity and confidentiality of Web services interactions and messages. Within this context, the J2EE platform currently addresses Web services security with the following two goals:

Transport-level security: Securing the message transport and the network layer forms the foundation for Web services security, because we know Web services operate across endpoints as point-to-point or intermediary-based multi-hop topology. J2EE Web services offer end-to-end security by securing sessions with authentication, data integrity, and confidentiality. J2EE adopts HTTP over SSL/TLS (HTTPS) for communication and uses digital certificates to secure the data being sent as encrypted and then decrypted upon receipt prior to processing. Both the J2EE-based Web services requestor and provider encrypt all traffic before sending and receiving any data. For authentication, J2EE Web services leverage Web-tier authentication schemes such as Basic Authentication over SSL and Client-Certificate/Mutual Authentication between the service provider and the requester.

Message-level security: Securing the SOAP messages that are transmitted across Web services end-points becomes very important to providing security of a message and its elements. J2EE leverages XML Encryption and XML Signature standards-based security mechanisms to provide message-level integrity and confidentiality. Using JAX-RPC security mechanisms, the message is secured by encrypting and signing, which ensures tamper-proof transmission to the intended recipient and vice versa.

Both transport-level and message-level security are provided by the JWSDP toolkit that includes a Web services security implementation. At the time of writing this book, JAX-RPC supported OASIS WSS 1.0, also referred to as the WS-Security Standard. For more information and further details about Web services security and applied techniques, refer to Chapter 6, "Web Services Security–Standards and Technologies," and Chapter 11, "Securing Web Services–Design Strategies and Best Practices."

Summary

In this chapter, we discussed the J2EE architecture's security concepts and applied mechanisms. We took an in-depth look at the different security mechanisms facilitated by the J2EE architecture and how they contribute to the end-to-end security of an overall J2EE application solution. In particular, we saw how the J2EE architecture facilitates end-to-end security mechanisms and how it spans across all logical tiers—from the presentation tier to the Business tier, and from the Business tier to the Back-end resources. We also looked at how to enforce security mechanisms at the J2EE application level as well as Java and J2ME clients. We studied the different security mechanisms available for the different J2EE components, including JSPs, Servlets, EJBs, J2EE Connectors, JMS, and JDBC. We discussed the security mechanisms for enforcing authentication, authorization, security communication, integrity, confidentiality, and so on, and how they can be applied to the tiers and components during the application development and deployment phases. In particular, we focused on the following:

- J2EE architecture and its logical tiers
- J2EE security infrastructure and mechanisms
- J2EE authentication and authorization
- Users, groups and realms
- J2EE Web-tier security mechanisms
- J2EE Business-tier security mechanisms

- J2EE Integration-tier security mechanisms
- J2EE application deployment and network topologies
- J2EE Web services security–overview

In general, this chapter provided a J2EE security reference guide that discussed the architectures security details and the available mechanisms for building end-to-end security in a J2EE-based solution. For more information about J2EE security design strategies and best practices, refer to Chapter 9, "Securing the Web Tier: Design Strategies and Best Practices," and Chapter 10, "Securing the Business Tier–Design Strategies and Best Practices."

In the next chapter, we will explore Web services security standards and technologies.

References

[LiGong] Li Gong. "Java Security Architecture," in "Java™ 2 SDK, Standard Edition Documentation Version 1.4.2." Sun Microsystems, 2003.

http://java.sun.com/j2se/1.4.2/docs/guide/security/spec/security-spec.doc1.html and http://java.sun.com/j2se/1.4.2/docs/guide/security/spec/security-spec.doc2.html

[J2EE-WS-Blueprints] J2EE Blueprints: Designing Web Services with the J2EE Platform, 2nd Edition–Guidelines, Patterns, and Code for Java Web services.

http://java.sun.com/blueprints/guidelines/designing_webservices/

[J2EE-Blueprints] J2EE Blueprints: Designing Enterprise Applications with the J2EE Platform, 2nd Edition–Guidelines, Patterns, and Code for End-to-End Java applications.

http://java.sun.com/blueprints/guidelines/designing_enterprise_applications_2e/

[JWS] Ramesh Nagappan, Robert Skoczylas, et al. *Developing Java Web Services: Architecting and Developing Java Web Services*. Wiley, 2002

[CJP] Deepak Alur, John Crupi, Dan Malks. *Core Security Patterns: Best practices and Design Strategies*, Sun Microsystems, 2003.

[EJBTier] Pravin V. Tulachan. Developing EJB 2.0 Components, Sun Microsystems, 2002.

[WebTier] Marty Hall. More Servlets and Java Server Pages, Sun Microsystems, 2002.

[EJBTier2] Kevin Boone. Applied Enterprise Java Beans Technology, Sun Microsystems, 2003.

Part III

Web Services Security and Identity Management

Web Services Security–Standards and Technologies

Topics in This Chapter

- Web Services Architecture and Its Building Blocks
- Web Services Security–Core Issues
- Web Services Security Requirements
- Web Services Security Standards
- XML Signature
- XML Encryption
- XML Key Management System (XKMS)
- OASIS Web Services Security (WS-Security)
- WS-I Basic Security Profile
- Java-Based Web Services Security Providers
- XML-Aware Security Appliances

Chapter 6

Web Services Security

The emergence of Web services introduced us to a new paradigm for enabling exchange of information across the Internet using open industry-standards and standards-based technologies. Adopting Web services and adhering to its standards facilitate building service-oriented and on-demand applications that can be discovered, subscribed to, and consumed over the Internet. The clients invoking these services do not need to be aware of their target service provider system environment or its underlying implementation model. Due to the flexibility of using platform-neutral standards, such as XML and adopting Internet-based protocols, Web services allow exposing application components such as services and making them available for access by any application, any platform, or any device—at any location. Web services enable services integration between the applications via interoperability and allow application-to-application communication for business collaboration and business process management across the Internet. With the increasing adoption, acceptance, and availability of Web services application infrastructure tools, Web services promise a new services industry that provides business services over the Internet.

Applying security and establishing trust among Web services or between a Web service and its consumer has caused new challenges, some of which remain unaddressed by traditional security methods and technologies. Because Web services can be dynamically located, subscribed to, and consumed using a wide range of platforms, including handheld devices, the Web services provider must facilitate a standardized security mechanism that can be accessed by the service requesters using heterogeneous platforms and devices. For example, patients viewing their medical records via Web services should not be constrained or impacted by whether they are using a Web browser client, a browser-capable device, or a stand-alone application as long as the service requester client on which patients view records is able to use the required message transport and apply relevant security mechanisms with the Web service provider.

Building a comprehensive security model for Web services requires the integration of currently available security technologies with the evolving set of XML security standards and technologies. This security model is an amalgamation of standards and technologies relevant to Web services security (such as message-level and transport-layer security) with application-specific security processes (such as authentication, access control, rules, and trust). Ensuring the integrity, confidentiality, and security of a Web service by applying a standards-based end-to-end security model from the ground up becomes important for both the Web services providers and their consumers.

In this chapter, we conduct an in-depth study of the architecture, the security threats and vulnerabilities, the security requirements, and the evolving standards for Web services that contribute to building end-to-end security in Web services. We also introduce the Java-based Web services infrastructure providers and their support to these evolving standards.

Web Services Architecture and Its Building Blocks

The Web services architecture is a technology stack that identifies standards-based application components, which ensures interoperability among Web services providers and requesters. It adopts service-oriented architecture (SOA) concepts using standards-based messages and communication protocols. Web-services architecture consists of many layers of interrelated logical components built using standards-based technologies. The logical components representing the layers provide standardized components and communication for defining and describing the services, discovering and subscribing to the services, transporting for service communication, aggregating a set of services, and collaborating with services. They also facilitate standards-based mechanisms for building end-to-end security, services provisioning and management, and delivering other QoS such as reliability, scalability, manageability, and availability.

Figure 6–1 depicts the Web services architecture technology stack with its different layers.

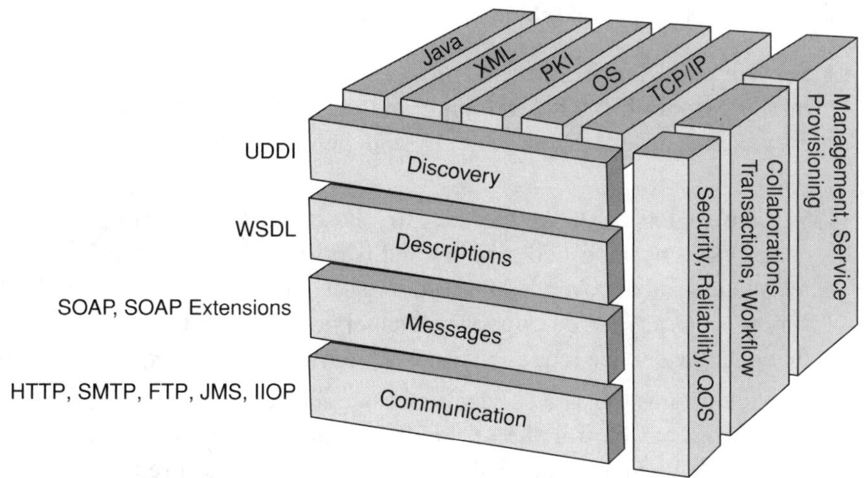

Figure 6–1 Technology stack of Web services architecture

Before jumping into the core standards and technologies of the technology stack, let's take a look at the fundamental operational model of Web services.

Web Services Operational Model

Web services can be conceptualized as a simple operational model with a standards-based communication model. The communication model uses three distinct roles and relationships that define Web-service providers and users. Figure 6–2, illustrates these relationships.

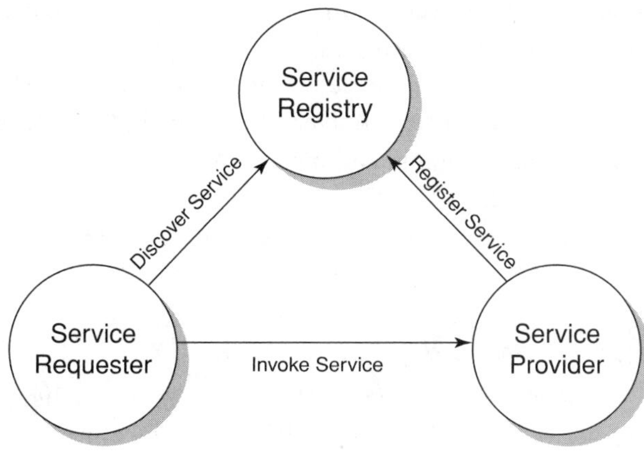

Figure 6–2 Web services operational model

The operational roles and relationships are defined as follows:

- **Service provider**: The service provider hosts the Web services and is primarily responsible for developing and deploying the Web services. The provider also defines the services and publishes them with the service registry.
- **Service registry**: The service registry hosts the lookup information and descriptions of published services and is primarily responsible for service registration and discovery of the Web services. The registry stores and lists the various service types, descriptions of the services, and locations of the services that help the service requesters find and subscribe to the required services.
- **Service requester**: The service requester acts as the Web services client, who is responsible for the service invocation. The requester locates the Web service using the service registry, invokes the required services, and executes them from the service provider.

Core Web Services Standards

A typical Web services architecture-based solution relies on de facto Web-services standards such as XML, SOAP, WSDL, and UDDI, and on industry-standard protocols such as HTTP and SMTP. These standards-based technologies form the foundation for building a Web services architecture and enabling Web services. Let's take a closer look at these standards, their role, and how they are represented in Web services architecture.

Extensible Markup Language (XML)

XML forms the basis for all Web-services standards. XML is endorsed by the W3C (World Wide Web Consortium) as a standard data format for structuring data and content, and for exchanging electronic documents. XML has already been widely accepted as the *de facto* universal language for exchanging information between applications, systems, and devices across the Internet. In the Web-services architectural model, XML plays a vital role as the common wire format in all forms of communication for expressing complex data structures. Another substantial benefit of XML is its ability to handle international character sets.

Simple Object Access Protocol (SOAP)

The Simple Object Access Protocol (SOAP) is a standard for a lightweight XML-based messaging protocol. In the core of Web-services communication, SOAP enables the exchange of information between two or more peers. SOAP enables them to communicate with each other in a decentralized, distributed application environment. SOAP provides transport bindings on top of various Internet protocols such as HTTP, SMTP, and FTP. SOAP uses XML as the message format and uses a set of encoding rules for representing data as messages. Although SOAP is used as a messaging protocol in Web services, it can also operate on a request-response model by exposing the application functionality using SOAP/RPC-based remote procedural calls. Like XML, SOAP is independent of the application object model, language, and running platforms or devices.

The structural format of a SOAP message contains the following elements, as illustrated in Figure 6–3:

- Envelope
- Header (optional)
- Body
- Attachments (optional)

Figure 6–3 represents the structure of a SOAP message with attachments. Typically, a SOAP message is represented by a SOAP envelope and with zero or more attachments. The SOAP message envelope contains the header and body of the message, and the SOAP message attachments enable the message to contain data such as XML and non-XML data (like text or binary files). In a SOAP message, the SOAP header represents the processing semantics and provides mechanisms

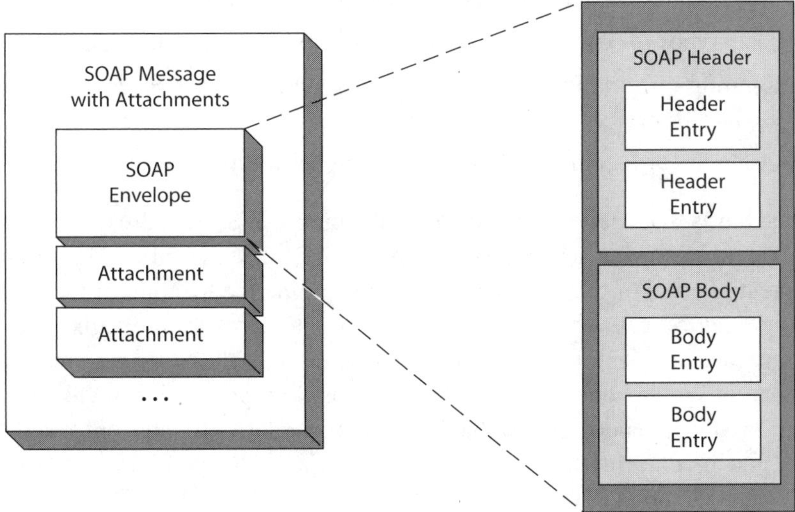

Figure 6–3 Structure of a SOAP message

for adding features and defining high-level functionalities such as security, transactions, priority, and auditing. The SOAP body contains information defining an RPC call or business documents in XML, and any XML data required to be part of the message during communication. It is important to note that a SOAP message package is constructed using the MIME Multipart/Related structure to separate and identify the different parts of the message.

SOAP is endorsed by the W3C and key industry vendors such as Sun Microsystems, IBM, HP, SAP, Oracle, and Microsoft. These vendors have announced their support by participating in the W3C's XML Protocol Working Group. To find out the current status of SOAP from the activities of this group, refer to the W3C Web site at http://www.w3.org/2000/xp/Group/.

Web Services Definition Language (WSDL)

The Web Services Definition Language (WSDL) standard is an XML representation for describing the services as a collection of operations and its access information. In the core of the Web services architecture, WSDL plays a vital role as a metadata language for defining Web services. It describes how service providers and requesters communicate with one another. WSDL describes the Web-services functionalities offered by the service provider, where the service is located, and how to access the service. Usually, the service provider creates Web services by generating WSDL from its exposed business applications. A WSDL definition represents the following about a Web service:

- Operations and interfaces describing the exposed functions.
- Data types to represent the requests and responses of messages.
- Binding information about the protocol to be used for accessing the specified Web service.
- Address for locating and invoking the specified Web service.

Once the WSDL definition is created, the public WSDL address for lookup is published in a Web-services registry such as UDDI (see the following section) so that potential users of the Web service can determine the location of the Web service, the function calls that it supports, and how to invoke these calls. The Web-service requesters use this WSDL information to build the SOAP requests or any other type of request based on the supported binding protocol to invoke the Web service. WSDL is endorsed by the W3C as a standard. To find out more about WSDL and its current status, refer to the official W3C Web site for WSDL at http://www.w3c.org/TR/wsdl/.

Universal Description, Discovery, and Integration (UDDI)

Universal Description, Discovery, and Integration (UDDI) defines standard interfaces and mechanisms for use by the electronic registries that store and publish descriptions of XML-based Web services. UDDI is quite similar to the "Yellow Pages" or a telephone directory in which business services and products are classified and listed. UDDI allows the registering and categorizing of Web services in a general-purpose registry that users communicate with to discover and locate registered services. Querying a UDDI registry for a service returns the location of the WSDL descriptions that set forth the service interfaces of a Web services provider. Using the WSDL description, the service requester can construct a SOAP client interface that can communicate with the service provider. By communicating with UDDI registries, the service requesters query for services, locate services, and then invoke them by sending SOAP messages. The UDDI registries can be either private (within an organization) or public (servicing the whole Internet community). UDDI is endorsed by OASIS as a standard. To find out more information about UDDI and its current status, refer to the official OASIS Web site for UDDI at http://www.oasis-open.org/committees/uddi-spec/tcspecs.

Web Services Communication Styles

The Web services architecture revolves around the interaction models based on the message representation and interaction. The message representation and interaction models focus on the message structure in terms of mechanisms for message routing and delivery using RPC or document-based communications. These interaction models use synchronous or messaging-based synchronous or asynchronous communication, which need to be understood before Web services are designed and implemented.

RPC Style Web Services

The RPC-based communication model defines a request–response-based synchronous communication. When the client initiates a request, the client sends a SOAP message that provides parameters in method calls to the services exposed by the server. The clients invoke the services by sending parameter values to the services that execute the required methods in the server, which then sends back the return values. The server receiving the request translates it into the back-end application method or object. The client waits until a response is sent back before continuing any operation. It is quite similar to implementing CORBA or RMI communication.

Document Style Web Services

With document style interaction, XML documents are transmitted between the client service requester and the services provider. The XML documents exchanged do not map to back-end method calls of the service provider or the requester. In a typical scenario, the client service requester sends a message that include the business document to the Web service provider rather than sending a set of parameters or procedural calls. The service provider receives the document, processes it, and then may or may not return a message. The document style communication is typically used in conjunction with asynchronous messaging protocols to provide guaranteed and reliable message delivery and to support multi-hop communication based on intermediaries.

Web Services Security–Core Issues

Security has become the most important focus in Web services because it is necessary to ensure that exposed Web services–based business transactions and processes are secure, reliable, and available to the service consumers. From a business perspective, it becomes mandatory to protect and safeguard the exposed services in order to achieve and maintain customer confidence as well as avoid the dangers of being a Web services provider or a consumer. To deliver Web services security, it becomes essential to adopt XML-based security standards and technologies to support security services such as authentication, authorization, trust policies, transport security, message-level security, single-sign-on, identity management, and identity federation.

Before delving into Web services security standards and technologies, it is important to understand the known security threats, vulnerabilities, and risks associated with Web services.

Web Services–Threats, Vulnerabilities, and Risks

As Web services have evolved, they have offered some compelling benefits over other Web-based applications. However, these advantages come along with known security threats and risks. These risks involve threats to the entire host network, including Web-services providers, consumers, intermediaries, data, users, applications, and systems infrastructure. While developing Web services architecture, it is important to proactively investigate and pinpoint known security loopholes. Then, mitigation strategies must be applied, and countermeasures must be implemented in order to fortify the exposed services.

Let's take a look at those known threats, vulnerabilities, and risk factors that will influence the decision on how to secure a Web services architecture and implementation.

Denial of Service (DoS) / XML Denial of Service (XML-DoS)

Denial of Service (DoS) attacks are attempts by an unauthorized user or a hacker to disrupt a Web-services provider and its exposed services by flooding them with useless traffic that consumes host system resources such as CPU, memory, network bandwidth, and so forth. These are fake service requests that are designed to take a long time to process, intended to generate faults, or targeted at preventing authorized users from accessing the service. DoS attacks result in significant losses due to outage of provider resources and exposed services. These attacks usually exploit the weaknesses in the application architecture and the host systems' infrastructure.

XML Web services were designed to use standard TCP/IP ports for XML traffic, port 80 for HTTP, and port 443 for SSL. Traditional firewalls are quite ineffective for inspecting XML traffic, because they do not provide support for detecting content-level threats. XML-DoS attacks are content-level vulnerabilities: an attacker makes use of malicious XML messages, manipulates parts of an XML document, or sends an oversized XML payload that can cause load-intensive operations at the target Web services endpoint. This causes those systems to crash or to consume an excessive amount of system resources, both of which result in the inability to respond to further requests or perform operations.

Man-in-the-Middle

Man-in-the-Middle (MITM) is an attack where the hacker acts as a Web-service intermediary that intercepts the communication and then accesses and modifies the messages between two communicating parties without the communicating parties knowing that the messages have been intercepted.

Message Injection and Manipulation

Message injection and manipulation is an attack on message integrity between a Web-service provider and the consumer. This is carried out by hackers who insert, modify, or delete parts of messages or attachments, which can push an XML parser to endless loops or transaction commit failures. The attacker also makes use of recursive elements or XML expressions (based on XPATH or XQUERY) or unrelated message attachments to perform unintended processing functions that lead to an endpoint failure. This attack usually comes after a MITM attack where the intruding intermediary generates forged service requests or sends forged server responses.

Session Hijacking and Theft

Some Web-services providers rely on using session identifiers during communication to identify service requesters. This usually leads to a potential security hole where a hacker can steal and use the session identifier information to hijack a session between the services provider and the consumer. In this attack, the hijacker sniffs the conversation or uses packet-capturing capabilities to obtain the session information from the communicating client peer. Based on the session identifier, the hijacker constructs forged service requests that affect the operational efficiency of a Web-services provider or a requester.

Identity Spoofing

Identity spoofing is an attack where a hacker uses the identity of a trusted service requester and sabotages the security of the services provider using forged service requests with malicious information. In this case, the services provider finds normal status and no security breach in the system. Although it is not trivial, from a business perspective, spoofing can cause significant losses due to false identity claims, refund fraud, and related issues.

Message Confidentiality

The threat to message confidentiality comes from eavesdroppers or after an intrusion attack by unauthorized entities. It is very important to use appropriate mechanisms to protect message confidentiality throughout the life cycle of Web services operations, including messages in transit or in storage. If these mechanisms are not used, messages will be available for viewing and interception by unintended recipients and intermediaries.

Replay Attacks

A replay attack is a form of DoS attack where an intruder forges a service request that has been previously sent to the service provider. In this case, the intruder fraudulently duplicates a previously sent request and repeatedly sends it for the purpose of causing the target Web services endpoint to generate faults that can cause failure and shutdown of the target's operations. Hackers usually use this attack as a first step in accessing the services provider in order to generate a fake session or to obtain critical information required for accessing services.

Message Validation Abuses

Most Web services security functions rely on XML–schema-based message validation for XML Encryption/decryption, XML Signature validation and security-tokens verification. These tasks generally require resource intensive XML processing. Hackers abuse message validation mechanisms by sending malformed messages or abnormal payload of encrypted content or non-compliant messages that can cause endless loops that compromise service performance and contribute to transaction failures.

XML Schema Tampering

In a Web services scenario, XML Schemas play a vital role in defining XML vocabularies in an XML message. They help to verify that an XML message is well-formed and valid. XML Schemas are liable to attacks because they are usually made publicly accessible. Using that as a potential loophole, the attacker alters the externally referenced XML schemas with erroneous and inconsistent information. This affects Web services endpoint with processing overheads and failures related to message validation and verification.

WSDL and UDDI Attacks

WSDL descriptions and public UDDI registries provide most service-related information in a self-describing XML format that reveals the service location and its exposed operations. The attacker makes use of publicly accessible UDDI or WSDL information to identify the service provider location and then performs a number of operations with arbitrary input and output parameters using malformed data. The attacker may also inflict changes by tampering with WSDL descriptions that affect creation of client-side artifacts to support service requesters.

Furthermore, from an end-to-end Web services perspective, the complexity of security threats and risks adds more difficulty to the tasks of user authentication, access control rules and policies, non-repudiation, identity management, service provisioning, and so forth. In real-world Web services, it becomes very important to address these security issues so that they do not interfere with the benefits and successes of Web services adoption in business organizations.

Web Services Security Requirements

The key factors related to security must be addressed in the Web services architecture as core security requirements. This ensures the ability to deliver a secure environment for conducting business transactions, processes, and collaboration. It is also important for Web services security to build on existing application security infrastructures and to integrate with them.

Based on those critical factors, the key requirements that must be addressed in order to be able to describe and deliver end-to-end security architecture for Web services solutions are discussed in the following sections. Each of these security requirements plays an important role in designing a Web services architecture and each is represented by an evolving set of Web-services security standards and security infrastructure providers.

Authentication

Authentication enforces the verification and validation of the identities and credentials exchanged between the Web-services provider and the consumer. The initiating service requester must be authenticated to prove its identity with reliable credentials. The credentials may be X.509 digital certificates, Kerberos tickets, or any security token used to validate the identity of the service requester. Depending upon the security requirements, it is also possible to deploy mutual authentication mechanisms where both service requester and the service provider exchange their credentials and validate them before initiating the communication. Using authentication mechanisms alleviates and mitigates the risks associated with man-in-the-middle, identity spoofing, and message-replay attacks.

Authorization and Entitlement

After authentication, it becomes crucial to control and monitor access to the service provider resources. Authorization defines the rules and policies associated with the required access control to the resources. Upon successful authentication, a service requester requiring access to business services should be provided with specific access rights to resources. Service requesters' rights to resources should be monitored, and they should be granted or denied as appropriate.

Auditability and Traceability

Auditing and tracing allow monitoring and recording of the relevant life-cycle events and transactions taken by the services provider based on the requests made by the consumer. Auditing and tracing ensure that the initiating clients are accountable for their requested operations and provide authentic proof of the originating request or response. The audit trail provides information that can be used to monitor resources, system break-ins, failed logins, and breach attempts. It also helps identify security loopholes, violations, spoofing, and those users who are attempting to circumvent security, either intentionally or unintentionally.

Data Integrity

Data integrity plays a vital role in ensuring that messages exchanged between the communicating parties are accurate, complete, and not modified or altered during transit or while in storage. The use of digital signature mechanisms ensures data integrity by securing Web services-based business transactions from modification. Ensuring data integrity guards Web-services communication across endpoints and intermediaries from MITM intrusions and interference that may damage data.

Data Confidentiality

Data privacy and confidentiality assure that the actual data transmitted are protected from the prying eyes of unintended recipients. Data privacy and confidentiality are made possible through cryptographic algorithms that convert the data to an encrypted form of message that unauthorized viewers aren't able to understand. Ensuring confidentiality guarantees that data transmitted is not accessible for viewing by interception or interference during transmission between endpoints and through intermediaries.

Non-repudiation

Non-repudiation ensures that the communicating parties accept a committed transaction. This prevents the service requesters from wrongfully claiming that the transaction has never occurred. Ensuring non-repudiation can be done using many approaches such as enabling logging and recording trails of the transaction exchanged, using timestamps on message requests and responses and using digital signatures to ensure that credentials of communicating parties are authentic.

Availability and Service Continuity

Availability and Service continuity are mandatory requirements to ensure the Web services infrastructure is capable of sustaining operations after a security breach or failure. These requirements can be achieved by introducing high-availability mechanisms such as load balancing, fault-tolerance and fail-over protection.

From a security standpoint, implementing high-availability mechanisms guarantees service continuity after failures.

Single Sign-on and Delegation

Single sign-on plays a vital role in Web Services environments. Because Web services allow integrating heterogeneous applications to communicate with each other using standards-based technologies, it becomes mandatory to facilitate a universal mechanism to support single sign-on, decentralized access control lists and delegated administration capabilities. In case of Web services aggregation scenario, it also becomes important to facilitate global sign-on that allows access to multiple Web services providers. This means all participating service providers share a common SSO token or a trusted credential that ensures global sign-on access and also a global logout for exiting from them.

Identity and Policy Management

Web services are required to make use of identities, trust policies, and their access privileges information from internal and external partner applications. This mandates a standardized way of sharing identities and policies information among disparate authentication and authorization systems spread across their trust boundaries. With federated identity management, a Web services provider can make its services available securely to their partners by establishing trusted partnerships and sharing their identities and policies. This ensures an authenticated identity to be recognized by partner service endpoints and enables the user associated with that identity to access privileged services across multiple partner services.

Security Interoperability

Ensuring and demonstrating security interoperability is another core Web services requirement to guarantee that the adopted security mechanisms and countermeasures seamlessly work together during communication. This means that the Web service providers and consumers are making use of standards-based protocols following security interoperability guidelines defined by the WS-I Security profile. The Web services and their security providers must allow security interoperability at all levels, including transport-level security, message-level security, and other supporting security infrastructures.

Web Services Security Standards

Because Web-services solutions are implemented using standards-based technologies, it is important to adopt standards-based security mechanisms that facilitate and support interoperability and remain independent of operating systems, application infrastructures, and programming languages.

With participation from leading technology companies, industry-standard initiatives on Web-services security specifications are under way. The most prominent XML security specifications for Web services, currently available as final or in progress with various standards bodies, are as follows:

- XML Signature (XML DSIG)
- XML Encryption (XML ENC)
- XML Key Management Services (XKMS)
- OASIS Web Services Security (WS-Security)

Based on these specifications, a long list of technology vendors provide security infrastructure solutions for XML-based Web services. In addition to the preceding standards, the following specifications provide support for Web services, particularly in identity management.

- Security Assertions Markup Language (SAML)
- XML Access Control Markup Language (XACML)
- Service Provisioning Markup Language
- Extensible Rights Management Language (XrML)
- XML Common Biometric Format (XCBF)

These supporting specifications on identity management are discussed in Chapter 7, "Identity Architecture and Its Technologies."

Let's now take an in-depth look at these core Web services security specifications and usage scenarios.

XML Signature

The XML signature specification forms the basis for securely exchanging XML documents and conducting secure business transactions. The goal of XML signature is to ensure data integrity, message authentication, and non-repudiation of services. It is an evolving standard for creating and representing digital signatures using XML syntax and processing for XML-based data communication. XML signature evolved from the joint effort by the W3C and IETF working groups. To find out the current status of the XML signature specification from the W3C working group activities, refer to the W3C Web site at www.w3.org/Signature.

Motivation of XML Signature

The process of applying digital signature is analogous to a physical handwriting signature. It ensures that a message recipient can verify that the signed message from a sender originated from the sender and has not been altered or tampered with during transit or storage. In XML-based data exchange and business transactions, applying digital signatures signs the complete message or XML document. This removes the flexibility of signing specific parts and applying changes to a document that has multiple recipients. In a business scenario involving multiple parties, applying a digital signature to a complete document restricts the document to one party, and adding any further modifications by that party invalidates the originally signed document.

To meet the above requirements, XML-based digital signature mechanisms are designed to facilitate data integrity in secure XML communication and to provide support for involving multiple parties. In a nutshell, XML signature defines the syntax and processing rules that provide the flexibility to add multiple signatures to the different fragments of an XML document. Signatures intended for multiple parties associated with the content of the document can thus be preserved.

The Anatomy of XML Signature

XML signature allows signing any sort of digital content or data objects, such as XML or HTML documents, binary data, and images. The signatures are applied to the content via an indirection. The content requiring signing is digested using a message digest algorithm (such as DSA-SHA1 or RSA-SHA1), and the resulting hash value is placed in an XML element. The XML element is digested and cryptographically signed. The signed form of the XML element represents the XML signature.

Representing XML Signatures

According to the XML signature specification, based on the data and associated XML signature, there are three ways to represent XML signatures.

- **Enveloped signatures**: The XML signature is embedded within the original XML content, where the XML signature is represented.

Example 6–1 Enveloped signature

```
<xmldocument no="xd001">
     <business-element/>
     <Signature>
          ...
          <Reference URI="xd001"/>
          ...
     </Signature>
</xmldocument>
```

- **Enveloping signatures**: The original XML content is embedded within the XML signature, where the XML content is represented as a child element within an <object> or identified as a URI <Reference> in the parent XML signature.

Example 6–2 Enveloping signature

```
<Signature>
     ...
     <Reference URI = "xyz"/>
     ...
     <Object Id="xd001">
          <xmldocument>
               <business-element/>
          </xmldocument>
     </Object>
</Signature>
```

- **Detached signatures**: The XML content resides external to the signature and is identified via a URI or transform. It applies to separate data objects external to the signature document and for the data objects residing within the original XML document as sibling elements.

Example 6–3 Detached signature

```
<xmldocument>
   <Signature>
       ...
         <Reference URI=
   "http://www.coresecuritypatterns.com/xmldocument/"/>
         ...
   </Signature>
     <business-elemt/>
</xmldocument>
```

Let's take a closer look at how to represent an XML signature, its structural elements, and its features.

Representation of XML Signature Structure and Elements

XML digital signatures are represented using XML elements. They are identified by a <Signature> element, where the original data is digested, signed, and embedded within the data structure. Example 6–4 is the structure of an XML signature represented by <Signature ?> as its root element. "?" in the element denotes zero or one occurrence, "+" denotes one or more occurrences, and "*" denotes zero or more occurrences).

Example 6–4 XML Signature–core structure and elements


```
<Signature ID?>
   <SignedInfo>
     <CanonicalizationMethod/>
        <SignatureMethod/>
          (<Reference URI?>
          (<Transforms>)?
            <DigestMethod>
               <DigestValue>
            </Reference>)+
        </SignedInfo>
    <SignatureValue>
    (<KeyInfo>)?
    (<Object ID?>)*
</Signature>
```

<Signature>

The <Signature> element is a parent element that identifies a complete XML signature within a given context. It contains the sequence of child elements: <SignedInfo>, <SignatureValue>, <KeyInfo>, and <Object>. Also, an optional Id attribute can be applied to the <Signature> element as an identifier. This is useful in the case of multiple <Signature> instances within a single context.

<SignatureValue>

The <SignatureValue> element contains the actual value of the digital signature, which is the digested value of <SignedInfo> element. The value is base64 encoded.

<SignedInfo>

The <SignedInfo> element contains the original data that is actually signed. The contents of this element also include a sequence of elements: <CanonicalizationMethod>, <SignatureMethod>, and one or more <Reference> elements. The <CanonicalizationMethod> and <SignatureMethod> elements describe the type of canonicalization and signature algorithms used in the generation of a <SignatureValue>. The <SignatureValue> element contains the digital signature value that is the digest of <SignedInfo> element. The <Reference> element defines the actual data using a data stream that is eventually hashed and transformed. The actual data stream is referenced by a URI.

<CanonicalizationMethod>

The <CanonicalizationMethod> element defines the representation of the physical structure by specifying the canonicalization algorithm applied to the <SignedInfo> element. To support security and interoperability, the XML signature specification recommends the use of XML-based canonicalization algorithms instead of text-based canonicalization algorithms (such as CRLF and charset normalization). It also mandates that the <SignedInfo> element be presented to the XML canonicalization methods as an XPath node set definition, mentioning the <SignedInfo>, its descendants, attributes, and namespace nodes of the <SignedInfo> element.

<SignatureMethod>

The <SignatureMethod> element specifies the cryptographic algorithm used for generating the signature. The algorithm also identifies other cryptographic functions involved in the signature operation, such as hash, public-key algorithms, MACs, and padding.

<Reference>

The <Reference> element contains the digest value of the data object. It optionally carries identifiers (URI) to the original data objects, including the list of transforms specifying transformations applied prior to computing the digest.

<Transforms>

The optional <Transforms> element contains an ordered list of <Transform> elements. It defines the steps required for obtaining the original data object that was digested. Each <Transform> serves as a transformation input to the next <Transform>. The input to the first <Transform> is the result of dereferencing the URI attribute of the <Reference> element. The output of the last <Transform> is the input for the <DigestMethod> algorithm.

<DigestMethod>

The <DigestMethod> contains the digest algorithm to be applied to the signed object. URIs identify the algorithms.

<DigestValue>

The <DigestValue> element contains the base64-encoded value of the digest.

<KeyInfo>

The optional <KeyInfo> element provides the ability to verify the signature using the packaged verification key. It contains keys, key names, certificates, and related information. This element also enables the integration of trust semantics within an application that utilizes XML signatures. The <KeyInfo> consists of a child element named <KeyValue>. The <KeyValue> element carries a raw RSA or DSA public key with child elements <RSAKeyValue> and <DSAKeyValue>, respectively. All information represented in the <KeyValue> element is represented in base64 encoding.

<Object>

The optional <Object> element is used mostly in enveloping signatures where the data object is part of the <Signature> element. The digest of the data object in this case would contain the <object> element along with its associated data objects. The <Object> elements also include optional MIME type, ID, and encoding attributes.

<Manifest>

The optional <Manifest> element is quite similar to the <SignedInfo> element in that it contains a list of <Reference> elements. In the case of the <Manifest> element, the processing of the <Reference> element is defined by the application.

<SignatureProperties>

The optional <SignatureProperties> element can contain additional information about the signature. This may include date, timestamp, serial number of cryptographic hardware, and other application-specific attributes.

Algorithms

In XML signature, algorithms are associated with an identifier attribute carrying a URI for <DigestMethod>, <SignatureMethod>, <CanonicalizationMethod>, and <Transform> elements. Most algorithms use implicit parameters such as key information for <SignatureMethod>. Some algorithms use explicit parameters with descriptive element names specific to the algorithm and within the XML signature or algorithm-specific namespace.

Let's take a brief look at the algorithms and their URIs discussed in the XML signature specification.

Signature Algorithms

Signature algorithms are used for creating the XML signature for given data objects. The algorithms used are a combination of message digests and public-key cryptography algorithms. The XML signature specification defines two signature algorithms, DSA and PKCS1 (RSA-SHA1), and their associated URIs. Both DSA and PKCS1 (RSA-SHA1) take no explicit parameters.

- **DSA**: DSA-SHA1, also referred to as DSA algorithm, is specified with a URI identifier, http://www.w3.org/2000/09/xmldsig#dsa-sha1. For example, DSA is represented in <SignatureMethod> element as shown in Example 6–5.

  Example 6–5 Signature method using DSA-SHA1

  ```
  <SignatureMethod>
       Algorithm=http://www.w3.org/2000/09/xmldsig#dsa-sha1
    </SignatureMethod>
  ```

  The output of the DSA algorithm consists of a pair of integers referred to as an r,s pair, and the signature value contains the base64-encoded value of the concatenation of two-octet streams of the octet-encoding of the r,s pair. The integer-to-octet stream conversion is done according to RFC2437 (PKCS1) specifications. The resulting <SignatureValue> element of the DSA algorithm will look as shown in Example 6–6.

  Example 6–6 Signature value output using the DSA algorithm

  ```
  <SignatureValue>
       BB4jRfH1bfJFj0JtFVtLotttzYyA==AyAorytrtur
    </SignatureValue>
  ```

- **RSA-SHA1**: The RSA-SHA1, also referred to as PKCS1, algorithm is specified with a URI identifier, http://www.w3.org/2000/09/xmldsig#rsa-sha1. For example, RSA is represented in <SignatureMethod> element as shown in Example 6–7.

Example 6–7 Signature method using RSA-SHA1

```
<SignatureMethod>
          Algorithm=http://www.w3.org/2000/09/xmldsig#rsa-sha1
        </SignatureMethod>
```


The <SignatureValue> element of the RSA-SHA1 is represented using base64 encoding, and the octet string is computed according to RFC 2437 [PKCS1, section 8.1.1: Signature generation for the RSASSA-PKCS1-v1_5 signature scheme].

Canonicalization Algorithms

Two equivalent XML documents can possibly differ on representations such as physical structure, attribute ordering, character encoding, or insignificant placing of white space. In an XML signature, it is extremely important to prove the equivalence of XML documents while representing digital signatures, checksums, identifiers, version control, and conformance. The XML Canonicalization algorithms allow generating the canonical form of an XML document, which can be correctly compared, byte-by-byte, to canonical forms of other documents. In XML signature, the XML documents need to be canonicalized before they are signed to ensure the representation is logically byte-by-byte identical with equivalent XML documents. If it is not canonicalized, the validation of an XML signature will potentially fail due to any difference in its physical structure or its representation. The XML signature specification defines two canonicalization algorithms:

- Canonical XML (omits comments)
  Identifier: http://www.w3.org/TR/2001/REC-xml-c14n-20010315
- Canonical XML with comments
  Identifier: http://www.w3.org/TR/2001/REC-xml-c14n- 20010315#WithComments

For example, the representation of the <CanonicalizationMethod> element in the signature will look as shown in Example 6–8.

Example 6–8 Canonicalization method using a canonicalization algorithm

```
<CanonicalizationMethod>
  Algorithm=http://www.w3.org/TR/2001/REC-xml-c14n-20010315
</CanonicalizationMethod>
```

Transform Algorithms

Applying transformations is mostly used to support canonicalization and to make sure the actual data object is processed, filtered, and represented in the right fashion before it is signed. Using transform algorithms, the XML signature can take an ordered list of transformations for a data object as required. Transform algorithms can be applied to the data objects referred to in the <Reference> element or the output of a previous <Transform> element. The XML signature specification defines three transform algorithms:

- XSLT Transform
  Identifier: http://www.w3.org/TR/1999/REC-xslt-19991116
- Xpath Transform
  Identifier: http://www.w3.org/TR/1999/REC-xpath-19991116
- Enveloped Signature
  Identifier: http://www.w3.org/2000/09/xmldsig#enveloped-signature

For example, the representation of <Transforms> element in the XML signature will look as shown in Example 6–9.

Example 6–9 Representing Transformation algorithms in XML signature

```
<Transforms>
 <Transform
  Algorithm="http://www.w3.org/TR/1999/REC-xpath-19991116">
 </Transform>
</Transforms>
```

XML Signature Examples

Let's consider an example scenario of a financial institution that hosts a Web-services-based solution for delivering banking services for its business customers. The business customer uses a service requester application that sends and receives messages from the service provider. Based on requests, the service provider responds with an account statement for the customer that includes critical information, such as account balances, credit card transactions, and other financial data. Using XML signature, the services provider guarantees that all Web-services-based transactions transmitted to and from the service requester remain authentic and have not been altered or tampered with during transit.

Let's use the XML document shown in Example 6–10, a financial statement of a business customer for applying XML signature and its types.

Example 6–10 XML Document representing a financial statement

```
<BusinessAccountSummary id="ABCD54321">
 <Customer id="45678943">
  <BusinessName>ABZ Company</BusinessName>
  <Address>1 ABZ Drive, Newton, CA</Address>
   <PrimaryContact>R Nagappan</PrimaryContact>
  <BusinessAccount id="BS-12345">
     <AccountBalance>950000.00</AccountBalance>
   </BusinessAccountNo>
   <CreditCard no="1233-3456-4567">
     <CreditBalance>45000.00</CreditBalance>
   </CreditCard>
    <CreditCard no="4230-3456-9877">
     <CreditBalance>6000.00</CreditBalance>
   </CreditCard>
      </Customer>
<BusinessAccountSummary>
```

Enveloped Signature

In the enveloped signature, the XML signature resides within the signed document. Example 6–11 represents the enveloped signature, where the XML signature is embedded as part of the signed XML document.

Example 6–11 Signed XML document using enveloped signature

```
<BusinessAccountSummary date="01/01/2004" id="ABCD54321">
  <Customer id="45678943">
    <BusinessName>ABZ Company</BusinessName>
     <Address>1 ABZ Drive, Newton, CA</Address>
      <PrimaryContact>R Nagappan</PrimaryContact>
     <BusinessAccount id="BS-12345">
        <AccountBalance>950000.00</AccountBalance>
      </BusinessAccountNo>
      <CreditCard no="1233-3456-4567">
        <CreditBalance>45000.00</CreditBalance>
      </CreditCard>
      <CreditCard no="4230-3456-9877">
        <CreditBalance>6000.00</CreditBalance>
      </CreditCard>
  </Customer>
    <Signature Id="xyz7802370"
             xmlns="http://www.w3.org/2000/09/xmldsig#">
  <SignedInfo>
```

```
  <CanonicalizationMethod
Algorithm="http://www.w3.org/TR/2001/REC-xml-c14n-20010315"/>
  <SignatureMethod
Algorithm=http://www.w3.org/2000/09/xmldsig#dsa-sha1 />
  <Reference URI="#ABCD54321">
    <Transforms>
    <Transform
   Algorithm="http://www.w3.org/2000/09/xmldsig#enveloped-signature">
  </Transform>
  </Transforms>
<DigestMethod
Algorithm="http://www.w3.org/2000/09/xmldsig#sha1" />
    <DigestValue>jav7lwx3rvLPO0vKVu8nk===</DigestValue>
  </Reference>
</SignedInfo>
   <SignatureValue>MC0E~LE=</SignatureValue>
 <KeyInfo>
   <X509Data>
<X509SubjectName>CN=RRN,O=CS,ST=BOSTON,C=MA</X509SubjectName>
   <X509Certificate>
     MIID5jCCA0+gA...lYZ==
   </X509Certificate>
  </X509Data>
  </KeyInfo>
</Signature>
</BusinessAccountSummary>
```

Web Services Security

In Example 6–11, the data object signed is the <BusinessAccountSummary> element that is identified by the URI attribute of the <Reference> element. As the XML signature is added, it changes the original document with the embedded <Signature> element. To verify the signature, it also becomes necessary to compare the original document without the signature. The XML digital signature recommendation defines an enveloped signature transformation algorithm for removing the <Signature> from the original document. The enveloped signature transform algorithm is defined in the specification with the URI identifier: http://www.w3.org/2000/09/xmldsig#enveloped-signature.

Enveloping Signature

In the enveloping signature, the XML signature encloses the signed XML document as its child element. Example 6–12 represents the enveloping signature, where the XML document is contained with the <Object> element within the XML signature.

Example 6–12 Signed XML document using enveloping signature

```
<Signature Id="abc76976343"
            xmlns="http://www.w3.org/2000/09/xmldsig#">
  <SignedInfo>
  <CanonicalizationMethod
Algorithm="http://www.w3.org/TR/2001/REC-xml-c14n-20010315"/>
  <SignatureMethod
Algorithm=http://www.w3.org/2000/09/xmldsig#dsa-sha1 />
  <Reference URI="#ABCD54321">
    <Transforms>
    <Transform
  Algorithm="http://www.w3.org/TR/1999/REC-xpath-19991116">
  </Transform>
    </Transforms>
<DigestMethod
Algorithm="http://www.w3.org/2000/09/xmldsig#sha1" />
<DigestValue>mnmasdvlwx3rvLP0vKVu8nk===</DigestValue>
</Reference>
</SignedInfo>
<SignatureValue>LMC0E~LE=</SignatureValue>
<KeyInfo>
<X509Data>
<X509SubjectName>CN=RRN,O=CS,ST=BOSTON,C=MA</X509SubjectName>
<X509Certificate>
  MIID5jCCA0+gA...lYZ==
</X509Certificate>
</X509Data>
</KeyInfo>
<Object id="ABCD54321">
<BusinessAccountSummary id="ABCD54321">
 <Customer id="45678943">
  <BusinessName>ABZ Company</BusinessName>
  <Address>1 ABZ Drive, Newton, CA</Address>
   <PrimaryContact>R Nagappan</PrimaryContact>
  <BusinessAccount id="BS-12345">
     <AccountBalance>950000.00</AccountBalance>
   </BusinessAccountNo>
   <CreditCard no="1233-3456-4567">
     <CreditBalance>45000.00</CreditBalance>
   </CreditCard>
    <CreditCard no="4230-3456-9877">
     <CreditBalance>6000.00</CreditBalance>
```

```
    </CreditCard>
      </Customer>
<BusinessAccountSummary>
 <Object>
</Signature>
```

Detached Signature

In the detached signature, both the XML document and XML signature reside independently—they are detached with external references or within the document as sibling elements. The URI attribute of the <Reference> element holds the identifier of the external reference, pointing to an external resource or pointing to an element id that is a sibling XML fragment residing as part of the same document. Example 6–13 represents a detached signature, where the XML signature <Signature> and the signed XML document <BusinessAccountSummary> are siblings of the main document.

Example 6–13 Signed XML document using detached signature

```
<Document>
<BusinessAccountSummary date="01/01/2004" id="ABCD54321">
  <Customer id="45678943">
    <BusinessName>ABZ Company</BusinessName>
    <Address>1 ABZ Drive, Newton, CA</Address>
<PrimaryContact>R Nagappan</PrimaryContact>
    <BusinessAccount id="BS-12345">
      <AccountBalance>950000.00</AccountBalance>
    </BusinessAccountNo>
    <CreditCard no="1233-3456-4567">
      <CreditBalance>45000.00</CreditBalance>
     </CreditCard>
     <CreditCard no="4230-3456-9877">
       <CreditBalance>6000.00</CreditBalance>
     </CreditCard>
   </Customer>
 </BusinessAccountSummary>
   <Signature Id="xyz7802370"
             xmlns="http://www.w3.org/2000/09/xmldsig#">
   <SignedInfo>
   <CanonicalizationMethod
Algorithm="http://www.w3.org/TR/2001/REC-xml-c14n-20010315"/>
  <SignatureMethod
     Algorithm=http://www.w3.org/2000/09/xmldsig#dsa-sha1 />
```

```
    <Reference URI="#ABCD54321">
   <Transforms>
     <Transform
   Algorithm="http://www.w3.org/TR/1999/REC-xpath-19991116">
   </Transform>
  </Transforms>
<DigestMethod
Algorithm="http://www.w3.org/2000/09/xmldsig#sha1" />
   <DigestValue>jav7lwx3rvLPO0vKVu8nk===</DigestValue>
    </Reference>
  </SignedInfo>
  <SignatureValue>MC0E~LE=</SignatureValue>
  <KeyInfo>
 <X509Data>
<X509SubjectName>CN=RRN,O=CS,ST=BOSTON,C=MA</X509SubjectName>
<X509Certificate>
    MIID5jCCA0+gA...lYZ==
   </X509Certificate>
  </X509Data>
  </KeyInfo>
  </Signature>
</Document>
```

In Example 6–13, the data object signed is the <BusinessAccountSummary>, and it is identified by the URI attribute of the <Reference> element.

Creating an XML Signature

The steps for creating an XML signature in compliance with the specification are as follows:

1. Identify the XML document, its parts of data objects, or other content resources that need to be signed. These data items are identified as a referenced resource through a URI. For example, a reference to an XML document with an HTTP URL will look like this: http://www.robmebank.com/statements/account.xml.
2. Apply transformations to the identified data object, specifying any encoding rules, canonicalization instructions, and XSLT transformations that need to be applied to the signed data. The <Transform> element identifies the transform algorithms to be applied.
3. After transformation, calculate the digest by applying message digest algorithms for each referenced URI resource identified by the <Reference>

element. The <DigestMethod> element identifies the applied algorithm and the <DigestValue> element holds the calculated digest.

4. Construct a <SignedInfo> element that collects all <Reference> elements, including the <DigestMethod> and <DigestValue>.
5. Canonicalize the <SignedInfo> element using the canonicalization algorithm specified through the <CananonicalizationMethod> element. If canonicalization is not applied, the validation of an XML signature may fail due to possible differences of the XML structure or its representation.
6. Calculate the digest of the <SignedInfo> element and sign it by applying the signature algorithm identified by the <SignatureMethod> element. The resulting signed value is represented under the <SignatureValue> element.
7. It is optional to include the <KeyInfo>, such as X.509 certificates and whether a public key is required for validating the signature.
8. Finally, construct the <Signature> element, including the <SignedInfo>, <SignatureValue>, and the <KeyInfo> that represent an XML signature of the given XML document or data objects.

Verifying and Validating an XML Signature

The following two steps are applied for verifying and validating an XML signature.

1. **Verify and validate the digests**: Recalculate the digests represented within the <Reference> elements. This includes applying transformations specified in the <Transforms> element and digesting the resulting value by applying the algorithm specified in the <DigestMethod> element. Compare the digested value against the value specified in the <DigestValue> element.
2. **Verify and validate the signature**: Recalculate the signature within the <SignedInfo> element using the key information included in the <KeyInfo> element or obtained from external sources. It is important to apply the canonicalized method and use the canonical form of the <SignatureMethod>, because the specified URI may be changed by the canonicalization of the <SignedInfo> element. Compare the signature value against the specified value in the <SignatureValue> element.

XML Encryption

XML Encryption specifications form the basis of securing the data and communication in order to conduct secure business transactions between partners. The goals of XML encryption is to provide data confidentiality and to ensure end-to-end security of messages transmitted between communicating parties. It is an evolving standard for encrypting and decrypting data and then representing that data using XML. XML encryption has emerged from the W3C as an industry-standard initiative for expressing encryption and decryption of digital content in XML. To find out the current status of XML encryption specifications from the W3C working group, refer to the W3C Web site at http://www.w3.org/Encryption.

Motivation of XML Encryption

Maintaining data confidentiality and privacy is made possible through encryption. The process of applying encryption involves converting a particular message into scrambled text (ciphertext) by applying cryptographic algorithms. These messages can be decrypted or unscrambled for viewing only by authorized parties who know the required secret key. This ensures that the data remains confidential during transit or at rest. Secure Sockets Layer (SSL) and Transport Layer Security (TLS) are the standard protocols typically used for encrypting communication and providing authentication using digital certificates over TCP/IP. SSL/TLS provides encryption for point-to-point communication, and during communication it facilitates encryption of the complete message or document in its entirety. It falls short of key mechanisms intended for XML-based business transactions, which require applying encryption for portions of a message, applying multiple encryptions to different parts of a message, and then leaving selected portions of message unencrypted. This mandates an XML-based digital encryption mechanism that meets the requirements of secure XML communication. These include message-level encryption and multiple encryptions to a message meant for multiple parties, a workflow, or a multi-hop communication.

XML encryption defines the syntax and processing rules that provide the flexibility of applying encryption or decryption to different fragments or a complete XML document while preserving the encrypted data intended for multiple parties in a workflow or a multi-hop communication involving intermediaries.

The Anatomy of XML Encryption

XML encryption allows encryption of any sort of digital content or data objects, such as XML, binary data, and images. It builds on existing industry-standard encryption algorithms and facilitates a standard XML-based representation and processing model for encryption and decryption.

In XML encryption, the resulting encrypted data are represented in an XML format identified by an <EncryptedData> element that contains the ciphertext of the content. The encrypted data can be an XML element or arbitrary data that include the complete document. The encryption key value is specified using an <Encrypted-Key> element.

Let's take a closer look at how to represent an XML encryption, its structural elements, and its features.

Structure of XML Encryption and Its Core Elements

XML encryption is represented and identified as an <EncryptedData> element, where the original data are encrypted and embedded within the data structure. Example 6–14 shows the structure of an XML Encryption represented by <EncryptedData ?> as its root element. The "?" in the element denotes zero or one occurrence, "*" denotes zero or more occurrences, and the empty element denotes the element must be empty).

Example 6–14 Structure of XML encryption and its core elements

```
<EncryptedData Id? Type? MimeType? Encoding?>
  <EncryptionMethod/>?
  <ds:KeyInfo>
    <EncryptedKey>?
    <AgreementMethod>?
    <ds:KeyName>?
    <ds:RetrievalMethod>?
    <ds:*>?
  </ds:KeyInfo>?
  <CipherData>
    <CipherValue>?
    <CipherReference URI?>?
  </CipherData>
  <EncryptionProperties>?
</EncryptedData>
```

<EncryptedData>

The <EncryptedData> element is the root element that contains all child elements, including the <CipherData> that contains the encrypted data. It replaces the encrypted content with the exception of the <EncryptedKey> element that contains the encrypted key. The <EncryptedData> elements contain four optional attributes: an Id attribute identifying the encrypted data with a unique id; a Type attribute defining the encrypted data, which is content or an element for the decrypting application; a MimeType attribute defining the content MIME type; and an Encoding attribute specifying the transfer encoding (e.g., Base64-encoded) of the encrypted data. See Example 6–15.

Example 6–15 Representation of EncryptedData element

```
<EncryptedData xmlns="http://www.w3.org/2001/04/xmlenc#"
  Id="MyXMLEncryption"
     Type="http://www.w3.org/2001/04/xmlenc#Element"
  MimeType= "text/xml"
  Encoding= "http://www.w3.org/2000/09/xmldsig#base64">
```

<EncryptionMethod>

The optional <EncryptionMethod> element specifies the applied encryption algorithm of the encrypted data. If it is not specified, the recipient would not be aware of the applied encryption algorithm and the decryption may fail. See Example 6–16.

Example 6–16 EncryptionMethod element specifying an encryption algorithm

```
<EncryptionMethod    xmlns="http://www.w3.org/2001/04/xmlenc#tripledes-cbc">
```

<ds:KeyInfo>

The <ds:KeyInfo> is a mandated element that specifies information about the key used for encrypting the data. It contains <ds:KeyName>, <ds:KeyValue>, and <ds:RetrievalMethod> as its child elements. The <ds:KeyName> element specifies the reference to the key or refers to a <CarriedKeyName> element of the <EncryptedKey> element. For example, the <ds:KeyInfo> element and <ds:KeyName> appears as shown in Example 6–17.

Example 6–17 Representing key information using <ds:KeyInfo> element

```
<ds:KeyInfo xmlns:ds="http://www.w3.org/2000/09/xmldsig#">
    <ds:KeyName>CSP-SecurityKey</ds:KeyName>
</ds:KeyInfo>
```

The <ds:RetrievalMethod> provides another way to retrieve the key information identified using a URI. Example 6–18 uses the <ds:RetrievalMethod> with a URL location to retrieve the key from the <EncryptedKey> element.

Example 6–18 Specifying RetrievalMethod for obtaining key information

```
<ds:KeyInfo xmlns:ds="http://www.w3.org/2000/09/xmldsig#">
  <ds:RetrievalMethod URI='#MYEK'
      Type="http://www.w3.org/2001/04/xmlenc#EncryptedKey"/>
       <ds:KeyName>CSP-SecurityKey</ds:KeyName>
 </ds:KeyInfo>
```

The <ds:KeyValue> is an optional element used to transport public keys.

<CipherData>

<CipherData> is a mandatory element that provides the encrypted data. It allows you to specify the encrypted value using <CipherValue> or <CipherReference> as child elements. Using the <CipherValue> element holds the value as an encrypted octet sequence using base64-encoded text as shown in Example 6–19.

Example 6–19 Representation of encrypted data as <CipherValue>

```
<EncryptedData Id="PYMT1"
    xmlns="http://www.w3.org/2001/04/xmlenc#"
    MimeType="text/xml"
    Type="http://www.w3.org/2001/04/xmlenc#Element">
    <CipherData>
      <CipherValue>gfgf-EncryptedText-u=gh#@hgh</CipherValue>
    </CipherData>
  </EncryptedData>
```

Alternatively, using the <CipherReference> element allows you to specify a URI that references an external location containing the encrypted octet sequence. In addition to URI, <CipherReference> can also contain an optional <Transforms> element to list the decryption steps required to obtain the cipher value. The <Transforms> element allows you to include any number of transformations specified by using the <ds:Transform> element. Example 6–20 illustrates the representation of the <CipherReference> and <Transforms> elements.

Example 6–20 Representing transforms to support decryption

```
<EncryptedData Id="PYMT1"
      xmlns="http://www.w3.org/2001/04/xmlenc#"
      MimeType="text/xml"
      Type="http://www.w3.org/2001/04/xmlenc#Element">
      <CipherData>
   <CipherReference
            URI="http://www.csp.com/cipher-payment.xml">
   <Transforms>
     <ds:Transform
      Algorithm="http://www.w3.org/TR/1999/REC-xpath-19991116">
      <ds:XPath xmlns:rep="http://www.my-xslt.org/xslt-dump/">
       self::text()[parent::rep:CipherValue[@Id="transformer"]]
       </ds:XPath>
      </ds:Transform>
      <ds:Transform
         Algorithm="http://www.w3.org/2000/09/xmldsig#base64"/>
    </Transforms>
```

```
</CipherReference>
</CipherData>
</EncryptedData>
```

<EncryptedKey>

The <EncryptedKey> element is used to transport encryption keys between the message sender and the message's ultimate recipients. It can be used within XML data or specified inside an <EncryptedData> element as a child of a <ds:KeyInfo> element. See Example 6–21.

Example 6–21 Representing encrypted keys using <EncryptedKey> element

```
<EncryptedKey Id="MYEK"
            xmlns="http://www.w3.org/2001/04/xmlenc#">
 <EncryptionMethod
    Algorithm="http://www.w3.org/2001/04/xmlenc#rsa-1_5"/>
 <ds:KeyInfo xmlns:ds="http://www.w3.org/2000/09/xmldsig#">
   <ds:KeyName>Isaac Newton</ds:KeyName>
 </ds:KeyInfo>
  <CipherData>
   <CipherValue>iutyuo</CipherValue>
 </CipherData>
   <ReferenceList>
    <DataReference URI="#DRL"/>
    </ReferenceList>
<CarriedKeyName>CSP SecurityKey</CarriedKeyName>
</EncryptedKey>
```

When <EncryptedKey> is decrypted, the resulting octets are made available to the EncryptionMethod algorithm without any additional processing.

<EncryptionProperties>

The optional <SignatureProperties> can contain all additional information about the creation of the XML encryption. This may include details such as date, timestamp, serial number of cryptographic hardware used for encryption, and other application-specific attributes.

XML Encryption Algorithms

The XML encryption specifications define a set of encryption and decryption algorithms and associate them with identifier URIs that can be used as the value of the <Algorithm> attribute of <EncryptionMethod>. In addition, an application can adopt an algorithm of its own choice provided by the XML encryption implementation. Based on the applied role, all algorithms take implicit parameters, such as encryption or decryption data, key information, and operations defining either encryption or decryption. Additional explicit parameters can be specified within the content of the element.

Let's take a closer look at those algorithms, their identifying URIs, and their implementation requirements.

Block Encryption

Block encryption algorithms are designed to provide encryption and decryption of data in fixed-size and multiple-octet blocks. The XML encryption specification defines four algorithms for block encryption, as follows:

- Algorithm name: TRIPLEDES
  Identifying URI: http://www.w3.org/2001/04/xmlenc#tripledes-cbc
  Implementation: Required
- Algorithm name: AES-128
  Identifying URI: http://www.w3.org/2001/04/xmlenc#aes128-cbc
  Implementation: Required
- Algorithm name: AES-256
  Identifying URI: http://www.w3.org/2001/04/xmlenc#aes256-cbc
  Implementation: Required
- Algorithm name: AES-192
  Identifying URI: http://www.w3.org/2001/04/xmlenc#aes192-cbc
  Implementation: Optional

Key Transport

Key transport algorithms are public-key algorithms designed for encrypting and decrypting keys. These algorithms are identified as the value of the <Algorithm> attribute of the <EncryptionMethod> element, representing the <EncryptedKey> element. The XML encryption specification defines two algorithms for key transport as follows:

- Algorithm name: RSA-v1.5
  Identifying URI: http://www.w3.org/2001/04/xmlenc#rsa-1_5
  Implementation: Required

- Algorithm name: RSA-OAEP
  Identifying URI: http://www.w3.org/2001/04/xmlenc#rsa-oaep-mgf1p
  Implementation: Required

Key Agreement

The key agreement algorithm is used to derive the shared secret key based on compatible public keys from both the sender and its recipient. This is represented using the <AgreementMethod> element as a child element of the <KeyInfo> element. The <AgreementMethod> element holds the information identifying the keys of the sender, key size information, and the computation procedure to obtain the shared encryption key. The XML encryption specification defines the following algorithm for key agreement:

- Algorithm name: Diffie-Hellman
  Identifying URI: http://www.w3.org/2001/04/xmlenc#dh
  Implementation: Optional

Symmetric Key Wrap

The symmetric key wrap algorithms are shared secret-key encryption algorithms specified for encrypting and decrypting symmetric keys. These algorithms are identified as the value of the <Algorithm> attribute of the <EncryptionMethod> element, representing the <EncryptedKey> element. The XML encryption specification defines four algorithms for symmetric key wrap as follows:

- Algorithm name: TRIPLEDES KeyWrap
  Identifying URI: http://www.w3.org/2001/04/xmlenc#kw-tripledes
  Implementation: Required
- Algorithm name: AES-128 KeyWrap
  Identifying URI: http://www.w3.org/2001/04/xmlenc#kw-aes128
  Implementation: Required
- Algorithm name: AES-256 KeyWrap
  Identifying URI: http://www.w3.org/2001/04/xmlenc#kw-aes256
  Implementation: Required
- Algorithm name: AES-192 KeyWrap
  Identifying URI: http://www.w3.org/2001/04/xmlenc#kw-aes192
  Implementation: Optional

Message Digest

The message digest algorithms are used to derive the hash value digest of a message or data. As part of the derivation, the <AgreementMethod> element is used to hold the information identifying the keys of the sender, key size information, and the computation procedure to obtain the digest. It can also be used as a hash function in the key transport RSA-OAEP algorithm. The XML encryption specification defines the following four algorithms for message digest:

- Algorithm name: SHA1
  Identifying URI: http://www.w3.org/2001/04/xmlenc#sha-1
  Implementation: Required
- Algorithm name: SHA256
  Identifying URI: http://www.w3.org/2001/04/xmlenc#sha256
  Implementation: Recommended
- Algorithm name: SHA512
  Identifying URI: http://www.w3.org/2001/04/xmlenc#sha512
  Implementation: Optional
- [blx]Algorithm name: RIPEMD-160
  Identifying URI: http://www.w3.org/2001/04/xmlenc#ripemd160
  Implementation: Optional

Message Authentication

For message authentication, the XML encryption specification uses the XML digital signature-based algorithm:

- Algorithm name: XML Digital Signature
  Identifying URI: http://www.w3.org/2000/09/xmldsig#
  Implementation: Recommended

Canonicalization

Prior to XML encryption, applying canonicalization allows you to consistently serialize the XML into an octet stream, which is an identical textual representation of the given XML document. XML encryption defines two kinds of canonicalization algorithms: inclusive canonicalization and exclusive canonicalization.

- **Inclusive Canonicalization**: The serialized XML includes both in-scope namespace and XML namespace attribute context from ancestors of the

XML being serialized. The specification defines two algorithms specific to inclusive canonicalization.

- Algorithm name: Canonical XML without comments
  Identifying URI: http://www.w3.org/TR/2001/REC-xml-c14n-20010315#
  Implementation: Optional
- Algorithm name: Canonical XML with comments
  Identifying URI: http://www.w3.org/TR/2001/REC-xml-c14n-20010315#WithComments
  Implementation: Optional

- **Exclusive Canonicalization**: The serialized XML provides the minimum requirement details about its namespace and associated XML namespace attribute context from ancestors of the XML being serialized. This helps a signed XML payload not to break its structural integrity when a sub element is removed from the original message and/or inserted into a different context. The specification defines two algorithms specific to exclusive canonicalization.
  - Algorithm name: Exclusive XML canonicalization without comments
    Identifying URI: http://www.w3.org/2001/10/xml-exc-c14n#
    Implementation: Optional
  - Algorithm name: Exclusive XML canonicalization with comments
    Identifying URI: http://www.w3.org/ 2001/10/xml-exc-c14n#WithComments
    Implementation: Optional

XML Encryption: Example Scenarios

Let's consider an example scenario: A wholesaler hosts a Web-services-based solution for delivering products, catalogs, and services for its business customers. The business customer uses a Web-services-based client application for sending purchase orders and receiving delivery confirmations from the service provider. The business customer sends purchase order information that includes some critical information, such as products, quantity, credit card number, and shipping address. Using XML encryption, both the service requester and service provider guarantee that all Web-services-based transactions transmitted between them remain secure and confidential.

Example 6–22 is a purchase order of a business customer that illustrates how to represent XML encryption.

Example 6–22 XML document representing a purchase order

```
<?xml version='1.0'?>
  <PurchaseOrder xmlns='http://speeding.com/online/pay'>
   <BusinessName>CSP Security</BusinessName>
    <OrderedProducts>
        <ProductDetails>
        <Name>Radar Detector</Name>
        <Quantity>1</Quantity>
        </ProductDetails>
        <TotalCost>75.00</TotalCost>
    <CreditCard>
     <Cardholder>R Nagappan</Cardholder>
     <Number>4000 2445 0277 5567</Number>
     <Currency>'USD'</Currency>
     <Issuer>American Generous Bank</Issuer>
    <Expiration>04/02</Expiration>
  </CreditCard>
  <ShipAddress>1 Bills Dr, Newton, MA01803</ShipAddress>
</PurchaseOrder>
```

Using the above example, let's take a look at the different scenarios of XML encryption and how XML encryption is represented.

XML Encryption: Element Level

In this scenario, let's consider the business customer that prefers to encrypt only the payment information such as cardholder name, credit card number, currency, and issuing bank as confidential. After applying XML encryption, the representation of the XML document appears as shown in Example 6–23.

Example 6–23 XML document using element-level XML encryption

```
<?xml version='1.0'?>
    <PurchaseOrder xmlns='http://speeding.com/online/pay'>
    <BusinessName>CSP Security</BusinessName>
    <OrderedProducts>
        <ProductDetails>
        <Name>Radar Detector</Name>
        <Quantity>1</Quantity>
        </ProductDetails>
```

```
            <TotalCost>75.00</TotalCost>
       <EncryptedData Id="PYMT1"
        xmlns="http://www.w3.org/2001/04/xmlenc#"
        MimeType="text/xml"
        Type="http://www.w3.org/2001/04/xmlenc#Element">
      <CipherData>
       <CipherValue>XHDDxyz=cArdDeTa3eNcrY==</CipherValue>
      </CipherData>
      </EncryptedData>
    <ShipAddress>1 Bills Dr, Newton, MA01803</ShipAddress>
</PurchaseOrder>
```


After encryption, the complete <CreditCard> element, including its child elements, are encrypted and represented within a <CipherData> element.

XML Encryption: Element Content Level

In this scenario, let's consider the business customer that prefers to encrypt only the credit card number element as confidential, leaving other payment related information readable. After applying XML encryption, the representation of XML document appears as shown in Example 6–24.

Example 6–24 XML document using content-level encryption

```
<?xml version='1.0'?>
    <PurchaseOrder xmlns='http://speeding.com/online/pay'>
    <BusinessName>CSP Security</BusinessName>
    <OrderedProducts>
        <ProductDetails>
        <Name>Radar Detector</Name>
        <Quantity>1</Quantity>
        </ProductDetails>
        <TotalCost>75.00</TotalCost>
<CreditCard>
   <Cardholder>R Nagappan</Cardholder>
   <EncryptedData Id="PYMT1"
    xmlns="http://www.w3.org/2001/04/xmlenc#"
    MimeType="text/xml"
    Type="http://www.w3.org/2001/04/xmlenc#Content">
<CipherData>
   <CipherValue>safDDxyzouyh</CipherValue>
  </CipherData>
  </EncryptedData>
     <Currency>'USD'</Currency>
```

```
<Issuer>American Generous Bank</Issuer>
<Expiration>04/02</Expiration>
</CreditCard>
<ShipAddress>1 Bills Dr, Newton, MA01803</ShipAddress>
</PurchaseOrder>
```

XML Encryption: Element Content (Character Data)

Let's consider the business customer that prefers to encrypt only the attribute value of the credit card number as confidential, leaving other information readable. In this scenario, the content value of the <Number> element will be encrypted as cipher data. After applying XML encryption, the representation of XML document appears as shown in Example 6–25.

Example 6–25 XML document using element data encryption

```
<?xml version='1.0'?>
<PurchaseOrder xmlns='http://sahara.com/online/pay'>
 <BusinessName>CSP Security</BusinessName>
   <OrderedProducts>
     <ProductDetails>
     <Name>Radar Detector</Name>
     <Quantity>1</Quantity>
     </ProductDetails>
     <TotalCost>75.00</TotalCost>
     <CreditCard>
 <Cardholder>R Nagappan</Cardholder>
   <Number>
   <EncryptedData Id="PYMT1"
    xmlns="http://www.w3.org/2001/04/xmlenc#"
    MimeType="text/xml"
    Type="http://www.w3.org/2001/04/xmlenc#Content">
<CipherData>
    <CipherValue>safDFFFuyh</CipherValue>
   </CipherData>
   </EncryptedData>
    </Number>
     <Currency>'USD'</Currency>
  <Issuer>American Generous Bank</Issuer>
  <Expiration>04/02</Expiration>
 </CreditCard>
   <ShipAddress>1 Bills Dr, Newton, MA01803</ShipAddress>
 </PurchaseOrder>
```

In Example 6–25, Both <CreditCard> and <Number> element names are readable, but the character data content of <Number> is encrypted.

XML Encryption: Arbitrary Content

Let's consider the business customer that prefers to encrypt the complete document as confidential. The whole document encrypted will become an octet sequence, as shown in Example 6–26.

Example 6–26 XML document using full document encryption


```
<?xml version='1.0'?>
<EncryptedData xmlns='http://www.w3.org/2001/04/xmlenc#'
 MimeType='text/xml'>
  <CipherData>
    <CipherValue>CSS#SDOUHDSajjn</CipherValue>
  </CipherData>
</EncryptedData>
```

Super Encryption: Encrypting the Encrypted Data

As we discussed earlier, XML encryption allows you to apply encryption to different parts of an XML document that may contain zero or more <EncryptedData> elements. But it is not possible to create an <EncryptedData> element within an existing <EncryptedData> element as a child or its parent.

Super encryption allows encryption of already encrypted content, including <EncryptedData> and <EncryptedKey> elements. To apply super encryption of an <EncryptedData> or <EncryptedKey> element, it is necessary to encrypt the entire element or it will be invalid.

Let's consider the business customer that prefers to encrypt the complete document as confidential. Example 6–27a shows the whole document encrypted and represented as a cipher data.

Example 6–27a XML document using full document encryption

```
<?xml version='1.0'?>
<EncryptedData Id="pd1"
          xmlns='http://www.w3.org/2001/04/xmlenc#'
          MimeType='text/xml'
            Type='http://www.w3.org/2001/04/xmlenc#Element'>
  <CipherData>
    <CipherValue>CSSSDOUHDSajjn</CipherValue>
  </CipherData>
</EncryptedData>
```

After Super encryption, the <EncryptedData Id="pd1"> would appear as follows in Example 6–27b:

Example 6–27b XML document using super encryption

```
<?xml version='1.0'?>
<EncryptedData Id="pd2"
          xmlns='http://www.w3.org/2001/04/xmlenc#'
          MimeType='text/xml'
            Type='http://www.w3.org/2001/04/xmlenc#Element'>
  <CipherData>
    <CipherValue>lkhjlkHDSajjn</CipherValue>
  </CipherData>
</EncryptedData>
```


The resulting cipher data is the base64-encoding of the encrypted octet sequence of the <EncryptedData> element with "Id1".

XML Key Management System (XKMS)

XML Key Management Service (XKMS) specifications form the basis for registration, subscription, and management of keys in XML Web services. XKMS facilitates PKI Key management functionality and services such as certificate issuance, processing, validation, revocation, status checking, and so forth. These services are suitable for use in conjunction with XML Signature and XML Encryption. XKMS enables offloading of PKI functionalities to remote trust service providers. XML Web services developers need to know only how to invoke these remote services by locating, registering, and subscribing to the services. XKMS has emerged from the W3C as an industry-standard initiative for defining protocols for distributing, registering, and processing public keys to support the use of XML Signature and XML Encryption in Web services.

To find out the current status of XKMS specifications from the W3C working group, refer to the W3C Web site at http://www.w3.org/TR/xkms.

Motivation of XKMS

PKI is based on public-private key pairs and has been used for securing business application infrastructures and transactions. Private keys are used by the service provider application and public keys can be distributed to the clients. In the case of Web services, the use of XML encryption and XML signature required integration with a PKI-based key solution to support related key management functionalities such as encryption, decryption, signature verification, and validation. There are a variety of PKI solutions, such as X.509, PGP, SPKI, and PKIX, available from multiple vendors.

In the case of Web services, using PKI solutions from multiple vendors mandates interoperability. For example, company A encrypts and signs its messages using an X.509 PKI solution from vendor A and communicates with company B using a different PKI solution from vendor B. In this scenario, company B's PKI solution fails to verify and is unable to decrypt the message sent by company A. This has become a problem in securing Web services due to the issues of interoperability and managing cryptographic keys.

XKMS introduces an easy solution for managing PKI-related functionalities by offloading PKI from applications to a trusted service provider. The trusted service provider facilitating XKMS service "under the hood" provides a PKI solution. This means that client applications and Web services relying on XKMS do not require a PKI solution. Instead, they delegate all PKI-related responsibilities to an XKMS provider (trusted service) and issue XML-based requests for obtaining PKI services from them.

XKMS Specification Overview

The XKMS specification defines an XML-based protocol for distributing and registering PKI-based cryptographic keys for use in Web services. It defines a set of PKI services that adopt standards-based protocol bindings, syntax, and processing rules. XKMS is implemented by a trust service provider that allows its subscribers to register and access its required PKI functions. To support the use of XML signature and XML encryption in Web services, XKMS allows an application or user using a public key to verify a digital signature, to encrypt data, or to locate that public key as well as other information pertaining to its communicating peer. The client application making the request does not need to know the details of the PKI solution hosted by the trust service.

The XKMS specification is made up of two parts: X-KISS (XML key information service specification) deals with retrieval and processing of key information and X-KRSS (XML key registration service specification) deals with registration of public keys.

XML Key Information Services (X-KISS)

X-KISS defines a protocol for delegating and processing of PKI-related functions associated with XML signature and XML encryption to a XKMS-based trust service provider. By delegating to a trust service, it reduces the complexity of using

PKI to establish trust relationships with a Web services provider or requesters and avoids interoperability-related issues. X-KISS supports processing of <ds:KeyInfo> elements that specify information about the key used for encrypting the data in an XML signature and an XML encryption. In an XML signature, the signer of the XML document includes <ds:KeyInfo> to specify the key identification details, such as the <ds:KeyName> element that specifies the key name and the <ds:RetrievalMethod> element for specifying the location of the key information.

X-KISS provides support for two types of service: locate service and validate service.

X-KISS Locate Service

The locate service allows you to locate and retrieve public keys by resolving the <ds:KeyInfo> element. The required key information may be available as part of the message as child elements <ds:KeyName> and <ds:RetrievalMethod> that specify the name and location of the key information, respectively.

Figure 6–4 is a sequence diagram illustrating the X-KISS locate service, where a Web service sends an XML request to a trust service provider to locate the key and obtains the key value. The Web services requester (or provider) receives a signed XML document from the XKMS trust service that contains a <ds:Keyinfo> element. The <ds:KeyInfo> element specifies a <ds:RetrievalMethod> child element that mentions the location of an X.509 certificate that contains the public key. The

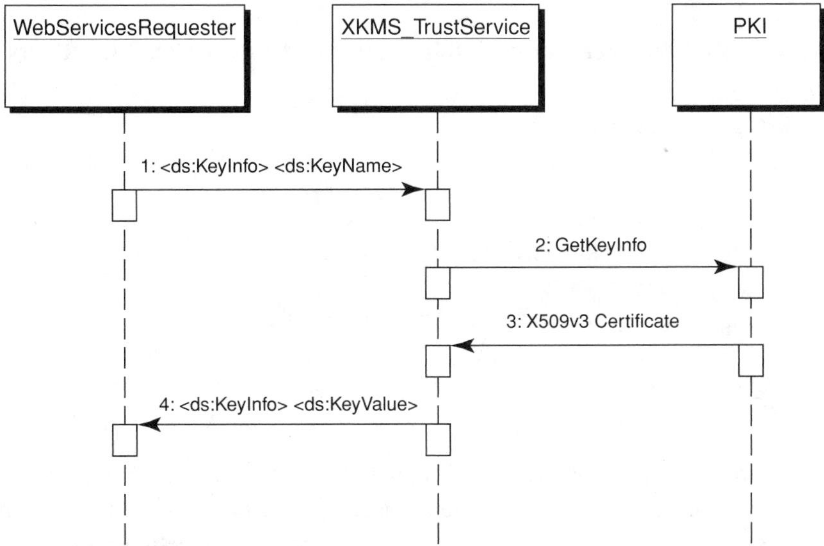

Figure 6–4 X-KISS locate service

application sends an XML request to the trust service that specifies the <ds:Keyinfo> element and in return, the trust service sends a response that specifies the <KeyName> and <KeyValue> elements.

Example 6–28 represents an XML request to a trust service to locate the key information. The <Locate> element contains the complete query for locating the key. The child element, <Query>, contains the <ds:KeyInfo> that may hold either a <ds:KeyName> or <ds:RetrievalMethod>. The <Respond> element specifies the required return values, such as the <KeyName> and the <KeyValue>.

Example 6–28 Representation of XML request to a XKMS trust service

```
<Locate>
   <Query>
        <ds:KeyInfo>
          <ds:KeyName>CSP Security</ds:KeyName>
        </ds:KeyInfo>
   </Query>
   <Respond>
        <string>KeyName</string>
        <string>KeyValue</string>
   </Respond>
</Locate>
```

Example 6–29 shows the representation of the XML response from the trust service, which provides the result, including the key name and key value.

Example 6–29 Representation of XML response from a XKMS trust service

```
<LocateResult>
   <Result>Success</Result>
     <Answer>
       <ds:KeyInfo>
            <ds:KeyName>
                 O=CSP, CN="CSP Services"
            </ds:KeyName>
            <ds:KeyValue>soijhfsdhsdf+h===</ds:KeyValue>
         </ds:KeyInfo>
       </Answer>
    </LocateResult>
```

In this response, the <LocateResult> element contains the complete response from the trust service, the child element <Result> contains the response; it can be either success or failure. The <Answer> element specifies the actual return values, such as the <KeyName> that mentions the name and the <KeyValue> holding an X.509 certificate.

X-KISS Validate Service

The X-KISS validate service searches the trust service provider for the public key defined in the <ds:KeyInfo> element. It returns a response that provides an assertion to the client about the validity of the binding between key name and key, and its trustworthiness. Let's take a look at a simple scenario in which the application sends a request that specifies the <ds:Keyinfo> element to the trust service and that requests validation of the status of the binding information. Example 6–30 shows the sample representation of the XML request to validate the binding status.

Example 6–30 Representation of XML request to validate the key status

```
<Validate>
     <Query>
         <Status>Valid</Status>
          <ds:KeyInfo>
               <ds:KeyName>CSP Security</ds:KeyName>
               <ds:KeyValue>...</ds:KeyValue>
          </ds:KeyInfo>
     </Query>
     <Respond>
<string>KeyName</string>
<string>KeyValue</string>
    </Respond>
</Validate>
```

In this representation, the <Validate> element contains the complete query for validating the binding information, and the child element <Query> contains the <ds:KeyInfo> or a <ds:KeyName>. The <Respond> element specifies the required return values, such as the <ds:KeyName> and the <ds:KeyValue>.

Example 6–31 shows the representation of the XML response from the trust service, which mentions the status of the binding between the <ds:KeyName> and <ds:KeyValue> and its validity.

Example 6–31 Representation of XML response about a key validity

```
<ValidateResult>
     <Result>Success</Result>
     <Answer>
          <KeyBinding>
               <Status>Valid</Status>
```

```
                <KeyID>
                  http://www.csp-xkms.org/assert/8676-986-80
                </KeyID>
                <ds:KeyInfo>
                    <ds:KeyName>...</ds:KeyName>
                    <ds:KeyValue>...</ds:KeyValue>
                </ds:KeyInfo>
                <ValidityInterval>
                    <NotBefore>
                        2000-09-20T12:00:00
                    </NotBefore>
                    <NotAfter>
                        2005-10-20T12:00:00
                    </NotAfter>
                </ValidityInterval>
            </KeyBinding>
        </Answer>
</ValidateResult>
```

In this response, the <ValidateResult> element contains the complete response from the trust service, and the child element, <Result>, contains the response, which can be either success or failure. The <Answer> element specifies the actual return values in the child element <KeyBinding>, defining the key id <KeyID>, key information <KeyInfo>, and validity <ValidityInterval> as its child elements.

XML Key Registration Service (X-KRSS)

The X-KRSS specification defines a protocol that provides public-key management services of an XKMS–based trust service provider. X-KRSS handles the entire life-cycle functions of a public key, including:

- **Registration**: The registration service registers a key pair and its associated binding information.
- **Revocation**: The revocation service revokes the status of previously issued keys (valid keys).
- **Recovery**: The recovery service recovers the private key associated with key binding.
- **Reissue**: The reissue service is quite similar to the registration service that allows the reissue of previously issued key bindings.

The ultimate goal of the X-KRSS specification is to deliver a complete XML-aware PKI management protocol providing these life-cycle operations.

X-KRSS Key Registration Service

The key registration service defines an XML-based protocol for registration of public-key information. It allows an XML-aware application to register its public-key pair and its associated binding information to an XKMS trust service provider. The key pair may be generated by the client application or by the XKMS trust service. To register a key pair, the client application typically sends a signed request to the XKMS trust service using an X-KRSS request format. The XKMS trust service responds and confirms the status of the registration. At the time of registration, the service may require the client application to provide a key pair along with additional information pertaining to authentication. Upon receipt of a registration request, the service verifies the authentication credentials and Possession of Private (POP) key information of the client and then registers the key and associated binding information.

Let's consider a scenario in which an application sends a request to register its client-generated public-key pair and binding information with an XKMS trust service provider. Example 6–32 shows the representation of the X-KRSS registration request to the XKMS trust service provider.

Example 6–32 X-KRSS registration request to an XKMS trust service

```
<Register>
     <Prototype Id="mykeybinding">
          <Status>Valid</Status>
<KeyID>
http://www.cspsecurity.com/myapplication
</KeyID>
          <ds:KeyInfo>
               <ds:KeyValue>
                    <ds:RSAKeyValue>
                         <ds:Modulus>...</ds:Modulus>
                         <ds:Exponent>...</ds:Exponent>
                    </ds:RSAKeyValue>
               </ds:KeyValue>
            <ds:KeyName>
http://www.cspsecurity.com/myapplication?company=csp;CN=web     </ds:KeyName>
          </ds:KeyInfo>
<PassPhrase>70lkjwer-94-09i-0</PassPhrase>
     </Prototype>
     <AuthInfo>
          <AuthUserInfo>
               <ProofOfPossession>
```

```
    <ds:Signature URI="#mykeybinding" [RSA-Sign (KeyBinding, Private)] />
                </ProofOfPossession>
                <KeyBindingAuth>
 <ds:Signature  URI="#mykeybinding" [HMAC-SHA1 (KeyBinding, Auth)] />
                </KeyBindingAuth>
          </AuthUserInfo>
    </AuthInfo>
    <Respond>
          <string>KeyName<string>
          <string>KeyValue</string>
          <string>RetrievalMethod</string>
    </Respond>
</Register>
```


In Example 6–32, the complete registration request is identified by the <Register> element. The <Prototype> element represents the prototype of the key and binding information. Because the request is intended for the registration of a client-generated key pair, it contains the key value information as part of the <ds:KeyInfo> element. The <PassPhrase> element provides the information for authenticating the client with the service provider. During registration, the <AuthInfo> element provides the data that authenticates the request, mentioning the authentication type and algorithm used. Because it is a client-generated key pair, it also includes the proof-of-possession of the private key using the <ProofOfPossession> element. The client uses a previously registered key to sign the <Prototype> element and represents the signature under the <KeyBindingAuth> element. The <Respond> element specifies the actual return values via the <KeyName>, <KeyValue>, and its <RetrievalMethod> elements. In the case of a service-generated key pair, the request does not contain the public-key information and the XKMS trust service provider responds to the requests with the private key along with the binding information.

Now, let's take a look at Example 6–33, the response obtained from the XKMS trust service provider after it registered the client-generated key-pair.

Example 6–33 X-KRSS registration response from an XKMS trust service

```
<RegisterResult>
    <Result>Success</Result>
    <Answer>
     <Status>Valid</Status>
    <KeyID>http://www.cspsecurity.com/myapplication</KeyID>
     <ds:KeyInfo>
    <ds:RetrievalMethod
    URI="http://trustservice.com/?company=csp;CN=web?sl-no='fju24jf'"
    Type = http://www.w3.org/2000/09/xmldsig#X509Data"/>
```

```
        <ds:KeyValue>
        <ds:RSAKeyValue>...</ds:RSAKeyValue>
         </ds:KeyValue
         <ds:KeyName> http://www.cspsecurity.com/myapplication</ds:KeyName>
        </ds:KeyInfo>
       </Answer>
</RegisterResult>
```

The complete response from the trust service is identified by the <RegisterResult> element. The <Answer> element contains the requested key binding information as the child element <KeyBinding>. The <KeyID> identifies the key registered and <ds:RetrievalMethod> provides the URI location of the key and its type.

X-KRSS Key Revocation Service

The X-KRSS key revocation service defines a protocol that allows revoking previously issued assertions. This protocol is quite similar to the registration services, except that the <Status> element in the request message will be specified Invalid and identify the <KeyID> and <ds:KeyInfo> elements. The revocation response from the service provider will be quite similar to the registration response message, except with the prototype <Status> element specified as Invalid. If the XKMS service provider does not possess the key information, it responds with the <Status> element specified as NotFound.

X-KRSS Key Recovery Service

The Key recovery service defines a protocol for recovery of a private key. When a client forgets or loses its previously registered private key, the key may be recovered by sending a recovery request. The request is quite similar to that of the registration services, except that the <Status> element will be specified Indeterminate, identifying the <KeyName> specified in the <ds:KeyInfo> element. When a recovery is requested, the trust service recovers the private key and the binding with the public key. The response from the XKMS service provider will be quite similar to the revocation response message. If more time to process the response is required, the XKMS trust service responds with a <ResultCode> as Pending.

If the XKMS service provider does not possess the key information, it responds with NotFound in the <Status> element.

X-KRSS Key Reissue Service

The key reissue service defines a protocol to reissue the previously issued assertions. It returns a similar response by sending a registration response with newer issuing credentials from the underlying PKI of the XKMS trust service.

X-BULK

X-BULK defines a single batch element that can contain multiple registration requests, responses, and status requests. The responding XKMS service processes the entire batch and returns a single response after processing. Without X-BULK support, XKMS would be limited to a single key registration and validation at a time. X-BULK operations are primarily meant for issuing multiple certificates to support deploying smart phone devices, smart cards, modems, and so forth.

X-BULK defines batch elements, such as <BulkRegister>, <BulkResponse>, <BulkStatusRequest>, and <BulkStatusResponse>, representing registration requests and responses, and status requests and responses. Each of these batch elements contains request or response messages that include requests or responses that are independently referenced. Example 6–34 is an X-BULK request made by a client application for running a bulk registration of certificates.

Example 6–34 X-BULK request for running volume registration of certificates

```
<BulkRegister xmlns="http://www.w3.org/2002/03/xkms-xbulk">
    <SignedPart Id="mybulkid">
        <BatchHeader>
            <BatchID>mybatch-0</BatchID>
            <BatchTime>...</BatchTime>
            <NumberOfRequests>2</NumberOfRequests>
        </BatchHeader>

        <xkms:Respond>
            <string xmlns="">X509Cert</string>
        </xkms:Respond>
        <Requests number="3">
            <Request>
                <xkms:KeyID>
                   mailto:admin@coresecuritypatterns.com
                </xkms:KeyID>
                <dsig:KeyInfo>
                    <dsig:X509Data>
                        <dsig:X509SubjectName>
                            CN=FirstName LastName
                        </dsig:X509SubjectName>
                    </dsig:X509Data>
                    <dsig:KeyValue>
                        <dsig:RSAKeyValue>
                            ...
```

```
                        </dsig:RSAKeyValue>
                    </dsig:KeyValue>
                </dsig:KeyInfo>
                <ClientInfo>
                    <userID
                    xmlns="urn:csp">
                        12345
                    </userID>
                </ClientInfo>
            </Request>
            <Request>...</Request>
          <Request>...</Request>
        </Requests>
    </SignedPart>
    <dsig:Signature>...</dsig:Signature>
</BulkRegister>
```


In Example 6–34, the <BulkRegister> element represents a bulk request message that contains the batch ID, the type of response from the XKMS service, the sequence of the requests, and the signature used to sign the bulk request. The <BatchHeader> child element consists of general batch-related information, such as the batch ID, batch creation date, and the number of requests included in the batch. The <Request> element carries the individual requests, including the <KeyID> and <ds:KeyInfo> elements for those requests. The <ClientInfo> element specifies client-specific information about each request that can be used by the trust services provider for bookkeeping. The <dsig:Signature> element specifies the digital signature used to sign the X-BULK message.

Example 6–35 is an example X-BULK response message received from the XKMS service provider after processing the bulk request containing three individual requests.

Example 6–35 X-BULK response after running volume registration of certificates

```
<BulkRegisterResult xmlns="http://www.w3.org/2002/03/xkms-xbulk">
   <SignedPart Id="mybulkid-0">
        <BatchHeader>
            <BatchID>mybatch-0</BatchID>
            ...
            <NumberOfRequests>3</NumberOfRequests>
        </BatchHeader>

        <RegisterResults number="2">
            <xkms:RegisterResult>
```

```
                <xkms:Result>
                    Success
                </xkms:Result>

                <xkms:Answer>
                    <xkms:Status>
                        Valid
                    </xkms:Status>

                    <xkms:KeyID>...</xkms:KeyID>

                    <dsig:KeyInfo>
                        ...
                    </dsig:KeyInfo>
                </xkms:Answer>
            </xkms:RegisterResult>
            <xkms:RegisterResult>
                ...
            </xkms:RegisterResult>
            <xkms:RegisterResult>
                ...
            </xkms:RegisterResult>
        </RegisterResults>
    </SignedPart>
    <dsig:Signature>...</dsig:Signature>
</BulkRegisterResult>
```

In Example 6–35, the <BulkRegisterResult> element represents the bulk response containing information such as the batch ID, the number of results included, the actual results to the registration requests, and the signature used to sign the given bulk response. The <BatchID> element identifies the relationship between the batch elements of the bulk request and bulk response. The <RegisterResults> element contains the individual <xkms:RegisterResult> elements, which hold the registration details of the individual requests.

OASIS Web Services Security (WS-Security)

The OASIS WS-Security (also referred to as OASIS WSS-SOAP Message Security) is an industry-standard effort to secure Web services by supporting and integrating multiple security standards and technologies. The OASIS WS-Security 1.0 specification has been accepted and approved by OASIS as an official standard. WS-Security forms the basis for building interoperable Web services security infrastructure by defining end-to-end message-level security mechanisms for SOAP messages. With industry support, currently WS-Security is emerging as a *de facto* standard for securing Web services and promoting security interoperability in Web services.

Motivation of WS-Security

In Web-services communication, SOAP defines the structure of an XML document and the rules and mechanisms that can be used to enable communication between applications. SOAP does not define or address any specific security mechanisms. Using SOAP headers provides a way to define and add features, enabling application-specific security mechanisms like digital signature and encryption.

Incorporating security mechanisms in SOAP headers poses several complexities and challenges in an end-to-end Web-services security scenario that mandates message-level and transport-level security features such as security context propagation, support for multiple security technologies, maintaining message integrity, and confidentiality across participating intermediaries. More importantly, incorporating security mechanisms in SOAP headers limits interoperability in certain aspects of addressing support for a variety of supporting security infrastructures, such as PKI, binary security tokens, digital signature formats, encryption mechanisms, and so forth.

The WS-Security specification incorporates a standard set of SOAP extensions required for securing Web services and implementing message authentication, message integrity, message confidentiality, and security token propagation. It also defines mechanisms for supporting a variety of security tokens, signature and encryption mechanisms, and standards-based security technologies, including PKI and Kerberos. The goal of WS-Security is to provide secure SOAP messages that support multiple security token formats for authentication or authorization, multiple signature formats, multiple encryption technologies, and multiple trust domains.

WS-Security Definitions

To understand WS-Security, it is important to know the terms and definitions specified in the WS-Security 1.0 specification. Let's take a look at some of the key terms and definitions.

- **Claim**: A declaration made by an entity. The entity can be a name, identity, key, group, privilege, capability, and so forth.
- **Claim Confirmation**: The process of verifying a claim belonging to an entity.
- **Security Token**: A security token (examples include username, X.509 certificate, and Kerberos token) represents a collection of one or more claims.
- **Signed Security Token**: A security token that is asserted and cryptographically signed by an authority.
- **Trust**: A characteristic that one entity is willing to accept and rely upon for another entity to execute a set of actions and/or to make a set of assertions about a set of subjects and/or scopes.

Using Digital Signatures in WS-Security

Applying a signature is critically important to Web services for the purpose of establishing the authenticity of a message and its sender's identity. With a digital signature applied in WS-Security, a recipient of a SOAP message is assured of the message's integrity and that the signed message and its elements have not been tampered with during transit.

WS-Security adopts and builds on the W3C XML signature specifications defining usage of various elements and a processing model for signing messages. However, XML signature better ensures that the message recipients at intermediaries or endpoints can verify the signature and validate the signer's identity.

Using Encryption in WS-Security

In Web-services communication, applying encryption can be done using standard SSL/TLS mechanisms, and the message can be encrypted in its entirety and sent confidentially to one or more recipients. Using SSL/TLS satisfies transport-level confidentiality requirements, but it does not solve message-level requirements when parts of an XML message must be made confidential by using selective encryption and then signed by different users.

WS-Security adopts and builds on XML encryption specifications for encrypting and decrypting messages. This facilitates encryption of messages in their entirety or as selected parts intended for multiple recipients based on their signed identity and privileges for viewing and consuming them. WS-Security also allows support use of SOAP intermediaries.

Using Security Tokens in WS-Security

WS-Security defines ways for sending security information as security tokens to its message recipients in order to provide support for authentication and representing identity in a SOAP message. WS-Security defines mechanisms for defining security tokens that include representing username and password combination, binary security tokens (e.g., X.509 certificate, Kerberos v5 ticket) and XML security tokens (e.g., SAML, REL).

The Role of SAML and REL in WS-Security

WS-Security allows representing XML-based security tokens by providing support for Security Assertions Mark-Up Language (SAML) and Rights Expression Language (REL).

SAML provides an XML-based framework for exchanging security-related information over networks, and thus over the Internet. SAML does not define newer mechanisms for authentication or authorization. Instead, it defines XML structures for representing information pertaining to authentication and authorization so that these structures can be marshaled across system boundaries and can be understood by the recipient's security systems. SAML is also designed to provide single sign-on for both automatic and manual interactions across security services. SAML is emerging as a de facto standard for securely exchanging XML-based security information regardless of the underlying security architectures and for promoting security interoperability. The OASIS WS-Security TC developed a SAML Token profile to define the rules for using SAML 1.1 assertions with WS-Security. OASIS endorsed SAML Token Profile 1.0 as a standard.

REL defines the rights, usage permissions, constraints, legal obligations, and license terms pertaining to an electronic document. Open Digital Rights Language (ODRL) and eXtensible Rights Markup Language (XrML) defines the XML vocabulary for representing REL. The OASIS WS-Security TC also developed a REL Token profile to define the rules and guidelines for using ISO/IEC 21000-5 Rights Expressions with WS-Security. OASIS ratified REL Token Profile 1.0 as a standard.

Refer to Chapter 7, "Identity Architecture and It's Technologies" for in-depth information about SAML and its applied scenarios.

WS-Security: The Anatomy of SOAP Message Security

WS-Security addresses the security of Web services by adopting existing standards and standards-based technologies in a platform-independent and transport-protocol–neutral way. As we discussed earlier, it adopts XML signature and XML encryption for protecting messages by applying digital signature and encryption-decryption specifications. To address authentication and authorization requirements, it uses standard mechanisms, including username-password tokens, binary security tokens, and XML-based security tokens. The WS-Security specification works with all SOAP versions since SOAP 1.1.

Let's take a closer look at the structural details and characteristics of a WS-Security-enabled SOAP message and its core elements.

Message Structure and Its Core Elements

WS-Security defines a set of security-specific extensions that are to be embedded in a SOAP message. It defines the structure and its core elements, processing rules, and mechanisms that can be used to enable SOAP message security. WS-Security–specific extensions are represented as child elements of the SOAP header element <soapenv:Header>. Figure 6–5 represents the structure of a SOAP message enabled with WS-Security elements representing security tokens, signature, and encryption.

Let's take a closer look at the WS-Security structural representation and its elements, illustrating the usage of security tokens, XML signature, and XML encryption.

Namespaces

The WS-Security 1.0 specification mandates the use of the following two XML namespaces in implementations. Using the following namespace URLs for obtaining the schema files is required. The prefix wsse identifies the namespace for WS-Security extensions, while wsu identifies the namespaces for global utility attributes. Table 6–1 shows the prefixes and namespaces for WS-Security extensions.

<wsse:Security>

The <wsse:Security> element is the parent element that represents a complete WS-Security–enabled SOAP message, including mechanisms for security tokens, applying signature, and encryption. A WS-Security–enabled SOAP message may contain one or more <wsse:Security> header elements.

Each <wsse:Security> element contains the security information applied to its intended message recipient or SOAP intermediaries. WS-Security headers representing multiple recipients should be specified with an optional role <S:role> attribute. It is optional to include a mustUnderstand="true" attribute, which forces the message recipient to generate a SOAP fault when the underlying implementation

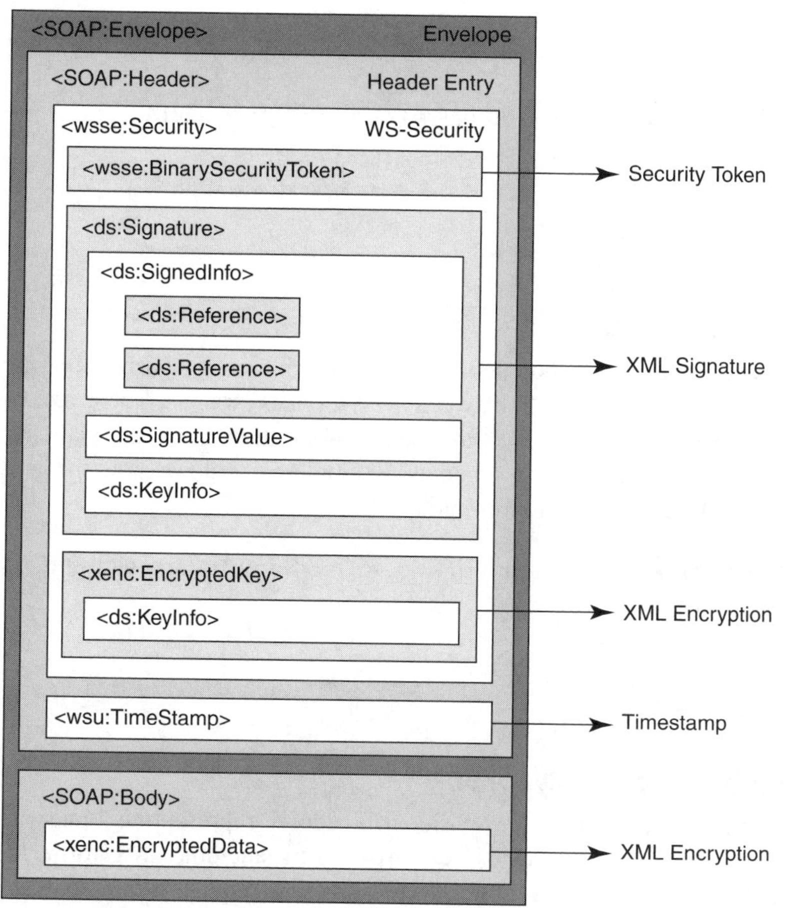

Figure 6–5 The WS-Security message structure and its core elements

Table 6–1 Namespaces for WS-Security Extensions

Prefix	*Namespaces*
wsse	http://docs.oasis-open.org/wss/2004/01/oasis-200401-wss-wssecurity-secext-1.0.xsd
wsu	http://docs.oasis-open.org/wss/2004/01/oasis-200401-wss-wssecurity-utility-1.0.xsd

does not support WS-Security specifications. Example 6–36 shows how a <wsse:Security> element can be represented.

Example 6–36 Representation of <wsse:Security> element

```
<wsse:Security S:role="IntendedRecipentEndpoint"
                             S:mustUnderstand="true">

. . .
</wsse:Security>
```


<wsse:UsernameToken>

The WS-Security specification defines how to attach security tokens for sending and receiving security information between Web-services partners. The <wsse:Username> element provides a way to insert username information and additional username-specific information based on schemas. Example 6–37 shows how the <wsse:UserNameToken> element can be represented.

Example 6–37 Representation of <wsse:UserNameToken> element

```
<wsse:Security>
  <wsse:UsernameToken>
      <wsse:Username>Nagappan</wsse:Username>
</wsse:UsernameToken>
```

<wsse:BinarySecurityToken>

Similar to username tokens, WS-Security allows representing binary security tokens such as X.509 certificates, Kerberos tickets, and non-XML format security information. For interpreting binary-formatted tokens, it uses two attributes, ValueType and EncodingType. The ValueType attribute indicates a security token, such as wsse:X509v3 or wsse:Kerberosv5ST. The EncodingType attribute specifies the encoding format of the binary data, such as Base64Binary. Example 6–38 shows how a wsse:BinarySecurityToken element indicating a X.509 certificate can be represented.

Example 6–38 Representation of <wsse:BinarySecurityToken> element

```
<wsse:BinarySecurityToken EncodingType="wsse:Base64Binary"
                             ValueType="wsse:X509v3"/>

JkFYGT9=...lhSE
</wsse:BinarySecurityToken>
```

<saml:Assertion> and <r:license>

WS-Security allows representing XML-based security tokens that are represented using Security Assertion Markup Language (SAML) or Extensible Rights

Markup language (XrML) as SAML assertions and REL security tokens, respectively. The SAML assertions and REL tokens are attached to WS-Security headers by placing them under the <wsse:Security> element.

Example 6–39 shows how a SAML 1.0 assertion can be represented using <saml:Assertion> element under <wsse:Security>.

Example 6–39 Representation of a SAML assertion in <wsse:Security>

```
<wsse:Security>
    <saml:Assertion
      AssertionID="_a75adf55-01d7-40cc-929f-dbd8372ebdfc"
      IssueInstant="2004-02-11T00:36:02Z"
      Issuer="www.sun.com/identity"
      MajorVersion="1"
      MinorVersion="1"
      . . .
     </saml:Assertion>
     . . .
</wsse:Security>
```

Example 6–40 show how a REL license can be represented using <r:license> element under <wsse:Security>.

Example 6–40 Representation of a REL license in <wsse:Security>

```
<wsse:Security xmlns:wsse="...">
    <r:license xmlns:r="."
       licenseId="urn:xyz:SecurityToken:sp8">
     <r:grant>
         <r:keyHolder>
           <r:info>
              <ds:KeyValue>...</ds:KeyValue>
           </r:info>
          </r:keyHolder>
          <r:possessProperty/>
          <sx:commonName '
            xmlns:sx="...">Sun Microsystems</sx:commonName>
          </r:grant>
      <r:issuer>       <ds:Signature>...</ds:Signature>
         </r:issuer>
       </r:license>
     . . .
</wsse:Security>
```

<wsse:SecurityTokenReference>

The <wsse:SecurityTokenReference> element defines a URI that locates where a security token can be found. This provides the flexibility to obtain a security token from named external locations accessible via URI. This element can also be used to refer to a security token contained within the same SOAP message header.

<ds:Signature>

The WS-Security specification builds on the W3C XML signature specification for representing digital signatures in the WS-Security headers. The <ds:Signature> element can represent the digital signature and other related information, including how the signature was generated. A typical instance of <ds:Signature> contains a <ds:SignedInfo> element describing the information being signed, a <ds:SignatureValue> element containing the bytes that make up the digital signature, a <ds:Reference> element identifying the information being signed along with transformations, and a <ds:KeyInfo> element indicating the key used to validate the signature. A <ds:SignedInfo> element contains the identifiers for canonicalization and signature method algorithms. The <ds:KeyInfo> element may contain where to find the public key that can be referenced using a <wsse:SecurityTokenReference> element.

Example 6–41 shows how a <ds:Signature> element can represent a WS-Security-enabled SOAP message.

Example 6–41 Representation of an XML signature in <wsse:Security>

```
<SOAP:Envelope>
        <SOAP:Header>
           <wsse:Security>
              ...
             <wsse:BinarySecurityToken>
              ...
              </wsse:BinarySecurityToken>
              <ds:Signature>
                   ...
                   <ds:SignedInfo>
                       <ds:Reference URI='#Body'>
                        ...
                        <ds:Transforms>
                           ...
                       </ds:Transforms>
                       <ds:DigestMethod>
                       . . .
                       </ds:DigestMethod>
                           ...
```

```
                    </ds:Reference>
                      <ds:CanonicalizationMethod  ...>

                  </ds:SignedInfo>
              <ds:SignatureValue>
                  ...
             </ds:SignatureValue>
           <ds:KeyInfo>
             <wsse:SecurityTokenReference>
           ...
         </wsse:SecurityTokenReference>
         </ds:KeyInfo>
      </ds:Signature>
    ...
         </wsse:Security>
      </SOAP:Header>
      <SOAP:Body Id='Body'>
          ...
      </SOAP:Body>
</SOAP:Envelope>
```

Refer to the "XML Signature" section earlier in this chapter for more information and details about generating and validating XML signatures.

<xenc:EncryptedData>

The WS-Security specification builds on the W3C XML encryption specification for representing encrypted data in SOAP messages. The <xenc:EncryptedData> element can represent the encrypted data and other related information, including the encryption method and the key information. A typical instance of <xenc:EncryptedData> contains an <xenc:EncryptionMethod> element specifying the applied encryption method, an <xenc:CipherData> element containing the cipher value of the encrypted data, and a <ds:KeyInfo> element indicating the key used for encryption and decryption. A <xenc:ReferenceList> element can be used to create a manifest of encrypted parts of a message envelope expressed using the <xenc:EncryptedData> elements.

Example 6–42 shows how an <xenc:EncryptedData> element is represented in a WS-Security-enabled SOAP message.

Example 6–42 Representation of XML encryption in <wsse:Security>

```
<SOAP:Envelope>
   <SOAP:Header>
       <wsse:Security>
```

```
          ...
      <wsse:BinarySecurityToken>
          ...
       </wsse:BinarySecurityToken>
            <ds:Signature>
          ...
        </ds:Signature>
     ...
        </wsse:Security>
     </SOAP:Header>
  <SOAP:Body Id="Body">
        ...
  <xenc:EncryptedData  Id="msgcontId"
      Type="http://www.w3.org/2001/04/xmlenc#Content">
   <xenc:EncryptionMethod Algorithm="..." />
    <ds:KeyInfo>
       <KeyName>...</KeyName>
   </ds:KeyInfo>
  <xenc:CipherData>
     <xenc:CipherValue
        ...
      </xenc:CipherValue>
     </xenc:CipherData>
 </xenc:EncryptedData>
 </SOAP:Body>
</SOAP:Envelope>
```

Refer to the "XML Encryption" section earlier in this chapter for more information and details about encryption and decryption using XML encryption.

<xenc:EncryptedKey>

The <xenc:EncryptedKey> element is used to represent encrypted keys. In usage, a SOAP message carries both encrypted data and the encrypted symmetric key needed to read that data. The symmetric key is encrypted using the recipient's public key. When the message is received, the recipient can use its private key to decrypt the encrypted symmetric key and then use this symmetric key to decrypt the actual data.

The structure of an <xenc:EncryptedKey> element is quite similar to an <xenc:EncryptedData> element with three sub-elements: an <xenc:EncryptionMethod> element specifying how the key was encrypted, an <xenc:CipherData> element containing the cipher value of the encrypted key, and a <ds:KeyInfo> element specifying the information about the key used.

Example 6–43 shows how an <xenc:EncryptedKey> element is represented in a WS-Security-enabled SOAP message.

Example 6–43 Representing encrypted key in <wsse:Security>

```
<SOAP:Envelope>
  <SOAP:Header>
   <wsse:Security>
     <xenc:EncryptedKey>
       ...
     <ds:KeyInfo>
       <wsse:SecurityTokenReference>
          <ds:X509IssuerSerial>
           <ds:X509IssuerName>
               DC=CSPSecurity, DC=com
               </ds:X509IssuerName>
          <ds:X509SerialNumber>87070953</ds:X509SerialNumber>
         </ds:X509IssuerSerial>
        </wsse:SecurityTokenReference>
      </ds:KeyInfo>
     ...
     </xenc:EncryptedKey>
     ...
    </wsse:Security>
    </SOAP:Header>
  <SOAP:Body>
   <xenc:EncryptedData Id="ContentID">
   <xenc:CipherData>
   </xenc:EncryptedData>
</SOAP:Body>
</SOAP:Envelope>
```

Again, refer to the "XML Encryption" section earlier in this chapter for more information and details about encryption and decryption using XML encryption.

<wsu:TimeStamp>

The WS-Security specification recommends the use of timestamps to determine the timelines and validity of security semantics. If a recipient receives two contradictory messages, the timestamps inserted in the message can be used to determine validity of one of them. The <wsu:TimeStamp> element allows you to define the message creation time and its expiration time.

Example 6–44 shows how a <wsu:Timestamp> element is represented in a WS-Security-enabled SOAP message.

Example 6–44 Representing time stamps in WS-Security

```
<SOAP:Envelope>
   <SOAP:Header>
      . . .
       <wsu:Timestamp wsu:Id="msgId1">
       <wsu:Created>2002-08-22T00:26:15Z</wsu:Created>
       <wsu:Expires>2002-08-22T00:31:15Z</wsu:Expires>
       </wsu:Timestamp>
       <wsse:Security>
          . . .
        </wsse:Security>
       . . .
     </SOAP:Header>
     <SOAP:Body>
   . . .
    </SOAP:Body>
 </SOAP:Envelope>
```


WS-I Basic Security Profile

The Web Services Interoperability Organization (WS-I) started as an industry initiative by leading technology vendors and organizations. Its ultimate goal is to promote interoperability in Web services implementations across platforms, applications, programming languages, and devices. As part of its deliverables plan, WS-I introduced the notion of WS-I profiles to address the interoperability issues due to specification versions, dependencies, requirements, and vendor interpretations. The WS-I Basic Security Profile Version 1.0 provides a set of requirements and guidelines to promote interoperability by adhering to standards and specifications that contribute to Web services security. In particular, it is intended to address the interoperability issues related to the following:

- SOAP Message Security
- Transport Layer Security (HTTP over SSL/TLS)
- Security Tokens (Username Tokens, Binary security tokens and XML security tokens)
- XML Signature

- XML Encryption
- Algorithms
- Relationship with WS-I Basic Profile
- SOAP Attachment Security
- Security considerations
- Usage scenarios

WS-I Basic Security Profile is an extension to the WS-I Basic profile that addresses the additional security-related functionalities without affecting interoperability. The security profile incorporates specifications based on the OASIS WS-Security 1.0 standard, the W3C XML signature, W3C XML encryption, and IETF-HTTP over SSL/TLS as an underlying protocol. It also identifies extensibility points to support additional cipher suites and algorithms that require private agreement between the peers involved in Web services.

At the time of writing this book, WS-I Basic security profile 1.0 is released as a working group draft, and conforming security provider implementations were not available. To find out the current status of WS-I Basic security profile from the WS-I Security profile working group, refer to the WS-I Web site at http://www.ws-i.org/deliverables/workinggroup.aspx?wg=basicsecurity.

Java-Based Web Services Security Providers

With the overwhelming success of Java in Web and pervasive applications running on a variety of platforms and devices, the Java platform has become the de facto run-time environment for multiplatform Web-services providers. With the release of J2EE 1.4, the J2EE platform allows development and deployment of Web services by enabling J2EE components to participate in Web services. Today there is a long list of technology vendors that provide Java-based infrastructure solutions for delivering Web services.

At the time of the writing of this book, the following vendors offered Java-based Web-services implementation based on the OASIS WS-Security specification.

Sun JWSDP

Java Web Services Developer Pack (JWSDP) is a Web services development kit that provides build, deploy, and test environments for Web-services applications and components. It brings together a set of Java APIs and reference implementations for building XML-based Java applications that support key XML Web services industry-standard initiatives such as SOAP, WSDL, UDDI, WS-I Profiles, XML Encryption, XML Digital Signature, and WS-Security. At the time of writing this book, Sun Microsystems released JWSDP 1.5, which includes the following APIs and tools for Web services:

- Java API for XML-based RPC (JAX-RPC)
- Java Architecture for XML Binding (JAXB)
- Java API for XML Registries (JAXR)
- XML and Web Services Security
- XML Digital Signature
- Java API for XML Processing (JAXP)
- SOAP with Attachments API for Java (SAAJ)

JWSDP 1.5 also implements the WS-I Basic profile 1.1 and WS-I Basic Attachment profile for enabling interoperability.

WS-Security in JWSDP

The JWSDP 1.5 provides full implementation of the OASIS Web Services Security 1.0 (WS-Security) specification as XWS-Security APIs for providing message-level security for SOAP messages. This allows representing message-level security mechanisms based on XML encryption and XML Digital signatures. It also provides support for applying authentication credentials such as username/password and certificates.

J2EE 1.4

With the release of J2EE 1.4, the J2EE platform allows enabling selected J2EE components to participate in Web-services communication. It adopts APIs and reference implementations from JWSDP. As a key requirement, it mandates the implementation of the JAX-RPC 1.1 and EJB 2.1 specifications that address the role of Web services and how to expose J2EE components as Web services. In compliance with WS-I Basic profile guidelines, J2EE ensures interoperability with all Web-services providers that adhere to WS-I specifications. The J2EE Web services security builds on the existing J2EE security mechanisms for securing Web-service interactions by adopting a flexible security model that uses both declarative and programmatic security mechanisms. In addition, it also allows incorporating security mechanisms used for Web services built using JAX-RPC and SAAJ.

Sun Java System Access Manager

The Sun Java System Access Manager is a standards-based authentication and authorization framework for securing resources that include applications and Web services. Based on J2EE architecture and API, it offers a Java-based implementation for providing Web-services security, including support for the OASIS WS-Security, SAML, and Liberty alliance specifications.

VeriSign TSIK and XKMS Services

The VeriSign Trust Services Integration Kit (TSIK) provides a Java API framework for XML Web-services security. It provides a set of Java APIs and reference implementations for securing XML Web services based on industry-standard initiatives such as XML Encryption, XML Digital signature, OASIS WS-Security, SAML, and XKMS.

VeriSign XKMS Services

The VeriSign XKMS service is a Web services interface to VeriSign-managed PKI. Based on Web-services security standards, the VeriSign XKMS service can be accessed in real time via Web services instead of via Java-based API mechanisms, RSA BSAFE, or Microsoft API. The service allows real-time authentication of Web services providers and requesters using digital certificates and PKI. The VeriSign XKMS Web services are publicly accessible at http://xkms.verisign.com. The VeriSign XKMS trust services offers the following PKI functions accessible to XML Web-services–based application solutions.

- Generating and registering the signing key pairs
- Locating the public key
- Verifying and validating the key
- Revocation and recovering keys

RSA BSAFE Secure-WS

The RSA BSAFE Secure-WS toolkit provides both Java and C implementations that allow encryption and decryption of SOAP messages as well as signing and validating digital signatures in accordance with the OASIS WS-Security specification. It allows representing security tokens that include username/password, X.509 certificates, RSA SecurID tokens, Kerberos tickets, and SAML assertions.

The Java version has full support for standard JCE providers in addition to BSAFE Crypto-J with FIPS-140 compliance.

In addition to the above products, there are a number of Java-based security toolkits from leading industry vendors, and open source initiatives are available that provide support for building Web services security. Before adopting these solutions, it is quite important to verify their support of the current and evolving Web-services security standards and specifications. Their meeting of architectural requirements, particularly with regard to interoperability, high-availability, reliability, manageability, auditability, and other QoS considerations is especially important.

XML-Aware Security Appliances

With the widespread adoption of Web services, the security appliance (firewall) vendors are addressing Web services security needs using XML-aware hardware appliances that ensure secure XML traffic and Web services transactions. Adopting hardware appliances for Web services is strongly recommended, particularly the substitution of hardware for resource-intensive XML processing tasks and the offloading of XML security processing from a Web services endpoint. These appliances are commonly referred to as XML firewall.

XML Firewall

XML firewall appliances will reside in the DMZ behind network firewall appliances and operate on the inbound and outbound XML traffic of a Web-services provider or requester. These appliances help in identifying XML content-level threats and vulnerabilities based on message compliance, payload, and attachments that are not detected by network firewalls. In addition, XML firewalls offer functionalities that support XML encryption, digital signatures, schema validation, access control, and SSL communication. An XML firewall appliance often will run at wire speeds that are superior to that of the traditional software infrastructure. Adopting XML firewall delivers significant performance gains in Web-services transactions that involve SSL communication, XML filtering, XML schema and message validation, signature validation, decryption, XML parsing, and transformation.

There is a growing list of XML-aware security appliances currently available, including XML firewalls and XML processing accelerators. It is noteworthy that some security hardware vendors provide support for Web-services security standards and specifications.

Summary

Web Services are gaining industry-wide acceptance because they can solve IT problems using standards and standards-based technologies. They deliver a promising solution that allows IT services to be interoperable and to integrate using XML-based messages and industry-standard protocols. With the involvement of leading industry vendors in XML Web-services standards initiatives, there is a growing list of standards and specifications for developing and deploying Web services. Web services form the basis for standards-based infrastructure, communication, and application development in the industry today. The security of Web services is the biggest concern today as the industry faces a continually growing list of requirements and challenges.

In this chapter, we began with a discussion about Web services' architectural concepts, building blocks, core security challenges and requirements, and standards and specifications. We looked at both the high-level and in-depth technical details of the key Web-services security specifications and standards that contribute to the end-to-end security of a Web-services infrastructure. In particular, we looked at the following:

- Web services architecture and its building blocks
- Web services threats and vulnerabilities
- Web services security requirements
- Web services security standards
- XML signature (XML DSIG)
- XML encryption (XML ENC)
- XML key management services (XKMS)
- OASIS Web services security (WS-Security)
- WS-I Basic Security profile

We discussed the critical security factors and considerations that need to be addressed with regard to the implementation of Web services. We also briefly looked at the Java-based Web-services infrastructure providers that offer solutions in compliance with Web-services standards and specifications.

In the next chapter, we will explore the identity architecture and its technologies.

References

[W3C] XML Signature–Syntax and Processing Rules. W3C Recommendation, February 12, 2002.

http://www.w3.org/TR/xmldsig-core/

[W3C] XML Encryption–Syntax and Processing Rules. W3C Recommendation, December 10, 2002.

http://www.w3.org/TR/xmlenc-core/

[OASIS] WS-Security 1.0 Standard and Specifications.

http://docs.oasis-open.org/wss/2004/01/oasis-200401-wss-soap-message-security-1.0.pdf

[WS-I] Web Services Security Basic Profile 1.0–Working Group Draft.

http://www.ws-i.org/Profiles/BasicSecurityProfile-1.0-2004-05-12.html

[W3C] Web Services Architecture. W3C Working Group Note, February 11, 2004.

http://www.w3.org/TR/ws-arch/

[Sun J2EE Blueprints] Designing Web Services with the J2EE Platform, 2nd Edition—Guidelines, Patterns, and Code for Java Web Services.

http://java.sun.com/blueprints/guidelines/designing_webservices/

[Ramesh Nagappan, Robert Skoczylas et al.] *Developing Java Web Services: Architecting and Developing Java Web Services,* Wiley 2002.

Identity Management Standards and Technologies

Topics in This Chapter

- Identity Management–Core Issues
- Understanding Network Identity and Federated Identity
- Introduction to SAML
- SAML Architecture
- SAML Usage Scenarios
- The Role of SAML in J2EE-Based Applications and Web Services
- Introduction to Liberty Alliance and Their Objectives
- Liberty Alliance Architecture
- Liberty Usage Scenarios
- The Nirvana of Access Control and Policy Management
- Introduction to XACML
- XACML Data Flow and Architecture
- XACML Usage Scenarios

Chapter 7

Identity management is one of the growing security concerns in enterprise IT services. According to Information Security Breaches Survey 2004 [SecurityBreach2004], security breaches due to identity management flaws are increasing. Confidentiality breaches can cause disruption to business services and may result in large financial losses, with 15 percent of cases costing £100,000 (Great British Pound, which is about US $250,000) in legal fees, investigation costs, and fines. They usually take at least 10 to 20 man-days to resolve. From the survey findings, 80 percent of the security attacks are from external sources. Identity is the key to unlocking access to business services, applications, and resources. It is extremely important to secure the identity by authenticating the user prior to that user accessing any resources within the enterprise. In addition, identity is a major piece of information security management that is addressed by compliance and regulatory requirements (such as Sarbanes-Oxley in the United States). It is a strategic area in the management of security risks that threaten mission-critical business applications.

This chapter will discuss the identity management technologies for single sign-on and policy management using standards such as SAML, Liberty, and XACML. It will also discuss their logical architecture.

Identity Management–Core Issues

As portals and Web-based applications proliferate, consumers tend to create new user accounts in different Web sites. Different online portals and Web sites have different security policies for creating user accounts and managing user passwords. Very often, consumers have to maintain a number of "digital" user identities (user account names and passwords). There are also information aggregators that extract user information from various Web sites and sell them to large corporations for database marketing. These digital user identities are often open to abuse or identity theft. Since these digital identities are managed by individual Web sites, and the security protection capability of individual Web sites varies, consumers have no control over the protection of their user identity and their privacy if these Web sites are attacked. According to the previously mentioned Information Security Breaches Survey 2004 [SecurityBreach2004], identity theft is becoming a major concern for consumers. Consumers want to be assured that their digital identity is reliable and secure so that they can shop securely online. This is fairly challenging, even with a robust and reliable identity management system.

Business corporations have different and complicated identity-related issues. Many of these organizations have customized user authentication and authorization mechanisms for their legacy systems, which may not share the same security implementation (such as authentication mechanisms and PKI operations) or infrastructure (such as authentication server, policy, and directory). Thus, users are often required to have individual user accounts and passwords for each application system. As the number of applications and systems grow, there is a need for using a single user identity for authentication and authorization across multiple systems and infrastructures. This can provide flexibility in collaborating with different business functions. However, achieving a single sign-on to multiple systems and infrastructures requires considerable security integration and interoperability. Areas involved include how to manage keys and certificates, and how to enable legacy systems to share the common user authentication mechanism or security provider infrastructure for authentication.

Another challenge is dealing with user identity for Business-to-Business (B2B) applications such as B2B workflow and supply chain applications. Users often require different user identities to sign on to each system hosted by the participating trading partners. Managing different user accounts and passwords among the trading partners adds complexity, particularly when any user password change needs to be synchronized in each system. Trading partners need to agree how to provision a new user account in each system that has its own security requirements. There are also integration issues if the trading partners want to adopt and implement a common user authentication and authorization infrastructure to streamline collaboration. Agreeing on a common user authentication mechanism among different security infrastructure and application systems is not trivial. If any of the vendor products or underlying technologies change (for example, by a product upgrade), all user authentication interfaces need to be retested again or the business-to-business workflow may have security related issues.

Compliance with United States federal regulations such as the Sarbanes-Oxley Act, HIPAA, and the Patriot Act also pose another challenge for identity management. Business corporations have to provide a reliable and thorough auditing capability to detect and manage any unusual or suspicious changes in user accounts or profiles. Building such capability is not trivial. This will require a sophisticated identity management infrastructure that can detect and manage any potential security vulnerabilities and threats, including identity spoofing and identity theft.

The security vulnerabilities and threats related to user identities are likely to impact more than one single application system, because user identities are used and processed across multiple systems, whether local or distributed. As discussed in Chapter 1, the following security vulnerabilities and threats will also apply to managing user identities:

- Denial of Service attacks on security infrastructures that handle user authentication and authorization
- Man-in-the-middle attacks to steal user identity and session information
- Session hijacking and theft from a "broken" or stolen user identity
- Spoofing with a faked or stolen user identity
- Identity theft by spoofing session information
- Data privacy and confidentiality violations
- Replay attacks with a stolen user identity
- Multiple sign-on issues while enabling aggregated access to disparate applications
- Broken authentication and authorization context propagation issues between applications

It is crucial for security architects and developers to understand the security issues that are related to managing user identities. The following sections introduce the concept of identity management, the associated industry standards, and their logical architecture. They also discuss how these standards and standards-based technologies can help address the challenges of managing user identities.

Understanding Network Identity and Federated Identity

Network Identity refers to a software solution that incorporates a set of network-concentric business processes and the supporting technology infrastructure to manage both the life cycle of identities and the relationship between these identities and business applications and information. The concept of network identity goes beyond simple user authentication or authorization for accessing applications and resources. It also entails the management aspects of the life cycle of identities and the implementation of business processes to support it. It is a useful distinction in the context of security breach issues and critical security flaws discussed in Chapter 1.

Federated Identity refers to the use of identity information between companies and applications or across different security infrastructures over a network. Management of these identities is inter-company and inter-dependent. Federated identity extends the use of network identity within a company or enterprise to multiple business entities or security infrastructures. This includes complicated processes and implementations of how identities are registered, revoked, and terminated with an identity provider. Federated identity is obviously subject to more security risks and integration challenges than network identity. Single sign-on across companies is an example of federated identity functionality. It enables a user to access remote applications and resources by authenticating only once. After that single sign-on, a user's identity authentication is shared among different authentication security infrastructures.

Identity management denotes the process of managing network identity and federated identity and provides the following functions:

- **User Provisioning**. This includes creating or administering user identities that can access enterprise resources and business applications.
- **Roles and Groups**. This refers to how user entities can be mapped to different roles or groups to access the enterprise resources. For example, creating a user role for managing the user profiles of low-volume mobile phone subscribers will be handy, instead of creating an individual user profile for each subscriber.

- **Account Service Provisioning**. This denotes how a user account service is provisioned in different systems according to the access rights and user profile. It also encompasses synchronizing user passwords among different applications and systems that can synchronize user passwords, and enforcing security policies for account passwords. Sometimes, provisioning a user account involves multistep management approval workflow processes.
- **Delegated Administration**. This allows local or distributed administrators to create or update a hierarchy of user identities and roles that grants access to applications and resources. This hierarchy allows an organization to delegate user administration, group and role administration, security administration, and application-specific functions to different roles or principals that are from sub-organizations within a network or dispersed geographically across multiple sub-domains of the network.
- **Audit Trails and Reporting**. It is becoming more important to track the history of the user identity life-cycle management, and detect any suspicious changes for risk management and compliance purposes.
- **Single Sign-on (SSO) and Global Logout**. Single sign-on (whether single domain, cross-domain, or across networks) addresses the issue of maintaining a silo authentication security infrastructure. By sharing the same user identity authentication, single sign-on provides for a lower cost of interoperating with other security domains and enhances the user experience. If the system invalidates the user identity or session in the presentation tier, global logout can automatically sign out from the rest of the sessions. Global logout is also critical to protecting user session integrity from security hackers and intruders.

OASIS [OASIS], as an industry effort, publishes a list of security standards supporting identity management. These standards include the following:

- Security Assertion Markup Language (SAML) [SAML-TC]
- eXtensible Access Control Markup Language (XACML) [XACML-TC]
- Service Provisioning Markup Language (SPML)[SPML-TC].

In addition, Liberty Alliance (http://www.projectliberty.org) is a consortium of more than 150 companies, nonprofit organizations, and government organizations worldwide that has developed open standards and specifications for enabling federated network identity architectures. These standards and specifications address key business requirements in terms of providing a single point of access to multiple resources. They also address enabling the integration and interoperability of legacy software products with an existing security infrastructure and other proprietary solutions.

This chapter focuses on SAML, Liberty, and XACML, while Chapter 13, "Secure Service Provisioning," will cover SPML in more detail.

The Importance of Identity Management

Identity management is becoming more important to application security, because security threats and identity fraud are becoming more common and complex, which makes it harder to prevent the related vulnerabilities. Having a robust identity management solution can lower administrative costs (via automated security service provisioning), enhance user productivity (via a streamlined user authentication process), and deliver strong and consistent security for end-to-end business applications (using a central, standards-based authentication point and shared credential management). In addition, it can foster new revenue opportunities through enhanced partnership opportunities.

Introduction to SAML

Security Assertion Markup Language (SAML) is derived from two previous security initiatives: Security Services Markup Language (S2ML) and Authorization Markup Language (AuthXML). SAML is an XML–based framework for exchanging security assertion information about subjects. Subjects are entities that have identity related information specific to a security domain. SAML plays a vital role in delivering standards-based infrastructure for enabling single sign-on without requiring the use of a single vendor's security architecture. However, SAML does not provide the underlying user authentication mechanism.

The Motivation of SAML

SAML provides a standards-based approach to the enabling of SSO among heterogeneous applications and to the supporting of identity management. Before we had the SAML standard, developers had to enforce a centralized security infrastructure using proprietary security mechanisms for heterogeneous application systems. That solution was not cost-effective and created many interoperability issues among different vendor products. In the worst case, developers used client-side screen-scraping or a keystroke-recorder solution that could enable the user to sign on to different applications. These solutions store user credentials locally in either cleartext or a proprietary data format. This created interoperability issues and also opened up many security loopholes and risks for hackers on the client side. In addition, these solutions made it difficult to manage deployment and troubleshooting in multiple application integration scenarios.

Another proprietary approach is to encapsulate encrypted user credentials (also referred to as a **security token**) in the HTTP-POST header and pass the security token to different applications via a secure transport protocol such as SSL. Once a user authenticates with an SSO-enabled application, the client application uses the SSO security token in the HTTP-POST headers, which helps to redirect the user to the target resource or application to which it has privileged access. Each resource or application needs to build a proprietary agent to intercept the HTTP header for SSO security token. To many business corporations and their trading partners, the use of proprietary agents is intrusive to the infrastructure. Although this approach looks similar to many vendor-defined mechanisms, it provides the basis of the SAML specification for representing authentication and authorization credentials in a standard security-token format.

The Role of SAML in SSO

SAML provides an XML standards-based representation of security information that allows security information to be shared among application security domains over the network. Using HTTP-POST or SOAP message headers, SAML allows applications to participate in SSO scenarios. To support SSO, SAML introduces the notion of **SAML Assertions**, a part of XML messages that can be transferred between security providers and service providers. SAML Assertions contain statements that applications and service providers use to make authentication and authorization decisions.

In addition, SAML provides many benefits. These include the absence of duplication of security mechanisms and their associated directory information. SAML messages and their underlying XML-based interactions also ensure interoperability and the use of scalable remote authorization services to support multiple applications. SAML requires the user to enroll with at least one SAML-enabled security provider that will provide authentication services to the user. However, SAML does not define how authentication and authorization services should be implemented.

SAML is also designed to be used with other standards; the Liberty Alliance Project, the Shibboleth project, and the OASIS WS-Security standards have all adopted SAML as a technological underpinning to support identity management. A number of security vendors currently provide SAML-compliant security products. These vendors include Sun Microsystems, CA-Netegrity, RSA Security,

Oracle-Oblix, Entrust, and so forth. OpenSAML [OpenSAML] and SourceID [SourceID] are open-source implementations. This is not an exhaustive list of SAML-compliant products. More examples of SAML-compliant products can be found at http://www.oasis-open.org/committees/download.php/11915/RSA2005-saml-interop-final.pdf.

SAML 1.0

SAML 1.0 was accepted as an OASIS standard in November 2002. It is endorsed by leading industry vendors for the support of single sign-on and interoperability among security infrastructures. SAML 1.0 addressed one key aspect of identity management: how identity information can be communicated from one domain to another.

SAML 1.1

OASIS released the SAML version 1.1 specification on September 2, 2003.

SAML 1.1 is similar to SAML 1.0 but adds support for "network identity," defined by Liberty Alliance specifications [Liberty]. SAML 1.1 support for Liberty Alliance specifications allows exchanging user authentication and authorization information securely between Web sites within an organization or between organizations over the Internet by Web account linking and role-based federation. SAML 1.1 also introduced guidelines for the use of digital certificates that allow signing of SAML assertions.

There are also changes in the digital signature guidelines, such as the recommended use of exclusive canonical transformation. For details about the differences, see the SAML 1.1 [SAML11Diff]. The specification did not address all of the problems in the single sign-on or identity management domain. For example, it did not provide a standard authentication protocol that supports a variety of authentication devices and methods. Although SAML provides a flexible structure for encapsulating user credentials, there is still a problem in integrating with a Kerberos-based security infrastructure such as Microsoft Windows Kerberos. SAML 2.0 currently includes a work item "Kerberos SAML Profiles" that addresses the integration requirement. This subject is discussed in the next section.

SAML 2.0

SAML 2.0 specifications were approved by OASIS as a standard in March 2005. SAML 1.1 defined the protocols for single sign-on, delegated administration, and simple policy management. Liberty's Identity Federation Framework (ID-FF) 1.2 was provided to the SAML committee, and SAML 2.0 was the result of converging previous SAML versions with Liberty ID-FF and with Shibboleth. SAML 2.0 fills in the gaps left in SAML 1.1 by including global sign-out, session management, and extension of identity federation framework for opt-in account linking across Web sites (used by Liberty).

Among the additions in SAML 2.0, there are several interesting items:

- Enhancement of SAML assertions and protocols in support of federated identity and global sign-out.
- Creation of new SAML attribute profiles, including the X.500/LDAP attribute and XACML. These attribute profiles simply the configuration and deployment of systems that exchange attribute data.
- Pseudonyms to provide a privacy-enabling "alias" for a global identifier to avoid collusion between service providers. SAML 2.0 uses an opaque pseudo-random identifier (with no discernible correspondence with meaning identifiers such as e-mail addresses) between service providers to represent principals.
- With the use of pseudonyms, SAML 2.0 defines how two service providers can establish and manage these pseudonyms for the principals they are working with.
- SAML meta-data specify how configuration and trust-related data can be more easily deployed in SAML systems. Identity providers and service providers often need to agree on data such as roles, identifiers, and supported profiles. SAML meta-data provides a structure for identifying the actors involved in the various profiles, such as single sign-on identity provider, attribute authority, and requester.
- Better support of mobile and active devices by adding more authentication contexts that accommodate new authentication requirements, such as including smart card-based PKI and Kerberos.
- Support of encryption for attribute statements, name identifiers, or entire assertion statements.
- Support for privacy using privacy policy and settings that service providers can obtain and use to express a principal's consent to particular operations.
- Discovery of multiple identity providers, using a provider discovery profile that uses a cookie written in a common domain between the identity provider and service providers.

- Use of an Authentication Request protocol (<AuthnRequest>), which enables an interoperable "destination-site-first" scenario. In other words, the <AuthnRequest> protocol allows a user to approach a service provider first and then be directed to log in at the identity provider if the service provider deems it to be necessary.
- Conformance requirements and interoperability details.

SAML 2.0 has some changes in the core specification as well. It has significant changes in scope, particularly with regard to extending the functionality and aligning itself with other related initiatives. Here are some examples of the functionalities:

- Support for global logout and time-out (session support)
- Discovery of SAML Web service through a WSDL file (meta-data exchange and protocol)
- Exchange of name identifier and pseudonyms between sites (identity federation, or federated name registration protocol)
- Multi-hop delegation and intermediaries (multi-participant transactional workflows)
- Liberty authentication context exchange and control (authentication context)
- Additional protocol binding for direct HTTP use (HTTP-based assertion referencing)
- Coordinating with IETF Simple Authentication and Security Layer effort (SASL support)
- Integrating and reconciling SAML 2.0 and XACML 2.0, including attribute usage, authorization decision requests and responses, and policy queries and responses.

In addition to the SAML assertion, SAML 2.0 introduces the following new message protocols: artifact protocol, federated name registration protocol, federation termination protocol, single logout protocol, and name identifier mapping protocol. [SAML2Core] has a full description of these new messaging protocols, which are not discussed here.

One new message protocol of interest is the logout request (specified by the <LogoutRequest> tag), which supports global logout. This new support means that if a principal (a user or a system entity) logs out as a session participant, then the session authority will issue a logout request to all session participants. The reason for the global logout can be "urn:oasis:names:tc:SAML:2.0:logout:user" (user decides to terminate the session), or "urn:oasis:names:tc:SAML:2.0:logout:admin" (administrator wishes to terminate the session, for example, due to timeout). These and other attributes will be discussed in later sections.

SAML Profiles

The SAML specification defines a standard mechanism for representation of security information. This mechanism allows security information to be shared by multiple applications so that they are able to address single sign-on requirements. The notion of a SAML profile addresses these core interoperability requirements. The SAML profile allows the protocols and assertions to facilitate the use of SAML for a specific application purpose. A **SAML profile** defines a set of rules and guidelines for how to embed SAML assertions into, and extract them from, a protocol or other context of use. Using a SAML profile, business applications would be able to exchange security information in SAML messages seamlessly and to easily interoperate between SAML-enabled systems.

SAML 2.0 defines the following SAML profiles:

- **Web browser SSO Profile**: Single sign-on using standard browsers to multiple service providers. The Web browser SSO profile uses the SAML Authentication Request protocol, in conjunction with the HTTP Redirect, HTTP POST, and HTTP Artifact bindings. SAML 2.0 combines the previous two Web browser profiles from SAML 1.1 into one single profile.
- **Enhanced Client and Proxy Profile**: This profile defines the rules for a system entity to contact the appropriate identity provider, possibly in a context-dependent fashion. It uses the Reverse SOAP (PAOS) binding.
- **Identity Provider Discovery Profile**: This profile defines how a service provider discovers the identity provider used by the Principal.
- **Single Logout Profile**: This profile defines how to terminate the sessions managed by the session authority (or identity provider).
- **Name Identifier Management Profile**: This profile defines how to exchange a persistent identifier for a principal with the service providers and how to later modify changes in the format or value.
- **Artifact Resolution Profile**: SAML 2.0 defines an Artifact Resolution protocol to dereference a SAML artifact into a corresponding protocol message. The HTTP Artifact binding can then leverage this Artifact Resolution protocol in order to pass SAML protocol messages by reference.

- **Assertion Query/Request Profile**: This profile defines a protocol for requesting existing assertions by reference or by querying on the basis of a subject and additional statement-specific criteria.

In addition, the SAML profile also defines rules for mapping attributes expressed in SAML to another attribute representation system. This type of SAML profile is known as *Attribute Profile*. SAML 2.0 defines five different Attribute Profiles [SAML2Profiles].

- **Basic Profile**: This profile defines simple string-based SAML attribute names.
- **X.500/LDAP Profile**: This profile defines a common standardized convention for SAML attribute-naming using OIDs (Object Identifiers) expressed as URNs (Uniform Resource Names) and accompanied by using the type xsi:type.
- **UUID Profile**: This profile defines SAML attribute names as UUIDs (Universal Unique Identifiers) expressed as URNs.
- **DCE PAC Profile**: This profile defines how to represent DCE realm, principal, and primary group, local group, and foreign group membership information in SAML attributes.
- **XACML Profile**: This profile defines how to map SAML attributes cleanly to XACML attribute representations.

To support Web services and usage of SAML tokens in Web services communication, the OASIS WS-Security TC developed a SAML Token profile. The SAML Token profile defines the rules and guidelines for using SAML assertions in Web services communication. OASIS also ratified SAML Token profile 1.0 as an approved standard. Refer to Chapter 6, "Web Services Security–Standards and Technologies," for information about the role of SAML token profiles and how to use them in WS-Security.

SAML Architecture

The original SAML specification introduced SAML using a domain model, which consists of **Credential Collector**, **Authentication Authority**, **Session Authority**, **Attribute Authority**, and **Policy Decision Point**. These are the key system entities in providing single sign-on service to service requesters.

- **Credential Collector**: A system object that collects user credentials to authenticate with the associated Authentication Authority, Attribute Authority, and Policy Decision Point.
- **Authentication Authority**: A system entity that produces authentication assertions.
- **Session Authority**: A system entity (for example, identity provider) that plays the role of maintaining the state related to the session.
- **Attribute Authority**: A system entity that produces attribute assertions.
- **Attribute Repository**: A repository where attribute assertions are stored.
- **Policy Repository (or Policy)**–A repository where policies are stored.
- **Policy Decision Point**: A system entity that makes authorization decisions for itself or for other system entities that request authorization.
- **Policy Enforcement Point**: A system entity that enforces the security policy of granting or revoking the access of resources to the service requester.
- **Policy Administration Point**: A system entity where policies (for example, access control rules about a resource) are defined and maintained.

SAML Assertions

A SAML *assertion* here resembles a piece of data produced by a SAML authority (for example, Authentication Authority) regarding either an authentication action performed on a subject (for example, service requester), attribute information about the subject, or an authorization request (for example, whether the service requester can access a resource).

There are three different SAML assertions:

- **Authentication Assertion**: An assertion that carries business data about successful authentication performed on a subject (for example, a service requester).
- **Authorization Decision Assertion**: An assertion that carries business data about an authorization decision. For example, the authorization decision may indicate that the subject is allowed to access a requested resource.
- **Attribute Assertion**: An assertion that carries business data about the attributes of a subject.

SAML Domain Model

Figure 7–1 depicts a SAML domain model (refer to [SAML11Core] for details) where a system entity (client) wants to send an application request to access a system resource. The system entity presents its user credentials to the Credentials Collector, who will authenticate with the associated Authentication Authority (authentication assertion), the Attribute Authority (attribute assertion), and Policy Decision Point (authorization decision assertion), before the system entity can be granted access (Policy). The Policy Enforcement Point will process the application request based on the access rights granted in the Policy. All assertion requests are represented in SAML.

Client requests for access (for example, credential or authentication assertion) come from a **System Entry Point** (refer to the System Entity in Figure 7–1) and are routed to different Authorities where authenticated and authorized requests will be routed to the relevant **Policy Enforcement Point** for execution.

These architectural entities resemble different instances of Certificate Authority, Registration Authority, and directory server in real life (within an enterprise, external Trust Service, or trading partners). For example, the **Credential Collector** is like a RADIUS protocol that front-ends the authentication process and passes

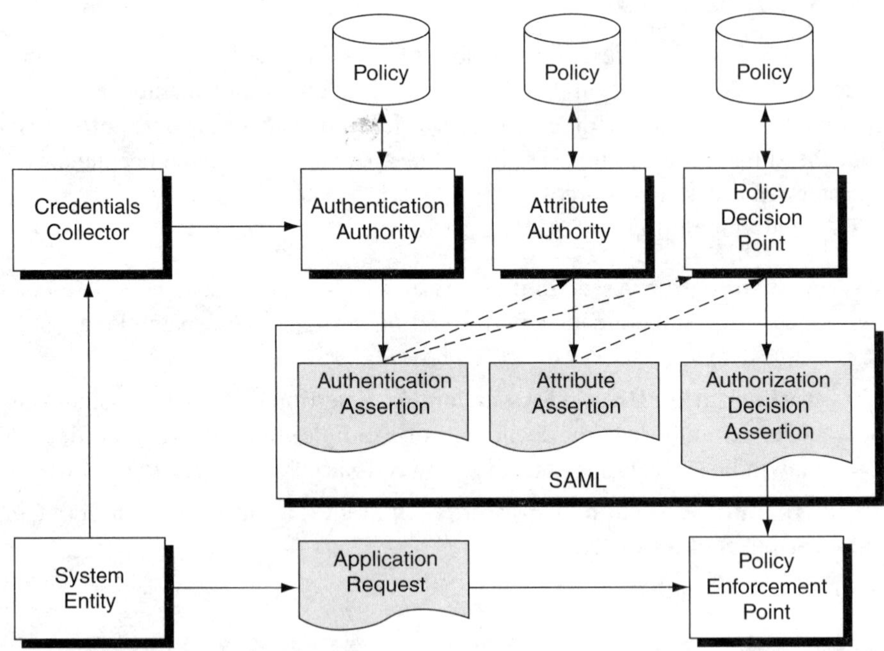

Figure 7–1 SAML domain model

to the directory server (or Authentication Authority) relevant user credentials for authentication.

Architecturally, SAML assertions are encoded in an XML package and consist of **Basic Information** (such as unique identifier of the assertion and issue date and time), **Conditions** (dependency or rule for the assertion), and **Advice** (specification of the assertion for policy decision).

SAML now supports a variety of protocol bindings when invoking different assertions. These include SOAP, reverse SOAP (multistage SOAP/HTTP exchange that allows an HTTP client to send an HTTP request containing a SOAP message), HTTP redirect (sending a SOAP message by HTTP 302 method), HTTP POST (sending a SOAP message in Base64-encoded HTML form control), HTTP artifact (way to transport an artifact using HTTP by a URI query string or by an HTML form control), and URI (retrieving a SAML message by resolving a URI).

SAML Architecture

Some architects and developers use the term "SAML architecture" to refer to the SAML entity model. This does not refer to the physical architecture. In the SAML architecture, the SAML domain model depicts the information entities (for example, System Entity) and their roles (for example, Policy Enforcement Point), but does not resemble any infrastructure-level component such as directory server or policy server. Thus, architects and developers need to map these domain entities into logical architecture components.

To illustrate how the SAML domain model is mapped to the SAML logical architecture, Figure 7–2 shows a scenario where a client requests access to remote resources under a single sign-on environment. Both the source site and the destination site collaborate to provide single sign-on security using SAML. The destination site has a number of remote resources and an existing authentication infrastructure with a custom-built authentication module (**Policy Enforcement Point**). It has implemented a SAML Responder (SAML-enabled agent) that can intercept application requests for resources and initiate SAML assertion requests. The source site has built an authentication service (**Authentication Authority**), directory server (**Attribute Authority** that stores the policy attributes), and a policy server (**Policy Decision Point** that determines what the client is entitled to). The SAML server (or authority) processes requests for SAML assertions and responds to the SAML Responder. These domain entities can easily map to the security architecture components. These architecture components may take more than one role; for example, the authentication module may act as Authentication Authority and Policy Enforcement Point.

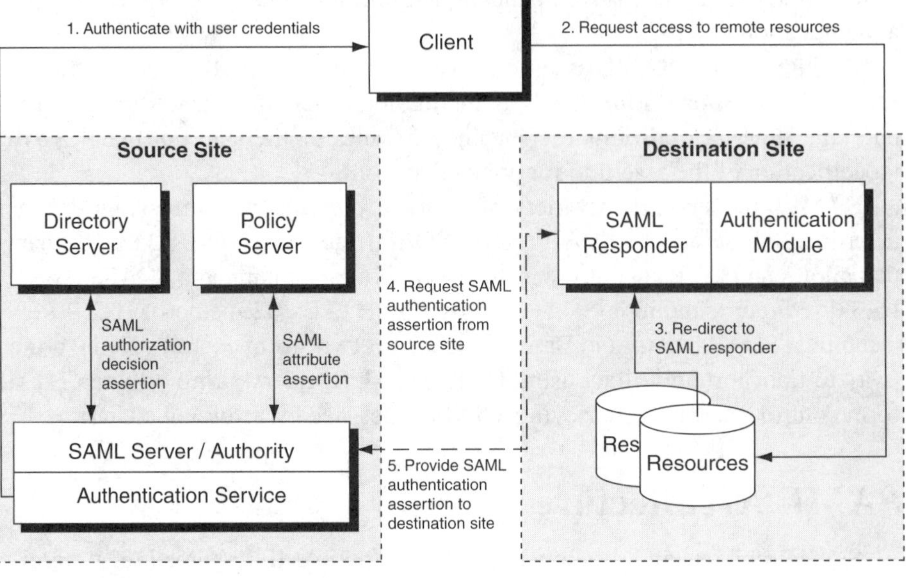

Figure 7–2 SAML logical architecture

The following describes the interaction between the system entities as per Figure 7–2:

- The client has already authenticated with the authentication service offered by the source site (Step 1).
- The client creates an application request (also called **Application Request**) to the remote sources at the destination site (Step 2). The destination site has a SAML responder (SAML-enabled agent) that uses an authentication module (for example, a JAAS authentication module using a local directory server) for generating authentication assertions.
- The remote destination redirects the application request to the SAML responder (Step 3).
- The SAML responder issues a SAML authentication assertion request to the source site (Step 4).
- The SAML-enabled authentication service processes the SAML authentication assertion request and provides a response to the destination site (Step 5).

Now the authentication module of the destination site knows that the client is already authenticated. It will not require the client to re-login again. The destination site will initiate a SAML attribute assertion request and an authorization decision assertion request to the source site to determine whether the client is entitled to access the remote resources.

Policy Enforcement Point

Policy Enforcement Point (PEP) is a system entity that enforces security policies so that unauthorized service requesters are not able to access or utilize the target resources. Many applications or security infrastructures play the role of PEP. For example, a custom-built Java application verifies the user authentication result, retrieves the attributes and access rights of the service requester from the directory server, and grants access to the service requester.

SAML does not specify how to build a PEP or how to implement the processing logic for authorization decisions. A PEP is in effect a SAML responder that processes the resource access request and communicates with the SAML authority for SAML authorization decision assertions. It issues a SAML assertion request to the SAML authority, which may provide user attributes (SAML attribute assertion) and access control policy information (SAML authorization assertion). Architects and developers can customize processing logic to enforce the policy information from SAML assertions. Many security vendor products for PEP provide scripting languages to implement PEP functionality.

Policy Administration Point

Policy Administration Point (PAP) is a system entity that provides administrative functions such as defining new policy information and modifying or deleting existing policy information centrally or remotely. SAML does not require a PAP; XACML introduces the use of PAP for administering policy information. The policy information may include actions, conditions, or dependencies that are associated with the access of resources. They reside in a policy repository, which is usually implemented in a database or directory server. PAP does not necessarily denote a sophisticated system front-end, although many security vendor products provide a browser-based administrative front-end. Architects and developers can also use a text-based editor to administer security policy information.

SAML Request-Reply Model

SAML uses a request-reply model to implement interaction between the SAML Responder and the SAML authority. It typically uses a SOAP protocol binding. Figure 7–3 shows a SAML request sent from a relying party (for example, the

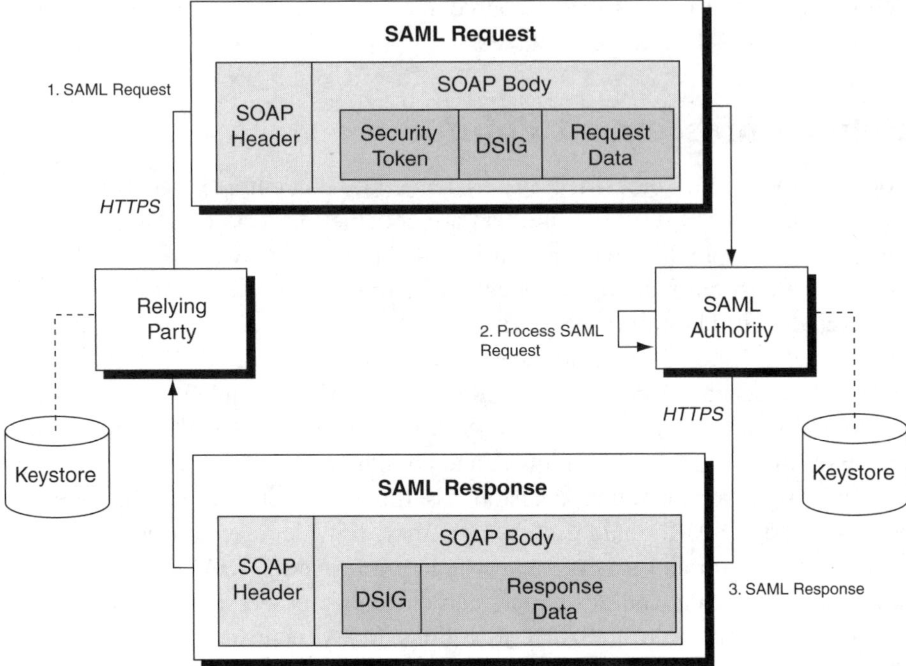

Figure 7–3 SAML request-reply model

destination site in Figure 7–2) that requests a SAML assertion (for example, password authentication) by the issuing party (for example, SAML Authority or the source site in Figure 7–2). The user credentials (for example, ID and password) are encapsulated in a security token together with a digital signature (using XML Signature), and the request data (for example, password authentication) are wrapped in a SOAP body and sent via HTTP. Once the SAML authority receives the SAML request, it will process the request and create the appropriate response, including the SAML assertion statements.

The SAML request consists of a SOAP envelope and a SOAP body that contain the SAML request <samlp:Request>. The SAML request element may contain the elements AuthenticationQuery, AttributeQuery, or AuthorizationDecisionQuery. A digital signature <ds:Signature> may also be generated and attached to the SOAP message, though this is not discussed here. Refer to Example 7–1 for an example of the SOAP message skeleton for a SAML request.

Example 7–1 SAML request message skeleton sample

```
<env:Envelope
xmlns:env="http://www.w3.org/2003/05/soap/envelope/">
```

```
<env:Body>
<samlp:AuthnRequest
   xmlns:samlp="urn:oasis:names:tc:SAML:2.0:protocol"
   ForceAuthn="true"
   AssertionConsumerServiceURL
      ="http://www.coresecuritypatterns.com/"
   AttributeConsumingServiceIndex="0"
   ProviderName="string"
   ID="skdfa7234"
   Version="2.0"
   IssueInstant="2005-06-01T01:00:00Z"
   Destination="http://www.coresecuritypatterns.com/"
   Consent="http://www.coresecuritypatterns.com/">
<saml:Subject
   xmlns:saml="urn:oasis:names:tc:SAML:2.0:assertion"
<saml:NameID
   Format=
"urn:oasis:names:tc:SAML:1.1:nameid-format:emailAddress">
      maryj@namredips.com
</saml:NameID>
</saml:Subject>
</samlp:AuthnRequest>
</env:Body>
</env:Envelope>
```

The SAML response will include the <Status> element with the SAML assertion statements, such as AuthenticationStatement, AttributeStatement, and AuthorizationDecisionStatement. Example 7–2 shows an example of the SOAP message skeleton for a SAML response.

Example 7–2 SAML response message skeleton sample

```
<SOAP-ENV:Envelope
xmlns:SOAP-ENV="http://schemas.xmlsoap.org/soap/envelope/">
<SOAP-ENV:Body>
   <samlp:Response xmlns:samlp="…" xmlns:saml="..."
          xmlns:ds="...">
      <Status>
         <StatusCode
     value="urn:oasis:names:tc:SAML:2.0:status:Success"/>
      </Status>
      <saml:Assertion>
         <saml:AuthenticationStatement>
           ...
```

```
      </saml:AuthenticationStatement>
    </saml:Assertion>
  </samlp:Response>
</SOAP-Env:Body>
</SOAP-ENV:Envelope>
```

SAML Authentication Assertion

The SAML authority (in this case, the SAML server of the source site in Figure 7–2) creates an authentication assertion to assert that the subject was authenticated by a particular authentication mechanism at a certain time. An authentication assertion statement AuthenticationStatement consists of the elements of AuthenticationMethod (for example, password), AuthenticationInstant (for example, timestamp of the authentication action), and optionally, SubjectLocality (for example, DNS domain name, IP address from which the subject was authenticated). Example 7–3 shows an example of an authentication assertion statement request.

Example 7–3 SAML message to request password authentication

```
<samlp:AuthnQuery
  xmlns:samlp="urn:oasis:names:tc:SAML:2.0:protocol"
  xmlns:ds="http://www.w3.org/2000/09/xmldsig#"
  xmlns:saml="urn:oasis:names:tc:SAML:2.0:assertion"
  xmlns:xsi="http://www.w3.org/2001/XMLSchema-instance"
  xsi:schemaLocation=
  "urn:oasis:names:tc:SAML:2.0:protocol" … >
<saml:Subject>
  <saml:SubjectConfirmation Method=
    "http://www.oasis-open.org/committees/security/docs/draft-sstc-core-25/
password">
      <saml:SubjectConfirmationData>
        cGFzc3dvcmQ=
      <saml:SubjectConfirmationData/>
    </saml:SubjectConfirmation>
</saml:Subject>
<samlp:RequestedAuthnContext Comparison="exact">
  <saml:AuthnContextClassRef>
    http://www.coresecuritypatterns.com
  </saml:AuthnContextClassRef>
</samlp:RequestedAuthnContext>
</samlp:AuthnQuery>
```

The SAML authority (or Issuing Authority) asserts that the client request has been authenticated and thus returns with a SAML response, as shown in Example 7–4.

Example 7–4 SAML response–password authenticated

```
<samlp:Response xmlns:samlp="urn:oasis:names:tc:SAML:2.0:protocol"
   xmlns:ds="http://www.w3.org/2000/09/xmldsig#"
   xmlns:saml="urn:oasis:names:tc:SAML:2.0:assertion"
   xmlns:xsi="http://www.w3.org/2001/XMLSchema-instance"
   IssueInstant="2005-06-01T09:30:47.0Z" Version="2.0"
   InResponseTo="NCName"
   Destination="http://www.coresecuritypatterns.com"
   ID="ID000065">
        ...
   <samlp:Status>
      <samlp:StatusCode
         Value="urn:oasis:names:tc:SAML:2.0:status:Success"/>
      <samlp:StatusMessage>status is successful</samlp:StatusMessage>
   </samlp:Status>
   <saml:Assertion
      IssueInstant="2005-06-01T09:30:47.0Z" Version="2.0" ID="ID000072">
      <saml:Issuer NameQualifier="String" Format="http://
www.coresecuritypatterns.com"
          SPProvidedID="MyServiceProvider" SPNameQualifier="String">CSP</
saml:Issuer>
      <saml:Subject>
      <saml:SubjectConfirmation
          Method="http://www.oasis-open.org/committees/security/docs/draft-
sstc-core-25/password">
         <saml:NameID NameQualifier="card:SQLDatabase">
            CoreSecurityPatterns
         <saml:NameID/>
      <saml:SubjectConfirmationData NotBefore="2005-06-01T09:30:47.0Z"
          InResponseTo="NCName"
          Recipient="http://www.coresecuritypatterns.com"
          NotOnOrAfter="2005-06-01T09:30:47.0Z"
          Address="String"/>
      </saml:SubjectConfirmation>
         </saml:Subject>
            <saml:Conditions NotBefore="2005-06-01T09:30:47.0Z"
               NotOnOrAfter="2005-06-01T09:30:47.0Z">
```

```
            <saml:Condition xsi:type="a type derived from
ConditionAbstractType"/>
          </saml:Conditions>
          <saml:Advice>
            <saml:AssertionIDRef>NCName</saml:AssertionIDRef>
          </saml:Advice>
      <saml:AuthnStatement>
          AuthnInstant="2005-06-0131T12:00:00Z"
          SessionIndex="67775277772">
          <saml:AuthnContext>
            <saml:AuthnContextClassRef>

urn:oasis:names:tc:SAML:2.0:ac:classes:PasswordProtectedTransport
            </saml:AuthnContextClassRef>
          </saml:AuthnContext>
      </saml:AuthnStatement>
   </saml:Assertion>
</samlp:Response>
```


SAML Attribute Assertion

The SAML authority (in this case, the SAML server of the source site in Figure 7–2) creates an attribute assertion to assert that the subject was associated with the specified attributes. Typically, the attributes are stored in the policy data store or a directory server. An attribute assertion statement AttributeStatement consists of the elements of Attribute, AttributeName, AttributeNamespace, and AttributeValue. For example, the SAML relying party is inquiring about the list of organization and user role attributes of the subject. It generates a SAML attribute assertion statement request to the SAML authority to retrieve a list of attributes. Example 7–5 shows an example of an attribute assertion statement request.

Example 7–5 SAML attribute assertion statement request

```
<samlp:AttributeQuery xmlns:samlp="urn:oasis:names:tc:SAML:2.0:protocol"
   xmlns:ds="http://www.w3.org/2000/09/xmldsig#"
   xmlns:saml="urn:oasis:names:tc:SAML:2.0:assertion"
   xmlns:xsi="http://www.w3.org/2001/XMLSchema-instance"
   IssueInstant="2005-06-01T09:30:47.0Z" Version="2.0"
   InResponseTo="NCName"
   Destination="http://www.coresecuritypatterns.com"
   ID="ID000065">
       ...
```

```
    <saml:Subject>
          ...
    </saml:Subject>
    <saml:Attribute Name="userRole">
       <saml:AttributeValue/>
    </saml:Attribute>
</samlp:AttributeQuery>
```

Example 7–6 shows the corresponding response. The list of attribute names and the associated values vary in customer implementations. They may resemble local resource names or policy mnemonics that may not be easily understandable to users.

Example 7–6 SAML attribute assertion statement response

```
<samlp:Response xmlns:samlp="urn:oasis:names:tc:SAML:2.0:protocol"
   xmlns:ds="http://www.w3.org/2000/09/xmldsig#"
   xmlns:saml="urn:oasis:names:tc:SAML:2.0:assertion"
   xmlns:xsi="http://www.w3.org/2001/XMLSchema-instance"
   IssueInstant="2005-06-01T09:30:47.0Z" Version="2.0"
   InResponseTo="NCName"
   Destination="http://www.coresecuritypatterns.com"
   ID="ID000065">
        ...
     <samlp:Status>
        <samlp:StatusCode
                Value="urn:oasis:names:tc:SAML:2.0:status:Success"/>
        <samlp:StatusMessage>status is successful</samlp:StatusMessage>
     </samlp:Status>
     <saml:Assertion IssueInstant="2005-06-01T09:30:47.0Z" Version="2.0"
ID="ID000072">
             ...
        <saml:Subject>
                 ...
        </saml:Subject>
        <saml:Conditions NotBefore="2005-06-01T09:30:47.0Z"
                  NotOnOrAfter="2005-06-01T09:30:47.0Z">
           <saml:Condition xsi:type="a type derived from
ConditionAbstractType"/>
        </saml:Conditions>
        <saml:Advice>
           <saml:AssertionIDRef>NCName</saml:AssertionIDRef>
        </saml:Advice>
```

```
            <saml:AttributeStatement>
               <saml:Attribute
                  NameFormat="http://www.coresecuritypatterns.com">
                  Name="PaymentStatus"
                  <saml:AttributeValue>
                     JustPaid
                  </saml:AttributeValue>
               </saml:Attribute>
               <saml:Attribute
                  NameFormat="http://coresecuritypatterns.com">
                  Name="CreditLimit"
                  <saml:AttributeValue
xsi:type="coresecuritypatterns:type">
                     <coresecuritypatterns:amount currency="USD">
                        1000.00
                     </coresecuritypatterns:amount>
                  </saml:AttributeValue>
               </saml:Attribute>
            </saml:AttributeStatement>
      </saml:Assertion>
</samlp:Response>
```


SAML Authorization Decision Assertion

An authorization decision assertion statement describes a resource access request for the specified subject. The requested resource is typically identified by a URI reference. The response to the resource request reflects the authorization decision (using the element <Decision>), which may be Permit, Deny, or Indeterminate. It usually includes the resulting actions (using the element <Action>) and a set of assertions (using the element <Evidence>) that the SAML authority relied on while making the decision.

Example 7–7 shows an authorization decision assertion statement request. For example, a user wants to access a remote printer resource. The authorization decision assertion statement request will describe a request about accessing the resource "Printer."

Example 7–7 SAML authorization decision assertion statement request

```
<samlp:AuthzDecisionQuery xmlns:samlp="urn:oasis:names:tc:SAML:2.0:protocol"
   xmlns:ds="http://www.w3.org/2000/09/xmldsig#"
   xmlns:saml="urn:oasis:names:tc:SAML:2.0:assertion"
   xmlns:xsi="http://www.w3.org/2001/XMLSchema-instance"
```

```
    IssueInstant="2005-06-01T09:30:47.0Z" Version="2.0"
    InResponseTo="NCName"
    Destination="http://www.coresecuritypatterns.com"
    ID="ID000065">
      <saml:Subject>
        <saml:BaseID xsi:type="a type derived from BaseIDAbstractType"/>
        <saml:SubjectConfirmation Method="http://
www.coresecuritypatterns.com">
                ...
        </saml:SubjectConfirmation>
      </saml:Subject>
      <saml:Action Namespace="http://
www.coresecuritypatterns.com">SomeAction</saml:Action>
      <saml:Evidence>
            ...
      </saml:Evidence>
</samlp:AuthzDecisionQuery>
```


Example 7–8 shows the corresponding response.

Example 7–8 SAML authorization decision assertion response

```
<samlp:Response xmlns:samlp="urn:oasis:names:tc:SAML:2.0:protocol"
    xmlns:ds="http://www.w3.org/2000/09/xmldsig#"
    xmlns:saml="urn:oasis:names:tc:SAML:2.0:assertion"
    xmlns:xsi="http://www.w3.org/2001/XMLSchema-instance"
    IssueInstant="2005-06-01T09:30:47.0Z" Version="2.0"
    InResponseTo="NCName"
    Destination="http://www.coresecuritypatterns.com"
    ID="ID000065">
      <saml:Issuer>IssuerName</saml:Issuer>
      <samlp:Status>
        <samlp:StatusCode
Value="urn:oasis:names:tc:SAML:2.0:status:Success"/>
        <samlp:StatusMessage>status is successful</samlp:StatusMessage>
      </samlp:Status>
      <saml:Assertion IssueInstant="2005-06-01T09:30:47.0Z" Version="2.0"
                ID="ID000072">
                ...
        <saml:Subject>
                ...
        </saml:Subject>
```

```
        <saml:Conditions NotBefore="2005-06-01T09:30:47.0Z"
                    NotOnOrAfter="2005-06-01T09:30:47.0Z">
           ...
        </saml:Conditions>
        <saml:Advice>
           <saml:AssertionIDRef>NCName</saml:AssertionIDRef>
        </saml:Advice>

            <saml:AuthzDecisionStatement Resource="Printer" Decision="Deny">

               <saml:Action Namespace="http://www.coresecuritypatterns.com">
                   SomeAction</saml:Action>
               <saml:Evidence>
                   ...
            </saml:Evidence>
            </saml:AuthzDecisionStatement>
     </saml:Assertion>
</samlp:Response>
```

The SAML core specification for assertions and protocols (refer to [SAML2Core], p. 25) indicates that the <AuthorizationDecisionStatement> feature has been frozen in version 2.0. Thus, architects and developers should consider using XACML for enhanced authorization decision features.

XML Signatures in SAML

The XML Signature defines mechanisms for embedding signatures in XML documents including SAML. XML Digital Signatures provide integrity and non-repudiation of SAML-based transactions. In SAML, XML Signature element is used to represent its authority who signs the message. The XML signature can be placed within the SAML assertion, request and response elements. The XML signature contains the X.509 certificate with a public key and also the signature value generated. When a signed message is received by a relying party, it verifies the message using the authority's public key. The verification process checks that the message has not been tampered during transmission, authenticity of the signer and identifies the content and portions of message signed.

For more information on XML signature and how to represent XML signature in XML messages, refer to Chapter 6, "Web Services Security–Standards and Technologies."

SAML Usage Scenarios

SAML was originally developed to meet single sign-on security requirements. It can enable a Web user who is visiting an Internet online store via a Web browser to pass identity information to a second Web site in the same security session without a second login. SAML can also support remote authorization, whereby a service provider asks another service provider to authenticate a user and perhaps retrieves some information or attributes about a user. Another usage of SAML would be authenticating Web services (asserting a user has been authenticated prior to using Web services). The following sections discuss the usage scenarios of SAML and provide examples.

Third-Party Authentication and Authorization

To provide a good user experience, many service providers (trading partners) affiliated with online stores and Internet portals rely on the primary service provider (online stores or Internet portals) for authentication and authorization. A typical scenario involves an Internet portal managed by a telecommunications service provider, where there are many trading partners that provide content and online store services. The benefit of using SAML is that service providers do not need to re-create a new authentication infrastructure. The primary service provider may be using its existing security infrastructure or a third-party service provider (for example, Trust Authority using XKMS) to authenticate the consumer's identity. In such a way, once the primary service provider authenticates the consumer, the affiliated service providers can take the SAML authentication or authorization assertion and allow the consumer to navigate and shop at their online stores or portals seamlessly. This enhances the user experience without requiring multiple logins.

To make use of third-party authentication and authorization, the affiliated service providers must be "federated" with the primary service provider. This denotes that each affiliated service provider trusts and relies on the authentication mechanism provided by the primary service provider. The primary service provider plays the role of the SAML authority, and the affiliated service providers are the SAML-relying parties. The affiliated service providers issue a SAML request for an authentication or authorization assertion. Once they receive the SAML response from the primary service provider, they process any online order or any order request from the consumer.

Global Logout

Corporations that have implemented single sign-on integration for legacy applications and heterogeneous security infrastructures will likely also need global logout capability. However, not all single sign-on implementations are capable of global logout. Single sign-on is usually initiated from a user sign-on action, but global logout can be initiated by a system event such as previous session invalidated or idle session time-out. Many developers have added a session time-out feature (for example, a session that is idle for five minutes will invalidate the previous sign-on session) to their single sign-on infrastructure so that idle user sessions exceeding the time-out limit will trigger a global logout. The global logout capability addresses potential security risks of replay or unauthorized access to resources from invalidated sessions.

In a Web portal that aggregates access to disparate applications, once consumers perform a single sign-on to a primary service provider, they can access any remote resources to which they are entitled with the affiliated service providers. If a consumer decides to sign out of the security session with one particular service provider, the global logout functionality should disconnect from all remaining security sessions with the other service providers. Similarly, if any of the service providers invalidate the user from one of the security sessions, then the primary service provider should also perform a global logout. Typically, a service provider issues a SAML 2.0 global logout request, and the SAML authority processes the global logout request.

Security Threats and Countermeasures

Architects and developers should be aware of the security threats and potential countermeasures associated with exchanging SAML messages. The OASIS SAML Technical Committee (refer to [SAML11Security] and [SAML11Core]) identify some security threats specific to applications that use SAML and discuss countermeasures. These security threats center around the SAML assertions, SAML protocol, SAML protocol bindings, and SAML profiles.

At the level of SAML assertions, once the issuer sends a SAML assertion, the assertion is out of his or her control. The issuer has no control over how other systems persist the SAML assertion or over how parties or trading partners will share the assertions with those systems. Either those systems or their trading partners may be exposed to security risks.

Denial of Service Attack

Security attackers may replay large numbers of SAML messages to launch a Denial of Service (DoS) attack on a SAML service provider. SAML protocol by nature is a request-response protocol model. It is possible that the service provider can check whether the SAML messages are from a valid requester at the origin by using the digital signature in order to filter or discard an influx of invalid incoming requests that may cause DoS. Requiring signed requests and use of XML Signature (for example, using the element <ds:SignatureProperties> with a timestamp to filter influx of the same request from a DoS attack) would help reduce the risk associated with a DoS attack. Requiring client authentication below the SAML protocol level with client-side certificates will help track the source of attacks for diagnosis.

Message Replay and Message Modification

SAML protocol binding using SOAP or HTTP POST is susceptible to eavesdropping, message replay, message insertion, message modification, and man-in-the-middle attack. It is possible for eavesdroppers to take a copy of the real user's SAML responses and included assertions and then compose an HTTP POST message that impersonates the user at the destination site. This is also known as a stolen artifact. For a stolen artifact scenario, hackers may add countermeasures to ensure confidentiality between a site and the user's browser. For example, architects and developers can set a time limit (such as a few minutes) for the time difference between generating a SAML artifact at the source site and placing it on a URL upon receiving the <samlp:Request> message from the destination site, or they can validate the IP address in the element <saml:SubjectLocality>.

Man-in-the-Middle Attack

In addition, SAML messages are also exposed to man-in-the-middle attacks (impersonating the assertion request using an HTML form) and forged assertions (altering an assertion). For a man-in-the-middle attack, architects and developers may want to use the SAML protocol binding that supports bilateral authentication, message integrity, and confidentiality—for example, digital signature. For forged assertion, architects and developers may enforce digital signing of the SAML response that carries the SAML assertions. The destination site can ensure message integrity and authentication by verifying the signature and authenticating the issuer. Man-in-the-middle attacks can also be mitigated by securing the message transport using SSL/TLS. This can ensure point-to-point tamperproof communication.

There are also security risks related to SAML profiles. SAML profiles refer to the rules that depict how to embed SAML assertions into an XML framework and how to extract them from the framework. For the Web Browser Single Sign-on profile, it is possible that hackers can relay service requests, capture the returned SAML assertions or artifacts, and relay back a falsified SAML assertion. To mitigate this security risk, we need to use a number of countermeasures together. First, we need to use a system with strong bilateral authentication. HTTP over

TLS/SSL is recommended for use with an appropriate cipher suite (strong encryption for confidentiality and for data integrity) and X.509v3 certificates (for strong authentication). These countermeasures will make man-in-the-middle attacks more difficult.

For the Enhanced Client and Proxy profile (ECP), it is possible for hackers to intercept AuthnRequest and AuthnResponse SOAP messages, which will allow subsequent Principal impersonation. The hackers may then substitute any URL of a responseConsumerServiceURL value in the message header block (PAOS message header) before forwarding the AuthnRequest on to the enhanced client. The inserted URL value may simply point back to itself so that the hackers are able to masquerade as the Principal as the legitimate service provider. To mitigate the security risk, the identity provider can specify to the enhanced client the address to which the enhanced client must send the :AuthnResponse. Thus, the responseConsumerServiceURL in the message header can only be used for error responses from the enhanced client.

The Role of SAML in J2EE-Based Applications and Web Services

J2EE-based applications can standardize the exchange of identities and access using SAML, which allows single sign-on across heterogeneous platforms within the enterprise (single domain) or across several security infrastructures (cross-domain). SAML becomes a common language or interface that allows users to sign on once to an application and to seamlessly access other applications to which they are entitled. The use of security patterns such as Assertion Builder (refer to the security patterns section later in this chapter) will be very handy. Architects and developers do not need to custom-build access control or authorization modules for each individual application or legacy system.

SAML does not replace the authentication service in J2EE-based applications and Web services. Developers still require the use of an authentication infrastructure, which may be a JAAS authentication module or a home-grown authentication framework using a directory server. After the system authenticates a user, a SAML authentication assertion is created. SAML also does not substitute for a policy manager or policy engine. Developers still need a policy manager that stores the access control rules and enforces the security policy rules using a Policy Enforcement Point. The policy manager evaluates the user and then creates a SAML attribute assertion based on the policies and rules defined.

There are two SAML usage scenarios in a J2EE-based application environment:

- Once the J2EE application authenticates a user, the J2EE components can create a SAML Authentication Assertion for that authentication event. This can be accomplished using a JAAS authentication module as part of the post-login process. In addition, it can implement the SAML Web Browser SSO profile, which defines how SAML Authentication Assertions are represented using the Authentication Query and Response messages to enable SSO for a user accessing via a Web browser.
- J2EE applications can make use of SAML assertions obtained from a user who is authenticated to an external security infrastructure (that acts as a SAML authority). Based on this authentication, the user receives SAML assertions and uses them to access J2EE applications. In this case, the J2EE applications can make use of a JAAS login module to verify the SAML assertions for authenticity. The JAAS login module can initiate callbacks to request the user's SAML assertions from the SAML authority using the SOAP protocol or HTTP POST. If the SAML assertions are found to be correct, then the JAAS login module can make use of the commit() method, which adds the Principal from the corresponding SAML assertion and populates the Subject with the Principal. If the authentication fails, the commit() method returns false and destroys the authentication state information and denies access to the requested application.

Without the use of SAML, J2EE-based applications are confined to proprietary mechanisms for passing authentication and authorization information between each other. This works well under an ideal, monolithic enterprise IT environment that has only J2EE-based applications. However, if there are custom-built applications, ERP, and legacy systems, architects and developers need to customize J2EE connectors and build session control for single sign-on. In such a case, the development effort is considerable, and the integration with these systems is fairly complex.

Introduction to Liberty Alliance and Their Objectives

The Liberty Alliance Project [Liberty] was formed in September 2001 to develop open standards for federated network identity management and identity-based services. Compared to W3C and OASIS, the Liberty Alliance has many industry participants (instead of many technology vendors), including American Express, Ericsson, Fidelity Investments, France Telecom, GM, HP, Intel, Nokia, Novell, NTT DoCoMo, Sony, Sun Microsystems, VeriSign, and Vodafone as management board members.

The business objective of Liberty Alliance is to address the management of network identity and federated network identity. According to [Liberty12FFArch], Liberty Alliance intends to enable consumers to protect the privacy and security of their network identity information and enable businesses to maintain their customer relationships without third-party participation. This requires the creation of a network identity infrastructure that supports all current and emerging network access devices and provides an open single sign-on standard to decentralize authentication and authorization from multiple service providers.

From this perspective, the scope of Liberty is different than the scope of SAML. Liberty's focus is on the identity provider for the authentication of federated network identity and the creation of network identity infrastructure. Liberty Phase 1's protocol extends SAML 1.1's protocol and provides support for a wide range of authentication methods associated with the identity provider and support of global logout protocol, which were out of scope in SAML 1.1. There has been some significant development in both Liberty and SAML since then. SAML is now under OASIS's governance. Liberty Alliance has recently contributed its Liberty Phase 2 to SAML 2.0, and Liberty will continue its work in developing its community network, the Liberty Web services framework (LD-WSF), and the useful starter service interfaces (LD-SIS). The scope of Liberty Phase 2 specifications are presented in detail at http://www.projectliberty.org/specs/index.html. [Liberty12Tutorial] provides a comprehensive tutorial for Phase 2 specifications.

Liberty introduces the following system entities in the Liberty specifications:

- **Principal**: An entity (for example, a user) that acquires a federated identity and makes decisions to which authenticated actions are done on its behalf.
- **Identity Provider**: A Liberty-enabled entity that creates, maintains, and manages identity information for principals and can authenticate principals for other service providers within a circle of trust.
- **Service Provider**: An entity that provides business services and/or goods to principals.
- **Circle of Trust**: A federation of service providers that have business relationships based on Liberty architecture and operational requirements. Within the circle of trust, users can transact business in a secure and seamless environment, say, using single sign-on.

- **Liberty-enabled Client**: A client who knows how to obtain knowledge about the identity provider that the principal wishes to use with the service provider.
- **Liberty-enabled Proxy**: An HTTP proxy that emulates a Liberty-enabled client.

Liberty Phase 1

Liberty Phase 1 introduced identity federation, which provides single sign-on and global sign-out to multiple application systems and infrastructures. This involves creating an identity-provider role that initiates federation of two or more identities. Using the Liberty protocol, users are able to sign on once to a Liberty-enabled Web site and be seamlessly signed on to another Liberty-enabled Web site without needing to reauthenticate.

In essence, Liberty Phase 1 delivers the Identity Federated Framework (ID-FF) version 1.1, which includes the following features:

- **Federated identity life cycle**: The lifecycle of identity federation begins with exchanging meta-data to federate an identity. A principal (for example, a user who can acquire a federated identity) can then perform a single sign-on to one or multiple Liberty-enabled Web sites. During the process of single sign-on, the federated identity needs to be registered (using the name registration protocol). Upon completion of user activity, the principal will perform a global logout and the federated identity will be terminated.
- **Meta-data**: The Liberty meta-data provides an extensible framework for describing cryptographic keys, service end-point information, and support protocols and profiles at run-time. The meta-data classes include entity provider, entity affiliation, and entity trust. The origin and the document that contain these meta-data will be verified using digital signatures.
- **Static conformance requirements**: The static conformance requirements define profiles for identity federation activities: identity provider, service provider basic, service provider complete, and Liberty-enabled Client or Proxy.
- **Interoperability conformance and validation**: There is a validation process for a vendor who wants to be licensed as Liberty-interoperable, where the vendor needs to participate in the Liberty Alliance Interop event to validate such a compliance assertion.

- **Security mechanisms**: Liberty's identity federated framework supports both channel security and message security. Channel security allows the service provider to authenticate the identity provider using server-side certificates. It also supports mutual authorization between the service providers and identity providers. Message security uses digital signatures for protecting the Liberty messages for data integrity and non-repudiation.

Liberty Phase 2

Liberty Phase 2 is a major enhancement to Phase 1. It delivers the following specifications:

- **Identity Federated Framework (ID-FF) version 1.2**. The ID-FF establishes identity federation under a circle of trust and supports single sign-on. Identity federation refers to linking all user accounts for the same user entity among different service providers and identity providers. Single sign-on denotes enabling a user to authenticate with the identity provider once in order to access remote services provided by multiple service providers under a circle of trust. The identity provider provides decentralized authentication of the user identity. The features of ID-FF include opt-in account linking, simplified sign-on, basic session management, user affiliation with Web sites, anonymity of user identities, and real-time discovery and exchange of meta-data.
- **Identity Service Interface Specification (ID-SIS) version 1.0**. The ID-SIS includes two profiles: personal identity and business identity. These profiles define important user attributes for exchanging identity information among service providers and identity providers on top of ID-WSF.
- **Identity Web Services Framework (ID-WSF) version 1.0**. The ID-WSF defines a framework to create, discover, or consume identity services. This includes permission-based attribute sharing, identity service discovery, interaction service, security profiles for securing the discovery, SOAP protocol binding for ID-FF, extended client support for non-HTTP devices, and identity service templates to implement identity services on top of ID-WSF.

It is important to understand the roles of Liberty and SAML in the identity management space. Liberty Phase 2 is primarily based on SAML version 2.0, and builds an extension on top of it. The additions in Phase 2 are ID-FF, ID-SIS, and ID-WSF. Liberty is not competing with SAML. SAML provides single sign-on and identity management specifications, and it does not provide custom profiles for specific scenarios or industry use. Security architects and developers have to build their own implementation and customize the profiles on top of SAML specifications. Another goal of Liberty Alliance is to share best practices of identity management, data privacy, and interoperability within the Liberty Alliance compliant products.

The number of commercial Liberty-enabled identity management products is growing. A full list of Liberty-enabled products is available at http://www.projectliberty.org/resources/enabled.html.

Liberty Alliance Architecture

The initial proposal of Liberty Alliance includes the following stages:

I. Single Sign-on for e-Wallet applications (which involves use of context-sensitive cookies and multi-authentication systems),

II. Federated Data Exchange (which uses extensive schema with mappings between partners and strong cryptographic mechanisms between trading partners),

III. B2B Transaction Support (which provides asynchronous communication and non-repudiation),

IV. Web Services as endpoints (distributed redundant data for identity theft protection).

There are three key actors in a Liberty-enabled single sign-on business scenario: User Agent (User, security agent), Service Provider (provider of services to users), and Identity Provider (provider for identifying user identity). The following describe these actors and their relationship.

- **User Agents**–Users or security agents that require signing on to the systems once to access the business services that they are entitled to.
- **Service Providers**–Service providers are organizations offering Web-based services to users. This includes a broad category of Internet portals, online stores, retailers, wholesalers, manufacturers, transportation service providers, financial service institutions, entertainment services, non-profit organizations, government agencies, and so forth.
- **Identity Providers**–Identity providers are service providers that specialize in providing authentication services. Any service provider affiliated with the identity provider will honor the authentication done by the latter.

For example, Hong Kong Post, who is also a Certificate Authority, provides authentication services to local service providers.

Relationships

Service providers are affiliated with an identity provider into circles of trust based on Liberty-enabled technology and on operational requirements that define trust relationships among themselves. In addition, users federate their accounts (also known as local identities) with these service providers so that the same user identity can link to multiple accounts under different service providers. Under the mutually trusted environment, if a user authenticates with the identity provider, these service providers will honor the authentication. Such a business relationship is also known as "Circle of Trust."

Figure 7–4 summarizes the Liberty concept in the use of cross-domain Single Sign-on and depicts the following interactions:

- User Agent sends an HTTP request to Service Provider for Single Sign-on (Step 1).
- Service Provider responds by redirecting the request to Identity Provider (Step 2).
- User Agent sends a request to Identity Provider (Step 3).
- Identity Provider responds by redirecting to Service Provider (Step 4).
- User Agent sends an authentication request to Service Provider with URI (Step 5).

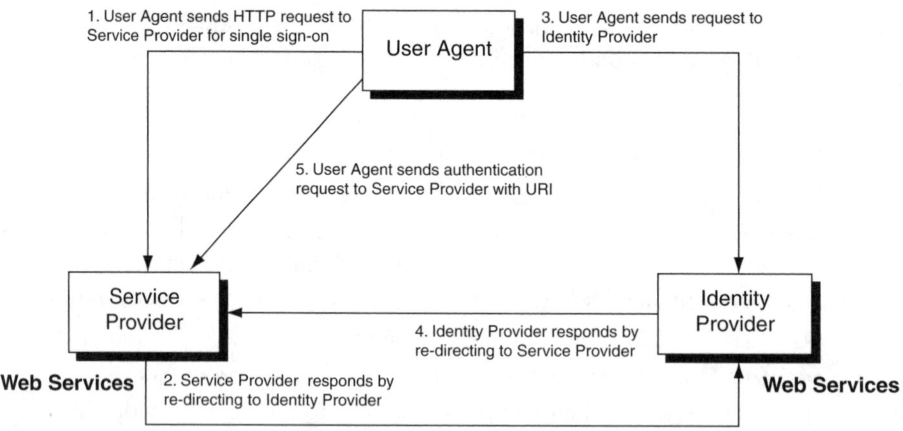

Figure 7–4 Liberty's logical architecture

Web Redirection

Web Redirection refers to actions that enable Liberty-enabled entities to provide services via user agents. It has two variants: HTTP-redirect-based redirection and Form-POST-based redirection. **HTTP-redirect-based redirection** uses HTTP redirection and the syntax of URIs to provide a communication channel between identity providers and service providers. For instance, the user clicks a link in the Web page displayed in the user agent. The user agent sends an HTTP request of resource access to the service provider using HTTP GET. The service provider responds with an HTTP response with a status code 302 (HTTP redirect) and an alternate URI (identity provider URI such as http://www.myidentityprovider.com/auth) in the Location header field. Then the user agent sends an HTTP request to the identity provider, and the identity provider can then respond with a redirect that specifies the service provider URI in the Location header field. Finally, the user agent sends an HTTP request to the service provider using HTTP GET with the complete URI from the identity provider's Location header field.

The flow of events in **form-POST-based redirection** is similar to the HTTP-redirect-based redirection, except that the service provider responds with an HTML form to the user agent with an action parameter pointing to the identity provider and a method parameter with the value of POST. The user needs to click on the Submit button, which sends the form and the data contents to the identity provider using HTTP POST.

Web Services

Web services here refer to business services provided by service providers using SOAP protocol profiles that enable Liberty-enabled entities to communicate to each other. Liberty currently supports RPC-style SOAP Web services.

Meta-Data and Schemas

Meta-data and schemas refer to a common set of classes of information and their formats that are exchanged between service providers and identity providers. They include user account identity information, authentication context (supporting a variety of authentication methods), and provider meta-data (meta-data schemas that need to be exchanged prior to exchanging authentication information, such as X.509v3 certificates and service endpoints).

Security Mechanisms

The Liberty ID-WSF specification defines security mechanisms that address the use-case scenarios intended for identity-based Web services. It mandates that the Liberty-provider implementation include security mechanisms that address the following requirements in order to secure the exchange of identity information between the applications and participants. The security mechanisms must address the following key requirements:

- Request Authentication
- Response Authentication
- Request/Response Correlation
- Replay Protection
- Integrity Protection
- Confidentiality Protection
- Privacy Protections
- Resource Access Authorization
- Proxy Authorization
- Mitigation of denial of service attack risks

In the Web redirection scenario, Liberty suggests the use of HTTPS for exchanging identity information and authentication assertions. This provides a secure transport mechanism between service providers and identity providers. In addition to the underlying secure transport, Liberty relies on strong authentication mechanisms used by the identity provider. Using cookies to maintain the local session state is often abused by unauthorized Web sites and hackers. If developers use cookies to persist identity and authentication information, it is possible that once a user exits the Web browser, another user may re-launch the Web browser using the same system, which may result in impersonating the first user. Using Web redirection and URL rewriting, identity providers do not need to send business data to service providers via cookies.

For details of the Liberty security mechanisms, please refer to [LibertyIDWSF].

Liberty Usage Scenarios

Liberty specifications primarily address identity federation, single sign-on, and global logout. Figure 7–5 shows a classic example of a business traveler authenticating with an airline and using a car rental service. In this example, JoeS joins a business travel service affinity group in which there are airline reservation services (Airline A), car rental services (Car Rental B), and hotel booking services (Hotel C). JoeS previously registers for online airline reservation services and car rental services. The business travel service affinity group runs a circle of trust under which service providers of airline reservation services, car rental services, and hotel booking services trust each other and share a common identity provider.

The following are the business events shown in Figure 7–5:

- Under the circle of trust, members like JoeS can authenticate once with the identity provider (Step 1).
- User JoeS accesses reservation service using single sign-on without duplicate logins to each service provider (Step 2).
- Airline A asks for consent to federate identity with the affiliated group, when previous sign-on has been detected (Step 3).
- User JoeS also accesses car rental service using single sign-on (Step 4).
- Car Rental B prompts for consent to federate identity with the affiliated group, with previous sign-on detected (Step 5).
- User JoeS accesses hotel reservation service using single sign-on (Step 6).
- Hotel C prompts for consent to federate identity with the affiliated group, with previous sign-on detected (Step 7).

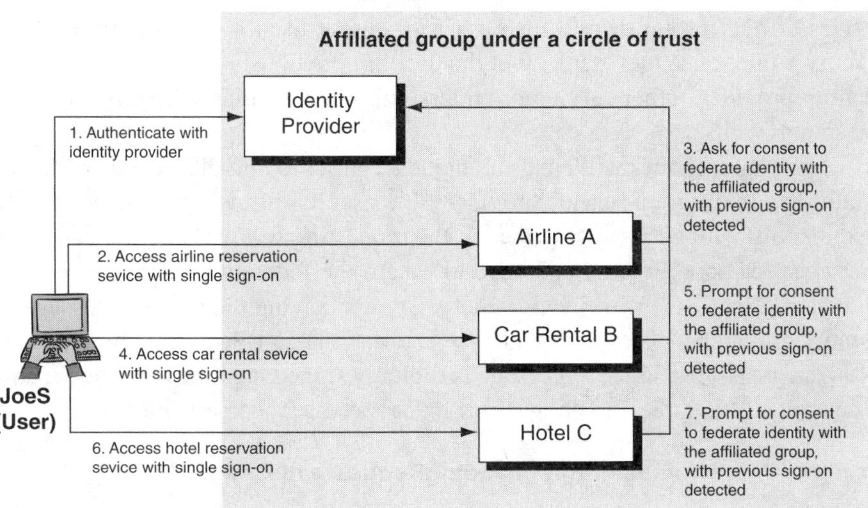

Figure 7–5 Liberty use case scenarios

The following sections discuss how architects and developers can use Liberty-enabled solutions to address the business challenges of federated identity management, single sign-on, and global logout.

Federation Management

Airlines, car rental companies, and hotels can federate themselves in an affinity group of business travel services. By federating themselves, they are able to rely on identity authentication services from an identity provider and share member identity information across different security infrastructures. In Figure 7–5, Airline A, Car Rental B, and Hotel C form an affiliated group under a circle of trust. They do not need to compromise or reengineer their security infrastructure for shared authentication or authorization. In other words, though their members (business travelers) may be using different user ids and account names in each service provider's system infrastructure, these service providers are able to link different user accounts to the same user identity anonymously under the circle of trust.

Identity Federation

Identity federation refers to linking accounts from distinct service providers and identity providers. The primary service provider (say, the airline reservation company A) will notify its eligible users (in this case, JoeS) of the possibility of federating their local identities among the service providers in the business travel service affinity group. It will also ask for consent to introduce the user into the affinity group, once they detect that the user has previously authenticated with the identity provider. Other service providers will make similar solicitations for permission as well.

Federating identities will create a unique identifier to link different user identities established in different service providers. If a user has already established a federated identity with an identity provider, the requesting service provider can issue a <NameIdentifierMappingRequest> message to obtain the federated identity when communicating with other service providers. Upon receiving the request message, the identity provider will respond with a <NameIdentifierMappingResponse> message. The <NameIdentifierMappingRequest> message is digitally signed, and the federated identity is encrypted. Example 7–9 shows a <NameIdentifierMappingRequest> message.

Example 7–9 <NameIdentifierMappingRequest> message

```
<NameIdentifierMappingRequest
    RequestID="a9c2-1b64-3bce-cb2e-3cbe ad118724"
```

```
    MajorVersion="1" MinorVersion="2"
    IssueInstant="2005-06-30T09:30:47Z">
  <ds:Signature>...</ds:Signature>
  <ProviderID>
   http://RequestingServiceProvider.com
  </ProviderID>
  <saml:NameIdentifier
     NameQualifier="http://www.coresecuritypatterns.com"
     Format="urn:liberty:iff:nameid:federated">
     d24 7128b
  </saml:NameIdentifier>
  <TargetNamespace>
     http://TargetServiceProvider.com
  </TargetNamespace>
</NameIdentifierMappingRequest>
```


Identity De-federation

Similarly, if the service provider is disassociated from the affinity group, it will also de-federate from the affinity group (**identity de-federation**) and notify the user. The federation termination notification (<FederationTerminationNotification>) is a specialized Liberty protocol to handle identity de-federation. Liberty-enabled architecture provides the capability of joining the identity federation or disassociating from the identity federation. Each of the service providers needs to implement a Liberty-enabled user agent so that it can reuse the user authentication service from the identity provider as well as federate the user identity of the users. The new ID-SIS personal or business profile defines the user profile and attributes for identity federation.

Identity Registration and Termination

Liberty Alliance introduces an **identity federated framework** (also known as ID-FF) to provide a solution for identity federation, cross-domain authentication, and session management using a set of protocols, bindings, and profiles. When a new user identity is created, the service provider needs to register with the identity provider. The **name registration protocol** in the ID-FF defines an optional-use protocol for the service provider to use to create an opaque handle to register and identify a user (principal) when communicating with the identity provider.

When a user is no longer allowed to access resources within the federated identity environment, the user identity needs to be revoked. This needs to be communicated from a service provider to the identity provider, or from the identity provider to all service providers within the federated identity environment. The

federation termination protocol in the ID-FF defines a notification protocol using one-way, asynchronous messages to indicate either the service provider or the identity provider will no longer accept authentication messages for the specific user (principal).

Liberty Single Sign-on

Once the registered user authenticates with the identity provider successfully, the identity provider will allow the user to use any business service within the affinity group. In Figure 7–5, JoeS authenticates with the identity provider, which verifies the user credentials for the right identity and grants access to business traveler services within the affinity group. Once JoeS signs on, he does not need to reauthenticate with any of the service providers in order to access other business traveler services.

Identity Provider Session State Maintenance

Liberty specifies how an identity provider handles user authentication via redirection. Identity providers can maintain local session information locally (that is, local to the identity provider) via an HTTP-based user agent (commonly known as Web browsers) using cookies. This is different from creating client-side cookies at the user's desktop whereby sensitive identity information may be persisted. Identity providers map local session state information to the participating user agent (Web browser). When a user (Principal) authenticates with the identity provider and accesses a primary service provider's resources, the identity provider will persist and keep track of the authentication state information using cookies. If the user decides to access another service provider, the primary service provider will issue an <AuthnRequest> to the identity provider. The identity provider will then check its local session state information and return an <AuthnResponse> message with an authentication assertion. This response message indicates that the current user agent (browser) session is still active.

Multi-tiered Authentication

With the nature of federated identity, Liberty allows authentication and authorization across different service providers, or across a multi-tier architecture. Some business services require more than one level of authentication to handle the varying nature of different business transactions. Some business transactions require sufficient quality of authentication mechanisms, in addition to plain user id and password. For example, a high-value funds transfer would require digital signing using an X.509v3 certificate. For risk-management purposes, service providers would not want any user with a user id and password to authorize a high-value funds transfer automatically without additional authentication. This type of reauthentication, or a second-tier authentication, is also known as **multi-tiered authentication**.

It is true that Liberty supports a wide range of authentication methods, but the actual authentication methods and their supporting protocol exchange are not specified in the Liberty specifications. To support multi-tiered authentication, the identity provider and the affiliated service providers need to make a mutual contractual agreement and the associated protocol exchange prior to the identity exchange (in other words, out of band, or a special mutual agreement outside the standard identity exchange process). The element <AuthenticationContextStatement> can encapsulate the identification process, technical protection, operational protection, authentication method, and government agreements. In addition, it is an implementation decision to determine which party is performing the reauthentication and how to select the appropriate authentication profile for the user. In addition, architects and developers need to customize the authentication policy associated with access to specific resources (for example, funds transfer services).

Credentials

Credentials contain security-related attributes that describe a user identity. Sensitive credentials require special protection from being stolen or tampered with, such as encryption and private cryptographic keys. These are used to prove an authentication or authorization assertion. For example, passwords and X.509v3 certificates are credentials. The Liberty artifact is a special form of credentials. The service provider can use a Liberty artifact profile to issue a query to the identity provider in order to get a SAML assertion. The Liberty artifact is an opaque user handle with a pseudo-random nonce that can be used only once. Thus, it serves the purpose of a credential and is a countermeasure against replay attacks.

Communication Security

Typically, the user communicates with the identity provider or any service provider within the affinity group under the circle of trust via HTTPS. This secures the communication channel between client and server, or between servers.

A service provider can reject communication with an identity provider if the security policy requires a credential over a communication protocol supporting bilateral authentication, integrity protection, and message confidentiality.

Federated Single Sign-on

Performing single sign-on across different security domains within an affinity group under a circle of trust is also known as **cross-domain single sign-on**. Liberty 1.2 specifications currently support cross-domain single sign-on. If the service providers are associated with more than one affinity group, then they can participate in multiple circles of trust, and users in the service providers can then benefit from single sign-on to multiple affinity groups. If a user who belongs to multiple circles of trust (affinity groups) wants to access multiple resources with single sign-on, this will require exchanging identity information between different identity providers. This scenario is also known as **federated single sign-on**. An example of federated single sign-on is accessing resources across two identity providers with two different identity infrastructures, such as Liberty-enabled infrastructure and Microsoft Passport.

At present, Liberty Phase 2 does not define any protocol or profile exchange between identity providers under the federated single sign-on scenario. In other words, users need to have an individual security session with each identity provider, and under each session they can enjoy single sign-on.

Global Logout

Liberty defines a logout request to enable a service provider to request global logout within the affiliated group under a circle of trust. This requires specifying the federated identity of the user and the session index. Example 7–10 shows a logout request. In this example, Airline A issues a global logout request for the federated identity (encrypted). The logout request comes with a digital signature.

Example 7–10 Liberty logout request

```
<LogoutRequest
   RequestID="efa4f215-5888-4312-cdf2-9872e32234223"
   MajorVersion="1" MinorVersion="2 "
   consent="urn:liberty:consent:obtained"
   IssueInstant="2004-09-16T12:30:47Z">
<ds:Signature>...</ds:Signature>
<ProviderID>http://AirlineA.com</ProviderID>
<saml:NameIdentifier
   NameQualifier="http://AirlineA.com"
   Format="urn:liberty:iff:nameid:federated">
   342ad3d8-93ee-4c68-be35-cc9e7db39e2b
</saml:NameIdentifier>
<SessionIndex>3</SessionIndex>
```

```
<RelayState>
231krjsdlfhsdffsda7sldfjsdl
</Relay State>
</LogoutRequest>
```

Example–SAML and Liberty Using Sun Java System Access Manager

Sun Java System Access Manager was the earliest Liberty-enabled solution; Sun has made considerable contributions to Liberty as well as SAML. Access Manager runs on top of Sun Java System directory server so it can benefit from the underlying LDAP-based infrastructure. Figure 7–6 depicts the high-level technical architecture of Access Manager. It has a common administration graphical user interface for its access management, identity administration, service management, and federation modules. There are SDK libraries available for customizing or building SAML- and Liberty-enabled solutions, respectively. The authentication service provides a login servlet template for customization. The authentication

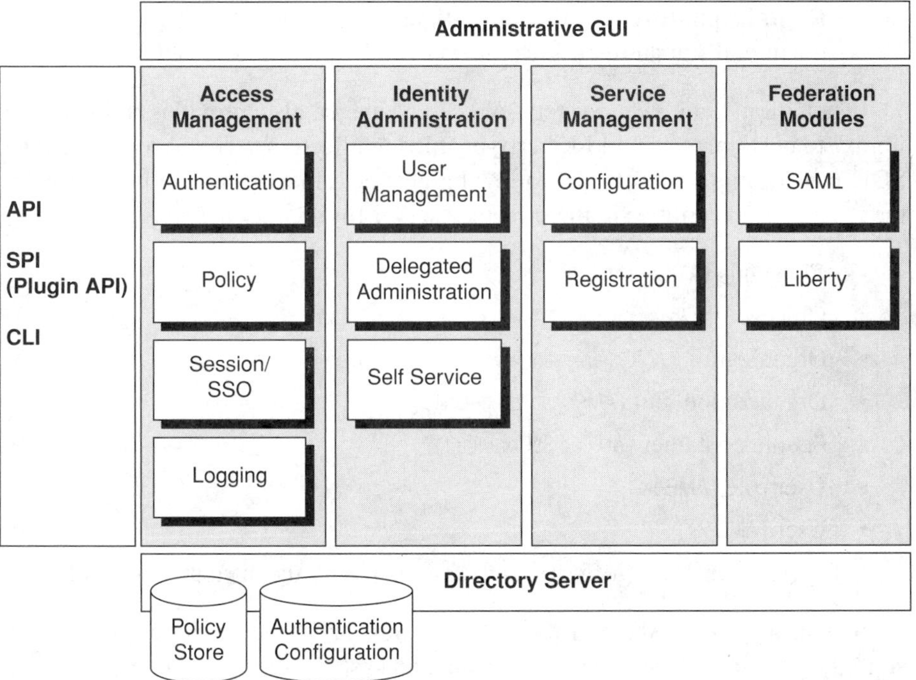

Figure 7–6 Sun Java System Access Manager architecture

mechanism reuses J2EE security APIs, including the JAAS authentication framework. It also has plug-ins for LDAP and X.509v3 certificates. The authorization or policy service includes a policy framework with a set of policy evaluation APIs and policy administration APIs.

Sun Java System Access Manager comes with a Java SDK library that supports SAML. The library includes:

- **SAML assertion statement (com.sun.identity.saml.assertion)**. This package creates and transforms SAML assertion statements, or accesses part of the attributes in the statements.
- **Common SAML functions (com.sun.identity.saml.common)**. This refers to XML attributes common to all elements.
- **Plug-in (com.sun.identity.saml)**. Currently, there are four Service Provider Interfaces (SPI) that are customizable. These APIs include AccountMapper, AttributeMapper, ActionMapper, and SiteAttributeMapper.
- **Protocol (com.sun.identity.saml.protocol)**. This package parses the request and response XML messages used to exchange assertions and their authentication, attribute, or authorization attribute information.
- **Digital signature (com.sun.identity.saml.xmlsig)**. This package refers to the digital signature utilities that sign and verify SAML messages.

In addition, Sun Java System Access Manager also provides a Java SDK library to customize or build Liberty-enabled applications. This Access Manager SDK provides interfaces to the following abstract objects that can be mapped to the resources and entities in the directory server for identity management:

- Constants (AMConstants)
- Objects (AMObject)
- Organization (AMOrganization)
- Organization unit (AMOrganizationUnit)
- People container (AMPeopleContainer)
- User role (AMRole)
- User (AMUser)
- Service template (AMTemplate) to associate with the attributes of AMObject.

Sun Java System Access Manager uses Sun Java System directory server to store the policy store, authentication data, and system configuration.

The Nirvana of Access Control and Policy Management

There are a number of initiatives in the industry related to access control and policy management, such as IETF, DMTF, and OASIS. Each of them produces specifications for policy and has corresponding industry support groups. Sometimes architects and developers are confused about whether they are related or whether they are competing. For example, a telecommunication service provider wants to build a generic policy engine for determining the security policy for service-on-demand home network services and network infrastructure services. IETF (http://www.ietf.org/html.charters/policy-charter.html) and DMTF (http://www.wbemsolutions.com/tutorials/CIM/dmtf-policies.html) have produced policy specifications. The Parlay Group (http://www.parlay.org/about/policy_management/index.asp) has also issued a framework specification on policy management, which is targeted for implementing security services and access-control policies in the telecommunications sector. Which policy management specification should the telecommunication service provider choose? This section summarizes each policy management specification and discusses how they are related.

It is important for security architects and developers to understand that although these standards and industry groups share the same term "policy," they use the term to denote different meanings. The term "policy" may refer to specific data formats, protocols, operational semantics, and logical architectural framework components. For example, many policy frameworks (such as IETF policy framework) specify operational components such as Policy Enforcement Point (PEP), Policy Decision Point (PDP), Policy Issuing Point (PIP), and Attribute Authorities. These policy operational components are not necessarily restricted to security access control; they can be applicable to general business services as well. There are also specific data flows between these architectural components. These architectural components are practically logical and agnostic to specific physical infrastructure.

There are two XML standards related to policy and access control: SAML and XACML. SAML provides specific data formats (also known as "assertions") and protocols (XML-based, and not network protocol) for communicating between architectural components using those data formats (for example, Attribute Query and Response, Authorization Decision Query and Response, and so forth). SAML describes a very basic (or primitive) assertion format and protocol for communicating between a PEP and a PDP, but does not specify the operation of a PDP (that is, how it reaches its decision). It also does not specify how a PDP gets the information on which its decision will depend (that is, the policies).

XACML (eXtensible Access Control Markup Language) provides specific data formats (for example, Request and Response Context, PolicySet or Policy, and so forth) and specifies how the PDP component must operate in order to process an authorization decision request from a PEP. XACML 2.0 defines a SAML profile to extend SAML for interoperation with SAML. Refer to the previous section on "Use of XACML 2.0 with SAML 2.0" for details.

IETF Policy Management Working Group

The IETF Policy Management Working Group defines a structure (also called **architecture**) to manage policies by a policy management service (for example, a graphical user interface administration console), a dedicated policy repository (for example, directory server), a policy decision point (for example, policy server), a policy enforcement point (for example, firewall, routers), and local policy decision points (aka scaled-down policy decision points). The IETF policy framework is widely referenced in network infrastructure products, such as Cisco Quality of Service Policy Manager and SOCKS v5 with IPSec. Another example is Common Open Policy Service (COPS), which is a network client-server protocol between policy decision points and policy enforcement points in the telecommunications sector. In summary, the IETF policy framework provides a good architecture framework, but it does not define any specific communication protocol or software component.

The IETF policy framework introduces key operational elements (for example, PDP) in the policy management area. There are two security patterns, Load Balancing PEP and Clustered PEP, that apply the principle of these operational elements to implement network perimeter security. Refer to Chapter 8, "The Alchemy of Security Design: Methodology, Patterns, and Reality Checks," for details. However, the IETF policy framework is too generic and does not provide details of the data formats or the underlying protocols that are necessary to support end-to-end security for distributed applications and business services, particularly for J2EE-based applications and Web services.

Distributed Management Task Force (DMTF)

DMTF collaborates with IETF to work on a policy architecture that includes more application infrastructure protocols (such as LDAP, FTP, and SOAP) and refines a declarative data model with details of a policyRule, policyGroup, policyAction, and policyCondition defined in a Common Information Model (CIM). IPSec policy is a direct result of the collaboration. DMTF also defines a set of CIM policy data models (CIM Policy version 2.6 and version 2.7) that are also available in XML Schema. There is wide support of Web-based Enterprise Management (WEBM) and CIM in the computer hardware component and system management areas.

DMTF has published a CIM data model for policy. With the XML Schema, the CIM data models can be used for Web-based application development. However, the CIM data model is fairly generic for policy definition. It does not provide a specific communication protocol or interaction mechanism that business applications (not systems management applications) can use.

Parlay Group

The Parlay Group has defined a framework for policy management related to secure access using a Parlay gateway. It has API definitions that can define new rules (createRule), define conditions (createCondition), retrieve actions (getAction) and action lists (setActionList), and commit transactions (commitTransactions). For example, architects and developers can create a set of policies that allow newly created users to access broadband Internet services upon successful provisioning of their service accounts. Unfortunately, there is no mature commercial implementation of the Parlay policy product available. In addition, the Parlay policy management API specification is very telecommunication-domain–specific, and it does not currently provide any integration mechanisms for use with other security specifications such as SAML.

Strictly speaking, the Parlay policy management API specification is not yet another policy framework, as is IETF and DMTF. It intends to provide APIs that can work on top of policy standards and frameworks. It does not create specific data formats or protocols. Nor does it create a policy language. Thus, it should not be confused with other policy standards that have their own architecture models.

Enterprise Privacy Authorization Language (EPAL)

EPAL is another policy markup language specification drafted by IBM (http://www.w3.org/Submission/2003/SUBM-EPAL-20031110/). It is designed to address data privacy, privacy audit, and enforcement requirements. EPAL allows privacy-rule administrators to define ruling, user category, action, data category, purpose, condition, and obligation. EPAL has some elements specific to data privacy but they are not necessarily relevant to access control. For example, the element <data-category> is an element that describes the type of resources (as in "resource" in XACML). The element <purpose> may be relevant to access control, but not always. EPAL requires a <purpose> element to describe both data privacy and access control, however, which makes it problematic for use as a general purpose access control language. The concept and usage of the elements <rule> and <condition> are similar to XACML. However, EPAL does not support sub-policies or the concept of combining algorithms (that is, combining multiple rule or policy results into a single overall response), which are often used in complex access-control environments. Instead, it can support a sequence of rules.

EPAL 1.1 reuses the <xacml:condition> element of the XACML condition language. In EPAL 1.2, IBM dropped any reference to XACML and submitted the draft specifications to W3C (http://www.w3.org/Submission/2003/SUBM-EPAL-20031110/). Currently, EPAL is in draft status and is not an approved standard or in pre-standard status yet.

For a detailed analysis on comparing EPAL and XACML refer to [Anne1]. Table 7–1 summarizes the comparison of EPAL and XACML from a Sun white paper (refer to [Anne1] for details and http://research.sun.com/projects/xacml for an updated comparison).

Table 7–1 High-Level Comparison of EPAL and XACML

Features	*EPAL*	*XACML*	*Remarks*
Decision request	X	X	EPAL is a functional subset of XACML.
Nested policies	Not Supported	X	
Policy references	Not Supported	X	
Rule	X	X	Functional equivalent.
Combining algorithm and precedence	X	X	EPAL is a functional subset of XACML.
Vocabulary	X	Not Supported	
Attribute values	X	X	Identical.
Attribute mapping	X	X	Functional equivalent.
Attribute retrieval	X	X	Identical.
XML attribute values	Not Supported	X	
Hierarchical entities	X	X	EPAL and XACML support different models for hierarchical entities.

Features	*EPAL*	*XACML*	*Remarks*
Subjects with multiple attributes	X	X	EPAL is a functional subset of XACML.
Multiple subjects	Not Supported	X	
Purpose attribute	X	X	EPAL is a functional subset of XACML.
Error handling	X	X	EPAL is a functional subset of XACML.
Targets or pre-conditions	X	X	EPAL is a functional subset of XACML.
Condition	X	X	Functional equivalent.
Revision number	X	X	Functional equivalent.
Data types	X	X	EPAL is a functional subset of XACML.
Functions	X	X	EPAL is a functional subset of XACML.
Obligations	X	X	EPAL is a functional subset of XACML.
Multiple responses	Not Supported	X	
Status as a standard	Proposal to W3C	OASIS standard	

EPAL introduces the concept of a policy vocabulary that is not available in XACML. Refer to the next section for the discussion of XACML. The element <vocabulary> points to a separate file that specifies the collection of attributes needed in order to evaluate the policy. Attributes in a vocabulary are grouped into containers. Each separate container specifies a collection of attributes that can be obtained together from a single source. It may also represent a subset of attributes that would be used by a given rule in a policy. However, there is a drawback when designing complex policies: The need to group attributes into containers in a vocabulary may actually add to complexity by requiring vocabulary managers to be aware of the structure of the rules in the policy.

In contrast, XACML provides a richer set of access-control and privacy features that are not available in EPAL version 1.2. This includes the following features:

- Combination of the results of multiple policies that are developed by potentially independent policy issuers
- The ability to reference other policies as part of a given policy
- The ability to specify conditions on multiple subjects that may be involved in making a request
- The ability to return multiple results when access to a hierarchical resource is being requested
- Support for subjects who must simultaneously be in multiple independent hierarchical roles or groups
- Clear handling of error conditions and missing attributes
- Support for attribute values that are XML schema elements
- Support for additional primitive data types (including X.500 Distinguished Names and RFC822 names)

Web Services Policy–WS-Policy and WSPL

Web services policies are necessary in order to specify the conditions or assertions regarding the interactions between two Web services endpoints, such as authentication, authorization, quality of protection, quality of service, privacy, reliable messaging, and service-specific options (such as bandwidth guarantee). There are two emerging policy-related specifications: WS-Policy and WSPL (Web services policy language).

Web Services Policy Framework (WS-Policy) is part of the Web Services roadmap and specifications (aka WS*) proposed by Microsoft, IBM, VeriSign, and others. It is primarily a policy language that defines policies for Web services; these policies are a collection of "policy alternatives" (a collection of policy assertions such as authentication scheme, privacy policy, and so forth). WS-Policy encodes the policy definition in XML using SOAP messages for data exchange.

The policy definitions in the WS-Policy specification are not restricted to access control or privacy, a fact that differentiates WS-Policy from XACML and EPAL. Security architects and developers can use WS-Policy to specify the type of security token, digital signature algorithm, and encryption mechanism for a SOAP message (for example, a payment message), or even partial contents of a

SOAP message (for example, credit card number). It can also specify data-privacy or data-confidentiality rules. However, WS-Policy does not specify how to discover policies or how to attach a policy to a Web service. It relies on other WS* specifications (for example, WS-PolicyAttachment) to provide full functionality of policy management.

The other necessary component of WS-Policy is the definition of a set of policy assertions for each policy domain. For example, the assertions for use with WS-Security are defined in WS-SecurityPolicy. Each specification or schema to be controlled or managed by WS-Policy will require definition of a new set of assertions. The authors suggest that in the future, assertions will be defined as part of the underlying specification or schema rather than in a separate document as was required for WS-SecurityPolicy.

Under the WS-Policy model, a policy for Web services denotes conditions or assertions regarding the interactions between two Web services endpoints. The service provider exposes a Web services policy for the services they provide. The service requester will decide, using the policies, whether they want to use the service, and if so, the "policy alternative" they wish to use. In other words, WS-Policy does not have the notion of a Policy Enforcement Point (which enforces policies) and a Policy Decision Point (which determines policies). It leaves the policy enforcement and decision to the service providers and service requesters.

WSPL (Web Services Policy Language) is based on XACML (refer to the next section for details) and is currently a working draft in the OASIS XACML technical committee. It uses a strict subset of XACML syntax (restricted to Disjunctive Normal Form) and has a different evaluation engine than XACML has. XACML evaluates the access-control policies with a given set of attributes and policies, while WSPL determines what the mutually acceptable sets of attributes are when given two policies. For a good introduction on WSPL refer to [Anne3].

WSPL has provided similar functionality to define policies for Web services. WSPL has the semantics of policy (set of rules) and operators (which allow comparison between an attribute of the policy and a value, or between two attributes of the policy). The policy syntax also supports rule preference. There are three distinctive features in WSPL. First, it allows policy negotiation, which can merge policies from two sources. Second, policy parameter allows fine-grained parameters such as time of day, cost, or network subnet address to be defined in a policy for Web services. Third, the design of WSPL is flexible enough to support any type of policy by expressing the policy parameters using standard data types and functions.

One main problem WSPL has addressed is the negotiation of policies for Web services. Negotiation is necessary when choices exist, or when both parties (Web services consumers and service providers) have preferences, capabilities, or requirements. In addition, it is necessary to automate service discovery and connection related to policies.

WSPL shares similar policy definition capabilities with WS-Policy. Example 7–11 shows a policy defined in WS-Policy, which specifies the security token usage and type for the Web services. It uses the element <ExactlyOne> to denote the security token usage.

Example 7–11 Policy for a security token usage and type defined in WS-Policy

```
<wsp:Policy>
   <wsp:ExactlyOne>
      <wsse:SecurityToken>
         <wsse:TokenType>wsse:Kerberosv5TGT
         </wsse:TokenType>
      <wsse:/SecurityToken>
      <wsse:SecurityToken>
         <wsse:TokenType>X509v3
         </wsse:TokenType>
      <wsse:/SecurityToken>
   </wsp:ExactlyOne>
</wsp:Policy>
```

Example 7–12 shows that the same policy can be expressed in WSPL. WSPL translates the policy requirements into two rules. This makes it more descriptive and extensible in the event that security architects and developers need to add more operators or constraints.

Example 7–12 Policy for security token usage and type using WSPL

```
<Policy PolicyId="policy:1" RuleCombiningAlgorithm="&permit-overrides;">
   <Rule RuleId="rule:1" Effect="Permit">
     Condition FunctionId="&function;string-is-in">
      <AttributeValue DataType="&string;">Kerberosv5TGT</AttributeValue>
      <ResourceAttributeDesignator
          AttributeId="&SecurityToken;"
          DataType="&string;"/>
     </Condition>
   </Rule>

  <Rule RuleId="rule:2" Effect="Permit">
     <Condition FunctionId="&function;string-is-in">
        <AttributeValue
            DataType="&string;">X509v3</AttributeValue>
```

```
      <ResourceAttributeDesignator
         AttributeId="&SecurityToken;"
         DataType="&string;"/>
    </Condition>
  </Rule>
</Policy>
```

The following are identified as technical limitations of WS-Policy when compared with WSPL (refer to [Anne2] for details):

- **Negotiation**. WS-Policy does not specify a standard merge algorithm or a standard way to specify policy negotiation (for example, for merging policies from two sources). Specifications for domain-specific WS-Policy Assertions may describe how to merge or negotiate assertions, but these methods are domain-specific.
- **Assertion Comparison**. Since there is no standard language for defining Assertions in WS-Policy, there is no standard way to describe requirements such as "fee > 25." Again, specifications for domain-specific WS-Policy Assertions may describe schema elements for such comparisons, but the implementation of these elements must be done on a domain-by-domain basis since there is no standard.
- **Dependency**. WS-Policy is designed to depend on extensions. Each extension must be supported by a custom evaluation engine.

Web services policy specifications are still evolving. Some of them have specific problems (for example, policy negotiation) to address. It is possible that these specifications may expand and converge into one single standard in the future. For security architects and developers, it is useful to understand the policy language design, architectural components, and differences behind these specifications and to determine whether these policy specifications meet their technical requirements before they adopt them for prototypes and implementations.

Introduction to XACML

eXtensible Access Control Markup Language (XACML) version 2.0 (refer to [XACML2] for details) is an approved security policy management standard under OASIS (http://www.oasis-open.org/committees/tc_home.php?wg_abbrev=xacml). It is both a policy language and an access-control decision request/response language encoded in XML. It defines a standard format for the expression of authorization rules and policies along with a standard way of evaluating rules and policies to produce authorization decisions. In addition, XACML defines an optional format for making authorization decision requests and responses.

There are many similarities between XACML and the other policy management initiatives discussed previously. XACML can handle both XML documents and non-XML systems, though it can also handle non-XML objects using a custom context handler. It uses a declarative data model similar to CIM policy. It is generic to all industry sectors, but flexible enough to include new functionalities. XACML is complementing SAML 2.0 by providing functionality that handles complex policy sets and rules.

There are a few business problems related to security access control today. Many customer environments have their own security policy governing which resources a service requester can access. To be flexible and adaptive to customer IT security requirements, commercial off-the-shelf vendor products intend to be "generic" enough to support different security access control requirements in heterogeneous or customized environments. For example, some vendor products choose to provide "maximum possible privilege" by default for accessing data and executing business functions and actions. In other words, every user can access all functions unless the access control policies are customized. Once these vendor products are implemented, customers can customize local administrative security policy and configure policy enforcement points. Unfortunately, customized security access control implementations are fairly expensive, and they are unreliable for modifying security policies manually due to their complexity. In addition, they are not scalable and timely if the number of applications or policy enforcement points is large. Thus, a flexible policy system for access control is required to address these problems.

Isn't SAML authorization decision assertion used in determining access rights for a service request? SAML provides a very basic assertion format and protocol between policy enforcement point and policy decision point. However, it does not specify any action or how a policy decision point should get information on which its decision will depend.

One major technology driver for creating XACML is the need to access partial content of XML documents. The current security method is to use encryption to control access to the entire XML document. Users are either authorized to view the entire XML document or denied access to any part of it. An example is an XML document containing a credit card payment transaction, where user A (call center personnel) is authorized to access the entire payment transaction except the full credit card number, while user B (claims department) is able to read the entire payment transaction. This is undesirable and very often this access control mechanism does not meet local business requirements.

In a typical application environment, a user wants to make request to access certain resources. The Policy Enforcement Point (PEP) is a system or application that protects the resources. The PEP needs to check whether the service requester is eligible to access the resources. It sends the resources request to the Policy Decision Point (PDP), which looks up the security access control policies. XACML provides both a policy language and an access-control decision request/ response language to meet the security access control requirements. With XACML, the PEP forms a query language to ask the PDP whether or not a given action should be allowed. The PDP responds by returning the value of either Permit, Deny, Indeterminate (decision cannot be made due to some errors or missing values), or Not Applicable (the request cannot be answered by this service).

XACML provides a rich policy language data model that is able to define sophisticated and flexible security policies. Figure 7–7 shows the full hierarchy of components of an XACML policy extracted from the XACML schema, which may be too complex for novice readers. The following are the key components that may be of interest to most readers:

- **Policies**. A Policy represents a single access control policy, expressed through a set of Rules. Policies are a set of rules together with a rule-combining algorithm and an optional set of obligations. *Obligations* are operations specified in a policy or policy set that should be performed in conjunction with enforcing an authorization decision. Each XACML policy document contains exactly one Policy or PolicySet root XML tag.
- **Policy Set**. A Policy Set is a set of policies or other Policy Sets and a policy-combining algorithm, along with a set of optional obligations.
- **Rules**. Rules are expressions describing conditions under which resource access requests are to be allowed or denied. They apply to the target (<Target>), which can specify some combination of particular resources, subjects, or actions. Each rule has an effect (which can be "permit" or "deny") that is the result to be returned if the rule's target and condition are true. Rules can specify a condition (<Condition>) using Boolean expressions and a large set of comparison and data-manipulation functions over subject, resource, action, and environment attributes.
- **Target**. A Target is basically a set of simplified conditions for the Subject, Resource, and Action that must be met for a PolicySet, Policy, or Rule to apply to a given request. These use Boolean functions (explained more in the next section) to compare values found in a request with those included in the Target. If all the conditions of a Target are met, then its associated PolicySet, Policy, or Rule applies to the request. In addition to being a way

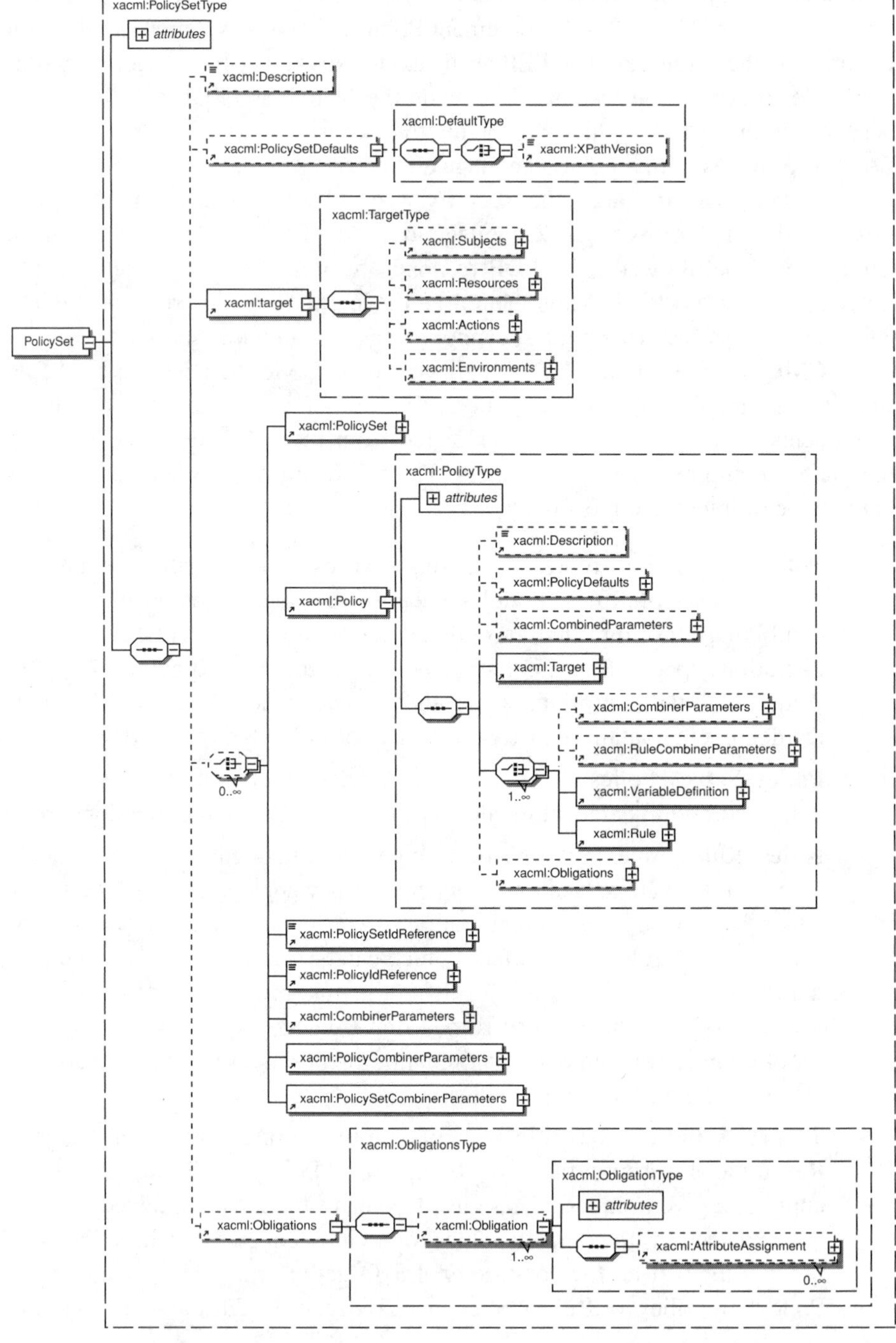

Figure 7–7 XACML policy language model

to check applicability, Target information also provides a way to index policies, which is useful if you need to store many policies and then quickly sift through them to find which ones apply.

- **Attributes**. Attributes are named values of known types that may include an issuer identifier or an issue date and time. Specifically, attributes are characteristics of the Subject, Resource, Action, or Environment in which the access request is made. For example, a user's name, their group membership, a file they want to access, and the time of day are all attribute values. When a request is sent from a PEP to a PDP, that request is formed almost exclusively of attributes, and they will be compared to attribute values in a policy in order to make the access decisions.

The XML Schema definition for XACML describes the input and output of policy decision points in an XACML context. A **context** denotes a canonical representation of a decision request and an authorization decision. Figure 7–8 shows the XACML context [XACML11] where a policy decision point makes reference to the attributes of a policy or identifies the attribute by subject, resource, action, or environment. The XACML context handler for requests converts the input format from domain-specific input, say, using XPath or any XSLT transformation mechanism. Upon processing the policy rules by the policy decision point, the XACML context handler for responses converts the authorization decision to a domain-specific output format. The shaded area that covers the XACML policy, policy decision point, and the XACML context handlers are the scope of XACML.

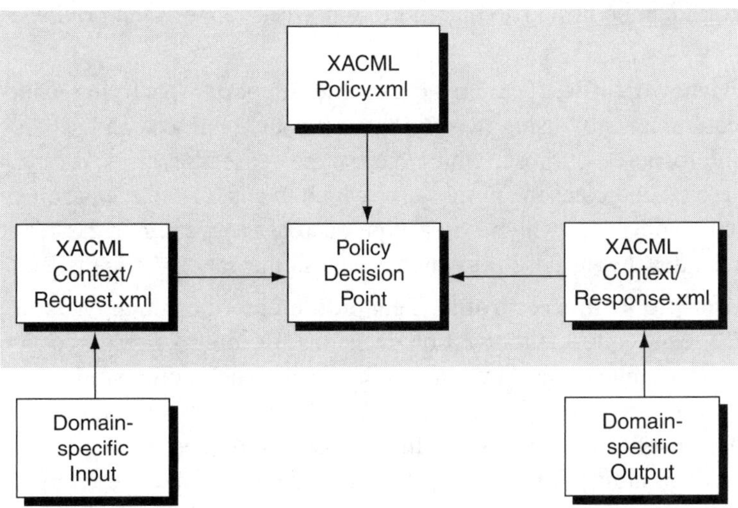

Figure 7–8 XACML context

Sun's XACML kit (http://sunxacml.sourceforge.net) is an open source implementation of XACML 1.1. There is also a C# implementation of XACML under http://mvpos.sourceforge.net/. Parthenon Computing's JiffyXACML (http://www.parthenoncomputing.com) is a free binary release that provides some specific functionality. A list of XACML implementations appears on the OASIS XACML TC home page (http://www.oasis-open.org/committees/tc_home.php?wg_abbrev=xacml), along with an XACML reference list that includes publicly announced adoptions of XACML.

XACML 2.0

XACML 2.0 [XACML2] does not have major functional changes. There are a few syntactic changes to make the policy language more flexible in its support of complex security requirements. Apart from the syntactic changes, the major change in XACML 2.0 is the introduction of six profiles:

- **SAML Profile**. The SAML profile defines how to use SAML 2.0 to protect, transport, and request XACML schema instances and other information needed by an XACML implementation. It supports six types of queries and statements: AttributeQuery, AttributeStatement, XACMLPolicyQuery, XACMLPolicyStatement, XACMLAuthzDecisionQuery, and XACMLAuthzDecisionStatement.
- **RBAC Profile**. The role-based access control profile allows policies to be specified in terms of subject roles instead of individual subject identities. Roles can be nested so that more senior roles inherit the privileges of junior roles.
- **Privacy Profile**. The privacy profile supports specifying data privacy requirements by using two attributes: resource purpose and action purpose. The resource purpose, which has a type "urn:oasis:names:tc:xacml:2.0:resource:purpose," indicates the purpose for which the data resource is collected. The action purpose, which has a type "urn:oasis:names:tc:xacml:2.0:action:purpose," indicates the purpose for which access to the data resource is requested.
- **Multiple Resource Profile**. This profile describes three ways in which a PEP can request authorization decisions for multiple resources in a single request context and how the result of each such authorization decision is represented in the single response context that is returned to the PEP. It also describes two ways in which a PEP can request a single authorization decision in response to a request for all the nodes in a hierarchy.

- **Hierarchical Resource Profile**. This profile specifies how XACML can provide access control for a resource (including files, XML documents, or organizations) that is organized as a hierarchy. For example, if the administrator wants to restrict certain segments of an XML document for access, he or she may want to treat the resource (in this case, the XML document) as a hierarchy in order to allow or deny access to particular nodes in the document.
- **DSIG Profile**. This profile uses XML Signature to provide authentication and integrity protection for XACML schema instances.

There are some new features to the policy language. For details, refer to [XACML2]. The following are new features that allow more flexibility in expressing policies and rules.

- The element <CombinerParameters> carries the parameters for use by the combining algorithms.
- A new optional attribute <Version> was added with default value "1.0" to denote the version of the Policy and PolicySet. Policy referencing allows developers to put constraints on the policy version.
- The element <VariableReference> is used to refer to a value by its <VariableDefinition> within the same policy.
- The element <EnvironmentMatch> was added to match the environment, similar to the elements <SubjectMatch>, <ResourceMatch>, and <ActionMatch>.
- A new substitution group called <Expression> was added, which contains the elements <Apply>, <AttributeSelector>, <AttributeValue>, <Function>, <VariableReference>, and all <FooAttributeDesignator>.
- There is a <RuleCombinerparameters> element, and likewise a <PolicyCombinerParameters> element, which are used to pass parameters to the combining algorithms. They are not used as a substitution model.

Some changes in XACML 2.0 are syntactical. They do not have a major impact on the core policy definition functionality. However, some changes are semantic changes. The following highlight the major syntactic changes in the context schema and the policy schema. For details, refer to [XACML2changes].

- The version number of XACML in the namespace has been updated as 2.0. For example, xmlns="urn:oasis:names:tc:xacml:2.0:context:schema:cd:04."
- The element <Status> in a <Result> statement is now optional in XACML 2.0.

- It is mandatory in XACML 2.0 to specify an <Environment> in a <Request> statement.
- For the elements <PolicySetIdReference> and <PolicyIdReference>, XACML 2.0 uses "type=xacml:IdReferenceType."
- The data type for "RuleId" attribute is now changed to "xs:String."
- Two syntactic changes are made to support SAML 2.0: The <Request> can contain more than one resource. The element <Attribute> can contain more than one <AttributeValue>.
- Two items are obsolete in XACML 2.0: the attribute <IssuesInstant> in the <Attribute> statement, and the elements <AnySubject>, <AnyResource>, and <AnyAction>.
- <VariableDefinition> and <VariableReference> elements support reuse of portions of a policy, which provides a macro capability.

XACML Data Flow and Architecture

XACML has a domain model expressed in XML Schema. A data flow diagram can better depict the logical components of XACML and how XACML interacts with other components. Figure 7–9 shows how XACML [XACML11] processes a service request to retrieve the attributes and policies. The following outlines the data flow in chronological sequence:

1. The policy administrator defines policies and policy sets at the policy administration point. <VariableDefinition> and <VariableReference> elements support reuse of portions of a policy, which provides a macro capability.
2. The service requester issues a request to the policy enforcement point to access the specified resource. This requires fetching the attributes and policies associated with the resource, the action, the environment, and the service requester.
3. The policy enforcement point sends the request for access to the XACML context handler in native request format. This may include the details of attributes of the subjects, resources, actions, and environment.
4. The context handler creates an XACML request context and sends a policy evaluation request to the policy decision point.
5. The policy decision point queries the context handler for attributes of the subject, resource, action, and environment needed to evaluate the policies.

6. The context handler obtains the attributes either from the request context created in Step 4, or it queries a policy information point for the attributes.
7. The policy information point returns the requested attributes to the context handler.
8. Optionally, the context handler includes the resource in the context.
9. The context handler returns the requested attributes to the policy decision point. The policy decision point continues evaluating the policy as attributes are made available.
10. The policy sends the response context (including the authorization decision) to the context handler.
11. The context handler responds to the policy enforcement point, after translating the response context to the native response format of the policy enforcement point.
12. The policy enforcement point executes any relevant obligations.

Once the policy is evaluated successfully, the policy enforcement point will either grant access to the service requester for the targeted resource or deny the access.

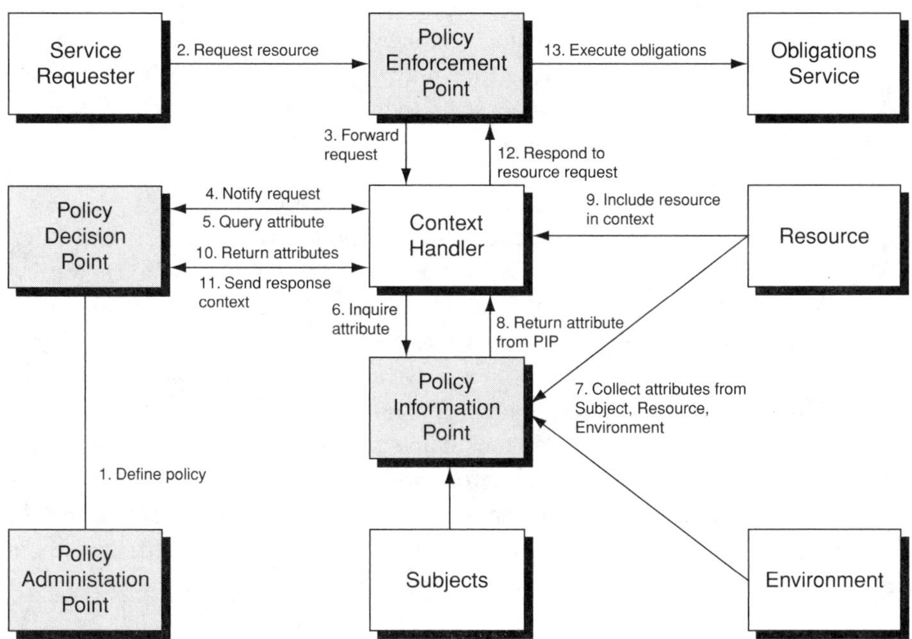

Figure 7–9 XACML data flow

XACML Architecture

XACML provides a standard virtual interface between the policy decision point and the service requester. Because XACML is a policy language set, it is difficult to define a specific technical architecture. XACML can support a variety of underlying infrastructures for policy stores. In summary, XACML has the following key logical architecture components:

- **Context Handler**. The context handler transforms service request formats into a format that XACML understands. Architects and developers may need to custom-build processing logic in the XACML context handler to handle the conversion between different service request formats.
- **Policy Decision Point**. The policy decision point (PDP) evaluates the resource access request against the relevant rules, policies, and policy sets. Architects and developers may customize their PDP by building a PDP application as reusable Java components (such as EJB) or simple servlets. Sun's XACML implementation provides a sample PDP.
- **Policy Repository**. The policy repository stores the rules, policies, and policy sets that XACML accesses. XACML does not define any standard interface, and leaves it to the implementation to provide an interface to create or retrieve policy objects from the policy repository. Architects and developers may use an existing directory server infrastructure to store all policy objects using LDAP, or they may opt to implement the policy repository using a relational database if their current entitlement application architecture is database-centric.

There are some distinctive architectural aspects in XACML. XACML stores the policy objects in a hierarchy relationship of policy sets, policies, and rules. XACML is defined to have the policy, rather than the rule, be the smallest retrievable policy object. This is different from a traditional rule engine where architects and developers can directly retrieve a specific rule or attribute element. Rules can be implemented as one-rule policies to achieve effective retrieval at the rule level.

In addition, an XACML solution can operate on a variety of infrastructures, depending on how customers implement the policy decision point, the policy enforcement point, and the policy information point. The XACML reference implementation from Sun can run on a Web container (Web server) or an EJB container (application server). These have created flexibility and agility for XACML solutions to interoperate with heterogeneous infrastructures.

XACML Usage Scenarios

The following sections identify a few scenarios where XACML can be used. XACML can be used as a centralized policy store for applications. It can also be used to provide access control for Web services. In addition, it can collaborate with SAML (using the SAML 2.0 profile of XACML 2.0) for implementation of single sign-on and sharing the same access control mechanisms with an enterprise.

Policy Store

XACML is an ideal technology candidate for use in implementing a centralized or distributed policy store because it can act as a data abstraction layer for the policy decision point. It can be implemented on top of any underlying data store platform, including directory server or relational database. If policy data are stored in a directory server or relational database directly, the policy retrieval will be strictly dependent on the underlying data store platform. If there are different policy store products running on heterogeneous data store platforms, then XACML will be a more flexible approach because it is shielded off from the underlying data store platform.

A distributed policy store refers to the scenario where customers partition the types of policies by geographical areas or by functional areas across different servers. This allows easier maintenance by the local administration. It is also possible to have multiple PEPs to process different types of policies by different partitions (for example, by geographical areas). This distributed architecture of the policy system is a common way to scale up the architecture and increase the capability of high-volume policy inquiries.

A centralized policy store refers to the scenario where customers have a single master policy store. This is useful for administering all types of security access control rules centrally. However, it also requires that the centralized policy store be highly available. Otherwise, any outage will be disruptive and impact all business services that rely on the access control policies.

Centralizing Security Policy for Web Services Security

Many Web services management products (such as AmberPoint, Actional, and Flamenco Networks) provide an access control mechanism for routing SOAP messages via a Web services proxy, or a Web services agent (refer to [WebServices-LifeCycle] for details). These proxies (Web services messaging intermediary) or agents (Web server or application server plug-in) usually act as a policy enforcement point that enforces access control policies for XML and SOAP messages. The associated Web services management server (aka policy administration point) allows defining and administering security policies for access to partial or full content of the SOAP messages by user groups or roles. These are ideal candidates for applying XACML technology.

Collaborating with SAML

SAML currently provides a mechanism for specifying policies and authorization decisions. There are constraints in the extensibility and flexibility of how to express rules and policies. In SAML 2.0, SAML enables collaborating with XACML, where SAML can share attributes and authorization decisions expressed in XACML. Details can be found at [SAML2Core] and [XACML2SAML2].

ebXML Registry

When service requesters discover and look up Web services from a service registry, there needs to be a reliable access control mechanism to protect the service registry. Many UDDI service registry implementations use database security for access control. However, the database-centric security approach usually provides primitive access control with read or write attributes. It does not support sophisticated rules, preferences, or even policy negotiation because it does not have a policy language.

ebXML registry open source implementation (http://sourceforge.net/projects/ebxmlrr/) uses XACML to implement an access control mechanism to discover and consume Web services. This allows more flexibility and extensibility in controlling who can access and under which condition the service requester can invoke the Web services. The ebXML registry stores the access-control policies and attributes in the registry and customizes a registry attribute finder module based on Sun's XACML kit.

Example–XACML Using Sun's XACML Kit

Sun Microsystems has created an implementation of XACML and released it as an open source project with the 1.0 release of XACML. It is available on sourceforge.net (http://sunxacml.sourceforge.net/). The current XACML Kit version 1.2 supports the XACML 1.x specifications (and most of the XACML 2.0 specification) with APIS for creating, validating, parsing, and evaluating policies and authorization requests. The code is broken into separate packages that support specific elements of the specification and is designed to make it easy to use or extend the XACML specification as needed. For more details, see the Sun XACML programmer's guide at http://sunxacml.sourceforge.net/guide.html.

Sample Scenario

To illustrate XACML kit, we use a sample scenario where a subscriber of an online portal tries to access their own account profile and check for credit card payment information. Here we have the following requirements:

- Only a premium member from "coresecuritypatterns.com" can access the URL http://www.onlinestore.com/sensitive/paymentinfo.html for their sensitive account information, including their own credit card payment information.
- Any other users who do not have the e-mail address domain ended with "coresecuritypatterns.com," or who are not a premium member, cannot access the credit card information.
- Successful access will be logged for audit control.
- Invalid access from users who do not have the valid e-mail address domain "coresecuritypatterns.com" will be also logged for audit control.

The online portal uses XACML for access control. This example will use the following features of XACML policies:

- Applying the constraint of premium member status for the account information access request. The element <condition> will be used to specify only premium member in the <target> can access the resource.
- Adding one of the conditions to enable only service requesters with an e-mail address domain "coresecuritypatterns.com" can access the resource.
- Illustrating the use of <obligation> element to log both successful read access as well as unsuccessful access for audit trail.

Sample Request

Example 7–13 shows a sample service request to access the URL http://www.onlinestore.com/sensitive/paymentinfo.html expressed in XACML. The request denotes a read request from a user maryj@coresecuritypatterns.com, who has a premium membership, to access the URL for her own account information. The subscriber clicks the URL, and the online portal (acting as a PEP) generates an XACML service request for a read request to the URL resource.

Example 7–13 Request to access sensitive payment resource

```
<?xml version="1.0" encoding="UTF-8"?>
<Request xmlns="urn:oasis:names:tc:xacml:1.0:context"
         xmlns:xsi="http://www.w3.org/2001/XMLSchema-instance">
    <Subject>
      <Attribute
          AttributeId=
   "urn:oasis:names:tc:xacml:1.0:subject:subject-id"
          DataType=
"urn:oasis:names:tc:xacml:1.0:data-type:rfc822Name">
        <AttributeValue>
           maryj@coresecuritypatterns.com
        </AttributeValue>
      </Attribute>
      <Attribute
          AttributeId="group"
               DataType=
             http://www.w3.org/2001/XMLSchema#string
                Issuer=
                   "admin@coresecuritypatterns.com">
        <AttributeValue>premiumMember</AttributeValue>
      </Attribute>
    </Subject>
    <Resource>
      <Attribute AttributeId=
      "urn:oasis:names:tc:xacml:1.0:resource:resource-id"
                DataType=
           "http://www.w3.org/2001/XMLSchema#anyURI">
        <AttributeValue>
http://www.onlinestore.com/sensitive/paymentinfo.html
</AttributeValue>
      </Attribute>
    </Resource>
    <Action>
      <Attribute
           AttributeId=
      "urn:oasis:names:tc:xacml:1.0:action:action-id"
           DataType=
      "http://www.w3.org/2001/XMLSchema#string">
```

```
      <AttributeValue>read</AttributeValue>
    </Attribute>
  </Action>
</Request>
```

Sample Policy

The XACML policy engine (acting as a PDP) receives the read request. It looks up any policies that are applicable to the request. Example 7–14 shows a sample policy to protect the sensitive payment resource. In plain English, the policy allows any subject with a group identifier "premiumMember" and with an e-mail address domain name "coresecuritypatterns.com" to have read access to the sensitive payment resource with the URI http://www.onlinestore.com/sensitive/paymentinfo.html. It also specifies that the policy will log any successful read action or any unsuccessful read with an invalid e-mail address domain name.

Example 7–14 Policy for the sensitive resource

```
<?xml version="1.0" encoding="UTF-8"?>
<Policy xmlns="urn:oasis:names:tc:xacml:1.0:policy"
   xmlns:xsi="http://www.w3.org/2001/XMLSchema-instance"
   PolicyId="AdminCanRead_ObligationPolicy"
   RuleCombiningAlgId=
   "urn:oasis:names:tc:xacml:1.0:rule-combining-algorithm:permit-overrides">

  <Description>
     This policy states that users with a domain name
     @coresecuritypatterns.com who are also premium members
     should be able to read the sensitive document
     http://www.onlinestore.com/sensitive/paymentinfo.html.
     Both successful and invalid read request are logged using Obligation.

     If users have a different domain name other than
     @coresecuritypatterns.com, this policy will deny access.
     If users with a domain name @coresecuritypatterns.com who
     are NOT premium members this policy also deny their access.

     This policy illustrates use of "Condition" within a
     "Target" element to apply constraints to the read access
     for the requester who are Administrator only. It also
     provides an example of "Obligation"
     to log successful read and log invalid access.
  </Description>
```

```
<Target>
  <Subjects>
    <Subject>
      <SubjectMatch MatchId=
          "urn:oasis:names:tc:xacml:1.0:function:rfc822Name-match">
        <AttributeValue
           DataType=
           "http://www.w3.org/2001/XMLSchema#string">
              coresecuritypatterns.com
        </AttributeValue>
        <SubjectAttributeDesignator
            DataType=
            "urn:oasis:names:tc:xacml:1.0:data-type:rfc822Name"
            AttributeId=
            "urn:oasis:names:tc:xacml:1.0:subject:subject-id"/>
      </SubjectMatch>
    </Subject>
  </Subjects>
  <Resources>
      <Resource>
        <ResourceMatch
           MatchId=
           "urn:oasis:names:tc:xacml:1.0:function:anyURI-equal">
          <AttributeValue
             DataType=
             "http://www.w3.org/2001/XMLSchema#anyURI">
             http://www.onlinestore.com/sensitive/paymentinfo.html
          </AttributeValue>
          <ResourceAttributeDesignator
             DataType=
             "http://www.w3.org/2001/XMLSchema#anyURI"
             AttributeId=
             "urn:oasis:names:tc:xacml:1.0:resource:resource-id"/>
        </ResourceMatch>
      </Resource>
  </Resources>
  <Actions>
    <AnyAction/>
  </Actions>
</Target>

<Rule RuleId="ReadRule" Effect="Permit">
  <Target>
```

```
    <Subjects>
      <AnySubject/>
    </Subjects>
    <Resources>
      <AnyResource/>
    </Resources>
    <Actions>
      <Action>
        <ActionMatch
           MatchId=
           "urn:oasis:names:tc:xacml:1.0:function:string-equal">
           <AttributeValue
               DataType="http://www.w3.org/2001/XMLSchema#string">
               read
            </AttributeValue>
          <ActionAttributeDesignator
             DataType=
             "http://www.w3.org/2001/XMLSchema#string"
             AttributeId=
             "urn:oasis:names:tc:xacml:1.0:action:action-id"/>
        </ActionMatch>
      </Action>
    </Actions>
  </Target>
        <Condition
           FunctionId=
           "urn:oasis:names:tc:xacml:1.0:function:string-equal">
      <Apply FunctionId=
      "urn:oasis:names:tc:xacml:1.0:function:string-one-and-only">
        <SubjectAttributeDesignator
           DataType="http://www.w3.org/2001/XMLSchema#string"
           AttributeId="group"/>
      </Apply>
      <AttributeValue
         DataType=
         "http://www.w3.org/2001/XMLSchema#string">
         premiumMember
      </AttributeValue>
    </Condition>
</Rule>

<Rule RuleId="DenyOtherActions" Effect="Deny"/>
```

Identity Management

```
  <Obligations>
    <Obligation
       ObligationId="LogSuccessfulRead"
       FulfillOn="Permit">
      <AttributeAssignment
         AttributeId="user"
         DataType=
         "http://www.w3.org/2001/
XMLSchema#anyURI">urn:oasis:names:tc:xacml:1.0:subject:subject-id
      </AttributeAssignment>
      <AttributeAssignment
         AttributeId="resource"
         DataType="http://www.w3.org/2001/XMLSchema#anyURI">
         urn:oasis:names:tc:xacml:1.0:resource:resource-id
      </AttributeAssignment>
    </Obligation>
    <Obligation
       ObligationId="LogInvalidAccess"
       FulfillOn="Deny">
      <AttributeAssignment
         AttributeId="user"
         DataType="http://www.w3.org/2001/XMLSchema#anyURI">
         urn:oasis:names:tc:xacml:1.0:subject:subject-id
      </AttributeAssignment>
      <AttributeAssignment
         AttributeId="resource"
         DataType="http://www.w3.org/2001/XMLSchema#anyURI">
         urn:oasis:names:tc:xacml:1.0:resource:resource-id
      </AttributeAssignment>
      <AttributeAssignment
         AttributeId="action"
         DataType="http://www.w3.org/2001/XMLSchema#anyURI">
         urn:oasis:names:tc:xacml:1.0:action:action-id
      </AttributeAssignment>
    </Obligation>
  </Obligations>

</Policy>
```

Example 7–15 shows the response to the read request. The PDP returns a status that indicates whether the read request is granted. If this is granted, the <Decision> element will indicate "Permit." If this is rejected, the <Decision> element will return "Deny." An error of any kind (such as missing attribute value) results in "Indeterminate." "NotApplicable" is the result if no available policies apply to the given request.

Example 7–15 Output from the PDP program

```
C:\XACML2\sunxacml-1.2\sample>java SimplePDP request\request.xml
policy\policy.xml
<Response>
  <Result ResourceID=
       "http://www.onlinestore.com/sensitive/paymentinfo.html">
    <Decision>Permit</Decision>
    <Status>
      <StatusCode
         Value="urn:oasis:names:tc:xacml:1.0:status:ok"/>
    </Status>
    <Obligations>
      <Obligation
          ObligationId="LogSuccessfulRead"
          FulfillOn="Permit">
        <AttributeAssignment
            AttributeId="user"
            DataType=
            "http://www.w3.org/2001/XMLSchema#anyURI">
            urn:oasis:names:tc:xacml:1.0:subject:subject-id
        </AttributeAssignment>
        <AttributeAssignment
            AttributeId="resource"
            DataType=
            "http://www.w3.org/2001/XMLSchema#anyURI">
            urn:oasis:names:tc:xacml:1.0:resource:resource-id
        </AttributeAssignment>
      </Obligation>
    </Obligations>
  </Result>
</Response>
```

Remark

These examples use Sun's XACML Kit version 1.2, which currently supports XACML 1.1. To run these examples in XACML 2.0, developers need to change the version number and the namespace (for example, xmlns="urn:oasis:names:tc:xacml:2.0:policy") in the XML header, and make any necessary XACML 2.0 changes.

Use of XACML 2.0 with SAML 2.0

XACML 2.0 and SAML 2.0 can be used together. In XACML 2.0, a SAML profile is defined. [XACML2SAML2] specifies OASIS-approved standard extensions to SAML for interoperation with XACML. The SAML profile in XACML 2.0 includes specifications for:

- Mapping SAML Attributes into XACML Attributes
- Sending a SAML authorization decision query to an XACML Policy Decision Point
- Receiving an XACML response in the form of a SAML authorization decision statement from an XACML Policy Decision Point
- Requesting one or more XACML policies from an online Policy Administration Point using a SAML policy query
- Receiving XACML policies from online Policy Administration Points in the form of a SAML policy statement in a SAML assertion
- Storing XACML policies in policy repositories in the form of SAML policy statements

Figure 7–10 illustrates the use of these SAML extensions with XACML (also refer to [XACML2SAML2] for more details):

- Service requester initiates request to access a specific resource. The Policy Enforcement Point sends the resource access request to an XACML Policy Decision Point in a SAML authorization decision query (XACMLAuthzDecisionQuery in Step 1).
  - The Policy Enforcement Point may obtain attributes in one of the following ways:
    - The Policy Enforcement Point may obtain attributes directly from an online Attribute Authority using an AttributeQuery (Step 1a). This query returns an AttributeStatement in the SAML response (Step 2a).
    - The Policy Enforcement Point may obtain attributes from a repository, where they were stored previously by an Attribute Authority in the form of SAML AttributeStatements (Step 4a).
- The XACML Policy Decision Point evaluates the resource access request and decides additional attributes are needed. It can obtain these in one of the following ways:

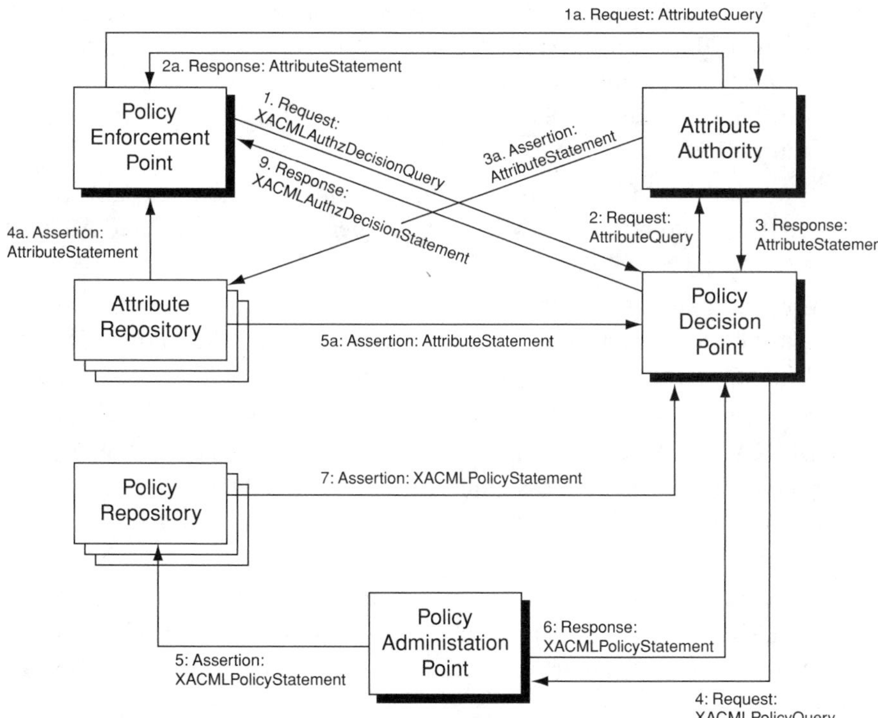

Figure 7–10 Use of SAML 2.0 in XACML 2.0

- The XACML Policy Decision Point may obtain attributes directly from an online Attribute Authority using an AttributeQuery (Step 2). This query returns an AttributeStatement in the SAML response (Step 3).
- The XACML Policy Decision Point may obtain attributes from a repository (Step 4), where they were stored previously by an Attribute Authority in the form of SAML AttributeStatements (Step 5a).

This allows the XACML Policy Decision Point to augment the resource access request with additional attributes.

- The Policy Enforcement Point may obtain attributes from the Attribute Authority or from the Attribute Repository that stores the attributes about the service requester or resource (AttributeQuery in Step 1a).
- The Attribute Authority returns attributes in a SAML attribute statement to the Policy Enforcement Point (AttributeStatement in Step 2a).

- The Attribute Authority creates an assertion of an attribute statement in the Attribute Repository (AttributeStatement in Step 3a), which also makes the attribute statement available to the XACML Policy Enforcement Point (AttributeStatement in Step 4a) or to the XACML Policy Decision Point (AttributeStatement in Step 5a).
- The XACML Policy Decision Point evaluates the resource access request and decides to make a SAML attribute query with the Attribute Authority (AttributeQuery in Step 2).
- The Attribute Authority returns with a SAML attribute statement (AttributeStatement in Step 3). This allows the XACML Policy Decision Point to augment the XACML Policy Enforcement Point's description of the resource access request with additional attributes.
- The XACML Policy Decision Point may need to retrieve any policies relevant to the resource access request from the XACML Policy Administration Point or from the XACML Policy Repository (XACMLPolicyQuery in Step 4).
- The XACML Policy Administration Point finds relevant policies from the XACML Policy Repository and creates a policy statement assertion (XACMLPolicyStatement in Step 5). These policies may be retrieved as follows:
  - The XACML Policy Administration Point responds to the policy query with a policy statement assertion (XACMLPolicyStatement in Step 6).
  - The XACML Policy Decision Point can also find relevant policies from the XACML Policy Repository (XACMLPolicyStatement in Step 7).
- With the availability of relevant policies and attributes, the XACML Policy Decision Point is able to respond to the XACML Policy Enforcement Point with a SAML authorization decision statement (XACMLAuthzDecisionStatement in Step 8).
- Alternatively, the XACML Policy Decision Point can retrieve necessary policies directly from the XACML Policy Repository.

Summary

Identity management is certainly becoming critical to preventing identity theft and addressing new security risks related to Java-based applications and Web services. Given the nature of distributed systems and Web-based applications, architects and developers need to secure the network identity in multiple tiers and across different security domains, not just in the Web tier. OASIS has published a set of identity management security standards, including SAML and XACML. The purpose of these security specifications is to address single sign-on, federated identity management, and access control issues.

SAML has become the definitive protocol for exchanging assertions that enable single sign-on and global logout. This security protocol allows different security infrastructures to exchange identity information without locking in specific-vendor architecture. SAML has gained wide industry support, including Liberty Alliance, which has reused and extended SAML for federated identity management.

XACML is a policy language for use in controlling access to XML documents or other resources. It provides a flexible and extensible mechanism for policy management and is consistent with the policy framework laid down by IETF and DMTF. XACML 2.0 is aligned with SAML 2.0 to allow the encapsulation and transmission of XACML attributes, policies, decision requests, and decisions in SAML assertions. It can also serve as a policy engine for many security infrastructures or vendor products.

Designing identity management using Java technology and Web services is complicated because multi-tier and multiple security domains are involved. Using J2EE design patterns for identity management would be helpful. In Chapter 12, "Securing the Identity," and Chapter 13, "Secure Service Provisioning," we will discuss design patterns that address SAML assertions, single sign-on, credential tokens, and security provisioning.

References

[Anne1] Anne Anderson. "A Comparison of EPAL and XACML." Sun Microsystems. July 12, 2004.

http://research.sun.com/projects/xacml/CompareEPALandXACML.html

[Anne2] Anne Anderson. "IEEE Policy 2004 Workshop 8 June 2004–Comparing WSPL and WS-Policy." IEEE Policy 2004.

http://www.policy-workshop.org/2004/slides/Anderson-WSPL_vs_WS-Policy_v2.pdf

[Anne3] Anne Anderson. "An Introduction to the Web Services Policy Language (WSPL)." Sun Microsystems Laboratories. 2004.

http://research.sun.com/projects/xacml/Policy2004.pdf

[KingPerkins1] Chris King and Earl Perkins. "The Role of Identity Management in Information Security: Part I–The Planning View."

http://techupdate.zdnet.com/techupdate/stories/main/Identity_Management_Information_Security_Part_1.html

[Liberty] Liberty Alliance Project–Official Web site

http://www.projectliberty.org/about/history.html

[Liberty12FFArch] Thomas Watson, et al. "Liberty ID-FF Architecture Overview." OASIS.

http://www.projectliberty.org/specs/liberty-idff-arch-overview-v1.2.pdf

[LibertyIDWSF] Liberty Alliance. Liberty ID-WSF Security Mechanisms. Version 1.2.

http://www.projectliberty.org/specs/liberty-idwsf-security-mechanisms-v1.2.pdf

[Liberty12Tutorial] Alexandre Stervinou. "Liberty Specifications Tutorial." Liberty Alliance.

http://www.itu.int/itudoc/itu-t/com17/tutorial/85606.html

[OASIS] OASIS–Official Web site

http://www.oasis-open.org/home/index.php

[OpenSAML] OpenSAML–Official Web site

http://www.opensaml.org/

[SecurityBreach2004] Information Security Breaches Survey 2004.

http://www.dti.gov.uk/industry_files/pdf/hardfacts.pdf

[SAML-TC] OASIS SAML–Technical Committee

http://www.oasis-open.org/committees/tc_home.php?wg_abbrev=security)

[SAML11Core] OASIS. Assertions and Protocols for the OASIS Security Assertion Markup Language (SAML) V1.1. September 2, 2003.

http://www.oasis-open.org/committees/download.php/3406/oasis-_sstc-saml-core-1.1.pdf

[SAML11Diff] OASIS. Differences between OASIS Security Assertion Markup Language (SAML) V1.1 and V1.0. May 21, 2003.

http://www.oasis-open.org/committees/download.php/3412/sstc-saml-diff-1.1-draft-01.pdf

[SAML11Security] OASIS. Security and Privacy Considerations for the OASIS Security Assertion Markup Language (SAML) V1.1. September 2, 2003.

http://www.oasis-open.org/committees/download.php/3404/oasis-_sstc-saml-sec-consider-1.1.pdf

[SAML2Core] OASIS. Assertions and Protocols for the OASIS Security Assertion Markup Language (SAML) V2.0. Working Draft 10. April 10, 2004.

http://www.oasis-open.org/committees/download.php/6347/sstc-saml-core-2.0-draft-10-diff.pdf

[SAML2Scope] OASIS. SAML Version 2.0 Scope and Work Items.

http://www.oasis-open.org/committees/download.php/6277/sstc-saml-scope-2.0-draft-17.pdf

[SAML2Profiles] OASIS. Profiles for the OASIS Security Assertion Markup Language (SAML) V2.0. March 15, 2005.

http://docs.oasis-open.org/security/saml/v2.0/saml-profiles-2.0-os.pdf

[SourceID] SourceID–Official Web site

http://www.sourceid.org/

[SPML-TC] OASIS SPML–Technical Committee

http://www.oasis-open.org/committees/tc_home.php?wg_abbrev=provision

[Systinet] Systinet article: SAML Support on Smartcard.

http://www.theserverside.com/resources/article.jsp?l=Systinet-Web services-part-6

[WebServicesLifeCycle] Ray Lai. "Web Services Life Cycle: Managing Enterprise Web Services." Sun Microsystems. October 2003.

http://wwws.sun.com/software/sunone/whitepapers/wp_mngwebsvcs.pdf

[XACML-TC] OASIS XACML–Technical Committee

http://www.oasis-open.org/committees/tc_home.php?wg_abbrev=xacml

[XACML11] OASIS. eXtensible Access Control Markup Language (XACML) Version 1.1. Committee Specification. August 7, 2003.

http://www.oasis-open.org/committees/xacml/repository/cs-xacml-specification-1.1.pdf

[XACML2] OASIS. eXtensible Access Control Markup Language (XACML) Version 2.0. Working Draft 09. April 16, 2004.

http://www.oasis-open.org/committees/download.php/6433/oasis-xacml-2.0-core-wd-09.zip

[XACML2changes] Daniel. "Differences Between XACML Versions 1.0 and 2.0." January 7, 2005.

http://blog.parthenoncomputing.com/xacml/archives/2005/01/the_differences.html

[XACML2SAML2] OASIS. SAML 2.0 Profile of XACML. Committee Draft 02. November 11, 2004.

http://docs.oasis-open.org/xacml/access_control-xacml-2.0-saml_profile-spec-cd-02.pdf

Part IV

Security Design Methodology, Patterns, and Reality Checks

The Alchemy of Security Design–Methodology, Patterns, and Reality Checks

Topics in This Chapter

- The Rationale
- Secure UP
- Security Patterns
- Security Patterns for J2EE, Web Services, Identity Management, and Service Provisioning
- Reality Checks
- Security Testing
- Adopting a Security Framework
- Refactoring Security Design
- Service Continuity and Recovery
- Conclusion

Chapter 8

In a typical application development environment, architects and developers share similar experiences. They deploy business applications in a highly compressed time frame—making the applications work, testing the functionality at all levels, ensuring that they meet expected system performance or service levels, and wrapping the applications with an attractive client presentation and user documentation. Ensuring the security of the application at all levels has usually been considered at the last phase of the development process. If this is your company's current application development process, then you are not alone.

End-to-end security should be adopted and accomplished as part of the early application design and development process. It should not be addressed at the end of the deployment phase or even considered just before the system testing in a preproduction environment. If you wait to consider security at either of these points, your options for reactive or post-mortem security fixes are very limited. And it is important to note the fact that there is no *rollback* for an application security breach.

In an enterprise application development life-cycle process, different architects may have different security architecture design perspectives for the same set of security requirements. Some assume that they can secure applications with infrastructure security protection (for example, firewall policy and proxy topology). Some would prefer to secure applications using a specific-vendor security framework and infrastructure solutions that are categorized as best-practice solutions for application security. Nevertheless, what was considered *secure* application design may appear to be *insecure* if someone discovers a loophole in the application that the security architects have overlooked in the early design stage. It would be challenging to create a quality application security design that is repeatable yet reliable, so that architects could ensure all aspects of application security are considered during the early design stage in a structured manner. In addition to that, there are industry best-practices for applying security that need to be put in place before the application design process. It is always accepted as a good practice to proactively check and verify the security design for risks, trade-offs, security policies, proactive defensive strategies, and reality checks upon completion of the application design phase. After production deployment, it is also important to adopt reactive security measures and defensive strategies to ensure service continuity and recovery in case of a security breach or malicious attack. These help in identifying and thwarting security-related threats and vulnerabilities in all facets of the application development life-cycle process, from use-cases to components, from components to prototypes, from prototypes to final implementation, from implementation to production deployment, and until retirement. With such a detailed verification process, architects and developers can reduce critical security risks within the software development life cycle and prior to production deployment. This mandates a security design methodology that provides a systematic approach and a well-defined process.

This chapter will discuss the prescription for a robust security architecture design, which is the *alchemy* of securing business applications end-to-end at all levels. In particular, it will cover the rationale for adopting a security methodology, the process steps of security methodology, and how to create and use security patterns within that methodology. It will also look at how and why to do a security assessment as well as adopting a security framework.

The Rationale

An application or service may consist of a single functional component or multiple sets of disparate components that reside locally or over a network. Security is often considered as a complex process, encompassing a chain of features and tasks related to computer system security, network security, application-level security, authentication services, data confidentiality, personal privacy issues, cryptography, and so forth. More importantly, these features must be designed and verified independently and then made to work together across the system. Applying a security feature often represents a unique function that can be a safeguard or a countermeasure, which guarantees the application or service by preventing or reducing the impact of a particular threat or vulnerability and the likelihood of its reoccurrence.

The Security Wheel

Security is represented as a set of features that fortifies the entire application or service with safeguards and countermeasures for potential risks and vulnerabilities. Each security feature is like a spoke in a wheel. This means that each functional component in the entire system must be secured or the wheel will not have structural integrity and may well break apart. In order to accomplish this, a methodical process must be put in place to ensure that security is addressed properly and integrated across all of these varying components. From the user who is accessing the application or service over the network to the routers and firewalls on the perimeter of the system and then up through the application or service and the OS on which it resides—a security design must identify the risks and address the safeguards and countermeasures of the system holistically. Incorporating fundamental security principles plays a vital role during the software design and architecture, and it also helps identifying and eliminating the risks and threats in the early phases of the software development cycle. The concept of a **Security Wheel** provides the basis for verifying the fundamental security principles mandated for securing an application or service.

Figure 8–1 illustrates the Security Wheel, which represents all of the fundamental principles of security.

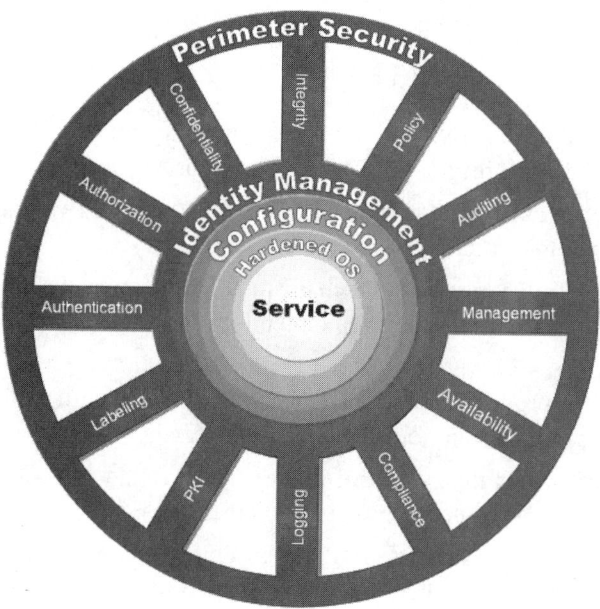

Figure 8–1 Security Wheel representing the fundamental security principles

The Security Wheel is a logical representation of the fundamental security principles required for establishing **Security by Default** in an application or a service. It provides guidelines that need to be taken into consideration during the entire software development life-cycle, and it can be applied across all or selected components of an application or a service.

The Hub

At the core of the hub of the Security Wheel sits the service or application that you are building. In this representation, it refers more to the business logic than the application as a whole. The service resides in a secured server host with minimized and hardened OS. (OS Minimization refers to fewer software components on a server infrastructure, and Hardened OS refers to a reconfigured OS that applies security measures specified by the OS vendor and retains no non-essential programs, protocols, or services.) The secured host includes storage devices and accessories. Both the service and the target host environment must be configured and deployed through a secure configuration management and reliable provisioning mechanisms. The service makes use of a common identity management solution that provides repository and supporting mechanisms for verifying an entity and its associated credentials, for logging, and for reporting all activities.

The Spokes

The spokes represent the following 12 core security services applicable to an application or a service.

- **Authentication** provides the process of verifying and validating the evidence and eligibility of an entity to carry out a desired action.
- **Authorization** provides the process of verifying and validating the rights and privileges granted to the authenticated entity.
- **Confidentiality** provides mechanisms of protecting the information during transit or in storage from intentional or unintentional unauthorized entities.
- **Integrity** provides the mechanisms for maintaining the information tamper-proof and unmodified by unauthorized entities.
- **Policy** provides the rules and procedures that can provide access control directives or a regulatory function to all entities.
- **Auditing** provides a series of records of events about an application or service activity. These records are maintained to support forensic investigation. It also helps in determining regulatory compliance.

- **Management** provides the mechanisms for centrally administering all security operations.
- **Availability** provides mechanisms for ensuring reliability and timely access to the application or service and also its prolonged continuity in the event of a disaster or service interruption.
- **Compliance** provides the assurance of a degree of constancy and accuracy by adherence to standards or regulatory requirements.
- **Logging** provides the mechanisms for recording events that can provide diagnostic information in case of errors, problems, and unexpected behaviors. The recording of these events is usually not driven by business requirements and is generally short-term and transient in nature. Failure to log such events will usually not necessitate cancellation of a transaction.
- **PKI** provides key management support for applying cryptographic mechanisms to protect data, transactions, and communication using a public-key infrastructure.
- **Labeling** is a process of classifying information based on roles and responsibilities to prevent unauthorized disclosure and failure of confidentiality.

The above-mentioned security services are the guiding security principles for providing a robust security architecture. Applications or services can be reviewed with these security measures during their design phases or at appropriate phases prior to deployment.

The Wheel Edge

The wheel edge represents the perimeter security: the network security components such as routers, firewalls, packet-filtering appliances, intrusion detection systems (IDS), crypto accelerators, and other devices that sit between the Internet and your network. They make up the solution for protecting the network perimeter from connection attacks based on IP addresses, TCP ports, protocols, and packet filters.

Across the service and OS and all the way to the perimeter security, every security principle must be addressed as a service that contributes to the overall security architecture. In some cases, many of these security principles, represented as spokes in the wheel, are only applicable to a few components of the overall application or a service. Nevertheless, each component within the system must be examined to determine the associated risks and trade-offs. Adopting a structured security methodology helps to ensure that all security principles are addressed and captured during the software development life cycle or prior to production.

Secure UP

To get started, we must first identify a process to guide us through the software development life cycle so that we can meet the business and security goals we set forth. Adopting the Unified Process (UP) provides a comprehensive approach for ensuring that business requirements are defined, implemented, and tested within the software development life cycle. UP is an industry standard process with a proven track record. It defines the development disciplines, along with an iterative approach, for gathering, analyzing, implementing, and testing functional business requirements. For these reasons, we have chosen it to achieve our business requirements. What UP fails to address are how to incorporate the non-functional requirements of the system. These requirements are assumed but never adequately defined as part of the process.

Security is a non-functional requirement, in particular, that must be baked into the process right from the beginning of the inception phase. Too often, it is retrofitted into the application at the end of the construction phase, leading to vulnerabilities and performance and/or usability impacts. To avoid this situation, it is necessary to extend UP with a security discipline that will ensure that all of the security requirements of the application are defined, designed appropriately, implemented, and thoroughly tested. We will refer to the incorporation of these security disciplines into the Unified Process as **Secure UP**.

Secure UP establishes the prerequisites for incorporating the fundamental security principles. It also defines a streamlined security design process within a software development life cycle. UP introduces a security discipline with a set of new security activities. At first glance, the security disciplines seem to overlap heavily with the standard UP disciplines. Why do we need to split hairs over the difference between business requirements and security requirements, or between implementing a functional use case and a security use case? The answer is that universally, for each of these disciplines, there is a wide gap between the people who know and understand the business needs of the application and those who know and understand the security needs. Figure 8–2 depicts Secure UP and the integrated security disciplines.

The Secure UP–Security disciplines define the following activities:

- Security Requirements
- Security Architecture
- Security Implementation
- White Box Testing
- Black Box Testing

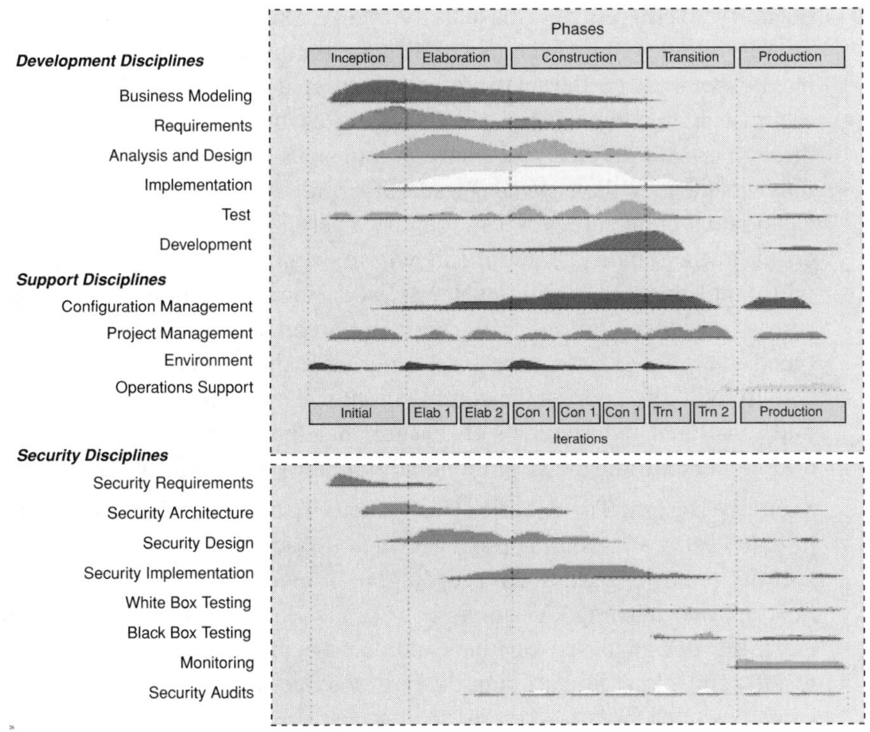

Figure 8–2 Secure UP: Security disciplines

- Monitoring
- Security Auditing

These activities coalesce to form the basis of a robust security infrastructure and deliver an end-to-end security solution for an application or service. The security discipline activities pertain to different phases of the software development cycle and do not include the sustaining functions in production, such as managing changes, updates, and patch management.

An overview of the activities in the security discipline is broken down as follows:

- **Security Requirements**: In this activity, one or more analysts will define the business-mandated security requirements of the system. This includes requirements based on industry regulations, corporate policies, and other business-specific needs. The analysts will be well-versed in regulatory compliance as well as corporate security policies.

- **Security Architecture**: This activity focuses on the creation of an overall security architecture. Architects will take the mandated security requirements specified by the analysts and then create a draft of the candidate security architecture. This activity qualifies the architectural decisions through a well-defined risk analysis and trade-off analysis processes in order to identify the risks and trade-offs and how to mitigate them. This candidate architecture will also identify a set of security patterns that covers all of the security requirements within the component architecture and will detail them in a high-level way, addressing the known risks, exposures, and vulnerabilities. The candidate architecture will then be prototyped and refined before the final security design activity is begun. This activity will also address the combination of security design with the other non-functional requirements to ensure that the security implementation does not compromise other functional or quality-of-service requirements.
- **Security Design**: The Security Design activity takes the security architecture and refines it using approaches such as factor analysis, tier analysis, security policy design, threat profiling, trust modeling, information classification, and labeling. A senior security developer will create and document the design based on the candidate security architecture, analysis results, and taking into account the best practices and pitfalls regarding the strategies of each of the patterns.
- **Security Implementation**: In this activity, security-aware developers will implement the security design. A good security design will decouple security components from the business components and therefore not require the security developers to have strong interaction or integration with business developers. The security developers will implement the security patterns by using the strategies defined in the security design and incorporating the best practices for securing the code.
- **White Box Testing**: The White Box Testing activity is for white box, or full knowledge, security testing of the code. In this activity, security testers will review the code and look for security holes or flaws that can be exploited. They will test a variety of security attacks aimed at compromising the system or demonstrating how the security requirements can be bypassed.
- **Black Box Testing**: This activity is for black box, or zero knowledge, security testing of the system. During this activity, security testers will attempt to break into the system without any knowledge of the code or its potential weaknesses. They will use a variety of tools and approaches to hack the system. They will use "out-of-the-box" techniques to break into

the system by all possible means at the application level and end-user level. This will provide an overall assessment of the security of the system.

- **Monitoring**: The monitoring activity is an ongoing activity for the system while it is in deployment. In this activity, operations personnel will monitor the application and all security facets of it. This consists of a broad range of areas, starting at the perimeter with the routers and firewalls and extending all the way back to the application itself. Monitoring is an integral part of security and an ongoing activity.
- **Security Auditing**: In this activity, security auditors will come in and audit the system for security. They assure that the systems are in compliance with all industry, corporate, and business regulations and that proper audit trails are being maintained and archived properly. These audit trails may also be reviewed for suspicious activity that may indicate a possible security breach.

These activities take place at different points in the application life cycle and have dependencies on each other. Figure 8–3 shows the roles and activities representing the Secure UP security discipline activities.

In the above activity diagram, we see the high-level view of the security specific software development life-cycle activities divided by swimlanes representing the different roles. At the start of the application life cycle, analysts gather the mandated security requirements. Once the requirements gathering process is complete, an architect will create a conceptual model of the security architecture. The architect will refine the model further and then define a candidate architecture. He or she will identify appropriate patterns, risks, and trade-offs. He or she will also represent the relevant security principles and perform some conceptual prototyping to validate the architectural decisions. Based on the results of the prototyping, the applicable patterns and the overall architectural approach will then be transitioned to the designer.

The designer will take the high-level candidate architecture, decompose it, and create a security design that addresses all component-level requirements and analyses. The resulting security design is a refinement of the architecture based on other functional requirements, non-functional requirements, factor analysis, security policy design, tier analysis, trust modeling, and threat profiling. Once complete, the design is transitioned to the developers to implement.

The developers implement the design with an eye on code-level security. Each security requirement is implemented and verified through unit testing, and all code is unit tested before being turned over to the test team for overall system-level tests, including security tests to verify the systemic qualities of architecture.

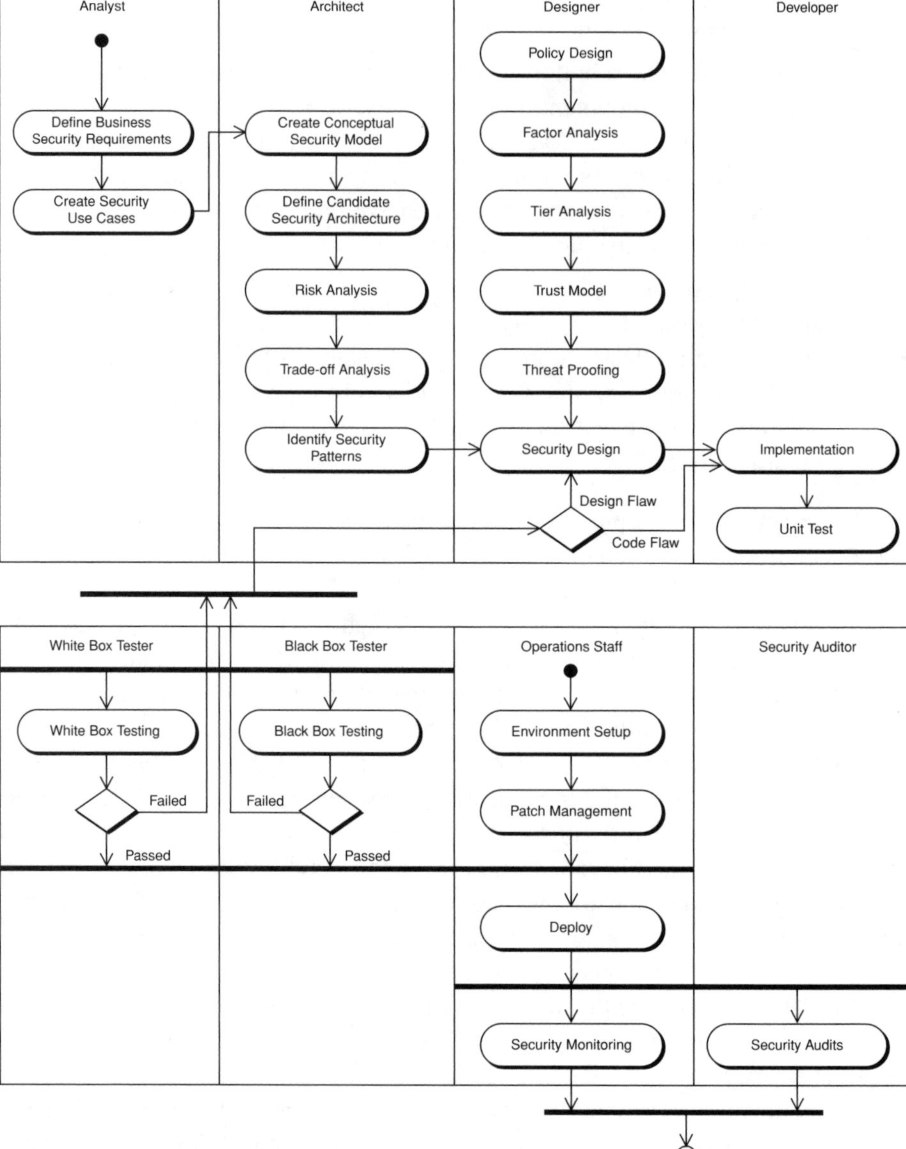

Figure 8–3 Secure UP Activity diagram

The designer takes the completed code and performs a variety of system tests to ensure that the functional requirements are met as well as the non-functional requirements. This includes application-specific regression tests and reality checks. The designer is responsible for ensuring the adequacy of all systemic qualities contributing to the QoS and SLA agreements of the system as a whole. Upon verification of the system tests, the designer transitions the application to the testers for further security testing, such as penetration tests, operational security testing, application-level scanning, and probing tests. Probing tests include network mapping, vulnerability scanning, password cracking, file integrity checking, malicious code testing, and so on. Two sets of security testers test in parallel. The White Box testers test the system based on a review of the code and full knowledge of the architecture, design, and implementation of the system. They usually find the most security holes. Black box testers test the security of the application from the outside, with no knowledge of the inner workings. They usually find holes in the system as a whole, not particularly in the application alone. If any holes are found, they are transitioned back to the system designer for security analysis. From there, they may require modification to the design and then go back through that particular flow again. If no holes are found, or if they are labeled as acceptable risks, the application is transitioned to the operations staff.

Operations will then deploy the application into production. Once in production, operations will be responsible for monitoring the system for security activity. This includes all aspects of the system from the router to the database and from the hardware to the application. It also means constantly checking for and applying hardware and software patches to keep the system available and secure. Once deployed, the system will also be transitioned to the security auditors for auditing. Like monitoring, auditors will perform routine security audits of the application for the duration of its lifetime. Finally, all activity ceases when the application is retired and pulled out of production.

Secure UP–Artifacts

For each of the security disciplines in our Secure UP, there is a mandated set of artifacts. These artifacts represent the work product of the discipline and serve as milestones that allow for transition to the start of another discipline within the software development life cycle. The following is a list of artifacts by security discipline.

- **Security Requirements**: The artifacts from the Security Requirements phase define the security requirements specific to the business, management, and operational security of the applications. Some of those business requirements are represented with organizational roles/rights, policies, and regulatory compliance requirements. These will be in document format with business-functional security requirements broken down and tracked by business-requirement identification number.

- **Create Security Use Cases**: The business security requirements are documented as a list of requirements with no real cohesion. To make sense of these requirements, they must be structured into developer-friendly use cases. These use cases will be in document format with business-functional security requirements broken down, combined into logical groups, and assigned use case numbers. The use cases then track back to any supporting business requirements or external policies that drove the use case.

- **Security Architecture**: The Security Architecture discipline has several artifacts. The first is a conceptual security model. This model represents the high-level security architecture that addresses the business security requirements defined in the use cases from the security requirements phase. The next artifact is the candidate security architecture. This architecture will be refined through the rest of the security activities in this phase, including risk analysis and trade-off analysis. Finally, a core set of security patterns will be chosen as part of the refined conceptual security model.

- **Security Design**: There are four significant artifacts of the Security Design discipline. The first is the policy design document. This document defines the policies for the application based on relevant industry, corporate, and business policies pertaining to the system. The second artifact is the trust model. This is created from factor and tier analyses of the policy design. The third artifact is the threat profile. This document defines the types of attacks and their associated risks based on the trust model, the policy design, and the refined security model. The last artifact of the Security Design discipline is the Security Design itself. This document or set of documents defines the detailed security design formulated from the union of all the artifacts. It will contain the patterns and other design material needed for implementation.

- **Security Implementation**: The four artifacts of Security Implementation are the source code, build/configuration, infrastructure, and the security unit tests. The source code in this case is the security-related code, such as the security patterns implementation and any security frameworks. The build artifacts are any security-related configurations (such as J2EE deployment descriptors) or documents for configuring security in third-party products. The infrastructure artifacts specify the firewall rules, minimization, hardening profiles, and so forth. The unit tests artifacts are those tests that developers use to test that their code complies with the use cases and provides the functionality specified in the design document.

- **White Box Testing**: This discipline has only one artifact, the test results document. This document will specify the tests performed, and their results identify the source code, configuration, and infrastructure failures/successes as well as status, and severity.
- **Black Box Testing**: Black Box Testing has only one artifact as well, the black box test results identifying the code flaws. This document will also contain the tests run, tools used, and any techniques found to exploit the application and its infrastructure weaknesses.
- **Environment Setup**: Environment Setup has several artifacts. To begin with, the first artifact is to have all of the hardware and software installed and configured. The next artifact is to have one or more Standard Operating Procedure (SOP) documents detailing how to install, configure, maintain, and troubleshoot the environment as well as how to manage crises in the operations center. Another artifact will be completion of a change management request (CMR) system for tracking and fulfilling change requests. Also, the infrastructure layout and design is an important artifact. This would consist of the network design (VLANs and DMZs), ACLs, and trust zones. In some instances, honey pots may be implemented in order to detect and observe and possibly capture intruders. System hardening, minimization, business continuity, and other system setup tasks may be treated as artifacts individually or as a whole. These and other artifacts are better described in a book focused on data center operations.
- **Patch Management**: The artifacts for Patch Management are similar to those for Environment Setup. A patch management tool in conjunction with the patch management procedures is the foremost artifact. This allows operations staff to patch and track all of the various systems within the data center. This is often a severely underestimated task. It is also the source of many production outages—just ask anyone whoever tracked down a random bug that turned out to be caused by a missing patch. Patch management is an ongoing task and therefore the artifacts are evolutionary in nature.

- **Monitoring**: Service-level agreement (SLA) is usually associated with monitoring. It is represented as an ongoing task using a logging mechanism that captures all the security-specific alerts and issues. This artifact could be a periodic activity report for designating monitoring tools and procedures used in production as well as a method of support for forensic investigation.
- **Security Auditing**: Security Auditing delivers many artifacts associated with SLAs, including organizational policies, verifying compliance requirements, application/host/network configuration, and user activity. These artifacts will be outlined in the policy design. Like monitoring, security auditing is an ongoing process.

Iterative Development

One of the major tenets of the Unified Process is iterative development. The activities stated thus far resemble a waterfall approach in terms of how they are tied together in sequence. This is merely a by-product of the representation of the activity diagram tool and not intended to imply that the process is not iterative. It therefore must be stated clearly that the security disciplines are intended to fit into the overall iterative approach to development. Each use case will be addressed in an incremental and iterative manner. While the swim lanes in the activity diagram illustrate some parallelism, the exact breakdown of what can be done in parallel and to what extent tasks are performed iteratively will vary from application to application. It is beyond the scope of this book to discuss the intrinsics of iterative development, and therefore we will simply state that the security activities should be performed iteratively, the same as any other Unified Process activities.

Risk Analysis (RA)

RA is the process of describing threats—their impacts, possible consequences, and their probability and frequency of occurrence. RA also helps determine how to mitigate those identified risks by establishing the selection criteria for safeguards and countermeasures meant for preventing or reducing those risks to an acceptable level. The acceptable risks are termed as transferred risks that are manageable. Depending upon the security requirements, the RA process may include a range of activities such as risk identification, risk assessment, risk characterization, risk communication, risk mitigation, and risk-specific policy definition. RA influences the security design process by helping the decision making process related to choosing applicable tools and mechanisms. This ensures that security measures are appropriate and fully commensurate with the risks to which the application or service is exposed.

A typical RA artifact will gather information based on the following techniques:

- **Asset Valuation**: This technique is the fundamental process of determining the value of an asset. An assessment of the overall business value of the application or service is made. Factors included are: initial and ongoing cost, insurance value and total estimated value, including the infrastructure and other intellectual properties. Asset valuation helps to justify the cost benefits in preventing or reducing the known risk and to satisfy the stakeholders, legal, and other regulatory requirements.
- **Quantitative Risk Analysis**: This technique identifies all key risk elements and estimates the value associated with each risk, such as infrastructure cost, potential threat, frequency, business impact, potential loss value, safeguard option, safeguard effectiveness, and safeguard value. Based on this information, it is possible to estimate the potential losses, analyze the potential threats, compute the Annual Loss Expectancy (ALE), and then identify countermeasures and safeguards. The formulas for computing the ALE are as follows:
  - Exposure Factor (EF) = Percentage of asset loss caused by the potential threat.
  - Single Loss Expectancy (SLE) = Asset value x Exposure Factor
  - Annualized Rate of Occurrence (ARO) = Frequency of threat per year.
  - Annual Loss Expectancy (ALE) = SLE x ARO
- **Qualitative Risk Analysis**: This technique identifies the threats and vulnerabilities specific to applicable scenarios identified through security reality checks. Based on the findings, it helps to mitigate the risks by identifying the appropriate safeguards and countermeasures to prevent them or to reduce the likelihood and effect of occurrence.

Table 8–1 represents an example template of a qualitative risk analysis artifact that identifies the known risks in aspects of *architecture tiers*, *possibility of occurrence* expressed in terms of number of prospects, *probability* expressed in terms of likelihood of possible occurrences, *Impact* expressed in terms of effect that affects the overall architecture, and *Exposure* expressed as the level of acceptability.

Table 8–1 Sample RA Template for Qualitative Risk Analysis

<table>
<tr><th>No</th><th>Known Risks</th><th>Tier/ Component</th><th>Possibility Of Occurrence (Single/Multiple)</th><th>Probability
1 – Low
5 – Medium
7 – High
10 – Extreme</th><th>Impact
1 – Low
5 – Medium
7– High
10–Extreme</th><th>Exposure
1 – Low
5 - Medium
7 – High
10–Unacceptable</th></tr>
<tr><td rowspan="2">1</td><td></td><td></td><td></td><td></td><td></td><td></td></tr>
<tr><td colspan="6">Issue:

Mitigation:</td></tr>
</table>

Trade-Off Analysis (TOA)

The purpose of trade-off analysis is to improve the quality of security architecture with explicit, efficient, and rational decisions. TOA provides stakeholders with a systematic way of improving and validating the security architecture with its use of multiple security criteria, options, alternatives, and recommendations. In the security architecture discipline, it helps to weigh choices of security features against potential threats or vulnerabilities. This assists in justifying a financial case or identifying alternative options.

A typical TOA artifact contains all of the security architecture criteria and safeguard options and alternatives. It will also include an **Effect Matrix**, where the security options/alternatives are represented in columns and security criteria are represented in rows. The cells have two values: the top value indicates the magnitude of impact on a scale from –10 to 10, and the bottom value indicates the relative importance of that security criterion on a scale from +1 to +10. Table 8–2 illustrates an example Effect Matrix.

Thus, TOA is a ranking index for making architectural security decisions with clear assumptions and for addressing associated uncertainties.

Table 8–2 Effect Matrix Table (An Example)

Trade-Off Analysis—Effect Matrix				
	Safeguard Option 1	***Safeguard Option 2***	***Safeguard Option 3***	***Safeguard Option 4***
Security Criterion A	+7	+6	+5	+8
	8	8	8	8
Security Criterion B	+2	0	0	+3
	9	9	9	9
Security Criterion C	–3	0	–2	+2
	7	7	7	7

Security Patterns

Good application design is often rooted in appropriate security design strategies and leverages proven best practices using design patterns. Design strategies determine which application security tactics or design patterns should be used for particular application security scenarios and constraints. **Security patterns** are an abstraction of business problems that address a variety of security requirements and provide a solution to the problem. They can be architectural patterns that depict how a security problem can be resolved architecturally (or conceptually), or they can be defensive design strategies upon which quality security protection code can later be built.

This section will note the existing security patterns available in the industry today and then introduce a new set of security patterns that are specific to J2EE-based applications, Web services, identity management, and service provisioning. These new security patterns will be further elaborated in the following chapters of this book.

Understanding Existing Security Patterns

There are a few known enterprise or information security patterns available on the Web. Most of them address generic information security issues related to the infrastructure of application security. Some of them are adapted from the Gang of Four [GoF] design patterns. They focus on security solutions dealing with the infrastructure or quality of services (for example, how to make the security service highly available), and are used as enterprise security design strategies. They do not delve into the feature and functional characteristics of using a security technology or how such technology can be incorporated to represent an end-to-end security model.

These known security patterns are summarized in the sections that follow. Table 8–3 through Table 8–6 outlines them.

Web Tier

Table 8–3 shows a list of known security patterns that support the Web Tier, which represents the components responsible for the presentation logic and delivery. The Web Tier accepts the client requests and handles access control to business service components. The security patterns shown in the table enable securing the client-to-server or server-to-server communication in the infrastructure as well as the application.

Table 8–3 Existing Security Patterns Supporting the Web Tier

Pattern Name	*Standards and Technologies*	*Description*	*Related Patterns*
Secure Communication	HTTPS; SSL (TLS), IPsec	This pattern describes the use of a secure data transport layer for client-to-server and server-to-server communication. Reference: [YoderBarcalow1997], p. 24; [OpenGroup], p. 27	Protected System; Login Tunnel; Secure Access Layer
Secure Association	SSL (TLS); Cryptographic standards supported by JSSE, JCE, and JGSS	This pattern shows how to make secure interactions between two entities; for example, protecting the session between the browser and Web server using SSL or TLS, and secure e-mail using encryption and proxies. Secure Communication pattern is more specific to encrypting the communication channel between the client and server. Typically, HTTPS is a means of implementing the pattern. Secure Association pattern is broader, and covers any secure interaction, including the session between the browser and Web server via HTTPS. Reference: [OpenGroup], p. 32.	Secure Communication

(*continues*)

Table 8–3 Existing Security Patterns Supporting the Web Tier (*continued*)

Pattern Name	*Standards and Technologies*	*Description*	*Related Patterns*
Single Access Point	HTTPS; SSL (TLS)	This pattern enforces a single point of entry to the business services and applications that provides a login prompt or login page. It is usually implemented by forms-based authentication and Secure Socket Layer (SSL) with J2EE declarative security. Reference: [Berry], pp. 203-204; [YoderBarcalow1997], p. 4; [WassermannBetty], p. 18	Protected System
Check Point	JAAS	This pattern centralizes the authentication and authorization process logic to a "checkpoint" entity. It assumes using JAAS to implement the checkpointed system. Reference: [Berry], p. 204; [Monzillo]; [YoderBarcalow1997], p. 7; [OpenGroup], p. 47; [WassermannBetty], p. 27	Authentication Gateway; Self Registration; Checkpointed System

(*continues*)

Table 8–3 Existing Security Patterns Supporting the Web Tier (*continued*)

Pattern Name	*Standards and Technologies*	*Description*	*Related Patterns*
Session		Secure applications need to track global information throughout the application life cycle. This pattern identifies session information (for example, HTTP session variables, RPC call information, service requester details in the JMS or the SOAP messages) that needs to be maintained for security tracking. This pattern differs from the Singleton pattern in that the session information needs to be maintained and shared in a multi-threaded, multi-user, or distributed environment. Reference: [YoderBarcalow1997], p. 14; [Amos], p. 3	Authenticated Session; User's Environment; Namespace; Threaded-based Singleton; Localized Globals
Security Provider		This pattern describes what a client should operate to perform authentication against the identity service provider for authentication or authorization assertion. It is part of the single sign-on process for enterprise identity management. Reference: [Romanosky2002], p. 11	Authoritative Source of Data; Enterprise Access Management; Enterprise Identity Management

Business Tier

Table 8–4 shows a list of known security patterns that support the security services in the Business Tier. The Business Tier represents the business data and business logic.

Table 8–4 Existing Security Patterns Supporting the Business Tier

Pattern Name	*Standards and Technologies*	*Description*	*Related Patterns*
Role	J2EE declarative security features	This pattern shows the disassociation of a specific user from their privileges by using roles. J2EE declarative security allows such role-based access control to be defined and managed in the ejb-jar.xml and Web.xml deployment descriptors. Reference: [Berry], p. 205; [Monzillo]; [YoderBarcalow1997], p. 11	Class-scoped Authorization
Subject Descriptor	J2EE Security Access Controller	This pattern allows access to the security attributes of a subject or principal via the operations. It corresponds to the javax.security.auth.Subject and java.security.Principal classes in JAAS. This pattern can be used to check rights or credentials. The Full View with Errors and Limited View patterns refer to the access rights of the application functionality, not to the subject or principal. Reference: [OpenGroup], p. 22	PEP

(*continues*)

Table 8–4 Existing Security Patterns Supporting the Business Tier (*continued*)

Pattern Name	*Standards and Technologies*	*Description*	*Related Patterns*
Security Context	J2EE Security Access Controller	This pattern provides a container for access to security attributes, such as effective user ID and group ID. In the context of J2EE technology, this pattern refers to the class AccessControlContext that provides a check permission API. Reference: [OpenGroup], p. 40	
Full View with Errors		This pattern provides a full view to users with errors incurred, including exceptions when necessary. Reference: [YoderBarcalow1997], p. 17	
Limited View		This pattern allows users to see what they can access. Reference: [YoderBarcalow1997], p. 19; [Amos], p. 4	Client Input Filter

(*continues*)

Table 8–4 Existing Security Patterns Supporting the Business Tier (*continued*)

Pattern Name	*Standards and Technologies*	*Description*	*Related Patterns*
Security Event Logging	JMX; Java API for Logging	This pattern is related to the capture and tracking of security-related events for logging and audit trail. Logged information can be used for risk assessment or analysis. A variant of this pattern is the Risk Analysis pattern, which relates the overall security risk to the sum of security threat, the cost of protecting the resources or losing the resources, and the vulnerability. Once the overall security risk is determined, then the priority will be allocated to protect resources appropriately. Reference: [Romanosky2001], p. 8; [Romanosky2002], p. 4; [Amos], p. 4; [Berry], p. 205	Risk Assessment and Management; Risk Analysis

Integration Tier

Table 8–5 shows a list of security patterns that facilitate integration with external data sources.

Infrastructure and Quality of Services

Table 8–6 shows a list of security patterns that describe enabling infrastructure capabilities and QoS requirements, such as availability, reliability, and scalability.

As you may be aware by now, the focus and scope of existing security patterns are mostly limited to the infrastructure level, and they do not address the core application-specific security issues and their associated challenges. Nor do they attempt to adopt the core security services such as authentication, authorization, auditing, confidentiality, non-repudiation, and other requirements mandated by enterprise-scale applications and Web services.

Table 8–5 Existing Security Patterns Supporting the Integration Tier

Pattern Name	*Standards and Technologies*	*Description*	*Related Patterns*
Authoritative Source of Data		This pattern verifies the data source for authenticity and data integrity. Reference: [Romanosky2001], p. 5; [Romanosky2002], p. 2; [Berry], p. 206	
Third-Party Communication		This pattern helps identify the risks of the third-party relationship and applies relevant security protection measures for the third-party communication. Reference: [Romanosky2001], p. 10; [Romanosky2002], p. 6	Enterprise Partner Communication

Table 8–6 Existing Security Patterns for Infrastructure Quality of Services

Pattern Name	*Standards and Technologies*	*Description*	*Related Patterns*
Load Balancing PEP		This pattern shows how to make horizontal scalable authentication components using load balancer and multiple instances of Policy Enforcement Points (PEPs). Reference: [OpenGroup], p. 18	Load Balancer; PEP; Subject Descriptor

(*continues*)

Table 8–6 Existing Security Patterns for Infrastructure Quality of Services (*continued*)

Pattern Name	*Standards and Technologies*	*Description*	*Related Patterns*
Clustered PEP		This pattern makes highly available authentication components over clustered Web containers. Reference: [OpenGroup], p. 46	Recoverable Component; Hot Standby; Cold Standby; Comparator-checked Fault Tolerant System
Layered Security		This pattern configures multiple checkpoints. Reference: [Romanosky2001], p. 7	Check Point; Authentication Gateway; Self Registration; Checkpointed System
Cold Standby		This pattern describes how to structure a security system or service to resume service after a system failure. The Cold Standby pattern typically consists of one active Recoverable Component and at least one standby Recoverable Component. The Cold Standby pattern differs from the Clustered PEP pattern in that the latter primarily provides an authentication service as a Policy Enforcement Point, while the former may be any security service (including PEP). Reference: [OpenGroup], p. 49	Disaster Recovery; Recoverable Component; Hot Standby; Cold Standby; Comparator-checked Fault Tolerant System

(*continues*)

Table 8–6 Existing Security Patterns for Infrastructure Quality of Services (*continued*)

Pattern Name	*Standards and Technologies*	*Description*	*Related Patterns*
Comparator-checked Fault Tolerant System		This pattern structures a system that enables the detection of independent failure of any component. It requires a fault-detecting mechanism to be in place to report or detect any system fault for a security system, for example, polling the state of the security device periodically, or checking the heartbeat of the Secure Service Proxy, Secure Daemon, or similar intermediaries. Reference: [OpenGroup], p. 51	Tandem System
Journaled Component		This pattern specifies how to capture changes to a security component's state for future system state recovery. Reference: [OpenGroup], p. 53	
Hot Standby		This pattern describes how to structure a security system or service to provide highly available security services, or to protect system integrity from system failure. This is usually done by synchronizing state updates to the replica or back-up security components without temporary loss of security services in case of full or partial system failure. Reference: [OpenGroup], p. 55	Synchronized Distributed System; Replicated Transaction

Security Patterns for J2EE, Web Services, Identity Management, and Service Provisioning

There are new security patterns specific to delivering end-to-end security in J2EE applications, Web services, identity management, and service provisioning. These security patterns differ from existing security design patterns in that they address the end-to-end security requirements of an application by mitigating security risks at the functional and deployment level, securing business objects and data across logical tiers, securing communications, and protecting the application from unauthorized internal and external threats and vulnerabilities.

A simple taxonomy by logical architecture tiers are made here: **Web Tier**, **Business Tier**, **Web Services Tier**, and **Identity Tier**. Ideally, these patterns and others like them will be maintained in a patterns catalog that will be consulted during the security architecture activity in order to feed patterns into the security design. Through many versions of the application and across applications, these patterns will continue to grow and their implementation will be refined.

These patterns are usually structured and represented using a standard pattern template that allows expressing a solution for solving a common or recurring problem. The template captures all the elements of a pattern and describes its motivation, issues, strategies, technology, applicable scenarios, solutions, and examples.

Security Pattern Template

To facilitate using the security patterns, we adopted a pattern template that consists of the following:

- **Problem**: Describes the security issues addressed by the pattern.
- **Forces**: Describes the motivations and constraints that affect the security problem. Highlights the reasons for choosing the pattern and provides justification.
- **Solution**: Describes the approach briefly and the associated mechanisms in detail.
- **Structure**: Describes the basic structure of the solution using UML sequence diagrams and details the participants.
- **Strategies**: Describes different ways a security pattern may be implemented and deployed.
- **Consequences**: Describes the results of using the security pattern as a safeguard and control measure. It also describes the trade-offs.

- **Security Factors and Risks**: Describes the factors and risks to be considered while applying the pattern.
- **Reality Checks**: Describes a set of review items to identify the feasibility and practicality of the pattern.
- **Related Patterns**: Lists other related patterns from the Security Patterns Catalog or from other related sources.

In the following sections, we will present the security **patterns catalog** and discuss each pattern and its logical tier. We will use sample scenarios and describe how these security patterns relate to each other and together contribute to the end-to-end security of an application.

Security Patterns Catalog

In this section we introduce the security design patterns that facilitate securing J2EE-based applications, Web services, identity management, and service provisioning technologies. We will identify the patterns based on their logical tier representations, such as Web Tier, Business Tier, Web Services Tier, Identity Tier, and Service Provisioning.

Web Tier Security Patterns

Table 8–7 shows a list of security patterns that are available in the Web Tier.

Table 8–7 Web Tier Security Design Patterns

Pattern Name	*Standards and Technologies*	*Description*	*Related Patterns*
Authentication Enforcer	HTTPS; SSL/TLS; IPsec JAAS; JSSE; JCE; JGSS;	This pattern shows how a browser client should authenticate with the server. It creates a base Action class to handle authentication of HTTP requests. Refer to Chapter 9, "Securing the Web Tier: Design Strategies and Best Practices," for details.	Context Object [CJP]; Intercepting Filter [CJP]

(continues)

Table 8–7 Web Tier Security Design Patterns (*continued*)

Pattern Name	*Standards and Technologies*	*Description*	*Related Patterns*
Authorization Enforcer	JACC JAAS; JSSE; JCE; JGSS;	This pattern creates a base Action class to handle authorization of HTTP requests. Refer to Chapter 9 for details.	Context Object; Intercepting Filter [CJP]
Intercepting Validator	JSP Servlets	This pattern refers to secure mechanisms for validating parameters before invoking a transaction. Unchecked parameters may lead to buffer overrun, arbitrary command execution, and SQL injection attacks. The validation of application-specific parameters includes validating business data and characteristics such as data type (string, integer), format, length, range, null-value handling, and verifying for character-set, locale, patterns, context, and legal values. Refer to Chapter 9 for details.	Message Inspector; Interceptor [POSA]

(*continues*)

Table 8–7 Web Tier Security Design Patterns (*continued*)

Pattern Name	*Standards and Technologies*	*Description*	*Related Patterns*
Secure Base Action	JSP; Servlets; and helper classes	The secure base action is a pattern for centralizing and coordinating security-related tasks within the Presentation Tier. It serves as the primary entry point into the Presentation Tier and should be extended, or used by a Front Controller. It coordinates use of the Authentication Enforcer, Authorization Enforcer, Secure Session Manager, Intercepting Validator, and Secure Logger to ensure cohesive security architecture throughout the Web Tier. Refer to Chapter 9 for details.	FrontController [CJP]; Command[GoF]; Authentication Enforcer; Authorization Enforcer; Secure Logger; Intercepting Validator
Secure Logger	JMX; Java API for logging	This pattern defines how to capture the application-specific events and exceptions in a secure and reliable manner to support security auditing. It accommodates the different behavioral nature of HTTP servlets, EJBs, SOAP messages, and other middleware events. Refer to Chapter 9 for details.	Abstract Factory Pattern[GoF]; Secure Pipe;

(*continues*)

Table 8–7 Web Tier Security Design Patterns (*continued*)

Pattern Name	*Standards and Technologies*	*Description*	*Related Patterns*
Secure Pipe	HTTPS; SSL/TLS; IPsec	This pattern shows how to secure the connection between the client and the server, or between servers when connecting between trading partners. In a complex distributed application environment, there will be a mixture of security requirements and constraints between clients, servers, and any intermediaries. Standardizing the connection between external parties using the same platform and security protection mechanism may not be viable. It adds value by requiring mutual authentication and establishing confidentiality or non-repudiation between trading partners. This is particularly critical for B2B integration using Web services. Refer to Chapter 9 for details.	Message Interceptor Gateway

(*continues*)

Table 8–7 Web Tier Security Design Patterns (*continued*)

Pattern Name	*Standards and Technologies*	*Description*	*Related Patterns*
Secure Service Proxy	Servlets JAX-RPC SAAJ	This pattern is intended to secure and control access to J2EE components exposed as Web services endpoints. It acts as a security proxy by providing a common interface to the underlying service provider components (for example, session EJBs, servlets, and so forth) and restricting direct access to the actual Web services provider components. The Secure Service Proxy pattern can be implemented as a Servlet or RPC handler for basic authentication of Web services components that do not use message-level security. Refer to Chapter 9 for details.	Proxy [GoF] Intercepting Web Agent; Secure Message Router; Message Interceptor Gateway; Extract Adapter [Kerievsky]

(continues)

Table 8–7 Web Tier Security Design Patterns (*continued*)

Pattern Name	*Standards and Technologies*	*Description*	*Related Patterns*
Secure Session Manager	Servlets EJB	This pattern defines how to create a secure session by capturing session information. Use this in conjunction with Secure Pipe. This pattern describes the actions required to build a secure session between the client and the server, or between the servers. It includes the creation of session information in the HTTP or stateful EJB sessions and how to protect the sensitive business transaction information during the session. The Session pattern is different from the Secure Session Manager pattern in that the former is generic for creating HTTP session information. The latter is much broader in scope and covers EJB sessions as well as server-to-server session information.	Context Object [CJP]
Intercepting Web Agent	Web server plug-in	This pattern helps protect Web applications through a Web Agent that intercepts requests at the Web Server and provides authentication, authorization, encryption, and auditing capabilities. Refer to Chapter 9 for details.	Proxy [GoF]

Business Tier Security Patterns

Table 8–8 shows a list of security patterns that are available in the Business Tier.

Table 8–8 Business Tier Security Design Patterns

Pattern Name	*Standards and Technologies*	*Description*	*Related Patterns*
Audit Interceptor	Java API for Logging	The Secure Logger pattern provides instrumentation of the logging aspects in the front, and the Audit Interceptor pattern enables the administration and manages the logging and audit in the back-end. Refer to Chapter 10, "Securing the Business Tier–Design Strategies and Best Practices," for details.	Secure Logger Intercepting Filter [CJP]
Container Managed Security	EJB	This pattern describes how to declare security-related information for EJBs in a deployment descriptor. Refer to Chapter 10 for details.	Secure Pipe
Dynamic Service Management	JMX	This pattern provides dynamically adjustable instrumentation of security components for monitoring and active management of business objects. Refer to Chapter 10 for details.	Secure Pipe; Secure Message Router

(*continues*)

Table 8–8 Business Tier Security Design Patterns (*continued*)

Pattern Name	*Standards and Technologies*	*Description*	*Related Patterns*
Obfuscated Transfer Object	JCE	This pattern describes ways of protecting business data represented in transfer objects and passed within and between logical tiers. Refer to Chapter 10 for details.	Transfer Object [CJP];
Policy Delegate	JACC EJB XACML	This pattern creates, manages, and administers security management policies governing how EJB tier objects are accessed and routed. Refer to Chapter 10 for details.	Secure Base Action; Business Delegate [CJP]
Secure Service Façade	EJB	This pattern provides a session façade that can contain and centralize complex interactions between business components under a secure session. It provides dynamic and declarative security to back-end business objects in the service façade. It shields off foreign entities from performing illegal or unauthorized service invocation directly under a secure session. Session information can be also captured and tracked in conjunction with the Secure Logger pattern. Refer to Chapter 10 for details.	Secure Service Proxy; Session Façade [CJP]

(*continues*)

Table 8–8 Business Tier Security Design Patterns (*continued*)

Pattern Name	*Standards and Technologies*	*Description*	*Related Patterns*
Secure Session Object	EJB	This pattern defines ways to secure session information in EJBs facilitating distributed access and seamless propagation of security context. Refer to Chapter 10 for details.	Transfer Object [CJP]; Session Façade[CJP]

Web Services Tier Security Patterns

Table 8–9 shows a list of security patterns that are available in the Web Services Tier.

Table 8–9 Web Services Tier Security Design Patterns

Pattern Name	*Standards and Technologies*	*Description*	*Related Patterns*
Message Inspector	XML Encryption; XML Signature; SAAJ; JAX-RPC; WS-Security; SAML; XKMS;	This pattern checks for and verifies the quality of XML message-level security mechanisms, such as XML Signature and XML Encryption in conjunction with a security token. The Message Inspector pattern also helps in verifying and validating applied security mechanisms in a SOAP message when processed by multiple intermediaries (actors). It supports a variety of signature formats and encryption technologies used by these intermediaries. Refer to Chapter 11, "Securing Web Services–Design Strategies and Best Practices," for details.	Message Interceptor Gateway, Secure Message Router

(*continues*)

Table 8–9 Web Services Tier Security Design Patterns (*continued*)

Pattern Name	*Standards and Technologies*	*Description*	*Related Patterns*
Message Interceptor Gateway	JAX-RPC; SAAJ; WS-Security XML Signature; XML Encryption; SAML XACML WS-*	This pattern provides a single entry point and allows centralization of security enforcement for incoming and outgoing messages. The security tasks include creating, modifying, and administering security policies for sending and receiving SOAP messages. It helps to apply transport-level and message-level security mechanisms required for securely communicating with a Web services endpoint. Refer to Chapter 11 for details.	Secure Access Point, Message Inspector, Secure Message Router
Secure Message Router	WSS-SMS XML Signature XML Encryption WS-Security Liberty Alliance SAML XKMS	This pattern facilitates secure XML communication with multiple partner endpoints that adopt message-level security and identity-federation mechanisms. It acts as a security intermediary component that applies message-level security mechanisms to deliver messages to multiple recipients where the intended recipient would be able to access only the required portion of the message and remaining message fragments are made confidential. Refer to Chapter 11 for details.	Secure Access Point, Message Inspector, Message Interceptor Gateway

Security Patterns for Identity Management and Service Provisioning

Table 8–10 shows a list of security patterns available for the Identity Tier and Secure Service Provisioning.

Table 8–10 Security Patterns for Identity Tier and Service Provisioning

Pattern Name	*Standards and Technologies*	*Description*	*Related Patterns*
Assertion Builder	SAML; Liberty Alliance	This pattern defines how an identity assertion (for example, authentication assertion or authorization assertion) can be built. Refer to Chapter 12, "Securing the Identity–Design Strategies and Best Practices," for details.	
Credential Tokenizer	SAML; Liberty Alliance	This pattern describes how a principal's security token can be encapsulated, embedded in a SOAP message, routed, and processed. Refer to Chapter 12 for details.	
Single Sign-on (SSO) Delegator	SAML; Liberty Alliance	This pattern describes how to construct a delegator agent for handling a legacy system for single sign-on (SSO). Refer to Chapter 12 for details.	
Password Synchronizer	SPML	This pattern describes how to securely synchronize principals across multiple applications using service provisioning. Refer to Chapter 13, "Secure Service Provisioning–Design Strategies and Best Practices," for details.	

Security Patterns and their Relationships

Security patterns can seem very complex before we know the role and context of how they are related to each other, how they are relevant to the scenario, and how to apply them end-to-end in a typical application design process. Figure 8–4 depicts how all the security patterns just presented work together in the Web Tier (interacting with the clients), the Business Tier (encapsulating business logic and related processes), the Web Services Tier (integrating with internal or external application infrastructure), and the Identity Tier (for signing-on the authenticated identity with identity infrastructure providers).

Applying Security Patterns

Let's consider a Web-based business portal as an example. The portal hosts business services from multiple business partner resources and provides member rewards redemption services. In a typical scenario, a subscriber logs in to the member rewards provider portal to check his membership award balance and submits a request to an affiliate content provider (a trading partner of the service provider) to redeem points and obtain a gift.

Web Tier

The subscriber uses a Web browser to sign on to the rewards portal. The portal initiates a secure communication channel between the client browser and the Web server using the Secure Pipe pattern. The Secure Pipe establishes the transport-layer security between the client and server using secure handshake protocols (such as SSL or TLS), which provide an encrypted data exchange and digital signatures for guaranteed message integrity.

Once the secure communication channel is established, the Front Controller pattern is used to process application requests (refer to http://java.sun.com/blueprints/patterns/FrontController.html for details). The Front Controller uses a Secure Base Action pattern that attempts to validate the session. Finding that the session information does not exist, the Secure Base Action uses the Authentication Enforcer pattern to authenticate the subscriber. The Authentication Enforcer prompts the subscriber for his user credentials. Upon successful authentication of the user credentials by the Authentication Enforcer, the Secure Base Action pattern uses the Secure Session Manager pattern to create a secure session for that user. It then applies the Authorization Enforcer pattern to perform access control on the request. Based on the user credentials and the relevant user provisioning information, it creates a secure session to access the required membership functions. During this process, the application uses the Secure Logger pattern to make

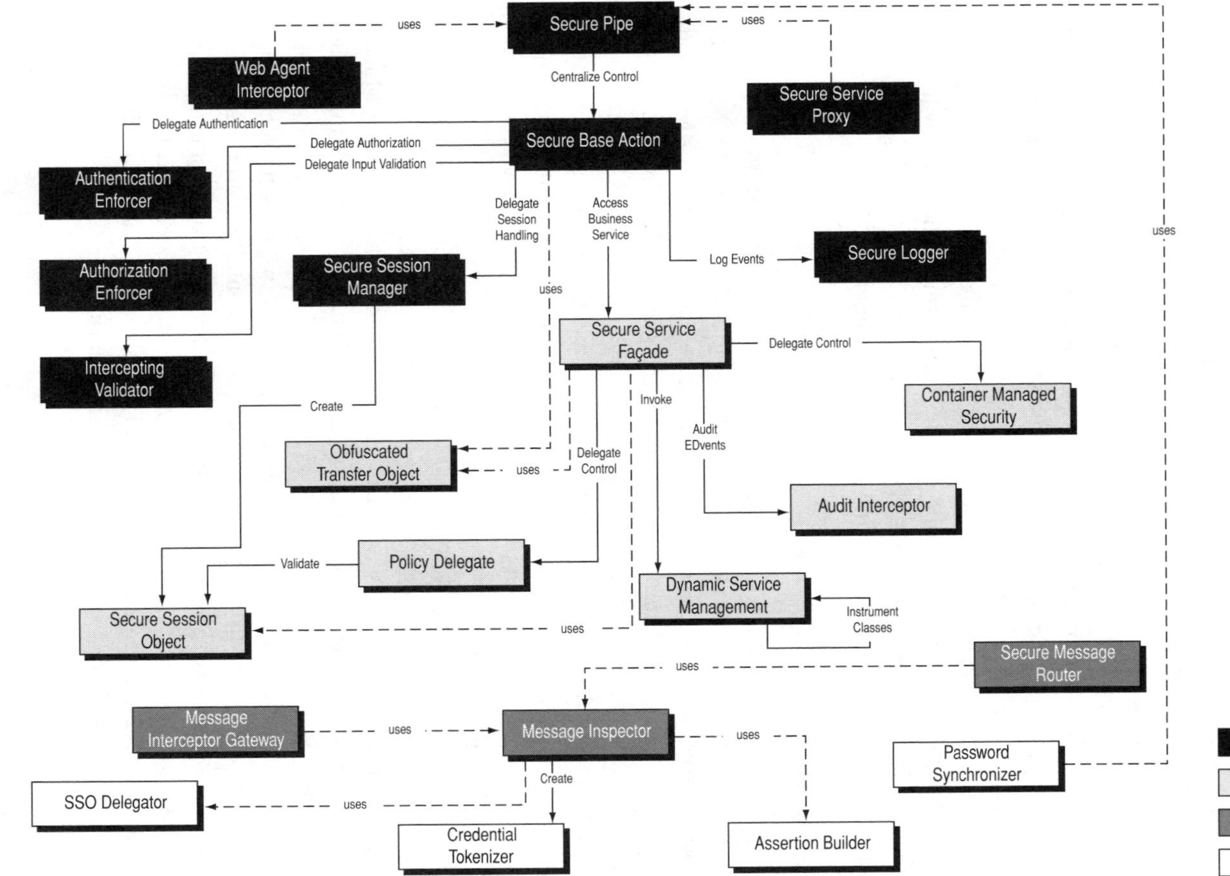

Figure 8–4 Security patterns and their relationships

use of the application logging infrastructure and initiates logging of all the user requests and responses by recording the sensitive business information and transactions, including success or failure attempts.

Figure 8–5 depicts the scenario with a sequence diagram showing the participants in the Web Tier.

In Figure 8–5, the actors denote the security patterns used. The Service Requester (or client) sends a request to initiate business services in the online portal. The Secure Pipe secures the service request in the transport layer. The Secure Base Action validates the session and uses the Authentication Enforcer to authenticate the session. The Authentication Enforcer will in turn request user credentials from the service requester and log the authentication result in the Secure Logger. Upon successful authentication, the Secure Base Action will create a secure session under the Secure Session Manager. It will also use the Authorization Enforcer to authorize the request and use the Intercepting Validator to validate the parameters in the request. Upon successful authorization processing, the Secure Base Action will log the events using the Secure Logger.

Business Tier

Under the secure session, a Container Managed Security pattern may be used to delegate authentication and authorization handling of the requests to the application server container. Policy can then be applied declaratively, in an XML deployment descriptor, or programmatically, using the container's J2EE security APIs.

In our example, the business portal architects and designers require a more dynamic policy framework for the Business Tier and choose not to use container managed security due to the relative static nature of the deployment descriptors. Instead they use a combination of Business Tier patterns to provide security in the back-end business portal services.

Once the request has been processed in the Web Tier, the application invokes the relevant Business Tier services. These services are fronted using the Secure Service Façade pattern. This pattern can be augmented by the Container Managed Security pattern and is used for authenticating, authorizing, and auditing requests from the Web Tier.

Anticipating a large user volume through the business portal, its Web Tier and Business Tier are placed on separate machines (horizontally scaling) in order to enable high-scalability. Since the Business Tier lives in a different application server instance, authentication and authorization must be enforced on the Business Tier via security context propagation. This may seem redundant, but were it not done this way, there would be a significant security risk.

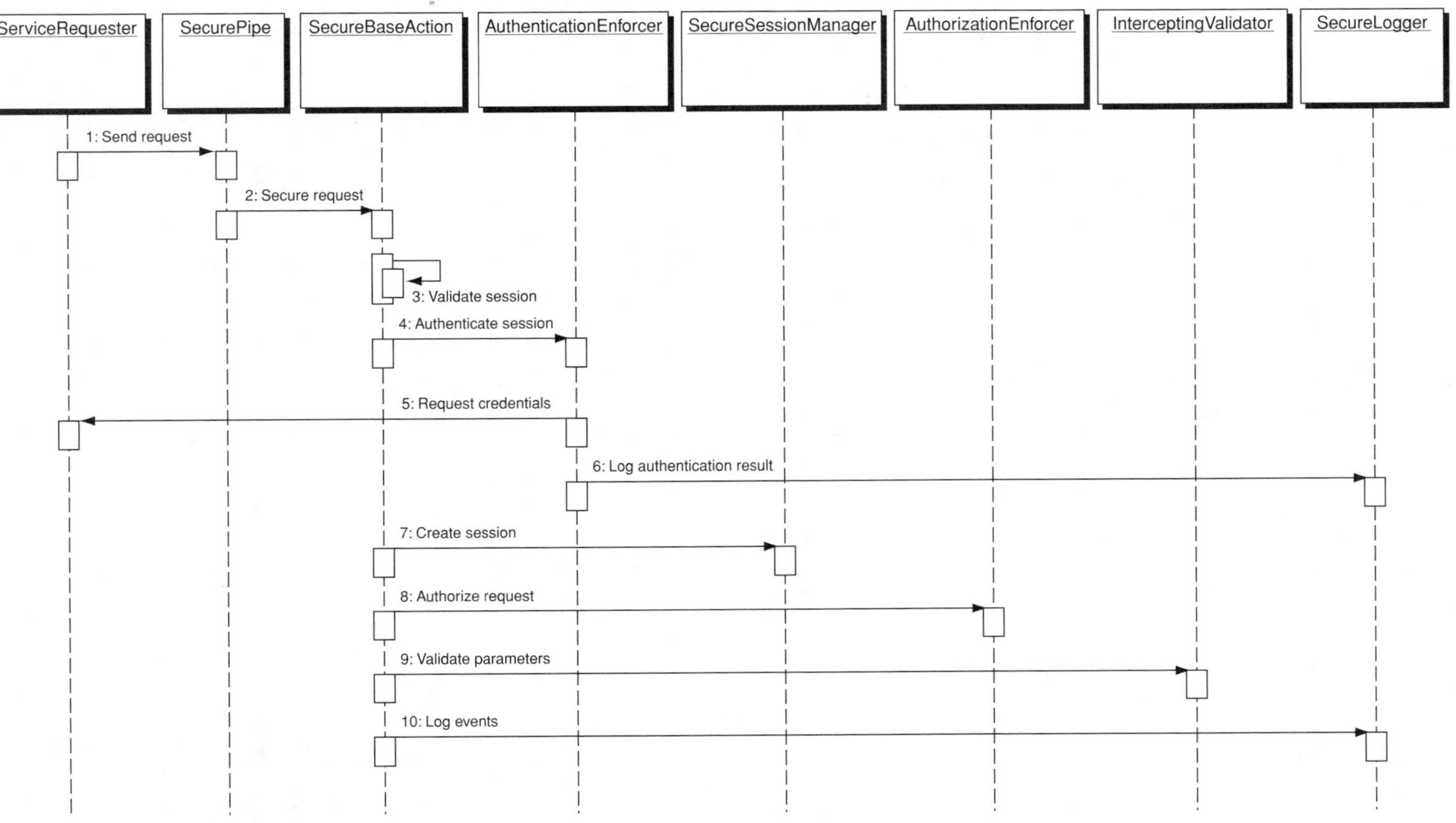

Figure 8–5 Web Tier security patterns sequence diagram

The Secure Service Façade represents the functional interface to the back-end application services. This may include a service to inquire about the membership award balance and the submission of the reward redemption request. These may be business functions to which the subscriber is not entitled. The Secure Service Façade will use the Policy Delegate pattern to determine and govern the business-related security policies for the services to which the requester is entitled. When a request is first made to the Secure Service Façade, it will use the Dynamic Service Management pattern to load and manage the Policy Delegate class and any security-related supporting classes. The Dynamic Service Management pattern allows the application to maintain up-to-date policy capabilities by providing the ability to dynamically load new classes at runtime. In addition, it provides JMX management interfaces to the Policy Delegate for management and monitoring of policy operations.

Once the Policy Delegate is loaded, it can provide authentication and authorization of requests. When the customer requests their rewards balance, the Policy Delegate authenticates and then authorizes the request. It then uses the Secure Session Object pattern to create a session object such as an SSO (Single Sign-on) token that can then be used in subsequent service calls or requests to verify the identity of the requester.

The Secure Service Façade provides business and security auditing capabilities by using the Audit Interceptor pattern. Upon invocation, it notifies the Audit Interceptor of the requesting service. The Audit Interceptor then determines if, when, and how to log the request. Different types of requests may be logged in different locations or through different mechanisms. For the membership award balance service, the Audit Interceptor disregards the balance inquiries and generates an audit entry message that gets logged each time a redemption request is made.

Since confidential material is passed via the Secure Service Façade and the back-end services, it is necessary to provide a means for securing data, such as account numbers, balances, and credit card information, which must be prevented from disclosure in log files and audit entries. The Secure Service Façade uses the Obfuscated Transfer Object pattern to obscure business data from potential unauthorized interception and intentional or unintentional access without authorization. In this case, our customer's credit card number, account number, and balance amount are obfuscated so that they will not show up in any logs or audit entries.

Figure 8–6 depicts a sequence diagram with some details about the scenario in the Business Tier.

In Figure 8–6, the actors denote the security patterns used. Typically, once the service request is processed by the Web Tier security patterns, a Business Delegate pattern (refer to http://java.sun.com/blueprints/corej2eepatterns/Patterns/BusinessDelegate.html for details) will be used to invoke Business Tier objects.

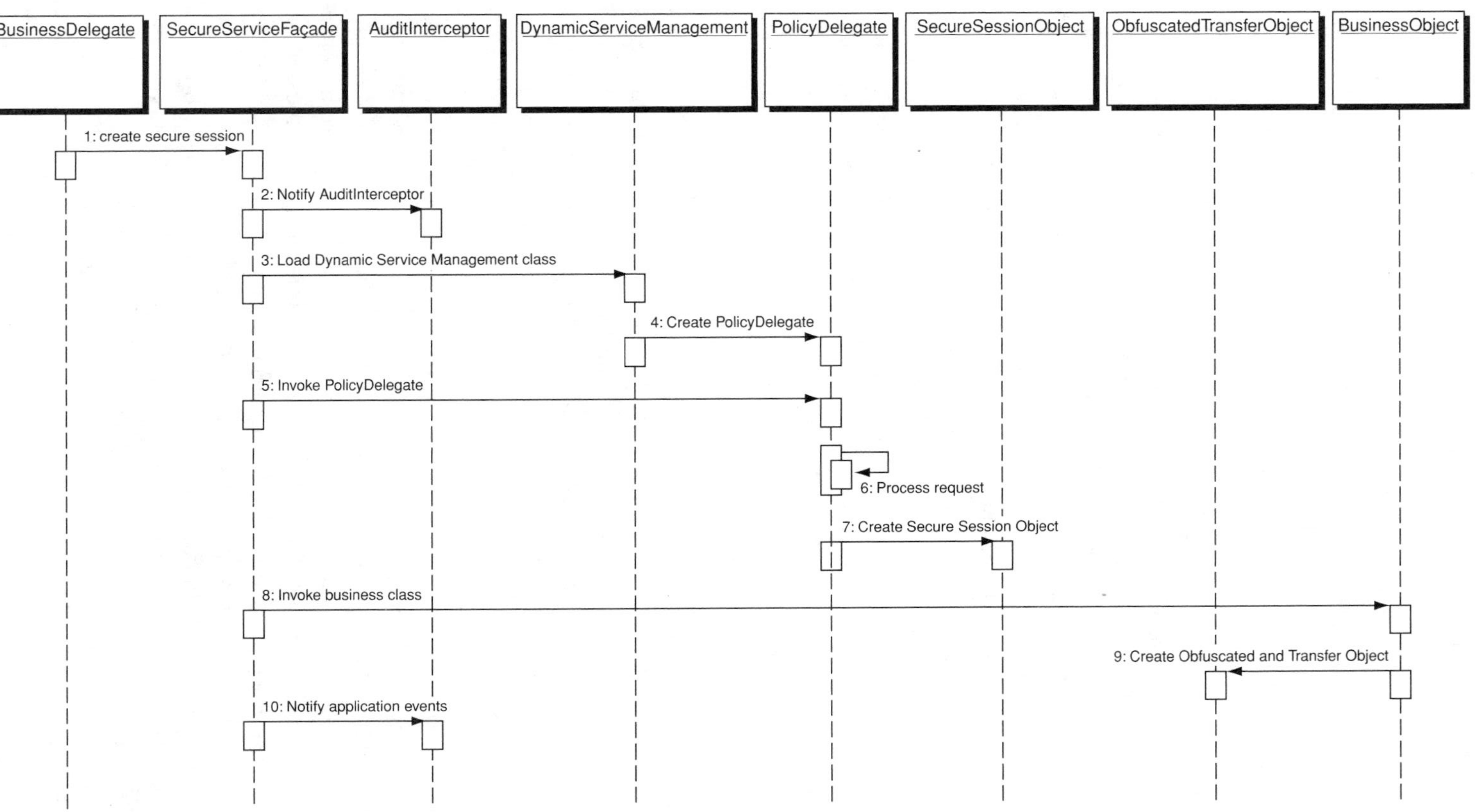

Figure 8–6 Business Tier security patterns sequence diagram

The Business Delegate will create a service session using the Secure Service Façade (either local or remote synchronous invocation). The Secure Service Façade will instruct the Audit Interceptor to initiate the auditing process either synchronously or asynchronously. It will also load the Dynamic Service Management pattern for forceful instrumentation of management and monitoring process for business components. The Dynamic Service Management creates an instance of the Policy Delegate. The Secure Service Façade will start processing the request and invoke the Policy Delegate functions to process the request with the relevant policies defined for the objects or the service requester. It creates an instance of a Secure Session Object for the online portal transactions. The Secure Service Façade will invoke the business object to process business data in the service request. This may involve accessing business information related to the membership reward balance or requesting reward redemption services, in our sample scenario. To protect the business data in the transfer object, the business object can create instances of Obfuscated Transfer Object for delivery. Upon completion of the service request, the Secure Service Façade instructs the Audit Interceptor to capture and verify application-related events.

Web Services Tier

To communicate with the content providers, the service provider portal acts as a Web Services requester using a SOAP/XML-based Web services backbone to send membership award catalog/redemption requests to service providers hosted via Web services. The Web services–based service provider intercepts the service request from the member portal using the Message Interceptor Gateway pattern. The SOAP service request (using RPC-style messaging or the request-reply model) is verified and validated for message-level security credentials and other information by applying the Message Inspector pattern. Then the underlying services apply the Secure Message Router pattern that securely routes the message to the appropriate service provider or recipients. Upon successful message verification and validation using the Message Inspector pattern, the response message will be routed back to the intending client application. If asynchronous messaging intermediaries (using document-style messaging) initiate the SOAP messages, the Message Interceptor Gateway pattern at each intermediary will process these SOAP messages and apply similar techniques. This process may also involve forwarding the request to an identity provider infrastructure for verification of the authenticity of the credentials.

Figure 8–7 depicts a sequence diagram with some details about the scenario for Web services.

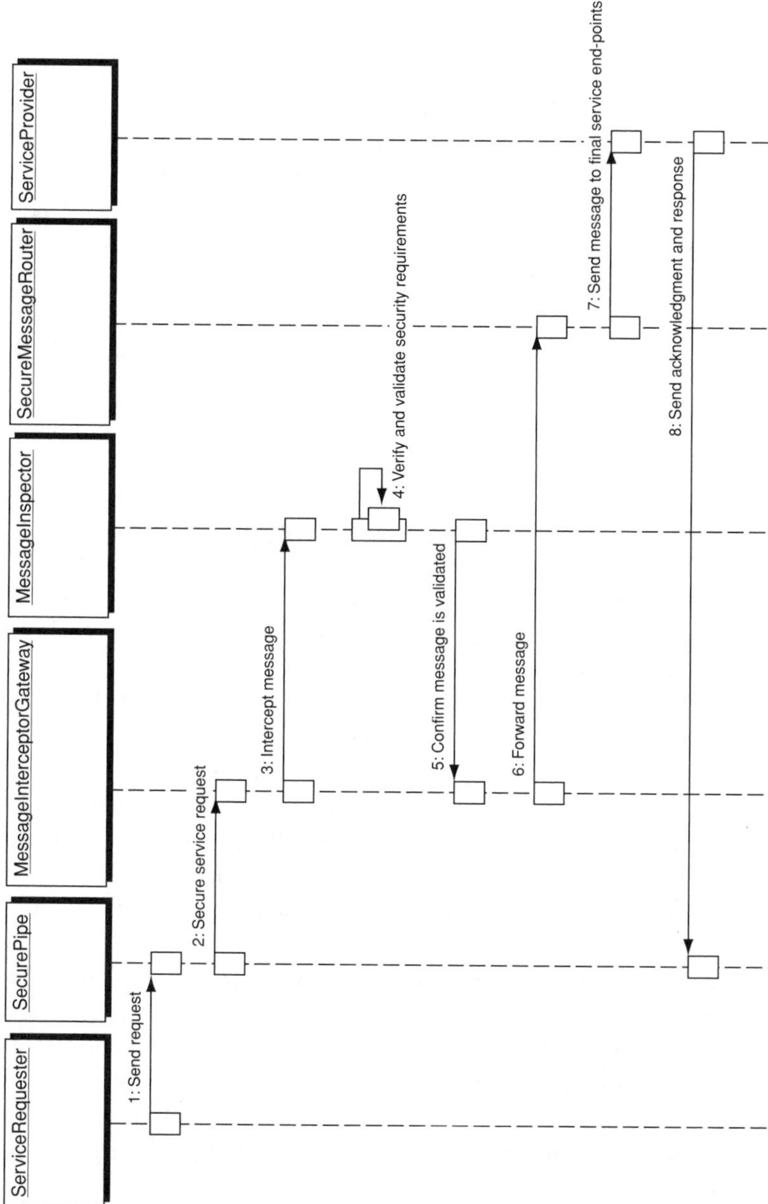

Figure 8–7 Web Services Tier security patterns sequence diagram

In Figure 8–7, the actors denote the security patterns used. The Service Requester sends a request to invoke business services for the membership award catalog or redemption requests with other content providers. The Secure Pipe secures the service request. The Message Interceptor Gateway intercepts the SOAP message and uses the Message Inspector to verify and validate the security elements in the SOAP message. The Message Inspector confirms with the Message Interceptor Gateway that the message is validated (or not validated). Upon successful validation, the Message Interceptor Gateway forwards the SOAP message to the Secure Message Router, which will send the SOAP message to the final service endpoints provided by the Service Provider. The Service Provider will process the service request and return the result of the membership award request to the Service Requester via the Secure Pipe.

Identity Tier

The member portal currently has the capability to allow subscribers to sign on with other underlying services, including the business applications hosted by the service provider or the remote business services provided by the content provider (trading partners). To establish identity and grant access to users to other business services to which they are entitled, the portal uses protocols based on SAML and Liberty Alliance specifications.

Using the Assertion Builder pattern, the application creates a SAML authentication assertion for each business service that the subscriber chooses to invoke from the Authorization Activator pattern. It then encapsulates the user credentials in the security token in the SAML assertion using the Credential Tokenizer pattern. Because the customer loyalty system runs on the legacy back-end systems, the SSO Delegator pattern can be applied to integrate with the legacy back-end EIS system to provide the single sign-on access. This also facilitates global logout capability.

Using the Password Synchronizer as a supporting infrastructure function, the application runs secure service provisioning to synchronize user accounts across service providers. It complements the single sign-on security functionality provided by the SSO Delegator pattern and the Assertion Builder pattern. The subscriber inquires about the account balance of his or her membership award.

Figure 8–8 depicts a sequence diagram with some details about the scenario in the Identity Tier.

In Figure 8–8, the actors denote the security patterns used. Before the subscriber can use different remote membership reward services, his or her user account and password need to be registered first, using the Password Synchronizer. Once the subscriber signs on to the Web portal, he or she initiates a single sign-on

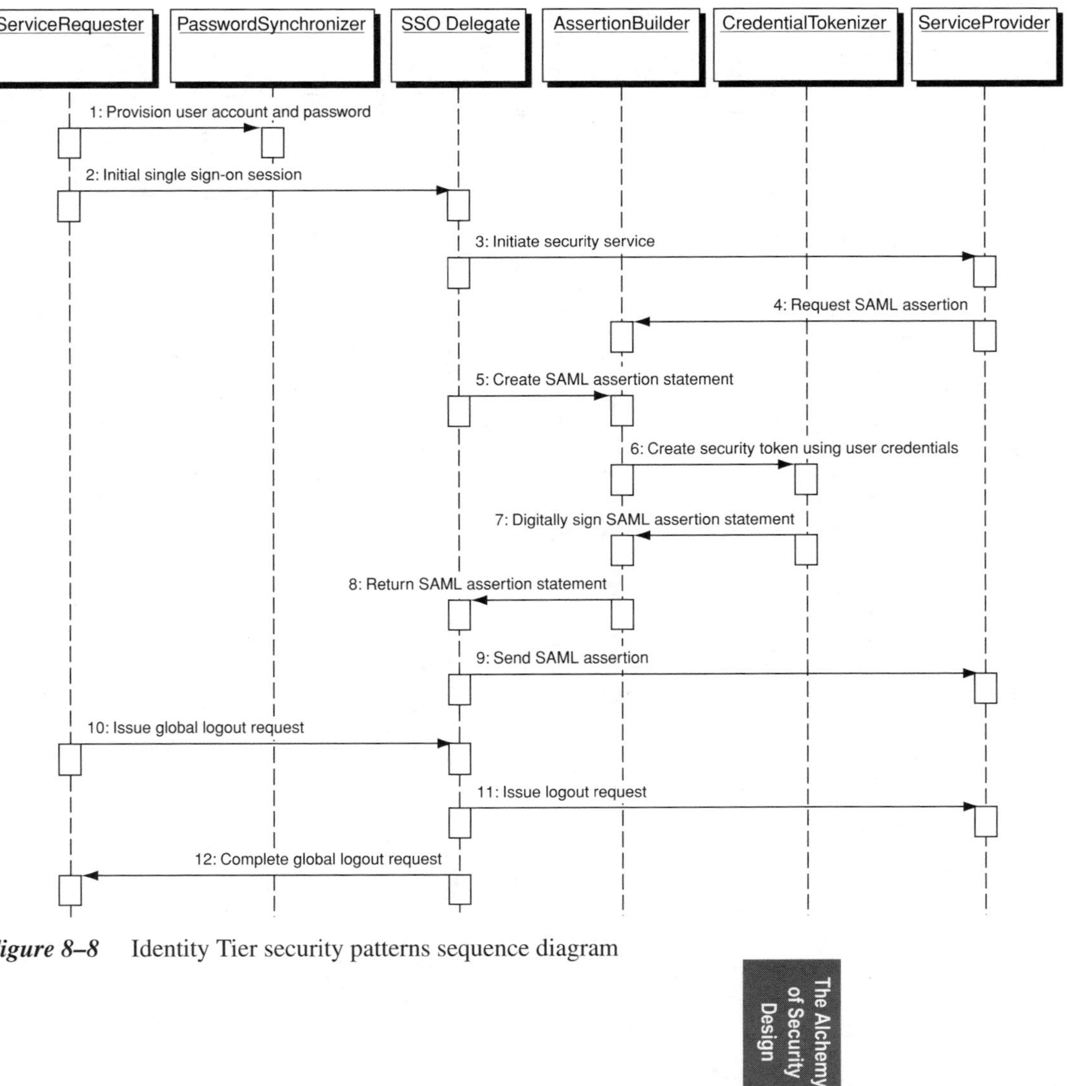

Figure 8–8 Identity Tier security patterns sequence diagram

request using the Single Sign-on (SSO) Delegator to the Web portal services and the associated service providers. The SSO Delegator will initiate remote security services. In order to process requests from the subscriber under the single sign-on environment, the service provider requires a SAML assertion (for example, a SAML authentication assertion). The SSO Delegator will then create a SAML assertion statement using the Assertion Builder, which will use the Credential Tokenizer to digitally sign the SAML assertion statement with the user credentials. Upon completion, the Assertion Builder will return the SAML assertion statement to the SSO Delegator, which will forward the SAML assertion statement to the service provider. After the subscriber has finished the membership reward request, he decides to log out from the online portal. He issues a global logout request to the SSO Delegator, which will issue the logout request to the service providers. Upon completion, the SSO Delegator notifies the service requester of the global logout result.

Patterns-Driven Security Design

As we discussed in the above example, a security design methodology is essential to any security-conscious service or application. Part of that methodology is adopting a patterns-driven security design process for addressing security requirements throughout the software development life cycle.

This security design process starts in the security architecture phase and continues into the security design phase. Figure 8–9 presents a patterns-driven security design process.

In Figure 8–9, in the architecture phase, the architects identify potential security patterns that can be used to satisfy the application-specific security requirements and rationalize the mitigated risks and trade-offs. Based on those inputs, the security design process will be carried out. The security designers perform factor analysis, tier analysis, trust models, threat profiling. They then create security policies that realize and validate the security use cases, architecture, and the identified patterns. During the design process, if there exists a security pattern that corresponds to the security use case requirements and it is architecturally significant, it can be incorporated into the security design. If there is no security pattern available, a new design approach must be taken. It can then be considered for reuse. If it is found to be reused enough, it can be classified as a pattern for inclusion into the Security Pattern Catalog.

In the build and integration portions of the development life cycle, architects and designers apply the relevant security patterns to the application design that satisfy the security use cases. They choose to use their preferred security framework tools to implement the application using the security patterns.

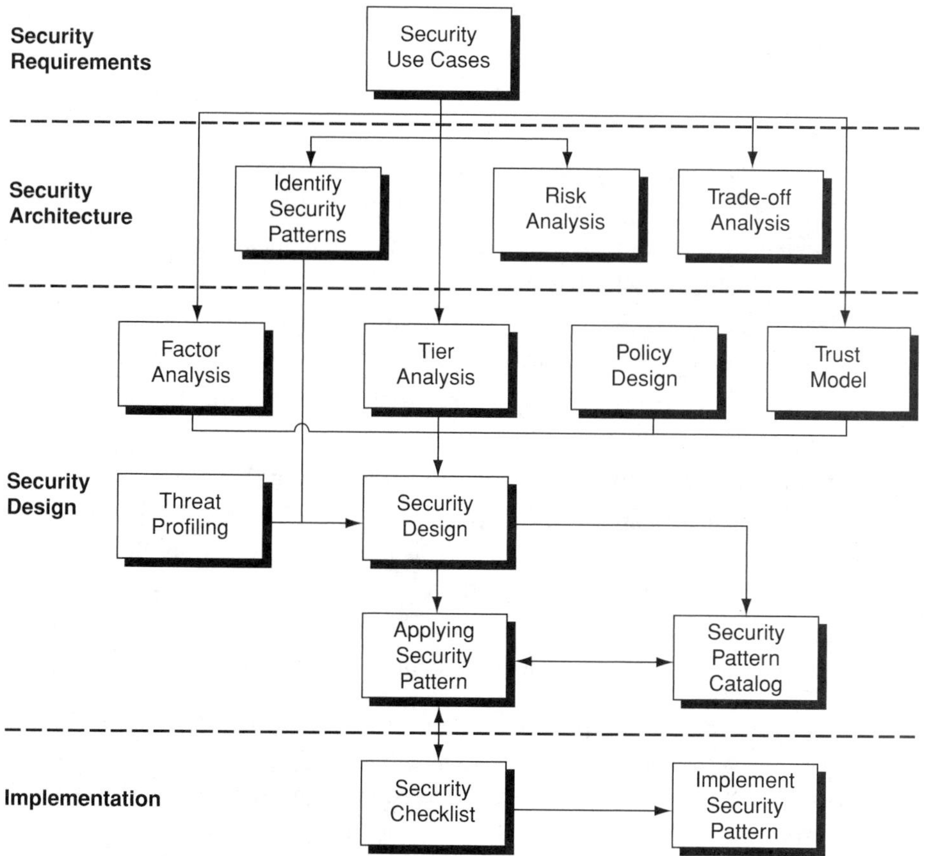

Figure 8–9 Patterns-driven security design

Prior to the deployment process, testers evaluate the application to ensure no security requirements or risk areas were overlooked. If a gap is identified that requires a change to the design, architects can revisit the security patterns to see if any additional security patterns or protection mechanisms are necessary. White and black box testing is an essential security measure that must be performed prior to deploying an application.

In summary, the security architecture and design process can be broken down into the following steps:

1. Identify the required security features based on the functional and non-functional requirements and organizational policies (Security Use Cases).
2. Create a conceptual security model based on architecturally significant use cases (Candidate Architecture).

3. Perform risk analysis and mitigate risks by applying security patterns (Risk Analysis).
4. Perform trade-off analysis to justify architectural decisions (Trade-off Analysis).
5. Identify the security factors for each component or service specific to the application or system infrastructure (Factor Analysis).
6. Review the factors that impact the security of applications or Web services elements under each logical architecture tier (Tier Analysis).
7. Define the object relationship for security protection and identify the associated trust models or security policies (Trust Model).
8. Identify any security risks or threats that are specific to the use case requirements (Threat Profiling).
9. Formulate a security policy (Security Policy Design).
10. Apply security patterns wherever appropriate. Sometimes, rearchitecting or reengineering may be required (Security Pattern Design, Security Pattern Catalog, Apply Security Pattern).
11. Prior to implementation, use Security Reality Checks to review and assess the security levels by logical architecture tiers (Security Reality Check).

By applying this design process within a structured methodology, architects should be able to complete a secure architecture design using security patterns and derive a secure application architecture addressing the known risks and vulnerabilities. They should also be able to maintain a customized security pattern catalog based on past design and implementation experience or known design patterns.

Security Design Processes

In this section, we will take a look at each of the design processes in detail as part of the security design.

Factor Analysis

The objective of end-to-end application security is to provide reliable and secure protection mechanisms in business applications that can support authentication, authorization, data integrity, data privacy (encryption), non-repudiation (digital signature), single sign-on (for better efficiency and cost-effective security administration), monitoring and audit control, and protection from various security threats or attacks. The related security attacks can be malicious code attacks, Denial of Service (DoS)/Distributed DoS attacks, dictionary attack, replay attacks, session hijacking, buffer overflow attacks, unauthorized intrusion, content-level attacks, session hijacking, identity spoofing, identity theft, and so on.

In an end-to-end security perspective, the security design will vary by a number of application-, platform-, and environment-specific requirements and factors, including the following.

Infrastructure

- Target deployment platform (and the underlying technologies and implementation constraints)
- Number or type of access points or intermediaries
- Service provider infrastructure (centralized, decentralized, distributed, or peer-to-peer), and the associated constraints of connecting to the infrastructure (for example, the data transport security requirement)
- Network security requirements

Web Tier

- Authentication-specific requirements (for example, multifactor authentication mechanism)
- Client devices or platform used (for example, Java card, Biometrics)
- Key management strategy (for example, whether key pairs are generated by a Certificate Authority and how the key pairs are stored)
- Authorization-specific requirements based on the sensitivity of the access requests.

Business Tier

- Nature of the business transaction (for example, non-sensitive information has a lower security protection requirement than sensitive, high-value financial transactions).

Web Services Tier

- Service invocation methods (RPC-style, document-style, synchronous, or asynchronous communication).
- Service aggregation requirements (for example, whether business services need to be intercepted, filtered, or aggregated from multiple service providers).

Identity Tier

- Identity management strategy (for example, how network identity is established, validated, and managed).
- Policy management strategy (for example, management policies for who can access the SOAP messages and whether the service requester can access the full or partial content).
- Legacy security integration constraints (for example, security credential propagation).
- Single sign-on and sign-out requirements.

Quality of Services

- Service-level requirements (for example, quality-of-services requirements for high availability, performance, and response time).

Relating the Factor Analysis to apply Security Patterns. The security factor analysis is a good practice to use to identify the important application-specific and environment-specific constraints of the target applications and the target clients in relation to the overall security requirements. This will also help with locating the appropriate security patterns that can be used to address the business problems.

For example, in a Web-services security design scenario, we address the application- and environment-specific security requirements and constraints by representing the following security patterns:

- Secure the transport layer (Secure Pipe pattern, Secure Message Router pattern).
- Validate the SOAP message for standards compliance, content-level threats, malicious payload, and attachments (Message Interceptor Gateway pattern, Message Inspector pattern).
- Validate the message at the element level and the requesting identity (Message Inspector pattern).
- Establish the Identity policies before making business requests (Assertion Builder pattern).
- Protect the exposed business services and resources by service masking (Secure Service Proxy pattern).
- Protect the service requests from untrusted hosts, XML DoS, Message replay, Message tampering (Message Interceptor Gateway pattern).

- Timestamping all service requests (Secure Message Router pattern).
- Log and audit all service requests and responses (Secure Logger and Audit Interceptor pattern).
- Route requesting to multiple service endpoints by applying message-level security and Liberty SSO mechanisms (Secure Message Router pattern).

Applying to the Media and Devices. The security factors will be different when applied to different media or client devices. Different media and client devices, ranging from a Web browser, Java card, J2ME phones, and a rich client to legacy systems, have different memory footprints. Some of them may have more memory capacity to store the key pairs, or some of them have less memory to perform required security checking.

For instance, Web browsers are able to store the certificates keys and provide a flexible way to download signed Java applets, establish client-certificate-based authentication, and use SSL communication. J2ME based mobile phones and client devices operate on a lesser memory footprint and lesser processing speed. It is harder to use encryption and signature mechanisms and to perform complex cryptographic processing with these phones and devices due to their memory capacity and environment constraints.

A possible security artifact for the factor analysis is to produce a summary of the security factors based on the application-specific, platform-specific security requirements and the technology constraints in the security requirements document. This can be a separate appendix or a dedicated section that highlights the key areas of security requirements. The factor analysis provides an important input to the security architecture document. From the factor analysis, security architects and developers can justify which security design patterns or security design decisions should be used.

Tier Analysis

Tier analysis refers to the analysis of the security protection mechanisms and design strategies based on the business applications residing in different logical architecture tiers. In particular, it identifies the intra-tier communication requirements and dependencies. For instance, architects can use the HTTPS protocol to secure the data transport for applications residing in the Web Tier, but the same security protection mechanism will not work for applications residing in the Business Tier or in the Integration Tier. Similarly, the security protection mechanisms for asynchronous Web services will not work for synchronous Web services due to the difference in the RPC-style service invocation and document-style messaging architecture. The security design strategies and patterns discussed in this book are grouped by tiers to reflect what security protection mechanisms are relevant for each logical architecture tier.

A possible security artifact for the tier analysis is to produce a **Tier matrix** of security features by architecture tiers and by application layers. This matrix identifies the key security capability and design elements and their relation to different architecture tiers and application layers. During the security review, security architects and developers can evaluate the appropriateness and reliability-availability-scalability of the security design based on the tier matrix.

Threat Profiling

Threat profiling denotes profiling of architecture and application configurations for potential security weaknesses. It helps to reveal the new or existing security loopholes and the weaknesses of an application or service. Thus, it enumerates the potential risks involved and how to protect the solutions built and deployed using them. This will involve defining and reinforcing security deployment and infrastructure management policies dealing with updating and implementing security mechanisms for the application security infrastructure on an ongoing basis. It can be applied to the newly designed application systems, existing applications, or legacy system environments.

A possible security artifact for threat profiling identifies and categorizes the types of threats, potential security vulnerabilities, or exposures that can attack the application systems. A use-case–driven data flow analysis can also be used to trace the potential risks. For example, a threat profile may identify and list the threats and vulnerabilities as follows:

- Actual or attempted unauthorized access
- Introduction of viruses, Trojan horses, and malicious code
- Actual or attempted unauthorized probing of content
- Denial of service attacks
- Arbitrary code execution
- Unauthorized alteration and deletion of data
- Unauthorized access
- Unauthorized disclosure
- Unauthorized privilege escalation

In addition, it would discuss the security considerations and risk management techniques for all the identified loopholes and flaws.

Trust Model

A trust model is the backbone of the security design. It provides mechanisms that establish a central authority of trust among the components of the security architecture and that verify the identity of participating user entities and their credentials, such as name, password, certificates, and so forth. In simpler terms, a trust-modeling process is defined as follows:

- A trust model identifies specific mechanisms meant for responding to a specific threat profile, where a threat profile is a set of threats or vulnerabilities identified through a set of security use cases.
- A trust model facilitates implicit or explicit validation of an entity's identity or the characteristics necessary for a particular event or transaction.

A trust model may contain a variety of systems infrastructure, business application, and security products. From a security design perspective, a trust model allows test-driving the patterns used, imposing a unique set of constraints, and determining the type and level of threat profiling required. Significant effort must go into the analysis preceding creation of the trust model to ensure that the trust model can be implemented and sufficiently tested. A trust model must be constructed to match business-specific requirements, because no generic trust model can be assumed to apply to all business or security requirements and scenarios.

Let's take a server-side SSL example in which we assume that an SSL session is initiated between a Web browser and a server. The Web browser determines the identity of the server by testing the credentials embedded in the SSL session by means of its underlying PKI. The testing of credentials proves a "one-way trust model" relationship; that is, the Web browser has some level of confidence that the server is who it claims to be. However, the server has no information for testing the Web browser. Essentially, the server is forced to trust the Web-browser–returned content after initiating its SSL session.

Two possible security artifacts from the trust model can be produced. First, the analysis of the trust model usually specifies the security requirements and system dependencies for authentication and authorization in the security requirements specification. This provides the basic design consideration for authentication and authorization and provides input to the definition of system use cases for authentication and authorization. Second, the trust model will identify the security risks associated with the trust relationship. These form an important component in the overall risk document. For an example of a trust model, refer to [Liberty1] and [XACML2].

Policy Design

Security policies are a set of rules and practices that regulate how an application or service provides services to protect its resources. The security policies must be incorporated into the security design in order to define how information may be accessed, what pre-conditions for access must be met, and by whom access can be permitted. In a typical security design artifact, security policies are presented in the form of rules and conditions that use the words *must*, *may*, and *should*. These rules and conditions are enforced on the application or service during the design phase by a security authority by defining the rights and privileges with respect to accessing an application resource or conducting operations.

Security policies applied to an application or service can be categorized as the following six types:

- **Identity policies**: Define the rules and conditions for verifying and validating the requesting entity's credentials. These include usage of username/passwords, digital certificates, smart cards, biometric samples, SAML assertions, and so forth. This policy is enforced during authentication, authorization, and re-verification requirements of an identity requesting access to an application.
- **Access control policies**: Define the rules and conditions applied to a requesting entity for accessing a resource or executing operations exposed by an application or service. The requesting entity can be a user, device, or another application resource. The access control policies are expressed as rights and privileges corresponding to the identity roles and responsibilities of the requesting entity.
- **Content-specific policies**: Define the rules and conditions for securing the content during communication or storage. This policy enforces the content-specific privacy and confidentiality requirements of an application or service.
- **Network and Infrastructure policies**: Define the rules and conditions for controlling the data flow and deployment of network and hosting infrastructure services for private or public access. This helps to protect the network and hosting infrastructure services from external threats and vulnerabilities.
- **Regulatory policies**: Define the rules and conditions an application or service must adhere to in order to meet compliance, regulation, and other legal requirements. These policies typically apply specifically to financial, health, and government institutions (for example, the SOX, GLBA, HIPAA, and Patriot Act).

- **Advisory and informative policies**: These rules and conditions are not mandated but they are strongly suggested with respect to an organization or to business rules. For example, these policies can be applied to inform an organizational management team about service agreements with external partners for accessing sensitive data and resources, or to establish business communication.

In addition, in some cases we need to design and apply target application environment and business-specific policies such as:

- User registration, revocation, and termination policy
- Role-based access control policy
- PKI management policy
- Service provider trust policy
- Data encryption and signature verification policy
- Service audit and traceability policy
- Password selection and maintenance policy
- Information classification and labeling policy
- DMZ Environment access policy
- Application administration policy
- Remote access policy
- Host and network administration policy
- Application failure notice policy
- Service continuity and recovery policy

The security policy artifacts must capture these policy requirements and define the roles and responsibilities of the stakeholders who are responsible for implementing and enforcing them. It is also important to incorporate updates based on the changes in the organization and the application environment.

Classification

Classification is a process of categorizing and designating data or processes according to an organization's sensitivity to its loss or disclosure. In an application or service, not all data has the same value to the requesting entity or to the business. Some data, such as trade-secrets, legal information, strategic military information, and so on, may be more sensitive or valuable than other data in terms of making business decisions. Classification is primarily adopted in information-sensitive applications or services in order to prevent the unauthorized disclosure of information and the failure of confidentiality and integrity.

The classification of data or processes in an application or service is typically represented as classes with five levels ranging from the lowest level of sensitivity to the highest. The least sensitive level is *1*, and the most sensitive is *5*.

1. **Unclassified**: The data or process represented with this classification is neither sensitive nor classified. The information is meant for public release and the disclosure does not violate confidentiality.
2. **Sensitive But Unclassified (SBU)**: The data or process represented with this classification may contain sensitive information but the consequences of disclosure do not cause any damage. Public access to this data or processes must be prevented. For example: General health care information such as medications, disease status, etc.
3. **Confidential**: The data or process in this classification must be protected within the organization and also from external access. Any disclosure of this information could affect operations and cause significant losses. For example: Loss of customer credit card information from a business data center.
4. **Secret**: The data or process in this classification must be considered as secret and highly protected. Any unauthorized access may cause significant damage. For example: Loss of strategic military information.
5. **Top Secret**: The data or process in this classification must be considered as highest secret. Any unauthorized disclosure will cause grave damage. For example: A country's national security information.

In a classified information system, all data has an owner and the owner is responsible for defining the sensitivity of the data depending on the organizational policies. If the owner is not sure about the sensitivity level, then the information must be classified as "3 - Confidential." The owner is also responsible for security of the data as per the organization security policy pertaining to the classification and for defining who can access the data. Classification also depends on organizational requirements related to information confidentiality. Organizations must define their classification terms and definitions.

Security Labeling

Security labels represent the sensitivity level of data or processes. They denote the type of classification assigned. During runtime access, the labels are verified and validated in accordance with an organization's security policy. To adopt classification and labeling of data processes, it is necessary to choose a highly secure operating system (for example, Trusted Solaris Operating system) that offers labeling of data and processes based on discretionary and mandatory access-control policies throughout the operating system, including all users, files, directories, processes, services, and applications. The label, once assigned, cannot be changed other than by an owner or authorized person in the classification hierarchy with higher privileges.

Classification and labeling requirements must be identified during the design phase. Classification and labeling must be adopted when an application or service is required to manage highly sensitive data or processes and the business or organization dictates classification requirements for its information with higher confidentiality.

Application Security Assessment Model

Before architects and developers decide on and adopt any security design strategies or patterns, they usually perform an assessment of the application security architecture and any security mechanisms in use. Typically, external security consultants or specialized security architects review the overall security requirements and the current security design in use. Based on their assessment, they will recommend a list of suggested security mechanisms to meet their application security goals as short-term and long-term implementations.

The assessment checklist has five columns in total. The first two columns enumerate the security services and the security mechanisms that provide them. The next three are checkboxes denoting if the mechanism is suggested for the architecture (that is, recommended for adoption based on best practices), if it is implemented in the current design, and/or whether it is planned for implementation in the future.

Let's consider an application architecture that delivers a Web-based business-to-consumer portal that integrates a variety of back-end applications. The application security architecture adopts a basic authentication using username and password for authenticating the user, authorizes the user as a customer or administrator to perform further operations, and captures all events and actions using a logging mechanism for accountability. The back-end applications running on heterogeneous platforms make use of a shared security context to provide single sign-on access and to participate in portal-initiated transactions.

Table 8–11 shows a simple assessment list for an example—a Web-based application architecture that has adopted a simple authentication using username and password mechanisms. The application is found to not be sufficient to address the security requirements because it is experiencing denial of service attacks using fake requests. After assessment, it is suggested to incorporate client-certificate–based mutual authentication to verify the originating source and to restrict forged requests from further processing. In terms of authorization mechanisms, the application architecture currently allows granting access based on user groups; the assessment suggests granting access based on roles, such as Web administrator, system administrator, and business manager.

Table 8–11 Simple Assessment Checklist for Application Security Architecture

Security Service	*Security Mechanism*	*Suggested*	*Current*	*Future*
Authentication	Username and password	✔	✔	
	Client-certificate	✔	✔	Yes
Authorization & Access Control	Group grants	✔	✔	Yes
	Role grants	✔		Yes
	Delegation	✔		Yes
	Access control lists	✔		
	Policy objects	✔		
	Rules	✔		
Secret Key	RSA	1024-bit	✔	Yes
Public Key	RSA - MD5	1024-bit	✔	Yes
	RSA - SHA-1	1024-bit	✔	Yes
	Audit logs	✔	✔	
Accountability	Centralized audit log	✔		
	Encrypted checksums on log records			
	Encrypted log records			
	Digital signature (non-repudiation)			

Reality Checks

In the design process, architects and developers may have chosen multiple security patterns to meet the application security requirements. They may need to make certain compromises in order to meet other application requirements, such as application performance throughput or cost constraints. However, any trade-off should not sacrifice the overall business security requirements without proper sign-off by the business owners.

Table 8–12 shows application-specific security reality checks intended for ensuring production-quality security protection measures prior to deploying the J2EE-based applications or Web services to production. It is not meant to be exhaustive, but can be very handy for self-assessment.

Table 8–12 Security Reality Checks

Areas	*Security Reality Check Item*	*Y/N*	*Remarks*
Policy	Are there any documented security policies for J2EE-based or Web-services–based applications?		A written security policy is a key ingredient in a well-formed security architecture. The security policy document should clearly define the application, its users, and environment-specific security policies for the security design, implementation, and deployment. It should also then document associated procedures for securing the applications or the underlying infrastructure until its retirement.

(*continues*)

Table 8–12 Security Reality Checks (*continued*)

Areas	*Security Reality Check Item*	*Y/N*	*Remarks*
Policy	Does the existing security policy cover the depth of application security that is associated with the following? Minimizing and hardening of the target operating system that runs the target applications Securing the application servers that run applications developed in J2EE or Web-services technologies Securing the business logic components and data objects Securing the production environment and the data center infrastructure.		
Policy	Does the security policy cover the organizational standards, procedures, and design processes for data encryption, cryptographic algorithms, and key management?		
Policy	Does the security policy cover any escalation procedure to manage security threats in case of security intrusion to the J2EE-based applications or Web services?		
Policy	Do you have a business continuity plan that includes the business continuity of the application infrastructure to protect the applications and the associated risks?		

(*continues*)

Table 8–12 Security Reality Checks (*continued*)

Areas	*Security Reality Check Item*	*Y/N*	*Remarks*
Policy	How is the Security Policy communicated throughout the organization?		Options are e-mail, bulletin board system, newsletter, training sessions, and so forth. Security functions should not be treated as only security personnel's job. It should be considered as everyone's responsibility.
Policy	Is senior management aware of and supportive of the security policy? This includes regulatory requirements such as SOX, FISMA, and so forth		If not, security policy is doomed to be ignored. If management is not supportive of the current policy, but look to you to provide a secure architecture, chances are you will be blamed for everything bad down the road that occurs because of their reluctance to enforce security. It is important to make management aware of their responsibility in enforcing the policy.
Policy	Is there an application and data access-control security policy? Are access policy roles and groups clearly documented?		These are the policies for establishing roles and groups. A simple system, for example, will have users and administrators. A more complex system requires remote access management, personnel management, access to server administration, and so forth.

(*continues*)

Table 8–12 Security Reality Checks (*continued*)

Areas	*Security Reality Check Item*	*Y/N*	*Remarks*
Policy	Are allowed and denied services and protocols documented? Is the network topology enabled with a firewall to protect the DMZ environment, including the hosts and applications?		
Policy	Are the locations of physical management points to support policy accessed through routers, gateways, and bridges identified on network topology documentation and how often is documentation updated?		These stress the importance of topology documentation, which is the guide to identifying where possible breaches in data access security could occur.
Policy	Does control of data access conform to policy? Is there a privacy/encryption policy?		Encryption is typically required for services involving personal information, for example, online banking. Although efforts are usually made to only encrypt sensitive payloads in order to avoid the computing overhead that encryption incurs, it is often (especially for Web-based applications) the case that the encryption overhead is minimal compared to the communications overhead. SSL carries noticeable performance issues; to counter these overheads, it should make use of hardware acceleration with key storage.

(*continues*)

Table 8–12 **Security Reality Checks (*continued*)**

Areas	*Security Reality Check Item*	*Y/N*	*Remarks*
Policy	How is data privacy ensured?		Online privacy is a very broad topic, but in our discussion we focus on the communication aspect, which is usually accomplished with encryption. It is important to pinpoint where the encryption is done, who is responsible for the product doing the encryption, and what technology/algorithm is being used. It is also important to know where the keys are stored and how they are managed. There are different methods for encrypting data between the client and a Web server, such as HTTP/SSL, which is transport-layer (or channel) encryption, and application-level encryption, which is encrypting data directly in the application. Data integrity can be accomplished through checksums or message digest algorithms. This is built into HTTPS, but at the application-level it must be implemented.
Policy	Are users aware of the need to ensure data privacy and follow information and data handling procedures. Are they aware of importance of using data sensitivity levels?		

(*continues*)

Table 8–12 Security Reality Checks (*continued*)

Areas	*Security Reality Check Item*	*Y/N*	*Remarks*
Policy	Is there an authentication and authorization policy?		These policies are more currently referred to as **trust management**. How is the trust established for a principal so that he or she is given authentication credentials and permitted authorization for certain functions? How is the trust maintained and terminated? Who is given the ability to give out these privileges? This portion of the security policy should lay these out in a step-by-step fashion.
Policy	Does policy prohibit sharing of authentication credentials, shared secrets, and so forth?		As stated previously, many headaches and finger-pointing episodes can be avoided by assuring a one-to-one relationship between each individual user and his or her authentication information. All actions and events should be traceable back to a unique credential (except for public access).
Policy	Does control of authentication and authorization conform to policy?		Password changes should be enforced regularly if a secure form of authentication such as S/KEY, smart cards, or biometrics are not used. This minimizes unauthorized users from borrowing or stealing passwords to access the system.

(*continues*)

Table 8–12 **Security Reality Checks (*continued*)**

Areas	*Security Reality Check Item*	*Y/N*	*Remarks*
Policy	Is there a change management policy?		There should be a process in place for change management on both a system and a data level.
Policy	Is access provided on a "need to know" or "need to have" basis?		If accessing different databases, authentication should be performed on a per-transaction level. Access Control Lists are one way to accomplish this task.
Policy	Is access to data controlled so that users can only change that which they should have access to?		In many systems, the middle tier accesses all the back-end databases as one user. A sufficiently savvy client with access to one database may try to access another database or someone else's records. This is why access control should be performed on a per-transaction basis with sufficiently fine-grained control.
Policy	Do procedures for changing production systems and data exist?		
Policy	Are access controls sufficiently flexible for users to do their jobs without compromising data confidentiality and integrity?		This can be accomplished in the ACL by specifying different levels of access (that is, read, write, append, modify, and create).
Policy	Does change management control conform to policy?		There should be a process in place to ensure that change management activities conform to a policy. This can be accomplished through routine reviews of log files.

(*continues*)

Table 8–12 Security Reality Checks (*continued*)

Areas	*Security Reality Check Item*	*Y/N*	*Remarks*
Administration	Do you have a secure protection mechanism and well-defined procedures for key management (storing the key pairs used for authentication or generating digital signatures)? How are the key pairs managed? Where are they stored? Who can create, update, and manage key pairs?		
Administration	Are the security design and administration control personnel separated?		Segregation of security design and administration is one of the security control best practices.
Administration	Do you have a regular security patch management process that applies to J2EE application servers, back-end application resources, and Web browsers?		There are new security threats discovered from time to time, especially for some operating systems and Web browsers.
Administration	How are security administration activities coordinated between locations?		Authorization databases may be mirrored; how is this process protected if separate systems are at separate locations or co-located using primary/secondary servers? Are the activities managed via delegated administration?
Administration	How is unauthorized access detected? Are automated detection tools in use? How are logs managed and reviewed?		Are repeated login failures detected and recorded? If repeated login failures are logged, there should be tools or mechanisms to monitor the logs and alert security personnel to possible hacking attempts.

(*continues*)

Table 8–12 Security Reality Checks (*continued*)

Areas	*Security Reality Check Item*	*Y/N*	*Remarks*
Administration	Are security monitoring processes in use?		Efficient monitoring requires the use of intrusion detection systems (IDS) and filtering software that flags potential problems in accordance with the security policy in place. It is important that the IDS and filtering mechanisms are not performed during the creation of the audit trail; when problems arise, the more detail available from the audit trail, the better.
Administration	Are audit trails of authentication and authorization generated and reviewed?		Audit trails should record as much as possible and be reviewed with a healthy dose of filtering. No one will catch any problem in the middle of 1000 pages of normal access logs. It is important that any changes to authorization of existing users/groups be scrutinized.
Administration	What is the content of the audit trails?		At a minimum, an audit trail record should contain activity identification, the time of the activity, user identification, requested transaction, and results. Audits of administration changes should ideally contain old and new data.

(continues)

Table 8–12 Security Reality Checks (*continued*)

Areas	*Security Reality Check Item*	*Y/N*	*Remarks*
Administration	Are audit trail mechanisms protected?		Most audit trail mechanisms, other than those that are directly related to a security product, are not protected from tampering. An attacker "covers his tracks" by removing incriminating entries from the audit trail and can foil detection. An authenticated audit trail can detect tampering; an audit trail to a write-only device (printer or CD-ROM) prevents tampering.
Quality of Services	Does your application security design support high availability of the security services, including the authentication of user credentials? In other words, have you included any design considerations to secure the application infrastructure, processes, and communications from loss or damage from disasters, accidents, or security attacks?		High availability of application security may include the use of hardware or software clustering of directory servers, Web Agents, Message Router Intermediaries, or any security service components.
Quality of Services	Do you have a recovery plan if your security components (such as Intercepting Web Agent and Secure Message Router Intermediary) are being compromised or fail to function? Do you have validation methods for verifying the integrity of those deployed components?		The recovery design of the security service component should be part of the design process. It should be represented in the infrastructure and/or application level.

(*continues*)

Table 8–12 Security Reality Checks (*continued*)

Areas	*Security Reality Check Item*	*Y/N*	*Remarks*
Quality of Services	Does your application security design include any plan to predetermine the tolerance of application security failure?		
Quality of Services	Does your application design include a recovery of the security services and provide an alternative infrastructure for the recovery while restoring the security services?		
Quality of Services	Do you have a checklist of Java objects, Web services, XML messages, or any application design elements for which you need to evaluate or identify security threats?		
Quality of Services	Do you have any risk management plan or any recovery strategies for each type of security breach?		
Client Device Tier	Do you check for any suspicious "footprint" in the client devices (for example, PDA)?		Hackers may leave a suspicious footprint in the client devices for future "replay" or "exploit."
Client Device Tier	Are the key pairs stored securely in the local client device? How is the security assured?		

(*continues*)

Table 8–12 Security Reality Checks (*continued*)

Areas	*Security Reality Check Item*	*Y/N*	*Remarks*
Presentation Tier	How does the J2EE-based application design support login authentication?		Clear text password is strongly not recommended. It is considered highly insecure because the password can be sniffed on the network, but it may be sufficient with adequate protection that guarantees there is no danger of interception; at any rate, architects need to weigh those risks. Encrypted password via Kerberos tickets or SSL mechanisms. One-time passwords using a token device (for example, SecureID). Certificates (used with SSL). Browsers using SSL normally support server authentication via certificates. Client authentication using passwords over an HTTP/SSL connection is often used, but using client-side certificates are highly recommended.

(*continues*)

Table 8–12 Security Reality Checks (*continued*)

Areas	*Security Reality Check Item*	*Y/N*	*Remarks*
Web Tier	How is the login information carried throughout the session execution: cookies, URL rewriting, or use of a security token?		Cookies in the clear-text form can be a source of attack. They should be encrypted, hashed, and timestamped to avoid session hijacking. URL rewriting must be protected using SSL and URL encoding/decoding mechanisms. Security tokens are set within the confines of an established security protocol such as SSL.
Web Tier	Does the session require encryption?		This is a measure of the importance of J2EE-based applications being dealt with. A positive answer means the bar has been raised for other security mechanisms, such as authentication, session state, and so forth.
Web Tier	Where is user authentication information stored?		Typically, there is a user lookup mechanism (database, LDAP, and so forth), which also holds authorization information about what the user is allowed to do now that we are confident he is who he says he is. However, certificate-based authentication may rely strictly on the certificate signature to ascertain authentication as well as authorization privileges.

(*continues*)

Table 8–12 Security Reality Checks (*continued*)

Areas	*Security Reality Check Item*	*Y/N*	*Remarks*
Web Tier	Are local resources accessed use signed JARs?		A trusted applet or application (from a signed JAR) may perform actions outside of the normal Java sandbox, such as writing to the local machine's hard drive. Take care that the client sanctions these actions and make sure there is obfuscation that hides the business logic to protect the middle-tier business abstraction.
Web Tier	How is authentication done? How is authorized access controlled and how is authentication and authorization administered?		
Web Tier	Is encryption hardware or software in use?		Hardware-based encryption is often more secure and has better performance. It provides a tamper-resistant solution. Software-based encryption is easier to install and change as necessary, but may be compromised if an attacker attains "root" access on the host machine.
Web Tier	How is encryption technology used?		It should be addressed in the application level, the network level, and at the host-environment level.

(*continues*)

Table 8–12 Security Reality Checks (*continued*)

Areas	*Security Reality Check Item*	*Y/N*	*Remarks*
Web Tier	Does encryption technology use standard encryption algorithms widely recognized as being effective (for example, FIPS approved)?		There is a standard set of accepted encryption algorithms, many of which are in the public domain, but there are security products that use unproven encryption technology. Standard algorithms include Triple-DES, RSA, Diffie-Hellman, IDEA, RC2, RC4, and Blowfish. The newsgroup sci.crypt regularly publishes a FAQ that identifies features to look out for when reviewing an encryption security product.
Web Tier	Are there U.S. export or international laws to be considered while using encryption?		U.S. federal law currently restricts export of products using encryption technology. For an intranet environment where U.S. businesses have a presence overseas, this is not an issue. For a U.S. company offering services to overseas clients, this is an issue.

(*continues*)

Table 8–12 Security Reality Checks (*continued*)

Areas	*Security Reality Check Item*	*Y/N*	*Remarks*
Web Tier	How is key management done?		Key management involves making sure each member of a communication has the correct key value to either encrypt or decrypt a data stream. Current encryption products involve the use of public-key technology, usually in the form of X.509 certificates. These are the certificates used by Web browsers from Netscape and Microsoft. The big problem today is finding out when a certificate has been revoked. A certificate always has an expiration date, but to date no standard method is in wide use for how to resolve premature certificate revocation; that is, revoking a fired employee's certificate.

(*continues*)

Table 8–12 Security Reality Checks (*continued*)

Areas	*Security Reality Check Item*	*Y/N*	*Remarks*
Web Tier	How are secret keys kept private?		Some options: token device (for example, smart card), or password-encrypted file. Use of a plaintext file to store a secret key is risky because the key is easily compromised if the machine is successfully attacked, but such a measure is necessary for machines that need the ability to cycle without human intervention (typing a password or inserting a smart card). If an LDAP database is used, encryption between the LDAP server and the authenticating party should be considered.
Web Tier	What other authentication mechanisms are in place (smart cards, biometrics)?		Multifactor authentication combining smart card and biometric authentication is often considered as a reliable personal authentication option.

(*continues*)

Table 8–12 Security Reality Checks (*continued*)

Areas	*Security Reality Check Item*	*Y/N*	*Remarks*
Web Tier	Is authentication tied to individual users?		Access can be granted to roles that can be assigned to individual users, thereby allowing user accounts to be tied to just one person. Efficiency is often realized by grouping similar types of users into one account. For some services (for example, the ubiquitous "anonymous" FTP account), it makes sense, but for most commercial services, an authenticated user should be an individual. This policy can assist clients with billing problems ("Who was logged on for 38 hours?") and help pinpoint liability when problems occur.
Web Tier	Are the Java security policy files and configuration files protected in the application server?		Is so, they should be protected with OS specific ACLs and residing on a read-only file system.
Web Tier	Do the application log files show the key-pair values and timestamps for troubleshooting?		
Web Tier	Are the log files and audit trails stored and secured in isolated systems and accessible by authorized personnel only?		

(*continues*)

Table 8–12 Security Reality Checks (*continued*)

Areas	*Security Reality Check Item*	*Y/N*	*Remarks*
Web Tier	Are the XML schemas (or DTDs) used to validate the data quality as well as to detect any invalid data or suspicious actions?		Someone could potentially send a valid schema with a petabyte of data in it. This could cause more trouble for the application than a small file that was malformed. The schemas should include restrictions on the amount of data being sent to prevent this type of attack.
Business Tier	Is authentication and authorization used to control access to particular applications? Is authentication and authorization used to control access to particular data within applications?		
Business Tier	Do users need to reauthenticate themselves for each type of access? Does the application make use of a shared security context propagation?		
Business Tier	Does user authentication expire based on inactivity? How are unauthenticated users prevented from accessing network facilities? Is an authenticated session terminated after a period of inactivity ?		This helps pinpoint the extent of resources a malicious, unauthorized user can use up.
Business Tier	Are the authentication and authorization databases properly protected?		For password-based authentication, encryption of passwords is prudent. Certificate-based authentication databases need only contain public keys, that are by nature secure.

(*continues*)

Table 8–12 Security Reality Checks (*continued*)

Areas	*Security Reality Check Item*	*Y/N*	*Remarks*
Business Tier	Are the EJB transfer objects obfuscated ?		
Business Tier	Do you use the system ID (or one superuser ID) to update or access business data?		Applications should not use superuser IDs. In required circumstances, it should make use of role-based access control mechanisms to get access to what they need.
Business Tier	Is the JDBC communication with remote databases protected? Does it use encrypted communication to transmit JDBC statements?		
Business Tier	Do you tightly couple the business logic with the security processing rules in the same application logic code?		N-tier application architecture design allows loose coupling of the business logic with security processing rules for better scalability.
Business Tier	Do you make use of role-based access to connect with back-end resources?		Role-based access is more secure, flexible, and scalable than user-based access.
Integration Tier	Are there any sensitive data encapsulated in a SOAP message?		Sensitive data in XML text encapsulated in a SOAP message can be easily snooped. Use of XML Signature and XML Encryption mechanisms to sign and encrypt sensitive payload in SOAP messages is often recommended.
Integration Tier	Are unused ports, OS services, and network devices disabled?		RPC ports are easily exploited for malicious attacks.

(*continues*)

Table 8–12 Security Reality Checks (*continued*)

Areas	*Security Reality Check Item*	*Y/N*	*Remarks*
Integration Tier	Do you have security appliances to scan and inspect SOAP payload content and attachments for suspected malicious action?		
Integration Tier	Are SOAP messages containing sensitive data or financial transaction encrypted and digitally signed during transit and storage?		
Integration Tier	Can the intermediary (SOAP proxies) modify the message contents in SOAP messages? Do intermediaries make use of XML Signature?		Intermediaries must make use of XML signatures to prove the authenticity and privileges to modify the message contents.
Integration Tier	Do you protect all direct access to the WSDL ?		No public access to WSDL should be permitted unless the requesting entity is authenticated and authorized to download them.
Integration Tier	Does your application mandate selected encryption of the contents of sensitive business data in the SOAP messages?		
Integration Tier	Do you encrypt SOAP messages that contain sensitive business data between SOAP proxies that route the messages?		SOAP proxies or intermediaries that route SOAP messages should be tamperproof, and unauthorized access should not change the data contents. One way to provide data integrity and confidentiality is the use of XML Signature and Encryption.

(*continues*)

Table 8–12 Security Reality Checks (*continued*)

Areas	*Security Reality Check Item*	*Y/N*	*Remarks*
Integration Tier	Have you properly set up individual user IDs for accessing the UDDI or ebXML service registry?		Some sites do not enforce access user IDs for the UDDI or ebXML service registry. Thus, hackers can easily hack in the service registry.
Integration Tier	Are your service registries highly available?		UDDI or ebXML service registries can be made highly available by hardware clustering or software clustering (for example, using vendor-specific replication features).
Integration Tier	Do you allow all users dynamic look-up of WSDL files and dynamic invocation of services?		WSDL can be dynamically looked up and then application can be invoked. The implication is that hackers may easily locate all Web services endpoints easily for future security attacks.
Integration Tier	Do you timestamp all SOAP messages?		Using timestamps allows identifying and preventing forged messages from further processing. It is also important to synchronize time throughout your environment.
Integration Tier	Do you set up any time-to-live token for all service requests?		Using time-to-live tokens helps detect DoS attacks using abnormal payloads and malicious messages requiring parsing with endless loops.

(*continues*)

Table 8–12 Security Reality Checks (*continued*)

Areas	*Security Reality Check Item*	*Y/N*	*Remarks*
Integration Tier	Do you associate access control and rights for all requesting resources?		
Integration Tier	Have you performed any security tests such as penetration tests or a regular host security scan for all intermediaries?		It is important to ensure that each of the host machines and network appliances is scanned for any suspicious footprint or unusual security-related activities. A security-host OS hardening and minimizing must be performed.

Security Testing

One of the most important and most frequently overlooked areas of application development is security testing. While we pay much heed to functional testing, it is surprising how little security testing we do. This may be attributed to many factors:

- Lack of understanding (of the importance of security testing)
- Lack of time
- Lack of knowledge (of how to do security testing)
- Lack of tools

Regardless of the reasons, it is not being done and it poses a serious security risk to the application.

Security testing is a time-consuming and tedious process, most often even more so than functional testing. It is also spread across a variety of disciplines. There are the functional business security requirements that the regular test team will perform. However, there are also non-business functional, or operational, tests that must be performed as well. These can be broken down into two categories, Black Box Testing and White Box Testing.

Black Box Testing

Zero knowledge or "black box" testing assumes no knowledge of the application. Black box testers approach the application as an attacker would, probing for information about the internals of the application and then attempting a mixture of different exploits based on that information. For example, if a URL of the application contained a ".cgi" extension, it might be inferred that the application was developed in CGI and therefore may be vulnerable to many well-known attacks.

Black box testers will employ a variety of tools for scanning and probing the application. There are hundreds of different tools out on the Internet for hacking into Web applications. These tools attempt everything from port scanning to attempting exploits for multiple implementation languages (Perl, CGI, C, PHP, and Java). Many such tools are quite sophisticated and provide comprehensive vulnerability scanning of any type of Web application. In fact, many operational groups will run such scans on their applications periodically to ensure that they are not vulnerable to the latest automated attacks.

Black box testing will generally not uncover application-code–specific vulnerabilities. It will, however, ferret out unanticipated vulnerabilities arising from the infrastructure that the application was built on. This could range from host or network misconfiguration (routers, services, and OS patches) to problems with the implementation language or version of the virtual machine that it runs on. All of these types of vulnerabilities are not easily foreseen by the developers or business owners and are usually only discovered during black box testing.

White Box Testing

The converse of black box testing is white box testing, where you have full knowledge of the application being tested. In this case, the testers will have access to all configuration information and the source code itself. They will perform code reviews, looking for possible weaknesses in the code and write test harnesses to try to take advantage of those weaknesses. White box testers are generally ex-developers or testers that have enough development background to understand the application's programming language and know the nuances of it.

White box testers have a toolbox of their own, albeit different from the black box testers. Their toolkit will contain tools that scan the code and can probe it internally. Debuggers and source code scanners are the most prevalent. These allow the testers to find very application-specific bugs and vulnerabilities. Problems such as race conditions and input parameter checking are specific to that application and will not be discovered through black box testing tools (hopefully). These tools will often find other problems with the application, such as memory leaks or performance issues. While these are not security vulnerabilities per se, they do contribute to the reliability and availability of the system, which is, after all, one of the main concerns of security.

Adopting a Security Framework

Most architects and developers adopt a security framework in order to build secure applications because it abstracts the complexity from many underlying security components and is built on proven best practices. The term **security framework** sometimes refers to a set of tools or mechanisms meant for designing and building secure applications. The J2EE platform security architecture builds on J2SE Security including Java Authentication and Authorization Service, Java Cryptography Architecture, and Java Crypto Services APIs (refer to Chapters 3 through 5 for details), do architects and developers really need a security framework in order to build secure Web applications? This section analyzes the logical components of a vendor-independent security framework that are common to many vendor products for building secure Web applications using J2EE-based applications and Web services.

Why do some architects and developers still want a security framework while there are Java API mechanisms? Different Java security APIs are designed to address specific or related problems; they do not necessarily intend to cover all aspects of application security. In addition, the Java security APIs define a large variety of classes and methods but provide no overall instructions about which subset to use in a particular application. An end-to-end security framework for building J2EE-based applications and Web services should be able to simplify the security code development complexity using an abstraction security layer instead of calling individual security components respectively. This should shorten the development life cycle and ease any debugging effort for numerous security components. It should encompass existing J2EE security components in order to meet the security requirements of authentication, authorization, traceability, data confidentiality, availability, data integrity, and non-repudiation. The security framework should also ensure messaging and transaction security across architecture tiers or layers instead of providing security for a stand-alone application or on a stand-alone host. More importantly, it should provide a structured approach to coding the messaging and transaction security using security patterns and best practices. Thus, a security framework is essential for building secure applications.

There are security framework software products available today that can provide security for J2EE-based applications and Web services. But this does not mean that we can choose one silver bullet to deliver end-to-end security that addresses all risks and vulnerabilities. Nevertheless, they are usually product-specific and may not provide a platform-independent structured methodology to build end-to-end application security. Thus, some architects and developers still prefer to pick a vendor-independent security framework first to address their security requirements rather than choosing a vendor-specific software product. Some enterprises that have a large IT development team may desire home-grown or custom-made security framework components based on open-source products and/or security vendor products. One possible reason is that they want to avoid vendor lock-in by proprietary security extension features, which may lead to compatibility issues with security standards or potential security risks if these security features are later exploited. Additionally, a customized security framework can be more agile in addressing specific security requirements or legacy system integration requirements, particularly when developers need to support both proprietary and open standards security specifications simultaneously during the transition. Most of these security framework software products or home-grown security frameworks share some similarities. Figure 8–10 depicts a generic logical security framework available from an application security infrastructure provider.

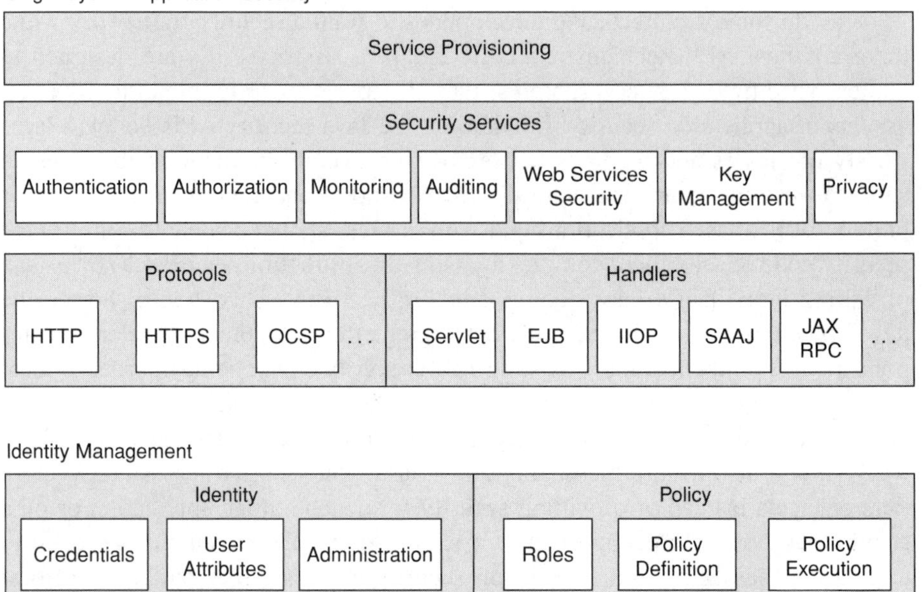

Figure 8–10 Logical security framework of an application security provider

Application Security Provider

The Application Security Provider infrastructure consists of single-system application security components that address security functions of organizational security requirements. They do this in terms of security infrastructure services and identity and policy management services. Let's take a look at the key components offered by an application security infrastructure provider.

Security Infrastructure Services

Security Services. This denotes a set of common security services that are reusable by many applications and system infrastructures. They include authentication, authorization, monitoring, auditing, WS-Security, and so forth. **Authentication** refers to the verification of the user identity and credentials using a mixture of security mechanisms. **Authorization** refers to the entitlement that allows a service requester to access resources as per the predefined security policies and access rights. **Monitoring** refers to the capability to observe and manage application-level security events or exceptions, especially suspicious security activities. Auditing refers to the capability to trace and track application events and exceptions for security auditing or troubleshooting. **Web Services Security** refers to the security functions required for protection of XML Web services messages—from message creation, routing, and message acknowledgement to the execution of SOAP-based service requests and responses. **Key management** denotes how key pairs are generated, maintained, or retrieved for authentication or producing digital signatures. Public Key Infrastructure is an example of key management service. **Privacy** denotes the management of personal or sensitive data by applying data policies to protect them from unauthorized access.

Protocols. The protocols denote the security protocols that are commonly used for security processing (for example, Online Certificate Status Protocol, or OCSP, for verifying user credentials with a Validation Authority in real-time), or securing the user session in the data transport layer with the server (for example, HTTPS).

Handlers. The handlers refer to the interface that interacts with each Java object or component for the access of the common security services or to the service provisioning layer (that ensures appropriate resources are allocated to each service request). Thus, developers can access any of the security services by making use of components such as JSP/Servlets, EJB, RMI/IIOP, SAAJ, or JAX-RPC calls.

Service Provisioning. This denotes the capability to provision and manage the resources to each authenticated service requester that has the proper access rights and security policies to access the resources. It implies that the resources are available and secure to each service requester and are properly provisioned according to the predefined security policies within a single system or the enterprise. This can be incremental (per usage), segmented (per usage), or transactional (per message or call), depending on the security infrastructure set-up or application system configuration.

Identity and Policy Management Services

Identity Management. This refers to the ability to define and manage user credentials and attributes, and to administer user identity by asserting the user credentials or attributes to the system resources. Single sign-on is a key objective of identity management. Typically, identity management includes a variety of authentication and authorization support mechanisms, including LDAP-based directory server and various security tokens such as user ID and password, Java card, and so forth.

Policy Management. This refers to the ability to define and manage user roles and security policies, and to execute security policies within a single system or across different security domains. It also allows administrators to map the users, groups, roles, and security policies to the protected system resources. In some implementations, they offer a policy management rule engine that facilitates security policy administration and execution.

Although there are vendor implementation differences among application security providers, architects and developers should choose a security framework that adheres to the J2EE security standards and open standards. It should also be able to easily migrate to the new security standards when available (for example, migrating legacy XML-based Security implementation to OASIS's WS-Security). Some common questions to consider are:

- Do they use proprietary implementation or security-standards–based implementations?
- Are they imposing a vendor-specific architecture, which may restrict the flexibility to apply security patterns and best practices?
- Does the security framework include a structured design methodology to secure applications right from the development phase?

More importantly, the chosen security framework should be flexible and follow security design best practices and patterns, and the vendor product architecture should not dictate how architects and developers tailor the security design. Instead, the framework should make use of the architecturally significant security use cases. A good security framework should enable building **vendor-independent** security solutions that adopt standards-based technologies, structured security methodology, security patterns, and industry best practices.

Refactoring Security Design

This book is mainly about patterns. It describes a set of security patterns and how, when, and why to use them. It also discusses a methodology for building secure applications using patterns. Often, though, you are not starting from scratch when attempting to secure an application. Furthermore, you rarely choose all of the right patterns and strategies in the design the first time around. To address this, we need to adopt **Refactoring**.

Refactoring is, as defined by Martin Fowler, "a change made to the internal structure of software to make it easier to understand and cheaper to modify without changing its observable behavior" [Fowler1]. So, why do we want to make a change to the software if we do not need to change its behavior? The answer is that we want to make the system easier to understand and maintain so that we can eliminate any unknown vulnerabilities hiding in the obscurity of a complex design or code implementation. Refactoring leads to simplicity, and security always favors simplicity over complexity.

As Joshua Kerievsky put it, "When you refactor, you relentlessly poke and prod your code to improve its design" [Kerievsky1]. He also goes on to state that the only way to refactor safely is to continuously test the changes. In the case of security pattern refactoring, this involves the functional, white box, and black box testing. Once the refactoring is complete and well-tested, you are left with a better overall design that will be more future-proof. Many of the security holes we see today are not the artifacts of a poor initial design or implementation. Instead, they are the result of series of add-ons and work-arounds that led to overly complex code and inevitably to bugs that are attributable to that complexity. Continuous refactoring protects applications from becoming buggy by continuing to simplify and refine the design and code.

Service Continuity and Recovery

No matter how elegant the security architecture is, if the application cannot sustain security attacks, or fails to recover to continuous business service, the application security design is still crippled. A robust and reliable security design should include design strategies for service continuity and recovery.

A preventive security design will also predetermine the tolerance level of potential security threats. This is usually done by estimating the capacity or sizing of the unexpected security threats and factoring them into the security design process. For example, security architects can benchmark (via simulation or system test) the tolerance level for handling a high influx of simultaneous authentication requests that may be a malicious denial of attack. They can then add any detection and exception-handling process logic in the authentication service security design. A robust security design will add processing logic to handle the service recovery scenarios when a security service is attacked and then restored to previous working condition. For example, the Secure Session Façade pattern should be able to handle session recovery after the application server is restored to normal working condition after security attacks or other non-security-related downtime. This security recovery design strategy typically goes hand in hand with implementing high availability of the security infrastructure for service continuity and requires a procedure to handle the service recovery in the IT security policy documentation.

Conclusion

Security must be omnipresent throughout your infrastructure in order for you to begin to feel your application or service is secure. In order to accomplish this, it is imperative that you follow a structured methodology. In this chapter, we looked at why this methodology must be baked into the development process right from the beginning. Security spans every aspect of your system—from the network perimeter to the service—as shown in the Security Wheel.

To incorporate security into the software development process, we extended the Unified Process to include several new security disciplines. These disciplines define the roles and responsibilities of the different security participants within the software life cycle. The Secure UP (as we called it) ensures that our security methodology can be supported within a software development process. Any security methodology must include this process or one like it. A secure methodology should also include how to adopt security patterns based on security use case requirements and design analysis as well as how to apply them in appropriate business scenarios.

In summary, we looked at what goes into a good security design. It starts with a methodology, leverages patterns and frameworks, and gets baked into the software development process from the ground up to deliver "Security by Default."

References

Unified Process

[Unified Process] Enterprise Unified Process:

http://www.enterpriseunifiedprocess.info

Security Principles

[NIST] NIST Security principles:

http://csrc.nist.gov/publications/nistpubs/

[Sun Blueprints] Trust Modeling for Security Architecture Development

http://www.sun.com/blueprints/1202/817-0775.pdf

Security Patterns

[Amos] Alfred Amos. "Designing Security into Software with Patterns." April 26, 2003.

http://www.giac.org/practical/GSEC/Alfred_Amos_GSEC.pdf

[Berry] Craig A. Berry, John Carnell, Matjaz B. Juric, Meeraj Moidoo Kunnumpurath, Nadia Nashi, and Sasha Romanosky. *J2EE Design Patterns Applied.* Wrox Press, 2002.

[CJP] Deepak Alur, John Crupi, Dan Malks. *Core J2EE Patterns: Best Practices and Design Strategies*. Prentice Hall, 2003.

[IBM] IBM. "Introduction to Business Security Patterns: An IBM White Paper." IBM, 2003.

http://www-3.ibm.com/security/patterns/intro.pdf

[Monzillo] Ron Monzillo and Mark Roth. "Securing Applications for the Java 2 Platform, Enterprise Edition (J2EE)." Java One 2001 Conference.

[OpenGroup] The Open Group. "Guide to Security Patterns." Draft 1. The Open Group, April 5, 2002.

[Romanosky2001] Sasha Romanosky. "Security Design Patterns, Part 1" Version 1.4. November 12, 2001.

[Romanosky2002] Sasha Romanosky. "Enterprise Security Patterns." June 4, 2002.

http://www.romanosky.net/papers/securitypatterns/EnterpriseSecurityPatterns.pdf

[WassermannBetty] Ronald Wassermann and Betty H. C. Cheng. "Security Patterns." Michigan State University (MSU-CSE-03-23). August 2003.

http://www.cse.msu.edu/cgi-user/Web/tech/document?ID=547

[YoderBarcalow1997] Joseph Yoder and Jeffrey Barcalow. "Architectural Patterns for Enabling Application Security." Pattern Languages of Programs Conference, 1997.

http://www.joeyoder.com/papers/patterns/Security/appsec.pdf

Others

[XACML2] OASIS. Extensible Access Control Markup Language–Version 2, Committee draft 04, December 6, 2004.

http://docs.oasis-open.org/xacml/access_control-xacml-2.0-core-spec-cd-04.pdf

[LIBERTY1] Liberty Alliance. Liberty Trust Models Guidelines, Version 1.0

http://www.projectliberty.org/specs/liberty-trust-models-guidelines-v1.0.pdf

[Fowler1] Martin Fowler. *Refactoring: Improving the Design of Existing Code*. Addison-Wesley, 2000.

[Kerievsky1] Joshua Kerievsky. *Refactoring to Patterns*. Addison-Wesley, 2005.

[Gof] Erich Gamma, Richard Helm, Ralph Johnson, John Vlissides. *Design Patterns: Elements of Reusable Object-Oriented Software*. Addison-Wesley, 1994.

Part V

Design Strategies and Best Practices

Securing the Web Tier–Design Strategies and Best Practices

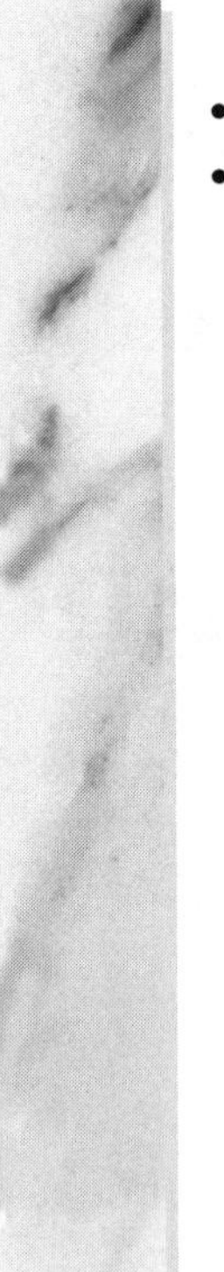

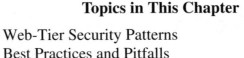

Topics in This Chapter

- Web-Tier Security Patterns
- Best Practices and Pitfalls

Chapter 9

For J2EE applications, the Web tier represents the front door—the entry point for all users. It is also the most frequently used initial point of attack for an adversary looking for security weaknesses in an application. This chapter will review the vulnerabilities associated with the Web tier and the patterns used to protect against them.

Web-Tier Security Patterns

Authentication Enforcer

Problem

You need to verify that each request is from an authenticated entity, and since different classes handle different requests, authentication code is replicated in many places and the authentication mechanism can't easily be changed.

Choice of user authentication mechanisms often require changes based on changes in business requirements, application-specific characteristics, and underlying security infrastructures. In a coexisting environment, some applications may use HTTP basic authentication or form-based authentication. In some applications, you may be required to use client certificate-based authentication or custom authentication via JAAS. It is therefore necessary that the authentication mechanisms be properly abstracted and encapsulated from the components that use them.

During the authentication process, applications transfer user credentials to verify the identity requesting access to a particular resource. The user credentials and associated data must be kept private and must not be made available to other users or coexisting applications. For instance, when a user sends a credit card number and PIN to authenticate a Web application for accessing his or her banking information, the user wants to ensure that the information sent is kept extremely confidential and does not want anyone else to have access to it during the process.

Forces

- Access to the application is restricted to valid users, and those users must be properly authenticated.
- There may be multiple entry points into the application, each requiring user authentication.
- It is desirable to centralize authentication code and keep it isolated from the presentation and business logic.

Solution

Create a centralized authentication enforcement that performs authentication of users and encapsulates the details of the authentication mechanism.

The Authentication Enforcer pattern handles the authentication logic across all of the actions within the Web tier. It assumes responsibility for authentication and verification of user identity and delegates direct interaction with the security provider to a helper class. This applies not only to password-based authentication, but also to client certificate-based authentication and other authentication schemes that provide a user's identity, such as Kerberos.

Centralizing authentication and encapsulating the mechanics of the authentication process behind a common interface eases migration to evolving authentication requirements and facilitates reuse. The generic interface is protocol-independent and can be used across tiers. This is especially important in cases where you have clients that access the Business tier or Web Services tier components directly.

Structure

Figure 9–1 shows a class diagram of the Authentication Enforcer pattern. The core Authentication Enforcer consists of three classes: AuthenticationEnforcer, RequestContext, and Subject.

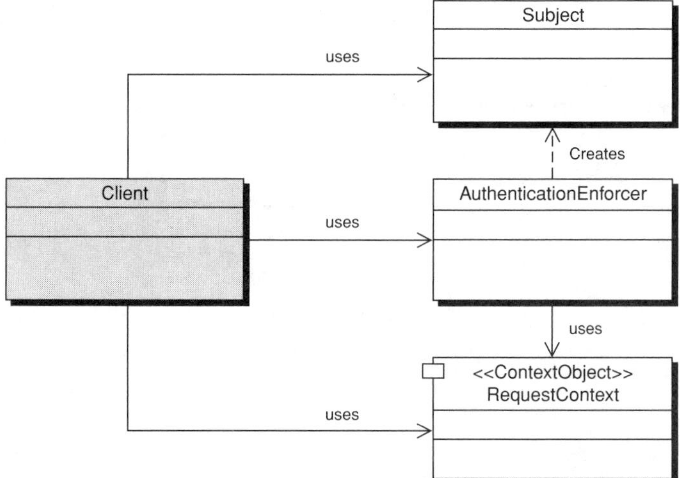

Figure 9–1 Authentication Enforcer class diagram

Participants and Responsibilities

Figure 9–1 is a class diagram of the Authentication Enforcer pattern participant classes. Their responsibilities are:

Client. A client uses the AuthenticationEnforcer to authenticate a user.

AuthenticationEnforcer. The AuthenticationEnforcer authenticates the user using the credentials passed in the RequestContext.

RequestContext. The RequestContext contains the user's credentials extracted from the protocol-specific request mechanism.

Subject. The AuthenticationEnforcer creates a Subject instance that represents the authenticated user.

Figure 9–2 is a sequence diagram representing the interaction of the participants.

Figure 9–2 depicts a typical client authentication using Authentication Enforcer. In this case, the Client is a SecureBaseAction that delegates to the AuthenticationEnforcer, which retrieves the appropriate user credentials from the UserStore. Upon successful authentication, the AuthenticationEnforcer creates a Subject instance for the requesting user and stores it in its cache.

- Client (such as a FrontController or ApplicationController) creates RequestContext containing user's credentials.

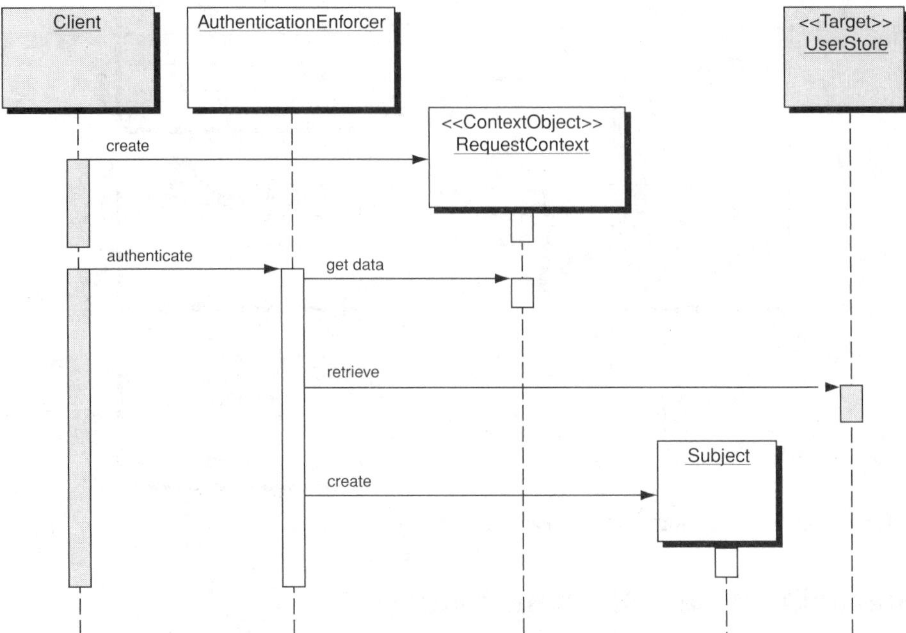

Figure 9–2 Sequence diagram for Authentication Enforcer

- Client invokes AuthenticationEnforcer's authenticate method, passing the RequestContext.

AuthenticationEnforcer retrieves the user's credentials from the RequestContext and attempts to locate user's Subject instance in its cache based upon the supplied user identifier in the credentials. This identifier may vary depending upon the authentication mechanism and may possibly require some form of mapping, for example, if an LDAP DN retrieved from a client certificate is used as a credential. Unable to locate an entry in the cache, the AuthenticationEnforcer retrieves the user's corresponding credentials in the UserStore. (Typically this will contain a hash of the password.) The AuthenticationEnforcer will verify that the user-supplied credentials match the known credentials for that user in the UserStore and upon successful verification will create a Subject for that user. The AuthenticationEnforcer will then place the Subject in the cache and return it to the SecureBaseAction.

Strategies

The Authentication Enforcer pattern provides a consistent and structured way to handle authentication and verification of requests across actions within Web-tier components and also supports Model-View-Controller (MVC) architecture without duplicating the code. The three strategies for implementing an Authentication Enforcer pattern include Container Authenticated Strategy, Authentication Provider Strategy (Using Third-party product), and the JAAS Login Module Strategy.

Container Authenticated Strategy

The Container Authenticated Strategy is usually considered to be the most straightforward solution, where the container performs the authentication process on behalf of the application. The J2EE specification mandates support for HTTP Basic Authentication, Form Based Authentication, Digest-based Authentication, and Client-certificate Authentication. The J2EE container takes the responsibility for authenticating the user using one of these four methods. These mechanisms don't actually define the method to verify the credentials, but rather they show how to retrieve them from the user. How the container performs the authentication with the supplied credentials depends on the vendor-specific J2EE container implementation. Most J2EE containers handle the authentication process by associating the current HTTPServletRequest object, and its internal session, with the user. By associating a session with the user, the container ensures that the initiated request and all subsequent requests from the same user can be associated with the same session until that user's logout or the authenticated session expires.

Once authenticated, the Web application can make use of the following methods provided by the HTTPServletRequest interface.

- getRemoteUser() Determines the user name with which the client authenticated.
- isUserInRole (String username) Determines the given user is in a specified security role.
- getUserPrincipal() Returns a java.security.Principal object.

Authentication Provider-Based Strategy

This Strategy adopts a third-party authentication provider for providing authentication for J2EE applications. Figure 9–3 illustrates how the Authentication provider is responsible for the authentication of the user, and the Authentication Enforcer extracts the user's Principal and creates a Subject instance with that Principal.

As you can see in Figure 9–3, the authentication provider takes care of the authentication and creation of the Principal. The Authentication Enforcer simply creates the Subject and adds the Principal and the Credential to it. The Subject then holds a collection of permissions associated with all the Principals for that user. The Subject object can then be used in the application to identify, and also to authorize, the user.

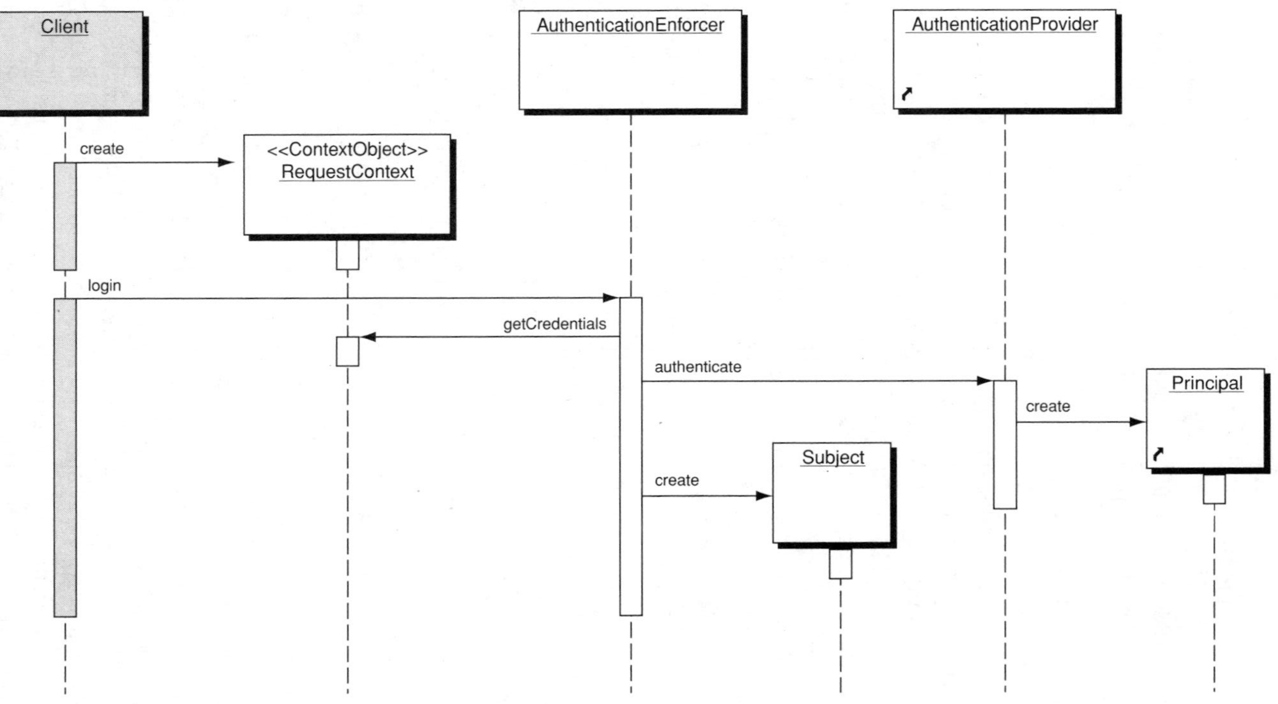

Figure 9–3 Sequence diagram for Authentication Provider strategy

JAAS Login Module Strategy

The JAAS Login Module Strategy is more involved, because it takes responsibility for authentication from the container and moves it to the application that uses an authentication provider. This provides a pluggable approach and more programmatic control offering more flexibility to applications that require additional authentication mechanisms not supported by the J2EE specification. In essence, JAAS provides a standard programmatic approach to nonstandard authentication mechanisms. It also allows incorporation of multifactor authentication using security providers based on smart cards and biometrics. Figure 9–4 shows the additional components required by this strategy.

In this strategy, the AuthenticationEnforcer is implemented as a JAAS client that interacts with JAAS LoginModule(s) for performing authentication. The JAAS LoginModules are configured using a JAAS configuration file, which identifies one or more JAAS LoginModules intended for authentication. Each LoginModule is specified via its fully qualified class name and an authentication *Flag* value that controls the overall authentication behavior. The flag values (such as Required, Requisite, Sufficient, Optional) defines the overall authentication process. The authentication process proceeds down the specified list of entries in the configuration file based on the flag values.

The AuthenticationEnforcer instantiates a LoginContext class that loads the required LoginModule(s), specified in the JAAS configuration file. To initiate authentication the AuthenticationEnforcer invokes the LoginContext.login() method which in turn calls the login() method in the LoginModule to perform the login and authentication. The LoginModule invokes a CallbackHandler to perform the user interaction and to prompt the user for obtaining the authentication credentials (such as username/password, smart card and biometric samples). Then the LoginModule authenticates the user by verifying the user authentication credentials. If authentication is successful, the LoginModule populates the Subject with a Principal representing the user. The calling application can retrieve the authenticated Subject by calling the LoginContext's getSubject method. Figure 9–5 shows the sequence diagram for JAAS Login Module strategy.

1. SecureBaseAction creates RequestContext containing user's credentials.
2. SecureBaseAction invokes AuthenticationEnforcer's login method, passing in the RequestContext.
3. AuthenticationEnforcer creates a CallbackHandler object that contains the username and password extracted from the RequestContext
4. AuthenticationEnforcer creates a LoginContext.

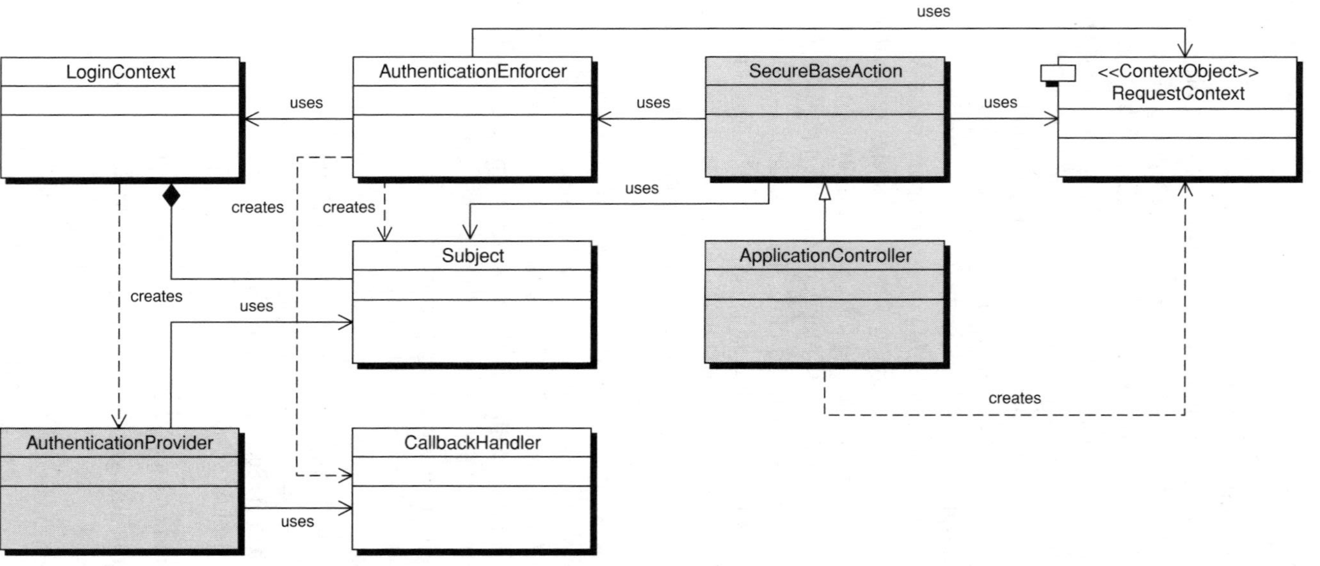

Figure 9–4 Class diagram for JAAS Login Module strategy

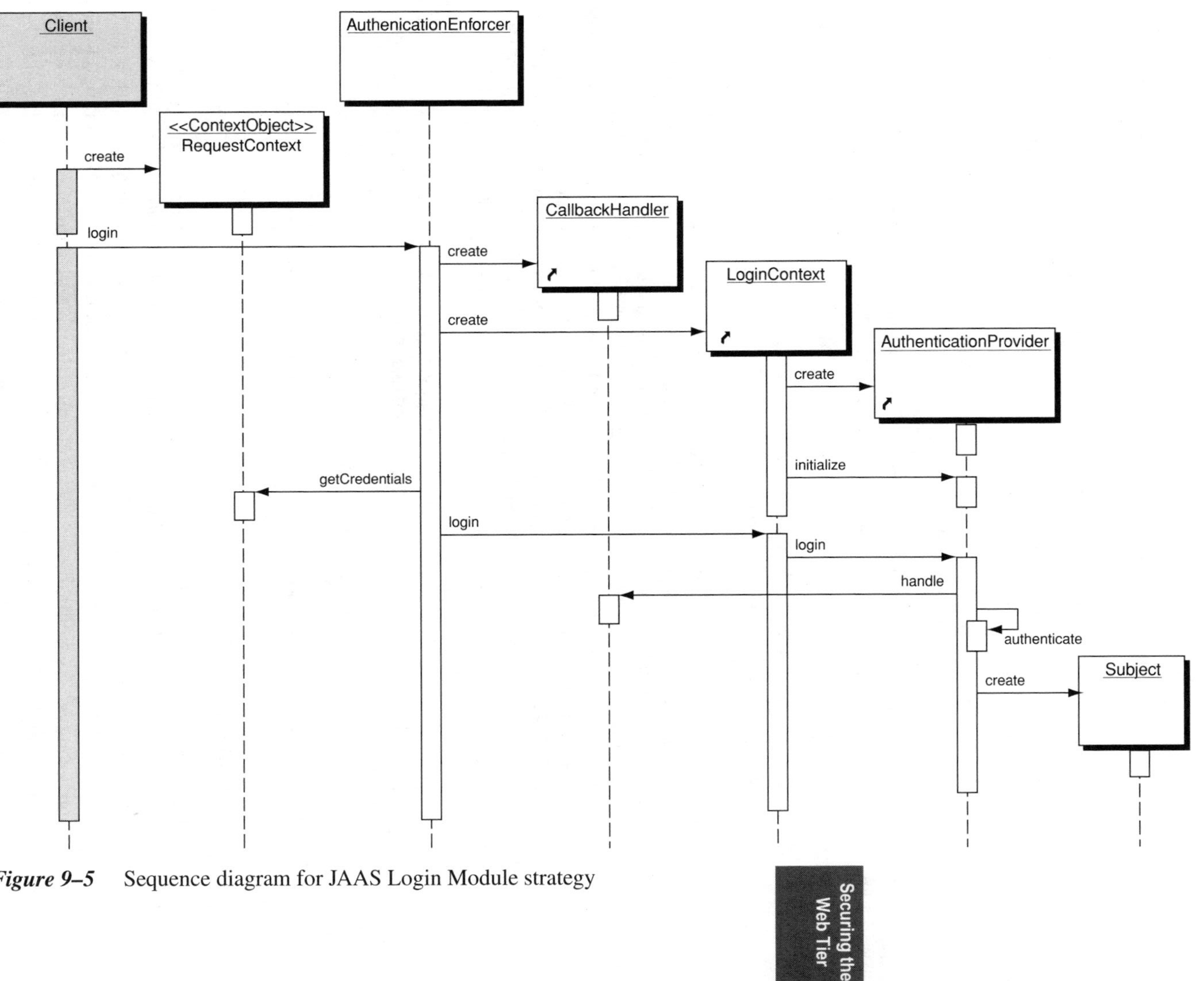

Figure 9–5 Sequence diagram for JAAS Login Module strategy

5. LoginContext loads the AuthenticationProvider implementation of a LoginModule.
6. LoginContext initializes the AuthenticationProvider.
7. AuthenticationEnforcer invokes login method on the AuthenticationProvider.
8. AuthenticationProvider retrieves the username and password by calling handle on the CallbackHandler.
9. AuthenticationProvider uses username and password to authenticate user.
10. Upon successful invocation AuthenticationProvider, upon commit, sets the Principal in the Subject and returns the Subject back up the request chain.

Design Note: Java GSS

Another option for securing communications is to use the Java GSS-API library, which is an implementation of the standard Generic Security Services API using Java bindings, as described in RFC 2853. GSS-API is typically used as an interface for the Kerberos protocol, a network authentication protocol that was developed in 1978 by Needham and Schroeder [Needham] to eliminate sending passwords in cleartext. The generic GSS-API was introduced in 1993 [RFC1508]; the latest update was made in 2000 [RFC2743]. Kerberos is often viewed as one of the first single sign-on (SSO) solutions and is still in wide use. Although GSS-API's design can support many other security protocols (for example, Simple Public Key Infrastructure), Kerberos is the most widely used with GSS-API.

The Java GSS-API is often used in coordination with JAAS, where the latter is used to establish the identity and credentials of the client (known in JAAS parlance as the Subject) for use by the former. Typically, one uses JAAS to get the username and password from the user; then JAAS converts that to credentials to be used by the Java GSS-API.

Consequences

By employing the Authentication Enforcer pattern, developers will be able to benefit from reduced code and consolidated authentication and verification to one class. The Authentication Enforcer pattern encapsulates the authentication process needed across actions into one centralized point that all other components can leverage. By centralizing authentication logic and wrapping it in a generic Authentication Enforcer, authentication mechanism details can be hidden and the application can be protected from changes in the underlying authentication mechanism. This is necessary because organizations change products, vendors, and platforms throughout the lifetime of an enterprise application.

A centralized approach to authentication reduces the number of places that authentication mechanisms are accessed and thereby reduces the chances for security holes due to misuse of those mechanisms. The Authentication Enforcer enables authenticating users by means of various authentication techniques that allow the application to appropriately identify and distinguish user's credentials. A centralized approach also forms the basis for authorization that is discussed in the Authorization Enforcer pattern. The Authentication Enforcer also provides a generic interface that allows it to be used across tiers. This is important if you need to authenticate on more than one tier and do not want to replicate code.

Authentication is a key security requirement for almost every application, and the Authentication Enforcer provides a reusable approach for authenticating users.

Sample Code

Examples 9–1, 9–2, and 9–3 illustrate different authentication configurations that can be specified in the web.xml file of a J2EE application deployment. Example 9–4 shows the programmatic approach to authentication.

Example 9–1 Basic HTTP authentication entry in the web.xml file

```
<login-config>
   <auth-method>BASIC</auth-method>
</login-config>
```

Example 9–2 Form-based authentication entry in the web.xml file

```
<login-config>
   <auth-method>FORM</auth-method>
</login-config>

<!-- LOGIN AUTHENTICATION -->
 <login-config>
 <auth-method>FORM</auth-method>
 <realm-name>default</realm-name>
    <form-login-config>
      <form-login-page>login.jsp</form-login-page>
      <form-error-page>error.jsp</form-error-page>
    </form-login-config>
  </login-config>
```

Example 9–3 Client certificate-based authentication entry in the web.xml file

```
<login-config>
   <auth-method>CLIENT-CERT</auth-method>
</login-config>
```

Example 9–4 JAAS authentication strategy code example

```
package com.csp.web;
public class AuthenticationEnforcer {

  public Subject login(RequestContext request)
       throws InvalidLoginException {

     // 1. Instantiate the LoginContext
     //    and load the LoginModule

     try {
        LoginContext ctx = new LoginContext("MyLoginModule",
                             new WebCallbackHandler(request));
     } catch(LoginException le) {
        System.err.println("LoginContext not created.
                                   "+ le.getMessage());
     } catch(SecurityException se) {
        System.err.println("LoginContext not created.
                                    "+ se.getMessage());
     }

     // 2. Invoke the Login method

     try {
        ctx.login();
     } catch(LoginException le) {
       System.out.println("Authentication failed");
     }

     System.out.println("Authentication succeeded");

     // Get the Subject

     Subject mySubject = ctx.getSubject();
     return mySubject;
  }
}
```

Security Factors and Risks

The following security factors and risks apply when using the Authentication Enforcer pattern and its strategies.

- **Authentication**. Keep all user login code in classes separate from your application classes so you can re-implement them if you port the application or change your user authentication mechanism. The J2EE platform expects that developers will not be writing authentication functionality directly into their applications; the authentication mechanisms must remain independent from the application functionality. However, developers will do so as long as the container-provided mechanisms aren't adequate to suit the needs of an application. If this is done, it would be wise for the developer to isolate the code so that it can be easily removed as containers become more capable [Sua]. The risk is this: As long as developers are writing authentication code in the application, they are opening up the possibility for bugs that attackers may be able to exploit.
- **Standardization**. Whenever possible, employ a JAAS Login Module Strategy. It promotes modularity and standardization. Most major application servers support JAAS, and it has become the industry-recognized standard. By using a proprietary approach, you increase the risk of creating security holes that can be exploited to subvert the application.
- **Web authentication**. Choose the right approach for your security requirements. Basic HTTP authentication is usually highly vulnerable to attacks and provides unacceptable exposure. On the other hand, requiring client certificates for authentication may deter potential users of the system, which is an abstract form of a denial of service attack.
- **Confidentiality**. During the authentication process, sensitive information is sent over the wire, so confidentiality becomes a critical requirement. Use a Secure Pipe pattern during the user login process to protect the user's credentials. Not securing transmission of the user credentials presents a risk that they may be captured and used by an attacker to masquerade as a legitimate user.

Reality Check

The following reality checks should be considered before implementing an Authentication Enforcer pattern.

Should you use the Authentication Enforcer programmatically or rely on container-managed security? That depends on the requirements of the application. If you are forced to integrate with a third-party security provider that does not plug into the container's underlying security SPI, then you may have to use a programmatic strategy.

Why would you use client certificate authentication? Client certificate authentication provides a high degree of authentication. It is a two-factor authentication mechanism, relying on what you have (client certificate) in addition to what you know (password).

Dependency on Secure Pipe. Most likely, you will be using the Form Based Authentication strategy. In order to protect privacy and prevent man-in-the-middle attacks, you will need to use a Secure Pipe pattern that will encrypt the password en route.

Related Patterns

The following are patterns related to the AuthenticationEnforcer.

ContextObject [CJP2]. A ContextObject is used to encapsulate protocol-specific request parameters.

Intercepting Filter [CJP2].

Authorization Enforcer

Problem

Many components need to verify that each request is properly authorized at the method and link level. For applications that cannot take advantage of container-managed security, this custom code has the potential to be replicated.

In large applications, where requests can take multiple paths to access multiple business functionality, each component needs to verify access at a fine-grained level. Just because a user is authenticated does not mean that user should have access to every resource available in the application. At a minimum, an application makes use of two types of users; common end users and administrators who perform administrative tasks. In many applications there are several different types of users and roles, each of them require access based on a set of criterion defined by the business rules and policies specific to a resource. Based on the defined set of criterion, the application must enforce that a user can be able to access only the resources (and in the manner) that user is allowed to do.

Forces

- You want to minimize the coupling between the view presentation and the security controller.
- Web applications require access control on a URL basis.

- Authorization logic required to be centralized and should not spread all over the code base in order to reduce risk of misuse or security holes.
- Authorization should be segregated from the authentication logic to allow for evolution of each without impacting the other.

Solution

Create an Access Controller that will perform authorization checks using standard Java security API classes.

The AuthorizationEnforcer provides a centralized point for programmatically authorizing resources. In addition to centralizing authorization, it also serves to encapsulate the details of the authorization mechanics. With programmatic authorization, access control to resources can be implemented in a multitude of ways. Using an AuthorizationEnforcer provides a generic encapsulation of authorization mechanisms by defining a standardized way for controlling access to Web-based applications. It provides fine-grained access control beyond the simple URL restriction. It provides the ability to restrict links displayed in a page or a header as well as to control the data within a table or list that is displayed, based on user permissions.

Structure

Figure 9–6 shows the AuthorizationEnforcer class diagram.

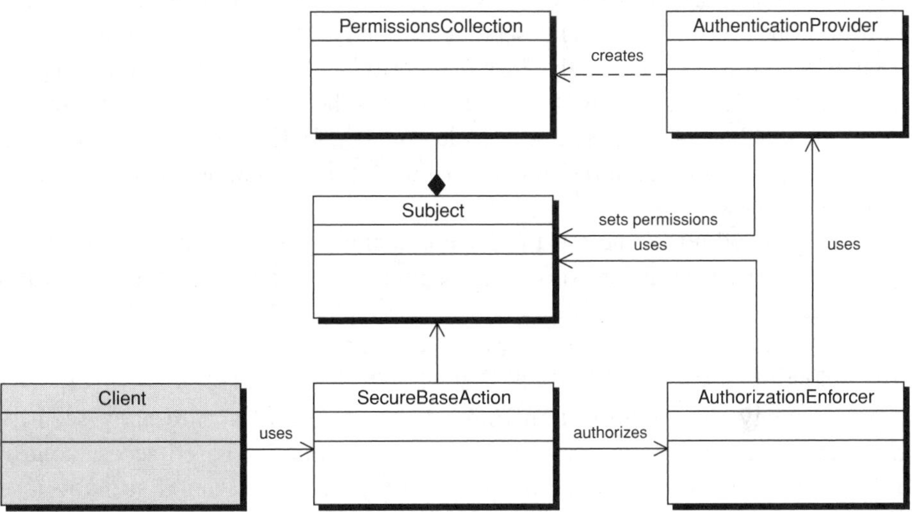

Figure 9–6 Authorization Enforcer class diagram

Participants and Responsibilities

Figure 9–7 shows a sequence diagram depicting the authorization of a user to a permission using the Authorization Enforcer.

SecureBaseAction. SecureBaseAction is an action class that gets the Subject from the RequestContext, and checks whether it is authorized for various permissions.

RequestContext. A protocol-independent object used to encapsulate protocol-specific request information.

AuthorizationEnforcer. An object used to generically enforce authorization in the Web tier.

Subject. A Subject class used to store a user's identities and credential information. [Java2]

AuthorizationProvider. A security provider that implements the authorization logic.

PermissionCollection. A PermissionCollection class used to store permissions, with a method for verifying whether a particular permission is implied in the collection. [Java2]

Strategies

There are three commonly adopted strategies that can be employed to provide authorization using Authorization Enforcer pattern. The first is using an authorization provider, using a third-party security solution that provides authentication and authorization services. The second is purely programmatic authorization strategy which makes use of the Java 2 security API classes and leveraging the Java 2 Permissions class. The third is a JAAS authorization strategy that makes use of the JAAS principal based policy files and takes advantage of the underlying JAAS programmatic authorization mechanism for populating and checking a user's access privileges.

Not discussed further here is the J2EE container-managed authorization strategy. This strategy, or more correctly, the implementation, was found to be too static and inflexible.

Authorization Provider Strategy

In this strategy, the Authorization Enforcer makes use of a third-party security provider which handles authentication and provides policy based access control to J2EE based application components. In a typical authorization scenario (see Figure 9–7), the client (an Application Controller or extended action class) wants to

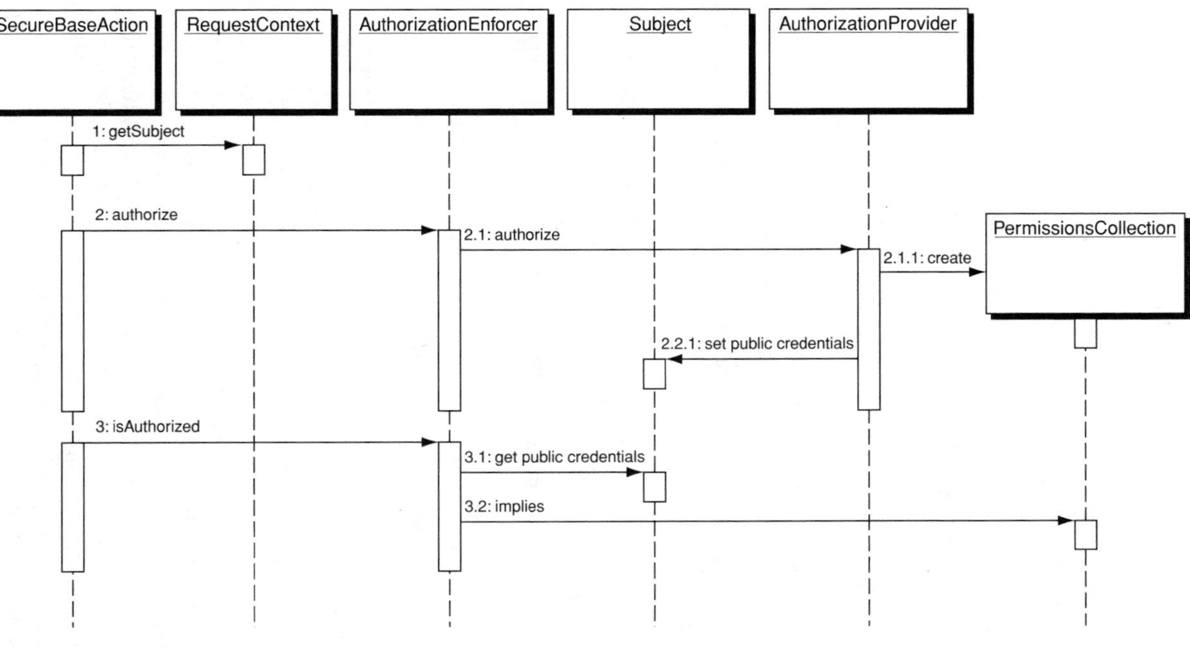

Figure 9–7 Authorization Enforcer sequence diagram

perform a permission check on a particular user defined in the Subject class retrieved from his or her session.

Prior to the illustrated flow, the SecureBaseAction class would have used the AuthenticationEnforcer to authenticate a user and then placed that user's Subject into the session. The Subject object can then be subsequently retrieved from the RequestContext. In the flow above through the following process:

1. SecureBaseAction retrieves the Subject from the RequestContext.
2. SecureBaseAction invokes AuthorizationEnforcer's authorize method, passing in the Subject.
3. AuthorizationEnforcer calls the AuthorizationProvider's authorize method, again passing the Subject.
4. AuthorizationProvider retrieves the appropriate permissions for the Principals defined in the Subject class and creates a PermissionsCollection.
5. AuthorizationProvider stores the PermissionsCollection in the Subject's public credential set.

Sometime later, the SecureBaseAction needs to check that a user has a specific Permission and calls the isAuthorized method of the AuthorizationEnforcer.

- AuthorizationEnforcer retrieves the PermissionsCollection from the Subject's public credential set.
- AuthorizationEnforcer calls the implies method of the PermissionCollection, which passes in the checked Permission and returns the response.

Design Note: J2EE Authorization

One of the problems with the J2EE authorization is its static model and its reliance on security constraints specified using deployment descriptors. This necessitates that an application be redeployed and the server restarted if the constraints change or a new role is added. Furthermore, the purpose of the role has been subverted into that of permission. Ideally, the purpose of a role is to reduce management by allowing users to be grouped into categories, with permissions assigned to those categories. The individual user is then decoupled from the permissions, allowing administrators to assign or restrict all of the necessary permissions for a user by just placing them in the appropriate role that has been assigned those permissions. This allows the administrator to more easily manage a large number of users and permissions: the users are grouped into small groups, or roles.

The J2EE model has broken this decoupling of users and permissions by eliminating the permissions and replacing it with a static role with resource mapping. Roles must be defined prior to deployment, in the deployment descriptor. In fact, it even defines the role as "an abstract name for the permission to access a particular set of resources." [WebAppSecurity]

The role has thus replaced the permission. This is further propagated to the programmatic interface. The J2EE specification defines an isCallerInRole method that allows developers to check if a user has authorization to a particular resource. A better approach would be to perform access control by checking permissions to resources. The permissions can be associated with roles, but now the roles themselves may be changed to include additional or different permissions. Alternatively, new roles can be created to correspond to different permission mappings without impacting the code that performs the access-control check. Another better approach is using Java Authorization Contract for Containers (JACC) which is part of J2EE 1.4-compliant application server platforms. Refer to Chapter 5, "J2EE Security Architecture," for more information about the role of JACC in the J2EE 1.4 platform.

Programmatic Authorization Strategy

The Programmatic Authorization Strategy has the advantage of being flexible enough to easily accommodate new types of permissions for the variety of resources that you want to protect. The programmatic authorization strategy is a purely programmatic approach to authorization. It allows developers to arbitrarily create permissions and store them in the PermissionsCollection class, as demonstrated in Figure 9–7. These permissions could be dynamically created at runtime as resources are created. For example, consider an application that allows administrators to upload new forms. Those forms may have access-control requirements that do not correspond to existing roles. You may need to create a resource permission that allows you to specify the name of the form and to then assign that permission to a user or group of users as necessary.

It is often necessary to not only deny access to a particular link on a page, but to hide it from the view of those users without appropriate permissions to view its contents. In this case, a custom tag library can be constructed to provide tags for defining permission-based access to links and other resources in the JSPs. Example 9–5 shows a code sample of a JSP utilizing such a library. In the example, we show a permission tag that protects the admin page from being accessed by anyone other than those with the "admin" permission and the application page from anyone without the "user" permission.

Example 9–5 JSP utilizing permission enforcement custom tag library

```
<TD>
<%-- display administration links --%>
<pg:permission forward="admin">
<strong>Administration</strong>
```

```
<ul>
<pg:permission forward="admin">
<li>
<pg:link forward="admin">
<pg:message bundle="common" key="text.admin"/>
</pg:link>
</li>
</pg:permission>
</ul>
</pg:permission>

<%-- display user links --%>
<pg:permission forward="user">
<strong>Application</strong>
<ul>
<pg:permission forward="user">
<li>
<pg:link forward="user">
<pg:message bundle="common" key="text.user"/>
</pg:link>
</li>
</pg:permission>
</ul>
</pg:permission>
</TD>
```


In Example 9–5, a table with admin and user links is rendered based on the requester's permissions. A user who has admin and user permissions will see both links. Regular users will only see the user link. Public users would see neither.

Example 9–6 shows the custom tag library used in Example 9–5 .

Example 9–6 Permission enforcement custom tag library

```
<?xml version="1.0" encoding="UTF-8"?>
<!DOCTYPE taglib PUBLIC "-//Sun Microsystems, Inc.//DTD JSP Tag Library 1.2/
/EN" "http://java.sun.com/dtd/web-jsptaglibrary_1_2.dtd">
<taglib>
 <tag>
 <name>permission</name>
        <tag-class>
      coresecuritypatterns.web.tags.PermissionTag
  </tag-class>
 <body-content>JSP</body-content>
 <attribute>
```

```
<name>require</name>
<required>false</required>
<rtexprvalue>false</rtexprvalue>
<type>java.lang.String</type>
</attribute>
<attribute>
<name>any</name>
<required>false</required>
<rtexprvalue>false</rtexprvalue>
<type>java.lang.String</type>
</attribute>
<attribute>
<name>deny</name>
<required>false</required>
<rtexprvalue>false</rtexprvalue>
<type>java.lang.String</type>
</attribute>
<attribute>
<name>action</name>
<required>false</required>
<rtexprvalue>false</rtexprvalue>
<type>java.lang.String</type>
</attribute>
<attribute>
<name>forward</name>
<required>false</required>
<rtexprvalue>false</rtexprvalue>
<type>java.lang.String</type>
</attribute>
<attribute>
<name>relative</name>
<required>false</required>
<rtexprvalue>false</rtexprvalue>
<type>java.lang.String</type>
</attribute>
</tag>
<tag>
</taglib>
```


JAAS Authorization Strategy

The JAAS Authorization Strategy is less flexible than a purely programmatic authorization strategy but provides the benefit of offering a standard JAAS Login-Module-based approach to authorization. It also utilizes a declarative means of mapping permissions to resources. This is a good approach for applications that do not support dynamic resource creation. Developers can map permissions to resources and roles to permissions declaratively at deployment time, thus eliminating programmatic mappings that often result in bugs and cause security vulnerabilities.

Figure 9-8 shows the sequence diagram of the Authorization Enforcer implemented using the JAAS Authorization Strategy. The key participants and their roles are as follows:

AuthorizationEnforcer. An object used to generically enforce authorization in the Web tier.

Subject. A Java 2 security class used to store a user's identities and security-related information. [Java2]

PrivilegedAction. A computation to be performed with privileges enabled.

Policy. It is JAAS Principal-based policy file, which defines the Principals with designated permissions to execute the specific application code or other privileges associated with the application or resources. [JAAS]

JAAS Module. The JAAS Module is responsible for enforcing access control by enforcing the JAAS Policy and verifying that the authenticated Subject has been granted the appropriate set of permissions before invoking the PrivilegedAction.

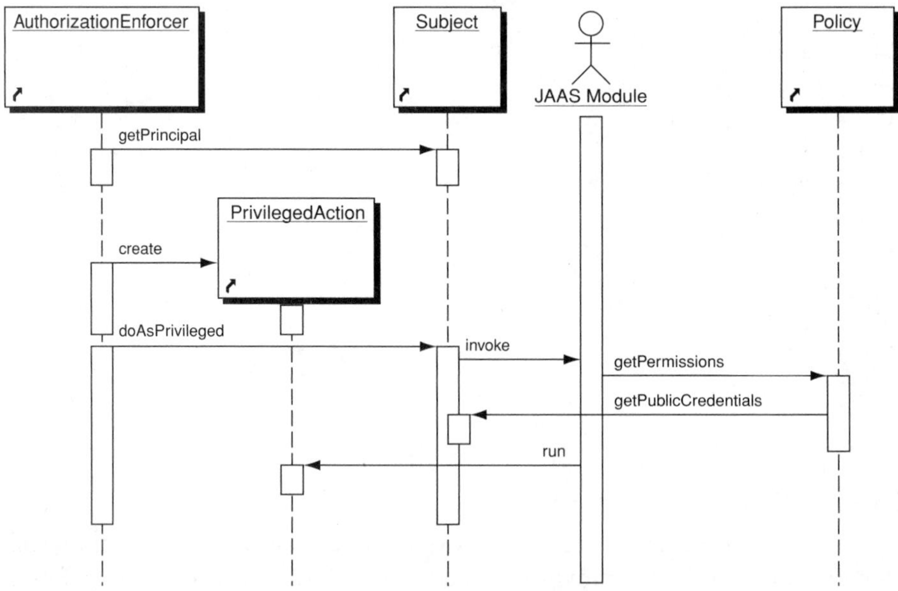

Figure 9–8 JAAS Authorization Enforcer Strategy sequence diagram

Example 9–7 shows a JAAS Authorization policy file (MyJAASAux.policy). Example 9–8 shows the source code for a JAAS-based authorization strategy (SampleAuthorizationEnforcer.java) and Example 9–9 shows the Java source code for PrivilegedAction implementation (MyPrivilegedAction.java).

Example 9–7 JAAS authorization policy file (MyJAASAux.policy)

```
//  grant the LoginModule for enforcing
//  authorization permissions

grant codebase "file:./MyLoginModule.jar" {
    permission javax.security.auth.AuthPermission
                                "modifyPrincipals";
};

grant codebase "file:./SampleAuthorizationEnforcer.jar" {

   permission javax.security.auth.AuthPermission
                                "doAsPrivileged";
};

/** User-Based Access Control Policy
 ** for executing the MyAction class
 ** instantiated by MyJAASAux.policy
 **/

grantcodebase "file:./MyPrivilegedAction.jar",

Principal csp.principal.myPrincipal "chris" {

   permission java.util.PropertyPermission
                               "java.home", "read";
   permission java.util.PropertyPermission
                               "user.home", "read";
   permission java.io.FilePermission "Chris.txt", "read";
};
```

Example 9–8 SampleAuthorizationEnforcer.java

```
import java.io.*;
import java.util.*;
import java.security.Principal;
import java.security.PrivilegedAction;
import javax.security.auth.*;
import javax.security.auth.callback.*;
```

```
public class SampleAuthorizationEnforcer {

   public void executeAsPrivileged(LoginContext lc) {
      Subject mySubject = lc.getSubject();

      // Identify the Principals we have

      Iterator principalIterator
             = mySubject.getPrincipals().iterator();

      System.out.println("Authenticated user - Principals:");
      while (principalIterator.hasNext()) {
         Principal p = (Principal)principalIterator.next();
    System.out.println("\t" + p.toString());
      }
      // Execute the required Action
      // as the authenticated Subject

      PrivilegedAction action = new MyPrivilegedAction();
      Subject.doAsPrivileged(mySubject, action, null);
   }
}
```


Example 9–9 MyPrivilegedAction.java

```
import java.security.PrivilegedAction;

public class MyPrivilegedAction implements PrivilegedAction {

   public Object run() {
      System.out.println("\nYour java.home property: "
            +System.getProperty("java.home"));
      System.out.println("\nYour user.home property: "
            +System.getProperty("user.home"));

      File f = new File("MyAction.txt");
      System.out.print("\nMyAction.txt does ");
      if (!f.exists())
         System.out.print("not ");
         System.out.println("exist in working directory.");
         return null;
      }
   }
```

Consequences

- *Centralizes control.* The Authorization Enforcer allows developers to encapsulate the complex intricacies of implementing access control. It provides a focus point for providing access control checks, thus eliminating the chance for repetitive code.
- *Improves reusability.* Authorization Enforcer allows greater reuse through encapsulation of disparate access-control mechanisms through common interfaces.
- *Promotes separation of responsibility.* Partitions authentication and access-control responsibilities, insulating developers from changes in implementations.

Security Factors and Risks

Authorization. Protect resources on a case by case basis. Fine-grained authorization allows you to properly protect the application without imposing a one-size-fits-all approach that could expose unnecessary security vulnerabilities. A common security vulnerability arises from access-control models that are too coarse-grained. When the model is too coarse-grained, you inevitably have users that do not fit nicely into the role-permission mappings defined. Often, administrators are forced to give these users elevated access due to business requirements. This leads to increased exposure. For instance, you have two groups of users that you break into two roles (staff and admin). The staff role only has the ability to read form data. The admin role has the ability to create, read, update, and delete (CRUD) form data. You find that you have a few users that need to update the form data, though they should not be able to create or delete it. You are now forced to put them into the admin role, giving them these additional permissions because your model is too coarse-grained.

Reality Check

Too complex. Implementing a JAAS Authorization Strategy and all but the most simplistic authorization strategies requires an in-depth understanding of the Java 2 security model and a variety of Java security APIs. As with any security mechanism, complexity can lead to vulnerabilities. Make sure you understand how your resources are being protected through this approach before diving in and implementing it.

Related Patterns

Context Object [CJP2]. The Authorization Enforcer uses a Context Object pattern to encapsulate handling and transferring of security-related request data. Refer to http://www.corej2eepatterns.com/Patterns2ndEd/ContextObject.htm for details.

Authentication Enforcer. The Authorization Enforcer relies on the Authentication Enforcer to first authenticate the user.

Intercepting Validator

Problem

You need a simple and flexible mechanism to scan and validate data passed in from the client for malicious code or malformed content. The data could be form-based, queries, or even XML content.

Several well-known attack strategies involve compromising the system by sending requests containing invalid data or malicious code. Such attacks include injection of malicious scripts, SQL statements, XML content, and invalid data using a form field that the attacker knows will be inserted into the application to cause a potential failure or denial of service. The embedded SQL commands can go further, allowing the attacker to wreak havoc on the underlying database.

These types of attacks require the application to intercept and scrub the data prior to its use. While some of the approaches for scrubbing the data are well known, it is a constant battle to keep up-to-date as new attacks are discovered.

Forces

- You want to validate a wide variety of data passed in by the client.
- You want a common mechanism for validating various types of data.
- You want to dynamically add validation logic as necessary to keep your application secure against newly discovered attacks.
- Validation rules must be decoupled from presentation logic.

Solution

Use an Intercepting Validator to cleanse and validate data prior to its use within the application, using dynamically loadable validation logic.

A good application will verify all input, for both business and security reasons. Similar to the Intercepting Filter pattern [CJP2], the Intercepting Validator makes use of a pluggable filter approach. The filters can then be applied declaratively based on URL, allowing different requests to be mapped to different filter chains. In the case of the Intercepting Validator, filtering would be restricted to preprocessing of requests and would primarily consist of validation (yes or no) logic that determines whether or not the request should continue as opposed to manipulation logic that would require business logic above and beyond the security concerns of the application.

While applications could incorporate security filters into an existing Intercepting Filter implementation, the preferred approach would be to employ both and keep them separate. Typically, the Intercepting Validator would be invoked earlier in the request-handling process than the Intercepting Filter and would consist of a more static and reusable set of filters because it is not tied to any particular set of business rules. Business rules are often tied to the business logic and must be performed in the Business tier, but security rules are often independent of the actual application and should be performed up front in the Web tier.

Client-side validations are inherently insecure. It is easy to spoof submitting a Web page and bypass any scripting on the original page. [Vau] For the application to be secure, validations must be performed on the server side. This does not detract from the value of client-side validations.

Client-side validations via JavaScript make sense for business rules and should be optionally supported. They provide the user with validation feedback before the form gets submitted. This increases the perceived performance by the end user and saves the server the cost of processing errors for the vast majority of cases. Input from malicious users who circumvent client-side validations must still be validated, though.

Therefore, to be prudent, validation checks must always be performed on the server side, whether or not client-side checking is done as well.

Structure

Figure 9-9 depicts a class diagram of the Intercepting Validator pattern.

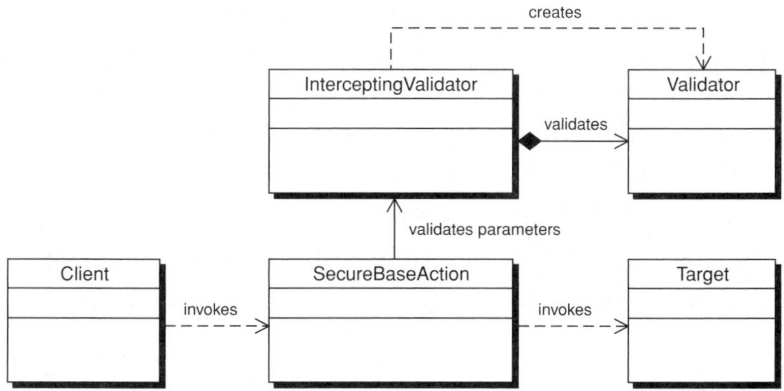

Figure 9–9 Intercepting Validator class diagram

Participants and Responsibilities

Figure 9-10 shows an Intercepting Validator sequence diagram.

Figure 9-10 illustrates a sequence of events for the Intercepting Validator pattern described by the following components.

Client. A client sends a request to a particular target resource.

SecureBaseAction. The SecureBaseAction is used by the client to generically enforce validating the request in the Web tier. SecureBaseAction delegates this responsibility to the InterceptingValidator.

InterceptingValidator. The InterceptingValidator is a specialized version of the InterceptingFilter pattern [CJP2], with some notable changes in strategy. Unlike the InterceptingFilter, it is solely responsible for data validation.

ParamValidator. The ParamValidator is responsible for validating all request parameters. Boundary checking, data formatting, and examining the parameters for cross-site scripting and malformed URL vulnerabilities are some of the validations it performs. Validations are specific to the Target.

SQLValidator. SQLValidator is responsible for validating the parameters for executing SQL statements. Examining the parameters for boundary checking, data size and format, and formatting are some of the validations it performs. Validations are specific to the database queries and transactions.

Target. The client requested resource.

Figure 9–10 depicts a use case scenario of how a request from a client to a resource gets properly validated to ensure against attacks based on malformed data. The scenario follows these steps:

1. Client makes a request to a particular resource, specified as the Target.
2. SecureBaseAction uses the InterceptingValidator to validate the data for the target service request.
3. InterceptingValidator retrieves the appropriate validators according to the configuration for the target.
4. InterceptingValidator invokes a series of validators as configured.
5. Each Validator validates and scrubs the request data, if necessary.
6. Upon successful validation, the SecureBaseAction invokes the target resource.

Strategies

Different validators are used to validate different types of data in a request or perform validation on that data in a different manner. For example, certain form

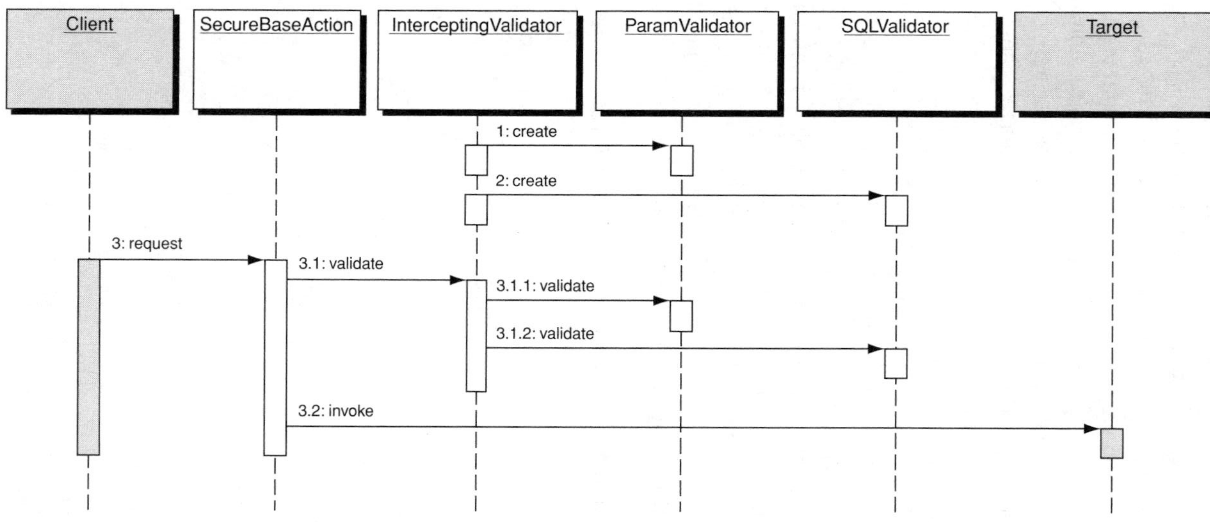

Figure 9–10 InterceptingValidator sequence diagram

fields need to be validated for size constraints. Form fields that will contain data that will be become part of an SQL query or update require SQL character validation to ensure that embedded SQL commands cannot be entered.

The logic to perform the validations can often be cumbersome. This logic can be simplified through use of the new J2SE 1.4 regular expressions package. This package contains classes that allow developers to perform regular expression matches as they would in the Perl programming language. These classes can be used for validation implementations.

Example 9–10 illustrates a simple action configuration in MVC architecture using Apache Struts. To implement a simple Intercepting Validator, the parameter attribute can define a key that can be used to apply a Validator against an ActionForm/HTTPRequest. Alternatively, a separate validation file, such as validator.xml as shown in Example 9–11 can define generic sets of validation rules to be applied to a form or other input request. Such XML-descriptive validation definitions can be leveraged by Intercepting Validator to dynamically apply over input requests; Validator instances that have been coded to be configured based on the XML content. Both these scenarios are illustrated in Figure 9–10.

Example 9–10 Web data validation using Apache Struts

```
<struts-config>
<!-- Action Form Beans -->
 <form-beans>
 <form-bean
 name="simpleForm"
 type="SimpleForm"/>
 </form-beans>
<!-- action mappings -->
 <action-mappings>
 <action
 path="/submitSimpleForm"
 type="SimpleFormAction"
 name="simpleForm"
 scope="request"
 validate="true"
 input="simpleForm.jsp"
 parameter="additional_security_validator_identifier">
 <forward
 name="continueWorkFlow"
 path="continue.jsp"/>
 </action>
 </action-mappings>
</struts-config>
```

Example 9–11 Form validation XML using Apache Struts

```
<form-validation>
 <formset>
 <form name="simpleForm">
 <field dataItemName="dataToSave" rule="preprocessorRule">
 <var name="minValue" value="1"/>
 <var name="maxValue" value="9999"/>
 <var name="maskingExpression"
  value="^\(?(\d{3})\)?[-| ]?(\d{3})[-| ]?(\d{4})$"/>
 <var msg="errors.dataToSave"/>
 </field>
 </form>
 </formset>
</form-validation>
```


Example 9–12 SecureBaseAction class using InterceptingValidator with Apache Struts

```
import org.apache.struts.action.Action;
import org.apache.struts.action.ActionMapping;
import org.apache.struts.action.ActionErrors;

/**
 * This code is based on Apache Struts examples.
 * It requires a working knowledge of Struts, not
 * explained here.
 */
public final class SecureBaseAction extends Action {

   public ActionErrors validate(ActionMapping actionmapping,
          HttpServletRequest request) {
      //perform basic input validation
      Validator validator =
    InterceptingValidator.getValidator (actionmapping);
      ValidationErrors errors = validator.process(request);
      if(errors.hasErrors())
    return InterceptingValidator.
        transformToActionErrors(errors);

      //For any additional externalized processing, use the
      //key 'additional_security_validator_identifier'
      //specified as 'parameter' attribute in action-mappings
```

```
      String externalizedProcessingKey =
                         actionmapping.getParameter();
      ExternalizedValidator validatorEx =
   InterceptingValidator.getExternalizedValidator(
         externalizedProcessingKey);
      errors = validatorEx.process(request);
      if(errors.hasErrors())
   return InterceptingValidator.transformToActionErrors(
                errors);
      // Alternatively,
      // use 'additional_security_validator_identifier' to
      //specify a class that implements command pattern
      //and invoke the 'process' method on the instantiation

      try {
   Class cls = InterceptingValidatorUtil.loadClass(
         externalizedProcessingKey);
        Method method = InterceptingValidatrUtil.
    getValidationActionMethod("process");
        InterceptingValidator.invoke(
    cls, method, new Object[] {request});
      }
      catch(Exception ex) {
        log("Invocation exception", ex);
        return
          InterceptingValidator.transformToActionErrors(ex);
      }
   }
}
```


An architect who is not inclined to use the Intercepting Validator pattern may end up forcing each developer to naively hardcode validation logic in each of the servlets/action classes/forms beans. Developers implementing business action classes (front controllers), who may not necessarily be security-aware, are prone to miss necessary validations. An example of this type of programmatic validation is illustrated in Example 9–13.

Example 9–13 SimpleFormAction using programmatic validation logic using Apache Struts

```
import org.apache.struts.action.Action;
import org.apache.struts.action.ActionErrors;
import org.apache.struts.action.ActionForm;
import org.apache.struts.action.ActionForward;
```

```
import org.apache.struts.action.ActionMapping;

/**
 * This code is taken from the Apache Struts examples.
 * It requires a working knowledge of Struts, not
 * explained here.
 */
public final class SimpleFormAction extends Action {
 public ActionForward perform(ActionMapping actionmapping,
        ActionForm actionform,
        HttpServletRequest httpservletrequest,
   HttpServletResponse httpservletresponse)
   throws IOException, ServletException {

 //perform explicit validation since
 // it is not implicitly taken care of by
 //the web application framework

 ActionErrors actionerrors = actionform.validate();

if(!actionerrors.empty()) {

 saveErrors(httpservletrequest, actionerrors);

 //redirect to input page with errors
 return new ActionForward(actionmapping.getInputForward());
 }
 else {
 return actionmapping.findForward("continueWorkFlow");
 }
 }
}
public class SimpleForm extends Form {
   //...
 public ActionErrors validate(ActionMapping actionmapping,
          HttpServletRequest request) {
   //for each request/form parameter, code for validation
   ActionErrors errs = new ActionErrors();
   if (request.getParameter("param1").indexOf("&")!=-1)
     errs.add(Action.ERROR_KEY,
      new ActionError("error_unacceptable_parameter1"));
   //...
   return errs;
 }
}
```

Consequences

Using the Intercepting Validator pattern helps in identifying malicious code and data injection attacks before the business logic processes the request. It ensures verification and validation of all inbound requests and safeguards the application from forged requests, parameter tampering, and validation failure attacks.

In addition, the Intercepting Validator offers developers several key benefits:

- *Centralizes security validations.* The Intercepting Validator pattern provides centralized security validation logic. By centralizing security validations, code is more maintainable and more reusable. Input validation is one of the most crucial aspects of securing Web applications, because there are so many vulnerabilities stemming from lack of validation. The Intercepting Validator ensures that such vulnerabilities can be addressed in a standardized way.
- *Decouples validations from presentation logic.* It is good programming practice to decouple the validation of the request data from the presentation logic. It promotes better software manageability and cleaner code. It also reduces redundancy.
- *Simplifies addition of new validators.* Developers have the ability to add new validators dynamically. As new data-based attacks are discovered, new validators can be implemented and installed without requiring redeployment of the application.

Security Factors and Risks

Processing Overhead: Failure to validate input data exposes an application to a variety of attacks, such as malicious code injection, cross-site scripting (XSS), SQL injection attacks, and buffer overruns. The validation process adds some processing overhead and can cause application failure if the application fails to detect a buffer overflow or endless-loop attack.

Reality Check

Is an elaborate security validation framework really needed? There are many known data attacks that can be prevented through proper data validation. A framework is needed to ensure that there is a mechanism in place to facilitate easy addition of new validation logic as future data attacks on the application become known.

Performance implications. The Intercepting Validator pattern could be competing with other Web server resources to read session data, which could lead to concurrency issues such as long wait times or deadlocks. A careful analysis of the Web requests traffic, performance requirements, dependencies, and other possible scenarios should bring forth appropriate resolutions and trade-offs.

Related Patterns

Intercepting Filter [CJP2]. The Intercepting Filter is similar but is used more as a filtering or transforming mechanism than a validation tool.

Message Inspector. The Message Inspector intercepts and processes XML requests, and in situations where custom validation mechanisms are required, it may need to use an Intercepting Validator.

Secure Base Action

Problem

You want to consolidate interaction of all security-related components in the Web tier into a single point of entry for enforcing security and integration of security mechanisms.

Security-related data and methods are used across many or most of the Web tier components. Operations such as verifying authentication, checking authorization, and storing and retrieving session information are prevalent throughout the servlets and JSPs. Due to the nature of security, these operations are often tied together through their implementation. When many normal application components are exposed to many of these security-related components, flexibility and reuse are reduced because of the inherent underlying coupling of security components.

For example, in many applications, several different components set cookies directly. If a new security mandate were to prohibit the use of cookies due to a newly found security hole in a popular Web browser, the application would have to be changed in many different areas. There is a possibility that some code would be missed and a security hole opened up. New authentication mechanisms and validation checks are other examples of changing code that is often exposed to many Web components.

Forces

- You want to enforce security by centralizing all security-related functionality.
- You want to reduce direct integration of presentation logic with security logic.

- You want to encapsulate the details of the security-related components so that those components can be enhanced without impact to presentation logic.
- You have several security components that you need to coordinate or orchestrate to ensure overall security requirements are met.

Solution

Use a Secure Base Action to coordinate security components and to provide Web tier components with a central access point for administering security-related functionality.

A Secure Base Action pattern can be used as a single point for security-related functionality within the Web tier. By having Web components such as Front Controllers [CJP2] and Application Controllers [CJP2] inherit from it, they gain access to all of the security operations that are necessary throughout the front end. Authentication, authorization, validation, logging, and session management are areas that the Secure Base Action encapsulates and provides centralized access to.

Structure

Figure 9–11 depicts a class diagram for the Secure Base Action.

As shown in Figure 9–11, the client is a FrontController or ApplicationController that allows delegation of the security handling of the request to the SecureBaseAction. The SecureBaseAction in turn delegates the individual tasks to the appropriate classes.

Participants and Responsibilities

Figure 9–12 shows a client invoking the execute method of SecureBaseAction.

Client. The client is a request handler that uses the SecureBaseAction to perform security processing of the request.

SecureBaseAction. A client sends a request to a particular target resource.

AuthenticationEnforcer. The AuthenticationEnforcer provides authentication and verification of requests.

AuthorizationEnforcer. The AuthorizationEnforcer authorizes users for requests.

InterceptingValidator. The InterceptingValidator handles validation of request parameters.

SecureLogger. The SecureLogger logs events for the request.

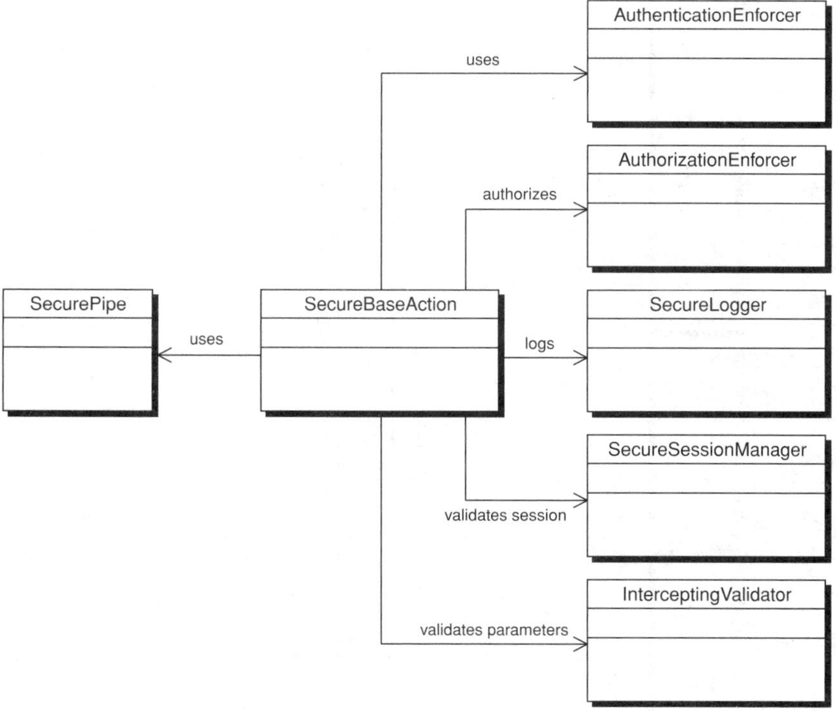

Figure 9–11 Secure Base Action class diagram

As shown in Figure 9–12, the SecureBaseAction invokes methods on all of the supporting security classes, ensuring that the request is authenticated, authorized, validated, and logged. The sequence is as follows:

1. Client invokes execute on SecureBaseAction.
2. SecureBaseAction gets the LoginContext from the session.
3. SecureBaseAction uses the AuthenticationEnforcer to verify the LoginContext.
4. SecureBaseAction authorizes the request using the AuthorizationEnforcer.
5. SecureBaseAction validates the request data using the InterceptingValidator.
6. SecureBaseAction logs the request using the SecureLogger.

Typically, the client would be a FrontController [CJP2] or an ApplicationController [CJP2] that would invoke and execute prior to delegating to any other classes. You would not want to make more than one call per request, because it would cause redundant processing.

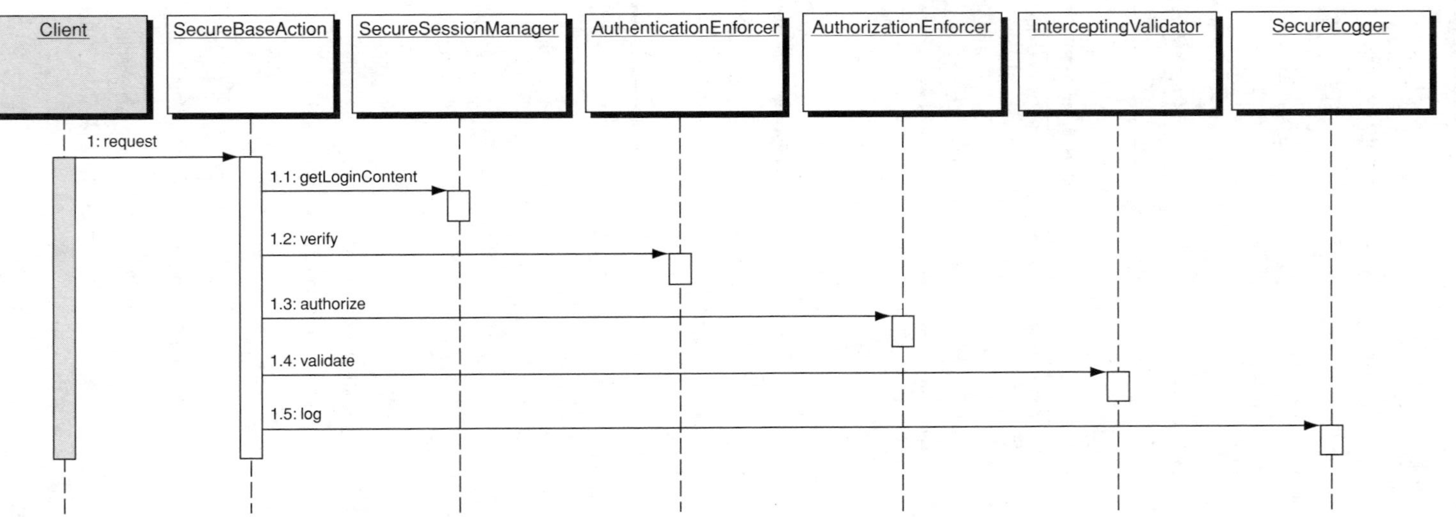

Figure 9–12 Secure Base Action sequence diagram

Strategies

MVC Style Secure Base Action Strategy

Secure Base Action class is well suited for the MVC frameworks (like Struts). Most MVC-based applications will have a base action class that provides the common services that all of the individual actions throughout the application need. It will often be this base action class that provides the operations specified in the Secure Base Action class. By consolidating a variety of security-related operations and separating them into the Secure Base Action, you achieve better segregation of responsibility. Developers who are responsible for the base action class in an application are usually not the same developers responsible for the security-related requirements. Secure Base Action provides a means for separating responsibility through inheritance or use of the Command [GoF] pattern.

Figure 9–13 illustrates the sequence of events for an MVC-style strategy using Struts.

Consequences

Using Secure Base Action helps in aggregating and enforcing security operations that include authentication, authorization, auditing, input validation, and other management functions before processing the request with presentation or business logic.

By employing the Secure Base Action pattern, developers will realize the following benefits:

- *Improved manageability of security requirements.* Architects and developers can improve management of security requirements by consolidating

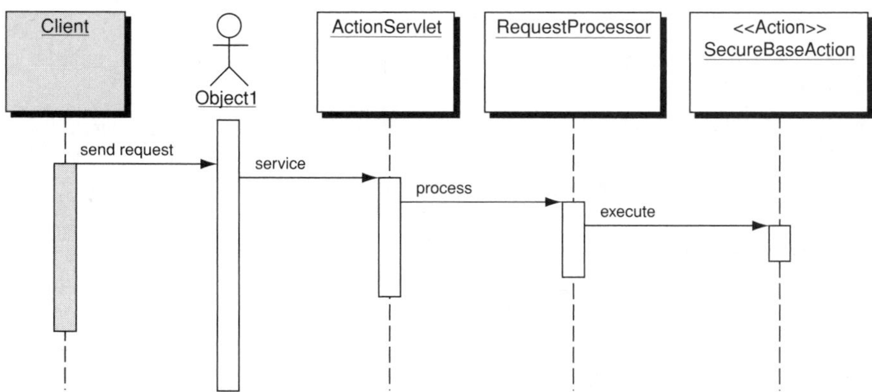

Figure 9–13 MVC style Secure Base Action strategy

enforcement of those requirements through a central class. This provides a single integration point between presentation code and security code. Therefore, presentation developers do not have to focus on security and have fewer chances for causing holes by not integrating security properly. Changes required for evolving security requirements are isolated from the rest of the application, reducing touchpoints in the application that could possibly be overlooked and result in security holes.

- *Improves reusability.* By consolidating security-related functionality behind one interface, developers gain better reuse of the functionality, since there are fewer touchpoints in the code base. All supporting security classes can be packaged together and reused, with the SecureBaseAction acting as the single interface for the Web tier components. The more components are reused, the more they are improved. The same goes for security. Reusing security code means that you are using code that has been security-tested and has many of the kinks already worked out.

Sample Code

Example 9–14 Secure base action class

```
Package com.csp.web;

import javax.servlet.http.HttpServletRequest;
import javax.servlet.http.HttpServletResponse;
import javax.security.auth.login.LoginContext;
import javax.security.auth.Subject;

public class SecureBaseAction {

    /**
     * Execute method called on each request. All exceptions will bubble up.
     */
     public void execute(HttpServletRequest req, HttpServletResponse)
    throws Exception {
        // Get an instance of ContextFactory
        ContextFactory factory = ContextFactory.getInstance();
        // Get LoginContext from factory
        RequestContext rc = factory.getContext(req,
         Constants.Request_CONTEXT);
        LoginContext lc = secureSessionManager.getLoginContext(rc);
        if(! authenticationEnforcer.verify(lc)) {
           lc = authenticationEnforcer.authenticate(rc);
```

```
            secureSessionManager.setLoginContext(lc);
        }
        // Authorize the request
        authorizationEnforcer.authorize(req, lc);
        // Validate request data
        interceptingValidator.validate(req);
        // Log data
        secureLogger.log(lc.getSubject().getPrincipals()[0] + rc);
    }

    /**
     * Set the subject in the login context
     */
     public void setLoginContext(ResponseContext resp, Subject s)
    throws Exception {
        // Get an instance of ContextFactory
        ContextFactory factory = ContextFactory.getInstance();
        // Get LoginContext from factory
        LoginContext lc = factory.getContext(Constants.LOGIN_CONTEXT);
        lc.setSubject(s);
        resp.setParameter(Constants.LOGIN_CONTEXT_KEY, lc);
    }
}
```


Security Factors and Risks

The Secure Base Action pattern acts as the focal point for enforcing security-related functionality within the Web tier. It is intended as a reusable base class that provides pluggable security functionality into the front end.

- **Authentication**. The Secure Base Action enforces authentication through use of an Authentication Enforcer.
- **Authorization**. The Secure Base Action enforces authorization of requests through use of an Authorization Enforcer.
- **Logging**. The Secure Base Action uses a Secure Logger to securely log request events.
- **Validation**. The Secure Base Action validates request data via an Intercepting Validator.

The Secure Base Action Pattern must adopt high-availability and fault-tolerance strategies to support the underlying security operations and to enhance reliability and performance of the infrastructure. When a failure is detected, it must securely failover to a redundant infrastructure without jeopardizing any existing inbound requests or its intermediate processing state.

Reality Check

Too inflexible. The Secure Base Action encapsulates all security-related functionality. This is great for shielding application components from changes to underlying security mechanisms, but it is also prohibitive in some cases where application components require access to those security mechanisms beyond what the Secure Base Action provides. For example, a web developer might want to implement password services that require direct access to the authentication provider, which is not accessible through the Secure Base Action.

Too much encapsulation? The Secure Base Action is not providing a lot of functionality on top of the other patterns that it delegates to. It is worthwhile, because it hides the detail of how the other security patterns are implemented from the presentation developer and reduces exposing integration points.

Related Patterns

Front Controller [CJP2]. A Front Controller inherits from or uses a Secure Base Action to provide and coordinate security-related functions.

Command [GoF]. Secure Base Action class makes use of the Command pattern for handling requests.

ContextObject [CJP2]. A Context Object is used by the Secure Base Action to hide the protocol-specific details of the requests, responses, and session information.

Authentication Enforcer. Secure Base Action uses the Authentication Enforcer to authenticate users.

Authorization Enforcer. Secure Base Action uses the Authorization Enforcer to authorize requests.

Secure Logger. The Secure Logger is used by the Secure Base Action to log request events.

Intercepting Validator. The Secure Base Action validates request data through use of an Intercepting Validator.

Secure Logger

Problem

All application events and related data must be securely logged for debugging and forensic purposes. This can lead to redundant code and complex logic.

All trustworthy applications require a secure and reliable logging capability. This logging capability may be needed for forensic purposes and must be secured against stealing or manipulation by an attacker. Logging must be centralized to avoid redundant code throughout the code base. All events must be logged appropriately at multiple points during the application's operational life cycle. In some cases, the data that needs to be logged may be sensitive and should not be viewable by unauthorized users. It becomes a critical requirement to protect the logging data from unauthorized users so that the data is not accessible or modifiable by a malicious user who tries to identify the information trail. Without centralized control, sometimes the code usually gets replicated, and it becomes difficult to maintain the changes and monitor the functionality.

One of the common elements of a successful intrusion is the ability to cover one's tracks. Usually, this means erasing any tell-tale events in various log files. Without a log trail, an administrator has no evidence of the intruder's activities and therefore no way to track the intruder. To prevent an attacker from breaking in again and again, administrators must take precautions to ensure that log files cannot be altered. Cryptographic algorithms can be adopted to ensure data confidentiality and the integrity of the logged data. But the application processing logic required to apply encryption and signatures to the logged data can be complex and cumbersome, further justifying the need to centralize the logger functionality.

Forces

- You need to log sensitive information that should not be accessible to unauthorized users.
- You need to ensure the integrity of the data logged to determine if it was tampered with by an intruder.
- You want to capture output at one level for normal operations and at other levels for greater debugging in the event of a failure or an attack.
- You want to centralize control of logging in the system for management purposes.
- You want to apply cryptographic mechanisms for ensuring confidentiality and integrity of the logged data.

Solution

Use a Secure Logger to log messages in a secure manner so that they cannot be easily altered or deleted and so that events cannot be lost.

The Secure Logger provides centralized control of logging functionality that can be used in various places throughout the application request and response. Centralizing control provides a means of decoupling the implementation details of the logger from the code of developers who will use it throughout the application. The processing of the events can be modified without impacting existing code. For instance, developers can make a single method call in their Java code or JSP code. The Secure Logger takes care of how the events are securely logged in a reliable manner.

Structure

Figure 9–14 depicts a class diagram for Secure Logger.

Participants and Responsibilities

Figure 9–15 shows a sequence diagram that depicts the structure of the Secure Logger pattern.

Client. A client sends a request to a particular target resource.

SecureLogger. SecureLogger is a class used to manage logging of data in a secure, centralized manner.

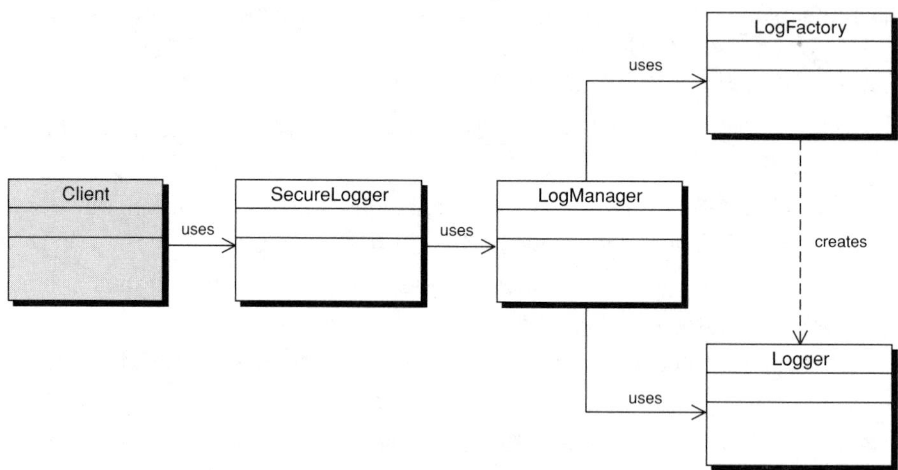

Figure 9–14 Secure Logger class diagram

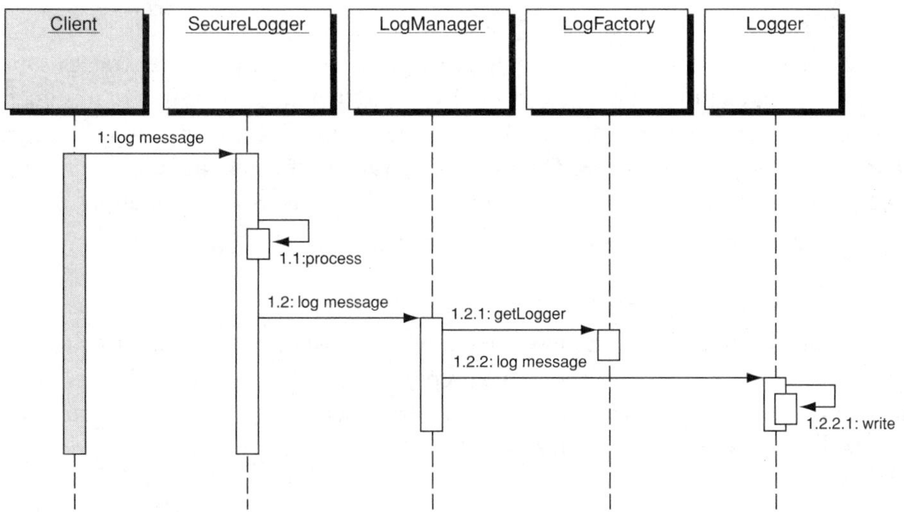

Figure 9–15 Secure Logger sequence diagram

LogManager. LogManager obtains a Logger instance from LogFactory and uses it to log messages.

LogFactory. A LogFactory is responsible for creating and returning Logger instances.

Logger. A Logger writes log messages to a target destination.

A client uses the SecureLogger to log events. The SecureLogger centralizes logging management and encapsulates the security mechanisms necessary for preventing unauthorized log alteration.

1. Client wants to log an event using SecureLogger.
2. SecureLogger generates a sequence number and prepends it to the message.
3. SecureLogger passes the LogManager the modified event string to log.
4. LogManager obtains a handle to a Logger instance from a LogFactory.
5. LogFactory creates a Logger instance.
6. LogManager delegates actual logging of the event to the Logger.

There are two parts to this logging process. The first part involves securing the data to be logged and the second part involves logging the secured data. The SecureLogger class takes care of securing the data and the LogManager class takes care of logging it.

Strategies

There are two basic strategies for implementing a Secure Logger. One strategy is to secure the log itself from being tampered with, so that all data written to it is guaranteed to be correct and complete. This strategy is the Secure Log Store Strategy. The other strategy, the Secure Data Logger Strategy, secures the data so that any alteration or deletion of it can be detected. This works well in situations where you cannot guarantee the security of the log itself.

Secure Data Logger Strategy

The Secure Data Logger Strategy entails preprocessing of the data prior to logging it. After the data is secured in the preprocessing, it is sent to the logger in the usual manner. There are four new classes introduced to help secure the data. Figure 9–16 illustrates the structure of the Secure Logger implemented using a Secure Data Logger Strategy.

We use the MessageDigest, Cipher, Signature, and UIDGenerator classes for applying cryptographic mechanisms and performing various functions necessary to guarantee the data logged is confidential and tamperproof.

Figure 9–17 shows the sequence of events used to secure the data prior to being logged.

When you have sensitive data or fear that log entries might be tampered with and can't rely on the security of the infrastructure to adequately protect those entries, it becomes necessary to secure the data itself prior to being logged. That way, even if the log destination (file, database, or message queue) is compromised, the data remains secure and any corruption of the log will become clearly evident.

There are three elements to securing the data:

- *Protect sensitive data.* Ensure all sensitive data are stored and remain confidential throughout the process. For example, Credit card numbers should not be viewed directly by unauthorized personnel.
- *Prevent data alteration.* Make sure that data is tamperproof. For example, user IDs, transaction amounts, and so forth should not be changed.
- *Detect deletion of data.* Detect if events have been deleted from the log, a tell-tale sign that an attacker has compromised the system.

To protect sensitive data, encrypt it using a symmetric key algorithm. Public-key algorithms are too CPU-intensive to use for bulk data. They are better for encrypting and protecting a symmetric key for use with a symmetric key algorithm. Properly protecting the symmetric key can ensure that attackers cannot access sensitive data even if they have access to the logs. For this, the SecureLogger

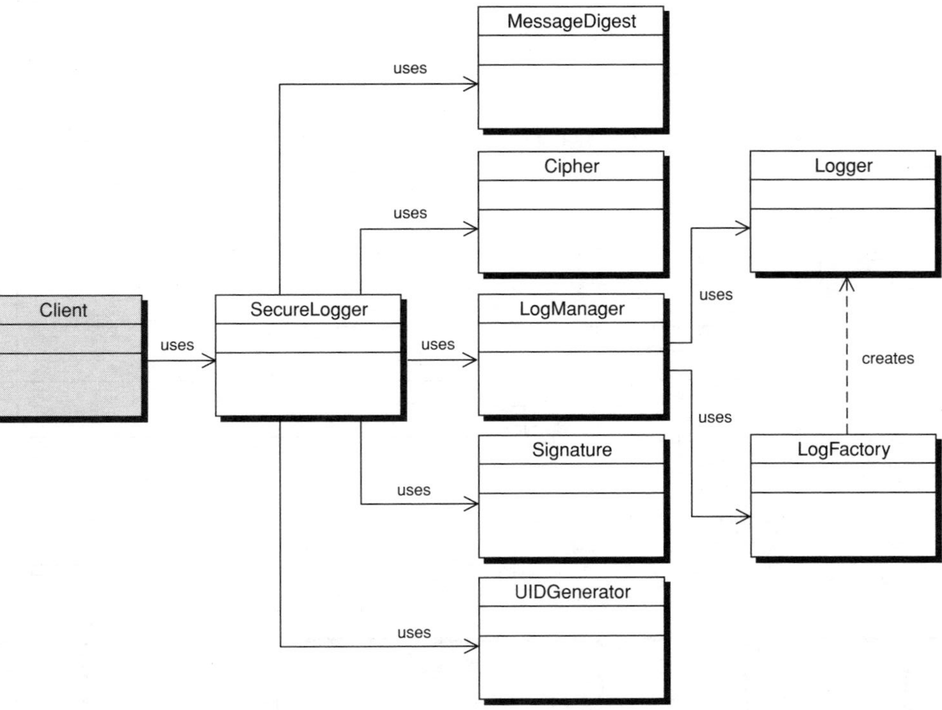

Figure 9–16 Secure Logger with Secure Data Logger Strategy class diagram

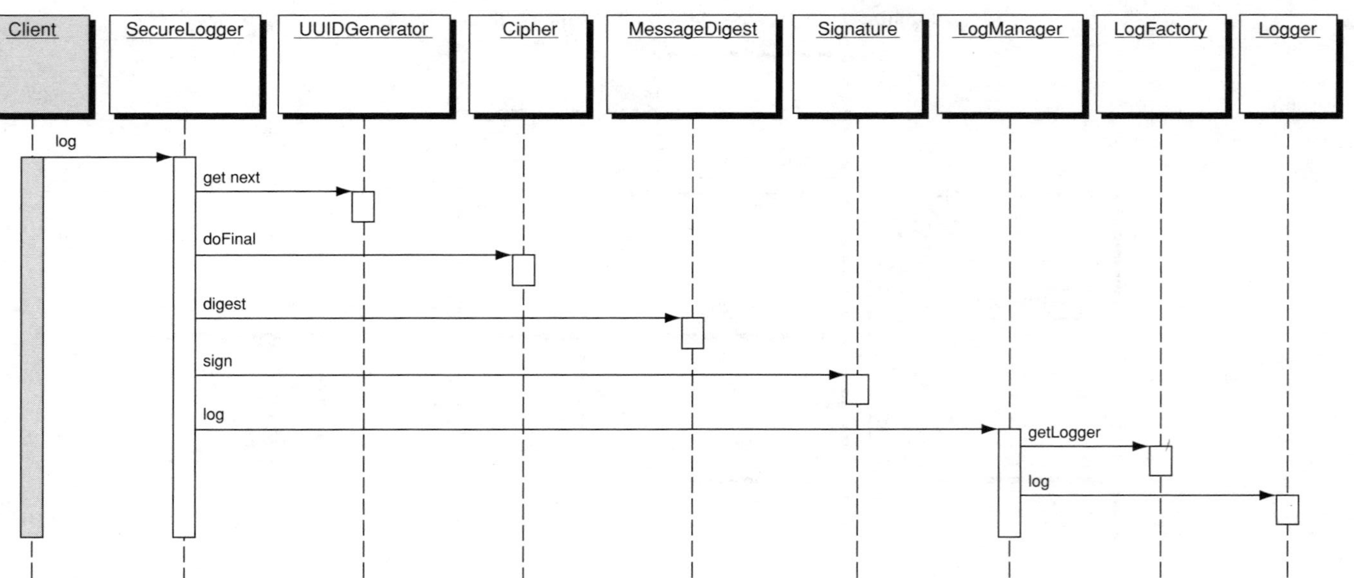

Figure 9–17 Secure Logger with Secure Data Logger Strategy sequence diagram

can use an EncryptionHelper class. This class is responsible for encrypting a given string but not for decrypting it. This is an extra security precaution to make it harder for attackers to gain access to that sensitive data. Decryption should only be done outside the application, using an external utility that is not accessible from the application and its residing host.

Data alteration can be prevented by using digitally signed message digests in the same manner that e-mail is signed. A message digest is generated for each message in the log file and then signed. The signature prevents an attacker from modifying the message and creating a subsequent message digest for the altered data. For this operation, the SecureLogger uses MessageDigestHelper and DigitalSignatureHelper classes.

Finally, to detect deletion of data, a sequence number must be used. Using message digests and digital signatures is of no use if the entire log entry, including the signed message, is deleted. To prevent deletion, each entry must contain a sequence number that is part of the data that gets signed. That way, it will be evident if an entry is missing, since there will be a gap in the sequence numbers. Because the sequence numbers are signed, an attacker would be unable to alter subsequent numbers in the sequence, making it easy for an administrator reviewing the logs to detect deletions. To accomplish this, the SecureLogger uses a UUID [Middleware] pattern.

Secure Log Store Strategy

In the Secure Log Store Strategy, the log itself is secured from tampering. A secure repository houses the log data and can be implemented using a variety of off-the-shelf products or various techniques such as a Secure Pipe. (See the "Secure Pipe Pattern" section later in this chapter.). A Secure Pipe pattern is used to guarantee that the data is not tampered with in transit to the Secure Store. Figure 9–18 illustrates the structure of the Secure Logger pattern implemented using a Secure Log Store Strategy.

The Secure Log Store strategy does not require the data processing that the Secure Data Logger Strategy introduced. Instead, it makes use of a Secure Pipe pattern and a secure datastore (such as a database), represented as the SecureStore object in Figure 9–18. In Figure 9–19, the only change from the main Secure Logger pattern sequence is the introduction of the Secure Pipe pattern.

In the Secure Log Store Strategy sequence diagram, depicted in Figure 9–19, Logger establishes a secure connection to the SecureStore using a SecurePipe. The Logger then logs messages normally. The SecureStore is responsible for preventing tampering with the log file. It could be implemented as a database with create-only permissions for the Logger user; a listener on a separate, secure box

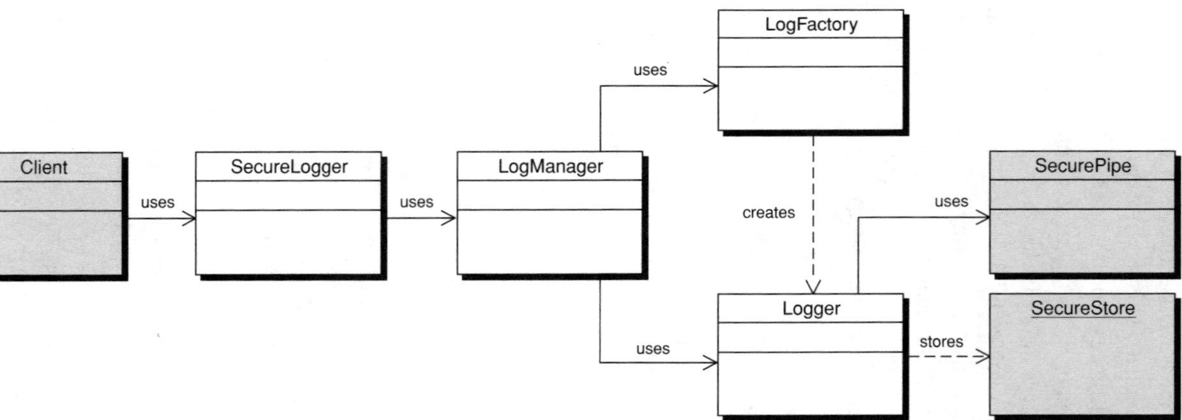

Figure 9–18 Secure Logger Pattern with Secure Log Store Strategy class diagram

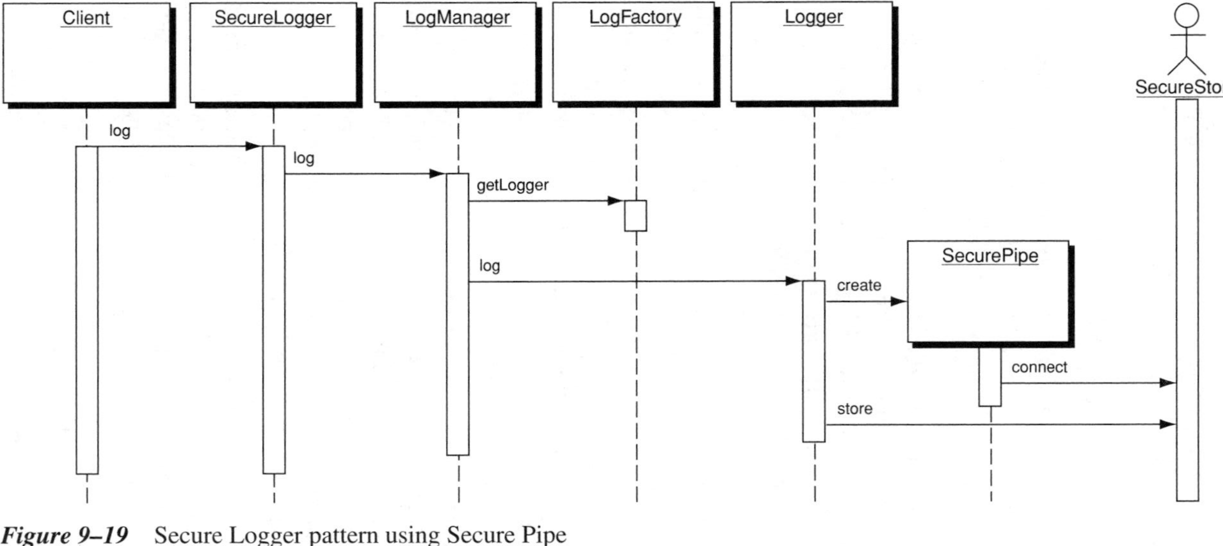

Figure 9–19 Secure Logger pattern using Secure Pipe

with write only capabilities; or any other solution that prevents deletion, modification, or unauthorized creation of log entries.

Consequences

Using the Secure Logger pattern helps in logging all data-related application events, user requests, and responses. It facilitates confidentiality and integrity of log files.

In addition, it provides the following benefits:

- *Centralizes logging control.* The Secure Logger improves reusability and maintainability by centralizing logging control and decoupling the implementation details from the API. This allows developers to use the logging facilities through the API independent of the security functionality built into the logger itself. This reduces the possibility that business developers will inadvertently circumvent security by misusing it.
- *Prevents undetected log alteration.* The key to successfully compromising a system or application is the ability to cover your tracks. This involves alteration of log files to ensure that an administrator cannot detect that a breach has occurred. By employing a Secure Logger, security developers can prevent log alterations, ensuring that a breach can be detected through log file forensics, which is the first step in tracking down an intruder and preventing security breaches.
- *Reduces performance.* The Secure Logger impacts performance due to the use of cryptographic algorithms. Operations such as message digests, digital signatures, and encryption are computationally expensive and add additional performance overhead. Use only the necessary functionality to avoid unwanted performance overhead. Reduced performance can lead to a self-inflicted denial of service attack.
- *Promotes extensibility.* Security is a constantly evolving process. To protect against both current and future threats, code must be adaptable and extensible. The Secure Logger provides the requisite extensibility by hiding implementation details behind a generic interface. By increasing the overall lifespan of the code, you increase its reliability by having tested it and worked out all of its bugs.
- *Improves manageability.* Since all of the logging control is centralized, it is easier to manage and monitor. The Secure Logger performs all of the necessary security processing prior to the actual logging of the data, which allows management of each function independently of the others without risk of impacting overall security.

Sample Code

Example 9–15 shows a sample signer class, Example 9–16 depicts a digest class, and Example 9–17 provides a sample encryptor class. These classes are used by the Secure Logger to sign, digest, and encrypt messages, respectively.

Example 9–15 Signer class

```
package com.csp.web;

import java.security.*;
import sun.misc.BASE64Encoder;

public class Signer {

    public String sign(String msg) throws Exception {
      // Create a Signature object to use for signing
      signer = Signature.getInstance(Constants.SIGNATURE_ALGORITHM);
      PrivateKey privateKey = keyPair.getPrivate();
      // Initialize the Signature object for signing
      signer.initSign(privateKey);
      signer.update(msg.getBytes());
      // Now sign the message
      byte[] signature = signer.sign();
      // Encode the signature using Base64 for logging.
      String encodedSignature = Base64Encoder.encode(signature);
      return encodedSignature;
    }

}
```

Example 9–16 Digester class

```
package com.csp.web;

import java.security.MessageDigest;
import sun.misc.BASE64Encoder;

public class Digester {

  public String digest(String msg) throws Exception {
    MessageDigest md =
      MessageDigest.getInstance(Constants.DIGEST_ALGORITHM);
    md.update(msg.getBytes());
    byte[] digest = md.digest();
```

```
        // Encode digest using Base64
        String encodedDigest =
          Base64Encoder.encode(digest);
        return encodedDigest;
    }

}
```

Example 9–17 Encryptor class

```
package com.csp.web;

import java.security.*;
import sun.misc.BASE64Encoder;

public class Encryptor {

   public String encrypt(String msg) throws Exception {
    // Create a Cipher and initialize it for encryption
    Cipher desCipher =
      Cipher.getInstance(Constants.CIPHER_ALGORITHM);
    // Retrieve DES key from storage such as Keystore
    desCipher.init(Cipher.ENCRYPT_MODE, desKey);
    // Create a message to send and encrypt it
    byte[] cipherText = desCipher.doFinal(msg.getBytes());
    String encodedCipher = Base64Encoder.encode(cipherText);
    return encodedCipher;
  }
}
```


Security Factors and Risks

The Secure Logger pattern provides the entry point for logging in the application. As such, it has the following security factors and risks associated with it.

- **Key Management**. The Secure Logger must either encrypt data itself or establish a secure channel to a secure log store. Either way, there are key management issues that must be addressed. If the key or password for retrieving the key (such as for a keystore) must be kept in code, make sure that the code is obfuscated. Failure to properly protect the key will render the Secure Logger useless.
- **Confidentiality**. The Secure Logger must provide confidentiality when communicating with the secure store in the Secure Data Store strategy. If

the communication channel is not secure, it opens up the possibility that an attacker can compromise the communication channel and modify the data in transit.

Reality Check

Should everything be logged from Web tier? No. The Secure Logger pattern is applicable across tiers. It should be implemented on each tier that requires logging.

Too much performance overhead. Using the Secure Data Store Strategy incurs severe performance overhead. Expect a significant slowdown due to the extensive use of cryptographic algorithms. The Secure Data Logger Strategy is the preferred strategy for performance, but it also incurs the same overhead associated with use of Secure Pipe.

How likely is log tampering? Log modifications to cover an attacker's tracks is not only common, it is the hallmark of a good hacker. It is difficult to determine how prevalent it is due to its very nature. Log files that have been successfully altered usually mean that the last trace of evidence that a system has been compromised is now gone.

Shouldn't log security be the responsibility of the system administrators? In many cases, system administrators can effectively secure the log, and additional security is unnecessary. It depends on the skill of your operations staff along with the requirements of the application. Like any other security, log security is only as strong as the weakest link. By consolidating and encapsulating log functionality using the Secure Logger, you provide the capability to add additional security, such as in the Secure Data Strategy, if and when you find external mechanisms are not sufficient.

Related Patterns

Abstract Factory Pattern [GoF]. An Abstract Factory, or Factory, provides an interface for creating objects with a common interface or base class that is responsible for the concrete implementation of the interface.

Secure Pipe [Web Tier]. Secure Pipe shows how to secure the connection between the client and the server, or between servers.

Universally Unique Identifier [Middleware]. A Universally Unique Identifier (UUID) provides an identifier that is unique.

Secure Pipe

Problem

You need to provide privacy and prevent eavesdropping and tampering of client transactions caused by man-in-the-middle attacks.

Web-based transactions are often exposed to eavesdropping, replay, and spoofing attacks. Anytime a request goes over an insecure network, the data can be intercepted or exposed by unauthorized users. Even within the confines of a VPN, data is exposed at the endpoint, such as inside of an intranet. When exposed, it is subject to disclosure, modification, or duplication.

Many of these types of attacks fall into the category of man-in-the-middle attacks. Replay attacks capture legitimate transactions, duplicate them, and resend them. Sniffer attacks just capture the information in the transactions for use later. Network sniffers are widely available today and have evolved to a point where even novices can use them to capture unencrypted passwords and credit card information. Other attacks capture the original transactions, modify them, and then send the altered transactions to the destination.

This is a common problem shared by all applications that do business over an untrusted network, such as the Internet. For simple Web applications that just serve up Web pages, it is not cost-effective to address these potential attacks, since there is no reason for attackers to carry out such an attack (other than for defacement of the pages) and therefore the risk is relatively low. But, if you have an application that requires sending sensitive data (such as a password) over the wire, you need to protect it from such an attack.

Forces

- You want to avoid writing application logic to provide the necessary protection; it is better to push this functionality down into the infrastructure layer to avoid complexity.
- You want to make use of hardware devices that can speed up the cryptographic algorithms needed to prevent confidentiality- and integrity-related issues.
- You want to adopt tested, third-party products for reliable data and communication security.
- You want to limit the protection of data to only sensitive data due to the large processing overhead and subsequent delay due to encryption.

Solution

Use a Secure Pipe to guarantee the integrity and privacy of data sent over the wire.

A Secure Pipe provides a simple and standardized way to protect data sent across a network. It does not require application-layer logic and therefore reduces the complexity of implementation. In some instances, the task of securing the pipe can actually be moved out of the application and even off of the hardware platform altogether. Because a Secure Pipe relies on encrypting and decrypting all of the data sent over it, there are performance issues to consider. A Secure Pipe allows developers to delegate processing to hardware accelerators, which are designed especially for the task.

Structure

Figure 9–20 depicts a class diagram of the Secure Pipe pattern in relation to an application.

Participants and Responsibilities

Figure 9–21 shows a sequence diagram depicting use of the Secure Pipe pattern.

The following participants are illustrated in the sequence diagram shown in Figure 9–20.

Client. Initiates a login with the application.

Application. Creates a system level SecurePipe over which to communicate with the client.

SecurePipe. A SecurePipe is an encrypted communications channel that provides data privacy and integrity between two endpoints.

In the sequence shown in Figure 9–21, a client needs to connect to an application over a secure communication line.

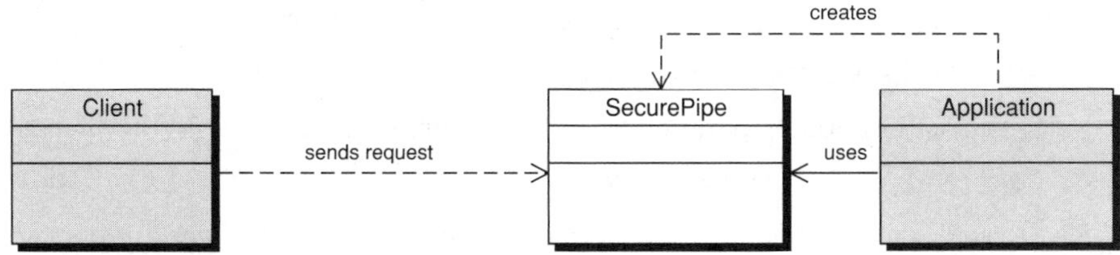

Figure 9–20 Secure Pipe Pattern class diagram

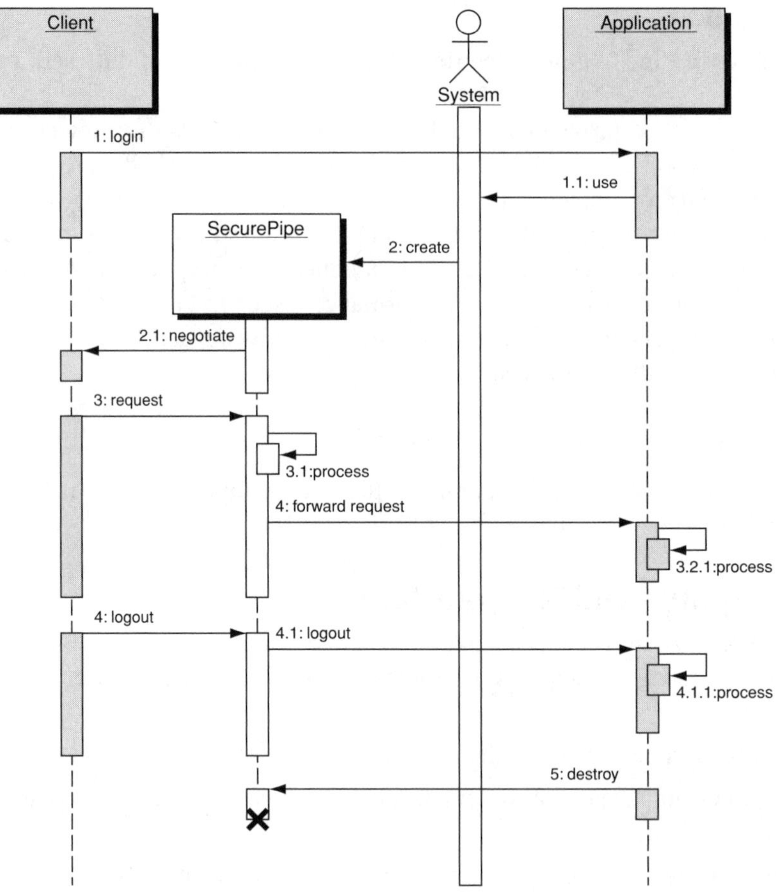

Figure 9–21 Secure Pipe sequence diagram

The sequence diagram shows how the client and the application communicate using the Secure Pipe. The interaction is as follows.

1. Client sends login request to the Application.
2. Application uses System to create a SecurePipe.
3. SecurePipe negotiates parameters of the secure connection with the Client.
4. Client sends request to the Application.
5. SecurePipe processes the request and creates a secure message by encrypting the data. It sends the message over the wire to the corresponding SecurePipe components on the Application.

6. SecurePipe on the Application processes the request received from the Client by decrypting it and then forwards the decrypted message to the Application.
7. Client sends a logout request.
8. Application destroys the SecurePipe.

There are two components of the Secure Pipe pattern: the client-side component and the server-side component. These components work together to establish a secure communication. Typically, these components would be SSL or TLS libraries that the client's Web browser and the application use for secure communications.

Strategies

There are several strategies for implementing a Secure Pipe pattern, each with its own set of benefits and drawbacks. Those strategies include:

- Web-server-based SSL/TLS
- Hardware-based cryptographic accelerator cards
- Application-layer encryption using the Java Cryptography Extension (JCE)

Web-Server-Based SSL

All major Web-server vendors support SSL. All it takes to implement SSL is to obtain or create server credentials from a CA, including the server X.509 certificate, and configure the Web server to use SSL with these credentials. Before enabling SSL, the Web server must be security-hardened to prevent compromise of the server's SSL credentials. Since these credentials would be stored on the Web server, if that server were compromised, an attacker could gain access to the server's credentials (including the private key associated with the certificate) and would then be able to impersonate the server.

Hardware-Based Cryptographic Card Strategy

To enhance SSL performance, a specialized hardware referred to as *SSL accelerators* can be used to assist with cryptographic computations. When a new SSL session is established, the Web server will use the SSL accelerator hardware to accept the SSL connection and perform the necessary cryptographic calculations for verifying certificates, encrypting session keys, and so forth instead of having the server CPU perform these calculations in software. SSL acceleration improves Web application performance by relieving servers of complex public key operations, bulk encryption, and high SSL traffic volumes.

Network Appliance Strategy

A network appliance is a stand-alone piece of hardware dedicated to a particular purpose. In this strategy, we refer to network appliances that act as dedicated SSL/TLS endpoints. They make use of hardware-based encryption algorithms and optimized network ports. Network appliances move the responsibility for establishing secure connections further out into the perimeter and provide greater performance. They sit out in front of the Web servers and promote a greater degree of reusability, since they can service multiple Web servers and applications. However, the security gap between the Secure Pipe endpoint and the application has widened as the appliance is moved logically and physically further away from the application endpoint on the network.

Application Layer Using JSSE Strategy

In some cases, Secure Pipe can be implemented in the application layer by making use of Java Secure Socket Extensions (JSSE) framework. JSSE allows enabling secure network communications using Secure Sockets Layer (SSL) and Transport Layer Security (TLS) protocols. It includes functionality for data encryption, server authentication, message integrity, and optional client authentication. Example 9–18 shows how to create secure RMI connections by implementing an RMI Secure Socket Factory that provides SSL connections for the RMI protocol, which provides a secure tunnel.

Consequences

- *Ensures data confidentiality and integrity during communication.* The Secure Pipe pattern enforces data confidentiality and integrity using a mixture of encryption and digital signatures. Using SSL/TLS mechanisms, all point-to-point communications links can be secured from man-in-the-middle attacks.
- *Promotes interoperability.* Using industry-standard infrastructure components to implement the Secure Pipe pattern allows application owners to achieve greater interoperability with clients and partners. By taking advantage of infrastructure products and standard protocols like SSL/TLS, IPSEC, application-level interoperability can be achieved between Web browser clients and Web-server-based applications.
- *Improves performance.* Delegating CPU-intensive cryptographic operations into hardware infrastructure often shows performance benefits. Strategies such as SSL accelerators and network appliances often demonstrated quadruple performance over application layer processing.

- *Reduces complexity.* The Secure Pipe pattern reduces complexity by separating complex cryptographic algorithms and procedures from application logic. The details associated with providing secure communications can be pushed down into the infrastructure, thus freeing up the application to focus on business logic rather than security.

Sample Code

Example 9–18 Creating a Secure RMI Server Socket Factory that Uses SSL


```
package com.csp.web.securepipe;

import java.io.*;
import java.net.*;
import java.rmi.server.*;
import java.security.KeyStore;
import javax.net.*;
import javax.net.ssl.*;
import com.sun.net.ssl.*;
import javax.security.cert.X509Certificate;


/**
 * This class creates RMI SSL connections.
 */
public class RMISSLServerSocketFactory
    implements RMIServerSocketFactory, Serializable {
   SSLServerSocketFactory ssf = null;

   /**
    * Constructor.
    */
   public RMISSLServerSocketFactory(char[] passphrase) {

      // set up key manager to do server authentication
      SSLContext ctx;
      KeyManagerFactory kmf;
      KeyStore ks;

      try {
         ctx = SSLContext.getInstance("SSL");
         // Retrieve an instance of an X509 Key manager
         kmf = KeyManagerFactory.getInstance("SunX509");
```

```
            // Get the keystore type.
            String keystoreType = System.getProperty(
              "javax.net.ssl.KeyStoreType");
            ks = KeyStore.getInstance(keystoreType);
            String keystoreFile = System.getProperty(
              "javax.net.ssl.trustStore");
            // Load the keystore.
            ks.load(new FileInputStream(keystoreFile), passphrase);
            kmf.init(ks, passphrase);
            passphrase = null;
            // Initialize the SSL context.
            ctx.init(kmf.getKeyManagers(), null, null);
            // Set the Server Socket Factory for getting SSL connections.
            ssf = ctx.getServerSocketFactory();
        }
        catch(Exception e) {
            e.printStackTrace();
        }
    }

    /**
     * Creates an SSL Server socketnad returns it.
     */
    public ServerSocket createServerSocket(int port)
            throws IOException {
        ServerSocket ss = ssf.createServerSocket(port);
        return ss;
    }
}
```

Example 9–19 Creating a secure RMI client socket factory that uses SSL

```
Package com.csp.web.securepipe;

import java.io.*;
import java.net.*;
import java.rmi.server.*;
import javax.net.ssl.*;

public class RMISSLClientSocketFactory
    implements RMIClientSocketFactory, Serializable {

    public Socket createSocket(String host, int port)
```

```
    throws IOException {
        SSLSocketFactory factory =
          (SSLSocketFactory)SSLSocketFactory.getDefault();
        SSLSocket socket =
          (SSLSocket)factory.createSocket(host, port)
        return socket;
    }
}
```

Security Factors and Risks

The Secure Pipe pattern is an integral part of most Web server infrastructures because we make use of SSL/TLS between the client and the Web Server. Without it, mechanisms for ensuring data privacy and integrity must be performed in the application itself, leading to increased complexity, reduced manageability, and the inability to push the responsibility down into the infrastructure.

Infrastructure

- *Infrastructure for ensuring data privacy and integrity.* Any communication over the Internet or an intranet are subject to attack. Attackers can sniff the wire and steal data, alter it, or resend it. Developers need to protect this data by encrypting it and using digitally signed timestamps, sequence numbers, and checksums. Using industry standards, such as SSL and TLS, developers can secure data that is interoperable with Web browsers and other client applications.
- *Data encryption performance.* Encryption is an expensive processing task. Hardware devices can increase throughput and response times by performing the necessary cryptographic functions in hardware, freeing up CPU cycles for the application.

Web Tier

- *Server certificates.* One of the requirements with SSL is public key management and trust models. To solve this problem, certificate authorities were established to act as trusted third parties responsible for the authentication and validation of public keys through the use of digital certificates. Several CA's certificates are packaged in Web browsers and in the Java Runtime Environment's cacerts file. This allows developers to take advantage of client certificate chains to ensure that the requesting client was properly authenticated by a trusted third party.

Reality Check

Will Secure Pipe impact performance? Using a Secure Pipe will certainly impact performance noticeably. Do not use it when it is not required. Many business cases dictate securing sensitive information and therefore a Secure Pipe must be used. If your Web application mandates the need for protecting passwords and sensitive information in transit, use a Secure Pipe (such as HTTPS) just for those operations. Otherwise, you may conduct all other transactions over standard HTTP communication.

Are there any compatibility issues with Secure Pipe? Implementing a Secure Pipe requires an agreement between the communicating peers. The client and the server must support the same cryptographic algorithms and key lengths as well as agree upon a common protocol for exchanges keys. SSL and TLS provide standard protocols for ensuring this compatibility by providing handshake mechanisms that allow clients and servers to negotiate algorithms and key lengths.

Related Patterns

Point-to-Point Channel [EIP]. A Secure Pipe is similar to a Point-to-Point Channel in its implementation. A Point-to-Point Channel ensures that only one receiver will receive a message from the sender. The Secure Pipe guarantees that only the intended receiver of the message will be able to successfully retrieve the message that was sent.

Secure Service Proxy

Problem

Integrating newer security protocols into existing applications can prove cumbersome and introduce risk, especially if the existing applications are legacy systems.

Often, you find that you need to adapt existing systems with integrated security protocols to newer security protocols. This is especially true when wrapping existing systems as services in a Service Oriented Architecture (SOA). You want to expose the existing system as a service that interacts with newer services, but the security protocols differ. You do not want to rewrite the existing system and therefore must integrate its existing security protocol.

Forces

- You want to support a legacy application's security protocols and can't modify the existing application.

- You want to completely decouple security tasks from applications so that you do not inadvertently break existing functionality.
- You want to leverage out-of-the-box security from reliable third-party vendors or reuse the J2EE security infrastructure developed for a different purpose that is less risky than a home-grown security solution.
- You want to protect Web service endpoints from malicious requests.

Solution

Use Secure Service Proxy to provide authentication and authorization externally by intercepting requests for security checks and then delegating the requests to the appropriate service.

A Secure Service Proxy intercepts all requests from the client, identifies the requested service, enforces the security policy as mandated by the specific service, optionally transforms the request from the inbound protocol to that expected by the destination service, and finally forwards the request to the destination service. On the return path, it transforms the results from the protocol and format used by the service to that format expected by the requesting client. It could also choose to maintain the security context, created in the initial request, in a session created for the client with the intent of using it in future requests.

The Secure Service Proxy can be configured on the corporate perimeter to provide authentication, authorization, and other security services that enforce policy to security-unaware lightweight or legacy enterprise services. While the Secure Service Proxy pattern acts similar to an Intercepting Web Agent pattern, it is more advanced because it does not require restricting HTTP URL-based access control, or delegating service requests to any service using any transport protocol. It externalizes the addition of security logic to existing applications that have been implemented and deployed already and integrates cleanly with newer applications that have been developed without security.

Structure

The Secure Service Proxy pattern allows developers to decouple the protocol details from the service implementation. This allows multiple clients using different network protocols to access the same enterprise service that expects one particular protocol. For instance, you may have an enterprise service that expects only HTTP requests. If you want to add additional protocol support, you can use a Secure Service Proxy, rather than building each protocol handler into the service. Each protocol may have its own way of handling security, and therefore the Secure Service Proxy can delegate security handling of each protocol to its appropriate protocol handler. For example, using a Secure Service Proxy in an enterprise

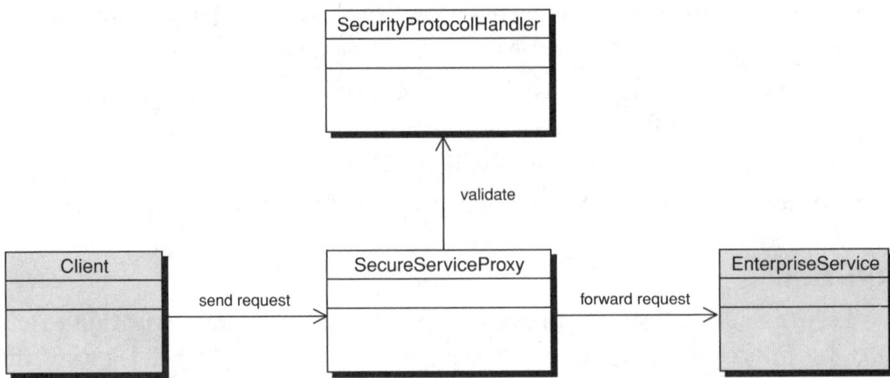

Figure 9–22 Secure Service Proxy class diagram

messaging scenario involves transforming message formats, such as converting a HTTP or an IIOP request from the client to a Java Messaging Service (JMS) message expected by a message-based service and vice versa. In so doing, the proxy can choose to use a channel that connects to the destination service, further decoupling the service implementation details from the proxy.

Figure 9–22 is a class diagram of a Secure Service Proxy pattern.

Participants and Responsibilities

Figure 9–23 shows the sequence diagram for Secure Service Proxy.

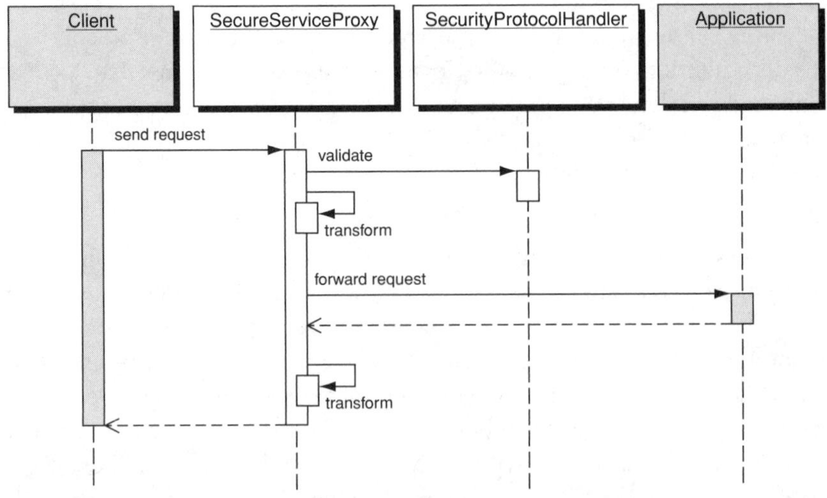

Figure 9–23 Secure Service Proxy sequence diagram

In the sequence shown in Figure 9–23, a Secure Service Proxy provides security to an Enterprise Service. The following are the participants.

Client. An end user making a request from a Web browser.

SecureServiceProxy. The SecureServiceProxy is responsible for intercepting and validating client requests and then forwarding them to an enterprise service.

SecurityProtocolHandler. The SecurityProtocolHandler validates requests based on the protocols supported by the enterprise service and the client.

EnterpriseService. An existing application or service that cannot or should not be modified to support additional security protocols.

In Figure 9–23, the following sequence takes place.

1. Client sends request to the EnterpriseService.
2. SecureServiceProxy intercepts request.
3. SecureServiceProxy uses SecurityProtocolHandler to validate the request.
4. SecureServiceProxy transforms request to a protocol suitable for EnterpriseService.
5. SecureServiceProxy forwards the request to EnterpriseService.
6. SecureServiceProxy transforms the response from the EnterpriseService to the Client's protocol.
7. SecureServiceProxy forwards response to the Client.

Strategies

The Secure Service Proxy can represent a single service or act as a service coordinator, orchestrating multiple services. A Secure Service Proxy may act as a façade exposing a coarse-grained interface to many fine-grained services, coordinating the interaction between those services, maintaining security context and transaction state between service invocations, and transforming the output of one service to the input format expected by any other service. This avoids having the client make any changes in the code if the service implementations and interfaces change over time.

Single-Service Secure Service Proxy Strategy

The Single-Service Secure Service Proxy Strategy acts as a router to a single service. It performs message authentication, authorization, and message translation. Upon receiving a message, it authenticates and authorizes it. Then, depending on the inbound protocol and the protocol expected by the service, it performs the necessary transformation. For example, the service may be expecting a SOAP message and the client may be sending an HTTP request. The Secure Service Proxy extracts the request parameters, generates a SOAP message with those parameters, and forwards the message to the service. In effect, the Secure Service Proxy has translated the security protocol used by the client to that expected by the service.

This is also useful for retrofitting newer security protocols to legacy applications. If you want to provide a Web service façade to an existing application that expects a security token in the form of a cookie, you need to adapt the Web services security protocol requirement (e.g., SAML token) to support the legacy format or rewrite the application. Since you may not be able to change the code for the legacy application, or it may prove too cumbersome, you are better off using the Single Service Secure Service Proxy Strategy. That way, the Secure Service Proxy can perform the necessary translation, independent of the existing service. This reduces effort and complexity and is less likely to introduce bugs or security holes.

Multi-Service Controller Secure Service Proxy Strategy

The Multi-Service Secure Service Proxy Strategy is similar to the Single Service Secure Service Proxy Strategy. However, it manages state between service calls and provides multi-protocol translation for multiple clients and services. Therefore, it needs to understand which service it is translating and to provide the appropriate transformation. In this case, you may have some services that expect SOAP messages, some services that expect HTTP requests, and some services that expect IIOP requests.

In the Multi-Service Secure Service Proxy Strategy, the Secure Service proxy becomes a state-based router. It may translate between several inbound and outbound protocols. Often, this is desirable if the work that goes into the translation is so complex that you do not want to create multiple single service secure proxies or deal with multiple code bases of largely redundant code. Doing so increases the risk of fixing a security hole in one codebase and then failing to migrate the fix to the other codebases.

Sample Code

Example 9–20 provides a sample service proxy single service strategy.

Example 9–20 Secure Service Proxy Single Service Strategy Sample Code

```
package com.csp.web;

public class ServiceProxyEndpoint extends HTTPServlet {
   /**
    * Process the HTTP Post request,
    */
```

```
    public void doPost(HttpServletRequest request,
                       HttpServletResponse response)
       throws ServletException, IOException {

       // Get the appropriate service proxy based on the request parameter
       // which contains the service identifier
       SecureServiceProxy proxy =
          ProxyFactory.getProxy(request.getQueryString());

       ((HTTPProxy)proxy).init(request, response);

       //Make the request pass through security validation
       if(!proxy.validateSecurityContext(request))

request.getRequestDispatcher("unauthorizedMessage").forward(request,
           response);
       //Have the proxy process the request
       proxy.process();
       //Finally, send the response back to the client
       proxy.respond();
    }
}

// This interface must be implemented by all service proxies.
public interface SecureServiceProxy {
   public boolean validateSecurityContext();
   public void process();
   public void respond();
}

// This interface, that caters to process and respond to HTTP requests,
// must be implemented by a HTTP Proxy
public interface HTTPProxy extends SecureServiceProxy {
   public void init(HttpServletRequest request,
      HttpServletResponse response);
}

/**
 * This is a sample proxy class that uses HTTP for client-to-proxy
 * communication and SOAP for proxy-to-service communication
 * It is responsible for security validations and message translations,
 * that involve marshalling and unmarshalling messages in one format to
 * another
 */
```

```
public class SimpleSOAPServiceSecureProxy implements HTTPProxy {
   private HttpServletRequest request;
   private HttpServletResponse response;
   private SOAPMessage input;
   private SOAPMessage output;

   public void init(HttpServletRequest request, HttpServletResponse
response)
   {
      this.request = request;
      this.response = response;
   }

   //validates the security credentials in the request
   public boolean validateSecurityContext(HttpServletRequest request) {
      HttpSession session = request.getSession();
      LoginContext lc = session.getAttribute("LoginContext");

      if(lc == null)
         Return false;

      if(!AuthenticationProvider.verify(lc))
         return false;

      if(!AuthorizationProvider.authorize(lc, request))
         return false;

      return true;
   }

   public void process() {
      MessageFactory factory = MessageFactory.newInstance();
      input = factory.createSOAPMessage(request);
      SOAPService service =
         SOAPService.getService(request.getParameter("action"));
      output = service.execute(input);
   }

   public void respond() {
      response.write(output.getHTTPResponse());
   }
}
```

Consequences

- *Application firewall capability.* Secure Service Proxy can act as an application firewall, curbing malicious requests and preventing them from reaching mission-critical, lightweight Web applications. It can also perform network address translation, shielding the Web infrastructure from the outside world. A smart Secure Service Proxy can monitor the number and frequency of requests from clients, potentially suppressing denial-of-service traffic from specific clients or determining the quality of service assigned to those clients.
- *Provides flexibility with a loosely coupled architecture.* The Secure Service Proxy pattern provides a loosely coupled approach to providing security across protocols. It translates protocol-specific security semantics between clients and existing services, allowing those services to be accessed by clients that otherwise would not have been able to use those services due to protocol impedance mismatch.
- *Enables integration of security mechanisms with legacy systems.* Security architects and developers can quickly implement a sufficient security solution for legacy applications using Secure Service Proxy, which acts as an adapter for non-J2EE applications while using the J2EE security infrastructure. Secure Service Proxy takes the responsibility of authentication and authorization before forwarding the request to security-unaware legacy applications.
- *Improves scalability.* Secure Service Proxy can delay input validation until the requester is authenticated and authorized, thus avoiding resource wastage caused by misuse of the system by attackers. The proxy can also store the session between requests from the client and manage the security context used in service calls, offloading that burden from lightweight, thin Web services. All these factors enhance scalability of the system.

Security Factors and Risks

Request Specification and Service Identifier. Since the Secure Service Proxy is intended to cater to multiple services with a common client interface, the specification of such an interface must be properly communicated to the clients along with the enumeration of exposed methods and operations.

Reality Check

Is Secure Service Proxy *really required?* If the Secure Service Proxy is written with the only goal of restricting access to applications differentiated by the URL pattern, an out-of-the-box product utilized with the Intercepting Web Agent pattern (mentioned later in this chapter) can serve the same needs without custom code development. The Secure Service Proxy is generally only required when you must integrate with an existing service's legacy security protocol.

Too service specific? A generic, multiprotocol Secure Service Proxy must be written in such a way that new applications and protocol mechanisms can be easily added to the existing proxy.

Related Patterns

Proxy [GoF]. A Proxy acts as a surrogate or placeholder. The Intercepting Web Agent acts as a security proxy for the Web application that it protects.

Intercepting Web Agent [Web Tier]. The Intercepting Web Agent can also retrofit security onto existing Web applications. However, it is not well suited for when your resources do not correspond to URLs or when you need fine-grained access control.

Secure Message Router [Web Services Tier]. The secure Message Router acts as an intermediary that applies and reapplies—or even transforms—the message-level security context before delivering the message to the destination service. The output of this pattern is a securely wrapped message that can traverse again in an insecure channel.

Extract Adapter [Kerievsky]. The Extract Adapter is similar to the Secure Service Proxy because it recommends using one class to adapt multiple versions of a component, library, or API.

Intercepting Web Agent

Problem

Retrofitting authentication and authorization into an existing Web application is cumbersome and costly.

It is often necessary to provide authentication and authorization for an existing application or to retrofit an application that has already been designed with a security architecture. Security is often overlooked or postponed until after the functional pieces of the application have been designed. After an application is deployed, or after it has been mostly implemented, it is very difficult to implement the authentication, authorization, and auditing mechanisms.

Forces

- You do not want to or cannot modify the existing application.
- You want to completely decouple the authentication and authorization from an existing application.
- You want to leverage out-of-the-box security from reliable third-party vendors rather than try to implement your own.

Solution

Use an Intercepting Web Agent to provide authentication and authorization external to the application by intercepting requests prior to the application.

Using an Intercepting Web Agent protects the application by providing authentication and authorization of requests outside the application. For example, you inherit an application with little or no security and you are tasked with providing proper authentication and authorization. Rather than attempt to modify the code or rewrite the Web tier, use an Intercepting Web Agent to provide the proper protection for the application. The Intercepting Web Agent can be installed on the Web server and provide authentication and authorization of incoming requests by intercepting them and enforcing access control policy at the Web server.

The decoupling of security from the application provides the ideal approach to securing existing applications that can't do so themselves or that are too difficult to modify. It also provides centralized management of the security-related components. Policy and the details of its implementation are enforced outside the application and can therefore be changed, usually without affecting the application. Third-party products from a variety of vendors provide security using the Intercepting Web Agent pattern.

The Intercepting Web Agent improves maintainability by isolating application logic from security logic. Typically, the implementation requires no code changes, just configuration. It also increases application performance by moving security-related processing out of the application and onto the Web server. Requests that are not properly authenticated or authorized are rejected at the Web server and thus use no extra cycles in the application.

Structure

Figure 9–24 is a class diagram of an Intercepting Web Agent.

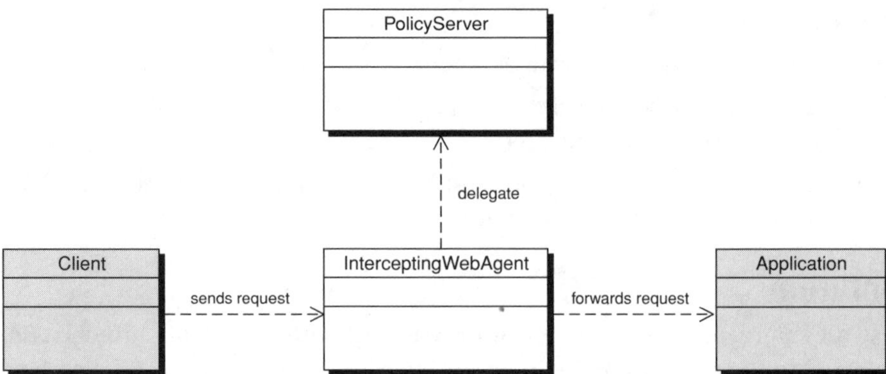

Figure 9–24 Intercepting Web Agent class diagram

Participants and Responsibilities

Figure 9–25 shows the sequence diagram for the Intercepting Web Agent.

Client. A client performs a login and then sends a request to the Application.

WebServer. The Web Server delegates handling of the request to the InterceptingWebAgent.

InterceptingWebAgent. The InterceptingWebAgent intercepts the request and checks that it is properly authenticated and authorized before forwarding it to the Application.

Application. The Application processes the request without needing to perform any security checks.

Figure 9–25 takes us through a typical sequence of events for an application employing an Intercepting Web Agent. The Intercepting Web Agent is located either on the Web server or between the Web server and the application, external to the application. The Web Server delegates handling of the requests for the application to the Intercepting Web Agent. It, in turn, checks authentication and authorization of the requests before forwarding to the application itself. When attempting to access the application, the client will be prompted by the Intercepting Web Agent to log in.

Figure 9–25 illustrates the following sequence of events:

1. Client sends a login request to the Application.
2. The WebServer delegates this request to the InterceptingWebAgent.
3. The InterceptingWebAgent performs authentication of the passed-in user credentials.

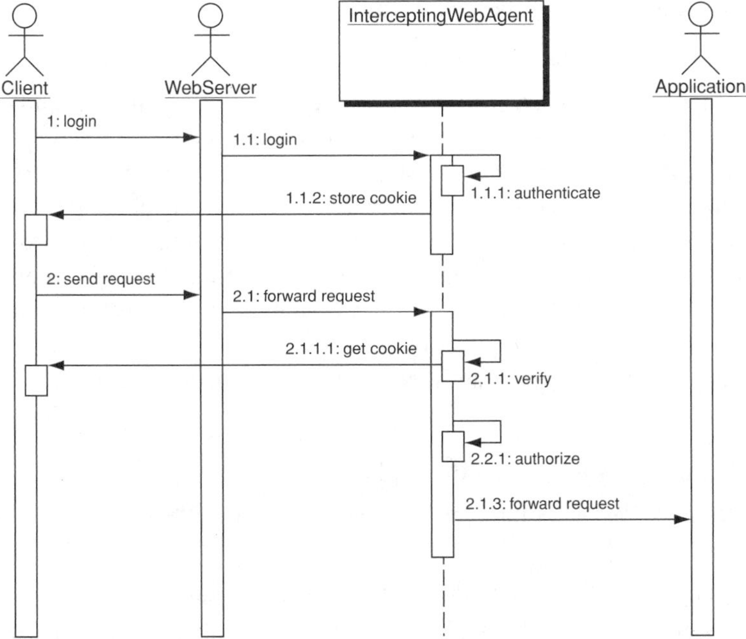

Figure 9–25 Intercepting Web Agent sequence diagram

4. The InterceptingWebAgent stores a cookie with encrypted session information on the Client.
5. The Client sends a request to the Application.
6. The WebServer delegates handling of the request to the InterceptingWebAgent.
7. The InterceptingWebAgent gets the cookie it stored on the Client and verifies it.
8. The InterceptingWebAgent checks that the Client is authorized to send the request (usually through a URL mapping).
9. The InterceptingWebAgent forwards the request to the Application for processing.

Strategies

External Policy Server Strategy

The External Policy Server Strategy is the strategy that most third-party vendors implement. With an External Policy Strategy, user and policy data are stored externally to the Web server. This is done for a variety of reasons.

- You have multiple Web servers, but only need one user and policy store.
- Web servers usually live in the DMZ, and you do not want user and policy information out where it is more susceptible to compromise.

- You want to segregate responsibility of authentication from enforcement of it.

The External Policy Server Strategy provides centralized storage and management of user and policy information that can be accessed by all Intercepting Web Agents on different Web servers. Using an external policy server, performance can be improved through caching. Load balancing and failover are possible due to the use of cookies and separation of authentication and authorization from particular Web Agent instances. The External Policy Server itself must be replicated.

Figure 9–26 depicts the interaction between a client and an Intercepting Web Agent that is protecting an application.

The sequence of events for an Intercepting Web Agent using and external Policy Server is:

1. Client attempts to log into the application.
2. Intercepting Web Agent intercepts request and authenticates the Client with the PolicyServer.
3. Upon successful authentication, Client sends a request to the Application.
4. Intercepting Web Agent intercepts request and authenticates it using the information stored in a cookie.
5. Intercepting Web Agent authorizes the request using the PolicyServer.
6. Upon successful authorization, Intercepting Web Agent forwards the request to the Application.

Consequences

Using the Intercepting Web Agent, developers and architects gain the following:

- *Helps defend Replay and DoS attacks.* Many of the vendor implementations perform tasks beyond just authentication and authorization. They provide auditing, reporting, and forensic capabilities as well. In addition, they perform filtering and weed out replay of forged requests and DoS attacks.
- *Provides more flexibility with a loosely coupled architecture.* The Intercepting Web Agent pattern provides a loosely coupled connection to remote security services. It also avoids specific-vendor product lock-in by disallowing clients to invoke the remote security services directly. This allows developers to quickly add authentication and authorization to their new or existing Web applications. Since the vendors provide the authentication and authorization implementation, you have a more tried and true security solution.

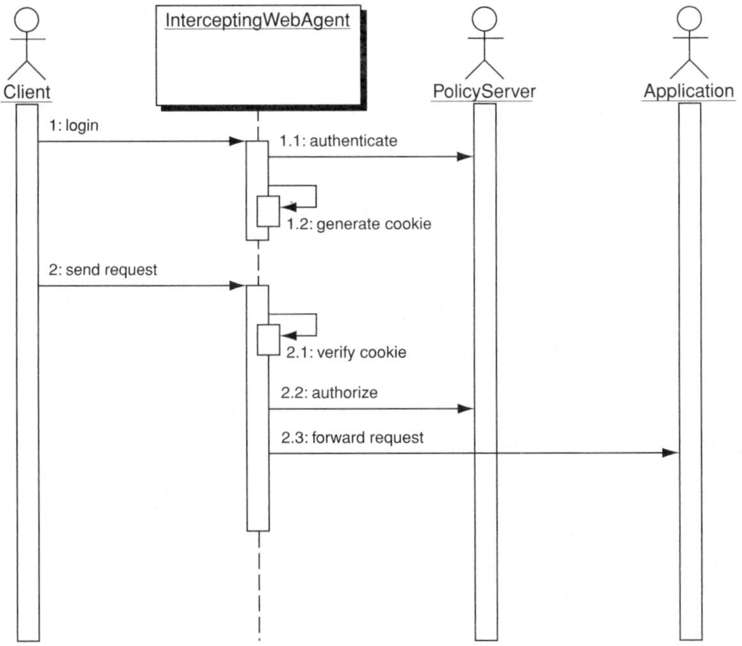

Figure 9–26 Intercepting Web Agent using External Policy Server sequence diagram

- *Supports legacy integration.* Security architects and developers can quickly implement a sufficient security solution for legacy Web applications by employing the Intercepting Web Agent. Because the Intercepting Web Agent can be used outside the application (usually on the Web server), legacy code does not have to be altered. This allows authentication and authorization to be retrofitted into an existing application.
- *Improves scalability.* Because the Intercepting Web Agent is typically implemented on the Web server, it scales horizontally. This scaling can be accomplished in a manner completely independent of the application, thus decoupling security overhead from application performance. This assumes of course that the matching components in the Identity tier can scale as well.

Sample Code

Example 9–21 is a sample obj.conf configuration file for a SiteMinder WebAgent running on a Sun Java System Web Server. Example 9–22 is the corresponding magnus.conf file for the WebAgent.

Example 9–21 Sun Java System Web Server obj.conf using CA SiteMinder Web Agent

```
<Object name="MyForms" ppath="*/MyForms/*">
  AuthTrans fn="SiteMinderAgent"
  NameTrans fn="document-root" root=""
  PathCheck fn="SmRequireAuth"
  PathCheck fn="unix-uri-clean"
  PathCheck fn="check-acl" acl="default"
  PathCheck fn="find-pathinfo"
  PathCheck fn="find-index" index-names="index.html,home.html"
  ObjectType fn="type-by-extension"
  ObjectType fn="force-type" type="text/plain"
  Service method="(GET|POST|HEAD)" type="magnus-internal/fcc" fn="SmLoginFcc"
  Service method="(GET|HEAD)" type="magnus-internal/scc" fn="smGetCred"
  Service method="(GET|HEAD)" type="magnus-internal/ccc" fn="smMakeCookie"
  Service method="(GET|POST|HEAD)" type="magnus-internal/sfcc"
    fn="SmSSLLoginFcc"
  Service method="(GET|HEAD|POST)" type="*~magnus-internal/*" fn="send-file"
  AddLog fn="flex-log" name="access"
</Object>
<Object name="default">
  NameTrans fn="pfx2dir" from="/smreportscgi" dir="/usr/siteminder/reports"
    name="cgi"
  NameTrans fn="pfx2dir" from="/sitemindercgi" dir="/usr/siteminder/admin"
    name="cgi"
  NameTrans fn="pfx2dir" from="/siteminder" dir="/usr/siteminder/admin"
  NameTrans fn="pfx2dir" from="/netegrity_docs" dir="/usr/siteminder/
    netegrity_documents"
  NameTrans fn="NSServletNameTrans" name="servlet"
  NameTrans fn="pfx2dir" from="/siteminderagent/pwcgi" dir="/usr/siteminder/
    webagent/pw" name="cgi"
  NameTrans fn="pfx2dir" from="/siteminderagent/pw" dir="/usr/siteminder/
    webagent/pw"
  NameTrans fn="pfx2dir" from="/siteminderagent/certoptional" dir="/usr/
    siteminder/webagent/samples"
  NameTrans fn="pfx2dir" from="/siteminderagent/jpw" dir="/usr/siteminder/
    webagent/jpw"
  NameTrans fn="pfx2dir" from="/siteminderagent" dir="/usr/siteminder/
    webagent/samples"
  NameTrans fn="pfx2dir" from="/servlet" dir="/usr/iplanet/web/docs/servlet"
    name="ServletByExt"
  NameTrans fn=pfx2dir from=/mc-icons dir="/usr/iplanet/web/ns-icons"
    name="es-internal"
```

```
  NameTrans fn="pfx2dir" from="/manual" dir="/usr/iplanet/web/manual/https"
    name="es-internal"
  NameTrans fn=document-root root="$docroot"
  PathCheck fn=unix-uri-clean
  PathCheck fn="check-acl" acl="default"
  PathCheck fn=find-pathinfo
  PathCheck fn=find-index index-names="index.html,home.html"
  ObjectType fn=type-by-extension
  ObjectType fn=force-type type=text/plain
  Service type="magnus-internal/jsp" fn="NSServletService"
  Service fn="send-cgi" type="magnus-internal/cgi"
  Service method=(GET|HEAD) type=magnus-internal/imagemap fn=imagemap
  Service method=(GET|HEAD) type=magnus-internal/directory fn=index-common
  Service method=(GET|HEAD|POST) type=*~magnus-internal/* fn=send-file
  AddLog fn=flex-log name="access"
</Object>
```


Example 9–21 Sun Java System Web Server magnus.conf with CA SiteMinder Web Agent

```
Init fn="load-modules" funcs="wl_proxy,wl_init" shlib=/usr/iplanet/web/
     plugins/nsapi/wls7/libproxy.so
Init fn="wl_init"
Init fn=flex-init access="$accesslog" format.access="%Ses->client.ip%
  - %Req->vars.auth-user% [%SYSDATE%] \"%Req->reqpb.clf-request%\"
  %Req->srvhdrs.clf-status% %Req->srvhdrs.content-length%"
Init fn=load-types mime-types=mime.types
Init fn="load-modules" shlib="/usr/iplanet/web/bin/https/lib/
  libNSServletPlugin.so" funcs=
  "NSServletEarlyInit,NSServletLateInit,NSServletNameTrans,NSServletService"
shlib_flags="(global|now)"
Init fn="NSServletEarlyInit" EarlyInit=yes
Init fn="NSServletLateInit" LateInit=yes
SSL2 off
SSL3 off
SSLClientCert off
Init fn="load-modules" shlib="/usr/siteminder/webagent/lib/NSAPIWebAgent.so"
funcs="SmInitAgent,SiteMinderAgent,SmRequireAuth,SmLoginFcc,smGetCred,smMake
Cookie,SmSSLLoginFcc" LateInit="no"
Init fn="SmInitAgent" config="/usr/iplanet/web/https-pluto/config/
  WebAgent.conf" LateInit="no"
Init fn="init-cgi" SM_ADM_UDP_PORT="44444" SM_ADM_TCP_PORT="44444"
```

Security Factors and Risks

The following are security factors and risks pertaining to use of the Intercepting Web Agent pattern.

- **Infrastructure**. This pattern assumes that the Web server is secured. If attackers are able to compromise the Web server, they may be able to modify the configuration files and disable or subvert the authentication and authorization process. It is therefore very important to harden the host machine and to implement an intrusion detection system on the Web server.
- **Authentication and authorization**. This pattern does not work well when your resources do not correspond to URLs or you need finer-grained access control that can only be accomplished at the application layer. For those instances, you should consider using a Secure Base Action and supporting patterns, which are discussed earlier in this chapter.
- **Legacy Integration**. It is often not possible for business reasons to add security mechanisms to a legacy application. The Intercepting Web Agent is a great pattern for retrofitting security onto existing Web applications. Several vendors provide mature products that implement this pattern. These third-party products are widely used and provide a variety of features out of the box.

Reality Check

Should I build or buy? Unless you have specific functional requirements that cannot be met by the products out there in the market today, consider buying. There are several third-party products that provide Intercepting Web Agent capabilities and many of them are mature, meaning that the bugs have been worked out. The products will generally provide more robust functionality and will typically scale better than a home-grown solution.

Too coarse-grained. The Intercepting Web Agent pattern is ideal for legacy applications, but often it is too coarse-grained for current business requirements. Assuming you purchase a third-party product, that product probably only allows access-control decisions down to the URL level. In today's Web applications, the URL level is too coarse-grained. With industry-standard frameworks such as Struts, it is necessary to go beyond just the URL level and into the request parameters for fine-grained access-control decisions. For those situations, an Intercepting Web Agent may not be an appropriate pattern.

Related Patterns

Secure Service Proxy [Web Tier]. A Secure Service Proxy acts as a security protocol translator. Like the Intercepting Web Agent, it intercepts requests and performs security validations. The Intercepting Web Agent on the other hand, performs all of the security functions itself, not relying on the services it protects for anything.

Proxy [GoF]. A Proxy acts as a surrogate or placeholder. The Intercepting Web Agent acts as a security proxy for the Web application that it protects.

Message Interceptor Gateway [Web Services Tier]. The Intercepting Web Agent is similar to the Message Interceptor Gateway. It acts as a translator in the same regard, the only difference being that its purpose is for security protocol translation and not message translation.

Best Practices and Pitfalls

Security is a goal that spans every tier and layer. To ensure a comprehensive security solution, best practices must span these tiers and layers as well. This section contains a summary of best practices that should be applied to the Web tier. They are categorized loosely by layer. Not all of them pertain specifically to the patterns outlined in this chapter, but they do pertain to securing the Web tier and therefore should be used in conjunction with the Web tier security patterns.

It is important to remember that deficiencies in one layer may invalidate all the other efforts in the other layers. An attacker only needs one hole to compromise the application. You can harden the operating system, construct a DMZ, use SSL, and audit every transaction, but if an attacker can guess an administrator's passwords, these efforts were in vain. Take care to review all of the following best practices to ensure a cohesive security approach.

Infrastructure

1. *Put Web Servers in a DMZ.* Secure the Internet-facing Web server host in a DMZ (Demilitarized Zone) using an exterior firewall. It is always a recommended option to use DMZ bastion hosts or switched connections to target Web servers. This will prevent attackers who have compromised the Web server from penetrating deeper into the application.
2. *Use Stateful Firewalls.* Use a stateful firewall inspection to keep track of all Web-tier transmissions and protocol sessions. Make sure it blocks all unrequested protocol transmissions.

3. *Drop Non-HTTP Packets*. Make sure your firewall is configured to drop connections except for HTTP and HTTP over SSL. This will help prevent Denial of Service (DoS) attacks and disallow malicious packets intended for back-end systems.
4. *Minimize and Harden the Web Server Operating System*. Make sure the operating system that is running the Web and application server is hardened and does not run any unsolicited services that may provide an opening for an attacker to compromise.
5. *Secure Administrative Communications*. Make sure all administration tasks on the server are done using encrypted communication. Disable remote administration of Web and application servers using system-level and root administrator access. All remote administration needs to be carried out using secure-shell connections from trusted machines and disallow administrator access from untrusted machines.
6. *Disallow Untrusted Services*. Disable telnet, remote login services, and FTP connections to the server machines. These are commonly attacked services and represent a strong security risk.
7. *Check Web Server User Permissions*. Make sure the running Web and application servers' configurations and their user privileges have no rights to access or to modify system files.
8. *Disable CGI*. Unless required, disable running CGI applications in the Web server or application server and accessing /cgi-bin directories. This is another common source of attacks.
9. *Enforce Strong Passwords*. Change all default passwords and use robust password mechanisms to avoid password-related vulnerabilities such as sniffing and replay attacks. For all application-level administrators, use password ageing, account locking, and password-complexity verification. Using one-time password mechanisms, dynamic passwords that use challenge-response schemes, smart card- and certificate-based authentication, and multifactor authentication are reliable practices.
10. *Audit Administration Operations*. Limit all Web administration access to the system to very few users. Monitor their account validity, log all their administration operations using encryption mechanisms, and make sure that system log files are written to a different machine that is secure from the rest of the network.
11. *Check Third-Party IPs*. All third-party supporting applications that are required to coexist with the Web and application servers have to be tested for their usage of IP and port addresses. Those applications must follow the maintained rules of the DMZ.

12. *Monitor Web Server Communications.* Monitor all transmissions and Web-server requests and responses for suspicious activity and misuse. Use watchdog macros or daemons to monitor and trap these activities. When detection of such abuses occurs, make sure you check the integrity of the application afterward and notify the system security administrator.
13. *Setup IDS.* Use intrusion detection systems to detect suspicious acts, abuses, and unsolicited system uses. Alert security administrators for such activities.
14. *Deny Outbound Traffic to Web Server.* Disallow all application requests to the IP addresses of the Web servers running in the DMZ.
15. *Distrust Servers in the DMZ.* Do not store any user or application-generated information in the DMZ. Store all sensitive information behind the DMZ interior firewall with the expectation that servers running in the DMZ will eventually be compromised. The exception would be a Honeypot, which is a server created specifically to lure attackers into what appears to be the real application. Their activities are then logged and analyzed to help stave offd future attacks.

Communication

16. *Secure the Pipe.* For all security-sensitive Web applications and Web-based online transactions, make sure the session and data exchanged between the server and client remain confidential and tamper-proof during transit. SSL/TLS is the de facto technology for securing communication on the wire. It allows Web-based applications to communicate over a secure communication channel. Using SSL communication with digital certificates offers confidentiality and integrity of data transmitted between the Web applications and client authentication.
17. *Segregate by Sensitivity.* Make sure that Web applications that contain sensitive information and Web applications that do not contain sensitive information run on different machines and different Web-server instances.
18. *Enforce Strong Encryption.* For applications that use classified or financial data, make sure that the Web server does not accept weak encryption. Disable or delete weak encryption cipher suites from the Web server and enforce adequate key lengths.
19. *Don't Flip Back to HTTP from HTTPS.* After switching to SSL communication, make sure the application no longer accepts non-SSL requests until logging out from the SSL session. In the event that the client is sending a non-SSL request, the application must enforce reauthentication of that

user over a new SSL session and then stop listening to non-SSL requests. Verifying SSL requests can be implemented using various Connection filter mechanisms.

20. *Capture Bad Requests.* Log and monitor all fake SSL and non-SSL requests using filters. For all such unsolicited requests, redirect the user to an authentication page to provide valid login credentials.
21. *Use Certificates for Server-to-Server Communications.* To support server-to-server or nonbrowser-based client communications that host secure transactions, always suggest using mutual or client certificate-based authentication over SSL. In this case, the server will authenticate the client using the client's X.509 certificate, a public-key certificate that conforms to a standard that is defined by X.509 Public Key Infrastructure (PKI). This provides a more reliable form of authentication than standard password-based approaches.
22. *Check Mutual Authentication.* Verify that mutual authentication is configured and running properly by examining debug messages. To generate debug messages from SSL mutual authentication, pass the system property javax.net.debug=ssl,handshake to the application, which will provide information on whether or not mutual authentication is working.
23. *Check Certification Expiration.* While authenticating a client using mutual authentication, be sure to check for certificate expiration or revocation.
24. *User SSL Accelerators.* Using hardware-based SSL accelerators enhances secure communication performance because it offloads the cryptographic processing load from the Web server.
25. *Use SGC When Possible.* Consider using Server Gated Cryptography (SGC) mechanisms when possible to ensure the highest level of security for Web applications regardless of browser clients or versions.
26. *Check Export Policies.* Before installing SSL server certificates, make sure that you understand and are in accordance with your country's export policies regarding encryption products containing cryptographic technology. Some countries and organizations may ban or require special licenses for using encryption technologies.

Application

27. *Disallow Direct Access.* Make sure that the application resides on a server accessed via reverse-proxy or Network Address Translation (NAT)-based IP addresses. Then rewrite the URLs of Web applications. This protects the application from direct access from unsolicited users.

28. *Encrypt Application-Specific Properties*. Make sure that all application-specific properties stored on local disks that are exposed to physical access are encrypted or digested using encryption or secure hash mechanisms. Decrypt these entries and verify them before use in the application. This will protect unauthorized access or modification of application-specific parameters.
29. *Restrict Application Administrator Privileges*. Do not create an application administrator user account (that is, admin or root) with explicit administration access and privileges. If someone steals the administrator's password and abuses the application with malicious motives, it is hard to find out who really abused the application. Use the security Principal of the user and assign role-based access by assigning users to the administrator role. This helps in identifying the tasks carried out by the associated Principal with an administrator role.
30. *Validate Request Data*. Verify and validate all user requests and responses and inbound and outbound data exchanged with the application. Apply constraints and verify the input data so that the data does not cause any undesirable side effects on the application.
31. *Validate Form Fields*. Ensure that any alteration, insertion, and removal of HTML form fields by the originating browser are detected, logged, and result in an error message.
32. *Use HTTP POST*. Use HTTP POST rather than HTTP GET and avoid using HTTP GET requests while generating HTML forms. HTTP GET requests reveal URL-appended information, allowing sensitive information to be revealed in the URL string.
33. *Track Sessions*. Identify the originating user and the host destination making the application request in the sessionid. Verify that all subsequent requests are received from that same user's host origin until the user logs out. This protects application sessions from hijacking and spoofing.
34. *Obfuscate Code*. Obfuscate all application-related classes to avoid code misuse. This protects the code from being easily reverse engineered. This should be done for stand-alone Java clients, helper classes, precompiled JSPs, and application JAR files.
35. *Sign JAR Files*. Make sure that all JAR files are signed and sealed before deployment. This includes signing JNLP files (Java Web Start), signed applets, and signed JARs for application server deployments.
36. *Audit All Relevant Security Tasks*. Securely log, audit, and timestamp all relevant application-level events. Audit events should include login

attempts and failures, logouts, disconnects, timeouts, administration tasks, user requests and responses, exceptions, database connections, and so forth. Redirect the log data to a file or database repository residing in another machine. Logging and auditing help to track and identify users with malicious intentions.

37. *Audit All Relevant Business Tasks*. Create audit trails for all identified user-level sessions and actions with timestamps and store them in a different log file with unique line identifiers. This helps in achieving nonrepudiation in both business and technical aspects of the application.

38. *Destroy HTTP Sessions on Logout*. Once a user logs out or exits a security-sensitive application resource, invalidate the HTTP Session and remove all state within the session. Leaving stale sessions on the server often leads to security breaches involving session hijacking, client-side Trojan horses, and eavesdropping on subsequent sessions.

39. *Set Session Timeouts*. Use HTTP session timeouts for all user sessions after a period of inactivity. Redirect the user back to the login page for reauthentication to enable the stored HTTP session state.

References

[Sua] Liz Blair. Build to Spec.

http://java.sun.com/developer/technicalArticles/J2EE/build/build2.html

[WebAppSecurity] Java Web Services Tutorial.

http://java.sun.com/webservices/docs/1.1/tutorial/doc/WebAppSecurity3.html

[Needham] R. M. Needham and M. D. Schroeder. "Using Encryption for Authentication in Large Networks of Computers." *Communications of the ACM*, Vol. 21 (12), pp. 993-99.

[Kerievsky] Joshua Kerievsky, *Refactoring to Patterns*. Addison-Wesley, 2004.

[Vau] David Winterfeldt and Ted Husted. *Struts in Action*, "Chapter 12: Validating User Input."

http://java.sun.com/developer/Books/javaprogramming/struts/struts_chptr_12.pdf

[POSA] Buschmann, Meunier, Rohnert, Sommerlad, and Stal. *Pattern-Oriented Software Architecture—A System of Patterns*. Wiley Press, 1996-2000.

[Gof] Gamma, Helm, Johnson, Vlissides. *Design Patterns: Elements of Reusable Object-Oriented Software*. Addison-Wesley, 1994.

[EIP] Hohpe, Woolf. *Enterprise Integration Patterns*. Addison-Wesley, 2004

[CJP2] Alur, Crupi, and Malks. *Core J2EE Patterns, Second Edition*. Prentice Hall, 2003.

[Java2] The Java™ 2 runtime environment

http://java.sun.com/java2

[RFC1508] RFC 1508–Generic Security Service Application Program Interface

http://www.faqs.org/rfcs/rfc1508.html

[RFC2743] RFC 2743–Generic Security Service Application Program Interface Version 2, Update 1

http://www.faqs.org/rfcs/rfc2743.html

[JAAS] Java Authentication and Authorization Service Developer Guide

http://java.sun.com/security/jaas/doc/api.html

Securing the Business Tier–Design Strategies and Best Practices

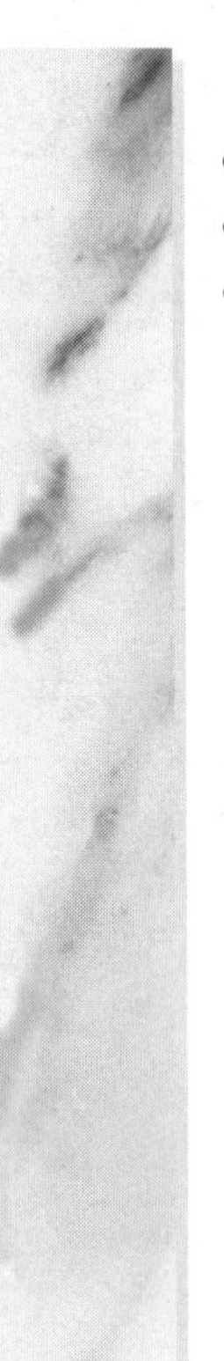

Topics in This Chapter

- Security Considerations in the Business Tier
- Business Tier Security Patterns
- Best Practices and Pitfalls

Chapter 10

In Chapter 9, we discussed the security patterns and best practices related to the Web tier. In this chapter, we will examine security patterns and best practices applicable to the Business tier. The Business tier comprises components responsible for implementing the business logic in the application. These patterns build upon those outlined in *Core J2EE Patterns* [CJP2]. They assume use of certain J2EE patterns and best practices mentioned there as well as industry-recognized approaches.

We will begin by briefly stating prominent security considerations relevant to the Business tier. These security considerations are the driving forces behind the security patterns. We will then dive into a detailed explanation of the security patterns. Finally, we will list some best practices and pitfalls for securing the Business tier.

Security Considerations in the Business Tier

Several security considerations pertain to the Business tier, most of which will be discussed alongside the security patterns that address them. One of them is whether or not your Business tier will be colocated with your Web tier. This can affect which of the patterns you use and the performance overhead related to those patterns. While it is generally a good idea to design for a remote Business tier in order to support scalability, the performance benefit and reduced complexity of a colocated design often outweigh the scalability concerns. If a distributed approach is required, there is an issue with propagating the security context from the Web tier to the Business tier. Propagation of the security context must also be addressed by applications that pass data across to other security-aware components, including J2EE connectors and message-oriented middleware via Java Message Service (JMS).

Auditing is a key security requirement for mission-critical applications as well as a general requirement for financial applications. The J2EE 1.4 specifications, while mentioning auditing, does not specify requirements for auditing [SPEC]. Thus, there is no standard approach to auditing prescribed in the specification; auditing must therefore be addressed by developers.

The Business tier contains the bulk of business processing logic. It will often contain large amounts of mature business functionalities as components or helper classes—legacy code from earlier versions of the application, framework code from internal projects, or even open source libraries. This code is usually reused across classes, and it is therefore a challenge to safeguard them. The J2EE platform facilitates a container-managed security mechanism, but it does not address code accessed in different security contexts and based on the data passed to it, or "instance-based" access control, as it refers to it.

Business Tier Security Patterns

Audit Interceptor

Problem

You want to intercept and audit requests and responses to and from the Business tier.

Auditing is an essential part of any security design. Most enterprise applications have security-audit requirements. A security audit allows auditors to reconcile actions or events that have taken place in the application with the policies that govern those actions. In this manner, the audit log serves as a record of events for the application. This record can then be used for forensic purposes following a security breach.

That record must be checked periodically to ensure that the actions that users have taken are in accordance with the actions allowed by their roles. Deviations must be noted from audit reports, and corrective actions must be taken to ensure those deviations do not happen in the future, either through code fixes or policy changes. The most important part of this procedure is recording the audit trail and making sure that the audit trail helps proper auditing of appropriate events and user actions associated. These events and actions are often not completely understood or defined prior to construction of the application. Therefore, it is essential that an auditing framework is able to easily support additions or changes to the auditing events.

Forces

- You want centralized and declarative auditing of service requests and responses.
- You want auditing of services decoupled from the applications themselves.
- You want pre- and post-process audit handling of service requests, response errors, and exceptions

Solution

Use an Audit Interceptor to centralize auditing functionality and define audit events declaratively, independent of the Business tier services.

An Audit Interceptor intercepts Business tier requests and responses. It creates audit events based on the information in a request and response using declarative mechanisms defined externally to the application. By centralizing auditing functionality, the burden of implementing it is removed from the back-end business component developers. Therefore, there is reduced code replication and increased code reuse.

A declarative approach to auditing is crucial to maintainability of the application. Seldom are all the auditing requirements correctly defined prior to implementation. Only through iterations of auditing reviews are all of the correct events captured and the extraneous events discarded. Additionally, auditing requirements often change as corporate and industry policies evolve. To keep up with these changes and avoid code maintainability problems, it is necessary to define audit events in a declarative manner that does not require recompilation or redeployment of the application. Since the Audit Interceptor is the centralized point for auditing, any required programmatic change is isolated to one area of the code, which increases code maintainability.

Structure

Figure 10–1 depicts the class diagram for the Audit Interceptor pattern. The Client attempts to access the Target. The AuditInterceptor class intercepts the request and uses the AuditEventCatalog to determine if an audit event should be written to the AuditLog.

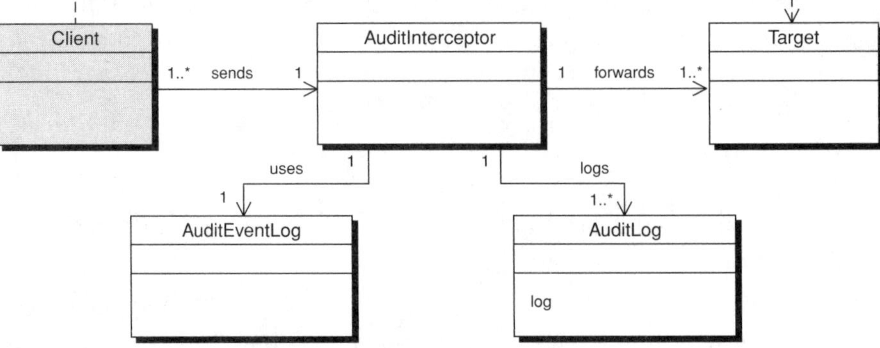

Figure 10–1 Audit Interceptor class diagram

Figure 10–2 shows the sequence of events for the Audit Interceptor pattern. The Client attempts to access the Target, not knowing that the Audit Interceptor is an intermediary in the request. This approach allows clients to access services in the typical manner without introducing new APIs or interfaces specific to auditing that the client would otherwise not care about.

The diagram in Figure 10–2 does not reflect the implementation of how the request is intercepted, but simply illustrates that the AuditInterceptor receives the request and then forwards it to the Target.

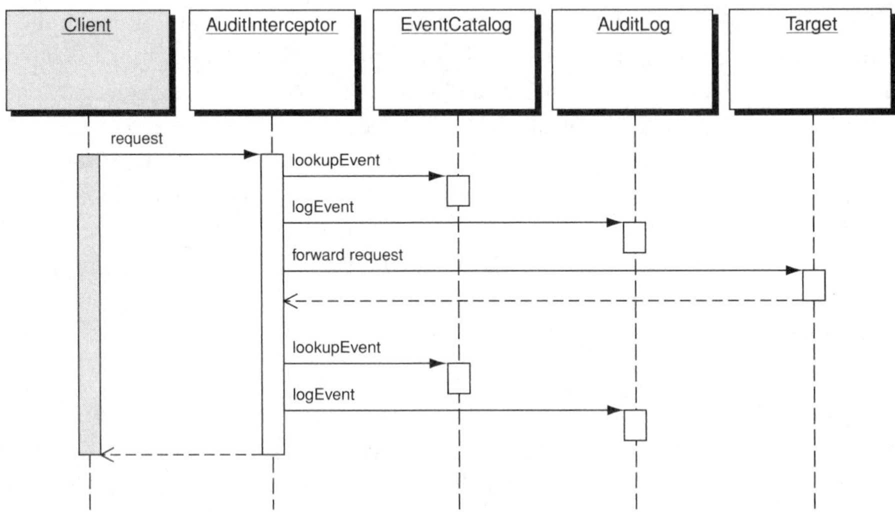

Figure 10–2 Audit Interceptor sequence diagram

Participants and Responsibilities

Client. A client sends a request to the Target.

AuditInterceptor. The AuditInterceptor intercepts the request. It encapsulates the details of auditing the request.

EventCatalog. The EventCatalog maintains a mapping of requests to audit events. It hides the details of managing the life cycle of a catalog from an external source.

AuditLog. AuditLog is responsible for writing audit events to a destination. This could be a database table, flat file, JMS queue, or any other persistent store.

Target. The Target is any Business-tier component that would be accessed by a client. Typically, this is a business object or other component that sits behind a SessionFaçade, but not the SessionFaçade itself, because it would mostly be the entry point that invokes the AuditInterceptor.

The Audit Interceptor pattern is illustrated in the following steps (see Figure 10–2):

1. Client attempts to access Target resource.
2. AuditInterceptor intercepts request and uses EventCatalog to determine which, if any, audit event to generate and log.
3. AuditInterceptor uses AuditLog to log audit event.
4. AuditInterceptor forwards request to Target resource.
5. AuditInterceptor uses EventCatalog to determine if the request response or any exceptions raised should generate an audit event.
6. AuditInterceptor uses AuditLog to log generated audit event.

Strategies

The Audit Interceptor pattern provides a flexible, unobtrusive approach to auditing Business tier events. It offers developers an easy-to-use approach to capturing audit events—by decoupling auditing from the business flow. This allows business developers to disregard auditing and defer the onus to the security developers, who then only deal with auditing in a centralized location. Auditing can easily be retrofitted into an application using this pattern. By making use of an Event Catalog, the Audit Interceptor becomes decoupled from the actual audit events and therefore can incorporate changes in auditing requirements via a configuration file. The following is a strategy for implementing the Audit Interceptor.

Intercepting Session Façade Strategy

The Audit Interceptor requires that it be inserted into the message flow to intercept requests. The Intercepting Session Façade strategy designates the Session Façade as the point of interception for the Intercepting Auditor. The Session Façade receives the request and then invokes the Audit Interceptor at the beginning of the request and again at the end of the request. Figure 10–3 depicts the class diagram for the Secure Service Façade Interceptor Strategy.

Using a Secure Service Façade Interceptor strategy, developers can audit at the entry and exit points to the Business tier. The SecureServiceFaçade is the appropriate point for audit interception, because its job is to forward to the Application Services and Business Objects. Typically, a request consists of several Business Objects or Application Services, though only one audit event is required for that request. For example, a credit card verification service may consist of one Secure Service Façade that invokes several Business Objects that make up that service, such as an expiration date check, a LUN10 check, and a card type check. It is unlikely that each individual check generates an audit event; it is likely that only the verification service itself generates the event.

In Figure 10–3, the SecureServiceFaçade is the entry to the Business tier. It provides the remote interface that the Client uses to access the target component, such as another EJB or a Business Object. Instead of forwarding directly to the target component, the SecureServiceFaçade first invokes AuditInterceptor. The AuditInterceptor then consults the EventCatalog to determine whether to generate an audit event and, if so, what audit event to generate. If an audit event is generated, the AuditLog is then used to persist the audit event. Afterward, the SecureServiceFaçade then forwards the request as usual to the Target. On the return of invocation of the Target, the SecureServiceFaçade again calls the AuditInterceptor. This allows auditing of both start and end events. Exceptions raised from the invocation of the Target also cause the SecureServiceFaçade to

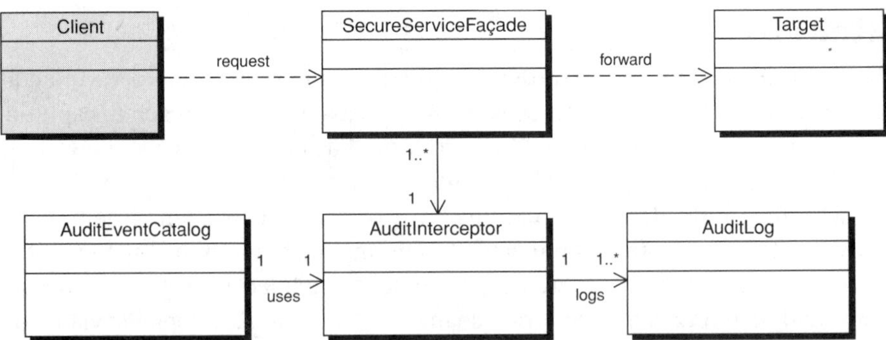

Figure 10–3 Secure Service Façade Interceptor strategy class diagram

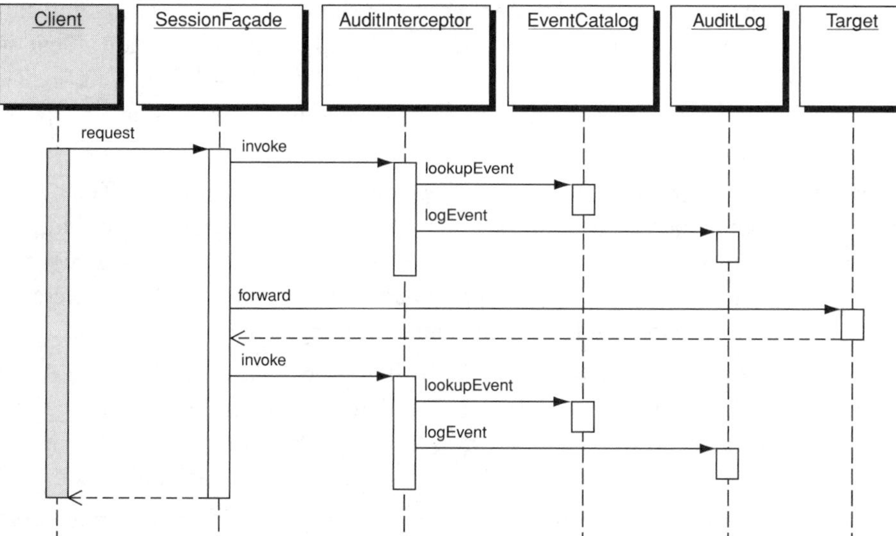

Figure 10–4 Secure Service Façade Interceptor strategy sequence diagram

invoke the AuditInterceptor. More often than not, you want to generate audit events for exceptions.

Figure 10–4 depicts the Secure Service Façade Interceptor strategy sequence diagram.

Consequences

Auditing is one of the key requirements for mission-critical applications. Auditing provides a trail of recorded events that can tie back to a Principal. The Audit Interceptor provides a mechanism to audit Business-tier events so that operations staff and security auditors can go back and examine the audit trail and look for all forms of application-layer attacks. The Audit Interceptor itself does not prevent an attack, but it does provide the ability to capture the events of the attack so that they can later be analyzed. Such an analysis can help prevent future attacks.

The Audit Interceptor pattern has the following consequences for developers:

- *Centralized, declarative auditing of service requests.* The Audit Interceptor centralizes the auditing code within the application. This promotes reuse and maintainability.
- *Pre- and post-process audit handling of service requests.* The Audit Interceptor enables developers to record audit events prior to a method call or after a method call. This is important when considering the business

requirements. Auditing is often required prior to the service or method call as a form of recording an "attempt." In other cases, an audit event is required only after the outcome of the call has been decided. And finally, there are cases where an audit event is needed in the event of an exception with the call.

- *Auditing of services decoupled from the services themselves.* The Audit Interceptor pattern decouples the business logic code from the auditing code. Business developers should not have to consider auditing requirements or implement code to support auditing. By using the Audit Interceptor, auditing can be achieved without impacting business developers.
- *Supports evolving requirements and increases maintainability.* The Audit Interceptor supports evolving auditing requirements by decoupling the events that need to be audited from the implementation. An audit catalog can be created that defines audit events declaratively, thus allowing different event types for different circumstances to be added without changing code. This improves the overall maintainability of the code by reducing the number of changes to it.
- *Reduces performance.* The cost of using an interceptor pattern is that performance is reduced anytime the interceptor is invoked. Every time that Audit Interceptor determines that a request or response does not require generation of an audit event, it unnecessarily decreases performance.

Sample Code

Example 10–1 is sample source code for the AuditRequestMessageBean class. This class is used subsequent to the AuditLog class placing audit events onto the JMS queue and is responsible for pulling audit messages off a JMS queue and writing them to a database using an AuditLogJdbcDAO class (not shown here). It is not reflected in the previous diagrams.

Example 10–1 AuditRequestMessageBean.java: AuditLog

```
package com.csp.audit;
import javax.jms.*;
/**
 * @ejb.bean transaction-type="Container"
 *           acknowledge-mode="Auto-acknowledge"
 *           destination-type="javax.jms.Queue"
 *           subscription-durability="NonDurable"
 *           name="AuditRequestMessageBean"
 *           display-name="Audit Request Message Bean"
```

```
 *          jndi-name=
 *      "com.csp.audit.AuditRequestMessageBean"
 *
 * @ejb:transaction type="NotSupported"
 *
 * @message-driven
 *      destination-jndi-name="Audit_Request_Queue"
 *      connection-factory-jndi-name="Audit_JMS_Factory"
 */
public class AuditRequestMessageBean
      extends MessageDrivenBeanAdapter {
   public void onMessage(Message msg) throws Exception {
      ObjectMessage objMsg = (ObjectMessage)msg;
     try {
         String message = (String)objMsg.getObject();
         JdbcDAOBase dao = (JdbcDAOBase)
            JdbcDAOFactory.getJdbcDAO(
               "com.csp.audit.AuditLogJdbcDAO");
         // The DAO is responsible for actually writing the
         // audit message in the database using the JDBC API.
         dao.executeUpdate(dto);
      }
      catch(Exception ex) {
         System.out.println("Audit event write failed: "
     + ex, ex);
      }
   }

// Other EJB Methods for MessageDrivenBean interface
        public void ejbCreate() {
        System.out.println("ejbCreate called");
      }

      public void ejbRemove() {
        System.out.println("ejbRemove called");
      }

      public void setMessageDrivenContext(MessageDrivenContext context) {
        System.out.println("setMessageDrivenContext called");
        this.context = context;
      }
}
```

Example 10–2 lists the sample source code for the AuditClient class, which is responsible for placing audit event messages on a JMS queue for persisting later. This class is used by the AuditLog class.

Example 10–2 AuditClient.java: Helper class used by AuditInterceptor

```
package com.csp.audit;

import javax.naming.*;
import javax.jms.*;

public class AuditClient {
   private static String JMS_FACTORY_NAME
                              = "Audit_JMS_Factory";
   private static String AUDIT_QUEUE_NAME
                             = "Audit_Request_Queue";
   private static QueueSender queueSender = null;
   private static ObjectMessage objectMessage = null;

  // Initialize the JMS Client
  //  1. Lookup JMS connection factory
  //  2. Create a JMS connection
  //  3. Create a JMS session object
  //  4. Lookup a JMS Queue and Create a JMS sender

  synchronized static void init() throws Exception {
      Context ctx = new InitialContext();
      QueueConnectionFactory cfactory =
         (QueueConnectionFactory) ctx.lookup(
            JMS_FACTORY_NAME);
       QueueConnection queueConnection = (QueueConnection)
          cfactory.createQueueConnection();
      QueueSession queueSession = (QueueSession)
         queueConnection.createQueueSession(
           false, javax.jms.Session.AUTO_ACKNOWLEDGE);
      Queue queue = (Queue)ctx.lookup(AUDIT_QUEUE_NAME);
      queueSender = queueSession.createSender(queue);
      objectMessage = queueSession.createObjectMessage();
   }


  // 5. Send the audit message to the Queue
```

```
    public static void audit(String auditMessage)
    throws Exception{
       try {
          if(queueSender == null || objectMessage == null){
             init();
             objectMessage.setObject(auditMessage);
             queueSender.send(objectMessage);
             return;
          }
          objectMessage.setObject(auditMessage);
          queueSender.send(objectMessage);
       }
       catch(Exception ex) {
          System.out.println("Error sending audit event: "
                             + ex, ex);
          throw ex;
       }
    }
}
```


Security Factors and Risks

The Audit Interceptor pattern provides developers with a standard way of capturing and auditing events in a decoupled manner. Auditing is an essential part of any security architecture. Audit events enable administrators to capture key events that they can later use to reconstruct who did what and when in the system. This is useful in cases of a system crash or in tracking down an intruder if the system is compromised.

Business Tier

Auditing. The Audit Interceptor pattern is responsible for providing a mechanism to capture audit events using an Interceptor approach. It is independent of where the audit information gets stored or how it is retrieved. Therefore, it is necessary to understand the general issues relating to auditing. Typically, audit logs (whether flat files or databases) should be stored separately from the applications, preferably on another machine or even off-site. This prevents intruders from covering their tracks by doctoring or erasing the audit logs. Audit logs should be writable but not updateable, depending on the implementation.

Distributed Security

JMS. The Audit Interceptor pattern is responsible for auditing potentially hundreds or even thousands of events per second in high-throughput systems. In these cases, a scalable solution must be designed to accommodate the high volume of messages. Such a solution would involve dumping the messages onto a persistent JMS queue for asynchronous persistence. In this case, the JMS queue itself must be secured. This can be done by using a JMS product that supports message-level encryption or using some of the other strategies for securing JMS described in Chapter 5. Since the queue must be persistent, you will also need to find a product that supports a secure backing store.

Reality Check

What is the performance cost? The Audit Interceptor adds additional method calls and checks to the request. Using a JMS queue to asynchronously write the events reduces the impact to the end user by allowing the request to complete before the data is actually persisted. The trade-off would be to insert auditing code only where it is required. But anticipating that requirements will change, and a lot of areas that require auditing, the benefits of decoupling and reduced maintenance outweigh the slight performance degradation.

Why not use Aspect Oriented Programming (AOP) techniques instead? AOP provides a new technique that reduces code complexity by consolidating code such as auditing, logging, and other functions that are spread across a variety of methods. It does this by inserting the (aspect) code into the methods either during the build process or through post-compile bytecode insertion. This makes it very useful when you require method-level auditing. The Audit Interceptor allows you to do service-level auditing. It can be as fine-grained as your Service Façade or other client allows, though usually not as fine-grained as AOP allows. The drawback to AOP is that it requires a third-party product and may introduce slight performance penalties, depending on the implementation.

Is auditing essential? In most cases, the answer is yes. It's essential—not just for record-keeping, but for forensic analyses purposes as well. You may not be able to detect—and most likely cannot diagnose—an attack if you do not maintain an audit log of events. The audit log can be used to detect brute-force password attacks, denial of service attacks, and many others.

Related Patterns

Intercepting Filter [CJP2]. The Audit Interceptor pattern is similar to the Intercepting Filter but is not as complex and is better suited for asynchronous writes.

Pipes and Filters [POSA1]. The Audit Interceptor pattern is closely related to the Pipes and Filters pattern.

Message Interceptor Gateway. It is often necessary to audit on the Web Services tier as well as the Business tier. In such cases, the Message Interceptor Gateway should employ the Audit Interceptor pattern.

Container Managed Security

Problem

You need a simple, standard way to enforce authentication and authorization in your J2EE applications and don't want to reinvent the wheel or write home-grown security code.

Using a Container Managed Security pattern, the container performs user authentication and authorization without requiring the developer to hard-wire security policies in the application code. It employs declarative security that requires the developer to only define roles at a desired level of granularity through deployment descriptors of the J2EE resources. The administrator or deployer then uses the container-provided tool to map the roles to the users and groups available in the realm at the time of deployment. A realm is a database of users and their profiles that includes at least usernames and passwords, but can also include role, group, and other pertinent attributes. The actual enforcement of authentication and authorization at runtime is handled by the container in which the application is deployed and is driven by the deployment descriptors. Most containers provide authentication mechanisms by configuring user realms for LDAP, RDBMS, UNIX, and Windows.

Declarative security can be supplemented by programmatic security in the application code that uses J2EE APIs to determine user identity and role membership and thereby enforce enhanced security. In cases where an application chooses not to use a J2EE container, configurable implementation of security similar to Container Managed Security can still be designed by using JAAS-based authentication providers and JAAS APIs for programmatic security.

Forces

- You need to authenticate users and provide access control to business components.
- You want a straightforward, declarative security model based on static mappings.
- You want to prevent developers from bypassing security requirements and inadvertently exposing business functionality.

Solution

Use Container Managed Security to define application-level roles at development time and perform user-role mappings at deployment time or thereafter.

In a J2EE application, both ejb-jar.xml and web.xml deployment descriptors can define container-managed security. The J2EE security elements in the deployment descriptor declare only the logical roles as conceived by the developer. The application deployer maps these application domain logical roles to the deployment environment.

Container Managed Security at the Web tier uses delayed authentication, prompting the user for login only when a protected resource is accessed for the first time. On this tier, it can offer security for the whole application or specific parts of the application that are identified and differentiated by URL patterns. At the Enterprise Java Beans tier, Container Managed Security can offer method-level, fine-grained security or object-level, coarse-grained security.

Structure

Figure 10–5 depicts a generic class diagram for a Container Managed Security implementation. Note that the class diagram can only be applicable to the container's implementation of Container Managed Security. The J2EE application developer would not use such a class structure, because it is already implemented and offered by the container for use by the developer.

Participants and Responsibilities

Figure 10–6 depicts a sequence of operations involved in fulfilling a client request on a protected resource on the Web tier that uses an EJB component on the Business tier. Both tiers leverage Container Managed Security for authentication and access control.

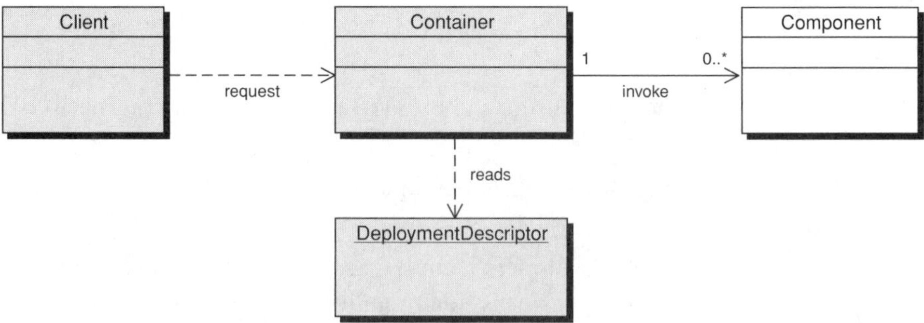

Figure 10–5 Container Managed Security class diagram

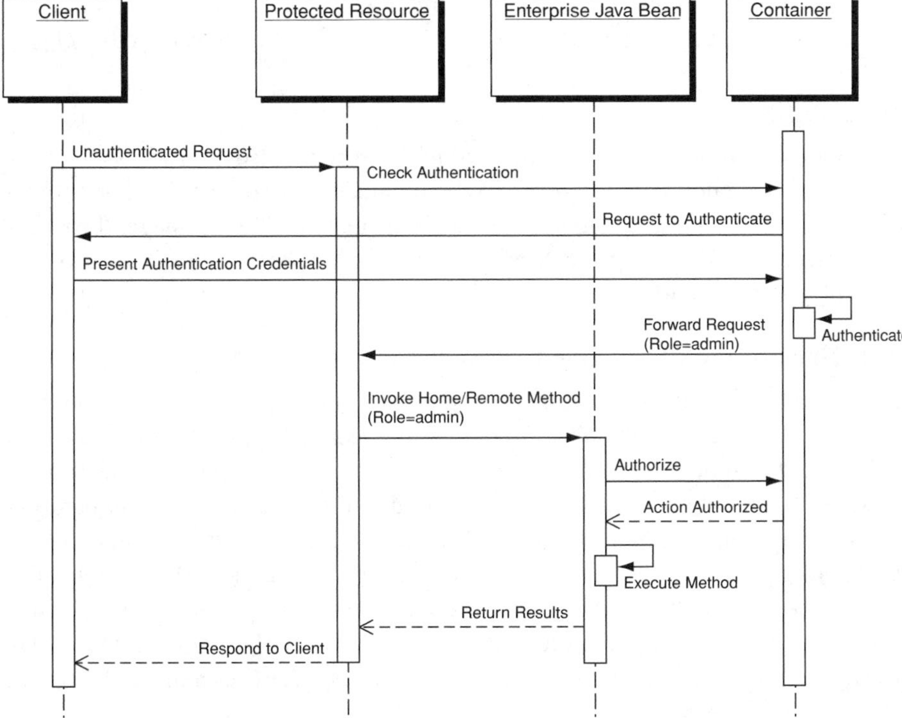

Figure 10–6 Sequence diagram leveraging Container Managed Security

Client. A client sends a request to access a protected resource to perform a specific task.

Container. The container intercepts the request to acquire authentication credentials from the client and thereafter authenticates the client using the realm configured in the J2EE container for the application.

Protected Resource. The security policy of the protected resource is declared via the Deployment Descriptor. Upon authentication, the container uses the Deployment Descriptor information to verify whether the client is authorized to access the protected resource using the method, such as GET and POST, specified in the client request. If authorized, the request is forwarded to the protected resource for fulfillment.

Enterprise Java Bean. The protected resource in turn could be using a Business Tier Enterprise Java Bean that declares its own security policy via the ejb.jar deployment descriptor. The security context of the client is propagated to the EJB container while making the EBJ method invocation. The EJB container intercepts the requests to validate against the security policy much like it did in the Web tier. If authorized, the EJB method is executed, fulfilling the client request. The results of execution of the request are then returned to the client.

Strategies

Container Managed Security can be used in the Web and Business tiers of a J2EE application, depending on whether a Web container, an EJB container, or both are used in an application. It can also be supplemented by Bean Managed/Programmatic Security for fine-grained implementations. The various scenarios are described in this section.

Web Tier Container Managed Security Strategy

In this strategy, security restraints are specified in the web.xml of the client/user-facing Web application (that is, the Web tier of the J2EE application). If this is the only security strategy used in the application, an assumption is made that the back-end Business tier is not directly exposed to the client for direct integration. The web.xml declares the authentication method via the <auth-method> node of the web.xml to mandate either BASIC, DIGEST, FORM, or CLIENT-CERT authentication modes whenever authentication is required. It also declares authorization for protected resources that are identified and distinguished by their URL patterns. The actual enforcement or security is performed by the J2EE-compliant Web container in this strategy.

Service Tier Container Managed Security Strategy

In this strategy, the developer configures the EJB's deployment descriptors to incorporate security into the service backbone of the application. A security role in EJB's ejb-jar.xml is defined through a <security-role-ref> element. These bean-specific logical roles can be associated to a security role defined with a different name in the <role-name> elements of the application deployment descriptor via a <role-link> element. The <assembly-descriptor> section of ejb-jar.xml, which is the application-level deployment descriptor, lists all the logical application-level roles via <role-name> elements, and these roles are mapped to the actual principals in the realm at the time of deployment.

Declarative Security for EJBs can either be at the bean level or at a more granular method level. Home and Remote interface methods can declare a <method-permission> element that includes one or more <role-name> elements that are allowed to access one or more EJB methods as identified by the <method> elements. One can also declare <exclude-list> elements to disable access to specific methods.

To specify an explicit identity that an EJB should use when it invokes methods on other EJBs, the developer can use <use-caller-identity> or <run-as>/<role-name> elements under the <security-identity> element of the deployment descriptor.

Container Manager Security in Conjunction with Programmatic Security

For finer granularity or to meet requirements unfulfilled by Container Managed Security, a developer could choose to use programmatic security in bean code or Web tier code in conjunction with Container Managed Security. For example, in the EJB code, the caller principal as a java.security.Principal instance can be obtained from the EJBContext.getCallerPrincipal() method. The EJBContext.isCallerInRole(String) method can determine if a caller is in a role that is declared with a <security-role-ref> element. Similarly, on the Web tier, HttpServletRequest.getUserPrincipal() returns a java.security.Principal object containing the name of the current authenticated user, and HttpServletRequest.isUserInRole(String) returns a Boolean indicating whether the authenticated user is included in the specified logical role. These APIs are very limited in scope and are confined to determining a user's identity and role membership.

This approach is useful where instance-level security is required, such as permitting only the admin role to perform account transfers exceeding a certain amount limit. A simple example is illustrated in Example 10–5 later in this chapter.

NOTE: EJB AND BUSINESS HELPER CLASSES

J2EE applications consist of a mixture of EJBs and business helper classes. EJBs are commonly used for remoting, transactionality, and state management. Business helper classes are used to provide utility or common functionality to the EJBs. The helper classes typically contain logic that is not called directly from a remote source, is not impacted by the context of a transaction, and does not maintain any state.

One of the benefits of J2EE is its robust security model. The container provides declarative and programmatic security to the Web tier resources and EJBs. Unfortunately, developers often do not design the Business tier with security in mind. They neglect to factor in the security considerations of separating business logic into EJBs and helper classes. The impact to security comes when helper classes are accessed from different EJBs in different contexts and have business logic that should be protected by the container. The container is unable to enforce access control on the helper classes because it does not recognize them—it only recognizes EJBs. It is therefore critical that developers understand the security ramifications of breaking logic into business helper classes.

For performance reasons, it is hard to avoid using helper classes. EJBs have a significant overhead; helper classes, which are plain old Java objects (POJOs), do not. Therefore, an architect or a developer responsible for designing Business tier objects must understand how security is enforced by the container and what implications business helper classes pose. In cases where a business helper class is only used by one EJB, or in one security context, there is no concern. Business helper classes that are used by different EJBs in different security contexts, allow their logic to be accessed in all of those contexts. This may or may not be desirable, but it is necessary that it be understood.

Consequences

Container Managed Security offers flexible policy management at no additional cost to the organization. While it allows the developer to incorporate security in the application by way of simply defining roles in the deployment descriptor without writing any implementation code, it also supports programmatic security for fine-grained access control. The pattern offers the following other benefits to the developer:

- *Straightforward, declarative security model based on static mappings.* The Container Managed Security pattern provides an easy-to-use and easy-to-understand security model based on declarative user-to-role and role-to-resource mappings.
- *Developers are prevented from bypassing security requirements and inadvertently exposing business functionality.* Developers often advertently or inadvertently bypass security mechanisms within the code. Using Container Managed Security prevents this and ensures that EJB methods are adequately protected and properly restricted at deployment time by the application deployer.
- *Less prone to security holes.* Since security is implemented by a time-tested container, programming errors are less likely to lead to security holes. However, the security functionality offered by the container could be too limited and inflexible to modify.
- *Separation of security code from business objects.* Since the container implements the security infrastructure, the application code is free of security logic. However, developers often end up starting with Container Managed Security and then using programmatic security in conjunction with it, which leads to mangled code with a mixture of declarative and programmatic security that is difficult to manage.

Sample Code

Sample code for each strategy described earlier is illustrated in this section. The samples could be used in conjunction with each other to implement multiple flavors of Container Managed Security.

Example 10–3 shows declarative security via a web.xml deployment descriptor.

Example 10–3 web.xml deployment descriptor

```
<web-app>
...
<security-constraint>
```

```
      <display-name>App Sec Constraints </display-name>
      <web-resource-collection>
      <web-resource-name>
         System Admin Resources
      </web-resource-name>
      <url-pattern>/sysadmin/*</url-pattern>
      <http-method>GET</http-method>
      <http-method>POST</http-method>
      </web-resource-collection>
      <auth-constraint>
         <role-name>CORPORATEADMIN</role-name>
         <role-name>CLIENTADMIN</role-name>
      </auth-constraint>
      <user-data-constraint>
         <transport-guarantee>
            NONE
         </transport-guarantee>
      </user-data-constraint>
   </security-constraint>

   <!-- Declare login configuration here -->
   <login-config>
      <auth-method>FORM</auth-method>
      <form-login-config>
         <form-login-page>
            /login.jsp
         </form-login-page>
         <form-error-page>
            /login.jsp
         </form-error-page>
      </form-login-config>
   </login-config>
   <security-role>
      <description>Corporate Administrators</description>
      <role-name>CORPORATEADMIN</role-name>
      </security-role>
   <security-role>
      <description>Client Administrators</description>
      <role-name>CLIENTADMIN</role-name>
   </security-role>
   ...
</web-app>
```

Example 10–4 shows declarative security via an ejb-jar.xml deployment descriptor.

Example 10–4 ejb-jar.xml deployment descriptor

```
    ...
<enterprise-beans>
...
   <session>
          <ejb-name>SecureServiceFacade</ejb-name>
          <ejb-class>SecureServiceFacade.class</ejb-class>
          ...
          <security-role-ref>
             <role-name>
                "admin_role_referenced_by_bean"
             </role-name>
             <role-link>
                admin_role_depicted_in_assembly_descriptor
             </role-link>
          </security-role-ref>
  ...
       </session>
</enterprise-beans>
...
<assembly-descriptor>
   <security-role>
          <description>
             Security Role for Administrators
          </description>
          <rolename>
             admin_role_depicted_in_assembly_descriptor
          </role-name>
       </security-role>
       ...
       <method-permission>
          <role-name>GUEST</role-name>
          <method>
             <ejb-name>PublicUtilities</ejb-name>
       <method-name>viewStatistics</method-name>
          </method>
       </method-permission>
      ...
       <exclude-list>
          <description>Unreleased Methods</description>
          <method>
```

```
            <ejb-name>PublicUtilities</ejb-name>
        <method-name>underConstruction</method-name>
          </method>
       </exclude-list>
       ...
  </assembly-descriptor>
      ...
```

Example 10–5 shows programmatic or bean-managed security in the bean code.

Example 10–5 EJB method employing programmatic security

```
//...
public void transfer(double amount, long fromAccount,
                     long toAccount){
   if (amount>1000000 &&
           !sessionContext.isCallerInRole("admin")){
      throw new EJBException(
           sessionContext.getCallerPrincipal().getName() +
           " not allowed to transfer amounts exceeding " +
           1000000.");
   }
      else {
      //perform transfer
   }
}
//...
```

Security Factors and Risks

The extent of security offered by this pattern is limited to the security mechanisms offered by the container where the application code is deployed. It is also constrained by the limited subset of security aspects covered in the J2EE specification. As a result, the pattern elicits several risks:

- **Limitations to fine-grained security**. Use of Container Managed Security limits the ability of the application to incorporate fine-grained security such as that based on an object's run-time attribute values, time of day, and physical location of the client. These deficiencies could be overcome by programmatic security inside business components, but the security context information accessible to the component code is limited to principal information and the role association.

- **Requires preconceived granularity of roles**. Container Managed Security necessitates a preestablished notion of roles at the granularity level required by the application over the foreseeable future. This is because roles need to be defined in the deployment descriptor for each Web tier resource, ejb-tier business objects, or business methods before the application is packaged and deployed. Retrofitting additional roles after deployment would require repackaging the application with new deployment descriptors.
- **Too limiting**. Container Managed Security of the J2EE specification omits many aspects of integration between the container and the existing security infrastructure and limits itself to authentication and role-based access control. This may be too limiting for certain requirements, making programmatic security inevitable.

Reality Check

Is Container Managed Security comprehensive at the Web tier? If the granularity of security enforcement is not matched by the granularity offered by the resource URL identifiers used by Container Managed Security to distinguish and differentiate resources, this pattern may not fulfill the requirements. This is particularly true in applications that use a single controller to front multiple resources. In such cases, the request URI would be the same for all resources, and individual resources would be identified only by way of some identifier in the query string (such as /myapp/controller?page=resource1). Container Manager Security by URL patterns is not applicable in such cases unless the container supports extensive use of regular expressions. Resource-level security in such scenarios requires additional work in the application.

Is Container Managed Security required at the service tier? If all the back-end business services are inevitably fronted by a security gateway such as Secure Service Proxy or Secure Service Façade, having additional security enforcement via Container Managed Security on EJBs may not add much value and may incur unnecessary performance overhead. The choice must be carefully made in such cases.

Related Patterns

Authentication Enforcer, Authorization Enforcer. Authentication Enforcer enforces authentication on a request that is antecedently unauthenticated, much like what Container Managed Security implementation can enforce on the Web tier resource of a J2EE application. Similarly, Authorization Enforcer behaves like the Business tier implementation of Container Managed Security

Secure Service Proxy. If security architecture was not planned in the initial phases of application development, utilization of Container Managed Security at later stages may seem chaotic. In such cases, Secure Service Proxy or Secure Service Façade can be used to offer a secure gateway exposed to the client that enforces security in lieu of such enforcement at the business service level.

Intercepting Web Agent. Rather than custom-building security via deployment descriptors and configuring the container as in Container Manager Security, one may delegate those tasks to a COTS product, with the application using Web Agent Interceptor to preprocess the security context of the requests before they are forwarded and fulfilled by the security-unaware application services.

Dynamic Service Management

Problem

You need to dynamically instrument fine-grained components to manage and monitor your application with the necessary level of detail.

Management is an important, if overlooked, aspect of security. There is the monitoring aspect that security administrators use to detect intrusions and other anomalies caused by malicious activity. Then there is the active management aspect that empowers administrators to proactively prevent intrusions by modifying objects or invoking operations before an attack can conclude.

Consider a scenario where an intruder launches a denial-of-service (DoS) attack against an LDAP server that causes the application to time out and drop the connection to the LDAP server, thus preventing new users from logging in. In many implementations, the only remedy to this scenario would be to restart the application, causing logged-in users to be dropped and forced to log in again. Ideally, an administrator would want to be able to monitor the connection, detect that it is not responding, determine why, take steps to stop the DoS attack, and then invoke an operation on the object responsible for connecting to LDAP that forces it to reestablish the connection.

Another scenario involves an authenticated user who is exhibiting malicious activity in the application. Security administrators would like the ability to detect such activity, log the user out, and disable that user's account. All of this requires a level of instrumentation not available in most applications today.

Forces

- You want to instrument POJO business objects that the container does not monitor for you.

- You have many business objects and want to adjust instrumentation at runtime as needed to provide security monitoring and real-time forensic data gathering.
- You want to monitor and actively manage business objects to tightly control security and proactively prevent attacks in progress.
- You want to use industry-standard Java Management Extension (JMX) technology to ensure a vendor-neutral solution.

Solution

Use a Dynamic Service Management pattern to enable fine-grained instrumentation of business objects at runtime on an as-needed basis using JMX.

Structure

Figure 10–7 illustrates a Dynamic Service Management pattern class.

Participants and Responsibilities

Figure 10-8 is a sequence diagram of the Dynamic Service Management pattern.

Client. A Client requests registration of an object as an MBean from the ServiceManager.

ServiceManager. The ServiceManager creates an instance of the MBeanServer and obtains an instance of an MBeanFactory. ServiceManager instantiates the Registry and

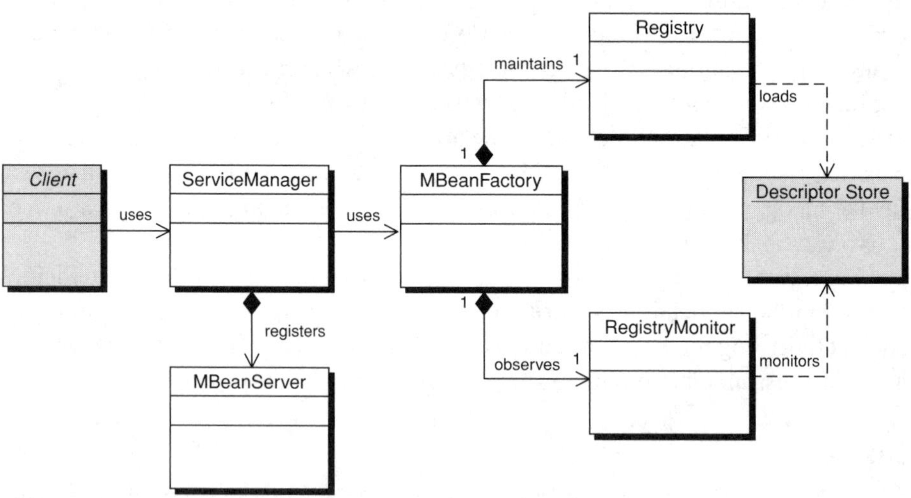

Figure 10–7 Dynamic Service Management class diagram

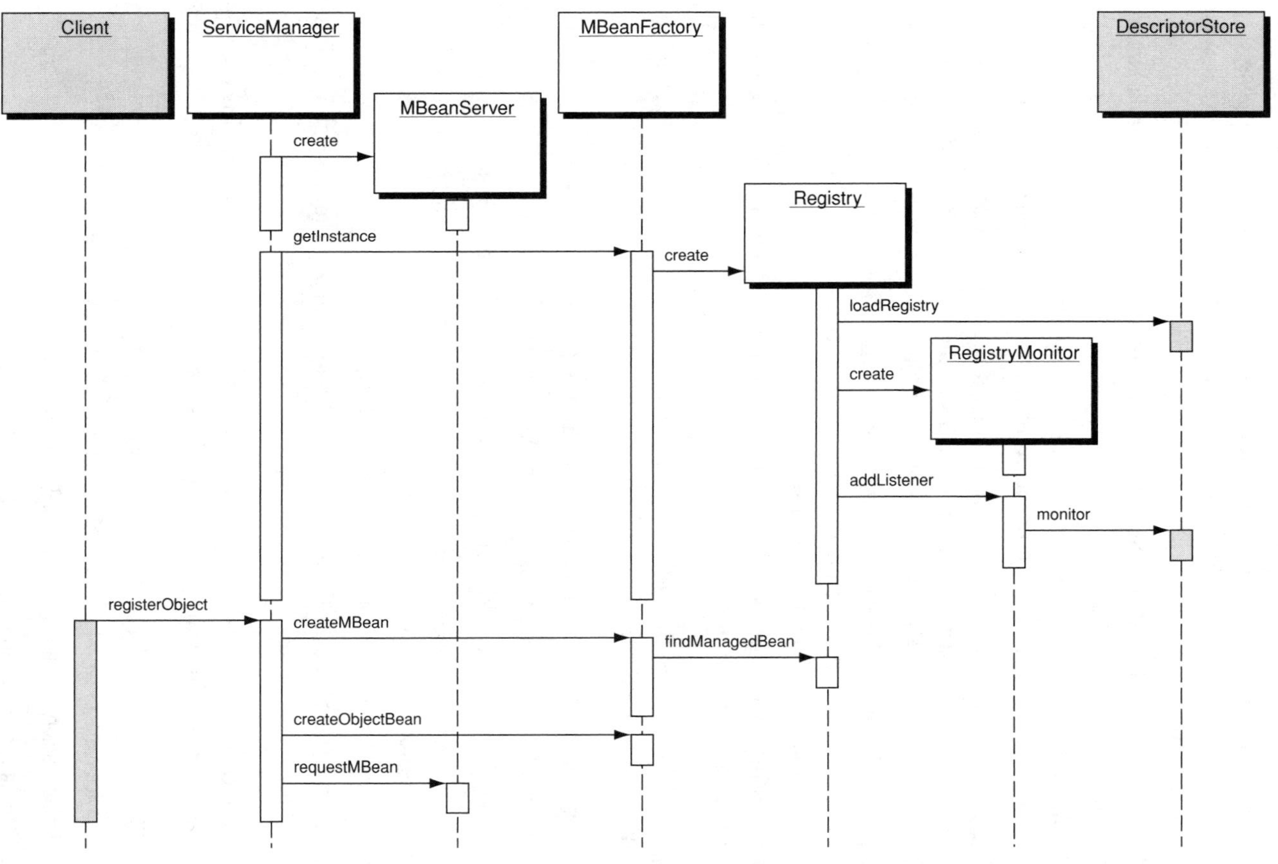

Figure 10–8 Dynamic Service Management sequence diagram

then uses the MBeanFactory to create an MBean for a particular object passed in by the Client. It creates an ObjectName for that object and then registers it with the MBeanServer.

MBeanServer. The MBeanServer exposes registered MBeans via adaptor-specific protocols.

MbeanFactory. The MBeanFactory creates the Registry and uses it to find managed MBean definitions, which it loaded from the Descriptor Store.

Registry. The Registry loads and maintains a registry of MBean descriptors. It creates a Registry Monitor to monitor changes to the DescriptorStore and reloads the definitions when the RegistryMonitor notifies it that the DescriptorStore has changed.

RegistryMonitor. The RegistryMonitor is responsible for monitoring changes to the DescriptorStore. It registers listeners and notifies those listeners when it detects a change to the DescriptorStore.

DescriptorStore. The DescriptorStore is an abstract representation of a persistent store of MBean descriptor definitions.

Figure 10–8 shows the following sequence for registering an object as an MBean using the Dynamic Service Management pattern.

1. ServiceManager creates an instance of an MBeanServer.
2. ServiceManager calls getInstance on MBeanFactory.
3. MBeanFactory, upon initial creation, creates an instance of Registry.
4. Upon creation, Registry calls its loadRegistry method, which loads MBean descriptors from the DescriptorStore.
5. Registry then creates an instance of RegistryMonitor.
6. Registry then adds itself as a listener to that DescriptorStore through a call to addListener method.

On call to addListener method, RegistryMonitor stores listener and begins polling DescriptorStore passed in as argument to addListener.

1. Client invokes registerObject on ServiceManager.
2. ServiceManager invokes createMBean on MBeanFactory.
3. MBeanFactory calls findManagedBean on Registry.
4. ServiceManager then calls createObjectName on MBeanFactory.
5. Once the MBean and an ObjectName for it have been created, the ServiceManager invokes registerMBean on the MBeanServer, passing in the MBean instance and its corresponding ObjectName.

Strategies

The Dynamic Service Management pattern provides dynamic instrumentation of business objects using JMX. JMX is a commonly used technology, present in all major application server products. There are several strategies for implementing this pattern, depending on what product you choose and what type of persistent store you require for your MBean Descriptors.

Model MBean Strategy

This strategy involves using JMX Model MBean loaded from an external configuration source. Model MBeans allow developers to define the attributes and operations they want to expose on their classes through metadata. This metadata can then be externalized from the class definition entirely. With a bit of work, the metadata can be reloaded at runtime to allow for just-in-time creation of MBeans as needed.

The Jakarta Commons subproject of the Apache Software Foundation is focused on building open source, reusable Java components. One of the components of the Commons project is the Commons-Modeler. Commons-Modeler provides a framework for creating JMX Model MBeans that allows developers to circumvent the creation of the metadata programmatically (as described in the specification) and instead defines that data in an XML descriptor file. This greatly reduces the amount of source code needed to create the Model MBeans.

The Model MBean Strategy utilizes the Commons-Modeler framework approach to simplify the task of creating MBeans and to leverage the file-based XML descriptor to implement dynamic reloading of MBeans based on changes to that descriptor file at runtime. This provides a mechanism that allows developers and operations staff to instrument components on an as-needed basis instead of incurring the run-time overhead of trying to instrument all of the components statically, most of which will never be used.

Figure 10-9 depicts a class diagram of a Dynamic Service Management pattern implemented using the Model MBean strategy.

Figure 10-10 is sequence diagram of the Dynamic Service Management pattern implemented using the Model MBean strategy. In this strategy, the Commons-Modeler framework supplies the Registry implementation and provides an XML DTD for the MBeans descriptor file. The Registry does all the work of creating the MBean from the data in the descriptor file, which is the bulk of the work overall. A simple file monitor can be implemented to detect changes to the XML file and the Registry can be told to reload from the changed file.

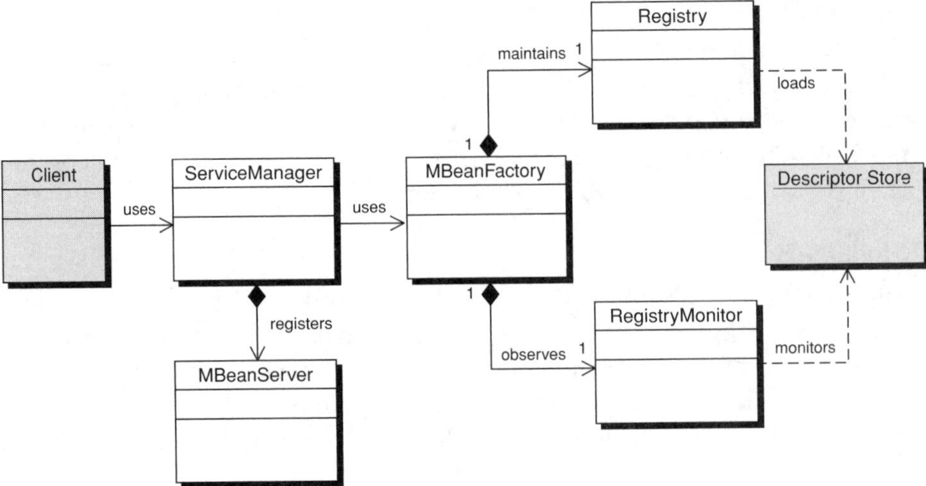

Figure 10–9 Model MBean Strategy class diagram

Consequences

The Dynamic Service Management pattern helps to identify and mitigate several types of threats. By enabling operations staff to monitor business components, they can readily identify an attack in progress, whether it is a denial-of-service attack or somebody trying to guess passwords using a dictionary attack. It also enables staff to manage those components so that they can take reactive action during an attack, such as setting a filter on an incoming IP or locking a user account. By employing the Dynamic Service Management pattern, developers can benefit from the following:

- *Instrumentation of POJO business objects.* Using a Dynamic Service Management pattern provides a means to instrument POJOs so that their attributes and operations can be managed and monitored based on definitions defined in a descriptor file. This allows operations staff to probe down into the business objects themselves to troubleshoot or collect data.
- *Adjust instrumentation at runtime as needed.* Today, systems are built with static management and monitoring capabilities. These capabilities incur a run-time cost in terms of performance, memory, and complexity. They also do not provide the ability to manage or monitor subsequent components or attributes at runtime as the needs arise. They require a large amount of upfront analysis and speculation to determine what to manage

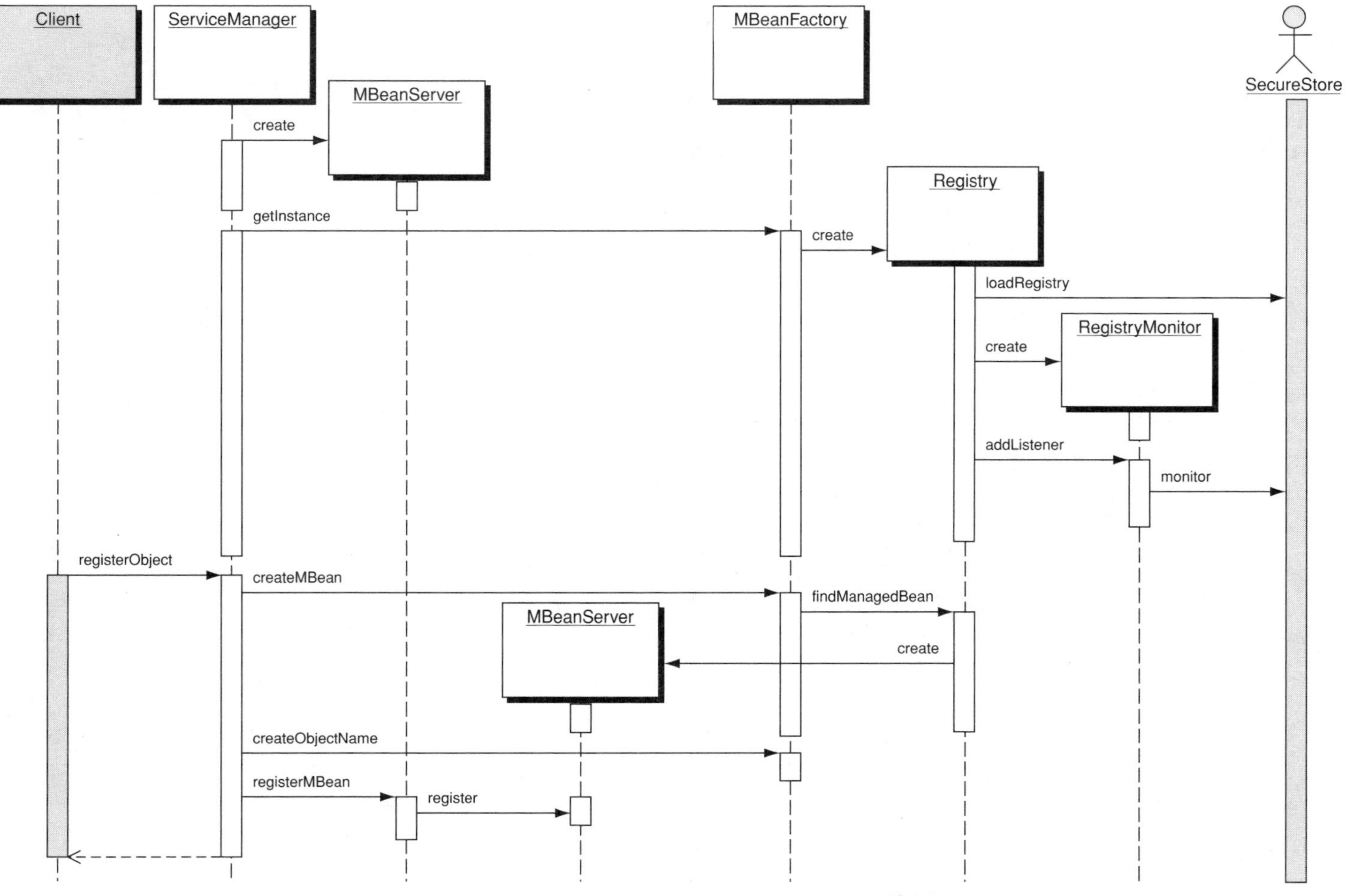

Figure 10–10 Model MBean Strategy sequence diagram

and monitor. The Dynamic Service Management pattern allows you to instrument thousands of business components on an as-needed basis.

- *Use industry-standard Java Management Extension (JMX) technology.* The Dynamic Service Management can be used in conjunction with JMX to ensure that a completely vendor-independent management and monitoring solution can be implemented.

Using a Dynamic Service Management pattern eliminates the need for upfront analysis and needless run-time overhead from monitoring or exposing components and attributes unnecessarily. Instead, components and attributes can be dynamically instrumented at runtime on an as-needed basis. When the need no longer exists, the instrumentation can be turned off, freeing up cycles and memory for business processing.

Sample Code

Example 10–6 is a sample source listing of a Service Manager class.

Example 10–6 MBeanManager.java: MBeanManager implementation

```
package com.csp.management;

import java.util.Enumeration;
import javax.management.MBeanServer;
import javax.management.ObjectName;
import javax.management.modelmbean.ModelMBean;
import javax.naming.Context;
import com.sun.jdmk.comm.HtmlAdaptorServer;

public class MBeanManager implements ManagedObject {
  private static MBeanManager instance = null;
  private HtmlAdaptorServer htmlServer = null;
  private MBeanFactory factory = null;
  private HashMap objNames = new HashMap();

  // This class returns an instance of MBeanManager
  public static MBeanManager getInstance() {
    if(instance == null) {
      instance = new MBeanManager();
      try {
          instance.registerObject(instance, "CSPM");
        }
        catch (Exception e) {
```

```
            log.error("Unable to register mbean.", e);
        }
    }
    return instance;
}

 // Create and initialize the MBeanManager
 private MBeanManager() {
init();
 }

// Initializes the adaptors and servers.
private void init() {
  htmlServer = new HtmlAdaptorServer();
htmlServer.setPort(4545);
String htmlServiceName = "Adaptor:name=html,
          port=" + port;
    // Create the Object name to register with.
ObjectName htmlObjectName =
               new ObjectName(htmlServiceName);

    objNames.put(htmlServiceName, htmlObjectName);
    htmlServer.start();
    // Load MBean factory
    factory = MBeanFactory.getInstance();
}

// Register a service object as an MBean.
public void registerObject(Object service,
     String serviceName) throws Exception {
   ModelMBean mbean =
      factory.createMBean(service, serviceName);
   if(mbean == null) {
      return;
   }
   // Create the ObjectName
   ObjectName objName = factory.createObjectName(
         mbeanDomain, service, serviceName);

   if (objName == null) {
      log.error("Could not create object name.");
      return;
   }
```

```
    // Get the MBeanServer
    MBeanServer wlsServer = getWLSMBeanServer();
    // Register the MBean with the server
    wlsServer.registerMBean(mbean, objName);
    // Add the ObjectName to the list of names
    objNames.put(serviceName, objName);
}

// Method to unregister an object as an MBean
public void unregisterObject(String serviceName) {
    try {
        if(serviceName != null && objNames != null) {
            // Remove the ObjectName from the list
            ObjectName oName =
             (ObjectName)objNames.remove(serviceName);
            if(oName != null) {
                MBeanServer server = getMBeanServer();
                // Unregister the bean from the server
                server.unregisterMBean(oName);
            }
        }
    }
    catch(Exception e) {
        log.error("Unable to unregister service.", e);
    }
}

// Method to reload the MBean descriptor from the registry
public void reloadMBeans() throws Exception {

// Unload previously registered mbeans
     unloadMBeans();

     // Tell factory to reload new MBeans.
     factory.loadRegistry();
}

// Unload the MBeans
public void unloadMBeans() throws Exception {
    // Get a handle to all of our registered MBeans
    Enumeration svcNames = objNames.keys();
    while(svcNames.hasMoreElements()) {
        String svc = (String) svcNames.nextElement();
```

```
         // Iterate through list unregistering each MBean
         unregisterObject(svc);
      }
   }
}
```

Example 10–7 is a sample source code listing of an MBeanFactory class.

Example 10–7 MBeanFactory.java: MBean factory implementation


```
package com.csp.management;

import java.io.IOException;
import java.io.InputStream;
import java.net.URL;
import java.io.FileNotFoundException;
import javax.management.modelmbean.ModelMBean;
import javax.management.ObjectName;
import org.apache.commons.modeler.ManagedBean;
import org.apache.commons.modeler.Registry;
import com.csp.logging.SecureLogger;
import com.csp.management.FileMonitor;
import com.csp.management.FileChangeListener;

/**
 * This class is responsible for creating, loading and
 * reloading the MBean descriptor registry.
 */
public class MBeanFactory implements FileChangeListener {
   private static SecureLogger log =
      (SecureLogger)SecureLogger.getLogger();
   private static MBeanFactory instance = null;
   private Registry registry = null;
   private String registryFileName =
      "mbeans-descriptors.xml";
   private FileMonitor fileMonitor = null;
   private static final Object lock = new Object();

   // Private constructor
   private MBeanFactory() {
      init();
   }
   // Initialization method for loading the MBean descriptor
   // registry and adding a file listener to detect changes.
```

```
private void init() {
   loadRegistry();
   try {
      fileMonitor.getInstance().addFileChangeListener(
        this, registryFileName);
   }
   catch (FileNotFoundException fnfe) {
      log.error("Unable to add listener.");
   }
}

// Load the MBean descriptor registry.
public void loadRegistry() {
   InputStream inputStream = null;
   try {
      inputStream = ClassLoader.getSystemClassLoader().
             getResourceAsStream(registryFileName);
      // Get the registry
      registry = Registry.getRegistry(null, instance);
      // Load the descriptors from the input stream.
      registry.loadDescriptors(inputStream);
   }
   catch (Exception e) {
      log.error("Unable to load file.", e);
   }
}

// Returns an MBeanFactory instance
public static MBeanFactory getInstance()
      throws Exception {
   if (instance == null) {
      instance = new MBeanFactory();
   }
   return instance;
}

// Create a ModelMBean given a service and name
public ModelMBean createMBean(Object service,
         String serviceName)
      throws Exception {

   ModelMBean mbean = null;
   // Create an MBean from the Registry
```

```
    ManagedBean managed =
   registry.findManagedBean(serviceName);
    if (managed != null) {
             mbean = managed.createMBean(service);
    }
    return mbean;
}

// Create an ObjectName for a service.
public ObjectName createObjectName(String domain,
     Object service, String serviceName)
      throws Exception {
   ObjectName oName = null;
   if(service instanceof ManagedObject) {
      ManagedObject svcImpl = (ManagedObject)service;
      // Set the JMX name to the input service name.
      svcImpl.setJMXName(serviceName);
      // Create the ObjectName
      oName = new ObjectName(domain + "Name:" +
                  svcImpl.getJMXName() + ",Type=" +
                  svcImpl.getJMXType());
   }
   else {
      oName = new ObjectName(domain + ":service=" +
         serviceName  + ",className=" +
         service.getClass().getName());
   }
   return oName;
}


public String getRegistryFileName() {
   return this.registryFileName;
}

public void setRegistryFileName(String fileName) {
   this.registryFileName = fileName;
}

public void fileChanged(String fileName) {
   try {
      loadRegistry();
   }
```

```
        catch(Exception e) {
            log.error("Failed to reload registry.");
        }
    }
}
```

Security Factors and Risks

The following are some of the security factors and risks related to the Dynamic Service Management pattern:

- **Authentication**. The Dynamic Service Management pattern allows operations staff to manage and monitor business components. This poses a security concern because unauthorized access to the components from outside the application could allow the application to be subverted. It is therefore necessary to implement a solution that requires proper authentication of users through the management interface.
- **Authorization**. It is necessary to control access and enforce authorization of users using the management interface. An access-control model needs to be incorporated into the solution to ensure that users only have the capabilities necessary to their roles. There is probably a need for different levels of access, such as monitor-only capabilities versus management *and* monitoring capabilities. A robust model needs to be implemented in the management interface in the same way that it needs to be incorporated into the application interface.
- **Confidentiality**. Communication via the management protocol needs to be secured to guarantee confidentiality.
- **Auditing**. Management of business objects during runtime can pose serious security concerns. It is therefore necessary to audit all such activities so that security personnel can determine what management operations were performed on the application and by whom.

Reality Check

What types of things need to be managed and monitored? What should be managed and monitored is very subjective and depends on the circumstances. The Dynamic Service Management pattern provides a means to transparently attach management and monitoring capabilities to business objects without prior consideration or elaboration of those objects. But to be effective, developers must at least understand what the approach provides and design their business objects to be taken advantage of by the JMX framework. If they do not implement member variables and choose to pass in only complex Objects as parameters to their method calls, they will be unable to make use of the framework in many cases.

Related Patterns

Secure Pipe. The Dynamic Service Management pattern makes use of the Secure Pipe pattern to provide confidentiality when communicating with the application via the management protocol.

Obfuscated Transfer Object

Problem

You need a way to protect critical data as it is passed within application and between tiers.

Transfer Objects [CJP2] provide a mechanism for transporting data elements across tiers and components. This is an efficient means of moving large sets of data without invoking multiple getter or setter methods on remote objects across tiers. You probably use strategies such as Updateable Transfer Objects or Multiple Transfer Objects when implementing the Transfer Object pattern. In many cases you then find yourself passing Transfer Objects across multiple components. This leads to a security concern.

By passing data in Transfer Objects across components, you unnecessarily expose data to components that may not require or should not have access to it. Consider an application that stores credit card information in a user's profile. The application passes the profile using a profile transfer object. This profile transfer object passes through many business and presentation tier components on its way to being stored in the database. Many of those components are not privy to the sensitive nature of the credit card data in the profile transfer object. They may print all of the data in the transfer object for debugging purposes or write it to an audit log that is not supposed to expose sensitive data. You do not want to modify all of those components just to handle that data differently. Instead, you want the transfer object itself to take responsibility for protecting that data.

Forces

- You want to protect sensitive data passed in Transfer Objects from being captured in console messages, log files, or audit logs.
- You want the Transfer Object to be responsible for protecting the data in order to reduce code and prevent business components from inadvertently exposing sensitive data.

- You want to specify which data elements are protected, since not all data should be protected and may need to be exposed.

Solution

Use an Obfuscated Transfer Object to protect access to data passed within and between tiers.

The Obfuscated Transfer Object allows developers to define data elements within it that are to be protected. The means of protection can vary between applications or implementations depending on the business requirements. The Obfuscated Transfer Object provides a way to prevent either purposeful or inadvertent unauthorized access to its data.

The producers and consumers of the data can agree upon the sensitive data elements that need to be protected and on their means of access. The Obfuscated Transfer Object will then take the responsibility of protecting that data from any intervening components that it is passed to on its way between producer and consumer. Credit card and other sensitive information can be protected from being accidentally dumped to a log file or audit trail, or worse, such as being captured and stored for malicious purposes.

Structure

Figure 10-11 is the class diagram for the Obfuscated Transfer Object.

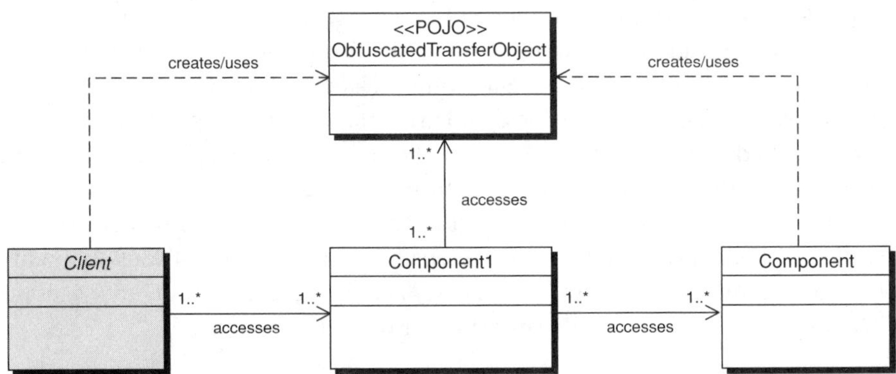

Figure 10–11 Obfuscated Transfer Object class diagram

Participants and Responsibilities

Figure 10-12 shows the sequence diagram of the Obfuscated Transfer Object pattern.

Client. The Client wants to send and receive data from a Target component via an intermediary Component. The Client can be any component in any tier.

Component. The Component is any application component in the message flow that is not the intended target of the Client. The Component can be any component in any tier that acts as an intermediary in the message flow between the Client and the Target.

Target. The Target is any object that is the intended recipient of the Client's request. It is responsible for setting the data that needs to be obfuscated.

Obfuscated Transfer Object. The ObfuscatedTransferObject is responsible for protecting access to data within it, as necessary.

Typically, the intermediary Component is not trusted or should not have access to any or all data in the Obfuscated Transfer Object. It then becomes the Obfuscated Transfer Object's responsibility to protect the data. The means of protection is dependent upon the business requirements and the level of trust of the intermediary components. Figure 10–12 takes us through a typical sequence of events for an application employing an ObfuscatedTransferObject.

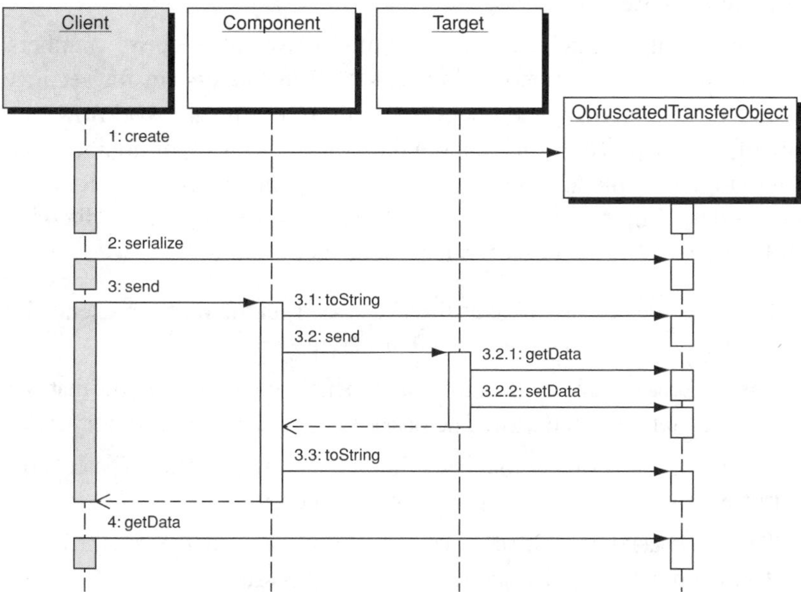

Figure 10–12 Obfuscated Transfer Object sequence diagram

1. Client creates an ObfuscatedTransferObject, setting the necessary request data.
2. Client serializes the ObfuscatedTransferObject and applies required obfuscation mechanisms.
3. Client sends the serialized ObfuscatedTransferObject to an intermediary Component.
4. The Component invokes toString on the ObfuscatedTransferObject and writes the output to a file. In this case, none of the protected data is listed in that output.
5. The Component sends the ObfuscatedTransferObject to the Target.
6. The Target retrieves the protected (obfuscated) data elements.
7. The Target sets new data that requires protection.
8. The Target logs the ObfuscatedTransferObject; again, the protected data is not output.
9. The Target returns the ObfuscatedTransferObject to the Client.
10. The Client retrieves the newly set data.

Strategies

A variety of strategies can implement the Obfuscated Transfer Object. A simple strategy is just to mask various data elements to prevent them from inadvertently being logged or displayed in an audit event. A more elaborate strategy is to encrypt the protected data within the Obfuscated Transfer Object. This entails a more complex implementation, but offers a higher degree of protection.

Masked List Strategy

Sensitive information like credit card numbers, Social Security numbers, and other personal information should not be stored in the system for security purposes. Since intermediary components within a request workflow may be unaware of the existence of such data in the Transfer Object, or do not know what data not to log, a simple Masked List Strategy prevents inadvertent storage or display of this data. Figure 10–13 shows a Masked List Strategy class diagram. Figure 10–14 shows a Masked List Strategy Sequence Diagram.

1. The Client creates an ObfuscatedTransferObject, sets the data, and sends it to the Target component via an intermediary Component.
2. The Component is any application component in the message flow that is not the intended target of the Client. The Component may log the ObfuscatedTransferObject.
3. The Target is any object that is the intended recipient of the Client's request. It retrieves the data that needs to be obfuscated.
4. The ObfuscatedTransferObject does not output data in the masked list. That data is only retrieved when specifically asked for.

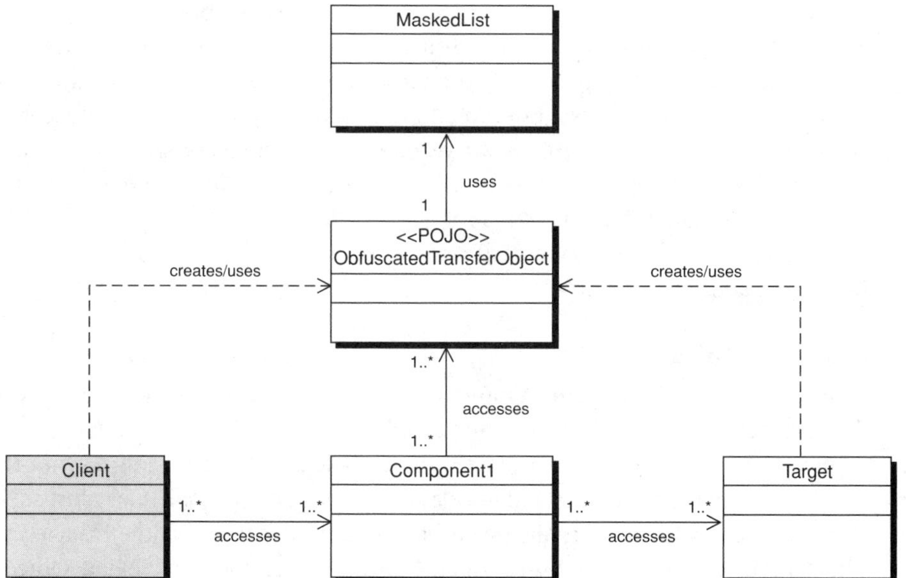

Figure 10–13 Masked List Strategy class diagram

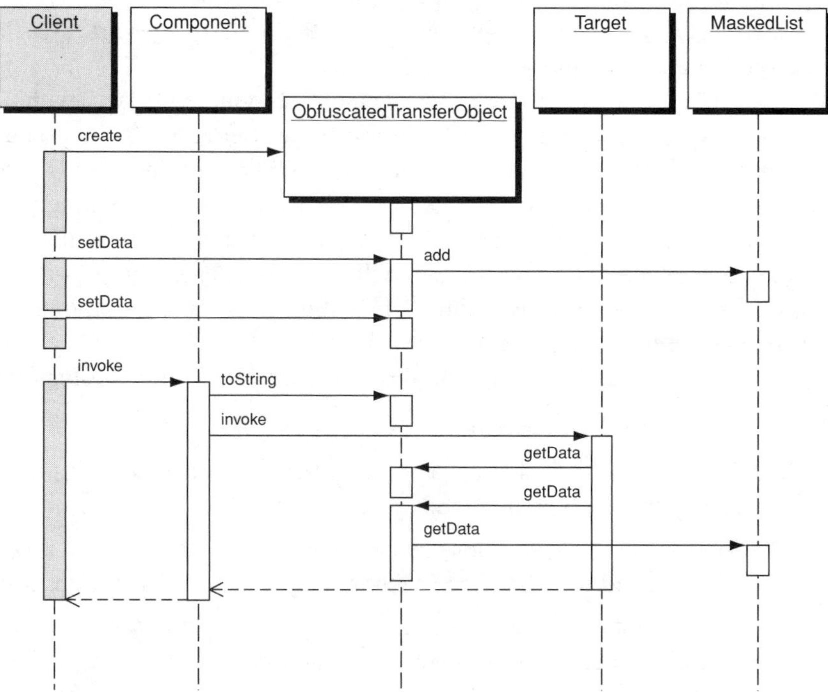

Figure 10–14 Masked List Strategy sequence diagram

In this strategy, the client sets data as name-value (NV) pairs in the Obfuscated Transfer Object. Internally, the Obfuscated Transfer Object maintains two maps, one for holding NV pairs that should be obfuscated and another for NV pairs that do not require obfuscation. In addition to the two maps, the Obfuscated Transfer Object contains a list of NV pair names that should be protected. Data passed in with names corresponding to names in the masked list, are placed in the map for the obfuscated data. This map is then protected. In the sequence above, when the Component logs the ObfuscatedTransferObject, the data in the obfuscated map is not logged, and thus it is protected.

Encryption Strategy

Using the Encryption Strategy for Obfuscated Transfer Object provides the highest level of protection for the data elements protected within. The data elements are stored in a Data Map, and then the Data Map as a whole is encrypted using a symmetric key. To retrieve the Data Map and the elements within it, the consumer must supply a symmetric key identical to the one used by the producer to seal the Data Map.

The Sun Java 2 Standard Edition (J2SE) runtime provides a Sealed Object class that allows developers to easily encrypt objects by passing in a serialized object and a Cipher object in the constructor. The serialized object can then be retrieved by either passing in an identical Cipher or a Key object that can be used to recreate the Cipher. This encapsulates all of the underlying work associated with encrypting and decrypting objects.

The only issue remaining is the management of symmetric keys within the application. This poses a significant challenge because it requires the producers and consumers to share symmetric keys without providing any intermediary components with access to those keys. This may be simple or overwhelmingly complex depending on the architecture of the application and the structure of the component trust model. Use this strategy with caution, because the key-management issues may be harder to overcome than architecting the application again to eliminate the need for the pattern.

Figure 10-15 is a sequence diagram illustrating the Encryption Strategy for an Obfuscated Transfer Object.

1. The Client creates an ObfuscatedTransferObject, sets the data, and sends it to the Target component via an intermediary Component.
2. The Component is any application component in the message flow that is not the intended target of the Client. The Component may log the ObfuscatedTransferObject.
3. The ObfuscatedTransferObject creates a Sealed object by encrypting the given serializable object using an encryption key. That data is only retrieved when the proper decryption key is supplied.

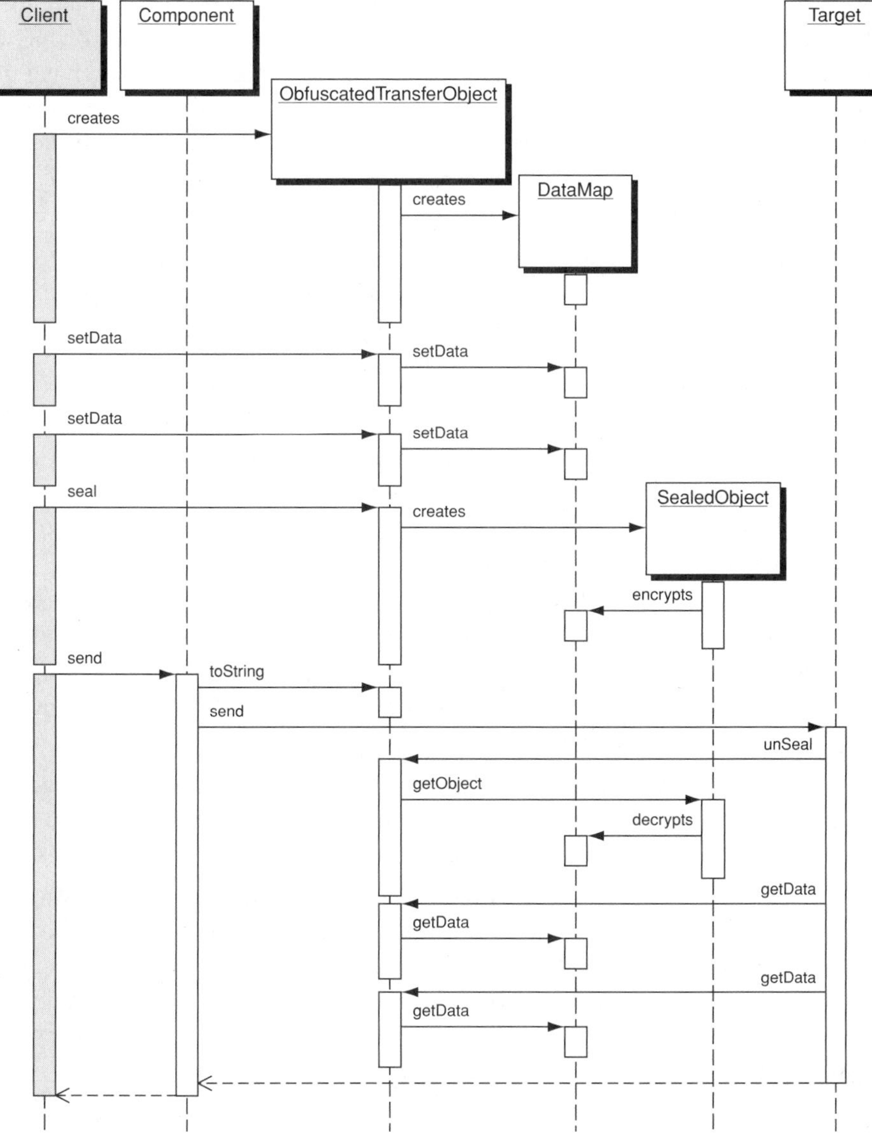

Figure 10–15 Encryption Strategy sequence diagram

4. The Target is any object that is the intended recipient of the Client's request. It retrieves the obfuscated data by supplying the key used to decrypt it.

The sequence diagram shown in Figure 10–15 illustrates implementation of the Obfuscated Transfer Object using an Encryption Strategy. The client creates the

Obfuscated Transfer Object and adds the data as name value pairs. The client then seals the data by passing in an encryption key. The intermediate components in the request flow are unable to access the data. The target object, upon receiving the Obfuscated Transfer Object, first unseals it by passing in the corresponding decryption key. It can then access the data as before, through the name-value pair keys.

Consequences

The Obfuscated Transfer Object protects against sniffing attacks and threats arising from log-file capture within the Business tier by ensuring that sensitive data is not passed or logged in the clear. By employing the Obfuscated Transfer Object pattern, the following consequences will apply:

- *Confidentiality: Generic protection of sensitive data passed in Transfer Objects.* The Obfuscated Transfer Object provides a means of generically protecting data passed between components and tiers from being improperly accessed—such as for logging or auditing, or purposefully, in the case of untrusted intermediary components.
- *Centralized encryption or obfuscation code.* The Obfuscated Transfer Object provides a central point for encrypting or obfuscating data that is passed in a Transfer Object. Moving the responsibility for protecting the data to the Transfer Object ensures that such code is then not required across all the components that use the Transfer Object.
- *Increased performance overhead.* The code necessary to obfuscate or encrypt has associated memory and processing overhead. For large amounts of data, this overhead may significantly reduce overall performance.
- *Specify which data elements are protected and which are not.* By using the Obfuscated Transfer Object, you can specify which data elements to protect and therefore only impact performance as necessary for security, which is better than alternative bulk encryption or obfuscation techniques.

Sample Code

Example 10–8 shows a sample listing of an Obfuscated Transfer Object implemented using an Encryption Strategy.

Example 10–8 Sample obfuscated TO using encryption implementation

```
package com.csp.business;

import java.io.Serializable;
import java.util.HashMap;
```

```
import javax.crypto.Cipher;
import javax.crypto.SealedObject;

public class GenericTO implements Serializable {
   final long serialVersionUID = -5831612260903682186L;
   private HashMap map;
   private SealedObject sealedMap;
   /**
    * Default constructor that initializes the object.
    */
   public GenericTO() {
      map = new HashMap();
   }
   public void seal(Cipher cipher) throws Exception {
      map = sealedMap.getObject(cipher);
   }
   public void unseal(Cipher cipher) throws Exception {
      sealedMap = new SealedObject(map, cipher);

      // Set the map to null so data can't be accessed.
      map = null;
   }
   public Object getData(Object key) throws Exception {
      return map.get(key(key);
   }
   public void setData(Object key, Object data)
   throws Exception {
      map.put(key, data);
   }
}
```


Security Factors and Risks

Confidentiality. The Obfuscated Transfer Object pattern provides a means to ensure varying degrees of confidentiality for data passed within the application, such as between components, across asynchronous message boundaries, and between tiers. This is necessary for applications that have sensitive data that should not be accidentally logged or displayed, or where data is passed through intermediary components that are not trusted and should not have access to that data.

Reality Check

Should we use a Masked List Strategy or an Encryption Strategy? It depends on your requirements and whether you trust your intermediary components not to access the data in the masked list. Using a Masked List Strategy, a component could access the data and dump it to a log if it wished, circumventing the intention of the masked list. By using an Encryption Strategy, the intermediary components cannot gain access to the sensitive data unless they obtain the Cipher used to protect that data. There is significant processing overhead to encrypting and decrypting the data, so you should only use this strategy when necessary and only for the data elements that require it.

Related Patterns

Transfer Object [CJP2]. The Obfuscated Transfer Object is similar to, and may be considered a strategy of, the *Core J2EE Patterns* Transfer Object pattern. It provides the additional capability of protecting data elements within it from unauthorized access.

Data Transfer HashMap (Middleware). The Obfuscated Transfer Object is similar to the Data Transfer HashMap pattern from the Middleware Company. Like the Data Transfer HashMap, it employs a strategy that makes use of an underlying HashMap for storing and retrieving data elements. In the case of the Obfuscated Transfer Object, that underlying map may be encrypted using a Sealed Object or may be divided into two maps, one containing data that can be dumped to a log or audit table and another containing sensitive data that should not be accessed.

Policy Delegate

Problem

You want to shield clients from discovery and invocation details of security services and to control client interactions by intercepting and administering policy on client requests.

You need an abstraction between enterprise security infrastructure and clients; hiding the intricacies of finding and invoking security services. It is desirable to abstract common framework specific code related to invocation of those services, thus reducing the coupling between clients and the security framework. As a result of the loose coupling, clients and services can then be easily replaced with alternate technologies, when appropriate, to increase the lifespan of the application.

Forces

- You want to reduce the coupling between the security framework and the client of security services offered by the framework and reduce the number of complex security interfaces exposed to the client in order to limit touchpoints that can give way to security holes.

- You need to manage the life cycle of a client's security context at the server and want to use it across multiple invocations by the same client.
- You need a way to centralize Business-tier security functions so that security can be enforced across business components without impacting business developers.

Solution

Use Policy Delegate to mediate requests between clients and security services, and to reduce the dependency of client code on implementation specifics of the service framework.

Policy Delegate is a coordinator of Business-tier security services that is akin to the Secure Base Action in the Web tier. The clients use the delegate to locate and mediate back-end security services. A delegate could in turn use a Secure Service Façade that offers a coarse-grained aggregate interface to fine-grained security services or business components and entities. This abstraction also offers a looser coupling and cleaner contract between clients and the secure services, reducing the magnitude of change required in the clients when the implementations of the security services change over time.

To use a delegate, the client need not be aware of the actual location of the service. A Policy Delegate uses a Service Locator to locate distributed security services. The client is unaware of the underlying implementation technology and the communication protocol of the service, which could be RMI, Web services, DCOM, CORBA, or another service.

While coordinating and mediating requests and responses between clients and the security framework, a delegate could also perform pertinent message translation to accommodate disparate message formats and protocols both expected and supported by the clients and individual services. In the same vein, the delegate could choose to perform error translation to encapsulate service-level security exceptions as user-friendly, application-level error messages.

The Policy Delegate can be a stateless delegate or a stateful delegate. A stateful delegate, identified and looked up by an appropriate ID, can cache the security context, service references, and transient state between multiple invocations by the client. This caching at the server side optimizes and reduces the number of object creations, service lookups, and security computations. The security context could be cached as a Secure Session Object.

The clients can retrieve a security delegate using a Factory pattern [GoF]. This is particularly useful when the application exposes multiple Policy Delegates rather than one aggregate delegate that mediates between multiple services.

Structure

Figure 10-16 shows a typical Policy Delegate class diagram. The Target in the diagram represents any security service, a Secure Service Façade, or a security-unaware Session Façade. The delegate uses a SecureSessionObject to maintain the transient state associated with a client session.

The single PolicyDelegate could maintain a one-to-many relationship with multiple targets, or multiple Policy Delegates could each map exactly to one of the several possible targets. In the latter case, it could make use of a Factory that returns an appropriate delegate, depending on the requested service.

Participants and Responsibilities

Figure 10-17 depicts a scenario where a client uses a Business Delegate retrieved from a Factory to invoke a security service on a SecureSessionFaçade, located using a Service Locator.

Client. A Client retrieves a PolicyDelegate through DelegateFactory to invoke a specific service.

PolicyDelegate. The PolicyDelegate uses ServiceLocator [CJP2] to locate the service.

SecureSessionObject. The PolicyDelegate maintains a SecureSessionObject to store transient client security context and service references between consecutive invocations by the same client.

SecureServiceFaçade, *Service2.* The back-end service could be implemented using any technology, such as a SecureServiceFaçade session bean or as a Web service depicted as Service2.

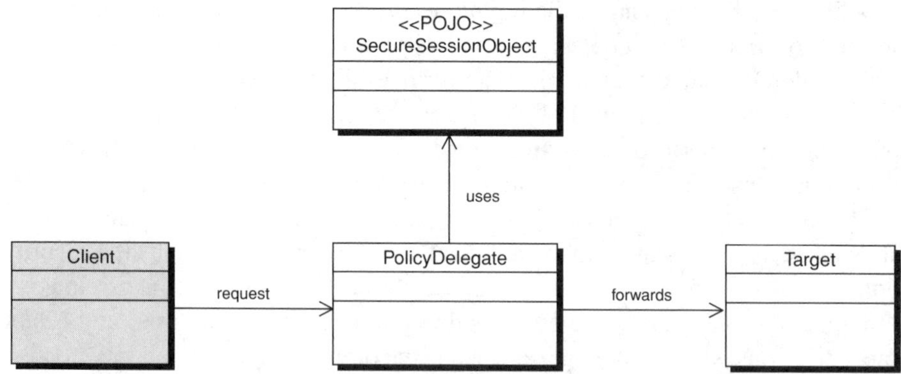

Figure 10–16 Policy Delegate pattern class diagram

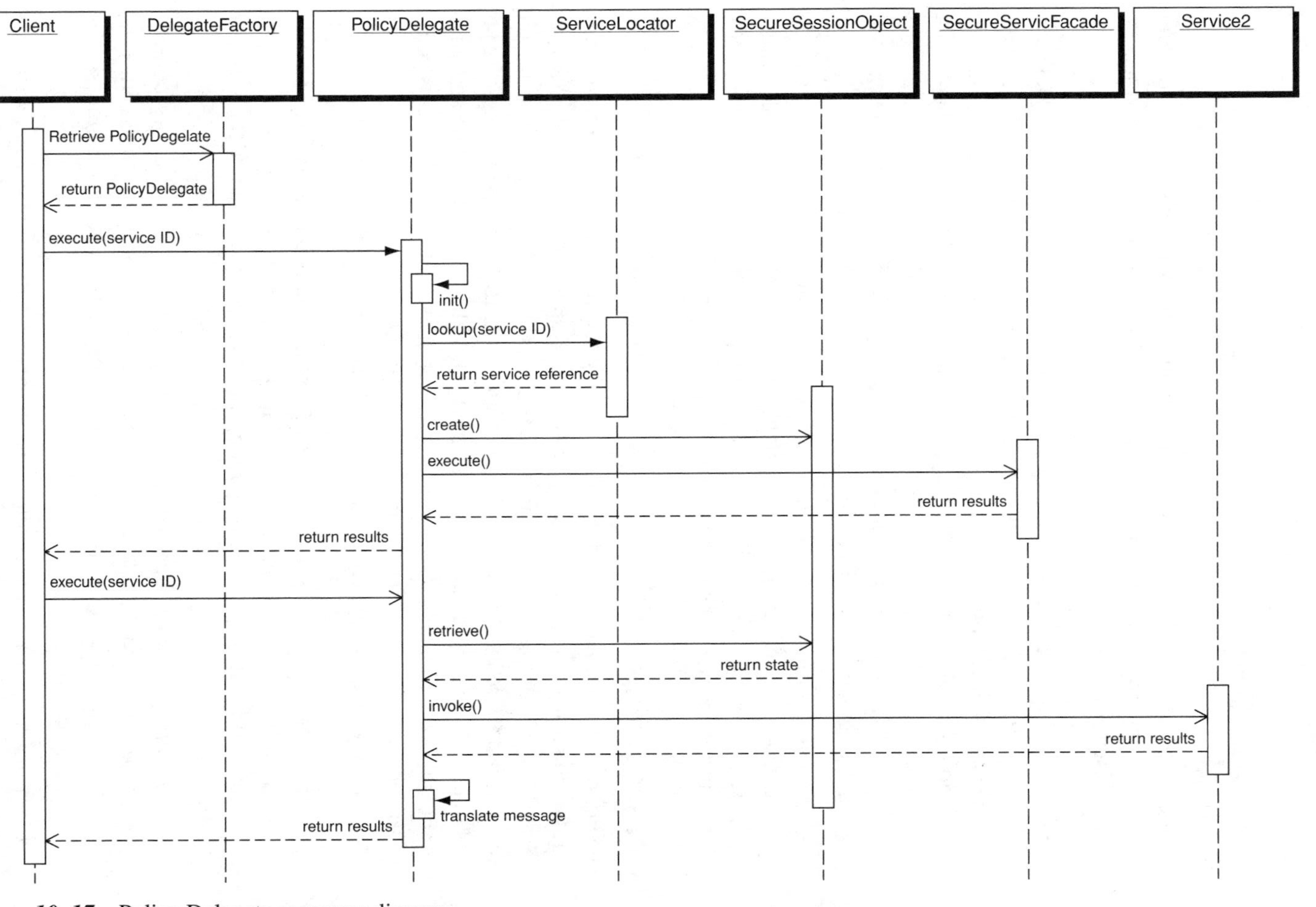

Figure 10–17 Policy Delegate sequence diagram

Strategies

The Policy Delegate pattern could be implemented in a variety of flavors depending on the magnitude of services it mediates and the approach to state management as discussed here.

- *One-to-many/one-to-one Policy Delegate.* In a one-to-one Policy Delegate, a delegate takes the responsibility of controlling one specific service, resulting in as many delegates as there are back-end services. This is a more granular approach than a one-to-many Policy Delegate, where a delegate controls multiple services offering a unified aggregate interface to a client. Remote references could be lazily loaded in such a delegate to avoid unnecessary service lookups and object creations.
- *Stateless/stateful Policy Delegate.* A stateful Policy Delegate maintains the state on the server side in a SecureSessionObject on behalf of the client. This is useful when clients are thin or are unaware of how security context must be preserved between invocations.

Consequences

The Policy Delegate pattern reduces the coupling between the security framework and the client of security services offered by the framework and thereby reduces the number of complex security interfaces exposed to the client. This has the overall effect of reducing complexity and therefore reducing potential software bugs that could lead to a variety of attacks. It also allows you to cache and manage the life cycle of a client's security context at the server and use it across multiple invocations by the same client, which enhances performance.

The Policy Delegate pattern benefits developers in the following ways:

- *Hides service complexity from client, exposes a cleaner interface.* The client only needs to be aware of the input and output messages of the delegate and not any implementation specifics or invocation details of the complex security services.
- *Optimizes performance.* By appropriate caching of the security context, the delegate could reduce repetitive computations associated with each individual request, thereby increasing the responsiveness of the system and scalability.
- *Performs message translation and error translation.* Security exceptions that are hard to decipher for a nonsecurity-aware client can be translated by the delegate to user-friendly exceptions before passing them to the client.
- *Performs service discovery, failover, and recovery.* Discovery and invocation details are abstracted to a central place, avoiding code duplication

among clients. The delegate, being aware of the location of each security service, can also perform application-level failover and recovery from catastrophic errors.

Sample Code

Example 10–9 lists the interface of the Policy Delegate that serves as the contract between security framework and clients.

Example 10–9 Policy Delegate interface

```
package com.csp.business;

import com.csp.*;
import com.csp.interfaces.*;

public interface PolicyDelegateInterface {
  // Alternative 1: Declare service specific methods
  public boolean authenticate(GenericTO  request)
          throws AuthenticationFailureException;

  public boolean authorize(GenericTO  request)
          throws AuthorizationFailureException;

  public SAMLMessage assertRequest(GenericTO  request)
          throws ApplicationException;
  // ...

  // Alternative 2: Declare a generic method (execute) with
  // with a generic transfer object as the inputs and outputs
  public GenericTO execute(String svcName, GenericTO input)
          throws ApplicationException;
}
```

Example 10–10 lists the implementation code of the Policy Delegate. The implementation code is not relevant to the client, which only relies on the Delegate Interface and a reference to the delegate.

Example 10–10 Sample Policy Delegate implementation code

```
package com.csp.business;

import com.csp.*;
import com.csp.interfaces.*;
```

```
public class PolicyDelegate implements PolicyDelegateInterface {
   private AuthenticationEnforcer authenticationEnforcer;
   private AuthorizationEnforcer authorizationEnforcer;
   private SecureSessionManager secureSessionManager;
   private SecureLogger secureLogger;
   private SecureServiceFacade secureServiceFacade;
   private RequestContext rc;

   //Manage lifecycle of the delegate
   public PolicyDelegate(RequestContext rc) {
      this.rc = rc;
      init(rc);
   }

   private void init(RequestContext rc) {
      // Look up and keep references to security
      // services/session facades/session beans...
      try {
         authenticationEnforcer = ServiceLocator.lookup(
               AuthenticationEnforcer.SERVICE_NAME);
         authorizationEnforcer = ServiceLocator.lookup(
               AuthorizationEnforcer.SERVICE_NAME);
         secureSessionManager = ServiceLocator.lookup(
               SecureSessionManager.SERVICE_NAME);
         secureLogger = ServiceLocator.lookup(
               SecureLogger.SERVICE_NAME);
         //...
         secureServiceFacade = ServiceLocator.lookup(
               SecureServiceFacade.SERVICE_NAME);
      } catch (Exception e) {
         throw new ApplicationException(e);
      }
   }

   public void destroy() {
      secureSessionManager.invalidate(rc);
  }

   //implement delegate methods
   // Alternative 1: Declare service specific methods
   public boolean authenticate(GenericTO request)
         throws AuthenticationFailureException {
      try {
         // Return the results of authentication
```

```
            return authenticationEnforcer.authenticate(request);
         } catch (SecurityFrameworkException e) {
            throw new AuthenticationFailureException(e);
         }
      }

      // Authorize the request.
      public boolean authorize(GenericTO request)
            throws AuthorizationFailureException {
         try {
            // Check the request is authenticated
            if(!request.authenticated()){
               if(!authenticationEnforcer.authenticate(request))
                  throw new AuthorizationFailureException(
                     new AuthenticationFailureException())
            }
            // Return the result of authorization
            return authenticationEnforcer.authorize(request);

         } catch (SecurityFrameworkException e) {
            throw new AuthorizationFailureException(e);
         }
      }

   // Alternative 2: Implement a generic method with generic
   // transfer object as input or output
   public GenericTO execute(String serviceName, GenericTO input) throws
ApplicationException{
     //Validate request as per security policy
     if(!input.authenticated()){
       if (!authenticationEnforcer.authenticate(input))
         throw new AuthenticationFailureException();
     }
     if(!input.authorized()){
       if (!authorizationEnforcer.authorize(input))
         throw new AuthorizationFailureException();
     }
     //process request
     GenericService service = ServiceLocator.lookup(serviceName);
     return service.execute(input);
   }
}
```

Example 10–11 lists a sample client code that uses a Policy Delegate.

Example 10–11 Client code using Policy Delegate

```
// ...
  try{
     // Get a dynamic proxy from the factory
     // This proxy will contain a populated GTO and overlay
     // the appropriate interface on top of it.
     PolicyDelegateInterface request =
        new PolicyDelegateFactory.getPolicyDelegate(
              PolicyDelegateFactory.AUTHENTICATION_ENFORCER);
     // This proxy is specific for Authentication and has
     // a method to retrieve the underlying GTO instance.

     // Retrieve the BusinessDelegate using the standard
     // technique outlined in the Core J2EE Patterns book
     // [CJP2].
     // BusinessDelegate delegate = ...
     GenericTO results = delegate.execute(
                           request.getGenericTO());
     // ... Do something with the results. You can use the
     // dynamic proxy to apply the appropriate interace.
  }
  catch (ApplicationException e){
     e.printStackTrace();
  }
// ...
```

Security Factors and Risks

The Policy Delegate simply acts as a central controller of security invocations. It is intended to be a helper class that provides seamless access to security functionality exposed in the Business tier. It eliminates the risks usually associated with business developers attempting to implement or integrate with security services. The fewer security touchpoints, the less potential for security holes. The Policy Delegate address the following security factors:

- **Authentication**. The Policy Delegate performs authentication through an Authentication Enforcer.
- **Authorization**. The Policy Delegate performs authorization of requests through an Authorization Enforcer.
- **Logging**. The Policy Delegate uses a Secure Logger to securely log request events.

- **Validation**. The Policy Delegate may validate request data via an Intercepting Validator.
- **Confidentiality**. The Policy Delegate relies on the underlying subsystems to provide confidentiality and data integrity.

Reality Check

Is Policy Delegate redundant? If the Web tier is already integrated with back-end security services in an implementation-specific manner without using Policy Delegate but using a Secure Service Façade, adding a Policy Delegate at that stage may not offer any benefit and will only cause rework. A thoughtful, careful design could avoid such scenarios.

Is the Policy Delegate interface too complex? If Policy Delegate usage becomes too complicated and requires too much knowledge of the underlying security framework by clients, it defeats the purpose of abstracting the complex logic in a simple helper as described in this pattern.

Related Patterns

Secure Base Action. Secure Base Action on the Web tier has a similar objective as the Policy Delegate on the Business tier. A Secure Base Action could in turn use a Policy Delegate to access security services.

Business Delegate [CJP2]. A Policy Delegate is similar to the Business Delegate pattern, but leverages other patterns discussed in this book related to security. Policy Delegate additionally makes use of a SecureSessionObject to protect the confidentiality and integrity of a client session.

Secure Service Façade

Problem

You need a secure gateway mandating and governing security on client requests, exposing a uniform, coarse-grained service interface over fine-grained, loosely coupled business services that mediates client requests to the appropriate services.

Having more access points in the Business tier leads to more opportunities for security holes. Every access point is then required to enforce all security requirements—from authentication and authorization to data validation and auditing. This becomes exacerbated in applications that have existing Business-tier services that are not secured.

Retrofitting security to security-unaware services is often difficult. Clients must not be made aware of the disparities between service implementations in terms of security requirements, message specifications, and other service-specific attributes. Offering a unified interface that couples the otherwise decoupled business services makes the design more comprehensible to clients and reduces the work involved in fulfilling client requests.

Forces

- You want to off-load security implementations from individual service components and perform them in a centralized fashion so that security developers can focus on security implementation and business developers can focus on business components.
- You want to impose and administer security rules on client requests that the service implementers are unaware of in order to ensure that authentication, authorization, validation, and auditing are properly performed on all services.
- You want a framework to manage the life cycle of the security context between interactive service invocations by clients and to propagate the security context to appropriate servers where the services are implemented.
- You want to reduce the coupling between fine-grained services but expose a unified aggregation of such services to the client through a simple interface that hides the complexities of interaction between individual services while enforcing all of the overall security requirements of each service.
- You want to minimize the message exchange between the client and the services, storing the intermittent state and context on the server on behalf of the client instead.

Solution

Use a Secure Service Façade to mediate and centralize complex interactions between business components under a secure session.

Use a Secure Session Façade to integrate fine-grained, security-unaware service implementation and offer a unified, security-enabled interface to clients. The Secure Service Façade acts as a gateway where client requests are securely validated and routed to the appropriate service implementations, often maintaining and mediating the security and workflow context between interactive client requests and between fine-grained services that fulfill portions of the client requests.

Structure

Figure 10-18 illustrates a Secure Service Façade class diagram. The Façade is the endpoint exposed to the client and could be implemented as a stateful session

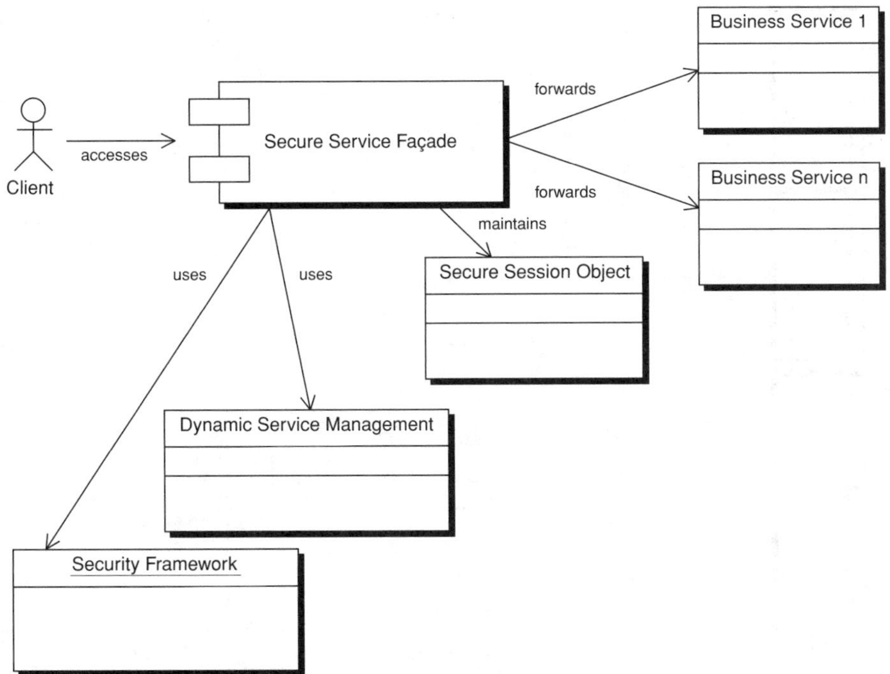

Figure 10–18 Secure Service Façade class diagram

bean or a servlet endpoint. It uses the security framework (implemented using other patterns) to perform security-related tasks applicable to the client request. The framework may request the client to present further credentials if the requested service mandates doing so and if those credentials were not found in the initial client request. The Façade then uses the Dynamic Service Management pattern to locate the appropriate service-provider implementations. The request is then forwarded to the individual services either sequentially, in parallel, or in any complex relationship order as specified in the request description.

If the client request represents an aggregation of fine-grained services, the return messages from previous sequential service invocations can be aggregated and delivered to the subsequent service to achieve a sequential workflow-like implementation. If those fine-grained services are independent of each other, then they can be invoked in parallel and the results can be aggregated before delivering to the client, thus achieving parallel processing of the client request.

Participants and Responsibilities

Figure 10-19 depicts a sequence diagram for a typical Secure Service Façade implementation that corresponds to the structure description in the preceding section.

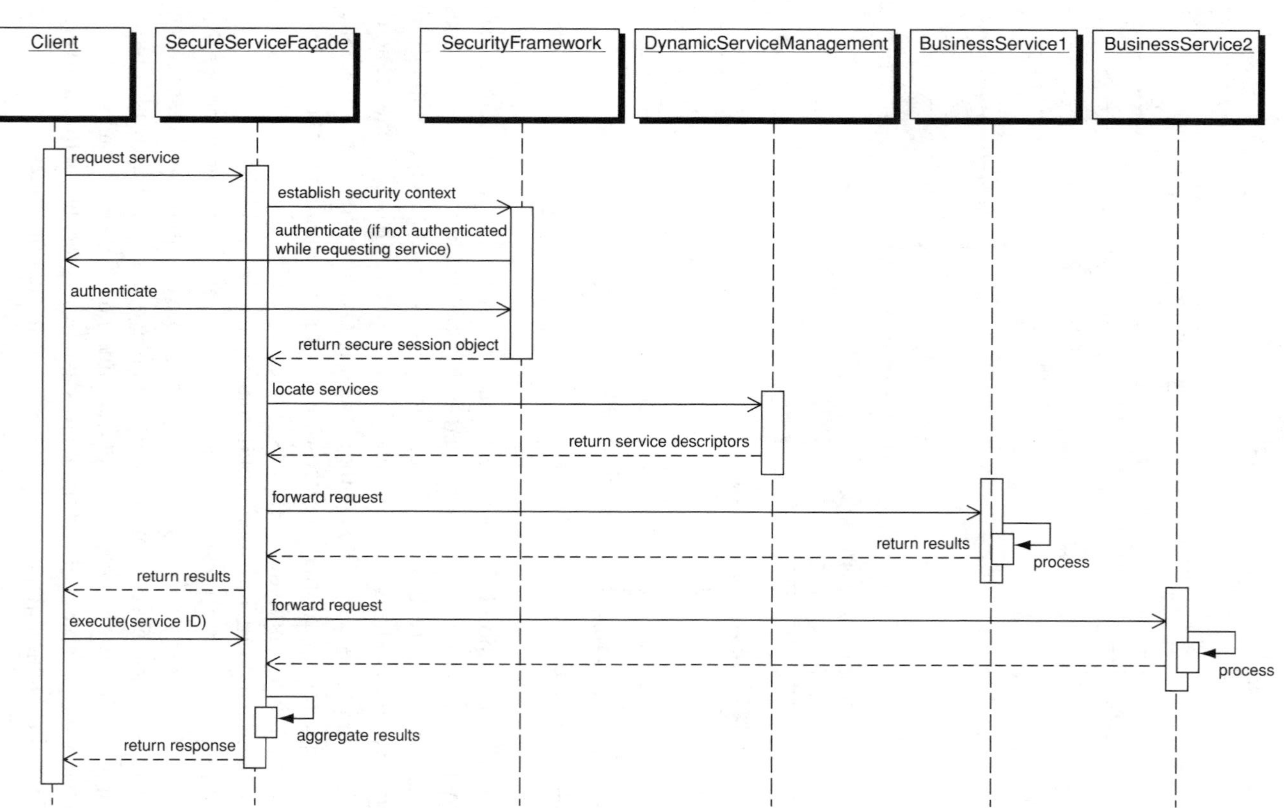

Figure 10–19 Secure Service Façade sequence diagram

- **Client**. A client sends a request to perform a specific task with the appropriate service descriptors to the Secure Service Façade, optionally incorporating the decision-tree predicates to determine the sequence services to be invoked.
- The Secure Service Façade deciphers the client request, verifies authentication, fulfills the request, and returns the results to the client. In doing so, it may use the following components:
  - **Security Framework**. The façade uses the existing enterprise-wide security framework implemented using other security patterns discussed in this book. Such a framework can be leveraged for authentication, authorization and access control, security assertions, trust management, and so forth. If the request is missing any credentials, the client request could be terminated or the client could be asked to furnish further credentials.
  - **Dynamic Service Framework/Service Locator**. The façade uses the Dynamic Service Framework or Service Locator to locate the services that are involved in fulfilling the request. The services could reside on the same host or be distributed throughout an enterprise. In either case, the façade ensures that the security context established using the security framework is correctly propagated to any service that expects such security attributes. The façade then establishes the execution logic and invokes each service in the correct order.

The fine-grained business services are not directly exposed to the client. The services themselves maintain loose coupling between each other and the façade. The façade takes the responsibility of unifying the individual services in the context of the client request. The service façade contains no business logic itself and therefore requires no protection.

Strategies

The Secure Service Façade manages the complex relationships between disparate participating business services, plugs in security to request fulfillment, and provides a high-level, coarse-grained abstraction to the client. The nature of such tasks opens up multiple choices for implementation flavors, two of which are briefly discussed now.

- *Façade with static relationships between individual service components.* The relationship between participating fine-grained services is permanently static in nature. In such cases, the façade can be represented by an interface that corresponds to the aggregate of the services and can be implemented by a session bean that implements the interface. The session bean life cycle method Create can preprocess the request for security validations.

- *Façade with dynamic, transient relationships between individual service components.* When the sequence of service calls to be invoked by the façade is dependent upon the prior invocation history in the execution sequence, the decision predicates can be specified in the request semantics and used in the façade implementations to determine the next service to be invoked. Such an implementation can be highly dynamic in nature, and the decision predicates can incorporate security class and compartment information to enable multilevel security in the façade implementation. A different flavor can use a simple interface in the façade, such as a command pattern implementation, and can mandate that the service descriptors be specified in the request message. This allows new services to be plugged-and-played without requiring changes to the façade interface and is widely used in Web services.

Consequences

The Secure Service Façade pattern protects the Business-tier services and business objects from attacks that circumvent the Web tier or Web Services tier. The Web tier and the Web Services tier are responsible for upfront authentication and access control. An attacker who has penetrated the network perimeter could circumvent these tiers and access the Business tier directly. The Secure Service Façade is responsible for protecting the Business tier by enforcing the security mechanisms established by the Web and Web Services tiers. By employing the Secure Service Façade pattern, developers and clients can benefit in the following ways:

- *Exposes a simplified, unified interface to a client.* The Secure Service Façade shields the client from the complex interactions between the participating services by providing a single unified interface for service invocation. This brings the advantages of loose coupling between clients and fine-grained business services, centralized mediation, easier management, and reduces the risks of change management.
- *Off-loads security validations from lightweight services.* Participating business services in a façade may be too lightweight to define security policies and incorporate security processing. Secure Service Façade off-loads such responsibility from business services and offers a centralized policy management and administration of centralized security processing tasks, thereby reducing code duplication and processing redundancies.
- *Centralizes policy administration.* The centralized nature of the Secure Service Façade eases security policy administration by isolating it to a single location. Such centralization also makes it feasible to retrofit infrastructure security to otherwise security-unaware or existing services.

- *Centralizes transaction management and incorporates security attributes.* As with a generic session façade, a Secure Service Façade allows applying distributed transaction management over individual transactions of the participating services. Since security attributes are accessible at the same place, transaction management can incorporate such security attributes, offering multilevel, security-driven transaction management.
- *Facilitates dynamic, rule-based service integration and invocation.* As explained in the preceding "Strategies" section, multiple flavors of façade implementations offer a very dynamic and flexible integration of business services. Integration rules can incorporate security and message attributes in order to dynamically determine execution sequence. An external Business Rules Engine can also be plugged into such a dynamic façade.
- *Minimize message exchange between client and services.* Secure Service Façade minimizes message exchange by caching the intermittent state and context on the server rather than on the client.

Sample Code

The sample code that follows illustrates a Stateful Session Bean approach to a Secure Service Façade implementation. Example 10–12 and Example 10–13 show the home and remote interfaces to the Façade Session bean.

Example 10–12 SecureServiceFaçade home interface

```
package com.csp.business;

import java.rmi.*;
import javax.ejb.*;
import com.csp.*;

public interface SecureServiceFacadeHome extends EJBHome {
  public SecureServiceFacade create(SecurityContext ctx)
     throws RemoteException,CreateException;
}
```

Example 10–13 SecureServiceFaçade remote interface

```
package com.csp.business;

import java.rmi.*;
import javax.ejb.*;
import com.csp.*;
```

```
public interface SecureServiceFacade extends EJBObject {
  public TransferObject execute(SecureMessage msg)
    throws RemoteException;
```

Example 10–14 lists a sample bean implementation code. The important item to notice is that the SecurityContext object is maintained as a state variable in the stateful session bean in order to facilitate propagation of the context to any individual service that expects it. The SecureMessage encapsulates the aggregate service description of the client request and is used to locate the appropriate services and optionally establish a dynamic sequence of participating service executions.

Example 10–14 SecureSessionFaçadeSessionBean.java sample implementation

```
package com.csp.business;

import java.rmi.*;
import javax.ejb.*;
import javax.naming.*;
import java.util.*;
import com.csp.*;

public class SecureServiceFacadeSessionBean implements SessionBean {
  private SessionContext context;
  private SecurityContext securityContext;
  // Remote references for the individual services
  // can be encapsulated as facade attributes
  // or made part of the message
  private ServiceMaps services = new HashMap();
  // Create the facade and initialize the security context
  public void ejbCreate(SecurityContext ctx)
      throws CreateException, ResourceException {
    securityContext = ctx;
  }
  // Locate the requested service and cache for
  // prospective future use and stickiness
  private SecureMessage execute(SecureMessage msg)
    throws SecureServiceFacadeException,
      ServiceLocatorException {
    SecureService svc = ServiceLocator.getService(
      msg.getRequestedServiceName());
    services.put(msg.getRequestedServiceName(), svc);
    return svc.execute(msg);
  }
```

```
    // ...
    // Other lifecycle methods
    public void ejbActivate() { ... }
    public void ejbPassivate() { ... }
    public void setSessionContext(SessionContext ctx) { ... }
    public void ejbRemove() { ... }
}
```

Security Factors and Risks

The Secure Service Façade pattern is susceptible to code bloating if too much interaction logic is incorporated. However, this can be minimized by appropriate design of the façade using other common design patterns. As the gateway into the Business tier, the Secure Service Façade serves to limit the touchpoints between the Web and Web Services tiers and the Business tier. This means that there are fewer entry points that need to be secured and therefore fewer opportunities for security holes to be introduced.

The following security factors are addressed by the Secure Service Façade:

- **Authentication**. The Secure Session Façade pattern authenticates requests coming into the Business tier. This is often necessary when clients connect directly to the Business tier through a remote interface or in cases where the Web tier cannot be trusted to perform authentication appropriately for the Business tier.
- **Auditing**. The Secure Session Façade enables developers to insert auditing at the entry and exit points of the Business tier. This enables them to put an Audit Interceptor pattern, discussed earlier in this chapter, in place and decouple auditing from business logic while ensuring that no requests can be initiated without first being audited.

Reality Check

Does the Service Façade need to incorporate security? The Secure Service Proxy uses the existing security framework while aggregating fine-grained services. However, security context validation may not be required if other means of authentication and access control are pertinently enforced on the client request before it reaches the façade.

Does the Secure Service Façade need to perform service aggregation? If the client requests will mostly be fulfilled by a single, fine-grained service component, there is no necessity for aggregation. In such cases, Secure Service Proxy may well suit the purpose.

Does the Secure Service Façade reduce security code duplication? If security context validation is performed by each service component, the validation at the façade level may turn out to be redundant and wasteful. A planned design could reduce such duplication.

Related Patterns

Secure Service Proxy. Secure Service Proxy, implemented as a Web service endpoint, acts as a mediator between the clients and the J2EE components with a one-on-one mapping between proxy methods and remote methods of J2EE components. Secure Service Façade, on the other hand, maintains complex relationships between participating services and exposes an aggregated uniform interface to the client.

Session Façade. The Secure Service Façade and the generic Session Façade [CJP2] offer the same benefits with respect to business object integration and aggregation. However, Secure Service Façade does not require that the participating components are EJBs. The participating services could use any framework and the façade would incorporate the appropriate invocation logic to use those services. In addition, Secure Service Façade emphasizes the security context life cycle management and its propagation to appropriate services.

Secure Session Object

Problem

You need to facilitate distributed access and seamless propagation of security context and client sessions in a platform-independent and location-independent manner.

A multi-user, multi-application distributed system needs a mechanism to allow global accessibility to the security context associated with a client session and secure transmission of the context among the distributed applications, each with its own address space. While many choices are possible, the developer must design a standardized structure and interface to the security context. The security context propagation is essential within the application because it is the sole means of allowing different components within the application to verify that authentication and access control have been properly enforced. Otherwise, each component would need to enforce security and the user would wind up authenticating on each request. The Secure Session Object pattern serves this purpose.

Forces

- You want to define a data structure for the security context that comprises authentication and authorization credentials so that application components can validate those credentials.
- You want to define a token that can uniquely identify the security context to be shared between applications to retrieve the context, thereby enabling single sign-on between applications.
- You want to abstract vendor-specific session management and distribution implementations.
- You want to securely transmit the security context across virtual machines and address spaces when desired in order to retain the client's credentials outside of the initial request thread.

Solution

Use a Secure Session Object to abstract encapsulation of authentication and authorization credentials that can be passed across boundaries.

You often need to persist session data within a single session or between user sessions that span an indeterminate period of time. In a typical Web application, you could use cookies and URL rewriting to achieve session persistence, but there are security, performance, and network-utilization implications of doing so. Applications that store sensitive data in the session are often compelled to protect such data and prevent potential misuse by malicious code (a Trojan horse) or a user (a hacker). Malicious code could use reflection to retrieve private members of an object. Hackers could sniff the serialized session object while in transit and misuse the data. Developers could unknowingly use debug statements to print sensitive data in log files. Secure Session Object can ensure that sensitive information is not inadvertently exposed.

The Secure Session Object provides a means of encapsulating authentication and authorization information such as credentials, roles, and privileges, and using them for secure transport. This allows components across tiers or asynchronous messaging systems to verify that the originator of the request is authenticated and authorized for that particular service. It is intended that this serves as an abstract mechanism to encapsulate vendor-specific implementations. A Secure Session Object is an ideal way to share and transmit global security information associated with a client.

Structure

Figure 10–20 is a class diagram of the Secure Session Object.

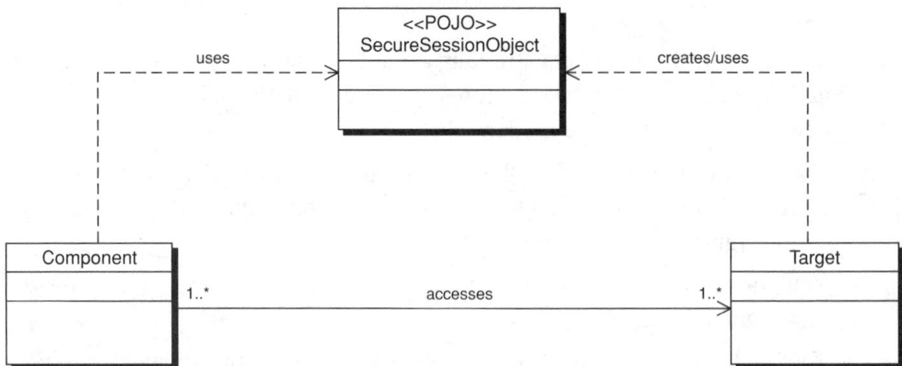

Figure 10–20 Secure Session Object class diagram

Participants and Responsibilities

Figure 10–21 contains the sequence diagram and illustrates the interactions of the Secure Session Object.

Client. The Client sends a request to a Target resource. The Client receives a SecureSessionObject and stores it for submitting in subsequent requests.

SecureSessionObject. SecureSessionObject stores information regarding the client and its session, which can be validated by consumers to establish authentication and authorization of that client.

Target. The Target creates a SecureSessionObject. It then verifies the SecureSessionObject passed in on subsequent requests.

The Secure Session Object is implemented through the following steps:

1. Client accesses a Target resource.
2. Target creates a SecureSessionObject.
3. Target serializes SecureSessionObject and returns it in response.
4. Client needs to access Target again and serialize SecureSessionObject from the last request.
5. Client accesses Target, passing the SecureSessionObject created previously in response to the request.
6. Target receives the request and verifies the SecureSessionObject before completing the request.

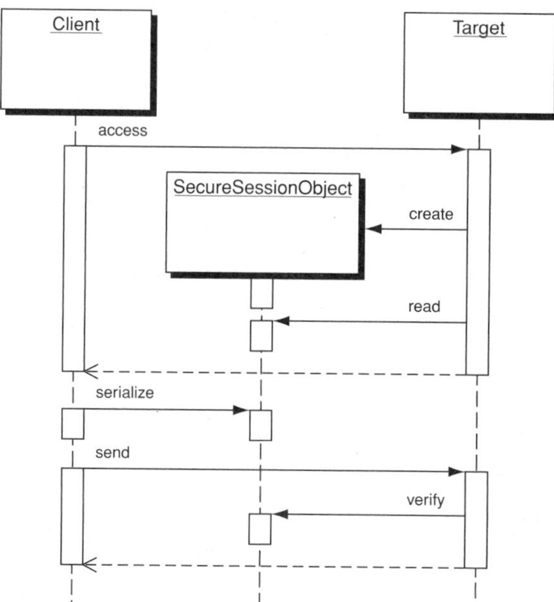

Figure 10–21 Secure Session Object sequence diagram

Strategies

You can use a number of strategies to implement Secure Session Object. The first strategy is using a Transfer Object Member, which allows you to use Transfer Objects to exchange data across tiers. The second strategy is using an Interceptor, which is applicable when transferring data across remote endpoints, such as between tiers.

Transfer Object Member Strategy

In the Transfer Object Member strategy, the Secure Session Object is passed as a member of the more generic Transfer Object. This allows the target component to validate the Secure Session Object wherever data is passed using a Transfer Object. Because the Secure Session Object is contained within the Transfer Object, the existing interfaces don't require additional instances of the Secure Session Object. This keeps the interfaces from becoming brittle or inflexible and allows easy integration of the Secure Session Object into existing applications with established interfaces.

Figure 10–22 is a class diagram of the Secure Session Object pattern implemented using a Transfer Object Member strategy.

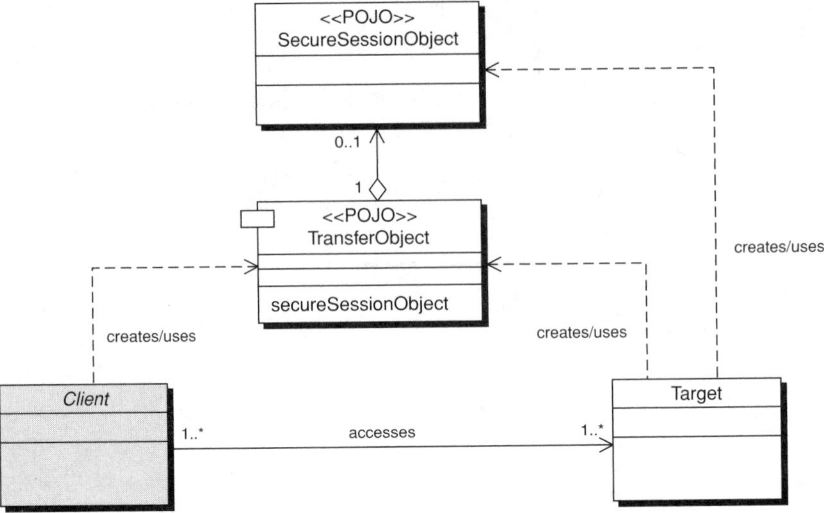

Figure 10–22 Transfer Object Member Strategy class diagram

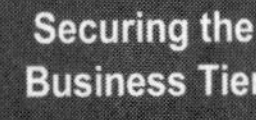

Interceptor Strategy

In the Interceptor Strategy, which is mostly applicable to a distributed client-server model, the client and the server use appropriate interceptors to negotiate and instantiate a centrally managed Secure Session Object. This session object glues the client and server interceptors to enforce session security on the client-server communication. The client and the server interceptors perform the initial handshake to agree upon the security mechanisms for the session object.

The client authenticates to the server and retrieves a reference to the session object via a client interceptor. The reference could be as simple as a token or a remote object reference. After the client has authenticated itself, the server interceptor uses a session object factory to instantiate the Secure Session Object and returns the reference of the object to the client. The client and the server interceptors then exchange messages marshalled and unmarshalled according to the security context maintained in the Secure Session Object.

Figure 10–23 is a class diagram of the Secure Session Object pattern implemented using an Interceptor Strategy.

This strategy offers the ability to update or replace the security implementations in the interceptors independently of one another. Moreover, any change in the Secure Session Object implementation causes changes only in the interceptors instead of the whole application.

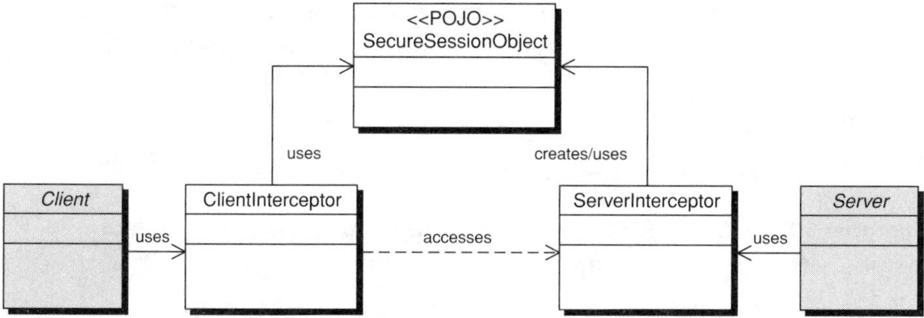

Figure 10–23 Interceptor Strategy class diagram

Consequences

The Secure Session Object prevents a form of session hijacking that could occur if session context is not propagated and therefore not checked in the Business tier. This happens when the Web tier is distributed from the Business tier. This also applies to message passing over JMS as well. The ramifications of not using a Secure Session Object are that impersonation attacks can take place from inside the perimeter. By employing the Secure Session Object pattern, developers benefit in the following ways:

- *Controlled access and common interface to sensitive information.* The Secure Session Object encapsulates all sensitive information related to session management and communication establishment. It can then restrict access to such information, encrypt with complete autonomy, or even block access to information that is inappropriate to the rest of the application. A common interface serves all components that need access to the rest of the session data and offers an aggregate view of session information.
- *Optimized security processing.* Since Secure Session Object can be reused over time, it minimizes repetition of security tasks such as authentication, secure connection establishment, and encryption and decryption of shared, static data.
- *Reduced network utilization and memory consumption.* Centralizing management and access to a Secure Session Object via appropriate references and tokens minimizes the amount of session information exchanged between clients and servers. Memory utilization is also optimized by sharing security context between multiple components.
- *Abstract vendor-specific session management implementations.* The Secure Session Object pattern provides a generic data structure for storing and

retrieving vendor-specific session management information. This reduces the dependency on a particular vendor and promotes code evolution.

Sample Code

Example 10–15 shows sample code for Transfer Object Member strategy.

Example 10–15 SecureSessionTransferObject.java: Transfer Object member strategy implementation


```
package com.csp.business;

public class SecureSessionTransferObject
     implements java.io.Serializable {
   private SecureSessionObject secureSessionObject;

   public SecureSessionObject getSecureTransferObject() {
      return secureSessionObject;
   }

   public void setSecureTransferObject(
            SecureSessionObject secureSessionObject) {
      this.secureSessionObject = secureSessionObject;
   }
   // Additional TransferObject methods...
}
```

A developer can implement a SecureSessionTransferObject whenever they want to pass credentials within a Transfer Object.

Security Factors and Risks

- **Authentication**. The Secure Session Object enforces authentication of clients requesting Business-tier components. Target components or interceptors for those components can validate the Secure Session Object passed in on request and therefore assure that the invoking client was properly authenticated.
- **Authorization**. The Secure Session Object can enforce authorization on Business-tier clients as well. While it provides a coarse-grained level of authorization, just by being in the request or not it can be extended to include and enforce fine-grained authorization.

Reality Check

Is Secure Session Object too bloated? Abstracting all session information into a single composite object may increase the object size. Serializing and de-serializing such an object quite frequently degrades performance. In such cases, one could revisit the object design or serialization routines to alleviate the performance degradation.

Concurrency implications. Many components associated with the client session could be competing to update and read session data, which could lead to concurrency issues such as long wait times or deadlocks. A careful analysis of the possible scenarios is recommended.

Related Patterns

Transfer Object [CJP2]. Secure Service Proxy, implemented as a Web service endpoint, acts as a mediator between the clients and the J2EE components with a one-on-one mapping between proxy methods and remote methods of J2EE components. Secure Service Façade, on the other hand, maintains complex relationships between participating services and exposes **an aggregated uniform interface to the client.**

Session Façade. The Secure Service Façade and the generic Session Façade [CJP2] offer the same benefits with respect to business object integration and aggregation. However, Secure Service Façade does not require that the participating components be EJBs. The participating components may be plain old java objects (POJOs) or any other object.

Best Practices and Pitfalls

This section discusses best practices and the associated pitfalls regarding securing the Business tier. The best practices have been broken down by layer and are followed by the pitfalls.

Infrastructure

1. *Agent-based policy enforcement.* Developers can use agents to enforce policies instead of writing custom code for policy enforcement. Application Server agents are good ways to take advantage of the J2EE container-managed security model while leveraging existing third-party security products.

2. *Access protection.* Make sure that a secure java.policy file is in place that enforces access privileges and permissions to protect the JAR components deployed by the application server. Make sure no untrusted JAR files are deployed. This secures JAR/Class files from downloading by hackers and external applications. Make use of digitally signed JAR files so that the code is downloaded by the coexisting application and the owner of the JAR file.
3. *Access restriction to Naming services.* Restrict anonymous access to the naming services. Secure the access to the naming services provider by defining only an administrator who can add or remove services from the JNDI registry. Allow application-level access to lookup, bind, and rebind with services.

4. *Error reporting.* Always return an error page or exception specific to the application error and the user's request. For example, you might use an application-specific InvalidUserException and NoAccessPrivilegesException. Do not expose remote, system-level, and naming service specific exceptions to the user accessing the applications. These exceptions to the end user expose weakness in the application and allow hackers to design potential attacks.
5. *Database communication.* Make use of the database provider's recommended security mechanisms for persisting data. Adopt possible options to improve the transport and data security, such as encrypting communication and sensitive data before writing it to the database. For example, store customer data in the database in plain text except for the encrypted credit card information.

Architecture

6. *Component protection.* Make sure all business components are protected with security roles and appropriate privileges before deployment. Avoid defining a global security role such as administrator unless it is warranted by the application.
7. *Role mappings.* Adopt dynamic role mappings based on business rules, the context of the request, or a condition such as access hours, time of day, group membership, specific assignment, or a caller member of the group. For example, a user may be allowed to be in an administrator role only while the actual administrator is away, as a temporary arrangement, by adding the user to a special role or group. You must be able to specify the hours between which the temporary administrator has special privileges.

These privileges are automatically revoked when the time expires or the actual administrator returns. You also want to avoid using the same role names in the application because application-specific roles are mapped in deployment descriptors and they should be different from LDAP roles.

8. *Rich-client authentication.* While accessing EJB components via rich Java clients, do not send username/password credentials of the user through a Java object. Adopt container-managed mechanisms and then use declarative or programmatic security mechanisms to obtain the associated principal from them.
9. *MDB access.* Restrict unauthorized access to the MDB and prevent it from sending and processing malicious messages. Make sure the message sender uses a unique message ID, correlation IDs, and custom message headers to verify the sender's authenticity before processing the message.
10. *Secure auditing.* Deploy a secure logging and auditing mechanism (Audit Interceptor) to record and to provide a means of identifying and auditing all direct access attempts, policy violations, failed authentication attempts, failed EJB access, and exceptions.
11. *Principal propagation.* In the case of defining delegated associations between EJBs and trust relationships between containers, it is necessary to analyze the consequences and potential risks of using the `runAs` technique for principal delegation and for propagating identity. SSL Mutual authentication is the best approach before initiating communication for exploring trust relationships between containers.
12. *Securing Business Tier components.* Use the Secure Session Façade to protect interactions and to mask the exposure of underlying business components and their methods.
13. *Data validation.* Adopt well-defined validation procedures in the business component for handling data-format and business data. This ensures data integrity and protects application components from the risk of processing overhead due to malicious data injection.
14. *Data obfuscation.* Adopt object obfuscation (Obfuscate Transfer Object) while using value objects that represent a snapshot of security-sensitive data in the database.

Policy

15. *Disallow unnecessary protocols.* In cases where rich clients are not being used to access business components, disallow all traffic from ports specific

to RMI/IIOP, IIOP-CSIv2, or J2EE vendor-preferred protocols. Also disallow all service requests, routing information, and packet content from external access to EJBs or business components.

16. *Restrict deployed components.* Do not store undeployed business components in the production environment.
17. *Restrict user access.* Configure user lockouts and access time limits to prevent attacks from potential hackers on user accounts that send malicious data. Avoid long-duration transactions that affect performance.
18. *Authentication enforcement.* Use a Secure Session Object to provide authentication enforcement in the Business tier. This prevents circumvention of Web-tier controls by preventing any communication with the Business tier (for example, a direct EJB invocation via RMI) from an external source without proper authentication.
19. *Use Audit Interceptor to audit events.* Properly audit events and have formal audit reviews to ensure the application has not been compromised. Have a process and procedures in place to diagnose the audit logs in the case of a disaster or attack.
20. *Monitor for malicious activity.* Use Dynamic Service Management to monitor security-related components. Build or buy a tool that provides automated monitoring of those components in a way that lets you detect malicious activity. For example, set a threshold with an alert on the number of incorrect logins per user client to detect a hacker using a brute force password attack or attempting to scan for weak passwords across accounts.

Pitfalls

21. *Build versus buy.* Developers tend to build versus buy solutions because doing so gives them maximum flexibility and allows them to maintain control. This is usually a bad practice, because the costs of additional time and resources outweigh the benefits of the flexibility. In the case of security, this is especially true. Most developers do not understand all of the security issues well enough to implement a security model better than a vendor. A vendor product has the added benefit of being time-tested in the real world with feedback from external sources.
22. *Performance risks.* The principle of conservation of energy demonstrates that you cannot get something for nothing. This holds true for security.

The cost for increased security usually comes at the price of performance. While it is necessary to achieve a certain level of security, introducing unnecessary security functionality usually reduces performance and increases complexity. Strive to balance security and performance in your applications.

References

[CJP2] Deepak Alur, John Crupi, and Dan Malks. *Core J2EE Patterns: Best Practices and Design Strategies*, Second Edition. Prentice Hall, 2003.

[SPEC] Java™ 2 Platform Enterprise Edition Specification, v1.4.
http://java.sun.com/j2ee/j2ee-1_4-fr-spec.pdf

[POSA1] Buschmann, Meunier, Rohnert, Sommerlad, and Stal. *Pattern-Oriented Software Architecture—A System of Patterns*. Wiley Press, 1996-2000.

[Gof] Gamma, Helm, Johnson, and Vlissides. *Design Patterns: Elements of Reusable Object-Oriented Software*. Addison-Wesley, 1994.

Securing Web Services–Design Strategies and Best Practices

Topics in This Chapter

- Web Services Security Protocols Stack
- Web Services Security Infrastructure
- Web Services Security Patterns
- Best Practices and Pitfalls

Chapter 11

Securing Web Services

Web services provide XML standards-based technology for developing and deploying application components. They provide an ideal infrastructure solution for delivering cross-platform application-to-application communication and integration. Web services are increasingly used for enabling inter-enterprise communication, workflow, and collaboration, and for integrating business applications over a network. Enabling XML Web services enables interoperability among applications developed using heterogeneous environments such as J2EE, Microsoft .NET, CORBA, and C++.

Security in Web services can be implemented from the ground up in a loosely coupled and platform-independent way, ensuring secure communication and controlled access via authentication and authorization. This is achieved by applying rules and policies for access to exposed services and establishing a circle of trust among service providers, identity providers, and service requesters. Adopting XML-based security and other standards-based technologies provides the mechanisms for achieving the goals of end-to-end Web services security and also enabling interoperability among infrastructure providers. Applying security and establishing trust among Web services or between a Web service and its consumer has created newer challenges, some of which remain un-addressed by traditional security methods and technologies. Because Web services can be dynamically located, subscribed, and consumed using a wide range of heterogeneous applications, system platforms, devices, and so on, it is also the responsibility of the Web services provider to facilitate a standardized security mechanism that can be accessed by the service requesters using heterogeneous platforms and devices.

For example, in a healthcare Web services scenario, a patient viewing his or her medical records via Web services should not be constrained or impacted by whether he or she is using a Web browser client, a network accessible device, or a stand-alone application as long as the service requester client is able to view the secured information using a network with the required standards, secure message transport, and relevant message-level security mechanisms required by the Web service provider. Similarly, a patient's record may be viewed in a workflow by multiple participants, including a physician, lab specialist, pharmacist, insurance provider, and so on. The problem is that each participant may require access to a selected portion of the document without compromising the security of the patient's health record.

In Chapter 6, we discussed the Web services architectural goals, Web services security threats and vulnerabilities, security requirements, and evolving standards and technologies. When implementing Web services applications, the known security risks and threats are usually considered as security challenges that need to be addressed with safeguards and countermeasures prior to deployment. Otherwise they can affect numerous aspects of the overall Web services architecture, including security, availability, reliability, scalability, and manageability. Many of these security challenges are captured and addressed using a proven set of security design patterns and best practices that are applicable during the architectural and design phases of Web services development.

This chapter explores the Web services security design strategies, applied patterns, and best practices that contribute to building end-to-end security of Web services. This chapter adheres to the XML security specifications derived from industry-standard efforts and compliant vendor implementations for building XML Web services.

Web Services Security Protocols Stack

The OSI 7-layer model provides the means to meaningfully discuss the rationale of Web services security protocols, security layers, and how they are partitioned. The OSI stack identifies seven distinct layers for the facilitation of data communication. Each layer provides services to the next higher layer, including its primitives and associated data. Each layer relies on the next lower layer.

Although the OSI stack is not reflected in reality, the representation of TCP/IP in the OSI structure forms the basis for any communication on the Internet. At the bottom, the Data Link and Physical layers represent the link between the host and the network. IP plays at the Network Layer and TCP/IP at the Transport layer, delivering the virtual circuit for transporting packets. On the top, the Application, Presentation, and Session layers facilitate the user exchange of data.

In a Web services communication, applying security protocol mechanisms is facilitated between the Network and Transport layers. In conjunction with OSI stack and its seven layers, the Web services security stack is shown in Figure 11–1.

Effectively, the end-to-end security of a Web services solution is addressed by three security layers that are clearly delineated with mechanisms and responsibilities for securing the Web services communication, messages, and their network infrastructure. The three security layers and their tasks and responsibilities are described in the following sections.

Network-Layer Security

Network-Layer Security works on the IP and TCP layers by providing perimeter security for the network infrastructure hosting the service and filtering out connections from unauthorized intruders. Network routers and firewall appliances make up this solution, and the protection is limited to connection attacks based on IP addresses, TCP ports, protocols, and packets.

Transport-Layer Security

Transport-Layer Security secures the communication and ensures data privacy, confidentiality, and integrity between the communicating endpoints. It ensures

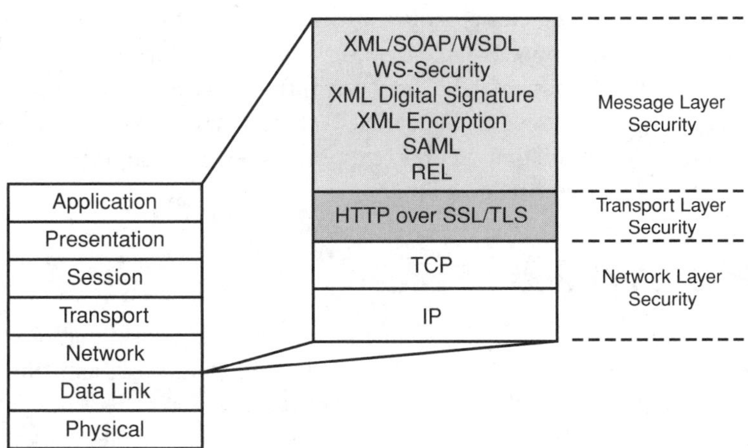

Figure 11–1 The OSI stack 7-layers and Web services security

that the data transmitted and the sessions are protected from eavesdropping by unintended recipients. Applying cryptographic algorithms and adopting two-way SSL/TLS mechanisms make up this solution, which allows securing the transport and data exchanged on the wire by encrypting messages. During transit, it also guarantees that data transmitted is not accessible for viewing by unintended recipients or intermediaries.

Message-Layer Security

Message-Layer Security secures the Web services endpoint with application-specific security information in the form of XML metadata. In Web services communication, XML messages may contain malicious content from unauthorized parties that can cause a threat to the service endpoint. Traditional security mechanisms such as firewalls and HTTP/SSL would not verify the XML content-level threats that can lead to a buffer overflow or SQL/XQUERY insertion, or XML-based denial-of-service (X-DoS). Incorporating message-level security allows defining application- or service-specific security as XML metadata or SOAP header blocks that represent information related to a user's identity, authentication, authorization, encryption/decryption, and digital signatures.

Web Services Security Infrastructure

In a Web services environment, the choice of deployment infrastructure is greatly influenced by the development and deployment environment, which is typically either the J2EE platform or Microsoft .NET. In both cases, the security infrastructure is expected to provide comparable run-time services for securing the services provider or a consumer's endpoint. These services must address all the mandated security layers, which include the network infrastructure, transport, and messages. Figure 11–2 illustrates a conceptual Web services infrastructure and components of an organization that securely exposes its business applications as XML Web services to a partner organization.

Network Perimeter Security

Network infrastructure security is provided by a network firewall, an IP router, or filtering gateways that can enforce access control by examining and filtering the inbound and outbound traffic routed between the networks. The firewall or IP router resides at the junction point or gateway between the two networks, usually a private network and a public network such as the Internet. Most network fire-

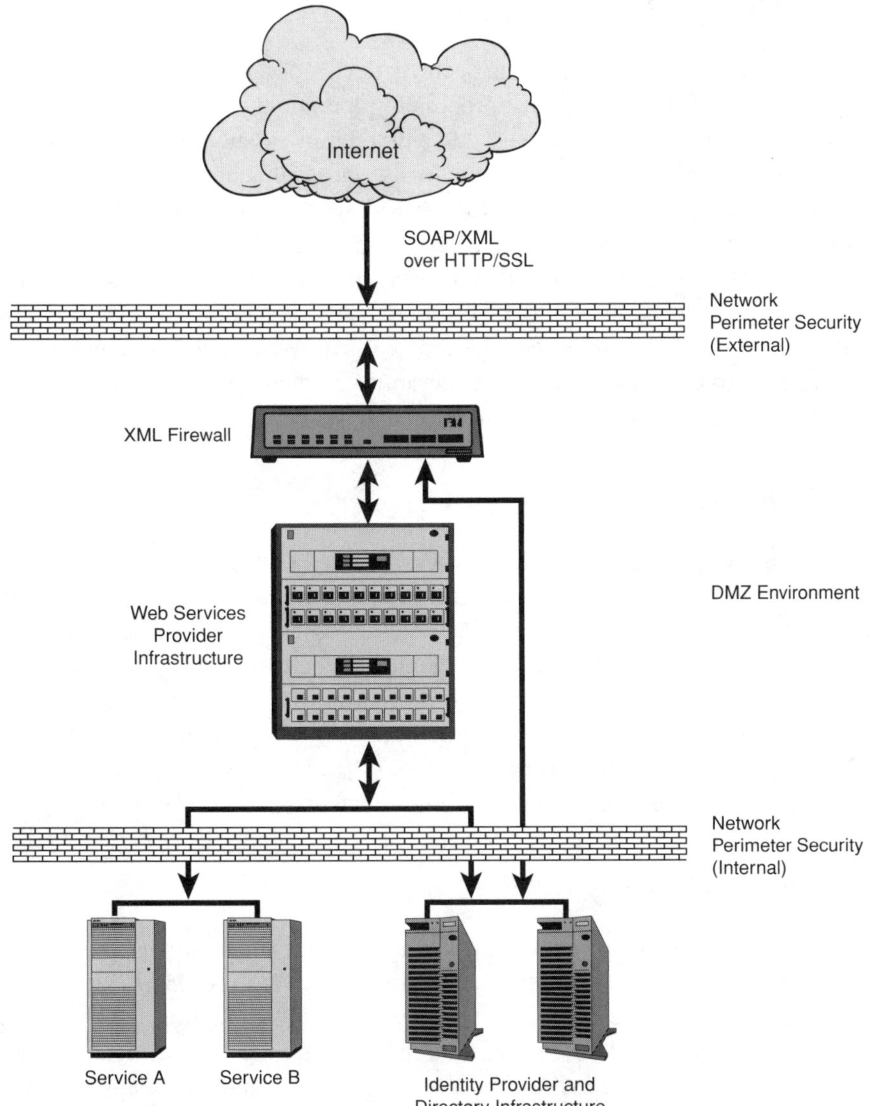

Figure 11–2 Conceptual Web services security infrastructure

walls can filter packets based on their source, protocols, destination addresses, and port numbers. At the protocol level, the network infrastructure security can filter and apply decisions to forward or reject traffic based on the protocol used, such as HTTP, SMTP, or FTP. It can also filter traffic by packet attribute or state of the request.

XML Firewall

The XML firewall is an XML-aware security device or a proxy infrastructure that can perform XML-based security processing operations. It helps in identifying and thwarting content-level threats and vulnerabilities such as malicious messages, buffer overflows, oversized payloads, virus attachments, and so on. It encapsulates access and enforces XML-based security mechanisms and access control policies to the underlying Web service endpoints and WSDL descriptions. Usually, XML firewalls are provided as specialized hardware or an XML-aware agent component that can be plugged in a Web server running on a bastion host. XML firewalls are also required to support XML Web services standards and specifications to enable message interoperability and compliance with the underlying Web services provider infrastructure.

Web Services Infrastructure

The Web services infrastructure is a standards-based platform that deploys application components as XML Web services. These services are accessible over the Internet using XML standards and XML standards-based technologies. In addition, the Web services infrastructure implements mechanisms for discovering and locating XML Web services, descriptions for defining how to use the exposed services, and representations of messages defining how to communicate with a Web services endpoint. For more information about Web services infrastructure basics, refer to Chapter 6, "Web Services Security–Standards and Technologies."

Identity Provider

The Identity Provider facilitates identity management, single sign-on (SSO), and identity federation for participating applications, service providers, and service requesters. Its primary responsibility is to provide authentication, authorization, and auditing services for all service interactions between the services provider and the requester. It also facilitates identity registration and termination services in conjunction with a user's repository. With Liberty standards compliance, it also enables interoperability and allows the establishment of trusted relationships between communicating service providers and identity providers.

Directory Services

The Directory Services provide mechanisms for storing and managing the user profiles, configuration, policies, and rules for accessing application and network resources. It features a specialized database, standard protocol, and APIs to store and retrieve information. LDAP is a de facto standard for implementing directory services. It defines a lightweight protocol that specifies the data model for representing information, naming, and security and functionalities for storing, accessing, and updating the LDAP information. Directory services provide support for application security mechanisms related to locating and managing PKI certificates and supporting other PKI life-cycle operations. For more information about LDAP, PKI, and digital certificates, refer to Chapter 2, "Basics of Security."

Web Services Security Patterns

Message Interceptor Gateway

Problem

You want to use a single entry point and centralize security enforcement for all incoming and outgoing XML messages.

In a Web services communication, allowing XML traffic to directly access the service endpoint creates the danger of content-level and XML-based external attacks from unauthorized parties. Web services traffic uses and tunnels through HTTP and HTTP/SSL ports of a firewall. Traditionally, network firewalls and intrusion detection systems provide protection to network traffic limited to connection attacks based on IP addresses, TCP ports, protocols, and packets. They do not offer application-endpoint security and lack support for providing protection against XML-based message attacks and content-layer vulnerabilities such as buffer overflow, malicious data injection, and virus attachments.

For the enforcement of XML-based security mechanisms and access control policies, it is very important to the exposed Web service endpoints and WSDL descriptions that a security entry point for all inbound requests and outbound responses is established. In addition, you should also require monitoring, logging, and recording of audit trails for the XML traffic. As a result, you need to intercept the XML traffic, look inside the XML content, and ensure that appropriate security and policy actions are taken based on the messages before letting them access the service endpoint. In most scenarios, you must intercept messages for performing content-level processing operations, including authentication, authorization, auditing, encryption/decryption, signature validation, compression/decompression, transformation, routing, and management functions mandated by the service endpoint.

Forces

- You want to block and prevent all direct access to the exposed service endpoints.
- You want to provide a single entry point, a centralized security point, and a policy enforcement point for invoking all target service endpoints.
- You want to intercept all XML traffic and inspect the complete XML message and attachments before processing at the service endpoint.
- You want to verify for message integrity and confidentiality during its transit, particularly for eavesdropping and tampering.
- You want to enforce transport-layer security using two-way SSL/TLS (mutual authentication) to achieve end-to-end data privacy and confidentiality of the communication.
- You want to protect the exposed WSDL descriptions from public access and prevent revealing operations.
- You want to apply message inspection and filter mechanisms on the XML traffic based on content, payload size, and message representation.
- You want to centralize enforcement of identity, role, and policy-based access control for all exposed services.
- You want to integrate existing identity-provider infrastructure for authentication and authorization.
- You want to monitor and identify XML-based replay and DoS attacks by tracking and verifying the IP addresses, hostnames, message timestamps, and other message sender-specific information.
- You want to verify and validate all incoming and outgoing messages for interoperability, current standards, and regulatory compliance.
- You want to enforce centralized logging, monitoring, and management of all XML-based transports, sessions, transactions, and exchanged data.
- You want to track usage, failures, and other service-level statistics, such as metering and billing.
- You want to provide support for verifying and validating incoming and outgoing messages based on XML security standards such as OASIS WS-Security, XML digital signatures, XML Encryption, SAML, XACML, and XrML.

Solution

The Message Interceptor Gateway pattern is a proxy infrastructure providing a centralized entry point that encapsulates access to all target service endpoints of a Web services provider. It acts as a controller that aggregates access and enforces security mechanisms on the XML traffic by making use of identity and access management infrastructure. It secures the incoming and outgoing XML traffic by securing the communication channels between the service endpoints.

The Message Interceptor Gateway accesses the network traffic using a packet sniffer mechanism that inspects the network packets for HTTP and XML headers. Once it encounters a packet with HTTP and XML headers, it off-loads the message to further processing using XML validation mechanisms. The XML validation mechanism is similar to the regular expression matching process for XML, which checks the given XML message against standard XML Schemas meant for verifying XML for well-formedness, structural integrity, and standards compliance. After validation and before allowing the user to access the service, the Message Interceptor Gateway communicates with the Message Inspector pattern for verification of mandated message-level security mechanisms, such as the user's identity and associated security policies that confirm the user's access privileges. Figure 11–3 illustrates the representation of a Message Interceptor Gateway in the Web services architecture.

The Message Interceptor Gateway pattern can be an XML-aware security appliance or a Web proxy infrastructure service that allows intercepting inbound

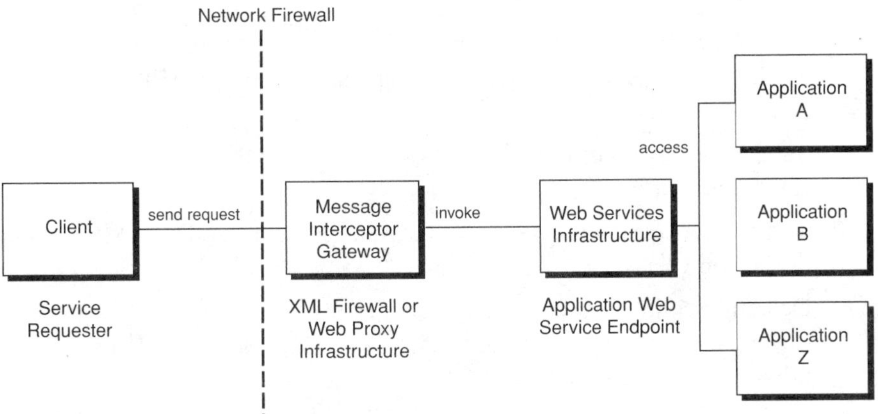

Figure 11–3 Message Interceptor Gateway pattern

and outbound XML Web services traffic and enforcing consistent security and policies to all its exposed service endpoints and targeting service requesters.

In effect, a Message Interceptor Gateway must handle tasks such as:

- Intercepting all incoming and outgoing XML traffic and verifying XML messages for integrity and confidentiality.
- Applying transport-level security mechanisms such as SSL/TLS for initiating secure communication.
- Identifying the communicating peer and authenticating them via X.509 server certificate or X.509 Mutual authentication of server and client.
- Applying data integrity at the transport-level using HTTP over SSL/TLS to ensure that the data in transit is not intercepted or tampered with by unauthorized parties.
- Applying data confidentiality at the transport-level using HTTP over SSL/TLS to ensure that the data in transit is not available for viewing or disclosed to unauthorized parties.
- Ensuring that a message received is unique and valid by verifying the IDs, timestamps, and receiving order, and making sure it is not resubmitted in a replay attack.
- Disallowing messages initiated from unauthorized parties and untrusted hosts by verifying IP addresses, protocols, service endpoints, message formats, and so on.
- Protecting access to WSDL descriptions with authentication and access control.
- Validating and verifying incoming XML messages for well-formedness, XML schema, and compliance with standards such as OASIS WS-Security and SAML Token profile.
- Validating and verifying the representation of XML digital signatures and XML Encryption.
- Verifying incoming messages for message correlation ID, timestamps, and expiration.
- Detecting content-based attacks such as virus attachments, abnormal messages, and malformed messages that can cause service endpoint crash or failure.
- Interfacing with the Message Inspector, identity provider, and PKI infrastructures to enforce authentication, authorization, and other security policies.
- Enforcing authentication and authorization decisions to the service callers.

- Initiating automated response that alert administrators of detected security breaches and malicious activities.
- Logging and recording auditable trails for monitoring and diagnosing activities.

Structure

Figure 11–4 shows a class diagram of the Message Interceptor Gateway pattern.

Participants and Responsibilities

Figure 11–5 shows the sequence diagram for Message Interceptor Gateway. It shows the interaction of the various participants of the Message Interceptor Gateway pattern for a basic operation that intercepts the XML traffic and then verifies XML data before processing at its service endpoint. The basic components of this pattern are discussed in the list that follows.

The key participants of the pattern are as follows:

Client. The client of the Message Interceptor Gateway is a Web service endpoint that initiates XML traffic or responds to a service request. In a Web services communication, the client can be a service provider or a requester endpoint that encapsulates an application or a Web browser that is capable of posting an XML message.

RequestMessage. The Request message represents a SOAP RPC message or an XML document that is subject to all the required security processing tasks

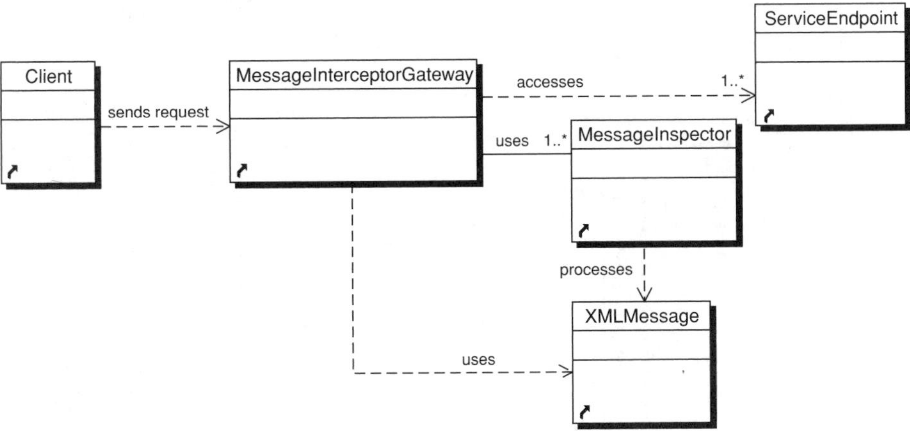

Figure 11–4 Message Interceptor Gateway class diagram

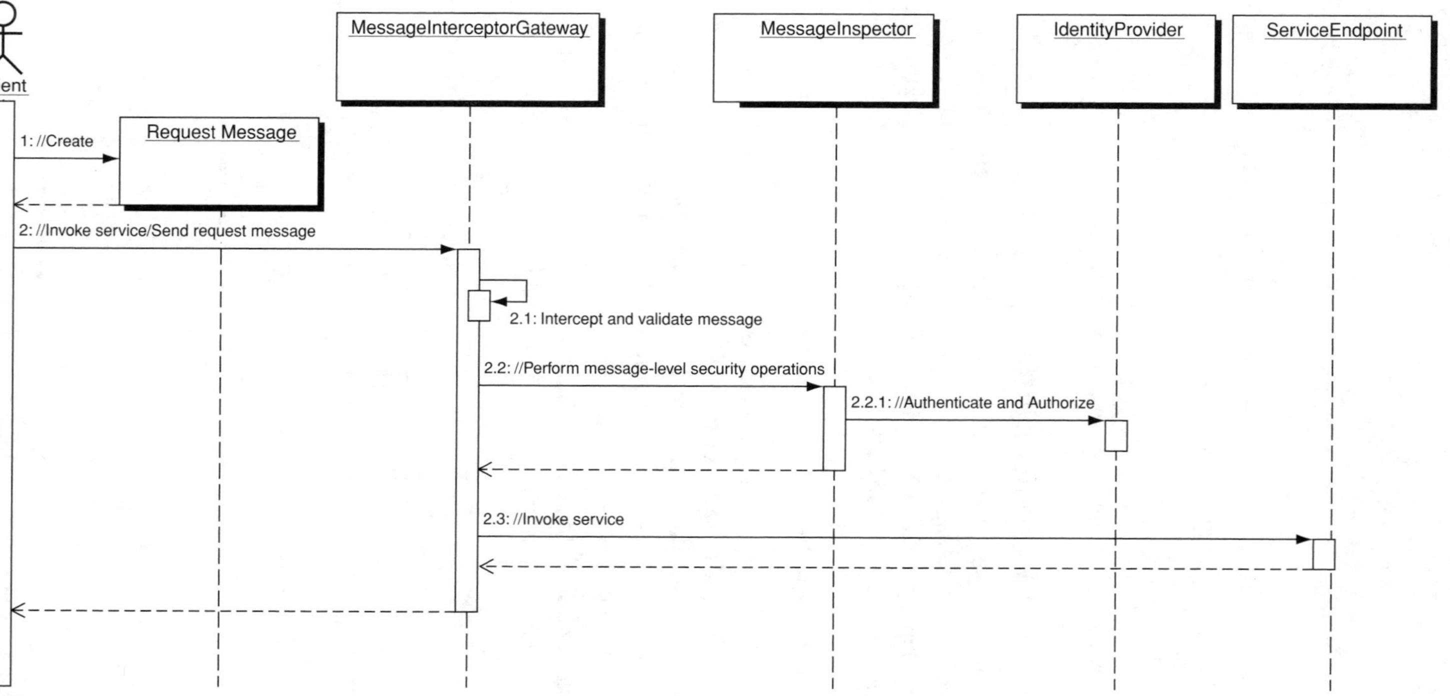

Figure 11–5 Sequence diagram for Message Interceptor Gateway

carried out by the Message Interceptor Gateway. Based on the request message, the service endpoint may allow or deny further processing of the message.

Message Interceptor Gateway. The Message Interceptor Gateway is the primary role object of this pattern. It acts as the security enforcement point by encapsulating access to all target service endpoints of a service provider or requester. It facilitates infrastructure services that can provide a secure single entry and exit point by intercepting inbound requests and outbound responses of Web services traffic. This ensures transport-layer security by addressing data integrity and confidentiality at the transport-level; identifying message uniqueness via timestamps, correlation and ordering; validating for standards compliance; and enforcing communicating peer authentication and authorization policies as required by the service endpoint infrastructure. It also ensures logging and recording audit trails of all incoming and outgoing messages.

Message Inspector. The Message Interceptor Gateway makes use of a Message Inspector pattern in a secondary role to provide message-level security processing. It also acts as a security decision point with the authentication and authorization policy decisions, message and element-level verification and validation, logging, and auditing that are required by the service provider endpoint or the message handler intermediary.

Identity Provider. The Identity Provider represents a service or user repository that contains all information required for authentication and authorization of an identity accessing a service.

ServiceEndpoint. The ServiceEndpoint represents the target object and the ultimate consumer of the message that the client asks to do message processing.

Response Message. The Response Message represents the SOAP RPC call or XML document that is sent by the Message Interceptor Gateway. It represents the results of processing the message or an acknowledgement message that lets the client know that the request was received.

Strategies

XML-Aware Security Appliance (XML Firewall) Strategy

The role of the Message Interceptor Gateway can be applied using an XML-aware security appliance referred to as an XML firewall. It complements the role of the network firewall infrastructure by adding support for securing XML message traffic that can be deployed downstream behind firewalls or load balancers. It resides in a DMZ environment and runs as an XML-aware firewall or proxy intermediary that encapsulates access to all exposed service endpoints and WSDL descriptions. The XML firewall appliance can provide functionalities by playing the role of a secure entry and exit point to incoming and outgoing XML traffic. It does this by enforcing secure communication using SSL/TLS, centralized security, and access control that protects the underlying service endpoints. Depending on the vendor solution, it provides support and services for the following: ensuring XML message well-formedness, XML schema validation, content-filtering for viruses and non-compliant messages, identifying and verifying user authentication tokens, signing and validating XML digital signatures, encrypting and decrypting using XML encryption, enforcing XML-based access control policies, ensuring WSDL protection, auditing, logging, providing standards-based security interoperability via compliance with Web services security specifications such as XML digital signature, XML Encryption, OASIS WS-Security, SAML Token profile, REL Token profile, WS-I security profile, and so on.

Intercepting Web Agent Strategy

Most Web services vendors provide pluggable agents that can act as a proxy infrastructure or a security intermediary to secure access to their exposed service endpoints and WSDL descriptions. The agent resides as a pluggable module configured on a Web server or an application server running on a bastion host in a DMZ environment. The agent interfaces with an underlying security provider infrastructure that manages the identity information and access control policies. The agent provides a security layer to the Web services endpoint by intercepting all incoming service requests and outbound responses and by enforcing centralized access control and policy rules for all exposed service endpoints. The identity information, roles, and access-control policies reside on an identity provider infrastructure. Figure 11–6 shows a conceptual representation of Web agent infrastructure strategy.

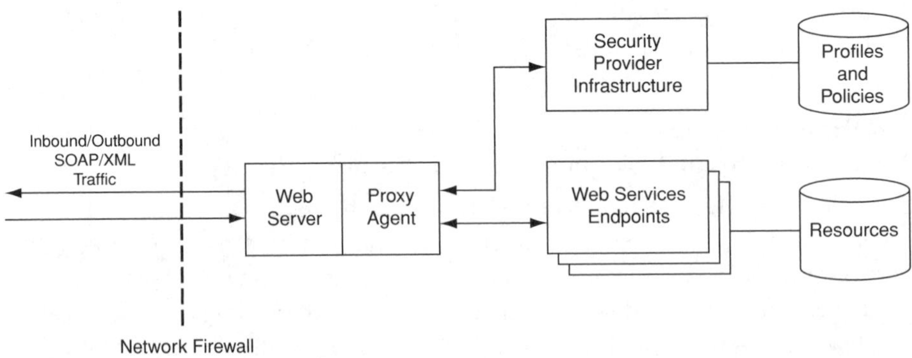

Figure 11–6 Intercepting Web agent strategy

In addition, depending on vendor implementation the agent may provide support and services for the following: ensuring XML message well-formedness, XML schema validation, content-filtering for viruses and noncompliant messages, identifying and verifying user authentication tokens, signing and validating XML digital signatures, encrypting and decrypting XML Encryption, enforcing XML-based access-control policies, ensuring WSDL protection, auditing, logging, enabling standards-based security interoperability, and ensuring conformance to Web services security specifications such as XML digital signature, XML Encryption, OASIS WS-Security, SAML Token profile, XACML, and WS-I security profile.

Consequences

Using the Message Intercept Gateway pattern helps in intercepting XML traffic in order to perform message-level security operations, including authentication, authorization, auditing, encryption/decryption, signature validation, compression/decompression, transformation, routing, and management. All these functions can be carried out before processing the message at its ultimate endpoint.

Message Interceptor Gateway ensures transport-level security and peer authentication, which verify message uniqueness and standards compliance. At the transport-level, it guarantees data integrity, data confidentiality, non-repudiation, auditability, and traceability. It also safeguards the service endpoint from attacks such as XML DoS, man-in-the-middle, untrusted hosts, brute-force message replay, malicious payloads, and non-compliant messages.

In addition to the above, the Message Interceptor Gateway pattern provides the following benefits to the service endpoint:

- *Centralized control.* The Message Interceptor Gateway acts as a controller offering a centralized control and processing subsystem for enforcing security-related tasks across all exposed service endpoints. It offers centralized management of related services, including authentication, authorization, faults, encryption, audit trails, metering, billing, and so on.
- *Modularity and maintainability.* Restricting direct access, centralizing all security mechanisms, enforcing access-control policies, and off-loading security tasks from the service endpoints keeps the underlying application interfaces unpolluted with security-handling methods and saves application processing time and resources. This enhances a service with a modular subsystem designated for security and reduces complex tasks, which results in better maintainability of the overall Web services security infrastructure.

- *Reusability.* The Message Interceptor Gateway pattern encapsulates and protects all direct access to underlying service endpoints, facilitating a common reusable solution that helps in protecting multiple service endpoints.
- *Extensibility.* The Message Interceptor Gateway pattern offers extensibility by allowing you to incorporate more mechanisms and functionalities related to transport-level and message-level security, thereby reducing tight coupling or integration with the underlying service endpoint infrastructure.
- *Ease of migration.* The security layer provided by the Message Interceptor Gateway pattern makes it easier for the underlying service endpoint to have a different security provider implementation. The service-requesting clients or the service provider have no knowledge about the security layer.
- *Improved testability.* The Message Interceptor Gateway pattern infrastructure separates the security architectural model from the underlying service endpoint. This improves ease of testability and extensibility of the security architecture.
- *Network responsiveness.* Implementing the Message Interceptor Gateway pattern with a combination of XML firewall and Web services security infrastructure often demonstrates significant performance gains in latency and message throughput. Using a software-only implementation has more processing overhead and impacts network performance.
- *Additional expertise required.* Implementing and managing the Message Interceptor Gateway pattern often requires strong familiarity and skills related to XML-aware and network appliances.

Security Factors and Risks

- **High availability**. The Message Interceptor Gateway pattern and every component that interacts with it must provide high availability. It becomes very important to ensure 100 percent availability so that it can be better than that of the weakest link in the overall Web services architecture. Failure to provide high availability may result in monetary loss and security vulnerabilities.
- **Fault tolerance**. The Message Interceptor Gateway pattern is also expected to be fault-tolerant in order to support security and to enhance reliability and performance of the infrastructure. When a failure is detected, it must be transparently replaced with a redundant infrastructure that does not jeopardize any existing inbound requests and any intermediate processing states. There must be a recovery mechanism that can perform all opera-

tions—without skipping or bypassing any security mechanisms that are currently in place—read all outstanding service requests and paused requests with intermediate state and forward them for further processing by the Message Interceptor Gateway pattern.

Reality Checks

Choosing the right strategy: XML firewall or an Intercepting Web agent? Using an Intercepting Web agent infrastructure provided by a Web services security provider could meet the target Web services endpoint-specific requirements for Web services security standards compliance as well as transport-level and message-level security mechanisms. Using software interfaces to incorporate SSL/TLS, signature validation, and encryption and decryption is usually resource-intensive and incurs processing overheads. It can also affect the performance of the overall architecture. Adopting a combination of an XML firewall appliance strategy and the Intercepting Web Agent strategy would help in achieving the performance and high-availability goals, particularly while handling a large number of connections, binary security tokens, and larger message payloads.

Is the Message Interceptor Gateway pattern performance too slow? Intercepting all XML traffic and handling security-related tasks within an intermediary often degrades performance. In such cases, one could revisit the Message Interceptor Gateway pattern with the Message Inspector pattern or use load-balancing strategies, adding multiple Interceptor gateways to alleviate the degradation.

Related Patterns

Message Inspector [Web Services Tier]. The Message Inspector pattern is used to verify and validate the quality of message-level security mechanisms applied to XML Web services.

Secure Message Router [Web Services Tier]. The Secure Message Router pattern allows secure communication with multiple partner endpoints using message-level security and identity-federation mechanisms.

Message Inspector

Problem

You want to verify and validate the quality of message-level security mechanisms applied to XML Web services.

In a Web-service communication, an incoming message should not be received unless it is confirmed and proven to be safe for further processing. The incoming messages may be client requests or response messages. These messages may contain malicious content or XML messages from unauthorized parties, which are a potential threat to the service provider.

Traditional security mechanisms such as firewalls and packet filtering systems do not secure and verify the content and cannot handle these threats. Message-level security mechanisms are required to secure the XML messages and to handle XML-related security attacks. It is necessary to adopt and deploy an XML standards-based security framework and consistently enforce it before processing messages. This involves pre- and post-processing XML messages by parsing the incoming content. This is done by verifying and validating for processing requirements and then making authentication and authorization decisions based on the message sender or receiver. As a result, it becomes mandatory to inspect the message, particularly for the purpose of identifying the sender and verifying whether the sender confirms its identity. Verification of whether the identity is authorized to send the message, the content has been secured and unaltered during transit, and the content is legitimate and does not contain any malicious information is also necessary.

Integrating message-level security mechanisms with an application service endpoint creates a direct dependency between the service and the XML security implementation. Such code dependencies in application components add complexity and make it tedious to process the application-specific content. It is also tedious when applying changes to security mechanisms in the content.

Thus, a common solution for implementing a series of message-level tasks related to identifying, verifying, and validating XML-based security before and after receiving the message is required. These tasks must be carried out as part of pre-processing or post-processing tasks to ensure that there are no security risks and vulnerabilities associated with the message. Some of these tasks determine whether it is necessary to process the message or to discontinue processing it based on required schemas, constraints, compliance, and specific processing requirements.

Forces

You want to use a common solution for message-level security tasks, such as examining the structure and content and verifying and determining the uniqueness, confidentiality, integrity, and validity of messages before the application endpoint starts processing them.

- You want to proactively identify and potentially limit messages upon receipt based on applied security token profiles and assertions representing the identity and policies.

- You want to monitor and identify message replay and XML-based DoS attacks by tracking and verifying encrypted communication, security tokens, XML digital signatures, message correlation, message expiry, or timestamps.
- You want to verify and validate messages at the element level to identify parameter tampering and message injection attacks via XPATH and XQUERY expressions.
- You want to verify messages for interoperability and standards compliance to guarantee that the applied security mechanisms of the incoming and outgoing messages work seamlessly in all usage scenarios.
- You want to enforce a centralized logging based on the security actions and decisions made on the received messages.
- You want to provide a uniform API mechanism for managing message-level security and processing the security headers in accordance with various XML security standards, such as OASIS WS-Security, XML digital signatures, XML Encryption, SAML Token profile, and REL Token profile.

Solution

Use the Message Inspector pattern as a modular or pluggable component that can be integrated with infrastructure service components that handle pre-processing and post-processing of incoming and outgoing SOAP or XML messages. The Message Inspector combines a chain of tasks intended for identifying message-level security headers, dissecting the header elements, and verifying the message for the key security requirements specified by the service provider. It acts as a Security Decision Point for enforcing all the security policies applicable to accessing a service endpoint, that is, a Web service provider or requester.

In effect, you are able to integrate a set of tasks, including:

- Verifying and validating a SOAP message and its populated headers for standards compliance, such as OASIS WS-Security, SAML Token profile, WS-I Basic Security Profile, REL Token profile, and so forth.
- Identifying the data origin by identification and authentication of the message payload and its elements using OASIS WS-Security and XML digital signature mechanisms.
- Verifying the message for data integrity and validating for accuracy and consistency (for example, that the message parts are not modified or deleted by unauthorized parties) using OASIS WS-Security or XML digital signature mechanisms.

- Verifying the message for data confidentiality to ensure that the message is not viewed by unauthorized parties during transit or processing at intermediaries using OASIS WS-Security or XML Encryption mechanisms.
- Validating and verifying the representation of XML digital signatures, including recalculating the digests by applying the digest algorithm and recalculating the signature using the key information.
- Decrypting and verifying the encrypted data to support the underlying service or prior to further processing by the service endpoint.
- Looking up an XKMS service provider to locate public keys intended for verifying and validating signatures.
- Verifying the messages for correlation IDs, timestamps, and expiration.
- Verifying and validating the business data for required length and data format to avoid buffer overflow attacks and to restrict malicious data insertion attacks.
- Interacting with the identity provider to enforce authentication and authorization.
- Enforcing authentication and authorization decisions based on the message sender's content (such as username/Password, SAML assertions, REL licenses and BinarySecurityTokens such as certificates and Kerberos tickets) and associated security policies.
- Ensuring the XML message conformity based on a given XML Schema, DTD, or XPATH expression to ensure that the content conforms to the security specifications.
- Detecting data injection attacks by identifying malicious schema definitions, XPATH/XQUERY expressions, SQL, cross-site scripting and malformed URLs.
- Initiating automated response upon detection of security breaches and malicious activities.
- Logging and recording audit trails for the monitoring and diagnosis of activities and for the reconstruction of events after a security issue.

Using the Message Inspector pattern eliminates the need for the service endpoint to perform complex message-level security operations, particularly looking up processes with an identity provider, accessing XKMS service, and creating decrypted business documents. These operations are quite resource-intensive (that is, they require excessive utilization of CPU, memory, and network bandwidth). To eliminate these overheads, this pattern provides a mechanism for offloading these tasks to an intermediary by abstracting all message-level security-specific dependencies required by the service provider application. The Message Inspector pattern can be implemented as a SOAP intermediary that integrates a set of message handlers working in sequence to perform a chain of message-level security tasks required by the service endpoint, such as identification, verification, validation, and extraction of security-specific headers and associated data represented in the message. An XML-aware security appliance that is capable of performing message-level and element-level validation and verification can also be incorporated. It is strongly recommended that the Message Inspector pattern does not cache any data during execution or any data from the message sender that might be needed later.

Structure

Figure 11–7 shows the class diagram for the Message Inspector pattern.

Participants and Responsibilities

Figure 11–8 shows the sequence diagram for the Message Inspector pattern and the various participants.

The key participants of the pattern are as follows:

- **Client**. The Client is any service requester that needs to invoke a Web-service endpoint. The client initiates a request message represented as method names with parameter values or XML documents. The client can be any type of application or a Web service that can create and send XML messages according to Web-services standards.
- **Request Message**. The Request message represents a SOAP RPC message or an XML document that is verifiable by all the required security

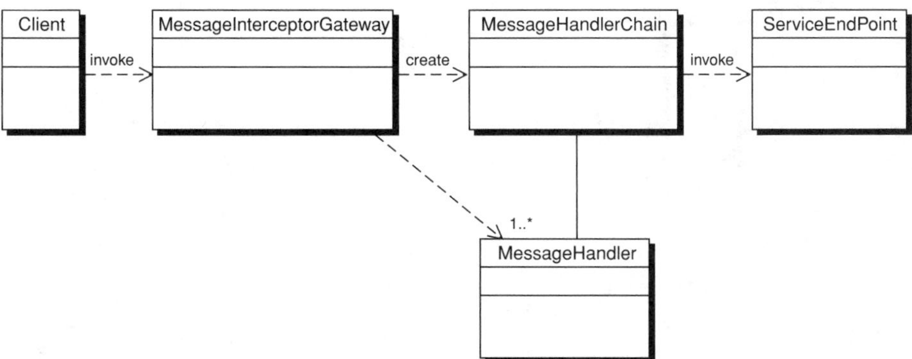

Figure 11–7 Message Inspector class diagram

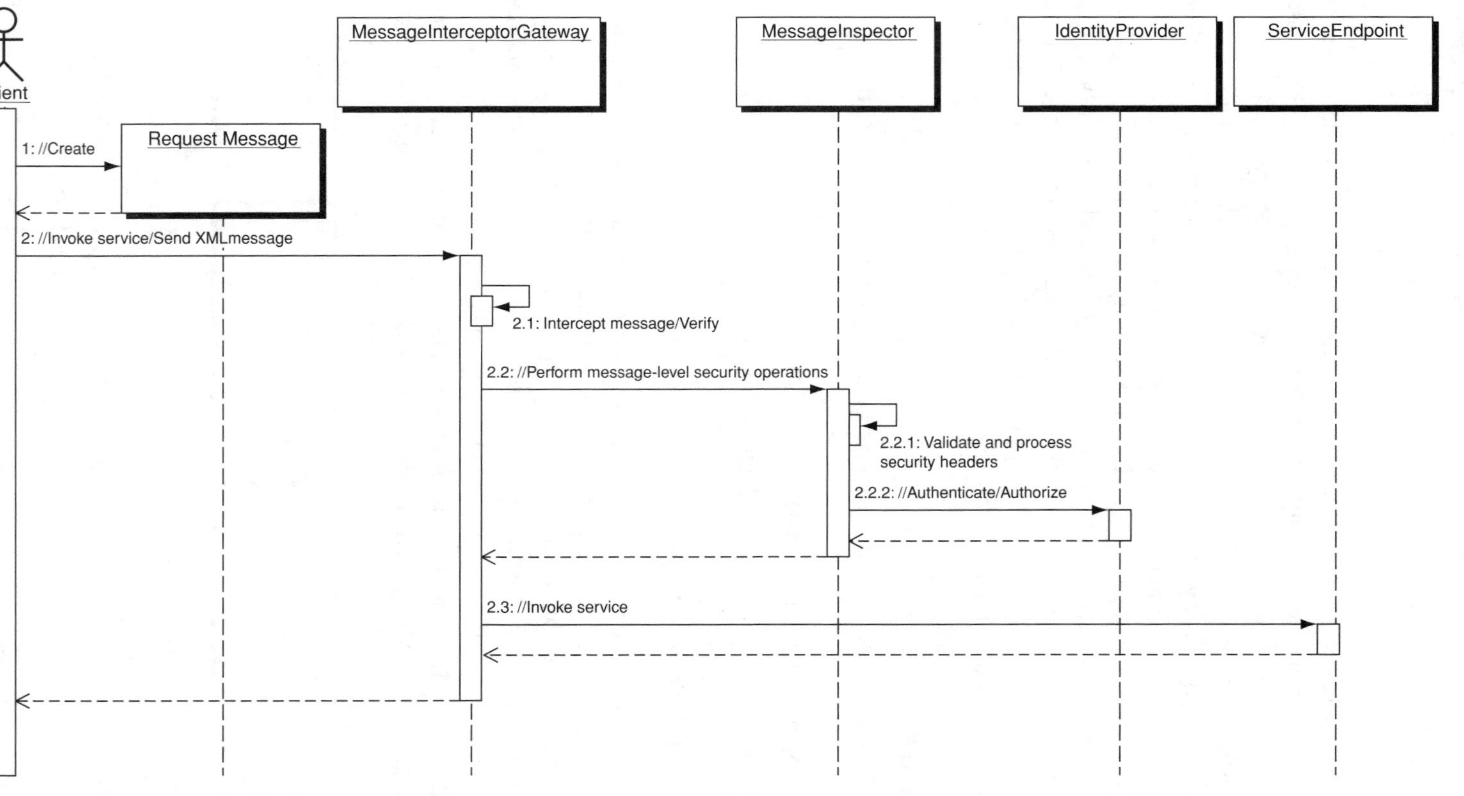

Figure 11–8 Message Inspector sequence diagram

processing tasks carried out by the Message Inspector. Based on the request message, the service provider endpoint may allow or deny further processing of the message.

- **Message Inspector**. The Message Inspector is the primary role object and main class of this pattern. It implements all the methods intended for message-level security processing. The Message Inspector parses the message requests to determine what needs to be done. It makes use of a series of operations to verify and validate the messages for all security-related processing. In a typical scenario, it acts as a security decision point that provides authentication and authorization policy decisions, message and element-level verification and validation, and logging and auditing functionalities required by the service-provider endpoint or the message-handler intermediary.
- **Message Interceptor Gateway**. The Message Interceptor Gateway is the secondary role object of this pattern. It provides infrastructure services that can intercept inbound requests and outbound responses to ensure transport-layer security, message integrity and confidentiality, standards compliance. It also enforces authentication and authorization policies required by the service-provider endpoint or the subsequent message-handler intermediary.
- **Identity Provider**. The Identity Provider represents a service or user repository that contains all information required for authentication and authorization of an identity accessing a service.
- **ServiceEndpoint**. The ServiceEndpoint represents the target object and the ultimate consumer of the message that the client asks to do message processing.
- **Response Message**. The Response Message represents the SOAP RPC call or XML document that is sent by the Message Interceptor Gateway or service endpoint. It represents the results after processing the message or an acknowledgement message that lets the client know that the request was received.

Strategies

XML-Aware Security Appliance Strategy

The role of Message Inspector can be off-loaded or delegated to an XML-aware security appliance (XML firewall or XML processing appliance) that is capable of verifying, validating, and processing XML security headers obtained from inbound and outbound Web services traffic. The XML appliance coexists with the

Message Interceptor Gateway and acts as a SOAP intermediary or a proxy infrastructure that enforces policies and makes security decisions on behalf of the underlying application service provider or requester. The XML appliance can provide all the Message Inspector functionality, including support and services for XML schema validation, XML parsing, XPath and XQuery handling, identifying and verifying user authentication tokens, applying and validating XML digital signatures, XML Encryption and decryption, XML-based access-control policies, auditing, and logging. It also enables security interoperability based on Web services security standards and specifications. The interoperability requirements must adhere to WS-I Basic Security Profile and associated security standards and specifications, such as XML digital signature, XML Encryption, OASIS WS-Security, SAML, REL, IETF, and so on.

Adopting XML-aware appliances and firewalls can ensure handling of multiple XML security operations at wire speed, which results in a performance gain over software-based solutions. In addition to an XML appliance, it is often good to have a programmatic interface (using the Message Handler Chain strategy discussed in the next section) to enforce verification and validation of messages at the element level for legitimate data, particularly its parameter length, type, and format. Doing this can detect and avoid replay of selected parts of messages, buffer overflows, infinite parsing loops, and malicious data injection using SQL, XSL, XPATH, and XQUERY expressions.

Figure 11–9 shows the sequence diagram for the XML-Aware Security Appliance Strategy.

Figure 11–9 illustrates a client sending a request to an endpoint. The request is intercepted by the Message Interceptor Gateway. After interception, the message is redirected to an XML appliance for verification, validation, and processing of message-level security information. In addition, the XML appliance may connect and interact with an identity provider to verify the request for authentication and authorization credentials.

Message-Handler Chain Strategy

Message Inspector can be represented by plugging in a message-handler chain that can represent a series of operations intended for enforcing message-level security in Web services. These operations include verifying user identity, validating messages for standards compliance, validating signatures, providing PKI lookups, encrypting and decrypting data, verifying timestamps, correlating messages, parsing XML, verifying element-level data, auditing, and logging.

In a Web services communication, each handler represents functionality such as pre-processing or post-processing of inbound requests or outbound responses. Each handler can be implemented to support a security operation that is configured

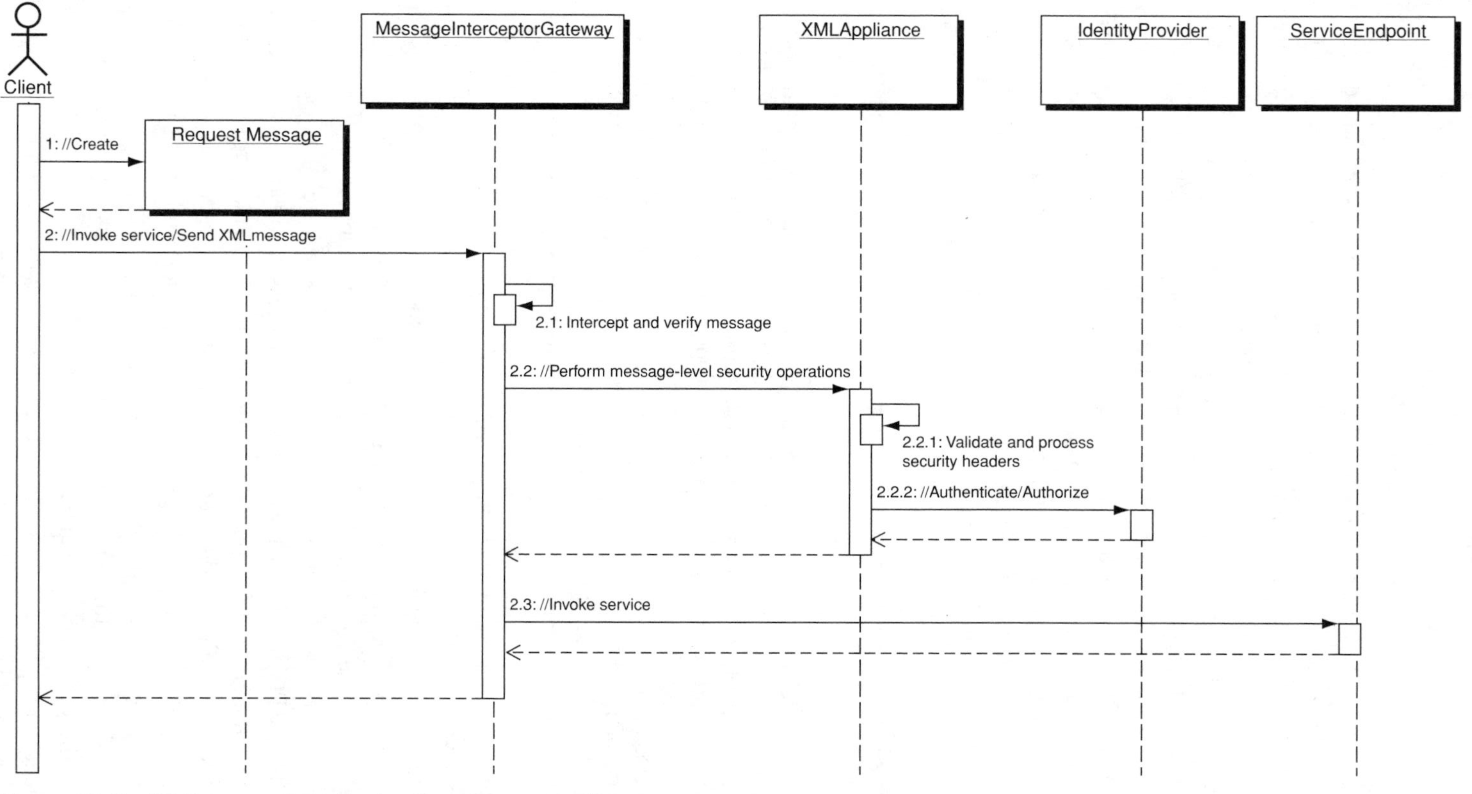

Figure 11–9 XML-aware Security Appliance sequence diagram

and associated with a service requester client or a services provider server, or both. At runtime, a handler has the ability to access the message header or its body and introduce an operation that can verify, validate, or modify the target message. Multiple message handlers can be grouped together as an ordered group or with a designated sequence representing a set of message processing operations and shared data. It is important that Message Handlers should make use of a dedicated Fault handler that captures all errors and exceptions from the respective operations and returns a response that sanitizes those exceptions in such a way that it does not reveal the internal functionalities and failures. All message handlers are implemented as stateless and they should not cache results of an operation or any data that the client might need at a later point. This helps message handlers to avoid potential threading and concurrency issues.

DESIGN NOTE:

In the Message Handler chain strategy, there is a known issue related to repeated XML processing in certain parts of XML parsing, DOM creation, and XML serialization functions. This issue usually impacts performance. A failure in one of the handler chains may result in a restart and it is a complex task to diagnose the data and the corresponding handler-specific errors. However, having the intermediate XML stored in database tables during the process has proved very valuable for troubleshooting purposes. Having intermediate XML storage helps the downstream processing without the need to restart or an extract from the beginning.

A message handler chain, including a series of security operations, can be represented as a Message Inspector for a service provider or service requester. During service invocation, each handler completes its operation and then passes the result to the next handler in the chain. When the handler chain completes processing, the message is delegated to the application service endpoint for further processing. In a J2EE-based Web services environment, message handlers can be built using JAX-RPC and SAAJ APIs. Message handlers can also be used for verifying SOAP attachments for potential virus or content-related vulnerabilities, Trojan horses, and malicious data attachments. The message handler chain strategy can make use of the Secure Logger Pattern (Web tier) and Audit Interceptor Pattern (Business tier) to ensure recording of audit trails.

Figure 11–10 shows the sequence diagram for the Message Handler Chain Strategy and the various participants.

The Client sends a request message to its intended service endpoint. The request message is intercepted using the Message Interceptor Gateway pattern for verification

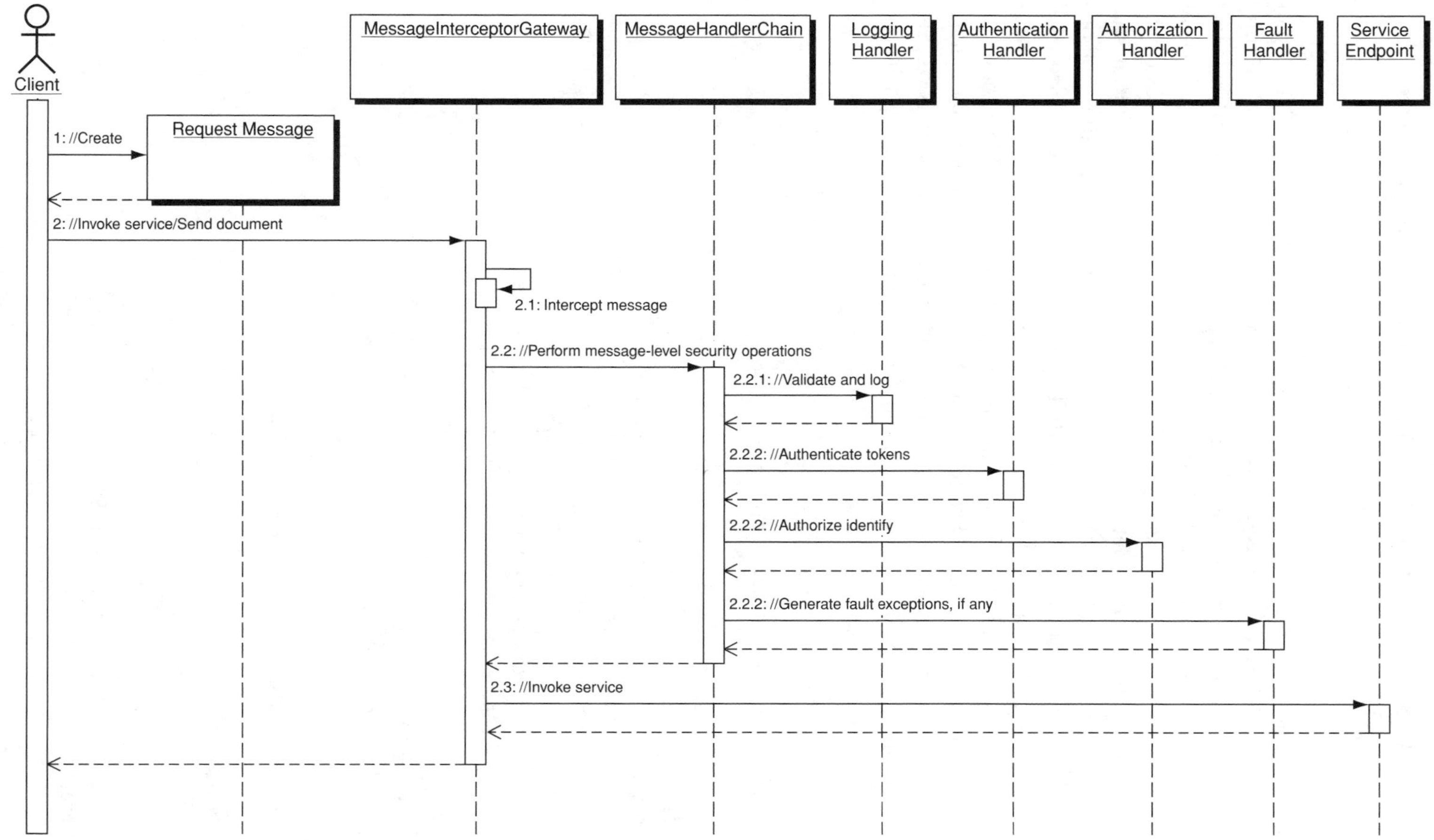

Figure 11–10 Message Handler Chain sequence diagram

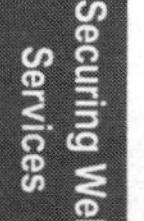

and validation of the message for security requirements. The Message Interceptor Gateway makes use of a Message Inspector for initiating message-level security processing. The Message Inspector is represented as a MessageHandlerChain that defines a series of message handlers tasked to apply and perform the sequence of message-level security processing required by the service endpoint. Once the defined operations are complete, the MessageHandlerChain returns a result that verifies all message-level security requirements, such as authentication, authorization, signature verification, and so forth. Based on the results, the message will be allowed or denied further processing.

Example 11–1 is a source code example (LoggingHandler.java) that shows the implementation of a Logging handler using Apache Axis. The logging handler receives all incoming message requests, verifies and validates them for XML Signature using Apache XML security kit, and then logs them using the Apache logging framework (log4j).

Example 11–1 LoggingHandler.java

```
package com.csp.inspector.handler;

import org.apache.axis.*;
import org.apache.axis.components.logger.LogFactory;
import org.apache.axis.handlers.BasicHandler;
import org.apache.axis.utils.Messages;
import org.apache.commons.logging.Log;
import
     org.apache.xml.security.signature.XMLSignature;
import org.apache.xml.security.utils.Constants;
import org.apache.xpath.CachedXPathAPI;
import org.w3c.dom.Document;
import org.w3c.dom.Element;
import java.io.FileWriter;
import java.io.PrintWriter;

public class LogHandler extends BasicHandler {

   // 1. Initialize the logger
    static Log log =
       LogFactory.getLog(LogHandler.class.getName());

   // 2. Initialize Apache XML Security library
   static {
        org.apache.xml.security.Init.init();
    }
```

```
      // 3. Initiate message verification
     public void invoke(MessageContext msgContext)
                                  throws AxisFault {
     try {
 System.out.println("Starting message verification");

 Message inMsg = msgContext.getRequestMessage();
 Message outMsg = msgContext.getResponseMessage();

  // 4. Verify the incoming message for XML signature

  Document doc =
    inMsg.getSOAPEnvelope().getAsDocument();
  String BaseURI = "http://xml-security";
  CachedXPathAPI xpathAPI = new CachedXPathAPI();

  Element nsctx = doc.createElement("nsctx");
  nsctx.setAttribute("xmlns:ds",
                    Constants.SignatureSpecNS);

 Element signatureElem
     = (Element) xpathAPI.selectSingleNode(doc,
                 "//ds:Signature", nsctx);

  // 5. Ensure that the document is digitally signed

   if (signatureElem == null) {
    System.out.println("The document is not signed");
      return;
   }

      // 6. Validate the signature
   XMLSignature sig =
       new XMLSignature(signatureElem, BaseURI);

     boolean verify =
sig.checkSignatureValue(sig.getKeyInfo().getPublicKey());
System.out.println("Message verification complete.");
System.out.println("The signature is" + (verify
                   ? " "
                   : " not ") + "valid");
```

```
 } catch (Exception e) {
          throw AxisFault.makeFault(e);
   }
}

// 7. Log messages to a file
public void onFault(MessageContext msgContext) {
try {
   Handler serviceHandler = msgContext.getService();
   String filename = (String) getOption("filename");

   if ((filename == null) || (filename.equals("")))
         throw new AxisFault("Server.NoLogFile",
       "No log file configured for the LogHandler!",
                      null, null);

   FileWriter fw = new FileWriter(filename, true);
   PrintWriter pw = new PrintWriter(fw);
   pw.println("====================");
   pw.println("= " + Messages.getMessage("fault00"));
   pw.println("====================");
      pw.close();
    } catch (Exception ex) {
          log.error(ex);
        }
    }
}
```


For more information about implementing and deploying message handlers using Apache Axis, refer to the architecture guide available at http://ws.apache.org/axis/java/architecture-guide.html. To implement XML security using Java, refer to the Apache XML security kit installation and API guide available at http://xml.apache.org/security/Java/. At the time of this writing, preparation of the JSR-105: XML Digital Signature APIs and JSR-106: XML Digital Encryption APIs specifications is still in progress; there are no current standard API mechanisms available for representing XML security using Java.

Identity Provider Agent Strategy

Most identity-provider vendors offer pluggable agents for enforcing XML-based security policies and rules on Web service endpoints. The agent plays the role of a Message Inspector pattern, performing message-level security tasks. These tasks include verifying user identity information, validating messages for standards compliance, validating signatures, making PKI lookups, encrypting and decrypting message elements, auditing, and logging. The agent resides as a modular component in the Web-services provider infrastructure or as a reverse proxy to a Web server that listens to inbound and outbound SOAP messages. The agent protects the service endpoint by intercepting the communication and processing the messages for security and access-control decisions by interacting with the underlying identity provider. The identity provider delivers all the access control and policy decisions made for the inbound requests and outbound responses.

Figure 11–11 shows the sequence diagram for the Identity Provider Agent Strategy and the various participants.

The Client sends a request message to its intended service endpoint. The request message is intercepted using the Message Interceptor Gateway in order to verify and validate the message for security requirements. The Message Interceptor Gateway delegates the request to an identity provider agent residing as a proxy infrastructure component that supports an underlying identity provider. The identity provider initiates the message-level security processing as required by the service endpoint. It takes responsibility for performing key security operations, such as authentication, authorization, signature verification, and so forth. Once the operations are complete, the identity provider issues a single sign-on token (SSO Token) that represents the authentication and authorization decisions to allow or deny the message for further processing at its intended endpoint.

In addition to processing for authentication and authorization decisions, the identity provider agent must be able to incorporate custom mechanisms for verifying selected elements of messages for the purpose of identifying message correlation, timestamps, and element-level data validation. These mechanisms help in detecting message-level attacks that can lead to forged requests, buffer overflow, malicious data injection, infinite parsing loops, and other content-level threats. It is highly recommended to install agents on Web-service infrastructure running on DMZ bastion hosts.

Consequences

Adopting Message Inspector facilitates message-level security processing capabilities and ensures message-level data integrity, confidentiality, non-repudiation, auditability, and traceability. It also safeguards the service endpoint from XML DoS attacks, forged tokens, malicious data injection, identity spoofing, message validation failure attacks, replay of selected parts, schema poisoning, and element/parameter tampering.

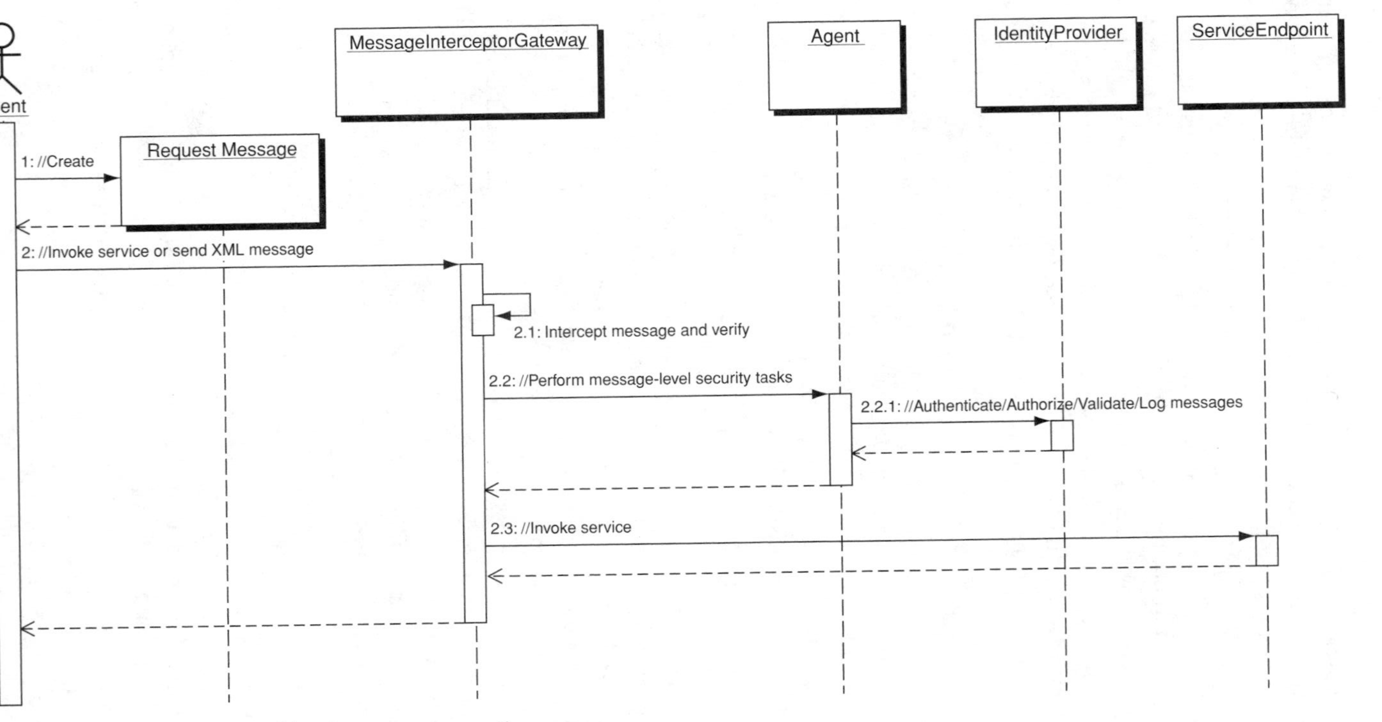

Figure 11–11 Identity Provider Agent sequence diagram

In addition, it provides the following benefits to the service endpoint:

- *Modularity and maintainability.* Separating message-level security mechanisms off-loads resource-intensive security processing tasks from the underlying application endpoint. This enhances the security architecture with a modular subsystem dedicated to processing security headers. It also reduces the complexity of maintaining security-related mechanisms at the service endpoint, which results in better maintainability of the overall Web-services security infrastructure.
- *Reusability.* Since a Message Inspector pattern encapsulates all the message-level security mechanisms, it facilitates a common reusable solution for protecting multiple service endpoints.
- *Extensibility.* A Message Inspector pattern offers extensibility by allowing you to incorporate more mechanisms and functionalities and by providing adherence to newer standards for enforcing message-level security. These mechanisms will also remain independent and reduce tight coupling with the underlying service endpoint infrastructure.

Security Factors and Risks

Confidentiality issues. The Message Inspector pattern provides a means to ensure verification and validation of applied message-level security mechanisms and to enforce security policies among communicating partners in Web services. Results returned from the Message Inspector pattern must remain confidential until they are consumed by their immediate or ultimate recipients. These results should not be accessed by, or pass through, intermediary components that are not trusted by the Web-services provider.

Reality Checks

Choosing the right strategy. XML-aware appliance, a message handler chain, or an identity provider agent? Your implementation choice depends on the application service endpoint requirements and the series of operations required for verification and validation of security headers of the message. Using a message handler chain or a vendor's identity provider agent strategy is extensible via programmatic interfaces. Using programmatic interfaces allows adapting to custom element-level data verification and achieving security standards compliance by handling newer content-level threats and vulnerabilities.

Message-level security processing. Tasks such as validating signatures and encrypting and decrypting the data are resource-intensive operations that often impact performance and result in processing overhead (for example, CPU, memory, and network bandwidth utilization). Adopting an XML-aware appliance strategy would help achieve performance and high-availability requirements, particularly while handling a large number of connections, binary security tokens, and larger message payloads by off-loading this processing to specialized hardware design specifically for these operations.

Concurrency implications. Many components associated with the Message Inspector pattern could be competing to update and read session data, which could lead to concurrency issues such as long wait times or deadlocks. A careful analysis of the XML traffic, message payloads, processing requirements, dependencies, and other possible scenarios should bring forth appropriate resolutions and trade-offs.

Related Patterns

Security Logger [Web Tier]. The Secure Logger is used by the Message Inspector to log request messages.

Audit Interceptor [Business Tier]. The Audit Interceptor is used to capture security-related events.

Message Interceptor Gateway [Web Services Tier]. Message Interceptor Gateway provides a single entry point by aggregating access to all service endpoints and centralizes security enforcement.

Secure Message Router

Problem

You want to securely communicate with multiple partner endpoints using message-level security and identity-federation mechanisms.

Using Web services communication in an organizational workflow or across the Internet with multiple partners poses a lot of challenges. If the message sender signs and encrypts the message in its entirety, the message sender restricts the possibility of further message changes by the message recipient in the workflow. This becomes a critical issue when each recipient of the message in a workflow has a responsibility for a selected portion of that message and must modify or add to it.

If the message-level security, such as signature and encryption, were applied to the entire message, any modification made by the initial recipient would invalidate the original message as well as expose the entire message, which was not intended for the initial recipient. In some cases, if a message is intended for multiple recipients and only selected fragments need to be revealed for each recipient, then it becomes more complex to convert each fragment as a message and then compile them together at the end of workflow.

Let's consider an example scenario; a patient visits a hospital that handles all documents and communication electronically using XML Web services. All patient information (for example, contact information, insurance data, health analysis, lab results, doctor observations, prescriptions, visit schedule, credit card information, and so on) is represented in XML. During the visit, the patient's health record is maintained via a workflow involving doctors, pharmacists, insurance providers, and so on. Each individual participating in the workflow does not require complete access to the patient's record. Only selected portions of the message are required and applicable to each workflow participant. For example, the billing department only requires knowing the insurance provider and the co-payment and credit card information; it does not need to know the patient's health history. Although the information workflow happens within an organization, it is a violation of specific legal regulations to unnecessarily disclose information to personnel.

Web services promise easier integration of applications, business partners, and consumers. With multiple parties involved, it often becomes more difficult to communicate with a standardized infrastructure representing a common scheme of authentication and authorization. Sometimes, each service needs a unique representation of credentials and message formats. In a trusted inter-organization or multi-partner communication scenario, eliminating point-to-point security and enabling interoperable mechanisms for single sign-on (SSO), global logout, identity registration, and termination are mandated. This is accomplished by adopting Liberty alliance standards, which define rules and guidelines for defining federated identities, identity registration and revocation, SSO with multiple partner services, global logout, and so forth.

Thus, it becomes very important to provide a security intermediary infrastructure that can handle multiple recipients using a standards-based framework, that can provide message-level configuration security mechanisms, and that can support SSO for accessing disparate security infrastructures.

Forces

- You want to use a security intermediary to support Web services–based workflow applications or to send messages to multiple service endpoints.
- You want to configure element-level security and access control that apply message-level security mechanisms, particularly authentication tokens and signatures and encrypted portions using XML digital signature or XML Encryption.

- You want to make sure to reveal only the required portions of a protected message to a target recipient.
- You want to implement SSO by interacting with an identity provider authority to generate SAML assertions and XACML-based access control lists for accessing Web services providers and applications that rely on SAML assertions.
- You want to incorporate a global logout mechanism that sends a logout notification to all participating service endpoints.
- You want to notify participating service providers when an identity is registered, revoked, and terminated.
- You want to dynamically apply security criteria through message transformations and canonicalizations before forwarding them to their intended recipients.
- You want to filter incoming message headers for security requirements and dynamically apply context-specific rules and other required security mechanisms before forwarding the messages to an endpoint.
- You want to support document-based Web services, particularly by checking document-level credentials and attributes.
- You want to enforce centralized logging for incoming messages, faults, messages sent, and intended recipients of the messages.
- You want to configure multiple message formats and support XML schemas that guarantee interoperability with intended service endpoints without compromising message security.
- You want to meet the mandated regulatory requirements defined by Web-services partners.
- You want to use a centralized intermediary that provides mechanisms for configuring message-level security headers supporting XML security specifications such as OASIS WS-Security, XML Signature, XML Encryption, SAML, XACML, and Liberty Alliance.

Solution

The Secure Message Router pattern is used to establish a security intermediary infrastructure that aggregates access to multiple application endpoints in a workflow or among partners participating in a Web-services transaction. It acts on incoming messages and dynamically provides the security logic for routing messages to multiple endpoint destinations without interrupting the flow of messages. It makes use of a security configuration utility to apply endpoint-specific security decisions and mechanisms, particularly configuring message-level security that protects messages in entirety or reveals selected portions to its intended recipients.

During operation, the Secure Message Router pattern works as a security enforcement point for outgoing messages before sending them to their intended recipients by providing endpoint-specific security services, including SSO, access control, and message-level security mechanisms. In addition, it can also provide identity-federation mechanisms that notify service providers and identity providers upon SSO, global logout, identity registration, and termination.

In effect, a Secure Message Router must handle tasks such as:

- Configuring message-level security that allows signing and encrypting an XML message or its selected elements intended for multiple service endpoints.
- Configuring SSO access with multiple Web-services endpoints using SAML tokens and XACML assertions that can act as SSO session tickets.
- Supporting the use of XKMS-based PKI services to retrieve keys for signing and encrypting appropriate message parts specific to a service endpoint or to participate in workflow.
- Notifying all participating service providers and identity providers of SSO and global logouts.
- Notifying all participating service providers and identity providers of identity registration, revocation, and termination.
- Dynamically applying message transformation and canonicalization algorithms to meet recipient endpoint requirements or standards compliance.
- Reconfiguring incoming messages to destination-specific message formats and supporting XML schemas that guarantee interoperability with the target service endpoint.
- Centralizing logging of messages and recording of auditable trails for incoming messages, faults, and their ultimate endpoints.
- Supporting use of a Liberty-compliant identity provider and agents for identity federation and establishing a circle of trust among participating service providers.

Structure

Figure 11–12 shows the class diagram of the Secure Message Router pattern.

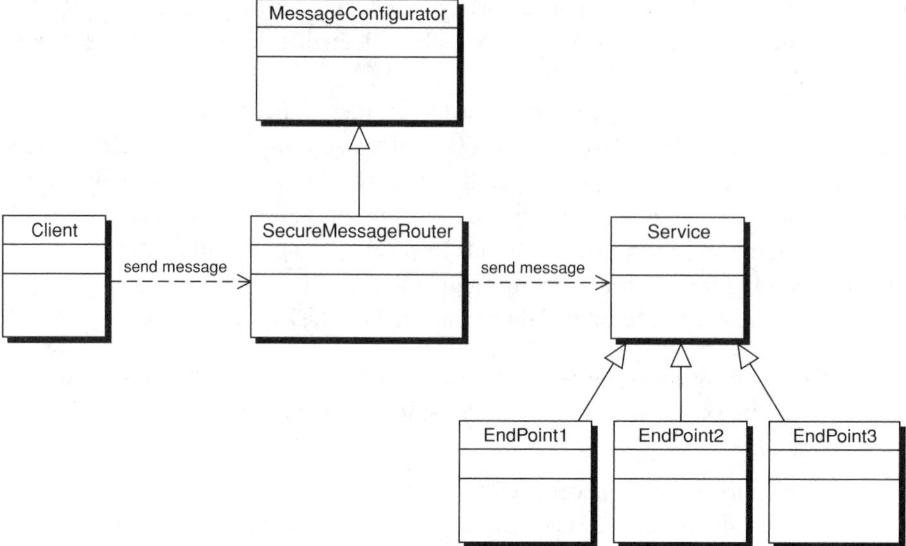

Figure 11–12 Secure Message Router class diagram

Participants and Responsibilities

Figure 11–13 shows the sequence diagram for the Secure Message Router. It illustrates the interactions of the various participants of the Secure Message Router pattern for a basic operation that receives an XML message, interacts with an identity provider, applies message-level security, and sends the message to a workflow or to multiple partner service endpoints over the Internet.

The key participants of the pattern are as follows:

- **Client**. The client of the Secure Message Router pattern can be any application that initiates a service request to access a single endpoint or multiple service endpoints. Typically, it can be any application component or a Message Interceptor Gateway that sends requests or responds to a Web-services transaction.
- **Secure Message Router**. The Secure Message Router allows configuring message-level security mechanisms and provides support for Liberty-enabled services such as Federated SSO, global logout, identity registration, and termination services by interacting with a Liberty-enabled identity provider.
- **Message Configurator**. The Message Configurator plays a secondary role as the Secure Message Router pattern. It implements all the methods

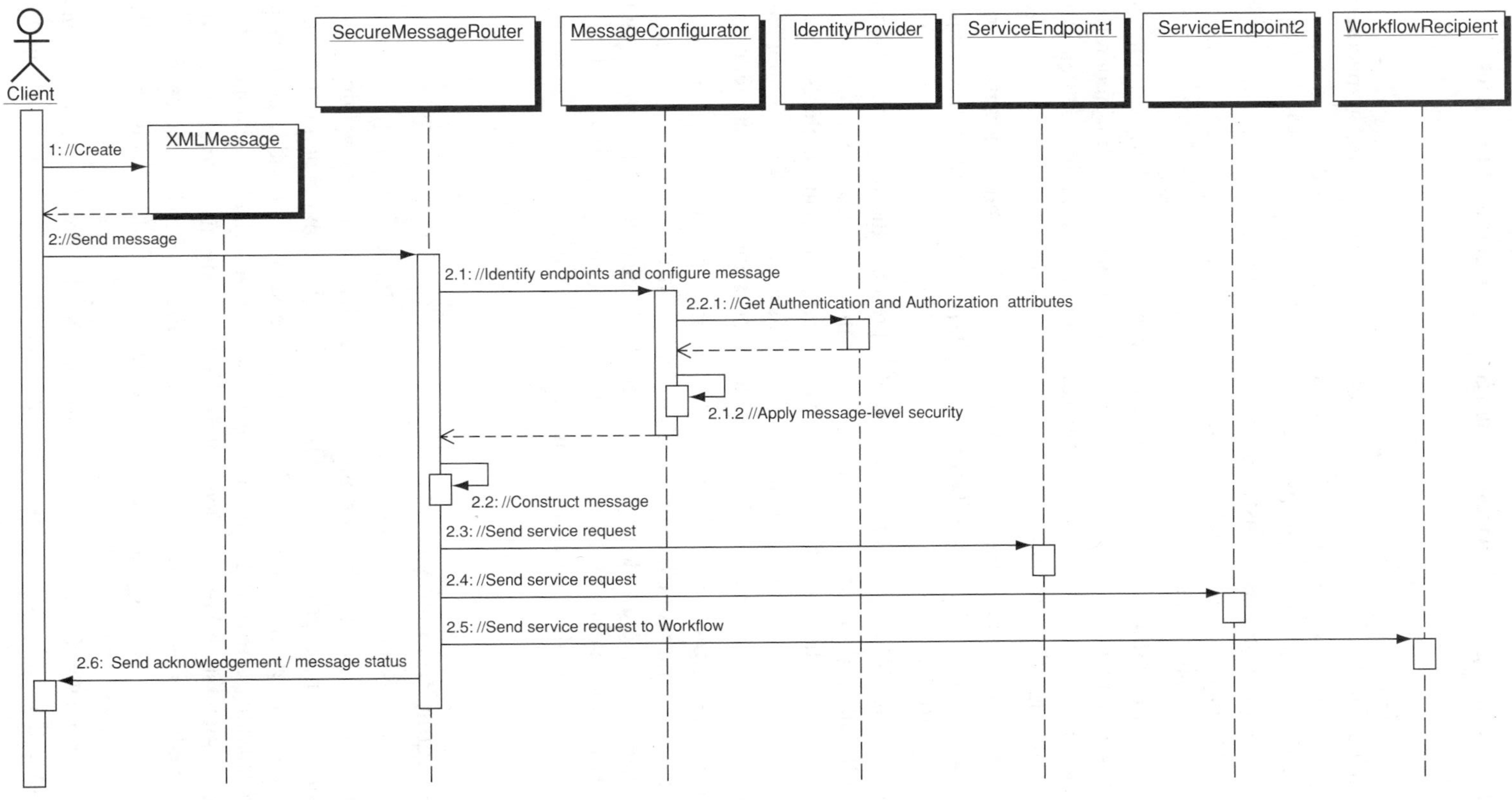

Figure 11–13 Secure Message Router sequence diagram

intended for configuring message-level security intended for a specified endpoint. It makes use of configuration tables that identify the message, service endpoint and intermediaries, message-level access privileges, validating XML schemas, transformations, and compliance requirements. It signs and encrypts messages in their entirety or selected portions, as specified in the configuration table.

- **Identity Provider**. The identity provider represents a Liberty-compliant service provider that delivers federated-identity services such as federated single sign-on, global logout, identity registration, termination, authentication, authorization, and auditing.
- **Request**. The Request message represents an XML document that is verified by all the required security-processing tasks carried out by the Secure Message Router.
- **ServiceEndpoint**. The ServiceEndpoint represents the target object and the ultimate consumer of the message that the client uses to do message processing. In the case of the Secure Message Router pattern, the Service-Endpoint can be a single provider or multiple service providers or applications that implement the business logic and processing of the client request.
- **WorkflowRecipient**. The WorkflowRecipient represents an endpoint that participates in a workflow or in collaboration. It is an intermediary endpoint representing an identity or business logic designated for processing the entire document or selected portions of an incoming message and then forwarding it to the next recipient in the workflow chain.

Strategies

XML Messaging Provider Strategy

In this strategy, the Secure Message Router pattern adopts an XML-based messaging provider or message-broker infrastructure that facilitates sending and receiving of XML messages (such as SOAP or ebXML) using synchronous and asynchronous delivery mechanisms. The XML messaging provider acts as a SOAP intermediary providing message-level security-mechanism support for RPC and document-style Web-services interactions among multiple service endpoints involved in a workflow or collaboration. Figure 11–14 represents the sequence diagram illustrating the Secure Message Router pattern using the XML Messaging Provider Strategy.

The Client initiates XML message requests intended for processing at multiple service endpoints in a Workflow. These messages are forwarded to the messaging

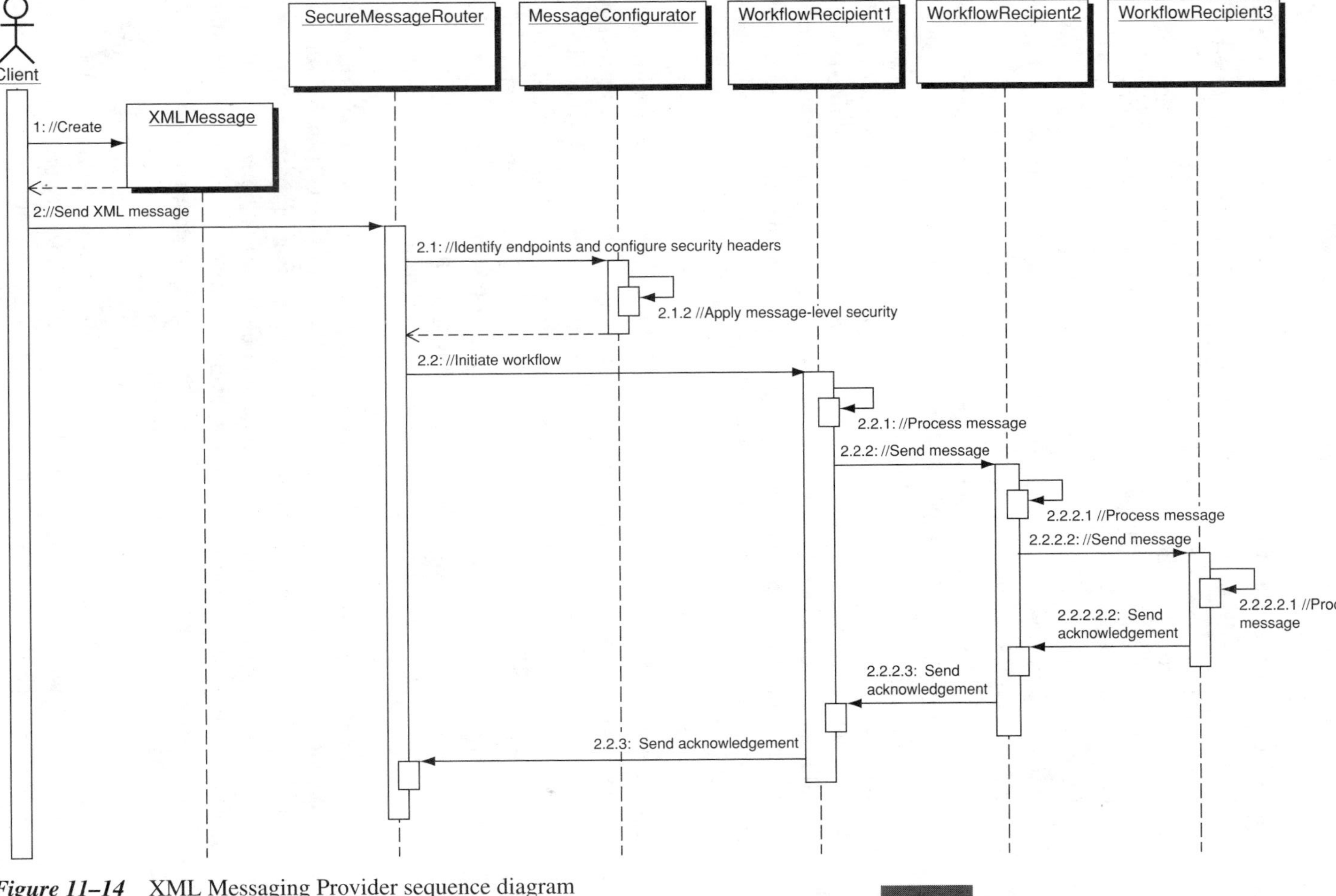

Figure 11–14 XML Messaging Provider sequence diagram

provider, which acts as a SOAP security intermediary that allows configuring and applying security-header mechanisms before sending the messages to its workflow participants. Upon receipt of a request message from the client, the messaging provider processes the message and then identifies and determines its intended recipients and their message-level security requirements. It makes use of a Message configurator that provides the required methods and information for applying the required message-level security mechanisms and defining endpoint-specific requirements. The Message configurator follows a security configuration table that specifies the message identifier, endpoints, and message-level security requirements related to representing the identity, signature, encryption, timestamps, correlation ID, and other endpoint-specific attributes. After configuring the message, the messaging provider initiates the workflow by dispatching configured message to its first intended endpoint (that is, a workflow participant). The dispatched message ensures that only the privileged portions of the message are allowed to be viewed or modified by workflow participants, based on their identities and other information; all other portions of the message remain integral and confidential throughout the workflow process.

Liberty SSO Strategy

The Liberty SSO Strategy adopts a federated network identity architecture based on the Liberty Alliance specifications. Using a Liberty-enabled identity provider, this strategy allows establishing circle-of-trust (CoT) relationships via identity federation to enable secure data communication among the service providers over the Internet. The service providers rely on a Liberty-enabled identity provider, which acts as a trust provider that defines and establishes identity federation-based trust relationships and also plays the role of an authority for issuing security assertions that represents authentication, authorization, and other attribute information.

In this strategy, the Secure Message Router pattern makes use of a Liberty-enabled identity provider to link service endpoints, and issue XML-based security assertions. Using the security assertions provided by the service provider, it initiates SSO with partner service endpoints and also uses authorization and other attribute assertions to support message-level security mechanisms for sending XML messages. Figure 11–15 represents the sequence diagram illustrating the Secure Message Router using the Liberty SSO strategy.

During operation, the client will make use of Secure Message Router to process the message, determine its intended endpoint recipients using a message Configurator, and then interact with a Liberty-enabled identity provider to establish SSO with partner endpoints. The Secure Message Router communicates with

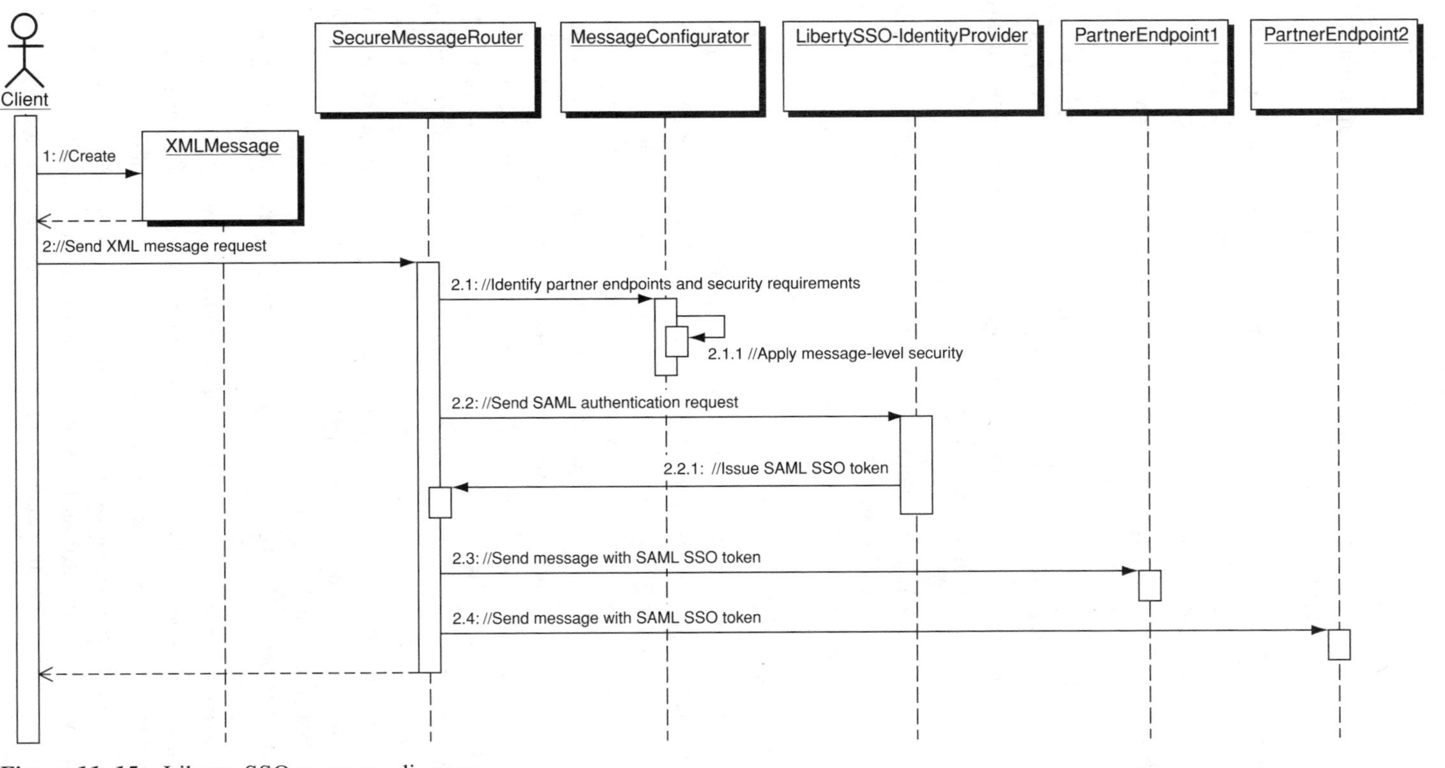

Figure 11–15 Liberty SSO sequence diagram

the Liberty-enabled identity provider using a Liberty-agent via a request and response protocol that works as follows:

1. The Secure Message Router initiates a request to the service provider, which sends a SAML authentication request to an identity provider that instructs the identity provider to provide an authentication assertion.
2. The identity provider responds with a SAML authentication response containing SAML artifacts or an error.
3. The Secure Message Router uses the SAML artifacts as an SSO token to interact with all partner endpoints and to initiate the transaction. The partner endpoints trust the SSO tokens issued by the Liberty-enabled identity provider that established the identity federation.

In addition to the above, the Secure Message Router also facilitates other Liberty-enabled services and tasks, such as notification of identity registration, termination, and global logout to all partner endpoints.

Consequences

Adopting the Secure Message Router pattern facilitates applying SSO mechanisms and trusted communication when the target message is exchanged among multiple recipients or intended to be part of a workflow. It also allows selectively applying XML Encryption and XML Signature at the element level by ensuring that content is not exposed to everyone unless the recipient has privileges to access the selected fragments of the message. This helps in securely sending messages to multiple recipients and ensuring that only selected fragments of the message are revealed or modified by the privileged recipients. With the support for Liberty-enabled identity providers, it establishes a circle of trust among participation endpoints and facilitates SSO by securely sharing identity information among the participating service endpoints. The Secure Message Router also ensures seamless integration and interoperability with all participating endpoints by sending destination-specific messages.

In addition, the Secure Message Router pattern provides the following benefits:

- *Centralized routing.* The Secure Message Router delivers a centralized message intermediary solution for applying message-level security mechanisms and enabling SSO access to multiple endpoints. This allows configuring a centralized access control and processing subsystem for incorporating all security-related operations for sending messages to multiple service endpoints. It offers centralized management of related services, including authentication, authorization, faults, encryption, audit trails, metering, billing, and so on.

- *Modularity and maintainability.* Centralizing all security mechanisms and configuring access-control policies using a single intermediary keep the message-sender application interfaces separated from security operations. This enhances a service with a modular subsystem designated for security and reduces complex tasks at the service endpoint of a Web services provider. This also saves significant application processing time and resources at the message-sending application endpoint.
- *Reusability and extensibility.* The Secure Message Router pattern encapsulates all direct access to participating service endpoints, facilitating a common reusable solution that is necessary for protecting multiple service endpoints. It also offers extensibility by allowing you to incorporate more message-level security mechanisms and functionalities specific to the target endpoints.
- *Improved testability.* The Secure Message Router infrastructure separates the security architectural model from the underlying message-sender's service endpoint. This improves ease of testability and extensibility of the security architecture.

Security Factors and Risks

- **High availability and reliability**. The Secure Message Router infrastructure and every component that interacts with it must provide high availability and reliability. It becomes very important to ensure 100 percent availability so that the message router can be better than the weakest link in the Web-services architecture. Failure to provide high availability may result in monetary loss and security vulnerabilities.

- **Fault tolerance**. The Secure Message Router is also expected to be fault tolerant in order to support security and to enhance reliability and performance of the infrastructure. When a failure is detected, it must be transparently replaced with a redundant infrastructure. The failure should not jeopardize any existing outbound requests or responses or their intermediate processing states. There must be a recovery mechanism that can read all outstanding service requests and paused requests with intermediate states and forward them for further processing with the Secure Message Router without skipping any existing security mechanisms.
- **Provider issues**. From an implementation standpoint, there are not many messaging providers that facilitate standards-based XML message workflow,

multi-hop Web-services communication, and Liberty SSO. Using non-standard implementations affects the secure message-router-based architecture with noticeable problems related to incompatible messages, routing failures, longer latencies, and lack of guaranteed message delivery. In general, these issues directly affect security and reliability of Web services or workflow communication using multiple Web-services endpoints. The adoption of emerging Web-services standards such as BPEL4WS, WS-Reliability, WS-Reliable Messaging, WS-*, and their compliant products is expected to provide interoperable workflow collaboration, reliability, and guaranteed message delivery protocols.

Reality Checks

Enabling interoperability in a workflow? The Secure Message Router must pre-verify the messages for interoperability before sending them to participants in a workflow or intended recipients. The interoperability requirements of the recipient endpoint with regard to WS-I profiles, XML schemas, transformations, canonicalizations, and other endpoint-specific attributes must be specified using the Message Configurator.

Scalability? It is important to verify the Secure Message Router solution architecture for scalability to eliminate bottlenecks when communicating with multiple endpoints. This is critical to the success of every Message Router to perform resource-intensive tasks such as applying signatures, encryptions, and transformations without the expense of scalability and overall performance.

Related Patterns

Message Inspector [Web services]. The Message Inspector pattern is used to verify and validate the quality of message-level security mechanisms applied to XML Web services.

Message Interceptor Gateway [Web services]. Message Interceptor Gateway provides a single entry point by aggregating access to all service endpoints and centralizes security enforcement.

Best Practices and Pitfalls

The following sections discuss the best practices and the associated pitfalls you should consider when implementing security in a Web-services infrastructure and in application services.

Best Practices

Web Services Infrastructure Security

1. *End-to-End Transport Layer Security.* During communication, secure the transport layer with appropriate message integrity and confidentiality mechanisms. The communication must be tamperproof and the messages in transit must not be intercepted or accessed. Adopting two-way SSL/TLS communication with the use of both server and client certificates is often considered the best-practice solution.
2. *Standards-Based Security and Infrastructure.* Web services are all about implementing standards-based messages and communication. They enable the adopted security mechanisms and countermeasures to seamlessly work together with architecture independence in all application layers and enable cross-platform support among Web-services providers and the client requesters. Thus, follow standards and adopt standards-based infrastructure providers to ensure security interoperability throughout the life cycle of the service. Using proprietary mechanisms affects interoperability with standards-based infrastructure providers.
3. *Network Perimeter Protection.* Use network firewalls and intrusion detection systems for identifying and protecting the Web-services infrastructure against connection attacks such as network spoofing, man-in-the-middle, and DOS attacks. Use router mechanisms for filtering incoming and outgoing traffic and use network access control lists (ACLs) for allowing authorized hosts and blocking traffic from unauthorized hosts based on IP addresses and protocols.
4. *Minimization and Hardening.* Prior to deployment testing of the host platform infrastructure, remove all unnecessary services, user accounts, OS/application libraries, and tools. All services that are considered to be insecure or vulnerable must be secured or replaced with alternatives (for example, SSH, SFTP, and so forth). Furthermore, it is important to consider adopting preventive measures such as securing file systems with encryption, tightened access control, and deploying host-based intrusion detection and monitoring systems that allow detection of suspicious events, policy violations, and abuses.
5. *IP Filtering.* Use IP filtering mechanisms to provide packet filtering based on IP addresses, port, protocol, network interface, and traffic direction. This helps to safeguard the Web-services endpoint host by allowing messages passed through authorized hosts and proxy servers.

6. *XML-Aware Security Infrastructure.* Adopt an XML-aware security infrastructure such as an XML firewall or Web-services security solution that can proactively detect and protect against XML DOS attacks, malformed or corrupted XML, malicious SOAP/XML payloads, and unsupported message attachments. These issues can disrupt the infrastructure by consuming excessive bandwidth and can degrade performance with infinite processing loops that can compromise availability of the service endpoint.
7. *Access Protection.* Make sure direct access to all service endpoints is disabled. Use an XML firewall or a Web-proxy infrastructure that masks all the underlying service endpoints and communicates through network address translation (NAT) or URL rewriting mechanisms. This helps in enforcing transport-layer security (such as two-way SSL/TLS) and in identifying all incoming traffic for XML and content-layer vulnerabilities before processing at the application service endpoint.
8. *XML Firewall Appliance Adoption for Performance.* XML firewall appliances can recognize and provide protection against XML-related malicious attacks. In particular, they can enhance message throughput significantly by reducing the processing time involved with resource-intensive tasks such as XML parsing, XML schema validation, XML Encryption and decryption, and XML Signature validation.
9. *Origin Host Verification.* Verify the host ID initiating the Web-services request before processing the message. This helps in identifying man-in-the-middle, message replay, impersonation, and illegitimate-request attacks initiated from unauthorized hosts. When it is determined that a request is from an unauthorized host, the service endpoint must drop those requests without further processing.
10. *Adopt Hardware Cryptographic Devices.* Cryptographic keys play a vital role in applying digital signatures and encryption mechanisms. It is important to safeguard the keys so that they are not accessible to hackers, because they are vulnerable to attack by modification, duplication, or substitution. Using hardware cryptographic devices ensures safer and more tamper-proof key management and helps in off-loading computationally intensive operations.
11. *VPN Access.* Consider using VPN-based limited access for Web-services solutions deployed within an intranet or an extranet (extended to potential consumers). Using VPN reduces security risks from external intrusions.
12. *Employ Honeypots.* Honeypots are intrusion detection decoys deployed with the intent to mislead potential attackers and thereby provide early warning to systems administrators. In-depth analysis of a honeypot's Web-

service traffic can yield useful knowledge for purposes of both research and defense against attacks.

Communication and Message Security

13. *Restrict direct WSDL Access.* WSDLs describe Web services providers in terms of their exposed operations, type and number of parameters, type and structure of returned results, protocol bindings, and so on. Protect WSDLs from public viewing and unauthorized access by disallowing all direct access to WSDL descriptions. Enforce an authentication and authorization mechanism that restricts access to viewing or downloading WSDL descriptions.

14. *UDDI Registration and Lookups.* UDDI registries allow registering WSDL information for public or private access and provide a repository for searching and sharing information about published services. While registering services in a public registry, ensure that the accessible methods and data types are subject to use after an agreement and mandated security policies. You should choose to register methods for providing inquiry transactions only. It is always recommended not to expose methods that allow critical business-transaction processing.
15. *Message Validation and Compliance.* Verify all incoming and outgoing messages for XML well-formedness, format, and syntax, and validate the messages against XML schemas or DTD-based rules mandated by the service endpoint. This ensures that the messages are not manipulated, are free from issues related to discontinuity or malformedness that affect parsing, and are compliant with valid XML schemas. XML-aware firewalls or hardware accelerators can be used for better performance and to reduce processing times.
16. *Message Inspection.* Make sure all incoming XML traffic is intercepted and filtered for performing message-level security operations before processing at its intended endpoint. These operations include authentication, authorization, auditing, validating signatures, encryption or decryption, compression or decompression, transformation, routing, and management of functions mandated by the service endpoint. This eliminates the risks and potential dangers of malicious content-level threats and XML-based attacks from unauthorized parties and hackers. Use the Message Inspector pattern and strategies for enforcing message inspection.
17. *WSDL Generation.* Using automated tools for generating WSDLs generally exposes all the methods provided by the underlying application component. Exposing all the methods available for Web services consumption

is prone to using unpublished methods, guess attacks, service abuses, and related vulnerabilities. Make sure the generated WSDL file exposes only specific operations intended for external access.

18. *Secure XML Schemas.* XML schemas help Web services requesters and services share rules and instructions for content, syntax, and semantics processing of XML documents. Storing XML schemas in a way that gives the public access to them invites manipulation that can compromise the security of the service endpoints and the exchanged data. Verify that all XML schemas are secured with appropriate rules and access privileges for public use.
19. *Timestamps.* Use timestamps in message headers to determine the timeliness and validity of security headers. Doing so also helps by providing non-repudiation evidence of the time of a transaction's execution. In addition, if a Web-services endpoint receives two contradictory messages, the timestamps inserted in the message can be used to determine its validity or its expiration. Timestamps help in identifying forged requests and message replay attacks.
20. *Correlation.* Identify correlated messages and service endpoints by tying a message sent from the requesting endpoint and the response message sent from the replying endpoint together using a unique identifier. The identifier, also referred to as correlation ID, identifies both the original request message from the sender and its response message from the receiver. Using message correlation helps to uniquely identify messages and their consumers from logs and recorded audit trails. It also helps when diagnosing issues in forensic investigations.
21. *Signing Messages.* Adopt XML signatures for signing messages and ensuring message-level integrity and authentication. Using XML signatures allows a message recipient to verify the signed messages from a sender. This proves that the signed messages originated by a sender are authentic and have not been altered or tampered with during their transit or storage. Using XML signatures also offers the flexibility of signing specific XML portions of a message and then applying changes to the message involving multiple parties during communication.
22. *Message and Element-Level Encryption.* Adopt XML encryption for maintaining message-level data confidentiality and privacy during transit or storage. Depending on the scenario, using XML Encryption allows encrypting XML messages in their entirety, applying encryption for portions of a message, or applying multiple encryptions to different parts of the message and leaving selected portions of the message unencrypted.

XML Encryption preserves the encrypted data intended for multiple parties in a workflow or a multi-hop communication involving intermediaries.

23. *XKMS Adoption*. XKMS defines a Web services interface to PKI services such as key registration, revocation, location, and validation. In Web-services communication, XKMS allows you to register, look up, and validate cryptographic keys used in XML signatures and XML Encryption. Adopting XKMS in Web services delegates all public-key lookup, registration, and verification tasks intended for XML signatures and XML Encryption. As a result, it delivers performance gains through reducing the message payload by off-loading all processing of key information to the XKMS trust service.

24. *Fault Handling*. When a Web services client request cannot be completed or fails, the service-provider endpoint must return an error as a SOAP Fault element. This is represented descriptively in the detail element that provides all of the error information provided by the service endpoint. In case of failures related to an application service, particularly exceptions from underlying application and services, the faults expose the weakness in the application and allow hackers to design potential vulnerabilities based on them. It is important to proactively identify those faults and redefine them with information that does not reveal the weakness of the underlying service endpoint.
25. *Logging and Recording of Audit Trails*. Create secure transaction logs and audit trails that can be used for forensic investigation about life-cycle events and transactions taken by the services provider based on the requests made by the consumer. This verifies that the initiating clients are accountable for their requested operations with an irrefutable proof of originating request or response. The audit trails provides information that can be used to monitor resources, system break-ins, failed login and breach attempts; to determine security loopholes, violations, and identity spoofing; and to identify users attempting to circumvent security, either intentionally or unintentionally.
26. *Avoiding Composability issues*. All exposed services must define the security requirements to the service-requester clients that relate to transport-level and message-level security mechanisms. It is important to verify the ability to compose the messages including the required security mechanisms and the endpoint-specific message payload. The composability of the message should not cause any unintentional functional side-effects.
27. *Identity and Policy Management*. Web services should use identity information, trust policies, and their access privileges from underlying applications

and should map them between service providers and consumers within a domain or multiple domains. The identity and policies associated with users can be used to define their roles and to access rules that are required as part of requests and responses between the communicating parties. Adopting a Liberty-enabled identity provider with the identity-federation capabilities required by Liberty Alliance specifications helps to aggregate Web services without compromising security by delivering a federated SSO, global logout, identity registration, and termination.

Testing and Deployment

28. *Service Penetration Tests.* The security-related vulnerabilities of Web services generally stem from improper handling of XML-based request messages or a lack of parameter validation checking that expose the service endpoint to buffer overflow, message injection, and malicious cross-site scripting attacks. It is important to identify these vulnerabilities by performing penetration tests on the service endpoint, hardening the underlying application code, and immunizing the host environment for these erroneous conditions. For example, the penetration test must draw out illicit conditions and anomalous behavior from the service endpoint by manipulating the request parameters and operations using special characters, large white spaces, missing tags, oversized requests, replay or recursive requests, malformed requests, malformed XML with discontinuity, schema poisoning, injecting malformed XML, SQL, Xquery, or Xpath expressions, and so forth. These tests identify known threats and vulnerabilities and help to fix the service endpoint through application-level hardening.
29. *Stress Testing.* Load testing with simulated users allows you to determine the Web-services provider scalability and number of supported concurrent users, to identify the breaking point, and to identify the acceptable service-level requirements. In a security context, it helps to validate the architecture capacity, scalability, and reliability and to identify potential security breaches after failures.
30. *Centralized Management.* Adopt a centralized control and administration solution for provisioning and monitoring all service endpoints. The solution includes deployment and monitoring of service endpoints, enabling content-based logging and auditing, enabling and disabling service endpoints, configuring authentication and security policies, and so forth.
31. *Monitoring and Alerting.* Monitor all security operations using automated monitoring of service components in a way that lets you detect malicious activities. For example, set a threshold with an alert on the number of authenti-

cation failures per client and to detect a hacker undergoing an XML DOS or WSDL descriptions attack. In such cases, the monitoring system must alert the security administrator that countermeasures and other corrective actions are needed.

32. *Fault Management and Self-Healing*. Fault management begins upon detection of an error or a security breach, and it is expected to capture sufficient data to diagnose the underlying problem. Once a diagnosis of a problem is determined, the fault-management solution should perform problem isolation and self-healing tasks. Adopting fault management and self-healing mechanisms improves the availability of the application infrastructure. Fault-management and self-healing solutions can be deployed using watchdog agents that automatically respond to the problem by disabling faulty components, restarting the services, issuing messages to alert administrators, and providing diagnostic information for forensic investigation.
33. *Fault Tolerance*. Mission-critical Web services demand fault-tolerance capabilities that provide reliability and solutions to support unpredictable and voluminous concurrent workloads. To handle such requirements requires a recovery mechanism that identifies the service failure, activates a new service-provider instance, and then reads the logs about the outstanding failed request to continue processing. Capturing the state of outstanding requests in order to repeat processing and restart a new service might degrade performance. To meet performance requirements, consider fault-tolerance capabilities for service requests that involve a business transaction—but not an inquiry transaction. Ensure all security tasks are processed as prescribed by the service provider, even though the service endpoint runs on a fault-tolerant mode.
34. *Configuration Management*. Follow a secure configuration management practice to administer all configuration information applied to the service endpoint. Make sure you adopt a security strategy that restricts access to configuration information to privileged users based on their roles. Any opening to unauthorized access to configuration information may cause a vulnerability that can compromise the security of all exposed services.

Pitfalls

35. *Vendor-Specific Security APIs*. Adopting vendor-specific API mechanisms often affects interoperability and integration of services across vendors due to failures related to message compliance, mismatched crypto algorithms, and schema validation. Choose API mechanisms evolved through

community processes and adopt a standards-based infrastructure that enables interoperability and seamless integration with other standards-based technology providers.

36. *Content Encryption.* Encrypting the messages in their entirety often results in abnormal payloads, increases network bandwidth utilization, and causes processing overheads. Consider adopting element-level encryption that allows encrypting selected portions of messages and then using secure communication channels that ensure data integrity and confidentiality during transit and storage.

References

[XML-DSIG] XML Signature–Syntax and Processing Rules. W3C Recommendation, February 12, 2002.

http://www.w3.org/TR/xmldsig-core/

[XML-ENC] XML Encryption–Syntax and Processing Rules. W3C Recommendation, December 10, 2002.

http://www.w3.org/TR/xmlenc-core/

[OASIS] WS-Security 1.0 Standard and Specifications.

http://docs.oasis-open.org/wss/2004/01/oasis-200401-wss-soap-message-security-1.0.pdf

[WS-I] Web Services Security Basic Profile 1.0–Working Group Draft.

http://www.ws-i.org/Profiles/BasicSecurityProfile-1.0-2004-05-12.html

[W3C] Web Services Architecture. W3C Working group Note, February 11, 2004.

http://www.w3.org/TR/ws-arch/

[CJP2] Alur, Crupi, and Malks. *Core J2EE Patterns*, Second Edition. Prentice Hall, 2003.

[Sun J2EE Blueprints] Designing Web Services with the J2EE Platform, 2nd Edition–Guidelines, Patterns, and Code for Java Web Services.

http://java.sun.com/blueprints/guidelines/designing_webservices/

[DWS] Nagappan, Skoczylas, et al. *Developing Java Web Services: Architecting and Developing Java Web Services*. Wiley, 2002

[SAML] OASIS Security Services TC–SAML Specifications.
http://www.oasis-open.org/committees/tc_home.php?wg_abbrev=security

[SAMLP] WS-I SAML Token Profile Version 1.0 Working Draft.
http://www.ws-i.org/Profiles/SAMLTokenProfile-1.0-2005-01-19.html

[REL] REL Token Profile.
http://www.ws-i.org/Profiles/RELTokenProfile-1.0-2005-01-19.html

[XKMS] W3C XML Key Management Specification 2.0.
http://www.w3.org/TR/xkms/

Securing the Identity–Design Strategies and Best Practices

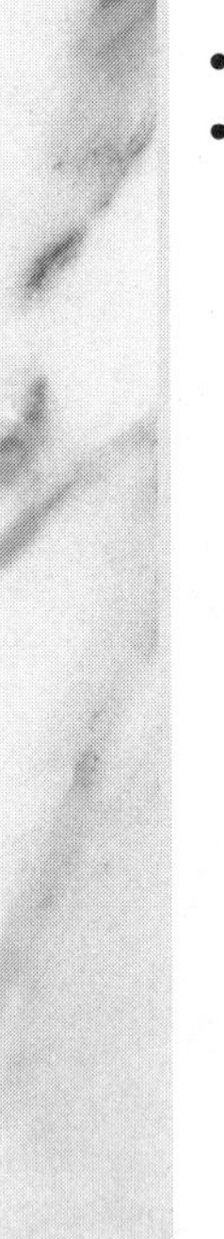

Topics in This Chapter

- Identity Management Security Patterns
- Best Practices and Pitfalls

Chapter 12

In Chapter 7, "Identity Management Standards and Technologies," we introduced the identity management and the relevant security standards, such as SAML, Liberty, and XACML. SAML is an XML protocol for representing authentication and authorization assertions and is used for single sign-on and global logout. Liberty reuses the security assertion framework from SAML and extends it with different identity profiles and framework. XACML provides a versatile policy management framework for administering access control rules and managing security policies. These security standards are important because they allow different security vendor products to interoperate with each other. Architects and developers are now able to work with different security infrastructures without rewriting most of the security components.

In a heterogeneous application infrastructure environment, each application system may have different user authentication mechanisms and customized authorization schemes. Enabling unified access with single sign-on and exit with global logout is a complex process. To handle this, architects and developers may need to build custom mechanisms or ensure that the current sign-on mechanisms support open standards such as SAML and Liberty. In either case, there is much similar processing logic and code in the Identity tier that can be refactored for reuse. You may also want to extract some commonly used security processing into helper classes instead of embedding the security processing logic into each of the authentication and authorization functions. If different versions of security packages are used simultaneously (for example, due to support for legacy systems), it would be useful to build an abstraction layer (using façade or delegate patterns) so that the identity management functionality can support multiple versions with backward compatibility. In these scenarios, adopting security patterns would be useful in addressing these requirements in the Identity tier.

In identity management, security patterns can provide a common design framework, unified SSO, and global-logout mechanisms for use with heterogeneous applications. They can also reduce significant design and development effort, because they simplify complexity while they capture many security best practices. Using abstraction, these security patterns can shield off custom-built or specific-vendor APIs, and this can reduce the impact of vendor lock-in if customers want to switch to another vendor product. Additionally, because security standards are still evolving, the abstraction layer in the security pattern can help mitigate the risk of migrating to new security standards.

There are many security vendor products and open source toolkits available in the market today that support SAML, Liberty, and XACML. Some security vendor products provide administrator-friendly agents or adapters so that you do not need to customize their applications by adding SAML protocols or Liberty identity profiles to their software program code. This is particularly useful for those who have a large amount of packaged applications purchased from vendors. Nevertheless, there are many of them who have home-grown applications that need to work with standards-based identity management architecture. This mandates a reusable identity management framework and security patterns to resolve the recurring problems and complexities.

Identity Management Security Patterns

Assertion Builder Pattern

Problem

You need a structured and consistent approach to gathering security information (for example, SAML assertions) about the authentication action performed on a subject, attribute information about the subject, or an authorization request from a trusted service provider.

Security assertions are authentication and authorization-related information exchanged between trusted service providers and requesters, and are used as a common mechanism for enabling applications to support SSO without requiring the client to login multiple times. To enable a trusted environment, we need to address the requirements of SSO with heterogeneous applications, discrete authentication schemes, authorization policies, and other related attributes in use. This requires having a generic mechanism for constructing and processing SAML-based assertions.

Forces

- You want to avoid duplicate program logic for building authentication assertion, authorization decision assertion, and attribute statements.
- You need to apply common processing logic to similar security assertion statements.
- You need a helper class to extract similar processing logic to build SAML assertion statements instead of embedding them into the authentication and authorization processes.
- You want the flexibility to support client requests from a servlet, EJB client, or a SOAP client.

Solution

Use an Assertion Builder to abstract similar processing control logic in order to create SAML assertion statements.

The Assertion Builder pattern encapsulates the processing control logic in order to create SAML authentication statements, authorization decision statements, and attribute statements as a service. Each assertion statement generation shares similar program logic of creating the SAML header (for example, schema version) and instantiating the assertion type, conditions, and subject statement information. The common program logic can also be used to avoid locking in with a specific product implementation. By exposing the Assertion Builder as a service, developers can also access SAML assertion statement creation using SOAP protocol binding without creating separate protocol handling routines.

Under a single sign-on environment (refer to Figure 12–3), a client authenticates with a single sign-on service provider (also known as the source site) and later requests access to a resource from a destination site. Upon successful authentication, the source site is able to redirect the client request to the destination site, assuming that the source site has a sophisticated security engine that determines the client is allowed to access the destination site. Then, the destination site will issue a SAML request to ask for an authentication assertion from the source site. The Assertion Builder will be used to assemble sign-on information and user credentials to generate SAML assertion statements. This is applicable for both the source site (processing SAML responses) and the destination site (processing SAML requests). The destination site will then respond to the client for resource access. Subsequently, the destination site will handle authorization decisions and attribute statements to determine what access level is allowed for the client request.

Figure 12–1 depicts a high-level architecture diagram of the Assertion Builder pattern. In a typical application scenario, developers can design an Assertion Builder to provide the service of generating SAML authentication statements, SAML authorization decision statements, and SAML attribute statements. The Assertion Builder creates a system context (Assertion Context) and produces a SAML assertion statement (Assertion), which can be an authentication statement, an authorization decision statement, or an attribute statement. An EJB client can perform a JNDI service look-up of the SAML Assertion Builder service and invoke the preliminary utilities to assemble the SAML headers. After that, it invokes the relevant statement generation function, such as authentication statement. Similarly, a servlet can perform service invocation by acting as an EJB client. For a SOAP client, the Assertion Builder service bean needs to be exposed as a WSDL. Upon service invocation, the Assertion Builder utilities will marshal and unmarshal the SOAP envelope when the protocol binding is set to SOAP.

Structure

Figure 12–2 shows a class diagram for Assertion Builder service. The core Assertion Builder service consists of two important classes: AssertionContext and Assertion. The AssertionContext class defines the public interfaces for managing the system

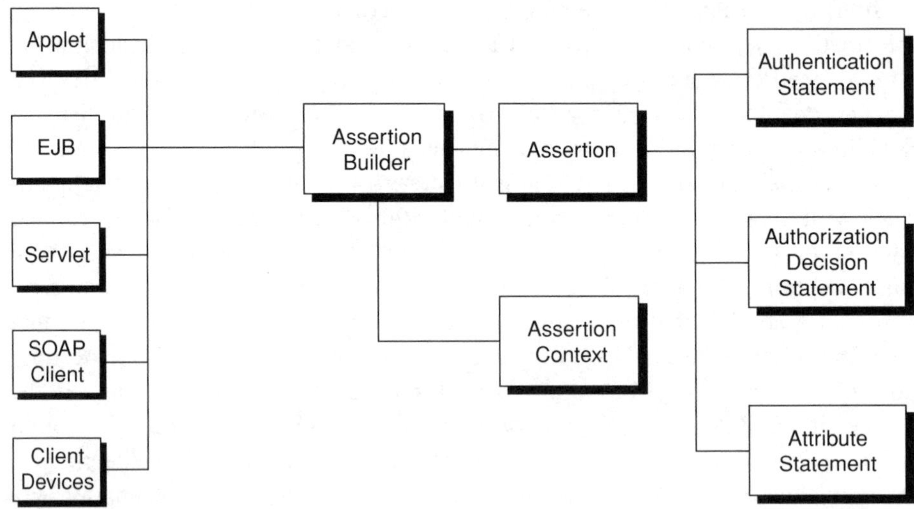

Figure 12–1 Assertion Builder logical architecture

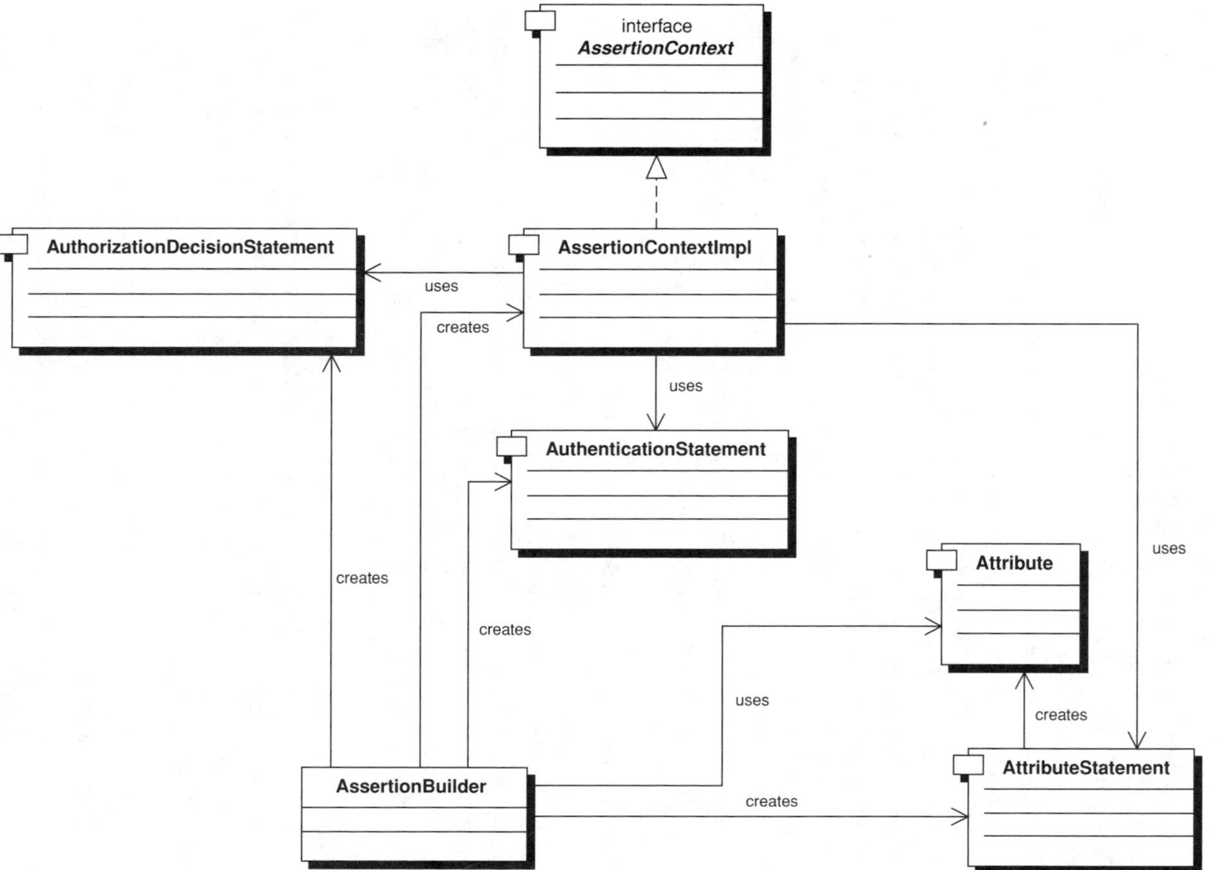

Figure 12–2 Assertion Builder class diagram

context when creating SAML assertion statements, SAML assertion types, and the protocol binding. If the SAML binding is set to be SOAP over HTTP, then the Assertion Builder service needs to wrap the SAML artifacts with a SOAP envelope instead of the HTTP header. It has a corresponding implementation class called AssertionContextImpl.

The Assertion class refers to the SAML assertion statement object. It contains basic elements of subject information (such as subject's IP address, subject's DNS address), source Web site, and destination Web site for the creation of SAML assertion statements. There is a corresponding data class called Subject, which refers to the principal for the security authentication or authorization. Each Assertion contains a Subject element. The Assertion class is also extended into AuthenticationStatement, AuthorizationDecisionStatement, and AttributeStatement. Each of these three assertion statement classes is responsible for creating SAML assertion statements, respectively, according to the SAML 2.0 specification. Attribute is a data class that encapsulates the distinctive characteristics of a subject and denotes the attributes in a SAML attribute statement.

Participants and Responsibilities

Figure 12–3 depicts a use case scenario where a client is requesting resource access from a destination site via the source site that acts as a single sign-on service provider. Client refers to a Web browser that initiates the resource access request. SourceSite denotes the single sign-on service provider that manages security information about which resources can be accessible in other affiliated sites, including DestinationSite. DestinationSite denotes the target site with resources that Client intends to access.

This is a scenario for a Web browser interacting with the source and destination sites with single sign-on (i.e., browser profile), and it is not applicable to a server-to-server single sign-on scenario. The Assertion Builder pattern is implemented for Steps 3 through 14. The other steps are provided here to provide a better context only.

1. Client accesses resources provided by the service provider (SourceSite).
2. SourceSite verifies if Client is authenticated already.
3. SourceSite creates an instance of AssertionBuilder. In this scenario, the instance is for creating a SAML authentication assertion request.
4. DestinationSite also creates an instance of AssertionBuilder. This is for creating a SAML authentication assertion response.
5. AssertionBuilder retrieves SAML protocol binding (for example, SOAP binding) for the interaction with SourceSite or DestinationSite.

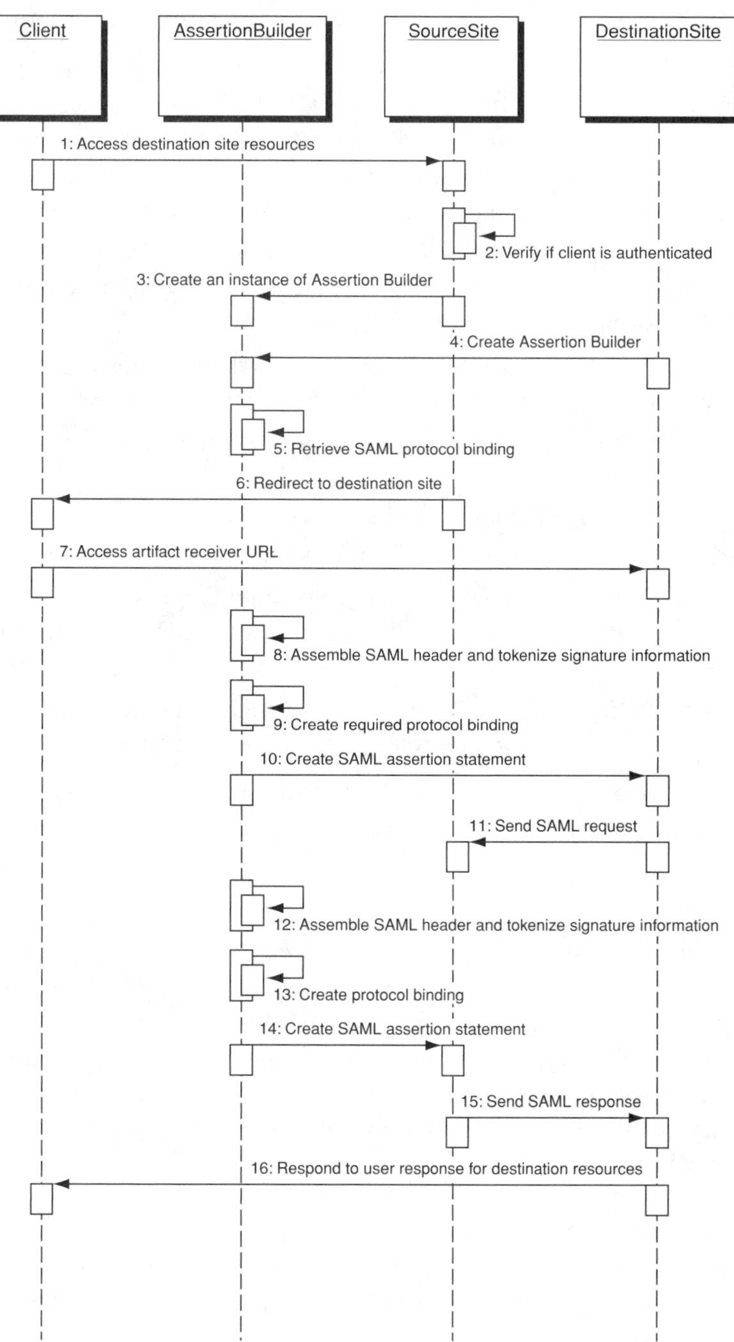

Figure 12–3 Assertion Builder sequence diagram

6. SourceSite redirects the resource access to the destination site DestinationSite via URL redirection.
7. Client accesses the artifact receiver URL.
8. AssertionBuilder assembles information to build the SAML header and tokenizes the user credentials (i.e., creates any security token from the user credentials) to facilitate the interaction with DestinationSite.
9. AssertionBuilder creates the relevant protocol binding. For example, if this is a SOAP binding, then AssertionBuilder creates the SOAP envelope and uses the SOAP binding protocol.
10. AssertionBuilder creates a SAML assertion statement (for example, SAML authentication assertion request) and sends it to DestinationSite.
11. DestinationSite issues a SAML request for any authentication assertion statement to SourceSite.
12. AssertionBuilder assembles information to build the SAML header and tokenizes the user credentials to facilitate interaction with SourceSite.
13. AssertionBuilder creates the relevant protocol binding. For example, if this is a SOAP binding, then AssertionBuilder creates the SOAP envelope and uses the SOAP binding protocol.
14. AssertionBuilder creates a SAML assertion statement (for example, SAML authentication assertion response) and sends it to SourceSite.
15. SourceSite issues a SAML response to DestinationSite.
16. DestinationSite responds to user response for resources at the destination site.

Strategies

Protocol Binding Strategy

It is possible that the same client may be using a mixture of SOAP over HTTP and SOAP over HTTPS SAML requests under different use case scenarios. It is important to be flexible about the protocol binding so that different protocols are supported. To accommodate such flexibility, developers can use a custom protocol binding look-up function to determine which SAML protocol binding is used for the SAML request.

Time Checking Strategy

Developers can add extra security control by adding timestamp comparison control for processing SAML responses in order to address the security risks of replay, message insertion, or message deletion. They can also compare the AuthenticationInstant timestamp in the SAML request and the SAML response. Typically, the timestamp in the SAML response is slightly behind the SAML request time. Another extension is to define a timeout strategy for the authentication timestamp. For example, a strategy might be that the destination site will not allow access for a client request if the authentication timestamp is over 120 minutes ago.

Audit Control Strategy

Although the subject IP and DNS addresses are optional in the current SAML 1.1 or 2.0 specifications, it is always a good design strategy to capture them for audit control purposes. For example, some hackers may be able to replay SAML assertion statements within the customer LAN. By tracking the subject IP and DNS addresses, security architects and developers are able to quickly detect any SAML assertion statements with unusual IP and DNS addresses.

Using Assertion Builder Pattern in Single Sign-on

The Assertion Builder pattern should be used in conjunction with the Single Sign-on Delegator (refer to next section for details). The Single Sign-on Delegator shields off the design complexity of remote communication with different assertion statement creation services and utilities of the Assertion Builder, as well as other single sign-on services such as Java Connector for legacy systems. This is particularly useful when these single sign-on services are provided in a variety of technologies, such as EJBs, servlets, Java Beans, and custom applications.

Consequences

By employing the Assertion Builder pattern, developers will be able to benefit in the following ways:

- *Addresses broken authentication flaw.* The Assertion Builder pattern can be used to build a helper class that creates and sends SAML authentication statements between trusted service providers. The SAML authentication statement denotes security information regarding authentication data about the subject. This helps to safeguard the authentication mechanisms from a potential broken authentication flaw.

- *Addresses broken access control risk.* The Assertion Builder pattern can be used to create SAML authorization decision and attribute statements. The SAML authorization decision statement denotes a critical decision about granting or denying resource access for a subject. This helps to safeguard the access control mechanisms from potential broken access control flaws.

- *Enables transparency by encapsulating the assertion statements.* The Assertion Builder pattern encapsulates three different assertion statement creation functionalities with similar processing logic. It is easier to maintain and use. In addition, architects and developers do not need to embed the processing logic of building SAML assertion statements in the business processing logic.

- *Reduces the complexity of integration.* The Assertion Builder pattern allows a flexible service invocation from a variety of clients, including servlets, EJB clients, and SOAP clients. It reduces the integration effort with different platforms.

Sample Code

Example 12–1 shows a sample code excerpt for creating an Assertion Builder for SAML assertion requests. The example creates a SAML authentication statement, a SAML authorization decision statement, and a SAML attribute statement. It defines the assertion type (using the setAssertionType method), initializes the assertion statement object, and sets relevant attributes (for example, setAuthenticationMethod for an authentication statement) for the corresponding assertion statement object. Then it uses the createAssertionStatement method to generate the SAML assertion statement in a document node object. It checks its validity upon completion of the SAML statement creation. It also retrieves the service configurations and protocol bindings (for example, SOAP over HTTP binding) before building SAML assertion statements.

Example 12–1 Sample Assertion Builder implementation

```
package com.csp.identity;

import java.util.ArrayList;
import java.util.Collection;

public class AssertionBuilder {

    // common variables and constants
    protected com.csp.identity.AssertionContextImpl
        assertionFactory;
    protected com.csp.identity.Subject subject;
    protected static final String authMethod =
        "urn:oasis:names:tc:SAML:1.0:am:password";
   protected static final String sourceSite = "www.coresecuritypattern.com";
    protected static final String destinationSite = "www.raylai.com";
```

```
protected static final String subjectDNS = "dns.coresecuritypattern.com";
protected static final String subjectIP = "168.192.10.1";
protected static final String subjectName = "Maryjo Parker";
protected static final String subjectQualifiedName = "cn=Maryjo,
     cn=Parker, ou=authors, o=coresecurity, o=com";

// authentication assertion specific
protected com.csp.identity.AuthenticationStatement
                              authenticationStatement;
protected org.w3c.dom.Document authAssertionDOM;

// authorization decision assertion specific
protected com.csp.identity.AuthorizationDecisionStatement
                                   authzDecisionStatement;
protected static final String decision = "someDecision";
protected static final String resource = "someResource";
protected java.util.Collection actions = new ArrayList();
protected java.util.Collection evidence = new ArrayList();
protected org.w3c.dom.Document authzDecisionAssertionDOM;

// attribute assertion specific
protected com.csp.identity.AttributeStatement
                                   attributeStatement;
protected com.csp.identity.Attribute attribute;
protected Collection attributeCollection = new ArrayList();;
protected org.w3c.dom.Document attributeStatementDOM;

/** Constructor - Creates a new instance of AssertionBuilder */
public AssertionBuilder() {

    // common
    assertionFactory =  new
       com.csp.identity.AssertionContextImpl();
    subject = new com.csp.identity.Subject();
    subject.setSubjectName(subjectName);
    subject.setSubjectNameQualifier(subjectQualifiedName);

    assertionFactory.setAssertionType
       (com.csp.identity.AuthenticationStatement
       .ASSERTION_TYPE);

    // ====create authentication statement=============
    // create authentication assertion object attribute
```

```
authenticationStatement = new
   com.csp.identity.AuthenticationStatement();
assertionFactory.setAuthenticationMethod(authMethod);
authenticationStatement.setSourceSite(sourceSite);
authenticationStatement
   .setDestinationSite(destinationSite);
authenticationStatement.setSubjectDNS(subjectDNS);
authenticationStatement.setSubjectIP(subjectIP);
authenticationStatement.setSubject(subject);

// create authentication statement
System.out.println("**Create authentication
                                        statement **");
authAssertionDOM =
   assertionFactory.createAssertionStatement
   ((com.csp.identity.AuthenticationStatement)
   authenticationStatement);

//===end of create authentication statement ========


//====create authorization decision statement=======
// create authorization decision assertion
// object attribute

authzDecisionStatement = new
   com.csp.identity.AuthorizationDecisionStatement();
authzDecisionStatement.setSourceSite(sourceSite);
authzDecisionStatement
   .setDestinationSite(destinationSite);
authzDecisionStatement.setSubjectDNS(subjectDNS);
authzDecisionStatement.setSubjectIP(subjectIP);
authzDecisionStatement.setResource(resource);
authzDecisionStatement.setDecision(decision);
authzDecisionStatement.setSubject(subject);
assertionFactory.setAssertionType
   (com.csp.identity.AuthorizationDecisionStatement
.ASSERTION_TYPE);

// Prepare evidence
this.evidence.add("Evidence1");
this.evidence.add("Evidence2");
this.evidence.add("Evidence3");
authzDecisionStatement.setEvidence(evidence);
```

```
    // Prepare action
    this.actions.add("Action1");
    this.actions.add("Action2");
    this.actions.add("Action3");
    authzDecisionStatement.setActions(actions);

    // create authorization decision statement
    System.out.println("**Create authorization
                                  decision statement **");
    authzDecisionAssertionDOM =
       assertionFactory.createAssertionStatement
       ((com.csp.identity.AuthorizationDecisionStatement)
       authzDecisionStatement);
    // ===end of create authorization statement ======

    // =====create attribute statement =============
    // create attribute  assertion object attribute
    attributeStatement = new
       com.csp.identity.AttributeStatement();
    attributeStatement.setSourceSite(sourceSite);
    attributeStatement.setDestinationSite(destinationSite);
    attributeStatement.setSubjectDNS(subjectDNS);
    attributeStatement.setSubjectIP(subjectIP);
    attributeStatement.setSubject(subject);
    assertionFactory.setAssertionType
       (com.csp.identity.AttributeStatement.ASSERTION_TYPE);

    // Prepare attribute
    attribute = new com.csp.identity.Attribute();
    this.attributeCollection.add("Attribute1");
    this.attributeCollection.add("Attribute2");
    this.attributeCollection.add("Attribute3");
    this.attribute.setAttribute(attributeCollection);
    attributeStatement.addAttribute(attribute);

    // create attribute statement
    System.out.println("**Create attribute statement **");
    attributeStatementDOM =
       assertionFactory.createAssertionStatement
       ((com.csp.identity.AttributeStatement)
                                attributeStatement);
    // ===end of create attribute statement ===
}
```

Securing the Identity

```
    public static void main(String[] args) {
        new AssertionBuilder();
    }
}
```


Example 12–2 shows how an authentication statement is implemented. An authentication statement extends the object Assertion, which is an abstraction of SAML assertion statements (including the SAML authentication statement, authorization decision statement, and attribute statement). This authentication statement is intended to implement how a SAML authentication assertion is created. The previous createAuthenticationStatement method in the last section will invoke the create method from the AuthenticationStatement class in order to create a SAML authentication statement. The create method can be implemented using custom SAML APIs, provided by a SAML implementation offered by open source or commercial vendor solution. In this example, the create method uses a constructor from the OpenSAML library to create a SAML authentication statement and checks for the validity of the SAML assertion statement.

Example 12–2 Sample AuthenticationStatement code

```
package com.csp.identity;

import java.util.Date;
import org.opensaml.*;

public class AuthenticationStatement extends com.csp.identity.Assertion {

    static final String ASSERTION_TYPE = "AUTHENTICATION";
    protected com.csp.identity.AuthenticationStatement
                                             authStateFactory;

    /** Constructor - Creates a new instance of AuthenticationStatement
     *
     */
    public AuthenticationStatement() {
    }

    /**
     *  Get instance of the existing authentication
     *  assertion statement
     *  If instance does not exist, create one
     *
     *  @return AuthenticationStatement instance of
```

```
 *  Authentication statement
 */
public com.csp.identity.AuthenticationStatement
   getInstance() {
    if (authStateFactory == null) {
        authStateFactory = new AuthenticationStatement();
        if (authStateFactory == null)
            System.out.println("WARNING -
                                authStat is null");
    }
    return this.authStateFactory;
}

/**
 * Create SAML authentication assertion statement
 *
 **/

public void create() {
    // This example uses OpenSAML 1.0
    // but you can use your custom SAML APIs or vendor APIs
    org.opensaml.SAMLSubject samlSubject;
    java.util.Date authInstant = new Date();
    String samlSubjectIP = this.getSubjectIP();
    String samlSubjectDNS = this.getSubjectDNS();
    org.opensaml.SAMLNameIdentifier samlNameIdentifier;

    try {
       // Create SAML Subject object using OpenSAML 1.0
       samlNameIdentifier =
            new org.opensaml.SAMLNameIdentifier
           (this.subject.getSubjectName(),
            this.subject.getSubjectNameQualifier(),"");
       samlSubject = new org.opensaml.SAMLSubject
          (samlNameIdentifier, null, null, null);

       // Create SAML authentication statement
       // using OpenSAML 1.0
       org.opensaml.SAMLAuthenticationStatement
         samlAuthStat =
            new org.opensaml.SAMLAuthenticationStatement
            (samlSubject, authInstant,
            samlSubjectIP, samlSubjectDNS, null);
```

```
            samlAuthStat.checkValidity();
      System.out.println("DEBUG
        - The current SAML authentication statement is valid!");
        }
        catch (org.opensaml.SAMLException se) {
            System.out.println("ERROR
              - Invalid SAML authentication assertion statement");
            se.printStackTrace();
        }
    }
}
```


Example 12–3 shows an example of creating a system context for the Assertion Builder pattern, which stores the service configuration and protocol binding information for creating and exchange SAML assertion statements. The AssertionContextImpl class is an implementation of the public interfaces defined in the AssertionContext class. This allows better flexibility in adding extensions or making program changes in the future.

Example 12–3 Sample AssertionContext implementation

```
package com.csp.identity;

public class AssertionContextImpl implements
                    com.csp.identity.AssertionContext {

    protected String authMethod;
    protected String assertionType;
    protected com.csp.identity.AuthenticationStatement
                                            authStatement;
    protected com.csp.identity.AuthorizationDecisionStatement
                                   authzDecisionStatement;
    protected com.csp.identity.AttributeStatement
                                        attributeStatement;
    protected org.w3c.dom.Document domTree;

    /** Constructor - Creates a new instance of
         AssertionContextImpl */

    public AssertionContextImpl() {
    }

    /** set assertion type
     *  @param String assertion type, for example authentication,
```

```
 * attribute
 **/
public void setAssertionType(String assertionType) {
    this.assertionType = assertionType;
}

/** create SSO token
 *
 *  @param Object security token
 **/
public void createSSOToken(Object securityToken) {
   ...
}

/** check for valid SAML statement
 *
 *  @return boolean true/false
 **/
public boolean isValidStatement() {
    // to be implemented
    return false;
}

/** set authentication method
 *
 *  @param String authentication method
 **/
public void setAuthenticationMethod(String authMethod) {
    this.authMethod = authMethod;
}

/** get authentication method
 *
 *  @return String authentication method
 **/
public String getAuthenticationMethod() {
    return this.authMethod;
}

/** create SAML assertion statement
 *
 *  Note - the @return has not been implemented.
 *
```

```
 *  @return org.w3c.dom.Document xml document
 **/
public org.w3c.dom.Document createAssertionStatement
    (Object assertObject) {

    System.out.println("DEBUG - Create SAML assertion
                                      in XML doc");
    if (this.assertionType.equals
       (com.csp.identity.AuthenticationStatement
        .ASSERTION_TYPE)) {

        // create SAML authentication statement
         //  using OpenSAML 1.0
         authStatement =
            (com.csp.identity.AuthenticationStatement)
             assertObject;

         authStatement.create();
    }
    else if (this.assertionType.equals
           (com.csp.identity.AuthorizationDecisionStatement
           .ASSERTION_TYPE)) {

        // create SAML authorization decision
         // statement using
        // OpenSAML 1.0

        authzDecisionStatement =
           (com.csp.identity.AuthorizationDecisionStatement)
            assertObject;

        authzDecisionStatement.create();
    }
    else if (this.assertionType.equals(
     com.csp.identity.AttributeStatement.ASSERTION_TYPE)) {

        // create SAML authorization decision statement
        // using
        // OpenSAML 1.0
        attributeStatement =
           (com.csp.identity.AttributeStatement)
           assertObject;
```

```
        attributeStatement.create();
    }
    return null;
}

/** get SAML assertion statement
 *
 *  @return org.w3c.dom.Document xml document
 **/
public org.w3c.dom.Document getAssertionStatement() {
    // to be implemented
    return null;
}

/** remove assertion statement
 *
 **/
public void removeAssertionStatement() {
    // to be implemented
}

/** create assertion reply
 *
 * @return org.w3c.dom.Document xml document
 **/
public org.w3c.dom.Document createAssertionReply(Object
      assertionRequest) {
    ...
    return null;
}

/** get assertion reply
 *
 * @return org.w3c.dom.Document xml document
 **/
public org.w3c.dom.Document getAssertionReply() {
    ...
    return null;
}

/** remove assertion reply
 *
 **/
```

```
    public void removeAssertionReply() {
        ...
    }

    /** set protocol binding
     *
     * @param String protocol binding
     **/
    public void setProtocolBinding (String protocolBinding){
       ...
    }

    /** get protocol binding
     *
     * @return String protocol binding
     **/
    public String getProtocolBinding() {
        ...
        return null;
    }
}
```


Security Factors and Risks

The Assertion Builder pattern is a reusable design that simplifies the creation of SAML assertion statements and can cater to either the synchronous or asynchronous mode of service invocation. The following discusses the security factors associated with the Assertion Builder pattern and the potential risk mitigation.

- **Configuration issues**. Assertion Builder relies on strong authentication by the identity provider. Improper configuration of authentication mechanisms and flawed credential management that compromises application authentication through password change will still lead to broken authentication.
- **Identity theft**. If a user identity is stolen by attackers who uses the user ID and password for proper authentication, Assertion Builder will not be able to address such a security risk. Use of XML Signature will help verifying the signer and also ensure the message is integral and tamper-proof during transit.
- **Confidentiality**. Using the HTTPS protocol to protect the client-to-server session is a stronger means of supporting confidentiality, because no unauthorized user can snoop the SAML assertion statements from the wire.

- **XML digital signature**. Using XML digital signature to the SAML assertion statements assures that no one can modify or tamper with the message content.
- **Reliability**. SAML assertion statements can be bound to a reliable data transport mechanism such as SOAP over JMS. This ensures that the recipient (either the source site or the destination site) can reliably get the SAML request or response.

Reality Check

Should we build assertion builder code from scratch? There are a few security vendor products that have out-of-the-box SAML assertion statement builder capability. In this case, architects and developers may either directly invoke the SAML assertion builder function or abstract them under the Assertion Builder pattern.

Capturing IP address. Although the SAML assertion statement allows capturing the source IP address, it is rather difficult to capture the real IP address in real life because real IP addresses can be translated into another virtual IP address or hidden from proxies. However, it is still a good practice to capture the IP address for verifying the origin host for authenticity, troubleshooting and other auditing purposes.

Dependency on authentication infrastructure. It is plausible to enable single sign-on security by using SAML assertions alone. However, SAML assertions depend on an existing authentication infrastructure.

Migration from SAML 1.1 to SAML 2.0. There are some deprecated items and changes in SAML 2.0. The SAML specifications do not provide guidance on how to migrate from SAML 1.1 to SAML 2.0, or how to make them compatible between trading partners running different SAML versions. Thus, it is important to cater to service versioning of SAML messages and to migrate the messaging infrastructure to SAML 2.0.

Related Patterns

Single Sign-on Delegator. Single Sign-on Delegator provides a delegate design approach to connect to remote security services and enables single sign-on within the same security domain or across multiple security domains. It is a good fit to use Assertion Builder in conjunction with Single Sign-on Delegator.

Single Sign-on (SSO) Delegator Pattern

Problem

You want to hide the complexity of interacting directly with heterogeneous service invocation methods or programming models of remote identity management or single sign-on service components.

In a heterogeneous security environment, you may need to use multiple vendor products to build their custom identity management functionality, such as account provisioning and authentication. Each vendor product may require different service invocation methods or programming models. If developers design the client to interact directly with remote identity management or single sign-on service interfaces, they probably need to add vendor-specific or fine-grained business logic in the client. This usually results in deploying a heavy client footprint or building rich clients that are loaded with complex security-specific business logic. Thus, such tight-coupling of the client directly with vendor-specific business logic creates many limitations for scalability in client-side performance, network connectivity, server-side caching, and support of a large number of simultaneous connections. In addition, you need to explicitly handle different types of network or system exceptions in the individual vendor-specific business logic while invoking the remote security services directly.

One related problem is software code maintenance and release control issues. If any identity management service interface changes, for example, due to a change in security standards or API specifications, developers have to maintain any corresponding client-side code changes. The client-side code also needs to be redeployed. This is quite a considerable software release control and maintenance issue because the tight-coupling architecture model is not flexible enough to accommodate software code changes.

Another problem is the lack of a flexible programming model for adding or managing new identity management functionalities if the existing vendor-specific APIs currently do not support them. For example, if the current security application architecture does not support global logout, it defeats the purpose of Single Sign-on in an integration environment, which may create authentication issues and session hijacking risks. At the worst, developers are required to rewrite the security application architecture every time they integrate a new application. Developers may also need to add newer functionalities in order to achieve Single Sign-on.

Forces

- You want to minimize the coupling between the clients and the remote identity management services for better scalability or for easier software maintenance.

- You want to streamline adding or removing identity management or single sign-on security service components (such as global logout), without reengineering the client or back-end application architecture.
- You want to hide the details of handling heterogeneous service invocation bindings (for example, EJB and asynchronous messaging) and service configuration of multiple security service components (for example, identity server and directory server) from the clients.
- You want to translate network exceptions caused by accessing different identity management service components into the application or user exceptions.

Solution

Use a Single Sign-on Delegator to encapsulate access to identity management and single sign-on functionalities, allowing independent evolution of loosely coupled identity management services while providing system availability.

A Single Sign-on Delegator resides in the middle tier between the clients and the identity management service components. It delegates the service request to the remote service components. It de-couples the physical security service interfaces and hides the details of service invocation, retrieval of security configuration, or credential token processing from the client. In other words, the client does not interact directly with the identity management service interfaces. The Single Sign-on Delegator in turn prepares for Single Sign-on, configures the security session, looks up the physical security service interfaces, invokes appropriate security service interfaces, and performs global logout at the end. Such loosely coupled application architecture minimizes the change impact to the client even though the remote security service interfaces require software upgrade or business logic changes.

A Business Delegate pattern would not be appropriate because it simply delegates the service request to the corresponding remote business components. It does not cater to configuring the security session or delegating to the remote security service components using the appropriate security protocols and bindings. Alternatively, developers can craft their own program construct to access remote service components. Using a design pattern approach to refactor similar security configuration (or preambles) for multiple remote security services into a single and reusable framework will enable higher reusability. The Single Sign-on Delegator pattern refactors similar security session processing logic and security configuration, and increases reusability.

To implement the Single Sign-on Delegator, you apply the delegator pattern that shields off the complexity of invoking service requests of building SAML assertions, processing credential tokens, performing global logout, initiating security service provisioning requests, and any custom identity management functions from heterogeneous vendor product APIs and programming models. They can create a unique service ID for each remote security service, create a service handler for each service interface, and then invoke the target security service. Under this delegator framework, it is easy to use the SAML protocol to perform single sign-on across remote security services. Similarly, it is also flexible enough to implement global logout by sending logout requests to each remote service because the delegator holds all unique service IDs and the relevant service handlers.

You can also use the Single Sign-on Delegator in conjunction with J2EE Connector Architecture. Single Sign-on Delegator can populate the security token or security context to legacy system environments, including ERP systems or EIS. If ERP systems have their own connectors or adapters, Single Sign-on Delegator can also exchange security tokens by encapsulating their connector APIs.

One major benefit of using the Single Sign-on Delegator is the convenience of encapsulating access to vendor-specific identity management APIs. Doing so shields the business components from changes in the underlying security vendor product implementation.

Structure

Figure 12–4 depicts a class diagram for the Single Sign-on Delegator. The client accesses the Single Sign-on Delegator component to invoke the remote security service components (SSOServiceProvider). The delegator (SSODelegator) retrieves security service configuration and service binding information from the system context (SSOContext) based on the client request. In other words, the client may be using a servlet, EJB, or Web services to access the identity management service. The delegator can also look up the service location via JNDI look-up or service registry look-up (if this is a Web service) according to the configuration details or service bindings. This can simplify the design construct for accommodating multiple security protocol bindings.

There are three important classes in Figure 12–4: SSOContext, SSODelegatorFactory and SSOServiceProvider. The SSOContext is a system context that encapsulates the service configuration and protocol binding for the remote service providers. It also stores the service status and the component reference (aka handler ID) for the remote service provider. The SSOContextImpl class is the implementation for the SSOContext class.

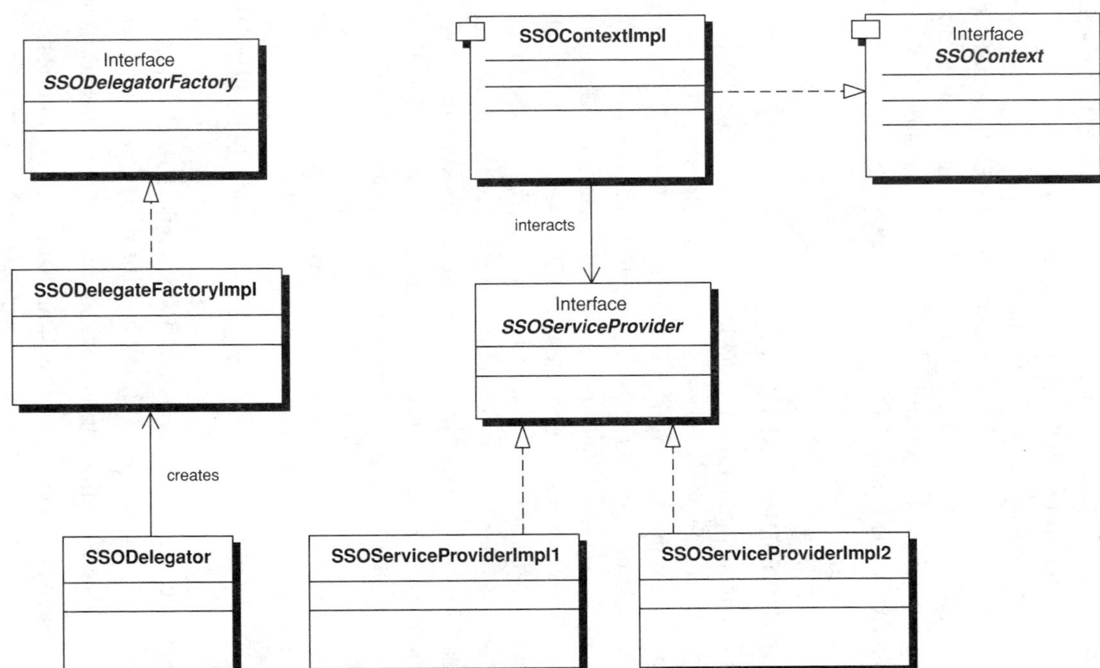

Figure 12–4 Single Sign-on Delegator class diagram

The SSODelegatorFactory defines the public interfaces to creating and closing a secure connection to the remote service provider. It takes a security token from the service requester so that it can validate the connection service request under a single sign-on environment. When a secure connection is established, the SSODelegatorFactory will also create a SSOToken used internally to reference it with the remote service provider. The SSODelegatorFactoryImpl class is the implementation for SSODelegatorFactory.

The SSOServiceProvider class defines the public interfaces for creating, closing, or reconnecting to a remote service. Figure 12–4 shows two examples of service providers (SSOServiceProviderImpl1 and SSOServiceProviderImpl2) that implement the public interfaces.

Participants and Responsibilities

Figure 12–5 shows a sequence diagram that depicts how to apply a delegator pattern to different identity management services via the Single Sign-on Delegator. In this scenario, the client wants to perform a single sign-on across different business services within the same domain (i.e., the same customer environment). The client (Client) refers to the service requester that initiates the service requests to multiple applications. The Single Sign-on Delegator (SSODelegator) connects to the remote business services. It retrieves the security service configuration information from the SSOContext service and looks up the service location via the naming service ServiceLocator. Finally, it keeps track of all connections using the service handlers and/or unique service IDs to perform single sign-on or global logout. The following shows the interaction between Client and SSODelegator:

1. Client wants to invoke remote services via SSODelegator. SSODelegator verifies if Client is authorized to invoke remote security services.
2. Upon successful verification, Client creates a delegator instance of SSODelegator.
3. SSODelegator retrieves service configuration (for example, EJB class name) and protocol bindings (for example, RMI method for EJB) from SSOContext.
4. SSOContext sends service configurations and protocol bindings to SSODelegator.
5. SSODelegator creates a single sign-on session using the method createSSODConnection and records the user ID and timestamp in the session information using the method setSessionInfo.
6. Client initiates a request to invoke a remote service.
7. SSODelegator creates a service connection to invoke the remote service provider using the method createService.

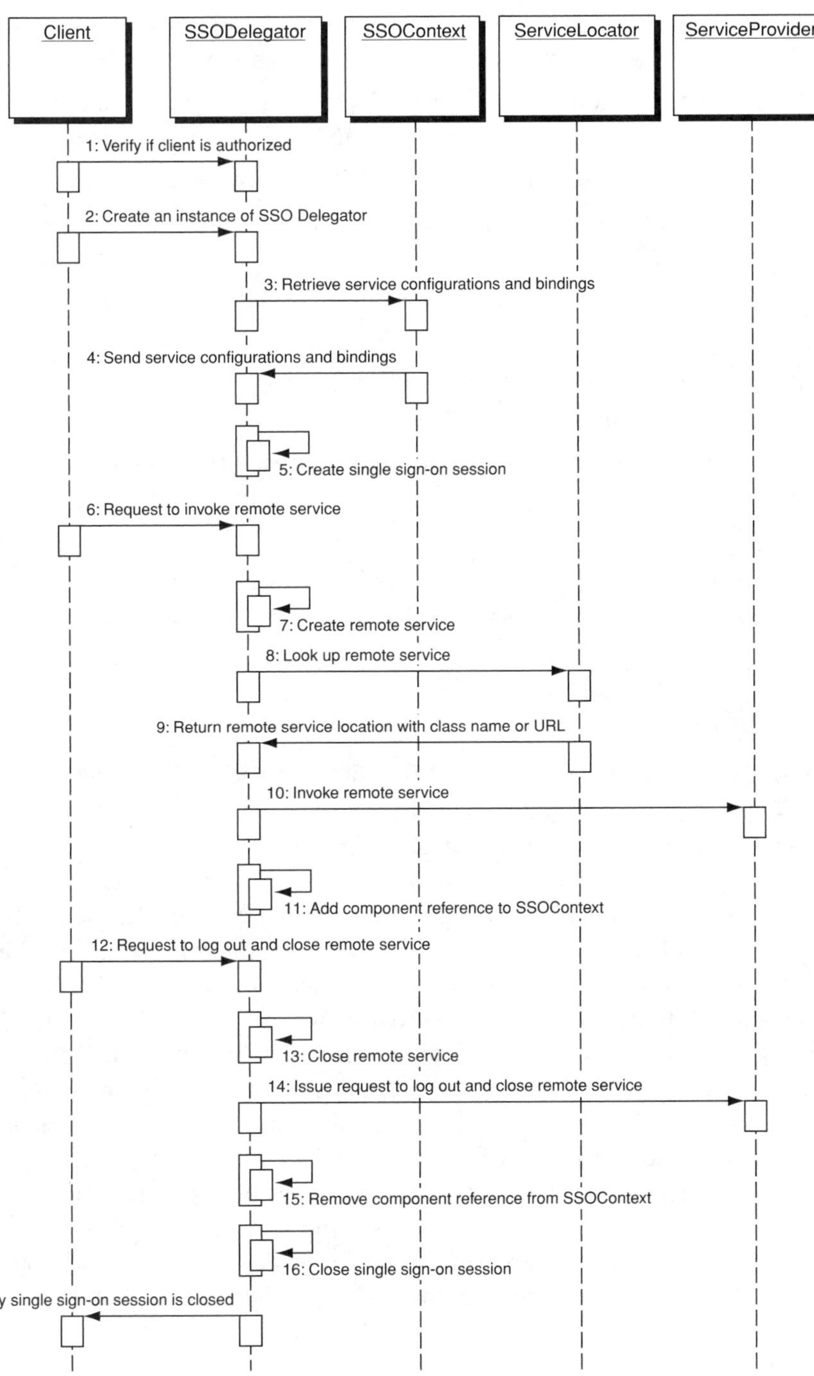

Figure 12–5 Single Sign-on Delegator sequence diagram

8. SSODelegator retrieves the service configuration details (for example, EJB class) and protocol bindings for the remote service.
9. SSODelegator looks up the service location of the remote security service using ServiceLocator (for example, via JNDI look-up for the remote EJB).
10. SSODelegator invokes the remote security service by class name or URI.
11. SSODelegator adds the component reference (also referred to as handler ID) to the SSOContext.
12. Client requests to log out and close the connection of existing remote security services.
13. SSODelegator begins to close the security service.
14. SSODelegator initiates a closeSSOConnection to close the remote service.
15. SSODelegator removes the component reference from SSOContext. It may also remove any existing session information by invoking the method removeSessionInfo.
16. SSODelegator now completes closing the single sign-on session.
17. SSODelegator notifies Client for successful global logout and closing security services.

Strategies

Using Single Sign-on Delegator and Assertion Builder Together

The Single Sign-on Delegator pattern provides a design framework for implementing single domain or cross-domain single sign-on using Liberty and SAML It also makes use of the Assertion Builder pattern to create SAML assertion statements for authentication, authorization, or attributes. Figure 12–6 depicts a use case scenario where a client (Client) needs to access multiple resources within the internal security domain. In order to access any resource, the client needs to authenticate with an identity service provider to establish the identity first. Once successful authentication is complete, it can initiate an authentication assertion request to access multiple resources within the single sign-on environment. The service provider (ServiceProvider) uses an identity server product to act as an identity service provider (IdentityProvider), which handles authentication for single sign-on purposes. The agent (WebAgent) is a Web server or application server plug-in that intercepts the authentication requests using the Liberty protocol to provide single sign-on. In this scenario, the service provider runs an application server with a Liberty-compliant agent. Both SSODelegator and AssertionBuilder refer to the

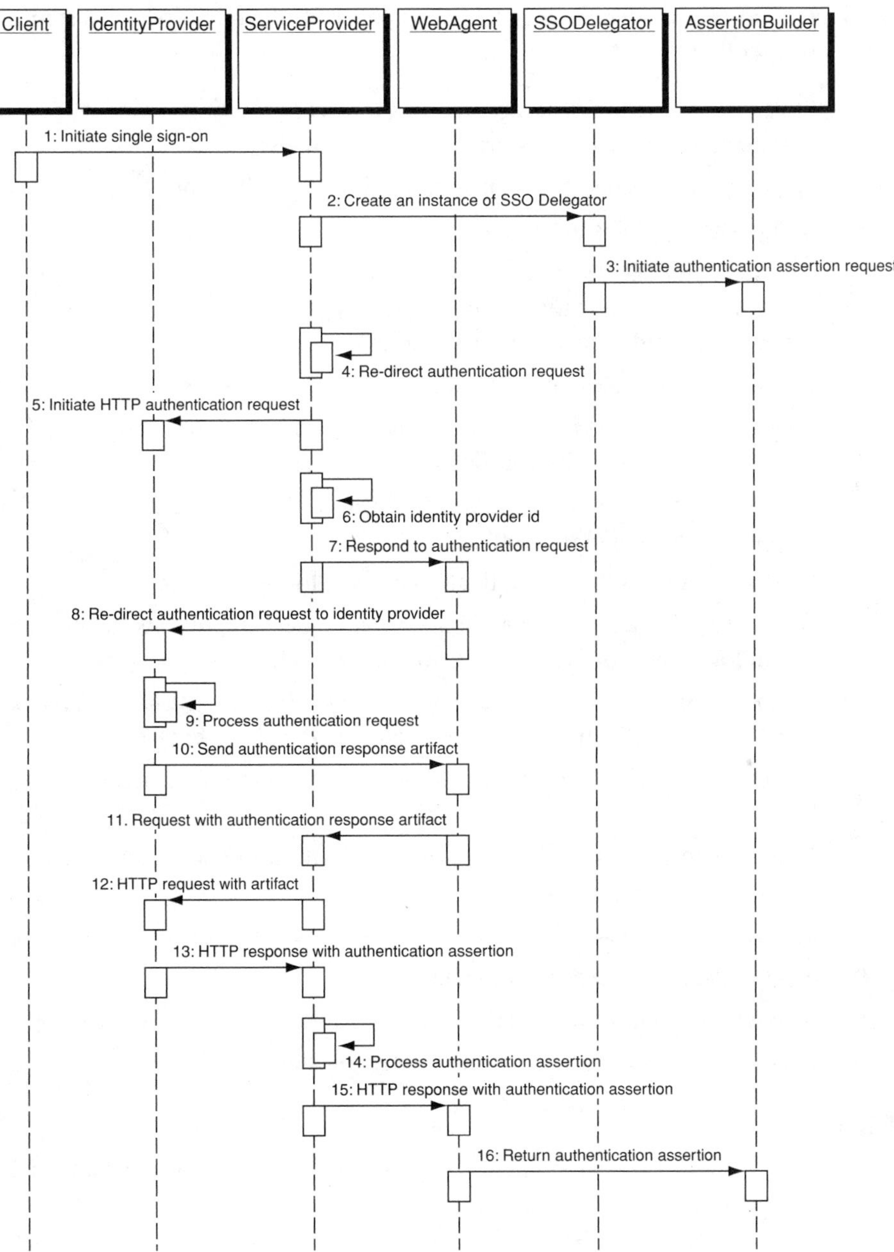

Figure 12–6 Single sign-on using Single Sign-on Delegator and Assertion Builder sequence diagram

design patterns discussed earlier in this chapter. The following provides a step-by-step description of the interaction:

1. Client initiates a single sign-on request to access resources under the internal identity provider (or external identity provider).
2. ServiceProvider creates an instance of single sign-on delegator.
3. SSODelegator initiates an authentication assertion request with AssertionBuilder.
4. Before AssertionBuilder creates an authentication assertion, Client needs to perform an authentication with the identity service provider first. Thus, ServiceProvider redirects the authentication request from Client.
5. ServiceProvider initiates an HTTP authentication request with IdentityProvider.
6. ServiceProvider obtains the relevant identity service provider identifier (there may be multiple identity service providers).
7. ServiceProvider uses WebAgent (running on top of the application server) to respond to the authentication request.
8. WebAgent redirects the authentication request to IdentityProvider.
9. IdentityProvider processes the authentication request. It presents the authentication login form or HTML page to Client.
10. Upon submission of the authentication login form by Client, IdentityProvider sends the authentication request response artifact to WebAgent.
11. WebAgent sends the request with authentication response artifact to ServiceProvider.
12. ServiceProvider processes the HTTP request with the authentication response artifact with IdentityProvider.
13. IdentityProvider sends the HTTP response with the authentication assertion.
14. ServiceProvider processes the authentication assertion.
15. ServiceProvider sends the HTTP response with the authentication assertion.
16. WebAgent returns the authentication assertion statement.

Global Logout Strategy

The Single Sign-on Delegator pattern can also act as a control mechanism for implementation of global logout, because it creates a connection to remote services and keeps track of each unique component reference to remote services (handle ID). If a client is invalidated in the presentation tier, the Single Sign-on Delegator can issue a timely global logout to ensure session integrity. Once a client decides to sign out from all remote security services, the Single Sign-on Delegator can simply retrieve the service configuration (from SSOContext) or service location information (from ServiceLocator). Then they relay the logout request to each security service. Figure 12–7 depicts a use case scenario for global logout:

1. Client initiates a request for global logout from all remote security services.
2. SSODelegator verifies if Client is authorized to log out from all remote services.
3. Upon successful verification, Client creates an instance of SSODelegator.
4. SSODelegator retrieves the service configurations and protocol bindings from SSOContext.
5. SSOContext sends the details of service configurations and protocol bindings to SSODelegator.
6. SSODelegator fetches all service identifiers from all existing security service connections.
7. SSODelegator looks up security service location from ServiceLocator.

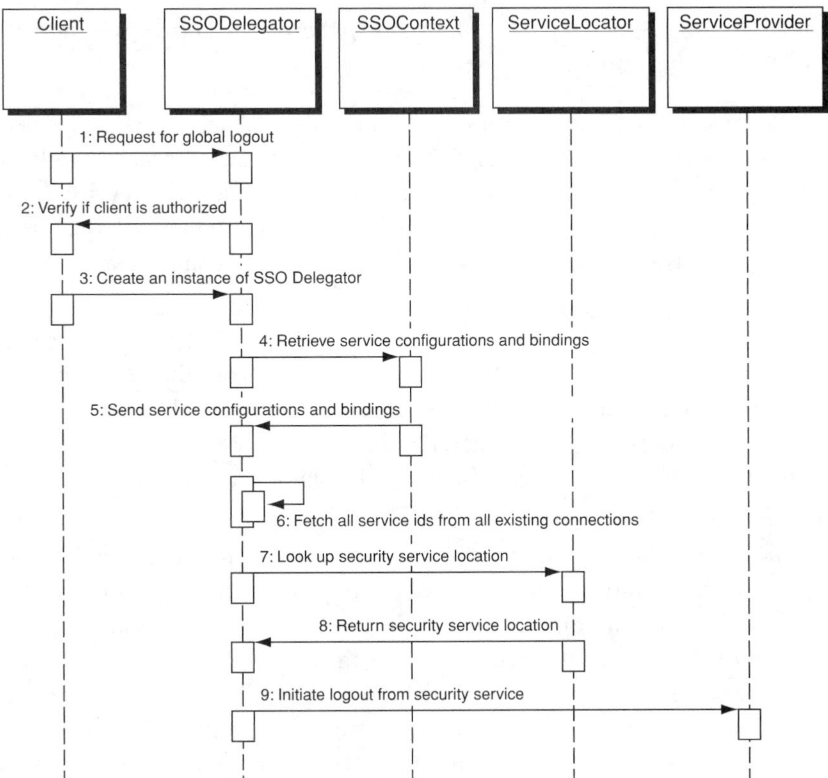

Figure 12–7 Global logout using Single Sign-on Delegator sequence diagram

8. ServiceLocator returns the service location of remote services.
9. SSODelegator initiates a global logout request to each remote service.

Identity Termination / Revocation Strategy

If the user identity is terminated or revoked by the identity provider or the service provider, the identity management system should not allow the user to continue to create a single sign-on session. Liberty Phase 2 defines a federation termination notification protocol for handling identity termination or revocation (refer to Chapter 7). The Single Sign-on Delegator should be able to subscribe to the federation termination notification protocol.

If a user identity is terminated by the identity provider or service provider in the midst of a single sign-on session, the Single Sign-on Delegator should be able to terminate the single sign-on session using the global logout strategy.

Consequences

By employing the Single Sign-on Delegator pattern, developers will be able to reap the following benefits:

- *Thwarting session theft.* Session theft is a critical security flaw to identity management. The Single Sign-on Delegator creates a secure single sign-on session and delegates the service requests to relevant security services. Client requests must be authenticated with an identity provider before they can establish a secure single sign-on session. This can mitigate the risk of session theft.
- *Addressing multiple sign-on issues.* The Single Sign-on Delegator pattern supports a standards-based single sign-on framework that does not require users to sign on multiple times. There are security attacks that target application systems that are vulnerable due to multiple sign-on actions being required. Thus, the Single Sign-on Delegator can mitigate the multiple sign-on issues.
- *More flexibility with a loosely coupled architecture.* The Single Sign-on Delegator pattern provides a loosely coupled connection to remote security services. It minimizes the coupling between the clients and the remote identity management services. It hides the details of the handling of heterogeneous service invocation bindings and the service configuration of multiple security service components from the clients. It also avoids specific-vendor product lock-in by disallowing clients to invoke the remote security services directly.

- *Better availability of the remote security services.* Architects and developers can implement or customize automatic recovery of the remote security services. They can also provide an alternate security services connection if the primary remote security service is not available.
- *Improves scalability.* Architects and developers can have multiple connections to the remote security services. Multiple instances of the remote security services will help improve scalability. In addition, architects and developers can cache some of the session variables or user identity information on behalf of the presentation tier components, which may help boost performance if there are a large number of simultaneous user connections.

Sample Code

Example 12–4 and Example 12–5 show a scenario where a service requester (for example, telecommunications subscriber) intends to access a variety of remote services via a primary service provider (for example, a telecommunication online portal). These sample code excerpts illustrate how to create a Single Sign-on Delegator pattern (using SSODelegatorFactoryImpl) to manage invoking remote security services using EJB. The Client creates an instance of the SSODelegatorFactoryImpl using the method getSSODelegator, and then invokes the method createSSOConnection to start a remote service. Upon completion, the Client invokes the method closeSSOConnection to close the remote service. The SSODelegatorFactoryImpl creates a single sign-on connection, invokes individual security service, and maintains session information. The code comment adds some annotation about how to add your own code to meet your local requirements or to extend the functionality.

In Example 12–4, the SSODelegatorFactoryImpl class initializes itself in the constructor by loading the list of "authorized" service providers (using the method initConfig). Then it creates a SSO token using the method createSSOToken to reference to all remote service connections. When the Client requests creating a single sign-on connection to a remote service, SSODelegatorFactoryImpl requires the Client to pass a security token for validation

Upon successful validation of the security token, the SSODelegatorFactoryImpl will look up the Java object class or URI of the remote service via the servicelocator method from the SSOContext. The SSOContext stores the service status and service configuration of the remote service. The service locator method is a service locator pattern that provides a few methods to look up the service location via EJB or Web services. The sample methods used in this code excerpt are examples only. The details can be found at [CJP2], pp. 315-340, or http://java.sun.com/blueprints/patterns/ServiceLocator.html.

The SSODelegatorFactoryImpl will then invoke the createService method of the remote service. It will update the service status "CREATED"). The component reference to the remote service will be added to SSOContext.

When the Client requests to close the remote service, the SSODelegatorFactoryImpl will invoke the closeService method of the remote service. It will update the service status to "CLOSED" and remove the component reference in the SSOContext.

Example 12–4 Sample SSODelegatorFactory implementation


```
package com.csp.identity;

import java.util.HashMap;
import com.csp.identity.*;

public class SSODelegatorFactoryImpl implements
com.csp.identity.SSODelegatorFactory {

    protected HashMap<String, com.csp.identity.SSOContextImpl>
       servicesMap = new HashMap(); // store serviceName, context
    protected HashMap<String, Object> SSOTokenMap = new HashMap();
       // store serviceName, SSOToken
    protected static com.csp.identity.SSODelegatorFactoryImpl
singletonInstance = null;
    protected String ssoToken;

    /** Constructor - Creates a new instance of
        SSODelegatorFactoryImpl */
    private SSODelegatorFactoryImpl() {
        // load config file for all security authorized service
        //  providers in Context
        initConfig();
        createSSOToken();
    }

    /**
     * Validate security token before creating, closing or
     * reconnecting to remote
     * service provider.
     * You can implement your security token validation process as
     * per local requirements.
     * You may want to reuse Credential Tokenizer to encapsulate
     * the security token.
     *
```

```
     * In this example, we'll always return true for demo purpose.
     */
    private boolean validateSecurityToken(Object securityToken) {
        ...
        return true;
    }

   /**
     * Create a SSO connection with the remote service provider
     * Need to pass a security token and the target service name.
     * The service locator will look up where the service name is.
     * And then invoke the remote object class/URI based on the
     * protocol binding.
     *
     * @param Object security token (for example, you can reuse
     * Credential Tokenizer)
     * @param String service name for the remote service provider
     */
    public void createSSOConnection(Object securityToken,
            String serviceName) throws
            com.csp.identity.SSODelegatorException {

        if (validateSecurityToken(securityToken) == true) {
            System.out.println("Security token is valid");
            try {
                // load Java object class (or URI) via
                // serviceLocator
               com.csp.identity.SSOContextImpl context =
                  servicesMap.get(serviceName);
               String className =
                  context.serviceLocator(serviceName);
               Class clazz = Class.forName(className);
               com.csp.identity.SSOServiceProvider serviceProvider
                 = (com.csp.identity.SSOServiceProvider)clazz.newInstance();
               // invoke remote security service provider
               serviceProvider.createService(context);

               // update status=CREATE
               context.setStatus(context.REMOTE_SERVICE_CREATED);
               // update servicesMap and context
               context.setCompRef(serviceProvider);
               servicesMap.remove(serviceName);
               servicesMap.put(serviceName, context);
```

```
            this.setSSOTokenMap(serviceName);

          }
          catch (ClassNotFoundException cnfe) {
              cnfe.printStackTrace();
             throw new com.csp.identity.SSODelegatorException("Class not
                                         found");
          }
          catch (InstantiationException ie) {
              ie.printStackTrace();
              throw new
                    com.csp.identity.SSODelegatorException("Instantiation
                                               exception");
          }
          catch (IllegalAccessException iae) {
              iae.printStackTrace();
              throw new com.csp.identity.SSODelegatorException("Illegal
                                        access exception");
          }
      }
      else {
          // update status=error
          System.out.println("Invalid security
                                       token presented!");
          throw new com.csp.identity.SSODelegatorException("Invalid
                                       securitiy token");
      }

  }

  /**
   * Close a SSO connection with the remote service provider
   * Need to pass a security token and the target
   * service name.
   * The service locator will look up where the
   * service name is.
   * And then invoke the remote object class/URI based on the
   * protocol binding.
   *
   * @param Object security token (for example, you can reuse
   * Credential Tokenizer)
   * @param String service name for the remote service provider
   */
```

```
public void closeSSOConnection(Object securityToken,
     String serviceName) throws
     com.csp.identity.SSODelegatorException {

    if (validateSecurityToken(securityToken) == true) {
        System.out.println("Security token is valid");

        // load Java object class (or URI)
        // via serviceLocator
        com.csp.identity.SSOContextImpl context =
            servicesMap.get(serviceName);
        com.csp.identity.SSOServiceProvider
            serviceProvider = context.getCompRef();

        if (serviceProvider == null) {
            throw new
          com.csp.identity.SSODelegatorException
                       ("SSO connection not made.");
        }
        // invoke remote security service provider
        serviceProvider.closeService();

        // update status=CLOSED
        context.setStatus(context.REMOTE_SERVICE_CLOSED);
        // update servicesMap and context
        context.removeCompRef();
        servicesMap.remove(serviceName);
        servicesMap.put(serviceName, context);
        this.removeSSOTokenMap(serviceName);

    }
    else {
        // update status=error
        System.out.println("Invalid security
                              token presented!");
        throw new
     com.csp.identity.SSODelegatorException("Invalid
                                   securitiy token");
    }
}

/**
 * Load the configuration into the SSODelegatorFactory
```

```
 * implementation so that
 * it will know which are the remote service providers
 * (including the
 * logical service name and the object class/URI for service
 * invocation.
 *
 * For demo purpose, we hard-coded a few examples here.
 * We can
 * also use
 * Apache Commons Configuration
 * to load a config.xml property
 * file.
 */
private void initConfig() {
    // load a list of "authorized" security
    // service providers
    // from the config file
    //    and load into an array of SSOContext
    try {
        // create sample data
       com.csp.identity.SSOContextImpl context1 = new
            com.csp.identity.SSOContextImpl();
       com.csp.identity.SSOContextImpl context2 = new
            com.csp.identity.SSOContextImpl();
       context1.setServiceName("service1");
       context1.setProtocolBinding("SOAP");

       context2.setServiceName("service2");
       context2.setProtocolBinding("RMI");

       this.servicesMap.put("service1", context1);
       this.servicesMap.put("service2", context2);
     }
     catch (com.csp.identity.SSODelegatorException se) {
         se.printStackTrace();
     }
}

 /**
  *
  * You need to pass a security token before you can get the
  * SSODelegator instance.
  * Rationale:
```

```
 * 1. This ensures that only authenticated/authorized
 *     subjects
 * can invoke the SSO Delegator.
 * (authentication and authorization requirements).
 * 2. No one can invoke the constructor directly (visibility
 * and segregation requirements).
 * 3. In addition, there is only a singleton copy (singleton
 * requirement).
 *
 * @param Object security token
 */
public static com.csp.identity.SSODelegatorFactoryImpl
    getSSODelegator(Object securityToken) {
    synchronized (com.csp.identity.SSODelegatorFactoryImpl.class) {
    if (singletonInstance==null) {
        singletonInstance = new
             com.csp.identity.SSODelegatorFactoryImpl();
    }
    return singletonInstance;
    }
}

/**
 * This private method creates a SSO token to resemble a SSO
 * session has been
 * created to connect to remote security service providers.
 * In practice, this security token should be implemented in
 * any object type
 * based on local requirements. You can also reuse the
 * SecurityToken object
 * type from the Credential Tokenizer.
 *
 * For demo purpose, we'll use a string.
 * You can also use the
 * String format
 * to represent a base64 encoded format of a SSO token.
 */
private void createSSOToken() {
    // to be implemented
    this.ssoToken = "myPrivateSSOToken";
}
```

```
/**
 * Register a SSOToken in the HashMap that a remote
 * service provider
 * connection has been made.
 *
 * @param String serviceName
 */
private void setSSOTokenMap(String serviceName) {
    this.SSOTokenMap.put(serviceName, this.ssoToken);
}

/**
 * Get a SSOToken in the HashMap that a remote service
 * provider
 * connection has been made.
 *
 * @param String serviceName
 * @return Object SSOToken (in this demo, we'll use a
 * String object)
 */
private Object getSSOTokenMap(String serviceName) {
    return (String)this.SSOTokenMap.get(serviceName);
}

/**
 * Remove a SSOToken from the HashMap that a remote
 * service provider
 * connection has been made.
 *
 * @param String serviceName
 */
private void removeSSOTokenMap(String serviceName) {
    this.SSOTokenMap.remove(serviceName);
}

/**
 * Get status from the remote service provider.
 * Need to pass a security token and the target service name.
 * The service locator will look up where
 * the service name is.
 * And then invoke the remote object class/URI based on the
 * protocol binding.
 *
```

```
     * @param Object security token
     * (for example, you can reuse Credential Tokenizer)
     * @param String service name for
     * the remote service provider
     */
    public String getServiceStatus(Object securityToken,
        String serviceName) throws
        com.csp.identity.SSODelegatorException {

        if (validateSecurityToken(securityToken) == true) {
            System.out.println("Security token is valid");

            // load Java object class (or URI)
            // via serviceLocator

            com.csp.identity.SSOContextImpl context =
                servicesMap.get(serviceName);
            return context.getStatus();
        }
        else {
            // update status=error
            System.out.println("Invalid security
                                token presented!");
            throw new
          com.csp.identity.SSODelegatorException("Invalid
                                     securitiy token");
        }
    }

}
```


Example 12–5 shows sample code for implementing the SSOContext. The SSOContextImpl class provides methods to add or get the service configuration and protocol binding for the remote service. When a new remote service is connected, the SSOContextImpl will add the component reference (aka handler ID) to the remote service using the method setCompRef and will update the status using the method setStatus.

Example 12–5 Sample SSOContext implementation

```
package com.csp.identity;

import java.rmi.RemoteException;
```

```
import java.util.HashMap;
import java.util.Properties;
import com.csp.identity.*;

public class SSOContextImpl
             implements com.csp.identity.SSOContext {

    protected String serviceName;
    protected Properties configProps;
    protected String protocolBinding;
    protected HashMap sessionInfo = new HashMap();
    protected com.csp.identity.SSOServiceProvider compRef;
    protected String status;
    protected final String REMOTE_SERVICE_CREATED = "CREATED";
    protected final String REMOTE_SERVICE_CLOSED = "CLOSED";
    protected final String REMOTE_SERVICE_ERROR = "ERROR";
    protected enum ServiceStatus { CREATED, CLOSED, ERROR };

    // Constructor - Creates a new instance
    // of SSOContextImpl

    public SSOContextImpl() throws
                com.csp.identity.SSODelegatorException {
    }

    /**
     * Set session information in a HashMap.
     * This stores specific
     * session variables
     * that are relevant to a particular remote secure service
     * provider
     *
     * @param String session variable name
     * @param String session variable value
     */
    public synchronized void setSessionInfo(String
        sessionVariable, String sessionValue) {
        this.sessionInfo.put(sessionVariable, sessionValue);
    }

    /**
     * Get session information from a HashMap. This stores
     * specific session variables
```

```
     * that are relevant to a particular remote secure service
     * provider
     * Need to cast the object type upon return
     *
     * @return Object  return in an Object (for example String).
     */
    public synchronized Object getSessionInfo(String
        sessionVariable) {
        return this.sessionInfo.get(sessionVariable);
    }

    /**
     * Remove session information from a HashMap. The HashMap
     * stores specific session variables
     * that are relevant to a particular remote secure service
     * provider
     *
     * @param String session variable name
     */
    public synchronized void removeSessionInfo(String
        sessionVariable) {
        this.sessionInfo.remove(sessionVariable);
    }

    /**
     * Get private configuration properties specific to a
     * particular
     * remote secure service provider. This object needs to be
     * loaded during
     * initConfig(), by the constructor or manually
     *
     * @return Properties  a Properties object
     */
    public java.util.Properties getConfigProperties() {
        return configProps;
    }

/**
     * Set private configuration properties specific to a
     * particular
     * remote secure service provider. This object needs to be
     * loaded during
     * initConfig(), by the constructor or manually
     *
```

```
 * @param Properties  a Properties object
 */
public void setConfigProperties(java.util.Properties
    configProps) {
    this.configProps = configProps;
}

/**
 * Get protocol binding for the remote security service
 * provider
 *
 * @return String protocol binding, for example SOAP, RMI
 * (arbitrary name)
 */
public String getProtocolBinding() {
    return this.protocolBinding;
}

 /**
 * Set protocol binding for the remote security service
 * provider
 *
 * @param String protocol binding, for example SOAP, RMI (arbitrary
 * name)
 */
public void setProtocolBinding(String protocolBinding) {
    this.protocolBinding = protocolBinding;
}

/**
 * Get service name of the remote security service provider.
 * This name needs to match the field 'serviceName' in the
 * SSOServiceProvider implementation classes
 *
 * @return String service name, for example service1
 */
public String getServiceName() {
    return this.serviceName;
}

/**
 * set service name
 *
```

```
 * @param String logical remote service name, for example service1
 *
 **/
public void setServiceName(String serviceName) {
    this.serviceName = serviceName;
}

/**
 * Get component reference
 *
 * @return SSOServiceProvider component
 *  reference to be stored
 * in the HashMap
 *   once a connection is created
 **/
public com.csp.identity.SSOServiceProvider getCompRef() {
    return this.compRef;
}

/**
 * Set component reference
 *
 * @param SSOServiceProvider component
 *  reference to be stored
 * in the HashMap
 *  once a connection is created
 **/
public void
   setCompRef(com.csp.identity.SSOServiceProvider compRef) {
    this.compRef = compRef;
}

/**
 * Remove component reference
 *
 **/
public void removeCompRef(){
    this.compRef = null;
}


/**
 * Look up the class name or URI by the service name
 *
```

```
     * This example hardcodes one class name for demo.
     * You may want to replace it by a Service Locator pattern
     *
     * @param String service name to look up
     * @return String class name (or URI) corresponding service
     **/
    public String serviceLocator(String serviceName) {

        // This example shows 2 remote
        // security service providers
        // hard-coded for demo purpose. Refer to the book's
        // website for sample code download.
        // You may want to use a Service Locator pattern here
        if (serviceName.equals("service1")) {
           return "com.csp.identity.SSOServiceProviderImpl1";
        } if (serviceName.equals("service2"))   {
             return "com.csp.identity.SSOServiceProviderImpl2";
        }
        return "com.csp.identity.SSOServiceProviderImpl2";
    }

    /**
     * set status of the remote service
     *
     * @param String status
     */
    public void setStatus(String status) {
        this.status = status;
    }

    /**
     * get status of the remote service
     *
     * @return String status
     */
    public String getStatus() {
        return this.status;
    }
}
```

Security Factors and Risks

- **Caching user identity information**. Caching user identity information in shared memory (for example, implemented in a hash table) is a mechanism used by the Single Sign-on Delegator to improve performance. However, there is also a security risk if any other application client can access the shared memory. Thus, architects and developers need to ensure that cached information is protected and is accessible to the Single Sign-on Delegator only.

- **Logging and audit risks**. Security compliance and local regulations often require all user login and security activities to be logged and audited throughout the user sign-on session. The logging and audit requirements can help to track down any unusual password changes or suspicious transaction changes under the single sign-on session. The security risk is extremely high if the single sign-on session control does not log all user authentication and access control changes throughout the session for audit control.

Reality Check

Too many abstraction layers. Single Sign-on Delegator brings the benefit of loosely coupled architecture by creating an abstraction layer for remote security services. However, if the remote security services have more than one abstraction layer, multiple abstraction layers of remote service invocations will create substantial performance overhead. From experience, one to two abstraction layers would be reasonable.

Supporting multiple circles of trust. Currently, Liberty specification 2.0 does not support integrating multiple circles of trust or interoperating with multiple identity service providers simultaneously (for example, when a client wants to perform single sign-on in two different circles of trust or in two different types of single sign-on environments). Single Sign-on Delegator is not designed to support multiple circles of trust, because it is a delegate design approach that simplifies the connection of remote security services. The support of interoperating with multiple identity service providers is dependent on the Liberty implementation or the remote security services.

Related Patterns

Assertion Builder. A Single Sign-on Delegator can delegate the creation of SAML assertion statements via the Assertion Builder to a remote security service provider that assembles and generates a SAML authentication or authorization decision statement. This does not require adding the business logic of managing SAML assertions in the Single Sign-on Delegator.

Credential Tokenizer. A Single Sign-on Delegator can delegate the encapsulation of user credentials to the Credential Tokenizer. This does not require building additional business logic to handle user credentials in the Single Sign-on Delegator. Architects and developers can also reuse the credential tokenizer functions for other applications (for example, EDI messaging applications) without using Single Sign-on Delegator.

Service Locator. The Single Sign-on Delegator pattern uses a Service Locator pattern to look up the service location of the remote security services. In other words, it delegates the service look-up function to a Service Locator, which can be implemented as a JNDI look-up or a UDDI service discovery. Refer to http://java.sun.com/blueprints/patterns/ServiceLocator.html and [CJP2] for details.

Credential Tokenizer Pattern

Problem

You need a flexible mechanism to encapsulate a security token that can be used by different security infrastructure providers.

There are different forms of user credentials (also referred to as security tokens), such as username/passwords, binary security tokens (for example, X.509v3 certificates), Kerberos tickets, SAML tokens, smart card tokens and biometric samples. Most security tokens are domain-specific. To encapsulate these user credentials for use with different security product architectures, developers have to modify the security token processing routine to accommodate individual security product architectures, which depends on the specific security specification the security product uses. A user credential based on a digital certificate will be processed differently than that of a Kerberos ticket. There is no consistent and flexible mechanism for using a common user credential tokenizer that supports different types of security product architectures supporting different security specifications.

Forces

- You need a reusable component that helps to extract processing logic to handle creation and management of security tokens instead of embedding them in the business logic or the authentication process.
- You want to shield off the design and implementation complexity using a common mechanism that can accommodate a security credential and interface with a supporting security provider that makes use of them.

Solution

Use a Credential Tokenizer to encapsulate different types of user credentials as a security token that can be reusable across different security providers.

A Credential Tokenizer is a security API abstraction that creates and retrieves the user identity information (for example, public key/X.509v3 certificate) from a given user credential (for example, a digital certificate issued by a Certificate Authority). Each security specification has slightly different semantics or mechanisms to handle user identity and credential information. These include the following characteristics:

- Java applications that need to access user credentials or security tokens from different application security infrastructures.
- Web Services security applications that need to encapsulate a security token, such as username token or binary token, in the SOAP message.
- Java applications that support SAML or Liberty that need to include an authentication credential in the SAML assertion request or response.
- Java applications that need to retrieve user credentials for performing SSO with legacy applications.

To build a Credential Tokenizer, developers need to identify the service, authentication scheme, application provider, and underlying protocol bindings. For example, in a SOAP communication model, the service requestor is required to use a digital certificate as a binary security token for accessing a service endpoint. In this case, the service configuration specifies the X.509v3 digital certificate as the security token and SOAP messages and SOAP over HTTPS as the protocol binding. Similarly, in a J2EE application, the client is required to use a Client-certificate for enabling mutual authentication. In this case, the authentication requirements specify an X.509v3 digital certificate as the security token and SOAP over HTTPS as the protocol binding, but the request is represented as HTML generated by a J2EE application using a JSP or a servlet.

Credential Tokenizer provides an API abstraction mechanism for constructing security tokens based on a defined authentication requirement, protocol binding, and application provider. It also provides API mechanisms for retrieving security tokens issued by a security infrastructure provider.

Structure

Figure 12–8 depicts a class diagram of the Credential Tokenizer. The Credential Tokenizer can be used to create different security tokens (SecurityToken), including username token and binary tokens (X.509v3 certificate. When creating a security token, the Credential Tokenizer creates a system context (TokenContext) that encapsulates the token type, the name of the principal, the service configuration, and the protocol binding that the security token supports.

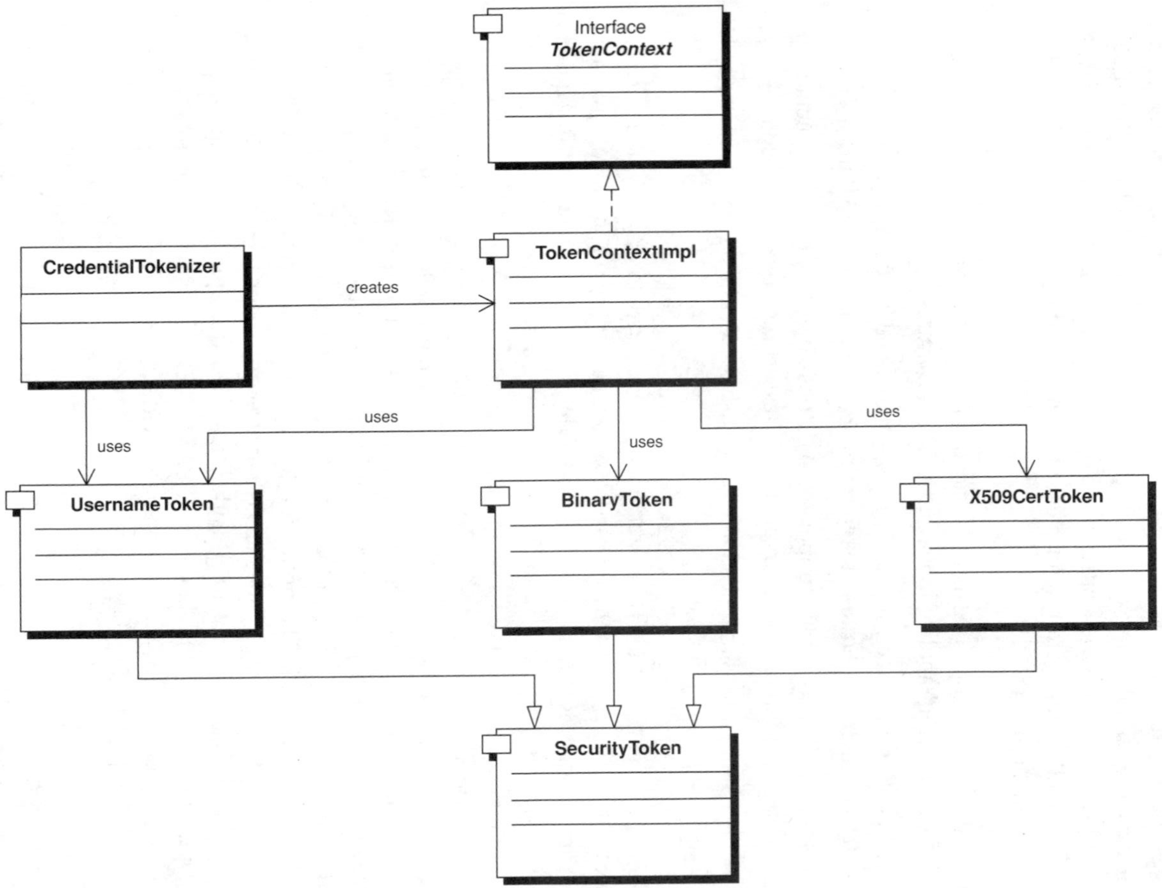

Interface
TokenContext

CredentialTokenizer

creates

TokenContextImpl

uses

uses

uses

uses

UsernameToken

BinaryToken

X509CertToken

SecurityToken

Figure 12–8 Credential Tokenizer class diagram

There are two major objects in the Credential Tokenizer: SecurityToken and TokenContext. The SecurityToken is a base class that encapsulates any security token. It can be extended to implement username token (UsernameToken), binary token (BinaryToken), and certificate token (X509v3CertToken). In this pattern, Username token is used to represent a user identity using Username Password. Binary tokens are used to represent a variety of security tokens that resemble a user identity using binary text form (such as Kerberos Tickets). Certificate tokens denote digital certificates issued to represent a user identity. An X.509v3 certificate is a common form of certificate token.

The TokenContext class refers to the system context used to create security tokens. It includes information such as the security token type, service configuration, and protocol binding for the security token. This class defines public interfaces only to set or get the security token information. TokenContextImpl is the implementation for TokenContext.

Participants and Responsibilities

Figure 12–9 depicts the Credential Tokenizer sequence diagram—how a client makes use of the Credential Tokenizer to create a security token. For example, the Client may be a service requester that is required to create the Username Password-token to represent in the WS-Security headers of a SOAP message. The CredentialTokenizer denotes the credential tokenizer that creates and manages user credentials. The UserCredential denotes the actual Credential Token, such as username/password or a X.509v3 digital certificate. The following sequences describe the interaction between the Client, CredentialTokenizer, and UserCredential:

1. Client creates an instance of CredentialTokenizer.
2. CredentialTokenizer retrieves the service configuration and the protocol bindings for the target service request.
3. CredentialTokenizer retrieves the user credentials from SecurityProvider according to the service configuration. For example, it extracts the key information from an X.509v3 certificate.
4. CredentialTokenizer creates a security token from the user credentials just retrieved.
5. Upon successful completion of creating the security token, CredentialTokenizer returns the security token to Client.

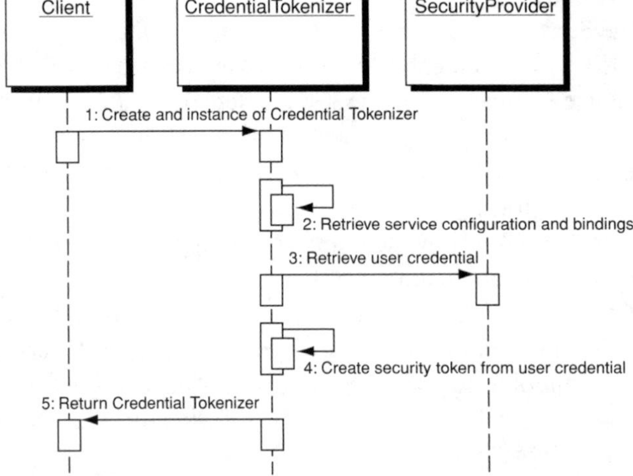

Figure 12–9 Credential Tokenizer sequence diagram

Strategies

Service Provider Interface Approach

Using a service provider interface approach to define the public interfaces for different security tokens will be more flexible and adaptive for different security tokens and devices. For example, certificate tokens may differ in vendor implementation. Developers can use the same public interfaces to support different credential token implementations and meet the requirements of different platforms and service providers without customizing the APIs for specific devices.

Protocol Binding Strategy

As with the Assertion Builder pattern, it is possible that the same client may be using the Credential Tokenizer to encapsulate user credentials as a security token in a SOAP message. To accommodate such use, developers can employ a custom service configuration look-up function (for example, refer to getProtocolBinding method in the SSOContext discussed in SSO Delegator pattern) to determine the data transport and application environment requirements. In this way, the common processing logic of the user credential processing and security token encapsulation can be reused.

Consequences

- *Supports SSO.* The Credential Tokenizer pattern helps in capturing authentication credentials for multifactor authentication. It also helps in using "shared state" (the "shared state" mechanism allows a login module to put the authentication credentials into a shared map and then passes it to other login modules) among authentication providers in order to establish single sign-on, where the Credential Tokenizer can be used for retrieving the SSO token and providing SSOToken on demand for requesting applications.

- *Provides a vendor-neutral credential handler.* The Credential Tokenizer pattern wraps vendor-specific APIs using a generic mechanism in order to create or retrieve security tokens from security providers.
- *Enables transparency by encapsulating multiple identity management infrastructures.* The Credential Tokenizer pattern encapsulates any form of security token as a credential token and thus eases integration and enables interoperability with different identity management infrastructures.

Sample Code

Example 12–6 shows a sample code excerpt for creating a Credential Tokenizer. The CredentialTokenizer creates an instance of TokenContextImpl, which provides a system context for encapsulation of the security token created. To create a security token, you need to define the security token type using the method setTokenType. Then you need to create the security token using the method createToken, which invokes the constructor of the target security token class (for example, UsernameToken).

Example 12–6 Sample Credential Tokenizer implementation

```
package com.csp.identity;

import java.io.FileInputStream;
import java.io.FileNotFoundException;
import java.io.IOException;
import java.io.InputStream;
import java.security.cert.CertificateException;
import java.security.cert.CertificateFactory;
import java.security.cert.X509Certificate;

public class CredentialTokenizer {

    protected com.csp.identity.TokenContextImpl   context;
    protected com.csp.identity.UsernameToken      usernameToken;
    protected java.security.cert.X509Certificate  cert;
    // in dev/production, you won't put the subject, principal
    // or password here
    protected final String testPrincipal = "username";
    protected final String testPassword = "password";
```

```
    /** Constructor - Creates a new instance of
        CredentialTokenizer */
    public CredentialTokenizer() {
       context = new com.csp.identity.TokenContextImpl();

       //------------For UsernameToken------------------------
       context.setTokenType
           (com.csp.identity.UsernameToken.TOKEN_TYPE);
       context.createToken(testPrincipal, testPassword);
       //-------------------------------------------------**/
    }

    public static void main(String[] args) {
        new CredentialTokenizer();
    }
}
```


Example 12–7 shows a sample implementation for the TokenContext. The TokenContextImpl is an implementation of the public interfaces defined in the TokenContext class. The former can provide methods to fetch the name of the principal (getPrincipal method) and the protocol binding for the security token (getProtocolBinding method).

Example 12–7 Sample TokenContext implementation

```
package com.csp.identity;

public class TokenContextImpl implements com.csp.identity.TokenContext {

    protected com.csp.identity.UsernameToken  usernameToken;
    protected com.csp.identity.BinaryToken    binaryToken;
    protected com.csp.identity.X509CertToken  x509CertToken;
    protected String                          tokenType;

    /** Constructor - Creates a new instance of
        CredentialTokenizer */
    public TokenContextImpl() {
        usernameToken = null;
        binaryToken = null;
        x509CertToken = null;
    }

    /**
     * Define token type
```

```
     * - use the constant in each security token subclass to
     * define
     *
     * @param tokenType  security token type, for example USERNAME_TOKEN,
     * X509CERT_TOKEN, BINARY_TOKEN, KERBEROS_TICKET
     **/
    public void setTokenType(String tokenType) {
        this.tokenType = tokenType;
    }

    /**
     * create security token based on the subject, principal
     *  and security token
     *
     * @param principal      principal
     * @param securityToken  security token can be
     *  binary,username, X.509v3 certificate,
     *  Kerberos ticket, etc
     *
     **/
    public void createToken(String principal, Object
         securityToken) {
        if (this.tokenType.equals
               (com.csp.identity.UsernameToken.TOKEN_TYPE)) {
            //System.out.println("create a usernametoken...");
            usernameToken
        = new com.csp.identity.UsernameToken(principal,
                                        (String)securityToken);
        }
        else if
(this.tokenType.equals(com.csp.identity.BinaryToken.TOKEN_TYPE)) {
     System.out.println("create a binary token...");
      binaryToken
     = new com.csp.identity.BinaryToken(principal,
                                       (String)securityToken);
        }
    }

    /**
     * get security token
     *
     * @return Object  any security token type,
     * for example String, X.509v3 certificate
     **/
```

```
    public Object getToken() {
       if (this.tokenType.equals(com.csp.identity.UsernameToken.TOKEN_TYPE)) {
            //System.out.println("get a usernametoken...");
            return (Object)usernameToken.getToken();
        }
        else if
(this.tokenType.equals(com.csp.identity.BinaryToken.TOKEN_TYPE)) {
            //System.out.println("get a binary token...");
            return (Object)binaryToken.getToken();
        }
        else return null;
    }

    /**
     * get principal
     *
     * @return principal  return principal in String
     **/
    public String getPrincipal() {
       if (this.tokenType.equals(com.csp.identity.UsernameToken.TOKEN_TYPE)) {
            //System.out.println("get principal...");
            return usernameToken.getPrincipal();
        }
        else if
(this.tokenType.equals(com.csp.identity.BinaryToken.TOKEN_TYPE)) {
            //System.out.println("get principal...");
            return binaryToken.getPrincipal();
        }
        else return null;
    }

    /**
     * get protocol binding for the security token
     *
     * @return protocolBinding  protocol binding in String
     **/
    public String getProtocolBinding() {
        return null;
    }
}
```


Example 12–8 shows a sample implementation of the username token used in previous code examples (refer to Figure 12–15 and Figure 12–16). The UsernameToken class is an extension of the base class SecurityToken. It provides methods to define and retrieve information regarding the principal name, subject's IP address, subject's DNS address and the password.

Example 12–8 Sample UsernameToken implementation

```
package com.csp.identity;

public class UsernameToken extends com.csp.identity.SecurityToken {

    protected static String                 password;
    static final String                     TOKEN_TYPE = "USERNAME_TOKEN";

    /** Constructor - create usernameToken
     *
     *  In future implementation, the constructor should be
     * private, and this class
     *  should provide a getInstance() to fetch the instance.
     */
    public UsernameToken(String principal, String password) {
        this.principal = principal;
        this.password = password;
    }

    /**
     * Get token ID from the binary token
     *
     * @return binaryToken security token in binary form
     */
    public String getToken() {
        return this.password;
    }
}
```

Security Factors and Risks

The Credential Tokenizer pattern is essential to encapsulating user credentials and user information to meet authentication and non-repudiation security requirements. One important security factor for building reliable credential tokenizers is the identity management infrastructure and whether the keys are securely managed prior to the credential processing. The following are security factors and risks associated with the Credential Tokenizer pattern.

- **Username password token**. Username password tokens are highly vulnerable to attacks by using a password dictionary.
- **X.509v3 certificate token**. Certificate token is a reliable security token and is stronger than Username Password token. However, it may be susceptible to human error during the management of the distribution of digital certificates and the timely revocation of certificates.
- **Key management strategy**. The security factor of key management strategy defines the process of generating key pairs, storing them in safe locations, and retrieving them. The generation of SAML assertion statements and signed SOAP messages using WS-Security is key management strategy. If the key management strategy and the infrastructures are not in place, the user credential token processing will be at risk.

Reality Check

Should we use username/password as a security token? Some security architects insist that the username/password pair is not secure enough and should not be used as a security token. To mitigate the potential risk of a weak password, security architects should reinforce strong password policies and adopt a flexible security token mechanism such as Credential Tokenizer to accommodate different types of security tokens for future extension and interoperability.

What other objects can be encapsulated as security token? You can embed different types of security tokens in the Credential Tokenizer, not just username/password or digital certificate. For example, you can embed binary security tokens, because they can be encapsulated as a SAML token for an authentication assertion statement. In addition, you can also add the REL token (which denotes the rights, usage permissions, constraints, legal obligations, and license terms pertaining to an electronic document) based on the eXtensible Rights Markup Language (XrML).

Related Patterns

Secure Pipe. The Secure Pipe pattern shows how to secure the connection between the client and the server, or between servers when connecting between trading partners. In a complex distributed application environment, there will be a mixture of security requirements and constraints between clients, servers, and any intermediaries. Standardizing the connection between external parties using the same platform and security protection mechanism may not be viable.

Best Practices and Pitfalls

Best Practices

1. *Externalizing Identity Management and Policy Functions.* It is important to de-couple the identity management and policy administration functions (i.e., policy administration point) from the application logic. Many applications build their own identity management and policy functions and then run without interacting with other systems. These identity management and policy functions provide similar or duplicate functions, and thus are difficult to integrate with other applications. It is beneficial to use a common policy system (for example, a standardized policy decision point) to standardize security control and ease audit control, for compliance reasons.
2. *Logging and Audit.* Filter and customize your logging mechanisms for any change in user credentials or creation of security tokens for audit control. For example, you can customize a logging handler (as in Java Logging API) or appender (as in log4j) to send details of user credential changes or creation of security tokens to a customized audit log. This can address local regulations and compliance requirements.
3. *High Availability.* Single sign-on and security token processing are critical security functions that need to be available to service requesters and service providers. Their application security designs should have high-availability design, either by deploying multi-master directory server topology (on which some identity server products run) or by clustering application containers. A failure to provide high availability for them may result in monetary loss and security vulnerabilities.
4. *SAML Single Sign-on Profile.* Developers can use SAML single sign-on profile to implement single sign-on. It is standards-based and is supported by many security vendor products. Developers should avoid using proprietary methods to implement cross-domain single sign-on. Because cross-domain single sign-on requires loosely coupled integration with different security infrastructures, SAML and Liberty provide a good security framework.
5. *Security Threat Mitigation.* [SAML11Security] defines some best practices of mitigating security threats for SAML messages. This includes the use of digital signatures, the combined use of secure transport layer (for example, HTTPS) and reliable messaging, and adding timestamp checking in the SAML server.

6. *Strong Password Policy.* Always reinforce strong password policies if username/password tokens are used.

Pitfalls

7. *Using Reusable Passwords in Creating Security Tokens.* Reusable passwords refer to Username Passwords that are constant and are used multiple times to gain access to a system resource. They are usually susceptible to dictionary attacks.
8. *Using Default Settings.* Some applications provide default settings that turn on all application functions as a convenience, which may open up security loopholes for unauthorized access. For example, a security product may have a default policy rule that grants anonymous access to the system. This type of default setting should be disabled.
9. *Using Minimal Security Elements.* When implementing SAML assertion statements according to the latest SAML specifications, developers may want to populate only the mandatory elements and leave all optional elements. Developers may assume that they should only use the minimal set of data elements, because they may not have a full understanding of how to use all of these optional elements. Some optional security elements such as IPAddress (IP address of the SAML responder) and DNSAddress (DNS address) are helpful information for identifying the message origin, troubleshooting, and tracking suspicious events. Without using these optional elements, the tracking of suspicious service requests or problem troubleshooting would be difficult.

References

Open SAML

http://www.opensaml.org

Sun Java System Access Manager

http://wwws.sun.com/software/products/identity_srvr/home_identity.html

Sun's XACML implementation

http://sunxacml.sourceforge.net/

VeriSign. Trust Gateway

http://www.verisign.com/products/trustgateway/index.html and http://www.verisign.com/products/trustgateway/download.html

[CJP2] Deepak Alur, John Crupi, and Dan Malks. *Core J2EE Patterns: Best Practices and Design Strategies, Second Edition*. Prentice Hall, 2003.

[SAML11Security] OASIS. Security and Privacy Considerations for the OASIS Security Assertion Markup Language (SAML) V1.1. September 2, 2003.

http://www.oasis-open.org/committees/download.php/3404/oasis-_sstc-saml-sec-consider-1.1.pdf

Secure Service Provisioning–Design Strategies and Best Practices

Topics in This Chapter

- Business Challenges
- User Account Provisioning Architecture
- Introduction to SPML
- Service Provisioning Security Pattern
- Best Practices and Pitfalls

Chapter 13

Service Provisioning refers to the software services that enterprises use to centralize and manage the process of supplying users with access to corporate systems and business data. Provisioning security service for user accounts (or user account provisioning) is a variant of service provisioning that is specific to security services, for example, creation of user accounts, password reset, and synchronization of user credentials (such as passwords) across application systems. Application service provisioning is a specialized form of service provisioning that simplifies complex software installation and policies to make the application service available in advance. Service provisioning has become one of the emerging technologies and industry interests.

When a business expands its IT infrastructure to meet increasing business needs, it builds and extends many home-grown applications or commercial off-the-shelf packages. These applications or packages have their own account management and services components. For example, they may have different security policy for the password or user ID length. Some legacy applications or packages that were developed in the past may not be flexible enough to support a centralized identity management infrastructure. Thus, provisioning services across a large number of servers, applications, or packages, such as manually managing the creation of user accounts or synchronizing heterogeneous user identities is highly complex and challenging.

Cryptocard Technology [cryptocard] reports that provisioning security service for a user costs from US$68 to US$102 on average. This is based on industry surveys and research about creating a new user account or managing password changes. The unit cost includes the staff resources to create the service request, the integration effort to create a user account or reset a password across heterogeneous systems, and the operating expenses for maintaining and sustaining the underlying service provisioning architecture. In practice, service provisioning is more complex than just resetting the password or creating a new user account for a single system manually.

This chapter outlines the functionality provided by secure service provisioning and describes the technologies and standards available today. It also defines a service provisioning architecture and discusses the differentiators for security vendor products that support secure service provisioning. In this chapter, we focus on user account provisioning, which is one important component in managing user identities and security policies. Application service provisioning is not in scope of this book.

Business Challenges

User provisioning is a preparatory action for supplying a new user prior to initiating the user specific business services. This has several implications. Provisioning a new user may require creating a new user account in multiple applications across many systems. The user account may have multiple user credentials for the same person. Account mapping and provisioning for heterogeneous applications and systems is often complex. Password management, for example, involves resetting user passwords or synchronizing the passwords across multiple systems. This requires sophisticated control processes that can manage secure system interfaces and connectivity between the centralized password management system and the remote application systems. Since some user passwords can access sensitive business data, the password management control process needs to be highly secure, reliable, and timely.

In case of application service provisioning, it poses a different challenge when installing and configuring a new instance of a software application. Many software applications require manual configuration (such as creation of specific user accounts) due to the complex system design and local system settings. The manual configuration may result in creating variants of application system instances based on different types of hardware and software configurations.

Scope of Service Provisioning

The OASIS Provisioning Service Technical Committee notes that there is no standard definition of the term *service provisioning* in the industry (refer to

[SPML10], p.10). In a broad sense, the term denotes the automation of managing and creating user accounts and its associated account services before and after the users can activate and use the business services. Service provisioning also include the preparation of the underlying operating system and server infrastructure, applications, the creation of user accounts and their associated service entitlement (for example, access rights and the entitled business functionality for the account), and the synchronization of user accounts and passwords across the rest of the enterprise architecture (including any large-scale vendor products such as PeopleSoft and SAP). Currently, Service Provisioning Markup Language (SPML) is an approved open standard for service provisioning to manage user accounts.

The scope of service provisioning may vary in different industry contexts. In the telecommunications industry, provisioning a subscriber account service means more than creating a user account in multiple business services (such as local call, distance call, or video-on-demand services) or creating user IDs in the online business systems. Some subscriber account services need to create account profiles for individual account services (such as a home video service bandwidth usage profile) based on product-specific business rules. Some subscriber account services have complex business rules and dependencies and may require some work-flow processes (such as credit approval and availability of local broadband cable infrastructure) to fulfill the account opening request. For example, provisioning a home video service account requires checking the credit, notifying the service provider to increase the network bandwidth dynamically for video streaming, creating a user profile that links up to existing business services, and so forth. Thus, there will be tight integration and complex interaction between business systems and the service provisioning system.

User account provisioning requires a tight integration with the application system (or application service provider) in order to create a new user account or identity. It may use a direct system interface that has a "root" or "super-user" access right in order to create or maintain the user account. Thus, user account provisioning needs to be extremely secure; if it is not secure, hackers or attackers will exploit any loophole in the system interface for harmful action or illegal access to business data.

Relationship with Identity Management

User account provisioning, a subset of secure service provisioning, is fairly different from single sign-on. The former denotes the creation of user accounts prior to using the business services and the management of passwords across systems. Single sign-on deals with the functionality to sign on to any system using a single user identity or a set of user credentials. It assumes that the user account and the associated account services are already in place; that is, service provisioning is complete. We should also differentiate the use of a directory server to provision user ID from secure service provisioning. The former is an implementation mechanism (or a means) for creating user accounts, but the latter implies a structured framework for creating as well as managing account services. Service provisioning may include using a directory server as one of the means to achieve security goals as well as other technologies and supporting service provisioning standards.

A Typical Scenario of User Account Provisioning

An employee may have multiple identities within the enterprise. For example, Figure 13–1 depicts a typical scenario in which Mary Jane Parker has recently joined the company. The IT administrator is going to create a user account for her in various application systems. The HR, CRM, and payroll systems require using her full name when creating a user account. Other computer systems have different user account creation rules. The ERP financial system uses her first and last name for her user account. The Messaging Server uses "maryj," and the directory server uses a mnemonic name, *retep4yram*. Mary may also be referred to as M_Jane or Mary.Jane when dealing with the Help Desk and external trading partners.

It is a nightmare for an IT administrator to provision a user account for a new employee across application systems with different user account creation rules and using multiple identities. The administrator also needs to determine whether

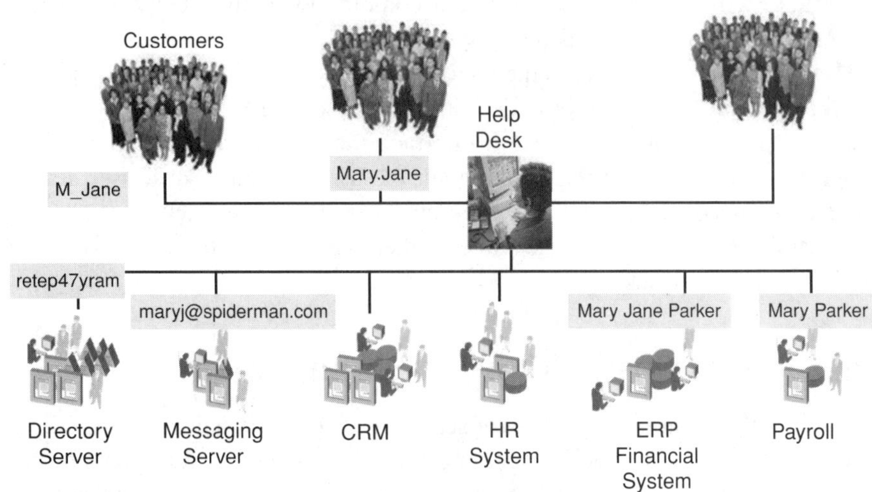

Figure 13–1 A typical scenario of user account provisioning

the user account has the same access rights for all of these application systems. If the user account has different access rights in each application system, a change in the user account attributes (for example, a change in the user's department) would probably require a change in the access rights in other systems. If there is no automated user account creation interface across application systems, this kind of a change will require considerable manual administrative processing. If there is an automated user account creation interface, it may expose a security risk (such as weak security token, broken authentication, or broken access control) when exchanging user credentials and synchronizing user passwords with external application systems. Additionally, it is challenging to synchronize all user passwords for these user accounts. Administering the security provisioning services—from creating user accounts to synchronizing user passwords—carries high administrative costs (refer to [Cryptocard] for details).

In the typical scenario shown in Figure 13–1, there are three implications to the security design and implementation. First, to provide a flexible identity management capability for multiple identities for different application systems requires reliability (for example, a failover mechanism in case the identity management infrastructure encounters problems), flexibility (for example, policy-based instead of hard-code rules), scalability (fit for a distributed environment), and maintainability (for example, reuse of security best practices and patterns). Unreliable user account provisioning will be exposed to potential security vulnerabilities such as insecure data transit, weak security token, broken authentication, or broken access control. Maintaining and administering identities and user accounts is more than a set of security administration procedures.

Second, to automate security service provisioning across application systems requires a standard interface (ideally, a standards-based interface) that works with the existing security infrastructure. If the interface is proprietary, there will be lots of integration and interoperability efforts required.

Third, there are needs for enabling proactive and reactive security protection measures to guard the user account creation interfaces among application systems or the password synchronization process among them. Message replay is a common security risk in such scenarios. Some service provisioning interfaces (such as an agent-based architecture) may require some software code changes in the underlying application infrastructure. Thus, they are "intrusive" to the security architecture. Some service provisioning interfaces may require sharing user credentials with external systems or trading partners, which may create a potential data privacy issue. Security architects need to understand the underlying mechanisms of these interfaces and ensure that the user account provisioning process and their interfaces do not expose new or unknown security risks.

Current Approaches to User Account Provisioning

To address the typical scenario illustrated in Figure 13–1, security architects commonly use the following approaches when building security service provisioning solutions:

- *User Account Mapping*. A mapping table can be created to map different user identities with different application systems. The authentication service component (for example, a directory server) may use an internal unique identifier to map to different user identity variants. When a user wants to access any application systems, the authentication service component looks up this mapping table and verifies whether the user can access any application systems. However, this is a tactical and proprietary solution. There is considerable customization effort required for the authentication service component and for integration with all application systems.
- *Password Synchronization*. Security architects use tactical and proprietary vendor solutions to synchronize user passwords in different application systems. These solutions usually have custom adapters or connectors that can populate user passwords into the target application systems. Synchronizing user passwords usually assumes that user accounts are created and provisioned in advance. The password synchronization products are specialized solutions and do not necessarily provision user accounts with different identities. Using tactical and proprietary vendor solutions can end up creating lock-in to a specific vendor's implementation and can make it fairly difficult to interoperate with new security infrastructure or emerging provisioning standards.
- *Single Sign-on*. A single sign-on security infrastructure allows a user to sign on to different security infrastructures. However, a single sign-on solution does not provide the functionality to provision user accounts in multiple application systems with different identities.
- *Point-to-Point Interfaces between Identity Management Products*. Custom point-to-point security interfaces can be built between identity management products (for example, a single sign-on or password synchronization product) to provision user accounts with different user identities. These interfaces are usually proprietary and require customization. If one of the identity management products has a version upgrade, the security interface needs to be upgraded as well in order to accommodate any necessary system changes.

- *Standards-Based Security Service Provisioning Interfaces.* The Service Provisioning Markup Language (SPML) is an XML specification for processing service requests for provisioning user accounts. The OASIS Provisioning Service Technical Committee approved it as a standard specification in October 2003. A number of security vendor products now support SPML. With SPML, security architects can define mappings between multiple identities and synchronize user passwords between application systems. SPML-based service provisioning systems can also work with single sign-on and portal server products.

Not all solution approaches address the entire problem of service provisioning. Most of these approaches are proprietary or vendor product-specific. They also may not be scalable enough to process user account requests for a large number of application systems simultaneously. SPML-enabled service provisioning is becoming more visible, especially after OASIS approved the SPML standard specification. Thus, customers can use a standards-based approach to address user account service provisioning. The following sections introduce the technical architecture of a service provisioning server and discuss how it can integrate with other infrastructure components, such as portal and identity service providers.

User Account Provisioning Architecture

Centralized Model versus Decentralized Model

Many service provisioning systems maintain a mapping of user identities and account services between application systems using a centralized provisioning server. The provisioning server can be a Java application that manages service provisioning requests and runs on top of a J2EE application server. Under the centralized model, the provisioning server can store user account profile information in multiple data stores (Profile Management Data Store). The provisioning server stores the user account information and user profile in the Profile Management Data Store in each application system. The Profile Management Data Store can be replicated and synchronized. This method allows better availability of user account provisioning services.

Figure 13–2 shows a sample centralized model. A client request from the help desk application intends to create a user account in PeopleSoft HRMS, SAP, and a home-grown application. The user account administration function of these applications should be able to process SPML requests to add, change, or delete user account requests.

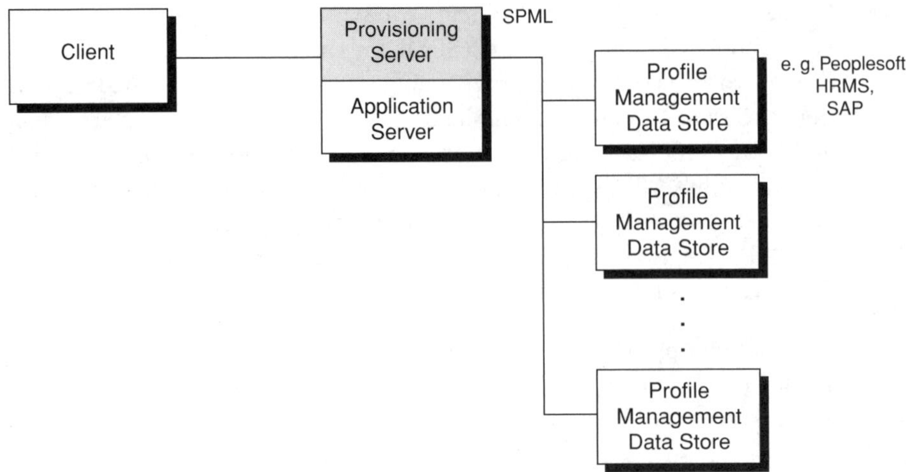

Figure 13–2 Centralized service provisioning model

Figure 13–3 depicts a decentralized model, where there is no centralized provisioning server or profile management data store. User account profile information can be stored in local application systems. When the help desk application receives a client request to create user accounts in local application systems, it issues an SPML request to all application systems.

Under the decentralized model, a local application system can be configured as the Primary Profile Management Data Store, which acts as the master or provider and synchronizes user account profiles with other Profile Management Data Stores. In the sample scenario in Figure 13–3, the help desk application sends the SPML request to PeopleSoft HRMS, which acts as the Principal Profile Management Data Store. PeopleSoft HRMS then replicates the user profile across all application systems, including Sun Java System Directory Server, RSA SecurID, and Microsoft Exchange Server.

Table 13–1 summarizes the pros and cons of centralized and decentralized service provisioning models. There is no definitive rule about whether a centralized or decentralized service provisioning model is ideal. Architects and developers need to decide on the service provisioning model to use based on local requirements and environment constraints. For example, if customers have a large investment in an ERP system such as PeopleSoft HRMS around different regional offices worldwide, they may have a requirement to reuse existing application infrastructure and user credential repositories. Thus, they may find it sensible to adopt a decentralized service provisioning model by leveraging the ERP system to be the principal profile management data store.

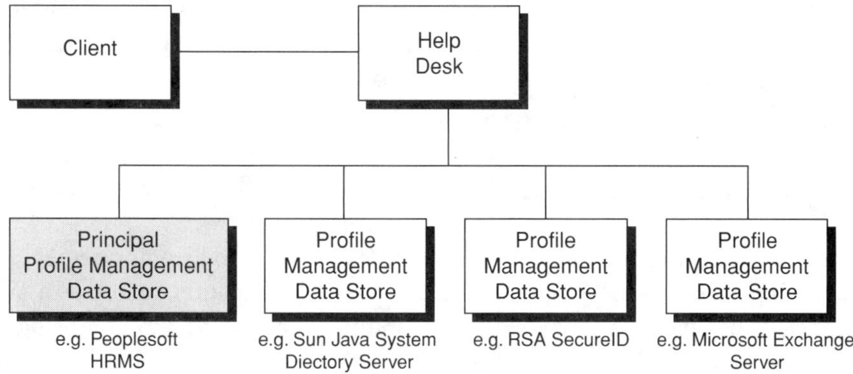

Figure 13–3 Decentralized service provisioning model

Table 13–1 Pros and Cons of Centralized and Decentralized Service Provisioning

	Pros	*Cons*
Centralized Service Provisioning	It provides a single point of control. It has a relatively consistent user interface. It allows an automated provisioning process.	Centralized service provisioning may become a single point of failure.
Decentralized Service Provisioning	It is useful for a highly decentralized business environment.	Synchronization between provisioning data stores is highly complex. The decentralized model may result in inconsistent user interface and provisioning processes. The failover design scheme and capability is fairly complex, because the decentralized model needs to cater to a multitude of data sources in which the data sources may have a very different data management nature, resilience, and failover requirements.

Many service provisioning products support centralized service provisioning, for example, Thor's Xellerate and Blockade's ManageID. Some products also support both centralized and decentralized service provisioning, such as Sun's Sun Java System Identity Manager.

Logical Architecture

Figure 13–4 depicts the logical architecture of a service provisioning server. The provisioning server usually runs on top of a J2EE application server or a Web container. It has workflow processing capabilities that create, modify, or delete user account services in each of the SPML-enabled application systems. The provisioning server stores user profile and user account provisioning details in the local Profile Management Data Store, which can be implemented in an RDBMS (Relational Database Management System) platform using JDBC (Java Database Connector).

There are two ways to issue service provisioning requests: from the client administrator and from an application system. The client administrator can use a Web browser to connect to the Web front-end of the provisioning server using the HTTP or HTTPS protocol. An application system, such as a help desk application, can also initiate service provisioning requests. It can connect to the provi-

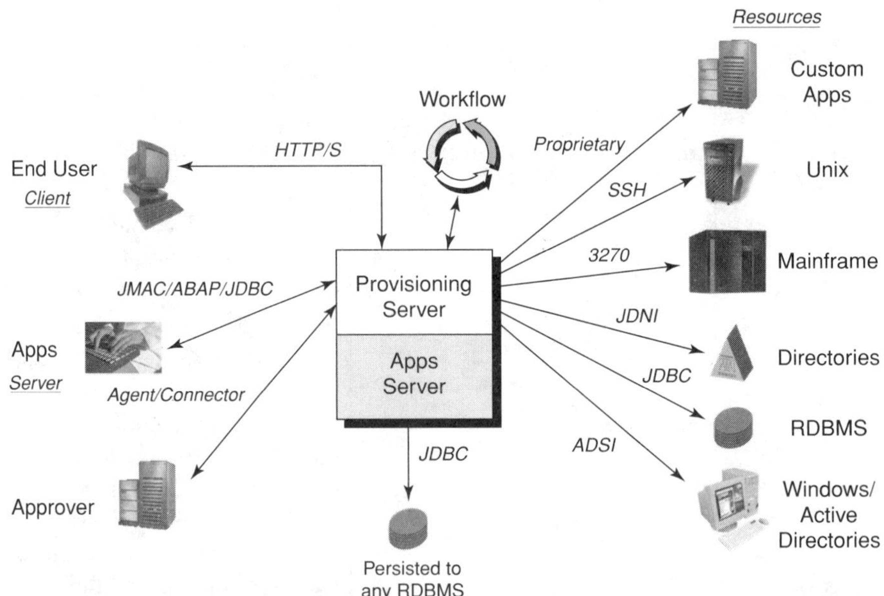

Figure 13–4 Service provisioning logical architecture for managing user accounts

sioning server using different protocols, such as JMAC, ABAP, or JDBC. It can also connect to the provisioning server using a custom SPML-enabled agent or connector. Some provisioning server products provide an SDK or API library to build a custom agent or connector.

The extensibility and interoperability of service provisioning is always dependent on the capability to interoperate with different underlying platforms and application infrastructures. These include a variety of operating systems (for example, UNIX, mainframe, and Windows), RDBMS, directories, and custom applications. Thus, the provisioning server should be able to create, modify, or delete user account service by remotely executing user account administration functions provided by the target application systems using standard protocols such as SSH, 3270, JNDI, JDBC, and ADSI. The target application systems need to establish a secure and reliable connection with the provisioning server and be able to process service provisioning requests in the standard protocol (that is, SPML). The ideal service provisioning logical architecture should be able to support multiple application platforms, including UNIX applications, legacy mainframe platforms (such as IBM), and directories (such as Microsoft Active Directory and LDAP-based directory server).

A provisioning server has a number of logical components that enable service provisioning services. Figure 13–5 depicts generic logical provisioning components and the underlying provisioning services. The underlying provisioning services provide common and reusable functions that support the core provisioning capability, including monitoring, password management, and connectivity capability. The provisioning components are specific programs or applications that can interact with provisioning administrators. Individual provisioning vendor

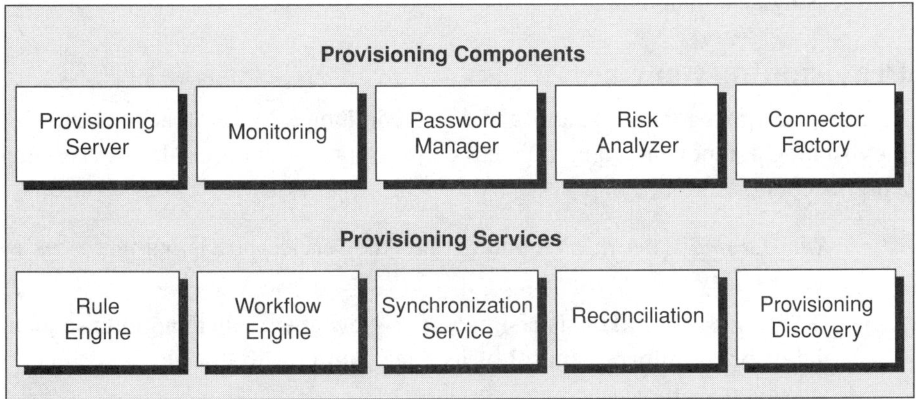

Figure 13–5 Service provisioning logical architecture components for managing user accounts

products have different names for these components, but most of them provide similar functionality.

Provisioning Components

There are several logical, reusable provisioning components in a service provisioning system:

- *Provisioning Server.* This is the core component that processes service provisioning requests.
- *Monitoring.* The monitoring component tracks the service requests received and processed, and provides statistics and logging information for audit control or administration support.
- *Password Manager.* This component provides an administration function that manages user passwords for the target application systems. It utilizes the underlying password synchronization service.
- *Risk Analyzer.* This administrative component analyzes any change impact from service provisioning requests or user account changes (for example, change of user roles) and provides system change information for security change risk analysis of the target application systems. It utilizes the processing rules and relationship defined in the rule engine (which is discussed later in this section).
- *Connector Factory.* This administrative component manages the connection or interfaces between the provisioning server and the target application systems. In other words, this is the middleware function of providing APIs to connect the provisioning server to the target application systems using custom adapters or connectors.

Provisioning Services

In a service provisioning system, there are common services that use multiple provisioning components to complete the task of provisioning or de-provisioning a user account.

- *Rule Engine.* This rule engine defines the service provisioning processes and security change impact.
- *Workflow Engine.* This is a simple workflow engine that supports sequential or programmatic control of user account creation or any account service changes for service provisioning.

- *Synchronization Service.* This is the underlying engine for synchronizing user passwords for the target application systems and for synchronizing the underlying Profile Management Data Stores.
- *Reconciliation.* This is a simple reporting infrastructure for reconciling the user account service profile (target service provisioning plan) with the provisioned user account services (actual provisioning result).
- *Provisioning Discovery.* This underlying service discovers whether there are SPML-enabled application systems in the network or infrastructure. Because there is no standard service provisioning discovery protocol yet, it may not be feasible for a provisioning server to discover different vendor-specific provisioning agents or proxies.

Provisioning server products have different levels of sophistication and functionality, and they may have logical architectures very different from this generic logical architecture. They may have several underlying provisioning services combined into one server component, or services that are split into more server components. Since an architect can craft the logical architecture in a variety of ways, provisioning server products may call these logical components by different names. It is not a trivial task to define a generic logical architecture for service provisioning servers.

Portal Integration

Administrators may sometimes have a special requirement to administer service provisioning requests via a portal server. The portal server provides a unified user interface for accessing different application systems using portal channels or portlets. Additionally, administrators can perform application administration from the same "console" without switching to different applications.

Figure 13–6 depicts how a provisioning server can integrate with a portal server. In this sample scenario, administrators can create a portal channel that connects to the system administration console of the provisioning server. Nevertheless, if the provisioning server has a fairly different user interface style, administrators might want to consider using the portlet approach. Using a portlet, administrators can customize a consistent user interface style for all applications and an administration front-end. The provisioning server needs to provide APIs that allow a portlet to initiate the administration console or process service provisioning requests. However, not every provisioning server supports portlet integration.

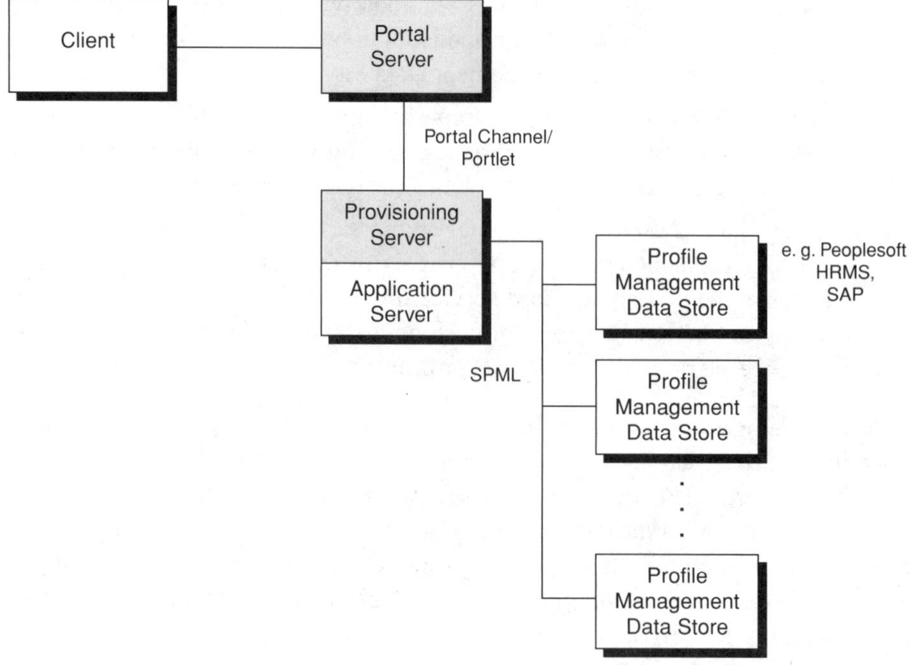

Figure 13–6 Integration with Portal Server

Integrating with an Identity Provider Infrastructure

Because administrators have a day-to-day need to administer multiple application systems, it is essential that they have the ability to access different administration consoles with a single sign-on capability. Administrators can also use a portal server to provide a unified user interface for performing system administration functions for multiple application systems. It is also beneficial to use an identity provider infrastructure that enables single sign-on to all application systems.

Here, the term "identity provider infrastructure" refers to software vendor products or application systems that enable single sign-on access and support single sign-on standard specifications, including SAML and Liberty. In other words, once the administrator provides user credentials to authenticate with a given identity provider, he or she can access the system administrative functions using the user interface provided by the portal server as well as any external systems outside the local system infrastructure (such as in a cross-domain single sign-on scenario). Even if the administrator is not performing service provisioning functions via a portal server, he or she can sign on once with the identity provider and access other application systems using an identity provider infrastructure.

Figure 13–7 depicts a single sign-on scenario where administrators authenticate their user credentials with an identity provider infrastructure. The identity provider infrastructure redirects the administrator to authenticate with an identity provider. Upon successful authentication, the administrator signs onto the portal server, which has an existing portal channel to connect to the administration console of the service provisioning server. The service provisioning server is configured to reuse the underlying directory server to store the user account profile and account information that are necessary to create or modify a user account.

Under the single sign-on security infrastructure, each of the target application systems supports the Liberty and SAML protocol. These application systems are able to integrate with the identity provider infrastructure using Liberty and SAML-enabled Web agents. User account mapping between the service provisioning server and the target application systems is defined and managed by the administrative function of the service provisioning server. The user account profile is stored in each individual Profile Management Data Store of the target application systems. These data stores are synchronized periodically.

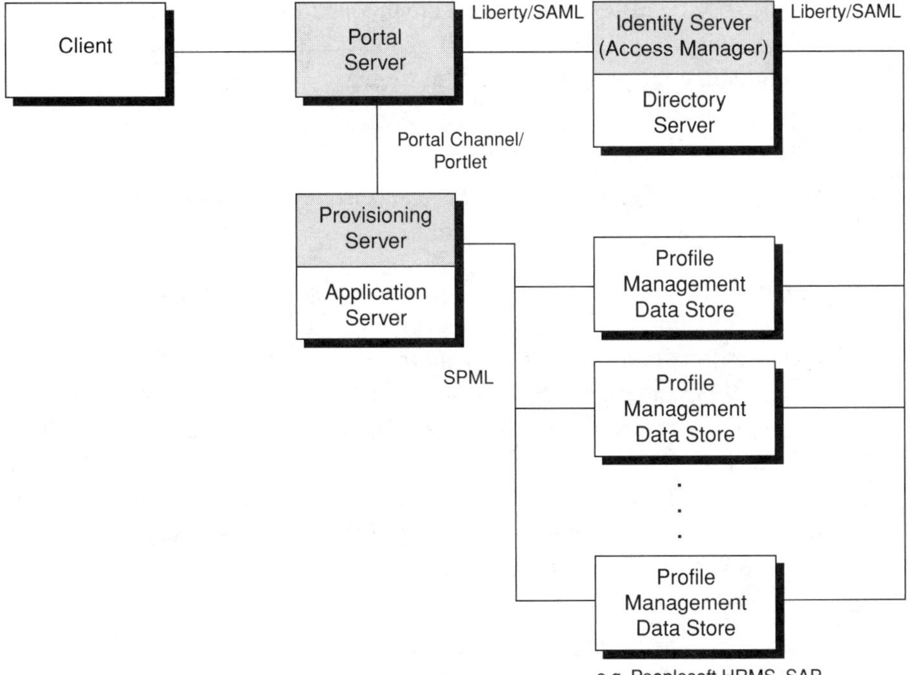

Figure 13–7 Integration with Identity Provider Infrastructure

When the administrator issues a service provisioning request to create a user account in these application systems, the provisioning server can ensure that the same user account that was just provisioned can sign on to all target application systems for which the user account has appropriate access rights.

Other Integration Capability

Some provisioning servers have a broader integration capability with legacy system infrastructure. For example, they can reuse the underlying security infrastructure for storing user credentials and user profiles in the directory server. LDAP-based directory servers are fairly commonly used in authenticating and storing sensitive user account data. Such use is ideal for enterprises whose security architecture is concentrated in directory servers. They can store all service provisioning data in the directory server.

Differentiators for Service Provisioning Products

There are many ways to set evaluation criteria for service provisioning products in terms of their system functionality, pricing, and support infrastructure. There are also some specific differentiators that are unique to service provisioning products. The following outlines a set of differentiators that can help architects and developers to define the product evaluation strategy.

Technology Differentiators

There are technology-related factors that can differentiate service provisioning products. The following identifies some of them:

- *Agent-based versus Agentless Architecture.* Some service provisioning products require installing a custom agent, which may need some software code modification, in their application infrastructure. This is also known as *agent-based* architecture. Agent-based architecture is generally not desirable and may require customization during software upgrades. Some products provide a nonintrusive connector that enables the target application system to intercept service provisioning requests. The connector may be a lightweight servlet running on top of the existing application server or Web server that doesn't require modification of the application system. This connector approach is sometimes called *agentless* architecture.
- *Data Model.* Some service provisioning products use an index-based data model to encapsulate the user account profile or provisioning data. They

implement the data model centrally in the Profile Management Data Store. Other provisioning products choose to implement the data model in distributed Profile Management Data Stores.

- *Extensibility.* It is important to have an SDK that can build custom adapters for application systems that do not support SPML or service provisioning requests. Such an SDK allows extending the system functionality to accommodate service provisioning requests.
- *Data Integration.* Some provisioning servers provide automated data integration with different Profile Management Data Stores or with the user account database of the target application systems. Some provisioning servers require manual data integration, such as creating data feeds to provision user accounts.

Introduction to SPML

Service Provisioning Markup Language (SPML) is an XML representation for creating service requests to provision user accounts or for processing service requests related to the management of user account services. As discussed earlier in this chapter, service provisioning is a loosely defined term. According to the OASIS SPML specification (refer to [SPML10], pp. 9-10), provisioning refers to "the automation of all the steps required to manage (set up, amend, and revoke) user or system access entitlements or data relative to electronically published services." The scope of service provisioning is primarily the management of user account services, not the underlying operating systems or application environment.

OASIS's service provisioning introduces the SPML domain model, which uses a *Requesting Authority* (a client requester that creates service provisioning requests to a known service point) to send service provisioning requests to the *Provisioning Service Point* (a service provider that intercepts service provisioning requests and processes them). The Provisioning Service Point handles the service provisioning request and creates or modifies user account information in the *Provisioning Service Targets* (target application systems where the service provisioning requests are executed and implemented).

SPML is different from SAML (refer to Chapter 12 for details). SPML defines the processes and steps that are required in order to prepare for user account services to be available, while SAML defines security assertions related to authentication or authorization after the user accounts are available. Directory Services Markup Language (DSML) is an XML specification for expressing directory queries, updates, and the results of directory operations. SPML is different from

DSML in that SPML may use directory servers (using DSML) as one of the underlying data store mechanisms to implement some of the user account service requests.

Like any SOAP-based messaging, SPML faces security threats such as message replay, message insertion, message deletion, and message modification. The security protection mechanisms discussed in Chapter 6, "Web Services Security–Standards and Techniques," is also applicable here.

Service Provisioning Operations

The SPML version 1.0 specification allows security architects and developers to perform the following operations:

- *Add Operation*. The add operation uses the message AddRequest (see Example 13–2) to allow the Requesting Authority (a special term used in SPML for a system that is authorized to make a service request for a resource) to add a new provisioning object, which may be a user account or user profile in the target system. It specifies the user account information in the element <attributes>. The service provisioning system will respond to the service request using a message AddResponse (see Example 13–1), where any error message will be returned in the element <errorMessage>.
- *Modify Operation*. The modify operation uses the message ModifyRequest to allow the Requesting Authority to make a change request to the provisioning object. It specifies the change request in the element <modifications>. The service provisioning system will respond to the change request using a message ModifyResponse, where any error message will be returned in the element <errorMessage>.
- *Delete Operation*. The delete operation uses the message DeleteRequest to allow the Requesting Authority to delete a unique identifier for a provisioning data set such as user account or managed data. It specifies the unique identifier (for example, e-mail address) in the element <identifier>. The service provisioning system will respond to the deletion request using the message DeleteResponse, where any error message will be returned in the element <errorMessage>.
- *Search Operation*. The search operation uses the message SearchRequest to allow an SPML client to perform a search of provisioning objects (user information defined or associated with the service provisioning system) by specifying partial user information, such as last name or part of the directory server objects (for example, "cn=raylai"). It specifies the starting

point in the element <searchBase>, the search criteria in the element <filter>, and the attributes to be returned in the element <attributes>. Upon completion of the search operation, the provisioning system will return the search result in the element <searchResultEntry> of the message SearchResponse. Similarly, any error message will be returned in the element <errorMessage> of the SearchResponse message.

- *Extended Operations*. The purpose of the extended operations is to specify additional or new operations for services that are not defined or provided in the existing protocol or specification. Security architects and developers can specify the custom operation in the elements <providerIdentifier> and <operationIdentifier>, and the user object details in the elements <identifier> and <attributes>. For example, if the security architects and developers want to define an extended operation to delete a mailbox, they may specify the service provider object identifier (such as 1.2.3.4.5.678.7.6.5.4.1.1.1.2.3456) in the element <providerIdentifer> and the operation identifier (such as urn:namredips.com.mailservice.ops:purge) in the element <operationIdentifier> with the mailbox ID (such as maryj@namredips.com) in the element <identifier>.

The SPML specification allows service provisioning products the flexibility to implement how to handle and process service provisioning requests. It defines the language semantics of add, delete, search, and extended operations. Nevertheless, it does not specify the underlying operations of how to create a user account in an application system.

Features in SPML

There are a few unique design features in the SPML version 1.0 specification that are worth discussing. They allow security architects and developers to build SPML-enabled interfaces or integrate SPML-enabled products with their existing architecture with more flexibility and extensibility. These unique design features include:

- *Flexible Request-Reply Model*. SPML supports both synchronous (or singleton request) and asynchronous (or multi-request batch) models to meet different technical requirements. In the synchronous request-reply model, the client (also known as the Requesting Authority) creates a session and issues a request to provision a user account. While it is waiting for the server to reply to the service provisioning request, the client will hold the session by using a "blocking" wait loop. In other words, it will not issue any new service provisioning request or handle other processing logic while waiting for the server response. The synchronous model is useful for legacy systems that support only synchronous communication. In the asynchronous request-reply model, the client and the server can freely exchange service provisioning requests and replies in any order or sequence. This allows the service provisioning system to manage a large volume of service provisioning transactions simultaneously.

- *Extensibility Using the Open Content Model.* The SPML schema follows an open content model in which architects and developers can add additional child elements or attributes to extend the service provisioning requests on top of standard schema. This allows individual service provisioning products to add custom information, such as additional user account profile details or configuration management details, in the SPML schema for the target application systems.
- *Custom Error Handling.* Error codes are important in handling error control for service provisioning requests. Different service provisioning systems usually have their own error code system that may not be shared and reusable by other systems. When returning an error to a service request, it is fairly helpful to use custom error handling that includes an error message that carries information other than just the specific error code. In SPML, errors are reported in the attribute "error" in the response message if the result of the SPML request shows a failure status in the attribute "result." For example, Example 13–1 illustrates an example of the message addResponse that shows a custom error status for a request to add the e-mail account raylai@namredips.com. The custom error status is a non-standard error code in SPML that provides an additional detailed description of the service request error. In the sample message, the attribute "Result" indicates whether this is a success, failure, or pending operation. The attribute "ErrorCode" details the reason for the failure. The attribute "errorMessage" further provides the description of the custom error code. This allows security architects and developers to define their custom error messages and descriptions.

Example 13–1 Sample SPML message for custom error handling

```
<addResponse
   requestID="ABC1234-5678-001"
    result="urn:oasis:names:tc:SPML:1.0#failure"
    error="urn:oasis:names:tc:SPML:1.0#customError"
    errorMessage="my custom error message">
```

```
  <identifier
      type="urn:oasis:names:tc:SPML:1.0#EMailAddress">
    <spml:id>raylai@namredips.com</id>
  </identifier>
  <attributes>
    <attr name="mailBoxLimit">
      <value>1000MB</value>
    </attr>
  </attributes>
</addResponse>
```


Adopting a SPML Implementation

There are a few SPML-compliant commercial service provisioning systems available, such as Sun Java System Identity Manager (previously known as Waveset Technologies' Lighthouse) and Thor's Xellerate. Refer to the "References" section for more vendor products. These service provisioning systems allow creating and managing user account information as well as synchronizing user passwords across systems. Some products come with an SPML API library that allows custom applications or legacy systems to intercept and process SPML service requests. If security architects and developers want to use an open source implementation, they can also download OpenSPML Toolkit from http://www.openspml.org as well.

Example 13–2 provides a sample SPML client using OpenSPML Toolkit (supporting SPML version 0.5). The OpenSPML Toolkit can be installed on any Web container (such as Apache Tomcat Web container or J2EE System Application Server).

Example 13–2 SPML client to add a user

```
package com.csp.provisioning;

import java.util.HashMap;
import org.openspml.client.SpmlClient;
import org.openspml.message.AddRequest;
import org.openspml.message.AddResponse;


public class AddUser {

    protected SpmlClient client = new SpmlClient();
    protected AddRequest request = new AddRequest();
    protected HashMap userAttr = new HashMap();
```

```
    protected AddResponse response;
    protected final String url = "http://localhost:8080/lighthouse/servlet/
rpcrouter2";
    protected final String firstName = "Mary";
    protected final String lastName = "Parker";
    protected final String fullName = "Mary Jane Parker";
    protected final String password = "peterIsSpidey123";
    protected final String email = "maryj@namredips.com";
    protected final String identifier = "maryjane";

    /**
     * Creates a new instance of AddUser
     */
    public AddUser() {
        try {
            System.out.println
            ("Creating a SPML request to add user");
            create();
            System.out.println
              ("SPML request generation is complete.");
        } catch (Throwable addUser) {
            // add your exception handling
            System.out.println(addUser.toString());
        }
    }

    /**
     * Create SPML request for add user
     *
     * @exception Exception ex
     */
    private void create() throws Exception {

        this.client.setTrace(true);
        // Use a generic SPML client
        // Assumptions
        // 1. SOAPRouter and TestSpmlHandler are registered using this URL below
        //    customize this URL for your local environment
        // 2. Lighthouse is a resource resembling your SPML server
        this.client.setUrl(this.url);

        this.request.setIdentifier(this.identifier);
        this.request.setObjectClass("user");
```

```
        // define user attributes
        this.userAttr.put("password", this.password);
        this.userAttr.put("email", this.email);
        this.userAttr.put("firstname", this.firstName);
        this.userAttr.put("lastname", this.lastName);
        this.userAttr.put("fullname", this.fullName);
        this.request.setAttributes(userAttr);

        // generate SPML request to add user
        response =
            (AddResponse)this.client.request(request);
        this.client.throwErrors(response);
    }

    public static void main(String args[]) {
        new AddUser();
    }
}
```


Executing the sample SPML client will create an SPML request, as depicted in Example 13–3. This is an add operation to create an e-mail user account for user Mary Jane Parker.

Example 13–3 Output from the sample SPML client

```
C:\Dev\OpenSPML\src>java -classpath
%SPML_LIB%\openspml.jar;%SPML_LIB%\soap.jar;
%SPML_LIB%\j2ee.jar;%SPML_LIB%\xercesImpl.jar;%SPML_LIB%\xmlParserAPIs.jar
com.csp.provisioning.AddUser

SpmlClient: sending to http://localhost:82/lighthouse/servlet/rpcrouter2
<spml:addRequest xmlns:spml='urn:oasis:names:tc:SPML:1:0'
xmlns:dsml='urn:oasis:
names:tc:DSML:2:0:core'>
  <spml:identifier type='urn:oasis:names:tc:SPML:1:0#GUID'>
    <spml:id>maryjane</spml:id>
  </spml:identifier>
  <spml:attributes>
    <dsml:attr name='objectclass'>
      <dsml:value>user</dsml:value>
    </dsml:attr>
    <dsml:attr name='fullname'>
      <dsml:value>Mary Jane Parker</dsml:value>
    </dsml:attr>
```

```
    <dsml:attr name='email'>
      <dsml:value>maryj@namredips.com</dsml:value>
    </dsml:attr>
    <dsml:attr name='password'>
      <dsml:value>peterIsSpidey123</dsml:value>
    </dsml:attr>
    <dsml:attr name='lastname'>
      <dsml:value>Parker</dsml:value>
    </dsml:attr>
    <dsml:attr name='firstname'>
      <dsml:value>Mary</dsml:value>
    </dsml:attr>
  </spml:attributes>
</spml:addRequest>
```


Service Provisioning Security Pattern

This section introduces a security pattern that synchronizes authentication and authorization credentials across different Provisioning Service Targets (application systems). Many application systems have their own user authentication and access control mechanisms. They may not share common user credentials. Users may have to use different user passwords for different application systems. Thus, it would be useful to synchronize all user credentials specific to application systems.

Password Synchronizer Pattern

Problem

You want to synchronize the user passwords (or user credentials used for authentication and authorization) across different application systems using a programmatic interface.

In a heterogeneous application security environment, different application systems use different user account management mechanisms. If security administrators need to modify the user account management policies or to reset user passwords for all application systems to which a user is entitled, it requires considerable administrative effort. This applies to user credentials (such as certificates, smart card tokens or even biometrics samples) used for authentication and authorization as well.

As discussed earlier, the administrative effort to reset user passwords is expensive. In earlier days, some security administrators built a proprietary programmatic interface with a text file to store the user passwords and the application system identifier. However, this is not easily scalable and maintainable for a system with a large number of user accounts and growing application systems. Additionally, it is highly insecure to store sensitive user account information in text files.

If all applications are home-grown, security architects and developers may want to standardize all user account management mechanisms and centralize the user account policy system. By standardizing and centralizing the user account policy, architects and developers can easily manage provisioning user accounts—they will not have a password synchronization issue. In reality, many organizations have a mix of home-grown applications, off-the-shelf packages, and legacy systems. Thus, this user account centralization approach would not be sufficient to process user account provisioning or password synchronization in the legacy systems without heavy customization.

Single sign-on security allows a user to sign on once and access application systems across a diverse security infrastructure using unique security assertions. However, this does not provide any mechanism to provision user accounts or to synchronize user passwords. If security administrators need to reset the user passwords for a user, they need to automate resetting user passwords in a programmatic manner instead of using a manual user password reset.

Forces

- You want to use a programmatic interface that can work with different password administration and management mechanisms of each application system to synchronize user account passwords.
- You want to hide the details of handling heterogeneous application protocols (for example, proprietary message format) and service configurations of multiple security service components (for example, directory server) that underlie password administration and management mechanisms.
- You want to standardize the processing control of the return codes and error codes. Different Provisioning Service Targets (application systems) may have their own style and naming convention for the return codes and error codes. When synchronizing user passwords with multiple Provisioning Service Targets, security architects and developers may want to use a common and standard interface to encapsulate these return codes and error codes or to translate different types of codes into a common code system. For example, application A may use "20" to denote service failure due to invalid user identifier, but application B may use "30" to denote the same error. The Password Synchronizer may translate these error codes (such as "20" and "30") into its common code system (such as "40").

Solution

Use a Password Synchronizer to centralize management of synchronizing user credentials (including user passwords) across different application systems via programmatic interfaces.

A Password Synchronizer is a convenient control center for synchronizing user account services across multiple application systems. It acts like a hub that issues user account password service commands (including password setting, password resetting, and synchronizing the user passwords) to all application systems that are connected to it. Each of the application systems receives the user account password service request, verifies the authenticity, and processes the request. If the request is successful, the application system will respond with a positive return code. Otherwise, it will return a response with the details of any unsuccessful condition or failure reason.

A Password Synchronizer can manage user credential (such as user account password) activities in a programmatic manner. All user account password service requests are logged and tracked. If the target application system is unavailable, the Password Synchronizer can reissue the service request. A Password Synchronizer is extremely important when there are a large number of target application systems and administrators need to synchronize the user account passwords within a short time window. Operational efficiency and accuracy are keys to success.

To provide a flexible user account password service, architects and developers may need a number of logical architecture components, as discussed earlier in this chapter. Figure 13–8 shows a simple adaptation of the logical components as they appear in the Password Synchronizer. These logical components are depicted as shown in the figure.

Password Synchronizer Manager. The Password Synchronizer Manager acts as a façade that directs user account password service requests to the provisioning service targets (that is, target application systems). It performs the roles of the provisioning server and password manager in Figure 13–6.

Ledger. The Ledger logs each user account password service request. Once the service request is complete, the ledger will mark the request as successful. If the provisioning service target (target application system) is not available, the Password Synchronizer Manager will reissue the service request after the provisioning service target resumes service. It also performs the role of the monitoring component as in Figure 13–6.

PSTID-ID Mapping Table. The provisioning service target ID (PSTID) to user ID mapping table references the unique user account ID with the target appli-

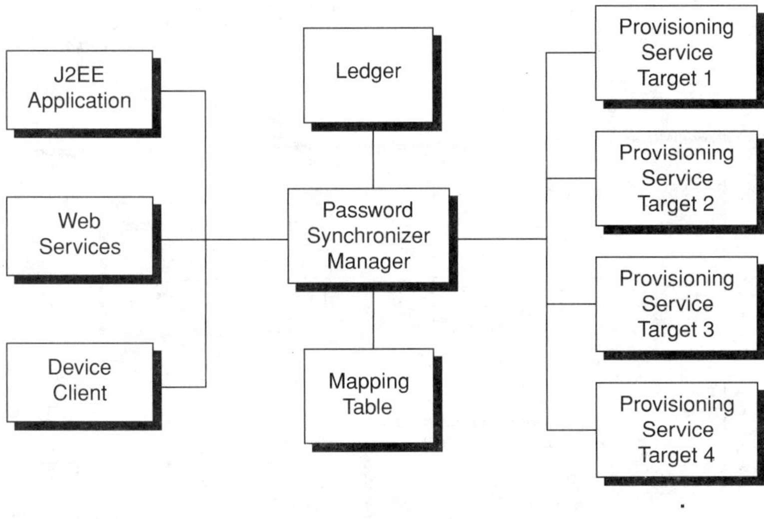

Figure 13–8 Password Synchronizer components

cation systems (provisioning service targets). This table provides information to the Password Synchronizer Manager for issuing any provisioning service requests to the target application systems.

For a large-scale deployment environment with a high volume of user account service requests, architects and developers would probably require the Password Synchronizer Manager to handle a large number of requests simultaneously using multithread processing. Typically, asynchronous messaging would be a good design approach. User account password service requests can be placed in a queue, where the Password Synchronizer Manager can create multiple threads to process these requests simultaneously.

Because each target application system may be running a different application protocol, the Password Synchronizer Manager must be flexible enough to handle multiple protocols by shielding the client tier from the underlying protocol. Doing this may require the use of connectors or adapters that can transform different underlying protocols.

Structure

Figure 13–9 shows a class diagram for the Password Synchronizer pattern. The core Password Synchronizer service consists of three important classes: PasswordSyncManager, ServiceConfig, PasswordSyncListener and PasswordSyncLedger.

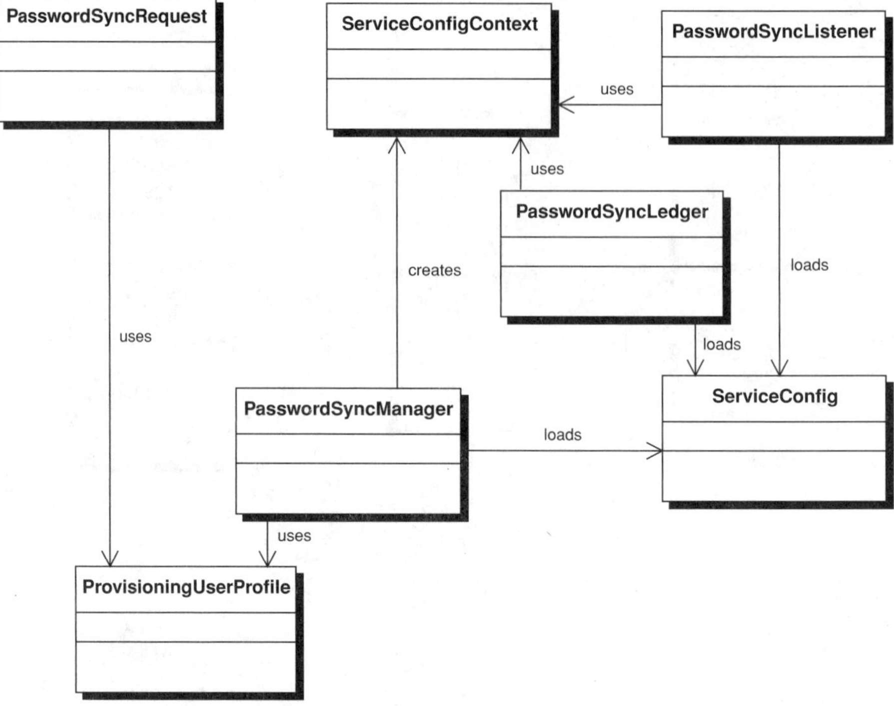

Figure 13–9 Password Synchronizer class diagram

The PasswordSyncManager class is the main process engine that handles user account password requests. The user account password request is created by the class PasswordSyncRequest, which loads the user profile (for example, user name, password) via the class ProvisioningUserProfile. The PasswordSyncManager creates a secure session, connects to each provisioning service target, and issues the relevant user account password request.

The ServiceConfig class loads the PSTID mapping file, which stores a list of the provisioning service targets and the underlying application protocol (in a context object called ServiceConfigContext for each provisioning target system) used to process the user account password service requests, such as RMI-IIOP and SOAP/HTTP. This avoids tightly coupling the data transport layer processing logic with the application processing logic in the program codes.

The PSTID Mapping file defines the mapping between the unique provisioning service target ID and the user IDs in each application system. Flexibility is increased by using a unique provisioning service target ID, which may be an arbitrary, system-generated reference number that references other user IDs. Using a unique provisioning service target ID allows user IDs to be added or removed from the mapping table without those actions impacting other systems or the application infrastructure. If architects and developers use any of the existing user IDs to map to other user IDs, any change to the user IDs will break the referential integrity (or mapping relationship). In that case, the PasswordSyncManager will not be able to complete the user account password service requests.

The PasswordSyncListener class resembles the target provisioning system that receives and processes the user account service request.

The PasswordSyncLedger class denotes the system entity that checks whether all user account service requests have been completed.

Participants and Responsibilities

Figure 13–10 depicts a use case scenario for synchronizing user account passwords across multiple provisioning service targets. The ProvisioningServicePoint denotes an administrative client that initiates a password synchronization request. The PasswordSyncManager is the core engine that issues user account password service requests to all provisioning service targets. The ServiceConfig is an internal table that indicates the underlying application protocol. The PasswordSyncManager writes unsuccessful service requests to a ledger, for example, when the provisioning service targets are offline and unavailable to process the service request. The Ledger records the outstanding service requests that need to be reprocessed, for example, after the provisioning service targets resume operation. The following sequence describes the password synchronization process:

1. ProvisioningServicePoint verifies if the client is authorized.
2. ProvisioningServicepoint creates an instance of the Password Synchronizer.
3. PasswordSyncManager retrieves service protocols and bindings.
4. ServiceConfig sends service protocols and bindings to PasswordSyncManager.
5. PasswordSyncManager creates session variables.
6. ProvisioningServicePoint initiates request to synchronize the user account password service.
7. PasswordSyncManager creates a handle for the password synchronization request.
8. PasswordSyncManager adds handle to the session information.
9. PasswordSyncManager issues an SPML add operation request to each individual ProvisioningServiceTarget.
10. ProvisioningServiceTarget returns the result.

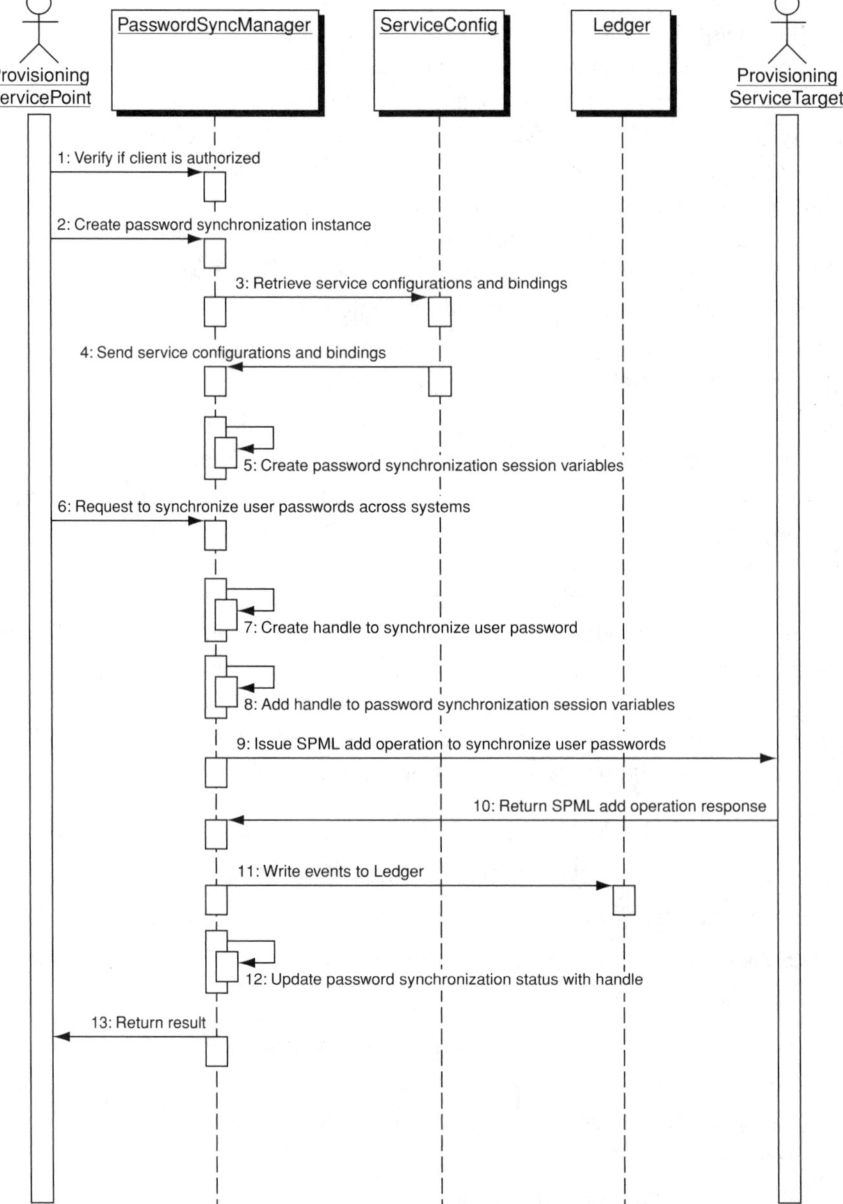

Figure 13–10 Password Synchronizer sequence diagram

11. PasswordSyncManager writes events to Ledger.
12. PasswordSyncManager updates status by the handle ID.
13. PasswordSyncManager returns the result to ProvisioningServicePoint.

Figure 13–11 shows how the Password Synchronizer pattern can reissue or reprocess the user account password service requests until they are successfully completed. This is useful if architects and developers require the reliability and resilience of handling provisioning requests. The capability of reprocessing service requests is essential for ensuring that all user passwords are synchronized, even if some of the target systems are offline. It is also important that the Password Synchronizer have the capability to roll back to the original user account password after any unsuccessful password synchronization operation. The following sequence shows the reprocessing capability of synchronizing user account passwords.

1. ProvisioningServicepoint creates an instance of the Password Synchronizer.
2. PasswordSyncManager retrieves service protocols and bindings.
3. ServiceConfig sends service protocols and bindings to PasswordSyncManager.
4. PasswordSyncManager creates session variables.
5. ProvisioningServicePoint initiates a request to synchronize user account password service.
6. ProvisioningServicePoint retrieves a list of outstanding user account password service requests from Ledger.
7. Ledger returns a list of outstanding requests.
8. PasswordSyncManager creates a handle for the password synchronization request.
9. PasswordSyncManager adds a handle to the session information.
10. PasswordSyncManager issues an SPML add operation request to each individual ProvisioningServiceTarget.
11. ProvisioningServiceTarget returns the result.
12. PasswordSyncManager writes events to Ledger.
13. PasswordSyncManager updates status by the handle ID.
14. PasswordSyncManager returns result to ProvisioningServicePoint.

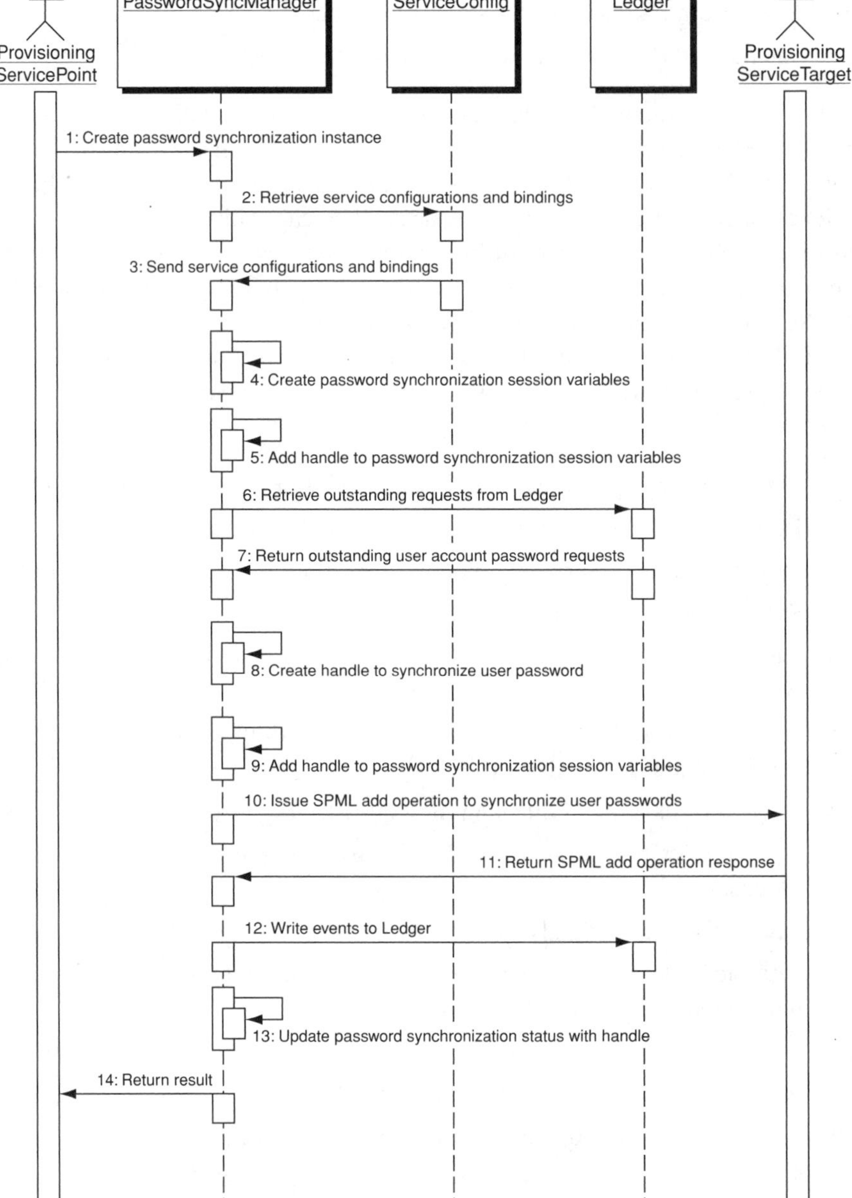

Figure 13–11 Reprocessing user account password requests after target system resumes operation

Strategies

A Password Synchronizer pattern provides a consistent and structured way to handle service provisioning functions and a flexible way to handle multiple protocol bindings. The following are scenarios discussing important design strategies for use with the Password Synchronizer pattern.

- *Multithreading strategy.* The Password Synchronizer should be flexible enough to support sequential and simultaneous processing. Sequential processing denotes that the Password Synchronizer processes each provisioning service target one at a time in a sequential order. However, this will not be scalable if there are a large number of provisioning service targets or service requests to handle. Simultaneous processing denotes the capability to create multiple threads for service request processing. Multiple threads require complex application design when implementing the Password Synchronizer to create them and handle synchronization among them.
- *Post-synchronization event strategy.* Architects and developers can invoke a script or a series of actions after processing the user account password service request. For example, the Password Synchronizer can invoke a user-defined service (for example, using EJB or a UNIX script) to notify the client that the password synchronization is unsuccessful and provide details of the problematic provisioning service target's status. This allows timely event notification or the alerting of the administrator upon completion of the service request. However, the Password Synchronizer should not be confused with a work-flow engine, which provides more flexibility of control processing.
- *Automated back-out strategy.* If the provisioning service target is unable to process any user account password service request after several attempts, architects and developers can define threshold parameters such as TIMEOUT and MAX_RETRIES to determine whether they want to back out of the user account password service request for the rest of the provisioning service targets. Backing out of the service request is similar to processing a user account password request and synchronizing the user passwords across systems.

  However, backing out of the user account password service request requires retrieving or storing the previous user account password temporarily. One challenge is that the Password Synchronizer pattern needs to retrieve the current user account password from the security infrastructure. Some security infrastructures (for example, the Solaris operating environment) do not allow retrieving user account passwords in clear text; they store the user account passwords in an encrypted format. Additionally, retrieving and storing the current user account password for a back-out operation may create several security risks. For example, security administrators need to determine a secure and safe mechanism for storing the user account password temporarily (for example, in encrypted text), which hackers may be able to access.

- *Protocol binding strategy.* It is possible that the administrative client may be using a mixture of protocols (SOAP, RMI) under different use case scenarios. Developers can build administrative clients for each different protocol, for example, a dedicated SOAP client for SOAP-based messaging and an EJB client for the RMI-IIOP protocol. However, it would be more desirable to separate the administrative processing logic from the underlying protocols. Doing so allows a single client to support more than one underlying protocol.

Consequences

By employing the Password Synchronizer pattern, developers can benefit in the following ways:

- *Addressing insecure data storage.* The Password Synchronizer pattern uses a secure data store such as Secure LDAP to store the ID mapping table. Using a secure data store is important for addressing any security vulnerability caused by insecure data storage.
- *Addressing broken authentication.* If each application system has its own user password, security hackers may easily break into an application system that uses weak user passwords. A possible risk mitigation is to synchronize the user passwords in a timely fashion across all application systems using a strong password policy. This measure can help in addressing the potential security vulnerability of broken authentication caused by weak user passwords.
- *Reusable programmatic interfaces that encapsulate different application protocols to set or reset user account passwords.* The Password Synchronizer pattern uses programmatic interfaces (such as SPML) to encapsulate the interface that instructs the provisioning service targets to set or reset user account passwords. It reduces the complexity by using standard interfaces, not custom-built proprietary connectors or interfaces. The program-

matic interfaces can be highly reusable for similar provisioning service targets.

- *Automated retry if the provisioning service target is offline.* The Password Synchronizer pattern will retry sending the user account service requests to the provisioning service targets using a ledger after they resume operations. It ensures that all provisioning service targets are synchronized. This is an essential feature of a reliable and resilient user account provisioning service.
- *Automated back-out during password synchronization.* After a number of retries (such as three times) of resending the requests to a specific provisioning service target, administrators can decide to back out of the user account password service request. It is an important design decision, because the back-out operation denotes undoing previously successful user account password service requests from a potentially large number of provisioning service targets. This may be implemented by archiving the user credential data store from each provisioning service target or by storing the current user account password securely and temporarily before executing the current service request. (Nevertheless, if the user account passwords are not securely maintained, they may be vulnerable to security exploits).

Sample Code

This section introduces sample program code for creating a Password Synchronizer to initiate user account password requests. The Password Synchronizer consists of two key components: *PasswordSyncManager* (administrative client that initiates a number of user password synchronization requests to the provisioning service targets) and *PasswordSyncLedger* (a manager component that monitors the status of the service provisioning requests from a predefined JMS topic). Each of the service provisioning requests is intercepted and processed by *PasswordSyncListener*, which resides in each provisioning service target. JMS is used because it provides a reliable message delivery mechanism and allows better scalability with multiple listeners processing the requests simultaneously.

PasswordSyncManager resembles a slight adaptation of the PasswordSyncManager in the Password Synchronizer Pattern section earlier in this chapter. Similarly, *PasswordSyncLedger* takes the role of Ledger. *pstidMapping.xml* is an adaptation of PSTIDMapping and is used by the methods in the class *ServiceConfig*.

Figure 13–12 shows the logical architecture for the sample program codes. In Step 1, *PasswordSyncManager* reads from the provisioning service target mapping

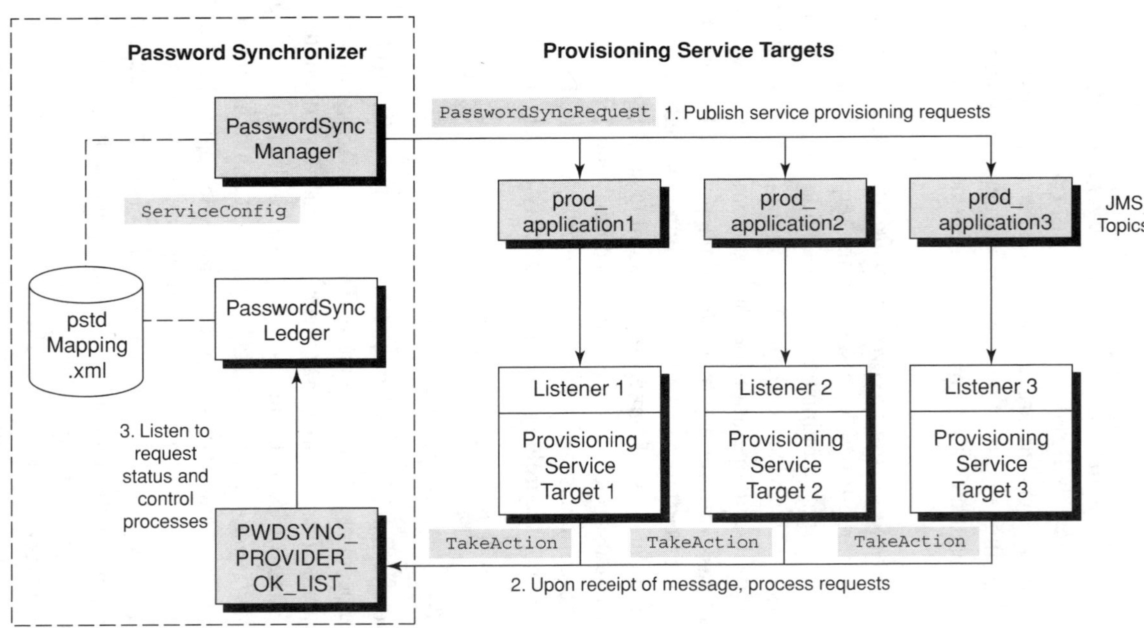

Figure 13–12 Sample code logical architecture

table *pstidMapping.xml* and publishes user password synchronization requests to different JMS topics. It renders the service provisioning request in SPML message format if the provisioning service target supports SOAP, according to the service configuration information defined in the mapping table using the methods defined in the class *ServiceConfig*. Otherwise, it generates a delimited text. *PasswordSyncManager* uses the utility *PasswordSyncRequest* to transform the SOAP message (or the delimited text) to an object and writes to the JMS topic name. Currently, the JMS topic name uses the application resource name of the provisioning service target.

In Step 2, each provisioning service target uses a JMS listener, *PasswordSyncListener. PasswordSyncListener* intercepts any JMS objects published to the associated JMS topic name. Upon receipt, the listener processes the service provisioning requests in the *takeAction* method and notifies the *PasswordSyncLedger* of successfully synchronized requests.

In Step 3, *PasswordSyncLedger* is a Password Synchronization Manager ledger process that listens to a predefined JMS topic (such as PASSWORDSYNC_PROVIDER_OK_LIST). It keeps track of the original list of provisioning service targets (from the mapping table *pstidMapping.xml*). If all passwords are synchronized, then Pass*wordSyncLedger* displays a message stating the completion of the user password synchronization requests.

The core component of the Password Synchronizer is the *PasswordSyncManager.* Example 13–4 shows a program excerpt for *PasswordSyncManager.* It uses a hash table (LinkedHashMap) to store the user password profile. Upon initialization and loading the system configuration, the *PasswordSyncManager* retrieves a list of applications from *pstidMapping.xml* using the class *ServiceConfig*. Then it publishes the user password synchronization requests in either SOAP or delimited text based on the service configuration information.

Example 13–4 Sample PasswordSyncManager

```
package com.csp.provisioning;

import java.util.Date;
import java.util.LinkedHashMap;


public class PasswordSyncManager {

    protected ProvisioningUserProfile userProfile = null;
    protected String protocolBinding;
    protected String topicName;
    protected String fullName;
```

```
protected String firstName;
protected String lastName;
protected String emailAddress;
protected String userId;
protected String password;
protected ServiceConfig serviceConfig;
protected ServiceConfigContext context;
protected LinkedHashMap<String,ServiceConfigContext>
    serviceConfigHashMap = new LinkedHashMap();
protected String timeStamp;


/** Creates a new instance of PasswordSyncManager */
public PasswordSyncManager() {
    setupDefaultUserProfile();
    this.serviceConfig = new ServiceConfig();
    this.serviceConfigHashMap = serviceConfig.getAllConfigContext();
    processPasswordSyncRequests();
}

/**
 * set up default user profile for the password sync requests
 *
 */
private void setupDefaultUserProfile() {
    // set up default user profile
    String fullName = "Mary Jo Parker";
    String firstName = "Mary Jo";
    String lastName = "Parker";
    String userId = "mjparker";
    String emailAddress = "mjparker@namredips.com";
    String password = "secret";
    this.userProfile = new
        ProvisioningUserProfile(fullName, firstName, lastName, userId,
        emailAddress, password);
}

/**
 * process password sync requests
 *
 */
private void processPasswordSyncRequests() {
    this.timeStamp = new Date().toString();
```

```
        for(ServiceConfigContext configContext:
this.serviceConfigHashMap.values()) {
            this.topicName = configContext.getTopicName();
            this.protocolBinding =
configContext.getProtocolBinding();
            System.out.println(this.timeStamp + "- " +
configContext.getApplicationId() +
" is being processed under " + this.topicName + " using " +
this.protocolBinding);
            new PasswordSyncRequest(this.userProfile, this.topicName,
this.protocolBinding);
        }
    }

    public static void main(String args[]) {
        new PasswordSyncManager();
    }
}
```


The service configuration for the Password Synchronizer allows different data transportation protocols to be used. Example 13–5 shows a program excerpt for *ServiceConfig*. The program first retrieves a list of applications from *pstidMapping.xml* using the class *ServiceConfig*. The service configuration is stored in a system properties file and is used to indicate the underlying data transport protocol for the password synchronization service, for example, SOAP or JMS.

Example 13–5 Sample ServiceConfig

```
package com.csp.provisioning;

import java.io.File;
import java.io.IOException;
import java.util.Iterator;
import java.util.LinkedHashMap;
import java.util.List;
import org.apache.commons.logging.Log;
import org.apache.commons.logging.LogFactory;
import org.jdom.Document;
import org.jdom.Element;
import org.jdom.JDOMException;
import org.jdom.input.SAXBuilder;
```

```
public class ServiceConfig {

    protected LinkedHashMap<String,ServiceConfigContext>
        serviceConfigHashMap = new LinkedHashMap();
    protected Document doc = null;
    private static final String configFile =
        "config/pstidMapping.xml";
    protected String requesterId = "passwordSynManagerUser";  // default
        // service requester id for audit log
    protected Log log;

    /** Creates a new instance of ServiceConfig */
    public ServiceConfig() {
        log = LogFactory.getLog(ServiceConfig.class
             .getPackage().getName());
        try {
            if (configFile == null) {
                log.fatal("Invalid Password Synchronizer"
                 + " configuration file name");
            } else {
                SAXBuilder builder = new SAXBuilder(false);
                doc = builder.build(new File(this.getConfigFile()));

                initConfig(doc);
// ensure we can get components config even components not initialized
            }
        } catch (IOException ie) {
            log.fatal("ServiceConfig constructor - cannot"
            + " find file/file not readable");
            ie.printStackTrace();
        } catch (JDOMException je) {
            log.fatal("cannot parse Password Synchronizer"
              + " config file");
            je.printStackTrace();
        }
    }

    /**
     * Get  config file from JVM options
     * if  the file does not exist, use the default one under config/config.xml
     *
     * @return String config file
     */
```

Secure Service Provisioning

```
private String getConfigFile() {
    String localConfigFile = new String();

    localConfigFile = System.getProperty("config.file");
    if (localConfigFile == null) {
        localConfigFile = this.configFile;
        return localConfigFile;
    } else {
        return localConfigFile;
    }
}

/**
 *  Initialize configuration by loading the ulyssesConfig.xml into the
 *  LinkedHashMap
 *  This will include:
 *  1. Load configFile
 *  2. Extract global config
 *  3. Extract private config for each component into UlyssesConfig
 *  4. Store private config info in LinkedHashMap
 *
 *  @param String configFile Ulysses config file
 */
private void initConfig(Document doc) {

    setComponentsConfig(doc);
}

/**
 * Create pstidMapping.xml from LinkedHashMap
 *
 * Assumption - must load pstd mapping file and create LinkedHashMap first
 *
 * @param Document doc
 */
private synchronized void setComponentsConfig(Document doc) {

    String parentElement = "service";
    String applicationIdElement = "applicationId";
    String applicationClassNameElement =
        "applicationClassName";
    String applicationURIElement = "applicationURI";
    String protocolBindingElement = "protocolBinding";
```

```
    String topicNameElement = "topicName";
    int state = com.csp.provisioning.ServiceConfigContext.UNKNOWN_STATE;

    String applicationId = new String();
    String applicationClassName = new String();
    String applicationURI = new String();
    String protocolBinding = new String();
    String topicName = new String();
    //String requesterId = new String();
    String requesterId = this.requesterId;
    ServiceConfigContext context = null;


    Element root = doc.getRootElement();
    List components = root.getChildren(parentElement);
    Iterator i = components.iterator();
    while (i.hasNext()) {
        Element component = (Element)i.next();
        applicationId = component.getChild
            (applicationIdElement).getText();
        applicationClassName = component.getChild
            (applicationClassNameElement).getText();
        applicationURI = component.getChild
            (applicationURIElement).getText();
        protocolBinding = component.getChild
            (protocolBindingElement).getText();
        topicName = component.getChild
            (topicNameElement).getText();

        //System.out.println("topic name = " + topicName);

        context = new ServiceConfigContext(applicationId,
          applicationClassName, applicationURI, protocolBinding, state,
            requesterId, topicName);

        this.serviceConfigHashMap.put(applicationId,
            context);
    }
}

/**
 * Retrieve private config in a list
 *
```

```
     * @param String componentName
     * @return List a list containing the private config of a Ulysses component
     */
    public ServiceConfigContext getContext
      (String applicationId) {
        ServiceConfigContext context;

        if (this.serviceConfigHashMap == null) {
            try {
                if (configFile == null) {
                    log.fatal("Invalid  configuration "
                     + "file name");
                } else {
                    SAXBuilder builder =
                       new SAXBuilder(false);
                    Document doc = builder.build
                       (new File(configFile));
                    initConfig(doc);
// ensure we can get components config even components not initialized
                    //dumpComponentMap();
                    context = this.serviceConfigHashMap.get(applicationId);
                    return context;
                }
            } catch (IOException ie) {
                log.fatal("ServiceConfig constructor - "
                 + " cannot find file/file not readable");
                ie.printStackTrace();
            } catch (JDOMException je) {
                log.fatal("cannot parse  config file");
                je.printStackTrace();
            }
            return null;
        } else {
            context = this.serviceConfigHashMap.get(applicationId);
            return context;
        }
    }

    /**
     * Fetch service config context of all components
     *
     * @return LinkedHashMap serviceConfigHashMap
     *
     **/
```

```
    public LinkedHashMap getAllConfigContext() {
        return this.serviceConfigHashMap;
    }
}
```

The Password Synchronizer pattern uses the SPML addRequest message to create a new user account and synchronize user passwords across application systems. Example 13–6 shows a program excerpt of *PasswordSyncRequest*, which creates a SPML service request. The method *createSPMLRequest* constructs a SOAP message encapsulating the SPML request. It can be modified to add or change user account details.

Example 13–6 PasswordSyncRequest

```
package com.csp.provisioning;

import java.net.URL;
import java.util.Hashtable;
import javax.activation.DataHandler;
import javax.jms.JMSException;
import javax.jms.Message;
import javax.jms.Session;
import javax.jms.TextMessage;
import javax.jms.Topic;
import javax.jms.TopicConnection;
import javax.jms.TopicPublisher;
import javax.jms.TopicSession;
import javax.xml.soap.AttachmentPart;
import javax.xml.soap.MessageFactory;
import javax.xml.soap.Name;
import javax.xml.soap.SOAPBody;
import javax.xml.soap.SOAPBodyElement;
import javax.xml.soap.SOAPElement;
import javax.xml.soap.SOAPEnvelope;
import javax.xml.soap.SOAPHeader;
import javax.xml.soap.SOAPMessage;
import javax.xml.soap.SOAPPart;
import com.sun.messaging.xml.MessageTransformer;
import com.sun.messaging.TopicConnectionFactory;
import com.csp.provisioning.ProvisioningUserProfile;
```

```
public class PasswordSyncRequest {

    protected TopicConnectionFactory
         topicConnectionFactory = null;
    protected TopicConnection          topicConnection
        = null;
    protected TopicSession             topicSession = null;
    protected Topic                    topic = null;
    protected TopicPublisher           topicPublisher
        =  null;
    protected Message                  msg = null;
    protected TextMessage              textMsg = null;

    protected ProvisioningUserProfile userProfile = null;
    protected String protocolBinding;
    protected String topicName;
    protected String fullName;
    protected String firstName;
    protected String lastName;
    protected String emailAddress;
    protected String userId;
    protected String password;

    /** Constructor - Creates a new instance of PasswordSyncRequest
     *  Default constructor to call. This default will use a default user
profile Mary Jo Parker for demo.
     *
     */
    public PasswordSyncRequest() {
        // default values if not specified
        this.protocolBinding = "SOAP";
        this.topicName = "PROD_FINANCIAL_FRONTOFFICE";
        this.fullName = "Mary Jo Parker";
        this.firstName = "Mary Jo";
        this.lastName = "Parker";
        this.userId = "mjparker";
        this.emailAddress = "mjparker@namredips.com";
        this.topicName = "prod_application1";
        this.password = "secret";

        init(topicName);
```

```
        try {
            createSPMLRequest();
            start();
        } catch (Exception ex) {
            ex.printStackTrace();
        }
    }


    /** Constructor - Creates a new instance of PasswordSyncRequest */
    public PasswordSyncRequest(ProvisioningUserProfile userProfile,
        String topicName, String protocolBinding) {

        this.protocolBinding = protocolBinding;
        this.topicName = topicName;

        this.fullName = userProfile.getFullName();
        this.firstName = userProfile.getFirstName();
        this.lastName = userProfile.getLastName();
        this.userId = userProfile.getUserId();
        this.emailAddress = userProfile.getEmailAddress();
        this.password = userProfile.getToken();

        init(this.topicName);

        try {
            createSPMLRequest();
            start();
        } catch (Exception ex) {
            ex.printStackTrace();
        }
    }

    /**
     * Initializes JMS settings
     *
     * @param String topicName JMS topic name
     * @exception JMSException ex    JMSException
     */
    private void init(String topicName) {

        try {
            // Create JMS topic and settings
```

```
        //  Can be replaced by ServiceLocator pattern when available
        topicConnectionFactory =
            new TopicConnectionFactory();
        topicConnection =
       topicConnectionFactory.createTopicConnection();
        topicSession = topicConnection
            .createTopicSession(false, Session.AUTO_ACKNOWLEDGE);
        // topic = null;
        topic = topicSession.createTopic(topicName);
    } catch (JMSException je) {
        je.printStackTrace();
        System.out.println("Cannot create topics "
           + " or topic names");
        System.out.println
         ("Connection problem: " + je.toString());
        if (topicConnection != null) {
            try {
                topicConnection.close();
            } // try
            catch (JMSException moreEx) {
                moreEx.printStackTrace();
            }
        } // catch
        System.exit(1);
    } // catch
} // init()

/**
 * Create SPML add request message in SOAP, and bind to JMS
 *
 *  This example uses SPML 1.0 syntax for illustration
 *
 * @param TopicSession session TopicSession JMS topic session
 * @param Message message Message JMS message
 * @param Hashtable PasswordUserProfile Hashtable user password info for
 * the SPML message
 * @exception JMSException ex Exception JAXM/SAAJ exception
 */
private void createSPMLRequest() throws Exception {

    try {
        // Create a SOAP envelope
        MessageFactory mf =
```

```
        MessageFactory.newInstance();
     SOAPMessage soapMessage = mf.createMessage();
     SOAPPart soapPart = soapMessage.getSOAPPart();
     SOAPEnvelope soapEnvelope =
        soapPart.getEnvelope();
     SOAPHeader soapHeader =
        soapMessage.getSOAPHeader();
     SOAPBody soapBody = soapEnvelope.getBody();

     // create addRequest SPML message
     Name name =
soapEnvelope.createName("addRequest", "spml",
      "http://www.coresecuritypattern.com");
     SOAPElement element =
       soapBody.addChildElement(name);
     SOAPBodyElement addRequest =
       soapBody.addBodyElement(name);
     Name childName =
       soapEnvelope.createName("xmlns");
     addRequest.addAttribute(childName,
       "urn:oasis:names:tc:SPML:1:0");

     childName = soapEnvelope.createName("spml");
     addRequest.addAttribute(childName,
        "urn:oasis:names:tc:DSML:2:0:core");

     // create identifier
     childName =
     soapEnvelope.createName("identifier");
     SOAPElement spmlIdentifier =
     addRequest.addChildElement(childName);
     childName = soapEnvelope.createName("type");
     spmlIdentifier.addAttribute(childName,
        "urn:oasis:names:tc:SPML:1:0#GUID");

     // create user account id
     childName = soapEnvelope.createName("id");
     SOAPElement spmlID =
     spmlIdentifier.addChildElement(childName);
     spmlIdentifier.addTextNode(this.userId);

     // create user account password
     childName =
```

```
 soapEnvelope.createName("attributes");
SOAPElement attributes =
 addRequest.addChildElement(childName);
childName = soapEnvelope.createName("attr", "dsml",
   "http://www.sun.com/imq");

childName = soapEnvelope.createName("name");
SOAPElement attr1 =
attributes.addChildElement(childName);
attributes.addAttribute(childName,
    "objectclass");

childName = soapEnvelope.createName("value");
SOAPElement attrObjclass = attr1.addChildElement(childName);
attrObjclass.addTextNode("user");

childName = soapEnvelope.createName("name");
SOAPElement attr2 =
attributes.addChildElement(childName);
attributes.addAttribute(childName,
"fullname");

childName = soapEnvelope.createName("value");
SOAPElement attrFullname = attr2.addChildElement(childName);
attrFullname.addTextNode(this.fullName);

childName = soapEnvelope.createName("name");
SOAPElement attr3 =
attributes.addChildElement(childName);
attributes.addAttribute(childName, "email");

childName = soapEnvelope.createName("value");
SOAPElement attrEmail = attr3.addChildElement(childName);
attrEmail.addTextNode(this.emailAddress);

childName = soapEnvelope.createName("name");
SOAPElement attr4 =
attributes.addChildElement(childName);
attributes.addAttribute(childName,
"password");

childName = soapEnvelope.createName("value");
SOAPElement attrPassword = attr4.addChildElement(childName);
```

```
            attrPassword.addTextNode(this.password);

            childName = soapEnvelope.createName("name");
            SOAPElement attr5 =
            attributes.addChildElement(childName);
            attributes.addAttribute(childName,
            "lastname");

            childName = soapEnvelope.createName("value");
            SOAPElement attrLastname = attr5.addChildElement(childName);
            attrLastname.addTextNode(this.lastName);

            childName = soapEnvelope.createName("name");
            SOAPElement attr6 =
            attributes.addChildElement(childName);
            attributes.addAttribute(childName, "firstname");

            childName = soapEnvelope.createName("value");
            SOAPElement attrFirstname = attr6.addChildElement(childName);
            attrFirstname.addTextNode(this.firstName);

            // Attach a local file
            URL url = new URL("http://localhost:8080");

            DataHandler dHandler = new DataHandler(url);
            AttachmentPart soapAttach =
            soapMessage.createAttachmentPart(dHandler);

            soapAttach.setContentType("text/html");
            soapAttach.setContentId("cid-001");

            //soapMessage.addAttachmentPart(soapAttach);
            soapMessage.saveChanges();

            // Convert SOAP message to JMS
            this.msg =
                MessageTransformer.SOAPMessageIntoJMSMessage(soapMessage,
                this.topicSession);
        } // try
        catch (Exception ex) {
            ex.printStackTrace();
            System.out.println("Exception occurred: " + ex.toString());
        } // catch
    }
```

```
/**
 * Create a string in plain text to encapsulate password sync request
 *
 * @return String a string that concatenates userId, fullName,
 * emailAddress, password, lastName, firstName
 */
private String createPasswordRequest() {

    String PasswordRequest = null;

    PasswordRequest = this.userId + ":" + this.fullName + ":" +
        this.emailAddress + ":" + this.password + ":" + this.lastName +
        ":" + this.firstName;
    return PasswordRequest;
}

/**
 * Start processing SPML message, given the JMS topic name,
 *    and the SPML user password info
 * It is intended that the start() will start and close JMS connection.
 * For better efficiency, create a batch loop to process multiple requests.
 *
 * @param String topicName String JMS topic name
 * @param Message message   Message JMS message content
 * @param Hashtable PasswordUserProfile Hashtable user password info for
 * the SPML message
 * @param String protocol
 */
private void start() {

    String PasswordRequestText = null;

    try {
        topicPublisher = this.topicSession.createPublisher(topic);

        if (this.protocolBinding.equals("SOAP")) {
            try {
                createSPMLRequest();
                this.topicPublisher.publish(this.msg);
            } catch (Exception ex) {
    System.out.println("Cannot create SOAP message");
    System.out.println("Message creation error: "
                                    + ex.toString());
```

```
    System.exit(1);
             } // catch
   } else if (this.protocolBinding.equals("JMS")) {
  this.textMsg = this.topicSession.createTextMessage();
             PasswordRequestText =
             createPasswordRequest();
             this.textMsg.setText(PasswordRequestText);
             this.topicPublisher.publish(textMsg);
         } else {
             System.out.println("Request protocol "
       + this.protocolBinding + " is not supported");
             System.exit(1);
         } // if protocol

     } // try
     catch (JMSException je) {
         je.printStackTrace();
         System.out.println("Cannot publish
                                SOAP message");
         System.out.println("Exception occurred: "
                                + je.toString());
     } finally {
         if (topicConnection != null) {
             try {
                 topicConnection.close();
             } // try topicConnection
             catch (JMSException jex) {
                 jex.printStackTrace();
   System.out.println("Cannot close topicConnection");
   System.out.println("Connection problem: "
                                + jex.toString());
             } // catch
         } // if topicConnection
     } // finally
 } // try

 /**
  * set protocol binding for the service request
  *
  * @param String protocolBinding
  */
 public void setProtocolBinding(String protocolBinding) {
     this.protocolBinding = protocolBinding;
 }
}
```

Using the JMS infrastructure, a small footprint listener program is required for each Provisioning Service Target to intercept the user password synchronization request. Example 13–7 shows a program excerpt of *PasswordSyncListener. PasswordSyncListener* listens to the predefined JMS topic. Once the password synchronization request is received, the listener processes the service request and notifies the *PasswordSyncLedger* when the service request is complete (or fails).

Example 13–7 Sample PasswordSyncListener

```
package com.csp.provisioning;

import java.io.IOException;
import java.io.InputStreamReader;
import javax.jms.JMSException;
import javax.jms.TopicConnection;
import javax.jms.TopicSession;
import javax.jms.Message;
import javax.jms.Session;
import javax.jms.TextMessage;
import javax.jms.Topic;
import javax.jms.TopicSubscriber;
import javax.xml.soap.MessageFactory;
import com.sun.messaging.TopicConnectionFactory;
import com.sun.messaging.xml.MessageTransformer;
import java.util.Date;
import java.util.Iterator;
import java.util.LinkedHashMap;
import javax.xml.soap.AttachmentPart;
import javax.xml.soap.Name;
import javax.xml.soap.Node;
import javax.xml.soap.SOAPBody;
import javax.xml.soap.SOAPElement;
import javax.xml.soap.SOAPFactory;
import javax.xml.soap.SOAPHeader;
import javax.xml.soap.SOAPHeaderElement;
import javax.xml.soap.SOAPMessage;
import javax.xml.soap.Text;


public class PasswordSyncListener implements javax.jms.MessageListener {

    protected TopicConnectionFactory
       topicConnectionFactory = null;
    protected TopicConnection
                    topicConnection = null;
```

```
    protected TopicSession
                    topicSession = null;
    protected Topic
                     topic = null;
    protected TopicSubscriber
                 topicSubscriber = null;
    protected TextMessage
                      message = null;
    protected InputStreamReader
                inputStreamReader = null;
    protected String
            topicName = "prod_application1";
    protected String
       notifyTopicName = "PASSWORDSYNC_PROVIDER_OK_LIST";
    protected MessageFactory
                    messageFactory = null;
    protected String timeStamp;
    protected ServiceConfig serviceConfig;
    protected ServiceConfigContext context;
    protected LinkedHashMap<String,ServiceConfigContext>
        serviceConfigHashMap = new LinkedHashMap();

    /**
     * Constructor - create new instance of Password Synchronizer listener
     * This is a default constructor if no param is given at run-time
     */
    public PasswordSyncListener() {
        serviceConfig = new ServiceConfig();
        serviceConfigHashMap =
           serviceConfig.getAllConfigContext();

        System.out.println("PasswordSyncListener - processing password
synchronization requests  from JMS topic '" + this.topicName + "'");
        System.out.println("Note - completed request will be notified under
the JMS topic '" + this.notifyTopicName + "'");
        init();  // initialize environment
        snoop(); // listen for SPML requests

    }

    /**
     * Constructor - create new instance of Password Synchronizer listener
     */
```

```
    public PasswordSyncListener(String newTopicName, String
newNotifyTopicName) {
        serviceConfig = new ServiceConfig();
        serviceConfigHashMap =
           serviceConfig.getAllConfigContext();

        this.topicName = newTopicName;
        this.notifyTopicName = newNotifyTopicName;
        System.out.println("PasswordSyncListener - processing password
synchronization requests from JMS topic '" + this.topicName + "'");
        System.out.println("Note - completed request will be notified under
the JMS topic '" + this.notifyTopicName + "'");
        init();
        snoop();
    }

  /*
   * Initializes the JMS settings
   * @exception ex  Exception
   */
    public void init() {

        // for future enhancement,
        // use serviceLocator pattern here
        try {
            this.messageFactory =
               MessageFactory.newInstance();
            this.topicConnectionFactory
                = new com.sun.messaging.TopicConnectionFactory();
            this.topicConnection
                = this.topicConnectionFactory.createTopicConnection();
            this.topicSession
                = this.topicConnection.createTopicSession(false,
            Session.AUTO_ACKNOWLEDGE);
            this.topic
                = this.topicSession.createTopic(this.topicName);
        } // try
        catch (Exception ex) {
            ex.printStackTrace();
            System.out.println("Cannot create
                               topics or topic names");
            System.out.println("Connection problem: "
                                   + ex.toString());
```

```
            if (topicConnection != null) {
                try {
                    topicConnection.close();
                } catch (JMSException moreEx) {
                    moreEx.printStackTrace();
                }
            } // if topicConnection
            System.exit(1);
        } // catch
    } // init()

  /*
   * Displays SOAP header
   * @param header SOAP header
   * @exception ex Exception
   */
    private void dumpHeaderContents(SOAPHeader header) {

        try {
            Iterator allHeaders
                = header.examineAllHeaderElements();

            while (allHeaders.hasNext()) {
                SOAPHeaderElement headerElement =
                        (SOAPHeaderElement)
                         allHeaders.next();
                Name headerName =
                   headerElement.getElementName();
                System.out.print("<" +
                     headerName.getQualifiedName() + ">");
                System.out.print("actor='"
                + headerElement.getActor() + "' ");
                System.out.print("mustUnderstand='" +
               headerElement.getMustUnderstand() + "' ");
                System.out.println("</" +
                 headerName.getQualifiedName() + ">");
            } // while addHeaders.hasNext
        } catch (Exception ex) {
            ex.printStackTrace();
        } // catch
    } // dumpHeaderContents
```

```
/*
 * Retrieves SOAP message contents, and displays
 *   in indented XML format
 *
 * @param iterator   Iterator for the SOAP message node
 * @param indent     indent space for displaying
 *  XML messages on screen
 */
  private void getContents(Iterator iterator,
      String indent) {

      while (iterator.hasNext()) {
          Node node = (Node) iterator.next();
          SOAPElement element = null;
          Text text = null;
          if (node instanceof SOAPElement) {
              element = (SOAPElement)node;
              Name name = element.getElementName();
              System.out.print(indent + "<" + name.getQualifiedName());
              Iterator attrs =
                  element.getAllAttributes();
              while (attrs.hasNext()){
                  Name attrName = (Name)attrs.next();
                  System.out.print(" "
                    + attrName.getQualifiedName() + "='" +
                    element.getAttributeValue(attrName) + "'");
              } // while attrs.hasNext
              System.out.println(">");

              Iterator iter2
                = element.getChildElements();
              getContents(iter2, indent + " ");
              System.out.println(indent + "</"
                   + name.getQualifiedName() + ">");
          } // if node instanceof
          else {
              text = (Text) node;
              String content = text.getValue();
              System.out.println(indent + " "
                   + content);
          } // else
      } // while
  } // getContents
```

```
 /*
  * Processes each JMS message when received
  * from the JMS topic
  * @param message   JMS message in SOAP format
  * @exception ex    Exception
  */
    public void onMessage(Message message) {

        try {
            this.timeStamp = new Date().toString();
            MessageFactory messageFactory =
                 MessageFactory.newInstance();

            // Should invoke other Web services messages
            //  to unmarshall encrypted SOAP messages,

            SOAPMessage soapMessage =
                    MessageTransformer
.SOAPMessageFromJMSMessage( message, messageFactory );
            System.out.println(timeStamp + "- Message received! Converting
the JMS message to SOAP message...");

            SOAPFactory soapFactory =
               SOAPFactory.newInstance();
            SOAPHeader thisSoapHeader =
               soapMessage.getSOAPHeader();
            dumpHeaderContents(thisSoapHeader);

            SOAPBody thisSoapBody =
                soapMessage.getSOAPBody();
            Iterator soapContent =
                thisSoapBody.getChildElements();

            System.out.println();
            System.out.println(timeStamp + "- Rendering SOAP Message
Content");
            getContents(soapContent, "");

            System.out.println("Attachment counts: " +
soapMessage.countAttachments());
            Iterator iterator =
               soapMessage.getAttachments();
            while ( iterator.hasNext() ) {
```

```
                AttachmentPart soapAttach =
                 (AttachmentPart) iterator.next();
                String contentType =
                  soapAttach.getContentType();
                String contentId = soapAttach.getContentId();

                if ( contentType.indexOf("text") >=0 ) {
                    String content = (String)
                           soapAttach.getContent();
                } // if contentType
            } // while

            // take action to notify Password Synchroniza
//tion Manager about OK status
            TakeAction action = new TakeAction();
            action.init(notifyTopicName);
            String tempTopicName =
                findApplicationId(topicName);

            if (tempTopicName != null) {
                action
.publishPasswordSyncResult(tempTopicName, "SOAP");
            } else {
              System.out.println("ERROR - Mismatch between applicationId and
topicName. Please check pstidMapping.xml");
            }


        } // try
        catch (Exception ex) {
            try {
                TextMessage textMessage = (TextMessage) message;
                String text = textMessage.getText();
                System.out.println(timeStamp + "- Password sync request in
delimited text: " + text);
                // take action to notify Password Synchronization Manager
about OK status
                TakeAction action = new TakeAction();
                action.init(notifyTopicName);
                String tempTopicName =
                   findApplicationId(topicName);

                if (tempTopicName != null) {
```

```
                    action.publishPasswordSyncResult(tempTopicName, "JMS");
                } else {
 System.out.println("ERROR - Mismatch between
     applicationId and topicName.
            Please check pstidMapping.xml");
                }


            } catch (Exception anotherEx) {
                anotherEx.printStackTrace();
            }
        } // catch
    }

/*
 * Starts listening to the JMS topic
 * @exception ex  JMSException
 */
   private void snoop() {

        char           answer = '\0';
        final boolean  NOLOCAL = true;

        try {
            topicSubscriber =
               topicSession.createSubscriber(topic,
                                   null, NOLOCAL);
            topicSession.createSubscriber(topic);


            topicSubscriber.setMessageListener(this);
            topicConnection.start();

            System.out.println("Command Option :
                     Q=quit, then <return>");
            System.out.println();
            inputStreamReader = new
               InputStreamReader(System.in);
            while (!((answer == 'q') || (answer == 'Q'))) {
                try {
                    answer = (char)
                      inputStreamReader.read();
                } catch (IOException e) {
```

```
                System.out.println("I/O exception: "
                        + e.toString());
            } // catch
        } // while !answer

    } // try
    catch (JMSException ex) {
        System.out.println("Cannot
                        subscribe message");
        System.out.println("Exception occurred: "
                        + ex.toString());
        System.exit(1);
    } finally {
        if (topicConnection != null) {
            try {
                topicConnection.close();
            } catch (JMSException ex) {
                System.out.println("Cannot
                      close topicConnection");
                System.out.println("Connection
                       problem: " + ex.toString());
                System.out.println.exit(1);
            }
        }  // if topicConnection
    }// finally
}

/**
 * Helper class to look up the applicationId
 * when given a topicName
 *
 * @param String targetTopicName
 * @return String applicationId
 */
private String findApplicationId(String
    targetTopicName) {

    for(ServiceConfigContext configContext:
this.serviceConfigHashMap.values()) {
        if (configContext.getTopicName()
.equals(targetTopicName)) {
            return configContext.getApplicationId();
        }
    }
```

```
            return null;
        }

        public static void main(String[] args) {

            String newTopicName = new String();
            String newNotifyTopicName = new String();

            // Command syntax helper
            if (args.length != 2) {
                // take default topic name and notify topic
                //name if no param is given at runtime
                new PasswordSyncListener();
            } else {
                newTopicName = args[0];
                newNotifyTopicName = args[1];
                new PasswordSyncListener(newTopicName,
                  newNotifyTopicName);
            }

        } // public main
    }
```


The listener (PasswordSyncListener) of each Provisioning Service Target uses a class called *TakeAction* to implement how the Provisioning Service Target should handle the user password synchronization request. This may include resetting the user password and notifying the service requester when completed. Example 13–8 shows an implementation of a simple notification action. The class *TakeAction* can be expanded and modified to include additional processes in the future.

Example 13–8 Sample TakeAction

```
package com.csp.provisioning;

import javax.jms.JMSException;
import javax.jms.Session;
import javax.jms.TextMessage;
import javax.jms.Topic;
import javax.jms.TopicConnection;
import javax.jms.TopicConnectionFactory;
import javax.jms.TopicPublisher;
import javax.jms.TopicSession;
```

```
public class TakeAction {
    protected TopicConnectionFactory  topicConnectionFactory = null;
    protected TopicConnection         topicConnection = null;
    protected TopicSession            topicSession = null;
    protected Topic                   topic = null;
    protected String                  topicName = null;


    /** Constructor - Creates a new instance of TakeAction */
    public TakeAction() {
    }

    /*
     * Set up the JMS topic connection
     *
     * @param String topicName String JMS topic name
     * @exception Exception ex
     */
    public  void init(String topicName) {

        try {
            this.topicConnectionFactory =
                new com.sun.messaging.TopicConnectionFactory();
            this.topicConnection =
                this.topicConnectionFactory.createTopicConnection();
            this.topicSession =
                this.topicConnection.createTopicSession(false,
                        Session.AUTO_ACKNOWLEDGE);
            this.topic = this.topicSession.createTopic(topicName);

        } // try
        catch (Exception ex) {
            ex.printStackTrace();
            System.out.println("Cannot create topics or
                               topic names");
            System.out.println("Connection problem: "
                            + ex.toString());
            if (this.topicConnection != null) {
                try {
                    this.topicConnection.close();
                } catch (JMSException moreEx) {
                    moreEx.printStackTrace();
                }
```

```
                System.exit(1);
            } // if topicConnection
        } // catch
    }  // init

   /*
    * Publish successfully completed application
    *    list to a pre-defined topic.
    *    The structure of the message is simply <application>
    *
    * @param String application application name where
    * password is synch
    * @param String protocol either SOAP or JMS
    * @exception JMSException ex
    */
    public void publishPasswordSyncResult(String application, String
       protocol) {

        TextMessage    sentMessage = null;
        TopicPublisher topicPublisher =  null;

        try {
            topicPublisher = this.topicSession.createPublisher(topic);
            sentMessage = this.topicSession.createTextMessage();
            sentMessage.setText(application);
            topicPublisher.publish(sentMessage);
        } // try
        catch (JMSException jmsex) {
            jmsex.printStackTrace();
            System.out.println("Cannot publish SOAP message");
            System.out.println("Exception occurred: " + jmsex.toString());
        } // catch
        finally {
            if (topicConnection != null) {
                try {
                    this.topicConnection.close();
                } catch (JMSException jmsex) {
                    jmsex.printStackTrace();
                    System.out.println("Cannot close topicConnection");
                    System.out.println("Connection problem: " +
jmsex.toString());
                } // catch
            } // if topicConnection
```

```
        } // finally
    }
}
```

A ledger (*PasswordSyncLedger*) is required to track the status of user password synchronization requests. Example 13–9 shows a program excerpt of using Java Message Service to implement the ledger.

Example 13–9 Sample PasswordSyncLedger

```
package com.csp.provisioning;

import java.io.IOException;
import java.io.InputStreamReader;
import java.util.LinkedHashMap;
import javax.jms.JMSException;
import javax.jms.MessageListener;
import javax.jms.TopicConnection;
import javax.jms.TopicSession;
import javax.jms.Message;
import javax.jms.Session;
import javax.jms.TextMessage;
import javax.jms.Topic;
import javax.jms.TopicSubscriber;
import javax.xml.soap.MessageFactory;
import com.sun.messaging.TopicConnectionFactory;
import java.util.Date;

public class PasswordSyncLedger implements MessageListener {

    protected TopicConnectionFactory  topicConnectionFactory;
    protected TopicConnection         topicConnection;
    protected TopicSession            topicSession;
    protected Topic                   topic;
    protected TopicSubscriber         topicSubscriber;
    protected TextMessage             inMessage;
    protected TextMessage             message;
    protected Message                 receivedMessage;
    protected InputStreamReader       inputStreamReader;
    protected String                  topicName;
    protected char                    answer = '\0';
    protected final boolean           NOLOCAL = true;
    protected ServiceConfig serviceConfig;
    protected ServiceConfigContext context;
```

```
protected LinkedHashMap<String,ServiceConfigContext>
    serviceConfigHashMap = new LinkedHashMap();
protected MessageFactory messageFactory = null;
protected String timeStamp;


/** Creates a new instance of PasswordSyncLedger */
public PasswordSyncLedger()  {
    // set default topic name
    this.topicName = "PASSWORDSYNC_PROVIDER_OK_LIST";

    // load Password Synchronizer config file
    serviceConfig = new ServiceConfig();
    serviceConfigHashMap =
        serviceConfig.getAllConfigContext();

    System.out.println("Password Synchronizer Ledger starts.");

    // set up JMS connection factory
    init(this.topicName);
    start();
}


/* Set up JMS topic connection, and
 *    initialize the JMS set-up
 *
 * @exception ex Exception
 */
public void init(String topicName) {

    try {
        this.topicConnectionFactory =
            new com.sun.messaging.TopicConnectionFactory();
        this.topicConnection =
            this.topicConnectionFactory.createTopicConnection();
        this.topicSession =
           this.topicConnection.createTopicSession(false,
            Session.AUTO_ACKNOWLEDGE);
        this.topic = this.topicSession.createTopic(topicName);

        messageFactory = MessageFactory.newInstance();
```

```
        } // try
        catch (Exception ex) {
            ex.printStackTrace();
            System.out.println("Cannot create topics or topic names");
            System.out.println("Connection problem: " + ex.toString());
            if (topicConnection != null) {
                try {
                    topicConnection.close();
                } catch (JMSException moreEx) {
                    //
                } // catch
            } // if topicConnection
            System.exit(1);
        } // catch
    }

   /*
    * Process each message received
    *    from the listener.
    *
    * @exception ex JMSException
    */
    public void onMessage(Message message) {

        int foundAny = -1;

        try {
            TextMessage textMessage = (TextMessage) message;
            String syncResult = textMessage.getText();

            // assume the application is synchronized
            this.timeStamp = new Date().toString();
            System.out.println(this.timeStamp + "- just complete password
synchronization for '" + syncResult + "'");

            if
(this.serviceConfig.getContext(syncResult).getApplicationId().equals
(syncResult)) {

                // set state to SYNC_STATE
               this.serviceConfig.getContext(syncResult).setState
(ServiceConfigContext.SYNC_STATE);
```

```
                viewResult();
            }

        } // try
        catch (JMSException jmsex) {
            jmsex.printStackTrace();
        }  // catch
    }

   /*
    * Start listening to the topic (passed in args[0])
    *    under a loop. It will only stop when users press Q
    *
    * @exception ex JMSException
    */
    public void start() {

        try {
          topicSubscriber = this.topicSession.createSubscriber(topic, null,
NOLOCAL);
           this.topicSession.createSubscriber(this.topic);

           this.topicSubscriber.setMessageListener(this);
           this.topicConnection.start();

           System.out.println("Command Option : Q=quit, then <return>");
           inputStreamReader = new
             InputStreamReader(System.in);
           while (!((answer == 'q') || (answer == 'Q'))) {
               try {
                   answer = (char) inputStreamReader.read();
               } catch (IOException e) {
                   e.printStackTrace();
                   System.out.println("I/O exception: " + e.toString());
               } // catch
           } // while
        } // try
        catch (JMSException ex) {
           ex.printStackTrace();
           System.out.println("Cannot subscribe message");
           System.out.println("Exception occurred: " + ex.toString());
        } finally {
           if (topicConnection != null) {
```

```
                try {
                    topicConnection.close();
                } catch (JMSException ex) {
                    ex.printStackTrace();
                    System.out.println("Cannot close topicConnection");
                    System.out.println("Connection problem: " +
ex.toString());
                } // catch
            }  // if topicConnection
        }// finally
    }

    /**
     * verify whether all provisioning target systems are synchronized
     */
    private void viewResult() {
        int totalSync = 0;

        for(ServiceConfigContext configContext:
this.serviceConfigHashMap.values()) {
            if (configContext.getState() != (configContext.SYNC_STATE)) {
               totalSync++;
            }
        }

        this.timeStamp = new Date().toString();
        if (totalSync == 0) {
            System.out.println(this.timeStamp + "- Notification - all
passwords are synchronized in all systems.");
            System.out.println("Password Synchronizer Ledger is stopped.");
            System.exit(0);
        }
        else {
            System.out.println(this.timeStamp + "- " + totalSync + "
applications need to be synchronized.");
        }
    }


    public static void main(String args[]) {
        new PasswordSyncLedger();
    }
}
```

Example 13–10 shows the screen display messages when invoking *PasswordSyncManager*. The system properties file specifies there are four password synchronization requests. There are three Java Message Service topics (prod_application1, prod_application2, prod_application3 and prod_application4) defined.

Example 13–10 Screen display message from PasswordSyncManager

```
circinus:~/work> java -cp ./PasswordSync_Lib.jar;./PasswordSync.jar com.
csp.provisioning.PasswordSyncManager

Password synchronization requests start.
Thu Jun 02 07:54:07 PDT 2005- application1 is being processed under
prod_application1 using SOAP
Thu Jun 02 07:54:07 PDT 2005- application2 is being processed under
prod_application2 using SOAP
Thu Jun 02 07:54:07 PDT 2005- application3 is being processed under
prod_application3 using JMS
Thu Jun 02 07:54:07 PDT 2005- application4 is being processed under
prod_application4 using JMS
Password synchronization requests completed.
```

Example 13–11 shows the screen display messages from a local instance of *PasswordSyncListener*. In this example, *PasswordSyncListener* subscribes to the Java Message Service topic "prod_application1," which corresponds to a specific Provisioning Service Target. Upon receipt of the SPML service request, *PasswordSyncListener* will display the content of the SOAP message on the screen.

Example 13–11 Screen display messages from PasswordSyncListener

```
circinus:~/work> java -cp ./PasswordSync_Lib.jar;./PasswordSync.jar com.
csp.provisioning.PasswordSyncListener prod_application1
PASSWORDSYNC_PROVIDER_OK_LIST

PasswordSyncListener - processing password synchronization requests from JMS
topic 'prod_application1'
Note - completed request will be notified under the JMS topic
'PASSWORDSYNC_PROVIDER_OK_LIST'
Command Option : Q=quit, then <return>

Thu Jun 02 07:51:18 PDT 2005- Message received! Converting the JMS message to
SOAP message...

Thu Jun 02 07:51:18 PDT 2005- Rendering SOAP Message Content
<spml:addRequest>
```

```
</spml:addRequest>
<spml:addRequest spml='urn:oasis:names:tc:DSML:2:0:core'
xmlns='urn:oasis:names:
tc:SPML:1:0'>
 <identifier type='urn:oasis:names:tc:SPML:1:0#GUID'>
  <id>
  </id>
   mjparker
 </identifier>
 <attributes name='firstname'>
  <name>
…
  </spml:addRequest>
Attachment counts: 1
```


Example 13–12 shows the notification messages from *PasswordSyncLedger*. This sample program excerpt acts as a console that shows the total number of Provisioning Service Targets whose passwords have been synchronized.

Example 13–12 Notification messages from PasswordSyncLedger

```
circinus:~/work> java -cp ./PasswordSync_Lib.jar;./PasswordSync.jar com.
csp.provisioning.PasswordSyncLedger

Password Synchronizer Ledger starts.
Command Option : Q=quit, then <return>
Thu Jun 02 07:51:19 PDT 2005- just complete password synchronization for
'application1'
Thu Jun 02 07:51:19 PDT 2005- 3 applications need to be synchronized.
Thu Jun 02 07:51:23 PDT 2005- just complete password synchronization for
'application2'
Thu Jun 02 07:51:23 PDT 2005- 2 applications need to be synchronized.
Thu Jun 02 07:51:25 PDT 2005- just complete password synchronization for
'application3'
Thu Jun 02 07:51:25 PDT 2005- 1 application needs to be synchronized.
Thu Jun 02 07:51:27 PDT 2005- just complete password synchronization for
'application4'
Thu Jun 02 07:51:27 PDT 2005- Notification - all passwords are synchronized
in all systems.
Password Synchronizer Ledger is stopped.
```

Security Factors and Risks

- **Infrastructure of the provisioning server (or the Password Synchronizer Manager)**. If the provisioning server or the Password Synchronizer Manager resides outside the demilitarized zone (DMZ), there is a higher risk of being attacked by unauthorized public intruders or internal hackers. Access to sensitive back-end processes such as password management and synchronization processing is more restrictive in the management LAN or behind the DMZ.
- **Infrastructure of provisioning service targets**. Interfacing with external provisioning service targets may impose high security risks depending on whether there is a strong trust relationship between the provisioning server and the provisioning service targets. Direct interface between external hosts and the provisioning server, if residing behind the DMZ or in the management LAN, is highly risky, because it opens itself to host scanning and unauthorized footprinting. A direct programmatic interface can also expose host information or infrastructure details to potential hackers or intruders via host scanning. To mitigate the risks, security architects can allow only the delegated administration function (the Password Synchronizer Manager), upon successful authentication and authorization, to initiate user account password service requests. The Password Synchronizer Manager should disallow any application system (service target) to initiate user account password service requests.
- **Client device interface**. If the client device (for example, user password token, mobile personal digital organizer, and so forth) is compromised, intruders or hackers may be able to exploit the current client device interface to access the provisioning server or the Password Synchronizer Manager. Security architects may review and assess the strength of a client device when securing the user account password—that is, how the client device stores the user credentials and initiates the interface to connect to the provisioning server (or the Password Synchronizer Manager).
- **Logging**. The log files for user account provisioning or user account password synchronization may contain sensitive user account information, which may be a target for host scanning or hacking. Security architects may want to segregate the provisioning event log from the normal system log and ensure the log files are only accessible to the administrative user account (for example, file attribute 700 on UNIX), or store the log events in a database or directory server (which has additional security protection of the logging data). The Secure Logger pattern would be useful in this

context. These security measures can reduce the risk of unauthorized access and potential security intrusion.

- **Processing logic of user account password changes**. The processing logic of creating or changing a user account password is usually customized in local provisioning service targets. This is typically implemented by reusing existing APIs or the delegated administration interface. The security interface to initiating a user account password change may incur security risks. Security architects need to understand the legacy security integration requirements, such as how the underlying interface connects to the application system and how the service requester is authenticated. It is possible that the provisioning service target exposes an API to handle the processing logic of creating or changing a user account password, but it does not authenticate the service requester. In such a case, security architects need to provide a custom authentication module that can mitigate the security risk of a legacy security environment. This is usually done on a case-by-case basis, and it is difficult to prescribe a specific security protection mechanism.
- **Integration with legacy environment**. Password Synchronizer (or the provisioning server) may have requirements for integrating with a legacy operating environment. These may include propagating security credentials in order to access systems in the legacy operating environment. The existing legacy operating environment may not have sophisticated or sufficient security protection. For example, it may not encrypt the data communication channel with external trading partners. Thus, the legacy operating environment will become a hacking target and will be exploited. Security architects may need to harden the legacy operating environment and allow only specific actions that can be performed by the Password Synchronizer (or provisioning server).
- **Protection for SOAP messaging**. If the programmatic interface for synchronizing user account passwords uses SOAP messaging, security architects may want to ensure that the SOAP message containing the user account password request is securely protected with a digital signature or encryption. XML encryption and XML digital signature would be essential to secure the SOAP messages.
- **Identity management strategy**. A sufficiently secure connection mechanism between the Password Synchronizer server (or the provisioning server) and the provisioning service targets is imperative. The trust relationship established determines whether the provisioning service target

(application system) should accept the user account password service requests from the service requester. An insufficient authentication or authorization mechanism between the server and the provisioning service targets may expose a high security risk of unauthorized access. Security architects may adopt an identity management strategy that authenticates the service requester with an identity provider (as discussed in Chapters 7 and 12) that uses a stronger authentication mechanism for user credentials. This can mitigate the security risks associated with user account provisioning services.

- **Single Sign-on and Sign-out**. If security architects use a Point-to-Point synchronous communication to connect the Password Synchronizer server to the provisioning service targets while synchronizing user account passwords, the Password Synchronizer will need to perform a sign-on and maintain a secure session with each system. In such a case, a single sign-on and single sign-out process control is essential. Security architects would need to consider any potential security risks that might allow the session information to be tampered with, or any hanging session that can be exploited. The Single Sign-on Delegator pattern discussed in Chapter 12 will be useful then. On the other hand, if the Password Synchronizer is implemented using asynchronous messaging, there is no need to sign on the provisioning service targets and maintain session information.

Reality Check

Should you build Password Synchronizer code from scratch? A few service provisioning vendor products (including OpenSPML initiatives) have an out-of-the-box service provisioning capability. These products provide some basic service provisioning application infrastructure such as error handling and logging. It may not be practical to build the password synchronization functionality from scratch.

Related Patterns

There are other design patterns that are related to the Password Synchronizer pattern. These include:

Single Sign-on Delegator. Single Sign-on Delegator provides a delegate design approach to connecting to remote security service providers. Using Password Synchronizer with Single Sign-on Delegator, architects and developers do not need to sign on to each provisioning service target individually in order to initiate user account password service requests.

Business Delegate. Business Delegate [CJP2] is a Business tier J2EE pattern that encapsulates access to a remote business service. Password Synchronizer shares some similarities with Business Delegate in encapsulating the complexity of invoking remote business services, but the former is specialized in dealing with user account password service requests using standards-based programmatic interfaces.

Best Practices and Pitfalls

This section discusses best practices and pitfalls that are related to implementing quality security service provisioning systems. Best practices for service provisioning include having a robust application design, achieving quality of services (such as reliability, availability, and scalability), having an appropriate server sizing, putting the right planning and management in place, and mitigating known security risks and threats.

Application Design

1. Adopt a lightweight provisioning solution architecture that avoids heavy data replication from the data store (maintained by the provisioning service targets) to the provisioning system (or Password Synchronizer). A database-centric replication architecture usually brings a relatively large data store overhead and potential data synchronization issues.
2. Cater to rule-based workflow requirements. Rule-based workflow is very useful for handling security service provisioning, including user account password synchronization. It is helpful to provide scripting support (for example, calling a UNIX shell script) to define rule-based work flow. Some software products may have a visual rule-based workflow user interface and drag-and-drop features for defining the work flow sequence.
3. Use standards-based integration protocols (such as JDBC, servlet, JNDI, or SMTP) for accessing resources. Avoid using proprietary application protocols.

Quality of Service

Quality of service refers to the service attributes of how reliable, available, and scalable a system is. This section discusses options that support reliability, availability, and scalability when implementing security service provisioning.

4. *Use persistent mode for processing service provisioning requests.* It increases reliability to persist service provisioning requests using an intermediary so that the service requests can be reprocessed after any server restart or service recovery. For example, service provisioning requests can be written to JMS in persistent mode for better reliability during message delivery or routing.
5. *Add availability options.* Service availability is essential for service provisioning functionality such as user password reset or password synchronization. Clustering the service provisioning server and enabling session failover for the service provisioning application in the application server provides high availability practices.
6. *Add scalability options.* When the volume of service provisioning requests or user password synchronization requests increases drastically, scalability becomes a concern. A simple rule of thumb for scaling up service provisioning servers is to deploy three instances of the service provisioning servers with a load balancer (sometimes known as "the rule of three"). When one service provisioning server is down, the other two servers are load balanced and are still in service.
7. *Use open standards for interoperability.* Interoperability between the service provisioning server and the back-end systems is important. Proprietary middleware or vendor-specific connector technology often requires a system rewrite or upgrade when the underlying operating system or product is upgraded or becomes obsolete. Thus, the use of open standards (such as SPML) or J2EE technology (such as JMS) is a key to interoperability between J2EE-based implementations.
8. *Define quality of service.* The quality of service (such as system response time) for the security service provisioning system depends on the system response time of the Provisioning Service Targets. It is fairly difficult to define the quality of service (such as a five-second response time) for the security service provisioning system if some of the depending Provisioning Service Targets have unpredictable system response times (such as if one has three seconds, but another has seven seconds). Thus, security architects and administrators may want to customize what key attributes (such as availability) are appropriate for the quality of service measurement.
9. *Customize your support strategy.* Traditional system support for an IT solution often requires that IT support staff only know the product details, because the software systems have been self-contained and do not usually have many external interfaces. Service provisioning solutions have multi-

ple external interfaces to a variety of back-end systems. The root cause of a service incident may span different back-end systems, which may make troubleshooting and diagnosis very complex. The IT support personnel need to be familiar with the dependency of the external interfaces for further escalation if necessary. Thus, security architects and administrators need to define and adopt a flexible support strategy that can accommodate the complexity of cross-product troubleshooting and the escalation procedures.

Server Sizing Consideration

Inappropriate server and application sizing can create considerable impact on the system performance. This is particularly critical when the service provisioning system stores all user profiles and the service configuration for a large number of Provisioning Service Targets. The following tips may be helpful:

10. Start with a small server sizing estimate. The nature of processing service provisioning requests does not require a heavyweight infrastructure. Thus, a service provisioning server does not usually require a high-end or heavy-duty server (four CPUs with 10 GB of memory). The server sizing can be estimated in the same way the size of an entry-level Directory Server (a single CPU with at least 2GB of memory) is estimated. Security architects and administrators need to consider additional storage and memory requirements (for example, LDAP calls to retrieve user credentials or to update user passwords), depending on the number of user accounts to be processed and the audit log requirements. For example, a storage requirement totaling seven years is fairly common for many companies for auditing or compliance reasons. The Sarbanes-Oxley Act (refer to [SOX1] for details) requires complex auditing reports and analysis for any user password changes. These data mining and reporting functionalities impose additional server memory and storage capacity requirements.
11. Check for the underlying container architecture. Some service provisioning solutions use servlets in a Web container instead of EJBs to implement the service provisioning engine and password synchronization component. Server sizing for a Web container architecture instead of an EJB container architecture is less demanding for hardware and storage requirements. A typical server sizing for a Web container architecture (as in Web servers) is a single CPU with 1 to 2 GB of memory. An EJB container architecture (as in application servers) requires multiple CPUs and additional physical memory.

Security Risk Mitigation

Data privacy and message replay are two major security risks to service provisioning. Risk mitigation measures that can address these security risks include:

12. Defining your privacy policy. There are potential privacy issues associated with the service provisioning solution. Each provisioning service target or resource needs to intercept service provisioning requests and may need to disclose user account profiles or information in responses. This unfolds a few privacy issues, such as what authorized or unauthorized disclosure of user account profile should be and what defines a minimal and consistent set of personal data (for example, just user name and ID) across users and systems for service provisioning processing requirements. For example, should the service provisioning system require personal data such as Social Security number or date of birth to provision a new user account? These personal data items are sensitive to data privacy issues and may be easily exploited for unauthorized use in the event that the service provisioning request is hijacked.
13. Adding preventive measures against message replay. Service provisioning requests are easily open to attacks by message replay techniques, such as message insertion, message deletion, and message modification. Use Web services security protection measures such as using timestamps, correlation ID, XML Encryption, and XML Digital Signature (refer to Chapter 11 for details on Web services security patterns) to mitigate the message replay security risk.

Summary

Security service provisioning addresses business problems related to account mapping, password synchronization, account provisioning, and so forth. These are operational tasks that incur high running costs and processing time. When designing secure service provisioning, architects need to consider the following design factors: centralized or decentralized architecture, integration strategy with existing infrastructure, and the associated security risk mitigation strategies.

Security service provisioning can lower the total cost of account provisioning. It can reduce the complexity of account mapping by providing a standard interface and XML schema using SPML. The standard interfaces allow easy interoperability between identity management systems. These business benefits are quantifiable—there are measurable cost savings in adopting service provisioning technologies.

The Service Provisioning Markup Language (SPML) is a standards-based interface between the client (requesting authority), resources (provisioning service target), and provisioning service point. A number of security vendor products in the market now support SPML. There is a growing interest in relating Web services provisioning to SPML.

The Password Synchronizer pattern is an example of security design patterns that use SPML to synchronize user passwords across heterogeneous platforms. It illustrates how Java Message Service can provide reliable messaging for password synchronization.

References

This section includes URLs and resources referenced in the chapter. In addition, leading vendor products for security service provisioning and password synchronization are listed.

General

Here are some URLs and resources referenced in this chapter.

[CJP2] Deepak Alur, Dan Malks and John Crupi. *Core J2EE Patterns, Second Edition*. Prentice Hall, 2003.

http://corej2eepatterns.com/Patterns2ndEd/BusinessDelegate.htm

[Cryptocard] Cryptocard Technology. "The Incredible Cost of 'Free' Passwords."

[FisherLai] Marina Fisher and Ray Lai. "Designing Secure Service Provisioning." RSA Conference 2004.

[OpenSPML] OpenSPML.

http://www.openspml.org

[PasswordSync] John Erik Setsaas. "Password Synchronization." EEMA's Directory Interest Group.

http://www.maxware.com/News_Reviews/182-Passw-Synch.pdf

[PasswordSyncAgent] Password Synchronization Agent.

https://pwsynch.dev.java.net/

[PasswordUsage] Protocom Development Systems. "Global Password Usage Survey." Version 1.0.0. October 23, 2003.

http://www.protocom.com/whitepapers/password_survey.pdf

[SOX1] US Congress. Sarbanes-Oxley Act. H.R. 3763. July 30, 2002.

http://www.law.uc.edu/CCL/SOact/soact.pdf

[SPML10] "Service Provisioning Markup Language (SPML) Version 1.0." OASIS. October 2003.

[SSOvsPasswordSync] Protocom Development Systems. "Single Sign-on Password Replay vs Password Synchronization." Version 1.0.0. 2003.

http://www.protocom.com/whitepapers/sso_vs_passwordsync.pdf

[Unix2Win] Microsoft. "How To: Install Password Synchronization on a UNIX Host for a UNIX-to-Windows Migration." February 2, 2004.

http://support.microsoft.com/default.aspx?scid=kb;EN-US;324542

[WS-Prov] IBM. "Web Services Provisioning (WS-Provisioning): Draft Version 0.7." October 17, 2003.

http://www-106.ibm.com/developerworks/library/ws-provis/

Some Security Service Provisioning Vendors

Here are some URLs that describe a few leading security service provisioning vendor products. They are not exhaustive, but are good starting points for further analysis.

Abridean (abrideanProvisor).

http://www.abridean.com/SubPage.php?parent=products&child=UserManagementModules&grandchild=UserManager

Blockade Systems (ManageID).

http://www.blockade.com/products/index.html

BMC Software (CONTROL-SA).

http://www.bmc.com/products/proddocview/0,2832,19052_19429_22855_1587,00.html

CA (eTrust).

http://2004.rsaconference.com/downloads/CAbroch.PDF

Entrust.

http://www.entrust.com/identity_management/specs.htm

IBM (Tivoli Identity Manager).

http://www-306.ibm.com/software/tivoli/products/identity-mgr/

Novell (Nsure Identity Manager).

http://www.novell.com/products/nsureidentitymanager/quicklook.html

Open Network (Universal IdP).

http://www.opennetwork.com/solutions/

Sun Microsystems (Sun Java System Identity Manager, or a.k.a Waveset Lighthouse).

http://wwws.sun.com/software/products/identity_mgr/index.html

Thor (Xellerate).

http://www.thortech.com/product/products_xell_architecture.asp

HP (OpenView Select Identity, or a.k.a. TruLogica).

http://www.managementsoftware.hp.com/products/select/index.html

Some Password Management or Password Synchronization Vendor Products

Here are some URLs that describe a few leading password management or password synchronization vendor products. They are not exhaustive, but are good starting points for further analysis.

Blockade Systems Corp's ManageID Syncserv

Overview of ManageID Suite.

http://www.blockade.com/products/index.html

ManageID Syncserv Architecture.

http://www.blockade.com/products/syncservarchitecture.html

Courion's Password Courier

Overview.

http://www.courion.com/products/pwc/sync.asp

Architecture.

http://www.courion.com/products/pwc/architecture.asp

IBM's Password Synchronization Service with Tivoli's Directory Integrator and Tivoli's Identity Manager

Technical Notes.

http://publib-b.boulder.ibm.com/Redbooks.nsf/RedbookAbstracts/tips0390.html?Open

M-Tech's P-synch

http://www.psynch.com/docs/psynch-overview.html

and

http://www.psynch.com/docs/psynch-white-paper.html

Proginet's SecurPass

Overview.

http://www.proginetuk.co.uk/products/securpass-home.htm

SecurPass-Syn.

http://www.proginetuk.co.uk/pdf/securpasssync.pdf

Protocom's SecureLogin

Overview.

http://www.protocom.com/html/securelogin_password_manage_suite.html

Self-service Password Reset.

http://www.protocom.com/html/securelogin_self_service_password_reset.html

Sun's Sun Java System Identity Manager

Overview.

http://www.sun.com/software/products/identity_mgr/index.xml

Part VI

Putting It All Together

Building End-to-End Security Architecture–A Case Study

Topics in This Chapter

- Overview
- Use Case Scenarios
- Application Architecture
- Security Architecture
- Design
- Development
- Testing
- Deployment
- Summary
- Lessons Learned
- Pitfalls
- Conclusion

Chapter 14

Building End-to-End Security Architecture

The objective of this case study is to use a simplified real-world example of a Web portal to illustrate how to define and implement an end-to-end security solution using the security design methodology, design patterns, and best practices introduced in this book. Real-life business scenarios are usually complex and may be full of many constraints that are difficult to generalize for a case study. This case study is intended to encapsulate the complexity of a typical multi-tier application environment that includes J2EE applications, Web services, identity management, and external integration with partner business services. It will articulate a software design process that proactively captures all security requirements and defines an end-to-end security design and implementation model addressing all required security considerations. It will also illustrate how to identify risks; balance trade-offs; identify and apply security patterns; and perform factor analysis, tier analysis, threat profiling, and reality checks. You will learn how to adopt a patterns-driven security design process, the best practices and pitfalls and how to align the security of the different logical tiers together to deliver end-to-end security of the entire Web portal solution.

This security architecture and its design patterns apply to generic J2EE-based and Web services applications and does not require any specific vendor implementations. Sample artifacts and Java program code excerpts for the security patterns relevant to the case study are available for download at http://www.coresecuritypatterns.com.

Overview

The case study analyzes a Web-based business application portal that hosts a set of merchant services from multiple business provider sources and provides member rewards redemption services. Figure 14–1 shows the conceptual representation of the Web-based business portal (eRewards). In a typical scenario, a subscriber logs in to the Web-based business portal to check his or her membership award balance and then submits a request to an affiliate content provider (a trading partner of the service provider) to redeem points and obtain a gift.

The portal permits access to users from Web browsers accessible via Internet- or intranet-based enterprise applications from trusted business corporations. To verify user identity, the portal relies on an external Identity Provider that provides user authentication functionality. Thus, the portal does not need to invest resources into the building of its own identity management infrastructure.

The eRewards Membership Service stores personal subscriber information and preferences in user profiles. It also keeps an account balance of the membership award points and tracks any redemption for merchandise. The eRewards Catalog Service provides a list of merchandise offered to subscribers in the Warehouse Database. Subscribers can browse through the catalog of merchandise, select specific items, and add them to the in-basket for membership award redemption. Upon user confirmation, the eRewards Order Management Service will process the order that was placed in the in-basket. It will verify the membership award account balance to see if the subscriber has sufficient points to redeem the merchandise. Eligible merchandise information will be forwarded to the affiliate trading partners for order fulfillment via the Merchant Service.

The eRewards portal adopts J2EE technology to build business applications. Both the Catalog Service and the Order Management Service are implemented using Java-based Web services technologies. The integration with external partners will be done by way of XML Web services. The trading partners use Web services to enable interoperability and to overcome integration issues related to platforms and technologies, such as C++ and Microsoft-based applications.

Understanding the Security Challenges

The security challenges surrounding the Web portal lie in the complexity of security requirements and in establishing a unified security model between J2EE applications and Web services. The J2EE security model defines transport-level security using HTTPS and role-based access control to protect the business data exchanged and the business components. In a Web portal scenario, this security model is not adequate, because the security does not guarantee the security of the processes or the

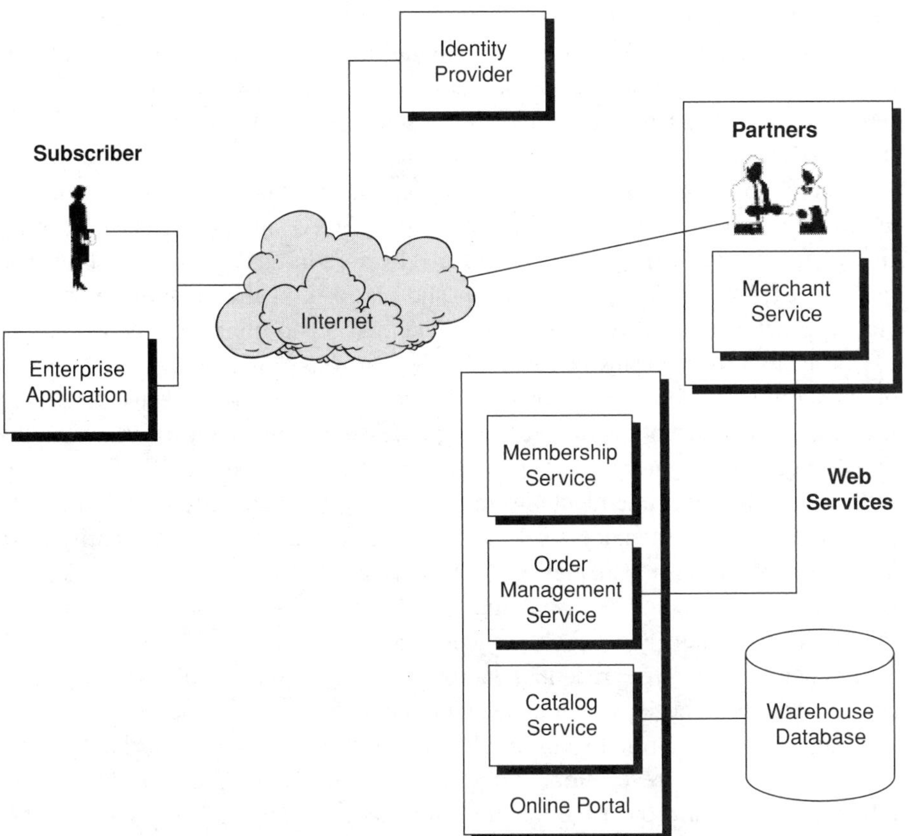

Figure 14–1 Conceptual model of the Web-based business portal (eRewards)

business data outside of the HTTPS session and user-based access control. This issue is even more complex when Web applications are distributed across different machines and there are many server-to-server processes. Thus designing end-to-end security for the eRewards portal is not trivial. A rigorous process that uses a well-defined methodology must be followed. This process includes gathering high-level requirements, implementing and testing the code, production deployment, and its final retirement. There are also other environment- and user-specific security factors that need to be considered and incorporated into the end-to-end security design. For example, each logical tier has its own associated risk in terms of development, deployment, and production. For example, there are risks involved in configuring the Web server plug-in to support the application server, building a custom login module to adopt a security provider, and in implementing the logging for capturing events and supporting security audit. Compliance and regulatory requirements such as the Sarbanes-Oxley Act, GLB Act, EU directives, and Patriot Act also define and add various security requirements in terms of auditing business transactions. In addition, they mandate traceability of business transactions for the detection of any suspicious activities or potential security threats. Refer to Chapters 9 and 10 [CSP] for details.

More importantly, security considerations differ widely from application to application. For example, Web services using SOAP messaging have security risks that are very different than those faced by a traditional Web application. The fact that SOAP messaging is language- and platform-neutral also makes it difficult to generalize security protection mechanisms or to implement generic security protection mechanisms that work on all platforms. Safeguarding synchronous or asynchronous Web services usually requires using Security tokens, XML signatures, XML Encryption, and enforcing access control for sensitive data in the SOAP messages. Security also becomes more complicated if the SOAP messages are routed to multiple intermediaries in a workflow or among external trading partners, where each of the nodes or servers exposes different levels of security risks and exposures. Refer to Chapters 6, "Web Services Security–Standards and Technologies," and Chapter 11, "Securing Web Services–Design Strategies and Best Practices," for details about Web services security and related patterns.

Exchanging identity credentials across security domains adds security risks and complexity in business communication among service providers. The services must also facilitate unified sign-on, global logout, and common mechanisms for identity registration, revocation, and termination. In addition to that, the identity infrastructure must protect the identity information against identity theft, spoofing, and man-in-the-middle attacks. Refer to Chapters 7, "Identity Management–Standards and Technologies," and Chapter 12, "Securing the Identity–Design Strategies and Best Practices," for details about identity management and related patterns.

Assumptions

First, we need to make some assumptions about our choice of platforms, client and server infrastructure options, and communication protocols in order to set the boundaries and constraints to the business application system environment. We also need to provide some context for the security requirements before we proceed with the case study. These requirements include:

- The eRewards online portal is accessible from a Web browser.
- We will address all business functionalities of the eRewards portal using J2EE platform-based application components.

- We will use synchronous and asynchronous protocols for invoking Web services via RPC and document-style Web services, respectively. Using Web services provides a standard interface for exposing business services previously implemented in Java (or .NET). The eRewards online portal has made prior arrangements with its trading partners by exchanging WSDL and XML schemas for representing the XML-based business document and by agreeing on the business data semantics. For external SOAP messaging, both the eRewards online portal—and its back-end integration with all trading partners—agree to sign and encrypt the XML messages.
- The identity management solution is provided by a third-party Identity Provider using a standards-based infrastructure using standards such as Liberty Alliance and SAML. This enables us to provide single sign-on access with different security domains over the Internet.
- User authentication is performed by a trusted Liberty-enabled security provider infrastructure that supports form-based authentication for J2EE over HTTPS as well as SSL client certificates (assuming that they were previously distributed via the eRewards online portal during the initial user or partner registration).

Use Case Scenarios

The following sections briefly discuss the business and security requirements of the eRewards portal followed by some detailed use cases represented by UML diagrams. We could devote a whole chapter to the requirements gathering processes and the creation of the architecture based on risk analysis, but because this book is focused more on security patterns, we have abbreviated the business requirements to highlight the importance of security in the portal.

Using use cases to analyze business requirements can help reduce the difficulty of building the application architecture and can help us to identify the required security features. Because the case study focuses on applying end-to-end security design techniques in different tiers, it will use a "micro-architecture" approach [CJP2], using appropriate security design patterns that were discussed in earlier chapters to illustrate the security design best practices (instead of the J2EE application design itself).

Choosing the Right Methodology

To get started on our eRewards portal case study, we must first identify a process methodology that gets us through the software development life cycle and meets both the business and security goals we set forth earlier. To accomplish our goals and to meet our deadlines while delivering a secure system, we chose to use the Secure UP as described in Chapter 8, "The Alchemy of Security Design: Methodology, Patterns, and Reality Checks." Doing so allows us to take advantage of the leading industry-recognized software development process and to extend it in order to ensure that our nonfunctional goals of security, reliability, and management are met.

Referring to the activity diagram (Figure 8–3) in Chapter 8, "The Alchemy of Security Design–Methodology, Patterns, and Reality Checks," we see that our first activity is to have a business analyst who defines the business and security requirements. Creating this definition is part of the business modeling and security requirements disciplines.

Identifying the Requirements

Let's assume that our business analysts have met with the business owners and derived the requirements for our eRewards portal. These would be broken out into business requirements and nonfunctional requirements, such as security, manageability, reliability, performance, high availability, and so forth. These functional and nonfunctional requirements are grouped into related sets of use cases for development and are tracked using a requirements management tool (for example, DOORS, RequisitePro, or another tool).

At a high level, the eRewards portal should be able to allow user self-registration by way of using a trusted Identity Provider. Upon successful registration, the portal subscribers (also referred to as **users**) can check their current account information, including their membership award point balance and the history of transactions. They can also update their personal information or access membership services. The portal also provides a selected list of merchandise for membership award redemption. It delivers an online product catalog system from a service provider hosted by the online portal. Subscribers can redeem merchandise by browsing the online product catalog, selecting the catalog product items, and placing the order in the online shopping cart. The internal order management system will fetch product details from the shopping cart and the corresponding item price by product ID and then retrieve the membership award status to see if the subscriber has sufficient membership award points to redeem for the merchandise. In the future, the eRewards portal will also allow the subscriber to purchase merchandise by credit card if the subscriber does not have enough membership award points for redemption.

The majority of the merchandise is supplied by trading partners by way of specialized merchant services. The eRewards online catalog maintains merchandise information and product details by taking a nightly offline data feed from the external trading partners. Fulfilling an order will require sending the delivery order from the internal order management system to the external systems of the trading partners. The order management system will send the subscriber's name, delivery address, and the merchandise details electronically in a secure manner. The order fulfillment system will also track the delivery status of the shipment.

Because the eRewards portal is intended to be available to subscribers around the clock, it has a high-availability service-level requirement of 99.99%. This suggests that the application servers running both the membership service and the merchant service should be almost "non-stop." Designing around merchant services operated by external trading partners (service providers) can be challenging, because the online portal does not have direct control over their availability. As an interim measure, the online portal requires notification of service exceptions if the external merchant service is not available. However, there is currently no service-level agreement (SLA) between the external trading partners and the eRewards portal about availability or the turnaround time for any service notification.

Identifying the Security Requirements

As mentioned earlier, we are focusing only on the security requirements of the portal—not the other nonfunctional requirements. End-to-end security is essential for the eRewards portal because security risks or threats do not come from a single source. Securing the Web server for the eRewards portal does not necessarily mean that the entire portal is secure. This is because business functions for membership services and merchant services do not come from a single server; they are distributed in different servers and different security domains. Each security domain has different fabrics or substrates of security elements that require specific security design considerations or security risk mitigation measures. A monolithic security model of using HTTPS or using traditional host security-hardening techniques will not be sufficient to handle a mixture of J2EE applications and Web services.

Security should never be an afterthought whose importance goes unnoticed until something unpleasant happens or a security loophole is reported. Security requirements are the key drivers for the reliability and availability of the business services provided by the online portal. These include authentication, authorization, traceability, data privacy or confidentiality, availability, data integrity, and non-repudiation.

The business-level security requirements gathered for the eRewards portal also include the following:

- *Identity Protection.* The Identity Provider infrastructure should be able to provide access management for authentication of valid subscribers to the portal. The Identity protection entails a variety of key management security protection mechanisms or risk mitigations that both secure the storage of key pairs (for example, the use of the Hardware Security Module (HSM) or a smart card device to store the private and public keys) and authenticate user identity (for example, the use of strong user authentication mechanisms such as smart cards, biometrics devices, or dynamic passwords) in a secure manner. Thus, the portal should be able to both accommodate various strong user authentication mechanisms on an as-needed basis and support key management operations for securing identity information.
- *Securing Web Servers and Application Servers.* The portal should provide security for the infrastructure hosting the Web servers and application servers. The hosting server infrastructure must make use of a trustworthy operating system and other required services.
- *Secure Client-to-Server Connection.* The portal should be able to secure the session and business data exchanged between the client and the server, using HTTP/SSL transport, for example. It should also make sure that the client is authenticated before establishing the user session.
- *Secure Server-to-Server Connection.* The portal should be able to secure the session and the business data exchanged with the service providers. Invoking Web services from external trading partners requires routing XML messages across different intermediaries or multiple processing nodes. Each external intermediary or trading partner node processing the business transaction or participating in the workflow should be secure. However, hosting servers should be able to authenticate each server before establishing the business data exchange.
- *Secure Transactions.* The portal should be able to support data privacy and confidentiality by securing the business transactions with encryption. Business transactions should be logged for traceability and audit control.
- *Message Level Protection.* Web services XML messages over a public network in clear text can be easily intercepted and tampered with. The XML messaging should make use of encryption and signature mechanisms that protect the data exchanged between the processing nodes. The message-level protection must ensure data integrity and non-repudiation of all business transactions.
- *Single Sign-on.* The portal should be able to provide single sign-on to merchant services hosted by external trading partners. Thus, subscribers can

provide user credentials to log in once, and they can then access both membership services and merchant services without re-login multiple times. In addition to single sign-on, the portal must facilitate a common mechanism for identity registration, revocation, and termination.

- *Security Considerations for High Availability.* No matter how secure and sophisticated the application infrastructure is, a DoS attack can cripple the online portal by making it unavailable for services. Thus, the portal should adopt appropriate preventive (such as load balancing, packet filtering, virus checking, failover, or backup) and service continuity measures that can defend against DoS attacks or other potential security breaches.
- *Security Risk Mitigation.* There should be a plan for identifying different security threats and the associated risk mitigation. Based on the security threat analysis, security architects can determine if additional security mitigation measures are necessary to cover any gaps in the security requirements or design elements.
- *Service Continuity and Recovery.* There should be an infrastructure plan that ensures the capability of delivering the services in the event of a security breach or human error. If such an event occurs, the Web portal infrastructure must have a recovery strategy for the worst-case scenario and must provide mechanisms for recovery from the event. Such mechanisms may even stop the event from occurring in the first place.

System Constraints

Based on our requirements, there are system constraints that may impact the security design. One main constraint is the identity management infrastructure. The eRewards portal has a previous investment in an identity management vendor solution and currently uses a trusted external Identity Provider. Thus, there will be no need to build or customize any single sign-on security solution.

Many Web services in the portal are created by exposing home-grown J2EE, .NET, and legacy applications as Web services. There may be no security built into these home-grown or legacy applications. Thus, there should be separate security considerations made for them during the design process.

Security Use Cases

Use cases are the end artifact of the requirements discipline. The use cases address one or more business requirements, defining the details of how those requirements must be implemented. Once a use case is complete, analysis and design for that functionality can begin. The following section presents some of the security use cases relevant to our eRewards portal case study. These use cases serve as the basis for defining the security design for our portal scenario. Typically, each use case would be defined in one or more documents, using a standard template. For our present purposes, we will skip an elaborate template and briefly summarize, using a use case diagram.

Use Case Diagram

Based on our business requirements, we have constructed our security use case diagram as shown in Figure 14–2.

In Figure 14–2, Client, a subscriber to the eRewards portal (OnlinePortal), needs to initiate and obtain secure login access to the portal. Upon successful authentication and authorization from the Identity Provider, Client can select different business services available from the portal. In this case study, Client intends to redeem merchandise (gifts offered by the portal and/or their affiliated merchants) using his or her membership award points. First, Client browses through the online catalog and selects the merchandise. Upon confirmation of his or her merchandise selection, Client chooses to redeem the merchandise by deducting membership award points from the available membership award balance. The portal retrieves the membership award balance and determines whether Client is eligible to redeem the merchandise. If Client is eligible to redeem the merchandise, the portal will place an order with the supplier merchant (TradingPartner) and issue an order to fulfill the order according to the pre-registered home address of the subscriber (Client).

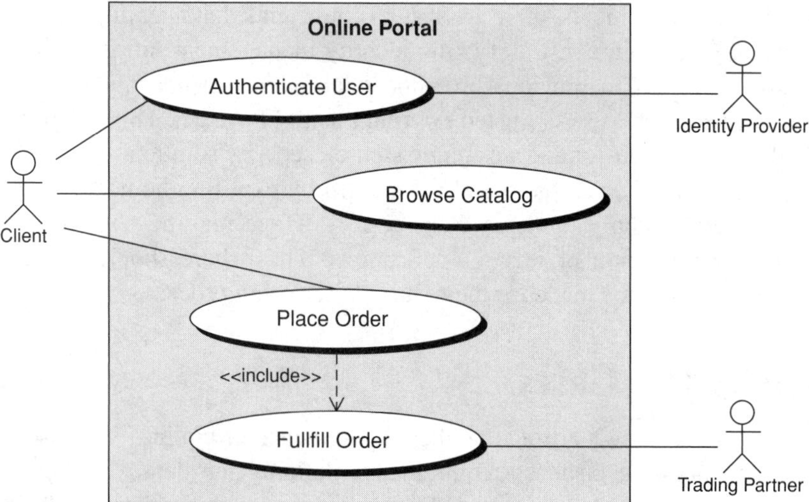

Figure 14–2 Security use cases for the eRewards portal

In this scenario, we primarily focus on the security-related use cases such as *User login*, *Secure Catalog service*, *Secure order placement*, and *Secure order fulfillment*.

- The *User login* use case refers to the user authentication process using an external Identity Provider.
- The *Secure catalog service* use case refers to the security mechanisms used to secure the catalog service. The portal catalog service component accesses a Web service provided by a partner service provider. Secure catalog service requires that the invocation of remote Web services is secure and that there is fully capable traceability that ensures there has been no unauthorized access to the catalog service and that supports audit trail or compliance reporting. Additionally, Client should not need to re-login to the catalog service, even though this is a remote Web service.
- The *Secure order placement* use case refers to the security mechanisms used to secure the order management process. The order management back-office function is currently implemented in J2EE. The J2EE component requires that the Client be authorized to invoke the order management functions. It is also necessary that this should reuse the logging infrastructure for traceability.
- The *Secure order fulfillment* use case refers to the security mechanisms used to secure the order fulfillment process. The order fulfillment is done by integrating external trading partners (TradingPartner) using document-style Web services. It is extremely important to authenticate with the external trading partners before routing XML messages in the Web Services tier. To address the risk of message interception or tampering, the XML messages should be secured by data encryption and digital signature for data integrity and confidentiality purposes.

Actors

The following Actors are the key entities that interact with the security use cases such as secure catalog service and secure order fulfillment. Here is a short description of each of the Actors:

Client	The subscriber to the online portal.
Online Portal	Also referred to as eRewards portal, a Web portal application that provides personalized access and a point of entry to multiple business services.

Trading Partner	A service provider organization that provides a business service to the service requester (Client).

eRewards Portal–Logical View

Based on the use cases, let's take a look now at what we have as a conceptual model of our Web-based business portal. Figure 14–3 illustrates the logical representation of the Web-based business portal.

In Figure 14–4, we see our three main services in the portal. They connect to the merchant service at our trading partner and use an external Identity Provider for identity management. All of the transactional data is stored in our warehouse database.

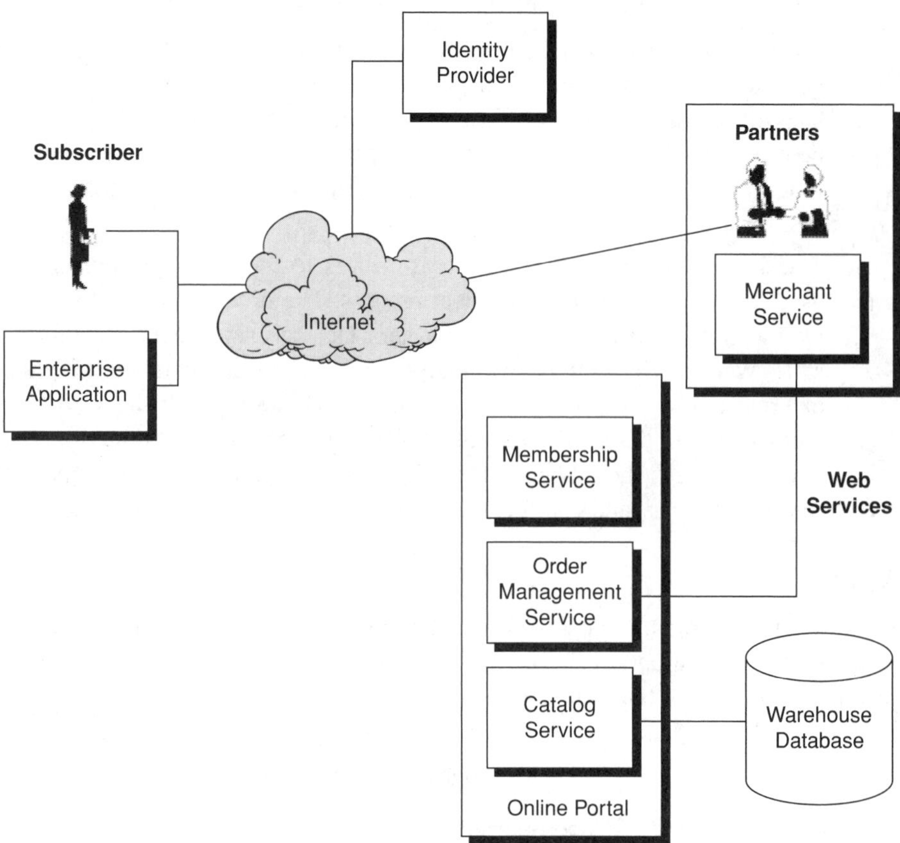

Figure 14–3 Logical View of eRewards portal

System Environment

We assume the eRewards portal and the service providers work together as a medium-scale business application hosted using heterogeneous platforms including Solaris, Linux, and Microsoft Windows. The portal runs on a J2EE 1.4-compliant application server that also provides support for RPC and document-style Web services. No vendor-specific application server extension features will be used. The portal and the underlying service providers make use of an external trusted Identity Provider for authentication, authorization, single sign-on, and identity management services.

Application Architecture

Figure 14-4 depicts the high-level application architecture for the eRewards portal. Because the focus of this case study is on building end-to-end security for the portal, we will not rationalize the details of how all the elements of the application architecture are derived. In a nutshell, the portal runs a J2EE 1.4-compliant application server using servlets and EJB components. The servlets make use of JAX-RPC or SAAJ handlers to invoke Web services provided by the service providers or external partners. The portal makes use of EJBs for processing orders. For identity management, the portal and the external trading partners have established a trusted relationship with service providers, making use of an external Liberty-enabled Identity Provider for user authentication, authorization, single sign-on, and identity management services. All server components of the portal and the service providers make use of a Liberty-enabled agent to communicate with the Identity Provider.

Technology Elements

The application architecture is represented using the following technology elements:

- Servlets are server-side MVC-style components that handle user presentation and control.
- EJBs are server-side components that encapsulate business logic to manipulate service requests, handle transaction processing, and retrieve or store business data in the database.
- JAX-RPC and SAAJ handlers integrate with service providers via XML Web services.

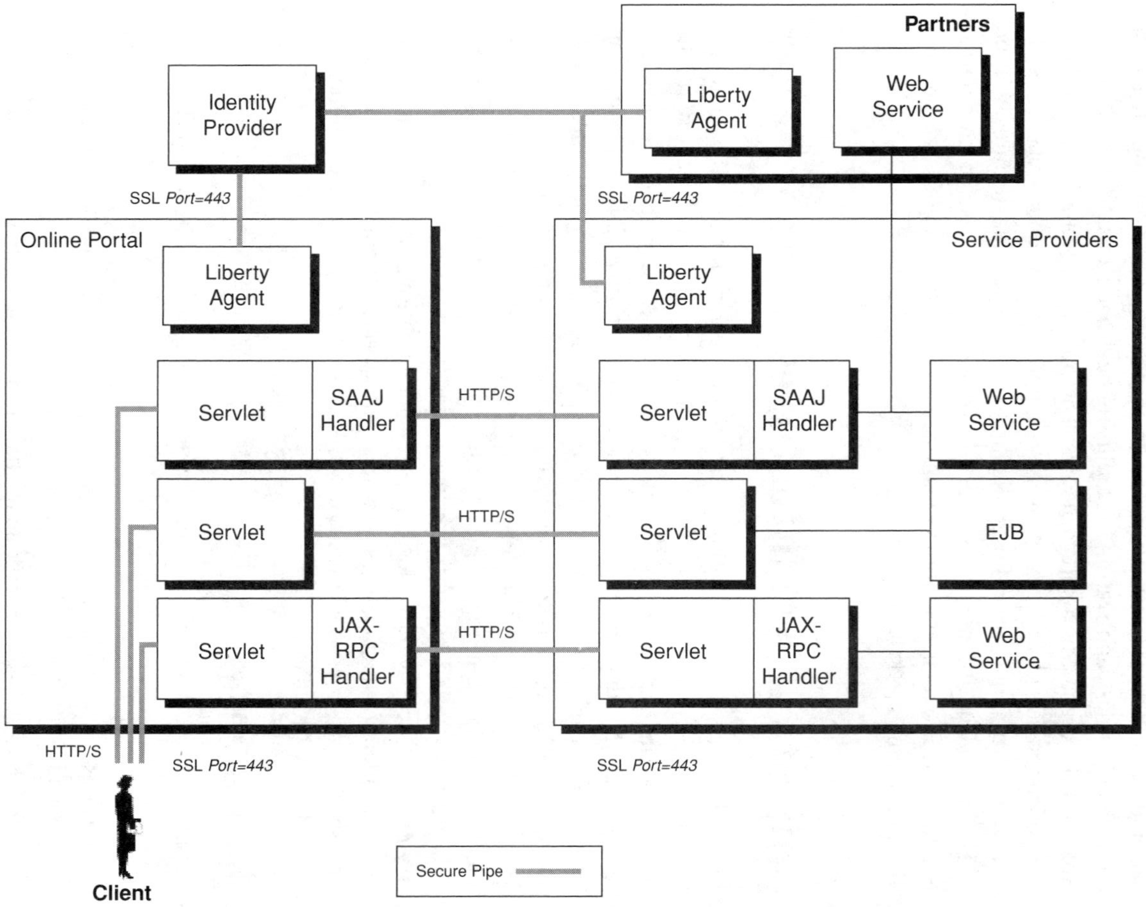

Figure 14–4 eRewards portal: high-level application architecture

- Java Data Objects are an implementation of data access objects that retrieve or store business data in the database using JDBC connectivity.

Security Prerequisites

Based on the application architecture, we need to define the following security prerequisites that will help us derive a conceptual security model.

1. Network perimeter security has historically been a critical requirement in any security architecture. This layer has been the most commonly attacked. Practices such as using a multi-tier firewall for the DMZ, NAT-ed proxies, and packet filters all fit into the security architecture.
2. Application infrastructure security represents safeguards and countermeasures for ensuring the security of enterprise applications, LDAP, and the database. Practices such as using HTTP/SSL to communicate with the application; limiting access to the application via authentication; and enabling role-based access control, digital signatures, and data encryption during transit must be addressed.
3. Using a Web services-based infrastructure for integration with service providers and exchanging XML messages introduces a newer set of security challenges both at the message and communication layers. Adopting XML-based security mechanisms for message-level security and SSL/TLS for transport-level security must be considered.
4. Identity protection is a key issue when securing applications and exchanging business data across multiple security domains and between trading partners. It becomes more complex when exchanging authentication and authorization information. Adopting single sign-on, global logout, common identity registration, revocation, and termination mechanisms must be considered using an external Identity Provider that establishes a chain of trust among all participating service providers.
5. Host security is another crucial requirement. Adopting a trusted or hardened OS, applying the appropriate patches, and installing an intrusion detection system are the key factors to consider to ensure that the host environment is secured.

Conceptual Security Model

We have enough information at this point to create a conceptual security model identifying the key security features that contribute to the end-to-end security of the eRewards portal. Creating a conceptual security model also entails defining some high-level components and technologies to fulfill our business security requirements. The following decisions here will help drive the design but are not set in stone, because there are several analyses yet to be performed. The major pieces of the conceptual model are:

- *Protecting the Identity Information.* The Identity Provider should be able to authenticate valid subscribers to the eRewards portal. Using PKI for protecting the identity information during transit and storage and using digital certificates for representing the identity is often considered as a recommended practice. Identity protection also entails secure storage of key pairs (for example, the use of Hardware Security Module (HSM) or a smart card device to store the private keys) and physical access control mechanisms such as biometric technologies. Thus, the portal should be able to provide support for different identity protection mechanisms and for adopting stronger authentication mechanisms.
- *Securing Web Servers and Application Servers.* Web servers and application servers may be the primary targets for security attacks or hacking. The portal should adopt and run on a hardened OS in the host application environment. A hardened OS ensures that all irrelevant and unused services that may be targets of threats are removed from the host environment. In addition, the Web servers and application servers must be securely deployed, with all default password configurations and sample applications completely removed.
- *Secure Client-to-Server Connection.* The portal should be able to secure the session and business data exchanged between the user client and the server by way of HTTP over SSL transport. Adopting a mutual authentication between the client and server before establishing the user session is recommended.
- *Secure Server-to-Server Connection.* The portal should be able to secure the Web services communication exchanged between the service providers. Establishing secure communication with external trading partners requires secure routing of XML messages. It is important to verify that the Web portal ensures transport-level data integrity and confidentiality during communication with service providers and other participating intermediaries.
- *Secure Transactions.* The portal should be able to support data privacy and confidentiality by securing the business transactions with encryption. Business transactions should be logged for traceability and should audit properly, but sensitive data should be obfuscated in the logging.

- *Securing Messages.* To communicate with service providers, the portal should adopt XML Web services using SOAP messages over HTTP/SSL. Although SSL ensures transport-level security, it does not facilitate message-level security that ensures that the message is received by only the intended recipient. Using message-level protection mechanisms such XML Signature and XML Encryption ensures message-level confidentiality and integrity during the Web services communication and also at the processing endpoints. This protection provides non-repudiation and trustworthy communication between the Web portal and the service providers.
- *Single Sign-on.* The portal should be able to provide single sign-on to merchant services hosted by external trading partners. Thus, subscribers can provide user credentials to login once and can access both membership services and merchant services without having to login multiple times.
- *Secure Logging and Auditing.* The portal must provide a full-fledged logging mechanism that captures and records all events with the corresponding identity as auditable trails. In addition to logging, the Web portal should provide an auditing mechanism to play back the recorded trails for forensic investigation.
- *Security Considerations for High Availability, Service Continuity, and Recovery.* No matter how secure and sophisticated the application infrastructure is, a denial-of-service attack can cripple the Web portal by making the portal offline and unavailable. Thus, the Web portal should adopt appropriate preventive measures (such as load balancing, fault-tolerance, failover recovery, and session persistence) that can help defend against a security breach and ensure further service continuity without disrupting legitimate user requests.
- *Risk Mitigation.* There should be a plan for identifying different security threats and the associated risk mitigation. Based on the security threat analysis, security architects can determine if additional security mitigation measures are necessary to cover any gaps in the security requirements or design elements. A cost/benefit analysis can then determine the legitimacy of the mitigation strategy.

Security Architecture

After formulating a conceptual security model identifying the key security features, we need to define candidate security architecture that represents an architect's view of the eRewards portal security. This means that we will make further architecture decisions to support development that allow us to start to tie together the security components in a cohesive application architecture. We will not bore down to the object level, but we will start to define services and subsystems that contribute to the end-to-end security. Upon identifying the candidate security architecture, we will perform a detailed risk analysis and identify mitigation strategies. We will also perform a trade-off analysis to meet the security criteria and support the business and architectural decisions.

Part of the job is already done. Due to business decisions, we have already decided to use a third-party identity management provider. This will drive a lot of the candidate architecture, because it imposes several constraints to begin with. Now we have to come up with a few high-level application components adopting security patterns. This will help us to illustrate candidate security architecture.

Figure 14–5 shows the logical representation of candidate security architecture for the eRewards portal. We adopted the core security patterns to represent the key security requirements in the logical tiers of the application architecture.

In the Web tier, we will use a *Secure Base Action* pattern for centralizing and coordinating all security-related tasks with Web components such as JSPs and Servlets. We will make use of an *Authentication Enforcer* pattern to authenticate Web requests and to verify authentication information established by our third-party Identity Provider.

In the Business tier, we will use a *Secure Session Façade* pattern that can contain and centralize all EJB interactions within a secure session. We will use an *Obfuscated Transfer Object* to protect the business data in a transfer object during transit.

To ensure Web service communication with service providers, we will make use of the *Secure Message Router* pattern, which facilitates applying message-level and transport-level security mechanisms before sending messages to Order management service and Membership service. To ensure secure sending and receipt of messages with service providers, we will make use of the *Message Interceptor Gateway* and *Message Inspector* patterns that allow us to enforce security mechanisms at the transport-level and the message-level, and to verify messages for standards compliance and other content-level vulnerabilities.

The candidate security architecture also consists of components at the network and host layers. Perimeter security design, DMZ architecture, patch management, and intrusion-detection systems are other key components that need to be part of the candidate security architecture artifacts. Because the scope of this book targets the application-level security solutions, we will assume that those tasks have been completed with as much due diligence, using known industry best practices.

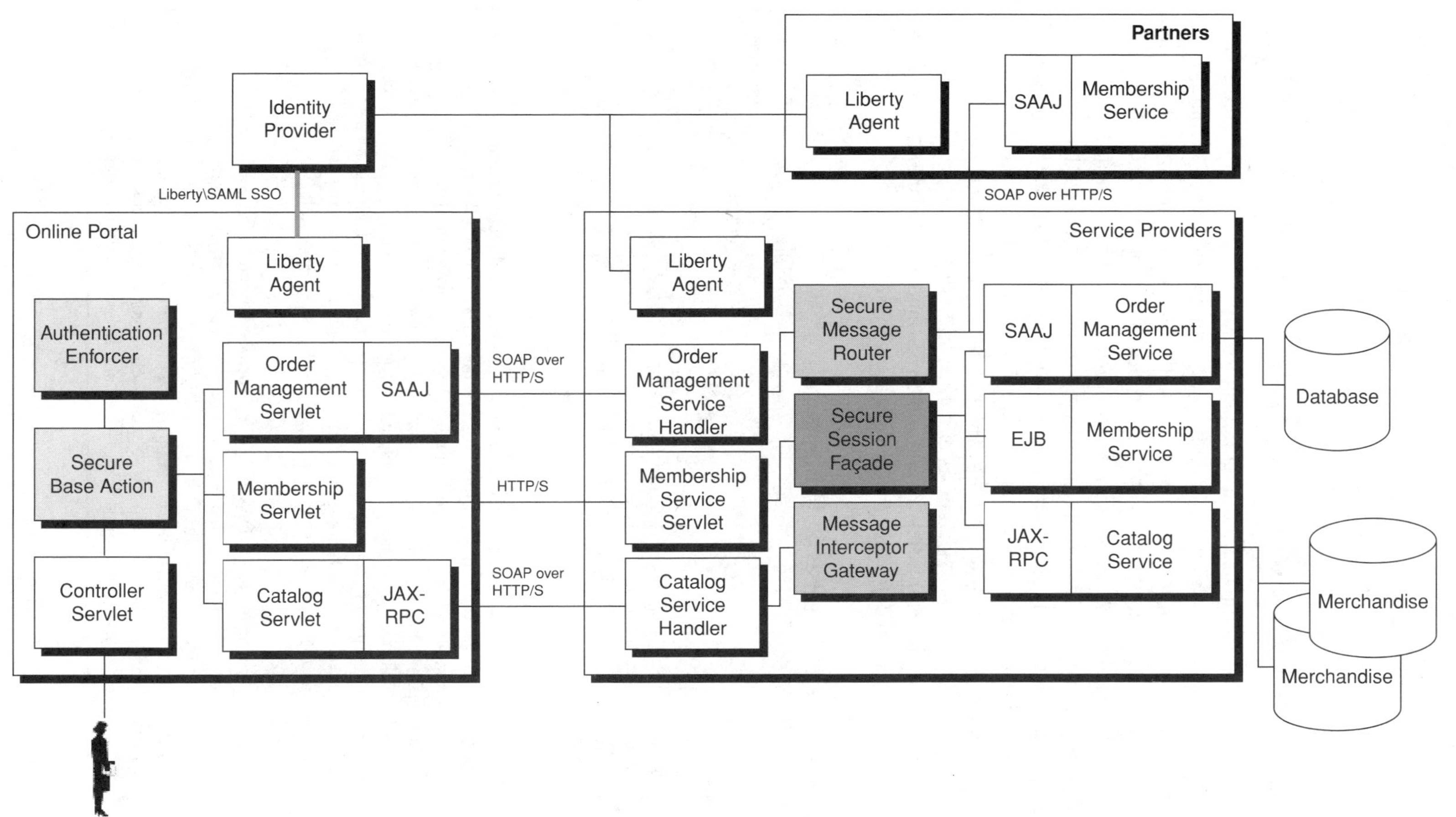

Figure 14–5 eRewards portal candidate security architecture

Risk Analysis and Mitigation

After deriving the candidate security architecture, we will analyze the architecture for known risks in terms of potential threats and vulnerabilities and identify mitigation strategies to avoid them. We will study the risks—both qualitative and quantitatively—in light of *architecture tiers*, *possibility of occurrence* (expressed in terms of the number of prospects), *probability* (expressed in terms of likelihood of possible occurrences), *impact* (expressed in terms of effect that affects the overall architecture), and *exposure* (expressed as the level of acceptability). We will also identify the issues that expose those potential risks and how to mitigate them by identifying potential security patterns, best practices, and solutions.

Table 14–1 shows the risk analysis and mitigation strategies for a partial list of known risks and vulnerabilities. A complete risk-analysis document is available at the companion Web site (http://www.coresecuritypatterns.com).

Table 14–1 Risk Analysis and Mitigation

No	*Known Risks*	*Tier/ Component*	*Possibility of Occurrence (Single / Multiple)*	*Probability* *1 – Low 3 – Medium 7 – High 10 – Extreme*	*Impact* *1 – Low 5 – Medium 7 – High 10 – Extreme*	*Exposure* *1 – Low 5 – Medium 7 – High 10 – Unacceptable*
1	DoS/ DDoS	Web tier	Multiple	10	10	10
	Issue: The portal is vulnerable to DoS/DDoS attacks because it is directly accessible over the Internet. There are many possibilities for carrying out DoS/DDoS by sending fake requests, initiating a flood of high-volume connections, malicious data injection causing buffer overflow, and exploiting application/configuration-specific weaknesses. These types of attacks usually consume Web/application server-specific system resources and deny accepting further user requests. During these attacks, if a legitimate user makes a portal access request, the request may fail completely or the page may take longer to download, and then making further transactions may not be possible. **Mitigation:** The preventive measures for DoS and DDoS include implementing router filtering to drop connections from untrusted hosts and networks and configuring fault-tolerant and redundant server resources. In addition, the Web/Application server must be configured to perform host-name verification, identifying fake requests and denying them from further processing. At the application level, the Web server may adopt security patterns such as Secure Pipe, Intercepting Web Agent, and Intercepting Validator.					

(*continues*)

Table 14–1 Risk Analysis and Mitigation (*continued*)

<table>
<tr><th>No</th><th>Known Risks</th><th>Tier/ Component</th><th>Possibility of Occurrence (Single / Multiple)</th><th>Probability
1 – Low
3 – Medium
7 – High
10 – Extreme</th><th>Impact
1 – Low
5 – Medium
7 – High
10 – Extreme</th><th>Exposure
1 – Low
5 – Medium
7 – High
10 – Unacceptable</th></tr>
<tr><td rowspan="2">2</td><td>XML-DoS</td><td>Web Services</td><td>Multiple</td><td>10</td><td>10</td><td>10</td></tr>
<tr><td colspan="6">Issue:
The Web service endpoints are vulnerable to XML-DoS, where an attacker can perpetuate XML-based and content-level attacks by sending malformed messages, replaying legitimate messages, sending abnormal payload size, and sending non-compliant messages. These attacks lead to resource-intensive XML parsing, causing endless loops, buffer overflow, endpoint crash, or denial of further service processing.
Mitigation:
The safeguards and preventive measures for XML-DoS can be carried out by adopting Message Interceptor Gateway and Message Inspector patterns. These patterns secure access to Web service endpoints from message-level threats and vulnerabilities.</td></tr>
<tr><td rowspan="2">3</td><td>Man-in-the-Middle</td><td>Web Tier
Web Services</td><td>Multiple</td><td>5</td><td>5</td><td>10</td></tr>
<tr><td colspan="6">Issue:
The Web portal and Web service endpoints are vulnerable to man-in-the-middle attacks, where an unauthorized user is able to read or modify the business transactions or messages sent between two endpoints. The service provider or requester is not aware that the communication channel, the business transaction, or the message exchange is being compromised.
Mitigation:
The preventive measures for safeguarding Web tier components and Web services communication is done by implementing transport-layer security using SSL/TLS or IPSEC protocols. At the application level, the components can make use of Secure Pipe pattern.</td></tr>
<tr><td rowspan="2">5</td><td>Message-Level Security</td><td>Web Tier
Web Services</td><td>Single</td><td>5</td><td>5</td><td>10</td></tr>
<tr><td colspan="6">Issue:
The messages exchanged between Web service endpoints is vulnerable to malicious data injection, identity spoofing, message validation failure attacks, replay of selected parts, schema poisoning, and element/parameter tampering.
Mitigation:
Protecting Web service endpoints from processing malicious messages is done by enforcing message-level security and processing messages for endpoint-specific security criterion. The Web service endpoint can make use of the Message Inspector pattern.</td></tr>
</table>

(*continues*)

Table 14–1 Risk Analysis and Mitigation (*continued*)

<table>
<tr><th>No</th><th>Known Risks</th><th>Tier/ Component</th><th>Possibility of Occurrence (Single / Multiple)</th><th>Probability
1 – Low
3 – Medium
7 – High
10 – Extreme</th><th>Impact
1 – Low
5 – Medium
7 – High
10 – Extreme</th><th>Exposure
1 – Low
5 – Medium
7 – High
10 – Unacceptable</th></tr>
<tr><td rowspan="2">6</td><td>Protecting Sensitive Information</td><td>Business Tier</td><td>Multiple</td><td>5</td><td>7</td><td>5</td></tr>
<tr><td colspan="6">Issue:
The data passed around in the Business tier is subject to logging and auditing. This data will often contain sensitive information such as a person's credit card number or personal bank information. If this data gets logged, it may be subject to inspection by unauthorized parties and leave open the possibility of identity theft.
Mitigation:
To ensure that sensitive data does not get inadvertently output to a log file or an audit table, the Web service endpoint can use an Obfuscating Transfer Object pattern.</td></tr>
<tr><td rowspan="2">7</td><td>Restricting Access to Business Components</td><td>Business Tier</td><td>Multiple</td><td>1</td><td>9</td><td>5</td></tr>
<tr><td colspan="6">Issue:
An attacker who has gained access to the internal network may attempt to communicate directly with the Business tier EJBs using RMI and thus by-pass the Web tier security protocols. This would allow the attacker to gain unauthorized access to Business tier services.
Mitigation:
Use a Secure Session Façade pattern to ensure that security is checked on the Business tier as well as on the Web tier. This can be done in conjunction with the Container Managed Security or Policy Delegate patterns.</td></tr>
</table>

In real-world scenarios, after the qualitative risk analysis, a quantitative risk analysis has to be performed. This helps identify all key risk elements and estimate the projected loss of value for each risk, such as infrastructure cost, potential threat, frequency, business impact, potential loss value, safeguard option, safeguard effectiveness, and safeguard value. Based on that information, we can estimate the potential losses and compute the annual loss expectancy (ALE), which helps to make a business case for identifying security countermeasures and safeguards. Refer to Chapter 8, "The Alchemy of Security Design–Methodology, Patterns, and Reality Checks," for more information about quantitative risk analysis.

Trade-Off Analysis (TOA)

After risk analysis, it becomes important to validate the quality of the security architecture, weighing the choices of security options, features, and alternatives. A trade-off analysis helps the security architect to make better decisions and allows justification of financial requirements that relate to the multiple security criteria, possible options, and recommendations.

For the Web tier, we need to perform a trade-off analysis of SSL Encryption options. The factors we need to consider are price and performance. Table 14–2 shows the trade-off analysis of the different SSL Encryption options.

Table 14–3 illustrates the TOA effect matrix for weighing different choices for identifying a load-balancing option for the eRewards portal.

On the Business tier, we need to examine different data obfuscation strategies. The considerations for data obfuscation strategies include performance, security, and implementation costs. Table 14–4 shows the comparisons of the data obfuscation strategies.

A TOA artifact is also available at the companion Web site (http://www.coresecuritypatterns.com). Refer to Chapter 8, "The Alchemy of Security Design: Methodology, Patterns, and Reality Checks," for more information about trade-off analysis.

Table 14–2 Trade-off Analysis—Effect Matrix for SSL Encryption

	In Software on Web Server	*Hardware Accelerator Web Server*	*Dedicated Hardware Device*	*Remarks*
SSL Encryption	–1	+1	+5	-
	2	2	2	-

Table 14–3 Trade-Off Analysis—Effect Matrix for Load Balancing

	Bastion Hosts with Web Server Reverse-Proxy Load Balancing	*Web Load-Balancer Appliances*	*Web Servers*	*Remarks*
Web application Load-balancing	+7	+8	+5	-
	8	8	8	-

Table 14–4 Load Data Obfuscation Trade-Off Analysis (Effect Matrix)

	Masked List Strategy	*Encryption Strategy*	*XML Encryption Strategy*	*Remarks*
Data Obfuscation Strategies	+1	–5	–8	-
	2	8	8	-

Applying Security Patterns

To address the key security requirements defined at the beginning of the chapter, and based upon the outcome of our risk analysis and trade-off analysis, we have identified a set of security patterns for use within the application. These patterns are identified as part of the mitigation strategy identified for the associated risks. These patterns are highlighted (in black boxes) in Figure 14–6.

To mitigate known risks, the application architecture, including the Web portal and service providers, will make use of the following security patterns:

- *Secure Pipe*: Provides transport-level data confidentiality and data integrity between the client, the portal, and the partners. Using client certificate-based mutual authentication also ensures non-repudiation.
- *Secure Base Action*: Acts as centralized security manager for the Web tier. It coordinates authentication, validation, and security logging for all Web requests.
- *Authentication Enforcer*: Authenticates clients by verifying identity information passed by third-party Identity Provider.
- *Intercepting Validator*: Validates input passed in from Client.
- *Secure Logger*: Logs all security-related activity to a secure store.
- *Secure Service Façade*: Provides security to all Service Provider components. Provides auditing facilities through the *Audit Interceptor*.
- *Audit Interceptor*: Captures audit events using the *Secure Session Façade* strategy.
- *Obfuscated Transfer Object*: Acts as a generic *Transfer Object* and employs a Masked List Strategy for obfuscating sensitive data written to logs and audit trails.
- *Secure Message Router*: Handles messages to multiple endpoints securely, applying message-level security and the SSO token.

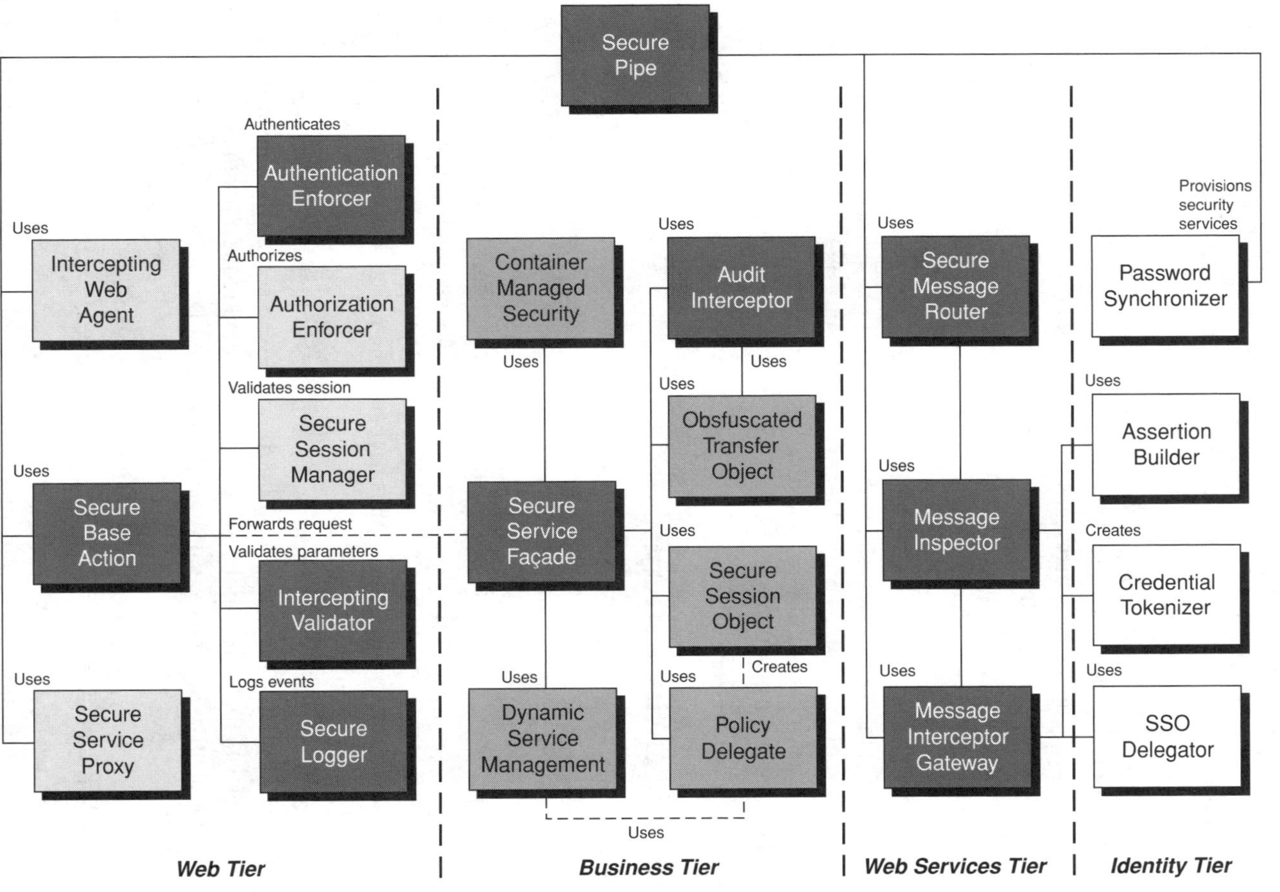

Figure 14–6 eRewards portal application: security patterns used

- *Message Inspector*: Verifies messages for message-level security mechanisms including authentication, authorization, signature, and encryption, and identifies content-level vulnerabilities.
- *Message Interceptor Gateway*: Acts as the entry point for enforcing security on the incoming and outgoing XML traffic. It ensures transport-level security and verifies messages for standards compliance, conformance to mandatory XML schemas, message uniqueness, and peer authentication of originating host. It makes use of the *Message Inspector* pattern for verifying message-level security threats and vulnerabilities.

These patterns address the key security requirements and mitigate those identified risks that span the Web-, business-, and Web Service tiers. We specifically chose not to address implementations of the Identity tier because such implementations are best performed by the third-party Identity Provider that is chosen by the eRewards portal owner. In this portal scenario, the Identity Provider is identified as a Liberty-enabled security infrastructure whose implementation is not discussed.

Other Security Patterns Used

To address other security requirements of data confidentiality, data integrity traceability, auditability, and accountability specific to the infrastructure, we chose to use the following application security design patterns:

- The *Secure Pipe* pattern ensures that the channel or transport layer between the client and the server or between servers is protected. For client-to-server communication, SSL is used to support communication privacy and integrity. This applies to the online portal as well as the back-end application infrastructure.
- The *Intercepting Web Agent* pattern applies to both the Web server and the application server when configuring the Web server plug-in to intercept requests for verifying the originating hosts and request parameters in order to identify fake or forged requests, potential DoS, and man-in-the-middle attacks.
- The *Intercepting Validator* pattern helps validate the input parameters prior to performing user authentication and service invocation.
- The *Secure Logger* pattern provides logging services capability to the Web tier application server infrastructure. It is used in both the Web portal and the back-end application server. It captures all events and messages, including the identity, requested operations, and results returned. This supports the security requirements of an audit trail and traceability of application requests, state of requests, and failures.

- The *Audit Interceptor* pattern is a Business tier security pattern that provides a centralized means for recording audit events. It allows developers to declaratively define events that will be captured to an audit log for long-term retention. It prevents developers from having to programmatically define audit events across the Business tier by intercepting service requests and auditing events based on a centralized event catalog. It is essential to support audit reporting and compliance security requirements in both the Web portal and the service provider's environment.

Security Architecture–Detailed Components

Security services associated with the business services in the Web, business, and Web Services tiers address the security requirements of authentication, authorization, data privacy or confidentiality, availability, data integrity, and non-repudiation. The Client logs in with the Web portal, and the controller servlet manages the user interaction. The *Authentication Enforcer* and *Secure Base Action* patterns handle the user authentication (authentication) and redirect the user to the Identity Provider for authentication services (and thus for single sign-on). Upon successful authentication, the Client makes selections for browsing the online catalog, placing an order, or requesting order fulfillment for the merchandise ordered (see Figure 14–7).

In the portal, each exposed business service is represented using a servlet to handle the business processing. To interact with service providers, the servlets use JAX-RPC handlers to invoke remote Web services. In cases of service providers using the J2EE environment, the servlets communicate with their presentation components, such as JSPs and servlets to invoke their business EJBs.

After enforcing authentication and authorization, the catalog servlet enables a Client to browse through the merchandise catalog and select specific product items to place into their shopping carts. The catalog servlet uses a JAX-RPC handler to invoke a remote catalog Web service over HTTPS. The *Secure Message Interceptor* pattern intercepts the SOAP message to examine the user credentials and signature in the SOAP service request (data privacy and data integrity).

The order management servlet takes a product or a group of product items selected in the catalog service and places an order with the back-end order management system using a membership service servlet. It uses a membership servlet to retrieve the membership award balance and verify if the requesting Client is eligible and entitled to redeem the merchandise (authorization). The membership servlet communicates with the membership service servlet over HTTPS, which uses the *Secure Session Façade* pattern to delegate to the back-end membership service, which is implemented in EJBs. Upon successful verification of the membership award balance, the order management servlet will issue a document-style

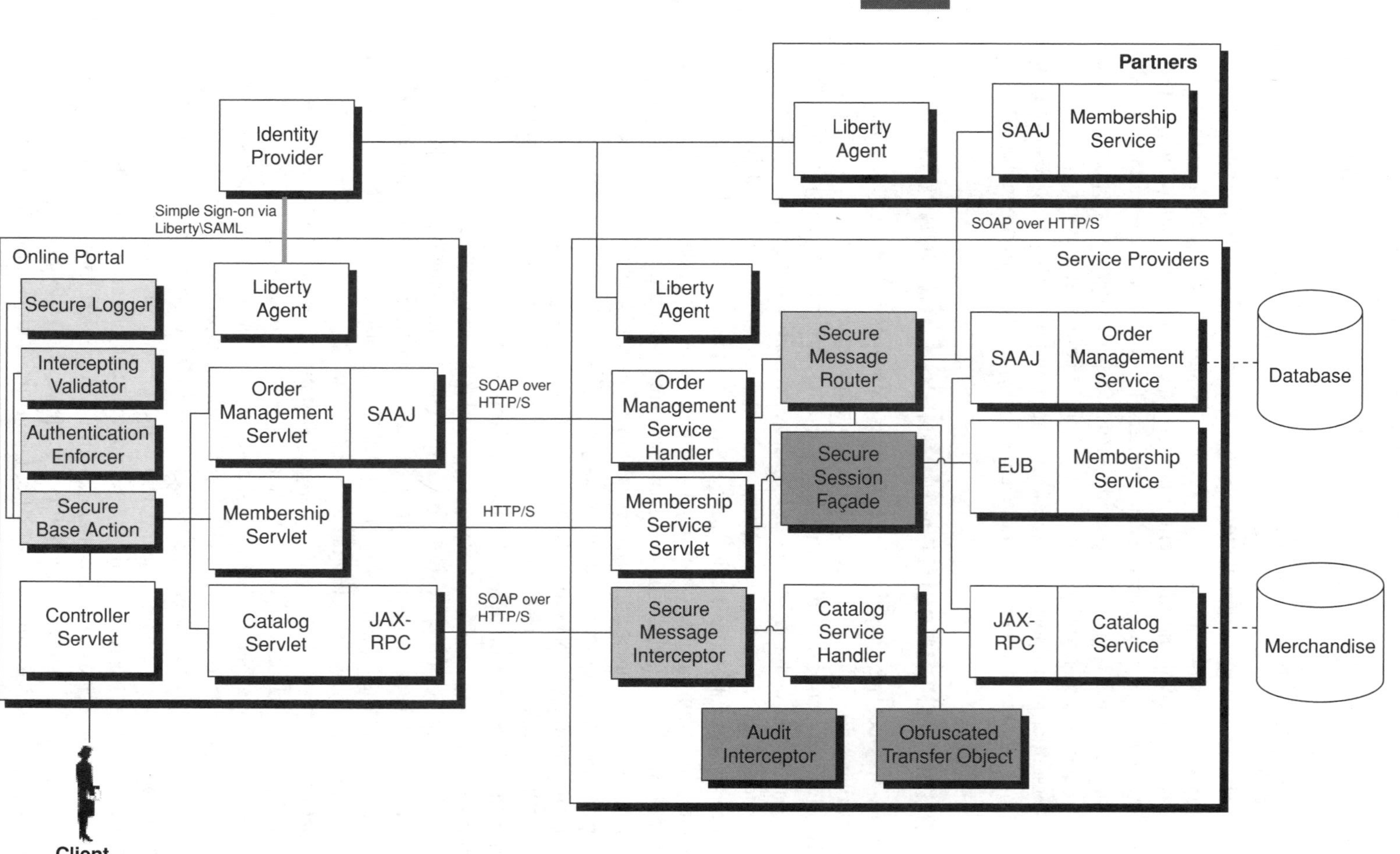

Figure 14–7 eRewards portal security architecture—detailed components

SOAP service request over HTTPS using a JAX-RPC handler to invoke the remote order management service. The handler will make use of a *Secure Message Router* pattern to route the SOAP messages to the relevant service providers or external partners, applying all required message-level security mechanisms. It ensures that the SOAP message is also encrypted and digitally signed to provide message-level confidentiality and integrity so that the message can be viewed only by the intended recipient.

Web Tier

On the Web tier, the *Secure Pipe* pattern was chosen to provide a secure communication channel. This protects communications between the client and the application from eavesdropping, man-in-the-middle attacks, and data injection or corruption. The *Secure Base Action* pattern is part of the entry point into the application and server to enforce security on the front-end in conjunction with other Web-tier security patterns. The *Authentication Enforcer* provides us with a means for encapsulating and decoupling the mechanism used for authentication from the actual establishment of the client's identity. Because the actual authentication is performed outside the application by a trusted external Identity Provider, the actual job of the *Authentication Enforcer* is simply to verify the trusted provider and its credentials. The encapsulation of the authentication mechanism assures us that if, in the future, authentication is moved back into the application, those changes will be isolated in one spot and not impact the rest of the Web tier. The *Intercepting Validator* is responsible for validating and cleansing the data passed in on the HTTP request. This provides protection from data corruption attacks such as SQL injection attacks, cross-site scripting attacks, and malformed requests aimed at crashing the site. Finally, the *Secure Logger* logs all of the relevant information about the request to a secure store so that if intruders did gain access to the application, they would not be able to alter the logs and conceal their attack.

Business Tier

On the Business tier, the Secure Session Façade pattern is used to provide a secure entry point into the business services. It has the responsibility of ensuring that auditing and any other security function is performed prior to service invocation. In this case, auditing is delegated to the *Audit Interceptor*, which audits service invocations, responses, and exceptions as defined declaratively. The *Obfuscated Transfer Object* is used to pass data between the Web tier and the Business tier and between service providers in the Business tier. It takes responsibility for obfuscating sensitive data passed back and forth, thereby removing that responsibility from service providers themselves. That way, credit card numbers, bank information, and other account details are not improperly written out to logs or the audit store.

Web Service Tier

The Web Service tier consists of the *Secure Message Router*, the *Message Inspector*, and the *Message Interceptor Gateway*. The *Secure Message Router* is used to provide message-level security between the portal and the trading partners. It configures the SSO capabilities between the partners and notifies them of global logout events. Additionally, it provides transformation of incoming messages to the message formats required by the service providers. The *Message Interceptor Gateway* sits in front of the Web Services interface to the application. It acts as a proxy and facilitates enforcement of channel-level security, including creation of SSL connections, IP verification, and some URL access control. It delegates data validations to the *Message Inspector*.

Design

This section illustrates the design process for the security use cases and applies the security architecture and those identified security design patterns. UML-style sequence diagrams are used to denote the flow of events and how each logical component interacts with specific security patterns. The security service design discussed here should be vendor-agnostic, and can be implemented in practically any language on any platform. We refer to J2EE-specific terminology because our security use cases and system constraints mandated the use of a J2EE environment, but those should not be misinterpreted as a necessary part of the security design.

Policy Design

Prior to the design elaboration phase, we need to document our policy design. In terms of security, the policy design must provide rules defining appropriate and inappropriate behavior, who and what to trust, level of control, communication requirements, procedures, and associated tools to support the security infrastructure. To do this as part of eRewards portal security architecture, we need to document the following security policy artifacts:

- User registration, revocation, and termination policy
- Role-based access control policy
- PKI management policy

- Service provider trust policy
- Data encryption and signature verification policy
- Service provider assessment policy
- Service Audit and traceability policy
- Proactive and Reactive risk-assessment policy
- Information disclosure and sensitivity policy
- Password selection and maintenance policy
- Information classification and labeling policy
- DMZ Environment access policy
- Application administration policy
- Host and network administration policy
- Application failure notice policy
- Service failure, continuity, and recovery policy

These policies serve as principal guidelines during implementation and deployment. They also contribute to the regulatory compliance requirements specific to the type of business handled by the eRewards portal. Sarbanes-Oxley (SOX) is one example of those business-related regulatory requirements.

Policy design is a tedious undertaking, and a full explanation could consume a chapter in and of itself. In this chapter, we are not able to bore down to the details of the above artifacts. The sample artifacts for policy design are available at http://www.coresecuritypatterns.com. Refer to Chapter 8, "The Alchemy of Security Design: Methodology, Patterns, and Reality Checks," for more information about Policy Design.

Factor Analysis

To begin construction of a security design, we must perform a factor analysis to identify the current system infrastructure-specific constraints and requirements. These constraints and requirements will drive the design decisions as we move forward. Forthcoming activities such as detailed security design and implementation will be based heavily on the analysis done here.

Infrastructure

- *Target Platform*: We need to establish the criteria for the host environment selection to provide a secure and reliable environment to run our Web portal applications. The key aspects to consider include operating systems, compatibility with applications/technologies, maintainability, security features, and deployment requirements. We need to identify the known security risks, preconditions, and vulnerabilities associated with the selected platform, OS, and software. To host our Web portal, we choose to use Trusted Solaris 8 as the OS environment for bastion hosts and for all the target hosts running the application server instances.

- *Number of Access Points*: We anticipate that our peak usage for the upcoming year will be around 1 million users from different geographic locations and time zones. So we need to facilitate a dedicated infrastructure to support different time zones. The access points should be geographically separated but colocated in the same network. The host infrastructure should provide fault-tolerance and failover capabilities in case of a service failure at one location.
- *Network Perimeter Security*: To design the network security and to control inter-tier traffic flows, we need to identify the routing/firewall appliances, multilayer Ethernet switches, and load-balancing devices. We choose to separate the Web tier and application server tier with a separate firewall. We choose to adopt a horizontally scalable solution including multiple server platforms running at different locations hosting many instances of the Web server at the Web tier and multiple server instances in the application server tier. The network design is composed of segregated networks, implemented physically using VLANs configured by network switches. We choose to use Foundry switches and Netscreen firewall devices. The internal network used the 10.0.0.0 private IP space for better security and portability advantages. Although several networks reside on a single active core switch, network traffic is segregated and secured using static routes, access control lists (ACLs), and VLANs. The trust zones are created using a Netscreen firewall and they map directly to the VLANs. The Netscreen firewall performs the Layer 3 routing. This configuration directs all traffic, resulting in firewall protection between each service tier.

Web Tier

- *Authentication Requirements*: Based on anticipated clients, we will support form-based authentication for our Web users and client certificate-based mutual authentication for our trading partners. All hosts are identified and trusted using peer authentication. All unauthorized connections from untrusted and IP addresses will be dropped.

- *Client Devices or Platform Used:* Our interactive clients will be Internet users who are using a variety of browsers on a variety of platforms. We therefore want to avoid any platform- or browser-specific code. We want to avoid or limit as much as possible the use of JavaScript. We also want to avoid requiring use of client-side mobile devices without browser support. Our trading partners will be connecting by way of server-to-server communication through trusted host authentication. The client devices and platforms are not a concern because the communication is all by way of standardized protocols that are device/platform-independent.
- *Web Agent:* The Web servers running on bastion hosts will make use of a Web agent to verify all incoming and outgoing Web requests for session tokens. Upon identification of fake or forged requests using a legitimate identity, the Web agent will log the request, initiate a request to the Identity Provider to revoke the user, and also send a notification to the administrator to audit those fake requests. This helps to identify and foil DoS and man-in-the-middle attacks on the Web tier.

Business Tier

- *Data Obfuscation*: To protect sensitive information such as credit card numbers, we need to obfuscate appropriate data in the Business tier. This allows us to log, audit, and transmit data without revealing sensitive information.
- *Auditing*: Due to the auditing requirements specified in the policy design, we need to audit our service transactions. Because the auditing requirements are expansive, this capability should be provided as part of the Business tier framework and not implemented on a service-by-service basis.

Web Services Tier

- *Restricting Direct Access to Endpoints*: The Web services communication with service providers makes use of the HTTP and HTTP/SSL protocols and standard ports of the firewall. This lacks support for providing protection against XML-based message attacks and content-layer vulnerabilities such as buffer overflow, malicious data injection, and virus attachments. We will introduce *Message Interceptor Gateway* and *Message Inspector* pattern-based mechanisms for enforcing XML-based security mechanisms and access control policies to the exposed Web service endpoints and WSDL descriptions.

Security Infrastructure

Based on the identified system requirements, we will evolve a tentative security infrastructure showing the security infrastructure, including application services, hosts, and network topology. Figure 14–8 shows a logical representation of the security infrastructure setup for our Web portal.

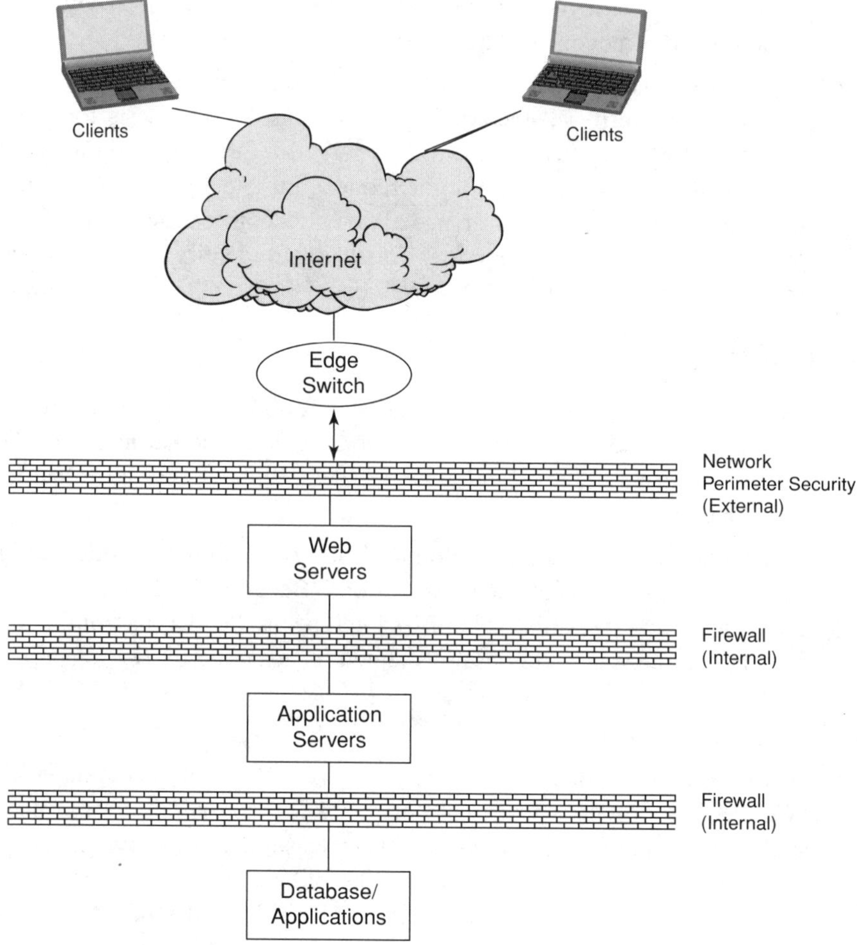

Figure 14–8 Logical representation of eRewards portal security infrastructure

Security Infrastructure–Detailed components

Figure 14–9 further elaborates on the security infrastructure with the physical representation of network security appliances, including switches, firewall, and load-balancer appliances. It also shows how the network topology is segregated physically by network switches as VLANs and how the Web server, application server, and back-end application traffic multiplexed on one VLAN.

Tier Analysis

A tier analysis becomes necessary because there are tier-specific factors and issues that will influence our design implementation. This analysis will then serve as the final analysis step in our design process.

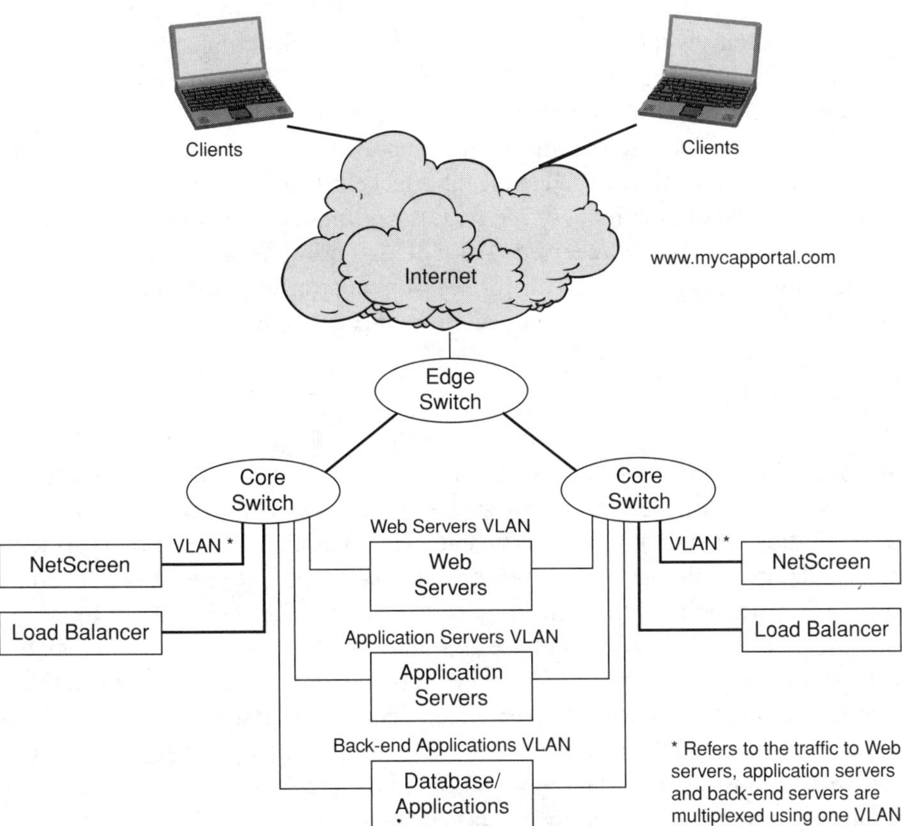

Figure 14–9 Physical representation of network security components

Web Tier

The decision was made early on to use an external Identity Provider for identity management and authentication. Because authentication will be done externally, we will need to secure the communication channel with the external Identity Provider using a *Secure Pipe* pattern. The portal will also need to collect the user credentials (username and password) from the client. To do so, we will need to use the *Secure Pipe* there as well in order to prevent the password being sniffed. We will implement the *Secure Pipe* using SSL hardware accelerator-based device mechanisms installed on the bastion hosts that run the Web servers. This will provide us with better SSL performance.

We chose to use the *Authentication Enforcer* pattern to represent the form-based authentication process in the Web tier. In our threat profile modeling, we determine that a hacker may try to guess a user's password. To prevent a hacker's success, we will configure our external Identity Provider to make use of strong password policies with minimum lengths and a mixture of alpha-numeric characters that make guessing impractical. We will also mandate account lockouts after a certain number of incorrect attempts.

One of the business requirements of the application is to provide the user with a form for reward selection. To prevent attackers from crashing the system by sending junk data in the request, we will use an *Intercepting Validator* pattern to scrub the data when it is received. We will also use a *Secure Logger* pattern to securely log all incoming requests for security monitoring and auditing. This will allow us to detect malicious activity and take preventive measures.

Business Tier

On the Business tier, we will address auditing and data obfuscation. We have identified the *Audit Interceptor* and *Obfuscated Transfer Object* patterns to address these factors. On the Business tier, we are only concerned with business-level auditing. We will not have sufficient insight into the incoming requests to do much security auditing. We can audit some business-level security audit events such as profile modification, but in general, security auditing will not be necessary on the Business tier. We will use an Intercepting Session Façade strategy that will provide us with an easy way to incorporate auditing into our Business tier without impacting our business object developers. This will reduce risk and provide a means to add or modify auditing requirements in parallel to other development.

We also must address data obfuscation on the Business tier. On this tier, that means obscuring application-layer data sent between business services. Our Business tier resides in a trusted environment, so we are not going to address securing data within the application, only obscuring sensitive information written to logs or sent from our Business tier outside our environment to our trading partners. We will use two strategies for data obfuscation. Internally, we will use the *Obfuscated Transfer Object* pattern. Because this is a protected tier and we are not concerned with host-level intrusions for this issue, we will use the Masked List strategy, which will provide data obfuscation for sensitive data written to a log or otherwise output.

Web Services Tier

To facilitate communication with service providers with a standardized infrastructure and to address the authentication and authorization requirements such as representation of credentials and message formats, we use the *Secure Message Router* pattern. Adopting this pattern eliminates point-to-point security intermediaries and makes use of a Liberty agent for enabling SSO, global logout, identity registration, and termination.

To address the message-level security requirements of the service providers and to support non-disclosure of message contents to unintended recipients, we will use element-level encryption and signatures. This will be accomplished by using a message configurator to facilitate configuration of messages applying XML Encryption and XML Signature.

Identity Tier

We elected to use an external Identity Provider for managing user identities and performing authentication and authorization for the Web portal and the participating trusted service providers. To meet our identity-management requirements and avoid the common pitfall of vendor lock-in, we will choose a vendor that provides a Liberty II protocol-based single sign-on and global logout mechanisms. Through the use of SAML assertions and a Liberty II protocol, we will deliver a vendor-neutral identity infrastructure and provide an industry-standard interface for identity federation and enabling SSO with service providers.

Trust Model

With the use of a trusted external Identity Provider, our trust modeling becomes quite straightforward. The trust model in this case is simply based on the vendor's product implementation, which allows establishing trusted relationships between the Web portal and service providers. The Web portal and the service providers trust the SAML assertions issued by the external Identity Provider for authentication and authorization decisions. The portal and service providers make use of Liberty-enabled agents to communicate with the Identity Provider.

Threat Profiling

For this case study, we will not perform exhaustive threat profiling. We will take a simple attack tree and look at two branches. Based on our use case scenario, we will assume that the goal (that is, the root node of the tree) is to gain an unearned reward from our partner service. One branch of the attack tree impacts the Web tier and the other impacts the Web Services tier.

The first branch involves an attacker trying to gain access to a legitimate user's account. From there, the attacker can modify the user's address information and order rewards for that user that will get shipped to the attacker. To do this, the attacker can use two approaches:

- Guess the user's password.
- Use a network-based packet sniffing tool to obtain the user's password.
- The second branch deals with an attacker trying to plagiarize a Web service request to the service provider. The two nodes under this goal in the branch are:
- Spoof a message from scratch.
- Alter a legitimate message en route.

Figure 14–10 is a diagram of the attack tree based on our modeling of this simple profile.

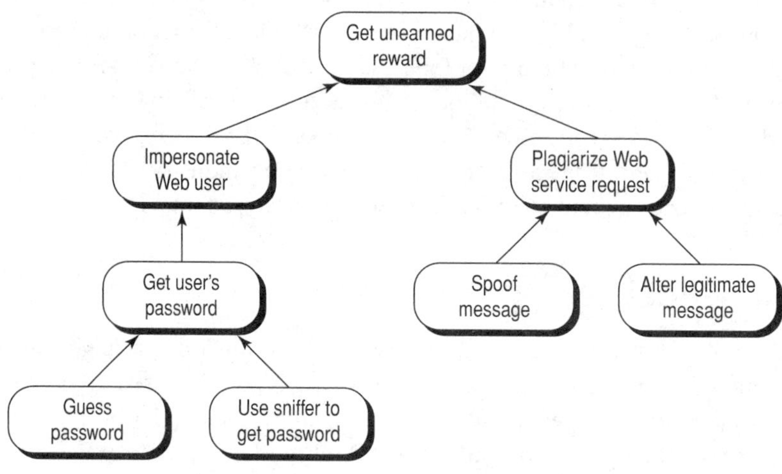

Figure 14–10 Threat profile attack tree

Security Design

The first step in our security design is to flesh out our patterns based on the analyses. As part of the architecture, we identified a set of initial security patterns to be used. We can now go back and validate that those patterns fit or choose others as necessary. We will then begin data modeling and create our business and data access objects and services.

Relating the Analyses to the Security Patterns

The security analyses we performed previously were necessary to identify the important security elements of the application in relation to the security requirements. This will also help with locating the appropriate security patterns that can be used to address the business problems. For example:

- Secure the transport layer (*Secure Pipe* pattern).
- Verify and validate the SOAP messages for message-level security, payload verification, virus attachments, fake or forged messages (*Message Inspector* and *Message Interceptor Gateway* patterns).
- Centralize, coordinate, and validate the Web requests (*Secure Base Action* pattern).
- Establish the identity policies before making business requests (*Assertion Builder* pattern).
- Protect the Web tier from denial of service or brute force fake request attacks (*Intercepting Web Agent* pattern).
- Validate Web requests and responses (*Intercepting Validator* pattern).
- Enabling Liberty SSO and applying message-level security for sending messages to service providers (*Secure Message Router* pattern).
- Obfuscate business information between objects (*Obfuscated Transfer Object* pattern).
- Log and timestamp all Web requests from a particular identity (*Secure Logger* pattern).
- Audit all service requests and responses (*Audit Interceptor* pattern).

Data Modeling and Objects

Now that the patterns have been established, the designer can set the stage for creating the application-level security design. The first step in this process is to perform data modeling tasks. Data modeling represents the relationship and dependencies of business data and objects in the application design. It is essential to abstract what business data should be accessible (for access rights control), cached (for example, for data look-up), or stored in the database (for traceability and reporting). From a security perspective of data privacy, we would also like to know whether the entire business data contents or a subset of it should be accessible by the service requester. This is particularly important when considering whether the data objects should encapsulate the entire membership record or not.

The following section describes the list of business data objects that we will use in the application design and the related data classes. Because this chapter is a case study of the security design, not the functional application design, this section will discuss the security implications of these data objects and classes only.

Business Data Objects

Several business data objects can be encapsulated, including the in-basket for the catalog service (for example, a list of the product items selected), product details, purchase order (a "manifest" or collection of the merchandise ordered), and membership record (personal information about the subscriber and the current membership award balance).

For data access, we have decided to use Java Data Objects (JDO). The JDO API is a standards-based interface for modeling business data and abstracting the data for persistence. It is a useful technology for implementing business data objects in a functional application architecture design. Refer to http://java.sun.com/products/jdo/index.jsp for details.

Data Class

Figure 14–11 depicts a class diagram of the classes represented in the eRewards portal application. The controller servlet uses the order management servlet, the membership servlet, and the catalog servlet. Each of these servlets has its corresponding helper class. Some of the methods or attributes are implementation-specific, and some are added to support specific security requirements. For example, the controller servlet has two methods that are specific to supporting single sign-on functions: redirectLogin (as used in the user login use case) and verifySSOToken (which is used for verifying the security token that is used by the Identity Provider for single sign-on).

Service Design

For our service design, we have elected to focus on four major services:

- User Login Service
- Catalog Service

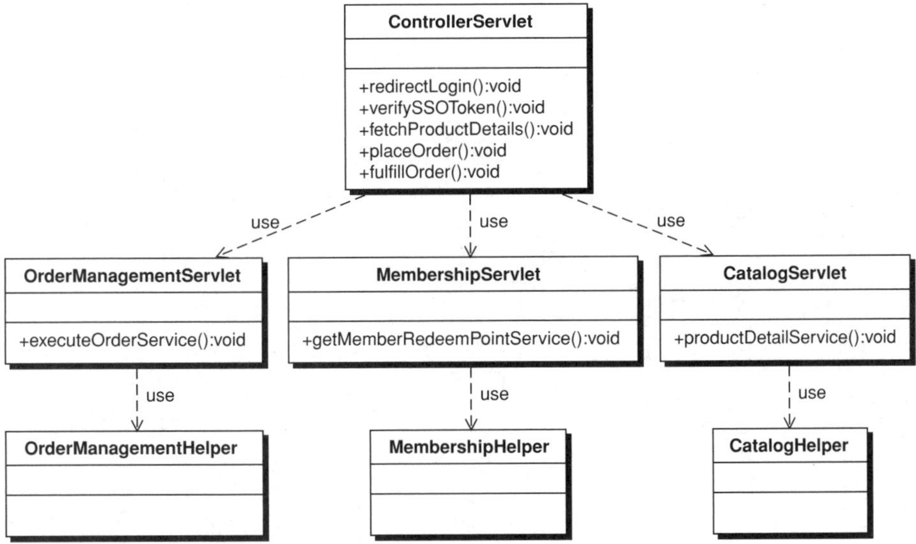

Figure 14–11 eRewards portal application: class diagram

- Order Management Service
- Order Fulfillment Service

These services represent the main services within the application. We will not address every possible service for the case study because there may be many auxiliary services in a good service-oriented architecture. These are the main services that will allow us to demonstrate the security process sufficiently.

User Login Service

The user login service allows a user to sign on to the eRewards portal and makes use of the external Identity Provider for user authentication and single sign-on. Client refers to the subscriber who wants to sign on to the online portal. IdentityProvider refers to the external Identity Provider who provides the user authentication service. The user login service is important in supporting the security requirements of authentication, identity protection, and single sign-on. Figure 14–12 depicts the detailed process between Client and IdentityProvider.

- Client initiates login.
- The online portal directs the user to the ControllerServlet, which redirects the service request from Client to SecureBaseAction.

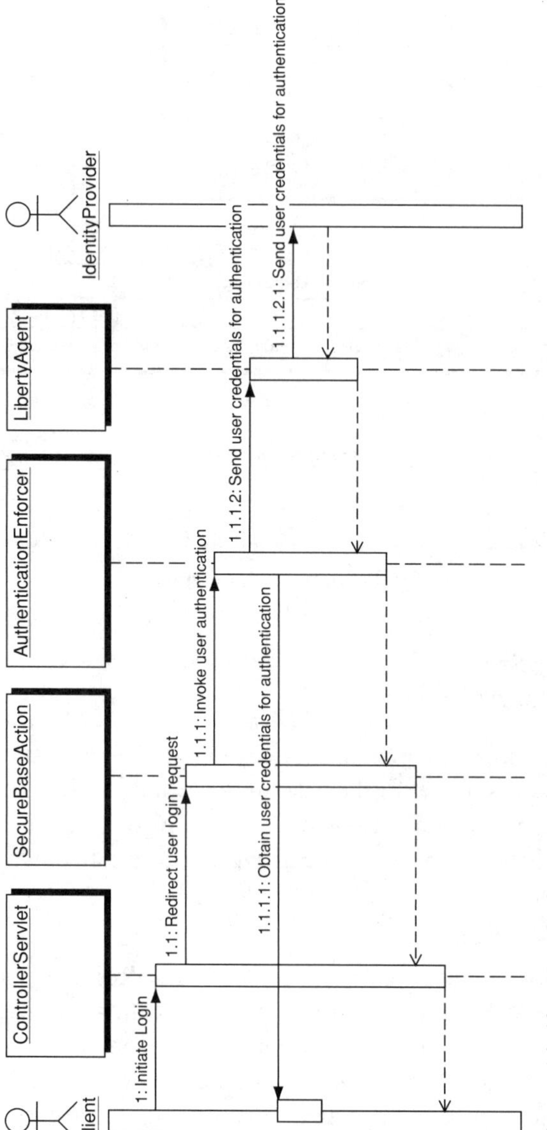

Figure 14–12 User login sequence diagram

- SecureBaseAction processes the login request and invokes the user authentication service using AuthenticationEnforcer.
- AuthenticationEnforcer prompts Client to obtain user credentials for user authentication.
- AuthenticationEnforcer sends user credentials to LibertyAgent for authentication.
- LibertyAgent sends user credentials to IdentityProvider for authentication.
- Upon successful (or unsuccessful) authentication, IdentityProvider returns status code to the service requester. LibertyAgent passes down the status code to ControllerServlet, which will respond to Client.

Catalog Service

The user browses the online catalog to select product items or merchandise for which rewards will be redeemed. The online catalog aggregates merchandise information from various sources, including external partners and service providers. It is essential that the Web servers and the application servers are secure and that the security service introduced here is able to protect the client-to-server or server-to-server session and business transactions associated with the catalog service. In other words, the security patterns here should be able to support authorization, traceability, data privacy or confidentiality, availability, data integrity, and non-repudiation.

Figure 14–13a and Figure 14–13b depict the detailed process of how security is used to protect the user while invoking the catalog service. Client refers to the subscriber who wants to sign on to the eRewards portal.

- Client sends a request to view the product catalog from the Web portal upon successful authentication and authorization.
- FrontController processes the request and dispatches Client to the Catalog page.
- The Catalog invokes CatalogAction to retrieve the data.
- CatalogAction first delegates to the SecureBaseAction for security processing.
- The SecureBaseAction invokes the verifySSOToken method on the AuthenticationEnforcer.
- The AuthenticationEnforcer verifies the SSOToken for assuring single sign-on.
- The SecureBaseAction then invokes SecureLogger to log the request.
- The SecureLogger writes the message out to a flat file log.
- The CatalogAction then invokes the SecureServiceFaçade on the Business tier to request the product details from the CatalogService.

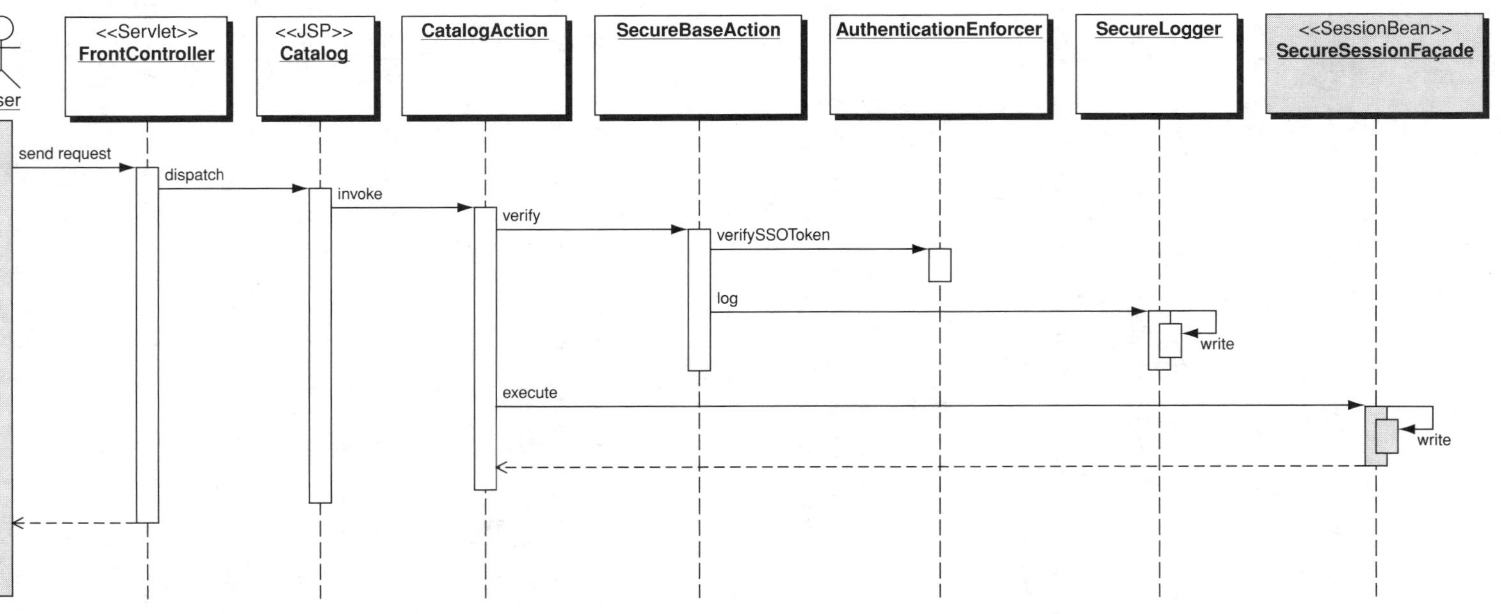

Figure 14–13a Catalog service front-end sequence diagram

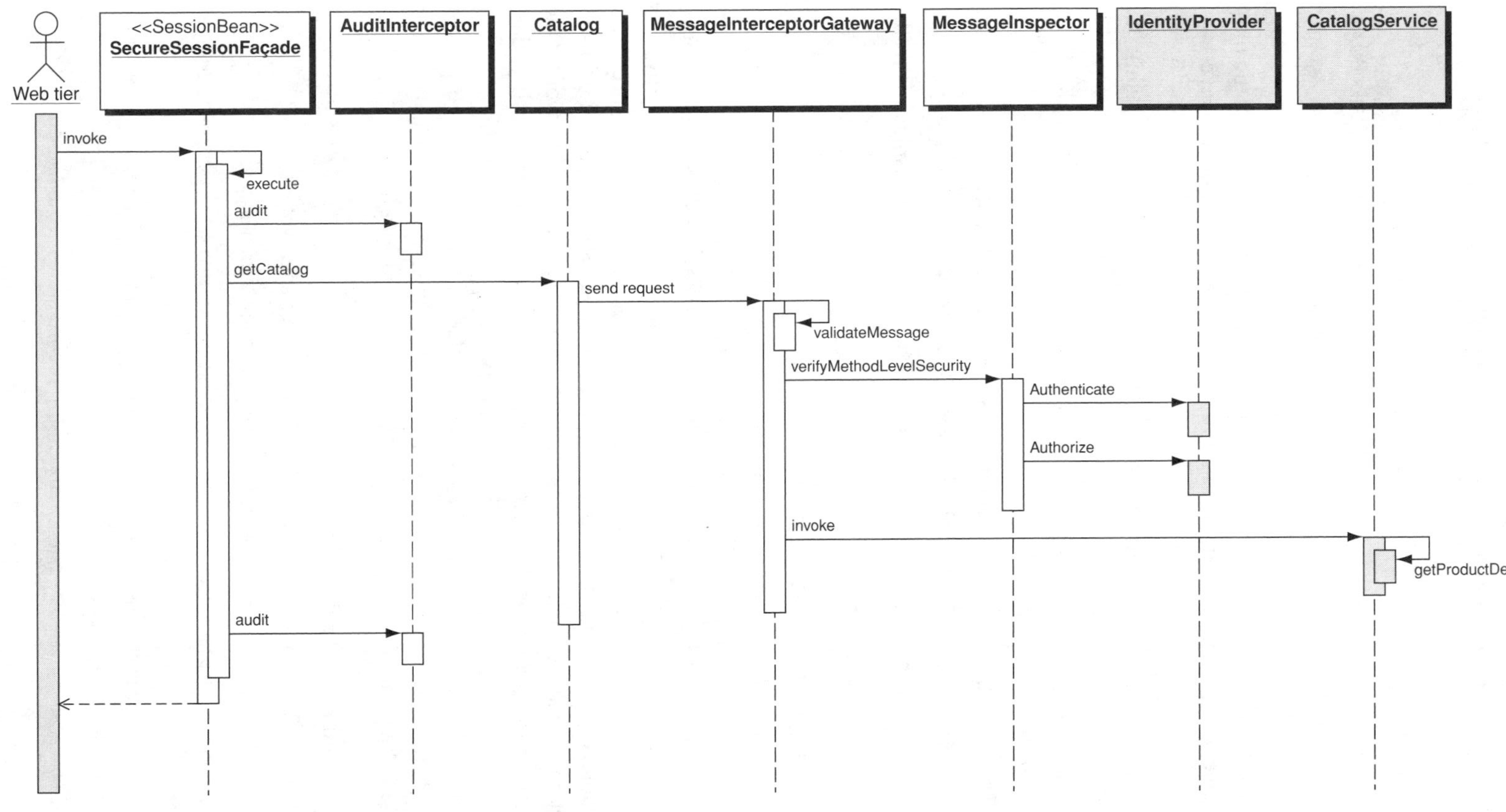

Figure 14–13b Catalog service back-end sequence diagram

- The SecureSessionFaçade invokes the getCatalog method on the CatalogBO.
- The CatalogBO, in turn, sends the request message to the MessageInterceptor-Gateway.
- The MessageInterceptorGateway makes use of MessageInspector to verify the message for authentication and authorization assertions and message-level security mechanisms.
- The MessageInspector authenticates and authorizes the request using the IdentityProvider.
- Once validated, the MessageInterceptorGateway then invokes getProductDetails on the CatalogService.
- The CatalogService retrieves and returns the product details.
- The product details are returned to the CatalogAction.
- The Catalog then gets the data from the CatalogAction and displays it to the user.

Order Management Service

Upon completion of merchandise selection in the catalog service, the user confirms placing an order with the order management service. The order management service also verifies that the user has a sufficient membership award balance before executing the order. Because the order management service involves retrieving personal information, it is essential that the security service introduced here is able to protect the client-to-server or server-to-server session and business transactions associated with the order management service. In other words, the security patterns here should be able to support authorization, traceability, data privacy or confidentiality, availability, data integrity, and non-repudiation.

Figure 14–14 depicts the detailed process of how security is used to protect the user while processing an order. Client refers to the subscriber who wants to sign on to the online portal.

- Client initiates placing an order.
- ControllerServlet places an order with OrderManagementServlet.
- OrderManagementServlet forwards request to SecureSessionFaçade.
- SecureSessionFaçade uses OrderManagementHandler to invoke order management service.
- OrderManagementHandler initiates remote order management service from OrderManagementService.
- OrderManagementService gets membership record status from MembershipServlet.

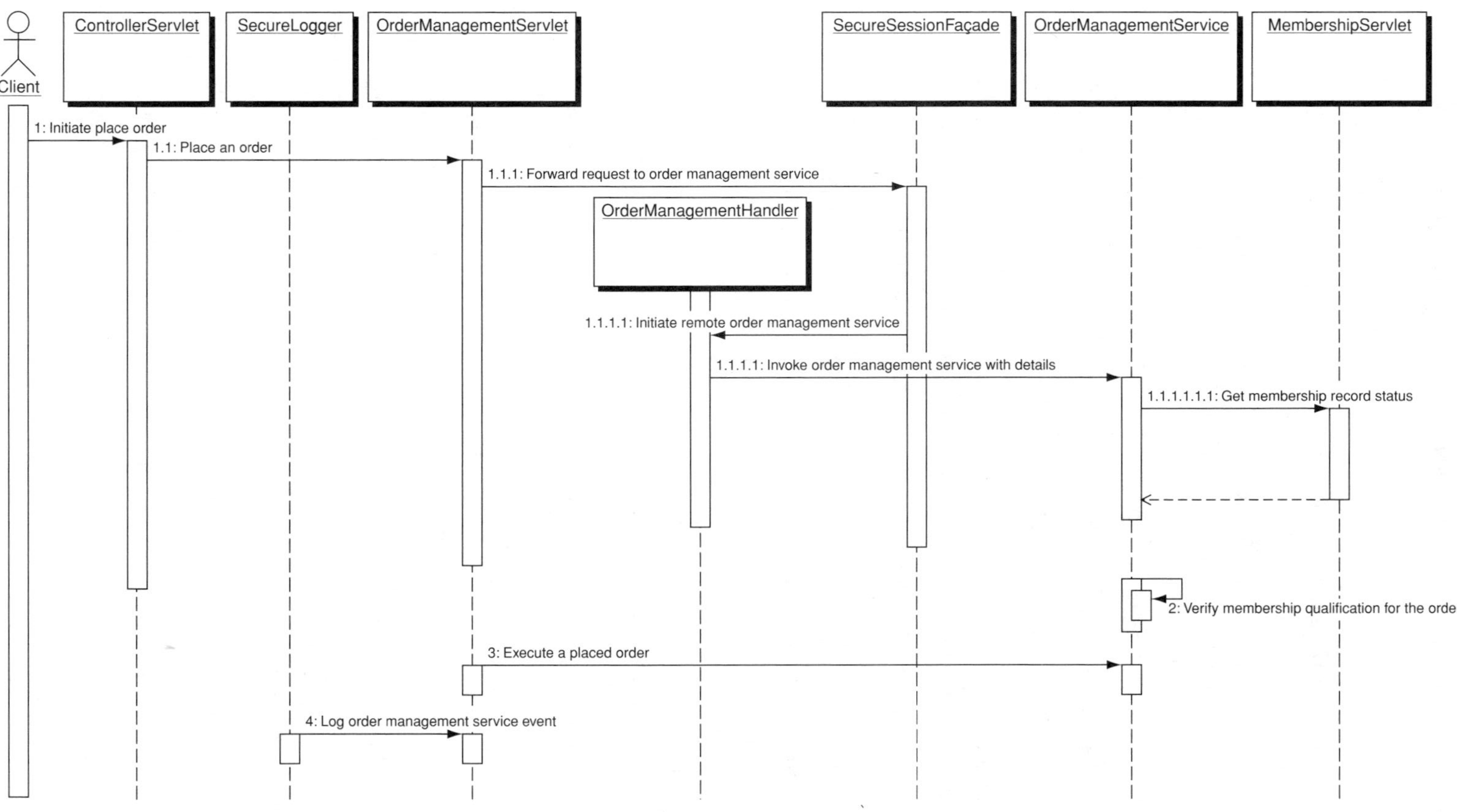

Figure 14–14 Order Management Service sequence diagram

- OrderManagementService verifies membership award status for eligibility before processing the order placement.
- Upon successful (or unsuccessful) verification, MembershipServlet returns status, membership award balance, and personal information (for example, delivery address).
- OrderManagementServlet processes the order if the status returned is positive.
- ControllerServlet logs the order management service request in the audit log.

Figure 14–15 depicts the details of processing the membership award record.

- OrderManagementService gets membership record status from MembershipServlet.
- MembershipServlet forwards request to SecureSessionFaçade.
- SecureSessionFaçade delegates the request to MembershipHandler to initiate remote membership Web service.
- MembershipHandler gets redemption points from MembershipService.
- MembershipService returns status and membership record to the service requester. Membershiphandler passes down the record to OrderManagementService.

Order Fulfillment Service

Upon completion of processing the order placement and membership balance verification, the online portal will proceed to send order details to external partners for order fulfillment. Because the order fulfillment service involves sending product details and personal information to external systems, it is essential that the security service introduced here is able to protect the server-to-server session and business transactions associated with the order fulfillment service. In other words, the security patterns here should be able to support authorization, traceability, data privacy or confidentiality, availability, data integrity, and non-repudiation.

Figure 14–16 depicts the detailed process of how security is applied to protect the user while fulfilling an order. Client refers to the subscriber who wants to sign on to the online portal. PartnerMerchantService represents the external system that handles order fulfillment requests.

- Client initiates order fulfillment service after confirming the order details with the recipient and the delivery address.
- ControllerServlet initiates order fulfillment service from OrderManagementService.
- OrderManagementService sends order fulfillment message in document-style SOAP messaging to SecureMessageRouter.

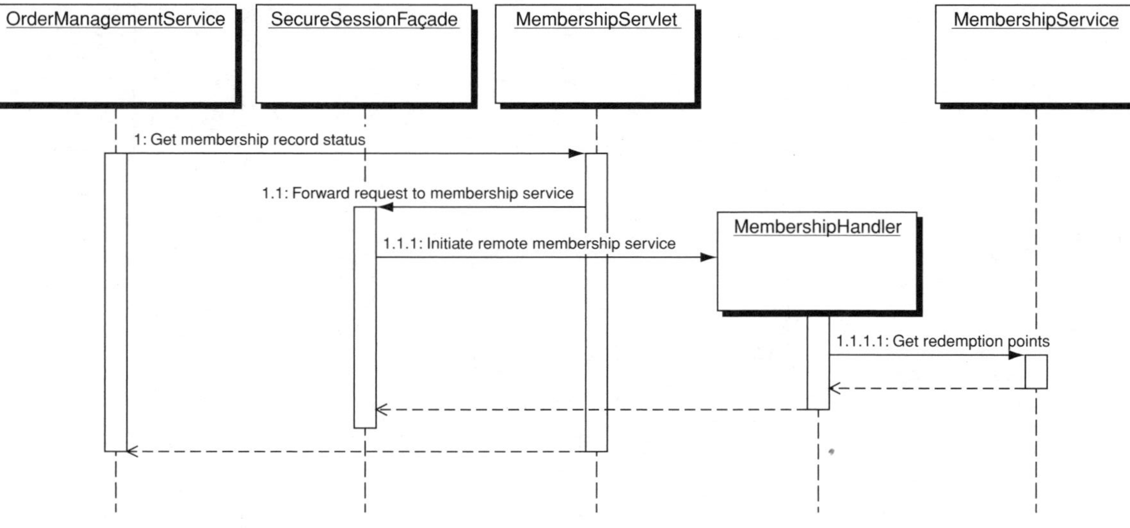

Figure 14–15 Fetching membership record status sequence diagram

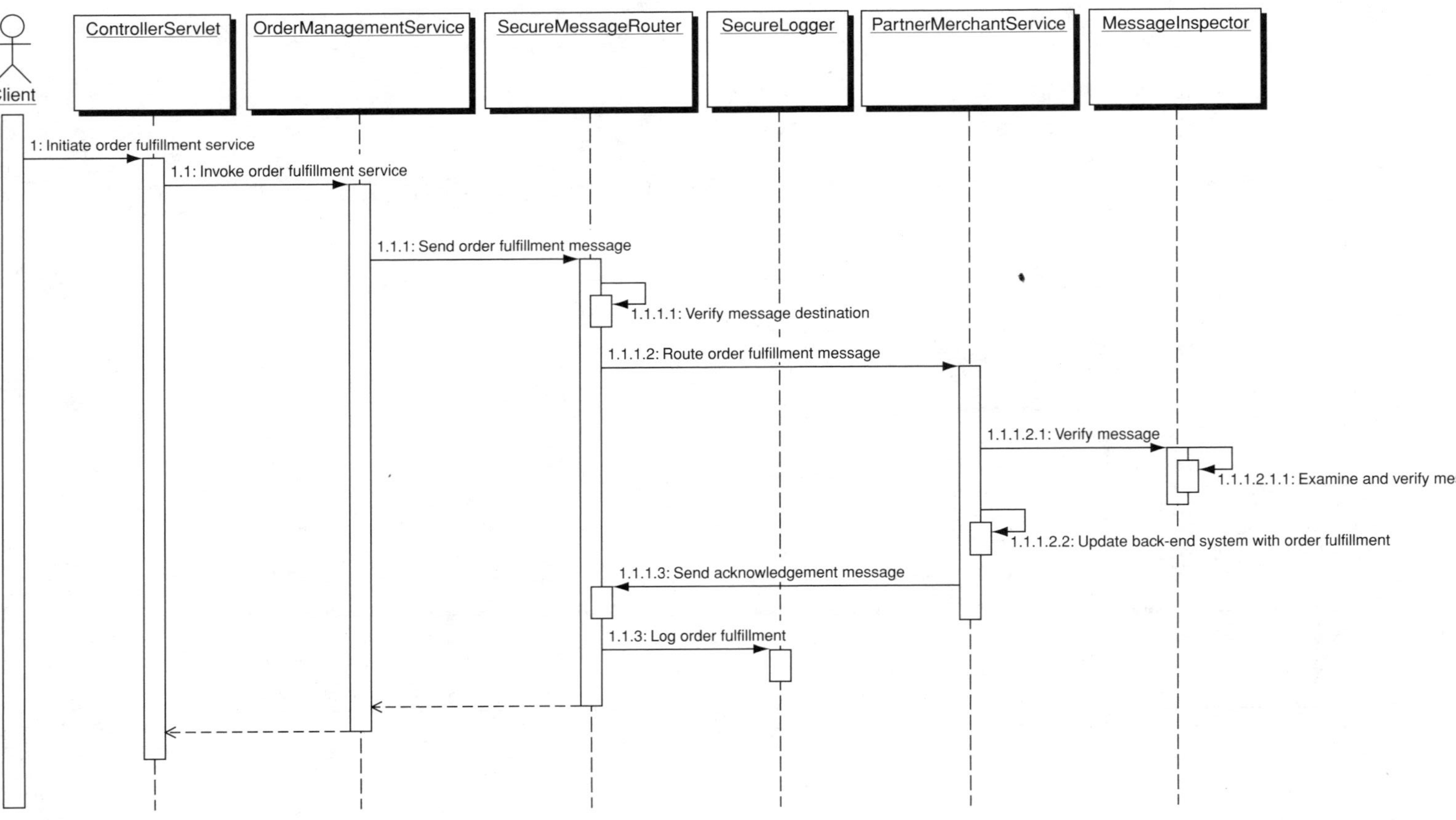

Figure 14–16 Order Fulfillment Service sequence diagram

- SecureMessageRouter defines the message destination endpoint and its message-level security mechanisms.
- SecureMessageRouter routes order fulfillment messages to PartnerMerchantService.
- PartnerMerchantService verifies the message routing information, credentials, and transaction type.
- MessageInspector examines and verifies the message for data integrity and non-repudiation.
- Upon completion of security checking, PartnerMerchantService updates the back-end system with order fulfillment details.
- PartnerMerchantService sends an acknowledgement to SecureMessageRouter.
- SecureMessageRouter logs the order fulfillment events to the audit log for traceability.
- Upon completion of order fulfillment processing, SecureMessageRouter returns status to the service requester, including ControllerServlet and Client.

These are our core services. Now that we have created the sequence diagrams and fleshed out the design details, we can turn them over to the developers for implementation.

Development

Based on the security architecture and design, we have to implement them as components and integrate them into the Web portal application. Because the scope of this chapter is limited to delivering end-to-end security architecture, we do not delve into the implementation details of the case study.

Unit and Integration Testing

One of the most important aspects of any development process is unit testing. Countless bugs, security holes, and system failures could have been prevented with a minimum amount of unit and integration testing. Like security, it is always paid lip service but seldom receives the time and resources necessary. When developers are behind schedule, the first shortcut they take is to skip writing the unit test. This often leads to bugs that the unit and integration testing would have readily revealed, and these bugs are what malicious hackers exploit.

In our scenario, we were careful to allot the proper amount of time to develop and execute unit tests throughout the code and then run integration test on executable subsystems. The unit tests themselves are an artifact of the construction phase, and code is not considered complete until the unit test is delivered and executed successfully. As a best practice, we recommend incorporating the unit tests into the build cycle. When weekly or nightly integration builds are performed, execution of the unit and integration tests should be part of the process, with the developers and development managers receiving reports of the results. This allows the development team to quickly identify when a change, either internal or external to a subsystem, causes an unintended failure elsewhere.

There are several unit and integration testing tools available in the industry and from open-source initiatives. One of the most popular is jUnit (http://junit.sourceforge.net/). JUnit is an open-source test framework that allows developers to easily write and execute unit tests. It is now integrated with many popular integrated development environments (IDEs) and provides a nice HTML reporting capability.

Testing

After successful unit and integration testing as part of the development cycle, the testers should already have completed their test cases and been exposed to development builds of the code. Now the testers will execute all functional and non-functional test cases. In particular, we will pay close attention to the security testing team. This team has the responsibility for performing security testing of the system, both white box and black box testing. Like our developers, these security testers will be hand-picked, dedicated to the security testing, and appropriately trained and mentored.

White Box Testing

The white box test team will perform white box or full knowledge testing of the system. They will examine the code, the configuration, and the environment for potential security vulnerabilities. They will make use of a variety of tools such as source code analyzers and debuggers to perform automated source code analysis, probing for security vulnerabilities.

Black Box Testing

In parallel to white box testing, a team of testers needs to be dedicated for black box or zero knowledge testing. These testers do not get to see the code or the configuration. They approach the application as a hacker would, probing for weaknesses to exploit using a variety of techniques and tools. There is a multitude of such tools out there, including the infamous SATAN (*Security Administrator Tool for Analyzing Networks*). These tools help probe the perimeter security, the host environment, and the application layers.

For our use case scenario, we used different tools to scan for network vulnerabilities that allow scanning our host and the application itself. The type of tool depends upon the type of testing. You can find anything from freeware port scanners to high-end enterprise tools with integrated reporting capabilities. The decision on which tools to use depends on how much you are willing to spend, how often they will be used, and the knowledge of the tool possessed by the test team.

Table 14–5 is a brief list of various black box tools for probing hosts, networks, and applications.

Our black box testing revealed an input parameter attack on our rewards payment page. This vulnerability opens up the application to a cross-site scripting attack. This was sent back to the designer who analyzed the risk and decided to have one of the security developers make a fix.

The security developer was able to quickly implement a fix by updating the *Intercepting Validator*'s validation rules. Once it was unit tested, it was sent back to testing. Further testing revealed no significant holes and therefore turned the code over for deployment.

Deployment

We have had our operations staff prepping the environment, setting up policies, procedures, and products. They have been testing development builds and are starting to track change management requests. We have set up our management and monitoring products and have hired an external security consulting firm to

Table 14–5 Sample Black Box Testing Tools

Black Box Testing Tools	
SATAN	http://www.fish.com/satan
Foundstone Enterprise	http://www.foundstone.com
Internet Scanner	http://www.iss.com
ITS4	http://www.cigital.com/its4/

perform a suite of penetration tests on our hosting environment. We have also applied all of the best practices mentioned throughout the book related to the environment. Everything is now locked down and ready for production support. We can now deploy our application to production.

Configuration

A critical step in securing the environment for production is configuration. Configuration management is always a tedious and time-consuming task. It applies to all aspects of the environment, just like security. It is also the basis of a security infrastructure because poor configuration is blamed for a large amount of security holes. A poorly configured router or firewall is more of a security problem than not having one at all, because it provides a false sense of security.

Intrusion Detection Systems (IDSs) are one way of managing host configurations. They do not necessarily provide configuration management, but they are good at reporting when a file in a file system has been added, changed, or deleted. Most host-based attacks involve changes to one or more files, either to open up additional holes or to compromise the system in a way that the initial penetration is unable to achieve. An IDS can detect this change and notify an administrator, who can then take corrective action.

Monitoring

We are also going to use our IDS to monitor our network for malicious activity. The IDS can detect an attack in progress and notify our administrators. Depending on your IDS, it may also be able to react to the attack and take proactive action such as blocking the IP address of the attacker.

In addition to network monitoring, we need to monitor our host and the application itself. For the host, we need to monitor log files, but we also need to monitor resource consumption. An application can often be taken down by the most mundane of factors, such as running out of hard disk space. There are many enterprise management tools. Many of these tools provide a range of sophisticated monitoring capabilities with the ability to set alarms and thresholds and the ability to provide a number of notification mechanisms.

Our eRewards portal application itself will be monitored using JMX interfaces of the J2EE platform. We built the ability to declaratively define the attributes and operations we want to monitor and to set alarms and notification options on the business components through the MBeans framework provided by the J2EE platform. This allows us to monitor various aspects, such as security, within our application.

Auditing

The last step in a successful deployment of our portal is ongoing audits of the system. Both financial and security audits are part of our business requirements and provide a sound means of ensuring security requirements are being met throughout the lifetime of the application.

For our auditing, we have brought in a security auditor to provide auditing of the network, host system, and application-level security mechanisms and infrastructure. This will provide us with the end-to-end security architecture verification that ensures we are adequately protected. We can now rest assured that our application is sufficiently secure and will remain so throughout its life cycle. While there is no guarantee that we are protected from all attacks, we are certain we have taken all the necessary steps to provide the level of security defined by our business requirements and all known threats and vulnerabilities

Summary

In this chapter, we put our security patterns, best practices, and strategies to the test. We began by looking at a real-world scenario. We derived the requirements and then we systematically put our new-found skills to use, creating a secure Web portal application. It wasn't easy, but we made it through. You now have some experience in architecting, designing, and implementing a secure Web portal application. We also understand how and when to apply the core security patterns in traditional J2EE Web applications as well as Web services.

We have also been introduced to using the Security Disciplines in the software development life cycle described in Chapter 8, "The Alchemy of Security Design: Methodology, Patterns, and Reality Checks." These disciplines define activities that need to take place within the software development process to ensure that security is baked, monitored, and kept up-to-date within the system throughout its lifetime.

Lessons Learned

There were several lessons learned as we worked our way through the case study. Overall, we learned that there are no silver bullets when it comes to security. Security is a holistic process that must begin at the start of the software development process and continue through the life cycle until the application is finally retired. It must be addressed at every stage and by a number of different roles.

We also learned that there are a number of factors that go into determining the patterns and strategies for securing an application. A good security design takes all the factors into account and derives the necessary security requirements from the business needs and other nonfunctional system requirements. Decisions and trade-offs must be made at every step of the process. We do this as part of the risk analysis and mitigation. The security design also holds true across the tiers of the system by verifying through factor analysis and tier analysis. Often, as is the case in our scenario, different patterns or strategies are used in different tiers, depending on external factors. In the Web tier, we chose to implement our own form-based authentication mechanism using the *Authentication Enforcer* pattern. In the Web Services tier, we chose to use authentication and authorization using SAML assertions for message-level security and SSL-based mutual client certificate authentication for ensuring transport-level security.

Pitfalls

We avoided many of the common pitfalls by adopting the security patterns and following the best practices mentioned earlier in this book. We chose to use a methodology that allowed us to address security throughout the development life cycle. This prevented us from being constrained by the architecture or design at the end, as often happens in real-world applications that fail to identify security requirements and incorporate them from the beginning.

We also have come close to falling into the pit of vendor lock-in. Our decision was to use a standards-based external identity provider and adopt standards-based mechanisms to demonstrate interoperability. The major difference is that in this case there were no vendor-specific APIs that would lock us in to a particular identity provider vendor. We have therefore employed the best practice of *buy versus build* over the slight drawback of using a vendor-specific identity provider. Throughout the case study, we followed a patterns-driven design process that helped us with a highly reusable solution approach and avoided our generating a vast number of unneeded security requirements from our business requirements.

Conclusion

This case study has provided us with a good example of the many factors that go into securing a real-world application. It has taught us some lessons, revealed some pitfalls, and provided a detailed example of how to use some of the core security patterns. If you have made it this far, then congratulations are in order. You are now ready to start putting your experience to the test in the real world.

When it comes to security, the devil is in the details. As you move forward and begin to bake security into your development process, remember the process itself and pay attention to the details. You simply can't take shortcuts. A good security implementation requires that you make it a part of your development culture and follow through on it thoroughly.

References

[CSP] Chris Steel, Ramesh Nagappan, and Ray Lai. *Core Security Patterns: Best Practices and Strategies for J2EE, Web Services and Identity Management.* Sun Microsystems Press.

[CJP2] Deepak Alur, John Crupi, and Dan Malks. *Core J2EE Patterns: Best Practices and Design Strategies, Second Edition*. Prentice Hall, 2003.

Part VII

Personal Identification Using Smart Cards and Biometrics

Secure Personal Identification Strategies Using Smart Cards and Biometrics

Topics in This Chapter

- Physical and Logical Access Control
- Enabling Technologies
- Smart Card-Based Identification and Authentication
- Biometric Identification and Authentication
- Multi-factor Authentication Using Smart Cards and Biometrics
- Best Practices and Pitfalls

Chapter 15

Secure Personal Identification Strategies

Secure personal identification enhances the confidence, accuracy, and reliability of verifying a human identity and its eligibility for physical or logical access to security-sensitive resources and restricted areas. Secure personal identification and verification technologies enable a high degree of access protection to restricted locations, network infrastructures, IDs, banking, financial transactions, law enforcement, healthcare, and social organizations' services. These resources include computer systems, applications, data, documents, business processes, ATM machines, personal devices, and doors to restricted locations.

Traditional identification and verification mechanisms often verify a person's knowledge of information such as passwords and PINs (magnetic stripe cards). These mechanisms are highly susceptible to fraud, because they can be forgotten, stolen, predicted, forged, manipulated, impersonated, and hacked while being used in trusted resources. Historically, it has been proven that passwords and PINs are inefficient and inaccurate when a trusted resource requires physical verification of an identity. Trustworthy personal identification requires verification of an individual beyond username/password and PINs; it requires a strong authentication similar to face-to-face interaction between the person and the verifying agent.

In Chapter 1, we discussed the importance of smart cards and biometrics technologies along with their increasing rate of use in the IT industry for the prevention of security issues related to personal identification and authentication. Adopting secure personal identification technologies using smart cards and biometrics facilitates a high degree of logical and physical verification and enables a stronger authentication process. Using secure personal identification technologies helps to identify and thwart identity fraud and impersonation crimes when an individual wrongfully obtains another individual's identity credentials and claims to be that other person. In secure personal identification, smart cards and biometrics provide a means of verifying an identity by verifying the person's proof of possession and proof of the person's physiological and behavioral properties, respectively.

This chapter explores the concepts, technologies, architectural strategies, and best practices for implementing secure personal identification and authentication. We discuss using smart cards and biometrics as well as enabling multifactor authentication with a combination of both methods. In particular, we will study how to incorporate smart cards and biometrics-based authentication in J2EE-based enterprise applications UNIX and Windows environments.

Physical and Logical Access Control

The security of an organization's assets involves protecting and safeguarding its physical and intellectual property from theft, vandalism, unauthorized access, and disasters.

Securing physical properties addresses the mandatory physical access control requirements for buildings, equipment, material inventory, and so forth. This defines the physical access control for a location in an organization or its infrastructure. Physical access control restricts unauthorized personnel from gaining entry and potentially causing theft, damage, disruption of an organization.

Securing intellectual property involves protecting business information, processes, data, and communications. This security defines the logical access control to computer and network infrastructures based on a person's identity information. Examples include authentication credentials and associated privileges set by the organization. Logical access control protects an organization from unauthorized access, intrusions, and electronic crimes that result in loss of sensitive information, disclosure of confidential data, policy breaches, data manipulation, identity theft, impersonation, regulatory violations, and so forth.

It is very common—historically, in most organizations—to find that physical and logical access control policies are addressed with two different approaches and managed as two different organizational silos. The physical access control of an organization is managed by the security department, which manages and monitors all physical entry and exit of personnel. The logical access control of an organization is managed by the IT department, which defines the policies and rules for accessing an information system. In reality, there are many critical issues unaddressed that impede an organization's efficiency in terms of impersonation and identity frauds, discrete security procedures, use of multiple credential tokens, disconnected enrollment/termination policies, and increased total cost of ownership.

The convergence and integration of physical and logical access control mechanisms brings remarkable benefits to an organization with a *unified credential token* solution. The integration aggregates an organization's physical and logical control mandates by offering the following:

- Centralized personal identification and authentication solution
- Single credential token for accessing disparate resources
- Single interface for identity enrollment and termination
- Single console for real-time monitoring and auditing
- Integration with business processes and IT operations
- Increased ROI

Adopting smart cards and biometric technologies helps deliver a trustworthy identification solution that addresses both logical and physical access control requirements. With a combination of smart card and biometrics-based identification, a smart card holder can present the card as proof of identification, insert the card into card readers, and then provide a PIN in order to obtain access to secure locations and systems. With biometrics, even stronger authentication is possible. This means that an identity can be proved by providing a biometric sample that is matched against the value stored on the card of a biometric sample presented at enrollment.

The Role of Smart Cards in Access Control

Smart cards provide a portable credential platform for proving an identity with a tamper-resistant token and for establishing a trustworthy interaction with a restricted resource. From an organization's security perspective, it provides a highly secure alternative for verifying proof of possession over traditional methods such as verifying driver's licenses, passports, visas, and so forth. The identity credentials stored in a smart card make use of cryptographic mechanisms. This assures the card holder that nobody would be able to forge or manipulate the credentials stored in a smart card, with the exception of the card-issuing authority. Smart cards are highly resistant to network-based attacks because they use local card readers, which do not interface directly with network resources. Storing biometric templates of an identity in a smart card requires the person's biometric samples to match what's on the card. This method assures a high degree of verification and multifactor authentication before allowing access to a restricted resource.

In general, smart card technologies are widely used to support strong authentication, on-card verification (such as PKI and biometrics), physical access control (such as access to buildings and restricted areas), personal data storage and management (such as storing confidential personal and medical information), and credit cards (storing credit/debit/payment information). To understand the basics of smart cards and their associated concepts, refer to the section entitled "Secure Personal Identification" in Chapter 1, "Security by Default."

The Role of Biometrics in Access Control

Biometric technologies provide a way to acquire and represent a person's unique physical traits or characteristics in order to verify an identity and offer a high-degree of assurance that a person is actually who he or she claims to be. Biometric samples are difficult to fabricate, which makes them much harder to share or steal than other authentication mechanisms such as passwords, tokens, certificates, or smart cards, which all have potential vulnerabilities due to credentials shared, forgotten, stolen, or used without the consent of the owner. Combining biometrics-based personal verification with two or more other authentication mechanisms is often considered a robust security approach for use where heightened security requirements are mandatory. This process, also referred to as multi-factor authentication, is gaining overwhelming acceptance in the IT industry for its ability to provide trustworthy and accurate personal verification and authentication solutions.

To understand the fundamental concepts of using biometric technologies, refer to the section entitled "Secure Personal Identification" in Chapter 1, "Security by Default."

Enabling Technologies

Before we delve into the mechanisms and architectural strategies, it is quite important to understand the enabling technologies that contribute to implementing and incorporating smart card and biometric authentication mechanisms in an IT environment.

Java Card API

The Java Card API framework provides a run-time environment and a set of class libraries for developing and deploying secure Java Card applets in Java Card-compliant smart cards. It includes a subset of cryptography and security packages from the J2SE platform. These cryptography and security packages support the smart card applet development and deployment operations with regard to implementing authentication and secure downloading, installing, and deleting of Java Card applets. To facilitate those operations, the Java Card API framework provides the following algorithms and supporting API mechanisms:

- Symmetric encryption and decryption algorithms
- Asymmetric encryption and decryption algorithms
- Key interfaces
- Signature generation and verification
- Message digests
- Random data generation
- PIN management

Most smart card vendors provide support for the Java Card API and the Java Card Virtual Machine. The Java Card API is available as part of the Java Card Runtime Environment (JCRE) from Sun Microsystems. For more information about security in the Java Card runtime environment, refer to Chapter 3, "The Java 2 Platform Security."

Global Platform

The Global Platform delivers standards for portable and interoperable infrastructure smart card solutions. It supports implementation on a wide range of systems, including card reader devices, PDAs, mobile phones, contactless chip technology, and infrared devices. The Global Platform-based Java Card delivers a hardware-neutral OS with compatibility and interoperability among smart cards, smart card readers, applications, devices, card personalization systems, and key management systems. Global Platform enables smart cards to run multiple applications as a multi-application enabled card. This helps a card holder to use his or her card as an authentication token in order to gain access to privileged areas. The smart card can also be used for personal data storage of medical and financial information. For more information about Global Platform, refer to the Web site located at http://www.globalplatform.org/.

The Global Platform Card Specification v2.1.1 is recognized by the ISO to support the ISO IEC* 7816 standard series for smart cards—the ISO/IEC 7816 part 13 standard, which is for application management in a multi-application environment. The Global Platform contribution was also supported by the U.S. International Committee for Information Technology Standards (INCITS) and the American National Standards Institute (ANSI).

PKCS#11

PKCS#11 is an RSA cryptographic token interface standard that defines an application programming interface (API) for performing cryptographic operations on hardware-based security devices, including smart cards. It defines device independence and resource sharing so that multiple applications can access the cryptographic token. Most operating systems and Web browsers provide support for integrating hardware-based cryptographic operations via PKCS#11 interfaces.

PKCS#15

PKCS#15 is an RSA cryptographic token format standard that defines storage of keys on smart cards, devices, and other conventional hardware tokens/IC cards. Most smart card-based National Ids (such as Belgium's eID, Finland's FINEID, Malaysia's MyKad, and Sweden's SEIS) conform to the PKCS#15 standard.

PC/SC Framework

PC/SC defines the architecture for the integration of smart card readers and the use of smart cards in a PC-based environment. PC/SC ensures interoperability through vendor independence among smart card readers and smart card products, PC applications, and card issuers. PC/SC also defines device-independent APIs and resource management to allow multiple applications to share smart card devices. This has led to a common interface for using smart cards and readers. Most vendors provide PC/SC-compliant drivers to support their smart card infrastructure.

For more information about understanding the PC/SC Framework, refer to the PC/SC Workgroup specifications available at http://www.pcscworkgroup.com/specifications/overview.php.

OpenCard Framework (OCF)

OCF provides standardized Java API mechanisms to facilitate the entire life cycle of smart card application development and deployment. It delivers an open architecture-based interoperable application environment and APIs for developing and deploying smart card applications meeting the needs of a wide range of smart card reader terminals (that is, card acceptance devices), card operating system providers, card issuers, and card holders. Using OCF helps smart card application developers and providers with a vendor-independent platform. This means that the developers follow the OpenCard interfaces for developing smart card applications, and providers adhere to OCF interfaces so that the smart cards and card reader devices can deploy and run OCF-based applications.

OCF plays a vital role in developing smart card authentication solutions and in managing biometric information to use with Match-on-the-Card scenarios that involves storing and matching biometric samples on the card. OCF supports all Java-enabled platforms and ISO 7816-compliant devices, such as Personal Computers (PCs), servers, automatic teller machines (ATMs), point-of-sales terminals, set-top boxes, and handheld devices. The OCF implementations also support existing PC/SC 1.0-supported reader devices. A reference implementation of OCF is publicly available for download at http://www.opencard.org. For more information about OCF, refer to the architecture and developer guide available at http://www.opencard.org/index-docs.shtml.

OpenSC

OpenSC is an open source framework initiative for enabling smart cards to support security operations. It provides a set of API libraries and tools for integrating smart card readers and accessing to smart cards. The OpenSC framework focuses on running cryptographic operations and facilitates smart card use in security applications such as mail encryption, authentication, and digital signature. OpenSC provides implements the PKCS#11 API so that applications supporting this API on operating systems such as Linux, Windows and Solaris and Web browsers/e-mail clients such as Mozilla, Firefox and Thunderbird can use it. OpenSC also implements the PKCS#15 standard.

For more information on using OpenSC framework, refer to the architecture and developer guide available at http://www.opensc.org/docs.php

BioAPI

The BioAPI is a standardized API for developing personal identification applications that interface with biometric verification devices such as fingerprint scanners, facial recognition devices, iris and retina scanners, voice recognition systems, and so forth. It was developed by a consortium consisting of industry vendors that support biometric technologies. The BioAPI Version 1.1 [refer BioAPI] is an approved standard that is compliant with the Common Biometric Exchange File Format (CBEFF). The BioAPI is also accepted by the American National Standards Institute (ANSI). BioAPI facilitates development and deployment of biometrics-based personal verification and authentication in a vendor-neutral way with standardized interfaces, modular access to biometric matching algorithms, and support for running across heterogeneous platforms and operating systems. For more information about BioAPI, refer to the Web site for the BioAPI Consortium located at http://www.bioapi.org/.

To support Biometrics Match-on-the-Card and Match-off-the-Card requirements, The Java Card Forum Biometric Task Force and the NIST Biometric Consortium Working Group have developed a Java Card Biometric API specification that defines API mechanisms to facilitate integration of the Java Card API with biometric authentication. This specification provides all required biometric authentication functions, such as enrollment, verification, and identification processes of a biometric service provider (BSP). For more information about the Java Card Biometric API, refer to the API specification located at http://www.javacardforum.org/Documents/JCFBioAPIV1A.pdf.

Pluggable Authentication Module (PAM)

PAM allows applications and OSs to be independent of authentication mechanisms in a UNIX environment, particularly Solaris and Linux. The PAM framework supports multiple authentication service modules configured as a authentication stack. The authentication service modules are a set of dynamically loadable objects invoked by the PAM API to provide a particular type of user authentication. PAM gives system administrators the flexibility to choose any authentication service available on the system to perform authentication. New authentication service modules can also be plugged in and made available without modifying the applications.

PAM allows implementing login modules for different authentication technologies, such as RSA, Kerberos, smart cards, biometrics, and so forth. PAM-based authentication modules can be plugged into the UNIX environment for system authentication, access control, and other related management tasks such as provider administration and account management. The core components of the PAM framework are the PAM API library (PAM API), PAM authentication module, and PAM Service provider interfaces (SPI). Applications implement PAM APIs to communicate with PAM modules for enabling authentication. Authentication service providers implement PAM modules using SPI. To initiate authentication, the application calls the PAM API that loads the appropriate authentication module defined in a configuration file. Then the request is forwarded to the underlying authentication module, which in turn communicates with the authentication service provider. The authentication module returns a response back to the application from the underlying authentication service provider. PAM allows a system administrator to add newer authentication methods simply by installing new PAM modules and to modify authentication policies by editing associated configuration files. In most UNIX environments, a PAM policy file is defined in a /etc/pam.conf or /etc/pam.d configuration file. This file specifies all the PAM policies for a system, such as terms of service name, facility name, control flag, module name, and module arguments:

```
login   auth    required    pam_biologin.so  bio_finger
```

The configuration fields are usually represented in the order of service name, facility name, control flag, module name, and module arguments. Any additional fields are interpreted as additional module arguments.

Smart card and Biometrics vendors provide PAM modules for integration with application and UNIX environments. PAM also facilitates multifactor authentication, which allows combining smart cards and biometrics—storing biometric samples of the person who is the smart card holder. During authentication, PAM acquires the biometric sample from the scanner and matches it with the value stored in the smart card of the sample presented at enrollment in order to allow or deny user access. For more information about PAM modules, refer to the Sun Web site at http://www.sun.com/software/solaris/pam.

Graphical Identification and Authentication (GINA)

GINA is a Windows dynamically linked library (DLL) in the Microsoft Windows environment that handles the default authentication process and initiates user interaction by presenting the Windows logon window. The default GINA library can be replaced with custom authentication mechanisms built using Microsoft authentication functions, interfaces, objects, structures, and other programming elements. This facilitates using a custom GINA library in the Windows environment to represent different authentication technologies, such as RSA, Kerberos, smart cards, biometrics, and so forth. Windows does not allow stacking of authentication modules, and therefore only a single GINA can be active at one time.

By default, Microsoft provides a GINA DLL in all their operating systems. In a typical Windows installation, the GINA DLL file called msgina.dll can be found by searching the Windows libraries (for example, in Windows XP, it is made available at C:\WINDOWS\systems). To load or replace the default GINA DLL with a custom GINA representing an authentication provider, it is necessary to change the appropriate registry key representing msgina.dll. The custom GINA is also responsible for setting itself up to receive secure attention sequence (SAS) events for logging and auditing. In Windows, SAS events define the key sequence for initiating the logging process (for example, CTRL+ALT+DEL SAS event).

The Windows CE environment provides support for smart cards by way of registering smart cards as CSPs (Cryptographic Service Providers). Refer to the Windows CE .NET documentation for using smart card subsystems (http://msdn.microsoft.com).

Java Authentication and Authorization Service (JAAS)

JAAS is a Java-based API framework that allows implementing authentication and authorization mechanisms in Java applications. It implements a Java technology version of the standard PAM framework. JAAS allows J2EE applications to remain independent from underlying authentication technologies. J2EE allows plugging in security providers as JAAS LoginModules for use with J2EE application components without requiring modifications to the application itself. JAAS is commonly used for integrating authentication technologies such as RSA SecurID, Kerberos, smart cards, biometrics, and so forth.

In a J2EE environment, JAAS LoginModules are usually configured as *Realms* that map applications and their user roles to a specific authentication process. Configuring realms is more vendor-specific; refer to the vendor documentation on how to configure realms using JAAS LoginModules in a J2EE application server.

For more information about using JAAS APIs and implementing JAAS login modules, refer to the section "Java Authentication and Authorization Service" in Chapter 4, "Java Extensible Security Architecture and APIs."

Smart Card-Based Identification and Authentication

To provide smart card-based identification and authentication for logical access control, the choice of technology and implementation model is greatly influenced by the environment-specific characteristics and dependencies in terms of client application type (Web-based, rich-client, or desktop login), platform implementation (Java or Microsoft), and host environment (UNIX or Windows). In this section, we discuss the tools of the trade, architectural strategies for enabling smart card-based identification and authentication for controlling access to J2EE-based applications, and Desktop Login for host systems such as UNIX and Windows workstations.

To enable smart card-based identification and authentication for physical access control, it is always recommended to use smart cards with dual interfaces for supporting contact and contactless readers. This allows the card to be inserted or presented for identification or authentication at both traditional smart card readers and contactless card readers (using proximity technologies) commonly used for door access in restricted locations and buildings.

Let's take a look now at the architecture and implementation model for enabling smart card-based authentication for J2EE applications in UNIX and Windows environments.

Architecture and Implementation Model

The basic principles behind the architecture and implementation of smart card authentication for J2EE applications are quite typical to integration of a security provider infrastructure with a J2EE application server. JAAS is the primary representative technology for enabling custom authentication in a J2EE environment. In UNIX and Windows environments, incorporating smart card authentication is done by plugging in PAM and GINA modules, respectively.

Let's take a closer look at the logical architecture and the infrastructure components necessary for building the smart card-enabled authentication in an enterprise IT infrastructure.

Logical Architecture

Figure 15–1 represents a logical architecture showing a smart card authentication-enabled application infrastructure involving J2EE applications, Solaris, Linux, and Windows environments.

Let's explore the logical architecture in terms of its infrastructure components and its role in enabling smart card-based authentication.

Smart Cards

Smart cards provided by a card vendor include the Smart Card OS and card management utilities. Most cards have the capability to run multiple applications and store personal and biometrics templates. It is also important that the card be PKCS#15-compliant so that it can support storing certificates and can execute PKI operations on the card. Most smart card vendors provide support for Global Platform, PC/SC, Java Card, and PKCS#11 interface specifications. The card also provides an adequate amount of memory to meet the storage requirements of the application. The card issuer usually pre-installs the card with Card Unique Identifier (CUID), Private Key, and a Certificate (X.509 certificate with public key). The user sets the PIN during enrollment.

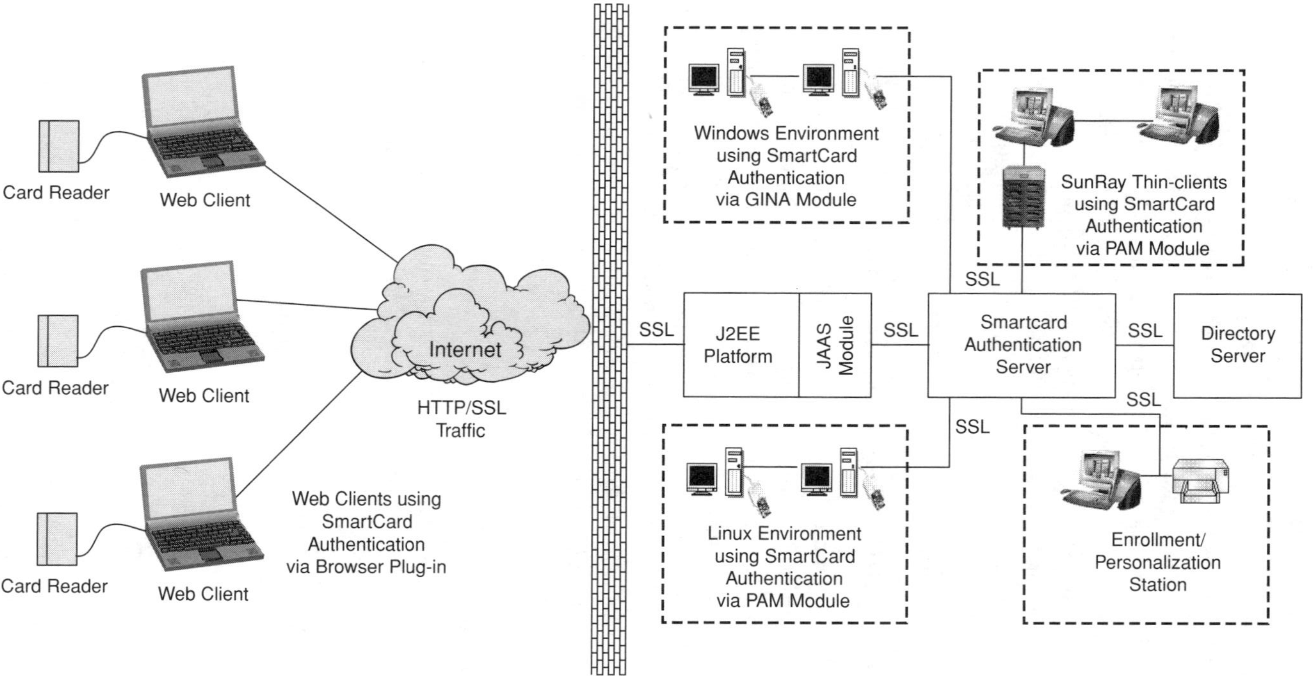

Figure 15–1 Smart card authentication—logical architecture

Smart Card Readers

Smart card readers (also referred to as *Card Acceptance Devices*) are usually provided by a card vendor, which also supplies drivers (for example. PC/SC drivers, PKCS#11 Modules) that support host operating systems such as Solaris, Linux, and Windows. The smart card readers interface with a desktop workstation or a notebook computer environment using standard connectors such as Serial, USB, or PCMCIA devices. The card reader device handles all card operations with the inserted card, such as card personalization, loading, and updating card applications and certificates.

Smart Card Enrollment/Personalization System

The smart card enrollment and personalization system is usually provided by a card vendor. The system facilitates enrolling a person to a smart card and registering the person's identification information. The system does this by capturing personal information, CUID, digitized photo, PIN, biometric sample, private key, certificate, and so forth. All enrollment information entries will be stored to a directory infrastructure. After enrollment, the system is responsible for securely loading the selected enrollment and personal information to the card by way of a Hardware Security Module (HSM) using PKCS#11 interfaces. After loading, the system then connects with a card printer to print the required personal information on the face of the card. The enrollment system is also responsible for deleting card applications, updating card information, and terminating or revoking an issued card by disabling the CUID in the directory.

Smart Card Authentication Server

The smart card authentication server provides services for verifying the identity of a person providing a smart card for authentication. It makes use of a challenge-response protocol to authenticate an identity who is trying to gain access to a resource. To verify the caller identity, the server generates a challenge string that is sent to the card to be encrypted using the private key stored in the card. As a response, the encrypted challenge is returned to the server with the CUID, which is used to locate the identity information corresponding to the CUID. The server uses the public key stored for the particular CUID to decrypt the response. If the decryption is successful and the response matches the original challenge, the user is considered as authenticated. The authentication server typically works as a security provider infrastructure for its target resource, which can be a network environment or business applications based on J2EE or Microsoft environments.

Browser Plug-in (for Web Clients)

To support Web browser-based client authentication, it is necessary to use a browser plug-in that allows interacting with a smart card reader and performing card operations. Most card vendors provide plug-ins based on Java, Mozilla, or Microsoft Active-X technologies to support popular Web browsers. The plug-in may implement PKCS#11-compliant interfaces to support cryptographic operations on smart cards such as accessing private keys, login using a PIN, signing e-mail documents, and other logical operations using a Web browser. The browser plug-in helps represent authentication callback and also prompts the user for smart card insertion during the authentication.

JAAS LoginModule (for J2EE and Java Applications)

To support smart card authentication for J2EE and Java applications, most smart card vendors provide JAAS LoginModules. In a J2EE environment, JAAS facilitates a pluggable authentication framework that allows incorporating authentication mechanisms from third-party security providers and custom authentication mechanisms specific to an application environment. JAAS LoginModules can also be built by encapsulating Global Platform or custom Java APIs provided by most smart card vendors. A JAAS LoginModule can be configured in a J2EE environment as a *realm* for authentication. All deployed applications and their associated user roles can be mapped into the realm. Once a realm is configured with a JAAS LoginModule for smart card authentication, it owns the responsibility of authenticating users within the defined realm and for populating a subject with the necessary principals, such as users and groups.

To understand the steps for implementing and configuring JAAS LoginModules for Java applications, refer to the section entitled "Java Authentication and Authorization Service" in Chapter 4, "Java Extensible Security Architecture and APIs."

J2EE-Compliant Application Server

The J2EE application server, also referred to as the J2EE platform, is a middleware environment capable of delivering multi-tier enterprise applications. It encompasses the architecture and programming model for building and deploying standards-based Java enterprise applications that span from client presentation to business logic and then integration with back-end databases and Enterprise Information Systems (EIS).

To enable smart card-based authentication, the J2EE platform requires an appropriate JAAS LoginModule that incorporates an authentication mechanism provided by a smart card authentication server.

PAM Module (for UNIX Applications and Desktop Login)

To support UNIX applications and desktop login, most smart card vendors provide PAM modules for enabling smart card authentication. PAM provides a set of shared libraries and a generalized API for enabling authentication services in the UNIX environment (for example, Solaris and Linux). PAM-based smart card authentication modules can be configured anytime and, once configured, all PAM-aware applications and the desktop environment (such as CDE, KDE, GNOME, and JDS) can immediately make use of smart card-based authentication services.

Refer to your UNIX provider administration guide for more information about configuring PAM modules.

GINA Module (for Windows Environment)

To support the Windows environment, most smart card vendors provide a GINA module that allows Windows Login using smart cards. GINA is a DLL that handles the default authentication and initiates the Window logon. Replacing the Microsoft default GINA with a smart card authentication-based GINA library allows the use of smart card-based authentication in a Windows environment.

Operational Model

Smart card-based security architecture has a lot in common with many authentication solutions. For a better understanding of the architecture and the relationships between the infrastructure components, we need to understand the different life-cycle operations managed by the architecture, such as card enrollment, authentication, and termination.

Smart Card Enrollment and Termination

To issue a smart card to a user, the card must be enrolled and registered with personal information from the prospective card holder. The entire enrollment process is usually carried out by a designated enrollment officer who is authorized to issue cards. Before enrollment, all required personal information such as digitized photo, biodata, biometric sample, and so forth must be collected and stored in a user directory (such as LDAP or RDBMS) that represents the smart card authentication process. During enrollment, the enrollment system associates the CUID of the card with the user entry stored in the directory. The enrollment system also extracts the public key certificate from the card and stores it to the corresponding user entry. If required, the enrollment system stores selected personal information to the card through a Hardware Security Module (HSM) using PKCS#11. During this process, the user will be asked to set a PIN on the card, which identifies his or her proof of possession. Once complete, the enrollment officer prints the required personal information on the face of the card using a card printer. After printing, the enrollment officer activates the card and the user's access control privileges. Now the card is enrolled to a user and ready for use.

To terminate the card from use, the enrollment officer deactivates the card by disabling the CUID and deleting the public key from the directory so that no further authentication can be done using the card. The card can also be temporarily revoked or blocked using PIN reset if a user enters an incorrect PIN too many times. The card cannot be used until the user resets the PIN, which requires the intervention of the enrollment officer to authorize the PIN reset. This PIN reset process is usually managed by the card OS itself and usually depends on the specific vendor solution.

Smart Card-Based Authentication

Let's consider a working scenario, assuming that a JAAS LoginModule for smart card authentication is installed and configured as the default authentication service for all the applications deployed using a J2EE application server. To support smart card authentication, the smart card authentication server and directory server are also installed as coexisting applications. All users entitled to access the J2EE applications are enrolled and issued a smart card. A user who attempts access to the applications using a Web browser must install a smart card browser plug-in that allows interacting with a smart card reader. During authentication, the client prompts the user to insert the smart card in order to submit credentials to the underlying JAAS LoginModule, which acts as a client to the smart card authentication server. The smart card authentication server authenticates the user based on the credentials and may allow or deny access to the requested application or resource.

The smart card authentication process is typically based on using a *Challenge-Response* protocol implemented by a smart card authentication server or using certificate validation through *Online Certificate Validation Protocol (OCSP).*

Smart Card Authentication Using Challenge-Response Protocol

In the Challenge-Response protocol-based authentication process, the server creates a random string (Challenge) requiring the smart card holder to encrypt the challenge using the card holder's private key. The encrypted challenge is sent back to the server as a Response. The server decrypts and verifies the response by means of a previously stored public key certificate. If the decrypted string matches the original string the authentication is considered successful.

Let's take a look at the core details of the Challenge-Response protocol-based authentication process using the sequence diagram shown in Figure 15–2.

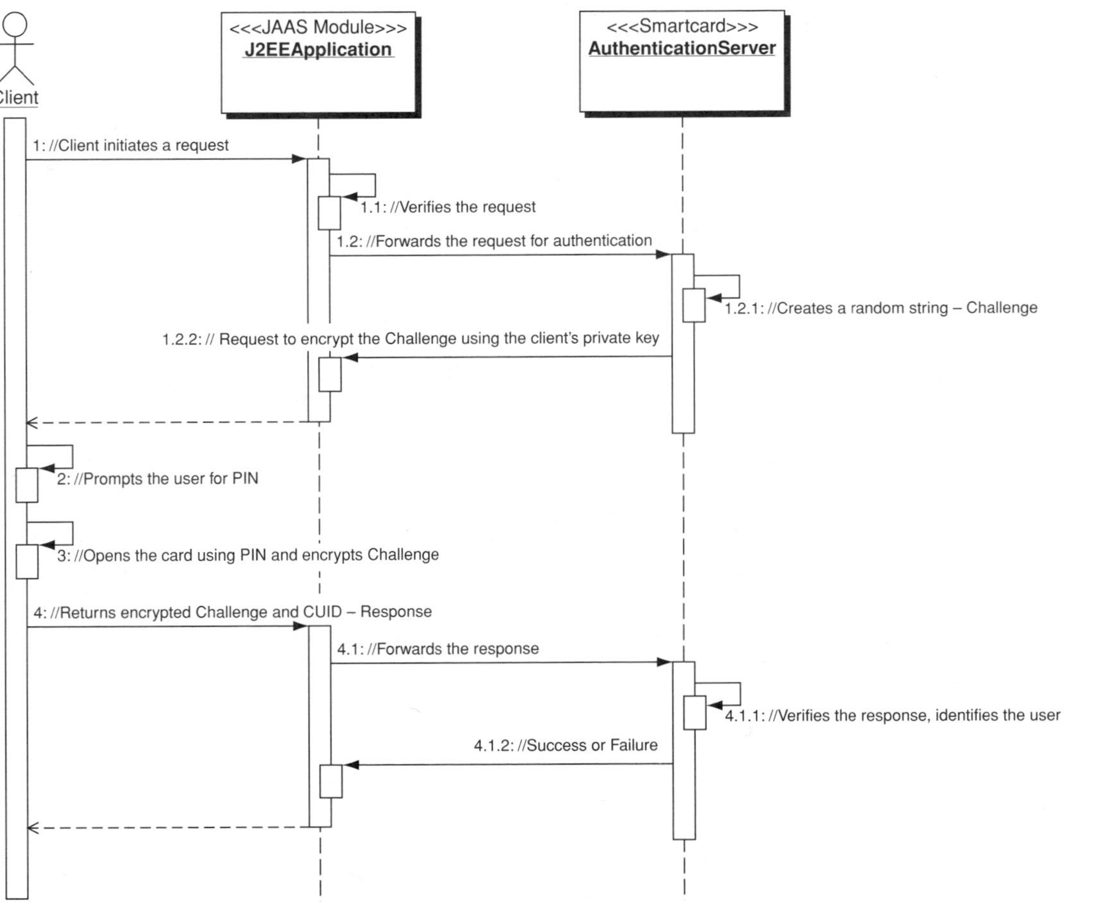

Figure 15–2 Sequence diagram for Smart Card authentication process (using Challenge-Response protocol)

The key participants and their activities involved in the authentication process are as follows:

1. The Client inserts the smart card and attempts to access the J2EE application using a Web browser.
2. The J2EE application verifies the request using the JAAS LoginModule and then initiates authentication by forwarding the request to the smart card authentication server.
3. The authentication server creates a random string (*Challenge*) and then requests the client to encrypt the *Challenge* using the client's private key.
4. The client opens the card using the PIN and then asks the card to encrypt the *Challenge* using the private key.
5. The encrypted *Challenge* and *CUID* of the card is sent back to the authentication server as *Response*.
6. The authentication server verifies the response identifying the user's CUID from the directory server and uses the public key for the corresponding CUID to decrypt the encrypted response.
7. If the decrypted string matches the original *Challenge*, the authentication is considered successful.
8. Based on the authentication result, the JAAS LoginModule allows or denies access to the requested application.

In UNIX and Windows environments, the PAM and GINA modules, respectively, play the role of JAAS LoginModule in the authentication process. The desktop login can be done using the smart card and the PIN. In desktop login, the removal of the card from the reader locks the window or logs the user out, depending upon the configuration.

Smart Card Authentication Using OCSP Responder

Using OCSP allows applications to determine the status and validity of smart card-based certificates. During the OCSP-based authentication process, the smart card authentication server (acting as an OCSP client) interacts with an OCSP responder by sending an OCSP request that includes the card holder certificate. The OCSP responder verifies the validity of the card holder certificate and returns the status information with a signed response from the OCSP responder. The OCSP responder returns the following state indicators about a certificate.

- "good": This state indicates that the requested certificate's status is valid and not revoked.

- "revoked": This state indicates that the requested certificate's status has been either permanently or temporarily revoked.
- "unknown": This state indicates that the responder doesn't know about the certificate being requested.

The OCSP responder provides real-time status checking and validation of certificates. The OCSP responder is designated by a Certificate Authority that maintains the status information of all issued certificates. The OCSP responder issues OCSP responses on behalf of that CA. HTTP is used as the preferred protocol to transport the OCSP request and the OCSP response between the smart card authentication client (server) and the OCSP responder.

Using Smart Cards for Physical Access Control

As we discussed earlier in this chapter, using a single credential token for providing unified access control is crucial to the success of any organization in providing both physical access control (building, locations, and so forth) and logical access control (computers, software applications, and so forth). This means that a smart card deployment must provide support for both physical and logical access control in terms of identification and authentication. This is accomplished by smart cards with dual-interfaces that meet the requirements of both physical access control systems using contactless readers (such as a proximity antenna) and logical access control systems using contact-based readers.

Biometric Identification and Authentication

Biometric identification and authentication solutions are based on pattern-recognition mechanisms for determining the authenticity and credibility of a living person's physiological or behavioral characteristics. This means using proof of physical properties of a human being; a person can be identified as "*Who am I*" and authenticated by verifying as "*Whom I claim to be.*" Biometric solutions are classified based on a variety of physical and behavioral characteristics. The physical characteristics include fingerprint scan, hand-geometry measurement, facial recognition, retinal scan, iris scan, and DNA verification. The behavioral characteristics include voice recognition, signature verification, and keystroke recognition. Using physiological characteristics-based biometrics is considered most reliable because they remain unaltered and unchanged unless there is illness or severe physical injury. Using behavioral characteristics are less reliable because they change according to a person's stress or health conditions.

Fingerprint-based identification and authentication are the oldest methods and are becoming more widely accepted in the IT industry to provide logical access control for security-sensitive systems and applications. Throughout this chapter, we discuss the fundamentals of fingerprint matching and how to make use of fingerprint-based biometric verification solutions.

Understanding the Biometric Verification Process

In a typical biometrics solution, a user submits multiple biometric samples (physiological or behavioral characteristics) during enrollment process that can be identifiable or recordable using a biometric acquisition device. Multiple biometric samples are acquired and processed to extract the unique features for creating a reference template. The reference template is equivalent to a user's password. Using a reference template, it is practically impossible to reverse engineer and reconstruct the original biometric sample. No two reference templates relate together or match each other as well.

During an identification or authentication process, the user submits a biometric sample that will be processed to create a template that is matched against the stored reference templates. The template matching will not be required to be 100%. The biometric verification process does not produce a success or failure result; instead, it is usually decided by a matching score that must exceed a predefined threshold limit. If the matching threshold limit is set to low, it is considered to be highly prone to impersonation; if it is set high, it is considered as robust against impersonation and fake claims.

Figure 15–3 illustrates the biometrics enrollment and identification process.

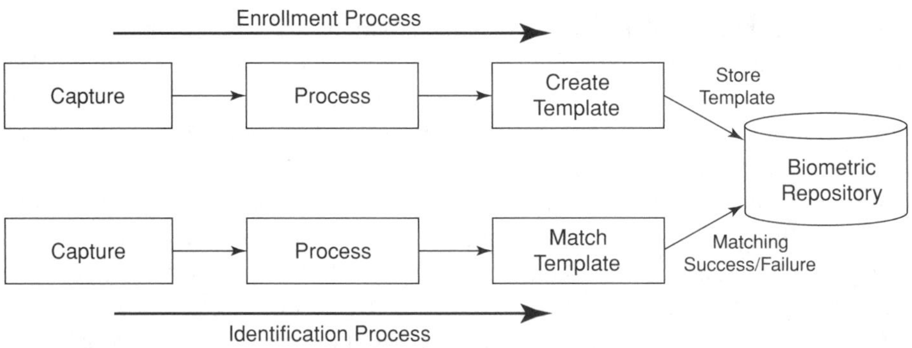

Figure 15–3 Biometrics enrollment and identification process

Identification and Authentication

The biometric verification process is usually done in two processes: *identification* and *authentication*. In the identification process (One-to-Many), the acquired biometric sample is matched against all the reference templates stored in a biometric template repository. In the authentication process (One-to-One), the acquired biometric sample is matched against a particular individual's reference templates obtained during enrollment.

Fingerprint Matching

A fingerprint consists of a series of furrows (shallow trenches) and ridges (crests) on the surface of a finger. The uniqueness of a fingerprint is determined based on the patterns of ridge-ending, bifurcations, divergences, and enclosures. These patterns are referred to as *minutiae* points, or *typica* (see Figure 15–4). A typical fingerprint can show from 30 to 40 minutiae points. A typical fingerprint template size ranges from 250 bytes to 1.2 Kbytes.

Fingerprint matching is usually done based on two common approaches: *minutiae-based* and *correlation-based*. In the minutiae-based approach, a fingerprint is identified with minutiae points and their relative placement on the finger is mapped (see Figure 15–4). In the correlation-based approach, the matching is done on the entire representation of the fingerprint based on location point. The minutiae approach is commonly adopted by most fingerprint scanner vendors.

Accuracy of a Biometric Verification Process

There are several factors and trade-offs that affect the biometric enrollment and verification process in terms of physical condition, positioning, location, weather, injury, biometric device condition, and so forth. These factors influence the accuracy of the biometric verification process because the submitted samples may

Figure 15–4 Sample fingerprint with minutiae

match incorrectly or fail to match with the reference templates. The accuracy of a biometric verification system is usually measured in terms of the concepts outlined in the following sections.

False Non-Match Rate (FNMR) or False Reject Rate (FRR)

The FRR reflects the probability that a biometric system will falsely reject a legitimate person and deny access to the restricted resource. This problem occurs when the submitted biometric information falls below the accepted threshold score. This can also occur due to the physical condition of the person's unique features at the time of submission. FRR is considered a Type-1 error.

False Acceptance Rate (FAR) or False Match Rate (FMR)

The FAR reflects the probability that a biometric system will falsely recognize an impostor as a verified person and grant them access to entry. This problem can be controlled by usually setting a high-threshold matching score, which lowers FAR and results in better security. FAR is considered a Type-2 error.

Failure to Enroll (FTE)

The FTE is a lack of unique features or sufficient biometric data to identify and enroll a person into a biometric verification system. If the fingerprint technology requires 200 minutiae points to enroll a person and a person requiring enrollment is only able to produce 190 minutiae points, this would cause an FTE issue. For example, construction workers use their hands for heavy work, which often causes worn out and hidden fingerprints. In such cases, a manual system must be in use for those who cannot enroll in the system.

Crossover Error Rate (CER) or Equal Error Rate (EER)

The CER determines the percentage by which the FAR and FRR are equal to each other. For example, it is important to strike a balance between the FAR and FRR so that we do not set the high threshold to lower FAR but end up affecting some legitimate persons by FRR.

Ability to Verify (ATV)

This defines the probability of the overall accuracy and performance of a biometric verification system. It is a combination of FTE and FRR, which provides the total percentage of persons successfully authenticated for access to a restricted resource. The lower the ATV, the greater the accuracy and reliability of the authentication. A higher ATV results in high FMR, which decreases the reliability of the verification. ATV can be computed as follows:

```
ATV = (1 - FTE) * (1 - FRR)
```

Architecture and Implementation

The architectural principles of biometric authentication are quite similar to smart card-based access control solutions. To enable biometric-based identification and authentication for physical and logical access control, the implementation model differs based on the technology options and the different approaches meant for representing the biometric samples, such as fingerprints, face (facial profile), hand geometry (shape of the hand), iris scan (colored ring of the eye), retina scan (blood vessel pattern), and others. Each option and approach has its own complexities and limitations.

The architecture is greatly influenced by the biometric environment-specific characteristics and dependencies in terms of biometric sensors to use, verification accuracy, client application type (Web-based, rich client, or desktop login), platform implementation (Java or Microsoft), and host environment (UNIX or Windows). More importantly, the architecture and implementation for enabling biometrics for physical and logical access control do not differ much from each other. This means the infrastructure components can be used for both physical and logical access in restricted locations and buildings, computers, sensitive business applications, and so forth.

In this section, we will discuss the architectural strategies for enabling biometrics-based authentication for controlling access to J2EE-based applications and desktop login for host systems such as UNIX and Windows workstations. We will use fingerprint matching as the technology of choice in our architecture discussion.

JAAS plays a vital role in incorporating biometric technology-based authentication in a J2EE environment. PAM and GINA modules enable implementation of biometrics-based desktop login in UNIX and Windows environments, respectively.

Let's take a closer look at the logical architecture and the infrastructure components necessary for building the biometrics-enabled J2EE architecture.

Logical Architecture

Figure 15–5 represents a logical architecture showing a fingerprint-based biometric authentication infrastructure involving J2EE applications, Solaris, Linux, and Windows environments.

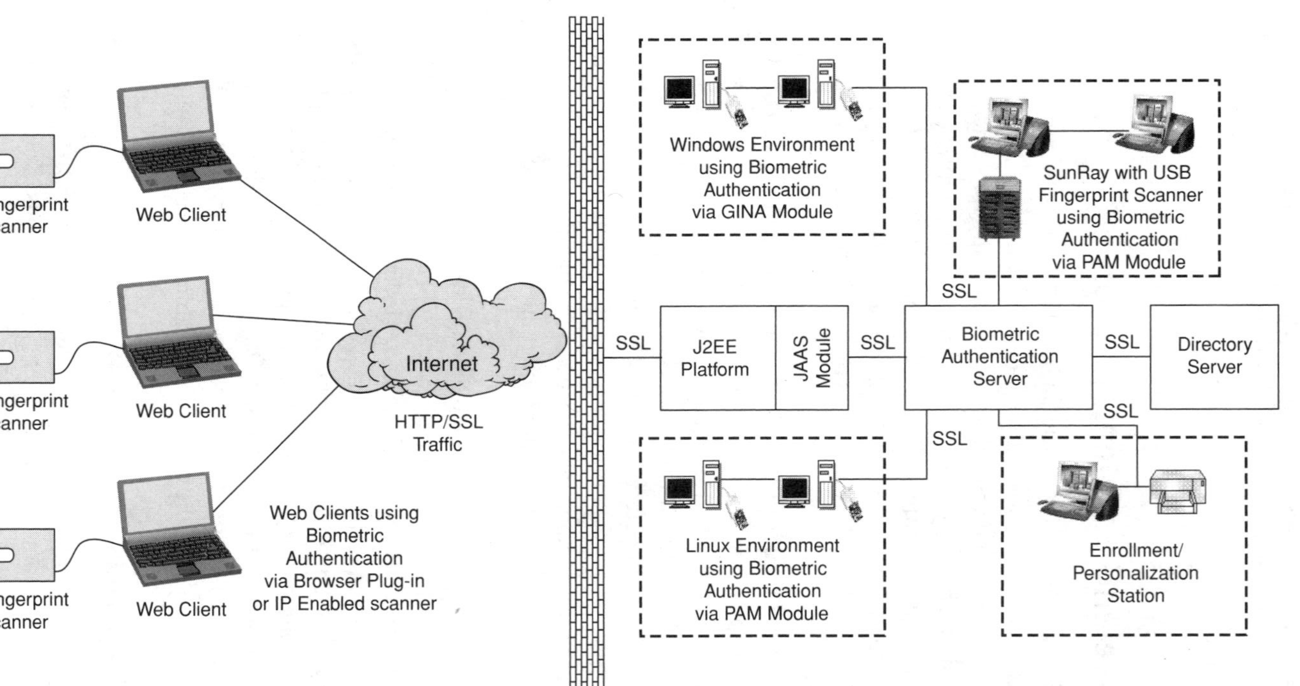

Figure 15–5 Fingerprint-based biometric authentication—logical architecture

Let's explore the logical architecture in terms of its infrastructure components and its role in enabling fingerprint technology-based authentication.

Fingerprint Scanner

A fingerprint scanner device scans the surface of a finger and identifies the patterns of the fingerprint in terms of valleys, ridges, ridge-ending, bifurcations, divergences, and enclosures. Using a device driver, the fingerprint scanner integrates with a computer by way of USB, Ethernet, or serial interfaces. The scanned fingerprint image is converted to a biometric template as part of enrolling a person's biometric profile, verifying against an existing template, or searching for a match against other templates. Because fingers can be soft, dry, hard, dirty, oily, or worn, it is important that the scanner is able to scan any fingerprint with a high degree of accuracy. There are a variety of devices that can acquire a fingerprint image; the most popular devices are optical scanners and capacitance scanners.

- **Optical Scanner**: The optical scanners are based on mechanisms quite typical to digital camera technology, which makes use of a charge-coupled device (CCD). The CCD is an array of light-sensitive photosites that generates an electrical signal in response to light. The photosite records the pixels once the light is flashed on the surface of a finger. The pixels represent the digital image of the scanned surface of the finger. The scanner also verifies the captured image for quality image definition; if the image is not dark enough, it rejects the image and attempts to scan it again.
- **Capacitance Scanner**: The capacitance-based scanners are sensors based on capacitors that use electrical current. The capacitors make use of two conductor plates insulated from each other. They are connected to an electrical circuit built around an inverting operational amplifier. Typical to any other amplifier, the inverting amplifier alters the supplied current based on fluctuations in another current. When a finger is placed on the scanner, the surface of the finger acts as a third capacitor plate, and it is insulated with a pocket of air. Capacitance-based scanners capture a fingerprint image as peaks and valleys that affect the electrical current. When a finger is placed on the scanner, only the peaks make contact with the scanner surface. Capacitors under the peaks thus have a higher capacitance, and the capacitance is lower in the valleys because of air pockets. Based on this difference, an image is electrically acquired.

Some fingerprint scanners provide an Ethernet interface that allows assigning an IP address to them. Using Ethernet-interface based scanners helps to identify the IP address and verify the initiating host machine and its domain. This also helps identify the user from the host machine who is privileged to access or not privileged. In addition, the scanner communication can also be secured using the SSL/TLS protocol using the certificate and keys stored in the scanner itself.

Biometrics Enrollment and Authentication System

The biometrics enrollment and authentication system is provided by a biometric vendor that facilitates enrollment, authentication, management, and integration of directory servers.

- The enrollment system is responsible for registering the personal identification information, including multiple biometric samples of a person. All enrollment information entries will be stored to an underlying directory infrastructure. The enrollment process is carried out by an enrollment officer who is authorized to register users, assign biometric scanners, set up roles and policies, and manage enrollment and termination of users.
- The authentication system is the biometric verification engine responsible for verifying an identity by matching the newly acquired image with the reference template stored in the directory. The authentication is termed successful if the matching score exceeds the predefined threshold limit. If the score is below the threshold, the authentication is considered unsuccessful. The authentication server is also responsible for monitoring and logging login attempts, access granted or denied, and user and machine information. All communication between the authentication system and the biometric scanner makes use of SSL/TLS protocols, which ensures the data transmitted is secure and tamperproof. The authentication server typically works as a security provider infrastructure for its target resource, which can be a network environment or business applications based on J2EE or Microsoft environments.

Browser Plug-in (for Web Clients)

To support Web browser-based client authentication, it is necessary to use a browser plug-in that allows interacting with a biometric scanner to acquire biometric samples (such as fingerprints). Most biometric vendors make use of plug-ins based on Java, Mozilla, or Microsoft Active-X technologies to support popular Web browsers. The plug-in may also implement native interfaces to integrate biometric scanners. The browser plug-in helps represent authentication callbacks and prompts the user for biometric samples during the authentication.

PAM Module (for UNIX Applications and Desktop Login)

To support UNIX applications and desktop login, most biometric vendors provide PAM modules for enabling biometric authentication. PAM-based biometric authentication modules can be configured to enable biometric authentication service for PAM-aware applications and the desktop environment (such as CDE, KDE, GNOME, and JDS). Refer to your UNIX provider administration guide for more information on configuring PAM modules.

GINA Module (for Windows Environment)

To support the Windows environment, most biometric vendors provide GINA modules that allow Windows Login using biometric authentication. Replacing the Microsoft-default GINA with biometric authentication-based GINA library enables biometric authentication in a Windows environment.

J2EE-Compliant Application Server

To enable biometric authentication, the J2EE platform requires an appropriate JAAS LoginModule that encapsulates the authentication mechanism provided by a biometric authentication server.

JAAS LoginModule (for J2EE and Java Applications)

To support biometric authentication for J2EE and Java applications, most vendors provide JAAS LoginModules. As we discussed earlier in this chapter, JAAS facilitates a pluggable authentication framework that allows incorporating authentication mechanisms in a Java or J2EE environment. JAAS LoginModules can also be built by encapsulating the BioAPI or custom Java APIs provided by most biometric authentication vendors.

Operational Model

The operational model of biometrics-enabled security architecture has a lot in common with smart card authentication solutions. Let's take a look at the different life-cycle operations such as biometric enrollment, authentication, and termination.

Biometric Enrollment and Termination

To enroll a user, the person to be registered must first provide the biometric samples and then personal and demographic information. The entire enrollment process is usually carried out by a designated enrollment officer who is authorized to acquire biometric samples. Before enrollment, all required personal information such as digitized photo, personal information such as address for communication, driver's license information, business responsibilities, and so forth must be collected and stored in a user directory (such as LDAP or RDBMS) that represents part of the biometric enrollment process.

Figure 15–6 shows the fingerprint-based biometric enrollment process using BiObex.

During enrollment, the system associates the biometric samples of a person (such as fingerprint images or face geometry) with the other personal information stored in the directory. Multiple samples may be acquired based on the biometric technology in use (for example, for fingerprint-based authentication, usually all fingers from both hands will be acquired). The acquired biometric samples are processed using relevant algorithms and then converted to a template format (referred to as a **reference template**). The enrollment system securely stores the templates in a directory. Once complete, the enrollment officer assigns the user to the privileged machines, scanners, and applications, specifying biometric authen-

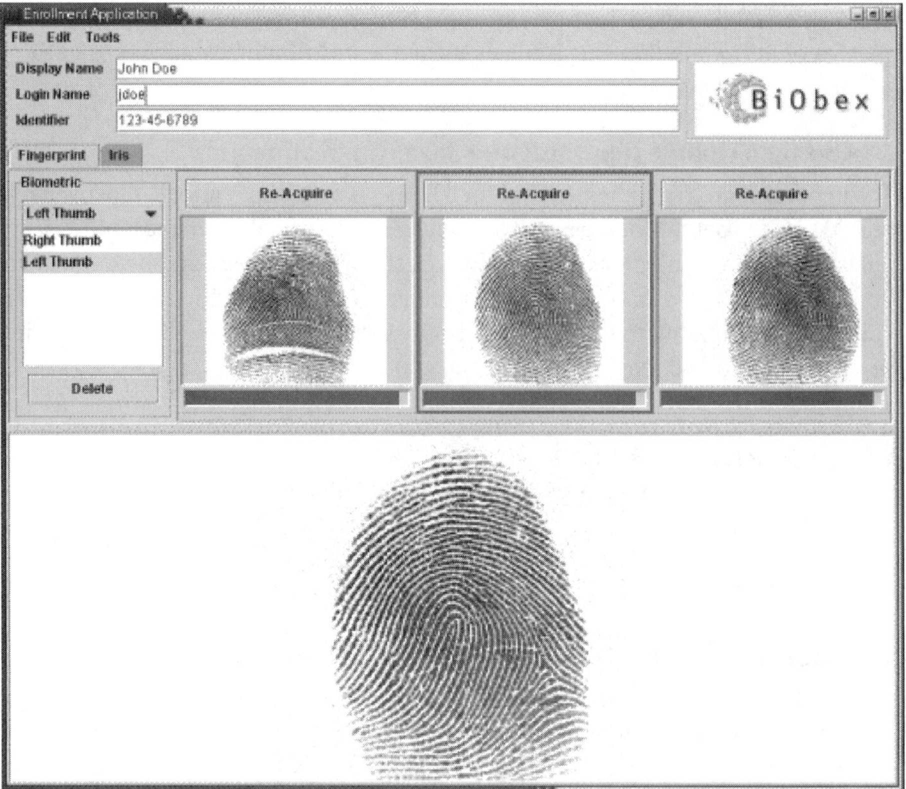

Figure 15–6 Biometric enrollment process using BiObex (Courtesy: AC Technology, Inc.)

tication for that user. The enrollment officer also activates the user's access control privileges, roles, and the authorized actions specific to the user's business responsibilities. This completes the user enrollment process with a biometric-enabled authentication system.

To terminate the user, the enrollment officer deactivates the user access by disabling the user account, scanner entry, and associated privileges so that no further authentication can be done using the assigned scanner (for example, the fingerprint scanner submission of images will no longer be accepted). The user's privileges can also be temporarily revoked if the user's biometric samples do not match after multiple attempts to obtain a match are made. A revoked user account cannot be accessed without the intervention of an enrollment officer.

Biometric Authentication Process

Let's consider a working scenario, assuming that a JAAS LoginModule for biometric authentication is installed and configured as the default authentication service for all the applications deployed using a J2EE application server. To support biometric authentication, the biometric authentication server and directory server are also installed as coexisting applications. All users entitled to access the J2EE applications are enrolled by providing their biometric samples, which are stored as reference templates. When a user attempts access to a protected application using a Web browser, the JAAS LoginModule initiates authentication. During authentication, the client prompts the user to submit the required biometric samples using the assigned biometric scanner. The biometric authentication server authenticates the user by processing the acquired image(s) (such as a fingerprint) and matching them with the reference templates. Based on the matching score, the authentication server may allow or deny access to the requested application or resource.

Let's take a look at the core details of the authentication process using the sequence diagram shown in Figure 15–7.

Figure 15–7 represents the sequence diagram for the biometric authentication process in a J2EE environment and identifies the key participants and their activities. The key steps involved in the process are as follows:

1. The Client requests access to a protected J2EE application using a Web browser.
2. The J2EE application verifies the request using the JAAS LoginModule and then initiates authentication by forwarding the request to the biometric authentication server.
3. The authentication server initiates a biometric callback.

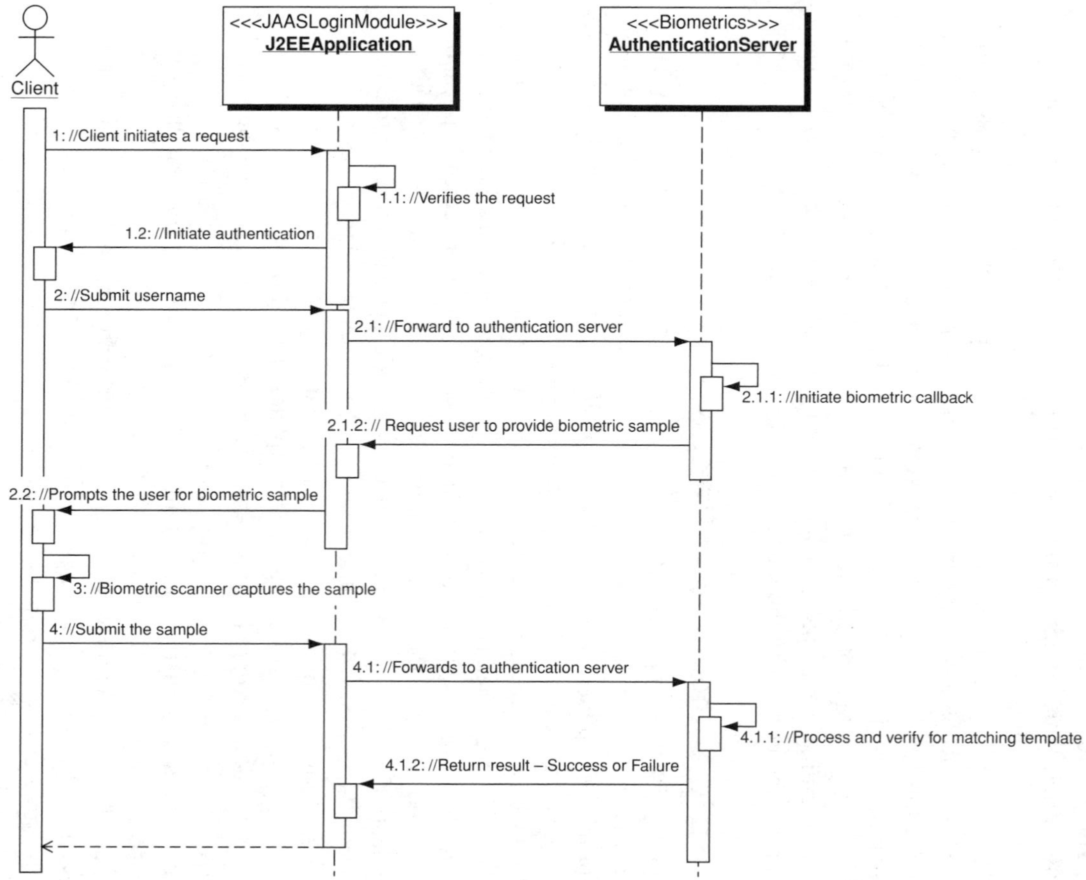

Figure 15–7 Biometric authentication for J2EE applications—sequence diagram

4. The client provides the biometric sample in the assigned biometric scanner and submits it for authentication.
5. The authentication server verifies the biometric sample by matching it with the reference template acquired during the enrollment process.
6. If the matching score exceeds the required threshold limit, the authentication is considered successful.
7. Based on the authentication result, the JAAS LoginModule allows or denies access to the requested application.

In the case of UNIX and Windows environments, using PAM and GINA modules, respectively, play the role of JAAS LoginModule in the authentication process.

Biometric SSO Strategy

Biometric SSO allows users to access multiple applications (for example, a Web portal aggregating access to multiple partner applications) after doing a single biometric authentication. In this case, the authentication is managed by the identity provider infrastructure that provides single sign-on services to support heterogeneous applications and system environments. The identity provider infrastructure is usually a vendor solution that encapsulates access to multiple resources by making use of pluggable authentication modules from security infrastructure providers. Upon authentication, the identity provider issues an SSO token that is trusted by all participating applications. This means the identity provider grants access to the secured application or resource by issuing an SSO token that represents the user's sign-on and session information. All partner applications trust the SSO token issued by the identity provider and grant the caller request to proceed for further processing based on the policies and privileges. Figure 15–8 represents the sequence diagram for the biometric SSO in a business portal that aggregates access to multiple partner applications.

Let's assume that a biometric authentication server is configured as the default authentication service in an identity provider infrastructure for providing access to a business portal. When a user attempts to access the business portal managed by an identity provider, the business portal redirects the user to a biometric login that requests submission by the user of biometric samples to the identity server, which acts as a client to the biometric authentication server. The biometric authentication server authenticates the user by acquiring one or more biometric samples from the user and matching them against the user's biometric reference template. If the biometric authentication is successful, the identity provider grants access to the business portal by issuing an SSO token that represents the user's

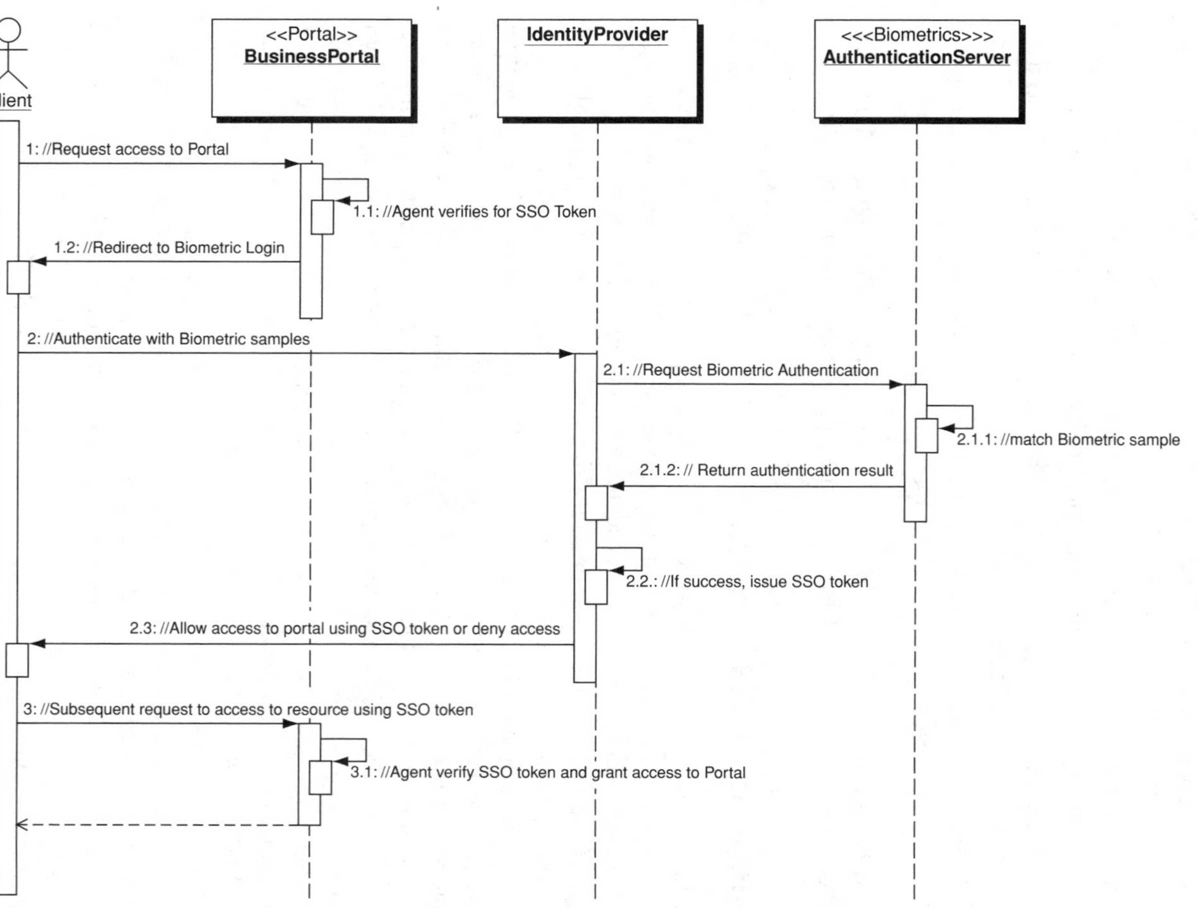

Figure 15–8 Biometric SSO for business portal—sequence diagram

sign-on and session information. If the authentication fails, the identity provider returns an error page to the user. The identity provider makes use of the policy agents for securing the business portal by intercepting requests from unauthorized intrusions, verifying and validating the user's SSO token if it exists, and controlling access to resources based on policies assigned to the user.

To learn more about building a biometric SSO for J2EE, Web, and enterprise applications using a vendor solution, refer to http://developers.sun.com/prodtech/identserver/reference/techart/bioauthentication.html.

Multi-factor Authentication Using Smart Cards and Biometrics

Security experts often recommend a multi-factor authentication approach in which security requirements are intended for highly secure installation and mandate a robust solution. Multi-factor authentication ensures verification and validation of a user identity using multiple authentication mechanisms. It often combines two or more authentication methods—for example, a three-factor authentication is based on password (what the user knows), smart card (what the user possesses), and fingerprints (who the user is).

Using smart cards delivers multi-factor authentication. For example, in addition to what the user knows (such as a PIN), the card can provide authentication using the card owner's digital certificate with the card owner's public key. The digital certificate associates the card owner's identity to the person's public key. The smart card also contains the card owner's private key, which can be used for digitally signing e-mail or documents, among other possible uses. With the support of biometric technologies, the smart card can also be used to store biometric templates of the card owner, which can be used to verify the card owner by acquiring a biometric sample (such as a fingerprint) and matching it to the reference template stored on the card or off the card using a biometric authentication server.

Combining smart card and biometrics technologies for multi-factor authentication helps verify an identity by authenticating for higher security requirements and in circumstances where physical verification is mandatory. Using biometric templates on a smart card eliminates the need for PIN verification in banking ATM machines, and it can also be considered for security-sensitive applications where PINs can be stolen.

Match-on-the-Card Biometrics Strategy

Match-on-the-card is a technique of verifying an identity by matching the live-scan biometric sample with the biometric reference template stored on the card. In this strategy, the biometric template is stored only on the card and the card owner's privacy is maintained by not storing the biometric sample externally. Because smart cards use cryptographic mechanisms, the biometric template can also be secured using the card owner's private key. This guarantees the card owner that the card cannot be used even if it is stolen or lost.

In this strategy, the reference template is stored directly into the smart card memory during the enrollment process. In the authentication process, the biometric scanner acquires the sample and submits it to the smart card. Using its processor, the smart card carries out the verification process by matching the newly acquired sample with the reference template stored in memory and finally delivers the authentication result. The stored template is not disclosed outside the card throughout the process.

Implementations of match-on-the-card that support fingerprint-based technologies are available from selected vendors. The Java Card Biometric API specification facilitates enrollment, verification, and termination functionalities that support match-on-the-card.

Match-off-the-Card Biometrics Strategy

Match-off-the-card is a technique of verifying an identity by matching the live-scan biometric sample with the biometric reference template stored on the card using an intermediary security infrastructure. Like the match-on-the-card strategy, the biometric template is stored only on the card and the card owner's privacy is maintained by not storing the biometric sample externally. The difference is that the authentication is performed by an intermediary system, which means that during the process, the reference template will be sent out for verification.

In this strategy, the reference template is directly stored into the smart card memory during the enrollment process. During authentication, the biometric scanner acquires the sample and submits it to an intermediary security infrastructure, which in turn requests the user's reference template from the smart card. Then the intermediary carries out the verification process by matching the newly acquired sample with the reference template obtained from the smart card and returns the authentication results. It is often noted that this implementation has security risks, because the reference template is verified off the card during authentication. Adopting encryption and digital signature mechanisms ensures the confidentiality and integrity of the reference template. This strategy usually helps overcome smart card limitations with regard to memory and performance.

Best Practices and Pitfalls

The following sections discuss best practices and the associated pitfalls you should consider when implementing security using smart cards and biometrics infrastructure-based authentication services.

Using Smart Cards

- *Unified credential token.* Adopt smart cards as a unified security token for both physical and access control. Dual-interface smart cards supporting both contact and contactless readers fulfills both purposes. Adopting a unified credential token also delivers increased ROI by way of a single token for accessing disparate physical and logical resources, a single console for monitoring and auditing, a single interface for identity enrollment and termination, and a centralized personal identification and authentication process.
- *Restrict post-issuance applet download.* In the case of smart cards used for identification and authentication purposes, it is important to restrict applet downloads after issuing the card. The master key must not be provided to the card holder. This protects the card from potential abuses resulting in running out of memory, downloading and processing untrusted applets, and fault injection.
- *Revoke access and reset PIN.* The card must be revoked or blocked using PIN reset if a user enters an incorrect PIN too many times. This protects the card from PIN guessing and dictionary attacks after it is stolen from the card holder. The card should be allowed to access the resource or other application after subject to verification by intervention of an enrollment officer or other authorized official.
- *Adopting card standards.* It is important to choose cards and card readers that support standards such as ISO, Java Card, Global Platform, Java Card Biometric API, and so forth. This avoids vendor lock-in and ensures interoperability when running multiple applications.
- *Strong authentication.* Smart cards allows two-factor authentication by making use of PINs (what you know) and digital certificates stored in the card (what you have). Combining both aspects ensures strong authentication by improving the security and privacy of the authentication process. As a result, it strengthens logical access to protected resources, signing electronic documents for authenticity, secure electronic payment through client authentication, and has other potential uses.

Using Biometrics

- *Use multiple biometrics samples for single authentication.* To reduce the possibility of fake or forged biometric sampling, use multiple biometric samples for single authentication. Use random sequences when acquiring samples (for example, with fingerprint authentication, request left-hand index finger first and then right-hand thumb). This helps thwart attacks using residual fingerprints obtained from previous authentication sessions, fingerprints from glasses, or latent fingerprints on scanners. This also helps in preventing gummy finger-based forged fingerprint attacks. [Gummy]
- *Assign biometric scanners to users.* Assign scanners to individuals and verify the originating host for all authentication requests to ensure that the biometric sample is transmitted from user-assigned scanners only. Authentication must be considered successful only if the matching sample is obtained from the assigned scanner of the individual. This helps make monitoring and logging of events easier.
- *Preventing mimic scanner attacks.* To thwart playback attacks mimicking scanners, use validation of scanner-stored certificates before processing the samples. This can be accomplished by establishing SSL/TLS communication between the scanner and the authentication server.
- *Control access to administration and enrollment system.* It is important to establish roles for privileged users who will be authorized for performing enrollment. To increase the level of access capabilities to a user with administration and enrollment, it is necessary to follow an authorization approval workflow involving multiple officials.
- *Multiple login attempts.* If a user attempts to log in multiple times and fails to generate a matching score, the user account pertaining to the user ID must be temporarily revoked and reported for further investigation by an administrator. It is important to verify the time of access and the device in use to identify the user.
- *Logging, auditing, and monitoring.* All enrollment, administration, and authentication events and related actions must be captured in secure logs that include timestamps, host, and user information. It is also important to store audit trails to identify fake attempts and the originating sources. The system must also be monitored for system activity and use alerts whenever a potential breach or violation occurs. It is also important to periodically inspect the scanners and their stored keys and certificates for validity.

- *Securing the biometric information repository.* It is important to secure the biometric information stored in a directory (LDAP) or relational database. It is strongly recommended to use encryption mechanisms during storage so that the information remains confidential.
- *Secure communication.* All network communication involved with a smart card or biometrics-based authentication must be secured using SSL/TLS protocols. This ensures the information is not intercepted or captured during transit by preventing man-in-the-middle attacks from reading CUID (smart cards) or fingerprint images (biometrics) and then impersonating using replay of previously recorded information.
- *Match-on-the-card biometrics.* Sizing the processor and memory capabilities of a smart card is necessary before test-driving match-on-the-card biometric authentication. For example, a typical fingerprint template size ranges from 250 bytes to 1.2 Kbytes and it differs from person to person. The smart card must be tested for storage performance and reliability when using multiple biometric samples.

Pitfalls

- *Architectural complexity.* The complexity of implementing a smart card and biometrics-based security infrastructure depends on the level of geographical dispersion and the systems requiring physical and logical access, the centralized or decentralized nature of administration, and the directory infrastructure. These factors result in potential scalability and performance issues with the overall architecture.
- *Lost, stolen, and revoked smart cards.* There is always a possibility of potential abuse of lost or stolen cards in terms of impersonation or gaining physical access to a location. If the card uses a biometric template for authentication, however, the card cannot be used.
- *False Acceptance Rate (FAR) and False Rejection Rate (FRR).* Biometric authentication systems are prone to err in terms of false acceptance and false rejection. Depending upon the security requirements, and using CER, it is important to strike a balance between the percentages of FAR and FRR. For example, you may not want to set a high score threshold to lower FAR but it may affect some legitimate persons as FRR. There are other factors, such as physical conditions, positioning, location, weather, injury, biometric device, and so forth that must be considered before deployment. These factors can directly influence the accuracy of the overall biometric authentication process.

Secure Personal Identification Strategies

References

[BioAPI] BioAPI Version 1.1 specifications

http://xml.coverpages.org/BIOAPIv11.pdf

[BioSSO] Ramesh Nagappan and Tuomo Lampinen. Building Biometric Authentication for J2EE, Web and Enterprise Applications.

http://developers.sun.com/prodtech/identserver/reference/techart/bioauthentication.htm

[GINA] Keith Brown. Customizing GINA

http://msdn.microsoft.com/msdnmag/issues/05/05/SecurityBriefs/default.aspx

[GlobalPlatform] Global Platform specifications and documents

http://www.globalplatform.org/

[Gummy] Impact of "Gummy" Fingers on Fingerprint Systems.

http://cryptome.org/gummy.htm

[JavaCard] Java Card 2.2.1 Specifications

http://java.sun.com/products/javacard/specs.html

[JavaCardForum] Biometric Application Programming Interface (API) for Java Card

http://www.javacardforum.org/Documents/Biometry/BCWG_JCBiometricsAPI_v01_1.pdf

[NIST] NIST Biometric Consortium Working Group

http://www.nist.gov/bcwg.

[OpenCard] OpenCard Framework specifications and documents

http://www.opencard.org

[PAM] Vipin Samar and Charlie Lai. Making Login Services Independent of Authentication Technologies.

http://www.sun.com/software/solaris/pam/pam.external.pdf

[PC/SC] PC/SC Working Group Specifications

http://www.pcscworkgroup.com/

[Smart Card Alliance] Smart Cards and Biometrics FAQ white paper

http://www.estrategy.gov/smartgov/information/smart_card_biometric_faq_final.pdf

Index

D

G

K

M

X

Y

Z